Business Law

TEXT & EXERCISES

EIGHTH EDITION

Business Law

TEXT & EXERCISES

EIGHTH EDITION

Roger LeRoy Miller

Institute for University Studies
Arlington, Texas

William Eric Hollowell

Institute for University Studies
Arlington, Texas
and Member of Florida State Bar
Minnesota State Bar
United States Supreme Court Bar

CENGAGE
Learning™

Australia • Brazil • Japan • Korea • Mexico • Singapore • Spain • United Kingdom • United States

Business Law
TEXT & EXERCISES
EIGHTH EDITION

Roger LeRoy Miller
William Eric Hollowell

Vice President for Social Science and Qualitative Business: Erin Joyner

Product Director: Michael Worls

Senior Product Manager: Vicky True-Baker

Content Development Manager: Rebecca von Gillern

Content Developer: Leah G. Wuchnick

Product Assistant: Ryan McAndrews

Marketing Manager: Katie Jergens

Marketing Director: Kristen Hurd

Marketing Coordinator: Christopher Walz

Production Director: Sharon Smith

Senior Content Project Manager: Ann Borman

Content Digitization Project Manager: Jennifer Chinn

Manufacturing Planner: Kevin Kluck

Senior Inventory Analyst: Terina Bradley

Senior IP Director: Julie Geagan-Chavez

IP Analyst: Jennifer Nonenmacher

IP Project Manager: Betsy Hathaway

Senior Art Director: Michelle Kunkler

Interior and Cover Designer: Liz Harasymczuk

Cover Images: Handshake: John Lund/Getty Images; Scales of Justice: DSGpro/Getty Images

Design Elements: Highlighting the Point: Galapagos Photo/ShutterStock.com; **Facing a Legal Problem:** Hans-Joerg Nisch/ShutterStock.com; **Linking Business Law:** cristapper/ShutterStock.com; **Real-World Case Example:** Artens/ShutterStock.com; **Using Business Law**, book icon: Kapreski/ShutterStock.com; **Unit Opener**, business abstract: Bruce Rolff/ShutterStock.com; **Unit Opener**, George Washington statue: pio3/ShutterStock.com; **Unit Opener**, U.S. stock market: iStockPhoto.com/stocknshares

Library of Congress Control Number: 2015947181

Student Edition ISBN: 978-1-305-50960-3

Cengage Learning
20 Channel Center Street
Boston, MA 02210
USA

Cengage Learning is a leading provider of customized learning solutions with employees residing in nearly 40 different countries and sales in more than 125 countries around the world. Find your local representative at **www.cengage.com.**

Cengage Learning products are represented in Canada by Nelson Education, Ltd.

To learn more about Cengage Learning Solutions, visit **www.cengage.com.**

Purchase any of our products at your local college store or at our preferred online store **www.cengagebrain.com.**

Printed in the United States of America

Print Number: 01   Print Year: 2015

Brief Contents

UNIT 1

THE LAW AND OUR LEGAL SYSTEM 1

Chapter 1   Introduction to the Law
              and Our Legal System 2
Chapter 2   Ethics in Business 15
Chapter 3   The Courts and Alternative Dispute
              Resolution 31
Chapter 4   Constitutional Law 49
Chapter 5   Tort Law 65
Chapter 6   Intellectual Property 81
Chapter 7   Internet Law, Social Media,
              and Privacy 93
Chapter 8   Criminal Law and Cyber Crime 107

UNIT 2

CONTRACTS 121

Chapter 9   Introduction to Contracts 122
Chapter 10   Offer and Acceptance 133
Chapter 11   Consideration 147
Chapter 12   Capacity 157
Chapter 13   The Legality of Agreements 169
Chapter 14   Voluntary Consent 179
Chapter 15   Written Contracts 189
Chapter 16   Third Party Rights 203
Chapter 17   Contract Discharge and Remedies 217

UNIT 3

SALES AND LEASES 233

Chapter 18   Introduction to Sales and Lease
              Contracts 234
Chapter 19   Title and Risk of Loss 247
Chapter 20   Performance and Breach 261

Chapter 21   Warranties and Product Liability 275
Chapter 22   Consumer Protection 289

UNIT 4

NEGOTIABLE INSTRUMENTS 303

Chapter 23   The Essentials of Negotiability 304
Chapter 24   Transferability and Liability 319
Chapter 25   Checks and Banking in the Digital
              Age 333

UNIT 5

AGENCY AND EMPLOYMENT 349

Chapter 26   Agency 350
Chapter 27   Employment, Immigration,
              and Labor Law 365
Chapter 28   Employment Discrimination 381

UNIT 6

BUSINESS ORGANIZATIONS 395

Chapter 29   Sole Proprietorships, Partnerships,
              and Limited Liability Companies 396
Chapter 30   Formation and Termination of a
              Corporation 411
Chapter 31   Management and Ownership of a
              Corporation 427

UNIT 7

CREDIT AND RISK 439

Chapter 32   Secured Transactions 440
Chapter 33   Creditors' Rights and Remedies 453
Chapter 34   Bankruptcy 465
Chapter 35   Insurance 481

UNIT 8

PROPERTY 493

Chapter 36   Personal Property and Bailments 494
Chapter 37   Real Property 509
Chapter 38   Landlord and Tenant Law 523
Chapter 39   Wills and Trusts 535

UNIT 9

SPECIAL TOPICS 549

Chapter 40   Administrative Law 550
Chapter 41   Antitrust Law 565
Chapter 42   International Law 579

APPENDICES

A   The Constitution of the United States A–1
B   Article 2 of the Uniform Commercial Code A–10
C   Answers to *Issue Spotters* A–29

GLOSSARY G–1

TABLE OF CASES TC–1

INDEX I–1

Contents

UNIT 1

THE LAW AND OUR LEGAL SYSTEM 1

CHAPTER 1
INTRODUCTION TO THE LAW AND OUR LEGAL SYSTEM 2

1–1 What Is Law? 2

1–2 Business Activities and the Legal Environment 3

Highlighting the Point 3

1–3 Sources of American Law 4

Real-World Case Example 6

Highlighting the Point 7

1–4 Civil Law versus Criminal Law 8

1–5 National Law around the World 9

1–6 International Law 9

Linking Business Law to Your Career
Consulting an Expert for Advice 10

CHAPTER 1—WORK SET 13

CHAPTER 2
ETHICS IN BUSINESS 15

2–1 The Importance of Business Ethics 15

2–2 Setting the Right Ethical Tone 16

2–3 The Sarbanes-Oxley Act 17

2–4 Business Ethics and the Law 17

Real-World Case Example 18

Highlighting the Point 19

2–5 Approaches to Ethical Reasoning 19

Highlighting the Point 21

2–6 Business Ethics and Social Media 22

2–7 Business Ethics on a Global Level 22

Highlighting the Point 23

Linking Business Law to Your Career
Managing a Company's Reputation 24

CHAPTER 2—WORK SET 29

CHAPTER 3
THE COURTS AND ALTERNATIVE DISPUTE RESOLUTION 31

3–1 Jurisdiction 31

3–2 The State Court System 32

3–3 The Federal Court System 34

3–4 The State Court Case Process 37

Highlighting the Point 37

Real-World Case Example 39

3–5 The Courts Adapt to the Online World 41

3–6 Alternative Dispute Resolution 42

CHAPTER 3—WORK SET 47

CHAPTER 4
CONSTITUTIONAL LAW 49

4–1 The Constitutional Powers of Government 49

Highlighting the Point 51

4–2 Business and the Bill of Rights 52

Highlighting the Point 54

4–3 Due Process and Equal Protection 55

Highlighting the Point 56

Real-World Case Example 57

4–4 Privacy Rights 57

Linking Business Law to Your Career
Pretexting and Marketing 59

CHAPTER 4—WORK SET 63

CHAPTER 5
TORT LAW 65

5–1 The Basis of Tort Law 65

5–2 Intentional Torts against Persons 67

Highlighting the Point 67

Highlighting the Point 68

5–3 Intentional Torts against Property 71

Real-World Case Example 72

5–4 Negligence 73

Highlighting the Point 74

Highlighting the Point 75

Highlighting the Point 76

5–5 Strict Liability 76

CHAPTER 5—WORK SET 79

CHAPTER 6
INTELLECTUAL PROPERTY 81

6–1 Trademarks and Related Property 81

Highlighting the Point 82

6–2 Patents 83

6–3 Copyrights 84

Real-World Case Example 85

Highlighting the Point 86

6–4 Trade Secrets 86

6–5 International Protection for Intellectual
Property 87

Linking Business Law to Your Career
Trademarks and Service Marks 88

CHAPTER 6—WORK SET 91

CHAPTER 7
INTERNET LAW, SOCIAL MEDIA, AND PRIVACY 93

7–1 Internet Law 93

Highlighting the Point 95

Highlighting the Point 96

Highlighting the Point 97

7–2 Social Media 98

Real-World Case Example 99

7–3 Privacy 100

CHAPTER 7—WORK SET 105

CHAPTER 8
CRIMINAL LAW AND CYBER CRIME 107

8–1 Civil Law and Criminal Law 107

8–2 What Constitutes Criminal Liability? 108

8–3 Constitutional Safeguards 109

Real-World Case Example 110

8–4 Crimes Affecting Business 110

Highlighting the Point 111

Highlighting the Point 112

8–5 Defenses to Criminal Liability 113

8–6 Cyber Crime 114

Linking Business Law to Your Career
Protect Your Company against Hacking 116

CHAPTER 8—WORK SET 119

UNIT 2

CONTRACTS 121

CHAPTER 9
INTRODUCTION TO CONTRACTS 122

9–1 The Definition of a Contract 122

Real-World Case Example 123

9–2 Types of Contracts 124

Highlighting the Point 124

Highlighting the Point 125

9–3 Interpretation of Contracts 127

CHAPTER 9—WORK SET 131

CHAPTER 10
OFFER AND ACCEPTANCE 133

10–1 Requirements of the Offer 133

Highlighting the Point 134

Real-World Case Example 135

10–2 Termination of the Offer 136

Highlighting the Point 136

10–3 Acceptance 138

10–4 E-Contracts—Offer and Acceptance 139

Highlighting the Point 140

CHAPTER 10—WORK SET 145

CHAPTER 11
CONSIDERATION 147

11–1 Elements of Consideration 147

Highlighting the Point 148

11–2 Adequacy of Consideration 148

11–3 Preexisting Duty 148

Highlighting the Point 149

11–4 Past Consideration 149

11–5 Problems with Consideration 150

Highlighting the Point 151

Real-World Case Example 151

CHAPTER 11—WORK SET 155

CHAPTER 12
CAPACITY 157

12–1 Minors 157

Real-World Case Example 158

Highlighting the Point 158

Highlighting the Point 159

12–2 Intoxicated Persons 160

12–3 Mentally Incompetent Persons 161

Highlighting the Point 162

Linking Business Law to Your Career
Contracts with Minors or Intoxicated Persons 162

CHAPTER 12—WORK SET 167

CHAPTER 13
THE LEGALITY OF AGREEMENTS 169

13–1 Contracts Contrary to Statute 169

13–2 Contracts Contrary to Public Policy 170

Real-World Case Example 171

Highlighting the Point 172

Highlighting the Point 173

13–3 The Effect of Illegality 173

Highlighting the Point 173

Highlighting the Point 174

CHAPTER 13—WORK SET 177

CHAPTER 14
VOLUNTARY CONSENT 179

14–1 Mistakes 179

Highlighting the Point 180

14–2 Fraudulent Misrepresentation 181

Highlighting the Point 182

Real-World Case Example 183

14–3 Undue Influence 184

14–4 Duress 184

CHAPTER 14—WORK SET 187

CHAPTER 15
WRITTEN CONTRACTS 189

15–1 The Statute of Frauds—Writing Requirement 189

Highlighting the Point 191

Highlighting the Point 192

Real-World Case Example 193

15–2 The Sufficiency of the Writing 194

15–3 The Parol Evidence Rule 195

Linking Business Law to Your Career
Enforceable E-Mail Contracts 197

CHAPTER 15—WORK SET 201

CHAPTER 16
THIRD PARTY RIGHTS 203

16–1 Assignments and Delegations 203

Highlighting the Point 206

Highlighting the Point 207

Highlighting the Point 208

16–2 Third Party Beneficiaries 208

Real-World Case Example 208

Linking Business Law to Your Career
Assignment and Delegation 211

CHAPTER 16—WORK SET 215

CHAPTER 17
CONTRACT DISCHARGE AND REMEDIES 217

17–1 Contract Discharge 217

Highlighting the Point 219

Real-World Case Example 221

17–2 Contract Remedies 222

Highlighting the Point 223

Highlighting the Point 224

17–3 Recovery Based on Quasi Contract 225

Linking Business Law to Your Career
Performance and Compromise 226

CHAPTER 17—WORK SET 231

UNIT 3

SALES AND LEASES 233

CHAPTER 18
INTRODUCTION TO SALES AND LEASE CONTRACTS 234

18–1 Sales of Goods 234

Real-World Case Example 235

18–2 Leases of Goods 236

18–3 Sales and Lease Contracts 236

Highlighting the Point 238

Highlighting the Point 239

Highlighting the Point 240

Highlighting the Point 241

CHAPTER 18—WORK SET 245

CHAPTER 19
TITLE AND RISK OF LOSS 247

19–1 Identification 247

Highlighting the Point 249

Highlighting the Point 251

19–2 Risk of Loss 251

Real-World Case Example 251

Highlighting the Point 252

19–3 Insurable Interest 254

Highlighting the Point 255

Linking Business Law to Your Career
Risk Management 256

CHAPTER 19—WORK SET 259

CHAPTER 20
PERFORMANCE AND BREACH 261

20–1 Obligations of the Seller or Lessor 261

Real-World Case Example 262

Highlighting the Point 263

Highlighting the Point 264

20–2 Obligations of the Buyer or Lessee 265

20–3 Anticipatory Repudiation 266

20–4 Remedies of the Seller or Lessor 266

Highlighting the Point 267

20–5 Remedies of the Buyer or Lessee 267

Highlighting the Point 268

CHAPTER 20—WORK SET 273

CHAPTER 21
WARRANTIES AND PRODUCT LIABILITY 275

21–1 Warranties 275

Highlighting the Point 277

Highlighting the Point 278

21–2 Product Liability 280

Real-World Case Example 282

Linking Business Law to Your Career
Quality Control Management 283

CHAPTER 21—WORK SET 287

CHAPTER 22
CONSUMER PROTECTION 289

22–1 Deceptive Advertising 289

Highlighting the Point 290

Real-World Case Example 291

22–2 Labeling and Packaging Laws 292

22–3 Consumer Sales 292

22–4 Credit Protection 293

Highlighting the Point 294

Highlighting the Point 295

Highlighting the Point 296

22–5 Protection of Health and Safety 297

Highlighting the Point 297

CHAPTER 22—WORK SET 301

UNIT 4

NEGOTIABLE INSTRUMENTS 303

CHAPTER 23
THE ESSENTIALS OF NEGOTIABILITY 304

23–1 Types of Instruments 304

23–2 What Is a Negotiable Instrument? 307

Real-World Case Example 308

Highlighting the Point 310

23–3 Transfer of Instruments 311

Highlighting the Point 311

Highlighting the Point 312

Linking Business Law to Your Career
Writing and Indorsing Checks 313

CHAPTER 23—WORK SET 317

CHAPTER 24
TRANSFERABILITY AND LIABILITY 319

24–1 Holder versus Holder in Due Course 319

24–2 Requirements for HDC Status 319

24–3 Signature Liability 321

   Highlighting the Point 325

24–4 Warranty Liability 325

   Highlighting the Point 325

24–5 Defenses 326

   Real-World Case Example 327

24–6 Discharge 328

CHAPTER 24—WORK SET 331

CHAPTER 25
CHECKS AND BANKING
IN THE DIGITAL AGE 333

25–1 Checks 333

25–2 The Bank-Customer Relationship 334

   Real-World Case Example 334

25–3 Honoring Checks 334

   Highlighting the Point 336

25–4 Accepting Deposits 337

   Highlighting the Point 338

25–5 Electronic Fund Transfers 341

25–6 E-Money and Online Banking 342

Linking Business Law to Your Career
Banking Risks 344

CHAPTER 25—WORK SET 347

UNIT 5

AGENCY AND EMPLOYMENT 349

CHAPTER 26
AGENCY 350

26–1 Agency Relationships 350

26–2 Agency Formation 351

   Highlighting the Point 352

26–3 Duties of Agents and Principals 353

26–4 Agent's Authority 354

   Highlighting the Point 354

   Highlighting the Point 355

26–5 Liability in Agency Relationships 356

   Real-World Case Example 357

26–6 Termination of Agency Relationships 357

   Highlighting the Point 358

Linking Business Law to Your Career
Independent Contractors 359

CHAPTER 26—WORK SET 363

CHAPTER 27
EMPLOYMENT, IMMIGRATION,
AND LABOR LAW 365

27–1 Employment at Will 365

   Highlighting the Point 366

27–2 Worker Health and Safety 366

   Highlighting the Point 367

27–3 Retirement Income and Security 367

   Highlighting the Point 369

27–4 Family and Medical Leave 369

   Real-World Case Example 369

27–5 Wage and Hour Laws 370

   Highlighting the Point 371

27–6 Immigration Law 371

27–7 Labor Law 372

   Highlighting the Point 373

CHAPTER 27—WORK SET 379

CHAPTER 28
EMPLOYMENT DISCRIMINATION 381

28–1 Title VII of the Civil Rights Act 381

   Highlighting the Point 382

   Highlighting the Point 384

   Real-World Case Example 385

   Highlighting the Point 386

28–2 Discrimination Based on Age 386

   Highlighting the Point 387

28–3 Discrimination Based on Disability 388

28–4 Defenses to Employment Discrimination 389

Linking Business Law to Your Career
Human Resources Management 390

CHAPTER 28—WORK SET 393

UNIT 6

BUSINESS ORGANIZATIONS 395

CHAPTER 29
SOLE PROPRIETORSHIPS, PARTNERSHIPS, AND LIMITED LIABILITY COMPANIES 396

29–1 Sole Proprietorships 396

29–2 Partnerships 397

Highlighting the Point 399

Highlighting the Point 399

Highlighting the Point 400

Highlighting the Point 401

Highlighting the Point 402

Highlighting the Point 403

Highlighting the Point 404

29–3 Limited Liability Companies 404

Real-World Case Example 405

Linking Business Law to Your Career
Business Formation 406

CHAPTER 29—WORK SET 409

CHAPTER 30
FORMATION AND TERMINATION OF A CORPORATION 411

30–1 Corporate Classifications 411

30–2 Formation of a Corporation 412

Real-World Case Example 414

30–3 Corporate Powers 415

30–4 Corporate Financing 415

30–5 Mergers and Consolidations 417

Highlighting the Point 417

30–6 Termination of a Corporation 420

Highlighting the Point 420

CHAPTER 30—WORK SET 425

CHAPTER 31
MANAGEMENT AND OWNERSHIP OF A CORPORATION 427

31–1 Corporate Management—Directors and Officers 427

Highlighting the Point 428

Highlighting the Point 429

Highlighting the Point 430

31–2 Corporate Ownership—Shareholders 431

Real-World Case Example 432

Highlighting the Point 432

Highlighting the Point 433

CHAPTER 31—WORK SET 437

UNIT 7

CREDIT AND RISK 439

CHAPTER 32
SECURED TRANSACTIONS 440

32–1 The Terminology of Secured Transactions 440

32–2 Creating a Security Interest 441

32–3 Perfecting a Security Interest 441

Highlighting the Point 442

32–4 The Scope of a Security Interest 443

Highlighting the Point 443

Highlighting the Point 444

Highlighting the Point 444

Highlighting the Point 444

32–5 Priorities among Security Interests 445

32–6 Rights and Duties of the Debtor and Creditor 446

32–7 Default 446

Real-World Case Example 447

CHAPTER 32—WORK SET 451

CHAPTER 33
CREDITORS' RIGHTS AND REMEDIES 453

33–1 Laws Assisting Creditors 453

Highlighting the Point 455

Highlighting the Point 456

Real-World Case Example 456

Highlighting the Point 458

Highlighting the Point 459

33–2 Laws Assisting Debtors 460

Highlighting the Point 460

CHAPTER 33—WORK SET 463

CHAPTER 34
BANKRUPTCY 465

34–1 The Bankruptcy Code 465
34–2 Chapter 7—Liquidation 466
  Highlighting the Point 467
  Highlighting the Point 468
  Highlighting the Point 470
34–3 Chapter 11—Reorganization 472
34–4 Chapter 13—Adjustment 473
  Real-World Case Example 474

CHAPTER 34—WORK SET 479

CHAPTER 35
INSURANCE 481

35–1 Insurance Terminology and Concepts 481
35–2 The Insurance Contract 483
  Highlighting the Point 484
  Real-World Case Example 485
  Highlighting the Point 486

Linking Business Law to Your Career
Risk Management in Cyberspace 487

CHAPTER 35—WORK SET 491

UNIT 8
PROPERTY 493

CHAPTER 36
PERSONAL PROPERTY AND BAILMENTS 494

36–1 The Nature of Personal Property 494
36–2 Property Ownership—Rights of Possession 495
  Highlighting the Point 495
36–3 Acquiring Ownership of Personal Property 496
36–4 Mislaid, Lost, and Abandoned Property 499
  Highlighting the Point 499
36–5 Bailments 500
  Real-World Case Example 502

CHAPTER 36—WORK SET 507

CHAPTER 37
REAL PROPERTY 509

37–1 The Nature of Real Property 509
37–2 Ownership Interest 511

  Highlighting the Point 511
  Highlighting the Point 512
  Real-World Case Example 513
  Highlighting the Point 514
37–3 Transfer of Ownership 514
  Highlighting the Point 514
  Highlighting the Point 515

Linking Business Law to Your Career
Eminent Domain and Commercial Development 517

CHAPTER 37—WORK SET 521

CHAPTER 38
LANDLORD AND TENANT LAW 523

38–1 Leasehold Estates 523
38–2 The Landlord-Tenant Relationship 524
  Real-World Case Example 525
  Highlighting the Point 525
  Highlighting the Point 527

CHAPTER 38—WORK SET 533

CHAPTER 39
WILLS AND TRUSTS 535

39–1 Wills 535
  Real-World Case Example 537
39–2 Intestacy Laws 539
  Highlighting the Point 540
39–3 Trusts 541

CHAPTER 39—WORK SET 547

UNIT 9
SPECIAL TOPICS 549

CHAPTER 40
ADMINISTRATIVE LAW 550

40–1 Agency Creation 550
40–2 The Administrative Process 552
  Highlighting the Point 554
40–3 Agency Powers 555
  Real-World Case Example 556
  Highlighting the Point 557
40–4 Public Accountability 558

Linking Business Law to Your Career
Dealing with Administrative Law 559

CHAPTER 40—WORK SET 563

CHAPTER 41

ANTITRUST LAW 565

41–1 The Sherman Act 565

   Highlighting the Point 567

   Highlighting the Point 568

   Highlighting the Point 569

41–2 The Clayton Act 569

   Real-World Case Example 570

41–3 Enforcement of Antitrust Laws 571

41–4 U.S. Antitrust Laws in the Global Context 572

CHAPTER 41—WORK SET 577

CHAPTER 42

INTERNATIONAL LAW 579

42–1 International Principles and Doctrines 579

42–2 Doing Business Internationally 580

42–3 International Contract Provisions 582

   Highlighting the Point 583

42–4 Payment on International Transactions 584

42–5 Regulation of International Business
      Activities 584

42–6 U.S. Laws in a Global Context 586

   Highlighting the Point 587

   Real-World Case Example 587

Linking Business Law to Your Career
Global Marketing Management 588

CHAPTER 42—WORK SET 593

APPENDICES

A   The Constitution of the United States A–1

B   Article 2 of the Uniform Commercial Code A–10

C   Answers to *Issue Spotters* A–29

GLOSSARY G–1

TABLE OF CASES TC–1

INDEX I–1

Preface to the Instructor

It is no exaggeration to say that today's legal world is changing at a pace never before experienced. In many instances, technology is both driving and facilitating this change. The expanded use of the Internet for both business and personal transactions has led to new ways of doing business and, as a result, to a changing legal environment for the twenty-first century. In the midst of this evolving environment, however, one thing remains certain: for students entering the business world, an awareness of the legal and regulatory environment of business is critical.

Even for those students who do not enter the business world, legal problems will arise. Thus, a solid background in business law is essential for everyone. In *Business Law: Text and Exercises*, Eighth Edition, we present business law in a straightforward, practical manner. The essential aspects of every important topic are covered without overburdening the reader with numerous details and explanations of arcane exceptions.

WHAT'S NEW IN THE EIGHTH EDITION

Instructors have come to rely on the coverage, accuracy, and applicability of *Business Law: Text and Exercises*. That is why in the Eighth Edition we continue to engage student interest and provide a basic understanding of business law. Consequently, we have incorporated significant new details, timely examples, helpful exhibits, and recent cases in every chapter. You will find that every chapter in the Eighth Edition includes several exciting new changes:

New Chapter Content *Chapter 7* on *Internet Law, Social Media, and Privacy* is completely new to this edition. Recognizing the significance of the Internet and social media in today's workplace, this chapter discusses issues such as spam, online defamation, domain name disputes, cybersquatting, digital copyright laws, and file sharing. In addition, we examine how social media have affected business policymaking and privacy issues.

Chapter 28 on *Employment Discrimination* has been reworked so that its entire content now focuses solely on issues regarding discrimination in the workplace. This chapter provides basic explanations and examples of the requirements under Title VII of the Civil Rights Act, as well as the Age Discrimination in Employment Act and the Americans with Disabilities Act.

Real-World Case Examples *Real-World Case Examples* are integrated appropriately throughout the text and present the facts, issues, and rulings from actual court cases. Students can quickly read through the *Real-World Case Examples* to see how courts apply legal principles to everyday scenarios. **Each *Real-World Case Example* is completely new to this edition and based on a 2013 or 2014 case.**

Highlighting the Point *Highlighting the Point* features help students understand how business law can apply to common situations. We have **added nearly forty new *Highlighting the Point* features,** and each chapter includes two or more of these helpful features.

Numbered Examples *Numbered Examples* are one of the more appreciated features of *Business Law: Text and Exercises* because they clarify legal principles for students. For the Eighth Edition, we have **added more than one hundred new Numbered Examples** throughout the chapters.

Real-World Case Problems All *Real-World Case Problems* are now based on cases from 2012, 2013, or 2014. Ninety-five percent of these case problems are new to this edition, and all of them have been condensed for an easier, more basic problem-solving process.

Terms and Concepts for Review The *Terms and Concepts for Review* sections with their lists of boldfaced terms help to increase student understanding of common business law terminology and concepts. For the Eighth Edition, we have **added fifty new Terms and Concepts to Review.** Each boldfaced term has a corresponding page number that directs students to its margin definition within a chapter. All boldfaced terms and their definitions can also be found in the book's **Glossary.**

PRACTICAL AND EFFECTIVE LEARNING TOOLS

To help students review chapter materials and prepare for testing, this text provides the following effective, practical features:

- *Learning Outcomes*—Every chapter starts with four to six *Learning Outcomes.* Within the body of the text, when the material being discussed relates to a specific *Learning Outcome,* we indicate this clearly in the page margin. Additionally, each *Chapter Summary* includes that chapter's *Learning Outcomes* with a succinct review of the major points students need to remember.

- *Facing (and Answering) a Legal Problem*—Each chapter opens with an appropriate and straightforward legal problem that is answered later in the text. The problem is set off in a distinctive manner that separates it from the text materials. At the end of the chapter, the problem is stated again, and the answer to the problem is given.

- *Linking Business Law to Your Career* features—Written in an easy-to-understand style, these features emphasize tips, pitfalls, and effective strategies for students to remember once they are working and applying their knowledge of basic business law to real-life workplace scenarios. In selected chapters, these features often reflect new business developments and examples. This edition added three new *Linking Business Law to Your Career* features.

- Exhibits—When appropriate, we have illustrated important aspects of the law in graphic or summary form in exhibits. These exhibits will help your students grasp the essential concepts pertaining to a specific area of the law or a particular legal doctrine.

- *Work Sets*—At the end of every chapter, there is a tear-out sheet called a *Work Set,* which features several true-false and multiple-choice questions, plus **an Answering More Legal Problems feature.** This in-text study guide helps students review the material covered in the chapter.

- *Issue Spotters*—The *Issue Spotters* provide students with two hypothetical situations that end with questions related to the topics discussed in the chapter. Students answer these questions by reviewing the topic material. They can then compare their answers with those provided in **Appendix C** at the end of this book.

- *Using Business Law*—These questions help students understand straightforward applications of the law.

- *Ethical Questions*—Located at the end of every chapter, these questions provide opportunities for critical thinking regarding ethical issues in a variety of actual business cases.
- *Appendices*—As a reference source for your students when studying chapter materials, we have included the following appendices:
  A—The Constitution of the United States
  B—Article 2 of the Uniform Commercial Code
  C—Answers to *Issue Spotters*

SUPPLEMENTS

Business Law: Text and Exercises, Eighth Edition, provides a comprehensive supplements package. The supplements were created with a single goal in mind: to make the tasks of teaching and learning more enjoyable and efficient. The following supplements are available for instructors.

MindTap Business Law for *Business Law: Text & Exercises*, Eighth Edition

MindTap™ is a fully online, highly personalized learning experience built upon authoritative Cengage Learning content. By combining readings, multimedia, activities, and assessments into a singular Learning Path, *MindTap* guides students through their course with ease and engagement. Instructors personalize the Learning Path by customizing Cengage Learning resources and adding their own content via apps that integrate into the *MindTap* framework seamlessly with Learning Management Systems.

Business law instructors have told us it is important to help students **Prepare** for class, **Engage** with the course concepts to reinforce learning, **Apply** these concepts in real-world scenarios, and use legal reasoning and critical thinking to **Analyze** business law content. Accordingly, the *Business Law MindTap* product provides a four-step Learning Path designed to meet these critical needs while also allowing instructors to measure skills and outcomes with ease.

- **Prepare**—Chapter review activities are guided readings designed to prepare students for classroom discussion by ensuring reading and comprehension.
- **Engage**—Real-world videos with related questions help engage students by displaying the relevance of business law in everyday life.
- **Apply**—Brief hypotheticals help students practice spotting issues and applying the law in the context of short factual scenarios.
- **Analyze**—Legal reasoning activities promote deeper critical thinking by building on acquired knowledge to truly assess students' understanding of legal principles.

Each and every item in the Learning Path is assignable and gradable. This gives instructors the knowledge of class standings and concepts that may be difficult. Additionally, students gain knowledge about where they stand—both individually and compared to the highest performers in class.

To view a demo video and learn more about *MindTap*, please visit **www.cengage.com/mindtap.**

Cengage Learning Testing Powered by Cognero

Cengage Learning Testing Powered by Cognero is a flexible, online system that allows instructors to do the following:

- Author, edit, and manage *Test Bank* content from multiple Cengage Learning solutions.

- Create multiple test versions in an instant.
- Deliver tests from their Learning Management System (LMS), classroom, or wherever they want.

Start Right Away! *Cengage Learning Testing Powered by Cognero* works on any operating system or browser.

- No special installs or downloads are needed.
- Create tests from school, home, the coffee shop—anywhere with Internet access.

What Instructors Will Find

- *Simplicity at every step.* A desktop-inspired interface features drop-down menus and familiar intuitive tools that take instructors through content creation and management with ease.
- *Full-featured test generator.* Create ideal assessments with a choice of fifteen question types—including true/false, multiple choice, opinion scale/Likert, and essay. Multi-language support, an equation editor, and unlimited metadata help ensure instructor tests are complete and compliant.
- *Cross-compatible capability.* Import and export content into other systems.

Instructor's Companion Web Site

The *Instructor's Companion Web Site* for *Business Law: Text and Exercises*, Eighth Edition, contains the following supplements:

- *Instructor's Manual.* The *Instructor's Manual* contains all of the answers to the *Issue Spotters, Using Business Law* questions, *Real-World Case Problems,* and *Ethical Questions.* In addition, it provides the answers to each chapter's *Work Set.*
- *Test Bank.* The comprehensive *Test Bank* contains multiple-choice, true-false, and short essay questions.
- *PowerPoint Slides.*

  For more details, contact your Cengage Learning sales representative.

ACKNOWLEDGMENTS

Business Law: Text and Exercises could never have been written without the extremely helpful criticisms, comments, and suggestions that we received from the following professors on the previous editions:

Helena Armour
Southwestern College of Business

David Blumberg
LaGuardia Community College–CUNY

Daniel Burnstein
Gibbs College

Jeffrey S. Chase
Clinton Community College

Jack R. Day
Sawyer College

Diamela delCastilla
University of Miami

Nancy K. Dempsey
Cape Cod Community College

Joseph L. DeTorres
Contra Costa College

Lucy Dorum
Clover Park Technical College

Greg Drummer
Stone Child College

John Elger
Georgia State University

Austin Emeagwai
Lemoyne Owen College

Linda Ferguson
Virginia Wesleyan College

Gary Grau
Northeast State Community College

Myrna Gusdorf
Linn-Benton Community College

Michael Harford
Morehead State University

James P. Hess
Ivy Technical State College

Sharon J. Kingrey
City College

Doris K. Loes
Dakota County Technical College

Margaret A. Lourdes
Cleary University–Howell/Ann Arbor

John F. Mastriani
El Paso Community College

Arin S. Miller
Keiser University

Seymour D. Mintz
Queens College

Karen S. Mozengo
Pitt Community College

Barb Portzen
Mid-State Technical College

Alan Questall
Richmond Community College

J. Kent Richards
Lake Superior College

Susan Rubisch-Gisler
Carlow University

Harold V. Rucker
Cuyamaca College

Steve Schneider
Lake Superior College

Mary T. Sessom
Cuyamaca College

Tom Severance
Mira Costa College

Gary T. Shara
California State University–Monterey Bay

Brenda A. Siragusa
Corinthian College

Deborah Vinecour
SUNY Rockland Community College

Al Walczak
Linn-Benton Community College

Ron Weston
Contra Costa College

Roger D. Westrup
Heald Business College

Frederick D. White
Indian River Community College

Timothy G. Wiedman
Thomas Nelson Community College

Tom Wilson
Remington College

The staff at Cengage Learning went out of their way to make sure that the Eighth Edition of *Business Law: Text and Exercises* came out in accurate form. In particular, we wish to thank Michael Worls and Vicky True-Baker for their countless new ideas, many of which have been incorporated into this new edition.

We also extend special thanks to Rebecca von Gillern, our managing content developer, for her many useful suggestions and for her efforts in coordinating reviews and ensuring the timely and accurate publication of all supplemental materials.

Our senior content project manager, Ann Borman, made sure that we had a visually attractive edition. We will always be in her debt. We are also indebted to the staff at Lachina Publishing Services, our compositor. Their ability to generate the pages for this text quickly and accurately made it possible for us to meet our ambitious printing schedule.

The copyediting services of Jeanne Yost will not go unnoticed. We also thank Vickie Reierson for her proofreading, project management, and other assistance, which helped to ensure a timely, error-free text. Thank you to Terry Casey for her detailed and thorough work on the Table of Cases and Index. Finally, our appreciation goes to Roxanna Lee and Suzanne Jasin for their special efforts on the project.

We know we are not perfect. If you find something you don't like or want us to change, write to us via e-mail, using the text's Web site. That is how we can make *Business Law: Text and Exercises* an even better book in the future.

R.L.M.
W.E.H.

DEDICATION

To Margaret and Jack,
It's just a wonderment
how we enjoy
so much.

—R. L. M.

Para mi esposa, Luisa,
y mi hijas, Sandra y Mariel,
con mucho amor.

—W. E. H.

THE LAW AND OUR LEGAL SYSTEM

UNIT CONTENTS

CHAPTER 1 Introduction to the Law and Our Legal System

CHAPTER 2 Ethics in Business

CHAPTER 3 The Courts and Alternative Dispute Resolution

CHAPTER 4 Constitutional Law

CHAPTER 5 Tort Law

CHAPTER 6 Intellectual Property

CHAPTER 7 Internet Law, Social Media, and Privacy

CHAPTER 8 Criminal Law and Cyber Crime

1 INTRODUCTION TO THE LAW AND OUR LEGAL SYSTEM

LEARNING OUTCOMES

The four Learning Outcomes below are designed to help improve your understanding of the chapter. After reading this chapter, you should be able to:

1. Answer the question "What is law?"

2. List the major sources of law in our legal system.

3. Identify the supreme law of the land.

4. Explain the difference between our legal system and the legal systems of other nations.

FACING A LEGAL PROBLEM

California passes a law that restricts carbon dioxide emissions from automobiles in that state. A group of automobile manufacturers files a suit against the state of California to prevent enforcement of the law. The automakers claim that a federal statute already sets national fuel economy standards. They assert that these standards are essentially the same as carbon dioxide emission standards.

Q Are the automakers seeking a legal remedy or an equitable remedy? What is the primary source of law at issue?

Persons entering the world of business today will find themselves subject to numerous laws and government regulations. An acquaintance with these laws and regulations is beneficial—if not essential—to anyone contemplating a successful career in business.

In this introductory chapter, we look at the nature of law in general. We also examine the history and sources—both domestic and international—of American law in particular.

 ## 1–1 WHAT IS LAW?

LEARNING OUTCOME 1

Answer the question "What is law?"

There have been, and will continue to be, different definitions of law. The Greek philosopher Aristotle (384–322 B.C.E.) saw law as a "pledge that citizens of a state will do justice to one another." Aristotle's teacher, Plato (427?–347 B.C.E.), believed that law was a form of social control. The Roman philosopher Cicero (106–43 B.C.E.) contended that law was the agreement of reason and nature, the distinction between the just and the unjust.

Later, the British jurist Sir William Blackstone (1723–1780) described law as "a rule of civil conduct prescribed by the supreme power in a state, commanding what is right, and prohibiting what is wrong." In America, the eminent judge Oliver Wendell Holmes, Jr. (1841–1935), contended that law was a set of rules that allowed one to predict how a court would resolve a particular dispute—"the prophecies of what the courts will do in fact, and nothing more pretentious, are what I mean by the law."

Although these definitions vary in their particulars, they all are based on the following general observation concerning the nature of **law:** *law consists of enforceable rules governing relationships among individuals and between individuals and their society.*

law
A body of rules of conduct with legal force and effect, set forth by the government of a society.

1–2 BUSINESS ACTIVITIES AND THE LEGAL ENVIRONMENT

Regardless of how law is defined, a knowledge of business law is essential for any businessperson. To make good business decisions, businesspersons must have a basic knowledge of the laws and regulations governing those decisions. Furthermore, in today's world, businesspersons are expected to make decisions that are ethical as well as legally sound. Thus, the study of business law involves an ethical dimension.

1–2a Many Different Laws May Affect a Single Business Transaction

As you will see, each chapter in this textbook covers a specific area of the law and shows how the legal rules in that area affect business activities. Dividing up the law in this manner makes learning easier. But it does not take account of an important fact: many different laws may apply to just one transaction.

Businesspersons should be aware of this and understand enough about the law to know when to hire an expert for advice. See the *Linking Business Law to Your Career* feature at the end of this chapter for more on this topic.

If a dispute cannot be resolved amicably, then a **lawsuit** may become necessary. At that point, it is also important to know about the laws and the rules concerning courts and court procedures that spell out the steps of a lawsuit.

lawsuit
A judicial proceeding for the resolution of a dispute between parties in which rights are enforced or protected, wrongs are prevented or redressed, or public offenses are prosecuted.

HIGHLIGHTING THE POINT

Bob is the president of NetSys, Inc., a company that creates and maintains computer network systems for its clients. NetSys also markets software for customers who need an internal computer network but cannot afford an individually designed intranet. One day, Janet, an operations officer for Southwest Distribution Corporation (SDC), contacts Bob by e-mail about a possible contract involving SDC's computer network. Bob and Janet appear to make a deal, but later, a dispute arises over the terms.

Do these parties have an enforceable contract? If so, does NetSys have any options if SDC breaches the contract? The answers to these questions are part of contract law and sales law. **How can NetSys guarantee that it will be paid? For example, if SDC pays with a check that is returned for insufficient funds, what are NetSys's options?** Answers to these questions can be found in the laws that relate to negotiable instruments (such as checks) and creditors' rights. **Who owns the rights to NetSys's software? Who is liable if the software is defective? Did Bob and Janet have the authority to make the deal in the first place?** Resolutions of these questions can be found in areas of the law that relate to intellectual property, e-commerce, torts, product liability, agency, and business organizations.

breach
The failure to perform a legal obligation.

1–2b The Role of the Law in a Small Business

Some of you may end up working in, or owning and operating, a small business. The small-business owner is the most general of managers. When you seek additional financing, you become a finance manager. As you go over the books, you become an accountant. When you direct an advertising campaign, you are the marketing manager. As you evaluate market trends and pricing, interest rates, and other macro phenomena, you take on the role of a managerial economist. Each of these roles has a link to the law.

Exhibit 1.1 shows some of the legal issues that can arise in managing a small—or large—business.

1–3 SOURCES OF AMERICAN LAW

To understand the law, you need to have some understanding of its origins. Thus, we begin our study with a discussion of the sources of American law. One major source is the *common law* tradition that originated in medieval England. Another is *constitutional law*, which includes the U.S. Constitution and the constitutions

EXHIBIT 1.1   Linking Business Law to the Management of a Small Business

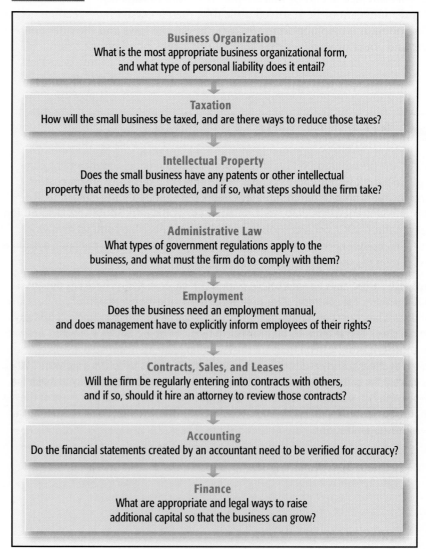

Business Organization
What is the most appropriate business organizational form,
and what type of personal liability does it entail?

Taxation
How will the small business be taxed, and are there ways to reduce those taxes?

Intellectual Property
Does the small business have any patents or other intellectual
property that needs to be protected, and if so, what steps should the firm take?

Administrative Law
What types of government regulations apply to the
business, and what must the firm do to comply with them?

Employment
Does the business need an employment manual,
and does management have to explicitly inform employees of their rights?

Contracts, Sales, and Leases
Will the firm be regularly entering into contracts with others,
and if so, should it hire an attorney to review those contracts?

Accounting
Do the financial statements created by an accountant need to be verified for accuracy?

Finance
What are appropriate and legal ways to raise
additional capital so that the business can grow?

of the states. The U.S. Constitution is the supreme law of the land. Within each state, the state constitution is supreme, so long as it does not conflict with the U.S. Constitution.

Statutes—the laws enacted by Congress and the state legislatures—comprise an additional source of American law. This source of the law is generally referred to as *statutory law.* Finally, yet another source of American law is *administrative law,* which consists of the numerous regulations created by administrative agencies (such as the U.S. Food and Drug Administration).

1–3a The Common Law Tradition

Because of our colonial heritage, much of American law is based on the English legal system. A knowledge of this tradition is necessary to understand the nature of our legal system today.

Early English Courts of Law In 1066, the Normans conquered England. William the Conqueror and his successors began the process of unifying the country under their rule. One of the means they used to this end was the establishment of the king's courts, or *curiae regis.* Before the Norman Conquest, disputes had been settled according to the local legal customs and traditions in various regions of the country. The king's courts sought to establish a uniform set of customs for the whole country. The body of rules that evolved in these courts was the beginning of the **common law**—a body of general rules that prescribed social conduct and was applied throughout the entire English realm.

common law
The body of law developed from custom or judicial decisions in English and U.S. courts.

Courts developed the common law rules from the principles behind the decisions in actual legal disputes. Judges attempted to be consistent. When possible, they based their decisions on the principles suggested by earlier cases. They sought to decide similar cases in a similar way. They considered new cases with care because they knew that their decisions would make new law. Each interpretation became part of the law on the subject and served as a legal **precedent** (a guide for future decisions). Later cases that involved similar legal principles or facts could be decided with reference to that precedent.

precedent
A court decision that furnishes an example or authority for deciding subsequent cases involving identical or similar facts.

Stare Decisis The practice of deciding new cases with reference to former decisions, or precedents, eventually became a cornerstone of the English and American judicial systems. It forms a doctrine called *stare decisis* (pronounced *ster*-ay dih-*si*-ses), which means "to stand on decided cases." Under this doctrine, judges are obligated to follow the precedents established within their jurisdictions.

stare decisis
A doctrine of the courts under which judges are obligated to follow the precedents established within their jurisdictions.

The doctrine of *stare decisis* performs many useful functions. It helps the courts to be more efficient, because if other courts have carefully reasoned through a similar case, their legal reasoning and opinions can serve as guides. *Stare decisis* also makes the law more stable and predictable, because if the law on a given subject is well settled, someone bringing an **action** usually can rely on the court to make a decision based on what the law has been.

action
A proceeding by one person against another in a court to obtain the enforcement or protection of a right, the redress or prevention of a wrong, or the punishment of a public offense.

Often, a court will depart from the rule of precedent if it decides that the precedent should no longer be followed. If a court decides that a precedent is simply incorrect or that technological or social changes have rendered the precedent inapplicable, the court might rule contrary to the precedent. Cases that overturn precedent often receive a great deal of publicity.

Sometimes, there is no precedent on which to base a decision, or there are conflicting precedents. In these situations, courts may consider a number of factors. Judges may consider legal principles and policies underlying previous court decisions. They also may take into account existing statutes, fairness, social values and customs, public policy, and data and concepts drawn from the social sciences. Which of these sources is chosen or receives the greatest emphasis will depend on the nature of the case being considered and the particular judge hearing the case.

remedy
The relief given to innocent parties, by law or by contract, to enforce a right or to prevent or compensate for a wrong.

damages
Money sought as a remedy for a harm suffered.

cause of action
A situation or state of facts that gives a person a right to initiate a judicial proceeding.

injunction
A court decree ordering a person to do or to refrain from doing a certain act.

Equity A person brings a case to a court of law seeking a **remedy**, or relief from a wrong. Usually, that remedy is **damages**—the payment of money. `EXAMPLE 1.1` Elena is injured because of Rowan's wrongdoing. If Elena files a lawsuit and is successful, a court can order Rowan to compensate Elena for the harm by paying her a certain amount of money (damages). The compensation is Elena's remedy. ◄

Money may not be enough to make the situation right, however. *Equity* is that branch of law, founded in justice and fair dealing, that seeks to supply a fairer and more adequate remedy than monetary damages.

Early History In medieval England, when individuals did not have a **cause of action** through which they could obtain an adequate remedy in a court of law, they petitioned the king for relief. Most of these petitions were decided by an adviser to the king, called the *chancellor*. The chancellor was said to be the "keeper of the king's conscience." When the chancellor thought that the claim was a fair one, new and unique remedies were granted. In this way, a body of chancery rules and remedies came into being.

Courts of Equity and Law Eventually, formal chancery courts were established. These became known as *courts of equity*, granting *remedies in equity*. Thus, two distinct court systems—courts of law and courts of equity—were created, each having a different set of judges and a different set of remedies.

A court of law could grant only damages as a remedy. A court of equity, however, could order a party to perform what was promised. A court of equity could also issue an **injunction** to direct a party to do or not to do a particular act. In certain cases involving contracts, when the legal remedy of the payment of money for damages was unavailable or inadequate, a court of equity might have allowed for the cancellation of the contract so that the parties would be returned to the positions that they held before the contract's formation.

Today, in most states, the courts of law and equity are merged. Thus, the distinction between the two courts has largely disappeared. A court may now grant both legal and equitable remedies in the same case. Yet the merging of law and equity does not diminish the importance of distinguishing legal remedies from equitable remedies. To request the proper remedy, one must know what remedies are available for specific kinds of harms suffered.

Real-World Case Example

Experience Hendrix, LLC, owns trademarks—including the name "Hendrix"—that it uses to sell and license merchandise related to the famous musician, Jimi Hendrix. Andrew Pitsicalis owns, or has licenses to use, photos and other art depicting Hendrix. Pitsicalis did business through his Web sites, hendrixlicensing.com and hendrixart work.com. Alleging trademark infringement, Experience Hendrix filed a suit in a federal court against Pitsicalis. From a judgment in Experience Hendrix's favor, both parties appealed.

Could Experience Hendrix obtain both an injunction and damages? Yes. In a 2014 decision, *Experience Hendrix, LLC v. Hendrixlicensing.com, Ltd.*, the U.S. Court of Appeals for the Ninth Circuit affirmed that Pitsicalis infringed the "Hendrix" trademark. Pitsicalis defended his use of the mark as *nominative fair use*—which is a defense that applies when a defendant uses a plaintiff's mark to describe the plaintiff's product. The court rejected this defense, however, concluding that Pitsicalis used "Hendrix" to sell his own products, not to refer to Experience Hendrix's products. The court issued an injunction prohibiting Pitsicalis from using "Hendrix" in his business and domain names. As for the damages, evidence showed a "significant" decline in Experience Hendrix's revenue during the period of Pitsicalis's infringing conduct.

The Common Law Today The body of law that was first developed in England is still used today in the United States. It consists of the rules of law announced in court decisions, including court interpretations of constitutional provisions, of statutes enacted by legislatures, and of regulations created by administrative agencies. Today, this body of law is referred to variously as the common law, judge-made law, and **case law.**

The common law governs all areas not covered by *statutory law,* which, as will be discussed shortly, generally consists of laws enacted by state legislatures and, at the federal level, by Congress. The body of statutory law has expanded greatly since the founding of this nation. This expansion has resulted in a reduction in the scope and applicability of the common law. Nonetheless, the common law remains a significant source of legal authority. Even when legislation has been substituted for common law principles, courts often rely on the common law as a guide to interpreting the legislation, on the theory that the people who drafted the statute intended to codify an existing common law rule.

case law
Rules of law announced in court decisions.

1–3b Constitutional Law

The federal government and the states have separate constitutions that set forth the general organization, powers, and limits of their governments. The U.S. Constitution is the supreme law of the land. A law in violation of the Constitution, no matter what its source, will be declared unconstitutional and will not be enforced.

The Tenth Amendment to the U.S. Constitution, which defines the powers and limitations of the federal government, reserves all powers not granted to the federal government to the states. Unless they conflict with the U.S. Constitution, state constitutions are supreme within their respective borders. The complete text of the U.S. Constitution is presented in Appendix A.

LEARNING OUTCOME 3
Identify the supreme law of the land.

HIGHLIGHTING THE POINT

Congress enacts a law prohibiting businesses engaged in interstate commerce from refusing to deal with the members of minority groups. Later, a state legislature enacts a law allowing businesses in the state to decline to deal with members of minority groups. Jill, a member of a minority, files a lawsuit against the state to stop the enforcement of this new state law. Jill explains that the commerce clause of the U.S. Constitution gives Congress the authority to regulate businesses involved in interstate commerce.

Is the state law valid? No. The U.S. Constitution is the supreme law of the land. A law in violation of the Constitution will be declared unconstitutional. The state law is in violation because it attempts to regulate an area over which the Constitution gives authority to the federal government (as well as infringing on some persons' constitutional rights). **Can the court grant Jill the remedy that she requests?** Yes. The court can order the state to stop its enforcement of the law.

1–3c Statutory Law

statutory law
Laws enacted by a legislative body.

Statutes enacted by Congress and the various state legislative bodies make up another source of law, which is generally referred to as **statutory law.** The statutory law of the United States also includes the ordinances passed by cities and counties. None of these can violate the U.S. Constitution or the relevant state constitution.

Today, legislative bodies and regulatory agencies assume an ever-increasing share of lawmaking. Much of the work of modern courts consists of interpreting what the rulemakers meant when a law was passed and applying the law to a present set of facts.

Uniform Laws No two states in the United States have identical statutes, constitutions, and case law. In other words, state laws differ from state to state. The differences among state laws were even more notable in the 1800s, when conflicting state statutes frequently made the rapidly developing trade and commerce among the states very difficult. To counter these problems, a group of legal scholars and lawyers formed the National Conference of Commissioners on Uniform State Laws (NCCUSL) in 1892 to draft uniform statutes for adoption by the states. The NCCUSL still exists today and continues to issue uniform statutes.

Adoption of a uniform law is a state matter. Furthermore, a state may reject all or part of the statute or rewrite it as the state legislature wishes. Hence, even when a uniform law is said to have been adopted in many states, those states' laws may not be entirely "uniform." Once adopted by a state, a uniform act becomes a part of the statutory law of that state.

The Uniform Commercial Code (UCC) The Uniform Commercial Code (UCC), which was created through the joint efforts of the NCCUSL and the American Law Institute, was issued in 1952. The UCC has been adopted in forty-nine states, the District of Columbia, and the Virgin Islands. Louisiana has adopted Articles 1, 3, 4, 5, 7, 8, and 9. The UCC facilitates commerce among the states by providing a uniform, yet flexible, set of rules governing commercial transactions. The UCC assures businesspersons that their contracts, if validly entered into, will be enforced.

1–3d Administrative Law

administrative law
A body of law in the form of rules, orders, and decisions created by administrative agencies in order to carry out their duties and responsibilities.

Administrative law consists of the rules, orders, and decisions of administrative agencies (government bodies, such as departments, commissions, and boards, charged by Congress or a state legislature with carrying out the terms of particular laws). Regulations issued by various administrative agencies affect virtually every aspect of a business's operation, including capital structure and financing, hiring and firing procedures, relations with employees and unions, and the way a firm manufactures and markets its products.

1–4 Civil Law versus Criminal Law

The huge body of the law is broken down into several classifications. One important classification divides law into *civil law* and *criminal law.*

civil law
The branch of law dealing with the definition and enforcement of all private and public rights, as opposed to criminal matters.

Civil law spells out the rights and duties that exist between persons and between citizens and their governments (*excluding* the duty not to commit crimes). In a civil case, one party (sometimes the government) tries to make the other party comply with a duty or pay for the damage caused by a failure to do so. Contract law is part of civil law. **EXAMPLE 1.2** If Craig fails to perform a contract with Mary, she may bring a lawsuit against Craig. The purpose of the lawsuit will be either to compel

Craig to perform as promised or, more commonly, to obtain monetary damages for Craig's failure to perform.◄

Criminal law has to do with a wrong committed against the public as a whole. Criminal acts are prohibited by local, state, or federal government statutes. In a criminal case, the government seeks to impose a penalty (a monetary penalty and/or imprisonment) on an allegedly guilty person.

criminal law
Law that governs and defines those actions that are crimes and that subject the convicted offender to punishment imposed by the government.

1–5 NATIONAL LAW AROUND THE WORLD

The common law system of England and the United States is one of the major legal systems of today's world. Generally, countries that were once colonies of Great Britain retained their English common law heritage after they achieved their independence. Today, common law systems exist in Australia, Canada, India, Ireland, and New Zealand.

In contrast to Great Britain and the other common law countries, most European nations base their legal systems on Roman civil law, or "code law." The term *civil law,* as used here, does not refer to civil as opposed to criminal law. It refers to *codified* law—an ordered grouping of legal principles enacted into law by a legislature or governing body.

In a **civil law system**, the primary source of law is a statutory code. Case precedents are not judicially binding, as they are in a common law system. This is not to say that precedents are unimportant in a civil law system. On the contrary, judges in such systems commonly refer to previous decisions as sources of legal guidance. The difference is that judges in a civil law system are not bound by precedent. The doctrine of *stare decisis* does not apply.

Today, the civil law system is followed in most of the continental European countries, as well as in the African, Asian, and Latin American countries that were once colonies of the continental European nations. In the United States, Louisiana, because of its historical ties to France, has a civil law system.

LEARNING OUTCOME 4
Explain the difference between our legal system and the legal systems of other nations.

civil law system
A system of law derived from that of the Roman Empire and based on a code rather than case law.

1–6 INTERNATIONAL LAW

International law can be defined as a body of written and unwritten laws observed by independent nations in their relations with other nations. It governs the acts of individuals as well as governments. International customs and treaties are generally considered to be two of the most important sources of international law.

The key difference between *national law* (the law of a particular nation) and international law is the fact that national law can be enforced by government authorities. What government can enforce international law, however? By definition, a *nation* is a sovereign entity, which means that there is no higher authority to which that nation must submit. If a nation violates an international law, the most that other countries or international organizations can do (if persuasive tactics fail) is resort to coercive actions against the violating nation. Coercive actions range from severance of diplomatic relations and boycotts to, as a last resort, war.

In essence, international law is the result of centuries-old attempts to reconcile the traditional need of each nation to be the final authority over its own affairs with the desire of nations to benefit economically from trade and harmonious relations with one another. Although no sovereign nation can be compelled to obey a law external to itself, nations can and do voluntarily agree to be governed in certain respects by international law for the purpose of facilitating international trade and commerce, as well as for civilized discourse.

international law
The law that governs relations among nations.

ANSWERING THE LEGAL PROBLEM

In the legal problem set out at the beginning of this chapter, a group of automakers files a suit against the state of California. They seek to prevent the enforcement of a state law that sets carbon dioxide emission standards for automobiles. They claim that a federal statute already sets such standards.

A **Is a legal remedy or an equitable remedy being sought here?** The automakers are seeking to have a court direct California not to enforce its carbon dioxide emission standards. This is an equitable remedy, not the legal remedy of payment of money for damages. **What is the primary source of law at the center of this dispute?** This problem involves a law passed by the California legislature and a federal statute (which, of course, was passed by the U.S. Congress). Thus, the primary source of law at issue is statutory law.

LINKING BUSINESS LAW to Your Career

CONSULTING AN EXPERT FOR ADVICE

Whether you own a business or work for one, you will face many issues that touch on subjects about which you know little. You are more likely to lack knowledge outside your area of expertise, but even within your career specialty, you cannot know everything. Not every manager is aware of all the information needed to manage a business. It is therefore necessary for you to know when to ask for advice from experts.

With respect to the law, as we point out in the text, it is important that you know enough to realize when to consult a lawyer. In some situations, you may know enough about the law to prevent a potential legal dispute simply by taking the appropriate action. In other circumstances, however, the best alternative will be to seek outside counsel or to recommend that your employer do so.

Why Consult a Legal Expert?

It is not possible for a businessperson to keep up with the variety of statutes, rules, and regulations that affect the conduct of business in the United States. This problem only gets worse with laws that concern doing business on a global scale. It is possible to break a law without knowing that a law has been broken.

The general standard for compliance with the law is "good faith," but this is not an excuse for a failure to seek an expert's advice when it is warranted. At any time, an issue may arise that can only be resolved with special expertise. When your business's reputation and profits are on the line, there is no substitute for the right advice.

How Can You Find an Attorney?

To choose an attorney for an issue that affects your employer's business, first ask for your employer's recommendations. There may be an advocate who works for your organization or with whom your employer consults on a regular basis.

To find an attorney for a question that concerns your own business, obtain the recommendations of your friends, relatives, or business associates who have had long-standing relationships with their attorneys.

Other sources of referrals include your local or state bar association and online directories.

TERMS AND CONCEPTS FOR REVIEW

action 5

administrative law 8

breach 3

case law 7

cause of action 6

civil law 8

civil law system 9

common law 5

criminal law 9

damages 6   law 2   remedy 6

injunction 6   lawsuit 3   *stare decisis* 5

international law 9   precedent 5   statutory law 8

CHAPTER SUMMARY—INTRODUCTION TO THE LAW AND OUR LEGAL SYSTEM

LEARNING OUTCOME	
1	**Answer the question "What is law?"** Definitions of law vary, but they are all based on the observation that law consists of enforceable rules governing relationships among individuals and between individuals and their society.
2	**List the major sources of law in our legal system.** The common law originated in medieval England with the creation of the king's courts. It consists of past judicial decisions and reasoning, and involves the application of the doctrine of *stare decisis*—the rule of precedent—in deciding cases. Common law governs all areas not covered by statutory law. Constitutional law is the law expressed in the U.S. Constitution and the various state constitutions.
	Statutory law consists of laws or ordinances created by federal, state, or local legislatures and governing bodies. Uniform statutes, when adopted by a state, become statutory law in that state. Administrative law is the branch of law concerned with the power and actions of administrative agencies at all levels of government.
3	**Identify the supreme law of the land.** The U.S. Constitution is the supreme law of the land. State constitutions are supreme within state borders to the extent that they do not violate a clause of the U.S. Constitution or a federal law. No federal, state, or local statute or ordinance can violate the U.S. Constitution or the relevant state constitution.
4	**Explain the difference between our legal system and the legal systems of other nations.** The U. S. common law system originated in England. It has been adopted by the United States and other former colonies of Great Britain, including Australia, Canada, India, Ireland, and New Zealand.
	The civil law system is a legal system in which the primary source of law is a statutory code—an ordered grouping of legal principles enacted into law by a legislature or governing body. Precedents are not binding in a civil law system. Most of the continental European countries have a civil law system, as do those African, Asian, and Latin American nations that were once colonies of the continental European countries.

ISSUE SPOTTERS

Check your answers to the *Issue Spotters* against the answers provided in Appendix C at the end of this text.

1. Under what circumstances might a judge rely on case law to determine the intent and purpose of a statute? (See *Sources of American Law.*)

2. The First Amendment of the U.S. Constitution protects the free exercise of religion. A state legislature enacts a law that outlaws all religions that do not derive from the Judeo-Christian tradition. Is this state law valid? Why or why not? (See *Sources of American Law.*)

USING BUSINESS LAW

1–1. Remedies. Arthur Rabe is suing Xavier Sanchez for breaching a contract in which Sanchez promised to sell Rabe a Van Gogh painting for $150,000. (See *Sources of American Law.*)

1. If Rabe wants Sanchez to perform the contract as promised, what type of remedy should Rabe seek?
2. Sanchez fraudulently misrepresented the painting as an original when in fact it is a copy. What type of remedy should Rabe seek?

1–2. *Stare Decisis.* Courts can depart from the rule of precedent and change the common law. For example, providing separate public educational facilities for whites and blacks was once legal, but the United States Supreme Court overturned this practice. Should judges have the same authority to overrule a statute? Should they be able to overturn an administrative rule? Explain. (See *Sources of American Law.*)

REAL-WORLD CASE PROBLEMS

1–3. Role of Law. Otto May, Jr., a pipefitter for Chrysler Group, LLC, was the target of racist, homophobic, and anti-Semitic remarks. He received death threats, his bike and car tires were punctured, and someone poured sugar into the gas tank of his car. A dead bird was placed at his workstation wrapped in toilet paper to look like a member of the Ku Klux Klan. Chrysler documented and investigated the incidents. Records were checked to determine who was in the building when the incidents occurred, the graffiti handwriting was examined, and employees were reminded that harassment was not acceptable. What role might the law play in these circumstances? Discuss. [*May v. Chrysler Group, LLC,* 716 F.3d 963 (7th Cir. 2013)] (See *Business Activities and the Legal Environment.*)

1–4. Constitutional Law. Under a Massachusetts statute, large wineries could sell their products through wholesalers or to consumers directly, but not both. Small wineries could use both methods. Family Winemakers of California filed a suit against the state, arguing that this restriction gave small wineries a competitive advantage in violation of the U.S. Constitution. Which source of law takes priority, and why? [*Family Winemakers of California v. Jenkins,* 592 F.3d 1 (1st Cir. 2010)] (See *Sources of American Law.*)

1–5. Law around the World. Karen Goldberg's husband was killed in a terrorist bombing in Israel. She filed a suit in a U.S. federal court against UBS AG, a Switzerland-based company. She claimed that UBS had aided in her husband's killing because it had provided services to the terrorists. UBS argued that the case should be transferred to another country. The United States has a common law system. Other nations have civil law systems. What are the key differences between these systems? [*Goldberg v. UBS AG,* 690 F.Supp.2d 92 (2010)] (See *National Law around the World.*)

1–6. The Common Law. AOL mistakenly made public personal information about 650,000 of its members. The members filed a suit, alleging violations of California law. AOL asked the court to dismiss the suit on the basis of a *forum-selection clause* in its member agreement that requires members to settle their disputes in Virginia courts. Under a decision of the United States Supreme Court, a forum-selection clause is unenforceable if its enforcement would violate a strong public policy of the forum in which the suit is brought. California courts have ruled the AOL clause violates a strong public policy. If the court applies the doctrine of *stare decisis,* will it dismiss the suit? Explain. [*Doe 1 v. AOL, LLC,* 552 F.3d 1077 (9th Cir. 2009)] (See *Sources of American Law.*)

ETHICAL QUESTIONS

1–7. Anticipation of Legal Problems. Should legal problems be anticipated? Why and why not? (See *Business Activities and the Legal Environment.*)

1–8. Good Faith. Good faith is a concept that applies in most, if not all, areas of the law. Persons generally are expected to act in good faith, which means being honest and observing reasonable commercial standards of fair dealing. Those who do not act in good faith are often considered to be in violation of the law. Why should good faith determine whether an act is legal or illegal? (See *Sources of American Law.*)

Chapter 1—Work Set

TRUE-FALSE QUESTIONS

_____ 1. Law consists of enforceable rules governing relationships among individuals and between individuals and their society.

_____ 2. *Stare decisis* refers to the practice of deciding new cases with reference to previous decisions.

_____ 3. The doctrine of *stare decisis* illustrates how unpredictable the law can be.

_____ 4. *Common law* is a term that normally refers to the body of law consisting of rules of law announced in court decisions.

_____ 5. Statutes are a primary source of law.

_____ 6. Administrative rules and regulations have virtually no effect on the operation of a business.

_____ 7. Each state's constitution is supreme within that state's borders even if it conflicts with the U.S. Constitution.

_____ 8. The Uniform Commercial Code was enacted by Congress for adoption by the states.

_____ 9. In most states, the same courts can grant both legal and equitable remedies.

MULTIPLE-CHOICE QUESTIONS

_____ 1. The doctrine of *stare decisis* performs many useful functions, including

a. efficiency.
b. uniformity.
c. stability.
d. all of the above.

_____ 2. In addition to case law, when making decisions, courts sometimes consider other sources of law, including

a. the U.S. Constitution.
b. state constitutions.
c. administrative agency rules and regulations.
d. all of the above.

_____ 3. Which of the following is a CORRECT statement about the distinction between law and equity?

a. Equity involves remedies different from those available at law.
b. Most states maintain separate courts of law and equity.
c. Damages may be awarded only in actions in equity.
d. None of the above.

_____ 4. Under the doctrine of *stare decisis*, a judge compares the facts in a case with facts in

a. another case.
b. a hypothetical case.
c. the arguments of the parties involved in the case.
d. none of the above.

_____ 5. To learn about the coverage of a statute and how the statute is applied, a person must

a. only read the statute.
b. only see how courts in his or her jurisdiction have interpreted the statute.
c. read the statute and see how courts in his or her jurisdiction have interpreted it.
d. none of the above.

_____ 6. Our common law system involves the application of legal principles applied in earlier cases

    a. with different facts.

    b. with similar facts.

    c. whether or not the facts are similar.

    d. none of the above.

_____ 7. The statutory law of the United States includes

    a. the statutes enacted by Congress and state legislatures.

    b. the rules, orders, and decisions of administrative agencies.

    c. both the statutes enacted by Congress and state legislatures and the rules, orders, and decisions of administrative agencies.

    d. none of the above.

_____ 8. The U.S. Constitution takes precedence over

    a. a provision in a state constitution or statute only.

    b. a state supreme court decision only.

    c. a state constitution, statute, or court decision.

    d. none of the above.

_____ 9. Civil law concerns

    a. duties that exist between persons or between citizens and governments.

    b. wrongs committed against the public as a whole.

    c. both a and b.

    d. none of the above.

_____ 10. In a civil law system, the primary source of law is

    a. case law.

    b. the decisions of administrative agencies.

    c. a statutory code.

    d. none of the above.

 ANSWERING MORE LEGAL PROBLEMS

1. Dark Brew and Sparkling Ale are competitors in the microbrewing industry. To market their competing wares, they use Facebook, Twitter, and other social media. A dispute arises between these parties over the statements each makes about the other through these sites. Dark Brew files a suit against Sparkling Ale. The parties argue their respective sides of the dispute, each citing earlier cases that appear to favor their contentions. Each party asks the court to consider the principles of law established in these cases to make a decision in this case.

    What is the term for these former decisions? Which decisions, if any, is the court obligated to follow? The earlier cases are known as _____. Later cases that involve similar principles or facts are decided with reference to those _____. Courts are obligated to follow the _____ established within their _____. The doctrine attempts to harmonize the results in cases with _____ facts. In other words, the objective is to decide similar cases in a similar way.

2. In Dark Brew and Sparkling Ale's case, the court follows a doctrine that requires it to review the rules of law established by other courts.

    What is the term for the doctrine under which a court reviews the principles suggested by the decisions of other courts in earlier cases? What are the advantages of this practice? The practice of deciding new cases by referring to earlier court decisions is known as the doctrine of _____ _____. This practice is a _____ of the U.S. judicial system. The reasoning in the other courts' opinions can serve as a guide, allowing a court reviewing the cases to be more _____. When the law on a subject is well settled, the application of this doctrine makes the law more _____.

ETHICS IN BUSINESS

2

FACING A LEGAL PROBLEM

The sales of some of Golden West's products are at an all-time low. Golden West sets up Four Oaks, a new company, and convinces employees involved with the poor-selling products to transfer their retirement benefits to Four Oaks. Golden West expects Four Oaks to fail within two years.

Q Would it be legal for Golden West to keep secret its expectations for Four Oaks from the employees? Would it be ethical for the firm to do so?

LEARNING OUTCOMES

The five Learning Outcomes below are designed to help improve your understanding of the chapter. After reading this chapter, you should be able to:

❶ Define business ethics, and explain its relationship to personal ethics.

❷ State how businesspersons can discourage unethical behavior.

❸ Explain the relationship between law and ethics.

❹ Compare and contrast duty-based ethics and utilitarian ethics.

❺ Identify examples of ethical problems in the global context.

One of the most complex issues that businesspersons and corporations face is ethics. Ethics is not as well defined as the law, and yet it can have a tremendous impact on a firm's finances and reputation. Consider, for instance, the experience of the Chick-fil-A restaurant chain in 2012, when its chief operating officer made several statements about the company's commitment to supporting traditional marriage. Opponents of same-sex marriage held support rallies, while supporters of same-sex marriage held "kiss-ins" at local Chick-fil-A restaurants. Today, Chick-fil-A no longer sponsors charities that discriminate against same-sex couples or those who identify themselves as gay, lesbian, bisexual, or transgendered. Even though Chick-fil-A was not accused of violating any laws, its actions raised questions about the effect of corporate ethics on profit.

Business ethics cannot be taken lightly. To help you gain a better understanding of business ethics, this chapter examines its definitions, its philosophical bases, and its application to today's global business situations.

2–1 THE IMPORTANCE OF BUSINESS ETHICS

Before we look at business ethics, we need to discuss what is meant by ethics generally. **Ethics** can be defined as the study of what constitutes right or wrong behavior. It is the branch of philosophy that focuses on morality and the way in which moral principles are derived or the way in which a given set of moral principles applies to conduct in daily life. Ethics has to do with questions relating to the fairness, justness, rightness, or wrongness of an action. What is fair? What is just? What is the right thing to do in this situation? These are essentially ethical questions.

ethics
Moral principles and values applied to social behavior.

LEARNING OUTCOME 1

Define business ethics, and define its relationship to personal ethics.

2–1a What Is Business Ethics?

Business ethics focuses on what constitutes right or wrong behavior in the business world and on how moral and ethical principles are applied by businesspersons to situations that arise in their daily activities in the workplace. Note that business ethics is not a separate *kind* of ethics. The ethical standards that guide our behavior as, say, mothers, fathers, or students apply equally well to our activities as businesspersons. Business decision makers, though, often must address more complex ethical issues and conflicts in the workplace than they do in their personal lives.

business ethics
A consensus of what constitutes right or wrong behavior in the world of business and how moral principles are applied by businesspersons.

2–1b Why Is Business Ethics Important?

A keen and in-depth understanding and application of business ethics are important to the long-run viability of a corporation. A thorough knowledge of business ethics is also important to the well-being of the individual officers and directors of the corporation, as well as to the welfare of the firm's employees. Certainly, corporate decisions and activities can significantly affect not only those who own and operate the company but also such groups as suppliers, the community, and society as a whole.

 ## 2–2 SETTING THE RIGHT ETHICAL TONE

LEARNING OUTCOME 2

State how businesspersons can discourage unethical behavior.

Many unethical business decisions are made simply because they *can* be made. In other words, the decision makers have the opportunity to make such decisions and are not too concerned about being seriously sanctioned for their unethical actions. Perhaps one of the most difficult challenges for business leaders today is to create the right "ethical tone" in their workplaces so as to deter unethical conduct.

2–2a The Importance of Ethical Leadership

Talking about ethical business decision making means nothing if management does not set standards. Moreover, managers must apply those standards to themselves and to the employees of the company.

One of the most important factors in creating and maintaining an ethical workplace is the attitude of top management. Managers who are not totally committed to maintaining an ethical workplace will rarely succeed in creating one. Employees take their cues from management. If a firm's managers do not violate obvious ethical norms in their business dealings, employees will be likely to follow that example. In contrast, if managers act unethically, employees will see no reason not to do so themselves. **EXAMPLE 2.1** Janice works at Granite Hardware. If Janice observes her manager cheating on his expense account, Janice quickly understands that such behavior is acceptable. ◄

2–2b Ethical Codes of Conduct

One of the most effective ways of setting the tone of ethical behavior within an organization is to create an ethical code of conduct. A well-written code of ethics explicitly states a company's ethical priorities.

For an ethical code to be effective, its provisions must be clearly communicated to employees. Most large companies have implemented ethics training programs in which management has face-to-face discussions with employees about the firm's policies and the importance of ethical conduct. Some firms hold periodic ethics seminars, during which employees can openly discuss any ethical problems that they may be experiencing and how the firm's ethical policies apply to those specific problems.

2–2c Corporate Compliance Programs

In large corporations, ethical codes of conduct are usually just one part of a comprehensive corporate compliance program. Other components of such a program include a corporation's ethics committee, ethical training programs, and internal audits to monitor compliance with applicable laws and the company's standards of ethical conduct.

To be effective, especially in large corporations, a compliance program must be integrated throughout the firm. Ethical policies and programs need to be coordinated and monitored by a committee that is separate from various corporate departments. Otherwise, unethical behavior in one department can easily escape the attention of those in control of the corporation and the corporate officials responsible for implementing and monitoring the company's compliance program.

2–2d Conflicts and Trade-offs

Firms have implied ethical (and legal) duties to a number of groups, including shareholders and employees. Because these duties may conflict, management is constantly faced with ethical trade-offs.

When a company decides to reduce costs by downsizing and restructuring, it may benefit shareholders, but it will harm those employees who are laid off or fired. When downsizing occurs, which employees should be laid off first? Cost-cutting considerations might dictate firing the most senior employees, who have had yearly raises, and retaining less senior employees, whose salaries are much lower. A company does not necessarily act illegally when it does so.

Yet the decision to be made by management clearly involves an important ethical question: Which group's interests—those of the shareholders or those of employees who have been loyal to the firm for a long period of time—should take priority in this situation?

 # 2–3 The Sarbanes-Oxley Act

Congress enacted the Sarbanes-Oxley Act to help reduce corporate fraud and unethical management decisions. Among other things, the act calls for a greater degree of government oversight of public accounting practices. To this end, the act created the Public Company Accounting Oversight Board. Generally, the duties of the board are as follows:

1. To oversee the audit of companies, or issuers, whose securities are sold to public investors in order to protect the interests of investors and the public interest.

2. To register public accounting firms that prepare audit reports for issuers.

The board also establishes standards relating to the preparation of audit reports for issuers.

To enforce compliance, the board can inspect registered public accounting firms, investigate firms that violate the act, and discipline those firms by imposing sanctions. Sanctions range from temporary or permanent suspension to civil penalties that can be as high as $15 million for intentional violations.

The Sarbanes-Oxley Act also prohibits the destruction or falsification of records with the intent to obstruct or influence a federal investigation or in relation to bankruptcy proceedings. Violation of this provision can result in a fine, imprisonment for up to twenty years, or both.

 # 2–4 Business Ethics and the Law

Today, legal compliance is regarded as a **moral minimum**—the minimum acceptable standard for ethical business behavior. Simply obeying the law does not fulfill all business ethics obligations, however. In the interests of preserving personal freedom, as well as for practical reasons, the law does not—and cannot—codify all ethical requirements. No law says, for instance, that it is illegal to tell a lie to one's family, but it may be unethical to do so.

moral minimum
The minimum degree of ethical behavior expected of a business firm.

Real-World Case Example

Rick Scott filed a lawsuit in a federal district court against Salvatore Carpanzano. Scott claimed that he had suffered a loss of about $2 million, which was in an account maintained by Carpanzano's company. Carpanzano failed to cooperate with the litigation process—he did not respond to attempts to contact him, he refused to appear before the court, and he did not finalize a settlement negotiated between the parties' attorneys. The court awarded Scott more than $6 million. Carpanzano appealed.

Did Carpanzano willfully default—that is, intentionally fail to respond to the litigation— and thereby justify the judgment against him? Yes. In a 2014 decision, *Scott v. Carpanzano,* the U.S. Court of Appeals for the Fifth Circuit affirmed the judgment. Carpanzano intentionally failed almost entirely to participate in the litigation in any way. This failure constituted a willful default. In this case, it is clear from the facts and the result that Carpanzano did not meet the minimum legal or ethical standard.

LEARNING OUTCOME 3

Explain the relationship between law and ethics.

It may seem that answering a question concerning the legality of a given action should be simple. Either something is legal or it is not. In fact, one of the major challenges businesspersons face is that the legality of a particular action is not always clear. In part, this is because there are so many laws regulating business that it is possible to violate one of them without realizing it. There are also numerous "gray areas" in the law, making it difficult to predict with certainty how a court may apply a given law to a particular action.

2–4a Laws Regulating Business

Today's business firms are subject to extensive government regulation. Nearly every action a firm undertakes—from going into business, to hiring and firing personnel, to selling products in the marketplace—is subject to statutory law and to numerous rules and regulations issued by administrative agencies. Furthermore, these rules and regulations change frequently.

Determining whether a planned action is legal thus requires that decision makers keep abreast of the law. Ignorance of the law will not excuse a business owner or manager from liability for violating a statute or regulation. Normally, large business firms have attorneys on their staffs to assist them in making key decisions. Small firms must also seek legal advice before making important business decisions because the consequences of just one violation of a regulatory rule may be costly.

2–4b "Gray Areas" in the Law

In many situations, business firms can predict with a fair amount of certainty whether a given action would be legal. In some situations, though, the legality of a particular action may be less clear. Uncertainties concerning how particular laws may apply to specific factual situations have been compounded in the cyber age. The widespread use of the Internet has given rise to legal and ethical questions in circumstances that never existed before.

In short, business decision makers need to proceed with caution and evaluate an action and its consequences from an ethical perspective. Generally, if a company can demonstrate that it acted in good faith and responsibly in the circumstances, it has a better chance of successfully defending its action.

HIGHLIGHTING THE POINT

Airway Airlines makes an online forum available to its pilots so that they can exchange ideas and information. Some Airway pilots publish on the forum a series of harassing, gender-based, false messages about Beth Jones, one of Airway's female pilots.

Could Airway be liable to Jones for any harm caused by these messages? Yes. An online forum can be considered similar to a company bulletin board, which is part of a workplace. If Airway knows about the messages and does nothing to stop them, the airline can be perceived as sending Jones the message that the harassment is acceptable. If the airline does not know about the postings or if it does attempt to stop them, however, it could argue that it is acting in good faith.

2–5 APPROACHES TO ETHICAL REASONING

Each individual, when faced with a particular ethical dilemma, engages in ethical reasoning—that is, a reasoning process in which the individual links his or her moral convictions or ethical standards to the particular situation at hand. Businesspersons do likewise when making decisions with ethical implications.

Ethical reasoning relating to business traditionally has been characterized by two fundamental approaches. One approach defines ethical behavior in terms of duty, which also implies certain rights. The other approach determines what is ethical in terms of the consequences, or outcomes, of any given action. We examine each of these approaches here.

LEARNING OUTCOME 4

Compare and contrast duty-based ethics and utilitarian ethics.

2–5a Duty-Based Ethics

Duty-based ethical standards often are derived from revealed truths, such as religious precepts. They can also be derived through philosophical reasoning.

Religion In the Judeo-Christian tradition, which is the dominant religious tradition in the United States, the Ten Commandments of the Old Testament establish fundamental rules for moral action. Other religions have their own sources of revealed truth. Religious rules generally are absolute with respect to the behavior of their adherents.

For instance, the commandment "Thou shalt not steal" is an absolute mandate for a person, such as a Jew or a Christian, who believes that the Ten Commandments reflect revealed truth. Even a benevolent motive for stealing (such as Robin Hood's) cannot justify the act, because the act itself is inherently immoral and thus wrong.

Ethical standards based on religious teachings also involve an element of *compassion*. **EXAMPLE 2.2** It might be profitable for Sun Valley Farms to lay off Lee, who is a less productive employee. If Lee would find it difficult to get employment elsewhere and his family would suffer as a result, however, this potential suffering would be given substantial weight by decision makers whose ethical standards were based on religion.◄ Compassionate treatment of others is also mandated—to a certain extent, at least—by the Golden Rule of the ancients ("Do unto others as you would have them do unto you"), which has been adopted by most religions.

Philosophy Duty-based ethical standards may also be derived solely from philosophical reasoning. The German philosopher Immanuel Kant (1724–1804), for instance, identified some general guiding principles for moral behavior based on what he believed to be the fundamental nature of human beings.

Kant held that it is rational to assume that human beings are qualitatively different from other physical objects in our world. Persons are endowed with moral integrity and the capacity to reason and conduct their affairs rationally. Therefore, their thoughts and actions should be respected. When human beings are treated merely as a means to an end, they are being regarded as the equivalent of objects and are being denied their basic humanity.

categorical imperative
An ethical framework in which an action is evaluated in terms of what would happen if everybody else in the same situation, or category, acted in the same way.

Kant believed that individuals should evaluate their actions in light of the consequences that would follow if *everyone* in society acted in the same way. This **categorical imperative** can be applied to any action. **EXAMPLE 2.3** Julie is deciding whether to cheat on an examination. If she adopts Kant's categorical imperative, she will decide not to cheat, because if everyone cheated, the examination would be meaningless.◄

The Principle of Rights Another view of duty-based ethics focuses on basic rights. The principle that human beings have certain fundamental rights, such as the rights to life, freedom, and the pursuit of happiness, is deeply embedded in Western culture.

principle of rights
The principle that human beings have certain fundamental rights. A key factor in determining whether an action is ethical is how it affects others' rights.

Those who adhere to this **principle of rights,** or "rights theory," believe that a key factor in determining whether a business decision is ethical is how that decision affects the rights of others. These others include the firm's owners, its employees, the consumers of its products or services, its suppliers, the community in which it does business, and society as a whole.

In general, rights theorists believe that the right with the strongest value in a particular circumstance takes precedence. **EXAMPLE 2.4** Murray Chemical has to decide whether to keep its Utah plant open—thereby saving the jobs of one hundred workers—or shut it down. Closing the plant will avoid contaminating a nearby river with pollutants that could endanger the health of tens of thousands of people. A rights theorist could easily choose which group to favor because the value of the right to health and well-being is obviously stronger than the basic right to work.◄

2–5b Outcome-Based Ethics: Utilitarianism

Utilitarianism is a philosophical theory developed by Jeremy Bentham (1748–1832) and then advanced, with some modifications, by John Stuart Mill (1806–1873)—both British philosophers. In contrast to duty-based ethics, utilitarianism is outcome oriented. It focuses on the consequences of an action, not on the nature of the action itself or on a set of moral values or religious beliefs.

utilitarianism
An approach to ethical reasoning in which an action is evaluated in terms of its consequences for those whom it will affect. A "good" action is one that results in the greatest good for the greatest number of people.

Those who apply utilitarian ethics believe that an action is morally correct, or "right," when, among the people it affects, it produces the greatest amount of good for the greatest number. When an action affects the majority adversely, it is morally wrong. Applying the utilitarian theory requires three steps:

1. A determination of which individuals will be affected by the action in question.

cost-benefit analysis
A decision-making technique that involves weighing the costs of a given action against the benefits of the action.

2. A **cost-benefit analysis**—an assessment of the negative and positive effects of alternative actions on these individuals.

3. A choice among alternative actions that will produce the greatest positive benefits for the greatest number of individuals.

HIGHLIGHTING THE POINT

International Foods Corporation (IFC) markets baby formula in developing countries. IFC learns that mothers in those countries often mix the formula with impure water, to make the formula go further. As a result, babies are suffering from malnutrition, diarrhea, and in some instances, even death.

Is IFC in violation of the law? No. **What is IFC's ethical responsibility in this situation?** If IFC's decision makers feel that they have an absolute duty not to harm others, then their response will be to withdraw the product from those markets. If they approach the problem from a utilitarian perspective, they will engage in a cost-benefit analysis. The cost of the action (the suffering and death of babies) will be weighed against its benefit (the availability of the formula to mothers). Having the formula available frees mothers from the task of breastfeeding and thus allows them to work to help raise their incomes and standards of living. The question in a utilitarian analysis focuses on whether the benefit outweighs the cost.

2–5c Corporate Social Responsibility

Groups concerned with employee safety, consumer protection, environmental preservation, and other causes often pressure corporations to behave responsibly with respect to these causes. That corporations have such an obligation is the concept of **corporate social responsibility.** (See this chapter's *Linking Business Law to Your Career* feature for more details on this topic.)

corporate social responsibility The idea that those who run corporations can and should act ethically and be accountable to society for their actions.

The Stakeholder Approach One view of corporate social responsibility stresses that corporations have a duty not just to shareholders but also to other groups affected by corporate decisions called stakeholders. These groups include employees, customers, creditors, suppliers, and the community. Sometimes, one of these groups may have a greater stake in a company decision than shareholders do.

EXAMPLE 2.5 To reduce labor costs without laying off its employees, Ellis, Inc., implements four-day workweeks, unpaid vacations and voluntary wage freezes, and flexible work schedules. These options can be in the best interests of many of Ellis's stakeholders, including its employees and the community in which it does business. ◄

Corporate Citizenship Another theory of social responsibility argues that corporations should promote goals that society deems worthwhile and take positive steps toward solving social problems. The idea is that business controls so much of a country's wealth and power that it should use that wealth and power in socially beneficial ways.

EXAMPLE 2.6 The Hitachi Group releases an Annual Corporate Social Responsibility Report that outlines its environmental strategy (including its attempts to reduce carbon dioxide emissions) and discusses its commitment to human rights awareness. ◄

A Way of Doing Business Corporate social responsibility attains its maximum effectiveness if it is treated as a way of doing business rather than as a special program.

The most successful activities are relevant and significant to the corporation's stakeholders.

EXAMPLE 2.7 Derek Industries is one of the world's largest diversified metals and mining companies. As a part of its business decision making, it invested more than $150 million in social projects involving healthcare, infrastructure, and education around the world. At the same time, it invested more than $300 million in environmental projects, including the rehabilitation of native species in the Amazon River Valley. ◄

2–6 BUSINESS ETHICS AND SOCIAL MEDIA

Most people think of social media simply as a way to communicate and network quickly with friends and family. Today, social media affect many areas of daily life, including the business world. As a result, businesses now face unique ethical issues with respect to all social media platforms. In particular, social media raise ethical questions in business hiring decisions.

Traditionally, to gain better insight into a job candidate, managers would ask for professional references from former employers, as well as character references from others who knew the candidate. Today, however, employers are likely to also conduct Internet searches to discover more about job candidates. Often, an online search can lead managers to several links regarding a candidate. With relative ease, managers can often view the prospective candidate's postings, photos, videos, blogs, and tweets.

Nevertheless, many people believe that judging a job candidate based on what she or he does outside the workplace is unethical. A person's personal opinions and activities should not factor into a manager's hiring decision. **EXAMPLE 2.8** After interviewing Penny for a cashier position at his country store, Parker does an online search on Penny. The search results reveal that Penny is politically active in an effort to ban off-road vehicles in a local wilderness area. An avid off-road enthusiast, Parker decides not to hire Penny. ◄

In contrast, given that so many people now use social media, some employers may decide that a candidate with no social media presence is somehow behind the times and is not a good employee choice. Some would consider this type of employer behavior to be unethical as well.

2–7 BUSINESS ETHICS ON A GLOBAL LEVEL

Given the various cultures and religions throughout the world, it should come as no surprise that frequent conflicts in ethics arise between foreign and U.S. businesspersons. In certain countries, the consumption of alcohol and specific foods is forbidden for religious reasons. Under such circumstances, it would be thoughtless and imprudent for a visiting U.S. businessperson to invite a local business contact out for a drink.

The role played by women in other countries also may present some difficult ethical problems for firms doing business internationally. Equal employment opportunity is a fundamental public policy in the United States, and Title VII of the Civil Rights Act of 1964 prohibits discrimination against women in the employment context. Some other countries, however, offer little protection for women against gender discrimination in the workplace, including sexual harassment.

2–7a Monitoring the Practices of Foreign Suppliers

Many U.S. businesses now contract with companies in developing nations to produce goods, such as shoes and clothing, because the wage rates in those nations

LEARNING OUTCOME 5

Identify examples of ethical problems in the global context.

are significantly lower than in the United States. Yet what if a foreign company exploits its workers—by hiring women and children at below-minimum-wage rates, for example, or by requiring its employees to toil long hours in a workplace full of health hazards? What if the company's supervisors routinely engage in workplace conduct that is offensive to women?

Given today's global communications network, few companies can assume that their actions in other nations will go unnoticed by "corporate watch" groups that discover and publicize unethical corporate behavior. As a result, U.S. businesses today usually take steps to avoid such adverse publicity—either by refusing to deal with certain suppliers or by making arrangements to monitor their suppliers' workplaces to make sure that the workers are not being mistreated.

2–7b The Foreign Corrupt Practices Act

Another ethical problem in international business dealings has to do with the legitimacy of certain side payments to government officials. In the United States, most contracts are formed within the private sector. In many foreign countries, however, decisions on major construction and manufacturing contracts are made by government officials because of extensive government regulation and control over trade and industry. Side payments (bribes) to government officials in exchange for favorable business contracts are not unusual in such countries, nor are they considered unethical.

In the past, U.S. corporations doing business in developing countries largely followed the saying, "When in Rome, do as the Romans do." In 1977, however, Congress passed the Foreign Corrupt Practices Act (FCPA), which prohibits U.S. businesspersons from bribing foreign officials to secure advantageous contracts.

Bribery of Foreign Officials The first part of the FCPA applies to all U.S. companies and their directors, officers, shareholders, employees, and agents. This part prohibits the bribery of most officials of foreign governments if the purpose of the payment is to get the official to act in his or her official capacity to provide business opportunities.

The FCPA does not prohibit payments made to minor officials whose duties are ministerial. (A ministerial action is a routine activity, such as the processing of paperwork with little or no discretion involved in the action.) These payments are often referred to as "grease," or facilitating payments. They are meant to speed up administrative services that might otherwise be performed at a slow pace. The act also does not prohibit payments to private foreign companies or other third parties unless the U.S. firm knows that the payments will be passed on to a foreign government in violation of the FCPA.

HIGHLIGHTING THE POINT

Joan Anderson, who is a representative for American Exports, Inc., makes a payment on American's behalf to a minor official in Nigeria to speed up an import licensing process.

Has either Anderson or her firm violated the Foreign Corrupt Practices Act? No, if the payment does not violate Nigerian law. Generally, the Foreign Corrupt Practices Act permits "grease" payments to foreign officials if such payments are lawful within the foreign country.

Accounting Requirements and Violations The second part of the FCPA is directed toward accountants, because in the past bribes were often concealed in corporate financial records. All companies must keep detailed records that "accurately and fairly" reflect their financial activities. In addition, their accounting systems must provide "reasonable assurance" that all transactions entered into by the companies are accounted for and legal. These requirements assist in detecting illegal bribes. The FCPA prohibits any person from making false statements to accountants or false entries in any record or account.

Business firms that violate the act may be fined up to $2 million. Individual officers or directors who violate the FCPA may be fined up to $100,000 (the fine cannot be paid by the company) and may be imprisoned for up to five years.

ANSWERING THE LEGAL PROBLEM

In the legal problem set out at the beginning of this chapter, Golden West wants employees involved with poor-selling products to transfer their retirement benefits to a new company, which Golden West expects to fail within two years.

A **Is it legal for Golden West to keep secret its expectations from the employees?** No. Under federal law, it is illegal for an employer that provides retirement benefits to deceive the recipients in order to save the employer money at the recipients' expense. **Is it ethical for Golden West to keep its expectations secret?** No. Although some groups, including the firm's owners and some current employees, could benefit in the short term from Golden West's actions, compliance with the law is regarded as the moral minimum.

LINKING BUSINESS LAW to Your Career

MANAGING A COMPANY'S REPUTATION

Some of you reading this text will major in accounting. Accounting is typically associated with developing balance sheets and profit-and-loss statements, but it can also provide information that helps managers do their jobs. The provision of accounting information for a company's internal use, called *managerial accounting*, helps in planning and decision making.

As a managerial accountant today, you might also use your skills to manage corporate reputations. More than 2,500 multinational companies now release large quantities of accounting information to the public.

Internal Reports
Designed for External Scrutiny

Some large companies refer to the managerial accounting information that they release to the public as corporate sustainability reports. Dow Chemical Company, for example, issues a sustainability report annually.

Other corporations call their published documents social responsibility reports. Symantec Corporation issues corporate responsibility reports to demonstrate its focus on environmental, social, and governance issues.

In its 2012 report, Symantec emphasized that the Leadership in Energy and Environmental Design (LEED) program had certified 88 percent of its facilities as environmentally friendly. LEED certification requires the achievement of high standards for energy efficiency, material usage in construction, and other environmental impacts.

Why Use Managerial Accounting to Manage Reputations?

We live in an age of information. Such sources as cable and online news networks, social media, and smartphones guarantee that any news, positive or negative, will be known throughout the world almost immediately after it happens.

Consequently, corporations want to manage their reputations by preparing and releasing company news themselves. In a world in which corporations are often blamed for anything bad that happens, managerial accounting information can be a useful counterweight.

To this end, some corporations have combined their social responsibility reports with their traditional financial accounting information. When a corporation's reputation is on the line, its future is at stake.

TERMS AND CONCEPTS FOR REVIEW

business ethics 15	cost-benefit analysis 20	principle of rights 20
categorical imperative 20	ethics 15	utilitarianism 20
corporate social responsibility 21	moral minimum 17	

CHAPTER SUMMARY—ETHICS IN BUSINESS

LEARNING OUTCOME	
1	**Define business ethics, and define its relationship to personal ethics.** Ethics can be defined as the study of what constitutes right or wrong behavior. Business ethics focuses on how personal moral and ethical principles are applied in the business context. An understanding of ethics is important to the long-term existence of a business, the well-being of its officers and directors, and the welfare of its employees and customers.
2	**State how businesspersons can discourage unethical behavior.** Managers must set and apply ethical standards to which they are committed. Employees will likely follow their example. Components of a comprehensive corporate compliance program include an ethical code of conduct, an ethics committee, training programs, and internal audits to monitor compliance. These components should be integrated throughout the firm. In making ethical trade-offs, a firm's management must consider which of the firm's constituent groups has a greater stake in the decision to be made.
3	**Explain the relationship between law and ethics.** The minimum acceptable standard for ethical business behavior is compliance with the law. The law reflects society's convictions of what constitutes right and wrong behaviors. The law has its limits, though, and some actions may be legal, yet not ethical. Because there are many laws regulating business, it is possible to violate one without realizing it, but ignorance of the law is no excuse. There are also many "gray areas," in which it can be difficult to determine the legality of an act.
4	**Compare and contrast duty-based ethics and utilitarian ethics.** Duty-based ethical standards are based on religious precepts or derived through philosophical reasoning. Religious rules can be absolute, when even a benevolent motive cannot justify an immoral act. Philosophical reasoning can lead to principles based on what is perceived to be fundamental human nature. These might include respect for others' thoughts and actions or the evaluation of an action in light of the consequences that would follow if everyone acted in the same way. Duty-based standards imply that human beings have basic rights. A key factor in determining whether a business decision is ethical is how it affects these rights.

Utilitarian ethics are outcome oriented, focusing on the consequences of an action, not its nature or a set of moral values or religious beliefs. Under this standard, an action is "right" when it produces the greatest amount of good for the greatest number of people. |

5	**Identify examples of ethical problems in the global context.** Laws governing workers in other countries have created some difficult ethical problems for U.S. sellers of goods made in those countries. A U.S. law that prohibits U.S. businesspersons from bribing foreign officials to obtain favorable business contracts also presents ethical problems in international business dealings.

ISSUE SPOTTERS

Check your answers to the *Issue Spotters* against the answers provided in Appendix C at the end of this text.

1. Mac Tools, Inc., markets a product that under some circumstances is capable of seriously injuring consumers. Does Mac have an ethical duty to remove this product from the market, even if the injuries result only from misuse? (See *Approaches to Ethical Reasoning.*)

2. Acme Corporation decides to respond to what it sees as a moral obligation to correct for past discrimination by adjusting pay differences among its employees. Does this raise an ethical conflict among Acme's employees? Between Acme and its employees? Between Acme and its shareholders? (See *Approaches to Ethical Reasoning.*)

USING BUSINESS LAW

2–1. Business Ethics. Some business ethicists maintain that whereas personal ethics has to do with right or wrong behavior, business ethics is concerned with appropriate behavior. In other words, ethical behavior in business has less to do with moral principles than with what society deems to be appropriate behavior in the business context. Do you agree with this distinction? Do personal and business ethics ever overlap? Should personal ethics play any role in business ethical decision making? (See *The Importance of Business Ethics.*)

2–2. Ethical Decision Making. Shokun Steel Co. owns many steel plants. One of its plants is much older than the others.

Equipment at that plant is outdated and inefficient, and the costs of production at the plant are twice as high as at any of Shokun's other plants. The company cannot raise the price of steel because of competition, both domestic and international. The plant is located in Twin Firs, Pennsylvania, which has a population of about 45,000, and currently employs over a thousand workers. Shokun is contemplating whether to close the plant. What factors should the firm consider in making its decision? Will the firm violate any ethical duties if it closes the plant? Analyze these questions from the two basic perspectives on ethical reasoning discussed in this chapter. (See *Approaches to Ethical Reasoning.*)

REAL-WORLD CASE PROBLEMS

2–3. Business Ethics. Stephen Glass made himself infamous as a dishonest journalist by fabricating material for more than forty articles for *The New Republic* and other publications. At the time, he was a law student at Georgetown University. Once suspicions were aroused, Glass tried to avoid detection. Later, Glass applied for admission to the California bar. The California Supreme Court denied his application, citing "numerous instances of dishonesty" during his "rehabilitation" following the exposure of his misdeeds. How do these circumstances underscore the importance of ethics? [*In re Glass*, 58 Cal.4th 500, 316 P.3d 1199 (2014)] (See *The Importance of Business Ethics.*)

2–4. Business Ethics. Mark Ramun worked as a manager for Allied Erecting and Dismantling Co., where he had a tense relationship with John Ramun, Allied's president and Mark's father. After more than ten years, Mark left Allied, taking 15,000 pages of Allied's documents (trade secrets) with him. Later, he joined Allied's competitor, Genesis Equipment & Manufacturing, Inc. Genesis soon developed a piece of equipment that incorporated design elements of Allied equipment. Who violated business ethics in these circumstances, and how? [*Allied Erecting and Dismantling Co. v. Genesis Equipment & Manufacturing, Inc.,* 2013 WL 85907 (6th Cir. 2013)] (See *The Importance of Business Ethics.*)

2–5. Ethical Misconduct. Frank Pasquale used his father's Social Security number to obtain a credit card. Later, pretending to act on behalf of his father's firm, Pasquale borrowed $350,000. When he defaulted on the loan and his father confronted him, he produced forged documents that showed the loan had been paid. Adams Associates, LLC, which held the unpaid loan, filed a suit against both Pasquales. Should the court issue a judgment against the father *and* the son? Discuss. [*Adams Associates, LLC v. Frank Pasquale Limited Partnership,* __ A.3d __ (N.J.Super A.D. 2011)] (See *Business Ethics and the Law.*)

2–6. Ethics and the Law. Prudential Insurance Co. of America has a company guideline not to change the amount of a salesperson's commission once a client has been quoted a price for insurance. Despite this principle, in order to reduce the quoted price for insurance offered to York International Corp., Prudential cut the fee that it paid to a broker. A competitive broker, Havensure, LLC, filed a suit, arguing that the reduced quote caused it to lose York as a potential customer. Is a company's violation of its own policy unethical? Is it a basis for legal liability? Explain. [*Havensure, LLC v. Prudential Insurance* Co. *of America,* 595 F.3d 312 (6th Cir. 2010)] (See *Business Ethics and the Law.*)

ETHICAL QUESTIONS

2–7. Ethical Workplace. What factors help to create an ethical workplace? (See *Setting the Right Ethical Tone.*)

2–8. Social Responsibility. Government entities spend time and money to find and destroy the labs in which methamphetamine (meth) is made, imprison meth dealers and users, treat addicts, and provide services for affected families. Meth cannot be made without ingredients that are also used in cold and allergy medications. To recoup the costs of fighting the meth epidemic, twenty counties in Arkansas filed a suit against Pfizer, Inc., which makes cold and allergy medications. What is Pfizer's ethical responsibility here, and to whom is it owed? Why? [*Ashley County, Arkansas v. Pfizer, Inc.,* 552 F.3d 659 (8th Cir. 2009)] (See *Approaches to Ethical Reasoning.*)

Chapter 2—Work Set

TRUE-FALSE QUESTIONS

_____ 1. Ethics is the study of what constitutes right and wrong behaviors.

_____ 2. A background in business ethics is as important as knowledge of specific laws.

_____ 3. The *minimum* acceptable standard for ethical behavior is compliance with the law.

_____ 4. According to utilitarianism, it does not matter how many people benefit from an act.

_____ 5. The best course for accomplishing legal and ethical behaviors is to act responsibly and in good faith.

_____ 6. The ethics of a particular act is always clear.

_____ 7. To foster ethical behavior among employees, managers should apply ethical standards to which they are committed.

_____ 8. If an act is legal, it is ethical.

_____ 9. Bribery of public officials is strictly an ethical issue.

MULTIPLE-CHOICE QUESTIONS

_____ 1. Beth is a marketing executive for Consumer Goods Company. Compared with Beth's personal actions, her business actions require the application of ethical standards that are

   a. more complex.
   b. simpler.
   c. the same.
   d. none of the above.

_____ 2. Pat, an employee of Quality Products, Inc., takes a duty-based approach to ethics. Pat believes that regardless of the consequences, he must

   a. avoid unethical behavior.
   b. conform to society's standards.
   c. place his employer's interests first.
   d. produce the greatest good for the most people.

_____ 3. Joy adopts religious ethical standards. These involve an element of

   a. compassion.
   b. cost-benefit analysis.
   c. discretion.
   d. utilitarianism.

_____ 4. Eve, an employee of Fine Sales Company, takes an outcome-based approach to ethics. Eve believes that she must

   a. avoid unethical behavior.
   b. conform to society's standards.
   c. place her employer's interests first.
   d. produce the greatest good for the most people.

_____ 5. In a debate, Ed's best criticism of utilitarianism is that it

   a. encourages unethical behavior.
   b. fosters conformance with society's standards.
   c. mandates acting in an employer's best interests.
   d. results in human costs many persons find unacceptable.

6. Ethical standards would most likely have been violated if Acme Services, Inc., represented to Best Production Company that certain services would be performed for a stated fee, but it was apparent to Acme at the time of the representation that

   a. Acme could not perform the services alone.
   b. the actual charge would be substantially higher.
   c. the actual charge would be substantially lower.
   d. the fee was a competitive bid.

7. Tina, the president of United Sales, Inc., tries to ensure that United's actions are legal and ethical. To achieve this result, the best course for Tina and United is to act in

   a. good faith.
   b. ignorance of the law.
   c. regard for the firm's shareholders only.
   d. their own self-interest.

8. Alan, an executive with Beta Corporation, follows the "principle of rights" theory. Under this theory, whether an action is ethical depends on how it affects

   a. the right determination under a cost-benefit analysis.
   b. the right of Alan to maintain his dignity.
   c. the right of Beta to make a profit.
   d. the rights of others.

9. Gamma, Inc., a U.S. corporation, makes a side payment to the minister of commerce of another country for a favorable business contract. In the United States, this payment would be considered

   a. illegal only.
   b. unethical only.
   c. illegal and unethical.
   d. none of the above.

 ANSWERING MORE LEGAL PROBLEMS

1. Carney & Deb, an accounting firm, performs a variety of tasks for its clients, including completing financial statements and tax returns. To accomplish these tasks, Carney & Deb collects personal and financial information from the clients.

   Does Carney & Deb have an ethical obligation to its clients with respect to this information? Ethics is the study of what constitutes right and wrong _____, focusing on morality and the way in which _____ principles are derived or the way in which such principles apply to conduct in daily life. Sometimes, the issues that arise concern fairness, justice, and "the right thing to do." To answer the question of the firm's ethical obligation, you should note that the confidentiality of its clients' sensitive personal and business information is at stake. The accountants have a(n) _____ duty to ensure that reasonable security precautions are taken to preserve this confidentiality and protect this information.

2. Carney & Deb can store the personal and financial information of its clients on any electronic device, including an iPhone, a flash drive, and a laptop. When Carney & Deb upgrades its storage media, the information is transferred between devices.

   What are the ethical concerns in this situation? Discuss. The _____ concerns in this situation relate to fairness, justice, "the right thing to do," personal honesty and integrity, and the duty to maintain the _____ of the clients' information. The accountants need to understand where they are putting the information, assess what the risks are of that location, and consider whether it is appropriate to put the _____ there. For example, putting sensitive information on an unencrypted flash drive would be a bad idea. When the storage media are upgraded, client confidentiality needs to be maintained. Any storage device should be sanitized, or wiped clean, of sensitive data before it is discarded.

THE COURTS AND ALTERNATIVE DISPUTE RESOLUTION

FACING A LEGAL PROBLEM

A dispute arises between Harry Koto, a resident of California, and Maria Mendez, a resident of Texas, over the ownership of the *Fairweather*, a sailboat in dry dock in San Diego, California.

Q Can a California state court exercise jurisdiction over the dispute?

LEARNING OUTCOMES

The five Learning Outcomes below are designed to help improve your understanding of the chapter. After reading this chapter, you should be able to:

1 List the basic parts of a state court system.

2 Identify when a lawsuit can be filed in a federal court.

3 Discuss the procedure of a trial.

4 Summarize the steps in a typical lawsuit.

5 Define the three basic traditional alternative methods for resolving disputes.

Every society needs to have an established method for resolving disputes. This is particularly true in the business world. Nearly every businessperson will face a lawsuit at some time in his or her career. For this reason, anyone involved in business needs to have an understanding of court systems in the United States, as well as of the various methods of dispute resolution that can be pursued outside the courts.

American law is based on numerous elements, including the following:

1. The case decisions and reasoning that form the common law.

2. Federal and state constitutions.

3. Statutes passed by federal and state legislatures—including uniform laws, such as the Uniform Commercial Code—that have been adopted by the various states.

4. Administrative law.

The function of the courts is to interpret and apply those laws.

Even though there are fifty-two court systems—one for each of the fifty states, one for the District of Columbia, plus a federal system—similarities abound. Keep in mind that the federal courts are not superior to the state courts. They are simply an independent system of courts. Both systems are examined in this chapter. The chapter concludes with an overview of some alternative methods of settling disputes, including online dispute resolution.

3–1 JURISDICTION

Jurisdiction refers either to the geographical area within which a court has the right and power to decide cases or to the right and power of a court to decide matters concerning certain persons, property, or subject matter. Before any court can hear a case, it must have jurisdiction over the person against whom the suit is brought or over the property involved in the suit, as well as jurisdiction over the subject matter.

3–1a Jurisdiction over Persons or Property

Generally, a court's power is limited to the territorial boundaries of the state in which it is located. Thus, a court can exercise personal jurisdiction (*in personam* jurisdiction) over residents of the state and anyone else within its boundaries. A

jurisdiction
The authority of a court to hear and decide a specific action.

court can also exercise jurisdiction over property (*in rem* jurisdiction) located within its boundaries.

Under a state **long arm statute**, a court can exercise jurisdiction over out-of-state defendants based on activities that took place within the state. The defendant must have had enough of a connection with the state for the court to conclude that it is fair to exercise its power over the defendant.

Courts apply a *minimum-contacts* test to determine if they can exercise jurisdiction over out-of-state corporations. The test is usually met if a corporation advertises or sells its products within the state. The test can also be met if the corporation has an ongoing business relationship with a party within the state, as shown by frequent transactions.

EXAMPLE 3.1 Allison, a Texas resident, was injured when the PowerFlex exercise machine she was using collapsed. Allison filed a lawsuit against PowerFlex in a Texas court. PowerFlex, which is headquartered in Chicago, argued that the state court lacked jurisdiction over it. Because PowerFlex sold its exercise products at many retail outlets in Texas, however, there was enough minimum contact within the state for the case to proceed.◄

3–1b Jurisdiction in Cyberspace

The Internet's capacity to bypass boundaries undercuts the traditional basis for jurisdiction. Generally, if a defendant's only connection to a state is through dealings with citizens of the state over the Internet, a "sliding-scale" standard determines when the exercise of jurisdiction is proper.

There are three types of Internet business contacts:

1. Substantial business done over the Internet (contracts and sales even using a smartphone).

2. Some interactivity through a Web site.

3. Passive advertising (such as an online ad with no interactivity).

Jurisdiction is proper for the first category, is improper for the third, and may or may not be appropriate for the second.

 3–2 THE STATE COURT SYSTEM

We turn now to the structure of state court systems. The typical state court system is made up of trial courts and appellate courts. Trial courts are exactly what their name implies—courts in which trials are held and testimony is taken. Appellate courts are courts of appeal and review. They review cases decided elsewhere.

Exhibit 3.1 shows how state court systems, as well as the federal court system, are structured. As the exhibit indicates, there are several levels of courts within state court systems:

1. State trial courts of limited jurisdiction.

2. State trial courts of general jurisdiction.

3. Appellate courts.

4. The state supreme court.

Any person who is a party to a lawsuit typically has the opportunity to plead the case before a trial court and then, if he or she loses, before at least one level of appellate courts. Finally, if a federal statute or constitutional issue is involved in the decision of the state supreme court, that decision may be further appealed to the United States Supreme Court.

long arm statute
A state statute that permits a state to exercise jurisdiction over nonresident defendants.

LEARNING OUTCOME 1

List the basic parts of a state court system.

3–2a Trial Courts

The state trial courts have either *general* or *limited* jurisdiction. Trial courts that have general jurisdiction as to subject matter may be called county, district, superior, or circuit courts. The jurisdiction of these courts is often determined by the size of the county in which the court sits. Many important cases involving businesses originate in these general trial courts.

Courts with limited jurisdiction as to subject matter are often called special inferior trial courts or minor judiciary courts. **Small claims courts** are inferior trial courts that hear only civil cases involving claims of less than a certain amount, usually $2,500. Most small claims are less than $1,000. Suits brought in small claims courts are generally conducted informally, and lawyers are not required. In a minority of states, lawyers are not even allowed to represent people in small claims courts for most purposes. Decisions of small claims courts may be appealed to a state trial court of general jurisdiction.

small claims court
A special inferior trial court in which parties litigate small claims (usually claims involving $2,500 or less).

Other courts of limited jurisdiction are domestic relations courts, local municipal courts, and probate courts. Domestic relations courts handle only divorce actions and child-custody cases. Local municipal courts mainly handle traffic cases, while probate courts handle the administration of wills and estate-settlement problems.

3–2b Appellate, or Reviewing, Courts

Every state has at least one appellate, or reviewing, court. About half of the states have intermediate appellate courts. The subject-matter jurisdiction of these courts is substantially limited to hearing appeals. Appellate courts normally examine the record of a case on appeal and determine whether the trial court committed an error. They look at questions of law and procedure, but usually not at questions of fact.

EXHIBIT 3.1   The State and Federal Court Systems

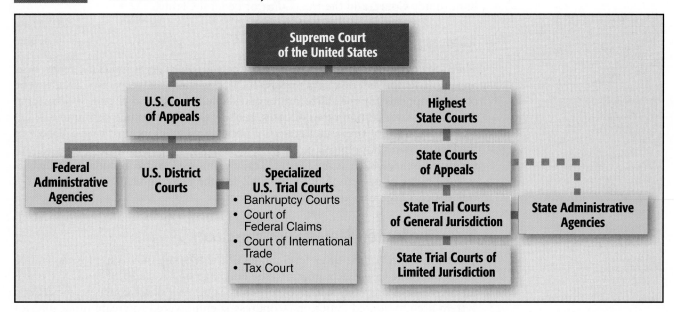

An appellate court will modify a trial court's finding of fact, however, when the finding is clearly erroneous—that is, when it is contrary to the evidence presented at trial—or when there is no evidence to support the finding. **EXAMPLE 3.2** A San Francisco trial jury finds Applied Mechanics, Inc., guilty of negligence for the harm suffered by Drew Crowston, who slipped and fell while visiting the company's manufacturing facility. No evidence was submitted to the court, however, that clearly proved the fall at the company's facility was the direct cause of Crowston's injury. A state appellate court later ruled that the trial court's verdict was erroneous. ◀

The highest appellate court in a state is usually called the supreme court but may be called by some other name. For instance, in both New York and Maryland, the highest state court is called the court of appeals. The decisions of each state's highest court on all questions of state law are final. Only when issues of federal law are involved can a state's highest court be overruled by the United States Supreme Court.

3–3 THE FEDERAL COURT SYSTEM

The federal court system is similar in many ways to most state court systems. It is a three-level model consisting of trial courts, intermediate courts of appeals, and the United States Supreme Court (see Exhibit 3.1).

3–3a U.S. District Courts

At the federal level, the United States is divided into thirteen federal judicial "circuits," and the circuits are subdivided into districts. A federal district court is the equivalent of a state trial court of general jurisdiction. There is at least one federal district court in every state. The number of judicial districts can vary over time, primarily owing to population changes and corresponding caseloads. The law now provides for ninety-four judicial districts.

U.S. district courts have original jurisdiction in federal matters. In other words, federal cases originate in district courts. There are other trial courts with original—although special (or limited)—jurisdiction, such as the U.S. Tax Court, the U.S. Bankruptcy Court, and the U.S. Court of Federal Claims.

3–3b U.S. Courts of Appeals

The U.S. courts of appeals for twelve of the thirteen federal judicial circuits hear appeals from the federal district courts located within their respective circuits. The court of appeals for the thirteenth circuit, called the federal circuit, has national jurisdiction over certain types of cases, such as those concerning patent law.

The decisions of the circuit courts of appeals are final in most cases. Appeal to the United States Supreme Court is possible, however. Appeals from federal administrative agencies, such as the Federal Trade Commission, are also made to the U.S. circuit courts of appeals. See Exhibit 3.2 for the geographical boundaries of the U.S. courts of appeals and U.S. district courts.

3–3c The United States Supreme Court

The highest level of the three-level model of the federal court system is the United States Supreme Court. According to the language of Article III of the U.S. Constitution, there is only one national Supreme Court. All other courts in the federal system are considered "inferior." Congress is empowered to create other inferior courts as it desires. The inferior courts that Congress has created include the second level in our model—the U.S. courts of appeals—as well as the district courts and any other courts of limited, or specialized, jurisdiction.

The Justices The United States Supreme Court consists of nine justices. These justices are nominated by the president of the United States and confirmed by the Senate. They (like all federal district and courts of appeals judges) receive lifetime appointments (because under Article III, they "hold their offices during Good Behavior").

How Cases Reach the Supreme Court Many people are surprised to learn that there is no absolute right of appeal to the United States Supreme Court. The Court has original, or trial court, jurisdiction in a small number of situations. In all other cases, its jurisdiction is appellate. The Court can review any case decided by any of the federal courts of appeals. It also has appellate authority over some cases decided in the state courts. Thousands of cases are filed with the Court each year, yet it hears, on average, fewer than one hundred.

Writ of *Certiorari* To bring a case before the United States Supreme Court, a party requests a **writ of *certiorari*** (pronounced *sir-she-a-rár-ee*). A writ of *certiorari* is an order issued by the Court to a lower court requiring the latter to send it the record of a case for review. Whether the Court will issue such a writ is entirely within its discretion. In no instance is the Court required to do so.

writ of *certiorari*
A writ from a higher court asking the lower court for the record of a case.

EXHIBIT 3.2   Boundaries of the U.S. Courts of Appeals and U.S. District Courts

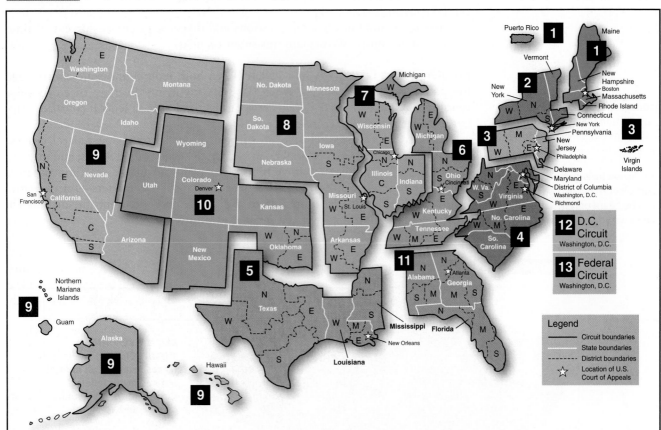

Source: Administrative Office of the United States Courts.

Rule of Four Most petitions for writs of *certiorari* are denied. A denial is not a decision on the merits of a case, nor does it indicate agreement with the lower court's opinion. Denial of the writ also has no value as a precedent. The Court will not issue a writ unless at least four justices approve. This is called the *rule of four.* Typically, only petitions that raise the possibility of important constitutional questions are granted.

3–3d Federal Court Jurisdiction

LEARNING OUTCOME 2

Identify when a lawsuit can be filed in a federal court.

The Constitution gives Congress the power to control the number and kind of inferior courts in the federal system. Except in those cases in which the Constitution gives the Supreme Court original jurisdiction (including cases involving ambassadors and controversies between states), Congress can also regulate the jurisdiction of the Supreme Court.

Federal Questions In general, federal courts have jurisdiction over cases involving federal questions. This jurisdiction arises from Article III, Section 2, of the Constitution. A **federal question** is an issue of law based, at least in part, on the Constitution, a treaty, or a federal law. Any lawsuit concerning a federal question can originate in a federal court.

federal question
A question that pertains to the U.S. Constitution, acts of Congress, or treaties. A federal question provides jurisdiction for federal courts.

Diversity of Citizenship Federal jurisdiction also extends to cases involving diversity of citizenship. **Diversity-of-citizenship** cases are those arising between (1) citizens of different states, (2) a foreign country and citizens of a state or of different states, or (3) citizens of a state and citizens or subjects of a foreign country. This jurisdiction arises from Article III, Section 2, of the Constitution as well. The amount in controversy in diversity cases must be more than $75,000 before a federal court can take jurisdiction.

Cases involving both federal questions and diversity of citizenship can also be heard in state courts. We explain this situation next.

diversity of citizenship
A basis for federal court jurisdiction over a lawsuit between citizens of different states and countries.

Exclusive versus Concurrent Jurisdiction When both federal and state courts have the power to hear a case, as is true in suits involving diversity of citizenship, **concurrent jurisdiction** exists. When cases can be tried only in federal courts or only in state courts, **exclusive jurisdiction** exists.

Federal courts have exclusive jurisdiction in cases involving federal crimes, bankruptcy, patents, and copyrights; in suits against the United States; and in some areas of admiralty law (law governing transportation on the seas and oceans). States also have exclusive jurisdiction over certain subject matters—for example, divorce and adoption. The concepts of exclusive and concurrent jurisdiction are illustrated in Exhibit 3.3.

concurrent jurisdiction
Jurisdiction that exists when two different courts have the power to hear a case.

exclusive jurisdiction
Jurisdiction that exists when a case can be heard only in a particular court or type of court.

EXHIBIT 3.3   Exclusive and Concurrent Jurisdictions

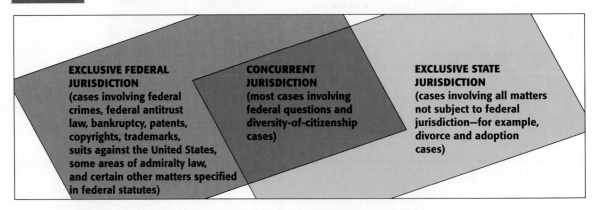

EXCLUSIVE FEDERAL JURISDICTION
(cases involving federal crimes, federal antitrust law, bankruptcy, patents, copyrights, trademarks, suits against the United States, some areas of admiralty law, and certain other matters specified in federal statutes)

CONCURRENT JURISDICTION
(most cases involving federal questions and diversity-of-citizenship cases)

EXCLUSIVE STATE JURISDICTION
(cases involving all matters not subject to federal jurisdiction—for example, divorce and adoption cases)

3–4 THE STATE COURT CASE PROCESS

Procedural law establishes the rules and standards for determining disputes in courts. The rules are complex, and they vary from court to court. There is a set of federal rules of procedure, and there are various sets of rules for state courts. In addition, procedural rules differ in criminal and civil cases. To clarify some of these procedural rules, we next follow a case through a typical state court system. The case we describe is a civil case, in which one party files a lawsuit against another party.

3–4a Standing to Sue

Before a person can bring a lawsuit before a court, the party must have **standing to sue,** or a sufficient stake in the matter to justify seeking relief through the court system. In other words, to have standing, a party must have a legally protected and tangible interest at stake in the litigation. The party bringing the lawsuit must have suffered a harm, or have been threatened by a harm, as a result of the action about which she or he has complained.

Standing to sue also requires that the controversy at issue be a *justiciable controversy*—a controversy that is real and substantial, as opposed to hypothetical or academic.

standing to sue
The requirement that an individual have a sufficient stake in a controversy before he or she can bring a lawsuit.

3–4b The Pleadings

The **pleadings** inform each party of the claims of the other and specify the issues (disputed questions) involved in the case. Pleadings remove the element of surprise from a case. They allow lawyers to gather the most persuasive evidence and to prepare better arguments, thus increasing the probability that a just and true result will be forthcoming from the trial. The pleadings include the complaint and summons (and a motion to dismiss or an answer.)

pleadings
Statements by the plaintiff and the defendant that detail the facts, charges, and defenses of a case.

Complaint A lawsuit begins when a lawyer files a **complaint** (sometimes called a petition or a declaration) with the clerk of the trial court with the appropriate jurisdiction. The party who files the complaint is known as the **plaintiff.** The party against whom a complaint is filed is the **defendant.** The complaint contains the following:

1. A statement alleging the facts necessary for the court to take jurisdiction.
2. A short statement of the facts necessary to show that the plaintiff is entitled to a remedy.
3. A statement of the remedy the plaintiff is seeking.

complaint
The pleading made by a plaintiff or a charge made by the state alleging wrongdoing on the part of the defendant.

plaintiff
A person who initiates a lawsuit.

defendant
A person against whom a lawsuit is brought.

HIGHLIGHTING THE POINT

Kevin Anderson, driving a Toyota Camry, is in an accident with Lisa Marconi, driving a Ford Focus. The accident occurs at the intersection of Wilshire Boulevard and Rodeo Drive in Beverly Hills, California. Marconi suffers personal injuries, incurring medical and hospital expenses as well as lost wages for four months. Anderson and Marconi are unable to agree on a settlement, and Marconi wants to sue Anderson.

After obtaining a lawyer, what is Marconi's next step? Marconi's suit commences with the filing of a complaint against Anderson. The complaint includes the facts that give rise to the suit and allegations concerning the defendant. Marconi's complaint may

(Continued)

state that Marconi was driving her car through a green light at the specified intersection, exercising good driving habits and reasonable care, when Anderson carelessly drove his car through a red light and into the intersection from a cross street, striking Marconi and causing personal injury and property damage. The complaint should state the relief that Marconi seeks—for example, $10,000 to cover medical bills, $9,000 to cover lost wages, and $6,000 to cover damage to her car.

Summons After the complaint has been filed, the sheriff or a deputy of the county or another person authorized by the law serves a summons and a copy of the complaint on the defendant. The *summons* notifies the defendant that he or she is required to prepare an answer to the complaint and to file a copy of the answer with both the court and the plaintiff's attorney within a specified time period (usually twenty to thirty days after the summons has been served). The summons also states that failure to answer will result in a **default judgment** for the plaintiff, meaning the plaintiff will be awarded the remedy sought in the complaint.

default judgment
A judgment entered by a court against a defendant who has failed to appear in court to answer or defend against the plaintiff's claim.

After Receipt of the Complaint and Summons Once the defendant has been served with a copy of the complaint and summons, the defendant must respond by filing a *motion to dismiss* or an *answer*. If a defendant does not respond, the court may enter a default judgment against him or her.

Motion to Dismiss A **motion to dismiss** is an allegation that even if the facts presented in the complaint are true, the defendant is not legally liable. The court may deny the motion to dismiss. If so, the judge is indicating that the plaintiff has stated a recognized cause of action—that is, if the facts are true, the plaintiff has a right to judicial relief—and the defendant is given an extension of time to file an answer. If the defendant does not do so, a judgment will normally be entered for the plaintiff.

motion to dismiss
A pleading in which a defendant admits the facts as alleged by the plaintiff but asserts that the plaintiff's claim has no basis in law.

If the court grants the motion to dismiss, the judge is saying that the plaintiff has failed to state a recognized cause of action. The plaintiff generally is given time to file an amended complaint. If the plaintiff does not file an amended complaint, a judgment will be entered against the plaintiff, who will not be allowed to bring suit on the matter again.

Answer If the defendant has chosen not to file a motion to dismiss or has filed a motion to dismiss that has been denied, then he or she must file an **answer**. This document either admits the allegations in the complaint or denies them and outlines any defenses that the defendant may have. If the defendant admits the allegations, the court will enter a judgment for the plaintiff. If the allegations are denied, the matter will proceed to trial.

answer
Procedurally, a defendant's response to a complaint.

The defendant can also use the answer to raise a *counterclaim*—any claim that he or she may have against the plaintiff arising out of the same transaction or occurrence that gave rise to the complaint. (In some circumstances, a defendant must bring up a counterclaim at this time or it will be lost, because the defendant will not be allowed to bring it up later.) In response to a counterclaim, the plaintiff can issue a *reply*.

3–4c Pretrial Motions

There are numerous procedural avenues for disposing of a case without a trial. Many of them involve one or the other party's attempts to get the case dismissed through the use of pretrial motions. We have already mentioned the motion to dismiss. Other important pretrial motions are the motion for a judgment on the pleadings and the motion for summary judgment.

Motion for Judgment on the Pleadings After the pleadings are closed—that is, after the complaint, answer, and any counterclaim and reply have been filed—either of the parties can file a *motion for judgment on the pleadings* (or *on the merits*). This motion may be used when no facts are disputed and, thus, only questions of law are at issue. On a motion for judgment on the pleadings, a court may not consider any evidence outside the pleadings.

Motion for Summary Judgment If there are no disagreements about the facts in a case and the only question is how the law applies to those facts, both sides can agree to the facts and ask the judge to apply the law to them. In this situation, it is appropriate for either party to move for **summary judgment.**

When the court considers a motion for summary judgment, it can take into account evidence outside the pleadings. The evidence may consist of sworn statements (affidavits) by parties or witnesses, as well as documents, such as a contract. The use of this additional evidence distinguishes this motion from the motion to dismiss and the motion for judgment on the pleadings.

summary judgment
A judgment entered by a trial court before trial that is based on the valid assertion by one of the parties that there are no disputed issues of fact that would necessitate a trial.

3–4d Discovery

Before a trial begins, the parties can use a number of procedural devices to obtain information and gather evidence about the case. The process of obtaining information from the opposing party or from other witnesses is known as **discovery.**

Discovery prevents surprises by giving parties access to evidence that might otherwise be hidden. This allows both parties to learn as much as they can about what to expect at a trial before they reach the courtroom. It also serves to narrow the issues so that trial time is spent on the main questions in the case.

discovery
A method by which opposing parties obtain information from each other to prepare for trial.

Real-World Case Example

Phillips Brothers, LP (a limited partnership), and Ray Winstead were two of the owners of Kilby Brake Fisheries, a Mississippi catfish farm. Winstead operated a hatchery for the firm, but after only two profitable years during an eight-year tenure, he was fired. He filed a suit in a Mississippi state court against Phillips Brothers, alleging a freeze-out. (A freeze-out occurs when some owners of a firm exclude others from participating in the firm.) In response, the defendants filed a counterclaim of theft and asked the court to allow them to obtain documents from Winstead regarding his finances. The court refused this discovery request. A jury awarded Winstead more than $1.7 million. The defendants appealed.

Were the defendants entitled to discovery of Winstead's personal finances? Yes. In a 2014 decision, *Brothers v. Winstead,* the Mississippi Supreme Court reversed the lower court's decision to deny discovery of Winstead's finances and remanded the case for a new trial. The refusal to allow discovery prevented the jury from finding out what happened to a certain load of fish, and this issue was central to both sides of the case. Discovery of Winstead's finances could reveal whether he was selling fish from Kilby Brake for his personal gain.

Depositions and Interrogatories Discovery can involve the use of depositions, interrogatories, or both. A **deposition** is sworn testimony by the opposing party or any witness, recorded by an authorized court official. The person deposed gives

deposition
A generic term that refers to any evidence verified by oath.

sworn testimony under oath and answers questions asked by the attorneys from both sides. The questions and answers are written down, sworn to, and signed.

An **interrogatory** is a series of written questions for which written answers are prepared and then signed under oath. The main difference between interrogatories and depositions with written questions is that an interrogatory is directed to the plaintiff or defendant, not to a witness, and the party can prepare answers with the aid of an attorney. In addition, the scope of interrogatories is broader, because parties are obligated to answer questions, even if it means disclosing information from their records and files.

interrogatory
A series of written questions for which written answers are prepared and then signed under oath by the plaintiff or the defendant.

Other Information A party can serve a written request to the other party for an admission of the truth of matters relating to the trial. An admission in response to such a request is the equivalent of an admission in court. A request for admission saves time at trial, because parties will not have to spend time proving facts on which they already agree.

A party can also gain access to documents and other items not in his or her possession in order to inspect and examine them. Likewise, a party can gain "entry upon land" to inspect premises relevant to the case.

When the physical or mental condition of one party is in question, the opposing party can ask the court to order a physical or mental examination. If the court is willing to make the order, the opposing party can obtain the results of the examination. The court will make such an order only when the need for the information outweighs the right to privacy of the person to be examined.

E-Evidence for Discovery Any relevant material, including information stored electronically, can be the object of a discovery request. Electronic evidence, or **e-evidence,** consists of all types of computer-generated or electronically recorded information, such as e-mail, voice mail, tweets, blogs, social media posts, and spreadsheets, as well as documents and other data stored on computers and mobile devices.

e-evidence
A type of evidence that consists of all computer-generated or electronically recorded information.

E-evidence can reveal significant facts that are not discoverable by other means. Computers, smartphones, cameras, and other devices automatically record certain information about files—such as who created the file and when, and who accessed, modified, or transmitted it—on their hard or flash drives. This information is called **metadata,** which can be thought of as "data about data." Metadata can be obtained only from the file in its electronic format, not from printed-out versions.

metadata
Data that are automatically recorded by electronic devices and provide information about who created a file and its history.

Compliance with Discovery Requests If a party refuses to cooperate with requests made by the opposing party during discovery, the court may compel the party to comply with the requests by a specific date. If the party still does not comply, he or she may be held in contempt of court and, as a consequence, may be fined or imprisoned and required to pay the opposing party's resulting expenses. The court might even enter a default judgment for the opposing party.

3–4e At the Trial

A trial commences with an opening statement by the attorney for each party. (The plaintiff's attorney goes first.) The plaintiff's attorney then calls and questions the first witness. This questioning is called **direct examination.** The defendant's attorney then questions the witness. This is known as **cross-examination.** The plaintiff's attorney may question the witness again, and the defendant's attorney may follow again.

direct examination
The examination of a witness by the attorney who calls the witness to testify on behalf of the attorney's client.

After the plaintiff's attorney has called all of the witnesses and presented all of the evidence for the plaintiff's side of the case, the defendant's attorney presents the defendant's witnesses and evidence. At the conclusion of the defendant's case, the plaintiff's attorney can present a *rebuttal*—that is, evidence and testimony refuting

cross-examination
The questioning of an opposing witness during the trial.

the defendant's case. After that, the defendant can respond with a *rejoinder*, which is evidence and testimony refuting the plaintiff's rebuttal. Each side then presents a *closing argument* (a final statement summarizing its version of the evidence). Finally, the court reaches a verdict.

Motions at the Trial   At every stage in a trial, the parties can file various motions, including a *motion to dismiss the case,* a *motion for summary judgment,* and a **motion for a directed verdict** (known in federal courts as a *motion for judgment as a matter of law*). With a motion for a directed verdict, the defendant's attorney asks the judge to direct a verdict for the defendant on the ground that the plaintiff has presented no evidence that would justify the granting of the plaintiff's remedy. The judge looks at the evidence in the light most favorable to the plaintiff and grants the motion only if there is insufficient evidence to prove that the parties disagree about the facts.

Posttrial Motions   At the end of the trial, a posttrial motion can be made to set aside the verdict and to hold a new trial. A *motion for a new trial* will be granted if the judge is convinced, after looking at all the evidence, that the jury was in error but does not feel it is appropriate to grant a judgment for the other side.

3–4f The Appeal

Either party can appeal the trial court's judgment to an appropriate court of appeals. A party who appeals is known as the **appellant,** or petitioner. His or her attorney files in the reviewing court the record on appeal, which includes trial testimony and the evidence. The party in opposition to the appellant is the **appellee,** or the respondent. Attorneys for both sides file **briefs** with the reviewing court. A typical brief has a written facts summary, law summary, and argument about how the law applies to the facts. The attorneys may also present oral arguments.

Types of Rulings   A court of appeals does not hear any evidence. Its decision in a case is based on the record and the briefs. In general, appellate courts review the record for errors of law. If the reviewing court believes that an error was committed, the judgment will be *reversed*. Sometimes, the case will be *remanded* (sent back to the court that originally heard the case) for a new trial. In most cases, the judgment of the lower court is *affirmed*, resulting in the enforcement of the court's judgment.

Final Review   If the reviewing court is an intermediate appellate court, the losing party normally may appeal to the state supreme court. If this court agrees to hear the case, new briefs must be filed, and there may again be oral arguments. The supreme court may reverse or affirm the appellate court's decision or remand the case. At this point, unless a federal question is at issue, the case has reached its end.

The events of a typical lawsuit are illustrated in Exhibit 3.4, which follows.

3–5 THE COURTS ADAPT TO THE ONLINE WORLD

We have already mentioned that the courts have attempted to adapt traditional jurisdictional concepts to the online world. Not surprisingly, the Internet has also brought about changes in court procedures and practices, including new methods for filing pleadings and other documents and issuing decisions and opinions. The federal courts and more than 60 percent of the state courts have implemented some form of electronic delivery, such as via the Internet.

Some jurisdictions are exploring the possibility of cyber courts, in which legal proceedings could be conducted totally online. In cyber courts, the parties to a case

---

LEARNING OUTCOME 3
Discuss the procedure of a trial.

motion for a directed verdict
A motion for the judge to direct a verdict for the moving party on the ground that the other party has not produced sufficient evidence to support his or her claim.

appellant
The party who takes an appeal from one court to another.

appellee
The party against whom an appeal is taken—that is, the party who opposes setting aside or reversing the judgment.

brief
A written summary or statement prepared by one side in a lawsuit to explain its case to the judge.

EXHIBIT 3.4   Stages in a Typical Lawsuit

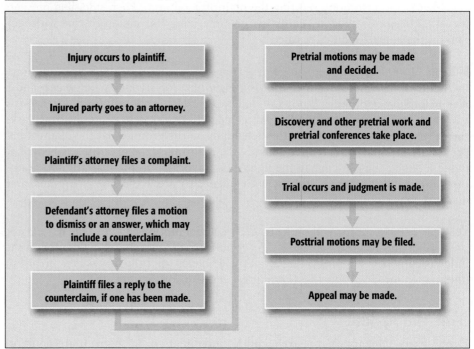

Injury occurs to plaintiff.

Injured party goes to an attorney.

Plaintiff's attorney files a complaint.

Defendant's attorney files a motion to dismiss or an answer, which may include a counterclaim.

Plaintiff files a reply to the counterclaim, if one has been made.

Pretrial motions may be made and decided.

Discovery and other pretrial work and pretrial conferences take place.

Trial occurs and judgment is made.

Posttrial motions may be filed.

Appeal may be made.

could meet online to make their arguments and present their evidence. This might be done, for instance, with e-mail submissions, through video cameras, in designated chat rooms, or at closed sites. These courtrooms could be efficient and economical. We might also see the use of virtual lawyers, judges, and juries—and possibly the replacement of court personnel with computers or software.

3–6 ALTERNATIVE DISPUTE RESOLUTION

Litigation is an expensive and time-consuming process. For this reason and others, most lawsuits do not go to trial. Instead, many businesses use methods of **alternative dispute resolution (ADR)** to settle their disputes. Methods of ADR range from the parties sitting down together and attempting to work out their differences to multinational corporations agreeing to resolve a dispute through a formal hearing before a panel of experts.

Normally, the parties themselves can control how they will attempt to settle their dispute, what procedures will be used, whether a neutral third party will be present or make a decision, and whether that decision will be legally binding or nonbinding. Most states require or encourage parties to undertake ADR before a trial. Many federal courts have instituted ADR programs as well.

The three traditional ADR methods are negotiation, mediation, and arbitration. A more recent ADR method is online dispute resolution.

3–6a Negotiation

The simplest form of ADR is **negotiation,** a process in which the parties attempt to settle their dispute informally, with or without attorneys to represent them. Attorneys frequently advise their clients to negotiate a settlement voluntarily before they proceed to trial. Parties may even try to negotiate a settlement during a trial or after the trial but before an appeal.

LEARNING OUTCOME 4

Summarize the steps in a typical lawsuit.

alternative dispute resolution (ADR)
The resolution of disputes in ways outside the traditional judicial process, such as negotiation, mediation, and arbitration.

LEARNING OUTCOME 5

Define the three basic traditional alternative methods for resolving disputes.

negotiation
A process in which parties attempt to settle their dispute without going to court, with or without attorneys to represent them.

3–6b Mediation

In **mediation,** a neutral third party acts as a communicating agent and works with both sides in the dispute to facilitate a resolution. The mediator talks with the parties and emphasizes their points of agreement to help them evaluate their options. The mediator may propose a solution, but he or she does not make a decision resolving the matter. States that require parties to undergo ADR before trial often offer mediation as one option or (as in Florida) the only option.

One of the main advantages of mediation is that it is not as adversarial as litigation. **EXAMPLE 3.3** Trevor and Julie, who are business partners, have a dispute over how the profits of their firm should be distributed. If the dispute is litigated, they will be adversaries, and their respective attorneys will emphasize how their positions differ, not what they have in common. In contrast, if the dispute is mediated, the mediator will emphasize the common ground shared by Trevor and Julie and help them work toward agreement. They can then work out the distribution of profits without damaging their continuing business relationship.◄

mediation
A method of settling disputes outside of court by using a neutral third party who acts as a communicating agent between the parties to help them negotiate a settlement.

3–6c Arbitration

A more formal method of ADR is **arbitration,** in which an *arbitrator* (a neutral third party or a panel of experts) hears a dispute and imposes a resolution on the parties. Usually, the parties in arbitration agree that the third party's decision will be *legally binding,* although they can also agree to *nonbinding* arbitration. Arbitration that is mandated by the courts often is not binding on the parties. In nonbinding arbitration, the parties can go forward with a lawsuit if they do not agree with the arbitrator's decision.

The arbitrator's decision is called an *award.* An award is usually the final word on the matter. A court will set aside an award only if one of the following occurs:

1. The arbitrator's conduct or "bad faith" substantially prejudiced the rights of one of the parties.

2. The award violates an established public policy.

3. The arbitrator exceeded her or his powers—that is, arbitrated issues that the parties did not agree to submit to arbitration.

Arbitration is unlike other forms of ADR because the third party hearing the dispute makes a decision for the parties. Exhibit 3.5 outlines the basic differences among the traditional forms of ADR.

arbitration
The settling of a dispute by submitting it to a disinterested third party who renders a decision.

EXHIBIT 3.5 Basic Differences in the Traditional Forms of Alternative Dispute Resolution

Type of ADR	Description	Neutral Third Party Present	Who Decides the Resolution
Negotiation	The parties meet informally with or without their attorneys and attempt to agree on a resolution.	No	The parties themselves reach a resolution.
Mediation	A neutral third party meets with the parties and emphasizes points of agreement to help them resolve their dispute.	Yes	The parties decide the resolution, but the mediator may suggest or propose a resolution.
Arbitration	The parties present their arguments and evidence before an arbitrator at a hearing, and the arbitrator renders a decision resolving the parties' dispute.	Yes	The arbitrator imposes a resolution on the parties that may be either binding or nonbinding.

3–6d Online Dispute Resolution

A number of companies and organizations offer dispute-resolution services using the Internet. The settlement of disputes in these online forums is known as **online dispute resolution (ODR)**. The disputes resolved in these forums have most commonly involved disagreements over the rights to *domain names* (see Chapter 7) or over the quality of goods sold via the Internet, including goods sold through online auction sites.

ODR may be best for resolving small- to medium-sized business liability claims, which may not be worth the expense of litigation or traditional ADR. Some local governments use ODR to resolve claims. Rules being developed in online forums may ultimately become a code of conduct for everyone who does business in cyberspace. Most online forums do not automatically apply the law of a specific jurisdiction. Instead, results are often based on general, universal legal principles. As with most offline methods of dispute resolution, any party may appeal to a court at any time.

online dispute resolution (ODR) The resolution of disputes with the assistance of organizations that offer dispute-resolution services via the Internet.

ANSWERING THE LEGAL PROBLEM

In the legal problem set out at the beginning of this chapter, Harry Koto, a resident of California, and Maria Mendez, a resident of Texas, are in a dispute over the ownership of the *Fairweather,* a boat in dry dock in San Diego, California.

A **Can a California state court exercise jurisdiction over the dispute?** Yes. The boat is located within the boundaries of California. A California court can exercise jurisdiction.

TERMS AND CONCEPTS FOR REVIEW

alternative dispute resolution (ADR) 42

answer 38

appellant 41

appellee 41

arbitration 43

brief 41

complaint 37

concurrent jurisdiction 36

cross-examination 40

default judgment 38

defendant 37

deposition 39

direct examination 40

discovery 39

diversity of citizenship 36

e-evidence 40

exclusive jurisdiction 36

federal question 36

interrogatory 40

jurisdiction 31

long arm statute 32

mediation 43

metadata 40

motion for a directed verdict 41

motion to dismiss 38

negotiation 42

online dispute resolution (ODR) 44

plaintiff 37

pleadings 37

small claims court 33

standing to sue 37

summary judgment 39

writ of *certiorari* 35

CHAPTER SUMMARY—THE COURTS AND ALTERNATIVE DISPUTE RESOLUTION

LEARNING OUTCOME	
1	**List the basic parts of a state court system.** A state court system includes trial courts and appellate courts. A *trial court* is where an action is initiated. An *appellate court* is a court of appeal and review. Many states have intermediate appellate courts. Each state has a high court, from which appeal to the United States Supreme Court is possible only if a federal question is involved.
2	**Identify when a lawsuit can be filed in a federal court.** Any lawsuit concerning a federal question can originate in a federal court. A federal question is an issue of law based, at least in part, on the Constitution, a treaty, or a federal law. A case involving diversity of citizenship can also be heard in a federal court. Diversity of citizenship exists between (1) citizens of different states, (2) a foreign country and citizens of a state or of different states, or (3) citizens of a state and citizens or subjects of a foreign country. The amount in controversy in a diversity case must be more than $75,000 for a federal court to take jurisdiction.
3	**Discuss the procedure of a trial.** A trial involves opening statements from both parties' attorneys, each party's presentation of its side of the case (with the introduction and examination of witnesses and evidence), the plaintiff's rebuttal, the defendant's rejoinder, closing arguments from both sides, various motions (such as a motion for a directed verdict) from both parties, and the court's verdict.
4	**Summarize the steps in a typical lawsuit.** An injury occurs to a party, who then goes to an attorney. The plaintiff's attorney files a complaint and a summons is issued. The defendant's attorney files a motion to dismiss or an answer. If the answer includes a counterclaim, the plaintiff files a reply. Pretrial motions may be made and decided. Discovery and other pretrial work and pretrial conferences take place. The trial occurs. A judgment is made. Posttrial motions may be filed. An appeal may be made.
5	**Define the three basic traditional alternative methods for resolving disputes.** The traditional method of resolving a legal dispute is through litigation. Alternative methods include negotiation, mediation, and arbitration. In negotiation, the parties attempt to settle their dispute informally without the involvement of a third party. In mediation, the parties attempt to come to an agreement with the assistance of a neutral third party, a mediator, who does not make a decision in the dispute. In arbitration, a neutral third party or a panel of experts hears a dispute and renders a decision.

ISSUE SPOTTERS

Check your answers to the *Issue Spotters* against the answers provided in Appendix C at the end of this text.

1. Ron wants to sue Art's Supply Company for Art's failure to deliver supplies that Ron needed to prepare his work for an appearance at a local artists' fair. What must Ron establish before a court will hear the suit? (See *Jurisdiction and The State Court Case Process.*)

2. Carlos, a citizen of California, is injured in an automobile accident in Arizona. Alex, the driver of the other car, is a citizen of New Mexico. Carlos wants Alex to pay Carlos's medical expenses and car repairs, which total $125,000. Can Carlos sue in federal court? Why or why not? (See *Federal Court System.*)

USING BUSINESS LAW

3–1. Jurisdiction. Marya Callais, a citizen of Florida, was walking along a busy street in Tallahassee when a large crate flew off a passing truck and hit her. She experienced a great deal of pain and suffering, incurred significant medical expenses, and could not work for six months. She wishes to sue the trucking firm for $300,000 in damages. The firm's headquarters are in Georgia, although the company does business in Florida. In what court may Callais bring suit—a Florida state court, a Georgia state court, or a federal court? What factors might influence her decision? (See *The Federal Court System.*)

3–2. Motion for a New Trial. Washoe Medical Center, Inc., admitted Shirley Swisher for the treatment of a fractured pelvis. During her stay, Swisher suffered a fall from her hospital bed. She filed an action against Washoe seeking

damages for the alleged lack of care in her treatment. During the trial, when her attorney returned a few minutes late from a break, the judge led the jurors in a standing ovation. The judge also joked with one of the jurors, whom he had known in college, about his fitness to serve as a judge and personally endorsed another juror's business. After the trial, the jury returned a verdict in favor of Washoe. Swisher moved for a new trial, but the judge denied the motion. Swisher appealed, arguing that the tone set by the judge prejudiced her right to a fair trial. Should the appellate court agree? Why or why not? (See *The State Court Case Process.*)

REAL-WORLD CASE PROBLEMS

3–3. Electronic Filing. Betsy Faden worked for the U.S. Department of Veterans Affairs. Removed from her position in April 2012, Faden had until May 29 of that year to appeal the removal decision. She submitted an appeal through the Merit Systems Protection Board's e-filing system seven days after the deadline. Ordered to show good cause for the delay, Faden testified about attempts to e-file the appeal when the board's system was down. The board acknowledged that its system had not been functioning on May 27, 28, and 29. Was Faden sufficiently diligent in ensuring a timely filing? Discuss. [*Faden v. Merit Systems Protection Board*, 2014 WL 163394 (Fed.Cir. 2014)] (See *The Courts Adapt to the Online World.*)

3–4. Discovery. Jessica Lester died from injuries suffered in an auto accident caused by the driver of a truck owned by Allied Concrete Co. Jessica's widower, Isaiah, filed a suit against Allied for damages. As part of discovery, Allied requested copies of all of Isaiah's Facebook photos and other postings. Before responding, Isaiah "cleaned up" his Facebook pages. Allied suspected that some of the items had been deleted, including a photo of Isaiah holding a beer can while wearing a t-shirt that declared "I love hot-moms." Can this material be recovered? If so, how? What effect might Isaiah's "misconduct" have on the result in this

case? [*Allied Concrete Co. v. Lester*, 285 Va. 40, 736 S.E.2d 899 (2013)] (See *The State Court Case Process.*)

3–5. Arbitration. Bruce Matthews played football for the Tennessee Titans. As part of his contract, he agreed to submit any dispute to arbitration. He also agreed that Tennessee law would determine all matters related to workers' compensation. After Matthews retired, he filed a workers' compensation claim in California. The arbitrator ruled that Matthews could pursue his claim in California but only under Tennessee law. Should this ruling be set aside? Explain. [*National Football League Players Association v. National Football League Management Council*, ___ F.Supp.2d ___ (S.D.Cal. 2011)] (See *Alternative Dispute Resolution.*)

3–6. Jurisdiction. Independence Plating Corp. (IPC) of New Jersey provides metal-coating services. It does not advertise or otherwise solicit business in North Carolina. Southern Prestige Industries, Inc., a North Carolina firm, contracted with IPC to ship parts from North Carolina to New Jersey for processing. After thirty-two transactions, Southern Prestige filed a suit in a North Carolina state court against IPC, alleging breach of contract. Can the court exercise jurisdiction? Explain. [*Southern Prestige Industries, Inc. v. Independence Plating Corp.*, 202 N.C.App. 372, 690 S.E.2d 768 (2010)] (See *Jurisdiction.*)

ETHICAL QUESTIONS

3–7. To Sue or Not to Sue? What ethical considerations might affect a decision to go to court?

3–8. The Ethics of Arbitration. Nellie Lumpkin, who suffered from dementia, was admitted to the Picayune Convalescent Center, a nursing home. Because of her diminished mental condition, her daughter, Beverly McDaniel, signed the

admissions agreement. It included a clause requiring the parties to submit any dispute to arbitration. After Lumpkin left the center two years later, she filed a suit against Picayune to recover damages for mistreatment and malpractice. Is it ethical for this dispute to go to arbitration? [*Covenant Health & Rehabilitation of Picayune, LP v. Lumpkin*, 23 So.2d 1092 (Miss.App. 2009)] (See *Alternative Dispute Resolution.*)

Chapter 3—Work Set

TRUE-FALSE QUESTIONS

_____ 1. Generally, a court can exercise jurisdiction over the residents of the state in which the court is located.

_____ 2. All state trial courts have general jurisdiction.

_____ 3. The decisions of a state's highest court on all questions of state law are final.

_____ 4. Federal courts may refuse to enforce a state or federal statute that violates the U.S. Constitution.

_____ 5. The United States Supreme Court can hear appeals on federal questions from state and federal courts.

_____ 6. Pleadings consist of a complaint, an answer, and a motion to dismiss.

_____ 7. If a party does not deny the truth of a complaint, he or she is in default.

_____ 8. In mediation, a mediator makes a decision on the matter in dispute.

MULTIPLE-CHOICE QUESTIONS

_____ 1. National Computers, Inc., was incorporated in Nebraska, has its main office in Kansas, and does business in Missouri. National is subject to the jurisdiction of

a. Nebraska, Kansas, and Missouri.
b. Nebraska and Kansas, but not Missouri.
c. Nebraska and Missouri, but not Kansas.
d. Kansas and Missouri, but not Nebraska.

_____ 2. Alpha, Inc., sues Beta, Inc., in a state court. Alpha loses and files an appeal with the state appeals court. The appeals court will

a. not retry the case, because the appropriate place for the retrial of a state case is a federal court.
b. not retry the case, because an appeals court examines the record of a case, looking at questions of law and procedure for errors by the trial court.
c. retry the case, because after a case is tried a party has a right to an appeal.
d. retry the case, because Alpha and Beta do not agree on the result of the trial.

_____ 3. A suit can be brought in a federal court if it involves

a. a question under the Constitution, a treaty, or a federal law.
b. citizens of different states, a foreign country and a U.S. citizen, or a foreign citizen and an American citizen, and the amount in controversy is more than $75,000.
c. either a or b.
d. none of the above.

_____ 4. Ace Corporation, which is based in Texas, advertises on the Web. A court in Illinois would be most likely to exercise jurisdiction over Ace if Ace

a. conducted substantial business with Illinois residents at its Web site.
b. interacted with any Illinois resident through its Web site.
c. only advertised passively at its Web site.
d. all of the above.

_____ 5. Ann sues Carla in a state trial court. Ann loses the suit. If Ann wants to appeal, the most appropriate court in which to file the appeal is

a. the state appellate court.
b. the nearest federal district court.
c. the nearest federal court of appeals.
d. the United States Supreme Court.

_____ 6. The first step in a lawsuit is the filing of pleadings, and the first pleading filed is the complaint. The complaint contains

   a. a statement alleging jurisdictional facts.
   b. a statement of facts entitling the complainant to relief.
   c. a statement asking for a specific remedy.
   d. all of the above.

_____ 7. The purposes of discovery include

   a. saving time.
   b. narrowing the issues.
   c. preventing surprises at trial.
   d. all of the above.

_____ 8. Jim and Bill are involved in an automobile accident. Sue is a passenger in Bill's car. Jim's attorney wants to ask Sue, as a witness, some questions concerning the accident. Sue's answers to the questions are given in

   a. a deposition.
   b. a response to interrogatories.
   c. a rebuttal.
   d. none of the above.

_____ 9. After the entry of a judgment, who can appeal?

   a. Only the winning party.
   b. Only the losing party.
   c. Either the winning party or the losing party.
   d. None of the above.

_____ 10. Cobb and Roberts submit their dispute to binding arbitration. A court can set aside the arbitrator's award if

   a. Cobb is not satisfied with the award.
   b. Roberts is not satisfied with the award.
   c. the award involves at least $75,000.
   d. the award violates public policy.

ANSWERING MORE LEGAL PROBLEMS

1. Bento Cuisine is a lunch-cart business. It occupies a street corner in Texarkana, a city that straddles the border of Arkansas and Texas. Across the street—and across the state line, which runs down the middle of the street—is Rico's Tacos. The two businesses compete for customers. Recently, Bento has begun to believe that Rico's is engaging in competitive behavior that is illegal.

   If Bento were to file a lawsuit against Rico's, in which type of court could Bento initiate the action? (Bento could file a suit against Rico's in a trial court of _____ jurisdiction in either the state of Bento's location or the state of Rico's location. Because there appears to be diversity of _____ in this situation, if the amount in controversy could conceivably exceed $75,000, a suit might instead be filed in a _____ district court, which is the equivalent of a state trial court of general jurisdiction.

2. Bento files a lawsuit against Rico's. Bento believes that it has both the law and the facts on its side. At the end of the trial, however, the jury decides against Bento, and the judge issues a ruling in favor of Rico's.

   If Bento is unwilling to accept this result, what are its options? Bento's first option might be to file a motion to set aside the verdict and hold a new _____. This motion will be granted if the judge is convinced, after examining the evidence, that the jury was in error but does not think it appropriate to issue a judgment for Bento's side. Bento's second option would be to appeal the trial court's judgment, including a denial of the motion for a new trial, to the appropriate court of _____. An appellate court is most likely to review the case for errors in _____, not fact. In any case, the appellate court will not hear new _____.

CONSTITUTIONAL LAW

4

FACING A LEGAL PROBLEM

Congress passed the Civil Rights Act of 1964 to prohibit racial discrimination in "establishments affecting interstate commerce." The owner of the Heart of Atlanta Motel refused to rent rooms to African Americans and filed a suit to have the Civil Rights Act declared unconstitutional.

The owner argued that his motel was not engaged in interstate commerce but was "of a purely local character." The hotel, however, was accessible to interstate highways, it was advertised nationally, and 75 percent of its guests were residents of other states.

 Did Congress exceed its power by enacting the Civil Rights Act?

LEARNING OUTCOMES

The five Learning Outcomes below are designed to help improve your understanding of the chapter. After reading this chapter, you should be able to:

1 State the constitutional clause that gives the federal government the power to regulate commercial activities among the states.

2 Identify the constitutional clause that allows federal laws to take priority over conflicting state laws.

3 Describe the Bill of Rights.

4 Locate the due process clause in the Constitution.

5 Outline the protection of individual privacy rights under the Constitution and federal statutes.

The U.S. Constitution is brief (see Appendix A at the end of this text). It contains only about seven thousand words—less than one-third of the number of words in the average state constitution. Perhaps its brevity explains why it has survived for more than two hundred years—longer than any other written constitution in the world.

Laws that govern business have their origin in the lawmaking authority granted by this document, which is the supreme law in this country. Neither Congress nor any state may pass a law that conflicts with the Constitution.

In this chapter, we first look at some basic constitutional concepts and clauses and their significance for business. Then we examine how certain freedoms guaranteed by the Constitution affect businesspersons.

4–1 THE CONSTITUTIONAL POWERS OF GOVERNMENT

Following the Revolutionary War, the states created a *confederal* form of government in which the power to govern rested largely with the states. This form of government caused serious problems. For one thing, laws passed by the various states hampered commerce. Also, the national government did not have the authority to demand revenues (by levying taxes, for example).

Because of these problems, a national convention was called. The delegates to the convention, now known as the Constitutional Convention, wrote the U.S. Constitution. This document, after its ratification by the states in 1789, became the basis for an entirely new form of government.

4–1a A Federal Form of Government

The new government created by the Constitution reflected a series of compromises. Some delegates wanted sovereign power to remain with the states. Others wanted the national government alone to exercise sovereign power. The end result was a compromise—a **federal form of government** in which the national government and the states *share* sovereign power.

The Constitution sets forth specific powers that can be exercised by the national government and provides that the national government has the implied power to undertake actions necessary to carry out its expressly designated powers. All other powers are "reserved" to the states. The broad language of the Constitution, though, leaves much room for debate over the specific nature and scope of these powers. Generally, it is the task of the courts to determine where the line between state and national powers lies.

4–1b The Separation of Powers

To prevent the national government from using its powers arbitrarily, the Constitution divides these powers among three branches of government. The legislative branch makes the laws, the executive branch enforces the laws, and the judicial branch interprets the laws. Each branch performs a separate function, and no branch may exercise the authority of another branch.

Additionally, a system of **checks and balances** allows each branch to limit the actions of the other two branches, thus preventing any one branch from exercising too much power. Some examples include the following:

1. The legislative branch (Congress) can enact a law, but the executive branch (the president) has the constitutional authority to veto that law.

2. The executive branch is responsible for foreign affairs, but treaties with foreign governments require the advice and consent of the Senate.

3. Congress determines the jurisdiction of the federal courts, and the president appoints federal judges with the advice and consent of the Senate, but the judicial branch has the power to hold actions of the other two branches unconstitutional.

4–1c The Commerce Clause

To prevent states from establishing laws and regulations that would interfere with trade and commerce among the states, the Constitution expressly delegated to the national government the power to regulate interstate commerce. Article I, Section 8, of the U.S. Constitution expressly permits Congress "[t]o regulate Commerce with foreign Nations, and among the several States, and with the Indian Tribes." This clause, referred to as the **commerce clause,** has had a greater impact on business than any other provision in the Constitution.

National Powers At least in theory, the power over commerce authorizes the national government to regulate every commercial enterprise in the United States. Federal (national) legislation governs nearly every major activity conducted by businesses. It can affect hiring and firing decisions, workplace safety, and how businesses compete and finance their enterprises. The commerce clause may not justify national regulation of noneconomic conduct, however.

The Regulatory Powers of the States State governments have the authority to regulate affairs within their borders. This authority stems in part from the Tenth Amendment to the Constitution, which reserves all powers not delegated to the national government to the states. State regulatory powers are often referred to as **police powers.** The term does not relate solely to criminal law enforcement but also to the right of state governments to regulate private activities to protect or promote the public order, health, safety, morals, and general welfare.

federal form of government
A system of government in which the states form a union and the sovereign power is divided between a central government and the member states.

checks and balances
The system by which each of the three branches of the national government exercises a check on the actions of the others.

State the constitutional clause that gives the federal government the power to regulate commercial activities among the states.

commerce clause
The provision in Article I, Section 8, of the U.S. Constitution that gives Congress the power to regulate interstate commerce.

police powers
Powers possessed by states as part of their inherent sovereignty.

Fire and building codes, antidiscrimination laws, parking regulations, zoning restrictions, licensing requirements, and thousands of other state statutes covering almost every aspect of life have been enacted based on a state's police powers. Local governments, including cities, also exercise police powers.

The "Dormant" Commerce Clause   The commerce clause gives the national government the *exclusive* authority to regulate commercial activities that substantially affects trade and commerce among the states. This express grant of authority to the national government, which is often referred to as the "positive" aspect of the commerce clause, implies a negative aspect of the clause—that the states do *not* have the authority to regulate interstate commerce. This negative aspect of the commerce clause is often referred to as the "dormant" (implied) commerce clause.

The dormant commerce clause comes into play when state regulations affect interstate commerce. In this situation, the courts normally weigh the state's interest in regulating a certain matter against the burden that the state's regulation places on interstate commerce.

4–1d The Supremacy Clause

Article VI of the Constitution provides that the Constitution, laws, and treaties of the United States are "the supreme Law of the Land." This article, commonly referred to as the **supremacy clause,** is important in the ordering of state and federal relationships. When there is a direct conflict between a federal law and a state law, the state law is rendered invalid. Because some powers are *concurrent* (shared by the federal government and the states), however, it is necessary to determine which law governs in a particular circumstance.

Preemption occurs when Congress chooses to act exclusively in a concurrent area. In this circumstance, a valid federal statute or regulation will take precedence over a conflicting state or local law or regulation on the same general subject.

supremacy clause
The provision in Article VI of the Constitution that the Constitution, laws, and treaties of the United States are "the supreme Law of the Land."

preemption
A doctrine under which certain federal laws preempt, or take precedence over, conflicting state or local laws.

HIGHLIGHTING THE POINT

Congress enacts a law that imposes certain rules for the labeling and packaging of pesticides. Later, a state legislature enacts a law that prescribes different requirements for pesticide package warnings. Pat, a farmer, uses Quik-Kil, a pesticide that damages her crops. Pat files a lawsuit against Royal Chemical Company, Quik-Kil's manufacturer, alleging a violation of the state law. Royal argues that the federal packaging rules preempt the state requirements.

Is the state law valid? No. Under the supremacy clause, when a state law conflicts with the federal law on the same subject, the federal law takes precedence. In some circumstances, a state can make the violation of a federal law a state offense, but it cannot permit something that the federal law prohibits or ban something that the federal law specifically allows.

LEARNING OUTCOME 2

Identify the constitutional clause that allows federal laws to take priority over conflicting state laws.

4–1e The Taxing and Spending Powers

Article I, Section 8, provides that Congress has the "Power to lay and collect Taxes, Duties, Imposts, and Excises." Section 8 further provides that "all Duties, Imposts and Excises shall be uniform throughout the United States." The requirement of uniformity refers to uniformity among the states. Thus, Congress may not tax some states while exempting others.

If a tax measure bears some reasonable relationship to revenue production, it is usually within the national taxing power. Also, the commerce clause almost always provides a basis for sustaining a federal tax.

Under Article I, Section 8, Congress has the power "to pay the Debts and provide for the common Defence and general welfare of the United States." Through the spending power, Congress disposes of the revenues accumulated from the taxing power. Congress can spend revenues to promote any objective it deems worthwhile, so long as it does not violate the Constitution.

4–2 BUSINESS AND THE BILL OF RIGHTS

Bill of Rights
The first ten amendments to the U.S. Constitution.

LEARNING OUTCOME 3

Describe the Bill of Rights.

indictment
A charge or formal accusation by a grand jury that a named person has committed a crime.

The Constitution's first ten amendments, commonly known as the **Bill of Rights,** embody a series of protections for the individual against various types of interference by the federal government. Some constitutional protections apply to business entities as well. Corporations exist as separate legal entities, or legal persons, and enjoy many of the same rights and privileges as natural persons do. Summarized here are the protections guaranteed by these ten amendments.

1. The First Amendment guarantees the freedoms of religion, speech, and the press and the rights to assemble peaceably and to petition the government.

2. The Second Amendment guarantees the right to keep and bear arms.

3. The Third Amendment prohibits, in peacetime, the lodging of soldiers in any house without the owner's consent.

4. The Fourth Amendment prohibits unreasonable searches and seizures of persons or property.

5. The Fifth Amendment guarantees the rights to **indictment** (pronounced in-*dite*-ment) by a grand jury, to due process of law, and to fair payment when private property is taken for public use. The Fifth Amendment also prohibits compulsory self-incrimination and double jeopardy (that is, a trial for the same crime twice).

6. The Sixth Amendment guarantees the accused in a criminal case the right to a speedy and public trial by an impartial jury and with counsel. The accused has the right to cross-examine witnesses against him or her and to solicit testimony from witnesses in his or her favor.

7. The Seventh Amendment guarantees the right to a trial by jury in a civil case involving at least twenty dollars.

8. The Eighth Amendment prohibits excessive bail and fines, as well as cruel and unusual punishment.

9. The Ninth Amendment establishes that the people have rights in addition to those specified in the Constitution.

10. The Tenth Amendment establishes that those powers neither delegated to the federal government nor denied to the states are reserved for the states.

Most of these rights also apply to state governments under the Fourteenth Amendment to the Constitution. That amendment provides in part that "[n]o State shall . . . deprive any person of life, liberty, or property, without due process of law." With respect to many of the rights and liberties set out in the Constitution, a law or other governmental action that limits one of these rights or liberties may violate the "due process of law." Here, we examine two important guarantees of the First Amendment—freedom of speech and freedom of religion.

4–2a The First Amendment—Freedom of Speech

Freedom of speech is a prized freedom that Americans have. Indeed, it forms the basis for our democratic form of government. Democracy could not exist if people could not freely express their political opinions and criticize government actions or policies. Also protected is **symbolic speech**—such as gestures, movements, articles of clothing, and other forms of nonverbal expressive conduct.

symbolic speech
Nonverbal expressive conduct.

The United States Supreme Court, for instance, has held that the burning of the American flag as part of a peaceful protest is a constitutionally protected form of expression. Similarly, wearing a T-shirt with a photo of a presidential candidate is a constitutionally protected form of expression. The test is whether a reasonable person would interpret the conduct as conveying some sort of message.

EXAMPLE 4.1 As a form of expression, Josh has gang signs tattooed on his torso, arms, and neck. If Rebecca would reasonably interpret this conduct as conveying a message, then the tattoos might be a protected form of symbolic speech. ◄

Reasonable Restrictions To protect citizens from those who would abuse the right to free expression, speech is subject to reasonable restrictions. Reasonableness is analyzed on a case-by-case basis. If a restriction imposed by the government is content neutral, then a court may allow it. To be content neutral, the restriction must be aimed at combatting a societal problem, such as crime, and not be aimed at suppressing the expressive conduct of the speech. **EXAMPLE 4.2** Roosevelt High School officials confiscated a banner, which read "Bong Hits 4 Jesus," from Russell Lende, a high school sophomore. Lende was suspended from high school and filed a lawsuit, claiming the banner was a protected form of expression. A federal court reasoned that the banner could be interpreted as promoting drugs and concluded that the restrictions were justified. ◄

Corporate Political Speech Political speech by corporations falls within the protection of the First Amendment. In a landmark case, *Citizens United v. Federal Election Committee*, the United States Supreme Court struck down a federal law that prohibited corporations from using their funds to advocate the election or defeat of a political candidate. The Court held that this prohibition violated the First Amendment.

Commercial Speech—Advertising The courts give substantial protection to "commercial" speech, which consists of communications—primarily advertising—by business firms. The protection given to commercial speech under the First Amendment is not as extensive as that afforded to noncommercial speech, however. A state may restrict certain kinds of advertising in the interest of protecting consumers from being misled. States also have a legitimate interest in the beautification of roadsides, and this interest allows states to place restraints on billboards.

A **substantial government interest** is a significant connection or concern of the government with respect to a particular matter. This requirement for a restriction on commercial speech limits the power of the government to regulate free speech.

substantial government interest
A significant connection or concern of the government that is required to justify restrictions on commercial speech.

Generally, a restriction on commercial speech is valid as long as it meets the following three criteria:

1. It must seek to implement a substantial government interest.

2. It must directly advance that interest.

3. It must go no further than necessary to accomplish its objective.

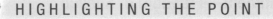

HIGHLIGHTING THE POINT

California enacts a statute that requires video game makers to attach labels to their games to warn parents of excessive violence. The statute defines a violent video game as one in which "the range of options available to a player include killing, maiming, dismembering, or sexually assaulting an image of a human being."

Does the California statute violate the First Amendment? Yes. Video games are entitled to First Amendment protection, and the statute's definition of a violent video game is too vague. Many games that are violent are based on popular novels or movies and have complex plots. They should not be treated differently than these novels and movies. The statute is not justified by a substantial government interest, and the law is not narrowly tailored to accomplish any particular objective.

Unprotected Speech Certain types of speech are not given any protection under the First Amendment. Speech that harms the good reputation of another, or defamatory speech, is not protected. Speech that violates criminal laws (such as threatening speech) is not constitutionally protected. Other unprotected speech includes "fighting words," or words that are likely to incite others to respond violently.

The First Amendment also does not protect obscene speech. Material is obscene if:

1. The average person finds that it violates contemporary community standards.

2. The work taken as a whole appeals to a *prurient* (arousing) interest in sex.

3. The work shows patently offensive sexual conduct.

4. The work lacks serious redeeming literary, artistic, political, or scientific merit.

Online Obscenity A significant problem is how to control the obscenity and child pornography that are disseminated via the Internet. Congress has attempted to protect minors from pornographic materials on the Internet by passing several laws. The Child Online Protection Act declares it a crime to communicate material over the Internet that is "harmful to minors" according to "contemporary community standards."

The Children's Internet Protection Act requires public schools and libraries to use **filtering software** to block children's access to adult content on Web sites. Such software is designed to prevent persons from viewing certain Web sites at certain times.

4–2b The First Amendment—Freedom of Religion

The First Amendment states that the government may neither establish any religion nor prohibit the free exercise of religious practices. The first part of this constitutional provision is referred to as the **establishment clause,** and the second part is known as the **free exercise clause.** Government action, both federal and state, must be consistent with this constitutional mandate.

The Establishment Clause The establishment clause prohibits the government from establishing a state-sponsored religion, as well as from passing laws that promote religion or that show a preference for one religion over another. The establishment clause does not require a complete separation of church and state, however. On the contrary, it requires the government to accommodate religions.

filtering software
A computer program that screens in order to block access to certain Web sites.

establishment clause
The provision in the First Amendment to the Constitution that prohibits Congress from creating any law "respecting an establishment of religion."

free exercise clause
The provision in the First Amendment to the Constitution that prohibits Congress from making any law "prohibiting the free exercise" of religion.

The establishment clause covers all conflicts about such matters as the legality of state and local government support for a particular religion, government aid to religious organizations and schools, the government's allowing or requiring school prayers, and the teaching of evolution versus fundamentalist theories of creation in public schools.

For a law or policy to be constitutional, it must be secular in aim, must not have the primary effect of advancing or inhibiting religions, and must not create an excessive government entanglement with religion. Generally, federal or state regulation that does not promote religion or place a significant burden on religion is constitutional, even if it has some impact on religion.

The Free Exercise Clause The free exercise clause guarantees that a person can hold any religious belief or no religious belief. When religious *practices* work against public policy and the public welfare, however, the government can act. For instance, regardless of a child's or a parent's religious beliefs, the government can require certain types of vaccinations as a condition for a child to attend public school.

For business firms, an important issue involves the accommodation that businesses must make for the religious beliefs of their employees. **EXAMPLE 4.3** Angela is hired as a waitress at Apple Spice Restaurant. A year later, Angela joins a church, which prohibits members from working on Saturdays. Apple Spice Restaurant must make a reasonable attempt—such as offering Angela other shifts or positions that require no Saturday work—to accommodate these religious beliefs. ◄ The beliefs need not be based on the tenets or dogma of a particular church, sect, or denomination. The only qualification is that the belief be religious in nature and sincerely held by the employee.

4–3 DUE PROCESS AND EQUAL PROTECTION

Two other constitutional guarantees of great significance to Americans come from the due process clauses of the Fifth and Fourteenth Amendments and the equal protection clause of the Fourteenth Amendment.

LEARNING OUTCOME 4
Locate the due process clause in the Constitution.

4–3a Due Process

Both the Fifth and the Fourteenth Amendments provide that no person shall be deprived "of life, liberty, or property, without due process of law." The **due process clause** of each of these amendments has two aspects—procedural and substantive.

due process clause
The provisions of the Fifth and Fourteenth Amendments to the Constitution that guarantee that no person shall be deprived of life, liberty, or property without due process of law.

Procedural Due Process Procedural due process requires that any government decision to take life, liberty, or property must be made fairly. Fair procedures must be used to determine whether a person will be subject to punishment or have some burden imposed on him or her.

Procedural due process requires that a person have at least an opportunity to object to a proposed action before a fair, neutral decision maker (who need not be a judge). **EXAMPLE 4.4** Sabrina, a nursing student, takes a selfie with an unconscious patient, who is a local celebrity. Sabrina is working her shift at the university hospital when she takes the photo. Although she quickly deletes the photo from her smartphone, it ends up on Facebook because before deleting it, she sent it to some fellow nursing students. When the director of nursing sees the photo online, Sabrina is expelled immediately from the university's nursing program. Sabrina may sue the university because it violated her due process rights by not giving her an opportunity to present her side to school authorities. ◄

Substantive Due Process Substantive due process focuses on the content, or substance, of legislation. If a law or other governmental action limits a *fundamental right*, it will be held to violate substantive due process unless it promotes a substantial government interest. Fundamental rights include interstate travel, privacy, voting, and all First Amendment rights.

Substantial government interests could include the public's safety. Thus, laws designating speed limits are valid, even though they affect interstate travel, if they are shown to reduce highway fatalities, because the state has a compelling interest in protecting the lives of its citizens.

In situations not involving fundamental rights, a law or action must rationally relate to a legitimate governmental end. Nearly every business regulation is upheld as reasonable against substantive due process challenges. These include insurance regulations, price and wage controls, banking controls, and controls of unfair competition and trade practices.

HIGHLIGHTING THE POINT

The state of Iowa enacts a law imposing a fifteen-year term of imprisonment without a trial on all businesspersons who appear in their own television commercials.

Is this law unconstitutional on either substantive or procedural grounds? Yes. Substantive review would invalidate the legislation because it abridges freedom of speech. Procedurally, the law is unfair because it imposes the penalty without giving the accused a chance to defend his or her actions.

4–3b Equal Protection

equal protection clause
The provision in the Fourteenth Amendment to the Constitution that guarantees that a state may not "deny to any person within its jurisdiction the equal protection of the laws."

Under the Fourteenth Amendment, a state may not "deny to any person within its jurisdiction the equal protection of the laws." This **equal protection clause** also applies to the federal government. Equal protection means that the government must treat similarly situated individuals in a similar manner.

Equal protection, like substantive due process, relates to the substance of a law or other governmental action. A law or action that limits the liberty of *all* persons may violate substantive due process, while a law or action that limits the liberty of *some* persons but not others may violate the equal protection clause. For instance, if a law prohibits all persons from buying contraceptive devices, it raises a substantive due process question. If it prohibits only unmarried persons from buying the same devices, it raises an equal protection issue.

Under the equal protection clause, when a law or action distinguishes between or among individuals, the basis for the distinction—that is, the classification—is examined.

The "Rational Basis" Test Generally, a law regulating economic or social matters is valid if there is any conceivable "rational basis" on which the classification might relate to any *legitimate government interest*. It is almost impossible for a law or action to fail the rational basis test.

Real-World Case Example

A Kentucky statute prohibits businesses that sell substantial amounts of groceries or gasoline from applying for a license to sell wine and liquor. An organization of convenience store operators, including Maxwell's Pic-Pac, Inc., filed a suit in a federal district court against Tony Dehner, the commissioner of the Kentucky Department of Alcoholic Beverage Control. The plaintiffs alleged that the statute was unconstitutional under the equal protection clause. The court issued a judgment in their favor, and Dehner appealed.

Is the statute rationally related to a legitimate government interest so as to be acceptable under the equal protection clause? Yes. In a 2014 decision, *Maxwell's Pic-Pac, Inc. v. Dehner*, the U.S. Court of Appeals for the Sixth Circuit reversed the judgment of the lower court. The federal appellate court cited the problems caused by alcohol, including drunk driving, as a rational basis for the state's legitimate interest in limiting access to these products to the general public. Grocery stores and gas stations pose a greater risk of exposing members of the public to alcohol—the average person spends more time in grocery stores and gas stations than in other retail establishments.

Intermediate Scrutiny A higher standard applies to laws involving gender discrimination or discrimination against illegitimate children (children born out of wedlock). Laws using these classifications must substantially relate to *important government objectives*. For example, an important government objective is preventing illegitimate teenage pregnancies. Because males and females are not similarly situated in this circumstance—only females can become pregnant—a law that punishes men but not women for statutory rape is valid.

Strict Scrutiny The highest standard applies to a law or an action that inhibits some persons' exercise of a fundamental right or is based on a *suspect trait* (such as race, national origin, or citizenship status). This will stand only if it is necessary to promote a *compelling government interest*. **EXAMPLE 4.5** A small town in New Jersey begins awarding construction contracts to Wyatt's Construction and several other minority-owned construction companies. The town is attempting to correct its long history of illegal discrimination against minority-owned construction companies. The preference program goes no further than necessary to correct the problem. Additionally, its guidelines mandate that it stop once there is success in balancing the number of city contracts awarded to Wyatt and other minorities. ◄

4–4 PRIVACY RIGHTS

The U.S. Constitution does not explicitly mention a general right to privacy. It was not until the 1960s that a majority on the United States Supreme Court endorsed the view that the Constitution indeed protects individual privacy rights.

LEARNING OUTCOME 5

Outline the protection of individual privacy rights under the Constitution and federal statutes.

In a landmark 1965 case, the Court invalidated a Connecticut law that effectively prohibited the use of contraceptives on the ground that it violated the right to privacy. The Court held that a constitutional right to privacy was implied by the First, Third, Fourth, Fifth, and Ninth Amendments. Today, privacy rights also receive protection under various state and federal statutes.

Important federal legislation relating to privacy rights includes the following:

1. *The Freedom of Information Act* (1966) provides that individuals have a right to access information about themselves collected in government files.

2. *The Privacy Act* (1974) protects the privacy of individuals about whom the federal government has information. Agencies that use or disclose personal information must ensure that the information is reliable and guard against its misuse.

3. *The Electronic Communications Privacy Act* (1986) prohibits the interception of information communicated by electronic means.

4. *The Health Insurance Portability and Accountability Act* (1996), or HIPAA, prohibits the use of a consumer's medical information for any purpose other than that for which such information was provided, unless the consumer expressly consents to the use.

For a discussion of two laws pertaining to the collection of personal information by businesses, see the *Linking Business Law to Your Career* feature at the end of this chapter.

ANSWERING THE LEGAL PROBLEM

In the legal problem set out at the beginning of this chapter, a motel owner challenged the Civil Rights Act of 1964, which bans racial discrimination in establishments of interstate commerce, as an unconstitutional exercise of Congress's power.

A **Did Congress exceed its authority by passing the Civil Rights Act?** No. Racial discrimination harms interstate travel when certain persons are denied equal access to "places of public accommodation," thus impeding interstate commerce. As for the motel's local character, under the Constitution's commerce clause, Congress has the power to regulate local activities that affect interstate commerce.

LINKING BUSINESS LAW to Your Career

PRETEXTING AND MARKETING

If you work in marketing or sales, gathering and obtaining information about your current and target customers will be a significant part of your position. There are many legitimate strategies for gleaning customer and market details, such as purchasing mailing lists, installing certain software on the company's Web site, and conducting social media and phone surveys.

Because of the rising concern over privacy rights as technology improves, however, you will need to be cautious how you conduct market research and gather personal information. One problematic research method that you should know about is pretexting.

What Is Pretexting?

A pretext is a false motive to hide the real motive. Thus, *pretexting* is the process of obtaining information by false means. For instance, a pretexter who claims that he is from a certain bank may ask an individual—via the phone or e-mail—for personal and banking data to assist him in updating that individual's account with a new security system. Once important details are given, the pretexter can sell it to a data broker who, in turn, can sell it to another party, such as your company or even an identity thief.

The Law and Pretexting

Congress has passed laws to help deal with the potential problems of pretexting, such as identity theft and the invasion of privacy. The Gramm-Leach-Bliley Act, for example, made pretexting to obtain financial information illegal. Another law—the Telephone Records and Privacy Protection Act—prohibits someone from using false representations to obtain another person's confidential phone records. The act also prohibits the buying or selling of such phone records without the owner's permission.

Despite these two laws, pretexting often skirts the boundary between legal and illegal. Thus, as a marketing professional, be careful not to violate any pretexting laws.

TERMS AND CONCEPTS FOR REVIEW

Bill of Rights 52

checks and balances 50

commerce clause 50

due process clause 55

equal protection clause 56

establishment clause 54

federal form of government 50

filtering software 54

free exercise clause 54

indictment 52

police powers 50

preemption 51

substantial government interest 53

supremacy clause 51

symbolic speech 53

CHAPTER SUMMARY—CONSTITUTIONAL LAW

LEARNING OUTCOME	
1	**State the constitutional clause that gives the federal government the power to regulate commercial activities among the states.** The commerce clause—Article I, Section 8, of the U.S. Constitution—expressly permits Congress to regulate commerce, authorizing the national government to regulate every commercial enterprise in the United States. A state government may regulate private activities within its borders to protect or promote the public order, health, safety, morals, and general welfare. But a state regulation that substantially interferes with interstate commerce violates the commerce clause.
2	**Identify the constitutional clause that allows federal laws to take priority over conflicting state laws.** The supremacy clause—Article VI of the U.S. Constitution—provides that the Constitution, laws, and treaties of the United States are "the supreme Law of the Land." Whenever a state law directly conflicts with a federal law, the state law is rendered invalid.
3	**Describe the Bill of Rights.** The Bill of Rights, which consists of the first ten amendments to the U.S. Constitution, embodies a series of protections for individuals—and in some situations, business entities—against various types of government interference.
4	**Locate the due process clause in the Constitution.** Both the Fifth and the Fourteenth Amendments to the U.S. Constitution provide that no person shall be deprived "of life, liberty, or property, without due process of law." The due process clause of each of these constitutional amendments has two aspects—procedural and substantive.
5	**Outline the protection of individual privacy rights under the Constitution and federal statutes.** A personal right to privacy is held to be so fundamental as to apply at both the state and the federal level. There is no specific guarantee of a right to privacy in the Constitution, but such a right has been derived from guarantees found in the First, Third, Fourth, Fifth, and Ninth Amendments. Federal statutes also protect privacy rights, including the Freedom of Information Act, the Privacy Act, the Electronic Communications Privacy Act, and the Health Insurance Portability and Accountability Act.

ISSUE SPOTTERS

Check your answers to the *Issue Spotters* against the answers provided in Appendix C at the end of this text.

1. Can a state, in the interest of energy conservation, ban all advertising by power utilities if conservation could be accomplished by less restrictive means? Why or why not? (See *Business and the Bill of Rights.*)

2. Would it be a violation of equal protection for a state to impose on out-of-state companies doing business in the state a tax that is higher than the tax on in-state companies if the only reason for the tax is to protect local firms from out-of-state competition? Explain your answer. (See *Due Process and Equal Protection.*)

USING BUSINESS LAW

4–1. Commerce Clause. A Georgia state law requires the use of contoured rear-fender mudguards on trucks and trailers operating within its state lines. The statute further makes it illegal for trucks and trailers to use straight mudguards. In thirty-five other states, straight mudguards are legal.

Moreover, in the neighboring state of Florida, straight mudguards are explicitly required by law. There is some evidence suggesting that contoured mudguards might be a little safer than straight mudguards. Discuss whether this Georgia statute violates any constitutional provisions. (See *The Constitutional Powers of Government.*)

4–2. Freedom of Speech. A mayoral election is about to be held in Bay City. One of the candidates is Donita Estrella, and her supporters wish to post campaign signs on streetlights and utility posts. A Bay City ordinance prohibits the posting of signs on public property. The purpose of the ordinance is to improve the appearance of the city. Estrella's supporters contend that the ordinance violates their rights to free speech. What factors might a court consider in determining the constitutionality of this ordinance? (See *Business and the Bill of Rights.*)

REAL-WORLD CASE PROBLEMS

4–3. Equal Protection. Abbott Laboratories licensed Smith-Kline Beecham Corp. to sell an Abbott human immuno-deficiency virus (HIV) drug. Abbott then increased the wholesale price of its drug. This forced SmithKline to increase its price and thereby drove business to Abbott, which continued to sell its product at a lower price. Smith-Kline filed a suit in a federal district court against Abbott, alleging breach of contract. During jury selection, Abbott eliminated the only self-identified gay person among the potential jurors. Could the equal protection clause be applied to prohibit discrimination based on sexual orientation in jury selection? Discuss. [*SmithKline Beecham Corp. v. Abbott Laboratories*, 740 F.3d 471 (9th Cir. 2014)] (See *Business and the Bill of Rights.*)

4–4. Freedom of Speech. Mark Wooden sent e-mail to an alderwoman for the city of St. Louis. Attached was a nineteen-minute audio. In a menacing, maniacal tone, Wooden said that he was "dusting off a sawed-off shotgun," called himself a "domestic terrorist," and referred to the assassination of President John Kennedy, the murder of federal Judge John Roll, and the shooting of Congresswoman Gabrielle Giffords. Feeling threatened, the alderwoman called the police. Wooden was convicted of harassment under a state criminal statute. Was this conviction unconstitutional under the First Amendment? Discuss. [*State v. Wooden*, 388 S.W.3d 522 (Mo. 2013)] (See *Business and the Bill of Rights.*)

4–5. Establishment Clause. Judge James DeWeese hung a poster in his courtroom showing the Ten Commandments. The American Civil Liberties Union filed a suit, alleging that the poster violated the establishment clause. DeWeese responded that his purpose was not to promote religion but to express his view about "warring" legal philosophies—moral relativism and moral absolutism. "Our legal system is based on moral absolutes from divine law handed down by God through the Ten Commandments." Does this poster violate the establishment clause? Why or why not? [*American Civil Liberties Union of Ohio Foundation, Inc. v. DeWeese*, 633 F.3d 424 (6th Cir. 2011)] (See *Business and the Bill of Rights.*)

4–6. Commerce Clause. Under the federal Sex Offender Registration and Notification Act (SORNA), sex offenders must register as sex offenders and must update their registration when they travel from one state to another. David Hall, a convicted sex offender in New York, moved to Virginia, where he did not update his registration. He was charged with violating SORNA. He claimed that the statute is unconstitutional, arguing that Congress cannot criminalize interstate travel if no commerce is involved. Is his argument reasonable? Why or why not? [*United States v. Hall*, 591 F.3d 83 (2d Cir. 2010)] (See *The Constitutional Powers of Government.*)

ETHICAL QUESTIONS

4–7. The Establishment Clause. Do religious displays on public property violate the establishment clause? Discuss. (See *Business and the Bill of Rights.*)

4–8. Free Speech. Aric Toll owns and manages the Balboa Island Village Inn, a restaurant and bar. Anne Lemen lives across from the inn. Lemen complained to the authorities about the inn's customers, whom she called "drunks" and "whores." Lemen told the inn's bartender Ewa Cook that Cook "worked for Satan." She repeated her statements to potential customers, and the inn's sales dropped more than 20 percent. The inn filed a suit against Lemen. Are her statements protected by the U.S. Constitution? Did she act unethically? Explain. [*Balboa Island Village Inn, Inc. v. Lemen,* 40 Cal.4th 1141, 156 P.3d 339 (2007)] (See *The Constitutional Powers of Government.*)

Chapter 4—Work Set

TRUE-FALSE QUESTIONS

_____ 1. A federal form of government is one in which a central authority holds all power.

_____ 2. The president can hold acts of Congress and of the courts unconstitutional.

_____ 3. Congress can regulate any activity that substantially affects commerce.

_____ 4. A state law that substantially interferes with interstate commerce is unconstitutional.

_____ 5. When there is a direct conflict between a federal law and a state law, the federal law is invalid.

_____ 6. If a tax is reasonable, it is within the federal taxing power.

_____ 7. The Bill of Rights protects individuals against various types of interference by the federal government only.

_____ 8. Any restriction on commercial speech is unconstitutional.

_____ 9. Due process and equal protection are different terms for the same thing.

_____ 10. The First Amendment protects individuals from speech that violates state criminal laws.

MULTIPLE-CHOICE QUESTIONS

_____ 1. Of the three branches of the federal government provided by the Constitution, the branch that makes the laws is
   a. the administrative branch.
   b. the executive branch.
   c. the judicial branch.
   d. the legislative branch.

_____ 2. Under the commerce clause, Congress can regulate
   a. any commercial activity in the United States.
   b. any noncommercial activity in the United States.
   c. both a and b.
   d. none of the above.

_____ 3. A business challenges a state law in court, claiming that it unlawfully interferes with interstate commerce. The court will consider
   a. only the state's interest in regulating the matter.
   b. only the burden that the law places on interstate commerce.
   c. the state's interest in regulating the matter and the burden that the law places on interstate commerce.
   d. none of the above.

_____ 4. A state statute that bans corporations from making political contributions that individuals can legally make is likely to be unconstitutional under
   a. the commerce clause.
   b. the First Amendment.
   c. the establishment clause.
   d. the supremacy clause.

5. A state statute that bans certain advertising practices for the purpose of preventing consumers from being misled is likely to be unconstitutional under

 a. the commerce clause.
 b. the First Amendment.
 c. the supremacy clause.
 d. none of the above.

6. Procedures that are used to decide whether to take life, liberty, or property are the focus of constitutional provisions covering

 a. equal protection.
 b. procedural due process.
 c. substantive due process.
 d. the commerce clause.

7. A law that limits the liberty of all persons to engage in a certain activity may violate constitutional provisions covering

 a. equal protection.
 b. procedural due process.
 c. substantive due process.
 d. the supremacy clause.

8. A law that restricts most vendors from doing business in a high-traffic area might be upheld under constitutional provisions covering

 a. equal protection.
 b. procedural due process.
 c. substantive due process.
 d. the free exercise clause.

9. Congress enacts a law covering airports. If a state enacts a law that directly conflicts with this federal law,

 a. both laws are valid.
 b. neither law is valid.
 c. the federal law takes precedence.
 d. the state law takes precedence.

 ## ANSWERING MORE LEGAL PROBLEMS

1. AgriCorp grows crops on farmland in three states. AgriCorp sells its harvests through USA Distributors, Inc., to Variety Mart and other national grocery chains. Small Potato Farm grows a limited crop on five acres chiefly for the personal use of its owners. The owners sell some of their produce on Saturdays at the Hector County Farmers' Market.

   Which of these growers is subject to federal regulation under the commerce clause? Both of these enterprises are subject to federal regulation under the commerce clause. The U.S. Constitution expressly delegates to the national government the power to regulate _____ commerce. This power over commerce authorizes the national government to regulate _____ commercial enterprise in the United States. Federal legislation governs nearly every major activity conducted by businesses. Here, both growers market their products, and their actions have an impact, however great or small, on interstate commerce.

2. Global Enterprises Corporation zealously advocates the election of Courtney Smith as the next president of the United States and the defeat of the incumbent, Herbert Dumpty. The corporation produces and distributes *Humpty Dumpty*, a film underscoring President Dumpty's shortcomings. The firm buys airtime on satellite and cable networks to broadcast *Courtney!*, an unabashed tribute to Dumpty's opponent.

   Has Global Enterprises violated the First Amendment? No. Freedom of _____ is Americans' most prized freedom. It forms the basis for our democratic form of government, which could not exist if we could not freely express our _____ opinions. The _____ Amendment to the U.S. Constitution guarantees the freedom of speech. Corporations exist as separate legal entities and enjoy many of the same rights as persons. Political speech by corporations falls under the protection of the First Amendment. Like persons, corporations can use their funds to advocate the election or defeat of a candidate.

TORT LAW

FACING A LEGAL PROBLEM

Joe, a supervisor at Standard Business Company, is walking down the street, minding his own business, when suddenly Albert, a former Standard employee, attacks him. In the ensuing struggle, Albert stabs Joe several times, seriously injuring Joe. A police officer restrains and arrests Albert. Albert is subject to criminal prosecution by the state.

 Can Albert also be subject to a civil lawsuit by Joe?

LEARNING OUTCOMES

The five Learning Outcomes below are designed to help improve your understanding of the chapter. After reading this chapter, you should be able to:

1 State the purpose of tort law.

2 Explain how torts and crimes differ.

3 Identify the types of intentional torts.

4 Name the four elements of negligence.

5 Define strict liability, and list circumstances in which it will be applied.

A **tort** is wrongful conduct—a civil wrong not arising from a breach of contract. Through tort law, society compensates those who have suffered injuries as a result of the wrongful conduct of others.

Tort law covers a wide variety of injuries. It provides remedies for acts that cause physical injury or that interfere with physical security and freedom of movement. Tort law provides remedies for acts that destroy or damage property. Society also recognizes an interest in protecting personal privacy, family relations, reputation, and dignity, and tort law provides remedies for invasion of these protected interests.

In this chapter, we discuss torts that can occur in any context, including the business environment.

tort
A civil wrong not arising from a breach of contract.

LEARNING OUTCOME 1

State the purpose of tort law.

5-1 THE BASIS OF TORT LAW

Tort law recognizes that some acts are wrong because they cause injuries to others. A tort is not the only type of wrong that exists in the law. Crimes also involve wrongs. A crime is an act so reprehensible that it is considered a wrong against society as a whole, as well as against the individual victim.

Therefore, the *state* prosecutes and punishes (through fines, imprisonment, and possibly death) persons who commit criminal acts. A tort action, in contrast, is a civil action in which one person brings a personal lawsuit against another to obtain compensation (monetary **damages**) or other relief for the harm suffered.

Society recognizes an interest in protecting property, and tort law provides remedies for acts that cause destruction of or damage to property. Note that in legal usage, the singular *damage* is used to refer to harm or injury to persons or property, and the plural *damages* is used to refer to monetary compensation for such harm or injury.

Sometimes the same wrongful act can result in both civil (tort) and criminal actions (see Chapter 8) against the wrongdoer. Exhibit 5.1 illustrates how this might occur.

LEARNING OUTCOME 2

Explain how torts and crimes differ.

damages
Money sought as a remedy for a breach of contract or for a tortious (wrongful) act.

EXHIBIT 5.1   Tort Lawsuit and Criminal Prosecution for the Same Act

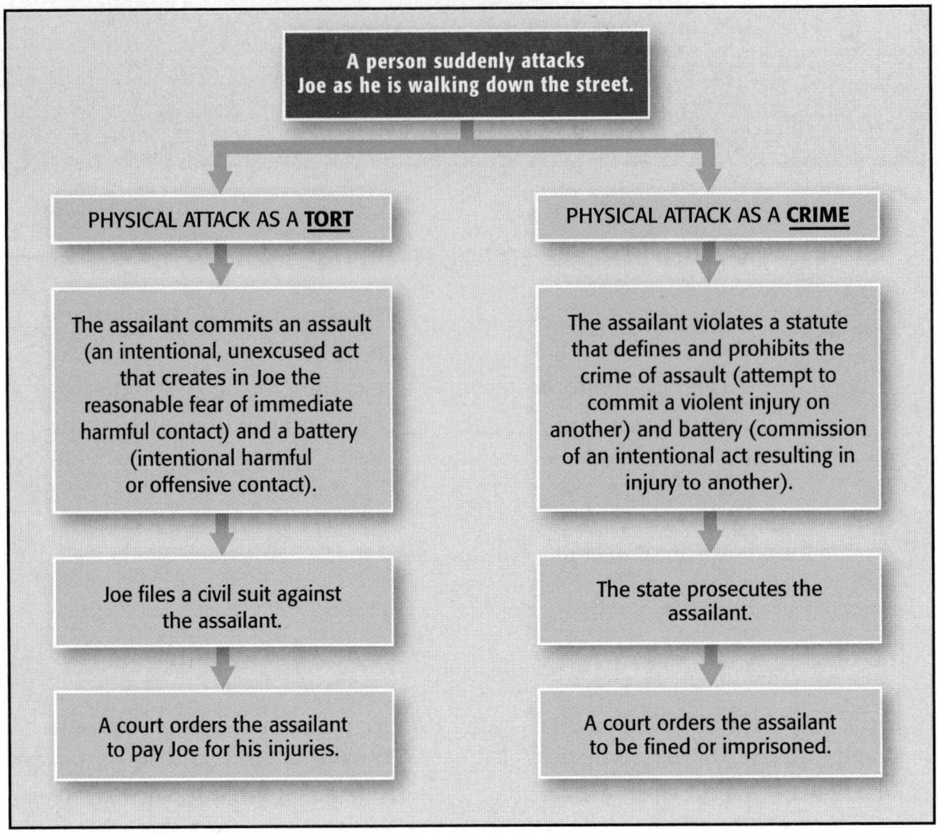

A person suddenly attacks Joe as he is walking down the street.

PHYSICAL ATTACK AS A **TORT**	PHYSICAL ATTACK AS A **CRIME**
The assailant commits an assault (an intentional, unexcused act that creates in Joe the reasonable fear of immediate harmful contact) and a battery (intentional harmful or offensive contact).	The assailant violates a statute that defines and prohibits the crime of assault (attempt to commit a violent injury on another) and battery (commission of an intentional act resulting in injury to another).
Joe files a civil suit against the assailant.	The state prosecutes the assailant.
A court orders the assailant to pay Joe for his injuries.	A court orders the assailant to be fined or imprisoned.

5–1a Tort Reform

Critics contend that tort law encourages too many trivial and unfounded lawsuits. These lawsuits clog the courts and create unnecessary costs. As an example of how tort lawsuits can be costly for society, consider medical malpractice actions, in which persons sue medical professionals for acts of *negligence* (discussed later in this chapter). Physicians who are worried about medical malpractice suits may order more tests than necessary, adding to the nation's health-care costs.

As a result, measures have been taken at various levels to reduce the number of tort cases in the nation's courts. They include limiting the amount of damages that can be awarded, limiting the amount that attorneys can collect in certain fees, and requiring the losing party to pay both the plaintiff's and the defendant's expenses.

At the federal level, the Class Action Fairness Act shifted jurisdiction over certain **class-action lawsuits** from the state courts to the federal courts. The intent of the act was to prevent plaintiffs' attorneys from *forum shopping*—that is, shopping around for a state court known to be sympathetic to their clients' cause and predisposed to award large damages.

class-action lawsuit
A suit in which a number of persons join together to bring an action.

5–1b Defenses

Even if a plaintiff proves all the elements of a tort, the defendant can raise a number of legally recognized **defenses**, which are reasons why the plaintiff should not obtain damages. The defenses available may vary depending on the specific tort involved.

A common defense to intentional torts against persons, for instance, is consent. When a person consents to the act that damages her or him, there is generally no

defense
A reason offered by the defendant in an action or lawsuit as to why the plaintiff should not recover or establish what he or she seeks.

liability. The most widely used defense in negligence actions, however, is *comparative negligence* (discussed later in this chapter). A successful defense releases the defendant from partial or full liability for the tortious act.

liability
The state of being legally responsible (liable) for something, such as a debt or an obligation.

5–2 INTENTIONAL TORTS AGAINST PERSONS

An **intentional tort** requires intent. The **tortfeasor** (the one committing the tort) must intend to commit an act, the consequences of which interfere with the interests of another in a way not permitted by law. An evil or harmful motive is not required. Intent means only that the actor intended the consequences of his or her act or knew with substantial certainty that particular consequences would result from the act.

It is assumed that individuals intend the *normal* consequences of their actions. Thus, forcefully pushing another—even if done in jest and without evil motive—is an intentional tort (if injury results) because the object of a strong push can ordinarily be expected to fall down.

This section discusses intentional torts against persons, which include assault and battery, false imprisonment, defamation, invasion of the right to privacy, fraudulent misrepresentation, and torts related to abusive litigation. It also discusses the business tort of wrongful interference.

intentional tort
A wrongful act knowingly committed.

tortfeasor
One who commits a tort.

LEARNING OUTCOME 3

Identify the types of intentional torts.

5–2a Assault and Battery

An intentional, unexcused act that creates in another person a reasonable apprehension or fear of immediate harmful or offensive contact is an **assault**. Apprehension is not the same as fear. If a contact is such that a reasonable person would want to avoid it, and there is a reasonable basis for believing that the contact will occur, the plaintiff suffers apprehension, whether or not he or she is afraid.

The *completion* of the act that caused the apprehension, if it results in harm to the plaintiff, is a **battery**—an unexcused and harmful or offensive physical contact *intentionally* performed.

assault
Any word or action intended to make another person fearful of immediate physical harm.

battery
The intentional touching of another.

HIGHLIGHTING THE POINT

Ivan enters Deli-Stop, a convenience store. He threatens Jean, the Deli-Stop clerk, with a gun, and then shoots her.

Which of these acts is an assault? Which is a battery? The pointing of the gun at Jean is an assault. The firing of the gun (if the bullet hits Jean) is a battery. The law concerning assault protects us from having to expect harmful or offensive contact. Apprehension of such contact is enough to justify compensation. The law concerning battery protects us from being subject to harmful or offensive contact. The contact can be made by another person or by some force the other person sets in motion— for example, a bullet fired from a gun.

The contact can be harmful, or it can be merely offensive (such as an unwelcome kiss). The contact can involve any part of the body or anything attached to it—for example, an item of clothing or a car in which one is sitting. Whether the contact is offensive is determined by the *reasonable person standard* (discussed shortly). The contact can be made by the defendant or by some force that the defendant sets in motion, such as a thrown rock.

5–2b False Imprisonment

False imprisonment is the intentional confinement or restraint of another person without justification. The confinement can be accomplished through the use of physical barriers, physical restraint, or threats of physical force. Moral pressure or threats of future harm do not constitute false imprisonment.

Businesspersons are often confronted with lawsuits for false imprisonment after they have attempted to confine a suspected shoplifter for questioning. In some states, a merchant can use the defense of *probable cause* to justify delaying a suspected shoplifter. Probable cause exists when the evidence to support the belief that a person is guilty outweighs the evidence against that belief. The detention, however, must be conducted in a reasonable manner and for only a reasonable length of time.

5–2c Defamation

defamation
Anything published or publicly spoken that causes injury to another's good name, reputation, or character.

libel
Defamation in written form.

slander
Defamation in oral form.

Defamation involves wrongfully hurting a person's good name, reputation, or character. Doing so in writing involves the tort of **libel**. Doing so orally involves the tort of **slander**. Defamation also occurs when a false statement is made about a person's product, business, or title to property.

To establish defamation, a plaintiff normally must prove the following:

1. The defendant made a false statement of fact. Simply making a negative statement about another person is not defamation, unless the statement is false and represents something as a fact rather than a personal opinion. **EXAMPLE 5.1** Kim's statement, "Lane cheats on his taxes," if false, can lead to liability for defamation. Kim's statement, "Lane is a jerk," however, cannot constitute defamation because it is an opinion. ◄

2. The statement was understood as being about the plaintiff and tended to harm the plaintiff's reputation.

3. The statement was published to at least one person other than the plaintiff.

4. If the plaintiff is a public figure, she or he must prove actual malice (discussed shortly).

The Publication Requirement The basis of the tort of defamation is the *publication* of a statement that holds an individual up to contempt, ridicule, or hatred. Publication means that a statement is communicated to a person other than the defamed party. **EXAMPLE 5.2** If Peters calls Gordon incompetent when no one else is around, the statement is not slander, because it was not communicated to a third party. ◄

Publication can take various forms, such as dictating a letter to another person, a third party overhearing a statement by chance, and making defamatory statements via the Internet. An individual who republishes or repeats defamatory statements is liable even if that person reveals the source of the statements.

HIGHLIGHTING THE POINT

Jack and Donna are exchanging thoughts online via Facebook. Donna falsely accuses her manager of sexual misconduct.

Does this statement constitute defamation? Yes. What may seem like a private online "conversation" between just two persons is, in fact, a very public exchange, potentially accessible to hundreds of people. The fact that Jack and Donna are unseen at the time the defamatory statement is made makes no difference. The person defamed (the manager) could suffer serious harm from the statement, such as loss of reputation and perhaps even the loss of a job. Donna also could be sued in court for damages.

Defenses Truth normally is an absolute defense against a defamation charge. In other words, if the defendant in a defamation suit can prove that his or her allegedly defamatory statements were true, most likely no tort has been committed.

Privileged Communications There may be a **privilege** involved in certain communications that will allow a person to avoid liability for defamation. For instance, statements made by attorneys and judges during a trial are privileged and cannot be the basis for a defamation charge. Statements made by members of Congress on the floor of Congress are also privileged.

privilege
In tort law, immunity from liability for an action that would otherwise be a tort.

Public Figures Special rules apply to statements about *public figures*—public officials who exercise substantial governmental power and any persons in the public limelight. In general, defamatory statements made in the press about public figures are privileged if they are made without **actual malice.**

To be made with actual malice, a statement must be made *with either knowledge of its falsity or a reckless disregard for the truth.* Public figures must prove actual malice because statements made about them are usually related to matters of public interest. Also, public figures generally have access to a public medium, such as television or radio, for answering falsehoods. Private individuals do not.

actual malice
A defamatory statement made about a public figure with knowledge of its falsity or with reckless disregard for the truth.

5–2d Invasion of the Right to Privacy

Four acts qualify as an invasion of privacy:

1. The use of a person's name, picture, or other likeness for commercial purposes without permission. This is the tort of *appropriation*.
2. Intrusion into an individual's affairs or seclusion in an area in which the person has a reasonable expectation of privacy. **EXAMPLE 5.3** Trevor secretly videos Janet while she is changing her clothes in her bedroom. He then posts the video on YouTube. Janet can sue Trevor for invasion of privacy.◄
3. Publication of information that places a person in a false light. This could be a story that a person did something that he or she did not actually do. (Publishing such a story could also constitute defamation.)
4. Public disclosure of private facts about a private individual that an ordinary person would find objectionable.

5–2e Fraudulent Misrepresentation

Misrepresentation leads another to believe in a condition that is different from the condition that actually exists. The tort of **fraudulent misrepresentation,** or fraud, involves intentional deceit for personal gain. The tort includes several elements:

fraudulent misrepresentation
Any misrepresentation, either by misstatement or by omission of a material fact, knowingly made with the intention of deceiving another and on which a reasonable person would and does rely to his or her detriment.

1. A misrepresentation of facts or conditions with knowledge that they are false or with reckless disregard for the truth.

2. An intent to induce another to rely on the misrepresentation.

3. A justifiable reliance on the misrepresentation by the deceived party.

4. Injuries suffered as a result of this reliance.

5. A causal connection between the misrepresentation and the injury.

For fraud to occur, more than mere **puffery,** or *seller's talk,* must be involved. Fraud exists only when a person represents as a fact something he or she knows is untrue. **EXAMPLE 5.4** Brandon commits fraud when he claims that a building does not leak when he knows it does.◄

Facts are objectively ascertainable, whereas seller's talk is not. **EXAMPLE 5.5** Betty, who is a certified public accountant, says, "I am the best accountant in town." This is seller's talk. Betty is not trying to represent something as fact, because the term *best* is a subjective, not an objective, term.◄

puffery
A salesperson's claims concerning the quality of property offered for sale. Such claims involve opinions rather than facts and are not legally binding promises or warranties.

5–2f Abusive or Frivolous Litigation

Tort law recognizes that people have a right not to be sued without a legally just and proper reason, and therefore it protects individuals from the misuse of litigation. If the party that initiated a lawsuit did so out of malice and without a legitimate legal reason, and ended up losing that suit, the party can be sued for *malicious prosecution.*

Abuse of process can apply to any person using a legal process against another in an improper manner or to accomplish a purpose for which it was not designed. Abuse of process does not require proof that the defendant acted out of malice or lost a prior legal proceeding.

5–2g Wrongful Interference—A Business Tort

Business torts involve wrongful interference with another's business rights. Wrongful interference is generally divided into two categories: wrongful interference with a contractual relationship and wrongful interference with a business relationship.

business tort
A tort occurring only within the business context.

Wrongful Interference with a Contractual Relationship Three elements are necessary for wrongful interference with a contractual relationship to occur:

1. A valid, enforceable *contract* (a promise constituting an agreement) must exist between two parties.

2. A third party must *know* that this contract exists.

3. The third party must *intentionally* cause either of the two parties to break the contract.

The contract may be between a firm and its employees or a firm and its customers. Sometimes, a firm's competitor may hire one of the firm's key employees. If the original employer can show that the competitor induced the former employee to break the contract, damages can be recovered from the competitor.

Wrongful Interference with a Business Relationship Businesspersons devise countless schemes to attract customers. They are forbidden by the courts, however, to interfere unreasonably in another's business in their attempts to gain a share of the market.

There is a difference between *competition* (which is legal) and *predatory behavior* (which is illegal). The distinction usually depends on whether a business is attempting to attract customers in general or to solicit only those customers who have shown an interest in a similar product or service of a specific competitor. **EXAMPLE 5.6** Northgate Shopping Center contains two shoe stores: Johnson's

Athletic Shoes and Lady Foot Locker. One day, Gordon, a Johnson's employee, stands near the Lady Foot Locker's entrance and tells incoming customers that his store will beat any Lady Foot Locker price on Nike running shoes. Gordon's actions constitute the tort of wrongful interference with a business relationship, which is commonly considered to be an unfair trade practice. ◄

Defenses In considering claims of wrongful interference, courts must strike a balance between competing policies. On the one hand, the courts seek to protect enforceable contracts. On the other, they wish to promote competition in the marketplace. The courts consider legitimate competitive behavior permissible even if it results in the breaking of a contract. Thus, a person will not be liable for the tort of wrongful interference if the interference results from legitimate competitive behavior.

EXAMPLE 5.7 If Antonio's Meats advertises so effectively that it induces Alex's Restaurant to break its contract with Alvarez Meat Company, Alvarez Meat Company will be unable to recover from Antonio's Meats for wrongful interference, because advertising is legitimate competitive behavior. ◄

5–3 INTENTIONAL TORTS AGAINST PROPERTY

Intentional torts against property include trespass to land, trespass to personal property, conversion, and disparagement of property. Land is *real property,* which also includes things "permanently" attached to the land. *Personal property* consists of all other items, which are basically movable. Thus, a house and lot are real property, whereas the furniture inside a house is personal property.

5–3a Trespass to Land

A **trespass to land** occurs when a person, without permission, (1) enters onto, above, or below the surface of land that is owned by another; (2) causes anything to enter onto the land; or (3) remains on the land or permits anything to remain on it. Actual harm to the land is not required.

Common types of trespass to land include walking or driving on the land, shooting a gun over the land, throwing rocks at a building, building a dam and thus causing water to back up on someone else's land, and placing part of one's building on an adjoining landowner's property.

trespass to land
The entry onto, above, or below the surface of land owned by another without the owner's permission or legal authorization.

Liability In some jurisdictions, a trespasser is liable for damage caused to the property and generally cannot hold the owner liable for injuries sustained on the premises. Other jurisdictions apply a "reasonable duty" rule. For example, a landowner may have a duty to post a notice that property is patrolled by guard dogs. Trespassers normally can be removed from the premises through the use of reasonable force without the owner's being liable for assault and battery.

Defenses A defense to charges of trespass exists if the trespass is warranted, as when a trespasser enters to assist someone in danger. Another defense is to show that the purported owner did not actually have the right to possess the land in question.

5–3b Trespass to Personal Property

When an individual unlawfully harms the personal property of another or otherwise interferes with the owner's right to exclusive possession and enjoyment of that property, **trespass to personal property** occurs. **EXAMPLE 5.8** Kelly takes Ryan's business law textbook as a practical joke. She hides it so that he cannot find it for

trespass to personal property
The unlawful taking or harming of another's personal property; interference with another's right to the exclusive possession of his or her personal property.

several days before a final examination. Kelly has committed trespass to personal property. (She has also committed the tort of *conversion*, discussed next.)◄ If it can be shown that trespass to personal property was warranted, however, then a complete defense exists.

5–3c Conversion

conversion
The wrongful taking, using, or retaining possession of personal property that belongs to another.

When personal property is wrongfully taken from its rightful owner or possessor and placed in the service of another, the act of conversion occurs. **Conversion** is any act depriving an owner of personal property (including electronic data) without that owner's permission and without just cause. Conversion is the civil side of crimes related to theft. A store clerk who steals merchandise from the store commits a crime and engages in the tort of conversion at the same time.

Real-World Case Example

Nicholas Mora worked for Welco Electronics, but he had also established his own company, AQM Supplies. Mora used his employer's credit card to obtain money—more than $375,000—from Welco through unauthorized charges to AQM. Money paid to AQM was electronically deposited into Mora's personal bank account. Welco filed a suit in a California state court against Mora, alleging conversion. From a judgment in Welco's favor, Mora appealed.

Can the use of a credit card to obtain money from a corporation constitute conversion? Yes. In a 2014 case, *Welco Electronics, Inc. v. Mora*, a state intermediate appellate court affirmed the lower court's judgment. "The tort of conversion has been adapted to new property rights and modern means of commercial transactions." The court reasoned that when Mora misappropriated Welco's credit card and used it, he was basically stealing part of Welco's credit balance with the credit-card company. The result was an unauthorized transfer to Mora of Welco's property rights (money).

When conversion occurs, trespass to personal property usually occurs as well. If the initial taking of the property is unlawful, there is trespass. Keeping the property is conversion. Even if the initial taking of the property is not a trespass, failing to return it may still be conversion. **EXAMPLE 5.9** Cheryl borrows Marik's iPad to use while traveling home from school for the holidays. When Cheryl returns to school, Marik asks for his iPad back. Cheryl tells Marik that she gave it to her little brother for Christmas. Marik can sue Cheryl for conversion, and she will have to either return the iPad or pay damages equal to its value.◄

5–3d Disparagement of Property

disparagement of property
Economically injurious falsehoods about another's product or property.

Disparagement of property occurs when economically injurious falsehoods (lies) are made about another's *product* or *property*. Disparagement of property is a general term for torts that can be more specifically referred to as *slander of quality* or *slander of title*.

slander of quality
Publication of false information about another's product, alleging it is not what its seller claims; also referred to as *trade libel*.

Slander of Quality Publication of false information about another's product, alleging that it is not what its seller claims, constitutes the tort of **slander of quality**. This tort has also been given the name *trade libel*. The plaintiff must prove that actual damages resulted from the slander of quality. That is, it must be shown not only that a third person refrained from dealing with the plaintiff because of the improper publication, but also that there were associated damages.

Slander of Title When a publication denies or casts doubt on another's legal ownership of any property, and when this results in financial loss to that property's owner, the tort of **slander of title** may exist. Usually, this is an intentional tort in which someone knowingly publishes an untrue statement about property with the intent of discouraging a third person from dealing with the person slandered.

slander of title
The publication of a statement that denies or casts doubt on another's legal ownership of any property, causing financial loss to that property's owner.

EXAMPLE 5.10 Skinner Autos and Lew's Used Cars are competitors for local auto sales. Larry, the manager at Skinner Autos, posts a notice on his company's Web site and on social media platforms, claiming that many of Lew's cars are stolen. As a result, customer traffic at Lew's dealership decreases drastically.◄

5–4 NEGLIGENCE

The tort of **negligence** occurs when someone suffers injury because of another's failure to live up to a required *duty of care*. It is not required that the tortfeasor wished to bring about the consequences of the act or believed that they would occur. It is required only that the actor's conduct created a *risk* of such consequences. If no risk was created, there is no negligence.

negligence
The failure to exercise the standard of care that a reasonable person would exercise in similar circumstances.

Many of the actions discussed in the section on intentional torts would constitute negligence if the element of intent were missing. **EXAMPLE 5.11** Gabe intentionally shoves Myah, who falls and breaks an arm as a result. Gabe has committed an intentional tort (assault and battery). If Gabe carelessly bumps into Myah, and she falls and breaks an arm as a result, his action constitutes negligence. In either situation, Gabe has committed a tort.◄

Negligence comprises four elements, which are addressed in the following questions:

1. *Duty*—Did the defendant owe a duty of care to the plaintiff?
2. *Breach*—Did the defendant breach that duty?
3. *Harm*—Did the plaintiff suffer a legally recognizable injury as a result of the defendant's breach of the duty of care?
4. *Cause*—Did the defendant's breach cause the plaintiff's injury?

LEARNING OUTCOME 4
Name the four elements of negligence.

5–4a The Duty of Care and Its Breach

The basic principle underlying the **duty of care** is that people are free to act as they please so long as their actions do not infringe on the interests of others. When someone fails to comply with the duty of exercising reasonable care, a tortious act may have been committed. Failure to live up to a standard of care may be an act (setting fire to a building) or an omission (neglecting to put out a campfire). It may be an intentional act, a careless act, or a carefully performed but nevertheless dangerous act that results in injury.

duty of care
The duty of all persons, as established by tort law, to exercise a reasonable amount of care in their dealings with others.

The Reasonable Person Standard In determining whether a duty of care has been breached, the courts ask how a reasonable person would have acted in the same circumstances. It is not necessarily how a particular person would act. It is society's judgment on how people *should* act. If the so-called reasonable person existed, he or she would be careful, conscientious, even tempered, and honest. What constitutes reasonable care varies with the circumstances.

Duty of Landowners Landowners are expected to exercise reasonable care to protect persons coming onto their property from harm. In some jurisdictions, landowners are held to owe a duty to protect even trespassers against certain risks. Landowners who rent or lease premises to tenants are expected to exercise reasonable care to ensure that the tenants and their guests are not harmed in common areas, such as stairways.

Retailers and other firms often explicitly or implicitly invite persons to come onto their premises. These persons are considered **business invitees.** Firms are usually charged with a duty to exercise reasonable care to protect business invitees.

business invitee
A person, such as a customer or a client, who is invited onto business premises by the owner for business purposes.

HIGHLIGHTING THE POINT

Don enters Select Foods, a supermarket. One of the employees has just finished cleaning the floor, but there is no sign warning that the floor is wet. Don slips on the wet floor and sustains injuries as a result.

Is Select Foods liable for damages? Yes. A court would hold that Select Foods was negligent because the employee failed to exercise reasonable care in protecting the store's customers against *foreseeable risks* (discussed shortly) that the employee knew or *should have known* about. That a patron might slip on a wet floor and be injured was a foreseeable risk, and the employee should have taken care to avoid this risk or to warn the customer of it. The store also has a duty to discover and remove any hidden dangers that might injure a customer or other invitee.

Some risks are so obvious that no warning is necessary. For instance, a business owner does not need to warn customers to open a door before attempting to walk through it. Other risks, however, may not be so obvious to some persons, such as children.

Duty of Professionals If an individual has knowledge, skill, or intelligence superior to that of an ordinary person, the individual's conduct must be consistent with that status. Professionals—including accountants, architects, physicians, and others—have a standard minimum level of special knowledge and ability.

In determining what constitutes reasonable care in the case of professionals, their training and expertise are taken into account. In other words, an accountant cannot defend against a lawsuit for negligence by claiming he was not familiar with that principle of accounting.

5–4b The Injury Requirement

For a tort to have been committed, the plaintiff must have suffered a *legally recognizable* injury. To recover damages—that is, receive compensation—the plaintiff must have suffered some loss, harm, wrong, or invasion of a protected interest. If no harm or injury results from an action, there is nothing to compensate—and no tort exists. **EXAMPLE 5.12** If Jack carelessly bumps into Lena, who stumbles and falls as a result, Jack may be liable in tort if Lena is injured in the fall. If she is unharmed, however, there normally could be no suit for damages, because no injury was suffered. ◄

5–4c Causation

Another element necessary to a tort is *causation*. If a person fails in a duty of care and someone suffers injury, the wrongful activity must have caused the harm for a tort to have been committed.

Causation in Fact and Proximate Cause In deciding whether there is causation, the court must address two questions:

1. *Is there causation in fact?* Did the injury occur because of the defendant's act? If an injury would not have occurred without the defendant's act, then there is causation in fact. **Causation in fact** can usually be determined by the use of the *but for* test. In other words, "but for" the wrongful act, the injury would not have occurred.

2. *Was the act the proximate cause of the injury?* As a practical matter, the law establishes limits on causation through the concept of proximate cause. **Proximate cause** exists when the connection between an act and an injury is strong enough to justify imposing liability.

> **causation in fact**
> An act or omission without which an event would not have occurred.

> **proximate cause**
> Legal cause that exists when the connection between an act and an injury is strong enough to justify imposing liability.

EXAMPLE 5.13 Randall carelessly leaves a campfire burning. The fire not only burns down the forest but also sets off an explosion in a nearby chemical plant. The explosion spills chemicals into a river, killing all the fish for a hundred miles downstream and ruining the economy of a tourist resort. Should Randall be liable to the resort owners? To the tourists whose vacations were ruined? These are questions of proximate cause that a court must decide. ◄

Foreseeability *Foreseeability* is the test for proximate cause. If the victim of the harm or the consequences of the harm are unforeseeable, there is no proximate cause. How far a court stretches foreseeability is determined in part by the extent to which the court is willing to stretch the defendant's duty of care.

HIGHLIGHTING THE POINT

Jim checks into Travelers Inn. During the night, a fire is started by an arsonist. The inn has a smoke detector, sprinkler system, and alarm system, which alert the guests, but there are no emergency lights or clear exits. Attempting to escape, Jim finds the first-floor doors and windows locked. He forces open a second-floor window and jumps out. To recover for his injuries, he files a suit against Travelers Inn, on the ground of negligence. Travelers Inn responds that harm caused by arson is not a reasonably foreseeable risk.

Is the harm caused by a fire set by an arsonist a reasonably foreseeable risk?
Yes. The duty to protect others against unreasonable risks of harm extends to risks arising from acts of third persons, even criminals. The inn foresaw the possibility of fire and guarded against it with smoke detectors and sprinkler and alarm systems. The inn's failure to provide adequate lighting and clear exits created a foreseeable risk that a fire, however it started, would harm its guests.

5–4d Defenses to Negligence

The basic defenses in negligence cases are *assumption of risk* and *comparative negligence.*

Assumption of Risk A plaintiff who voluntarily enters into a risky situation, knowing the risk involved, will not be allowed to recover. This is the defense of **assumption of risk.** The requirements of this defense are (1) knowledge of the risk and (2) voluntary assumption of the risk. For instance, a driver entering a car race knows there is a risk of being injured in a crash. The driver assumes this risk. Of course, a person does not assume a risk different from or greater than a risk normally carried by an activity.

> **assumption of risk**
> A defense against negligence that can be used when the plaintiff is aware of a danger and voluntarily assumes the risk of injury from that danger.

Comparative Negligence Most states allow recovery based on the doctrine of **comparative negligence.** Under this doctrine, both the plaintiff's negligence and the defendant's negligence are computed and the liability distributed accordingly. Some

> **comparative negligence**
> A doctrine in tort law under which the liability for injuries resulting from negligent acts is shared by all parties who were negligent (including the injured party), on the basis of each person's proportionate negligence.

jurisdictions have a "pure" form of comparative negligence that allows a plaintiff to recover even if the extent of his or her fault is greater than that of the defendant.

For example, if a plaintiff is 80 percent at fault and a defendant 20 percent at fault, the plaintiff may recover 20 percent of his or her damages. Many states, however, have a "50 percent" rule by which the plaintiff recovers nothing if he or she was more than 50 percent at fault.

HIGHLIGHTING THE POINT

Brian is an experienced all-terrain-vehicle (ATV) rider. Without putting on a helmet, Brian takes his ATV for a drive. It flips, and Brian strikes his head, sustaining injuries. He files a suit against the ATV's manufacturer, American ATV Company. During the trial, it is proved that Brian's failure to wear a helmet was responsible for essentially all of his injuries. Brian's state has a "50 percent" rule.

Under these circumstances, is the manufacturer liable for any of the damage sustained? No. In a 50-percent-rule state, if a plaintiff is found to be at least equally responsible for whatever damage is sustained, he or she can recover nothing. The evidence that Brian's failure to wear a helmet is responsible for essentially all of the damage is fatal to his case.

5–5 STRICT LIABILITY

strict liability
Liability regardless of fault.

LEARNING OUTCOME 5

Define strict liability, and list circumstances in which it will be applied.

Another category of torts is **strict liability,** or *liability without fault.* Strict liability for damages proximately caused by an abnormally dangerous activity is one application of this doctrine. Strict liability applies in such a case because of the extreme risk of the activity. Balancing that risk against the potential for harm, it is fair to ask the person engaged in the activity to pay for any injury caused by it. A significant application of strict liability is in the area of *product liability*—liability of manufacturers and sellers for harmful or defective products (see Chapter 21).

ANSWERING THE LEGAL PROBLEM

In the legal problem set out at the beginning of this chapter, Joe is attacked and stabbed by Albert. Joe is seriously injured. A police officer arrests Albert, who is subject to criminal prosecution by the state.

A **Can Albert also be subject to a civil lawsuit by Joe?** Yes. Albert has committed the torts of assault and battery. Some torts, such as assault and battery, provide a basis for a criminal prosecution as well as a tort (civil) action.

TERMS AND CONCEPTS FOR REVIEW

actual malice 69	assumption of risk 75	business invitee 74
assault 67	battery 67	business tort 70

causation in fact 75

class-action lawsuit 66

comparative negligence 75

conversion 72

damages 65

defamation 68

defense 66

disparagement of property 72

duty of care 73

fraudulent misrepresentation 69

intentional tort 67

liability 67

libel 68

negligence 73

privilege 69

proximate cause 75

puffery 70

slander 68

slander of quality 72

slander of title 73

strict liability 76

tort 65

tortfeasor 67

trespass to land 71

trespass to personal property 71

CHAPTER SUMMARY—TORT LAW

LEARNING OUTCOME	
1	**State the purpose of tort law.** Through tort law, society compensates those who have suffered injuries or harm as a result of others' wrongful conduct.
2	**Explain how torts and crimes differ.** A tort is wrongful conduct not arising from a breach of contract that proximately causes harm or injury to another. A tort action is a civil action in which one person brings a personal suit against another to obtain damages (compensation) or other relief for the harm or injury. A crime is an act that is considered a wrong against society as a whole, as well as against the individual victim. The state prosecutes and punishes—through fines, imprisonment, and possibly death—a person who commits a crime.
3	**Identify the types of intentional torts.** An intentional tort is an act committed with the intent that its consequences interfere with another's interests in a way not permitted by law. Intentional torts against persons include assault, battery, false imprisonment, defamation, invasion of the right to privacy, fraudulent misrepresentation, abusive or frivolous litigation, and wrongful interference. Intentional torts against property include trespass to land, trespass to personal property, conversion, and disparagement of property.
4	**Name the four elements of negligence.** Negligence is the failure to exercise the standard of care that a reasonable person would exercise in similar circumstances. Intent to bring about certain consequences is not required. It is required only that the failure to exercise care create a risk of such consequences. The elements of negligence are (1) the existence of a legal duty of care, (2) a breach of the duty, and (3) an injury, harm, or damage to another (4) caused by the breach.
5	**Define strict liability, and list circumstances in which it will be applied.** Strict liability is liability without fault. This doctrine applies when an injury or damage is proximately caused by an abnormally dangerous activity. The theory also applies in the area of product liability—the liability of manufacturers and sellers for harmful or defective products.

ISSUE SPOTTERS

Check your answers to the *Issue Spotters* against the answers provided in Appendix C at the end of this text.

1. Adam kisses the sleeve of Eve's blouse, an act to which she did not consent. Is Adam guilty of a tort? Why or why not? (See *Intentional Torts against Persons.*)

2. After less than a year in business, Elite Fitness Club surpasses Good Health Club in number of members. Elite's marketing strategies attract many Good Health members, who then change clubs. Does Good Health have any recourse against Elite? Explain your answer. (See *Intentional Torts against Persons.*)

USING BUSINESS LAW

5–1. Trespass. Gerrit is a former employee of ABC Auto Repair Co. He enters ABC's repair shop, claiming that the company owes him $800 in back wages. Gerrit argues with ABC's general manager, Steward, and Steward orders him off the property. Gerrit refuses to leave, and Steward tells two mechanics to throw him off the property. Gerrit runs to his truck, but on the way, he grabs some tools valued at $800. Then he drives away. Gerrit refuses to return the tools. Discuss whether Gerrit has committed any torts. (See *Intentional Torts against Property.*)

5–2. Wrongful Interference. Bombardier Capital, Inc., provides financing to boat and recreational vehicle dealers.

Bombardier's credit policy requires dealers to forward the proceeds of boat sales immediately to Bombardier. When Howard Mulcahey, Bombardier's vice president of sales and marketing, learned that a dealer was not complying with this policy, he told Frank Chandler, Bombardier's credit director, of his concern. Before Chandler could obtain the proceeds, Mulcahey falsely told Jacques Gingras, Bombardier's president, that Chandler was, among other things, trying to hide the problem. On the basis of Mulcahey's statements, Gingras fired Chandler and put Mulcahey in charge of the credit department. Under what business tort theory discussed in this chapter might Chandler recover damages from Mulcahey? Explain. (See *Intentional Torts against Persons.*)

REAL-WORLD CASE PROBLEMS

5–3. Negligence. Ronald Rawls and Zabian Bailey were in an auto accident in Bridgeport, Connecticut. Bailey rear-ended Rawls at a stoplight. The evidence showed that Bailey had failed to apply his brakes in time to avoid the collision, failed to turn his vehicle to avoid the collision, failed to keep his vehicle under control, and was inattentive to his surroundings. Because Bailey's auto insurance did not cover all of the costs, Rawls filed a suit in a Connecticut state court against his own insurance company, Progressive Northern Insurance Co. Rawls wanted to obtain benefits under an underinsured motorist clause. Rawls claimed that Bailey had been negligent. Could Rawls collect from Progressive because of Bailey's negligence? Discuss. [*Rawls v. Progressive Northern Insurance Co.*, 310 Conn. 768, 83 A.3d 576 (2014)] (See *Negligence.*)

5–4. Proximate Cause. Galen Stoller was killed at a railroad crossing when a train hit his car. The crossing was marked with a stop sign and a railroad-crossing symbol. The sign was not obstructed by vegetation, but there were no flashing lights. Galen's parents filed a suit against Burlington

Northern & Santa Fe Railroad Corp. The plaintiffs accused the defendant of negligence in the design and maintenance of the crossing. The defendant argued that Galen had not stopped at the stop sign. Was the railroad negligent? What was the proximate cause of the accident? Discuss. [*Henderson v. National Railroad Passenger Corp.*, ___ F.3d ___ (10th Cir. 2011)] (See *Negligence.*)

5–5. Business Torts. Medtronic, Inc., competes for customers with St. Jude Medical S.C., Inc. James Hughes worked for Medtronic as a sales manager. His contract prohibited him from working for a competitor for one year after leaving Medtronic. Hughes sought a position as a sales director for St. Jude. St. Jude told Hughes that his contract with Medtronic was unenforceable and offered him a job. Hughes accepted. Medtronic filed a suit, alleging wrongful interference. Which type of interference was most likely the basis for this suit? Did this interference take place in the situation described above? Explain. [*Medtronic, Inc. v. Hughes*, ___ N.W.2d ___ (Minn.App. 2011)] (See *Intentional Torts against Persons.*)

ETHICAL QUESTIONS

5–6. Duty of Care. Does a person's duty of care include a duty to come to the aid of a stranger in peril? (See *Negligence.*)

5–7. Trespass to Personal Property. Who should be liable for computer viruses? Why? (See *Intentional Torts against Property.*)

Chapter 5—Work Set

TRUE-FALSE QUESTIONS

_____ 1. To be guilty of an intentional tort, a person must intend the consequences of his or her act or know with substantial certainty that those consequences will result.

_____ 2. Immediate harmful or offensive contact is an element of assault.

_____ 3. Legitimate competitive behavior does not constitute wrongful interference with a contractual relationship.

_____ 4. Slander of title requires publication of false information that denies or casts doubt on another's legal ownership of any property.

_____ 5. The tort of defamation does not occur unless a defamatory statement is made in writing.

_____ 6. Ed tells customers that he is "the best plumber in town." This is fraudulent misrepresentation, unless Ed actually believes that he is the best.

_____ 7. A person who borrows a friend's car and fails to return it at the friend's request is guilty of conversion.

_____ 8. All individuals—regardless of their knowledge, skill, or intelligence—must exercise the same duty of care if they wish to avoid liability for negligence.

_____ 9. Under the doctrine of strict liability, liability is imposed for reasons other than fault.

MULTIPLE-CHOICE QUESTIONS

_____ 1. Tom owns Tom's Computer Store. Tom sees Nan, a customer, pick up software from a shelf and put it in her bag. As Nan is about to leave, Tom tells her that she can't leave until he checks her bag. If Nan sues Tom for false imprisonment, Nan will

a. win, because a merchant cannot delay a customer on a mere suspicion.
b. win, because Nan did not first commit a tort.
c. lose, because a merchant may delay a suspected shoplifter for a reasonable time based on probable cause.
d. lose, because Tom did not intend to commit the tort of false imprisonment.

_____ 2. Walking in Don's air-conditioned market on a hot day with her sisters, four-year-old Silvia drops her ice cream on the floor near the dairy case. Two hours later, Jan stops to buy milk, slips on the ice cream puddle, and breaks her arm. Don is

a. liable, because a merchant is always liable for customers' actions.
b. liable, if Don failed to take all reasonable precautions against Jan's injury.
c. not liable, because Jan's injury was her own fault.
d. not liable, because Jan's injury was Silvia's fault.

_____ 3. Gus sends a letter to José in which he falsely accuses José of embezzling. José's secretary, Tina, reads the letter. If José sues Gus for defamation, José will

a. win, because Tina's reading of the letter satisfies the publication element.
b. win, because Gus's writing of the letter satisfies the publication element.
c. lose, because the letter is not proof that José is an embezzler.
d. lose, because the publication element is not satisfied.

_____ 4. Online Services Company (OSC) is an Internet service provider. Ads Unlimited, Inc., sends spam to OSC's customers, and some of them then cancel OSC's services. Ads Unlimited is most likely liable for

a. appropriation.
b. disparagement of property.
c. trespass to personal property.
d. wrongful interference with a business relationship.

_____ 5. Bio Box Company advertises so effectively that Product Packaging, Inc., stops doing business with Styro Cartons, Inc. Bio is

    a. liable to Styro for wrongful interference with a contractual relationship.

    b. liable to Styro for wrongful interference with a business relationship.

    c. liable to Styro for disparagement of property.

    d. not liable.

_____ 6. Al, a landlord, installs two-way mirrors in his tenants' rooms through which he watches them without their knowledge. Al is guilty of

    a. using another's likeness for commercial purposes without permission.

    b. public disclosure of private facts about another.

    c. publication of information that places another in a false light.

    d. intrusion into another's affairs or seclusion.

_____ 7. Fred returns home from work to find Barney camped in Fred's backyard. Fred says, "Get off my property." Barney says, "I'm not leaving." Fred forcibly drags Barney off the property. If Barney sues Fred, Barney will

    a. win, because Fred used too much force.

    b. win, because Barney told Fred that he was not leaving.

    c. lose, because Fred used only reasonable force.

    d. lose, because Barney is a trespasser.

_____ 8. Driving his car negligently, Paul crashes into a light pole. The pole falls, smashing through the roof of a house onto Karl, who is killed. But for Paul's negligence, Karl would not have died. Regarding Karl's death, Paul's crash is the

    a. cause in fact.

    b. proximate cause.

    c. intervening cause.

    d. superseding cause.

 ANSWERING MORE LEGAL PROBLEMS

1. During a professional hockey game, Derek, a player for the Devils, collides with Alexei, a player for the Bruins, and falls, hitting his head hard against the ice. Dazed, Derek tells his coach that he thinks he might have a concussion. The coach orders him to "man up" and get back in the game. Derek suffers a second collision with Alexei and is removed from the game unconscious. He is later diagnosed with a brain injury.

Has a tort been committed? If so, what is it, and who committed it? What is this party's best defense? The tort that has most likely been committed is _____. The elements are (1) a duty of care, (2) a breach of the duty, and (3) the breach's causation of (4) an injury. The coach has a duty to exercise _____ care within the context of the game. Ordering a player with a possible concussion to "man up" is likely not an exercise of reasonable care. This breach leads to further injuries to Derek. The coach's best defense is _____ _____. A party who voluntarily enters into a situation—such as a hockey game—knowing the risk involved cannot recover if he or she suffers an injury as a consequence. The requirements are knowledge of the risk and a voluntary assumption of it. As a player of the game, Derek most likely meets both requirements.

2. Marty, who also plays for the Devils, watches Derek being removed from the game unconscious. As soon as his teammate is off the ice, Marty swings his stick at Alexei but misses. Alexei jumps Marty and slams him into the ice. Brock, a Devil, cross-checks Alexei and kicks him on the top of the helmet.

Which tort or torts have these parties most likely committed? What are the elements, and how do they apply to these facts? The torts most likely committed by these parties are assault and _____. Assault involves an intentional, unexcused act that creates in another person a reasonable apprehension or fear of immediate harmful or offensive _____. The completion of the act, if it results in harm, is a _____. The contact can involve anything attached to the body. Whether the contact is offensive is determined by the _____ person standard. Defenses include consent and self-defense. Here, Marty's swing at Alexei would be an assault. Alexei's slam of Marty could be construed as a battery, but his best defense would be self-defense. Brock's acts would constitute assault and battery. His best defense would be consent—that Alexei consented to play a game in which the players often come to blows.

INTELLECTUAL PROPERTY

6

FACING A LEGAL PROBLEM

By 1910, the Coca-Cola Company was selling its soft drink, Coca-Cola, throughout Canada, Europe, Mexico, and the United States. Coca-Cola's competitors included Koke Company of America, which sold beverages named Koke, among other things.

Q Did Koke's marketing of products with names that were similar to Coca-Cola constitute an infringement of Coca-Cola's trademark?

LEARNING OUTCOMES

The four Learning Outcomes below are designed to help improve your understanding of the chapter. After reading this chapter, you should be able to:

1 Identify intellectual property.

2 Discuss the law's protection for trademarks.

3 Describe the protection that the law provides for patents.

4 State the law's protection for copyrights.

Intellectual property is any property resulting from intellectual, creative processes—the products of an individual's mind. It is familiar to everyone. The information in books and on computers is intellectual property—as are the apps on your smartphone, the movies you watch, and the music you hear.

Although the need to protect creative works was first recognized in Article I, Section 8, of the U.S. Constitution (see Appendix A), statutory protection of these rights began in the 1940s and continues to evolve to meet the needs of modern society. Of significant concern to businesspersons is the need to protect their rights in intellectual property, which may be more valuable than their physical property, such as machines and buildings. Thus, company trademarks, patents, copyrights, and trade secrets need legal protection, both in the United States and globally.

intellectual property
Property resulting from intellectual, creative processes.

LEARNING OUTCOME 1
Identify intellectual property.

6–1 TRADEMARKS AND RELATED PROPERTY

A **trademark** is a distinctive word, symbol, sound, or design that identifies the manufacturer as the source of particular goods and distinguishes its products from those made or sold by others. Clearly, if one manufacturer uses the trademark of another, consumers will be misled. For instance, an independent athletic clothing manufacturer that uses the trademarked Nike "swoosh" will confuse consumers. Consumers would believe that this manufacturer's products were Nike brand clothing, even though they were not. The law seeks to avoid this kind of confusion.

Once a trademark is established, the owner has exclusive use of it and has the right to bring a legal action against anyone who infringes on the trademark protection. The tort of *trademark infringement* occurs when one who does not own a trademark copies it to a substantial degree or uses it in its entirety.

trademark
A word, symbol, sound, or design that has become sufficiently associated with a good or has been registered with a government agency.

6–1a Trademark Protection

The Lanham Act of 1946 protects manufacturers from losing business to competitors that use confusingly similar trademarks. Protection under the act was given only when the unauthorized use of the mark would likely confuse consumers. In 1995, however, Congress amended the Lanham Act by passing the Federal Trademark Dilution Act. This act allows trademark owners to bring a suit in federal court for trademark dilution.

Dilution occurs when a trademark is used, without permission, in a way that diminishes the distinctive quality of the mark. Unlike trademark infringement, dilution does *not* require proof that consumers are likely to be confused by a connection between the unauthorized use and the mark. The products involved do not have to be similar. Dilution does require, however, that a mark be famous when the dilution occurs.

EXAMPLE 6.1 Samantha opens a small coffee shop in her hometown of Astoria, Oregon. She names her business "Sambuck's Coffeehouse." Starbucks Corporation—the largest coffeehouse chain in the United States—could sue Samantha over the use of the similar mark (Sambuck's). Starbucks would have a strong dilution claim against Sambuck's because her mark reduces the value (distinctive quality) of Starbucks' famous mark—even though most consumers would likely not be confused about the coffee products offered by each company. ◄

LEARNING OUTCOME 2

Discuss the law's protection for trademarks.

Distinctiveness of the Mark A central objective of the Lanham Act is to reduce the likelihood that consumers will be confused by similar marks. For that reason, only those trademarks that are deemed sufficiently distinctive from all competing trademarks will be protected.

Strong Marks Fanciful, arbitrary, or suggestive trademarks are generally considered to be the most distinctive (strongest) trademarks. Because they are normally taken from outside the context of the particular product, strong marks provide the best means of distinguishing one product from another. Fanciful trademarks include invented words, such as *Xerox* for one manufacturer's copiers and *Google* for a search engine.

In addition, arbitrary trademarks use common words that would not ordinarily be associated with the product, such as *Dutch Boy* as a name for paint. Sometimes, a single letter used in a particular style can be deemed an arbitrary trademark.

HIGHLIGHTING THE POINT

Quiksilver, Inc., a maker of surfer clothing, uses a stylized X on its products. Sports entertainment company ESPN, Inc., uses a similarly styled X in connection with its X Games, which are competitions in extreme action sports. ESPN filed a suit against Quiksilver, claiming trademark infringement. Quiksilver countered with its own claim against ESPN for trademark infringement. ESPN argued that Quiksilver's X was a design, not a trademark, and asked the court to dismiss the counterclaim.

Can a single letter, such as an X, that is used in a particular style be an arbitrary trademark? Yes. The court refused to dismiss Quiksilver's claim, holding that the X on Quiksilver's products was clearly an arbitrary mark. The court found further that the two Xs were similar enough that a consumer might well confuse them.

Lastly, suggestive trademarks bring to mind something about a product without describing the product directly. For instance, "Dairy Queen" suggests an association between its products and milk, but it does not directly describe ice cream. Likewise, "Blu-ray" is a suggestive mark that is associated with the high-quality, high-definition video contained on a particular optical data storage disc.

Secondary Meaning Descriptive terms, geographical terms, and personal names are not inherently distinctive and do not receive protection under the law until they acquire a secondary meaning. A secondary meaning may arise when customers begin to associate a specific trademark with the source of the trademarked product.

For example, even though it is a personal name, *Calvin Klein* is a distinctive trademark because consumers associate that name with designer clothing and goods marketed by Calvin Klein or licensed distributors of Calvin Klein products.

Trademark Registration and Infringement The state and federal governments provide for the registration of trademarks. Once a trademark has been registered, a firm is entitled to its exclusive use for marketing purposes. The owner of the trademark need not register it to obtain protection from the tort of trademark infringement, but registration does furnish proof of the date of inception of its use.

To register for protection under federal trademark law, a person must file an application with the U.S. Patent and Trademark Office. This registration gives national notice that the trademark belongs exclusively to the registrant. Whenever someone else uses that trademark in its entirety or copies it to a substantial degree, intentionally or unintentionally, the trademark has been *infringed*—that is, used without authorization. When a trademark has been infringed, the owner has a cause of action against the infringer.

6–1b Counterfeit Goods

Counterfeit goods copy or otherwise imitate trademarked goods. It is estimated that nearly 7 percent of the goods imported into the United States are counterfeit. In addition to having negative financial effects on legitimate businesses, sales of certain counterfeit goods, such as pharmaceuticals and nutritional supplements, can present serious public health risks.

It is a crime to intentionally traffic, or attempt to traffic, in counterfeit goods or services or to knowingly use a counterfeit mark on or in connection with goods or services. It is also a crime to knowingly traffic, or attempt to traffic, in counterfeit labels, stickers, packaging, and the like—regardless of whether the item is attached to any goods.

6–1c Service Marks and Trade Names

A **service mark** is similar to a trademark but used to distinguish the services of one person or company from those of another. For example, each commercial airline has a particular mark or symbol associated with its name. Titles and character names used in radio and television are frequently registered as service marks. Service marks are protected the same way as trademarks.

Trademarks also apply to *products*. The term **trade name** is used to indicate part or all of a *business's name,* whether the business is a sole proprietorship, a partnership, or a corporation. Generally, a trade name is directly related to a business and its goodwill. As with trademarks, words must be unusual or fancifully used if they are to be protected as trade names. For instance, the word *Safeway* was held by the courts to be sufficiently fanciful to obtain protection as a trade name for a grocery store chain.

service mark
A mark used in the sale or advertising of services to distinguish the services of one person or company from the services of others.

trade name
A name used in commercial activity to designate a particular business.

 6–2 PATENTS

A **patent** is a grant from the government that gives an inventor the exclusive right to make, use, and sell an invention for a period of twenty years. Patents for fourteen years are given for designs, as opposed to inventions. For either a regular patent or a design patent, the applicant must demonstrate to the satisfaction of the U.S. Patent and Trademark Office that the invention, discovery, or design is *novel, useful,* and *not obvious* in light of current technology. Almost anything is patentable, including artistic methods, certain business processes, and storyline structures and patterns.

patent
A government grant that gives an inventor the exclusive right or privilege to make, use, or sell his or her invention for a limited time period.

Under the America Invents Act, the first person to file an application for a patent on the product or process receives patent protection. In addition, under the act there is a nine-month limit for challenging a patent on any ground. The words *Patent* or *Pat.* with a patent number gives notice to the world that the article or design is patented.

6–2a Patent Infringement

Describe the protection that the law provides for patents.

If a firm makes, uses, or sells another's patented design, product, or process without the patent owner's permission, the tort of patent infringement exists. Patent infringement of a design or product may exist even though not all features or parts of an invention are copied. (With respect to a patented process, however, all steps or their equivalent must be copied for infringement to exist.) In many cases of patent infringement, the costs of detection, prosecution, and monitoring are so high that the patents become valueless to their owners, because the owners cannot justify the costs of protecting them.

6–2b Licensing

license
An agreement permitting the use of a trademark, patent, copyright, or trade secret for certain limited purposes.

Because patent infringement litigation can be so costly, many patent holders will instead offer to sell a **license** to the infringer. A license for a patent, for instance, allows the use of the patented design, product, or process for certain specified purposes to another party. Licensing is one of the best ways to protect patents—as well as trademarks, copyrights, and trade secrets—and avoid costly litigation. Also, a license can limit the use of the patent to the *licensee* (the person gaining the licensing rights).

EXAMPLE 6.2 West Coast Beverage Company produces Blast Off, its newly patented sports drink, at its headquarters in California. Gordon, one of West Coast's founding partners, is moving to Vermont and wants to sell and distribute Blast Off there. To avoid costly litigation and expand their product's territory, the other partners enter into a licensing agreement with Gordon, allowing him to use the patented soft drink formula to produce and distribute Blast Off in Vermont.◄

6–3 COPYRIGHTS

copyright
The exclusive right of an author to publish, print, or sell an intellectual production for a statutory period of time.

A **copyright** is an intangible right granted by statute to the author or originator of certain literary or artistic productions. These works are protected by the federal government's Copyright Act. Works created after January 1, 1978, are automatically given copyright protection for the life of the author, plus 70 years. For copyrights owned by publishing houses, the copyright expires 95 years from the date of publication or 120 years from the date of creation, whichever is first. For works by one or more authors, the copyright expires 70 years after the death of the last surviving author.

Copyrights can be registered with the U.S. Copyright Office. This registration is evidence that the copyright is valid. A copyright owner no longer needs to place a © or an ® on the work to have the work protected against infringement. Chances are that if somebody created it, somebody owns it. **EXAMPLE 6.3** Rusty Carroll operated an online term paper business, R2C2 Inc., that offered up to 300,000 research papers for sale. Some individuals whose work had been posted without their permission sued. The court prohibited Carroll and R2C2 from selling any term paper without proof that the paper's author had given his or her permission.◄

6–3a What Is Protected Expression?

Works that are copyrightable include books, records, films, artworks, architectural plans, menus, music videos, and product packaging. To obtain protection under the

Copyright Act, a work must be original and fall into one of the following categories: (1) literary works; (2) musical works; (3) dramatic works; (4) pantomimes and choreographic works; (5) pictorial, graphic, and sculptural works; (6) motion pictures and other audiovisual works; (7) sound recordings; and (8) computer software.

To be protected, a work must be "fixed in a durable medium" from which it can be perceived, reproduced, or communicated. Protection is automatic. Registration is not required.

The Copyright Act excludes copyright protection for any "idea, procedure, process, system, method of operation, concept, principle or discovery, regardless of the form in which it is described, explained, illustrated, or embodied." Note that it is not possible to copyright an *idea*. The underlying ideas embodied in a work may be freely used by others. What is copyrightable is the particular way in which an idea is *expressed*. Whenever an idea and an expression are inseparable, the expression cannot be copyrighted. (A standard calendar, for instance, cannot be copyrighted.)

Real-World Case Example

Inhale, Inc., held a copyright on a hookah—a device for smoking tobacco by filtering the smoke through water—that included skull-and-crossbones images on its outside. Inhale filed a suit in a federal district court against Starbuzz Tobacco, Inc., alleging copyright infringement for the sale of identically shaped hookahs (without the skull-and-crossbones images). The court determined that the shape of the water container on Inhale's hookahs was not copyrightable and issued a judgment in Starbuzz's favor. Inhale appealed.

Was Inhale's copyright infringed by Starbuzz's sale of hookahs with identically shaped water containers? No. In the 2014 case, *Inhale, Inc. v. Starbuzz Tobacco, Inc.*, the U.S. Court of Appeals for the Ninth Circuit affirmed the lower court's judgment. The water container on a hookah is a "useful article," and thus its shape is copyrightable only if it incorporates sculptural features that are separate from its useful aspect. In this case, the shape of the container was not independent of its utilitarian function—to hold water within its shape—and thus the shape was not copyrightable.

6–3b Copyright Infringement

Whenever the form or expression of an idea is copied, an infringement of copyright occurs. The production does not have to be exactly the same as the original, nor does it have to reproduce the original in its entirety. Penalties or remedies can be imposed on those who infringe copyrights. These include requiring the payment of damages and subjecting an infringer to criminal proceedings for willful violations (which may result in fines, imprisonment, or both).

An exception to liability for copyright infringement is made under the "fair use" doctrine. A person or organization can reproduce copyrighted material without paying *royalties* for purposes such as criticism, comment, news reporting, teaching (including multiple copies for classroom use), scholarship, and research. (*Royalties* are fees paid to the copyright holder for the privilege of reproducing the copyrighted material.)

LEARNING OUTCOME 4

State the law's protection for copyrights.

In determining whether the use of a work in a particular case is a fair use, a court considers the following:

1. The purpose of the use.
2. The nature of the copyrighted work.
3. How much of the original is copied.
4. The effect of the use on the market for the copyrighted work.

Once a copyright owner sells or gives away a copy of a work, the copyright owner no longer has the right to control the distribution of that copy. **EXAMPLE 6.4** Lisa buys a copyrighted book, such as *The Hunger Games* by Suzanne Collins. Lisa can then legally sell it to another person. ◄

6–3c Copyright Protection for Software

In 1980, Congress passed the Computer Software Copyright Act to include computer programs in the list of creative works protected by federal copyright law. Generally, copyright protection extends not only to those parts of a computer program that can be read by humans, such as the high-level language of a source code, but also to the binary-language object code of the program, which is readable only by the computer. Additionally, such elements as the overall structure, sequence, and organization of a program have been deemed copyrightable.

Not all aspects of software may be protected by copyright law, however. For the most part, courts have not extended copyright protection to the "look and feel"— the general appearance, command structure, video images, menus, windows, and other screen displays—of computer programs. Note, however, that copying the look and feel of another's product may be a violation of trademark laws.

HIGHLIGHTING THE POINT

MyTek, LLC, developed architectural-blueprint software that, among other things, indicated the size and location of wood trusses on the walls of a structure under construction. Contractor Associates, Inc., created and marketed a different architectural-blueprint program that accomplished the same tasks, such as the layout of wood trusses, and included similar elements, such as the menu and submenu command structures.

Did Contractor Associates commit copyright infringement? No. MyTek could not successfully sue Contractor Associates for copyright infringement because the idea of an architectural-blueprint software program is not copyrightable and copyright law does not protect the command structure of software.

6–4 TRADE SECRETS

Some business processes and information that are not, or cannot be, patented, copyrighted, or trademarked are nevertheless protected as trade secrets. A **trade secret** consists of customer lists, plans, research and development, pricing information, marketing techniques, or production techniques. Generally, anything that makes an individual company unique and that would have value to a competitor is considered a trade secret.

EXAMPLE 6.5 Norman is a salesman for Rockford Textiles Company. If he tries to solicit Rockford's competitors for noncompany business, or if he copies Rockford's unique method of manufacture, he has appropriated a trade secret. ◄ Theft

trade secret
Information or a process giving a business an advantage over competitors who do not know the information or process.

of confidential business data by industrial espionage, as when a business taps into a competitor's computer, is also a theft of trade secrets.

The Economic Espionage Act of 1996 made the theft of trade secrets a federal crime. An individual who violates the act can be imprisoned for up to ten years and fined up to $500,000. If a corporation or other organization violates the act, it can be fined up to $5 million. Any property acquired as a result of the violation and any property used in the commission of the violation is subject to forfeiture—meaning that the government can take the property.

6–5 INTERNATIONAL PROTECTION FOR INTELLECTUAL PROPERTY

Various international agreements relate to intellectual property rights. One of the first was the Paris Convention of 1883, to which 174 countries are signatories. The Paris Convention allows parties in one country to file for patent and trademark protection in any of the other member countries.

6–5a The Berne Convention

Under the Berne Convention of 1886, an international copyright agreement, every member country must recognize the copyrights of authors who are citizens of other member countries. If a citizen of a country that has not signed the convention first publishes a book in a country that has signed, all other countries that have signed the convention must recognize that author's copyright.

6–5b The TRIPS Agreement

More than one hundred countries have signed the agreement on Trade-Related Aspects of Intellectual Property Rights (TRIPS). Under this agreement, a member nation cannot give its citizens more favorable treatment, in terms of the administration, regulation, or adjudication of intellectual property rights, than it offers to the citizens of other member countries.

TRIPS specifically provides copyright protection for computer programs by stating that compilations of data, databases, or other materials are "intellectual creations" and that they are to be protected as copyrightable works. Other provisions relate to patents, trademarks, trade secrets, and the rental of computer programs and cinematographic works.

6–5c The Anti-Counterfeiting Trade Agreement

Eight countries—Australia, Canada, Japan, Korea, Morocco, New Zealand, Singapore, and the United States—signed the Anti-Counterfeiting Trade Agreement (ACTA) in 2011. This international treaty's goals are to increase international cooperation, facilitate the best law enforcement practices, and provide a legal framework to combat counterfeiting. ACTA applies to counterfeit physical goods, such as medications, and pirated, copyrighted works being distributed online.

ANSWERING THE LEGAL PROBLEM

In the legal problem set out at the beginning of this chapter, the Coca-Cola Company's competitors included Koke Company of America, which sold beverages named Koke, among other things.

A Did Koke's marketing of products with names that were similar to Coca-Cola constitute an infringement of Coca-Cola's trademark? Yes. The name *Coke* was so common a term for the trademarked product that Koke Company's use of the similar-sounding *Koke* as a name for its beverages was not acceptable. Trademarks and trade names (and their nicknames) that are in common use are protected under the law.

LINKING BUSINESS LAW to Your Career

TRADEMARKS AND SERVICE MARKS

You might plan on having a career in marketing. As a marketing manager, you will be involved with creating trademarks or service marks for your firm and protecting the firm's existing marks.

The Broad Range of Trademarks and Service Marks

The courts have held that trademarks and service marks consist of much more than well-known brand names, such as Sony™. Be aware that parts of a brand or other product identification often qualify for trademark protection. Keep the following examples of branding in mind when working in a marketing department:

- **Catchy Phrases**—Certain brands have established phrases that are associated with them, such as Nike's "Just Do It!"
- **Abbreviations**—Sometimes, the public abbreviates a well-known trademark. For example, Budweiser™ is also known as Bud.
- **Shapes**—The shape of a brand name, service mark, or even a container can take on exclusivity if these shapes clearly aid in product or service identification, such as the shape of a Coca-Cola bottle.
- **Ornamental Colors**—Color combinations can become part of a service mark or trademark. For instance,

FedEx established its identity with the use of bright orange and purple.

- **Ornamental Designs**—Symbols and designs associated with a mark normally are protected.

When to Protect Your Trademarks and Service Marks

Once your company has established a trademark or a service mark, if you fail to protect it, your company faces the possibility that it will become generic. Always include the trademark symbols in your advertising. Both online and off. You want to take every opportunity to have your trademark on all company documents too.

TERMS AND CONCEPTS FOR REVIEW

copyright 84

intellectual property 81

license 84

patent 83

service mark 83

trademark 81

trade name 83

trade secret 86

CHAPTER SUMMARY—INTELLECTUAL PROPERTY

LEARNING OUTCOME	
1	**Identify intellectual property.** Trademarks, patents, copyrights, and trade secrets are forms of intellectual property. (1) A *trademark* is a distinctive word, symbol, sound, or design that identifies the manufacturer as the source of particular goods and distinguishes its products from those made or sold by others. (2) A *patent* is a grant from the government that gives an inventor the exclusive right to make, use, and sell an invention for twenty years (fourteen years for a design). (3) A *copyright* is an exclusive right granted by statute to the author or originator of certain literary or artistic work to publish, print, or sell the work for a period of time. (4) *Trade secrets* include anything (such as customer lists, plans, and pricing information) that makes a company unique and would have value to a competitor.
2	**Discuss the law's protection for trademarks.** To be protected, a trademark must be sufficiently distinctive from other trademarks. State and federal governments provide for the registration of trademarks, but a trademark does not need registration to be protected. Trademark infringement occurs when one who does not own a trademark copies it to a substantial degree or uses it in its entirety.
3	**Describe the protection that the law provides for patents.** To be patentable, an invention, discovery, process, or design must be novel, useful, and not obvious in light of current technology. Patent infringement occurs when one makes, uses, or sells another's patented design, product, or process without the patent owner's permission.
4	**State the law's protection for copyrights.** Copyright infringement occurs when the form or expression of an idea is copied without the permission of the copyright owner. The copy does not have to be exactly the same as the original to infringe. There is an exception for copying deemed a "fair use."

ISSUE SPOTTERS

Check your answers to the *Issue Spotters* against the answers provided in Appendix C at the end of this text.

1. Global Products develops, patents, and markets software. World Copies, Inc., sells Global's software without the maker's permission. Is this patent infringement? If so, how might Global save the cost of suing World for infringement and at the same time profit from World's sales? (See *Patents*.)

2. Roslyn is a food buyer for Organic Cornucopia Food Company when she decides to go into business for herself as Roslyn's Kitchen. She contacts Organic's suppliers, offering to buy their entire harvest for the next year, and Organic's customers, offering to sell her products for less than her ex-employer. Has Roslyn violated any of the intellectual property rights discussed in this chapter? Explain. (See *Trade Secrets*.)

USING BUSINESS LAW

6–1. Copyright Infringement. In which of the following situations would a court likely hold Maruta liable for copyright infringement? (See *Copyrights*.)

1. At the library, Maruta photocopies ten pages from a scholarly journal relating to a topic on which she is writing a term paper.

2. Maruta makes leather handbags and sells them in her small leather shop. She advertises her handbags as "Vutton handbags," hoping customers might mistakenly assume that they were made by Vuitton, the well-known maker of high-quality luggage and handbags.

3. Maruta owns a small country store. She purchases one copy of several popular movie DVDs from various DVD manufacturers. Then, using blank DVDs, she makes copies to rent or sell to her customers.

4. Maruta teaches Latin American history at a small university. She has a digital video recorder and frequently records television programs relating to Latin America and puts them on DVDs. She then takes the DVDs to her classroom so that her students can watch them.

6–2. Trademark Infringement. Alpha Software, Inc., announced a new computer operating system to be marketed under the name McSoftware. McDonald's Corp. wrote Alpha a letter stating that the use of this name infringed on the McDonald's family of trademarks characterized by the prefix "Mc" attached to a generic term. Alpha claimed that "Mc" had come into generic use as a prefix and therefore McDonald's had no trademark rights to the prefix itself. Alpha filed an action seeking a judgment from the court that the mark McSoftware did not infringe on McDonald's federally registered trademarks or its common law rights to the marks and that its use would not constitute an unfair trade practice. What factors must the court consider in deciding this issue? What will be the probable outcome of the case? Explain. (See *Trademarks and Related Property.*)

REAL-WORLD CASE PROBLEMS

6–3. Patents. The U.S. Patent and Trademark Office (PTO) denied Raymond Gianelli's application for a patent for a "Rowing Machine"—an exercise machine that requires a user to *pull* on handles to perform a rowing motion against a selected resistance in order to strengthen the back muscles. The PTO considered the device obvious in light of a previously patented "Chest Press Apparatus for Exercising Regions of the Upper Body"—a chest press exercise machine on which a user *pushes* on handles to overcome a selected resistance. On what ground might this result be reversed on appeal? Discuss. [*In re Gianelli*, 739 F.3d 1375 (Fed. Cir. 2014)] (See *Patents.*)

6–4. Theft of Trade Secrets. Hanjuan Jin, a Chinese citizen, worked at Motorola in the United States as a software engineer in a division that created proprietary standards for cellular communications. After a few years, she started corresponding with a company in China about a possible full-time job. During this period, she took several leaves of absence from Motorola to go to China. After one of these leaves, she returned to Motorola and downloaded thousands of company documents onto her personal laptop. While at the airport to board a flight to China, U.S. officials search her belongings and discovered the Motorola documents. Under which federal law could Jin be prosecuted for theft of trade secrets? What are the penalties under this

law? [*United States v. Hanjuan Jin*, 833 F.Supp.2d 977 (N.D.Ill. 2012)] (See *Trade Secrets.*)

6–5. Copyright Infringement. Universal Music Group (UMG) regularly ships free, unsolicited promotional CDs to music critics and others. The labels state that they are "the property of the record company" and for "Promotional Use Only—Not for Sale." When Troy Augusto sold some of the CDs through online auction sites, UMG filed a complaint in a federal district court, alleging copyright infringement. UMG argued that it had only licensed the CDs to the recipients and that ownership had not transferred to Augusto. Could Augusto sell, or otherwise dispose of, the CDs? Explain. [*UMG Recordings, Inc. v. Augusto*, 628 F.3d 1175 (9th Cir. 2011)] (See *Copyrights.*)

6–6. Copyright Infringement. United Fabrics International, Inc., bought a fabric design from an Italian designer and registered a copyright to it with the U.S. Copyright Office. When Macy's, Inc., began selling garments with a similar design, United filed a copyright infringement suit against Macy's. Macy's argued that United did not own a valid copyright to the design and so could not claim infringement. Does United have to prove that the copyright is valid to establish infringement? Explain. [*United Fabrics International, Inc. v. C & J Wear, Inc.*, 630 F.3d 1255 (9th Cir. 2011)] (See *Copyrights.*)

ETHICAL QUESTIONS

6–7. Copyright Infringement. Custom Copies, Inc., prepares and sells coursepacks, which contain compilations of readings for college courses. A teacher selects the readings and delivers a syllabus to the copy shop, which obtains the materials from a library, copies them, and binds the copies.

Blackwell Publishing, Inc., which owns the copyright to some of the materials, filed a suit, alleging copyright infringement. Does the "fair use" doctrine apply in these circumstances? Discuss. [*Blackwell Publishing, Inc. v. Custom Copies, Inc.*, ___ F.Supp.2d ___ (N.D. Fla. 2007)] (See *Copyrights.*)

Chapter 6—Work Set

TRUE-FALSE QUESTIONS

_____ 1. To obtain a patent, a person must prove to the patent office that his or her invention is novel, useful, and not obvious in light of contemporary technology.

_____ 2. To obtain a copyright, an author must prove to the copyright office that a work is novel, useful, and not a copy of another copyrighted work.

_____ 3. A personal name can be trademarked if it has acquired a secondary meaning.

_____ 4. Service marks are covered by the same policies and restrictions that apply to copyrights.

_____ 5. Dilution occurs when a trademark is used, without permission, in a way that diminishes the distinctive quality of the mark.

_____ 6. A copyright is infringed only if a work is copied in its entirety.

_____ 7. A formula for a chemical compound is not a trade secret.

_____ 8. A copy must be exactly the same as an original work to infringe on its copyright.

_____ 9. A license permits the use of another's intellectual property for certain limited purposes.

MULTIPLE-CHOICE QUESTIONS

_____ 1. For years, Mark Corporation has used a monkey symbol in marketing its jeans but has not registered the symbol with a government office. Quick, Inc., recently decided to import jeans made abroad and sell them with the monkey symbol, which it also has not registered. Mark sues Quick. Quick is

a. liable, because it had no right to trade on Mark's goodwill.
b. not liable, because Mark did not register the symbol with the government.
c. not liable, because it did not manufacture the jeans; it only imported them.
d. not liable, because a monkey symbol cannot be a trademark.

_____ 2. Ken invents a light bulb that lasts longer than ordinary bulbs. To prevent others from making, using, or selling the bulb or its design, he should obtain

a. a trademark.
b. a copyright.
c. a patent.
d. none of the above.

_____ 3. Standard Products, Inc., obtains a patent on a laser printer. This patent is violated if the printer is copied

a. in its entirety only.
b. in part.
c. not at all.
d. none of the above.

_____ 4. Bob works for Consolidated Manufacturing Company under a contract in which he agrees not to disclose any process he uses while in Consolidated's employ. When Bob goes into business for himself, he copies some of Consolidated's unique production techniques. Bob has committed

a. trademark infringement.
b. patent infringement.
c. copyright infringement.
d. theft of a trade secret.

_____ 5. To identify its goods, Nationwide Products uses a red, white, and blue symbol that combines the letter N and a map of the United States. This symbol is protected by

a. trademark law.
b. copyright law.
c. patent law.
d. all of the above.

_____ 6. The graphics used in "Grave Raiders," a computer game, are protected by

a. copyright law.
b. patent law.
c. trademark law.
d. trade secrets law.

_____ 7. Sales Track, Inc., creates, makes, and sells inventory control software for businesses. Generally, copyright protection extends to

a. no parts of the software.
b. the "look and feel" of the software.
c. those parts of the software that can be read by humans.
d. all of the above.

_____ 8. Realty Markets Corporation allows Sam, an independent real estate salesperson, to use Realty's trademark to advertise the properties that Sam represents for sale. This is

a. a license.
b. likely to confuse consumers.
c. counterfeiting.
d. dilution.

_____ 9. Ordinarily, you may not reproduce a copyrighted object without the owner's permission. The exception to this general rule is contained in the

a. Lanham Act.
b. appropriation doctrine.
c. "fair use" doctrine.
d. "fair copy" doctrine.

ANSWERING MORE LEGAL PROBLEMS

1. Apple, Inc., obtains design patents on its iPhones and iPads that cover the devices' graphical user interface, shell, and screen and button design. Other patents cover the way the information is displayed, the way the windows pop open, the way the information is scaled and rotated, and other aspects.

What is a patent? A patent is a grant from the government that gives an inventor the exclusive _____ to make, use, and sell an invention for a period of twenty years. For designs, patents are given for _____ years. How is a patent obtained? To obtain a patent, an applicant must show to the satisfaction of the patent office that the invention, discovery, or design is novel, useful, and not _____ in light of current technology. The word _Patent_ or _Pat._ with the patent number gives notice to the world that the article or design is patented.

2. Apple, Inc., files a suit in a federal district court against Samsung Electronics Company, alleging that Samsung's Galaxy mobile phones and tablets infringe on Apple's patents. Apple claims that the features of these phones and tablets violate all of Apple's design patents on the features of its iPhones and iPads.

What is patent infringement? The tort of patent infringement exists when a firm makes, uses, or sells another's patented design, product, or process without the patent owner's _____. Can patent infringement exist even though not all features of a design or parts of an invention are copied? _____. Only with respect to a patented process must all of the steps, or their equivalent, be copied to constitute infringement.

INTERNET LAW, SOCIAL MEDIA, AND PRIVACY

7

FACING A LEGAL PROBLEM

Hasbro, Inc., the maker of the children's board game Candyland, owns the Candyland trademark. A nonaffiliated company—the Internet Entertainment Group (IEG)—uses <u>candyland.com</u> as a domain name for a sexually explicit Internet site. Any person who performs an online search for "candyland" is directed to this adult Web site.

Q Has IEG violated Hasbro's rights in the Candyland trademark?

LEARNING OUTCOMES

The four Learning Outcomes below are designed to help improve your understanding of the chapter. After reading this chapter, you should be able to:

❶ Define cybersquatting, and indicate when it is illegal.

❷ Identify the federal legislation that significantly protects copyrights in the digital age.

❸ Explain the law that governs whether Internet service providers are liable for online defamatory statements made by users.

❹ State when the law protects a person's electronic communications from being intercepted or accessed.

The Internet has changed our lives and our laws. Technology has put the world at our fingertips and now allows even the smallest business to reach customers around the globe. Courts are often in uncharted waters when deciding disputes that involve the Internet, social media, and online privacy. There may not be any common law precedents for judges to rely on when resolving a case. Long-standing principles of justice may be inapplicable. New rules are evolving, as we discuss in this chapter, but often not as quickly as technology.

7–1 INTERNET LAW

A number of laws specifically address issues that arise only on the Internet. Three such issues are spam, domain names, and cybersquatting. We also discuss how the law is dealing with problems of online trademark infringement and dilution, as well as copyright law for digital information.

7–1a Spam

Spam is the unsolicited "junk e-mail" that floods virtual mailboxes with advertisements, solicitations, and other messages. Businesses and individuals alike are targets of spam. Considered relatively harmless in the early days of the Internet, spam now accounts for roughly 75 percent of all e-mails.

spam
Bulk, unsolicited (junk) e-mail.

State Regulation In an attempt to combat spam, thirty-six states have enacted laws that prohibit or regulate its use. Many state laws that regulate spam require the senders of e-mail ads to instruct the recipients on how they can "opt out" of further e-mail ads from the same sources. **EXAMPLE 7.1** Knife River Industries sends unsolicited e-mails to residents offering a special on driveway paving services. These e-mails must include a toll-free phone number or return e-mail address that the recipients can use to ask Knife River to send no more unsolicited e-mails.◄

The CAN-SPAM Act On the federal level, the Controlling the Assault of Non-Solicited Pornography and Marketing (CAN-SPAM) Act applies to any e-mail that is sent to promote a commercial product or service. Generally, the CAN-SPAM Act permits the sending of unsolicited commercial e-mails, but it prohibits certain types of spamming activities. Prohibited activities include the use of false, misleading, or deceptive information in such e-mails. It also prohibits the "harvesting" of e-mail addresses using specialized software. This federal statute often preempts state antispam laws.

The U.S. Safe Web Act The federal U.S. Safe Web Act is also known as the Undertaking Spam, Spyware, and Fraud Enforcement with Enforcers beyond Borders Act. The act allows the Federal Trade Commission, a federal regulatory agency, to cooperate and share information with foreign agencies in investigating and prosecuting those individuals and groups involved in spamming, spyware, and various Internet frauds and deceptions.

7–1b Domain Names

domain name
The series of letters and symbols used to identify site operators on the Internet; Internet "addresses."

A **domain name** is an Internet address, such as www.google.com or www.sandiego.edu. The top-level domain (TLD) is the part of the name to the right of the period. The TLD indicates the type of entity that is using the name; for example, "com" is an abbreviation for "commercial" and "edu" stands for "education." The second-level domain (SLD) often consists of the name of the entity that owns the site, such as Google, Inc., or the University of San Diego.

In the real world, one business can often use the same name as another without causing any conflict, particularly if the businesses are small, their goods or services are different, and the geographical areas within which they do business are separate. In cyberspace, however, no two businesses can use the same domain name. **EXAMPLE 7.2** Acme Truck Rentals in Oklahoma and Acme Plumbing in Maine can own the trademark "Acme," but only one business can operate on the Internet with the domain name acme.com. ◄

Because of this restrictive feature of domain names, the courts have held that the unauthorized use of another's mark in a domain name constitutes trademark infringement, if the use would likely cause customer confusion (see Chapter 6). The Internet Corporation for Assigned Names and Numbers (ICANN) oversees the distribution of domain names and operates an online arbitration system to handle complaints and disputes.

7–1c Cybersquatting

cybersquatting
The act of registering a domain name that is the same as, or confusingly similar to, the trademark of another and then offering to sell that domain name back to the trademark owner.

Cybersquatting occurs when a person registers a domain name that is the same as, or confusingly similar to, the trademark of another and then offers to sell the domain name back to the trademark owner.

Because cybersquatting has led to so much litigation, Congress enacted the Anticybersquatting Consumer Protection Act (ACPA), which amended the Lanham Act—the federal law protecting trademarks. The ACPA makes cybersquatting illegal when both of the following are true:

1. The name is identical or confusingly similar to the trademark of another.
2. The one registering, trafficking in, or using the domain name has a "bad faith intent" to profit from that trademark.

The ACPA applies to all domain name registrations of trademarks. Successful plaintiffs in suits brought under the act can collect actual damages and profits, or they can elect to receive statutory damages ranging from $1,000 to $100,000.

Tracking Domain Names Despite the ACPA, cybersquatting continues to present a problem for businesses, largely because more TLDs are now available and domain

LEARNING OUTCOME 1

Define cybersquatting, and indicate when it is illegal.

name registrars have proliferated. Registrar companies charge a fee to businesses and individuals to register new names and to renew annual registrations, as well as buy and sell expired domain names.

All domain name registrars are supposed to relay information about these transactions to ICANN and other companies that keep a master list of domain names, but this does not always occur. The speed at which domain names change hands and the difficulty in tracking mass automated registrations have created an environment where cybersquatting can flourish.

Typosquatting Cybersquatters have also developed new tactics, such as **typosquatting,** or registering a name that is a misspelling of a popular brand, such as googl.com or appple.com. Because many Internet users are not perfect typists, Web pages using these misspelled names receive a lot of traffic. Also, if the misspelling is significant, the trademark owner may have difficulty proving that the name is identical or confusingly similar to the trademark of another as the ACPA requires. As a result, cybersquatting is costly for businesses that want to protect their domain name rights from would-be cybersquatters and typosquatters.

typosquatting
A form of cybersquatting that relies on mistakes, such as typographical errors, made by Internet users when inputting information into a Web browser.

7–1d Trademark Infringement

As discussed in Chapter 6, trademark infringement occurs when one party who does not own a trademark copies it to a substantial degree or uses the mark in its entirety. Trademark infringement can also occur online, most notably through the use of *meta tags.*

Meta Tags Search engines compile their results by looking through a Web site's keywords coding. **Meta tags,** or key words, may be inserted in this coding to increase the frequency with which a site appears in search engine results, even if the site has nothing to do with the inserted words. Using this same technique, one site may appropriate the key words of more popular sites, so that the appropriating site appears in the same search engine results as the other sites. Using another's trademark in a meta tag without the owner's permission constitutes trademark infringement.

meta tag
A key word used in online coding that gives Internet browsers specific information about a Web site, often increasing its frequency in search engine results.

HIGHLIGHTING THE POINT

Michael and Lisa Tabot are auto brokers—that is, a personal car-shopping service. In their services, they contact dealers, solicit bids, and arrange for customers to buy from the dealer offering the best combination of location, availability, and price. The Tabots offer this service at their Web site that includes "lexus" in its key-words coding. Toyota Motor Sales, Inc., is the exclusive distributor of Lexus vehicles and the owner of the Lexus mark.

Does the Tabots' use of the Lexus mark as a meta tag, without Toyota's permission, constitute trademark infringement? Yes. Toyota owns the rights to the Lexus mark, and "lexus" is not a name by which the Tabots' service is known. The Tabots' use of the "lexus" mark to attract Internet users to their Web site creates a likelihood of confusion. Thus, the Tabots could be ordered to stop using the mark.

Licenses A company may permit another party to use a trademark under a license, or licensing agreement. A license, for example, may allow the use of a trademark within a domain name or meta tag. In addition, whenever an app or software program is downloaded, individuals usually enter into a licensing agreement. **EXAMPLE 7.3** Liam downloads a popular app to his iPhone. Before the download begins, he is prompted to agree to a licensing agreement. Once Liam clicks that he agrees, he gains the right to use the app, but not ownership rights.◄

Licensing agreements frequently include restrictions that prohibit others from sharing the file and using it to create similar software applications. The license may also limit the use of an application to a specific device or user for a certain time period.

7–1e Trademark Dilution

Trademark *dilution* occurs when a trademark is used, without authorization, in a way that diminishes the distinctive quality of the mark. Trademark dilution can occur online.

EXAMPLE 7.4 Brookie Cookies, a popular dessert franchise on the West Coast, owns the mark, "Brookie." The company is well-known throughout the West Coast and advertises regularly on radio and television. Brookie Cookies discovers that an outdoor footwear business in Washington State called "Brookie Boots" is using its mark in their domain name, www.brookieboots.com. Thinking that this unauthorized online use of its mark will diminish the quality of the mark, Brookie Cookies can sue Brookie Boots for trademark dilution.◄

Unlike trademark infringement, a claim of dilution does not require proof that consumers are likely to be confused by a connection between the unauthorized use and the mark. For this reason, the products involved need not be similar.

7–1f Copyrights in Digital Information

LEARNING OUTCOME 2

Identify the federal legislation that significantly protects copyrights in the digital age.

Copyright law is probably the most important form of intellectual property protection on the Internet. This is because much of the material on the Internet (including software and database information) is copyrighted, and in order to transfer that material online, it must be "copied." Generally, whenever a party downloads software or music into a computer's random access memory, or RAM, without authorization, a copyright is infringed. Technology has vastly increased the potential for copyright infringement.

HIGHLIGHTING THE POINT

Bridgeport Music, Inc., and Westbound Records, Inc., own the copyright to the song "Get Off Your Ass and Jam," which opens with a three-note solo guitar riff that lasts four seconds. The rap song "100 Miles and Runnin'" contains a two-second sample from that guitar solo, but at a lower pitch. The guitar riff is also looped and extended to sixteen beats in five places in the song, with each looped segment lasting about seven seconds.

Does the use of the guitar riff in "100 Miles and Runnin'" without the permission of Bridgeport and Westbound constitute copyright infringement? Yes. Digitally sampling a copyrighted sound recording of any length is copyright infringement. Even when a small part of a sound recording is sampled, the part taken is something of value.

The Digital Millennium Copyright Act The Digital Millennium Copyright Act (DMCA) gives significant protection to owners of copyrights in digital information. The act established civil and criminal penalties for anyone who circumvents (bypasses) encryption software or other technological antipiracy protection. Also prohibited are the manufacture, import, sale, and distribution of devices or services for circumvention.

The "Fair Use" Exception The DMCA provides for exceptions to fit the needs of libraries, scientists, universities, and others. In general, the law does not restrict the "fair use" of circumvention methods for educational and other noncommercial purposes. For instance, circumvention is allowed to test computer security, to conduct encryption research, to protect personal privacy, and to enable parents to monitor their children's use of the Internet.

ISP Limited Liability The DMCA also limits the liability of **Internet service providers (ISPs)**. Under the act, an ISP is not liable for copyright infringement by a subscriber *unless* the ISP is aware of the subscriber's violation. An ISP may be held liable only if it fails to take action to shut down the subscriber after learning of the violation. A copyright holder must act promptly, however, by pursuing a claim in court, or the subscriber has the right to be restored to online access.

Methods of File-Sharing The issue of file-sharing infringement is an ongoing debate. File-sharing can be accomplished in the following ways:

1. *Peer-to-peer networking*—**Peer-to-peer (P2P) networking** uses numerous personal computers that are connected to the Internet. Individuals on the same network can access files stored on one another's computers through a **distributed network**. Persons scattered throughout the country or the world can work together on the same project by using file-sharing programs.

2. *Cloud computing*—A newer method of sharing files via the Internet is **cloud computing,** which is essentially a subscription-based or pay-per-use service that extends a computer's software or storage capabilities. Cloud computing can deliver a single application through a browser to multiple users. Alternatively, cloud computing might be a utility program to pool resources and provide data storage and virtual servers that can be accessed on demand.

The DMCA plays a role in protecting copyrights when file-sharing technology is used. One area in which file-sharing technology is most prevalent in copyright disputes is in the music industry.

When file-sharing is used to download others' stored music files, copyright issues arise. For instance, recording artists and their labels stand to lose large amounts of royalties and revenues if relatively few digital downloads or CDs are purchased and then made available on distributed networks. Anyone can get the music for free on these networks, which has prompted recording companies to pursue individuals for file-sharing copyrighted works.

Internet service provider (ISP)
A business or organization that offers users access to the Internet and related services.

peer-to-peer (P2P) networking
The sharing of resources (such as files, hard and flash drives, and processing styles) among multiple computers without the requirement of a central network server.

distributed network
A network that can be used by persons located (distributed) around the country or the globe to share computer files.

cloud computing
The delivery to users of on-demand services from third-party servers over a network.

HIGHLIGHTING THE POINT

Marilyn Harper shared digital audio files of songs with others through a P2P network. Mason Recording Company filed a suit against Harper for copyright infringement. Harper argued that her infringement was "innocent"—that is, she was not aware that the songs were copyrighted and thus had no reason to believe that sharing them was infringement.

Can an "innocent" infringer violate an owner's copyright? Yes. Each of Mason's songs included a copyright notice. Harper's contention that she was too naive to understand that the copyrights on published music applied to downloaded music is irrelevant. Harper is liable to pay damages per infringed work to Mason.

File-sharing also creates problems for the motion picture industry, which loses significant amounts of revenue annually as a result of pirated DVDs.

7–2 SOCIAL MEDIA

social media
Forms of communication through which users create and share information, ideas, messages, and other content via the Internet.

Social media provide a means by which people can create, share, and exchange ideas and comments via the Internet. Social networking sites, such as Facebook, Google+, LinkedIn, Pinterest, and Twitter, have become ubiquitous. Studies show that Internet users spend more time on social networks than at any other sites. The amount of time people spend accessing social networks on their smartphones and other mobile devices has increased every year.

7–2a Legal Issues

The emergence of Facebook and other social networking sites has created a number of legal and ethical issues for businesses. For instance, a firm's rights in valuable intellectual property may be infringed if users post trademarked images or copyrighted materials on these sites without permission.

Criminal Litigation Social media posts now are routinely included in discovery in litigation because they can provide damaging information that establishes a person's intent or what she or he knew at a particular time. **EXAMPLE 7.5** One day in May, Jackson tweets that he was unjustly fired from his job with Bradley Trucking Company. He predicts that the company is going to regret firing him, noting that "A burning building can be sweet revenge." In June, Bradley becomes a victim of arson when its offices are destroyed by fire. Jackson is arrested and tried for the crime. At trial, among other evidence, Jackson's tweets and text messages are offered as evidence that he intended to do harm to Bradley.◄

Criminal Investigations Law enforcement can use social media to detect and prosecute criminals. **EXAMPLE 7.6** Colin, a nineteen-year-old, posts a message on Facebook bragging about how drunk he was on New Year's Eve. He apologizes to the owner of the parked car that he hit. The next day, police officers arrest Colin for drunk driving and leaving the scene of an accident.◄ Administrative agencies and their federal regulators can also use social media posts in their investigations into illegal activities.

Workplace Social Media Policies It is no surprise that work-related topics and issues get discussed on social media. Consequently, numerous companies have provided strict guidelines for employees about what is and is not appropriate when posting on social media. Some companies have even fired employees for such activities as criticizing other employees or managers through social media outlets.

Courts and administrative agencies usually uphold an employer's right to terminate an employee based on his or her violation of a social media policy. Despite this trend in the courts, however, there is likely to be an ongoing debate about how to balance employees' right to free expression against an employer's right to prevent inaccurate and negative statements being spread via social media.

Company Social Media Networks Many companies form their own internal social media networks. Posts on these internal networks are quite different from the typical posts on Facebook, LinkedIn, and Twitter, for example. Because employees use these internal networks to exchange messages about topics related to their work, the tone is businesslike. Advantages to using an internal system for employee communications include the following:

1. The company can better protect its trade secrets by deciding which employees can see particular intranet files.

2. The employer can offer real-time information about important company issues, such as product details and sales tips.

3. The use of e-mail overall is significantly reduced because workers read only e-mails and postings that apply to their particular field or projects.

7–2b Online Defamation

Cyber torts are torts that arise from online conduct. One of the most prevalent cyber torts is online defamation. Defamation is wrongfully hurting a person's reputation by communicating false statements about that person to others. The Internet enables individuals to communicate with large numbers of people simultaneously via social media platforms, such as Twitter, blogs, and Facebook. As a result, online defamation has become a problem for many businesses.

cyber tort
A tort committed via the Internet.

Identifying the Author of Online Defamation An initial issue raised by online defamation is simply discovering who is committing it. Online forums allow others—customers, employees, and crackpots—to complain about a firm that they dislike while remaining anonymous. An ISP can disclose personal information about its customers only when ordered to do so by a court. Using the authority of the courts, plaintiffs can then obtain from the ISPs the identity of the persons responsible for the defamatory messages.

Real-World Case Example

Seven users of Yelp—a social-networking consumer review Web site—each posted negative reviews of Hadeed Carpet Cleaning of Alexandria, Virginia. Hadeed brought an action in a Virginia state court against the users, claiming defamation. Hadeed alleged that the Yelp reviewers were not actual customers and thus their comments were defamatory because they falsely stated that Hadeed had provided shoddy service to each reviewer. When Yelp failed to comply with a subpoena seeking documents revealing the users' identities, the court held the Web site in contempt. Yelp appealed.

Does requiring Yelp to reveal the identities of its anonymous users violate those users' rights under the First Amendment? No. In a 2014 case, *Yelp v. Hadeed Carpet Cleaning*, a state intermediate appellate court affirmed the lower court's judgment. "Without the identity of the . . . defendants, Hadeed cannot move forward with its defamation lawsuit. There is no other option. The identity of the . . . defendants is not only important, it is necessary."

Liability of Internet Service Providers Normally, one who repeats or otherwise republishes a defamatory statement is subject to liability as if he or she had originally published it. Thus, newspapers, magazines, and television and radio stations are subject to liability for defamatory content that they publish or broadcast, even though the content was prepared or created by others.

Under the Communications Decency Act (CDA), however, ISPs are not liable with respect to such material. The CDA states, "No provider or user of an interactive computer service shall be treated as the publisher or speaker of any information

LEARNING OUTCOME 3

Explain the law that governs whether Internet service providers are liable for online defamatory statements made by users.

provided by another information content provider." Thus, ISPs usually are treated differently than publishers in print and other media and are not liable for publishing defamatory statements that come from a third party.

7–3 PRIVACY

Facebook, Google, and Yahoo have all been accused of violating users' privacy rights. The courts have held that the right to privacy is guaranteed by the Bill of Rights, and some state constitutions guarantee it as well. To maintain a suit for the invasion of privacy, though, a person must have a reasonable expectation of privacy in the particular situation.

Clearly, people have a reasonable expectation of privacy when they enter their personal banking or credit-card information online. They also have a reasonable expectation that online companies will follow their own privacy policies. But it is probably not reasonable to expect privacy in statements made on Twitter—or photos posted on any social media platform, for that matter.

EXAMPLE 7.7 Jennifer, a college swimmer, creates a profile on an online dating Web site and uploads a photo of herself in a bikini. Gary sees her profile photo and tweets it to his followers. It ultimately goes viral once a well-known news magazine features Jennifer's photo in an article on the "Ten Most Beautiful College Swimmers." ◄

7–3a The Electronic Communications Privacy Act

LEARNING OUTCOME 4

State when the law protects a person's electronic communications from being intercepted or accessed.

The Electronic Communications Privacy Act (ECPA) was enacted to amend federal wiretapping law to cover electronic forms of communications. Specifically, the ECPA prohibits the intentional interception of any wire, oral, or electronic communication, as well as the intentional disclosure or use of information obtained by the interception. Today, the ECPA also applies to online communications, including e-mail, social media postings, and smartphone text conversations.

Exceptions to the ECPA Excluded from the ECPA's coverage, however, are any electronic communications through devices—such as a cell phone, computer, or tablet—that an employer provides for its employee to use "in the ordinary course of its business." Consequently, if a company provides an electronic device to the employee for ordinary business use, the company is allowed to intercept and monitor all business communications made on that device.

This "business-extension exception" permits employers to monitor employees' electronic communications made in the ordinary course of business, but not their personal communications. Another ECPA exception allows an employer to avoid liability under the act if employees give their consent to having their electronic communications monitored by the employer on these company devices.

Reasonable Expectation of Privacy When determining whether an employer should be held liable for violating an employee's privacy rights, the courts generally weigh the employer's interests against the employee's reasonable expectation of privacy. In most situations, if an employer has informed its employees that their electronic communications on company devices and equipment are being monitored, they cannot reasonably expect their exchanges and messages to be private. Most employers who engage in electronic monitoring notify their employees about the policy.

EXAMPLE 7.8 Springleaf Financial Services provides each of its certified public accountants with a company cell phone, which they can use at any time for business and personal purposes. Under the ECPA, Springleaf can intercept any business-related communications from the employees' phones, but any personal communications on the phones are off limits. Several months later, Springleaf notifies its employees that all communications conducted on company equipment and devices will be monitored. Employees then should not expect privacy in their personal electronic communications.◄

Stored Communications Part of the ECPA is known as the Stored Communications Act (SCA). The SCA prohibits intentional and unauthorized access to stored electronic communications and sets forth criminal and civil sanctions for violators. A person can violate the SCA by intentionally accessing a stored electronic communication. The SCA also prevents "providers" of communication services (such as cell phone companies and social media networks) from divulging private communications to certain entities and individuals.

7–3b Data Collection

Whenever a consumer purchases items from an online retailer, such as Amazon.com, or a retailer that sells both offline and online, such as Best Buy, the retailer collects information about the consumer. **Cookies** are invisible files that computers, smartphones, and other mobile devices create to track a user's Web-browsing activities. Cookies provide detailed information to marketers about an individual's behavior and preferences, which is then used to personalize online services.

> Over time, the retailer can amass considerable data about a person's shopping habits. This can give rise to certain questions about privacy. For instance, does collecting this information violate a consumer's right to privacy? Should retailers be able to pass on the data they have collected?

cookie
A small file sent from a Web site and stored in a user's Web browser to track the user's Web-browsing activities.

7–3c Internet Companies' Privacy Policies

The Federal Trade Commission (FTC) investigates consumer complaints of privacy violations. The FTC has forced many companies, including Google, Facebook, Twitter, and MySpace, to enter into a consent decree that gives the FTC broad power to review their privacy and data practices. It can then sue companies that violate the terms of the decree.

> Google recently settled a suit brought by the FTC alleging that it had misused data. Google allegedly had used cookies to trick the Safari browser on iPhones and iPads so that it could monitor users who had blocked such tracking. This violated the consent decree with the FTC. Google agreed to pay $22.5 million to settle the suit without admitting liability.

> Facebook has had a number of complaints about its privacy policy and has changed the policy several times to satisfy its critics and ward off potential government investigations. Other companies, including mobile app developers, have also changed their privacy policies to provide more information to consumers. Consequently, it is frequently the companies, rather than courts or legislatures, that are defining the privacy rights of their online users.

ANSWERING THE LEGAL PROBLEM

In the legal problem set out at the beginning of this chapter, the Internet Entertainment Group (IEG), used <u>candyland.com</u> as a domain name for a sexually explicit Internet site without the permission of Hasbro, Inc., the maker of the children's game Candyland and owner of the Candyland trademark.

A **Does IEG's use of the Candyland trademark violate Hasbro's rights?** Yes. Hasbro's mark is famous, IEG is using it without permission, and that use arguably diminishes the quality of the mark. If Hasbro can show that IEG's use of the mark and the domain name candyland.com in connection with its site is causing irreparable injury to Hasbro, a court will likely order IEG to remove all content from the candyland.com site and stop using the Candyland mark. This would be trademark dilution.

TERMS AND CONCEPTS TO REVIEW

cloud computing 97
cookie 101
cybersquatting 94
cyber tort 99

distributed network 97
domain name 94
Internet service provider (ISP) 97
meta tag 95

peer-to-peer (P2P) networking 97
social media 98
spam 93
typosquatting 95

CHAPTER SUMMARY: INTERNET LAW, SOCIAL MEDIA, AND PRIVACY

LEARNING OUTCOME	
1	**Define cybersquatting, and indicate when it is illegal.** Cybersquatting occurs when a person registers a domain name that is the same as, or confusingly similar to, the trademark of another and then offers to sell the domain name back to the trademark owner. Cybersquatting is illegal under the Anticybersquatting Consumer Protection Act when both of the following circumstances exist: (1) the name is identical or confusingly similar to the trademark of another, and (2) the one registering, trafficking in, or using the domain name has a "bad faith intent" to profit from that trademark.
2	**Identify the federal legislation that significantly protects copyrights in the digital age.** The Digital Millennium Copyright Act (DMCA) is one of the most significant pieces of federal legislation to provide protection to owners of copyrights in digital information. The DMCA provides a "fair use" exception to certain institutions and limited liability to Internet service providers for copyright infringement by its users. The act also plays a role in protecting copyrights when file-sharing technology is used.
3	**Explain the law that governs whether Internet service providers are liable for online defamatory statements made by users.** The Communications Decency Act (CDA) sets out the liability of Internet service providers (ISPs) for online defamatory statements made by users. Under the CDA, "No provider or user of an interactive computer service shall be treated as the publisher or speaker of any information provided by another information content provider." Thus, an ISP is usually not liable for the publication of a user's defamatory statement.
4	**State when the law protects a person's electronic communications from being intercepted or accessed.** The Electronic Communications Privacy Act (ECPA) covers electronic forms of communications. The ECPA prohibits the intentional interception of any wire, oral, or electronic communication. Excluded from the ECPA's coverage are communications through devices that an employer provides for its employees to use "in the ordinary course of its business." Monitoring employees' personal communication is not permitted, however. An employer can avoid liability under the act if employees consent to having their electronic communications monitored by the employer on their company devices.

ISSUE SPOTTERS

Check your answers to the *Issue Spotters* against the answers provided in Appendix C at the end of this text.

1. Karl self-publishes a cookbook titled *Hole Foods,* in which he sets out recipes for donuts, Bundt cakes, tortellini, and other foods with holes. To publicize the book, Karl designs the Web site <u>holefoods.com</u>. Karl appropriates the key words of other cooking and cookbook sites with more frequent hits so that <u>holefoods.com</u> will appear in the same search engine results as the more popular sites. Has Karl done anything wrong? Explain. (See *Internet Law.*)

2. Theft Guard Corporation began marketing software in 2005 under the mark "Theft Guard." In 2014, Theftwatch.com, Inc., a different company selling different products, begins to use *theftguard* as part of its URL and registers it as a domain name. Can Theft Guard Corporation stop this use of *theftguard?* If so, what must the company show? (See *Internet Law.*)

USING BUSINESS LAW

7–1. Domain Names. Tony owns Antonio's, a pub in a small town in Iowa. Universal Dining, Inc., opens a chain of pizza parlors in California called "Antonio's." Without Tony's consent, Universal uses "antoniosincalifornia" as part of the domain name for the chain's Web site. Has Universal committed trademark dilution or any other violation of the law? Explain. (See *Internet Law.*)

7–2. Internet Service Providers. CyberConnect, Inc., is an Internet service provider (ISP). Pepper is a CyberConnect subscriber. Market Reach, Inc., is an online advertising company. Using sophisticated software, Market Reach directs its ads to those users most likely to be interested in a particular product. When Pepper receives one of the ads, she objects to the content. Further, she claims that CyberConnect should pay damages for "publishing" the ad. Is the ISP regarded as a publisher and therefore liable for the content of Market Reach's ad? Why or why not? (See *Social Media.*)

REAL-WORLD CASE PROBLEMS

7–3. Copyrights in Digital Information. When she was in college, Jammie Thomas-Rasset wrote a case study on Napster, the online peer-to-peer (P2P) file-sharing network, and knew that it was shut down because it was illegal. Later, Capitol Records, Inc., which owns the copyrights to a large number of music recordings, discovered that "tereastarr"—a user name associated with Thomas-Rasset's Internet protocol address—had made twenty-four songs available for distribution on KaZaA, another P2P network. Capitol notified Thomas-Rasset that she had been identified as engaging in the unauthorized trading of music. She replaced the hard drive on her computer with a new drive that did not contain the songs in dispute. Is Thomas-Rasset liable for copyright infringement? Explain. [*Capitol Records, Inc. v. Thomas-Rasset,* 692 F.3d 899 (8th Cir. 2012)] (See *Internet Law.*)

7–4. Domain Names. Austin Rare Coins, Inc., buys and sells rare coins, bullion, and other precious metals through eight Web sites with different domain names. An unknown individual took control of Austin's servers and transferred the domain names to another registrant without Austin's permission. The new registrant began using the domain names to host malicious content—including hate letters to customers and fraudulent contact information—and to post customers' credit-card numbers and other private information, thereby tarnishing Austin's goodwill. Austin filed a suit in a federal district court against the new registrant under the Anticybersquatting Consumer Protection Act. Is Austin entitled to a transfer of the domain names? Explain. [*Austin Rare Coins, Inc. v. Acoins.com,* 2013 WL 85142 (E.D.Va. 2013)] (See *Internet Law.*)

7–5. File-Sharing. Dartmouth College professor M. Eric Johnson, in collaboration with Tiversa, Inc., a company that monitors peer-to-peer networks to provide security services, wrote an article titled "Data Hemorrhages in the Health-Care Sector." In preparing the article, Johnson and Tiversa searched the networks for data that could be used to commit medical or financial identity theft. They found a document that contained the Social Security numbers, insurance information, and treatment codes for patients of

LabMD, Inc. Tiversa notified LabMD of the find in order to solicit its business. Instead of hiring Tiversa, however, LabMD filed a suit in a federal district court against the company, alleging trespass, conversion, and violations of federal statutes. What do these facts indicate about the security of private information? Explain. How should the court rule? [*LabMD, Inc. v. Tiversa, Inc.,* 2013 WL 425983 (11th Cir. 2013)] (See *Internet Law.*)

7–6. Social Media. Mohammad Omar Aly Hassan and nine others were indicted in a federal district court on charges of conspiring to advance violent *jihad* (holy war against enemies of Islam) and other offenses related to terrorism. The evidence at Hassan's trial included postings he made on Facebook concerning his adherence to violent jihadist ideology. Convicted, Hassan appealed, contending that the Facebook items had not been properly authenticated (established as his comments). How might the government show the connection between postings on Facebook and those who post them? Discuss. [*United States v. Hassan,* 742 F.3d 104 (4th Cir. 2014)] (See *Social Media.*)

ETHICAL QUESTIONS

7–7. File-Sharing. From an ethical perspective, is it important to protect copyrighted music from unauthorized file-sharing and other forms of distribution online? Why or why not? (See *Internet Law.*)

7–8. Criminal Litigation and Investigations. After the unauthorized release and posting of classified U.S. government documents to WikiLeaks.org, involving Bradley Manning, a U.S. Army private first class, the U.S. government began a criminal investigation. The government obtained a court order to require Twitter, Inc., to turn over subscriber information and communications to and from the e-mail addresses of Birgitta Jonsdottir and others. The court sealed the order and the other documents in the case, reasoning that "there exists no right to public notice of all the types of documents filed in a . . . case." Jonsdottir and the others appealed this decision. How does law enforcement use social media to detect and prosecute criminals? Is this use of social media an unethical invasion of individuals' privacy? Discuss. [*In re Application of the United States of America for an Order Pursuant to 18 U.S.C. Section 2703(d),* 707 F.3d 283 (4th Cir. 2013)] (See *Social Media.*)

Chapter 7—Work Set

TRUE-FALSE QUESTIONS

_____ 1. Using a domain name that is identical or similar to the trademark of another is legal.

_____ 2. Using another's trademark in a meta tag does not normally constitute trademark infringement, even if it is done without the owner's permission.

_____ 3. When you download an application to your laptop, you are typically entering into a licensing agreement.

_____ 4. Downloading music onto a computer is not copyright infringement, even if it is done without authorization.

_____ 5. An Internet service provider is liable for any act of copyright infringement by its customer.

_____ 6. There are no penalties for circumventing encryption software or other technological antipiracy protection.

_____ 7. Federal law does not permit the intentional accessing of stored electronic communication unless the accessing is authorized.

_____ 8. Cookies are invisible files that computers, smartphones, and other mobile devices create to track a user's Web-browsing activities.

_____ 9. Online defamation is a cyber tort that involves wrongfully hurting a person's reputation by communicating false statements about that person to others.

MULTIPLE-CHOICE QUESTIONS

_____ 1. Security Solutions, Inc., registers a domain name that is the same as, or confusingly similar to, the trademark of Security Services Corporation and then offers to sell the domain name back to Security Services. This is

a. cybersquatting.
b. typosquatting.
c. trademark infringement.
d. trademark dilution.

_____ 2. Fullprice Corporation uses the trademark of Dollar Stores, Inc., in a meta tag without Dollar Stores' permission. This is called

a. cybersquatting.
b. typosquatting.
c. trademark infringement.
d. trademark dilution.

_____ 3. Coffee & Donuts Corporation allows its trademark to be used as part of a domain name for Coffee & Donuts California, Inc., an unaffiliated company. Coffee & Donuts California does not obtain ownership rights in the mark. This is

a. a cookie.
b. a license.
c. copyright infringement.
d. trademark dilution.

_____ 4. To test the security of a network operating system, Tech Tests, Inc., circumvents the encryption software of Standard Business Corporation's software. This is

a. a "fair use" exception to copyright protection.
b. a violation of copyright law.
c. cloud computing.
d. typosquatting.

5. Bob posts copyrighted materials on Click + View, a social networking site, without the permission of the copyright owners. This is
   a. a "fair use" exception to copyright protection.
   b. a violation of copyright law.
   c. cloud computing.
   d. spam.

6. CostCut Discount Stores discovers that defamatory statements about its products are being posted in an online forum. Buy & Tell, the forum whose users are posting the messages, can be ordered to disclose the identity of the person or persons responsible by
   a. any consumer confused by a post on the site.
   b. any user of the site.
   c. a court.
   d. CostCut.

7. Pico (a songwriter, musician, and recording artist), Quality Music, and other recording artists and their labels, have lost significant revenue through
   a. the "fair use" exception to copyright protection.
   b. cloud computing.
   c. goodwill.
   d. unauthorized file-sharing.

8. Galaxy Corporation uses invisible files created on the computers and mobile devices of visitors to its Web sites to track the users' browsing activities. These files are
   a. cookies.
   b. goodwill.
   c. licenses.
   d. spam.

ANSWERING MORE LEGAL PROBLEMS

1. Lucy, an emergency medical technician (EMT), was issued a cell phone by her employer, Mercy Ambulance Service. Mercy had a policy that prohibited employees from using work phones and other devices for personal matters. Lucy exceeded Mercy's limit on text messages for the month, so without Lucy's knowledge, Mercy management read her stored messages to determine whether all of the text messages were indeed work-related.

   Did Mercy's action violate Lucy's privacy rights? No. When an employer provides an employee with a cell phone or other tech device and has a stated policy about its use, the employee is not considered to have a reasonable expectation of _____ in the data. The employee should anticipate that anything in the device, including texts, is subject to _____. The employer can avoid potential legal restrictions by telling the employees that they are subject to such _____. Because Mercy had a stated policy that limited employees' use of tech devices to work-related matters, Lucy had no reasonable expectation of _____ in her use of the phone.

2. Offshore Oil Corporation's social media policy bans employees' "public comments that adversely affect co-workers." One violation is a ground for discipline. Two violations can result in being fired. Pete, an Offshore supervisory employee, posts unfavorable comments about his subordinates on Q&A.com, a social networking site. Rita, Pete's manager, disciplines him for the posts. He immediately goes on Q&A to post angry, critical comments about Rita. Offshore fires Pete.

   Was Offshore's firing of Pete within the company's rights as an employer? Yes. Many companies have established guidelines on their employees' use of social media. Employees who use social media in a way that violates their employer's social media _____ can be disciplined or fired from their jobs. Courts usually _____ an employer's right to discipline or terminate an employee based on his or her violation of a stated social media policy. Here, Pete was first disciplined and then fired for violations of Offshore's social media policy, an outcome that was set out in the company's guidelines. If Pete challenged those actions in court, the court would most likely rule in favor of _____.

CRIMINAL LAW AND CYBER CRIME

8

FACING A LEGAL PROBLEM

Ray steals a purse from an unattended car at a gas station. Because the purse contains money and a handgun, Ray is convicted of grand theft of property (cash) and grand theft of a firearm. On appeal, Ray claims that he is not guilty of grand theft of a firearm because he did not know that the purse contained a gun.

Q Can Ray be convicted of the crime of grand theft of a firearm even though he did not know that a gun was in the purse?

LEARNING OUTCOMES

The six Learning Outcomes below are designed to help improve your understanding of the chapter. After reading this chapter, you should be able to:

1 Explain the difference between crimes and other types of wrongful conduct.

2 Indicate the essential elements of criminal liability.

3 Describe the constitutional safeguards that protect the rights of persons accused of crimes.

4 List the crimes that affect business.

5 Summarize the defenses to criminal liability.

6 Discuss how the Internet has expanded opportunities for crime, and outline the protection that the law provides for online victims.

Criminal law is an important part of the business world. Various sanctions are used to bring about a society in which individuals engaging in business can compete and flourish. These sanctions include damages for torts and damages for breaches of contract. Other sanctions are imposed under criminal law.

In this chapter, following a brief summary of the major differences between criminal and civil law, we look at how crimes are classified and what elements must be present for criminal liability to exist. We then examine criminal procedural law. Finally, we focus on crimes affecting business and the defenses that can be raised to avoid liability for criminal actions. We conclude the chapter with an overview of cyber crime.

8–1 CIVIL LAW AND CRIMINAL LAW

Civil law spells out the duties that exist between persons or between citizens and their governments, excluding the duty not to commit crimes. Contract law, for example, is part of civil law. The whole body of tort law, which deals with the infringement by one person on the legally recognized rights of another, is also an area of civil law. When a civil wrong is committed, the person who suffered the harm can bring a lawsuit for damages.

Criminal law, in contrast, has to do with crime. A **crime** is a wrong against society proclaimed in a statute and punishable by society through fines, imprisonment, or, in some cases, death. Because crimes are *offenses against society as a whole,* they are prosecuted by a public official, such as a district attorney, rather than by the crime victims.

8–1a Burden of Proof and Sanctions

In a civil case, the plaintiff usually must prove his or her case by a *preponderance of the evidence.* Under this standard, the plaintiff must convince the court that, based on the evidence presented by both parties, it is more likely than not that the plaintiff's allegation is true.

In a criminal case, in contrast, the state must prove its case *beyond a reasonable doubt.* Note also that in a criminal case, the jury's verdict normally must be

LEARNING OUTCOME 1

Explain the difference between crimes and other types of wrongful conduct.

crime
A wrong against society proclaimed in a statute and punishable by society through fines, imprisonment, or death.

unanimous—that is, agreed to by all members of the jury—to convict the defendant. (In a civil trial by jury, however, typically only three-fourths of the jurors need to agree.)

The sanctions—fines, imprisonment, or death—imposed on criminal wrongdoers are also harsher than those in civil cases. The purpose of tort law is to allow persons harmed by the wrongful acts of others to obtain compensation from (and not punish) the wrongdoer. In contrast, criminal sanctions are designed to punish those who commit crimes and to deter others from committing similar acts in the future.

Exhibit 8.1 presents additional ways in which criminal and civil law differ.

8–1b Classification of Crimes

Crimes are classified as felonies or misdemeanors. **Felonies** are serious crimes punishable by death or by imprisonment in a federal or state penitentiary for more than a year.

Under federal law and in most states, any crime that is not a felony is a **misdemeanor.** Misdemeanors are crimes punishable by a fine or by confinement for up to a year. If imprisoned, the guilty party goes to a local jail instead of a penitentiary. Disorderly conduct and trespass are common examples of misdemeanors.

felony
A crime that carries the most severe sanctions, usually ranging from one year in prison to death.

misdemeanor
A lesser crime than a felony, usually punishable by a fine or imprisonment for up to one year.

8–2 WHAT CONSTITUTES CRIMINAL LIABILITY?

Two elements must exist for a person to be convicted of a crime: (1) the performance of a prohibited act and (2) a specified state of mind, or intent, on the part of the actor.

8–2a The Criminal Act

Every criminal statute prohibits certain acts. Most crimes require an act of *commission*—that is, a person must do something to be accused of a crime. In some cases, an act of *omission* can be a crime, but only when a person has a legal duty to perform the omitted act. Failure to file a tax return is an example of an omission that is a crime.

8–2b The Intent to Commit a Crime

A wrongful mental state is as necessary as a wrongful act in establishing criminal liability. What constitutes such a mental state varies according to the wrongful

LEARNING OUTCOME 2

Indicate the essential elements of criminal liability.

EXHIBIT 8.1   Key Differences between Civil Law and Criminal Law

Issue	Civil Law	Criminal Law
Party who brings suit	The person who suffered harm.	The state.
Wrongful act	Causing harm to a person or to a person's property.	Violating a statute that prohibits some type of activity.
Burden of proof	Preponderance of the evidence.	Beyond a reasonable doubt.
Verdict	Three-fourths majority (typically).	Unanimous (almost always).
Remedy	Damages to compensate for the harm or a decree to achieve an equitable result.	Punishment (fine, imprisonment, or death).

action. For murder, for instance, the act is the taking of a life, and the mental state is the intent to take a life. For theft, the guilty act is the taking of another person's property, and the mental state involves both the knowledge that the property belongs to another and the intent to deprive the owner of it.

8–3 CONSTITUTIONAL SAFEGUARDS

LEARNING OUTCOME 3
Describe the constitutional safeguards that protect the rights of persons accused of crimes.

Criminal law brings the force of the state, with all its resources, to bear against the individual. The U.S. Constitution provides safeguards to protect the rights of individuals and to prevent the arbitrary use of power on the part of the government. The United States Supreme Court has ruled that most of these safeguards apply not only in federal but also in state courts. They include the following:

1. The Fourth Amendment protection from unreasonable searches and seizures.

2. The Fourth Amendment requirement that no warrants for a search or an arrest can be issued without probable cause.

3. The Fifth Amendment requirement that no one can be deprived of "life, liberty, or property without due process of law."

4. The Fifth Amendment prohibition against **double jeopardy**—that is, trying someone twice for the same criminal offense.

double jeopardy
A situation occurring when a person is tried twice for the same criminal offense.

5. The Fifth Amendment requirement that no person can be forced to be a witness against (incriminate) himself or herself.

6. The Sixth Amendment guarantees of a speedy trial, a trial by jury, a public trial, the right to confront witnesses, and the right to a lawyer at various stages in some proceedings.

7. The Eighth Amendment prohibitions against excessive bail and fines and against cruel and unusual punishment.

8–3a Searches and Seizures

Before searching or seizing private property, a law enforcement officer must obtain a **search warrant**—an order from a judge or other public official authorizing the search or seizure. To obtain the warrant, the officer must convince the judge that there is **probable cause** to believe a search will reveal a specific illegality. Probable cause requires evidence that would convince a reasonable person that the proposed search or seizure is more likely justified than not. The officer must describe what is to be searched or seized.

search warrant
An order from a judge or other public official that authorizes a search or seizure of particular property.

probable cause
Reasonable grounds for believing that a search will reveal a specific illegality.

Whether the search of a person is reasonable requires a consideration of the need for the search against the invasion of personal rights that the search would involve. In an emergency—a terrorist attack, for instance—there might be an immediate need to search for weapons or other evidence. This need could justify what in other circumstances could be an unreasonable invasion of personal rights.

Businesses are also protected against unreasonable searches. Government inspectors do not have a right to search business premises without a warrant, although the standard of probable cause is not the same as that required in non-business contexts. The existence of a general and neutral plan of enforcement will justify the issuance of a warrant. A warrant normally is not required for a seizure of spoiled or contaminated food. Nor are warrants required for searches of businesses in such highly regulated industries as those dealing with liquor, guns, and strip mining.

The Fourth Amendment only protects against searches that violate a person's reasonable expectation of privacy. This exists if an individual actually expects privacy and the expectation is one that society, as a whole, thinks is legitimate.

Real-World Case Example

Angela Marcum was the drug court coordinator responsible for collecting money for the District County Court of Pittsburg County, Oklahoma. She was romantically involved with James Miller, an assistant district attorney. The state charged Marcum with obstructing an investigation of suspected embezzlement and offered in evidence text messages sent and received by her and Miller. Marcum filed a motion to suppress the messages, which the court granted. The state appealed.

Did Marcum have a reasonable expectation of privacy in texts stored in Miller's account with his cell phone company? No. In a 2014 case, *State of Oklahoma v. Marcum*, a state intermediate appellate court reversed the lower court's judgment. Marcum had no reasonable expectation of privacy in U.S. Cellular's records of her text messages in Miller's account. "Once the messages were both transmitted and received, the expectation of privacy was lost."

8–3b The Exclusionary Rule

exclusionary rule
Evidence obtained in violation of rights under the Fourth, Fifth, and Sixth Amendments—and evidence derived from illegally obtained evidence—is not admissible in court.

Under the **exclusionary rule,** all evidence obtained in violation of the constitutional rights spelled out in the Fourth, Fifth, and Sixth Amendments usually must be excluded, as well as all evidence derived from the illegally obtained evidence. Evidence derived from illegally obtained evidence is known as "fruit of the poisonous tree." If a confession is obtained after an illegal arrest, the arrest is "the poisonous tree," and the confession, if "tainted" by the arrest, is the "fruit." The purpose of the exclusionary rule is to deter police from misconduct.

EXAMPLE 8.1 Oliver hacked personal information from various parties. He then filed for and received unemployment benefits in their names. Oliver was later arrested, along with his friend John, who told the police about a laptop computer that Oliver kept at Erica's apartment. Police searched this laptop and found more evidence of the crime. Oliver argued that this post-arrest evidence was "fruit of the poisonous tree," and it should be excluded. ◄

8–3c Informing Suspects of Their Rights

Individuals who are arrested must be informed of certain constitutional rights, including their right to remain silent and their right to legal counsel. If the arresting officer fails to inform a criminal suspect of these rights, any statement the suspect makes normally will not be admissible in court.

There are some exceptions. In federal cases, for example, a voluntary confession can be used in evidence even if the accused was not informed of his or her rights. In some cases, juries may accept confessions without being convinced that they were made voluntarily.

LEARNING OUTCOME 4

List the crimes that affect business.

white-collar crime
Nonviolent crime committed by individuals or corporations to obtain a personal or business advantage.

8–4 Crimes Affecting Business

Numerous forms of crime occur in a business context. Many of these are referred to as **white-collar crimes.** The term is used to mean an illegal act or series of acts committed by an individual or business using some nonviolent means to obtain a personal or business advantage. In this section, we focus on white-collar property crimes, and violations of the Racketeer Influenced and Corrupt Organizations Act that affect business.

8–4a Forgery

The fraudulent making or altering of any writing in a way that changes the legal rights and liabilities of another is **forgery**. **EXAMPLE 8.2** Without authorization, Severson signs Bennett's name to the back of a check made out to Bennett. Severson is committing forgery. ◄ Forgery also includes changing trademarks, falsifying public records, counterfeiting, and altering a legal document.

forgery
The fraudulent making or altering of any writing in a way that changes the legal rights and liabilities of another.

8–4b Robbery

Robbery is forcefully and unlawfully taking personal property of any value from another. The use of force or intimidation is usually necessary for an act of theft to be considered a robbery. Thus, picking pockets is not robbery, because the action is unknown to the victim.

robbery
The act of forcefully and unlawfully taking personal property of any value from another.

8–4c Larceny

The crime of **larceny** involves the unlawful taking and carrying away of someone else's personal property with the intent to permanently deprive the owner of possession. In short, larceny is stealing or theft. As noted, robbery involves force or fear, but larceny does not. So pickpocketing is larceny, not robbery.

larceny
The wrongful taking and carrying away of another person's personal property with the intent to permanently deprive the owner of the property.

8–4d Embezzlement

When a person who is entrusted with another person's property or money fraudulently appropriates it, **embezzlement** occurs. Typically, this involves an employee who steals money. Banks face this problem, and so do businesses in which company officers or accountants "doctor" the books to cover up the fraudulent conversion of money for their own benefit. Embezzlement is not larceny, because the wrongdoer does not physically take the property from the possession of another, and it is not robbery, because no force or fear is used.

embezzlement
The fraudulent appropriation of money or other property by a person to whom the money or property has been entrusted.

HIGHLIGHTING THE POINT

While hauling a load of refrigerators from San Diego to New York in a truck owned by National Appliance Company, Fred departs from his route and stops in Las Vegas, where he tries to sell some of the refrigerators. No one buys them, and they never leave the truck, but to display them Fred breaks the truck's seals, enters the cargo compartment, and opens two refrigerator cartons. Fred is arrested and charged with embezzlement. Fred claims that there are no grounds for the charge, because he never took anything off the truck.

Does the charge of embezzlement apply when property is not physically removed from the owner's possession? Yes. If a person has control over the property of another and has the intent of converting the goods to his or her own use, then embezzlement occurs. By leaving his route to sell the refrigerators and keep the proceeds, Fred exercised control over the property with the intent to convert it to his own use.

Generally, the intent to return the embezzled property—or its actual return—is *not* a defense to the crime of embezzlement.

8–4e Mail and Wire Fraud

One of the most potent weapons against white-collar criminals is the Mail Fraud Act. Under this act, it is a federal crime to use the mails to defraud the public. Illegal use of the mails must involve the following:

1. Mailing or causing someone else to mail a writing—something written, printed, or photocopied—for the purpose of executing a scheme to defraud.

2. A contemplated or an organized scheme to defraud by false pretenses.

Federal law also makes it a crime to use wire, radio, or television transmissions to defraud. Violators may be fined up to $1,000, imprisoned for up to five years, or both. If the violation affects a financial institution, the violator may be fined up to $1 million, imprisoned up to thirty years, or both.

HIGHLIGHTING THE POINT

Franklin Systems offers a warranty program to authorized resellers of Franklin parts. George Taylor and Robert Singer devise a scheme to intentionally defraud Franklin using this reseller program to obtain replacement parts to which they are not entitled. The two men plan and use specific language in numerous e-mails and Internet service requests that they send to Franklin to convince the company to ship them new parts via commercial carriers.

Does Taylor and Singer's use of e-mail and the Internet constitute mail and wire fraud? Yes. They sent e-mails with the intent to obtain goods by false pretenses and to which they were not entitled. They have committed mail and wire fraud, as well as conspiracy to commit mail and wire fraud.

8–4f Bribery

Basically, three types of bribery are considered crimes: bribery of public officials, commercial bribery, and bribery of foreign officials.

Bribery of Public Officials The attempt to influence a public official to act in a way that serves a private interest is a crime. The bribe can be anything the recipient considers to be valuable. The commission of the crime occurs when the bribe is offered. The recipient does not have to agree to perform whatever action is desired by the person offering the bribe, nor does the recipient have to accept the bribe.

Commercial Bribery Typically, people make commercial bribes to obtain proprietary information, cover up an inferior product, or secure new business. Industrial espionage sometimes involves commercial bribes. **EXAMPLE 8.3** Rosemary works for Telecom. She offers Craig, an employee at QMC Services (a Telecom competitor), some type of payoff in exchange for QMC trade secrets and pricing schedules. ◄ So-called kickbacks, or payoffs for special favors or services, are a form of commercial bribery in some situations.

Bribery of Foreign Officials Bribing foreign officials to obtain favorable business contracts is a crime. The Foreign Corrupt Practices Act was passed to prevent U.S. businesspersons from using bribery to secure foreign contracts.

8–4g Racketeer Influenced and Corrupt Organizations Act

The purpose of the Racketeer Influenced and Corrupt Organizations Act (RICO) was to curb the apparently increasing entry of organized crime into the legitimate business world. Under RICO, it is a federal crime to do the following:

- Use income obtained from racketeering activity to purchase any interest in an enterprise.
- Acquire or maintain an interest in an enterprise through racketeering activity.
- Conduct or participate in the affairs of an enterprise through racketeering activity.
- Conspire to do any of the preceding acts.

Racketeering activity is not a new type of crime created by RICO. Rather, RICO incorporates twenty-six separate types of federal crimes and nine types of state felonies. It stipulates that if a person commits two or more of these offenses, he or she is guilty of "racketeering activity." Most of the criminal RICO offenses have little, if anything, to do with normal business activities, for they involve gambling, arson, and extortion.

Securities fraud (involving the sale of stocks and bonds) and mail fraud, however, can also be criminal violations under RICO. The act has become an effective tool in attacking these white-collar crimes. Under criminal provisions of RICO, any individual found guilty of a violation is subject to a fine of up to $25,000 per violation, imprisonment for up to twenty years, or both.

 # 8–5 DEFENSES TO CRIMINAL LIABILITY

LEARNING OUTCOME 5

Summarize the defenses to criminal liability.

Two elements must be present for a person to be convicted of a crime: the performance of a prohibited act and the intent to commit that act. Even if both elements are present, however, there are defenses that the law deems sufficient to excuse a defendant's criminal behavior.

Among the most important defenses to criminal liability are infancy, insanity, and entrapment. Also, in some cases, defendants are given *immunity* and thus relieved, at least in part, of criminal liability for crimes they committed.

8–5a Mistakes

Everyone has heard the saying, "Ignorance of the law is no excuse." Ordinarily, a *mistake of law*—that is, ignorance of the law or a mistaken idea about what the law requires—is not a valid defense. In contrast, a *mistake of fact* can often excuse criminal responsibility, if it negates the mental state necessary to commit a crime. **EXAMPLE 8.4** Wyatt mistakenly walks off with Julie's briefcase at a popular restaurant because he thinks it is his. Wyatt has not committed a crime because theft requires knowledge that the property belongs to another. (If Wyatt's act causes Julie to incur damages, however, she may sue him in a civil action for conversion.)◄

8–5b Insanity

Someone suffering from a mental illness is sometimes judged incapable of the state of mind required to commit a crime. Different courts use different tests for legal insanity. Almost all federal courts and some state courts hold that a person is not responsible for criminal conduct if, as a result of mental disease or defect, the person lacked the capacity to appreciate the wrongfulness of the conduct or to obey the law.

Some states use a test under which a criminal defendant is not responsible if, at the time of the offense, he or she did not know the nature and quality of the act or did not know that the act was wrong. Other states use the irresistible-impulse test. A person operating under an irresistible impulse may know an act is wrong but cannot refrain from doing it.

8–5c Entrapment

entrapment
A claim that a defendant was induced by a police officer or other public official to commit a crime that he or she would not otherwise have committed.

Entrapment is a defense designed to prevent police officers or other government agents from encouraging crimes in order to apprehend persons wanted for criminal acts. In the typical entrapment case, an undercover agent *suggests* that a crime be committed and somehow pressures or induces an individual to commit it. The agent then arrests the individual for the crime. The crucial issue is whether a person who committed a crime was predisposed to commit the crime or did so because the agent induced it.

8–5d Immunity

Accused persons cannot be forced to give information if it will be used to prosecute them. This privilege is granted by the Fifth Amendment to the U.S. Constitution. To obtain information from a person accused of a crime, the state can grant immunity from prosecution or agree to prosecute for a less serious offense in exchange for the information.

 # 8–6 Cyber Crime

computer crime
Any act that is directed against computers and computer parts or that uses computers as instruments of crime.

The American Bar Association defines **computer crime** as any act that is directed against computers and computer parts or that uses computers as instruments of crime. Because much of the crime committed with computers occurs in cyberspace, many computer crimes are referred to as **cyber crimes.** In this section, we look at some of the ways in which computers are used in criminal activity.

cyber crime
A crime that occurs in the virtual community of the Internet, as opposed to the physical world.

8–6a Cyber Fraud

cyber fraud
Any misrepresentation knowingly made over the Internet with the intention of deceiving another for the purpose of obtaining property or funds.

Fraud is any misrepresentation knowingly made with the intention of deceiving another and on which a reasonable person would and does rely to her or his detriment. **Cyber fraud** is fraud committed over the Internet. Fraud that was once conducted solely by mail or phone can now be found online, and new technology has led to increasingly creative ways to commit fraud.

EXAMPLE 8.5 Gary selects four different online auction sites and creates bogus seller accounts on each. He then creates an auction page on each site for a rare antique clock, complete with a detailed description, authentication papers, and photos. His minimum starting bid is $500. The clock sells for more than $500 on each site. Gary sends two buyers a clock, but it is not the one advertised in the auction and is worth much less than $500. The other two buyers receive nothing from Gary.◄

8–6b Identity Theft

identity theft
The act of stealing another's identifying information and using that information to access the victim's financial resources.

A form of cyber crime that has become particularly troublesome is identity theft. **Identity theft** occurs when the wrongdoer steals a form of identification—such as a name, date of birth, or Social Security number—and uses the information to access the victim's financial resources.

The Internet has turned identity theft into a prevalent cyber crime. From the identity thief's perspective, the Internet provides those who steal information offline with an easy medium for using items such as stolen credit-card or Social Security numbers while protected by anonymity.

Phishing is a distinct form of identity theft (and cyber fraud). In a phishing attack, the perpetrators "fish" for financial data and passwords from consumers by posing as a legitimate business and asking for personal data that help them steal a user's identity.

EXAMPLE 8.6 Virginia City Bank customers receive official-looking e-mails from the bank, requesting they click on a link and input personal account information on an online form to ensure their online accounts are secure. The Web site, however, is bogus. When the customers complete the form, their computers are infected and funnel their data to a computer server. The cyber criminals then sell the data. ◄

phishing
An e-mail scam in which the message appears to be from a legitimate business to induce individuals to reveal personal financial data, passwords, or other information.

8–6c Hacking

A person who uses one computer to break into another is referred to as a **hacker**. (Smartphones can be hacked, too.) Hackers who break into computers and mobile devices without authorization often commit cyber theft. The goals of a hacking operation might include a wholesale theft of data, such as a merchant's customer files, or the monitoring of a computer to discover a business firm's plans and transactions.

In particular, retail companies take risks by storing their customers' debit- and credit-card numbers and personal information online. The electronic warehouses that store these data are attractive targets for cyber thieves and hackers. (See the *Linking Business Law to Your Career* feature at the end of this chapter.)

EXAMPLE 8.7 Amy hacks into Urban Mix Boutique's Web site, a popular clothing outlet in her community. Customers can purchase items at the retail store or online. After hacking into the site, Amy installs malware that sends her the financial data of Urban Mix customers. Amy can then sell the stolen data to other cyber thieves or use the information to make fraudulent purchases herself. ◄

hacker
A person who uses one computer to break into another.

8–6d Cyberterrorism

A **cyberterrorist** is a hacker who exploits computers to create a serious impact. For instance, false code entered into the processing control system of a food manufacturer could alter the levels of ingredients so that consumers of the food would become ill. Computer viruses could also cripple communications networks. A prolonged disruption of computer, cable, satellite, or telecommunications systems would have serious effects on business operations—and national security—on a global level.

cyberterrorist
A hacker whose purpose is to exploit a target computer to create a serious impact.

8–6e Prosecuting Cyber Crime

Cyberspace has raised new issues in the investigation of crimes and the prosecution of offenders. A threshold issue is jurisdiction. For example, a person who commits an act against a business in California, where the act is a cyber crime, might never have set foot in California but might instead reside in New York, where the act may not be a crime. Identifying the wrongdoer can also be difficult. Cyber criminals do not leave physical traces, such as fingerprints or DNA samples, as evidence of their crimes.

At the federal level, the Counterfeit Access Device and Computer Fraud and Abuse Act, as amended by the National Information Infrastructure Protection Act, provides that a person who accesses a computer online without authority to obtain classified, restricted, or protected data, or attempts to do so, is subject to criminal

LEARNING OUTCOME 6

Discuss how the Internet has expanded opportunities for crime, and outline the protection that the law provides for online victims.

prosecution. The theft is a felony if it is committed for a commercial purpose or for private financial gain or if the value of the stolen data (or computer time) exceeds $5,000. Penalties include fines and imprisonment for up to twenty years.

ANSWERING THE LEGAL PROBLEM

In the legal problem set out at the beginning of this chapter, Ray steals a purse that contains money and a handgun. He is convicted of grand theft of property (cash) and grand theft of a firearm. He appeals, arguing that he is not guilty of grand theft of a firearm because he did not know that a gun was in the purse.

A **Can Ray be convicted of the crime of grand theft of a firearm even though he did not know that a gun was in the purse?** No. Separate crimes would have occurred only if there had been separate acts. Ray committed the crime of grand theft because of the value of the property in the purse, including the value of the gun. Only one crime of theft occurred, however. Ray saw the purse and took it without knowing what it contained: there was one intent and one act.

LINKING BUSINESS LAW to Your Career

PROTECT YOUR COMPANY AGAINST HACKING

If you are planning a career in accounting or business management, you need to know how to protect your company from hackers. Each year, millions of dollars are hacked from the bank accounts of small- to mid-sized businesses. This is because most of these businesses do not take steps to reduce the risk of hacking. Their accounts are often in local banks or credit unions, which tend to have inadequate security measures (if any) and lack the services of cyber security experts.

Know What Is "Commercially Reasonable"

Many small-business owners believe that if their bank accounts are hacked

and disappear, their banks will reimburse them. That is not always the case, however. Just ask Mark Patterson, the owner of Patco Construction in Maryland. He lost more than $350,000 to hackers. When People's United Bank would not agree to a settlement, Patterson sued, claiming that the bank should have monitored his account. So far, federal judges have agreed with the bank—that its protections were "commercially reasonable," which is the only standard that banks have to follow.

Know Your Insurance Coverage Policy

Similarly, small-business owners often think that their regular insurance

policy will cover cyber losses at their local banks. In reality, unless there is a specific "rider" to a business's insurance policy, its bank accounts are not covered.

So, just because your business will be reimbursed if thieves break in and steal your machines and network servers, that does not mean you will be covered if hackers break into your bank account.

TERMS AND CONCEPTS FOR REVIEW

computer crime 114	cyber fraud 114	embezzlement 111
crime 107	cyberterrorist 115	entrapment 114
cyber crime 114	double jeopardy 109	exclusionary rule 110

felony 108

forgery 111

hacker 115

identity theft 114

larceny 111

misdemeanor 108

phishing 115

probable cause 109

robbery 111

search warrant 109

white-collar crime 110

CHAPTER SUMMARY—CRIMINAL LAW AND CYBER CRIME

LEARNING OUTCOME	
1	**Explain the difference between crimes and other types of wrongful conduct.** A *crime* is a wrong against society proclaimed in a statute and punishable by society through fines, imprisonment, or sometimes death. Crimes are prosecuted by public officials. In contrast, a civil wrong violates a duty between persons or between citizens and their governments, excluding the duty not to commit crimes. Civil wrongs are remedied through damages awarded in lawsuits brought by the persons who suffered the harm.
2	**Indicate the essential elements of criminal liability.** The elements of criminal liability are (1) the performance of a prohibited act and (2) a specified state of mind, or intent.
3	**Describe the constitutional safeguards that protect the rights of persons accused of crimes.** The rights of accused persons are protected under the U.S. Constitution, particularly by the Fourth, Fifth, Sixth, and Eighth Amendments. Under the exclusionary rule, evidence obtained in violation of the constitutional rights of the accused will not be admissible in court. Individuals must be informed of their constitutional rights, including their right to counsel and their right to remain silent, when taken into custody.
4	**List the crimes that affect business.** Crimes affecting business include forgery, robbery, larceny, embezzlement, mail and wire fraud, and bribery. The Racketeer Influenced and Corrupt Organizations Act helps to curb organized crime.
5	**Summarize the defenses to criminal liability.** The most important defenses to criminal liability include mistakes, insanity, and entrapment. In some cases, defendants can be granted immunity from prosecution, or be prosecuted for a less serious offense, in exchange for information.
6	**Discuss how the Internet has expanded opportunities for crime, and outline the protection that the law provides for online victims.** The Internet provides easy access to private data, and Web users often surrender information about themselves without knowing it. Criminals find it easy to assume multiple identities online and thereby commit traditional fraud through the Internet. The Counterfeit Access Device and Computer Fraud and Abuse Act prohibits cyber theft, which is accessing, or attempting to access, a computer without authority to obtain classified or protected data. Penalties include fines and imprisonment for up to twenty years.

ISSUE SPOTTERS

Check your answers to the *Issue Spotters* against the answers provided in Appendix C at the end of this text.

1. Without Jim's permission, Lee signs Jim's name to several checks that were issued to Jim and then cashes them. Jim reports that the checks were stolen and receives replacements. Has Lee committed forgery? Why or why not? (See *Crimes Affecting Business.*)

2. Carl appears on television talk shows touting a cure for AIDS that he knows is fraudulent. He frequently mentions that he needs funds to make the cure widely available, and donations pour into local television stations to be forwarded to Carl. Has Carl committed a crime? If so, what? (See *Crimes Affecting Business.*)

USING BUSINESS LAW

8–1. Types of Crimes. Determine from the facts below what type of crime has been committed in each situation.

1. Carlos is walking through an amusement park when his wallet, with $2,000 in it, is "picked" from his pocket. (See *Crimes Affecting Business*.)
2. Carlos walks into a camera shop. Without force and without the owner's noticing, Carlos walks out with a camera. (See *Crimes Affecting Business*.)

8–2. Theft. The head of CompTac's accounting department, Roy Olson, has to pay his daughter's college tuition within a week or his daughter will not be able to continue taking classes. The payment due is more than $20,000. Roy would be able to make the payment in two months but cannot do so until then. The college refuses to wait that long. In desperation, Roy—through a fictitious bank account and some clever accounting—"borrows" funds from CompTac. Before Roy can pay back the borrowed funds, an auditor discovers what Roy did. CompTac's president alleges that Roy has "stolen" company funds and informs the police of the theft. Has Roy committed a crime? If so, what crime did he commit? Explain. (See *Crimes Affecting Business*.)

REAL-WORLD CASE PROBLEMS

8–3. White-Collar Crime. Matthew Simpson and others created and operated a series of corporate entities to defraud telecommunications companies, creditors, credit-reporting agencies, among others. Through these entities, Simpson and the others used routing codes and spoofing services to make long-distance calls appear to be local. They stole other firms' network capacity and diverted payments to themselves. They leased goods and services without paying for them. They also assumed false identities, addresses, and credit histories, and issued false bills, invoices, financial statements, and credit references, to hide their real identities. Did these acts constitute mail and wire fraud? Discuss. [*United States v. Simpson*, 741 F.3d 539 (5th Cir. 2014)] (See *Crimes Affecting Business*.)

8–4. Criminal Liability. David Green threw bottles and plates from a twenty-sixth-floor hotel balcony overlooking a street in New York City. He suspended his antics when he saw police on the street below and on the roof of the building across the street. He resumed tossing objects off the balcony after the police left, however. Later, he admitted that he could recall what he had done, but he claimed to have been intoxicated and that his only purpose had been to amuse himself and his friends. Did Green have the mental state required to establish criminal liability? Discuss. [*State of New York v. Green*, 104 A.D.3d 126, 958 N.Y.S.2d 138 (1 Dept. 2013)] (See *What Constitutes Criminal Liability?*)

8–5. Search. Charles Byrd was in a minimum-security jail awaiting trial. A team of sheriff's deputies wearing T-shirts and jeans took several inmates into a room for a strip search without any apparent justification. Byrd was ordered to remove all his clothing except his boxer shorts. A female deputy searched Byrd while several male deputies watched. One of the male deputies videotaped the search. Byrd filed a suit against the sheriff's department. Did the search violate Byrd's rights? Discuss. [*Byrd v. Maricopa County Sheriff's Department*, 629 F.3d. 1135 (9th Cir. 2011)] (See *Constitutional Safeguards*.)

8–6. Embezzlement. Lou Sisuphan was the director of finance at a Toyota dealership. To cause trouble for a subordinate, Sisuphan kept a payment of nearly $30,000 from one of the subordinate's customers. Later, Sisuphan told the dealership what he had done and returned the payment, adding that he had "no intention of stealing the money." Did Sisuphan take the funds with the intent to defraud his employer? Did he commit embezzlement? Explain. [*People v. Sisuphan*, 181 Cal.App.4th 800, 104 Cal.Rptr.3d 654 (1 Dist. 2010)] (See *Crimes Affecting Business*.)

ETHICAL QUESTIONS

8–7. Informing Suspects of Their Rights. Should there be any exceptions to the rule that suspects be informed of their rights? Discuss. (See *Constitutional Safeguards*.)

8–8. Identity Theft. Twenty-year-old Davis Omole worked at a cell phone store. He stole customers' personal information and used the stolen identities to create a hundred different accounts on eBay. Omole held more than three hundred auctions on eBay, listing sale items that he did not own. From these auctions, he collected $90,000. Charged with identity theft, Omole displayed contempt for the court and ridiculed his victims, calling them stupid for having been cheated. What does this behavior suggest about Omole's ethics? Discuss. [*United States v. Omole*, 523 F.3d 691 (7th Cir. 2008)] (See *Cyber Crime*.)

Chapter 8—Work Set

TRUE-FALSE QUESTIONS

_____ 1. A crime is a wrong against society proclaimed in a statute.

_____ 2. A person can be convicted simply for intending to commit a crime.

_____ 3. If a crime is punishable by death, it must be a felony.

_____ 4. Ordinarily, "ignorance of the law" is a valid defense to criminal liability.

_____ 5. A person who has been granted immunity from prosecution cannot be compelled to answer any questions.

_____ 6. Robbery is the taking of another's personal property from his or her person or immediate presence.

_____ 7. Stealing a computer program is not a crime.

_____ 8. Fraudulently altering a public document can be forgery.

_____ 9. Racketeering activity is a new type of crime created by RICO.

_____ 10. Persons suffering from mental illness are sometimes judged incapable of the state of mind required to commit a crime.

MULTIPLE-CHOICE QUESTIONS

_____ 1. Which of the following statements is true?
a. Criminal defendants are prosecuted by the state.
b. Criminal defendants must prove their innocence.
c. Criminal law actions are intended to give the victims financial compensation.
d. A crime is never a violation of a statute.

_____ 2. Crime requires
a. the performance of a prohibited act.
b. the intent to commit a crime.
c. both a and b.
d. none of the above.

_____ 3. Helen, an undercover police officer, pressures Pete to buy stolen goods. When he does so, he is arrested and charged with dealing in stolen goods. Pete will likely be
a. acquitted, because he was entrapped.
b. acquitted, because Helen was entrapped.
c. acquitted, because both parties were entrapped.
d. convicted.

_____ 4. Police officer Berry arrests John on suspicion of embezzlement. Berry advises John of his rights. He informs John
a. that John has the right to remain silent.
b. that John has the right to consult with an attorney.
c. of both a and b.
d. of none of the above.

_____ 5. In a jewelry store, April takes a diamond ring from the counter and puts it in her pocket. She walks three steps toward the door before the manager stops her. April is arrested and charged with larceny. She will likely be
a. acquitted, because she was entrapped.
b. acquitted, because she took only three steps.
c. acquitted, because she did not leave the store.
d. convicted.

6. Kevin takes home the company-owned laptop computer that he uses in his office. He has no intention of returning it. Kevin has committed

   a. larceny.
   b. embezzlement.
   c. robbery.
   d. none of the above.

7. Police detective Howard suspects Carol of a crime. Howard may be issued a warrant to search Carol's premises if he can show

   a. probable cause.
   b. proximate cause.
   c. causation in fact.
   d. intent to search the premises.

8. Adam signs Beth's name, without her consent, to the back of a check payable to Beth. This is

   a. burglary.
   b. embezzlement.
   c. forgery.
   d. larceny.

9. Police officer Katy obtains a confession from criminal suspect Bart after an illegal arrest. At Bart's trial, the confession will likely be

   a. admitted as proof of Bart's guilt.
   b. admitted as evidence of Bart's crime.
   c. admitted as support for Katy's suspicions.
   d. excluded.

ANSWERING MORE LEGAL PROBLEMS

1. Sylvia requires her students, including Ralph, to submit their written assignments to CopyCat Detection Agency. CopyCat compares the work to the universe of material online to expose plagiarism. Ralph obtains another person's password, log-in ID, and credit-card number via the Internet to submit papers to CopyCat, misrepresenting himself as a student at a different school.

   What is a cyber crime? Has Ralph committed such a crime? If so, which one? Crimes committed with computers in _____ are referred to as cyber crimes. One of the cyber crimes that Ralph has committed is _____ _____. This occurs when a wrongdoer steals a form of identification, such as a name, and uses it to access the victim's financial resources. Here, Ralph obtained another's password, log-in ID, and credit-card number via the Internet. By using the credit-card number without the other's _____, Ralph accessed that person's financial resources.

2. CopyCat quickly discovers what Ralph has done. The company files a suit against him, alleging that he has gained unauthorized access to its online services in violation of a certain federal statute.

   Which statute mentioned in this chapter has Ralph most likely violated? The Counterfeit Access Device and Computer _____ and Abuse Act is one of the statutes that Ralph has violated. Under this act, a person who accesses a computer online without authorization to obtain classified, restricted, or protected data commits _____. Here, Ralph used another's identity to access _____ data on CopyCat's Web site. If the company's loss, in terms of the cost to verify its security and other expenses, exceeds $5,000, this act is a _____.

CONTRACTS

UNIT CONTENTS

CHAPTER 9   Introduction to Contracts

CHAPTER 10   Offer and Acceptance

CHAPTER 11   Consideration

CHAPTER 12   Capacity

CHAPTER 13   The Legality of Agreements

CHAPTER 14   Voluntary Consent

CHAPTER 15   Written Contracts

CHAPTER 16   Third Party Rights

CHAPTER 17   Contract Discharge and Remedies

9 INTRODUCTION TO CONTRACTS

promise
A declaration that binds the person who makes it (promisor) to do or not to do a certain act.

promisor
A person who makes a promise.

promisee
A person to whom a promise is made.

contract
A set of promises constituting an agreement between parties, giving each a legal duty to the other and also the right to seek a remedy for the breach of the promises or duties.

objective theory of contracts
The view that contracting parties shall be bound only by terms that can objectively be inferred from promises made.

FACING A LEGAL PROBLEM

Jack, Barry, and Simone are visiting San Francisco during Spring Break. Jack offers to pay Simone $100 if she walks across the entire span of the Golden Gate Bridge.

Q If Simone says nothing but simply walks across the bridge, do she and Jack have a contract? If Simone says no and turns and walks away, are there any legal consequences? If, without saying a word, Barry rather than Simone starts to walk across, do Jack and Barry have a contract?

Contract law assures the parties to private agreements that the promises they make will be enforceable. A **promise** is a declaration that something either will or will not happen in the future. Sometimes, the promises exchanged create *moral* rather than *legal* obligations. Failure to perform a moral obligation, such as an agreement to take a friend to lunch, usually does not create a legal liability.

Some promises may create both a moral and a legal obligation. **EXAMPLE 9.1** Nolan and Pam are getting a divorce. Nolan's promise to pay a set amount of child support and alimony to Pam every month creates both a moral and a legal obligation.◄

Clearly, many promises are kept because of a sense of duty or because keeping them is in the mutual self-interest of the parties involved, not because the **promisor** (the person making the promise) or the **promisee** (the person to whom the promise is made) is conscious of the rules of contract law. Nevertheless, the rules of contract law are often followed in business agreements to avoid potential problems.

9–1 THE DEFINITION OF A CONTRACT

A **contract** is an agreement that can be enforced in a court. It is formed by two or more parties who agree to perform or refrain from performing some act now or in the future. Generally, contract disputes arise when there is a promise of future performance. If the contractual promise is not fulfilled, the party who made it is subject to the sanctions of a court. That party may be required to pay monetary damages for failing to perform. In limited instances, the party may be required to perform the promised act.

9–1a The Objective Theory of Contracts

The element of intent is of prime importance in determining whether a contract has been formed. In contract law, intent is determined by what is called the **objective theory of contracts,** not by the personal or subjective intent, or belief, of a party. The theory is that a party's intention to enter into a contract is judged by outward, objective facts as interpreted by a *reasonable* person, rather than by the party's own secret, subjective intentions. Objective facts include the following:

1. What the party said when entering into the contract.

2. How the party acted or appeared.

3. The circumstances surrounding the transaction.

As will be discussed later in this chapter, intent to form a contract may be manifested not only in words (oral or written) but also by conduct.

Real-World Case Example

Pan Handle Realty, LLC, and Robert Olins signed a lease for a new home in Westport, Connecticut. Olins gave Pan Handle a check for the first year's rent. A few days later, however, Olins stopped payment on the check and told Pan Handle that he no longer had an "interest in the property." Pan Handle was unable to secure a new tenant and filed a suit in a Connecticut state court against Olins. The defendant argued that when he signed the lease, he did not intend to be bound by it. The court ruled in Pan Handle's favor. Olins appealed.

When Pan Handle and Olins signed the lease, did each party intend to be bound to it? Yes. In a 2013 case, *Pan Handle Realty, LLC v. Olins*, a state intermediate appellate court affirmed the lower court's ruling. There was nothing to support Olins's contention that he did not intend to be bound by the lease when he signed it. His apparent "change of heart" did not negate the parties' "meeting of the minds" that occurred at the time the lease was signed. This mutual assent was indicated by their signatures on the lease and Olins's payment of the first year's rent.

9–1b The Basic Requirements of a Contract

The following list briefly describes the four requirements that must be met before a valid contract exists. If any of these elements is lacking, no contract will have been formed.

1. *Agreement.* An agreement includes an *offer* and an *acceptance*. One party must offer to enter into a legal agreement, and another party must accept the terms of the offer.

2. *Consideration.* Any promises made by the parties must be supported by legally sufficient and bargained-for *consideration* (something of value received or promised to convince a person to make a deal).

3. *Capacity.* Both parties entering into the contract must have the legal *capacity* to do so. The law must recognize them as possessing characteristics that qualify them as competent parties.

4. *Legality.* The contract's purpose must be to accomplish some goal that is legal and not against public policy.

Even if all of these requirements are satisfied, a contract may be unenforceable if the following requirements are not met. These requirements typically are raised as *defenses* to the enforceability of an otherwise valid contract.

1. *Voluntary consent.* The apparent consent of both parties must be voluntary. For example, if a contract was formed as a result of fraud, undue influence, mistake, or duress, the contract may not be enforceable.

2. *Form.* The contract must be in whatever form the law requires. For instance, some contracts must be in writing to be enforceable.

9–2 TYPES OF CONTRACTS

There are many types of contracts, and they are categorized according to differences in formation, enforceability, or performance. The best method of explaining each is to compare one type of contract with another.

9–2a Bilateral versus Unilateral Contracts

offeror
A person who makes an offer.

offeree
A person to whom an offer is made.

bilateral contract
A contract that includes the exchange of a promise for a promise.

Every contract involves at least two parties. The **offeror** is the party making the offer. The **offeree** is the party to whom the offer is made. The offeror always promises to do or not to do something and thus is also a promisor. Whether the contract is classified as *unilateral* or *bilateral* depends on what the offeree must do to accept the offer and to bind the offeror to a contract.

Bilateral Contracts If, to accept the offer, the offeree must only *promise* to perform, the contract is a **bilateral contract.** Hence, a bilateral contract is a "promise for a promise." No performance, such as the payment of money or delivery of goods, need take place for a bilateral contract to be formed. The contract comes into existence at the moment the promises are exchanged. **EXAMPLE 9.2** Brian offers to buy Tara's Android-based smartphone for $250. Brian tells Tara that he will give her the $250 next Friday, when he gets paid. Tara accepts his offer and promises to give him the smartphone when he pays her on Friday. They have formed a bilateral contract.◄

unilateral contract
A contract that includes the exchange of a promise for an act.

Unilateral Contracts If the offer is phrased so that the offeree can accept only by completing the contract performance, the contract is a **unilateral contract.** Hence, a unilateral contract is a "promise for an act." In other words, the contract is not formed at the moment when promises are exchanged but rather when the contract is *performed*.

Contests, lotteries, and other competitions for prizes are examples of offers for unilateral contracts. If a person complies with the rules of the contest—such as by submitting the right lottery number at the right place and time—a unilateral contract is formed, binding the organization offering the prize to a contract to perform as promised in the offer.

A problem arises in unilateral contracts when the promisor attempts to *revoke* (cancel) the offer after the promisee has begun performance but before the act has been completed. The promisee can accept the offer only on full performance, and offers normally are *revocable* (capable of being canceled) until accepted. The modern-day view, however, is that the offer becomes irrevocable once performance has begun. Thus, even though the offer has not yet been accepted, the offeror is prohibited from revoking it for a reasonable time.

HIGHLIGHTING THE POINT

Margo offers to buy Harry's sailboat, moored in San Francisco, on delivery of the boat to Margo's dock in Newport Beach, three hundred miles south of San Francisco. Harry rigs the boat and sets sail. Shortly before his arrival at Newport Beach, Harry receives a radio message from Margo withdrawing her offer.

Does Margo's message terminate the offer or—because Harry has begun performing—is the offer irrevocable? Margo's offer is part of a unilateral contract, and only Harry's delivery of the sailboat at her dock is an acceptance. Ordinarily, her revocation would terminate the offer. In the modern view, however, the offer is irrevocable, because Harry has undertaken performance (and has in fact sailed almost three hundred miles). Harry can thus deliver the boat and bind Margo to the contract.

9–2b Express versus Implied Contracts

An **express contract** is one in which the terms of the agreement are fully and explicitly stated in words, oral or written. For instance, a signed lease for an apartment or a house is an express written contract. **EXAMPLE 9.3** Katie and her friend Laura are talking to each other using FaceTime. During the online conversation, Katie agrees to buy Laura's used Macbook Pro computer for $750 on the first day of the following month. They have an express oral contract.◄

A contract that is implied from the conduct of the parties is called an **implied contract**. This contract differs from an express contract in that the *conduct* of the parties, rather than their words, creates and defines the terms of the contract. The following three steps normally establish an implied contract:

1. A party furnishes some goods or services.

2. That party expects to be paid for those goods or services, and the party to whom the goods or services were provided knows, or should know, payment is expected (based on the objective theory of contracts test).

3. The party to whom the goods or services were provided has a chance to reject them but does not.

EXAMPLE 9.4 Ted needs an accountant to complete his tax return. He drops by a local accountant's office, explains his situation to the accountant, and learns what fees she charges. The next day, he returns and gives the receptionist all of the necessary documents to complete his return. Then he walks out without saying anything further to the accountant. In this situation, Ted has entered into an implied contract to pay the accountant the usual fees for her services. The contract is implied because of Ted's conduct and hers. She expects to be paid for completing the tax return, and by bringing in the records she will need to do the job, Ted has implied an intent to pay her.◄

9–2c Quasi Contracts

Quasi contracts are wholly different from actual contracts. Express contracts and implied contracts are actual, or true, contracts. Quasi contracts, as their name suggests, are not true contracts. They do not arise from any agreement, express or implied, between the parties themselves. Rather, quasi contracts are fictional contracts implied by courts and imposed on parties in the interests of fairness and justice. Usually, quasi contracts are imposed to avoid the *unjust enrichment* of one party at the expense of another.

> **express contract**
> A contract that is stated in words, oral or written.
>
> **LEARNING OUTCOME 3**
> Contrast express and implied contracts.
>
> **implied contract**
> A contract formed in whole or in part from the conduct of the parties.
>
> **quasi contract**
> An obligation or contract imposed by law, in the absence of agreement, to prevent unjust enrichment.

HIGHLIGHTING THE POINT

Freshwater Services operates a water-distribution system that serves a residential area, including Joe and Carol Green's home. The Greens do not have an express contract with Freshwater, but the couple pays the firm's monthly charges for water. When Freshwater increases the monthly price, however, the Greens refuse to pay more. Freshwater files a suit against the Greens to collect the additional charge.

(Continued)

> **Can a quasi contract be imposed for the value of Freshwater's services?** Yes. A quasi contract can be imposed when a person knowingly receives a benefit from another party and it would be unjust for the person not to pay for its value. Here, the Greens enjoy the benefits of Freshwater's water services and would be unjustly enriched if they did not pay for those services.

There are situations in which the party obtaining the unjust enrichment is not liable. Basically, a quasi-contract cannot be invoked by a party who has conferred a benefit on someone else unnecessarily or as a result of misconduct or negligence. **EXAMPLE 9.5** Rhonda leaves her 2015 Camry at the Northgate Toyota dealership for its regular oil and lube service. When she returns to pick up the car, she learns that a Northgate employee mistakenly performed a coolant fluid exchange service in addition to the requested oil and lube service. Rhonda does not have to pay for the additional service that she did not request. ◄

9–2d Formal versus Informal Contracts

formal contract
A contract that by law requires a specific form for its validity.

Formal contracts require a special form or method of creation (formation) to be enforceable. They include negotiable instruments and letters of credit. *Negotiable instruments* include checks, notes, drafts, and certificates of deposits. *Letters of credit* are often used in international sales contracts.

informal contract
A contract that does not require a specific form for its validity.

Informal contracts include all contracts other than formal contracts. No special form is required (except for certain types of contracts that must be in writing), because the contracts are usually based on their substance rather than on their form. **EXAMPLE 9.6** Southwest Grocers Association signs an agreement to lease a warehouse from Commercial Properties for a certain term. In turn, United Trucking Company signs a contract to transport goods to and from the warehouse for Southwest for the same period of time. These are informal contracts. ◄

9–2e Executed versus Executory Contracts

executed contract
A contract that has been completely performed by both parties.

executory contract
A contract that has not yet been fully performed.

Contracts are also classified according to their state of performance. A contract that has been fully performed on both sides is called an **executed contract**. A contract that has not been fully performed on either side is called an **executory contract**. If one party has fully performed but the other has not, the contract is said to be executed on the one side and executory on the other, but the contract is still classified as executory.

EXAMPLE 9.7 MTM Incorporated agreed to buy ten tons of coal from Western Coal Company. Western has delivered the coal to MTM's steel mill, where it is now being burned. At this point, the contract is an executory contract—it is executed on the part of Western and executory on MTM's part. After MTM pays Western for the coal, the contract will be executed on both sides. ◄

LEARNING OUTCOME 4
Summarize the difference between executed and executory contracts.

9–2f Valid, Voidable, Unenforceable, and Void Contracts

valid contract
A properly constituted contract having legal strength or force.

A **valid contract** has the necessary elements to entitle at least one of the parties to enforce it in court. Those elements consist of an offer and an acceptance that are supported by legally sufficient consideration and are made for a legal purpose by parties who have the legal capacity to enter into the contract. As you can see in Exhibit 9.1, valid contracts may be enforceable, voidable, or unenforceable.

voidable contract
A contract that may be legally avoided at the option of one of the parties.

Voidable Contracts A **voidable contract** is a valid contract that can nevertheless be avoided by one or both of the parties. The party having the option can elect to avoid any duty to perform or can elect to *ratify* (make valid) the contract. If the contract is avoided, both parties are released from it. If it is ratified, both parties must fully perform their respective legal obligations.

As a general rule, but subject to exceptions, contracts made by minors are voidable at the option of the minor. Contracts entered into under fraudulent conditions are voidable at the option of the innocent party. In addition, contracts entered into because of mistakes and those entered into under legally defined duress or undue influence are voidable.

Unenforceable Contracts An **unenforceable contract** is one that cannot be enforced because of certain legal defenses against it. It is not unenforceable because a party failed to satisfy a legal requirement of the contract. Rather, it is a valid contract rendered unenforceable by law. For instance, certain contracts must be in writing. If they are not, they will not be enforceable except under certain exceptional circumstances.

Void Contracts In contrast to a valid contract, a **void contract** is no contract at all. The terms *void* and *contract* are contradictory. A void contract produces no legal obligations on the part of any of the parties. For example, a contract can be void because one of the parties was adjudged by a court to be legally insane or because the purpose of the contract was illegal.

9–2g E-Contracts

E-contracts are contracts entered into online. Most courts apply traditional common law principles to cases arising in cyberspace, including disputes involving e-contracts. New laws have been drafted, however, to apply in situations in which old laws have been thought inadequate. The Uniform Electronic Transactions Act, or UETA, for example, removes barriers to e-contracts by giving the same legal effect to electronic records and signatures as is given to paper documents and signatures. Throughout Unit 2, we consider some of the circumstances and laws that exist for contracts in the online environment.

9–3 INTERPRETATION OF CONTRACTS

When a contract dispute arises, a court is sometimes asked to interpret contract terms. Whether the court will do so depends on whether the terms are clear or ambiguous.

LEARNING OUTCOME 5
State the differences among valid, voidable, unenforceable, and void contracts.

unenforceable contract
A valid contract having no legal effect because of a statute or law.

void contract
A contract having no legal force or binding effect.

e-contract
A contract entered into online.

EXHIBIT 9.1 Enforceable, Voidable, Unenforceable, and Void Contracts

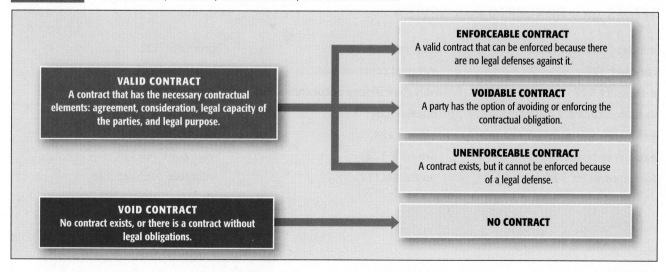

If what is written in a contract is clear, a court will enforce the contract according to its obvious terms. This is sometimes referred to as the *plain meaning rule*. Under this rule, if the words in a contract appear clear and unambiguous, a court cannot consider any evidence not contained in the document itself. The words—and their plain, ordinary meanings—determine the intent of the parties at the time that they entered into the contract. A court is bound to give effect to the contract according to this intent.

If a contract is ambiguous, however, the court may have to consider outside evidence to determine the parties' intent. A contract may be ambiguous under the following circumstances:

1. The intent of the parties cannot be determined from the contract's language.

2. The contract lacks a provision on a disputed issue.

3. A contract term can be interpreted in more than one way.

4. There is uncertainty about a particular provision.

Outside evidence may include oral testimony, additional agreements or communications between the parties, and other relevant information. If this evidence fails to make the ambiguous term or provision clear, the court may interpret the ambiguity against the party who was responsible for creating it.

ANSWERING THE LEGAL PROBLEM

In the legal problem set out at the beginning of this chapter, Jack offers to pay Simone $100 if she walks across the Golden Gate Bridge.

A **If, without saying a word, Simone walks across the bridge, do she and Jack have a contract?** Yes. They have a unilateral contract, which can be accepted only by performance. **If Simone tells Jack no and turns and walks away, are there any legal consequences?** No. A unilateral contract is a "promise for an act." Without the act, there is no contract and thus no consequences for not acting. **If no one says anything more, but Barry rather than Simone starts to walk across, do Jack and Barry have a contract?** No. Only the person to whom the offer is made can accept it.

TERMS AND CONCEPTS FOR REVIEW

bilateral contract 124	implied contract 125	promisor 122
contract 122	informal contract 126	quasi contract 125
e-contract 127	objective theory of contracts 122	unenforceable contract 127
executed contract 126	offeree 124	unilateral contract 124
executory contract 126	offeror 124	valid contract 126
express contract 125	promise 122	void contract 127
formal contract 126	promisee 122	voidable contract 126

CHAPTER SUMMARY—INTRODUCTION TO CONTRACTS

LEARNING OUTCOME	
1	**Define the objective theory of contracts.** The objective theory of contracts holds that a party's intent to enter into a contract is judged by outward, objective facts as interpreted by a reasonable person, rather than by the party's secret, subjective intent. Objective facts include what the party said when entering into the contract, how the party acted or appeared, and the circumstances surrounding the transaction.
2	**List the basic requirements of a contract.** The requirements of a contract are (1) *agreement,* which includes an offer and an acceptance; (2) *consideration,* which must be legally sufficient and bargained for—the promises made by the parties must be supported by something of value received or promised to convince a person to make a deal; (3) *capacity,* which means that the parties are competent to enter into the contract; and (4) *legality,* which means that the contract's purpose must be legal and not against public policy.
3	**Contrast express and implied contracts.** The terms of an *express contract* are fully and explicitly stated in words, oral or written. The terms of an *implied contract* are implied from the conduct of the parties. An implied contract differs from an express contract in that the conduct of the parties, rather than their words, creates and defines the terms.
4	**Summarize the difference between executed and executory contracts.** A contract that has been fully performed is an *executed contract.* A contract that has not been fully performed is an *executory contract.* If one party has fully performed but the other has not, the contract is executory.
5	**State the differences among valid, voidable, unenforceable, and void contracts.** A *valid contract* has the basic contractual requirements of offer and acceptance, consideration, the parties' capacity, and a legal purpose, which entitles at least one of the parties to enforce it in court. A *voidable contract* is a valid contract that can be avoided by one or both of the parties. An *unenforceable contract* is a valid contract rendered unenforceable by law because of certain legal defenses against it. A *void contract* is no contract, with no legal obligations on the part of any party.

ISSUE SPOTTERS

Check your answers to the *Issue Spotters* against the answers provided in Appendix C at the end of this text.

1. Molly tells Nick that she will pay him $10,000 to set fire to her store, so that she can collect the money from her fire insurance policy. Nick sets fire to the store, but Molly refuses to pay him. Can Nick recover the $10,000 from Molly? Why or why not? (See *Types of Contracts.*)

2. Alison receives a notice of property taxes due from the local tax collector. The notice is for tax on Jerry's property, but Alison believes that the tax is hers and pays it. Can Alison recover from Jerry the amount that she paid? Why or why not? (See *Types of Contracts.*)

USING BUSINESS LAW

9–1. Express versus Implied Contracts. Suppose that McDougal, a local businessperson, is a good friend of Krunch, the owner of a local candy store. Every day on his lunch hour, McDougal goes into Krunch's candy store and spends about five minutes looking at the candy. After examining Krunch's candy and talking with Krunch, McDougal usually buys one or two candy bars. One afternoon, McDougal goes into Krunch's candy shop, looks at the candy, and picks up a $1 candy bar. Seeing that Krunch is very busy, he waves the candy bar at Krunch without saying a word and walks out. Is there a contract? If so, classify it within the categories presented in this chapter. (See *Types of Contracts*.)

9–2. Contract Classification. High-Flying Advertising, Inc., contracted with Big Burger Restaurants to fly an advertisement above the Connecticut beaches. The advertisement offered $5,000 to any person who could swim from the Connecticut beaches to Long Island across the Long Island Sound in less than a day. McElfresh saw the streamer and accepted the challenge. He started his marathon swim that same day at 10 A.M. After he had been swimming for four hours and was about halfway across the sound, McElfresh saw another plane pulling a streamer that read, "Big Burger revokes." Is there a contract between McElfresh and Big Burger? If there is a contract, classify it by types. (See *Types of Contracts*.)

REAL-WORLD CASE PROBLEMS

9–3. Implied Contracts. Ralph Ramsey insured his car with Allstate Insurance Co. He also owned a house on which he maintained a homeowner's insurance policy with Allstate. Bank of America had a mortgage on the house and paid the insurance premiums on the homeowner's policy from Ralph's account. After Ralph died, Allstate cancelled the car insurance. Ralph's son, Douglas, inherited the house. The bank continued to pay the premiums on the homeowner's policy, but from Douglas's account, and Allstate continued to renew the insurance. When a fire destroyed the house, however, Allstate denied coverage, claiming that the policy was still in Ralph's name. Douglas filed a suit in a federal district court against the insurer. Was Allstate liable under the homeowner's policy? Explain. [*Ramsey v. Allstate Insurance Co.*, 2013 WL 467327 (6th Cir. 2013)] (See *Types of Contracts*.)

9–4. Quasi Contract. Kim Panenka asked to borrow $4,750 from her sister, Kris, to make a mortgage payment. Kris deposited a check for that amount into Kim's bank account. Hours later, Kim asked to borrow another $1,100. Kris took a cash advance on her credit card and deposited this amount into Kim's account. When Kim did not repay her, Kris filed a suit, arguing that she had loaned Kim the money. Can the court impose a contract between the sisters? Explain. [*Panenka v. Panenka*, 331 Wis.2d 731, 795 N.W.2d 493 (2011)] (See *Types of Contracts*.)

9–5. Interpretation of Contracts. Lisa and Darrell Miller had a son, Landon. When the Millers divorced, they entered into a "Joint Plan" (JP). Under the JP, Darrell agreed to "begin setting funds aside for Landon to attend college." After Landon's eighteenth birthday, Lisa asked a court to order Darrell to pay the boy's college expenses based on the JP. Darrell contended that the JP was not clear on this point. Do the rules of contract interpretation support Lisa's request or Darrell's contention? Explain. [*Miller v. Miller*, 1 So.3d 815 (La.App. 2009)] (See *Interpretation of Contracts*.)

ETHICAL QUESTIONS

9–6. Quasi Contract. Should any enrichment always be considered unjust? Discuss. (See *Types of Contracts*.)

9–7. Unilateral Contract. International Business Machines Corp. (IBM) hired Niels Jensen as a software sales representative. According to IBM's "Sales Incentive Plan" (SIP), "the more you sell, the more earnings for you." But "the SIP program does not constitute a promise by IBM. IBM reserves the right to modify the program at any time." Jensen closed a deal worth more than $24 million to IBM. When IBM paid him less than $500,000 as a commission, Jensen filed a suit. He argued that the SIP was a unilateral offer that became a binding contract when he closed the sale. Would it be fair to rule in Jensen's favor? Discuss. [*Jensen v. International Business Machines Corp.*, 454 F.3d 382 (4th Cir. 2006)] (See *Types of Contracts*.)

Chapter 9—Work Set

TRUE-FALSE QUESTIONS

_____ 1. All contracts involve promises, and every promise is a legal contract.

_____ 2. An agreement includes an offer and an acceptance.

_____ 3. Consideration, in contract terms, refers to a party's competency to enter into a contract.

_____ 4. A unilateral contract involves performance instead of promises.

_____ 5. Formal contracts are contracts between parties who are in formal relationships—employer-employee relationships, for example.

_____ 6. An unenforceable contract is a contract in which one or both of the parties have the option of avoiding their legal obligations.

_____ 7. A court imposes a quasi contract to avoid one party's unjust enrichment at another's expense.

_____ 8. An express contract is one in which the terms are fully stated in words.

_____ 9. An oral contract is an implied contract.

MULTIPLE-CHOICE QUESTIONS

_____ 1. Don contracts with Jan to paint Jan's townhouse while she's on vacation. By mistake, Don paints Mick's townhouse. Mick sees Don painting but says nothing. From whom can Don recover?

a. Jan, because she was the party with whom Don contracted.
b. Jan, under the theory of quasi contract.
c. Mick, because his house was painted.
d. Mick, under the theory of quasi contract.

_____ 2. Brian offers to sell Ashley his vintage vinyl records collection, forgetting that he does not want to sell some of the records. Unaware of Brian's forgetfulness, Ashley accepts. Is there a contract including all of Brian's records?

a. Yes, according to the objective theory of contracts.
b. Yes, according to the subjective theory of contracts.
c. No, because Brian did not intend to sell his favorite records.
d. No, because Ashley had no reason to know of Brian's forgetfulness.

_____ 3. Greg promises to imprint four thousand T-shirts with Rona's logo. Rona pays in advance. Before Greg delivers the shirts, the contract is classified as

a. executory, because it is executory on Greg's part.
b. executory, because it is executory on Rona's part.
c. executed, because it is executed on Greg's part.
d. none of the above.

_____ 4. Without mentioning payment, Mary accepts the services of Lee, a contractor, and is pleased with the work. Is there a contract between them?

a. Yes, there is an express contract.
b. Yes, there is an implied contract.
c. No, because they made no agreement concerning payment.
d. Yes, there is a quasi contract.

_____ 5. The requirements of a contract include

    a. agreement only.

    b. consideration only.

    c. agreement and consideration only.

    d. agreement, consideration, and other elements.

_____ 6. Sam contracts with Hugo's Sports Equipment to buy a jet ski and to pay for it in installments. Sam is a minor, and so he can choose to avoid his contractual obligations. The contract between Sam and Hugo is

    a. valid.

    b. void.

    c. voidable.

    d. both a and c.

_____ 7. A contract consists of promises between two or more parties to

    a. refrain from performing some act.

    b. perform some act in the future.

    c. perform some act now.

    d. any of the above.

_____ 8. Donny tells Elise that he will pay her $2,000 to hack into the database of Filipe, Donny's competitor, so that Donny can obtain the names and credit-card numbers of Filipe's customers, as well as other trade secrets. This deal is

    a. an enforceable contract.

    b. a voidable contract.

    c. a void contract.

    d. an executed contract.

_____ 9. Rita calls Rick on the phone and agrees to buy his antique rocking chair for $200. This is

    a. an express contract.

    b. an implied contract.

    c. a quasi contract.

    d. no contract.

 ANSWERING MORE LEGAL PROBLEMS

1. Rocky Mountain Races, Inc., sponsors the Pioneer Trail Ultramarathon, which has an advertised first prize of $10,000. The rules require the competitors to run one hundred miles from the floor of Blackwater Canyon to the top of Pinnacle Mountain. The rules also provide that Rocky reserves the right to change the terms of the race at any time. Monica enters the race and is declared the winner. Rocky offers her a prize of $1,000 instead of $10,000.

    Did Rocky and Monica have a contract? Yes. These parties had a contract. Contests, lotteries, and other competitions for prizes are offers for contracts. Here, the _____ is phrased so that each competitor can accept only by completing the run. At that point, a contract is formed—a _____ contract—binding its sponsor to perform as promised. **By changing the prize, did Rocky breach this contract?** No. Rocky did not breach the contract when the prize was changed. Under the rules, Rocky could _____ the terms at any time.

2. For employment with the Firestorm Smokejumpers— a crew of elite paratroopers who parachute into dangerous situations to fight fires—applicants must complete a series of tests. The crew chief sends the most qualified applicants a letter stating that they will be admitted to Firestorm's training sessions if they pass a medical exam. Scott receives one of the letters and passes the exam, but a new crew chief changes the selection process and rejects him.

    Did the letter from Firestorm to Scott constitute a contract? Yes. Firestorm and Scott had a contract. The letter was a unilateral offer phrased so that the offeree could accept only by completing the required performance. The contract was formed when the _____ was complete. This was a _____ contract. Scott accepted the offer by passing the medical exam. **Did Firestorm breach this contract?** Yes. Firestorm breached the contract when the new crew chief rejected Scott, who had already received the offer and _____ it. The appropriate remedy would be to allow Scott to attend Firestorm's training sessions.

OFFER AND ACCEPTANCE

10

FACING A LEGAL PROBLEM

Debbie and Julio ride to college each day in Julio's automobile, which has a market value of $12,000. One cold morning, they get into the car, but Julio cannot get it started. He yells in anger, "I'll sell this car to anyone for $500!" Debbie writes a check for $500 and drops it in his lap.

 Is the car Debbie's?

LEARNING OUTCOMES

The five Learning Outcomes below are designed to help improve your understanding of the chapter. After reading this chapter, you should be able to:

1 Identify the requirements of an offer.

2 Recognize a counteroffer.

3 Identify the requirements of a valid acceptance.

4 Describe how an offer can be accepted.

5 Compare shrink-wrap and click-on agreements.

Essential to any contract is that the parties agree on the terms of the contract. **Agreement** exists when an offer made by one party is accepted, or assented to, by the other. Ordinarily, agreement is evidenced by an *offer* and an *acceptance*. One party offers a certain bargain to another party, who then accepts that bargain.

Because words often fail to convey the precise meaning intended, the law of contracts generally adheres to the *objective theory of contracts* (see Chapter 9). Under this theory, a party's words and conduct are held to mean whatever a reasonable person in the offeree's position would think they mean.

10–1 REQUIREMENTS OF THE OFFER

An **offer** is a promise or commitment to perform or refrain from performing some specified act in the future. The party making an offer is called the *offeror*, and the party to whom the offer is made is called the *offeree*. Three elements are necessary for an offer to be effective:

1. The offeror must have a *serious intention* to become bound by the offer, and this intention must be *objectively* ascertainable—that is, readily recognizable by others.

2. The terms of the offer must be reasonably *certain* or *definite* so that the parties and the court can ascertain the terms of the contract.

3. The offer must be communicated to the offeree.

10–1a Intention

The first requirement for an effective offer is a serious intention on the part of the offeror. Furthermore, this intention must be objectively clear to others. Serious intent is not determined by the *subjective* (personal, unspoken) intentions, beliefs, or assumptions of the offeror. It is determined by what a reasonable person in the offeree's position would conclude that the offeror's words and actions meant. Offers made in obvious anger, jest, or undue excitement do not meet the serious-intent test. Because these offers are not effective, an offeree's acceptance does not create an agreement.

agreement
A meeting of two or more minds in regard to the terms of a contract.

offer
A promise or commitment to perform or refrain from performing some specified act in the future.

LEARNING OUTCOME 1
Identify the requirements of an offer.

133

Expressions of Opinion An expression of opinion is not an offer. An expressed opinion does not evidence an intention to enter into a binding agreement. **EXAMPLE 10.1** Henry takes his daughter, Miranda, to Dr. Ryan and asks him to operate on her hand, which has been scarred in an accident. Ryan says Miranda will be in the hospital three or four days and that the hand will *probably* heal within a few days. Miranda's hand becomes infected, and she is hospitalized for nearly two weeks. Normally, Henry could not sue Ryan for breach of contract because Ryan's words did not constitute an offer to heal Miranda's hand in three or four days. Rather, Ryan simply expressed an opinion as to when the hand would heal. ◄

Preliminary Negotiations A request or invitation to negotiate is not an offer. It is only an expression of a willingness to discuss the possibility of entering into a contract. For instance, statements such as "Will you sell your three-bedroom house?" and "I wouldn't sell my car for less than $8,000" are not offers. A reasonable person in the offeree's position would not conclude that these statements show an intention to enter into a binding obligation.

Similarly, when the government and private firms need to have construction work done, contractors are invited to submit bids. The *invitation* to submit bids is not an offer, and a contractor does not bind the government or private firm by submitting a bid. The bids that the contractors submit are offers, however, and the government or private firm can bind the contractor by accepting the bid.

Advertisements In general, advertisements, catalogues, price lists, and circular letters (meant for the general public) are considered invitations to negotiate. They are not considered evidence of an intention to enter into a contract.

HIGHLIGHTING THE POINT

An ad on *ScienceNOW's* Web site asks for "news tips." Erik submits a manuscript in which he claims to have solved a famous mathematical problem. *ScienceNOW* declines to publish the manuscript. Erik files a lawsuit, alleging breach of contract. He asserts that *ScienceNOW's* ad is an offer, which he has accepted.

Is the ad on *ScienceNOW's* Web site an offer? No. Most courts would dismiss this suit. Ads are not offers—they invite offers. Responses to ads are not acceptances—they are offers. Thus, Erik's submission of the manuscript for publication is the offer, which *ScienceNOW* did not accept.

Price lists are another form of invitation to negotiate or trade. A seller's price list is not an offer to sell at that price. It merely invites the buyer to offer to buy at that price. In fact, a seller usually puts "prices subject to change" on a price list. Only in rare circumstances will a price quotation be construed as an offer.

Auctions In a live auction, a seller "offers" goods for sale through an auctioneer, but this is not an offer to form a contract. Rather, it is an invitation, asking bidders to submit offers. In the context of an auction, a bidder is the offeror, and the auctioneer is the offeree.

Auctions with and without Reserve Auctions traditionally have been referred to as either "with reserve" or "without reserve." In an auction with reserve, for instance, the seller may withdraw the goods at any time before the auctioneer closes the sale by announcement or by the fall of the hammer. All auctions are assumed to be auctions with reserve unless the terms of the auction are explicitly stated to be *without reserve*. In an auction without reserve, the goods cannot be withdrawn by the seller and must be sold to the highest bidder.

Online Auctions Online auctions are the most familiar type of auction today. Sites, such as eBay, provide a forum for buyers and sellers to sell almost anything. Like an advertisement or an auction with reserve, an "offer" to sell an item on one of these sites is generally treated as an invitation to negotiate.

10–1b Definiteness of Terms

The second requirement for an effective offer concerns the definiteness of its terms. An offer must have reasonably definite (determined or fixed) terms— such as the names of the parties, quantity of items, how work will be performed, and payment details. In short, the terms should be specific and definite so that a court can determine if a breach has occurred and give an appropriate remedy.

An offer may invite an acceptance to be worded in such specific terms that the contract is made definite. **EXAMPLE 10.2** Soccer World, Inc., e-mails Gary's Athletic Store and offers to sell "from one to twenty-five Kwik Goal heavy-duty anchor bags for $200 each. State the number desired in acceptance." In his e-mail reply, Gary, the store's owner, agrees to buy one dozen of the bags. Because the quantity is specified in the acceptance, the terms are definite. The contract is enforceable. ◄

10–1c Communication

The third requirement for an effective offer is communication. The offer must be communicated to the offeree, thus resulting in his or her knowledge of the offer.

Real-World Case Example

Adwoa Gyabaah was hit by a bus owned by Rivlab Transportation Corp. Gyabaah filed a suit in a New York state court against the bus company. Rivlab's insurer offered to tender the company's policy limit of $1 million in full settlement of Gyabaah's claims. On the advice of her attorney, Jeffrey Aronsky, Gyabaah signed a release in order to obtain the settlement funds. The release, however, was not forwarded to Rivlab or its insurer, National Casualty. Two months later, Gyabaah changed lawyers, as well as her mind about the release. In reaction to this, Aronsky filed a motion to enforce the release so that he could obtain his fee from the settlement funds. The court denied the motion. Aronsky appealed.

Was the release that was signed by Gyabaah—but never communicated to Rivlab and National Casualty—binding? No. In a 2013 case, *Gyabaah v. Rivlab Transportation Corp.,* a state intermediate appellate court affirmed the lower court's order to deny Aronsky's motion. There was no binding settlement because the release was not delivered to Rivlab or its insurer, who were thus not informed that the offer had been accepted. In other words, the lack of communication was fatal to Aronsky's claim of a settlement.

10–2 TERMINATION OF THE OFFER

The communication of an effective offer to an offeree gives the offeree the power to transform the offer into a binding legal obligation (a contract). This power of acceptance, however, does not continue forever. It can be terminated by *action of the parties* or by *operation of law*.

10–2a Termination by Action of the Parties

An offer can be terminated by the action of the parties in any of the three ways discussed next.

revocation
In contract law, the withdrawal of an offer by an offeror. Unless the offer is irrevocable, it can be revoked at any time before acceptance without liability.

Revocation of the Offer The offeror's act of withdrawing an offer is called **revocation.** Unless an offer is irrevocable, the offeror usually can revoke the offer (even if he or she promises to keep the offer open), as long as the revocation is communicated to the offeree before she or he accepts. The offeror can revoke the offer by expressly repudiating it or by performing acts inconsistent with the existence of the offer, which are made known to the offeree. For example, a statement such as "I withdraw my previous offer of October 17" is an express repudiation.

The general rule followed by most states is that a revocation becomes effective when the offeree or offeree's agent actually receives it. Therefore, a revocation sent via FedEx on April 1 and delivered at the offeree's residence or place of business on April 3 becomes effective on April 3.

Similarly, an offer made to the public can be revoked in the same manner in which the offer was originally communicated. **EXAMPLE 10.3** Al's Cycle Shop offers a reward for information leading to the arrest and conviction of persons who burglarized it. Al's publicizes the offer by advertising it on its Facebook page and on two local radio stations for four days. To revoke the offer, Al's normally must publish the revocation in the same media for the same number of days.◄

Irrevocable Offers Although most offers are revocable, some can be made *irrevocable*—that is, they cannot be revoked. Increasingly, courts refuse to allow an offeror to revoke an offer when the offeree has changed position because of justifiable reliance on the offer.

option contract
A contract under which the offeror cannot revoke his or her offer for a stipulated time period and the offeree can accept or reject the offer during this period.

Another form of irrevocable offer is an **option contract.** An option contract is created when an offeror promises to hold an offer open for a specified period of time in return for a payment (consideration) given by the offeree. An option contract takes away the offeror's power to revoke the offer for the period of time specified in the option. If no time is specified, then a reasonable period of time is implied.

HIGHLIGHTING THE POINT

You are in the business of writing movie scripts. Your agent contacts the head of development at New Line Cinema and offers to sell New Line your latest script. New Line likes the script and agrees to pay you $5,000 for an option to buy it within the next six months. According to the terms, for the next six months you cannot sell the script to anyone without offering it to New Line first. In this situation, you (through your agent) are the offeror, and New Line is the offeree.

Can you revoke your offer to sell New Line your script within the next six months? No. The offer to sell the script has become a contract—an option contract. If after six months no contract to buy the script is formed, however, New Line loses the $5,000, and you are free to sell the script to another firm.

Rejection of the Offer The offer may be rejected by the offeree, in which case the offer is terminated. A rejection is ordinarily accomplished by words or by conduct showing an intent not to accept the offer. As with revocation, rejection of an offer is effective only when it is actually received by the offeror or the offeror's agent.

Simply inquiring about an offer does not constitute rejection. When the offeree merely inquires as to the firmness of the offer, there is no reason to presume that he or she intends to reject it. **EXAMPLE 10.4** Raymond offers to buy Jasmine's iPhone6 for $250, and Jasmine responds, "Is that your best offer?" or "Will you pay me $300 for it?" A reasonable person would conclude that Jasmine did not reject the offer but merely made an inquiry about it. She can still accept and bind Raymond to his offered $250 purchase price.◄

Counteroffer A **counteroffer** usually is a rejection of the original offer and the simultaneous making of a new offer, giving the original offeror (now the offeree) the power of acceptance. **EXAMPLE 10.5** Jessica offers to sell her home to Bradley for $225,000, and Bradley says, "The price is too high. I'll pay $200,000." Bradley's response is a counteroffer—it terminates the original offer and creates a new offer.◄

At common law, the **mirror image rule** requires that the offeree's acceptance match the offeror's offer exactly. In other words, the terms of acceptance must "mirror" those of the offer. If the acceptance materially changes or adds to the terms of the original offer, it will be considered not an acceptance but rather a counteroffer.

10–2b Termination by Operation of Law

The offeree's power to transform an offer into a binding obligation can be terminated by the operation of law in the following circumstances.

Lapse of Time An offer terminates automatically by law when the period of time specified in the offer has passed. The time period normally begins to run when the offer is actually received by the offeree, not when it is sent or drawn up. When receipt of the offer is delayed, the period begins to run from the date the offeree would have received the offer, but only if the offeree knows or should know that the offer is delayed. For instance, an offer specifying that it will be held open for twenty days will lapse at the end of twenty days. If the offeror mails the offer to the wrong address, and the offeree knows it, the offer will lapse twenty days after the day the offeree would have received the offer if the offeror had mailed it correctly.

If no time for acceptance is specified in the offer, the offer terminates at the end of a *reasonable* period of time. A reasonable period of time is determined by the subject matter of the contract, business and market conditions, and other relevant circumstances. For example, an offer to sell farm produce terminates sooner than an offer to sell farm equipment, because farm produce is perishable and subject to greater fluctuations in market value.

Destruction or Death An offer is automatically terminated if the specific subject matter of the offer (such as an iPad or a house) is destroyed before the offer is accepted. An offeree's power of acceptance is also terminated when the offeror or offeree dies or becomes legally incapacitated, *unless the offer is irrevocable.* (Legal capacity will be discussed in Chapter 12.)

Supervening Illegality A statute or court decision that makes an offer illegal automatically terminates the offer. **EXAMPLE 10.6** Lee offers to lend Kim $10,000 at an annual interest rate of 15 percent. Before Kim can accept Lee's offer, a state law is enacted that prohibits interest rates higher than 12 percent in personal loans. Lee's offer is automatically terminated.◄

LEARNING OUTCOME 2
Recognize a counteroffer.

counteroffer
An offeree's response to an offer in which the offeree rejects the original offer and at the same time makes a new offer.

mirror image rule
A common law rule that requires, for a valid contractual agreement, that the terms of the offeree's acceptance adhere exactly to the terms of the offeror's offer.

10–3 ACCEPTANCE

acceptance
A voluntary act by the offeree that shows assent, or agreement, to the terms of an offer.

Acceptance is a voluntary act (which may consist of words or conduct) by the offeree that shows assent, or agreement, to the offer. An acceptance has three requirements:

1. An offer must be accepted by the offeree, not by a third party.

2. The acceptance must be unequivocal.

3. In most situations, the acceptance must be communicated to the offeror.

LEARNING OUTCOME 3

Identify the requirements of a valid acceptance.

10–3a Offeree Acceptance Only

Generally, a third party cannot substitute for the offeree and effectively accept the offer. After all, the identity of the offeree is as much a condition of a bargaining offer as any other term. Thus, except in special circumstances, only the person to whom the offer is made (or that person's agent) can accept the offer and create a binding contract. **EXAMPLE 10.7** Lotte makes an offer to Paul. Paul is not interested, but Paul's friend José says, "I accept the offer." No contract is formed.◄

10–3b Unequivocal Acceptance

To exercise the power of acceptance effectively, the offeree must accept without adding or changing any terms. This is the mirror image rule previously discussed. If the acceptance is subject to new conditions, or if the terms of the acceptance materially change the original offer, the acceptance may be deemed a counteroffer that implicitly rejects the original offer.

Ordinarily, silence cannot constitute acceptance, even if the offeror states, "By your silence and inaction, you will be deemed to have accepted this offer." This general rule applies because an offeree should not be put under a burden of liability to act affirmatively in order to reject an offer. No consideration has passed to the offeree to impose such a liability.

10–3c Communication of Acceptance

LEARNING OUTCOME 4

Describe how an offer can be accepted.

Whether the offeror must be notified of the acceptance depends on the nature of the contract. In a unilateral contract, the full performance of some act is called for. Acceptance is usually evident, and notification is therefore unnecessary (unless the law requires it or the offeror asks for it).

In a bilateral contract, in contrast, communication of acceptance is necessary, because acceptance is in the form of a promise. The bilateral contract is formed when the promise is made rather than when the act is performed.

In addition, in a bilateral contract, acceptance must be timely. The general rule is that acceptance is timely if it is effective before the offer is terminated. Problems arise, however, when the parties involved are not dealing face to face. In such situations, the offeree may use an authorized mode of communication.

mailbox rule
A rule providing that an acceptance of an offer becomes effective on dispatch.

The Mailbox Rule Acceptance takes effect, thus completing formation of the contract, at the time the communication is sent via the mode expressly or impliedly authorized by the offeror. This is the **mailbox rule**, also called the "deposited acceptance rule," which the majority of courts uphold.

Under this rule, if the authorized mode of communication is via the U.S. mail, then an acceptance becomes valid when it is dispatched—not when it is received by the offeror. (This is an exception to the rule that acceptance requires a completed communication in bilateral contracts.)

The mailbox rule does not apply to instantaneous forms of communication, such as face-to-face, phone, and e-mail communication. E-mail is considered sent when it either leaves the control of the sender or is received by the recipient. Either circumstance allows an e-mail acceptance to become effective when sent.

Authorized Means of Acceptance When an offeror specifies how acceptance should be made, such as by overnight delivery, the contract is not formed unless the offeree uses that mode of acceptance. Both the offeror and the offeree are bound in contract the moment the specified means of acceptance is employed. **EXAMPLE 10.8** Motorola Mobility, Inc., offers to sell 144 Atrix 4G smartphones and 72 Lapdocks to Call Me Plus phone stores. The offer states that Call Me Plus must accept the offer via FedEx overnight delivery. The acceptance is effective (and a binding contract is formed) the moment that Call Me Plus gives the overnight envelope containing the acceptance to the FedEx driver. ◄

If the offeror does not expressly specify a certain mode of acceptance, then acceptance can be made by *any reasonable means*. The prevailing business usages and the surrounding circumstances determine whether a mode of acceptance is reasonable. Usually, the offeror's choice of a particular means in making the offer implies that the offeree can use the *same or a faster* means for acceptance. For instance, if the offer is made via Priority U.S. Mail, it would be reasonable to accept the offer via Priority Mail or a faster method, such as FedEx or an e-mail.

Substitute Method of Acceptance If the offeror authorizes a particular method of acceptance, but the offeree accepts by a different means, the acceptance may still be effective if the substituted method serves the same purpose as the authorized means. The use of a substitute method of acceptance is not effective on dispatch, though. No contract will be formed until the acceptance is received by the offeror.

Thus, if an offer specifies FedEx overnight delivery but the offeree accepts by overnight delivery from another carrier, such as UPS, the acceptance will still be effective, but not until the offeror receives it.

 ## 10–4 E-CONTRACTS—OFFER AND ACCEPTANCE

An e-contract—one entered into online—has the same basic requirements as a valid paper contract. Most often, e-contracts are formed for the sale of goods and services offered online. Disputes regarding e-contracts tend to center on the terms and whether the parties voluntarily consented to those terms.

10–4a Online Offers

To avoid legal disputes, offerors should make sure that online offers are conspicuous and easy to view and read. On a Web site, this requirement can be accomplished with a link to a separate page that contains the contract's full details. Usually, these details include specific provisions regarding the acceptance of the terms, payment, disclaimers, the seller's return policy, remedy limitations, and dispute resolution. **EXAMPLE 10.9** Iowa-based Baxter Wholesalers offers up-scale office equipment on its Web site. Susan, a Florida retailer, enters into an e-contract with Baxter to buy fifteen desks. The e-contract, among other terms, contains a *forum-selection clause*, which stipulates that any dispute resulting from the contract must be settled in Iowa. If a dispute arises, Susan will have to settle the dispute in Iowa and not in her home state of Florida. ◄

10–4b Online Acceptances

As with traditional paper contracts, acceptance of e-contracts must show that the offeree voluntarily assented to the offer's terms. Such an action can be indicated by accepting the terms inside a product's packaging (a *shrink-wrap agreement*) or by clicking on an "I agree" box while ordering online (a *click-on agreement*).

Shrink-Wrap Agreement Consumers today are buying more products online and thus are often receiving shrink-wrap agreements with their purchases. A **shrink-wrap agreement** is an agreement whose terms are expressed on the inside or outside of a box in which goods are packaged. In most situations, the agreement is between the product's manufacturer and its user. The terms generally concern warranties, remedies, and other issues associated with the product's use of the product.

Generally, the terms of a shrink-wrap agreement are enforceable if they are conspicuous and accessible, and the buyer had an opportunity to read them before using the product. Once the offeree uses the product, the agreement is binding.

Click-on Agreement The online equivalent of a shrink-wrap agreement is called a **click-on agreement**. This may consist of a box that includes the words "I agree." If the offeree can click on the box to indicate acceptance, a binding contract can be created.

Courts normally have enforced the terms of these agreements in the same way as terms of other contracts. Under the common law of contracts, a binding contract can be created by conduct—including conduct such as using a product or clicking on an online box—that indicates consent to the terms in a shrink-wrap or a click-on agreement.

shrink-wrap agreement
An agreement expressed on the inside or the outside of a box in which goods are packaged.

LEARNING OUTCOME 5
Compare shrink-wrap and click-on agreements.

click-on agreement
An agreement entered into online when a buyer indicates his or her acceptance of an offer by clicking on a button that reads "I agree."

HIGHLIGHTING THE POINT

Facebook, Inc., is headquartered in Santa Clara County, California. The "Terms of Use" that govern Facebook users' accounts include a forum-selection clause stating that all disputes will be resolved in a court in Santa Clara County. Potential Facebook users cannot become actual users unless they click on an acknowledgment that they have agreed to this term.

Is the forum-selection clause in Facebook's user click-on agreement binding? Yes. A binding contract can be created online by clicking on a button that indicates agreement to the contract's terms. Here, a user is informed of the result of his or her click to agree. In short, by clicking on the acknowledgment button and then using Facebook, the user agrees to resolve all disputes according to this term.

10–4c The Uniform Electronic Transactions Act

The Uniform Electronic Transactions Act (UETA), which has been enacted in most states, applies to some e-contracts. The UETA does not create new rules for e-contracts but does support their enforcement.

Before the UETA applies, each party to a transaction must agree to conduct it by electronic means. The agreement may be implied by the conduct of the parties and the circumstances. **EXAMPLE 10.10** Jonas gives out his business card with an e-mail address on it. Jonas has consented to do business electronically.◄

ANSWERING THE LEGAL PROBLEM

In the legal problem set out at the beginning of this chapter, Julio angrily yelled that he would sell his $12,000 car to anyone for $500.

A Would a reasonable person conclude that Julio's statement was a serious offer? No. A reasonable person, taking into consideration Julio's frustration and the obvious difference between the car's market price and the purchase price, would conclude that his offer was not made with serious intent. Thus, even if Debbie dropped $500 in Julio's lap at the moment of his angry "offer," she and Julio would not have had an agreement.

TERMS AND CONCEPTS FOR REVIEW

acceptance 138	mailbox rule 138	revocation 136
agreement 133	mirror image rule 137	shrink-wrap agreement 140
click-on agreement 140	offer 133	
counteroffer 137	option contract 136	

CHAPTER SUMMARY—OFFER AND ACCEPTANCE

LEARNING OUTCOME	
1	**Identify the requirements of an offer.** The elements of an effective offer are (1) the offeror's serious, objectively ascertainable *intent* to be bound by the offer; (2) terms that are reasonably *definite* so that a court can determine if a breach has occurred; and (3) *communication* of the offer to the offeree.
2	**Recognize a counteroffer.** A counteroffer is a response to an offer in which an offeree rejects the original offer and at the same time makes a new offer. The mirror image rule requires that an offeree's acceptance match an offer exactly. Therefore, a response that materially changes or adds to the terms of the original offer is not an acceptance but a counteroffer.
3	**Identify the requirements of a valid acceptance.** The requirements of a valid acceptance are (1) acceptance *by the offeree*, not a third party; (2) no new material terms, conditions, or changes—the acceptance must be *unequivocal*, or it will be deemed a counteroffer; and (3) *communication* of the acceptance to the offeror.
4	**Describe how an offer can be accepted.** Acceptance of a unilateral offer is effective on performance of the contract, with no communication necessary. Acceptance of a bilateral offer can be communicated by any authorized mode of communication and is effective on dispatch. If the offeror does not specify a mode of communication, acceptance can be made by any reasonable means. Usually, the same means used by the offeror or a faster means can be used. If an unauthorized substitute means of acceptance is used, it is effective if it serves the same purpose as the authorized method. It is effective on the offeror's receipt of the acceptance, however, not the offeree's dispatch.
5	**Compare shrink-wrap and click-on agreements.** In a shrink-wrap agreement, the terms are expressed on the inside or the outside of a box in which goods are packaged. By using the goods, the user accepts the terms. A click-on agreement arises when a buyer, completing a transaction online, is required to indicate his or her consent to the terms by clicking on a button or a box that says, for example, "I agree."

ISSUE SPOTTERS

Check your answers to the *Issue Spotters* against the answers provided in Appendix C at the end of this text.

1. Fidelity Corporation offers to hire Ron to replace Monica, who has given Fidelity a month's notice of intent to quit. Fidelity gives Ron a week to decide whether to accept. Two days later, Monica signs an employment contract with Fidelity for another year. The next day, Monica tells Ron of the new contract. Ron immediately sends a formal letter of acceptance to Fidelity. Do Fidelity and Ron have a contract? Why or why not? (See *Termination of the Offer*.)

2. While visiting the Web site of Cyber Investments, Dani encounters a pop-up box that reads, "Our e-mail daily newsletter *E-Profit* is available by subscription at the rate of one dollar per issue. To subscribe, enter your e-mail address below and click on 'SUBSCRIBE.'" Dani enters her e-mail address and clicks on "SUBSCRIBE." Has Dani entered into an enforceable contract? Explain. (See *E-Contracts—Offer and Acceptance*.)

USING BUSINESS LAW

10–1. Offer. Chernek, operating a sole proprietorship, has a large piece of used farm equipment for sale. He offers to sell the equipment to Bollow for $10,000. Discuss the legal effects of the following events on the offer. (See *Termination of the Offer*.)

1. Chernek dies prior to Bollow's acceptance. At the time she accepts, Bollow is unaware of Chernek's death.

2. Bollow pays $100 for a thirty-day option to purchase the farm equipment. During this period, Chernek dies. Later, Bollow accepts the offer, knowing of Chernek's death.

3. Bollow pays $100 for a thirty-day option to purchase the equipment. During this period, Bollow dies.

Bollow's estate accepts Chernek's offer within the stipulated time period.

10–2. Revocation and Acceptance. On Thursday, Dennis mailed a letter to Tanya's office offering to sell his car to her for $3,000. On Saturday, having changed his mind, Dennis sent a fax to Tanya's office revoking his offer. Tanya did not go to her office over the weekend and thus did not learn about the revocation until Monday morning, just a few minutes after she had mailed a letter of acceptance to Dennis. When Tanya demanded that Dennis sell his car to her as promised, Dennis claimed that no contract existed because he had revoked his offer prior to Tanya's acceptance. Is Dennis correct? Explain. (See *Termination of the Offer*.)

REAL-WORLD CASE PROBLEMS

10–3. Offer. While riding her motorcycle, Amy Kemper was seriously injured when Christopher Brown hit her with his vehicle. Kemper wrote to Statewide Claims Services, the administrator for Brown's insurer, asking for "all the insurance money that Mr. Brown had under his insurance policy." In exchange, Kemper agreed to sign a limited release that could not contain "any language saying that [she would] have to pay Mr. Brown or his insurance company any of their incurred costs." Statewide sent a check and a demand that Kemper "place money in an escrow account in regards to any and all liens pending." Kemper refused the demand. Did Statewide and Kemper have an enforceable agreement? Discuss. [*Kemper v. Brown*, 325 Ga.App. 806, 754 S.E.2d 141 (2014)] (See *Termination of the Offer*.)

10–4. Acceptance. Kathy Wright and real estate agent Jennifer Crilow orally agreed to a contract with a

"protection period." Under this provision, if Wright's property sold after the contract expired to a party who had been shown the property during the term of the contract, Crilow would still receive a commission. Crilow sent Wright a written copy of the agreement. Wright crossed out the protection-period provision and then signed and returned the copy. Before the contract expired, Crilow showed Wright's property to Michael Ballway. After the contract expired, Ballway bought the property. Does Wright owe Crilow a commission? Why or why not? [*Crilow v. Wright*, __ Ohio App.3d __ (2011)] (See *Acceptance*.)

10–5. Acceptance. Troy Blackford smashed a slot machine while he was gambling at Prairie Meadows Casino. He was banned from the premises. Despite the ban, he later gambled at the casino and won $9,387. When he tried to collect his winnings, the casino refused to pay. He filed a suit for breach of contract, arguing that he and the casino had a contract because he had accepted its offer to gamble. Is there a contract between the casino and Blackford? Discuss. [*Blackford v. Prairie Meadows Racetrack and Casino*, 778 N.W.2d 184 (Iowa 2010)] (See *Acceptance*.)

10–6. Communication of Acceptance. The Baton Rouge Crime Stoppers (BCS) offered a reward for information about the "South Louisiana Serial Killer." The

information was to be provided via a hotline. Dianne Alexander had survived an attack by a person suspected of being the killer. She identified a suspect in a police photo line-up and later sought to collect the reward. BCS refused to pay because she did not provide information to them via the hotline. Did Alexander comply with the terms of the offer? Explain. *Alexander v. Lafayette Crime Stoppers, Inc.*, 28 So.3d 1252 (La.App. 3 Dist. 2010) (See *Acceptance*.)

 ## ETHICAL QUESTIONS

10–7. Intent. Should promises of prizes in ads and circulars always be enforced? Discuss. (See *Requirements of the Offer*.)

10–8. Definiteness. Kenneth McMillan obtained a judgment against Laurence Hibbard for $52,972.74. When Hibbard did not pay, McMillan offered him an option. He could pay the judgment outright, or he could maintain an insurance policy on McMillan's life and the policy's proceeds would

pay the debt. Hibbard agreed. More than a year later, however, Hibbard had not paid the debt or maintained the policy. McMillan filed another lawsuit against him. Hibbard argued that the terms of the option agreement were not sufficiently definite or fair. Is he correct? Discuss. [*Hibbard v. McMillan*, 284 Ga.App. 753, 645 S.E.2d 356 (2007)] (See *Requirements of the Offer*.)

Chapter 10—Work Set

TRUE-FALSE QUESTIONS

_____ 1. The seriousness of an offeror's intent is determined by what a reasonable offeree would conclude was meant by the offeror's words and actions.

_____ 2. A contract providing that Joe is to pay Bill "a fair share of the profits" will be enforced.

_____ 3. A simple rejection of an offer will terminate it.

_____ 4. Offers that must be kept open for a period of time include advertisements.

_____ 5. The mirror image rule is an old rule that no longer applies.

_____ 6. If an offeree is silent, he or she can never be considered to have accepted an offer.

_____ 7. An offer terminates when the time specified in the offer has passed and the offeror has given one last chance to the offeree to accept.

_____ 8. Anyone who is aware of an offer can accept it and create a binding contract.

_____ 9. Acceptance is timely if it is made before an offer terminates.

_____ 10. There is no such thing as an irrevocable offer.

MULTIPLE-CHOICE QUESTIONS

_____ 1. Julio offers to sell Christine a used iPad for $400. Which of the following replies would constitute an acceptance?

  a. "I accept. Please send a written contract."
  b. "I accept, if you send a written contract."
  c. "I accept, if I can pay in monthly installments."
  d. None of the above.

_____ 2. Vern offers to sell his car to Lee, stating that the offer will stay open for thirty days. Vern

  a. cannot revoke the offer for thirty days.
  b. can revoke the offer after any reasonable period of time.
  c. can revoke the offer any time before Lee accepts.
  d. can revoke the offer any time within thirty days, even after Lee accepts.

_____ 3. Digit Electronics places an ad announcing a sale of its inventory at public auction. At the auction, Digit's auctioneer points to an eighty-inch 3D HDTV and asks, "What am I bid for this item?" Which of the following is true?

  a. The first bid is an acceptance if no other bid is received.
  b. Each bid is an acceptance if no higher bid is received.
  c. Each bid is an offer that may be accepted or rejected.
  d. Each bid is an offer that must be accepted if no higher bid is received.

_____ 4. Ed sends to Sax, Inc., a written order for software to be specially designed, offering a certain amount of money. If Sax does not respond, it can be considered to have accepted the offer

  a. after a reasonable time has passed.
  b. if Ed knows that Sax accepts all offers unless it sends notice to the contrary.
  c. only when Sax begins the work.
  d. in none of the above situations.

5. Paul makes an offer to Lynn in a written purchase order, saying nothing about how her acceptance should be sent. Lynn indicates her acceptance by signing and returning the purchase order. Lynn's acceptance is effective

   a. when Lynn decides to accept.
   b. when Lynn sends the signed purchase order.
   c. when Paul receives the signed purchase order.
   d. in none of the above situations.

6. Strike Force Games includes a shrink-wrap agreement with its products. Tom buys a Strike Force game. The agreement is likely enforceable if Tom plays the game

   a. *after* having had an opportunity to read the agreement.
   b. *before* having had an opportunity to read the agreement.
   c. only after having actually read the agreement.
   d. under any circumstances.

7. Garfield Company agrees to sell software to Holly from its Web site. To complete the deal, Holly clicks on a button that, with reference to certain terms, reads, "I agree." The parties have

   a. a binding contract that does not include the terms.
   b. a binding contract that includes only the terms to which Holly later agrees.
   c. a binding contract that includes the terms.
   d. no contract.

8. Icon Properties, Inc., makes an offer to Bob to sell a certain lot for $30,000, with the offer to stay open for thirty days. Bob would prefer to pay $25,000 if Icon would sell at that price. What should Bob reply to Icon to leave room for negotiation without rejecting the offer?

   a. "I will not pay $30,000."
   b. "Will you take $25,000?"
   c. "I will pay $25,000."
   d. "I will pay $27,500."

ANSWERING MORE LEGAL PROBLEMS

1. Nils bargains with the city of Fargo, North Dakota, concerning a contract to design a waste-to-energy incinerator that is to double as a tourist attraction. Integrated into the structure will be a ski slope with areas for skiers of all skill levels. On January 12, the city sends a written offer that states, "Acceptance of this offer must be made by registered or certified mail and received no later than January 22." Nils responds with a note accepting the offer via an overnight delivery service. The city receives the note January 23.

   Do Nils and Fargo have a contract? No. Fargo received Nils's note one day after its deadline had expired. For this reason, his response to the city's offer is a counteroffer—a new _____. When an offeror specifies a date for acceptance, an offer automatically _____ on that specified date. This _____ the offeree's power to accept the offer. An attempted acceptance after the expiration constitutes a new offer.

2. The University of Connecticut offers Jordana an assistant coaching position on its women's basketball team. The offer states that it will expire thirty days from May 1. Jordana rejects the offer on May 12.

   Can Jordana change her mind and accept the offer within what remains of the thirty days? Jordana can change her mind, but she _____ accept the school's offer. An offer is terminated when, within its terms, the _____ rejects it. An attempt to accept an offer after its termination is not an acceptance, but a new _____ to enter into a contract.

   (Exceptions to this rule are explained in Chapters 11 and 18. For example, if an offeree gives consideration to have an offer held open for a stated period, the offeree can change a rejection into an acceptance within that period. Also, a "firm offer" to a merchant may remain open. But those exceptions do not apply here.)

CONSIDERATION

11

FACING A LEGAL PROBLEM

Antonio says to his son, "When you finish painting the garage, I will pay you $100." Antonio's son paints the garage. The act of painting the garage is the consideration that creates the contractual obligation of Antonio to pay his son $100.

Q If, instead, Antonio had said to his son, "In consideration of the fact that you are not as wealthy as your brothers, I will pay you $500," would this promise have been enforceable?

Just because a party has made a promise does not mean the promise is enforceable. In every legal system, there are promises that will be enforced and promises that will not be enforced. Under the common law, a primary basis for the enforcement of promises is **consideration,** which is usually defined as the value (such as money) given in return for a promise (in a bilateral contract) or in return for a performance (in a unilateral contract).

consideration
The value given in return for a promise or performance in a contractual agreement.

 ## 11–1 ELEMENTS OF CONSIDERATION

Often, consideration is broken down into two parts:

1. Something of *legally sufficient value* must be given in exchange for the promise.

2. There must be a *bargained-for exchange*.

11–1a Legally Sufficient Value

To be legally sufficient, consideration must be something of value in the eyes of the law. The "something of legally sufficient value" may consist of any of the following:

1. A promise to do something that one has no prior legal duty to do (to pay on receipt of certain goods, for example).

2. The performance of an action that one is otherwise not obligated to undertake (such as providing accounting services).

3. The refraining from an action that one has a legal right to undertake (called a **forbearance**).

forbearance
The act of refraining from an action that one has a legal right to undertake.

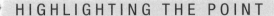

HIGHLIGHTING THE POINT

James Garvin promises his fifteen-year-old nephew, William, that if he refrains from drinking alcohol, using tobacco, and gambling until he reaches the age of twenty-one, James will pay him $5,000. William agrees. Following his twenty-first birthday, William writes to his uncle that he has performed his part of the bargain and is thus entitled to the $5,000. They agree that James will invest the funds for William.

Four years later, when James dies, the executor of his estate refuses to pay William, contending that the contract is invalid. The executor argues that there is no consideration, and therefore no contract, because James received nothing of value and William actually benefited by fulfilling James's wishes.

Did James and William have an enforceable contract? Yes. The funds belong to William. Before James's intervention, William had used tobacco and drunk liquor. On the strength of his uncle's promise, William dropped his bad habits. This performance was the consideration that made the contract—on the faith of the agreement, William refrained from doing something that he was otherwise entitled to do (a forbearance).

11–1b Bargained-for Exchange

The second element of consideration is that it must provide the basis for the bargain struck between the contracting parties. The item of value must be given or promised by the promisor (offeror) in return for the promisee's promise, performance, or promise of performance.

This element of bargained-for exchange distinguishes contracts from gifts. **EXAMPLE 11.1** Peggy says to Mariah, "Since you have been my friend for most of my life, I will pay you $5,000 when you turn seventy years old." Peggy's promise is not enforceable because Mariah need not do anything to receive the promised $5,000. Because Mariah does not need to give Peggy something of legal value in return for her promise, there is no bargained-for exchange. Peggy has simply stated her motive for giving her longtime friend a gift.◄

 ## 11–2 ADEQUACY OF CONSIDERATION

Legal sufficiency is distinct from *adequacy* of consideration, which refers to "how much" consideration is given. Essentially, adequacy of consideration concerns the fairness of the bargain.

On the surface, fairness would appear to be an issue when the values of items exchanged are unequal. In general, however, courts do not question the adequacy of consideration if the consideration is legally sufficient. Under the doctrine of freedom of contract, parties are usually free to bargain as they wish. If people could sue merely because they entered into an unwise contract, the courts would be overloaded with frivolous suits.

Sometimes, one of the parties (or both parties) to an agreement may think that consideration has been exchanged when, in fact, it has not. Preexisting duty and past consideration are two situations in which agreements lack consideration.

 ## 11–3 PREEXISTING DUTY

LEARNING OUTCOME 2

State the preexisting duty rule.

Under most circumstances, a promise to do what one already has a legal duty to do is not legally sufficient consideration, because no legal detriment or benefit has been incurred. This is the *preexisting duty rule*. The preexisting legal duty may be imposed by law or may arise out of a previous contract. For instance, a sheriff cannot collect a reward for information leading to the capture of a criminal if the sheriff already has a legal duty to capture the criminal. Thus, if a party is already bound by contract to perform a certain duty, that duty cannot serve as consideration for a second contract.

HIGHLIGHTING THE POINT

Bauman-Bache, Inc., begins construction on a seven-story office building. After three months, the company demands an extra $75,000 payment on its contract. If the extra $75,000 is not paid, it will stop working. The owner of the land, finding no one else to complete construction, agrees to the extra $75,000.

If the owner later refuses to pay the extra amount, could Bauman-Bache successfully sue to enforce the agreement? No. The agreement is not enforceable, because it is not supported by legally sufficient consideration. Bauman-Bache had a preexisting duty to complete the building under the original contract.

In the interests of fairness, the courts sometimes allow exceptions to the preexisting duty rule. These exceptions include *unforeseen difficulties* and *rescission*.

11–3a Unforeseen Difficulties

A court may decide not to apply the preexisting duty rule when a party to a contract confronts extraordinary difficulties that were totally unforeseen at the time the contract was formed. **EXAMPLE 11.2** Batzer Construction contracts with Jacob Kant to build a house. Batzer runs into extraordinary difficulties—it finds an underground tank full of hazardous materials. Kant then agrees to pay extra compensation to cover the cost of the clean-up. A court may enforce the agreement to pay more under these circumstances.◄ If the difficulties are the types of risks ordinarily assumed in business, however, the court will likely assert the preexisting duty rule (and not enforce the agreement to pay more).

LEARNING OUTCOME 3
Identify the exceptions to the preexisting duty rule.

11–3b Rescission and New Contract

The law recognizes that two parties can mutually agree to rescind their contract, at least to the extent that it is *executory*—that is, still to be carried out. **Rescission** is defined as the unmaking of a contract so as to return the parties to the positions they occupied before the contract was made.

Sometimes, parties rescind a contract and make a new contract at the same time. When this occurs, it is often difficult to determine whether there was consideration for the new contract, or whether the parties had a preexisting duty under the previous contract. If a court finds there was a preexisting duty, then the new contract will be invalid because there was no consideration. When rescission is ordered by a court, it is intended to bring about substantial justice by adjusting the equities between the parties.

rescission
A remedy whereby a contract is terminated and the parties are returned to the positions they occupied before the contract was made.

11–4 PAST CONSIDERATION

Promises made in return for actions or events that have already taken place are unenforceable. These promises lack consideration because the element of

past consideration
An act completed in the past, which ordinarily, by itself, cannot be consideration for a later promise to pay for the act.

bargained-for exchange is missing. In short, you can bargain for something to take place now or in the future, but not for something that has already taken place. Therefore, **past consideration** is no consideration.

EXAMPLE 11.3 Elsie, a real estate agent, does her friend Judy a favor by selling Judy's house and not charging a sales commission. Later, Judy says to Elsie, "In return for your generous favor, I will pay you $1,000." Judy's promise is made in return for past consideration and is thus unenforceable. In reality, Judy is stating her intention to give Elsie a gift. ◄

Additionally, in a variety of situations, an employer will often ask an employee to sign a noncompete agreement. Under such an agreement, the employee agrees not to compete with the employer for a certain period of time after the employment relationship ends. When a current employee is required to sign a noncompete agreement, his or her employment is not sufficient consideration for the agreement because the individual is already employed. To be valid, the agreement requires new consideration.

11–5 PROBLEMS WITH CONSIDERATION

Problems concerning consideration usually fall into one of the following categories:

1. Promises exchanged when total performance by the parties is uncertain (illusory).
2. Settlement of claims.
3. Promises enforceable without consideration (under the doctrine of *promissory estoppel*).

The courts' solutions to these types of problems can give you insight into how the law views the complex concept of consideration.

11–5a Illusory Promises

If the terms of the contract express such uncertainty of performance that the promisor has not definitely promised to do anything, the promise is said to be *illusory*. Such a promise is without consideration and unenforceable.

EXAMPLE 11.4 Liam Dodson, president of Tuscan Corporation, says to his employees, "All of you have worked hard, and if profits remain high, a 10 percent bonus at the end of the year will be given—if management thinks it is warranted." Dodson's words constitute an illusory promise, or no promise at all, because performance depends solely on the discretion of Dodson and the management. There is no bargained-for consideration. Dodson's statement declares merely that management may or may not do something in the future. ◄

Option-to-cancel clauses in contracts for specified time periods sometimes present problems in regard to consideration. **EXAMPLE 11.5** Abe contracts to hire Chris for one year at $5,000 per month, reserving the right to cancel the contract at any time. Abe has not actually agreed to hire Chris, however, because Abe can cancel Chris's employment without liability at any time and has not given up the possibility of hiring someone else. This contract is therefore illusory. ◄

11–5b Settlement of Claims

There are several ways in which businesspersons or others can settle legal claims, and it is important to understand the nature of consideration given in these kinds of settlement agreements, or contracts. A common means of settling a claim is through an *accord and satisfaction*, in which one who owes a debt offers to pay a lesser amount than the amount owed. Two other methods are also commonly used to settle claims: a *release* and a *covenant not to sue*.

Release A **release** is an agreement in which one party gives up the right to pursue a legal claim against another party. The release bars any recovery other than that specified in its own terms. Releases are generally binding if they are (1) given in good faith, (2) stated in a signed writing (required by many states), and (3) accompanied by consideration.

release
An agreement in which one party gives up the right to pursue a legal claim against another party.

HIGHLIGHTING THE POINT

Suppose that you are involved in an automobile accident caused by Raoul's negligence. Raoul offers to give you $4,000 if you will release him from further liability resulting from the accident. You believe that this amount will cover your damages, so you agree to the release. Later, you discover that it will cost $5,000 to repair your car.

Can you collect the balance from Raoul? The answer is normally no. You are limited to the $4,000 specified in the release. **Why not?** Because the release is a valid contract. You and Raoul both agreed to the bargain, and sufficient consideration was present. The consideration was the legal detriment you suffered—by releasing Raoul from liability, you forfeited your right to sue to recover damages, should they be more than $4,000.

Covenant Not to Sue A **covenant not to sue,** unlike a release, does not always bar further recovery. The parties simply substitute a contractual obligation for some other type of action.

covenant not to sue
An agreement to substitute a contractual obligation for some other type of action.

Real-World Case Example

Nike, Inc., sells a line of athletic shoes known as Air Force 1. Already, LLC, markets athletic shoe lines known as Sugar and Soulja Boy. Nike filed a suit in a federal district court against Already, alleging that Soulja Boy and Sugar infringed the Air Force 1 trademark. Already filed a counterclaim, contending that the Air Force 1 trademark was invalid. While the suit was pending, Nike issued a covenant not to sue, promising not to raise any trademark claims against Already based on Already's footwear designs. Nike then filed a motion to dismiss its claims and Already's counterclaim. The court granted the motion. The U.S. Court of Appeals for the Second Circuit affirmed this decision. Already appealed.

Did Nike's covenant not to sue prevent Already from suing Nike to establish that Nike's trademark was invalid? Yes. In a 2014 case, *Already, LLC v. Nike, Inc.,* the United States Supreme Court affirmed the lower court's judgment. The Court held that "this case is moot." Under the covenant not to sue, Nike could not file a claim for trademark infringement against Already, and Already could not assert that Nike's trademark was invalid.

11–5c Promissory Estoppel

Sometimes, individuals rely on promises, and such reliance may form a basis for contract rights and duties. Under the doctrine of **promissory estoppel** (also called

promissory estoppel
A doctrine that can be used to enforce a promise when the promisee has justifiably relied on it, and justice will be better served by enforcing it.

detrimental reliance), a person who has reasonably relied on the promise of another can often obtain some measure of recovery. When this doctrine is applied, the promisor is *estopped*, or barred, from revoking the promise. For the doctrine of promissory estoppel to be applied, a number of elements are required:

1. There must be a clear and definite promise.
2. The promisee must justifiably rely on the promise.
3. The reliance normally must be of a substantial and definite character.
4. Justice will be better served by the enforcement of the promise.

EXAMPLE 11.6 Jay Bailey, the owner of a local machine shop, employs six employees. As part of their employment, Bailey orally promises to pay each of them $2,000 per month for the remainder of their lives after they retire. Sal Hernandez, one of Bailey's employees, retires. Hernandez receives the $2,000 monthly amount for two years, but after that, Bailey stops paying Hernandez. Under the doctrine of promissory estoppel, Hernandez can sue Bailey in an attempt to enforce Bailey's promise. ◄

ANSWERING THE LEGAL PROBLEM

In the legal problem set out at the beginning of this chapter, Antonio said to his son, "When you finish painting the garage, I will pay you $100." Antonio's son painted the garage. This act is the consideration that creates Antonio's obligation to pay the $100.

A If Antonio had instead said to his son, "In consideration of the fact that you are not as wealthy as your brothers, I will pay you $500," would this promise have been enforceable? No. Antonio's son would not have given any consideration for it. Antonio would simply have stated his motive for giving his son $500. Using the word *consideration* in an agreement does not, alone, create consideration.

TERMS AND CONCEPTS FOR REVIEW

consideration 147

covenant not to sue 151

forbearance 147

past consideration 150

promissory estoppel 151

release 151

rescission 149

CHAPTER SUMMARY—CONSIDERATION

LEARNING OUTCOME	
1	**List the elements of consideration.** The elements of consideration are (1) something of legally sufficient value given in exchange for a promise and (2) a bargained-for exchange. The something of legally sufficient value may consist of (1) a promise to do something that one has no prior legal duty to do, (2) the performance of an action that one is otherwise not obligated to undertake, or (3) the refraining from an action that one has a legal right to undertake (a forbearance). The second element of bargained-for exchange distinguishes contracts from gifts.
2	**State the preexisting duty rule.** A promise to do what one has a preexisting legal duty to do is not legally sufficient consideration. This is because no new legal detriment or benefit has been incurred.
3	**Identify the exceptions to the preexisting duty rule.** The preexisting duty rule may not apply when (1) a party to a contract confronts extraordinary difficulties that were totally unforeseen at the time the contract was formed and are not ordinary business risks, or (2) the parties to a contract mutually agree to rescind it and, possibly, make a new contract at the same time.
4	**Understand the concept of promissory estoppel.** Promissory estoppel is a doctrine that applies when (1) there is a clear and definite promise, (2) the promisee justifiably relies on the promise, (3) the reliance is of a substantial and definite character, and (4) justice is better served by enforcing the promise.

ISSUE SPOTTERS

Check your answers to the *Issue Spotters* against the answers provided in Appendix C at the end of this text.

1. In September, Sharon agrees to work for Cole Productions, Inc., at $500 a week for a year beginning January 1. In October, Sharon is offered the same work at $600 a week by Quintero Shows, Ltd. When Sharon tells Cole about the other offer, they tear up their contract and agree that Sharon will be paid $575. Is the new contract binding? Why or why not? (See *Preexisting Duty.*)

2. Before Maria starts her first year of college, Fred promises to give her $5,000 when she graduates. She goes to college, borrowing and spending far more than $5,000. At the beginning of the spring semester of her senior year, she reminds Fred of the promise. Fred sends her a note that says, "I revoke the promise." Is Fred's promise binding? Explain. (See *Problems with Consideration.*)

USING BUSINESS LAW

11–1. Preexisting Duty. Ben hired Lewis to drive his racing car in a race. Tuan, a friend of Lewis, promised to pay Lewis $3,000 if he won the race. Lewis won the race, but Tuan refused to pay the $3,000. Tuan contended that no legally binding contract had been formed because he had received no consideration from Lewis for his promise to pay the $3,000. Lewis sued Tuan for breach of contract, arguing that winning the race was the consideration given in exchange for Tuan's promise to pay the $3,000. What rule of law discussed in this chapter supports Tuan's claim? Explain. (See *Preexisting Duty.*)

11–2. Consideration. Healthy Heart Clinic is a medical practice that provides comprehensive cardiology services. Its physician-owners, including Kevin, are all cardiologists. Several years after joining the practice, Kevin signed an agreement that provided Healthy Heart would pay him $5,000 per month for twelve months following his separation from employment with the clinic as long as he did not compete with its cardiology practice. Is this agreement unenforceable for lack of consideration? Discuss. (See *Past Consideration.*)

REAL-WORLD CASE PROBLEMS

11–3. Bargained-for Exchange. On Brenda Sniezek's first day of work for the Kansas City Chiefs Football Club, she signed a document that compelled arbitration of any disputes that she might have with the Chiefs. In the document, Sniezek promised that on the arbitrator's decision, she would release the Chiefs from any related claims. Nowhere in the document did the Chiefs agree to do anything in return for Sniezek's promise. Was there consideration for the arbitration provision? Explain. [*Sniezek v. Kansas City Chiefs Football Club*, 402 S.W.3d 580 (Mo.App. W.D. 2013)] (See *Elements of Consideration*.)

11–4. Rescission. Farrokh and Scheherezade Sharabianlou agreed to buy a building owned by Berenstein Associates for $2 million. They deposited $115,000 toward the purchase. Before the deal closed, an environmental assessment of the property indicated the presence of chemicals used in dry cleaning. This substantially reduced the property's value. Do the Sharabianlous have a good argument for the return of their deposit and rescission of the contract? Explain. [*Sharabianlou v. Karp*, 181 Cal.App.4th 1133, 105 Cal.Rptr.3d 300 (1 Dist. 2010)] (See *Preexisting Duty*.)

ETHICAL QUESTIONS

11–5. Legally Sufficient Value. Can a moral obligation satisfy the requirements of consideration? Why or why not? (See *Elements of Consideration*.)

11–6. Promissory Estoppel. Claudia Aceves borrowed from U.S. Bank to buy a home. Two years later, she could no longer afford the monthly payments. The bank notified her that it planned to foreclose on her home. Aceves filed for bankruptcy. The bank offered to modify Aceves's mortgage if she would forgo bankruptcy. She agreed. Once she withdrew the filing, however, the bank foreclosed. Could Aceves succeed on a claim of promissory estoppel? Why or why not? Did Aceves or U.S. Bank behave unethically? Discuss. [*Aceves v. U.S. Bank, N.A.*, 129 Cal.App.4th 218, 120 Cal. Rptr.3d 507 (2 Dist. 2011)] (See *Problem with Consideration*.)

Chapter 11—Work Set

TRUE-FALSE QUESTIONS

_____ 1. Ordinarily, courts evaluate the adequacy or fairness of consideration even if the consideration is legally sufficient.

_____ 2. A promise to do what one already has a legal duty to do is not legally sufficient consideration under most circumstances.

_____ 3. Promises made with consideration based on events that have already taken place are fully enforceable.

_____ 4. Rescission is the unmaking of a contract so as to return the parties to the positions they occupied before the contract was made.

_____ 5. A promise has no legal value as consideration.

_____ 6. A covenant not to sue is an agreement to substitute a contractual obligation for some other type of action.

_____ 7. Consideration is the value given in return for a promise.

_____ 8. Promissory estoppel may prevent a party from using lack of consideration as a defense.

_____ 9. The doctrine of promissory estoppel requires a clear and definite promise.

MULTIPLE-CHOICE QUESTIONS

_____ 1. Dwight offers to buy a book owned by Lee for $40. Lee accepts and hands the book to Dwight. The transfer and delivery of the book constitute performance. Is this performance consideration for Dwight's promise?

a. Yes, because performance always constitutes consideration.
b. Yes, because Dwight sought it in exchange for his promise, and Lee gave it in exchange for that promise.
c. No, because performance never constitutes consideration.
d. No, because Lee already had a duty to hand the book to Dwight.

_____ 2. Max agrees to supervise a construction project for Al for a certain fee. In midproject, without an excuse, Max removes the plans from the site and refuses to continue. Al promises to increase Max's fee. Max returns to work. Is going back to work consideration for the promise to increase the fee?

a. Yes, because performance always constitutes consideration.
b. Yes, because Al sought it in exchange for his promise.
c. No, because performance never constitutes consideration.
d. No, because Max already had a duty to supervise the project.

_____ 3. Shannon contracts with Dan to build two houses on two lots. After the first house is finished, they decide to build a garage instead of a house on the second lot. Under these circumstances,

a. they must build the second house—a contract must be fully executed.
b. they can rescind their contract and make a new contract to build a garage.
c. the contract to build two houses is illusory.
d. none of the above is true.

_____ 4. Ed has a cause to sue Mary in a tort action but agrees not to sue her if she will pay for the damage. If she fails to pay, Ed can bring an action against her for breach of contract. This is an example of

a. promissory estoppel.
b. a release.
c. a covenant not to sue.
d. an unenforceable contract.

5. John's car is hit by Ben's truck. A doctor tells John that he will be disabled only temporarily. Ben's insurance company offers John $5,000 to settle his claim. John accepts and signs a release. Later, John learns that he is permanently disabled. John sues Ben and the insurance company. John will

   a. win, because John did not know when he signed the release that the disability was permanent.
   b. win, because Ben caused the accident.
   c. lose, because John signed a written release—no fraud was involved, and consideration was given.
   d. do none of the above.

6. Mike promises that next year he will sell Kim a certain house. Meanwhile, he allows her to live in the house. Kim completely renovates the house, repairs the heating system, and entirely landscapes the property. The next year, Mike tells Kim he's decided to keep the house. Who is entitled to the house?

   a. Kim, under the doctrine of promissory estoppel.
   b. Kim, because Mike's decision to keep the house is an unforeseen difficulty.
   c. Mike, because his promise to sell Kim the house was illusory.
   d. Mike, because he initially stated only his intention to sell.

7. Deb has a cause to sue Jim in a tort action. Jim offers Deb $5,000 not to sue, and she agrees. This an example of

   a. promissory estoppel.
   b. a release.
   c. a covenant not to sue.
   d. an unenforceable contract.

8. Green Energy Company files a suit against First Bank, claiming that the consideration for a contract between them was inadequate. The court likely will not evaluate the adequacy of consideration unless it is

   a. somewhat unbalanced.
   b. grossly inadequate.
   c. legally sufficient.
   d. willfully unfair.

 ANSWERING MORE LEGAL PROBLEMS

1. RiotGear contracts with Standard Transit, Inc., to distribute RiotGear's "Occupy Earth/Global Movement" line of apparel to retail outlets for a certain price. With the goods in transit, RiotGear receives this tweet from Standard: "Price increase of 99 percent or no delivery." RiotGear agrees and pays, but later sues Standard for the increase over the original price.

   Is RiotGear entitled to the difference in price? Yes. Under the _____ _____ rule, if a party is already bound by contract to perform a certain duty, that duty cannot serve as _____ for a second contract. A party to a contract is not bound to a modification of the contract unless there is additional consideration for the change. In this set of facts, there is no new consideration, so RiotGear's agreement to the change is _____ _____.

2. RiotGear promises to donate a share of the proceeds from the sale of the "Occupy Earth/Global Movement"

line to The Cause, a charitable organization dedicated to supporting those who seek social and economic change through protest. In reliance on the expected donation, The Cause contracts for medical and other supplies. When Standard increases the distribution cost, RiotGear tells The Cause that there will be no donation.

   Can The Cause enforce RiotGear's original promise despite the lack of consideration? Yes. Under the doctrine of _____ _____, a party who makes a promise can be estopped from revoking it. For the doctrine to be applied, (1) there must be a _____, (2) the promisee must reasonably rely on it, (3) the reliance must be substantial and definite, and (4) justice must be better served by the enforcement of the _____. It is reasonable to expect that a charitable organization will incur obligations in reliance on a _____ of a donation. Failing to enforce it would be unjust.

CAPACITY

FACING A LEGAL PROBLEM

Josh, a minor, is shot in the head at point-blank range by another boy. Josh receives life-saving medical services from Yale Diagnostic Radiology (and others). Yale bills Josh's mother for its services, but she declares bankruptcy, and the debt is discharged. When Josh receives money for medical care from the shooter's family, Yale files a suit to recover from him.

 Can Yale collect for its services from Josh?

The first two requirements for a valid contract are agreement and consideration. The third requirement is **contractual capacity**—the legal ability to enter into a contractual relationship. Although the parties to a contract must assume certain risks, the law indicates that neither party should be allowed to benefit from the other party's lack of contractual capacity. For this reason, contracts entered into by persons lacking the contractual capacity to do so may be unenforceable.

Courts generally presume the existence of contractual capacity. In some situations, however, capacity is lacking or questionable. For instance, a person *adjudged by a court* to be mentally incompetent cannot form a legally binding contract with another party. In other situations, a party may have the capacity to enter into a valid contract but also have the right to avoid liability under it. In this chapter, we look at the effects of youth, intoxication, and mental incompetence on contractual capacity.

contractual capacity
The legal ability to enter into a contractual relationship.

12–1 MINORS

Minors—or *infants,* as they are commonly referred to in the law—usually are not legally bound by contracts. Under the common law, a *minor* was defined as a male who had not attained the age of twenty-one or a female who was not yet eighteen years old. Today, in most states the *age of majority* (when a person is no longer a minor) for contractual purposes is eighteen years for both genders. In addition, some states provide for the termination of minority on marriage.

The general rule is that a minor can enter into any contract an adult can, provided that the contract is not one prohibited by law for minors (for example, the sale of alcoholic beverages). Subject to certain exceptions, however, the contracts entered into by a minor are voidable at the option of that minor. The minor has the choice of *ratifying* (accepting and validating) the contract, thus making it enforceable, or *disaffirming* (avoiding) the contract and setting aside all legal obligations arising from it. An adult who enters into a contract with a minor, however, cannot avoid his or her contractual duties on the ground that the minor can do so. Unless the minor exercises the option to disaffirm the contract, the adult party is bound by it.

disaffirmance
The repudiation (avoidance) of an obligation.

Understand the right of minors to disaffirm their contracts.

12–1a Disaffirmance

The technical definition of **disaffirmance** is the legal avoidance, or setting aside, of a contractual obligation. For a minor to exercise the option to disaffirm a contract, he or she need only show an intention not to be bound by it. Words or conduct may serve to show this intent.

Real-World Case Example

S.L., a sixteen-year-old minor, worked at a KFC Restaurant operated by PAK Foods Houston, LLC. PAK Foods' policy was to resolve any dispute with an employee through arbitration. At the employer's request, S.L. signed an acknowledgment of this policy. S.L. was injured on the job, and subsequently terminated her employment. Marissa Garcia, S.L.'s mother, filed a suit on her daughter's behalf in a Texas state court against PAK Foods to recover for the injury. PAK Foods filed a motion to compel arbitration. The court denied the motion. PAK Foods appealed.

Did S.L. disaffirm the agreement to arbitrate? Yes. In a 2014 case, *PAK Foods Houston, LLC. v. Garcia,* a state intermediate appellate court affirmed the decision of the lower court. A minor may disaffirm a contract at his or her option. S.L. opted to disaffirm the agreement to arbitrate by terminating her employment and filing the lawsuit.

The contract can ordinarily be disaffirmed at any time during minority or for a reasonable time after the minor comes of age. It is important that disaffirmance be timely. Suppose an individual wishes to disaffirm a contract made as a minor but fails to do so until two years after he or she has reached the age of majority. A court will likely hold that the contract has been *ratified* (discussed shortly).

HIGHLIGHTING THE POINT

Darlo's great-grandmother dies and leaves him a small rented house. As a minor, Darlo is not prepared to manage the property, so he agrees to let his grandmother do so on his behalf. Five years after reaching his majority, Darlo sells the house. His grandmother asks to be reimbursed for funds she has spent to maintain the property. Darlo refuses.

Can Darlo disaffirm the management agreement with his grandmother? No. A minor is bound by his or her contracts unless they are disaffirmed within a reasonable time after the minor reaches majority. What is a reasonable time depends on the circumstances. Here, Darlo's disaffirmance takes place five years after he reaches majority. It has not occurred within a reasonable time.

Duty of Restitution When a contract has been executed, minors cannot disaffirm it without returning whatever goods they received or paying for their reasonable use. The majority of courts hold that the minor need only return the goods (or other consideration), provided the goods are in the minor's possession or control.

A few states, however, either by statute or by court decision, place an additional duty on the minor—the duty of **restitution.** This rule recognizes the legitimate interests of those who deal with minors. The theory is that the adult should be returned to the position he or she held before the contract was made.

If a minor disaffirms a contract, he or she must disaffirm the *entire* contract. The minor cannot decide to keep part of the goods contracted for and return the remainder. When a minor disaffirms, all property that he or she has transferred to the adult as consideration (or its equivalent in money) can be recovered.

restitution
A remedy under which a person is restored to his or her original position prior to the formation of a contract.

Exceptions to a Minor's Right to Disaffirm State courts and legislatures have carved out a few exceptions to a minor's right to disaffirm contracts. Two notable exceptions include age misrepresentation and necessaries.

Misrepresentation of Age Suppose that a minor tells a seller she is twenty-one years old when she is really only seventeen. Ordinarily, the minor can disaffirm the contract even though she has misrepresented her age.

Many jurisdictions, however, do find circumstances under which a minor can be bound by a contract when he or she has misrepresented his or her age. Several states have enacted statutes for precisely this purpose. In these states, misrepresentation of age is enough to prohibit disaffirmance.

Additionally, some courts refuse to allow minors to disaffirm executed (fully performed) contracts unless they can return the consideration received. The combination of the minors' misrepresentations and their unjust enrichment has persuaded several courts to *estop* (prevent) minors from asserting contractual incapacity. Some courts allow a misrepresenting minor to disaffirm the contract, but they hold the minor liable for damages.

Basically, a minor's ability to avoid a contractual obligation is allowed by the law as a shield for the minor's defense, not as a sword for his or her unjust enrichment.

HIGHLIGHTING THE POINT

Jennifer Lee, a minor, contracts to purchase an automobile from Haydocy Pontiac, Inc., but she tells the salesperson that she is twenty-one. Lee finances most of the purchase price. Immediately following delivery of the automobile, she turns the car over to a third person and thereafter never has possession. She makes no further payments on the contract and attempts to rescind (cancel) it. She makes no offer to return the car. Haydocy sues Lee for the balance owed.

Can Haydocy recover the balance, given the fact that Lee is a minor who misrepresented her age? Haydocy should be allowed to recover the fair market value of the automobile from Lee—although the fair market value could not exceed the original purchase price of the automobile. Lee is barred from rescinding the contract on the ground that she is a minor. She made the sale possible by misrepresenting her age.

Liability for Necessaries A minor who enters into a contract for **necessaries** (such items as food, clothing, and shelter) may disaffirm the contract but remains liable for the reasonable value of the goods. The legal duty to pay a reasonable value does not arise from the contract itself but is imposed by law under a theory of quasi contract. Under this theory, a minor should not be unjustly enriched and should therefore be liable for purchases that fulfill basic needs. Also, a minor's right to disaffirm a contract might cause a seller to refuse to deal with minors. If minors can at least be held liable for the reasonable value of the goods, the seller

necessaries
Necessities required for life, such as food, shelter, clothing, and medical attention.

LEARNING OUTCOME 2
Identify obligations that minors cannot avoid.

might be less reluctant to enter into contracts with them. This theory explains why the courts narrow the subject matter to necessaries—without such a rule, minors might not be able to purchase necessary goods.

12–1b Ratification

ratification
The act of accepting and giving legal force to an obligation that previously was not enforceable.

In contract law, **ratification** is the act of accepting and giving legal force to an obligation that previously was not enforceable. A minor who has reached the age of majority can ratify a contract expressly or impliedly. *Express* ratification occurs when the individual, on reaching the age of majority, states orally or in writing that she or he intends to be bound by the contract. *Implied* ratification takes place when the minor, on reaching the age of majority, indicates an intent to abide by the contract.

EXAMPLE 12.1 Lin enters into a contract to sell her electronic piano to Andrew, a minor. Andrew does not disaffirm the contract. If, on reaching the age of majority, he writes an e-mail to Lin stating that he still agrees to buy the piano, he has expressly ratified the contract. If, instead, Andrew takes possession of the piano as a minor and continues to use it well after reaching the age of majority, he has impliedly ratified the contract. ◄

If a minor fails to disaffirm a contract within a reasonable time after reaching the age of majority, then a court must determine whether the conduct constitutes implied ratification or disaffirmance. Generally, courts presume that a contract that is *executed* (fully performed by both sides) was ratified. A contract that is still *executory* (not yet performed by both parties) is normally considered to be disaffirmed.

12–1c Parents' Liability

As a general rule, parents are not liable for the contracts made by their minor children acting on their own. This is why businesses ordinarily require parents to sign any contract made with a minor. The parents then become personally obligated under the contract to perform the conditions of the contract, even if their child avoids liability.

Generally, a minor is held personally liable for the torts he or she commits. Therefore, minors cannot disaffirm their liability for their tortious conduct. The parents of the minor can *also* be held liable under certain circumstances. **EXAMPLE 12.2** Jessie works for her father, Karl, in the family restaurant. She is working under Karl's supervision when she negligently drops a hot bowl of soup on Lorena, a customer, causing an injury. Lorena can hold Karl liable for Jessie's negligence. ◄ In addition, parents are liable in many states up to a statutory amount for malicious acts committed by a minor living in the parents' home.

12–1d Emancipation

emancipation
In regard to minors, the act of being freed from parental control.

The release of a minor by his or her parents is known as **emancipation.** Emancipation involves completely relinquishing the right to the minor's control, care, custody, and earnings. It is a repudiation of parental obligations. Emancipation may be express or implied, absolute or conditional, total or partial. A number of jurisdictions permit minors to petition for emancipation themselves. In addition, a minor may petition a court to be treated as an adult for business purposes. If the court grants the minor's request, it removes the lack of contractual capacity, and the minor no longer has the right to disaffirm business contracts.

12–2 Intoxicated Persons

A contract entered into by an intoxicated person can be either voidable or valid. If the person was sufficiently intoxicated to lack mental capacity, the transaction is voidable at the option of the intoxicated person, even if the intoxication was purely voluntary. For the contract to be voidable, it must be proved that the intoxicated person's reason and judgment were impaired to the extent that he or she did not comprehend the legal consequences of entering into the contract. If the person was intoxicated but understood these legal consequences, the contract is enforceable. Under any circumstances, an intoxicated person is liable for the reasonable value of any necessaries he or she receives.

Problems often arise in determining whether a party was sufficiently intoxicated to avoid legal duties. Many courts prefer looking at factors other than the intoxicated party's mental state (for example, whether the other party fraudulently induced the person to become intoxicated). **EXAMPLE 12.3** Bill offers to buy Serengeti, a prime commercial property, from Nick. Nick refuses to sell. Bill encourages Nick to quickly down a couple of strong alcoholic drinks "to celebrate your resolve." Bill then persuades Nick to sell Serengeti. If a court finds that Bill fraudulently induced Nick to become intoxicated, and that Nick was sufficiently intoxicated to lack mental capacity, Nick can avoid the sale.◄

12–3 MENTALLY INCOMPETENT PERSONS

Contracts made by mentally incompetent persons can be void, voidable, or valid. Specific circumstances determine when these classifications apply.

LEARNING OUTCOME 4

Discuss the effects of mental incompetence on contractual liability.

12–3a When a Contract Is Void

If a person has been adjudged mentally incompetent by a court of law and a guardian has been appointed, any contract made by the mentally incompetent person is void—no contract exists. Only the guardian can enter into a binding legal duty on the person's behalf.

12–3b When a Contract Is Voidable

The situation is somewhat different when mentally incompetent persons who have not been adjudged incompetent by a court enter into contracts. Such contracts are voidable if the incompetent persons did not know they were entering into a contract or if they lacked the mental capacity to comprehend its subject matter, nature, and consequences. In such situations, the contracts are voidable at the option of the mentally incompetent person but not the other party. The key issue is whether the party was able to understand the nature, purpose, and consequences of his or her act at the time of the transaction.

EXAMPLE 12.4 Larry agrees to sell his stock in Google, Inc., to Sergey for substantially less than its market value. At the time of the deal, Larry is confused about the purpose and details of the transaction, but he has not been declared incompetent. If a court finds that Larry did not understand the nature and consequences of the contract due to a lack of mental capacity, he can avoid the sale.◄

As with minors, voidable contracts made by mentally incompetent persons may be disaffirmed or ratified. Ratification must occur after the person is mentally competent or after a guardian is appointed and ratifies the contract. Like intoxicated persons, mentally incompetent persons are liable for the reasonable value of any necessaries they receive.

12–3c When a Contract Is Valid

A contract entered into by a mentally incompetent person may also be valid. A person can understand the nature and effect of entering into a certain contract yet simultaneously lack capacity to engage in other activities. In such situations, the contract is valid because the person is not legally mentally incompetent for contractual purposes.

HIGHLIGHTING THE POINT

Rhonda is diagnosed with manic depression, but a court has not declared her mentally incompetent. One afternoon, wearing shabby clothes and with her hair uncombed, she arrives at Classic Automotive. After two hours of negotiations, she trades in her Honda Civic and signs a lease for a BMW. She does not test-drive the new car, she has difficulty removing the Civic's keys from her key ring, and the payments on the BMW are more than she can afford.

Can Rhonda disaffirm the lease agreement because of mental incompetence?
No. A party cannot avoid a contract on the ground of mental incompetence unless at the time of the contract's execution, the person did not reasonably understand the nature and terms of the contract. In this situation, nothing—including Rhonda's disheveled appearance, her difficulty with the keys, her failure to test-drive the car, or its price—indicates that she did not understand she was executing an auto lease. After all, she negotiated more than two hours with Classic Automotive.

ANSWERING THE LEGAL PROBLEM

In the legal problem set out at the beginning of this chapter, Josh, a minor, is shot. He receives life-saving medical services from Yale Diagnostic Radiology. Yale bills his mother for its services, but she does not pay because she has declared bankruptcy.

A **Can Yale collect the unpaid amount from Josh?** Yes. A minor who receives life-saving medical services is liable for their reasonable value on a theory of *quasi contract*, as well as for necessaries. When necessary medical services are provided to a minor whose parents do not pay for the services, a contract is imposed by law between the provider and the minor so that the minor is not unjustly enriched.

LINKING BUSINESS LAW to Your Career

CONTRACTS WITH MINORS OR INTOXICATED PERSONS

Some of you have been or will be involved in retail careers at the managerial level. Sometimes, sales personnel must deal with minors or intoxicated persons, both of whom have limited contractual capacity. As a sales manager, you should introduce your employees to the law governing contracts with minors and intoxicated persons.

Contracts with Minors

If your business involves selling consumer durables, such as large-screen televisions, entertainment centers, appliances, furniture, or automobiles, your employees must be careful in forming contracts with minors and should heed the adage "When in doubt, check." Remember that a contract signed by a minor (unless it is for

necessaries) normally is voidable, and the minor may exercise the option to disaffirm the contract. Employees should demand proof of legal age when they have any doubt about whether a customer is a minor. If the customer is a minor, employees should insist that an adult (such as a parent) be the purchaser or at least the co-signer on any sales contract.

Because the law governing minors' rights varies from state to state, you should check with an attorney concerning the laws governing disaffirmance in your state. You and those who sell your products should know, for example, what the consequences are if a minor disaffirms a sale or misrepresents his or her age in forming a sales contract. Similarly, you need to find out whether and in what circumstances a minor, on disaffirming a contract, can be required to pay for damage to goods sold under the contract.

Contracts with Intoxicated Persons

Little need be said about a salesperson's dealings with obviously intoxicated persons. If the customer, despite intoxication, understands the legal consequences of the contract being signed, the contract is enforceable.

Nonetheless, it may be extremely difficult to establish that the intoxicated customer understood the consequences of entering into the contract if the customer claims that she or he did not understand it. Therefore, the best advice is "When in doubt, don't do it." In other words, if you suspect that a customer may be intoxicated, do not sign a contract with him or her.

TERMS AND CONCEPTS FOR REVIEW

contractual capacity 157

disaffirmance 158

emancipation 160

necessaries 159

ratification 160

restitution 159

CHAPTER SUMMARY—CAPACITY

LEARNING OUTCOME

1 **Understand the right of minors to disaffirm their contracts.** Contracts with minors are voidable at the option of the minor. Disaffirmance can take place (in most states) at any time during minority and within a reasonable time after the minor has reached the age of majority. If a minor disaffirms a contract, the entire contract must be disaffirmed. When disaffirming an executed contract, the minor has a duty of restitution to return the received goods if they are still in the minor's control and (in some states) to pay for any damage to the goods.

2 **Identify obligations that minors cannot avoid.** A minor who has committed an act of fraud (such as misrepresentation of age) will be denied the right to disaffirm by some courts. A minor may disaffirm a contract for necessaries but remains liable for the reasonable value of the goods.

3 **Explain how intoxication affects the liability on a contract.** A contract entered into by an intoxicated person is voidable at the option of the intoxicated person if the person was sufficiently intoxicated to lack mental capacity, even if the intoxication was voluntary. A contract with an intoxicated person is enforceable if, despite being intoxicated, the person understood the legal consequences of entering into the contract.

4 **Discuss the effects of mental incompetence on contractual liability.** A contract made by a person adjudged by a court to be mentally incompetent is void. A contract made by a mentally incompetent person not adjudged by a court to be mentally incompetent is voidable at the option of the mentally incompetent person. A contract made by a mentally incompetent person who nevertheless understands the nature and effect of entering into the contract is valid.

ISSUE SPOTTERS

Check your answers to the *Issue Spotters* against the answers provided in Appendix C at the end of this text.

1. Joan, who is sixteen years old, moves out of her parents' home and signs a one-year lease for an apartment at Kenwood Apartments. Joan's parents tell her that she can return to live with them at any time. Unable to pay the rent, Joan moves to her parents' home two months later. Can Kenwood enforce the lease against Joan? Why or why not? (See *Minors.*)

2. Cedric, a minor, enters into a contract with Diane. How might Cedric effectively ratify this contract? (See *Minors.*)

USING BUSINESS LAW

12–1. Intoxication. After Kira had had several drinks one night, she sold Charlotte a diamond necklace worth thousands of dollars for one hundred dollars. The next day, Kira offered the one hundred dollars to Charlotte and requested the return of her necklace. Charlotte refused to accept the money or return the necklace, claiming that she and Kira had a valid contract of sale. Kira explained that she had been intoxicated at the time the bargain was made and thus the contract was voidable at her option. Was Kira correct? Explain. (See *Intoxicated Persons.*)

12–2. Mental Incompetence. Two physicians, Devito and Burke, leased an office suite for five years and agreed to share the rent payments equally—even if one of them moved out or was unable to occupy his part of the premises as a result of disability or for any other reason. Two weeks later, Devito consulted a neurologist about his increasing absentmindedness and forgetfulness and discussed the possibility of giving up his practice. A few months later, Devito was diagnosed as suffering from presenile dementia (premature deterioration of the brain). The condition had been developing slowly for a matter of years, resulting in the progressive loss of memory and other mental abilities. The following year, Devito was so impaired mentally that he had to close his practice and retire. Burke later sued Devito for his share of the remaining rent under the lease. Devito claimed that he had been mentally incompetent at the time he signed the agreement to share the rent and hence the agreement was voidable at his option. Will Devito prevail in court? Discuss. (See *Mentally Incompetent Persons.*)

REAL-WORLD CASE PROBLEMS

12–3. Minors. D.V.G. (a minor) was injured in a one-car auto accident in Hoover, Alabama. The vehicle was covered by an insurance policy issued by Nationwide Mutual Insurance Company. Stan Brobston, D.V.G.'s attorney, accepted Nationwide's offer of $50,000 on D.V.G.'s behalf. Before the settlement could be submitted to an Alabama state court for approval, D.V.G. died from injuries received in a second, unrelated auto accident. Was Nationwide bound to the settlement or, as the insurance company argued, does a minor lack the capacity to contract and so cannot enter into a binding settlement without court approval? Explain. [*Nationwide Mutual Insurance Co. v. Wood*, 121 So.3d 982 (Ala. 2013)] (See *Minors.*)

12–4. Mental Incompetence. William Zurenda was disabled by post-traumatic stress disorder (PTSD), but had not been adjudged mentally incompetent. During divorce proceedings, he agreed to pay his spouse $5,000 within six months. The settlement was read aloud in court, and the judge asked William if he understood that the settlement was binding. He answered that he did. Later, he argued that he should not have to pay the $5,000, because the stress of the divorce had made his PTSD worse. Is the settlement void on the basis of mental incompetence? Explain. [*Zurenda v. Zurenda*, 85 A.D.3d 1283, 925 N.Y.S.2d 221 (3 Dept. 2011)] (See *Mentally Incompetent Persons.*)

12–5. Mental Incompetence. Dorothy Drury suffered from dementia and chronic confusion. When she became unable to manage her own affairs, including decisions about medical and financial matters, her son arranged for her to move into an assisted-living facility. During admission, she signed a residency agreement, which included an arbitration clause. After she sustained injuries in a fall at the facility, a suit was filed to recover damages. The facility asked the court to compel arbitration. Was Dorothy bound to the residency agreement? Discuss. [*Drury v. Assisted Living Concepts, Inc.,* 245 Or.App. 217, 262 P.3d 1162 (2011)] (See *Mentally Incompetent Persons.*)

12–6. Disaffirmance. J. T., a minor, is a motocross competitor. At Monster Mountain MX Park, he signed a waiver of liability to "hold harmless the park for any loss due to negligence." Riding around the Monster Mountain track, J. T. rode over a blind jump, became airborne, and crashed into a tractor that he had not seen until he was in the air. To recover for his injuries, J. T. filed a suit against Monster Mountain, alleging negligence for its failure to remove the tractor from the track. Does the liability waiver bar this claim? Explain. [*J. T. v. Monster Mountain, LLC,* 754 F.Supp.2d 1323 (M.D.Ala. 2010)] (See *Minors.*)

ETHICAL QUESTIONS

12–7. Minors. Should the goal of protecting minors from the consequences of unwise contracts ever outweigh the goal of encouraging minors to behave in a responsible manner? Discuss. (See *Minors.*)

12–8. Capacity. Joe Riley shattered the bones above his left ankle in an accident at Ingalls Shipbuilding, Inc. In the hospital, Riley met with Caty Suthoff, an insurance claims adjuster. Riley answered her questions about his injury accurately and clearly, and signed a form consenting to the release of his medical records. Later, Riley complained of back pain, which he blamed on the accident, but his physician made a note that the pain was not work related. To prevent the insurance company from seeing this note—which would reduce the amount of his monetary recovery—Riley filed a suit against the adjuster. He contended that he had signed the consent form while incapacitated by medication. Did Riley show a lack of capacity when he signed the form? Did he show a lack of ethics when he filed the suit? Discuss. [*Riley v. F. A. Richards & Associates, Inc.,* 16 So.3d 708 (Miss.App. 2009)] (See *Mentally Incompetent Persons.*)

Chapter 12—Work Set

TRUE-FALSE QUESTIONS

_____ 1. An adult who enters into a contract with a minor generally cannot avoid the contract.

_____ 2. When a minor disaffirms a contract, whatever the minor transferred as consideration (or its value) normally must be returned.

_____ 3. A person who is so intoxicated as to lack mental capacity when he or she enters into a contract must perform the contract.

_____ 4. Emancipation has no effect on a minor's contractual capacity.

_____ 5. If an individual who has not been judged mentally incompetent understands the nature and effect of entering into a certain contract, the contract is normally valid.

_____ 6. The age of majority for contractual purposes is twenty-one years for males and eighteen years for females.

_____ 7. Some states' statutes restrict minors from avoiding certain contracts, including for necessaries.

_____ 8. Generally, parents are liable for contracts made by their minor children.

_____ 9. In most cases, a person, to disaffirm a contract entered into when he or she was intoxicated, must return any consideration received.

_____ 10. A minor may disaffirm a contract entered into with an adult.

MULTIPLE-CHOICE QUESTIONS

_____ 1. Troy, a minor, sells his collection of sports memorabilia to Vern for $250. On his eighteenth birthday, Troy learns that the collection may have been worth at least $2,500. Troy

   a. can disaffirm, because the contract has not been fully performed.
   b. can disaffirm, if he does so within a reasonable time of attaining majority.
   c. cannot disaffirm, because he has already attained majority.
   d. cannot disaffirm, because the contract has been fully performed.

_____ 2. Doug has been drinking heavily. Joe offers to buy Doug's farm for a fair price. Believing the deal is a joke, Doug writes and signs an agreement to sell and gives it to Joe. Joe believes the deal is serious. The contract is

   a. enforceable, if the circumstances indicate that Doug understands what he did.
   b. enforceable, because Joe believes that the transaction is serious.
   c. unenforceable, because the intoxication permits Doug to avoid the contract.
   d. unenforceable, because Doug thinks it is a joke.

_____ 3. Ed is adjudged mentally incompetent. Irwin is appointed to act as Ed's guardian. Irwin signs a contract to sell some of Ed's property to pay for Ed's care. On regaining competency, Ed

   a. can disaffirm, because he was mentally incompetent.
   b. can disaffirm, because he is no longer mentally incompetent.
   c. cannot disaffirm, because Irwin could enter into contracts on his behalf.
   d. cannot disaffirm, because he may become mentally incompetent again.

_____ 4. Adam, a sixteen-year-old minor, enters into a contract for necessaries, which his parents could provide but do not. Adam disaffirms the contract. Adam's parents

   a. must pay the reasonable value of the goods.
   b. must pay more than the reasonable value of the goods.
   c. can pay less than the reasonable value of the goods.
   d. do not have to pay anything for the goods.

5. First Bank loans money to Patty, a sixteen-year-old minor. Patty must repay the loan

  a. if the loan is made for the express purpose of buying necessaries.
  b. if First Bank makes sure the money is spent on necessaries.
  c. if both a and b are true.
  d. in none of the above circumstances.

6. Eve, a fifteen-year-old minor, buys from EZ Spyware a smartphone app that remotely monitors calls. The contract is fully executed. Eve now wants to disaffirm it. To do so, she

  a. must return only the app to EZ.
  b. must return the smartphone with the app to EZ.
  c. must return just the smartphone to EZ.
  d. need do none of the above.

7. Neal is adjudged mentally incompetent, and a guardian is appointed. Neal later signs an investment contract with Mary. This contract is

  a. valid.
  b. voidable.
  c. void.
  d. none of the above.

8. Jeff, a fifteen-year-old minor, contracts with Online, Inc., for Internet access services. Considering that Jeff is a minor, which of the following is true?

  a. Online can disaffirm the contract.
  b. Jeff can disaffirm the contract.
  c. Both a and b.
  d. None of the above.

ANSWERING MORE LEGAL PROBLEMS

1. After sipping half a glass of wine at a meeting with Vineyard Valley Adventures, Esmé buys a discounted tour package. The time of the trip is approaching, and Vineyard's costs to provide the package have doubled. Vineyard tries to avoid honoring the agreement with Esmé on the ground that she was intoxicated when the agreement was made.

   Can Vineyard avoid the contract on the basis of Esmé's lack of capacity? No. A contract entered into by an intoxicated person is _____ if the person was sufficiently intoxicated to lack mental capacity. But the transaction is _____ only at the option of the _____ person. Furthermore, if the person was intoxicated but understood the legal consequences, the contract is enforceable. In this problem, Vineyard cannot avoid the contract.

2. Lucrezia is diagnosed with chronic, severe schizoaffective psychosis. Experiencing hallucinations, she is hospitalized in a psychiatric ward and placed on medication. On a furlough a month later, she signs an agreement at the insistence of her spouse, Cesare. The agreement states that Cesare has exclusive rights to all of their finances and property, and Lucrezia has the sole duty to pay all of their debts. Cesare files for divorce.

   Can Lucrezia avoid this agreement? Yes. When a mentally incompetent person not previously so adjudged by a court enters into a contract, the contract is _____ if he or she lacks the capacity to comprehend its subject matter, nature, and consequences at the time of the _____. At the time of this agreement, Lucrezia had been diagnosed with schizoaffective psychosis. She was experiencing hallucinations, and she was on medication. Based on these facts, she lacked the mental capacity to manage her own affairs and to make decisions in her own best interest.

THE LEGALITY OF AGREEMENTS

FACING A LEGAL PROBLEM

Each of five co-workers receives a free lottery ticket from a customer. The co-workers orally agree to split the jackpot if one of the tickets turns out to be the winning one. When one of the tickets is a winner, its holder decides not to share the proceeds. The other co-workers file a suit to collect.

Q Is the agreement to split the lottery winnings among the co-workers enforceable?

LEARNING OUTCOMES

The four Learning Outcomes below are designed to help improve your understanding of the chapter. After reading this chapter, you should be able to:

❶ Identify contracts that are contrary to federal or state statutes.

❷ Identify contracts that are contrary to public policy.

❸ State circumstances in which covenants not to compete are enforceable.

❹ Understand the consequences of entering into an illegal agreement.

To this point, we have discussed three of the requirements for a valid contract to exist—agreement (offer and acceptance), consideration, and contractual capacity. Legality is the fourth requirement. For a contract to be valid and enforceable, it must be formed for a legal purpose. A contract to do something that is prohibited by federal or state statutory law is illegal. As such, it is void from the outset and thus unenforceable. Also, a contract that is tortious (pronounced *tor*-shus) or calls for an action contrary to public policy is illegal and unenforceable.

13–1 CONTRACTS CONTRARY TO STATUTE

Statutes often set forth rules affecting the terms of contracts. Statutes may specify clauses that must be included in certain contracts, for example, or may prohibit certain contracts based on their subject matter. In this section, we examine several ways in which contracts may be contrary to statute and thus illegal.

LEARNING OUTCOME 1
Identify contracts that are contrary to federal or state statutes.

13–1a Contracts to Commit a Crime

Any contract to commit a crime is contrary to statute. Thus, a contract to sell illegal drugs in violation of criminal laws is unenforceable. Similarly, a contract to smuggle undocumented workers from another country into the United States for an employer is illegal, as is a contract to dump hazardous waste in violation of environmental laws. If the object or performance of a contract is rendered illegal by statute after the contract has been formed, the contract is considered to be discharged by law.

13–1b Usury

Almost every state has a statute that sets the maximum rate of interest that can be charged for different types of transactions, including ordinary loans. A lender who makes a loan at an interest rate above the lawful maximum commits **usury**. The maximum rate of interest varies from state to state.

usury
Charging an illegal rate of interest.

13–1c Gambling

In general, wagers and games of chance are illegal. All states have statutes that regulate *gambling*—defined as any scheme that involves distribution of property by chance among persons who have paid valuable consideration for the opportunity to receive the property. Nearly all states operate lotteries, allow horse racing, or permit games of chance (such as bingo) for charitable purposes. A few states allow casino gambling. But in any state, a gambling-related contract may be illegal.

EXAMPLE 13.1 Video poker machines are legal in Louisiana, but their use requires the approval of the state video gaming commission. Gaming Venture, Inc., did not obtain this approval before agreeing with Tastee Restaurant Corporation to install poker machines in some of its restaurants. Later, Tastee allegedly backed out of the deal. Because of the failure to obtain approval, the state held that the agreement between Tastee and Gaming Venture was an illegal gambling contract and therefore void.◄

13–1d Licensing Statutes

All states require members of certain professions—including physicians, lawyers, real estate brokers, architects, electricians, and stockbrokers—to have licenses. Some licenses require extensive schooling and examinations, which indicate to the public that a special skill has been acquired. Others require only that the particular person be of good moral character and pay a fee.

Generally, business licenses provide a means of regulating and taxing certain businesses and protecting the public against actions that could threaten the general welfare. **EXAMPLE 13.2** Beth is a stockbroker in New York City. In New York—as in nearly all states—Beth must be licensed and file a *bond* (a promise obtained from a professional bonding company to pay a certain amount of money if Beth commits theft). The bond is filed with the state to protect the public from Beth's performing fraudulent stock transactions.◄

When a person enters into a contract with an unlicensed individual, the contract may still be enforceable depending on the nature of the licensing statute. Some states expressly provide that the lack of a license in certain occupations bars the enforcement of work-related contracts. If the statute does not expressly state this, it is necessary to look to the underlying purpose of the licensing requirements for a particular occupation.

If the purpose is to protect the public from unauthorized practitioners, a contract involving an unlicensed individual is illegal and unenforceable. If, however, the underlying purpose of the statute is to raise government revenues, a contract entered into with an unlicensed practitioner is enforceable—although the unlicensed person is usually fined.

 ## 13–2 Contracts Contrary to Public Policy

LEARNING OUTCOME 2

Identify contracts that are contrary to public policy.

Although contracts involve private parties, some are not enforceable because of the negative impact they would have on society. These contracts are said to be *contrary to public policy*. Examples include a contract to commit an immoral act, such as selling a child, and a contract that prohibits marriage.

13–2a Contracts in Restraint of Trade

Restraint of trade involves interfering with free competition. Contracts in restraint of trade usually adversely affect the public (which favors competition in the economy) and typically violate one or more federal or state statutes.

An exception is recognized when the restraint is reasonable and an integral part of a contract. Many such exceptions involve a type of restraint called a **covenant not to compete.**

Covenants Not to Compete and the Sale of an Ongoing Business Covenants not to compete are often contained in contracts concerning the sale of an ongoing business. In this situation, a covenant not to compete is created when a seller agrees not to open a new store in a certain geographical area surrounding the old store. Such agreements enable the seller to sell, and the purchaser to buy, the "goodwill" and "reputation" of an ongoing business.

EXAMPLE 13.3 For more than twenty years, Ryan has been operating his specialty art supply store, Central District Art Shop, in the rural town of Ashville. Customers come from other cities to shop at Central. He decides to sell the business to Barbara, who includes a provision in the sales agreement stating that Ryan will not open an art store within one hundred miles of Ashville. By requiring Ryan to not compete in business near Ashville, Barbara is protecting her investment in Central's goodwill and reputation with its loyal customers. ◄

Covenants Not to Compete in Employment Contracts Agreements not to compete can also be contained in employment contracts. It is common for people in middle-level and upper-level management positions to agree not to work for competitors or not to start a competing business for a specified period of time after terminating employment. Such agreements are legal so long as the specified period of time is not excessive in duration and the geographical restriction is reasonable. Basically, the restriction on competition must be reasonable—that is, no greater than necessary to protect a legitimate business interest.

> **covenant not to compete**
> A contractual promise of one party to refrain from competing in business with another party for a certain period of time and within a specified geographical area.

> **LEARNING OUTCOME 3**
> State circumstances in which covenants not to compete are enforceable.

Real-World Case Example

Brown & Brown, Inc., an insurance agency, hired Theresa Johnson to provide actuarial (financial) analysis. On Johnson's first day of work, she was asked to sign a nonsolicitation covenant, which prohibited her from soliciting or servicing any client of Brown's New York offices for two years after the termination of her employment. Less than five years later, Johnson was terminated and went to work for Lawley Benefits Group. Brown filed a suit in a New York state court against Johnson, alleging breach of contract. The court ruled in Johnson's favor. Brown appealed.

Was Brown's covenant not to compete too broad to be enforced? Yes. In a 2014 case, *Brown & Brown, Inc. v. Johnson,* a state intermediate appellate court affirmed the lower court's judgment. The nonsolicitation covenant was "overbroad"—meaning that it prohibited Johnson from soliciting or providing services to clients with whom she had never acquired a relationship through her employment. Additionally, Johnson was not presented with the covenant until her first day of work, nor did she receive any benefit for signing it beyond her continued employment.

Covenants Not to Compete and Reformation On occasion, when a covenant not to compete is unreasonable in its essential terms, the court may *reform* the covenant, converting its terms into reasonable ones. Instead of declaring the covenant not to compete illegal and unenforceable, the court reasons that the parties intended their contract to contain reasonable terms and changes the contract so that this basic intent can be enforced.

reformation
A court-ordered correction of a written contract so that it reflects the true intentions of the parties.

This practice, called contract **reformation**, presents a problem, however. By rewriting the contract, the judge becomes a party to it. Consequently, a court usually will reform a contract only when it is necessary to prevent undue burdens or hardships.

13–2b Unconscionable Contracts or Clauses

Ordinarily, a court does not look at the fairness, or equity, of a contract. In other words, it does not inquire into the adequacy of consideration. Persons are assumed to be reasonably intelligent, and the court does not come to their aid just because they have made an unwise or foolish bargain.

unconscionable contract or clause
A contract or clause that is void because one party is forced to accept terms that are unfairly burdensome and that unfairly benefit the other party.

In certain circumstances, however, bargains are so oppressive that the courts relieve innocent parties of part or all of their duties. Such a bargain may be evidenced by an **unconscionable contract or clause.** (*Unconscionable* means grossly unethical or unfair.) An unconscionable contract is one in which the terms of the agreement are so unfair as to "shock the conscience" of the court. Court decisions have distinguished between *procedural* and *substantive unconscionability*.

Procedural Unconscionability Procedural unconscionability has to do with how a term becomes part of a contract. It relates to factors bearing on a party's lack of knowledge or understanding of the contract terms because of inconspicuous print, unintelligible language (legalese), lack of opportunity to read the contract, lack of opportunity to ask questions about the contract's meaning, and other factors.

Substantive Unconscionability Substantive unconscionability describes contracts, or portions of contracts, that are oppressive or overly harsh. Courts generally focus on provisions that deprive one party of the benefits of the agreement or leave that party without a remedy for nonperformance by the other.

adhesion contract
A standard-form contract in which the stronger party dictates the terms.

Contracts entered into because of one party's vastly superior bargaining power may be deemed unconscionable. These situations usually involve an **adhesion contract,** which is a contract drafted by one party (such as a dishonest retail dealer) and then presented to another (such as an uneducated consumer) on a take-it-or-leave-it basis.

HIGHLIGHTING THE POINT

Smith, a welfare recipient with a fourth-grade education, agrees to purchase a fifty-five-inch flat-screen TV from A-Plus Appliances for $3,000. Smith signs a two-year *installment contract*. The same type of TV usually sells for $1,000. After paying $900, Smith refuses to pay more, and A-Plus sues to collect the balance.

Is Smith required to pay the remaining $2,100? No. This type of contract would be considered unconscionable because of the buyer's lack of education, the disparity of bargaining power between the parties, and the price of the goods (despite the general rule that courts will not inquire into the adequacy of consideration).

13–2c Exculpatory Clauses

exculpatory clause
A clause that releases a party to a contract from liability for his or her wrongful acts.

Closely related to the concept of unconscionability are **exculpatory clauses.** These are clauses that release a party from liability in the event of monetary or physical injury, *no matter who is at fault*. (*Exculpatory* means tending to avoid blame.) Indeed, some courts refer to such clauses in terms of unconscionability.

Exculpatory clauses are often held to be unenforceable. For example, exculpatory clauses that relieve a party from liability for harm caused by simple negligence normally are unenforceable when they are asserted by an employer against an employee.

HIGHLIGHTING THE POINT

Madison Manufacturing Company asks Juan, a new employee, to sign a contract that includes a clause absolving Madison from liability for harm caused "by accidents or injuries in the factory, or which may result from defective machinery or carelessness or misconduct of himself or any other employee in service of the employer."

If Juan is injured in a factory accident, can Madison use the clause to avoid responsibility? Probably not. The provision attempts to remove Madison's potential liability for injuries occurring to employees, and it would ordinarily be held contrary to public policy.

13–3 THE EFFECT OF ILLEGALITY

In general, an illegal contract is void. The contract is deemed never to have existed, and the courts will not aid either party. In most illegal contracts, both parties are considered to be equally at fault—*in pari delicto*. If a contract is *executory* (not yet fulfilled), neither party can enforce it. If it is executed, there can be neither contractual nor quasi-contractual recovery.

What if one wrongdoer in an illegal contract is unjustly enriched at the expense of the other? That is generally of no concern to the law. The major justification for this hands-off attitude is that it is improper to place the machinery of justice at the disposal of a plaintiff who has broken the law by entering into an illegal bargain. Another justification is the hoped-for deterrent effect of this general rule. A plaintiff who suffers a loss because of an illegal bargain should presumably be deterred from entering into similar illegal bargains in the future.

Some persons are excluded from the general rule that neither party to an illegal bargain can sue for breach and neither can recover for performance rendered. We discuss these exceptions next.

> **LEARNING OUTCOME 4**
> Understand the consequences of entering into an illegal agreement.

13–3a Justifiable Ignorance of the Facts

When one of the parties is relatively innocent, that party can often obtain restitution (recovery of benefits conferred) in a partially executed contract. The courts do not enforce the contract but do allow the parties to return to their original positions. It is also possible for an innocent party who has fully performed under the contract to enforce the contract against the guilty party.

HIGHLIGHTING THE POINT

Debbie contracts with Tucker to purchase ten crates of goods that legally cannot be sold or shipped. Tucker hires a trucking firm to deliver the shipment to Debbie and agrees to pay the trucking firm the normal fee of $500.

(Continued)

If the trucking firm delivers the goods as agreed, but Tucker fails to pay, can the firm recover the $500 from Tucker? Yes. Although the law specifies that the shipment and sale of the goods were illegal, the carrier, being an innocent party, can legally collect the $500 from Tucker.

13–3b Members of Protected Classes

When a statute protects a certain class of people, a member of that class can enforce an illegal contract even though the other party cannot. For instance, statutes prohibit certain employees (such as flight attendants) from working more than a specified number of hours per month. An employee who works more than the maximum can recover for those extra hours of service.

Other examples of statutes designed to protect a particular class of people are **blue sky laws**, which are state laws that regulate and supervise investment companies for the protection of the public. Such laws are intended to stop the sale of stock in fly-by-night concerns, such as nonexistent oil wells and gold mines. Investors are protected as a class and can sue to recover the purchase price of stock issued in violation of such laws. Most states also have statutes regulating the sale of insurance. If an insurance company violates a statute when selling insurance, the purchaser can nevertheless enforce the policy and recover from the insurer.

blue sky law
State law that regulates the offer and sale of securities.

13–3c Withdrawal from an Illegal Agreement

If the illegal part of a bargain has not yet been performed, the party tendering performance can withdraw from the bargain and recover the performance or its value.

HIGHLIGHTING THE POINT

Martha and Francisco decide to wager (illegally) on the outcome of a boxing match. Each deposits money with a stakeholder, who agrees to pay the winner of the bet. Before the boxing match is held, Francisco changes his mind about the bet.

Can Francisco get his money back? Yes. At this point, each party has performed part of the agreement, but the illegal part of the agreement will not occur until the money is paid to the winner. Before such payment occurs, either party is entitled to withdraw from the agreement by giving notice to the stakeholder.

ANSWERING THE LEGAL PROBLEM

In the legal problem set out at the beginning of this chapter, five co-workers agreed to split the winnings from their individual lottery tickets, but a worker with a winning ticket later refused to share the proceeds.

A **Is the co-workers' agreement enforceable?** No. At first glance, this agreement might seem entirely legal. The contract here, however, is an exchange of promises to share winnings from the parties' individually owned lottery tickets in the uncertain event that one of the tickets wins. Consequently, the agreement is founded on a gambling consideration and is therefore void.

TERMS AND CONCEPTS FOR REVIEW

adhesion contract 172

blue sky law 174

covenant not to compete 171

exculpatory clause 172

reformation 172

unconscionable contract
or clause 172

usury 169

CHAPTER SUMMARY—THE LEGALITY OF AGREEMENTS

LEARNING OUTCOME	
1	**Identify contracts that are contrary to federal or state statutes.** Any contract to commit a crime is contrary to statute. It is also illegal to make a loan at an interest rate that exceeds the maximum rate established by state law. Gambling contracts that violate state statutes are illegal. A contract entered into by a person who does not have a license, when one is required by statute, is not enforceable if the underlying purpose of the statute is to protect the public from unlicensed practitioners.
2	**Identify contracts that are contrary to public policy.** Contracts that have a negative impact on society are contrary to public policy. These include contracts to commit immoral acts and contracts that prohibit marriage. Contracts in restraint of trade are generally prohibited by statute, unless the restraint is reasonable. When a contract or clause is so unfair that it is oppressive to one party, it can be deemed unconscionable by a court and will be unenforceable.
3	**State circumstances in which covenants not to compete are enforceable.** A covenant not to compete is enforceable if its terms are reasonable as to time and area of restraint. Covenants not to compete are often contained in contracts for the sale of an ongoing business and in certain employment contracts.
4	**Understand the consequences of entering into an illegal agreement.** An illegal contract is void, and the courts will aid neither party when both parties are equally at fault. If the contract is executory, neither party can enforce it. If it is executed, neither party can recover for its breach or on a quasi-contract theory.

ISSUE SPOTTERS

Check your answers to the *Issue Spotters* against the answers provided in Appendix C at the end of this text.

1. Diane bets Tex $1,000 that the Green Bay Packers will win the Super Bowl. A state law prohibits gambling. Do Diane and Tex have an enforceable contract? Explain. (See *Contracts Contrary to Statute.*)

2. Potomac Airlines prints on the backs of its tickets that it is not liable for any injury to a passenger caused by

Potomac's negligence. Ron buys a ticket and boards the plane. On takeoff, the plane crashes, and Ron is injured. If the cause of the accident is found to be Potomac's negligence, can Potomac use the clause as a defense to liability? Why or why not? (See *Contracts Contrary to Public Policy.*)

USING BUSINESS LAW

13–1. Covenants Not to Compete. Joseph, who owns the only pizza parlor in Middletown, learns that Giovanni is about to open a competing pizza parlor in the same small town,

just a few blocks from Joseph's restaurant. Joseph offers Giovanni $10,000 in return for Giovanni's promise not to open a pizza parlor in the Middletown area. Giovanni accepts the $10,000 but goes ahead with his plans, in spite of the agreement. When Giovanni opens his restaurant for business, Joseph sues to enjoin (prevent) Giovanni's continued operation of his restaurant or to recover the $10,000. The court denies recovery. On what basis? (See *Contracts Contrary to Public Policy.*)

13–2. Licensing Statutes. State X requires that persons who prepare and serve liquor in the form of drinks at commercial establishments be licensed by the state to do so. The only requirement for obtaining a yearly license is that the person be at least twenty-one years old. Mickey, aged thirty-five, is hired as a bartender for the Southtown Restaurant. Gerald, a staunch alumnus of a nearby university, brings twenty of his friends to the restaurant to celebrate a football victory one afternoon. Gerald orders four rounds of drinks, and the bill is nearly $500. Gerald learns that Mickey has failed to renew his bartender's license, and Gerald refuses to pay, claiming that the contract is unenforceable. Discuss whether Gerald is correct. (See *Contracts Contrary to Statute.*)

REAL-WORLD CASE PROBLEMS

13–3. Adhesion Contracts. David Desgro hired Paul Pack to inspect a house that Desgro wanted to buy. Pack had Desgro sign a standard-form contract that included a twelve-month limit for claims based on the agreement. Pack reported that the house had no major problems, but after Desgro bought it, he discovered issues with the plumbing, insulation, heat pump, and floor support. Thirteen months after the inspection, Desgro filed a suit in a Tennessee state court against Pack. Was Desgro's complaint filed too late, or was the contract's twelve-month limit unenforceable? Discuss. [*Desgro v. Pack*, 2013 WL 84899 (Tenn.Ct.App. 2013)] (See *Contracts Contrary to Public Policy.*)

13–4. Licensing Statutes. PEMS Co. International, Inc., agreed to find a buyer for Rupp Industries, Inc. Using PEMS's services, an investment group bought Rupp for $20 million and changed its name to Temp-Air, Inc. PEMS asked Temp-Air to pay a commission on the sale. Temp-Air refused, arguing that PEMS had acted as a broker in the deal without a license. The applicable statute defines a broker as any person who deals with the sale of a business. If this statute was intended to protect the public, can PEMS collect its commission? Explain. [*PEMS Co. International, Inc. v. Temp-Air, Inc.*, __ N.W.2d __ (Minn.App. 2011)] (See *Contracts Contrary to Statute.*)

13–5. Unconscionable Contracts or Clauses. Erica Bishop's apartment lease listed her and her children as members of the household and required her to notify the landlord if any of them moved out. The lease also held her responsible for the acts of all members. Any criminal act was a ground for eviction. When Bishop's son, Derek, was convicted of the robbery of a nearby store, she was given thirty days to vacate the apartment. Bishop responded that Derek had moved out, but she had forgotten to tell the landlord. Besides, she contended, the lease was unconscionable. Is she correct? Discuss. [*Bishop v. Housing Authority of South Bend*, 920 N.E.2d 772 (Ind.App. 2010)] (See *Contracts Contrary to Public Policy.*)

13–6. Unconscionable Contracts or Clauses. Geographic Expeditions, Inc. (GeoEx), which guided climbs up Mount Kilimanjaro, required climbers to sign a release to participate in an expedition. The form mandated the arbitration of any dispute in San Francisco and limited damages to the cost of the trip. GeoEx told climbers that the terms were nonnegotiable and were the same as terms imposed by other travel firms. Jason Lhotka died on a GeoEx climb. His mother filed a suit against GeoEx. GeoEx sought arbitration. Was the arbitration clause unconscionable? Why or why not? [*Lhotka v. Geographic Expeditions, Inc.*, 181 Cal.App.4th 816, 104 Cal.Rptr.3d 844 (1 Dist. 2010)] (See *Contracts Contrary to Public Policy.*)

ETHICAL QUESTIONS

13–7. Gambling. How can states enforce gambling laws in the age of the Internet? (See *Contracts Contrary to Statute.*)

13–8. Contracts in Restraint of Trade. Brendan Coleman created and marketed Clinex, a software billing program. Later, Retina Consultants, P.C., a medical practice, hired Coleman as a software engineer. Together, they modified the Clinex program to create Clinex-RE. Coleman signed an agreement to the effect that he owned Clinex, Retina owned Clinex-RE, and he would not market Clinex in competition with Clinex-RE. After Coleman quit Retina, he withdrew funds from a Retina bank account and marketed both forms of the software to other medical practices. Was the covenant not to compete in this case enforceable? Was Coleman's behavior after leaving Retina unethical? Explain. [*Coleman v. Retina Consultants, P.C.*, 286 Ga. 317, 687 S.E.2d 457 (2009)] (See *Contracts Contrary to Public Policy.*)

Chapter 13—Work Set

TRUE-FALSE QUESTIONS

_____ 1. An exculpatory clause may or may not be enforced.

_____ 2. An adhesion contract will never be deemed unconscionable.

_____ 3. An illegal contract is valid unless it is executory.

_____ 4. If the purpose of a licensing statute is to protect the public from unlicensed practitioners, a contract entered into with an unlicensed practitioner is unenforceable.

_____ 5. Covenants not to compete are never enforceable.

_____ 6. Usury is charging an illegal rate of interest.

_____ 7. There is no difference between gambling and the risk that underlies most contracts.

_____ 8. All states have statutes that regulate gambling.

MULTIPLE-CHOICE QUESTIONS

_____ 1. At the start of the football season, Bob and Murray make a bet about the results of the next Super Bowl. Adam holds their money. Just as the divisional play-offs are beginning, Bob changes his mind and asks for his money back. Gambling on sports events is illegal in their state. Can Bob be held to the bet?

a. Yes. It would be unconscionable to let Bob back out so late in the season.
b. Yes. No party to the contract is innocent, and thus no party can withdraw.
c. No. If an illegal agreement is still executory, either party can withdraw.
d. No. The only party who can be held to the bet is Murray.

_____ 2. Al sells his business to Dan and, as part of the agreement, promises not to engage in a business of the same kind within thirty miles for three years. Competition within thirty miles would hurt Dan's business. Al's promise

a. violates public policy, because it is part of the sale of a business.
b. violates public policy, because it unreasonably restrains Al from competing.
c. does not violate public policy, because it is no broader than necessary.
d. does none of the above.

_____ 3. Luke practices law without an attorney's license. The state requires a license to protect the public from unauthorized practitioners. Clark hires Luke to handle a legal matter. Luke cannot enforce their contract because

a. it is illegal.
b. Luke has no contractual capacity.
c. Luke did not give consideration.
d. none of the above.

_____ 4. Amy contracts to buy Kim's business. Kim agrees not to compete with Amy for one year in the same county. Six months later, Kim opens a competing business six blocks away. Amy

a. cannot enforce the contract because it is unconscionable.
b. cannot enforce the contract because it is a restraint of trade.
c. can enforce the contract because all covenants not to compete are valid.
d. can enforce the contract because it is reasonable in scope and duration.

_____ 5. Sam signs an employment contract that contains a clause absolving the employer of any liability if Sam is injured on the job. If Sam is injured on the job due to the employer's negligence, the clause will

a. protect the employer from liability.
b. likely not protect the employer from liability.
c. likely be held unconscionable.
d. do both b and c.

_____ 6. Fred signs a covenant not to compete with his employer, General Sales Corporation. This covenant is enforceable if it

    a. is not ancillary to the sale of a business.

    b. is reasonable in terms of geographic area and time.

    c. is supported by consideration.

    d. requires both parties to obtain business licenses.

_____ 7. Ann contracts with Bob, a financial planner who is required by the state to have a license. Bob does not have a license. Their contract is enforceable if

    a. the purpose of the statute is to protect the public from unlicensed practitioners.

    b. the purpose of the statute is to raise government revenue.

    c. Bob does not know that he is required to have a license.

    d. Ann does not know that Bob is required to have a license.

_____ 8. A contract that is full of inconspicuous print and unintelligible language and that is presented to someone without giving him or her an opportunity to read it is

    a. always unenforceable.

    b. always enforceable.

    c. unenforceable under some circumstances.

    d. void.

_____ 9. In an exculpatory clause, which of the following statements is true?

    a. One party agrees that the other party is not mentally incompetent.

    b. One party releases the other party from liability in the event of monetary or physical injury, no matter who is at fault.

    c. One party is able to sue the other party based on the clear fault of the other party.

    d. Both parties agree to use arbitration, not adjudication, to settle any disputes arising under the contract containing the clause.

ANSWERING MORE LEGAL PROBLEMS

1. To protect professional boxers, California law requires that their managers be licensed by the state. José, who was not licensed by the state, assumed the management of Marco, a professional boxer. José negotiated a contract for Marco with Everlast Promotions, Inc. José helped Marco resolve three lawsuits and unrelated tax problems so that he could continue boxing. When Marco stopped talking to José, the latter filed a suit in a California court.

    Is this management contract enforceable? No. A contract with an unlicensed practitioner is not enforceable if the underlying purpose of the state's licensing statute is to protect the _____ from unauthorized _____. Here, the manager of a professional boxer must be licensed by the state. The purpose is to protect boxers. The state did not license José as a boxing manager, yet he conducted himself as the manager of a professional boxer. Because he acted without a _____, the alleged contract with Marco is _____.

2. Roberto, who did not speak or read English, visited Dart Dodge, a car dealership. Aware that Roberto was monolingual, Dart's staff transacted a deal in Spanish. They explained the English-language contract, except for one clause. This clause limited the buyer's right to seek damages in court to less than $5,000, but did not limit Dart's right to ask for damages. Roberto bought a Dodge Ram truck and signed the contract.

    Is the damages clause in this contract enforceable? No. The clause is unconscionable. _____ unconscionability concerns the manner in which a contract is entered into. _____ unconscionability can occur when a contract unfairly limits one party's remedy for the other's breach. Having undertaken to explain the contract in Spanish, Dart's staff was obliged to do so accurately so Roberto would have a meaningful opportunity to bargain. The failure to do so made the contract _____ unconscionable. The unfair limit to the buyer's damages was _____ unconscionable.

VOLUNTARY CONSENT

14

FACING A LEGAL PROBLEM

David signs a contract with William to purchase ten acres of land in Idaho. If David believes that the land is owned by William, when it actually belongs to Jenny, a court may allow David to avoid the contract with William because David made a mistake of fact.

Q Suppose, however, that David instead makes a contract with Jenny, who owns the land. David believes he can sell the land to Harcourt for a profit of 30 percent. Later, he finds that Harcourt is not willing to pay what he expected. Can David escape his contractual obligations because of his mistaken expectation?

An otherwise valid contract may still be unenforceable if the parties have not genuinely agreed to its terms. This lack of **voluntary consent** can be used as a *defense* to the contract's enforceability. Voluntary consent may be lacking if one or more of the parties is mistaken about an important fact concerning the subject matter of the contract. Parties are also considered to lack voluntary consent if they have entered into a contract as a result of fraudulent misrepresentation, undue influence, or duress.

 ## 14–1 MISTAKES

We all make mistakes, and it is not surprising that mistakes are made when contracts are formed. In certain circumstances, contract law allows a contract to be avoided on the basis of mistake. It is important to distinguish between *mistakes of fact* and *mistakes of value or quality*, however. Only a mistake of fact makes a contract voidable.

14–1a Mistakes of Fact

Mistakes of fact can occur in two forms—*unilateral* and *bilateral* (mutual). A unilateral mistake is made by only one of the contracting parties. A bilateral mistake is made by both. These two types of mistakes are illustrated in Exhibit 14.1. In either case, the mistake must involve a *material fact*—a fact that is important and central to the subject matter of the contract, such as the identity of the parties.

Unilateral Mistakes A **unilateral mistake** is made by only one of the parties. In general, a unilateral mistake does not give the mistaken party any right to relief from the contract. In other words, the contract normally is enforceable against the mistaken party. **EXAMPLE 14.1** Elena intends to sell her personal jet ski for $6,500. When she learns that Derek is interested in buying a used personal jet ski, she sends him a text offering to sell the jet ski to him. When writing the text, however, she mistakenly keys in the price of $5,600. Derek immediately sends Elena a text

LEARNING OUTCOMES

The four Learning Outcomes below are designed to help improve your understanding of the chapter. After reading this chapter, you should be able to:

① State the difference between mistakes of fact and mistakes of value or quality.

② List the elements of fraudulent misrepresentation.

③ Contrast misrepresentation of a material fact and misrepresentation of law.

④ Recognize the difference between undue influence and duress.

voluntary consent
The knowledge of, and genuine assent to, the terms of a contract.

LEARNING OUTCOME 1

State the difference between mistakes of fact and mistakes of value or quality.

unilateral mistake
A mistake that occurs when one party to a contract is mistaken as to a material fact.

EXHIBIT 14.1   Mistakes of Fact

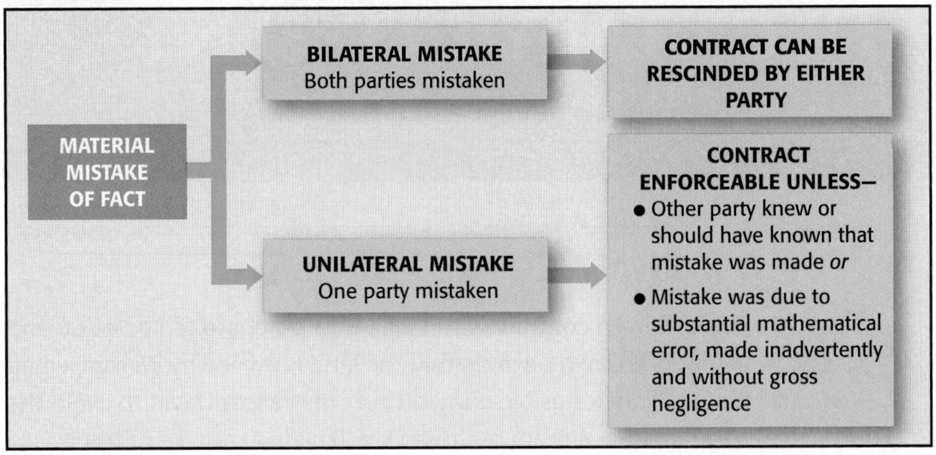

reply accepting her offer. Even though Elena intended to sell her personal jet ski for $6,500, she has made a unilateral mistake and is bound by the contract to sell it to Derek for $5,600.◄

There are at least two exceptions to this rule. The contract may not be enforceable if:

1. The *other* party to the contract knows or should have known that a mistake was made.
2. The error was due to a substantial mathematical mistake in addition, subtraction, division, or multiplication and was made inadvertently and without *gross negligence*—that is, the intentional failure to perform a duty in reckless disregard of the consequences.

Of course, the mistake must still involve some material fact.

HIGHLIGHTING THE POINT

Odell Construction Company makes a bid to install the plumbing in an apartment building. Herbert Odell, the president, adds up his costs, but his secretary forgets to give him the figures for the pipe fittings. Because of the omission, Odell's bid is $6,500 below that of the other bidders. The prime contractor, Sunspan, Inc., accepts and relies on Odell's bid.

Is the bid enforceable? If Sunspan is not aware of Odell's mistake and could not reasonably have been aware of it, the bid will be enforceable, and Odell will be required to install the plumbing at the bid price. If, however, it can be shown that Odell's secretary mentioned the error to Sunspan, or if Odell's bid was so far below the others that, as a contractor, Sunspan should reasonably have known the bid was a mistake, the bid can be rescinded (canceled). Sunspan would not be allowed to accept the offer knowing it was made by mistake. The law of contracts protects only *reasonable* expectations.

Bilateral (Mutual) Mistakes When both parties are mistaken about the same material fact, a **bilateral mistake** has occurred, and the contract can be rescinded by either party. Normally, the contract is voidable by the adversely affected party. Note that, as with a unilateral mistake, the mistake must be about a material fact.

One type of bilateral mistake can occur when a word or term in a contract is subject to more than one reasonable interpretation. In that situation, if the parties

bilateral mistake
A mistake that occurs when both parties to a contract are mistaken as to a material fact.

to the contract attach materially different meanings to the term, their mutual misunderstanding may allow the contract to be rescinded.

14–1b Mistakes of Value or Quality

If a mistake concerns the future market value or quality of the object of the contract, the mistake is one of *value*, and the contract normally is enforceable. Mistakes of value can be bilateral or unilateral. Either way, they do not serve as a basis for avoiding a contract. **EXAMPLE 14.2** Carlos buys a violin from Beverly for $250. Although the violin is very old, neither party believes that it is valuable. Later, however, an antiques dealer informs Carlos and Beverly that the violin is rare and worth thousands of dollars. Here, both parties were mistaken, but the mistake is a mistake of value rather than a mistake of fact. Therefore, Beverly cannot cancel the contract.◄

The reason that mistakes of value or quality have no legal significance is that value is variable. Depending on the time, place, and other circumstances, the same item may be worth considerably different amounts. When parties form a contract, their agreement establishes the value of the object of their transaction—for the moment. Each party is considered to have assumed the risk that the value will change in the future or prove to be different from what he or she thought. Without this rule, almost any party who did not receive what she or he considered a fair bargain could argue mistake.

 ## 14–2 Fraudulent Misrepresentation

Although fraudulent misrepresentation is a tort, the presence of fraud also affects the authenticity of the innocent party's consent to the contract. When an innocent party consents to a contract with fraudulent terms, the contract usually can be avoided because the innocent party has not *voluntarily* consented to the terms. Normally, the innocent party can either cancel the contract and be restored to his or her original position, or enforce the contract and seek damages for injuries resulting from the fraud.

Typically, there are three elements of fraud:

1. A misrepresentation of a material fact must occur.
2. There must be an intent to deceive.
3. The innocent party must justifiably rely on the misrepresentation.

To recover damages, the innocent party must also suffer an injury.

14–2a Misrepresentation Has Occurred

The first element of proving fraud is to show that *misrepresentation of a material fact* has occurred. This misrepresentation can be through words or actions. For instance, an art gallery owner's statement that a painting is a Picasso is an express misrepresentation if the painting was done by another artist.

Misrepresentation by Words A *statement of opinion* generally is not subject to a claim of fraud. Claims such as "This investment will be worth twice as much next year" and "This car will last for years and years" are statements of opinion, not fact. Contracting parties should recognize them as such and not rely on them. A fact is objective and verifiable, whereas, an opinion usually is subject to debate. Therefore, sellers are allowed to tout their wares without being liable for fraud.

In certain cases, however—particularly when a naïve purchaser relies on a so-called expert's opinion—the innocent party may be entitled to rescission or reformation. Reformation is an equitable remedy granted by a court in which the terms of a contract are altered to reflect the true intentions of the parties. **EXAMPLE 14.3** At a dancing school, Brian, an instructor, praised Audrey for her potential to be an excellent dancer. She contracted for more than $100,000 of dancing lessons before realizing that, in fact, she did not have the potential to be an excellent dancer. Brian's superior knowledge about dance potential made the statement to Audrey one of fact rather than one of opinion. ◄

Misrepresentation by Conduct Misrepresentation need not be expressly made through the words or writings of another. It can also occur by conduct. **EXAMPLE 14.4** Tom contracted to buy a horse named Zorro from Dolores. Through various actions, Dolores led Tom to believe that the horse was fit to ride in competition, but it actually suffered from a medical condition that made it unsuitable for this use. Wrongfully concealing the horse's condition was misrepresentation by conduct. ◄

Misrepresentation by conduct can also involve denial. Suppose that one party requests information concerning facts that are material to a contract. If the other party has knowledge concerning these facts but falsely denies it, misrepresentation by conduct occurs.

Misrepresentation of Law Misrepresentation of law does not ordinarily entitle the party to be relieved of a contract. People are assumed to know the law.

LEARNING OUTCOME 3

Contrast misrepresentation of a material fact and misrepresentation of law.

HIGHLIGHTING THE POINT

Mercedes has a parcel of property that she is trying to sell to Carlos. Mercedes knows that a local ordinance prohibits building anything higher than three stories on the property. Nonetheless, she tells Carlos, "You can build an office building fifty stories high if you want to." Carlos buys the land and later discovers that Mercedes's statement is false.

Can Carlos avoid the contract? Normally, Carlos cannot avoid the contract, because under the common law, people are assumed to know easily researched state and local laws. Today, these laws are readily available on the Internet.

In general, a person should not rely on a nonlawyer's statement about a point of law. Exceptions to this rule occur when the misrepresenting party is in a profession known to require greater knowledge of the law than the average citizen possesses.

Misrepresentation by Silence Ordinarily, neither party to a contract has a duty to come forward and disclose facts, and a contract normally will not be set aside because certain pertinent information is not volunteered. **EXAMPLE 14.5** Norah does not have to tell potential buyers that a car she is selling has been in an accident unless they ask. ◄

If a serious defect or a serious potential problem is known to the seller but cannot reasonably be suspected by the buyer, however, the seller may have a duty to speak. **EXAMPLE 14.6** If River City fails to disclose to bidders subsoil conditions that will cause great expense in constructing a sewer system, the city is guilty of fraud. ◄

14–2b Intent to Deceive

The second element of fraud is knowledge on the part of the misrepresenting party that facts have been falsely represented. This element, normally called *scienter* (pronounced sy-*en*-ter), or "guilty knowledge," usually signifies that there was an *intent to deceive*.

Scienter clearly exists if a party knows that a fact is not as stated. **EXAMPLE 14.7** Robert applied for a position as a business law professor. He said

scienter

The knowledge by the misrepresenting party that material facts have been falsely represented or omitted with an intent to deceive.

that he had been a corporate president for several years and had taught business law at another college. Neither claim was true. After he was hired, his probation officer alerted the school to his criminal history. The school immediately fired him. Robert sued for breach of his employment contract. Robert is unlikely to win his suit because he clearly engaged in an attempt to deceive the college. Furthermore, the college justifiably relied on his misrepresentations. ◄

Scienter also exists if a party makes a statement that he or she believes not to be true or makes a statement recklessly, without regard to whether it is true or false. Finally, this element is met if a party says or implies that a statement is made on some basis, such as personal knowledge or personal investigation, when it is not.

14–2c Reliance on the Misrepresentation

The third element of fraud is reasonably *justifiable reliance* on the misrepresentation of fact. The deceived party must have a justifiable reason for relying on the misrepresentation. The misrepresentation must also be an important factor (but not necessarily the sole factor) in inducing the party to enter into the contract.

Real-World Case Example

Clifford Cronkelton negotiated with Patrick Shivley to buy a car wash in Bellefontaine, Ohio. Before the sale closed, Shivley told Cronkelton that the property had been winterized. When Cronkelton opened the door, however, it was clear that the entire facility had frozen up. Cronkelton filed a suit in an Ohio state court against Shivley—and Guaranteed Construction Services, LLC, which had been hired to winterize the property—claiming fraud. Based on a jury verdict in Cronkelton's favor, and an award of more than $140,000 in damages, the defendants appealed.

Did Cronkelton justifiably rely on Shivley's representation that the car wash had been winterized? Yes. In a 2013 case, *Cronkelton v. Guaranteed Construction Services, LLC,* a state intermediate appellate court affirmed the lower court's judgment. The jury found that Cronkelton had reasonably relied on Shivley's representations, and that the lower court's finding was supported by "competent, credible evidence," including Shivley's guaranty by e-mail that everything had been taken care of.

Reliance is not justified if the innocent party knows the true facts or relies on obviously extravagant statements. If the defects in a piece of property are obvious, the buyer cannot justifiably rely on the seller's misrepresentations concerning those defects. **EXAMPLE 14.8** Dylan, a used-car salesman, tells Shelby, "This old Chevy Trailblazer SUV will get more than sixty miles per gallon." Shelby cannot justifiably rely on Dylan's statement because the fact is obviously not accurate. ◄

If the defects are hidden or *latent*—that is, not apparent on examination—the buyer is justified in relying on the seller's statements. **EXAMPLE 14.9** Michael and Ruth are directors at North Country Bank. Michael induces Ruth to sign a statement saying their bank has sufficient assets to meet its financial obligations by telling her, "We have plenty of assets to satisfy our creditors." This statement is false, however. If Ruth knows the true facts, or as bank director, should know the true facts, she is not justified in relying on Michael's statement. If Ruth does not know the true facts, and has no way of finding them out, she may be justified on her reliance of the statement. ◄

14-2d Injury to the Innocent Party

For a person to recover damages based on fraud, proof of an injury is required. The measure of damages is ordinarily equal to the property's value had it been delivered as represented, less the actual price paid for the property. In actions based on fraud, courts also often award punitive, or exemplary, damages. Punitive damages are granted to a plaintiff over and above the proved, actual compensation for the loss. These damages are based on the public-policy consideration of *punishing* the defendant or setting an example for similar wrongdoers.

Most courts do not require a showing of injury when the action is to rescind (cancel) the contract. Because rescission returns the parties to the position they were in prior to the contract, a showing of injury to the innocent party is unnecessary.

 ## 14-3 UNDUE INFLUENCE

undue influence
Persuasion that is less than actual force but more than advice and that induces a person to act according to the will or purposes of the dominating party.

Undue influence arises from relationships in which one party can greatly influence another party, thus overcoming that party's free will. Minors and elderly people are often under the influence of guardians. **EXAMPLE 14.10** Susan has been Edith's in-home caregiver for several years. Edith is nearly eighty years old and in frail health. One afternoon, Susan convinces Edith to review her will. Together, they rework the will so that Susan will receive a large portion of Edith's estate. Susan convinces Edith that she, and not Edith's two sons, deserves the money more. Susan also implies that she will quit her job if she cannot be a beneficiary of Edith's will. Susan has used undue influence to make Edith act in a way that she would not have done ordinarily. ◄

Undue influence can arise from a number of confidential relationships or relationships founded on trust, including attorney-client, doctor-patient, and trustee-beneficiary relationships. The essential feature of undue influence is that the party being taken advantage of does not, in reality, exercise free will in entering into a contract. A contract entered into under excessive or undue influence lacks voluntary consent and is therefore voidable.

LEARNING OUTCOME 4

Recognize the difference between undue influence and duress.

 ## 14-4 DURESS

duress
Unlawful, forceful pressure brought to bear on a person, overcoming that person's free will and causing him or her to do what he or she otherwise would not have done.

Consent to the terms of a contract is not voluntary if one of the parties is *forced* into the agreement. Recognizing this, the courts allow that party to rescind the contract. Forcing a party to enter into a contract under the fear of threats is legally defined as **duress.** Duress is both a defense to the enforcement of a contract and a ground for rescission of a contract. Therefore, the party on whom the duress is exerted can choose to carry out the contract or to avoid the entire transaction. (The wronged party usually has this choice when consent is not voluntary.)

Economic need generally is not sufficient to constitute duress, even when one party exacts a very high price for an item that the other party needs. If the party exacting the price also creates the need, however, *economic duress* may be found.

 ### ANSWERING THE LEGAL PROBLEM

In the legal problem set out at the beginning of this chapter, David signed a contract to buy ten acres of land in Idaho.

A If David wanted to buy the land because he believed that he could resell it at a profit to Harcourt, could David avoid the contract if it later turned out that he was

mistaken? Not likely. David's overestimation of the value of the land or of Harcourt's desire to buy it is an ordinary risk of business. Thus, a court normally will not provide relief for David.

TERMS AND CONCEPTS FOR REVIEW

bilateral mistake 180	*scienter* 182	unilateral mistake 179
duress 184	undue influence 184	voluntary consent 179

CHAPTER SUMMARY—VOLUNTARY CONSENT

LEARNING OUTCOME	
1	**State the difference between mistakes of fact and mistakes of value or quality.** A mistake of fact involves a material fact—one that is important to the subject matter of the contract. Only a mistake of fact can give a party the right to relief under a contract. If the mistake is unilateral, the mistaken party is bound unless (1) the other party knows or should have known of the mistake or (2) the mistake is an inadvertent mathematical error. If the mistake is mutual, either party can rescind the contract. In contrast to a mistake of fact, a mistake that concerns the future market value or quality of the object of the contract normally does not serve as a basis for avoiding a contract.
2	**List the elements of fraudulent misrepresentation.** The elements of fraud are (1) a misrepresentation of a material fact, (2) an intent to deceive, and (3) an innocent party's reliance on the misrepresentation. To recover damages, the innocent party must suffer an injury.
3	**Contrast misrepresentation of a material fact and misrepresentation of law.** A material fact is objective and verifiable (in contrast to an opinion, which is subject to debate). A misrepresentation of a material fact can serve as the basis for relief under a contract. A misrepresentation of law usually does not entitle a party to be relieved of a contract. People are assumed to know the law.
4	**Recognize the difference between undue influence and duress.** Undue influence—persuasion that is less than force but more than advice—can occur in a confidential relationship or a relationship founded on trust, in which one party can greatly influence another party, overcoming the other's free will. Duress—unlawful pressure through the fear of a threat—causes a party to do what he or she would not otherwise have done. A contract entered into under undue influence or duress is voidable.

ISSUE SPOTTERS

Check your answers to the *Issue Spotters* against the answers provided in Appendix C at the end of this text.

1. Brad, an accountant, files Dina's tax returns. When the Internal Revenue Service assesses a large tax against Dina, she retains Brad to contest the assessment. The day before the deadline for replying to the IRS, Brad tells Dina that unless she pays a higher fee, he will withdraw. If Dina agrees to pay, is the contract enforceable? Explain your answer. (See *Duress*.)

2. In selling a house, Matt tells Ann that the wiring, fixtures, and appliances are of a certain quality. Matt knows nothing about the quality, but it is not as specified. Ann buys the house. On learning the true quality, Ann confronts Matt. He says he wasn't trying to fool her, he was only trying to make a sale. Can she rescind the deal? Why or why not? (See *Fraudulent Misrepresentation*.)

USING BUSINESS LAW

14–1. Undue Influence. Jerome is an elderly man who lives with his nephew, Philip. Jerome is totally dependent on Philip's support. Philip tells Jerome that unless Jerome transfers a tract of land he owns to Philip for a price 15 percent below market value, Philip will no longer support and take care of him. Jerome enters into the contract. Discuss fully whether Jerome can set aside this contract. (See *Undue Influence*.)

14–2. Fraudulent Misrepresentation. Grano owns a forty-room motel on Highway 100. Tanner is interested in purchasing the motel. During the course of negotiations, Grano tells Tanner that the motel netted $30,000 last year

and that it will net at least $45,000 next year. The motel books, which Grano turns over to Tanner before the purchase, clearly show that Grano's motel netted only $15,000 last year. Also, Grano fails to tell Tanner that a bypass to Highway 100 is being planned that will redirect most traffic away from the front of the motel. Tanner purchases the motel. During the first year under Tanner's operation, the motel nets $18,000. At this time, Tanner learns of the previous low profitability of the motel and the planned bypass. Tanner wants his money back from Grano. Discuss fully Tanner's probable success in getting his money back. (See *Fraudulent Misrepresentation*.)

REAL-WORLD CASE PROBLEMS

14–3. Fraudulent Misrepresentation. Joy Pervis and Brenda Pauley worked together as talent agents in Georgia. When Pervis "discovered" actress Dakota Fanning, Pervis sent Fanning's audition tape to Cindy Osbrink, a talent agent in California. Osbrink agreed to represent Fanning in California and to pay 3 percent of Osbrink's commissions to Pervis and Pauley, who agreed to split the payments equally. Six years later, Pervis told Pauley that their agreement with Osbrink had expired and there would be no more payments. Nevertheless, Pervis continued to receive payments from Osbrink. Each time Pauley asked about commissions, however, Pervis replied that she was not receiving any. Do these facts evidence fraud? Explain. [*In re Pervis*, 512 Bankr. 348 (N.D.Ga. 2014)] (See *Fraudulent Misrepresentation*.)

14–4. Bilateral Mistake. When Steven Simkin divorced Laura Blank, they agreed to split their assets equally. At the time, they owned an account with Bernard L. Madoff Investment Securities estimated to be worth $5.4 million.

Simkin kept the account and paid Blank more than $6.5 million, which included $2.7 million specifically to offset the amount of the funds that they both believed were in the Madoff account. Later, they learned that the account had no funds due to fraud on the part of Madoff. Could their divorce agreement be rescinded on the basis of a mistake? Discuss. [*Simkin v. Blank*, 80 A.D.3d 401, 915 N.Y.S.2d 47 (1 Dept. 2011)] (See *Mistakes*.)

14–5. Fraudulent Misrepresentation. Charter One Bank owned a fifteen-story commercial building. A fire inspector identified a number of defects in the building's drinking-water and fire-suppression systems. Without disclosing this information, Charter sold the building to Northpoint Properties, Inc. Northpoint spent $280,000 to repair the water and fire-suppression systems and filed a suit against Charter One. Is the seller liable for not disclosing the building's defects? Discuss. [*Northpoint Properties, Inc. v. Charter One Bank*, __ N.E.2d __ (Ohio App. 8 Dist. 2011)] (See *Fraudulent Misrepresentation*.)

ETHICAL QUESTIONS

14–6. Fraudulent Misrepresentation. Is honesty an implicit duty of every employee? Discuss. (See *Fraudulent Misrepresentation*.)

14–7. Fraudulent Misrepresentation. Radiah Givens was involved romantically with Joseph Rosenzweig. She moved into an apartment on which he made the down payment. She signed the mortgage, but he made the payments and paid household expenses. They later married. She had

their marriage annulled, however, when she learned that he was married to someone else. Rosenzweig then filed a suit against her to collect on the mortgage. Did Rosenzweig commit fraud? Was he deceitful? If so, should his deceitfulness affect the decision in this case? Discuss. [*Rosenzweig v. Givens*, 62 A.D.3d 1, 879 N.Y.S.2d 387 (2009)] (See *Fraudulent Misrepresentation*.)

Chapter 14—Work Set

TRUE-FALSE QUESTIONS

_____ 1. A contract involving a mistake of fact can sometimes be avoided.

_____ 2. When both parties to a contract are mistaken as to the same material fact, the contract cannot be rescinded by either party.

_____ 3. To commit fraudulent misrepresentation, one party must intend to mislead another.

_____ 4. In an action to rescind a contract for fraudulent misrepresentation, proof of injury is required for damages to be awarded.

_____ 5. The essential feature of undue influence is that the party taken advantage of does not exercise free will.

_____ 6. If a person makes a statement that he or she believes to be true, he or she cannot be held liable for misrepresentation.

_____ 7. A seller has no duty to disclose to a buyer a defect that is known to the seller but could not reasonably be suspected by the buyer.

_____ 8. When both parties make a mistake as to the future market value of the object of their contract, the contract can be rescinded by either party.

_____ 9. A contract entered into under duress is voidable.

MULTIPLE-CHOICE QUESTIONS

_____ 1. Metro Transport asks for bids on a construction project. Metro estimates that the cost will be $200,000. Most bids are about $200,000, but EZ Construction bids $150,000. In adding a column of figures, EZ mistakenly omitted a $50,000 item. Because Metro had reason to know of the mistake

  a. Metro can enforce the contract.
  b. EZ can increase the price and enforce the contract at the higher price.
  c. EZ can avoid the contract.
  d. none of the above.

_____ 2. To induce Sam to buy a lot in Mel's development, Mel tells Sam that he intends to add a golf course. The terrain is suitable, and there is enough land, but Mel has no intention of adding a golf course. Sam is induced by the statement to buy a lot. Sam's reliance on Mel's statement is justified because

  a. Mel is the owner of the development.
  b. Sam does not know the truth and has no way of finding it out.
  c. Sam did not buy the golf course.
  d. the golf course had obviously not been built yet.

_____ 3. Bob agrees to sell ten shares of Black Bear Corporation stock to Pam. Neither party knows whether the stock will increase or decrease in value. Pam believes that it will increase in value. If she is mistaken, her mistake will

  a. justify voiding the contract.
  b. not justify voiding the contract.
  c. justify a refund to her from Bob of the difference.
  d. justify a payment from her to Bob of the difference.

_____ 4. In an e-mail message offering to sell amplifiers to Gina for her theater, Dick describes the 120-watt amplifiers as "210 watts per channel." This is fraudulent misrepresentation if

   a. the number of watts is a material fact.
   b. Dick intended to deceive Gina.
   c. Gina relies on the description.
   d. all of the above are true.

_____ 5. Ken, who is not a real estate broker, sells Global Associates some land. Which of the following statements by Ken, with the accompanying circumstance, would be a fraudulent misrepresentation in that sale?

   a. "This acreage offers the most spectacular view of the valley." From higher up the mountain, more of the valley is visible.
   b. "You can build an office building here." The county requires the property to be exclusively residential, but neither Ken nor Global knows that.
   c. "This property includes ninety acres." Ken knows it includes only eighty acres.
   d. "The value of this property will triple in five years." Ken does not know whether the value of the property will triple in five years.

_____ 6. Adam persuades Beth to contract for his company's services by telling her that his employees are "the best and the brightest." Adam's statement is

   a. duress.
   b. fraud.
   c. opinion.
   d. undue influence.

_____ 7. In selling a warehouse to A&B Enterprises, Ray does not disclose that the foundation was built on unstable pilings. A&B may later avoid the contract on the ground of

   a. misrepresentation.
   b. undue influence.
   c. duress.
   d. none of the above.

 ## ANSWERING MORE LEGAL PROBLEMS

1. Trulov.com is an online dating site. Trulov allows subscribers to create profiles, browse other profiles, take a relationship test, use the site's computerized matching system, and exchange messages. Browsing through profiles, Sophia, a subscriber, notices that many use the same phrases and photos. She files a suit against Trulov, alleging that the site created and posted false profiles of nonexistent "potential matches" to attract subscribers.

   Has Trulov committed fraudulent misrepresentation? Yes. Fraud requires (1) a _____ of a material fact, (2) an intent to deceive, and (3) an innocent party's justifiable reliance on the _____. To recover damages, the innocent party must also suffer an injury. Trulov created and posted bogus user profiles to entice new subscribers and retain old ones. This constituted _____ of material facts with an intent to deceive. Some new subscribers and some renewing subscribers relied on Trulov's _____. Damages include the expense of initiating or continuing subscriptions.

2. Lionel, a Trulov subscriber, browses other profiles and contacts some of the subscribers. He discovers that the profiles many of the members created for themselves exaggerate their physical appearance, intelligence, experiences, accomplishments, and occupations. Trulov's policy is to remove a subscriber's profile when such deception is revealed.

   Is Trulov liable for fraud in these circumstances? No. Fraud requires a _____ of a material fact, as well as an intent to deceive. The intent is knowledge on the part of the _____ party that facts have been falsely represented. There is clearly _____ in these circumstances. It occurred through the exaggerated profiles created and posted by individual subscribers. Unless Trulov knew that the profiles were false and allowed them to remain despite its stated policy, however, there is no _____ nor intent to deceive on its part.

WRITTEN CONTRACTS

FACING A LEGAL PROBLEM

Regional Community College forms a contract with Yolanda to teach three courses in business law during the next academic year (September 15 through June 15). Janine enters into a contract to provide security for the college's student center as long as the college needs the service.

  Q Do these two contracts have to be in writing to be enforceable? Why or why not?

A contract that is otherwise valid may be unenforceable if it is not in the proper **form**—that is, in writing. Certain types of contracts are required by law to be in writing. If there is no written evidence of the contract, it may not be enforceable. In this chapter, we examine the kinds of contracts that require a writing under what is called the *Statute of Frauds*. We conclude the chapter with a discussion of the *parol evidence rule*, under which courts determine the admissibility at trial of evidence extraneous (external) to written contracts.

15–1 THE STATUTE OF FRAUDS— WRITING REQUIREMENT

Every state has a statute that stipulates what types of contracts must be in writing. We refer to such a statute as the **Statute of Frauds.** The actual name of the Statute of Frauds is misleading because the statute does not apply to fraud. Rather, it denies enforceability to certain contracts that do not comply with its requirements. The primary purpose of the statute is to prevent harm to innocent parties by requiring written evidence of agreements concerning important transactions.

Essentially, the Statute of Frauds requires certain contracts to be in writing or be evidenced by a written memorandum. A contract that is oral when it is required to be in writing will not, as a rule, be enforced by the courts. Although the statutes vary slightly from state to state, all require the following types of contracts to be in writing or evidenced by a written memorandum:

1. Contracts involving interests in land.
2. Contracts that cannot *by their terms* be performed within one year from the day after the contract's formation.
3. Collateral contracts, such as promises to answer for the debt or duty of another.
4. Promises made in consideration of marriage.
5. Under the Uniform Commercial Code, contracts for the sale of goods priced at $500 or more.

LEARNING OUTCOMES

The four Learning Outcomes below are designed to help improve your understanding of the chapter. After reading this chapter, you should be able to:

1 Identify contracts that must be in writing under the Statute of Frauds.

2 Describe what satisfies the writing requirement under the Statute of Frauds.

3 State the parol evidence rule.

4 List circumstances in which parol evidence is admissible.

form
The manner observed in creating a legal agreement, as opposed to the substance of the agreement.

Statute of Frauds
A state statute under which certain types of contracts must be in writing to be enforceable.

LEARNING OUTCOME 1

Identify contracts that must be in writing under the Statute of Frauds.

15–1a Contracts Involving Interests in Land

Under the Statute of Frauds, a contract involving an interest in land must be in writing. Land is real property and includes all physical objects that are permanently attached to the land, such as buildings, plants, and trees. A contract calling for the sale of land is not enforceable unless it is in writing or evidenced by a written memorandum. **EXAMPLE 15.1** Lewis is a party to an oral contract with Maria involving a vineyard. Neither Lewis nor Maria can force the other to buy or sell the land that is the subject of their contract. The Statute of Frauds is a defense to the enforcement of this contract. ◂

A contract for the sale of land ordinarily involves the entire interest in the real property, including buildings, growing crops, vegetation, minerals, timber, and anything else affixed to the land. Therefore, a **fixture** (personal property so affixed or so used as to become a part of the real property) is treated as real property. Anything else, however, such as a couch, is treated as personal property.

fixture
Personal property attached to real property in such a way that it is part of that real property.

15–1b The One-Year Rule

A contract that cannot, *by its own terms,* be performed within one year *from the day after* the contract is formed must be in writing to be enforceable. Because disputes over such contracts are unlikely to occur until some time after the contracts are made, resolution of these disputes is difficult unless the contract terms have been put in writing. The one-year period begins to run *the day after the contract is made.* **EXAMPLE 15.2** Isabella enters into a contract with Diamond Auto Body & Paint in August, stating that she will provide accounting services to Diamond during the firm's coming fiscal year, which begins October 1 and continues until September 30. Because the contract is formed in August, it must be in writing to be enforceable—because it cannot be performed within one year. ◂

Exhibit 15.1 graphically illustrates the one-year rule. The idea behind this rule is that a witness's memory is not to be trusted for longer than a year.

If Performance Is Objectively Impossible Note that for a particular contract to fall under the one-year rule, contract performance must be *objectively impossible* to complete within a year. For instance, a contract to provide five crops of tomatoes

EXHIBIT 15.1   The One-Year Rule

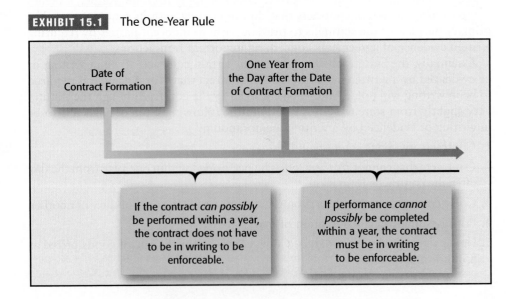

to be grown on a specific farm in Illinois would be impossible to perform within a year. It is impossible to grow five crops of tomatoes on the same farmland in a single year in Illinois.

If Performance Is Possible If the contract, by its terms, makes performance within the year *possible* (even if not probable), the contract does not fall within the Statute of Frauds and need not be in writing. **EXAMPLE 15.3** Jason agrees to provide office-cleaning services for Omar's Imports for as long as the company needs his services. This means the contract could be fully performed within a year because Omar's could go out of business within twelve months. Thus, the contract need not be in writing to be enforceable. ◄

15–1c Collateral Promises

A **collateral promise** is one that is secondary to a principal transaction or primary contractual relationship. In other words, a collateral promise is one made by a third party to assume the debts or obligations of a primary party to a contract if the primary party does *not* perform. Any collateral promise of this nature falls under the Statute of Frauds and therefore must be in writing to be enforceable.

collateral promise
A secondary promise, such as a promise made by one person to pay the debts of another if the latter fails to perform.

Primary versus Secondary Obligations To understand this concept, it is important to distinguish between primary and secondary promises and obligations. You commit yourself to a primary obligation when you agree to pay for something. You commit yourself to a secondary obligation when you agree to pay for something *on the condition that* a certain other party does not make the payment.

HIGHLIGHTING THE POINT

Pablo contracts with Joanne's Floral Boutique to send his mother a dozen roses for Mother's Day. Pablo promises to pay for the roses when he receives the bill. On the same day, Pablo's mother borrows $10,000 from the Medford Bank. Pablo promises the bank that he will pay the $10,000 if his mother does not repay the loan on time.

Which of these promises must be in writing to be enforceable under the Statute of Frauds? In contracting for the roses, Pablo incurs a *primary* obligation. This contract does not fall under the Statute of Frauds and does not have to be in writing to be enforceable. If Pablo fails to pay the florist and the florist sues him for payment, Pablo cannot raise the Statute of Frauds as a defense. He cannot claim that the contract is unenforceable because it was not in writing.

Pablo's promise to repay his mother's debt is a *secondary* obligation and must be in writing if the bank wants to enforce it. Pablo, in this situation, becomes a *guarantor* of the loan—that is, he guarantees that he will pay back the loan if his mother fails to do so.

An Exception—The "Main Purpose" Rule An oral promise to answer for the debt of another is covered by the Statute of Frauds *unless* the guarantor's main purpose in accepting secondary liability is to secure a personal benefit. This type of contract need not be in writing. The assumption is that a court can infer from the circumstances of a case whether the main, or "leading," objective of the promisor was to secure a personal benefit and thus, in effect, to answer for his or her own debt.

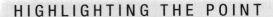

HIGHLIGHTING THE POINT

Frances contracts with Machio Manufacturing Company to have some machines made to detailed specifications for her factory. She promises Allrite Supply Company, Machio's supplier, that if Allrite continues to deliver materials to Machio, Frances will guarantee payment.

Under the Statute of Frauds, does this promise need to be in writing to be enforceable? No. This promise need not be in writing, even though the effect may be to pay the debt of another, because Frances's main purpose is to secure a benefit for herself.

Another typical application of the so-called main purpose doctrine occurs when one creditor guarantees a debtor's debt to another creditor to prevent litigation. This allows the debtor to remain in business long enough to generate profits sufficient to pay *both* creditors.

15–1d Promises Made in Consideration of Marriage

A unilateral promise to pay a sum of money or to give property in consideration of a promise to marry must be in writing. **EXAMPLE 15.4** Ralph promises to pay Stewart $10,000 if he agrees to marry Ralph's daughter Taylor. This promise must be in writing. ◄

The same rule applies to **prenuptial agreements.** These agreements are made before marriage and define each partner's ownership rights in the other partner's property. Prenuptial arrangements made in consideration of marriage must be in writing to be enforceable.

Generally, courts tend to give more credence to prenuptial agreements that are accompanied by consideration. **EXAMPLE 15.5** Maureen, who is not wealthy, marries Kaiser, who has a net worth of $300 million. Kaiser has several children, and he wants them to receive most of his wealth on his death. Before their marriage, Maureen and Kaiser draft and sign a prenuptial agreement in which Kaiser promises to give Maureen $100,000 per year for the rest of her life if they divorce. As consideration for consenting to this amount, Kaiser offers Maureen $1 million. If Maureen consents to the agreement and accepts the $1 million, very likely a court would hold that this prenuptial agreement is valid, should it ever be contested. ◄

prenuptial agreement
An agreement entered into in contemplation of marriage, specifying the rights and ownership of the parties' property.

15–1e Contracts for the Sale of Goods

The UCC includes Statute of Frauds provisions that require written evidence or an electronic record of a contract. Section 2–201 requires a writing or memorandum for a sale of goods priced at $500 or more. (Section 2–201 of the UCC is included in Appendix B.) A writing that will satisfy the UCC requirement need only state the quantity term. Other terms need not be stated "accurately" in the writing, as long as they adequately reflect both parties' intentions.

The contract will not be enforceable for any quantity greater than that set forth in the writing. In addition, the writing must have been signed by the person to be charged—that is, by the person who refuses to perform or the one being sued. Beyond these two requirements, the writing need not designate the buyer or the seller, the terms of payment, or the price.

15–1f Exceptions to the Statute of Frauds

Exceptions to the applicability of the Statute of Frauds are made in certain situations. These include partial performance, admissions, and promissory estoppel.

Partial Performance In cases involving contracts for the transfer of interests in land, partial performance may create an exception. If the purchaser has paid part of the price, taken possession, and made permanent improvements to the property (such as by building a house on the land), a court may grant *specific performance*—that is, performance of the contract according to its precise terms. In such situations, the parties cannot be returned to the positions they held before their contract was formed.

Whether the courts will enforce an oral contract for an interest in land when partial performance has taken place is usually determined by the degree of injury that would be suffered if the court did not enforce the oral contract. In some states, mere reliance on an oral contract is enough to remove it from the Statute of Frauds.

Under the UCC, an oral contract is enforceable to the extent that a seller accepts payment or a buyer accepts delivery of the goods. **EXAMPLE 15.6** Natural Grocers orders twenty bushels of apples from Valley Orchards. After ten bushels have been delivered and accepted, Natural Grocers cancels the contract. Valley Orchards could enforce the contract to the extent of the ten bushels accepted by Natural Grocers. ◄

Partial performance can unmistakably indicate an understanding that a contract is in effect. Clearly, the party who provides performance believes that there is a contract. So, too, does the party who accepts that performance.

Real-World Case Example

NYKCool A.B. is one of the world's largest operators of maritime transportation for hire with a fleet of more than fifty ships. Pacific Fruit, Inc., exports cargo from Ecuador. NYKCool and Pacific entered into an oral contract, under which NYKCool agreed to transport weekly shipments of bananas from Ecuador to California and Japan. After more than two years of performance, a dispute arose between the parties. An arbitrator held Pacific liable for nearly $9 million for breach of contract. Pacific appealed.

Did the parties' performance establish that they had formed a binding agreement? Yes. In a 2013 case, *NYKCool A.B. v. Pacific Fruit, Inc.,* the U.S. Court of Appeals for the Second Circuit affirmed the arbitrator's award. "The parties' substantial partial performance on the contract weighs strongly in favor of contract formation." NYKCool transported thirty million boxes of cargo for Pacific during more than one hundred trips for which Pacific paid $70 million. Both parties believed themselves to be subject to a binding agreement.

Admissions In some states, if a party against whom enforcement of an oral contract is sought "admits" in pleadings, testimony, or otherwise in court that a contract for sale was made, the contract will be enforceable. A contract subject to the UCC will be enforceable, but only to the extent of the quantity admitted.

EXAMPLE 15.7 Rachel, the president of Bistro Corporation, admits under oath that an oral agreement was made with Commercial Kitchens, Inc., to buy certain equipment for $10,000. A court will enforce the agreement only to the extent admitted ($10,000), even if Commercial Kitchens claims that the agreement involved $20,000 worth of equipment. ◄

Promissory Estoppel In some states, an oral contract that would otherwise be unenforceable under the Statute of Frauds may be enforced under the doctrine of promissory estoppel, or detrimental reliance. If a promisor makes a promise on which the promisee justifiably relies to his or her detriment, a court may *estop* (prevent) the promisor from denying that a contract exists. In these circumstances, an oral promise can be enforceable if two requirements are met:

1. The person making the promise must foresee that the promisee will rely on it.
2. There must be no way to avoid injustice except to enforce the promise.

EXAMPLE 15.8 John orally promises to give Ann, the manager of his farm, a certain plot of land if she achieves a specific level of success with the farm. Once Ann has performed, John normally will be held to the promise.◄

Special Exceptions under the UCC Special exceptions to the applicability of the Statute of Frauds apply to sales contracts. Oral contracts for customized goods may be enforced in certain circumstances. Another exception has to do with oral contracts *between merchants* that have been confirmed in writing (see Chapter 18).

 # 15–2 THE SUFFICIENCY OF THE WRITING

All contracts should be fully set forth in a writing signed by all of the parties. This ensures that if any problems arise concerning performance of the contract, a written agreement fully specifying the performance promised by each party can be introduced into court. The Statute of Frauds requires either a written contract or a written memorandum signed by the party against whom enforcement is sought.

15–2a Memorandums

A *written memorandum* can consist of any confirmation, invoice, sales slip, check, or e-mail. Any one or any combination of these items may constitute a writing that satisfies the Statute of Frauds. In addition, a written contract need not consist of a single document to constitute an enforceable contract. One document may incorporate another document by expressly referring to it. Several documents may form a single contract if they are physically attached by staple, paper clip, or glue, or even if they are only placed in the same envelope.

15–2b Essential Terms

A memorandum evidencing an oral contract must contain the essential terms of the contract. Under the UCC, for a sale of goods the writing need only name the quantity term and be signed by the party being charged. Under most provisions of the Statute of Frauds, the writing must name the parties, subject matter, consideration, and quantity. Contracts for the sale of land must state the *essential* terms of the contract (such as location and price) and describe the property with sufficient clarity to allow the terms to be determined from the memo, without reference to any outside sources.

15–2c Signatures

A party's signature need not be placed at the end of a written memorandum but can be anywhere in the writing. It can even be initials rather than the full name. Only the party to be held liable on the contract need have signed the writing. Therefore, a contract may be enforceable by one of its parties but not by the other. **EXAMPLE 15.9** Troy, who signs a memo setting out the essential terms of an oral contract, can be held to those terms. The other party, Wilma, who signed nothing, can plead the Statute of Frauds as a defense. Thus, the contract cannot be enforced against Wilma.◄

e-signature
An electronic sound, symbol, or process attached to or logically associated with a record and executed or adopted by a person with the intent to sign the record.

An **e-signature** is "an electronic sound, symbol, or process attached to or logically associated with a record and executed or adopted by a person with the intent to sign the record," according to the Uniform Electronic Transactions Act (UETA). A party's name typed at the end of an e-mail note, for instance, meets this signature requirement.

Under the UETA—as well as under the Electronic Signatures in Global and National Commerce Act (E-SIGN Act), which is a federal law—a record or signature may not be denied legal effect solely because it is in electronic form. In other words, an e-signature is as valid as a signature on paper, and an e-document is as enforceable as a paper one. (See the *Linking Business Law to Your Career* feature at the end of the chapter.)

15–3 THE PAROL EVIDENCE RULE

Sometimes, a written contract does not include—or contradicts—an oral understanding reached by the parties before or at the time of contracting. When a dispute arises in such situations, the courts look to a common law rule governing the admissibility of oral evidence in court, or *parol evidence*.

Under the **parol evidence rule,** if a court finds that the parties intended their written contract to be a complete and final statement of their agreement, then it will not allow either party to present *parol evidence*—that is, testimony or other evidence of communications between the parties not contained in the contract itself. In other words, a party normally cannot introduce evidence of the parties' prior negotiations—nor any existing oral agreements—to a court if that evidence contradicts or varies the terms of the parties' written contract.

LEARNING OUTCOME 3
State the parol evidence rule.

parol evidence rule
A rule of contracts under which a court will not receive into evidence oral statements that contradict a written agreement.

15–3a Exceptions to the Parol Evidence Rule

Because of the rigidity of the parol evidence rule, courts make several exceptions. These exceptions are discussed next.

Contracts Subsequently Modified Evidence of a *subsequent modification* of a written contract can be introduced into court. Keep in mind that the oral modifications may not be enforceable if they come under the Statute of Frauds—for example, if they increase the price of the goods for sale to $500 or more or increase the term for performance to more than one year. Also, oral modifications will not be enforceable if the original contract provides that any modification must be in writing.

LEARNING OUTCOME 4
List circumstances in which parol evidence is admissible.

Voidable or Void Contracts Oral evidence can be introduced in all cases to show that the contract was voidable or void (for example, induced by mistake or fraudulent misrepresentation). If deception led one of the parties to agree to the terms of a written contract, oral evidence attesting to fraud should not be excluded. Courts frown on bad faith and are quick to allow such evidence when it establishes fraud.

Ambiguous Terms When the terms of a written contract are ambiguous or not clear, evidence is admissible to show the meaning of the terms.

Incomplete Contracts Evidence is admissible when the written contract is incomplete in that it lacks one or more of the essential terms. The courts allow evidence to "fill in the gaps."

Customary Practices Under the UCC, evidence can be introduced to explain or supplement a written contract by showing a *prior dealing, course of performance,* or *usage of trade.* It is sufficient to say that when buyers and sellers deal with each other over extended periods of time, certain customary practices develop. The parties often overlook these practices when writing the contract, so courts allow the introduction of evidence to show how the parties have acted in the past.

An Orally Agreed-on Condition The parol evidence rule does not apply if the existence of the entire written contract is subject to an orally agreed-on condition. Proof of the condition does not *alter* or *modify* the written terms but involves the *enforceability* of the written contract.

EXAMPLE 15.10 A lease between the city of Cheddar Bay and Romano, the owner of Monterey Corporate Office Suites, is subject to the approval of the city council. This approval is a condition required for the formation of the lease. If a dispute arises over the lease, the parol evidence rule will not apply. Oral evidence will be admissible to show whether the council has approved the terms and thus whether the lease is enforceable. ◄

Obvious Errors When an obvious clerical error exists that clearly would not represent the agreement of the parties, parol evidence is admissible to correct the error. For instance, a written lease provides for monthly rent of $300 rather than the $3,000 orally agreed to by the parties. Thus, parol evidence will be admissible to correct the obvious mistake.

15–3b Integrated Contracts

integrated contract
A written contract that constitutes the final expression of the parties' agreement.

The key in determining whether parol evidence will be allowed is whether the written contract is intended to be a complete and final embodiment of the terms of the agreement. If it is so intended, it is referred to as an **integrated contract,** and outside evidence is excluded. If it is only partially integrated, evidence of consistent additional terms is admissible to supplement the written agreement. Exhibit 15.2 illustrates the relationship between integrated contracts and the parol evidence rule.

EXHIBIT 15.2 The Parol Evidence Rule

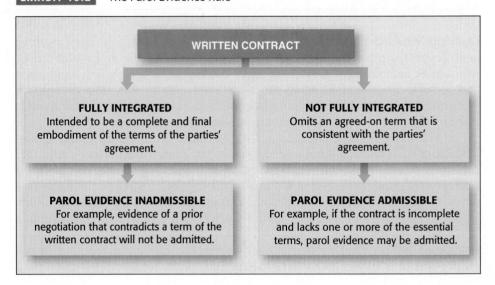

WRITTEN CONTRACT

FULLY INTEGRATED
Intended to be a complete and final embodiment of the terms of the parties' agreement.

NOT FULLY INTEGRATED
Omits an agreed-on term that is consistent with the parties' agreement.

PAROL EVIDENCE INADMISSIBLE
For example, evidence of a prior negotiation that contradicts a term of the written contract will not be admitted.

PAROL EVIDENCE ADMISSIBLE
For example, if the contract is incomplete and lacks one or more of the essential terms, parol evidence may be admitted.

ANSWERING THE LEGAL PROBLEM

In the legal problem set out at the beginning of this chapter, Regional Community College contracted with Yolanda to teach courses in business law during the next academic year, which ends June 15, and with Janine to provide security for the student center as long as the college needs it.

A **Do these two contracts have to be in writing to be enforceable?** Under the Statute of Frauds, a contract that cannot, by its own terms, be performed within one year from the day after the contract is formed must be in writing to be enforceable. Thus, if Yolanda's contract were formed before June 14 of the preceding year, it would need to be in writing to be enforceable, because it could not be performed within one year. If the contract were formed after June 14, however, it would not need to be in writing, because it would be performed within one year. Similarly, Janine's contract does not need to be in writing, because it could be performed within one year—the college's need for her services could run out within twelve months.

LINKING BUSINESS LAW to Your Career

ENFORCEABLE E-MAIL CONTRACTS

At any point in your business career, you may represent yourself or your company in contract negotiations for a transaction as simple as a purchase of office supplies or as complex as a sale of the firm's assets. These negotiations may involve oral and written contacts, including communication online. Be aware that an enforceable contract can be created via e-mail.

Voluntary Consent and Mistakes

As discussed in Chapter 14, lack of voluntary consent is a defense to contract enforceability. Sometimes, lack of voluntary consent is due to a mistake. But when a mistake is unilateral, the contract may be enforced. Consequently, an e-mail can result in an enforceable contract even if it contains a typographical error in, say, a dollar amount. If you are making an offer or acceptance via e-mail, you must draft it as carefully as

if you were typing it on paper. Reread it several times before you hit the "Send" button.

Sufficiency of the Writing

A series of e-mail exchanges can comprise a writing that constitutes a contract. In other words, five e-mail messages between two parties may collectively form a single contract. If the e-mails name the parties, identify the subject matter, and state the consideration, a court normally will hold that they satisfy the writing requirement under the Statute of Frauds.

Precise Language

E-mail is a medium that may increase the possibility for ambiguities. After all, we often compose e-mails quickly and use casual language that may be imprecise. When e-mailing business contacts, you should:

1. *Include an informative subject line.* Specify the subject exactly—such as "Change in Delivery Date for XYZ Portable Generators."
2. *Repeat the subject within the body of the message.* That way, if the recipient skips reading the subject line, the message will still be clear.
3. *Focus on a limited number of subjects.* Send separate e-mails to discuss different topics.
4. *Be clear.* If you do not phrase your communication carefully to say what you intend, you may create an enforceable contract without intending to do so.
5. *Proof your writing.* E-mail text with misspellings, incorrect punctuation, and other errors creates a bad impression. Reviewing your e-mails before you send them may be the most important step in avoiding misinterpretations.

TERMS AND CONCEPTS FOR REVIEW

collateral promise 191

e-signature 194

fixture 190

form 189

integrated contract 196

parol evidence rule 195

prenuptial agreement 192

Statute of Frauds 189

CHAPTER SUMMARY—WRITTEN CONTRACTS

LEARNING OUTCOME	
1	**Identify contracts that must be in writing under the Statute of Frauds.** Contracts that must be in writing to be enforceable under the Statute of Frauds include the following: (1) Contracts involving interests in land. (2) Contracts that cannot by their terms be performed within one year from the day after the contract's formation. (3) Collateral contracts, such as promises to answer for the debt or duty of another. (4) Promises made in consideration of marriage. (5) Contracts for sales of goods priced at $500 or more.
2	**Describe what satisfies the writing requirement under the Statute of Frauds.** To constitute an enforceable contract under the Statute of Frauds, a writing must be signed by the party against whom enforcement is sought and state with reasonable certainty the essential terms of the contract. Generally, it must name the parties, subject matter, consideration, and quantity. A contract for the sale of land must also describe the property. A contract for a sale of goods is not enforceable beyond the quantity of goods stated.
3	**State the parol evidence rule.** The parol evidence rule prohibits the introduction at trial of testimony or other evidence of oral communications between the parties that is not contained in the contract itself. The written contract is assumed to be the complete embodiment of the parties' agreement.
4	**List circumstances in which parol evidence is admissible.** Evidence that would not otherwise be admissible under the parol evidence rule is admissible for the following purposes: (1) To show that the contract was subsequently modified. (2) To show that the contract was voidable or void. (3) To clarify the meaning of an ambiguous term. (4) To clarify the terms of a written contract that lacks one or more of its essential terms. (5) To explain the meaning of a term in a sales contract in light of the parties' prior dealing, course of performance, or usage of trade. (6) To show that an entire contract is subject to an orally agreed-on condition. (7) To correct an obvious clerical or typographical error.

ISSUE SPOTTERS

Check your answers to the *Issue Spotters* against the answers provided in Appendix C at the end of this text.

1. GamesCo orders $800 worth of game pieces from Midstate Plastic, Inc. Midstate delivers, and GamesCo pays for $450 worth. GamesCo then says it wants no more pieces from Midstate. GamesCo and Midstate have never dealt with each other before and have nothing in writing. Can Midstate enforce a deal for $350 more? Explain your answer. (See *The Statute of Frauds—Writing Requirement*.)

2. Paula orally agrees to work with Next Corporation in New York City for two years. Paula moves her family and begins work. Three months later, Paula is fired for no stated cause. She sues for reinstatement or pay. Next Corporation argues that there is no written contract between them. What will the court say? (See *The Statute of Frauds—Writing Requirement*.)

USING BUSINESS LAW

15–1. Collateral Promises. Gemma promises a local hardware store that she will pay for a lawn mower that her brother is purchasing on credit if the brother fails to pay the debt. Must this promise be in writing to be enforceable? Why or why not? (See *The Statute of Frauds—Writing Requirement.*)

15–2. The One-Year Rule. On May 1, by telephone, Yu offers to hire Benson to perform personal services. On May 5, Benson returns Yu's call and accepts the offer. Discuss fully whether this contract falls under the Statute of Frauds in the following circumstances: (See *The Statute of Frauds—Writing Requirement.*)

1. The contract calls for Benson to be employed for one year, with the right to begin performance immediately.

2. The contract calls for Benson to be employed for nine months, with performance of services to begin on September 1.

3. The contract calls for Benson to submit a written research report, with a deadline of two years for submission.

REAL-WORLD CASE PROBLEMS

15–3. Promises Made in Consideration of Marriage. After twenty-nine years of marriage, Robert and Mary Lou Tuttle were divorced. They admitted in court that before they were married, they had signed a prenuptial agreement and had agreed on its general term that each would keep his or her own property and anything derived from that property. But a copy of the prenuptial agreement could not be found. Can the court enforce the agreement without a writing? Why or why not? [*In re Marriage of Tuttle*, 2013 WL 164035 (5 Dist. 2013)] (See *The Statute of Frauds—Writing Requirement.*)

15–4. Sufficiency of the Writing. Newmark & Co. Real Estate, Inc., contacted 2615 East 17 Street Realty, LLC, to lease certain real property on behalf of a client. Newmark e-mailed the landlord a separate agreement for the payment of Newmark's commission. The landlord e-mailed it back with a request to pay the commission in installments. Newmark revised the agreement and e-mailed a final copy to the landlord. Does this exchange qualify as a writing under the Statute of Frauds? Explain. [*Newmark & Co. Real Estate Inc. v. 2615 East 17 Street Realty, LLC,* 80 A.D.3d 476, 914 N.Y.S.2d 162 (1 Dept. 2011)] (See *The Sufficiency of the Writing.*)

15–5. The Parol Evidence Rule. Evangel Temple Assembly of God leased a facility from Wood Care Centers, Inc., to house evacuees who had lost their homes in a hurricane. The lease agreement stated that Evangel could end the lease at any time by giving notice and paying 10 percent of the rent that would otherwise have been paid over the rest of the term. The lease agreement also stated that if the facility did not retain its tax exemption—which was granted to it on Evangel's behalf as a church—Evangel could end the lease without making the 10 percent payment. Is parol evidence admissible to interpret this lease? Why or why not? [*Wood Care Centers, Inc. v. Evangel Temple Assembly of God of Wichita Falls,* 307 S.W.3d 816 (Tex.App.—Fort Worth 2010)] (See *The Parol Evidence Rule.*)

15–6. The Parol Evidence Rule. Pamela Watkins bought a home from Sandra Schexnider. Their agreement stated that Watkins would make payments on the mortgage until the note was paid in full, when "the house" would become hers. The agreement also stipulated that she would pay for insurance on "the property." The home was destroyed in a hurricane, and the insurance proceeds satisfied the mortgage. Watkins claimed that she owned the land, but Schexnider asserted that she had sold only the house. Is parol evidence admissible to resolve this dispute? Explain. [*Watkins v. Schexnider,* 31 So.3d 609 (La.App. 3 Cir. 2010)] (See *The Parol Evidence Rule.*)

ETHICAL QUESTIONS

15–7. Prenuptial Agreements. Should prenuptial agreements be enforced if one party did not have the advice of counsel? Discuss. (See *The Statute of Frauds—Writing Requirement*.)

15–8. The Parol Evidence Rule. Robert Shelborne asked William Williams to represent him in a deal with Robert Tundy. Shelborne expected to receive $31 million from the deal and agreed to pay Williams a fee of $1 million. Tundy said that a tax of $100,000 would have to be paid first. Shelborne asked James Parker to loan him $50,000. Parker, Shelborne, and Williams wired the funds to Tundy. They never heard from him again. No $31 million was transferred. Shelborne then disappeared. Parker filed a suit against Williams, alleging breach of contract. Parker offered as evidence a recording of a phone conversation in which Williams guaranteed Shelborne's loan. Does Williams have a defense under the Statute of Frauds? In this case, who, if anyone, behaved ethically? Discuss. [*Parker v. Williams*, 977 So.2d 476 (Ala. 2007)] (See *The Parol Evidence Rule*.)

Chapter 15—Work Set

TRUE-FALSE QUESTIONS

_____ 1. Contracts for transfers, other than sales, of interests in land need not be in writing to be enforceable under the Statute of Frauds.

_____ 2. A contract for a sale of goods of over $300 must be in writing to be enforceable under the Statute of Frauds.

_____ 3. An oral contract that should be in writing to be enforceable under the Statute of Frauds may be enforceable if it has been partially performed.

_____ 4. The only writing sufficient to satisfy the Statute of Frauds is a typewritten form, signed at the bottom by all parties, with the heading "Contract" at the top.

_____ 5. Under the parol evidence rule, virtually any evidence is admissible to prove or disprove the terms of a contract.

_____ 6. A promise to answer for the debt of another must be in writing to be enforceable, unless the guarantor's main purpose is to obtain a personal benefit.

_____ 7. A contract that makes performance within one year possible need not be in writing to be enforceable.

_____ 8. A promise to pay a sum of money in consideration of a promise to marry must be in writing.

_____ 9. Under the Statute of Frauds, any contract that is not in writing is void.

MULTIPLE-CHOICE QUESTIONS

_____ 1. Walt sells his pickup truck to Bob. When Walt starts to remove its camper shell, Bob says, "Wait. We agreed the camper shell was included." Walt points to their written contract and says, "No, we didn't." The contract says nothing about the camper shell. The camper shell is

   a. part of the deal under the parol evidence rule.
   b. not part of the deal under the parol evidence rule.
   c. part of the deal, because Bob thought it was.
   d. not part of the deal, because Walt thought it was not.

_____ 2. On March 1, the chief engineer for the software design division of Uni Products orally contracts to hire Lee for one year, beginning March 4. Lee works for Uni for five months. When sales decline, Lee is discharged. Lee sues Uni for reinstatement or seven months' salary. Lee will

   a. win, because the contract can be performed within one year.
   b. win, because employment contracts need not be in writing to be enforceable.
   c. lose, because the contract cannot be performed within one year.
   d. lose, because employment contracts must be in writing to be enforceable.

_____ 3. National Properties, Inc., orally contracts for a sale of its lot and warehouse to U.S. Merchants, Inc., but later decides not to go through with the sale. The contract is most likely enforceable against

   a. both National and U.S. Merchants.
   b. National only.
   c. U.S. Merchants only.
   d. neither National nor U.S. Merchants.

_____ 4. Hans owes Bell Credit Company $10,000. Chris orally promises Bell that he will pay Hans's debt if Hans does not. This promise is

   a. not enforceable, because it is not in writing.
   b. enforceable under the "main purpose rule" exception.
   c. not enforceable, because the debt is Hans's.
   d. enforceable under the partial performance exception.

5. Which of the following constitutes a writing that satisfies the Statute of Frauds?

    a. A signed sales slip.

    b. A blank invoice.

    c. An empty envelope.

    d. All of the above.

6. Terry signs a letter setting out the essential terms of an oral contract with Adrian. Those terms are most likely enforceable against

    a. both Terry and Adrian.

    b. Terry only.

    c. Adrian only.

    d. neither Terry nor Adrian.

7. Jim orally promises to work for Pat, and Pat orally promises to employ Jim at a rate of $500 a week. This contract must be in writing to be enforceable if Jim promises to work for

    a. his entire life.

    b. at least five years.

    c. five years, but either party may terminate the contract on thirty days' notice.

    d. either a or c.

8. Tom orally agrees to be liable for Meg's debt to Ace Loan Company. If Tom's purpose for this guaranty is to obtain a personal benefit, the guaranty is

    a. enforceable whether or not it is in writing.

    b. enforceable only if it is in writing.

    c. unenforceable if it is in writing.

    d. unenforceable unless it is in writing.

ANSWERING MORE LEGAL PROBLEMS

1. On June 1, Mel, the owner of Fresco Organico, asks Ray to deliver Fresco's menu items to customers on State University's campus until June 15, which is the final day of the spring semester. Ray says he'll do it if Mel agrees to pay him a certain hourly wage or $500 plus tips, whichever is more. Mel agrees. Nothing is put in writing.

Is this oral agreement enforceable? Yes. A contract that is oral when it is required to be in writing will not, as a rule, be enforced by the courts. Mel and Ray's agreement does not fall into any of the categories listed below and is thus enforceable despite the lack of a writing.

The following types of contracts must be in writing or be evidenced by a written memorandum: (1) contracts involving interests in _____, (2) contracts that cannot by their terms be performed within one _____ from the day after the contract's formation, (3) _____ promises, (4) promises made in consideration of _____, and

(5) contracts for the sale of _____ priced at $500 or more.

2. Sushi Yo! makes ready-to-eat Asian seafood dishes that are sold in grocery stores. Sushi Yo! and Dragonfly Tea Company comarket their products in Milwaukee. Due to their success, the two firms negotiate a new comarketing agreement for Chicago. Sushi Yo! e-mails a proposed multiyear contract to Dragonfly, but Dragonfly does not sign it or respond.

Is this deal enforceable against Dragonfly? No. Under the Statute of Frauds, a contract that cannot, by its own terms, be performed within one _____ from the day after the contract is formed must be in writing to be enforceable. Because Sushi Yo!'s proposed contract could not be performed within a _____, it was not enforceable without a writing _____ by Dragonfly. Because Dragonfly did not _____ the proposal, it was not enforceable.

THIRD PARTY RIGHTS

FACING A LEGAL PROBLEM

Wayne attends Metro Community College in Riverside. To pay tuition, buy books, and meet other expenses, Wayne obtains a loan from the First National Bank of Riverside. Six months later, Wayne receives a letter from the bank, which states that the bank has transferred its rights to receive Wayne's payments on the loan to the Educational Loan Collection Agency (ELCA). The letter tells Wayne that when he begins making payments, he should make them directly to the ELCA.

 What is this transfer called? Should Wayne pay the bank or the ELCA?

Because a contract is a private agreement between the parties who have entered into it, it is fitting that these parties alone should have rights and liabilities under the contract. This is referred to as **privity of contract.** *Privity* refers to the parties' relationship, which is considered sufficiently direct to uphold a legal claim between them.

Privity of contract establishes the basic concept that third parties have no rights in contracts to which they are not parties. **EXAMPLE 16.1** Jean offers to sell Ben her watch and he accepts, but she later refuses to deliver it. If Ben decides to overlook the breach, his mother, Edith, who is outraged by Jean's behavior, cannot successfully sue her because Edith was not a party to the contract. ◄

You may be convinced by now that for every rule of contract law, there is an exception. As times change, so must the laws. When justice cannot be served by adherence to a rule of law, exceptions to the rule must be made. In this chapter, we look at some exceptions to the rule of privity of contract. These exceptions include *assignments* and *delegations,* as well as *third party beneficiary contracts.*

privity of contract
The relationship that exists between the promisor and the promisee of a contract.

16–1 ASSIGNMENTS AND DELEGATIONS

When third parties acquire rights or assume duties arising from a contract to which they were not parties, the rights are transferred to them by *assignment,* and the duties are transferred by *delegation.* Assignment and delegation occur *after* the original contract is made, when one of the parties transfers to another party a right or duty under the contract.

LEARNING OUTCOME 1
Describe a contract assignment.

16–1a Assignments

In a bilateral contract, the two parties have corresponding rights and duties. One party (the obligee) has a *right* to require the other to perform some task, and the other party (the obligor) has a *duty* to perform it. The transfer of *rights* to a third person is known as an **assignment.**

assignment
The act of transferring to another all or part of one's rights arising under a contract.

203

Assignments are important because they are often used in business financing. Lending institutions, such as banks, frequently assign the rights to receive payments under their loan contracts to other firms, which pay for those rights. **EXAMPLE 16.2** Chelsea obtains a loan from Downtown Credit to purchase a car. She may later receive a notice stating that Downtown has transferred (assigned) its rights to receive payments on the loan to another firm and that she should make her payments to that other firm.◄

In addition, lenders that make mortgage loans often assign their rights to collect the mortgage payments to a third party, such as Chase Home Mortgage Lending. Following an assignment, the home buyer is notified that future payments must be made to the third party, rather than to the original lender. Billions of dollars change hands daily in the business world in the form of assignments of rights in contracts.

Effect of an Assignment In an assignment, the party assigning the rights to a third party is known as the *assignor* (pronounced uh-*sye*-nore). The party receiving the rights is the *assignee* (pronounced uh-*sye*-nee). Other terms traditionally used to describe the parties in assignment relationships are the *obligee* (the person to whom a duty, or obligation, is owed) and the *obligor* (the person who is obligated to perform the duty).

Extinguished Rights When rights under a contract are assigned unconditionally, the rights of the *assignor* (the party making the assignment) are extinguished. The third party (the *assignee,* or the party receiving the assignment) has a right to demand performance from the other original party to the contract (the obligor). **EXAMPLE 16.3** Brent, the obligor, owes Alex $1,000, and Alex, the obligee, assigns to Carmen the right to receive the $1,000 (thus, Alex is now the assignor). Here, a valid assignment of a debt exists. Carmen, the assignee, can enforce the contract against Brent, the obligor, if Brent fails to perform (pay the $1,000).◄ Exhibit 16.1 illustrates assignment relationships.

Defenses The assignee's rights are subject to any defenses that the obligor has against the assignor. **EXAMPLE 16.4** Alex leases an apartment from Brent for one year but fails to pay the seventh month's rent. If Alex then assigns the lease to Carmen, Brent can evict Alex and Carmen, even though Carmen is innocent of the failure to pay the rent.◄

EXHIBIT 16.1   Assignment Relationships

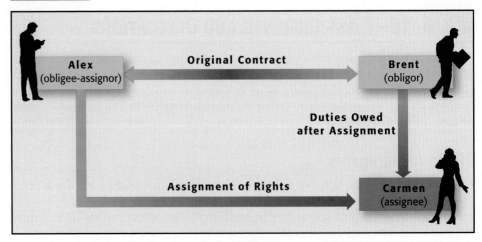

Rights That Cannot Be Assigned As a general rule, all rights can be assigned, except in the following special circumstances:

When a Statute Expressly Prohibits Assignment If a statute expressly prohibits assignment, the particular right in question cannot be assigned. For instance, if a state statute prohibits the assignment of future workers' compensation benefits, a worker cannot assign all benefits due her should she be injured on the job.

When a Contract Is Personal in Nature When a contract is *personal* in nature, the rights under the contract cannot be assigned unless all that remains is a monetary payment. **EXAMPLE 16.5** Brent signs a contract to tutor Alex's children. Alex then attempts to assign his right to Brent's tutoring services to Carmen for her children. Carmen, however, cannot enforce the contract against Brent. Brent may not like Carmen's children or for some other reason may not want to tutor them. Because personal services are unique to the person rendering them, rights to receive personal services cannot be assigned.◄

When an Assignment Changes a Risk or Duty A right cannot be assigned if assignment will significantly increase or alter the risks to or the duties of the obligor (the person owing performance under the contract). **EXAMPLE 16.6** Alex has a hotel, and to insure it, he takes out a policy with Coast Insurance. The policy insures against fire, theft, and floods. Alex attempts to assign the insurance policy to Carmen, who also owns a hotel. The assignment is ineffective because it may substantially alter the insurance company's duty of performance and the risk that the company undertakes. An insurance company evaluates the particular risk of a certain party and tailors its policy to fit that risk. If that policy is assigned to a third party, the insurance risk is materially altered.◄

When the Contract Prohibits Assignment If a contract stipulates that the rights cannot be assigned, then *ordinarily* they cannot be assigned. **EXAMPLE 16.7** Brent agrees to build a house for Alex. The contract between Brent and Alex states, "This contract cannot be assigned by Alex without Brent's consent. Any assignment without such consent renders this contract void, and all rights hereunder will thereupon terminate." Alex then assigns his rights to Carmen, without first obtaining Brent's consent. Carmen cannot enforce the contract against Brent.◄ Despite such a provision, however, if Carmen consents to the assignment by accepting Brent's performance, the contract will remain valid.

This rule, however, has some exceptions:

1. A contract cannot prevent an assignment of the right to receive money. This exception exists to encourage the free flow of money and credit in modern business settings.

2. The assignment of rights in real estate often cannot be prohibited, because such a prohibition is contrary to public policy. These prohibitions are called restraints against *alienation*—that is, against transferring land out of one's possession, thus "alienating" the land from oneself.

3. The assignment of *negotiable instruments* cannot be prohibited.

4. In a contract for the sale of goods, the right to receive damages for breach of contract or for payment of an account owed may be assigned even though the sales contract prohibits such assignment.

Notice of Assignment Once a valid assignment of rights has been made to a third party, the third party should notify the obligor—the original party to the contract—of the assignment. This is not legally necessary to establish the validity of the assignment because an assignment is effective immediately, whether or not notice is given. Two major problems arise, however, when notice of the assignment is not given to the obligor:

1. If the assignor assigns the same right to two different persons, the question arises as to which one has priority—that is, the right to performance by the obligor. Although the rule most often observed in the United States is that the first assignment in time is the first in right, some states follow the English rule, which basically gives priority to the first assignee who gives notice. **EXAMPLE 16.8** If Brent owes Alex $1,000 and Alex assigns the claim first to Carmen without notice to Brent and then assigns it to Dorman, who notifies Brent, in most states Carmen would have priority to payment. In some states, though, Dorman would have priority because Dorman gave first notice. ◄

2. Until the obligor has notice of assignment, the obligor can discharge his or her obligation by performance to the assignor, and performance by the obligor to the assignor constitutes a discharge to the assignee. Once the obligor receives proper notice, only performance to the assignee can discharge the obligor's obligations.

HIGHLIGHTING THE POINT

Pryor owes Tomás $1,000 on a contractual obligation. Tomás assigns this monetary claim to Maria. No notice of assignment is given to Pryor. Pryor pays Tomás the $1,000.

Was the assignment valid? Did Pryor's payment discharge the debt, or does Pryor also have to pay Maria? Although the assignment was valid, Pryor's payment to Tomás discharged the debt, and Maria's failure to give notice to Pryor of the assignment caused Maria to lose the right to collect the $1,000 from Pryor. If Maria had given Pryor notice, Pryor's payment to Tomás would not have discharged the debt, and Maria would have had a legal right to require payment from Pryor.

16–1b Delegations

delegation
The transfer of a contractual duty to a third party.

Just as a party can transfer rights through an assignment, a party can also transfer duties. A transfer of duties is called a **delegation**. Normally, a delegation of duties does not relieve the party making the delegation (the *delegator*) of the obligation to perform in the event that the party to whom the duty has been delegated (the *delegatee*) fails to perform. No special form is required to create a valid delegation of duties. As long as the delegator expresses an intention to make the delegation, it is effective. The delegator need not even use the word *delegate*.

Delegation relationships are graphically illustrated in Exhibit 16.2. In the delegation relationship illustrated in the exhibit, Brent delegates his *duties* under a contract that he made with Alex to a third party, Carmen. Brent thus becomes the *delegator* and Carmen the *delegatee* of the contractual duties. Carmen now owes performance of the contractual duties to Alex. Note that a delegation of duties normally does not relieve the delegator (Brent) of liability if the delegatee (Carmen) fails to perform the contractual duties.

LEARNING OUTCOME 2

Define a contract delegation.

Duties That Cannot Be Delegated As a general rule, any duty can be delegated. This rule has some exceptions, however. Delegation is prohibited in the following circumstances:

1. *When the duties are personal in nature.* **EXAMPLE 16.9** Megan is known for her expertise in finance. She is hired to teach the various aspects of financial underwriting and investment banking. Megan's duty could not be delegated. ◄

EXHIBIT 16.2 Delegation Relationships

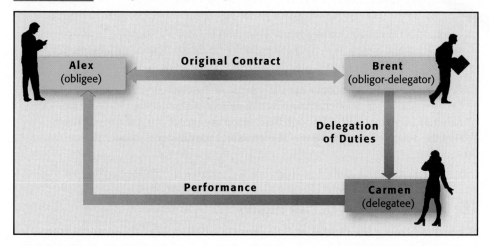

2. *When performance by a third party will vary materially from that expected by the obligee under the contract.* **EXAMPLE 16.10** Jared, a wealthy investor, established Heaven Sent, LLC, to provide capital in the form of grants to struggling but potentially successful businesses. Jared contracted with Merilyn, whose judgment Jared trusted, to select the recipients of the grants. Later, Merilyn delegated this duty to Donald. Jared, who did not approve of Donald, claimed that the delegation was not effective because it materially altered his expectations under the contract with Merilyn.◄

3. *When the contract expressly prohibits delegation.* **EXAMPLE 16.11** Dakota Company contracted with Belisario, a certified public accountant, to perform its audits. Because the contract prohibited delegation, Belisario could not delegate the duty to perform the audits to another accountant—not even an accountant at the same firm.◄ As with an anti-assignment clause, however, the obligor can consent to the delegation by accepting the delegatee's performance.

HIGHLIGHTING THE POINT

Sue contracts with Karl to pick up and deliver some heavy construction machinery. Sue delegates this duty to Frank, who is in the business of delivering heavy machinery.

Is the delegation effective? Yes. The performance required is of a routine and nonpersonal nature and does not change Karl's expectations under the contract.

Effect of a Delegation If a delegation of duties is enforceable, the obligee must accept performance from the delegatee. The obligee can legally refuse performance from the delegatee only if the duty is one that cannot be delegated. A valid delegation of duties does not relieve the delegator of obligations under the contract. If the delegatee fails to perform, the delegator is still liable to the obligee.

Liability of the Delegatee Can the obligee hold the delegatee liable if the delegatee fails to perform? If the delegatee has made a promise of performance that will directly benefit the obligee, there is an "assumption of duty." Breach of this duty makes the delegatee liable to the obligee.

16–1c Assignment of "All Rights"

When a contract provides for an "assignment of all rights," this wording may also be treated as providing for an "assumption of duties" on the part of the assignee. Therefore, when general words are used (for example, "I assign the contract" or "I assign all my rights under the contract"), the contract is construed as implying both an assignment of rights and a delegation of duties.

16–2 THIRD PARTY BENEFICIARIES

To have contractual rights, a party normally must be a party to the contract. An exception exists, however, when the original parties to the contract intend at the time of contracting that the contract performance directly benefit a third person. In this situation, the third person becomes a *beneficiary* of the contract and has legal rights. The law distinguishes between two types of **third party beneficiaries:** *intended* beneficiaries and *incidental* beneficiaries.

16–2a Intended Beneficiaries

An **intended beneficiary** can sue the promisor directly for breach of a contract made for the beneficiary's benefit. Who, however, is the promisor? In bilateral contracts, both parties to the contract are promisors, because they both make promises that can be enforced. In third party beneficiary contracts, courts will determine the identity of the promisor by asking which party made the promise that benefits the third party—that person is the "promisor." Allowing a third party to sue the promisor directly in effect circumvents the "middle person" (the promisee) and thus reduces the burden on the courts. Otherwise, a third party would sue the promisee, who would then sue the promisor.

Real-World Case Example

Neumann Homes, Inc., contracted with the Village of Antioch, Illinois, to make public improvements in two residential subdivisions. Neumann subcontracted the grading work to Lake County Grading Company. When the work was done, Neumann did not pay Lake and declared bankruptcy. Lake filed a suit in an Illinois state court against the Village to recover, alleging that the Village breached its contract with Neumann by failing to require Neumann to post a sufficient bond to pay Lake. The court issued a judgment in Lake's favor. The Village appealed.

Was Lake an intended third party beneficiary of the contract between the Village and Neumann? Yes. In a 2013 case, *Lake County Grading Co. v. Village of Antioch*, a state intermediate appellate court affirmed the lower court's judgment. "A subcontractor is a third-party beneficiary of a contract between a public entity and a general contractor." The court further held that the Village breached the contract and Lake had a right to bring an action for the breach.

Creditor Beneficiaries Only intended beneficiaries acquire legal rights in a contract. One type of intended beneficiary is a *creditor beneficiary*. A creditor beneficiary benefits from a contract in which one party (the promisor) promises another party (the promisee) to pay a debt that the promisee owes to a third party (the creditor beneficiary). As an intended beneficiary, the creditor beneficiary can sue the promisor directly to enforce the contract.

Donee Beneficiaries Another type of intended beneficiary is a *donee beneficiary*. When a contract is made for the express purpose of giving a gift to a third party, the third party (the donee beneficiary) can sue the promisor directly to enforce the promise. The most common donee beneficiary contract is a life insurance contract.
       EXAMPLE 16.12 Al (the promisee) pays premiums to Standard Life Insurance Company (the promisor), which promises to pay a certain amount on Al's death to Julia, Al's wife and his donee beneficiary. Under the life insurance policy, Julia can enforce the promise made by the insurance company to pay her the certain amount on Al's death.◄

16–2b Vested Intended Beneficiary Rights

An intended third party beneficiary cannot enforce a contract against the original parties until the rights of the third party have **vested**. Until these rights have vested, the original parties to the contract—the promisor and the promisee—can modify or rescind the contract without the consent of the third party. When do the rights of third parties vest? Generally, the rights of an intended beneficiary vest when one of the following occurs:

1. When the third party demonstrates *manifest assent* to the contract, such as by sending a letter or note consenting to a contract formed for his or her benefit.

2. When the third party materially alters his or her position in *detrimental reliance* on the contract.

3. When the conditions for vesting are satisfied. For example, the rights of a beneficiary under a life insurance policy vest when the insured person dies.

   If the original parties to the contract expressly reserve the right to cancel or modify the contract, the rights of the third party beneficiary are subject to any changes that result. In such a case, the vesting of the third party's rights does not terminate the power of the original contracting parties to alter their legal relationships. This is particularly true in most life insurance contracts, in which the right to change the beneficiary is reserved to the policy owner.

16–2c Incidental Beneficiaries

The benefit that an **incidental beneficiary** receives from a contract between two parties is *unintentional*. Therefore, an incidental beneficiary cannot enforce a contract

vested
The condition in which rights have taken effect and cannot be taken away.

LEARNING OUTCOME 4

Explain when a third party beneficiary's rights in a contract vest.

incidental beneficiary
A third party who incidentally benefits from a contract but has no rights in it and cannot sue the promisor if it is breached.

to which he or she is not a party. Exhibit 16.3 illustrates the distinction between intended and incidental beneficiaries.

In determining whether a third party beneficiary is an intended or an incidental beneficiary, the courts generally use the *reasonable person* test—that is, a beneficiary will be considered an intended beneficiary if a reasonable person in the position of the third party beneficiary would believe that the promisee *intended* to confer on the beneficiary the right to bring suit to enforce the contract.

Several other factors must also be examined to determine whether a party is an intended or an incidental beneficiary. The presence of one or more of the following factors strongly indicates an *intended* (rather than an incidental) benefit to a third party:

1. Performance is rendered directly to the third party.

2. The third party has the right to control the details of performance.

3. The third party is expressly designated as a beneficiary in the contract.

EXHIBIT 16.3   Third Party Beneficiaries

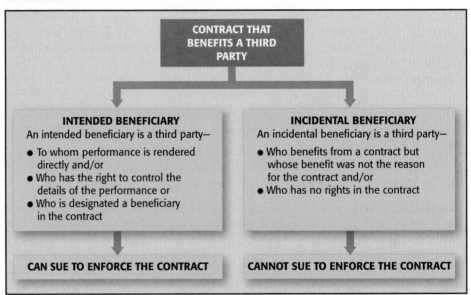

CONTRACT THAT BENEFITS A THIRD PARTY

INTENDED BENEFICIARY
An intended beneficiary is a third party—
- To whom performance is rendered directly and/or
- Who has the right to control the details of the performance or
- Who is designated a beneficiary in the contract

INCIDENTAL BENEFICIARY
An incidental beneficiary is a third party—
- Who benefits from a contract but whose benefit was not the reason for the contract and/or
- Who has no rights in the contract

CAN SUE TO ENFORCE THE CONTRACT

CANNOT SUE TO ENFORCE THE CONTRACT

ANSWERING THE LEGAL PROBLEM

In the legal problem set out at the beginning of this chapter, Wayne obtains a student loan from a bank and is later notified that the bank has transferred its right to receive Wayne's payments to a collection agency.

A **What is this transfer called? Should Wayne pay the bank or the ELCA?** The transfer is an assignment. The agency may have purchased the right to receive Wayne's payments. The agency can insist that Wayne make his payments directly to the ELCA.

LINKING BUSINESS LAW to Your Career

ASSIGNMENT AND DELEGATION

In the majority of businesses, most sales are based on open accounts. This means that the buyer is obligated to pay, but the seller agrees to accept payment within thirty, sixty, or ninety days, depending on the industry and the parties involved.

During that time, the seller has no cash to show for the sale. To obtain working capital, the seller generally can assign the right to payment to a lender. The assignments of such rights—and the delegations of duties—are common in the business world.

Contract Rights and Duties

Any contract right or duty can be assigned or delegated unless this is prohibited by the contract, a statute, or another limitation. For example, a manufacturer can assign or delegate the production of goods to a third party unless prohibited by a buyer's contract.

Similarly, without a clause specifying otherwise, a tenant under a lease may assign it to another party.

Contract Restrictions

In certain situations, businesses may wish to prohibit third parties from acquiring contract rights. For instance, a property owner can prohibit the assignment of a lease for the balance of its term without the property owner's consent. Most purchase orders (contracts) have clauses that prohibit the sellers' assignments or delegations of performance with respect to the subject of the contract without the buyers' consent.

Contract Review

When you are a party to a business contract, be aware of the possibility of its assignment or delegation. With this in mind, you should:

1. *Read the contract.* Review the terms to learn whether you or the other contracting party can assign or delegate rights or duties under the contract to a third party.
2. *Permit or prohibit these rights.* If you do not want your contract rights or duties to be assigned or delegated, insert a clause that prohibits assignment or delegation without your consent.
3. *Identify the terms.* If you or the other party can assign or delegate the contract rights or performance, then pinpoint the benefits and obligations, such as notice to customers.
4. *Follow the requirements.* To avoid unwanted liability and other negative consequences, carefully adhere to the requirements for a contract's assignment or delegation.

TERMS AND CONCEPTS FOR REVIEW

assignment 203

delegation 206

incidental beneficiary 209

intended beneficiary 208

privity of contract 203

third party beneficiary 208

vested 209

CHAPTER SUMMARY—THIRD PARTY RIGHTS

LEARNING OUTCOME	
1	**Describe a contract assignment.** An *assignment* is the transfer of rights under a contract to a third party. The person assigning the rights is the *assignor*. The party to whom the rights are assigned—the *assignee*—has a right to demand performance from the other original party to the contract (the *obligor*). Generally, any right can be assigned except when (1) a statute prohibits assignment, (2) a contract calls for the performance of personal services, (3) the assignment will materially increase or alter the obligor's risks or duties, or (4) the contract stipulates that the rights cannot be assigned.
	If the assignor assigns the same right to two different persons, generally the first assignment in time is the first in right (in some states, the first assignee to give notice takes priority). Until the obligor is notified of the assignment, she or he can tender performance to the assignor. If the assignor accepts the performance, the obligor's duties under the contract are discharged without benefit to the assignee.
2	**Define a contract delegation.** A *delegation* is the transfer of duties under a contract to a third party—the *delegatee*—who assumes the obligation of performing the duties previously held by the one making the delegation—the *delegator*. Generally, any duty can be delegated except when (1) the duties are personal in nature, (2) performance by a third party will vary materially from that expected by the *obligee*—the one to whom the duty is owed, or (3) the contract expressly prohibits delegation.
	If the delegatee fails to perform, the delegator is liable to the obligee. An "assignment of all rights" is construed to mean that both the rights and the duties under a contract are transferred to a third party.
3	**Identify noncontracting parties who have rights in a contract.** A third party beneficiary contract is made for the purpose of benefiting a third party. An *intended beneficiary* is one for whose benefit a contract is created. When the *promisor*—the one making the contractual promise that benefits a third party—fails to perform as promised, the third party can sue the promisor directly. An *incidental beneficiary* is a third party who indirectly benefits from a contract but for whose benefit the contract was not specifically intended. Incidental beneficiaries have no rights to the benefits received and cannot sue to have the contract enforced.
4	**Explain when a third party beneficiary's rights in a contract vest.** An intended third party beneficiary cannot enforce a contract against the original parties until the third party's rights *vest*, which means that they take effect and cannot be taken away. The rights vest (1) when the third party manifests assent to the contract, (2) when the third party materially alters his or her position in detrimental reliance on the contract, or (3) when the conditions for vesting are satisfied.

ISSUE SPOTTERS

Check your answers to the *Issue Spotters* against the answers provided in Appendix C at the end of this text.

1. Brian owes Jeff $100. Ed tells Brian to give him the $100 and he'll pay Jeff. Brian gives Ed the $100. Ed never pays Jeff. Can Jeff successfully sue Ed for the $100? Why or why not? (**See** *Third Party Beneficiaries.*)

2. A&B Construction Company contracts to build a house for Mike. The contract states that "any assignment of this contract renders the contract void." After A&B builds the house, but before Mike pays, A&B assigns its right to payment to Ace Credit Company. Can Ace enforce the contract against Mike? Explain your answer. (**See** *Assignments and Delegations.*)

USING BUSINESS LAW

16–1. Third Party Beneficiaries. Wilken owes Rivera $2,000. Howie promises Wilken to pay Rivera the $2,000 in return for Wilken's promise to give Howie's children guitar lessons. Is Rivera an intended beneficiary of the Howie-Wilken contract? Explain. (See *Third Party Beneficiaries.*)

16–2. Delegation. Inez has a specific set of plans to build a sailboat. The plans are detailed in nature, and any boat builder can build the boat. Inez secures bids, and the low bid is made by the Whale of a Boat Corp. Inez contracts with Whale to build the boat for $4,000. Whale then receives unexpected business from elsewhere. To meet the delivery date in the contract with Inez, Whale delegates its obligation to build the boat, without Inez's consent, to Quick Brothers, a reputable boat builder. When the boat is ready for delivery, Inez learns of the delegation and refuses to accept delivery, even though the boat is built to specifications. Discuss fully whether Inez is obligated to accept and pay for the boat. Would your answer be any different if Inez had not had a specific set of plans but had instead contracted with Whale to design and build a sailboat for $4,000? Explain. (See *Assignments and Delegations.*)

REAL-WORLD CASE PROBLEMS

16–3. Third Party Beneficiary. David and Sandra Dess contracted with Sirva Relocation, LLC, to assist in selling their home. In their contract, the Desses agreed to disclose all information about the property on which Sirva "and other prospective buyers may rely in deciding whether and on what terms to purchase the Property." The Kincaids contracted with Sirva to buy the house. After the closing, they discovered dampness in the walls, defective and rotten windows, mold, and other undisclosed problems. Can the Kincaids bring an action against the Desses for breach of their contract with Sirva? Why or why not? [*Kincaid v. Dess*, 48 Kan.App.2d 640, 298 P.3d 358 (2013)] (See *Third Party Beneficiaries.*)

16–4. Notice of Assignment. Arnold Kazery was the owner of a hotel leased to George Wilkinson. The lease included renewal options of ten years each. When Arnold transferred his interest in the property to his son, Sam, no one notified Wilkinson. For the next twenty years, Wilkinson paid the rent to Arnold and renewed the lease by notice to Arnold. When Wilkinson wrote to Arnold that he was exercising another option to renew, Sam filed a suit against him, claiming that the lease was void. Did Wilkinson give proper notice to renew? Discuss. [*Kazery v. Wilkinson*, 52 So.3d 1270 (Miss.App. 2011)] (See *Assignments and Delegations.*)

16–5. Duties That Cannot Be Delegated. Bruce Albea Contracting, Inc., the contractor on a highway project, subcontracted the asphalt work to APAC-Southeast, Inc. The contract prohibited delegation without Albea's consent. In mid-project, APAC delegated its duties to Matthews Contracting Co. Albea allowed Matthews to finish the work. But Albea did not pay APAC for its work on the project, arguing that APAC had violated the anti-delegation clause, rendering their contact void. Is Albea correct? Explain. [*Western Surety Co. v. APAC-Southeast, Inc.*, 302 Ga.App. 654, 691 S.E.2d 234 (2010)] (See *Assignments and Delegations.*)

16–6. Intended Beneficiary. Autumn Allan owned a condominium directly beneath Aslan Koraev's condominium. The properties' governing documents formed a contract between the owners and the Condominium Owners Association. The documents made each owner liable for his or her damage to other units and provided that "an aggrieved owner" could maintain an action to enforce this provision. After eight incidents of water and sewage "incursion" from Koraev's unit, could Allan file a suit against Koraev for breach of contract? Explain. [*Allan v. Nersesova*, 307 S.W.3d 564 (Tex.App.—Dallas 2010)] (See *Third Party Beneficiaries.*)

ETHICAL QUESTIONS

16–7. Incidental Beneficiaries. Should incidental beneficiaries have any legal recourse against parties who do not perform their contracts? Why or why not? (See *Third Party Beneficiaries*.)

16–8. Notice of Assignment. James Grigg's mother was killed in a car accident. As the beneficiary of her insurance policy, Grigg was entitled to a payment of $50,000 from Safeco Life Insurance Co. Grigg assigned this payment to Howard Foley. Neither Grigg nor Foley notified Safeco. Later, Grigg assigned the payment to Settlement Capital Corp., which filed notice with a court. Still later, Grigg assigned the payment to Timothy Johnson, who assigned it to Robert Chris, who used it as collateral for a loan from Canco Credit Union. Under the rule most often observed in the United States, who is entitled to the $50,000? Regardless of this rule, has a violation of ethics occurred? Explain. [*Foley v. Grigg*, 144 Idaho 530, 164 P.3d 180 (2007)] (See *Assignments and Delegations*.)

Chapter 16—Work Set

TRUE-FALSE QUESTIONS

_____ 1. Intended beneficiaries have no legal rights under a contract.

_____ 2. The party who makes an assignment is the assignee.

_____ 3. All rights can be assigned.

_____ 4. If a contract contains a clause that prohibits assignment of the contract, then ordinarily the contract cannot be assigned.

_____ 5. A right to the payment of money may be assigned.

_____ 6. An assignment is not effective without notice.

_____ 7. No special form is required to create a valid delegation of duties.

_____ 8. Only intended beneficiaries acquire legal rights in a contract.

_____ 9. A transfer of duties is called a delegation.

_____ 10. If a delegatee fails to perform, the delegator must do so.

MULTIPLE-CHOICE QUESTIONS

_____ 1. Gary contracts with Dan to buy Dan a new car manufactured by General Motors Corporation (GMC). GMC is
   a. an intended beneficiary.
   b. an incidental beneficiary.
   c. not a third party beneficiary.
   d. both a and b.

_____ 2. Bernie has a right to $100 against Holly. Bernie assigns the right to Tom. Tom's rights against Holly
   a. include the right to demand performance from Holly.
   b. are subject to any defenses Holly has against Bernie.
   c. do not vest until Holly assents to the assignment.
   d. include both a and b.

_____ 3. Frank owes Jim $100. Frank contracts with Ron to pay the $100 and notifies Jim of the contract by fax. Jim replies by fax that he agrees. After Frank receives Jim's reply, Ron and Frank send Jim a fax stating that they have decided to rescind their contract. Jim's rights under the contract
   a. vested when Jim learned of the contract and manifested assent to it.
   b. vested when Frank and Ron formed their contract.
   c. will not vest, because Ron and Frank rescinded their contract.
   d. could never vest, because Jim is an incidental beneficiary.

_____ 4. Jenny sells her Value Auto Parts store to Burt and makes a valid contract not to compete. Burt wants to sell the store to Discount Auto Centers and assign to Discount the right to Jenny's promise not to compete. Burt can
   a. sell the business and assign the right.
   b. sell the business but not assign the right.
   c. assign the right but not sell the business.
   d. neither assign the right nor sell the business.

_____ 5. Dick contracts with Jane to mow Jane's lawn. Dick delegates performance of the duty to Sally with Jane's assent. Who owes Jane a duty to cut her grass?

   a. Dick, but not Sally.
   b. Sally, but not Dick.
   c. Both Dick and Sally.
   d. Neither Dick nor Sally.

_____ 6. Nick contracts with Kathy to paint Nick's portrait. Kathy's right to receive payment for the work

   a. cannot be assigned.
   b. can be assigned if the duty to paint the portrait is delegated.
   c. can be assigned if Nick agrees.
   d. can be assigned under any circumstances.

_____ 7. A contract for a sale of goods between John and Mary provides that the right to receive damages for its breach cannot be assigned. This clause

   a. is not effective.
   b. is effective only before the contract is executed.
   c. is effective only after the contract is executed.
   d. is effective under all circumstances.

_____ 8. Fred unconditionally assigns to Ellen his rights under a contract with Paul. Fred's rights under the contract

   a. continue until the contract is fully executed.
   b. continue until Paul performs his obligations under the contract.
   c. continue until Ellen receives Paul's performance.
   d. are extinguished.

_____ 9. Ann has a right to receive payment under a contract with Bill. Without notice, Ann assigns the right first to Carl and then to Diane. In most states, the party with priority to the right would be

   a. Ann.
   b. Bill.
   c. Carl.
   d. Diane.

ANSWERING MORE LEGAL PROBLEMS

1. Eli develops and patents the technology behind the VuYu, which allows its users to stream high-definition video from online video services directly to a television set. Eli assigns the rights to Bright Lights, Inc. In exchange, Bright Lights agrees to make and market the device, and assigns a right to receive a percentage of the gross sales revenue to Eli.

   Can these rights be assigned? Yes. As a general rule, all rights can be assigned, except in special circumstances. If a _____ expressly prohibits the assignment of a certain right, the right cannot be assigned. When a contract is _____ in nature, the rights in the contract cannot be assigned except for the payment of money. A right cannot be assigned if its assignment will significantly _____ the risks to or the duties of the obligor. If a _____ provides that certain rights cannot be assigned, then they cannot be assigned (except for the right to receive money, rights in real estate, negotiable instruments, and the right to damages on a breach or to payment of

an account). The rights in this contract do not fall into any of these categories.

2. To begin to manufacture the VuYu, Bright Lights buys equipment from Crest Labs, Inc. Because Bright Lights does not have the funds to finance the purchase, Crest grants the buyer credit in exchange for monthly payments of the amount owed. Later, the owners of Bright Lights sell the firm to Playback, LLC, which agrees in their contract to make the remaining payments to Crest.

   If Playback fails to make the payments, can Crest sue Playback directly? Yes. An _____ beneficiary can sue the promisor directly for breach of a contract made for the benefit of the _____. The contract between Bright Lights and Playback includes a provision for the continuation of payments to Crest. This provision is clearly for the benefit of _____. Thus, Crest can sue Playback directly to enforce the contract and obtain payment on the amount owed for the equipment.

CONTRACT DISCHARGE AND REMEDIES

17

LEARNING OUTCOMES

The five Learning Outcomes below are designed to help improve your understanding of the chapter. After reading this chapter, you should be able to:

❶ Explain the difference between complete and substantial contractual performance.

❷ Describe how parties can discharge their contract by agreement.

❸ Identify different types of damages.

❹ Define the remedy of rescission and restitution.

❺ Explain the remedy of specific performance.

FACING A LEGAL PROBLEM

The DeLeons contract with a construction company to build a house. The contract specifies Brand X plasterboard. The builder cannot obtain Brand X, and the DeLeons are on vacation hiking in the mountains of Peru and are unreachable. The builder decides to install Brand Y instead, which she knows is identical in quality and durability to Brand X. All other aspects of construction conform to the contract.

Q Does this deviation constitute a breach of contract? Can the DeLeons avoid their obligation to pay the builder because Brand Y plasterboard was used instead of Brand X?

Parties to a contract need to know when their contract is terminated. In other words, the parties need to know when their contractual duties are at an end. This chapter deals first with the *discharge* of a contract, which is normally accomplished when both parties have performed the acts promised in the contract. We look at the degree of *performance* required and at some other ways in which discharge can occur.

When it is no longer advantageous for a party to fulfill his or her contractual obligations, breach of contract may result. A **breach of contract** occurs when a party fails to perform part or all of the required duties under a contract. Once this occurs, the other party—the nonbreaching party—can choose one or more of several remedies. These remedies are discussed later in this chapter.

breach of contract
Failure, without legal excuse, of a promisor to perform the obligations of a contract.

17–1 CONTRACT DISCHARGE

The most common way to **discharge** (terminate) contractual duties is by **performance** (fulfillment) of those duties. In addition to discharge by performance, a contract can be discharged in numerous other ways. These include discharge by failure of a condition, by agreement, and by operation of law.

discharge
The termination of one's obligation under a contract.

performance
The fulfillment of one's duties arising under a contract.

17–1a Discharge by Failure of a Condition

In most contracts, promises of performance are not conditioned. They must be performed, or the party promising the act will be in breach of contract. **EXAMPLE 17.1** If Home Farms contracts to sell Bagels & Bytes a truckload of organic produce for $1,000, the promises are unconditional. Bagels & Bytes does not have to pay Home Farms if the produce is not delivered. ◄

In some situations, however, the duty to perform may be conditioned on the occurrence or nonoccurrence of a certain event. If the condition is not satisfied, the obligations of the parties are discharged. **EXAMPLE 17.2** If Restoration Motors offers to buy Charlie's 1960 Cadillac limousine only if an expert appraiser estimates that it can be restored for less than a certain price, their obligations are conditioned on the outcome of the appraisal. If the condition is not satisfied—if the appraiser deems the cost to be above that price—their obligations are discharged. ◄

17–1b Discharge by Performance

A contract comes to an end when both parties fulfill their respective duties by performance of the acts they have promised. Performance can also be accomplished by tender. **Tender** is an unconditional offer to perform by a person who is ready, willing, and able to do so.

For instance, a seller who places goods at the disposal of a buyer has tendered delivery and can demand payment according to the terms of the agreement. A buyer who offers to pay for goods has tendered payment and can demand delivery of the goods. **EXAMPLE 17.3** Custom Renovations orders bathroom fixtures from Budget Plumbing Company, which places the fixtures on its warehouse loading dock for Custom to pick up on May 1. According to the terms of their agreement, Budget has tendered delivery and can demand payment from Custom. ◄

Once performance has been tendered, the party making the tender has done everything possible to carry out the terms of the contract. If the other party refuses to perform, the party making the tender can consider the duty discharged and sue for breach of contract.

It is important to distinguish between *complete performance* and *substantial performance*.

Complete Performance When a party performs exactly as agreed, there is no question as to whether the contract has been performed. When a party's performance is perfect, it is said to be complete.

Normally, conditions expressly stated in the contract must fully occur in all aspects for complete (or strict) performance to take place. Any deviation breaches the contract and discharges the other party's obligation to perform.

Although in most contracts the parties fully discharge their obligations by complete performance, sometimes a party fails to fulfill all of the duties or completes the duties in a manner contrary to the terms of the contract. The issue then arises as to whether the performance was sufficiently substantial to discharge the contractual obligations.

Substantial Performance To qualify as substantial, the performance must not vary greatly from the performance promised in the contract. It must result in substantially the same benefits as those promised in the contract. If performance is substantial, the other party's duty to perform remains absolute (minus damages, if any, for the minor deviations). If performance is not substantial, there is a *material breach*—the nonbreaching party is excused from performance and can sue for damages caused by the breach.

EXAMPLE 17.4 Clay sold an apartment building in San Francisco to Montgomery. The building's plumbing did not meet the standards of the city's building code. The contract between Clay and Montgomery provided that Clay would have the plumbing fixed within six months. A year later, the repairs had not been made, the city had fined Montgomery for the code violations, and the building's tenants were moving out. Clay's failure to fix the plumbing was a material breach. Montgomery was no longer obligated to make payments under the contract. ◄

Performance to the Satisfaction of Another Contracts often state that completed work must personally satisfy one of the parties or a third person.

When the subject matter of the contract is personal, performance must actually satisfy the party whose satisfaction is required. Contracts for portraits, works of art, medical or dental work, and tailoring are personal. Only the personal

---

tender

A timely offer or expression of willingness to pay a debt or perform an obligation.

LEARNING OUTCOME 1

Explain the difference between complete and substantial contractual performance.

satisfaction of the party is sufficient to fulfill the contract—unless the party expresses dissatisfaction just to avoid payment or otherwise is not acting in good faith. **EXAMPLE 17.5** Teresa hires Raymond to take a minimum of one hundred photos of her wedding and create an online wedding photo album within two weeks of her wedding day. Teresa's personal satisfaction with the results of Raymond's performance is required to successfully complete the contract. ◂

Contracts that involve mechanical fitness, utility, or marketability (such as "the pump must be mounted on a platform") need only be performed to the satisfaction of a reasonable person unless they *expressly state otherwise*. When contracts require performance to the satisfaction of a third party (such as "the road must be graded to the satisfaction of the supervising engineer"), the courts are divided. A majority of courts require the work to be satisfactory to a reasonable person, but some courts hold that the personal satisfaction of the third party must be met.

17–1c Discharge by Agreement

Any contract can be discharged by the agreement of the parties. This agreement can be part of the original contract, or the parties can form a new contract for the express purpose of discharging the original contract.

Mutual Rescission *Rescission* is a process in which the parties cancel the contract and are returned to the positions they occupied before the contract's formation. For *mutual rescission* to take place, the parties must make another agreement that also satisfies the legal requirements for a contract—there must be an *offer*, an *acceptance*, and *consideration*.

Ordinarily, if the parties agree to rescind the original contract, their promises *not* to perform the acts promised in the original contract will be legal consideration for the second contract. This occurs when the contract is executory on *both* sides—that is, neither party has completed performance. Contracts that are executed on *one* side (one party has performed) can be rescinded only if the party who has performed receives consideration for agreeing to call off the deal.

Novation The process of **novation** substitutes a new contract for an old one, terminating the rights under the old contract. A third party takes the place of one of the original parties. Essentially, the parties to the original contract and one or more new parties all get together and agree to the substitution. The requirements of a novation are as follows:

1. The existence of a previous, valid obligation.
2. Agreement by all the parties to a new contract.
3. The extinguishing of the old obligation (discharge of the prior party).
4. A new, valid contract.

LEARNING OUTCOME 2
Describe how parties can discharge their contract by agreement.

novation
The substitution, by agreement, of a new contract for an old one, with the rights under the old one being terminated.

HIGHLIGHTING THE POINT

Glasso Corporation contracts to sell its pharmaceutical division to Phistar Pharma, Ltd. Before the transfer is completed, Glasso, Phistar, and a third company, HealthCare Industries, Inc., execute a new agreement to transfer all of Phistar's rights and duties in the transaction to HealthCare.

Is the original contract discharged and replaced with the new contract? Yes. As long as the new contract is supported by consideration, the novation will discharge the original contract (between Glasso and Phistar) and replace it with the new contract

(Continued)

(between Glasso and HealthCare). Phistar prefers a novation instead of an assignment because the novation discharges all of the liabilties associated with its contract with Glasso. If Phistar had simply assigned the contract to HealthCare, Phistar would have remained liable to Glasso for any payments under the contract if HealthCare defaulted.

accord and satisfaction
An agreement and payment (or other performance) between two parties, one of whom has a right of action against the other.

Accord and Satisfaction In an **accord and satisfaction,** the parties agree to accept performance different from the performance originally promised. An *accord* is defined as an executory contract (one that has not yet been performed) to perform some act in order to satisfy an existing contractual duty. The duty is not yet discharged. A *satisfaction* is the performance of the accord. An *accord* and its *satisfaction* (performance) discharge the original contractual obligation.

Once the accord has been made, the original obligation is merely suspended. The obligor can discharge the original obligation by performing the obligation agreed to in the accord. Likewise, if the obligor refuses to perform the accord, the obligee can bring an action on the original obligation.

EXAMPLE 17.6 Shep obtains a judgment against Marla for $8,000. Later, both parties agree that the judgment can be satisfied by Marla's transfer of her automobile to Shep. This agreement to accept the auto in lieu of $8,000 is the accord. If Marla transfers her automobile to Shep, the accord agreement is fully performed (satisfied), and the $8,000 obligation is discharged. If Marla refuses to transfer her car, the accord is breached. Because the original obligation is merely suspended, Shep can sue to enforce the judgment for $8,000 or bring an action for breach of the accord. ◄ See this chapter's *Linking Business Law to Your Career* feature for more on performance and compromise.

17–1d Discharge by Operation of Law

Under some circumstances, contractual duties may be discharged by operation of law. These circumstances include the running of the relevant statute of limitations and impossibility of performance.

statute of limitations
A statute setting the maximum time period during which a certain action can be brought.

Statute of Limitations A **statute of limitations** limits the time during which a party can sue on a particular cause of action. After the time has passed, a suit based on that cause can no longer be brought. The statutory period for bringing a suit for breach of a written contract is typically four or five years.

impossibility of performance
A doctrine under which a party to a contract is relieved of the duty to perform when performance becomes impossible or totally impracticable.

When Performance Is Impossible or Impracticable After a contract has been made, performance may become impossible in an objective sense. This is known as **impossibility of performance** and may discharge a contract. This *objective impossibility* ("It cannot be done.") must be distinguished from *subjective impossibility* ("I'm sorry, I personally cannot do it."). Examples of *subjective* impossibility include contracts in which goods cannot be delivered on time because of freight car shortages and contracts in which payments cannot be made on time because the bank is closed.

In effect, the party in these cases is saying, "It is impossible for *me* to perform," not "It is impossible for *anyone* to perform." Accordingly, such excuses do not discharge a contract, and the nonperforming party is normally held in breach of contract.

Impossibility of Performance. Certain situations generally qualify under the objective-impossibility rules to discharge contractual obligations:

1. *When one of the parties to a personal contract dies or becomes incapacitated before a performance.* **EXAMPLE 17.7** Fred, a famous dancer, contracts with Ethereal Dancing Guild to play a leading role in its new ballet. Before the ballet can be performed, Fred becomes ill and dies. His personal performance was essential to the completion of the contract. Thus, his death discharges the contract.◄

2. *When the specific subject matter of the contract is destroyed.* **EXAMPLE 17.8** Ace Farm Equipment agrees to sell Gudgel a specific tractor on its lot and promises to have it ready for Gudgel to pick up on Saturday. On Friday night, a bus veers off the nearby highway and smashes into the tractor, destroying it beyond repair. The accident renders Ace's performance impossible.◄

3. *When a change in the law renders performance illegal.* **EXAMPLE 17.9** T-Square Construction enters into a contract to build a row of townhouses for Uptown Homes at a certain location. When the zoning laws are changed to prohibit the construction of residential property at the planned location, the contract becomes impossible to perform.◄

Real-World Case Example

Hilary Kolodin, a jazz singer, was involved personally with John Valenti, the president of Jayarvee, Inc., which manages artists, produces recordings, and owns and operates Birdland. Kolodin contracted professionally with Jayarvee. When Kolodin and Valenti's personal relationship deteriorated, they agreed to have contact only through legal counsel. Later, Kolodin filed a suit in a New York state court against Valenti, alleging breach of her Jayarvee contracts and seeking their rescission. The court issued a judgment in Kolodin's favor. Valenti appealed.

Did Kolodin and Valenti's agreement render objectively impossible the performance of Kolodin's Jayarvee contracts? Yes. In a 2014 case, *Kolodin v. Valenti*, a state intermediate appellate court affirmed the lower court's judgment. Performance of the contracts was rendered objectively impossible by the stipulation prohibiting contact between the parties except through legal counsel. Performance would require Valenti's input because of his position with Jayarvee, and "the [legal counsel] stipulation was not foreseeable, such that the parties could have contracted around it."

Commercial Impracticability. Performance becomes *commercially impracticable* when it turns out to be significantly more difficult or expensive than anticipated. A party may sometimes be excused from performing a contract under the doctrine of **commercial impracticability.** **EXAMPLE 17.10** Sanchez Excavation Company contracts with Energy Fuel to bury a pipeline. Several days into the work, Sanchez encounters unforeseen difficulties in the subsurface that significantly increases its original excavation costs. Both parties agree to discharge the contract on the ground of commercial impracticability.◄

Caution should be used in invoking the doctrine of commercial impracticability. The added burden of performing must be *extreme* and must *not* have been foreseeable by the parties at the time the contract was made.

Temporary Impossibility. An occurrence or event (such as a war) that makes it temporarily impossible to perform the act for which a party has contracted

commercial impracticability
A doctrine that may excuse the duty to perform a contract when it becomes much more difficult or costly due to forces neither party could control at the time of contract formation.

operates to suspend performance until the impossibility ceases. Then, ordinarily, the parties must perform the contract as originally planned.

EXAMPLE 17.11 Estelle contracted to sell her house to Marrero for $200,000. Five days later, the house was damaged in a hurricane. Estelle refused to pay the estimated $50,000 required to repair the house. If Marrero filed a suit to enforce the contract, a court would hold that the natural disaster had not discharged the contract on the ground of impossibility, but only suspended performance on the ground of temporary impossibility. The court most likely would order Estelle to repair the house and then perform the contract with Marrero. ◄

If, however, the lapse of time and the change in circumstances make it substantially more burdensome for the parties to perform the promised acts, then the contract can be discharged. For a visual summary of all the ways in which a contract can be discharged, see Exhibit 17.1.

17–2 CONTRACT REMEDIES

A **remedy** is the relief provided for an innocent party when the other party has breached the contract. It is the means employed to enforce a right or to redress an injury. The most common remedies are *damages, rescission and restitution,* and *specific performance.*

17–2a Types of Damages

A breach of contract entitles the nonbreaching party to sue for damages (money). **Damages** are designed to compensate the nonbreaching party for the loss of the bargain. Generally, innocent parties are to be placed in the position they would have occupied had the contract been performed. Several types of damages are discussed in the sections that follow.

Compensatory Damages Damages compensating the nonbreaching party for the loss of the bargain are known as **compensatory damages.** These damages compensate the injured party only for injuries actually sustained and proved to have arisen

---

remedy
The relief given to innocent parties, by law or by contract, to enforce a right or to prevent or compensate for the violation of a right.

damages
Money sought as a remedy for a breach of contract or for a tortious act.

compensatory damages
A money award equivalent to the actual value of injuries or damages sustained by the aggrieved party.

EXHIBIT 17.1   Contract Discharge

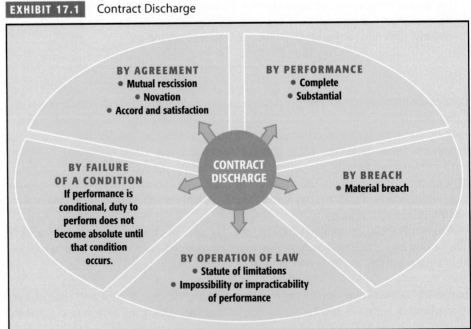

directly from the loss of the bargain due to the breach of contract. Compensatory damages simply replace the loss caused by the wrong or injury.

LEARNING OUTCOME 3
Identify different types of damages.

The amount of compensatory damages is the difference between the value of the breaching party's promised performance and the value of his or her actual performance. This amount is reduced by any loss that the injured party has avoided. **EXAMPLE 17.12** If Mary is hired to perform certain services during August for $3,000, but her employer breaches the contract and she finds another job that pays only $500, she can recover $2,500 as compensatory damages. She can also recover expenses she incurred in finding the other job. These are *incidental damages*—damages directly resulting from a breach of contract, including expenses incurred because of the breach.◄

The measurement of compensatory damages varies by type of contract. In a contract for a sale of goods, the usual measure of compensatory damages is the difference between the contract price and the market price at the time and place of delivery.

Consequential Damages Consequential damages, also referred to as *special damages*, are foreseeable damages that result from a party's breach of contract. They differ from compensatory damages in that they are caused by special circumstances beyond the contract itself. When a seller does not deliver goods, knowing that a buyer is planning to resell those goods immediately, consequential damages are awarded for the loss of profits from the planned resale.

consequential damages
Special damages that compensate for a loss that is not direct or immediate.

EXAMPLE 17.13 Marty contracts to buy a certain quantity of Quench, a specialty sports drink, from Nathan. Nathan knows that Marty has contracted with Ruthie to resell and ship the Quench within hours of its receipt. The beverage is then to be sold to fans attending the Super Bowl. Nathan fails to deliver the Quench. Marty can recover the consequential damages—the loss of profits from the planned resale to Ruthie—caused by the nondelivery.◄

For a nonbreaching party to recover consequential damages, the breaching party must know (or have reason to know) that special circumstances will cause the nonbreaching party to suffer an additional loss.

HIGHLIGHTING THE POINT

Gilmore contracts to have a specific item shipped to her—one that she desperately needs to repair her printing press. Gilmore tells the shipper that she must receive the item by Monday or she will not be able to print her paper and will lose $750.

If the shipper is late, what can Gilmore recover? Gilmore can recover the consequential damages caused by the delay (the $750 in losses).

Punitive Damages Punitive damages, also known as *exemplary damages*, generally are not recoverable in an action for breach of contract. Punitive damages are designed to punish and make an example of a wrongdoer for the purpose of deterring similar conduct in the future. Such damages have no legitimate place in contract law because they are, in essence, penalties, and a breach of contract is not unlawful in a criminal sense. A contract is, after all, a civil relationship between the parties. The law may compensate one party for the loss of the bargain—no more and no less.

punitive damages
Compensation in excess of actual or consequential damages awarded to punish the wrongdoer.

In a few situations, a person's actions can cause both a breach of contract and a tort, and punitive damages may be available. Overall, though, punitive damages are almost never available in contract disputes.

liquidated damages
An amount, stipulated in a contract, that the parties to the contract believe to be a reasonable estimate of the damages that will occur in the event of a breach.

penalty
A sum named in a contract as punishment for a default.

Liquidated Damages A **liquidated damages** provision in a contract specifies a certain amount to be paid in the event of a future default or breach of contract. (*Liquidated* means determined, settled, or fixed.) Liquidated damages differ from penalties. A **penalty** specifies a certain amount to be paid in the event of a default or breach of contract and is *designed to penalize* the breaching party. Liquidated damages provisions normally are enforceable, but penalty provisions are not.

To determine whether a particular provision is for liquidated damages or for a penalty, answer two questions:

1. When the contract was formed, were the potential damages that would be incurred if the contract was not performed on time difficult to estimate?
2. Was the amount set as damages a reasonable estimate of those potential damages?

If both answers are yes, the provision is for liquidated damages and will be enforced. If either answer is no, the provision is for a penalty and normally will not be enforced.

17–2b Mitigation of Damages

In most situations, when a breach of contract occurs, the injured party has a duty to mitigate, or reduce, the damages that he or she suffers. Under this doctrine of **mitigation of damages,** the required action depends on the nature of the situation.

mitigation of damages
A rule requiring a plaintiff to have done whatever was reasonable to minimize the damages caused by the defendant.

In the majority of states, for example, a person whose employment has been wrongfully terminated has a duty to mitigate damages incurred because of the employer's breach of the employment contract. In other words, a wrongfully terminated employee has a duty to take a similar job if one is available. If the person fails to do this, the damages received will be equivalent to the person's former salary less the income he or she would have received in a similar job obtained by reasonable means.

17–2c Rescission and Restitution

LEARNING OUTCOME 4

Define the remedy of rescission and restitution.

restitution
The restoration of goods, property, or funds previously conveyed; necessary to rescind a contract.

Rescission is essentially an action to undo, or cancel, a contract and to return non-breaching parties to the positions that they occupied before the transaction. When fraud, mistake, duress, or failure of consideration is present, rescission is available. The failure of one party to perform entitles the other party to rescind the contract. The rescinding party must give prompt notice to the breaching party. To rescind a contract, the parties must make **restitution** to each other by returning goods, property, or funds previously conveyed.

If the property or goods can be returned, they must be. If the property or goods have been consumed, restitution must be an equivalent amount of money. Basically, restitution refers to the recapture of a benefit conferred on the defendant through which the defendant has been unjustly enriched.

HIGHLIGHTING THE POINT

Alima pays $10,000 to Milos in return for Milos's promise to design a house for her. The next day, Milos calls Alima and tells her that he has taken a position with a large architectural firm in another state and cannot design the house. Alima decides to hire another architect that afternoon.

If Alima sues Milos for restitution, what can Alima recover? Alima can obtain restitution of $10,000, because an unjust benefit of $10,000 was conferred on Milos.

17–2d Specific Performance

The equitable remedy of **specific performance** calls for the exact performance of the act promised in the contract. This remedy is quite attractive to the nonbreaching party because it provides the exact bargain promised in the contract. It also avoids some of the problems inherent in a suit for money damages, such as collecting a judgment and arranging another contract. Moreover, the actual performance may be more valuable than the monetary damages.

Although the equitable remedy of specific performance is often preferable to other remedies, it is not granted unless the party's legal remedy (monetary damages) is inadequate. Contracts for the sale of goods, such as wheat or corn, that are readily available on the market rarely qualify for specific performance. Damages ordinarily are adequate in such situations because substantially identical goods can be bought or sold in the market.

Sale of Land If the goods are rare or unique, such as a painting or parcel of land, a court of equity will decree specific performance because obtaining substantially identical goods in the market is nearly impossible. **EXAMPLE 17.14** Levy contracted to sell twelve acres to Solano for $65,000. Solano paid for a survey and other costs, and gave Levy $1,000 as a demonstration of intent to fulfill the contract. Before the sale closed, Levy died. His heir, Herschel, refused to go through with the deal. Solano filed a suit against Herschel. Because Solano had substantially fulfilled his duties under the contract and stood ready to perform the rest, a court would issue an order of specific performance in his favor. ◄

Contracts for Personal Services Personal-service contracts require one party to work personally for another party. Courts normally refuse to grant specific performance of personal-service contracts. This is because ordering a party to perform personal services against his or her will amounts to involuntary servitude, which is against public policy.

EXAMPLE 17.15 Terrence needs brain surgery so he contracts with Elizabeth, a local physician, to perform the procedure. A week later, Elizabeth refuses to perform the surgery. A court would not compel (nor would Terrence want) Elizabeth to perform under the circumstances. There is no way that a court could ensure meaningful performance in such a situation. ◄

17–3 RECOVERY BASED ON QUASI CONTRACT

In some situations, when no actual contract exists, a court may step in to prevent one party from being unjustly enriched at the expense of another party. *Quasi contract* is a legal theory under which an obligation is imposed in the absence of an agreement.

The courts can also use this theory when the parties entered into a contract, but it is unenforceable for some reason. **EXAMPLE 17.16** Norman Ericson contracts to build two oil derricks for Petro Industries. The derricks are to be built over a period of three years, but the parties do not create a written contract. Therefore, the writing requirement of the Statute of Frauds will bar the enforcement of the contract. After Ericson completes one derrick, Petro informs him that it will not pay for the derrick. Ericson can sue Petro under the theory of quasi contract. ◄

To recover on a quasi contract theory, a party must show the following:

1. The party conferred a benefit on the other party.

2. The party conferred the benefit with the reasonable expectation of being paid.

3. The party did not act as a volunteer in conferring the benefit.

4. The party receiving the benefit would be unjustly enriched by retaining the benefit without paying for it.

specific performance
An equitable remedy requiring exactly the performance that was specified in a contract.

LEARNING OUTCOME 5

Explain the remedy of specific performance.

ANSWERING THE LEGAL PROBLEM

In the legal problem set out at the beginning of this chapter, a contract specified Brand X plasterboard, but the builder substituted Brand Y, which is identical in quality and durability.

A **Does this deviation from the contract constitute a breach? Can the DeLeons avoid the contract on this basis?** Very likely, a court will hold that the builder has substantially performed her end of the bargain, and the buyers are therefore obligated to pay. **What if the plasterboard substituted for Brand X had been inferior in quality, reducing the value of the house by $20,000?** A court would likely hold that the contract had been substantially performed and the contract price should be paid, less the $20,000.

LINKING BUSINESS LAW to Your Career

PERFORMANCE AND COMPROMISE

In any career field, if you become a contractor, you may take on a job that you cannot or do not wish to perform. Simply walking away from the job and hoping for the best normally is not the most effective way to avoid litigation, which can be costly, time consuming, and emotionally draining. Instead, you should consider various options that may reduce the likelihood of litigation.

Suppose that you are a building contractor and you sign a contract to build a home for the Andersons. Performance is to begin on June 15. On June 1, Central Enterprises offers you a position that will yield you two and a half times the amount of income you could earn as an independent builder. To take this new job, you would have to start on June 15.

Consider Your Options When You Cannot Perform

What can you do in this situation? One option is to subcontract the work on the Andersons' home to another builder and oversee the work to make sure it conforms to the contract. Another option is to negotiate with the Andersons for a release. You can offer to find another contractor who will build a house of the same quality at the same price. Or you can offer to pay any additional costs if another builder takes the job but is more expensive.

In any event, this additional cost would be one measure of damages that a court would impose on you if the Andersons prevailed in a lawsuit for breach of contract (in addition to any costs the Andersons suffered as a

result of the breach, such as costs due to the delay in construction). Thus, by making the offer, you might be able to avoid the expense of litigation—if the Andersons accept.

What to Consider When You Make an Offer

Often, parties are reluctant to propose compromise settlements because they fear that what they say will be used against them in court if litigation ensues. Generally, offers for settlement will not be admitted in court to prove liability for a breach of contract, but at times, they are admissible to prove that a party breached the duty of good faith. For this reason, the best course might be to work with your attorney in making an offer unless only an insignificant amount of money is involved.

TERMS AND CONCEPTS FOR REVIEW

accord and satisfaction 220

breach of contract 217

commercial impracticability 221

compensatory damages 222

consequential damages 223

damages 222

discharge 217

impossibility of performance 220

liquidated damages 224

mitigation of damages 224

novation 219

penalty 224

performance 217

punitive damages 223

remedy 222

restitution 224

specific performance 225

statute of limitations 220

tender 218

CHAPTER SUMMARY—CONTRACT DISCHARGE AND REMEDIES

LEARNING OUTCOME

1   **Explain the difference between complete and substantial contractual performance.** A contract may be discharged by complete (strict) performance or by substantial performance. Complete performance takes place when conditions expressly stated in a contract fully occur in all aspects. Substantial performance does not vary greatly from the performance promised in a contract and must result in substantially the same benefits. If performance is substantial, the other party's duty to perform remains absolute (less damages for the deviation). Totally inadequate performance constitutes a material breach of the contract—the other party is excused from performance and can sue for damages caused by the breach.

2   **Describe how parties can discharge their contract by agreement.** Any contract can be discharged by an agreement of the parties. This may occur as part of the original contract, or the parties may form a new contract that expressly or impliedly discharges the original contract. Parties may also agree to discharge their contract by:

(1) *Mutual rescission*—Canceling their contract and returning to the positions they held before its formation.
(2) *Novation*—Substituting a new new contract for the old one, with a new party taking the place of one of the original parties.
(3) *Accord and satisfaction*—Agreeing to accept performance different from what was originally promised.

3   **Identify different types of damages.** Damages are designed to compensate a nonbreaching party for the loss of a bargain on the breach of a contract. Damages attempt to place the parties in the positions they would have occupied had the contract been performed. Types of damages include the following:

(1) *Compensatory damages*—Damages that compensate a nonbreaching party for injuries actually sustained from a breach and proved to have arisen directly from the loss of a bargain, which is the difference between the value of the promised performance and the value of the actual performance.
(2) *Consequential damages*—Damages that result from special circumstances beyond a contract, which a breaching party knew or had reason to know would cause a nonbreaching party to incur an additional loss.
(3) *Punitive damages*—Damages that punish a breaching party but are normally awarded only in a case of willful or malicious misconduct involving a tort.
(4) *Liquidated damages*—Damages that a contract specifies as the amount to be paid on its breach as a reasonable estimate of potential damages.

4   **Define the remedy of rescission and restitution.** *Rescission* is an action to cancel a contract and return the parties to the positions that they occupied before the transaction. The rescinding party must give prompt notice to the breaching party. When a contract is rescinded, the parties must make *restitution*—return to each other the goods, property, or money previously conveyed.

5   **Explain the remedy of specific performance.** *Specific performance* is an equitable remedy requiring the exact performance of an act promised in a contract. It is available when monetary damages would be an inadequate remedy and the subject matter of the contract is unique. It usually is not available as a remedy on the breach of a contract for personal services.

ISSUE SPOTTERS

Check your answers to the *Issue Spotters* against the answers provided in Appendix C at the end of this text.

1. George contracts to build a storage shed for Ron. Ron pays George in full, but George completes only half the work. Ron pays Paula $500 to finish the shed. If Ron sues George, what would be the measure of recovery? (**See** *Contract Remedies.*)

2. Amy contracts to sell her ranch to Mark, who is to take possession on June 1. Amy delays the transfer until August 1. Mark incurs expenses in providing for cattle that he bought to stock the ranch. When they made the contract, Amy had no reason to know of the cattle. Is Amy liable for Mark's expenses in providing for the cattle? Explain your answer. (**See** *Contract Remedies.*)

USING BUSINESS LAW

17–1. Compensatory Damages. Ken owns and operates a famous candy store and makes most of the candy sold in the store. Business is particularly heavy during the Christmas season. Ken contracts with Sweet, Inc., to purchase ten thousand pounds of sugar to be delivered on or before November 15. Ken has informed Sweet that this particular order is to be used for the Christmas season. Because of problems at the refinery, the sugar is not tendered to Ken until December 10. Ken refuses to accept the sugar, saying it is too late. Ken has been unable to purchase the quantity of sugar needed to meet his Christmas orders and has had to turn down numerous regular customers, some of whom have indicated that they will purchase candy elsewhere in the future. What sugar Ken has been able to purchase has cost him 10 cents per pound more than the price contracted for with Sweet. Ken sues Sweet for breach of contract, claiming as damages the higher price paid for sugar from others, lost profits from this year's lost Christmas sales, future lost profits from customers who said that they will stop doing business with him, and punitive damages for failure to meet the contracted delivery date. Sweet claims Ken is limited to compensatory damages only. Discuss who is correct, and why. (**See** *Contract Remedies.*)

17–2. Objective Impossibility of Performance. Millie contracted to sell Frank 1,000 bushels of corn to be grown on her farm. Owing to drought conditions during the growing season, Millie's yield was much less than anticipated, and she could deliver only 250 bushels to Frank. Frank accepted the lesser amount but sued Millie for breach of contract. Can Millie defend successfully on the basis of objective impossibility of performance? Explain. (**See** *Contract Discharge.*)

REAL-WORLD CASE PROBLEMS

17–3. Specific Performance. Russ Wyant owned Humble Ranch in South Dakota. Edward Humble was Wyant's uncle and held a two-year option to buy the ranch from Wyant. The option included specific conditions. Once it was exercised, for instance, the parties had thirty days to enter into a purchase agreement and the seller could become the buyer's lender by matching the terms of the proposed financing. After the option was exercised, Wyant and Humble engaged in lengthy negotiations. Humble, however, did not respond to Wyant's proposed purchase agreement nor did Humble advise him of available financing terms before the option expired. Six months later, Humble filed a suit against Wyant to enforce the option. Is Humble entitled to specific performance? Explain. [*Humble v. Wyant*, 843 N.W.2d 334 (S.Dak. 2014)] (**See** *Contract Remedies.*)

17–4. Damages. Before buying a house, Dean and Donna Testa hired Ground Systems, Inc. (GSI), to inspect the sewage and water disposal system. GSI reported a split system with a watertight septic tank, a wastewater tank, a distribution box, and a leach field. The Testas bought the house. Later, Dean discovered that the system was not as GSI described. There was no distribution box or leach field, and there was only one tank, which was not watertight. The Testas arranged for the installation of a new system and sold the house. Assuming that GSI is liable for breach of contract, what is the measure of damages? [*Testa v. Ground Systems, Inc.*, 206 N.J.Super. 330, 20 A.3d 435 (App.Div. 2011)] (**See** *Contract Remedies.*)

17–5. Liquidated Damages. Planned Pethood Plus, Inc. (PPP), a veterinary clinic, borrowed $389,000 from KeyBank. The term of the loan was ten years. A "prepayment penalty" clause provided a formula to add an amount to the balance due if PPP offered to repay its loan early. The additional amount depended on the time of the prepayment. Such clauses are common in loan agreements. After one year, PPP offered to pay its loan. KeyBank applied the formula to add $40,525.92 to the balance due. Is this a penalty or liquidated damages? Explain. [*Planned Pethood Plus, Inc. v. KeyCorp, Inc.*, 228 P.3d 262 (Colo.App. 2010)] (See *Contract Remedies*.)

17–6. Liquidated Damages. B-Sharp Musical Productions, Inc., contracted with James Haber to provide a sixteen-piece band at Haber's son's bar mitzvah for $30,000. Their contract stipulated payment of half of the price if Haber canceled more than ninety days before the performance and payment of the entire price if he canceled less than ninety days before. Haber canceled the deal less than ninety days before the bar mitzvah, but refused to pay the price. Is the provision for the payment of the entire price enforceable? Explain. [*B-Sharp Musical Productions, Inc. v. Haber*, 27 Misc.3d 41, 899 N.Y.S.2d 792 (2010)] (See *Contract Remedies*.)

ETHICAL QUESTIONS

17–7. Impossibility of Performance. Should the courts allow the defense of impossibility of performance to be be used more often? (See *Contract Discharge*.)

17–8. Liquidated Damages. Should liquidated damages clauses be enforced when no actual damages have been incurred? (See *Contract Remedies*.)

17–9. Discharge by Performance. On a weekday, Tamara Cohen, a real estate broker, showed a townhouse owned by Ray and Harriet Mayer to Jessica Seinfeld, the wife of comedian Jerry Seinfeld. On the weekend, Cohen was

unavailable because her religious beliefs prevented her from working, but the Seinfelds revisited the townhouse on their own and agreed to buy it. The contract stated that the "buyers will pay buyer's real estate broker's fees." Is Cohen entitled to payment even though she was not available on the weekend? What obligation do parties in business owe to each other with respect to their religious beliefs? How might the situation in this case have been avoided? [*Cohen v. Seinfeld*, 15 Misc.3d 1118(A), 839 N.Y.S.2d 432 (Sup. 2007)] (See *Contract Discharge*.)

Chapter 17—Work Set

TRUE-FALSE QUESTIONS

_____ 1. Complete performance occurs when a contract's conditions are fully satisfied.

_____ 2. A material breach of contract does not discharge the other party's duty to perform.

_____ 3. An executory contract cannot be rescinded.

_____ 4. Damages compensate a nonbreaching party for the loss of the contract or give a nonbreaching party the benefit of the contract.

_____ 5. Punitive damages are usually not awarded for a breach of contract.

_____ 6. Liquidated damages are uncertain in amount.

_____ 7. Consequential damages are awarded for foreseeable losses caused by special circumstances beyond the contract.

_____ 8. Specific performance is available only when damages are also an adequate remedy.

_____ 9. Objective impossibility discharges a contract.

MULTIPLE-CHOICE QUESTIONS

_____ 1. Sam owes Lyle $100. Sam promises, in writing, to give Lyle a video-game machine in lieu of payment of the debt. Lyle agrees, and Sam delivers the machine. Substituting and performing one duty for another is

a. a rescission.
b. an accord and satisfaction.
c. a novation.
d. none of the above.

_____ 2. C&D Services contracts with Ace Concessions, Inc., to service Ace's vending machines. Later, C&D wants Dean Vending Services to assume the duties under a new contract. Ace consents. This is

a. a rescission.
b. an accord and satisfaction.
c. an alteration of contract.
d. a novation.

_____ 3. Kate contracts with Bob to transport Bob's goods to his stores. If this contract is discharged as most contracts are, it will be discharged by

a. performance.
b. agreement.
c. operation of law.
d. none of the above.

_____ 4. Alan contracts with Pam to build a shopping mall on Pam's land. Before construction begins, the city enacts a law that makes it illegal to build a mall in Pam's area. Performance of this contract is

a. not affected.
b. temporarily suspended.
c. discharged.
d. discharged on Pam's obligations only.

5. Mix Corporation contracts to sell to Frosty Malts, Inc., eight steel mixers. When Mix refuses to deliver, Frosty buys mixers from MaxCo for 25 percent more than the contract price. Frosty is entitled to damages equal to

a. what Mix's profits would have been.
b. the price Frosty would have had to pay Mix.
c. the difference between what Frosty would have had to pay Mix and what Frosty did pay MaxCo.
d. what Frosty paid MaxCo.

6. Dave contracts with Paul to buy a delivery truck. Dave tells Paul that if the truck is not delivered on Monday, he will lose $12,000 in business. Paul does not deliver the truck on Monday. Dave is forced to rent a truck on Tuesday. Dave is entitled to

a. compensatory damages.
b. incidental damages.
c. consequential damages.
d. all of the above.

7. Jay agrees in writing to sell a warehouse and the land on which it is located to Nora. When Jay refuses to go through with the deal, Nora sues. Jay must transfer the land and warehouse to Nora if she is awarded

a. rescission and restitution.
b. specific performance.
c. novation.
d. none of the above.

8. Jake agrees to hire Teresa. Their contract provides that if Jake fires Teresa, she is to be paid whatever amount would have been payable if she had worked for the full term. This clause is

a. a liquidated damages clause.
b. a penalty clause.
c. both a and b.
d. none of the above.

ANSWERING MORE LEGAL PROBLEMS

1. Russo contracts with Playlist, Inc., to create a Web site through which users can post and share movies, music, and other forms of digital entertainment. Russo goes to work. Before the site is online, however, Congress passes the No Online Piracy in Entertainment (NOPE) Act. The NOPE act makes it illegal to operate a Web site on which copyrighted works are posted without the copyright owners' consent.

   Is Russo and Playlist's contract discharged? Yes. The contract was discharged by operation of law. After a contract has been made, performance may become impossible in an _____ sense. This impossibility of performance may discharge a contract. Certain situations qualify under the _____-impossibility rules to discharge contractual obligations, such as when a change in law renders performance of a contract illegal. Here, the purpose of the contract has been rendered illegal. The contract is discharged for _____ impossibility on the ground of illegality.

2. Marketshare, Inc., contracts with Ogle, a popular search engine, to use the searches conducted by Ogle's users to compile data that will accurately pinpoint the users' interests and provide advertisers with a precisely targeted audience. Marketshare promises that the result will be worth $5 billion, but its data produce incorrect assumptions about Ogle's users and mistargeted ads. The value of this effort to Ogle is actually $1 billion. Ogle files a suit for breach of contract.

   What is the measure of compensatory damages for this breach? The measure of compensatory damages generally is the difference between the value of the breaching party's promised _____ and the value of his or her actual _____. Compensatory damages compensate the nonbreaching party for the loss of a _____. They compensate the injured party only for injuries actually sustained and proved to have arisen directly from the loss of the _____ due to the breach of contract. The amount of compensatory damages for this breach could be as much as $4 billion.

SALES AND LEASES

UNIT CONTENTS

CHAPTER 18 Introduction to Sales and Lease Contracts

CHAPTER 19 Title and Risk of Loss

CHAPTER 20 Performance and Breach

CHAPTER 21 Warranties and Product Liability

CHAPTER 22 Consumer Protection

LEARNING OUTCOMES

The five Learning Outcomes below are designed to help improve your understanding of the chapter. After reading this chapter, you should be able to:

1. State the scope of Article 2 of the UCC.

2. Identify how the UCC deals with open contract terms.

3. Explain whether a contract under the UCC contains any additional terms included in the offeree's acceptance.

4. Discuss the UCC exceptions to the Statute of Frauds.

5. Describe what a court can do when confronted with an unconscionable contract or clause.

sales contract
A contract to sell goods.

State the scope of Article 2 of the UCC.

sale
The passing of title to property from the seller to the buyer for a price.

FACING A LEGAL PROBLEM

Gene sold Festival Foods, a well-established concessions business, to Lindsey for $150,000. The deal involved numerous pieces of equipment, including a truck and trailer. Lindsey took the equipment and began to use it immediately. After six events, however, she wanted to return the equipment and get out of the deal entirely. Gene argued that Lindsey could not reject the deal because the contract was primarily a sale of goods and was subject to Article 2 of the UCC. Under Article 2, Gene argued, Lindsey had waited too long to reject the deal. Lindsey claimed that the UCC did not apply to the sales transaction because she had primarily bought the services of the business.

 Does the UCC cover this deal? Why or why not?

When we turn to contracts for the sale and lease of goods, we move away from common law principles and into the area of statutory law. The state statutory law governing such transactions is based on the Uniform Commercial Code (UCC). The primary goal of the UCC is to simplify and streamline commercial transactions, allowing parties to form sales and lease contracts without observing the same degree of formality used in forming other types of contracts.

18–1 SALES OF GOODS

A contract for a sale of goods, or **sales contract**, is governed by the common law principles applicable to all contracts, and you should reexamine these principles when studying sales. The law of sales is based on Article 2 of the UCC. (Article 2 of the UCC is included as Appendix B in this text.)

18–1a What Is a Sale?

The UCC states that Article 2 "applies to transactions in goods." This implies a broad scope—covering leases, gifts, bailments (temporary deliveries of personal property), and purchases of goods. In this chapter, however, we (as would most authorities and courts) treat Article 2 as being applicable only to an actual sale.

A **sale** is officially defined as "the passing of title from the seller to the buyer for a price," where *title* refers to the formal right of ownership of property. The price may be payable in cash (or its equivalent) or in other goods or services.

Real-World Case Example

Nautilus Insurance Company provided commercial property insurance to Blasini, Inc., doing business as the Attic Bar & Grill in Omaha, Nebraska. Following a fire at the bar, Nautilus filed an action in a Nebraska state court against several defendants, including Cheran Investments, LLC, to determine who was entitled to the insurance proceeds for the personal property damage at the bar. Under a sales agreement with Cheran, Blasini had agreed to buy the Attic's business assets but had failed to pay the full purchase price. Blasini was making monthly payments on the purchase price. The court declared Cheran the owner of the personal property, and Blasini appealed.

Did the sale of the Attic's assets pass title to those goods to Blasini? Yes. In a 2014 case, *Nautilus Insurance Co. v. Cheran Investments LLC*, a state intermediate appellate court reversed the lower court's ruling. Under Section 2–401 of the UCC, title to the Attic's assets passed to Blasini at the time the company contracted with Cheran, and Blasini became the owner—regardless of whether the purchase price had been fully paid.

18–1b What Are Goods?

To be characterized as a good, an item of property must be tangible, and it must be movable. **Tangible property** has physical existence—it can be touched or seen. **Intangible property**—such as corporate stocks and bonds, patents and copyrights, and ordinary contract rights—has only conceptual existence and thus does not come under Article 2. A movable item can be carried from place to place.

tangible property
Property that has physical existence (such as a car).

intangible property
Property that cannot be seen or touched but exists only conceptually (such as corporate stocks).

Goods Associated with Real Estate Real estate is excluded from Article 2. Real estate includes land, interests in land, and things permanently attached to the land. For example, a contract for the sale of minerals (including oil and gas) or a structure (such as a building) is a contract for a sale of goods *if they are to be severed from the land by the seller.* A sale of growing crops or timber to be cut is a contract for a sale of goods *regardless of who severs them.* Other "things attached" to realty but capable of severance without material harm to the realty (such as a window air conditioner) are considered goods *regardless of who severs them from the land.*

Goods and Services Combined The majority of courts treat contracts for services as being excluded from Article 2 of the UCC. In cases in which goods and services are combined, however, courts disagree. For example, is the blood furnished to a patient during an operation a sale of goods or the performance of a medical service? Some courts say it is a good, but others say it is a service.

Because the UCC does not provide the answer, the courts generally use the *predominant-factor test* to determine whether a contract is primarily for the sale of goods or for the sale of services. This determination is important. If a court decides that a mixed contract is primarily a goods contract, any dispute, even a dispute over the services portion, will be decided under the UCC.

18–1c Who Is a Merchant?

Article 2 governs the sale of goods in general. It applies to sales transactions between all buyers and sellers. In a limited number of instances, however, the UCC

merchant
A person who is engaged in the purchase and sale of goods.

presumes that in certain phases of sales transactions involving **merchants,** special business standards ought to be imposed because of the merchants' relatively high degree of commercial expertise. Such standards do not apply to the casual or inexperienced seller or buyer (consumer). Under the UCC, a merchant is a person who deals in goods of the kind involved in the sales contract or who, by occupation, *holds himself or herself out as having knowledge and skill* unique to the practices or goods involved in the transaction.

 ## 18–2 LEASES OF GOODS

Consumers and business firms lease automobiles, industrial equipment, and many other types of goods. Article 2A of the UCC covers any transaction that creates a lease of goods. Article 2A is essentially a repetition of Article 2, except that it applies to leases of goods, rather than sales of goods, and thus varies to reflect differences between sale and lease transactions.

lease agreement
An agreement in which one person (the lessor) agrees to transfer the right to the possession and use of the property or goods to another person (the lessee) in exchange for rental payments.

Article 2A defines a **lease agreement** as the lessor's and lessee's bargain, as found in their language and as implied by other circumstance. A **lessor** is one who transfers the right to the possession and use of goods under a lease. A **lessee** is one who acquires the right to the possession and use of goods under a lease.

lessor
A person who transfers the right to the possession and use of goods to another in exchange for rental payments.

 ## 18–3 SALES AND LEASE CONTRACTS

Note that sales and lease contracts are not governed exclusively by Articles 2 and 2A of the UCC. They are also governed by general contract law whenever it is relevant and has not been modified by the UCC. Exhibit 18.1 illustrates the relationship between general contract law and statutory law—UCC Articles 2 and 2A—governing contracts for the sale and lease of goods.

lessee
A person who acquires the right to the possession and use of another's goods in exchange for rental payments.

The following sections summarize the ways that UCC provisions *change* the effect of the general law of contracts. It is important to remember that parties to sales and lease contracts are free to establish whatever terms they wish. The UCC comes into play when the parties have left a term out of their contract and that omission later gives rise to a dispute.

EXHIBIT 18.1   Law Governing Contracts

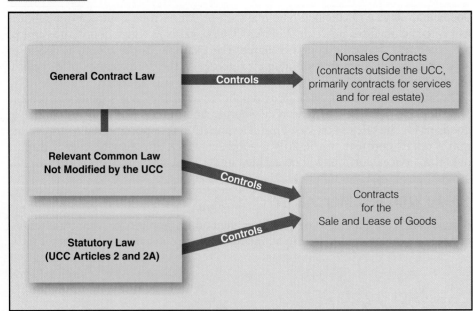

18–3a The Offer

In general contract law, the moment a definite offer is met by an unqualified acceptance, a binding contract is formed. In commercial sales transactions, the verbal exchanges, the correspondence, and the actions of the parties may not reveal exactly when a binding contract arises. The UCC states that an agreement sufficient to constitute a contract can exist even if the moment of its making is undetermined.

Open Terms According to contract law, an offer must be definite enough for the parties (and the courts) to ascertain its essential terms when it is accepted. The UCC states that a sales or lease contract will not fail for indefiniteness even if one or more terms are left open as long as (1) the parties intended to make a contract and (2) there is a reasonably certain basis for the court to grant an appropriate remedy.

LEARNING OUTCOME 2
Identify how the UCC deals with open contract terms.

Although the UCC has radically lessened the requirements for definiteness of terms, it has not removed the common law requirement that the contract be at least definite enough for the court to identify the agreement, so as to enforce the contract or award appropriate damages in the event of breach.

The UCC provides numerous *open-term* provisions that can be used to fill the gaps in a contract. Thus, in the case of a dispute, all that is necessary to prove the existence of a contract is an indication (such as a purchase order) that there is a contract. Missing terms can be proved by evidence, or it will be presumed that what the parties intended was whatever is reasonable. The *quantity* of goods involved must be expressly stated, however. If the quantity term is left open, the courts will have no basis for determining a remedy.

Merchant's Firm Offer Under regular contract principles, an offer can be revoked at any time before acceptance. The UCC has an exception that applies only to **firm offers** for the sale or lease of goods made by a *merchant* (regardless of whether or not the offeree is a merchant).

firm offer
An offer (by a merchant) that is irrevocable without consideration for a period of time (not longer than three months). A firm offer by a merchant must be in writing and must be signed by the offeror.

A firm offer exists if a merchant gives *assurances* in a *signed writing* that his or her offer will remain open. A firm offer is irrevocable without the necessity of consideration for the stated period or, if no definite period is stated, for a reasonable period (neither to exceed three months).

EXAMPLE 18.1 Chad, a car dealer, writes an e-mail to Ricardo from his business account on January 1 stating, "I have a 2016 Toyota RAV4 on the lot that I'll sell you for $20,500 any time between now and January 31." This writing creates a firm offer, and Chad will be liable for breach if he sells that Toyota RAV4 to someone other than Ricardo before January 31.◄

18–3b Acceptance

The following sections examine the UCC provisions covering acceptance. As you will see, acceptance of an offer to buy, sell, or lease goods generally may be made in any reasonable manner and by any reasonable means.

Methods of Acceptance The common law rule is that an offeror can specify a particular means of acceptance, making that means the only one effective for contract formation. Nonetheless, unauthorized means are effective as long as the acceptance is received by the specified deadline. When the offeror does not specify a means of acceptance, the UCC provides that acceptance can be made by any means of communication reasonable under the circumstances.

The UCC permits acceptance of an offer to buy goods for current or prompt shipment by either a *promise* to ship or the *prompt shipment* of the goods to the buyer. If the seller does not promise to ship the goods that the buyer ordered but instead ships goods that differ from the buyer's order in some way (a different color or size, for example), this shipment constitutes both an *acceptance* (a contract) and a *breach*. This rule does not apply if the seller seasonably (within a reasonable amount of time) notifies the buyer that the nonconforming shipment is offered only as an *accommodation* or as a favor. The notice of accommodation must clearly indicate to the buyer that the shipment does not constitute an acceptance and that, therefore, no contract has been formed.

HIGHLIGHTING THE POINT

McIntosh orders five thousand *blue* headphones from Halderson. Halderson ships five thousand *black* headphones to McIntosh, notifying McIntosh that, as Halderson has only black headphones in stock, these are sent as an accommodation.

Is the shipment of black headphones an acceptance or an offer? The shipment is an offer. A contract will be formed only if McIntosh accepts the black headphones. If Halderson ships black *without* notifying McIntosh that the goods are being sent *as an accommodation*, Halderson's shipment is both an acceptance of McIntosh's offer and a breach of the resulting contract. McIntosh may sue Halderson for any appropriate damages.

Notice of Acceptance Under the common law, because a unilateral offer invites acceptance by performance, the offeree need not notify the offeror of the performance unless the offeror would not otherwise know about it. Under the UCC, however, if a sales contract is unilateral, the offeror must be notified of the offeree's performance (acceptance) within a reasonable time, or the offeror can treat the offer as having lapsed.

LEARNING OUTCOME 3

Explain whether a contract under the UCC contains any additional terms included in the offeree's acceptance.

Additional Terms Under the common law, variations in terms between the offer and the offeree's acceptance violate the mirror image rule, which requires that the terms of an acceptance exactly mirror the offer. This rule causes considerable problems in commercial transactions, particularly when different standardized purchase order forms are used.

To avoid these problems, the UCC dispenses with the mirror image rule. Under the UCC, a contract is formed if the offeree makes a definite expression of acceptance (such as signing the form in the appropriate location), even though the terms of the acceptance modify or add to the terms of the original offer. What happens to these new terms? The answer depends on whether the parties are nonmerchants or merchants.

When One or Both Parties Are Nonmerchants If one (or both) of the parties is a nonmerchant, the contract is formed according to the terms of the original offer submitted by the original offeror and not according to the additional terms of the acceptance.

EXAMPLE 18.2 Tanya, a public school employee in Idaho, purchases five hundred red LED flashlights from Kool Gadgets, an online retailer based in Michigan. When the flashlights arrive, the accompanying invoice includes an additional term that states any dispute between the parties will be settled in Michigan. When a dispute arises regarding payment, Kool files a suit in Michigan. The school district, however, is not legally bound to the dispute-resolution clause because the added term was included in an invoice delivered by a seller-merchant (Kool) to a nonmerchant buyer (the school district). ◄

When Both Parties Are Merchants When both parties to the contract are merchants, the additional terms automatically become part of the contract unless (1) the original offer expressly required acceptance of its terms, (2) the new or changed terms materially alter the contract, or (3) the offeror rejects the new or changed terms within a reasonable time.

Modifications Subject to the Offeror's Consent Regardless of merchant status, the offeree's expression cannot be construed as an acceptance if the modifications are subject to the offeror's assent. **EXAMPLE 18.3** Farmland Harvest Company offers to sell ninety bales of hay at a certain price to Cattle Valley Ranch. Doris, the owner of Cattle Valley, says, "I accept your offer if you agree to include ten more bales." This is not an acceptance because it includes a modification (ten more bales) subject to Farmland's consent. ◄

18–3c Consideration

The UCC radically changes the common law rule that contract modification must be supported by new consideration. Under the UCC, an agreement modifying a contract needs no consideration to be binding.

Modifications Must Be Made in Good Faith Of course, contract modification must be sought in good faith. Good faith in the case of a merchant means honesty in fact and the observance of reasonable commercial standards of fair dealing in the trade. Modifications *extorted* from the other party are in bad faith and unenforceable.

HIGHLIGHTING THE POINT

Jim agrees to manufacture and lease certain goods to Louise for a stated price. Subsequently, a sudden shift in the market makes it difficult for Jim to lease the items to Louise at the agreed-on price without suffering a loss. Jim tells Louise of the situation, and Louise agrees to pay an additional sum for leasing the goods.

Can Louise later refuse to pay more than the original lease price? No. A shift in the market is a good faith reason for contract modification. Under the UCC, Louise's promise to modify the contract needs no consideration to be binding. Thus, Louise is bound to the modified contract.

When Modification without Consideration Requires a Writing In some situations, modification without consideration must be written to be enforceable. The contract may prohibit any changes unless they are in a signed writing. Also, any modification that brings a sales contract under the Statute of Frauds—which requires that a contract for a sale of goods priced at $500 or more must be in writing to be enforceable—usually will require that the modification be written.

EXAMPLE 18.4 Cosby Renovators enters into an oral contract with Anderson Plumbing Supply for the sale of four kitchen sinks for a total of $400. Later, if the contract is modified so that the four sinks cost $650, the modification must be in writing to be enforceable. ◄

18–3d The Statute of Frauds

The UCC contains a Statute of Frauds provision that applies to contracts for the sale or lease of goods. As mentioned, this requires that if the price is $500 or more, there must be a writing for the contract to be enforceable. The parties can have an initial oral agreement, however, and satisfy the Statute of Frauds by having a subsequent written memorandum of their oral agreement. In each case, the writing must be signed by the party against whom enforcement is sought.

Sufficiency of the Writing A writing or a memorandum will be sufficient as long as it indicates that the parties intended to form a contract and as long as it is signed by the party against whom enforcement is sought. The contract will not be enforceable beyond the quantity of goods shown in the writing, but all other terms can be proved in court by oral testimony. For leases, the writing must reasonably identify and describe the goods leased and the lease term.

Written Confirmation between Merchants Merchants can satisfy the requirements of a writing for the Statute of Frauds if, after the parties have agreed orally, one of the merchants sends a signed written confirmation to the other merchant. Unless the merchant who receives the confirmation gives written notice of objection to its contents within ten days after receipt, the writing is sufficient against the receiving merchant, even though he or she has not signed anything.

HIGHLIGHTING THE POINT

Alfonso is a merchant buyer in Cleveland. He contracts over the telephone to purchase $4,000 worth of goods from Goldstein, a New York City merchant seller. Two days later, Goldstein sends written confirmation detailing the terms of the oral contract, and Alfonso subsequently receives it.

Is Alfonso bound to the contract? If Alfonso does not give Goldstein written notice of objection to the contents of the written confirmation within ten days of receipt, Alfonso cannot raise the Statute of Frauds as a defense against the enforcement of the contract. Alfonso will be bound by the contract.

LEARNING OUTCOME 4

Discuss the UCC exceptions to the Statute of Frauds.

Exceptions There are three other exceptions to the UCC's Statute of Frauds requirement. An oral contract for a sale of goods priced at $500 or more or a lease of goods involving total payments of $1,000 or more will be enforceable despite the absence of a writing in the following circumstances.

Specially Manufactured Goods An oral contract is enforceable if (1) it is for goods that are specially manufactured for a particular buyer or specially manufactured or obtained for a particular lessee, (2) these goods are not suitable for resale or lease to others in the ordinary course of the seller's or lessor's business, and (3) the seller or lessor has substantially started to manufacture the goods or has made commitments for the manufacture or procurement of the goods. In this situation, once the seller or lessor has taken action, the buyer or lessee cannot repudiate the agreement claiming the Statute of Frauds as a defense.

Admissions An oral contract is enforceable if the party against whom enforcement of a contract is sought admits in pleadings (written answers), testimony, or other court proceedings that a contract was made. In this case, the contract will be enforceable even though it was oral, but enforceability is limited to the quantity of goods admitted.

Partial Performance An oral contract is enforceable if payment has been made and accepted or goods have been received and accepted. This is the "partial performance" exception. The oral contract will be enforced at least to the extent that performance *actually* took place.

18–3e The Parol Evidence Rule

If the parties to a contract set forth its terms in a confirmatory memorandum (a writing expressing the offer and acceptance of the deal) or in a writing intended as their final expression, the terms of the contract cannot be contradicted by evidence of any prior agreements or contemporaneous oral agreements. This is called the parol evidence rule. The terms of the contract may, however, be explained or supplemented by *consistent additional terms* or by *course of dealing, usage of trade,* or *course of performance.*

Consistent Additional Terms If the court finds an ambiguity in a writing that is supposed to be a complete and exclusive statement of the agreement between the parties, it may accept evidence of consistent additional terms to clarify or remove the ambiguity. The court will not, however, accept evidence of contradictory terms. This is the rule under both the UCC and the common law of contracts.

Course of Dealing and Usage of Trade The UCC has determined that the meaning of any agreement, evidenced by the language of the parties and by their actions, must be interpreted in light of commercial practices and other surrounding circumstances. In interpreting a commercial agreement, the court will assume that the *course of dealing* between the parties and the *usage of trade* were taken into account when the agreement was phrased.

A **course of dealing** is a sequence of previous actions and communications between the parties to a particular transaction that establishes a common basis for their understanding. A course of dealing is restricted, literally, to the sequence of actions and communications between the parties that occurred *prior* to the agreement in question.

Usage of trade is any practice or method of dealing having such regularity of observance in a place, vocation, or trade as to justify an expectation that it will be observed with respect to the transaction in question. Further, the express terms of an agreement and an applicable course of dealing or usage of trade will be interpreted to be consistent with each other whenever reasonable. When such interpretation is *unreasonable,* however, the express terms in the agreement will prevail.

course of dealing
A sequence of previous conduct between the parties to a particular transaction that establishes a common basis for their understanding.

usage of trade
Any practice or method of dealing having such regularity of observance in a place, vocation, or trade as to justify an expectation that it will be observed.

HIGHLIGHTING THE POINT

Franklin Loans hires American Title Company to search public records for prior claims on potential borrowers' assets. American's invoice to Franklin states, "Liability limited to amount of $150 fee." In the title search industry, liability limits are common. After conducting many searches for Franklin, American reports that there are no claims with respect to Skinner Autos. So Franklin loans $100,000 to Skinner, with payment guaranteed by Skinner's assets. When Skinner defaults on the loan, Franklin learns that another lender has priority to Skinner's assets under a previous claim. Franklin sues American for breach of contract to recover their $100,000.

Can Franklin recover $100,000 in damages from American? American's liability is limited to the amount of its $150 fee. The statement in the invoice was part of the contract between Franklin and American, according to the usage of trade in the title search industry, as well as the parties' course of dealing.

Course of Performance A **course of performance** is the conduct that occurs under the terms of a particular agreement. The parties know best what they meant by their words, and the course of performance actually undertaken is the best indication of what they meant.

course of performance
The conduct that occurs under the terms of a particular agreement indicating what the parties to an agreement intended it to mean.

18–3f Unconscionability

An unconscionable contract is one that is so unfair and one-sided that it would be unreasonable to enforce it. The UCC allows a court to evaluate a contract or any

LEARNING OUTCOME 5

Describe what a court can do when confronted with an unconscionable contract or clause.

clause in a contract, and if the court deems it to be unconscionable *at the time it was made*, the court can do one of the following:

1. Refuse to enforce the contract.

2. Enforce the contract without the unconscionable clause.

3. Limit the application of any unconscionable clauses to avoid an unconscionable result.

ANSWERING THE LEGAL PROBLEM

In the legal problem set out at the beginning of this chapter, Gene sold Festival Foods, a concessions business, to Lindsey. The deal included a variety of equipment. Later, Lindsey wanted out of the deal. Gene argued that Lindsay could not cancel the deal because the sale of goods was within Article 2 of the UCC. Lindsey claimed that the UCC did not apply.

A **Does the UCC cover this deal?** Most likely, yes. The UCC governs sales of goods. When a contract combines both goods and services, the UCC is not definitive. So courts use the predominant-factor test to determine if a contract is primarily for goods or services. Under this test, the primary value of the contract between Gene and Lindsey was in the goods, not the intangible (nonphysical) value of the business. And because Lindsey took possession of those goods and kept them too long, under the UCC, she could not cancel the deal.

TERMS AND CONCEPTS FOR REVIEW

course of dealing 241	lease agreement 236	sale 234
course of performance 241	lessee 236	sales contract 234
firm offer 237	lessor 236	tangible property 235
intangible property 235	merchant 236	usage of trade 241

CHAPTER SUMMARY—INTRODUCTION TO SALES AND LEASE CONTRACTS

LEARNING OUTCOME	
1	**State the scope of Article 2 of the UCC.** Article 2 of the UCC governs contracts for sales of goods. Under the UCC, a sale is "the passing of title"—the formal right of ownership—"from the seller to the buyer for a price." The price may be payable in cash (or its equivalent), or in other goods or services.
	To be characterized as a *good,* an item of property must be tangible and movable. Tangible property has physical existence—it can be touched or seen—unlike intangible property such as stocks and bonds. A movable item can be carried from place to place. Real estate is excluded, but items attached to the land that can be severed and moved are included.

2   **Identify how the UCC deals with open contract terms.** Under the UCC, a sales or lease contract will not fail for indefiniteness even if one or more terms are left open as long as (1) the parties intended to make a contract and (2) there is a reasonably certain basis for the court to grant an appropriate remedy. The UCC offers numerous open-term provisions that can be used to fill the gaps in a contract. To determine a remedy, however, the quantity of goods must be expressly stated. Otherwise, the courts have no basis for determining a remedy.

3   **Explain whether a contract under the UCC contains any additional terms included in the offeree's acceptance.** A contract is formed if an offeree makes a definite expression of acceptance, even though the terms of the acceptance modify or add to the terms of the offer. If one or both of the parties are nonmerchants, the contract is formed according to the terms of the offer and does not include the additional terms of the acceptance.

If both parties are merchants, the additional terms become part of the contract unless:

(1) The original offer expressly required acceptance of its terms.
(2) The new or changed terms materially alter the contract.
(3) The offeror rejects the new or changed terms within a reasonable time.

Regardless of the parties' merchant status, an offeree's response to an offer is not an acceptance if its terms are subject to the offeror's assent ("I accept your offer if you agree to sell me two items for the price of one").

4   **Discuss the UCC exceptions to the Statute of Frauds.** An oral contract for a sale of goods priced at $500 or more or a lease of goods involving total payments of $1,000 or more will be enforceable despite the absence of a writing if:

(1) It is for goods that are specially manufactured for a particular buyer or specially manufactured or obtained for a particular lessee.
(2) These goods are not suitable for resale or lease to others in the ordinary course of the seller's or lessor's business.
(3) The seller or lessor has substantially started to manufacture the goods or has made commitments for their manufacture or procurement.

An oral contract for a sale or lease of goods is enforceable if the party against whom enforcement of the contract is sought admits in pleadings, testimony, or other court proceedings that a contract for sale was made. An oral contract for a sale or lease of goods is enforceable if payment has been made and accepted or goods have been received and accepted.

5   **Describe what a court can do when confronted with an unconscionable contract or clause.** An unconscionable contract is one that is so unfair and one-sided that it would be unreasonable to enforce it. The UCC allows a court to evaluate a contract or any clause in a contract, and if the court deems it to have been unconscionable at the time it was made, the court can refuse to enforce the contract, enforce the contract without the unconscionable clause, or limit the application of the clause to avoid an unconscionable result.

ISSUE SPOTTERS

Check your answers to the *Issue Spotters* against the answers provided in Appendix C at the end of this text.

1. Brad orders 150 computer desks. Fred ships 150 printer stands. Is this an acceptance of Brad's offer or a counteroffer? If it is an acceptance, is it a breach of the contract? What if Fred told Brad that he was sending printer stands as an accommodation? (See *Sales and Lease Contracts*.)

2. Smith & Sons, Inc., sells truck supplies to J&B, which services trucks. Over the phone, J&B and Smith negotiate for the sale of eighty-four sets of tires. Smith sends a letter to J&B detailing the terms. Smith ships the tires two weeks later. J&B refuses to pay. Is there an enforceable contract between them? Explain why or why not. (See *Sales and Lease Contracts*.)

USING BUSINESS LAW

18–1. The Statute of Frauds. Fresher Foods, orally agreed to purchase from Vernon, a farmer, one thousand bushels of corn for $1.25 per bushel. Fresher Foods paid $125 down and agreed to pay the remainder of the purchase price on delivery, which was scheduled for one week later. When Fresher Foods tendered the balance of $1,125 on the scheduled day of delivery and requested the corn, Vernon refused to deliver it. Fresher Foods claimed Vernon had breached their oral contract. Can Fresher Foods recover? If so, to what extent? (See *Sales and Lease Contracts*.)

18–2. Merchant's Firm Offer. On May 1, Jennings, a car dealer, wrote a letter to Wheeler and stated, "I have a 1955 Thunderbird convertible in mint condition that I will sell you for $13,500 at any time before June 9. [Signed] Peter Jennings." By May 15, having heard nothing from Wheeler, Jennings sold the car to another. On May 29, Wheeler accepted Jennings's offer and tendered $13,500. When told Jennings had sold the car to another, Wheeler claimed Jennings had breached their contract. Is Jennings in breach? Explain. (See *Sales and Lease Contracts*.)

REAL-WORLD CASE PROBLEMS

18–3. The Statute of Frauds. Kendall Gardner agreed to buy from James Bowen and Richard Cagle—doing business as B&C Shavings—a specially built shaving mill to produce wood shavings for poultry processors. B&C sent an invoice to Gardner reflecting a purchase price of $86,200, with a 30 percent down payment and the "balance due before shipment." Gardner paid the down payment. B&C finished the mill and wrote Gardner a letter, telling him to "pay the balance due or you will lose the down payment." By then, Gardner had lost his customers for the wood shavings and could not pay the balance due. He asked for the return of his down payment. Did these parties have an enforceable contract under the Statute of Frauds? Explain. [*Bowen v. Gardner*, 2013 Ark.App. 52, 425 S.W.3d 875 (2013)] (See *Sales and Lease Contracts*.)

18–4. Additional Terms. B.S. International, Ltd. (BSI), makes costume jewelry. JMAM, LLC, is a wholesaler of costume jewelry. JMAM sent a letter with the terms for its orders to BSI, including the necessary procedure for obtaining credit for items that customers rejected. The letter stated, "By signing below, you agree to the terms." Steven Baracsi, BSI's owner, signed the letter and returned it. For six years, BSI made jewelry for JMAM, which resold it. Items rejected

by customers were sent back to JMAM, but were never returned to BSI. BSI filed a suit against JMAM, claiming $41,294.21 for the unreturned items. BSI showed the court a copy of JMAM's terms. Across the bottom had been typed a postscript (P.S.) requiring the return of rejected merchandise. Was this "PS" part of the contract? Discuss. [*B.S. International, Ltd. v. JMAM, LLC*, 13 A.3d 1057 (R.I. 2011)] (See *Sales and Lease Contracts*.)

18–5. Offer and Acceptance. Continental Insurance Co. issued a policy to cover shipments by Oakley Fertilizer, Inc. Oakley agreed to ship three thousand tons of fertilizer to Ameropa North America on barges. Oakley sent Ameropa a contract form that stated Oakley would be responsible for any damage to the goods until Ameropa paid for them. Ameropa e-mailed a different form that indicated that Ameropa would be responsible for any damage once the fertilizer was loaded onto barges. The cargo was loaded onto barges but had not been paid for when it was damaged in a hurricane. Oakley filed a claim for the loss. Continental denied coverage on the basis of Ameropa's form. Is Continental correct? Explain. [*Oakley Fertilizer, Inc. v. Continental Insurance Co.*, 276 S.W.3d 342 (Mo. App.E.D. 2009)] (See *Sales and Lease Contracts*.)

ETHICAL QUESTIONS

18–6. Sales of Goods. Should merchants be required to act in good faith? Why or why not? (See *Sales of Goods*.)

18–7. The Statute of Frauds. Daniel Fox owned Fox & Lamberth Enterprises, Inc., a kitchen remodeling business. Fox leased a building from Carl Hussong. When Fox planned to close his business, Craftsmen Home Improvement, Inc., expressed an interest in buying his assets. Fox set a price of $50,000. Craftsmen's owners agreed and gave Fox a list of

the desired items and "Bill of Sale" that set the terms for payment. Craftsmen expected to negotiate a new lease with Hussong and modified the premises, including removal of some of the displays. When Hussong and Craftsmen could not agree on new terms, Craftsmen told Fox that the deal was off. Is this deal enforceable under the Statute of Frauds? If so, is it fair to Craftsmen? Discuss. [*Fox & Lamberth Enterprises, Inc. v. Craftsmen Home Improvement, Inc.*, __ N.E.2d __ (2006)] (See *Sales and Lease Contracts*.)

Chapter 18—Work Set

TRUE-FALSE QUESTIONS

_____ 1. If the subject of a sale is goods, Article 2 of the UCC applies.

_____ 2. A contract for a sale of goods is subject to the same traditional principles that apply to all contracts.

_____ 3. If the subject of a transaction is a service, Article 2 of the UCC applies.

_____ 4. The UCC requires that an agreement modifying a contract be supported by new consideration to be binding.

_____ 5. Under the UCC's Statute of Frauds, a writing must include all material terms except quantity.

_____ 6. An unconscionable contract is a contract so one sided and unfair, at the time it is made, that enforcing it would be unreasonable.

_____ 7. A lease agreement is a bargain between a lessor and a lessee, as shown by their words and conduct.

_____ 8. Under the UCC, acceptance can be made by any means of communication reasonable under the circumstances.

_____ 9. No oral contract is enforceable under the UCC.

MULTIPLE-CHOICE QUESTIONS

_____ 1. Adam pays Beta Corporation $1,500 for a laptop. Under the UCC, this is

a. a bailment.
b. a consignment.
c. a lease.
d. a sale.

_____ 2. Morro Beverage Company has a surplus of carbon dioxide (which is what puts the bubbles in Morro beverages). Morro agrees to sell the surplus to the Rock Ale Company. Morro is a merchant with respect to

a. carbon dioxide but not Morro beverages.
b. Morro beverages but not carbon dioxide.
c. both Morro beverages and carbon dioxide.
d. neither Morro beverages nor carbon dioxide.

_____ 3. Marina Shipyard agrees to build a barge for MaxCo Shipping. The contract includes an option for up to five more barges, but states that the prices of the other barges could be higher. Marina and MaxCo have

a. a binding contract for at least one barge and up to six barges.
b. a binding contract for one barge only.
c. no contract, because the terms of the option are too indefinite.
d. no contract, because both parties are merchants with respect to barges.

_____ 4. Mike and Rita orally agree to a sale of one hundred pairs of hiking boots at $50 each. Rita gives Mike a check for $500 as a down payment. Mike takes the check. At this point, the contract is enforceable

a. to the full extent, because it is for specially made goods.
b. to the full extent, because it is oral.
c. to the extent of $500.
d. as described by none of the above.

_____ 5. Med Labs sends Kraft Instruments a purchase order for scalpels. The order states that Med will not be bound by any additional terms. Kraft ships the scalpels with an acknowledgment that includes an additional, materially different term. Med is

a. not bound by the term, because the offer expressly states that no other terms will be accepted.
b. not bound by the term, because the additional term constitutes a material alteration.
c. both a and b.
d. bound by the term.

_____ 6. Under the parol evidence rule, evidence of contradictory prior agreements or contemporaneous oral agreements is inadmissible except

a. that consistent terms can clarify or remove an ambiguity in the writing.
b. that commercial practices can be used to interpret the contract.
c. both a and b.
d. none of the above.

_____ 7. Lena, a car dealer, writes to Sam that "I have a 2002 Honda Civic that I will sell to you for $4,000. This offer will be kept open for one week." Six days later, Todd tells Sam that Lena sold the car that morning for $5,000. Who violated the terms of the offer?

a. Lena.
b. Sam.
c. Todd.
d. No one.

_____ 8. Stron Cellphones agrees to buy an unspecified quantity of microchips from SmartCorp. The quantity that a court would order Stron to buy under this contract is

a. the amount that Stron would buy during a normal year.
b. the amount that SmartCorp would make in a normal year.
c. the amount that SmartCorp actually makes this year.
d. none of the amounts above.

ANSWERING MORE LEGAL PROBLEMS

1. Western Horse, Inc., agreed to buy hay from AgriSales, Inc. They signed a "Purchase Order" for "26 tons (880 bales)" that left other details blank. AgriSales loaded and weighed a trailer and dispatched it. Before delivery, however, Western told AgriSales to cancel the order—it had arranged to buy the hay for a lower price and faster delivery from Orchard Alfalfa Fields.

   Can AgriSales recover the cost of attempting to fill Western's order? Yes. AgriSales will have to show that the parties had an enforceable contract despite the details left "blank." The UCC states that a sales contract will not fail for indefiniteness even if one or more terms are left open as long as (1) the parties _____ to make a contract and (2) there is a _____ certain basis for the court to grant an appropriate remedy. Missing terms can be proved, or it can be presumed that the parties _____ whatever is _____, as long as the quantity is not left open.

2. Mountain Stream Trout, Inc., agreed to buy *market size* trout from trout grower Lake Farms, LLC. Their five-year contract did not define *market size*. At the time, in the trade *market size* referred to fish of one-pound live weight. After three years, Mountain Stream began taking fewer, smaller deliveries of larger fish, claiming that *market size* varied according to whatever its customers demanded. Lake Farms filed a suit for breach of contract.

   Is outside evidence admissible to explain *market size*? Yes. Under the UCC, in interpreting a commercial agreement, a court will assume that the usage of _____ between the parties was considered when the contract was formed. Also, the conduct that occurs under an agreement, the course of _____, is the best indication of what the parties meant. Here, the _____ usage at the time of the contract indicated that *market size* referred to fish of one-pound live weight. This was the standard for the course of _____ between the parties over the first three years of the contract.

246

TITLE AND RISK OF LOSS

19

FACING A LEGAL PROBLEM

Anselm, Brad, and Cord are farmers. They deposit, respectively, 5,000 bushels, 3,000 bushels, and 2,000 bushels of the same grade and quality of grain in a bin. The three become owners in common, with Anselm owning 50 percent of the 10,000 bushels, Brad 30 percent, and Cord 20 percent.

Q If Anselm contracts to sell 5,000 bushels of grain to Tarey, do those bushels have to be removed from the bin?

LEARNING OUTCOMES

The five Learning Outcomes below are designed to help improve your understanding of the chapter. After reading this chapter, you should be able to:

1 Explain the concept of identifying goods to a contract.

2 Identify when title passes under a contract for a sale of goods.

3 State what happens when persons who acquire goods without title attempt to resell the goods.

4 Discuss who bears the loss if goods are damaged, destroyed, or lost, or if the contract is breached.

5 Pinpoint who has an insurable interest in goods.

Anything can happen between the time a contract is signed and the time the goods are transferred to the buyer's or lessee's possession. For example, in a sale of oranges to be delivered after the harvest, fire, flood, or frost may destroy the orange groves. Or, the oranges may be damaged or lost in transit. Because of these possibilities, it is important to know the rights and liabilities of the parties.

The rules of the Uniform Commercial Code (UCC) about the rights and liabilities of the parties to a contract are discussed in the sections that follow. In most situations, rights and liabilities are determined not by who has *title*—the right of ownership—but by three other concepts: (1) identification, (2) risk of loss, and (3) insurable interest.

19–1 IDENTIFICATION

Before any interest in specific goods can pass from the seller or lessor to the buyer or lessee, the goods must exist and be identified as the specific goods designated in the contract. **Identification** takes place when specific goods are designated as the subject matter of a sales contract.

Title and risk of loss cannot pass from seller to buyer unless the goods are identified to the contract. (Title to leased goods does not pass to a lessee.) Identification is significant because it gives the buyer or lessee the right to insure the goods and the right to recover from third parties who damage the goods.

The parties can agree in their contract on when identification will take place. If the parties do not so specify, however, the UCC provisions discussed next determine when identification takes place.

19–1a Existing Goods

If the contract calls for the sale or lease of specific goods that are already in existence, identification takes place at the time the contract is made. **EXAMPLE 19.1** Dmitri's Autoplex contracts to purchase or lease a fleet of five cars designated by their vehicle identification numbers (VINs). Because the cars are identified by their VINs, identification has taken place. ◄

identification
In the sale or lease of goods, the express designation of the goods provided for in the contract.

LEARNING OUTCOME 1

Explain the concept of identifying goods to a contract.

247

19–1b Future Goods

Goods that are not both existing and identified to the contract are called *future goods*. For instance, if a sale involves unborn animals to be born within twelve months after contracting, identification takes place when the animals are conceived. If a sale involves crops that are to be harvested within twelve months (or the next harvest season occurring after contracting, whichever is longer), identification takes place when the crops are planted. Otherwise, identification takes place when they begin to grow.

In a sale (or lease) of any other future goods, identification occurs when the goods are shipped, marked, or otherwise designated by the seller (or lessor) as the goods to which the contract refers.

19–1c Goods from a Larger Mass

Goods that are part of a larger mass are identified when the goods are marked, shipped, or somehow designated by the seller or lessor as the particular goods to pass under the contract. **EXAMPLE 19.2** McKee, the buyer, orders 1,000 cases of beans from a 10,000-case lot. Until Adhir, the seller, separates the 1,000 cases of beans from the 10,000-case lot, title and risk of loss remain with Adhir. If anything happens to the beans, Adhir will have to pay for them. ◀

fungible goods
Goods that are alike by physical nature, by agreement, or by trade usage.

The most common exception to this rule deals with fungible goods. **Fungible goods** are goods that are alike naturally or by agreement or trade usage. Examples are wheat and oil that are of like grade and quality. If these goods are held or intended to be held by *owners in common*—that is, owners with an undivided share of the whole—a seller-owner can pass title and risk of loss to the buyer without a separation. The buyer replaces the seller as an owner in common.

19–1d Passage of Title

LEARNING OUTCOME 2

Identify when title passes under a contract for a sale of goods.

Once goods exist and are identified, title can be determined. Under the UCC, any explicit understanding between the buyer and the seller determines when title passes. If there is no such agreement, title passes to the buyer at the time and the place the seller *physically* delivers the goods. The delivery arrangements determine when this occurs.

In lease contracts, of course, title to the goods is retained by the lessor-owner of the goods. Hence, the UCC's provisions relating to passage of title do not apply to leased goods.

shipment contract
A contract for the sale of goods in which the buyer assumes liability for any losses or damage to the goods on the seller's delivery of the goods to a carrier.

Shipment Contracts and Passage of Title In a **shipment contract**, the seller is required or authorized to ship goods by carrier, such as a trucking company or an air freight company. Under a shipment contract, the seller is required only to deliver the goods into the hands of a carrier. Title passes to the buyer at the time and place of shipment. Generally, *all contracts are assumed to be shipment contracts if nothing to the contrary is stated in the contract.*

destination contract
A contract for the sale of goods in which the seller assumes liability for any losses or damage to the goods until they are tendered at the destination specified in the contract.

Destination Contracts and Passage of Title In a **destination contract**, the seller is required to deliver the goods to a particular destination, usually directly to the buyer. Title passes to the buyer when the goods are *tendered* at that destination. A tender of delivery is the seller's placing or holding of the goods at the buyer's disposition (with any necessary notice) so that the buyer can take delivery. **EXAMPLE 19.3** Jackson Tools, a seller in New York, agrees to deliver goods to Spencer Hardware's warehouse in Los Angeles by truck. When the truck arrives in Los Angeles, Jackson calls Spencer to tell it that the goods are in the city and to ask that the warehouse be opened so that delivery can take place. ◀

Delivery without Movement of the Goods Some contracts of sale do not call for the seller's shipment or delivery (the buyer is to pick up the goods). The passage of title in this situation depends on whether the seller must deliver a **document of title,** such as a bill of lading or a warehouse receipt, to the buyer. A *bill of lading* is a receipt for goods that is signed by a carrier and that serves as a contract for the transportation of the goods. A *warehouse receipt* is a receipt issued by a warehouser for goods stored in a warehouse.

When a document of title is required, title passes to the buyer *when and where the document is delivered.* Thus, if the goods are stored in a warehouse, title passes to the buyer when the appropriate documents are delivered to the buyer. The goods never move.

When no documents of title are required and delivery is made without moving the goods, title passes at the time and place the sales contract was made, if the goods have already been identified. If the goods have not been identified, title does not pass until identification occurs. **EXAMPLE 19.4** Norton Timber Company sells some lumber to Byron. They agree that Byron will pick up the lumber at the company's sorting yard. If the lumber has been identified—that is, segregated or distinguished from the other lumber—title passes to Byron when the contract is signed. If the lumber is still in storage buildings, however, title does not pass to Byron until the particular pieces of lumber to be sold under this contract are identified. ◄

Sales or Leases by Nonowners Problems relating to passage of title occur when persons who acquire goods with imperfect titles attempt to sell or lease the goods. What are the rights of two parties who lay claim to the same goods when those goods are sold or leased with imperfect titles? Generally, the buyer acquires at least whatever title the seller has to the goods sold.

Void Title A buyer may unknowingly purchase goods from a seller who is not the owner of the goods. If the seller is a thief, the seller's title is *void*—legally, no title exists. Thus, the buyer acquires no title, and the real owner can reclaim the goods from the buyer. (Of course, the buyer can then try to recover from the thief!)

> ## HIGHLIGHTING THE POINT
>
> Jim steals a Nikon digital camera owned by Margaret. He sells the camera to Sandra, who acts in good faith and honestly was not aware that the camera was stolen.
>
> **Can Margaret reclaim the camera from Sandra?** Yes. Jim had void title to the camera. Margaret can reclaim it from Sandra even though Sandra acted in good faith and honestly was not aware that the camera was stolen. Sandra can seek damages from Jim.

The same result would occur if the goods were leased. Generally, a lessee acquires only whatever right to possess and use the goods that the lessor has or has the power to transfer, subject to the lease contract. If the lessor has no rights to transfer, the lessee acquires no rights.

Voidable Title A seller has *voidable title* if the goods that he or she is selling were obtained by fraud, paid for with a check that is later dishonored, purchased from a minor, or purchased on credit when the seller was **insolvent.** (Under the UCC, a person is insolvent when that person ceases to pay his or her debts, cannot pay the

document of title
Paper exchanged in the regular course of business that evidences the right to possession of goods.

LEARNING OUTCOME 3
State what happens when persons who acquire goods without title attempt to resell the goods.

insolvent
A condition in which a person's liabilities exceed the value of his or her assets.

debts as they become due, or is insolvent within the meaning of federal bankruptcy law.) Purchasers of such goods acquire all title that their transferors either had or had the power to transfer, but no more.

In contrast to a seller with void title, a seller with *voidable title* has the power to transfer good title to a good faith purchaser. A **good faith purchaser** is a buyer who is unaware of circumstances that would make an average person inquire about the validity of the seller's title to the goods. The real owner cannot recover goods from a good faith purchaser. If the buyer of the goods is not a good faith purchaser, then the actual owner of the goods can reclaim them from the buyer (or from the seller, if the goods are still in the seller's possession). Exhibit 19.1 illustrates these concepts.

The same rules apply in circumstances involving leases. A lessor with voidable title has the power to transfer a valid leasehold interest to a good faith lessee for value. The real owner cannot recover the goods, except as permitted by the terms of the lease. The real owner can, however, receive all proceeds arising from the lease, as well as a transfer of all rights, title, and interest as lessor under the lease, including the lessor's interest in the return of the goods when the lease expires.

The Entrustment Rule Entrusting goods to a merchant *who deals in goods of that kind* gives the merchant the power to transfer all rights to a *buyer in the ordinary course of business*. This is known as the **entrustment rule.** Entrusting includes both delivering the goods to the merchant and leaving the goods with the merchant for later delivery or pickup. A buyer in the ordinary course of business is a person who, in good faith and without knowledge that the sale violates the ownership rights of a third party, buys in the normal course of business from a person (other than a pawnbroker) in the business of selling goods of that kind. The entrustment rule basically allows innocent buyers to obtain legitimate title to goods purchased from merchants even if the merchants do not have good title.

good faith purchaser
A purchaser who buys without notice of any circumstance that would cause a person of ordinary prudence to inquire as to whether the seller has valid title to the goods being sold.

entrustment rule
A rule stating that transferring goods to a merchant who deals in goods of that kind gives that merchant the power to transfer those goods and all rights to them to a buyer in the ordinary course of business.

EXHIBIT 19.1   Void and Voidable Titles

If goods are transferred from their owner to another by theft, the thief acquires no ownership rights. Because the thief's title is *void,* a later buyer can acquire no title, and the owner can recover the goods. If the transfer occurs by fraud, the transferee acquires a *voidable* title. A later good faith purchaser for value can acquire good title, and the original owner cannot recover the goods.

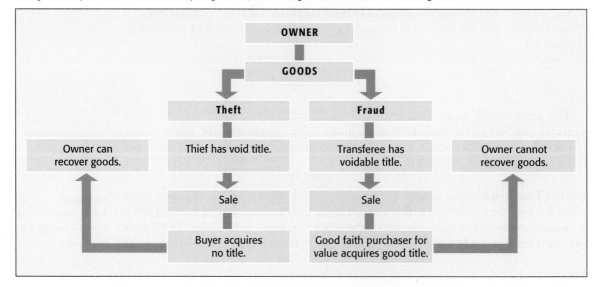

HIGHLIGHTING THE POINT

Selena steals Jan's watch and leaves it with a jeweler for repairs. The jeweler sells the watch to Ben, who does not know that the jeweler has no right to sell it.

Against whom does Ben get good title? Ben gets good title against Selena, who entrusted the watch to the jeweler, but not against Jan, who neither entrusted the watch to Selena nor authorized Selena to entrust it. Therefore, Ben is a buyer in the ordinary course of business as to Selena but not as to Jan, who can recover the watch from Ben.

The UCC provides a similar rule for leased goods. If a lessor entrusts goods to a lessee-merchant who deals in goods of that kind, the lessee-merchant has the power to transfer all of the rights the lessor had in the goods to a buyer or sublessee in the ordinary course of business.

19–2 RISK OF LOSS

Under the UCC, the question of who suffers a financial loss if goods are damaged, destroyed, or lost is not necessarily determined by title. Who bears the risk of loss can be determined by the parties in their contract. Who suffers the loss may also depend on whether the sales or lease contract has been breached at the time of loss.

LEARNING OUTCOME 4
Discuss who bears the loss if goods are damaged, destroyed, or lost, or if the contract is breached.

Real-World Case Example

Tammy Herring and Stacy Bowman signed a "Bill of Sale—Purchase Agreement" that required Herring to pay $2,200 for a horse named Toby. Before the price was fully paid, Herring's minor daughter, Alex, was driving a buggy drawn by Toby when the horse reared and threw its passenger, Diana Person, from the buggy. To recover for her injuries, Person filed a suit in a Washington state court against Bowman, claiming that Bowman owned the horse. The court, however, ruled that Herring owned the horse. Person appealed.

For purposes of the passage of risk, did Herring own the horse? Yes. In a 2013 case, *Person v. Bowman,* a state intermediate appellate court affirmed the lower court's ruling. Herring may have believed that she would not own Toby until she had paid the full price and that this was a "lease-like" agreement. But "the parties' objective manifestations are consistent with this being a sale not a lease."

19–2a Delivery with Movement of the Goods—Carrier Cases

When the contract involves movement of the goods through a common carrier but does not specify when risk of loss passes, the courts first look for specific delivery terms in the contract.

The terms that have traditionally been used in contracts within the United States are listed and defined in Exhibit 19.2. These terms determine which party will pay the costs of delivering the goods and who bears the risk of loss. If the contract does

Contract Terms—Definitions

The contract terms listed below help determine which party will bear the costs of delivery and when risk of loss will pass from the seller to the buyer.

Term	Definition
F.O.B. (free on board)	Indicates that the selling price of goods includes transportation costs to the specific F.O.B. place named in the contract. The seller pays the expenses and carries the risk of loss to the F.O.B. place named. If the named place is the place from which the goods are shipped (for example, the seller's city or place of business), the contract is a shipment contract. If the named place is the place to which the goods are to be shipped (for example, the buyer's city or place of business), the contract is a destination contract.
F.A.S. (free alongside ship)	Requires that the seller, at his or her own expense and risk, deliver the goods alongside the vessel in the manner usual in that port or on a dock designated and provided by the buyer. An F.A.S. contract is essentially an F.O.B. contract for ships.
C.I.F. or C.&F. **(cost, insurance, and freight** **or just cost and freight)**	Requires, among other things, that the seller "put the goods in the possession of a carrier" before risk passes to the buyer. (These are basically pricing terms, and the contracts remain shipment contracts, not destination contracts.)
Delivery ex-ship **(delivery from the carrying vessel)**	Means that risk of loss does not pass to the buyer until the goods are properly unloaded from the ship or other carrier.

not include these terms, then the courts must decide whether the contract is a shipment contract or a destination contract.

Shipment Contracts and Risk of Loss In a shipment contract, if the seller or lessor is required or authorized to ship goods by carrier (but not required to deliver them to a particular destination), risk of loss passes to the buyer or lessee when the goods are delivered to the carrier. (Buyers and lessees have recourse against carriers, and they also usually buy insurance to cover the goods.)

HIGHLIGHTING THE POINT

Russell Orchards, a seller in Houston, Texas, sells five hundred cases of grapefruit to Grocers Fruit Brokers, a buyer in New York. The contract states that the sale is "F.O.B. Houston" (*free on board* in Houston—that is, the *buyer* pays the transportation charges from Houston). The contract authorizes a shipment by carrier. It does not require that the seller tender the grapefruit in New York.

If the goods are damaged in transit, who suffers the loss—the seller or the buyer? The loss is the buyer's. Risk passes to the buyer when conforming goods are placed in the possession of the carrier.

Destination Contracts and Risk of Loss In a destination contract, the risk of loss passes to the buyer or lessee when the goods are *tendered* to the buyer or lessee at that destination. In the preceding *Highlighting the Point* feature, for instance, if the contract had been F.O.B. New York, risk of loss during transit to New York would have been the seller's.

19–2b Delivery without Movement of the Goods

The UCC also addresses situations in which the seller or lessor is required neither to ship nor to deliver the goods. Frequently, the buyer or lessee is to pick up the goods from the seller or lessor, or the goods are held by a **bailee.** For example, a warehousing company or a trucking company that normally issues documents of

bailee
One to whom goods are entrusted by a bailor.

title for goods it receives is a bailee. Under the UCC, a *bailee* is a party who, by a bill of lading, warehouse receipt, or other document of title, acknowledges possession of goods and contracts to deliver them.

Goods Held by the Seller or Lessor If the goods are held by the seller or lessor, a document of title is usually not used. If the seller or lessor is a merchant, risk of loss to goods held by the seller or lessor passes to the buyer or lessee when he or she *takes physical possession of the goods*. If the seller or lessor is not a merchant, the risk of loss passes to the buyer or lessee on *tender of delivery*.

Goods Held by a Bailee When a bailee is holding goods for a person who has contracted to sell them and the goods are to be delivered without being moved, the goods are usually represented by a document of title (a bill of lading or a warehouse receipt), as mentioned earlier. This document may be negotiable or nonnegotiable.

Negotiable and *nonnegotiable* refer to the capability of a document of title to transfer the rights to goods that the document covers. With a negotiable document of title, a party can transfer the rights by signing and delivering, or in some situations simply delivering, the document. For example, when a seller signs a negotiable document of title that covers certain goods and delivers it to a buyer, the buyer may acquire *all* rights to the goods (and, by signing and delivering the document, transfer those rights to someone else).

When goods are held by a bailee, risk of loss passes to the buyer when one of the following occurs:

1. The buyer receives a negotiable document of title for the goods.
2. The bailee acknowledges the buyer's right to possess the goods.
3. The buyer receives a nonnegotiable document of title *and* has had a *reasonable time* to present the document to the bailee and demand the goods. If the bailee refuses to honor the document, the risk of loss remains with the seller.

In respect to leases, if goods held by a bailee are to be delivered without being moved, the risk of loss passes to the lessee on acknowledgment by the bailee of the lessee's right to possession of the goods.

19–2c Conditional Sales

Buyers and sellers sometimes form sales contracts that are conditioned either on the buyer's approval of the goods or on the buyer's resale of the purchased goods. The UCC states that (unless otherwise agreed) if the goods are for the buyer to use, the transaction is a *sale on approval*. If the goods are for the buyer to resell, the transaction is a *sale or return*.

Sale on Approval When a seller offers to sell goods to a buyer and permits the buyer to take the goods on a trial basis, a **sale on approval** is made. Title and risk of loss (from causes beyond the buyer's control) remain with the seller until the buyer accepts (approves) the offer. Acceptance can be made expressly, by any act inconsistent with the *trial* purpose or the seller's ownership (such as reselling the goods), or by the buyer's decision not to return the goods within the trial period. If the buyer does not wish to accept, the buyer must return the goods to the seller. The return is at the seller's expense and risk. Goods held on approval are not subject to the claims of the buyer's creditors until acceptance.

sale on approval
A conditional sale that becomes absolute only when the buyer approves, or is satisfied with, the goods sold.

EXAMPLE 19.5 Brad orders a Bowflex TreadClimber online, and the manufacturer allows him to try it risk-free for thirty days. If Brad decides to keep the TreadClimber, then the sale is complete. If he returns it within thirty days, however, there is no sale, and he is not charged. If Brad files for bankruptcy within the thirty-day period and still has the TreadClimber in his possession, his creditors may not attach (seize) the TreadClimber, because he has not accepted it yet.◄

sale or return
A conditional sale wherein title and possession pass from the seller to the buyer. The buyer, however, retains the option to rescind or return the goods during a specified period even though the goods conform to the contract.

Sale or Return   In a **sale or return**, the sale is completed but the buyer has an option to return the goods and undo the sale. Sale-or-return contracts often arise when a merchant purchases goods primarily for resale, but has the right to return part or all of the goods in lieu of payment if the goods are not resold. Basically, a sale or return is a sale of goods in the present that may be undone at the buyer's option within a specified time period.   **EXAMPLE 19.6**   Curtis, Inc., a diamond wholesaler, delivers gems to Shane Company, a jewelry retailer. Their understanding is that Shane can return any unsold gems at the end of six months. This transaction is a sale or return. ◄

When the buyer receives possession at the time of sale, the title and risk of loss pass to the buyer. Both remain with the buyer until the buyer returns the goods to the seller within the specified time. If the buyer fails to return the goods within this time, the sale is finalized. The return of the goods is at the buyer's risk and expense. Goods held under a sale-or-return contract are subject to the claims of the buyer's creditors while they are in the buyer's possession.

19–2d Risk of Loss When a Contract Is Breached

There are many ways to breach a sales or lease contract. The transfer of risk operates differently depending on which party breaches. Generally, the party in breach bears the risk of loss.

cure
The right of a party who tenders nonconforming performance to correct his or her performance within the contract period.

When the Seller or Lessor Breaches   If the seller or lessor breaches by supplying goods that are so nonconforming that the buyer has the right to reject them, the risk of loss does not pass to the buyer until the defects are **cured** (until the goods are repaired, replaced, or discounted in price by the seller) or until the buyer accepts the goods in spite of their defects (thus waiving the right to reject).   **EXAMPLE 19.7**   David orders blue iPhone6 cases, but Nikki, the seller, ships red ones. The risk of loss remains with Nikki unless David accepts the cases in spite of their color. ◄

If a buyer accepts a shipment of goods and later discovers a defect, acceptance can be revoked. Revocation allows the buyer to pass the risk of loss back to the seller, at least to the extent that the buyer's insurance does not cover the loss.

There is a similar rule for leases. If the lessor or supplier tenders goods that are so nonconforming that the lessee has the right to reject them, the risk of loss remains with the lessor or the supplier until cure or acceptance. If the lessee, after acceptance, revokes his or her acceptance of nonconforming goods, the revocation passes the risk of loss back to the seller or supplier, to the extent that the lessee's insurance does not cover the loss.

When the Buyer or Lessee Breaches   When a buyer or lessee breaches a contract, the general rule is that the risk of loss *immediately* shifts to the buyer or lessee. There are three important limitations to this rule:

1. The seller or lessor must already have identified the goods under the contract.
2. The buyer or lessee bears the risk for only a *commercially reasonable time* after the seller or lessor learns of the breach. What is a commercially reasonable time depends on the circumstances.
3. The buyer or lessee is liable only to the extent of any *deficiency* in the seller's insurance coverage.

19–3 INSURABLE INTEREST

LEARNING OUTCOME 5

Pinpoint who has an insurable interest in goods.

Parties to sales or lease contracts often obtain insurance coverage to protect against damage, loss, or destruction of goods. Any party purchasing insurance, however, must have a "sufficient interest" in the insured item to obtain a valid policy. Insurance laws—not the UCC—determine "sufficiency." The UCC is helpful, however, because it contains certain rules regarding the buyer's and seller's insurable interest in goods.

19–3a Insurable Interest of the Buyer or Lessee

Buyers and lessees have an **insurable interest** in *identified goods*. The moment goods are identified to the contract by the seller or lessor, the buyer or lessee has an interest that allows him or her to obtain necessary insurance coverage for those goods even before the risk of loss passes. Buyers obtain an insurable interest in crops at the time of identification.

insurable interest
A property interest in goods that is sufficiently substantial to permit a party to insure against damage to the goods.

HIGHLIGHTING THE POINT

In March, Hillcrest Farms sells a cotton crop that it hopes to harvest in October. After the crop is planted, Simpson Textiles, the buyer, insures it against hail damage. In September, a hailstorm ruins the crop. Simpson files a claim under its insurance policy. The insurer—Liberty Insurance Company—refuses to pay, asserting that Simpson has no insurable interest in the crop.

Is Liberty Insurance correct? No. Simpson acquired an insurable interest when the crop was planted, because it had a contract to buy it.

19–3b Insurable Interest of the Seller or Lessor

A seller has an insurable interest in goods as long as he or she retains title to the goods. Even after title passes to a buyer, a seller who has a *security interest* (a right to secure payment) in the goods still has an insurable interest and can insure the goods. Hence, a buyer and a seller can have an insurable interest in identical goods at the same time. Of course, the buyer or seller must sustain an actual loss to have the right to recover from an insurance company. Any loss or damage in transit falls on the seller because the seller has control until proper tender has been made.

In regard to leases, a lessor retains an insurable interest in leased goods until an option to buy has been exercised by the lessee and the risk of loss has passed to the lessee.

ANSWERING THE LEGAL PROBLEM

In the legal problem set out at the beginning of this chapter, farmers Anselm, Brad, and Cord deposit, respectively, 5,000 bushels, 3,000 bushels, and 2,000 bushels of the same grade and quality of grain in a bin. As owners in common, Anselm owns 50 percent of the 10,000 bushels, Brad 30 percent, and Cord 20 percent.

A **If Anselm contracts to sell his bushels of grain to Tarey, do those 5,000 bushels need to be removed?** No. Because the goods are fungible, title and risk of loss can pass to Tarey without physical separation of the bushels. Tarey becomes an owner in common with Brad and Cord.

LINKING BUSINESS LAW to Your Career

RISK MANAGEMENT

If you go into business or work for a company as a manager, you may be in charge of shipping goods. The shipment of goods is a major aspect of many commercial transactions. Issues of liability can arise when an event such as fire or theft damages goods in transit. Before a loss occurs, it is important that a company assess the risk of potential liability and take steps to guard against it.

Liability Provision

Businesses almost always allocate the risk of liability for a loss in their contracts. Reviewing a contract for a liability allocation provision is thus the most important first step in managing risk. When your company is allocated the risk, the next step is to obtain insurance to protect against it.

Delivery Terms

If a sales or lease contract does not refer to liability for damaged or lost goods and the goods are to be shipped or delivered, then the risk is borne by the party having control of the goods. The delivery terms in a contract can serve as a basis for determining control. Thus, under "F.O.B. buyer's business"—a destination-delivery term—the risk of loss does not pass to the buyer until there is a tender of delivery at the point of destination. The seller is liable for any damage in transit because the seller has control until tender is made.

Most sellers prefer "F.O.B. seller's business" as a delivery term. Once the goods are delivered to the carrier, the buyer bears the risk of loss. Thus, if conforming goods are lost in transit, the buyer suffers the loss.

Breach of Contract

If a contract is silent as to risk and either party breaches the contract, the breaching party is liable for any loss. For example, if a buyer orders fifteen cooling fans to be installed at a certain location in a manufacturing facility, and the seller ships the wrong size, the risk of loss does not pass to the buyer until this defect is cured.

Before a loss occurs, you should determine at which point your company will have an insurable interest in the goods and obtain insurance to cover any potential liability for the damage, loss, or destruction of the goods.

TERMS AND CONCEPTS FOR REVIEW

bailee 252

cure 254

destination contract 248

document of title 249

entrustment rule 250

fungible goods 248

good faith purchaser 250

identification 247

insolvent 249

insurable interest 255

sale on approval 253

sale or return 254

shipment contract 248

CHAPTER SUMMARY—TITLE AND RISK OF LOSS

LEARNING OUTCOME

1 **Explain the concept of identifying goods to a contract.** Before an interest in goods can pass from a seller or lessor to a buyer or lessee, the goods must exist and be identified as the specific goods designated in the contract. Identification occurs when specific goods are designated as the subject matter of a sales or lease contract. Title and risk of loss cannot pass from seller to buyer unless the goods are identified to the contract. (Title to leased goods does not pass to the lessee.) Identification gives the buyer or lessee the right to insure the goods and the right to recover from third parties who damage the goods.

2	**Identify when title passes under a contract for a sale of goods.** Unless the parties agree otherwise, title passes from the seller to the buyer at the time and place the seller physically delivers the goods. Under a shipment contract, this occurs when the seller delivers the goods into the hands of a carrier. Under a destination contract, title passes when the goods are delivered to that destination. If the contract does not require the seller to ship or deliver the goods, title passes to the buyer when and where a document of title is delivered. When no documents of title are required, title passes at the time and place the contract is made if the goods have been identified. If the goods have not been identified, title passes on identification.
3	**State what happens when persons who acquire goods without title attempt to resell the goods.** When a person who acquires goods with an imperfect title attempts to sell the goods, a buyer acquires at least whatever title the seller has. If the seller is a thief, the seller's title is void, the buyer acquires no title, and the real owner can reclaim the goods. A seller with voidable title can transfer good title to a good faith purchaser for value, and the real, or original, owner cannot recover the goods. Entrusting goods to a merchant who deals in goods of that kind gives the merchant the power to transfer all rights to a buyer in the ordinary course of business.
4	**Discuss who bears the loss if goods are damaged, destroyed, or lost, or if the contract is breached.** Unless the parties agree otherwise, the risk of loss passes from the seller or lessor to the buyer or lessee at the time and place the seller or lessor physically delivers the goods. Under a shipment contract, this occurs when the seller or lessor delivers the goods into the hands of a carrier. Under a destination contract, the risk passes when the goods are tendered at that destination. If the contract does not require the seller to ship or deliver the goods, the risk passes to the buyer when and where (1) a negotiable document of title is delivered, (2) a bailee who holds the goods acknowledges the buyer's right to them, or (3) a nonnegotiable document of title is delivered and the buyer has had a reasonable time to present the document and demand the goods. When no document of title is required, the risk passes (1) when the buyer or lessee takes physical possession of the goods if the seller or lessor is a merchant or (2) on tender if the seller or lessor is not a merchant. If the goods are so nonconforming that the buyer or lessee has the right to reject them, the risk does not pass until the defects are cured or the buyer or lessee accepts the goods in spite of their defects. If a buyer or lessee breaches a contract, the risk of loss immediately shifts to the buyer or lessee for a commercially reasonable time after the seller or lessor learns of the breach, but only to the extent of any deficiency in the seller's or lessor's insurance.
5	**Pinpoint who has an insurable interest in goods.** A buyer or lessee has an insurable interest in goods that are identified to the contract. A seller or lessor has an insurable interest in goods if he or she has title to them or a security interest in them.

ISSUE SPOTTERS

Check your answers to the *Issue Spotters* against the answers provided in Appendix C at the end of this text.

1. Adams Textiles in Kansas City sells certain fabric to Silk & Satin Stores in Oklahoma City. Adams packs the fabric and ships it by rail to Silk. While the fabric is in transit across Kansas, a tornado derails the train and scatters and shreds the fabric across miles of cornfields. What are the consequences if Silk bore the risk? If Adams bore the risk? (See *Insurable Interest*.)

2. Paula boards her horse, Blaze, at Gold Spur Stables. She sells the horse to George and calls Gold Spur to say, "I sold Blaze to George." Gold Spur says, "Okay." That night, Blaze is kicked in the head by another horse and dies. Who pays for the loss? (See *Risk of Loss*.)

USING BUSINESS LAW

19–1. Sales by Nonowners. In the following situations, two parties lay claim to the same goods sold. Discuss which of the parties would prevail in each situation. (See *Identification*.)

1. Terry steals Dom's television set and sells the set to Blake, an innocent purchaser, for value. Dom learns that Blake has the set and demands its return.

2. Karlin takes her television set for repair to Orken, a merchant who sells new and used television sets. By accident, one of Orken's employees sells the set to Grady, an innocent purchaser-customer, who takes possession. Karlin wants her set back from Grady.

19–2. Risk of Loss. When will risk of loss pass from the seller to the buyer under each of the following contracts, assuming the parties have not expressly agreed on when risk of loss would pass? (See *Risk of Loss*.)

1. A New York seller contracts with a San Francisco buyer to ship goods to the buyer F.O.B. San Francisco.

2. A New York seller contracts with a San Francisco buyer to ship goods to the buyer in San Francisco. There is no indication as to whether the shipment will be F.O.B. New York or F.O.B. San Francisco.

3. A seller contracts with a buyer to sell goods located on the seller's premises. The buyer pays for the goods and makes arrangements to pick them up the next week at the seller's place of business.

4. A seller contracts with a buyer to sell goods located in a warehouse.

REAL-WORLD CASE PROBLEMS

19–3. Risk of Loss. Ethicon, Inc., entered into an agreement with UPS Supply Chain Solutions, Inc., to transport pharmaceuticals. Under a contract with UPS's subsidiary, Worldwide Dedicated Services, drivers were provided by International Management Services Co. During the transport of a shipment from Ethicon's facility in Texas to buyers "F.O.B. Tennessee," one of the trucks collided with a concrete barrier, damaging the goods. Who was liable for the loss, and why? [*Royal & Sun Alliance Insurance, PLC v. International Management Services Co.*, 703 F.3d 604 (2d Cir. 2013)] (See *Risk of Loss*.)

19–4. Delivery without Movement of the Goods. Aleris International, Inc., signed a contract to buy a John Deere loader from Holt Equipment Co. The agreement provided that "despite physical delivery of the equipment, title shall remain in the seller until" Aleris paid the full price. The next month, Aleris filed for bankruptcy. Holt filed a claim with the court to repossess the loader. Holt asserted that it was the owner. Who is entitled to the loader, and why? [*In re Aleris International, Ltd.*, ___ Bankr ___ (D.Del. 2011)] (See *Identification*.)

19–5. Goods Held by the Seller or Lessor. Douglas Singletary bought a manufactured home from Andy's Mobile Home and Land Sales. The contract stated that the buyer accepted the home "as is where is." Singletary paid the full price, and his crew began to ready the home to relocate it to his property. The night before the home was to be moved, however, it was destroyed by fire. Who suffered the loss? Explain. [*Singletary, III v. P&A Investments, Inc.*, 712 S.E.2d 681 (N.C.App. 2011)] (See *Risk of Loss*.)

ETHICAL QUESTIONS

19–6. Risk of Loss. If the parties to a contract do not specify when the risk of loss passes, the risk generally rests with the party who has possession of the goods or the right to their possession. Why is this the rule?

19–7. Shipment Contracts. Professional Products, Inc. (PPI), bought three pallets of computer wafers from Omneon Video Graphics. (A computer wafer is a thin, round slice of silicon from which microchips are made.) Omneon agreed to ship the wafers to the City University of New York "FOB Omneon's dock." Shipment was arranged through Haas Industries, Inc. The "conditions of carriage" on the back of the bill of lading stated that Haas's liability for lost goods was limited to fifty cents per pound. When the shipment arrived, it included only two pallets. Who suffers the loss? Is it fair for a carrier to limit its liability for lost goods? Discuss. [*OneBeacon Insurance Co. v. Haas Industries, Inc.*, 634 F.3d 1092 (9th Cir. 2011)] (See *Risk of Loss*.)

Chapter 19—Work Set

TRUE-FALSE QUESTIONS

_____ 1. Identification occurs when goods are shipped by the seller.

_____ 2. Unless the parties agree otherwise, title passes at the time and place that the buyer accepts the goods.

_____ 3. Unless a contract provides otherwise, it is normally assumed to be a shipment contract.

_____ 4. A buyer and a seller cannot both have an insurable interest in the same goods at the same time.

_____ 5. In a sale on approval, the risk of loss passes to the buyer as soon as the buyer takes possession.

_____ 6. A buyer can acquire valid title to stolen goods if he or she does not know that the goods are stolen.

_____ 7. Under a destination contract, title passes at the time and place of shipment.

_____ 8. If a seller is a merchant, the risk of loss passes when a buyer takes possession of the goods.

MULTIPLE-CHOICE QUESTIONS

_____ 1. Bob contracts to sell to the Marcos University Bookstore 10,000 black USB flash drives. Bob identifies the flash drives by boxing up the order, attaching labels with Marcos's address to the cartons, and leaving the boxes on the loading dock for shipping. Between Bob and Marcos,

  a. the risk of loss has passed with respect to all of the flash drives.
  b. the risk of loss has passed with respect to half of the flash drives.
  c. the risk of loss has passed with respect to the flash drives with labels on the boxes.
  d. none of the above has occurred.

_____ 2. Sam defrauds his Aunt Claire out of her antique clock. He then sells the clock to Jill. If Jill does not know that the clock was acquired by fraud, what title does she take?

  a. Jill takes voidable title, based on Sam's voidable title.
  b. Jill takes good title because she was a good faith purchaser.
  c. Jill takes valid title but may be subject to a tort claim for embezzlement.
  d. Jill has no title because Sam's title was void.

_____ 3. On Monday, Stan buys a mountain bike from Tom, his neighbor, who says, "Take the bike." Stan says, "I'll leave it in your garage until Friday." On Tuesday, Rosie steals the bike from Tom's garage. Who bore the risk?

  a. Stan.
  b. Tom.
  c. Both a and b.
  d. None of the above.

_____ 4. On Monday, Craft Computers in Seattle delivers five hundred Dell LED-Lit Monitors to Pac Transport to take to Portland under a destination contract with Connecting Point Stores. The monitors arrive in Portland on Tuesday, and Pac tells Connecting Point they are at Pac's warehouse. On Thursday, the warehouse burns down. On Friday, Connecting Point learns of the fire. The risk of loss passed to Connecting Point on

  a. Monday.
  b. Tuesday.
  c. Friday.
  d. none of the above days.

5. Foster Wholesalers agrees to sell one hundred Toshiba Tablets to Beta Electronics. Foster identifies the goods by marking the crates with red stripes. Title has not yet passed to Beta. Who has an insurable interest in the goods?

   a. Only Foster.
   b. Only Beta.
   c. Both Foster and Beta.
   d. None of the above.

6. Under a contract with QT Corporation, Gold Medical ships an assortment of medical supplies. When QT opens the crates, it discovers that the supplies are the wrong assortment, but agrees to accept them anyway. The risk of loss passed to QT when

   a. Gold shipped the supplies.
   b. QT opened the crates.
   c. QT discovered that the goods were the wrong assortment.
   d. QT accepted the supplies.

7. Apple Bike Makers agrees to sell forty mountain bikes to Orange Mountain Recreation under a shipment contract. Apple delivers the goods to Sugar Trucking to take to Orange Mountain. Sugar delivers the goods. Title to the goods passed

   a. when Apple agreed to sell the goods.
   b. when Apple delivered the goods to Sugar.
   c. when Sugar delivered the goods to Orange Mountain.
   d. at none of the above times.

8. Nora leaves her car with OK Auto Sales & Service for repairs. OK sells the car to Pete, who does not know that OK has no right to sell the car. Nora can recover from

   a. OK only.
   b. Pete only.
   c. OK and Pete.
   d. none of the above.

ANSWERING MORE LEGAL PROBLEMS

1. Hank bought a twelve-foot, four-by-four beam at Econo Lumber. An Econo employee loaded the beam onto Hank's truck but did not secure it. A sign at the lumber-yard stated that the store did not secure loads. Hank did not secure the beam, either. As he drove on the highway, the beam fell from the truck. While trying to retrieve it, Hank was struck by a car and injured.

   Who held title to the beam at the time of the accident? Hank held the title. Unless the parties agree otherwise, when delivery is made without moving the goods—when the buyer picks them up—title passes at the time and place the _____ was made, if the goods have been _____. Here, title to the beam passed when Hank selected it and paid for it at Econo. Who bore the risk of loss when the beam fell from Hank's truck? Hank bore the risk of loss at the time of the accident. If a buyer is to pick up goods, and the seller is a merchant, the risk of loss to the goods passes to the buyer when he takes _____ _____ of the goods. The risk of loss passed from Econo to Hank when the beam was loaded onto his truck.

2. Price-Cut Markets ordered strawberries, blueberries, and raspberries from Driscoll County Harvest Distribution Cooperative. Driscoll employees designated the berries for Price-Cut, loaded them onto a truck, and dispatched it. En route, the truck overturned, and the berries were damaged.

   When could Price-Cut obtain insurance on the berries? Once _____ of the berries as the subject matter of the contract between Price-Cut and Driscoll occurred, Price-Cut could insure against their loss or damage. When did identification of the berries as the subject matter of the contract take place? Identification occurred when Driscoll employees _____ the berries for Price-Cut. Unless a buyer and seller agree otherwise, identification takes place when goods are marked, shipped, or somehow _____ by the seller as the goods to pass under a contract.

PERFORMANCE AND BREACH

20

LEARNING OUTCOMES

The four Learning Outcomes below are designed to help improve your understanding of the chapter. After reading this chapter, you should be able to:

1 Explain the seller's or lessor's major obligation under a contract.

2 Identify the buyer's or lessee's major duties under a contract.

3 List the remedies available to a seller or lessor when the buyer or lessee is in breach.

4 State the remedies available to a buyer or lessee when the seller or lessor is in breach.

FACING A LEGAL PROBLEM

In San Francisco, Roger contracts to sell Arturo five used trucks, which both parties know are located in a warehouse in Chicago. The parties expect that Arturo will pick up the trucks, but nothing about a place of delivery is specified in the contract.

Q What is the place for delivery of the trucks? Can Roger "deliver" the trucks without moving them? If so, how?

To understand the *performance* that is required of the parties under a sales or lease contract, it is necessary to know the duties and obligations each party has assumed under the terms of the contract. The basic obligations of good faith and commercial reasonableness underlie every contract under the Uniform Commercial Code (UCC). These standards are read into every contract. They also provide a framework in which the parties can specify particulars of performance.

For example, a contract may specify the city in which goods are to be delivered but leave open the particular address. The buyer is obliged to specify the address before the delivery date. If he or she fails to do so, the seller is excused from any resulting delay.

In this chapter, we examine the basic performance obligations of the parties under a sales or lease contract. Sometimes, circumstances make it difficult for a person to carry out the promised performance. In this situation, the contract may be breached. When a breach occurs, the aggrieved party looks for remedies—which are dealt with in the second half of this chapter.

20–1 OBLIGATIONS OF THE SELLER OR LESSOR

The seller's or lessor's major obligation under a sales contract is to tender **conforming goods** to the buyer or lessee.

20–1a Tender of Delivery

Tender of delivery requires that the seller or lessor hold *conforming* goods at the buyer's or lessee's disposal and give the buyer or lessee whatever notification is reasonably necessary to enable the buyer or lessee to take delivery.

Tender must occur at a *reasonable hour* and in a *reasonable manner.* **EXAMPLE 20.1** Dairy Products, Inc., the seller, cannot call Grocers Supply, the buyer, at 2:00 A.M. and say, "The goods are ready. I'll give you twenty minutes to get them." ◄ Unless the parties have agreed otherwise, the goods must be tendered for delivery at a reasonable hour and kept available for a reasonable period of time to enable the buyer to take possession of them.

LEARNING OUTCOME 1

Explain the seller's or lessor's major obligation under a contract.

conforming goods
Goods that conform to contract specifications.

tender of delivery
A seller's or lessor's act of placing conforming goods at the disposal of the buyer or lessee and providing whatever notification is reasonably necessary to enable the buyer or lessee to take delivery.

Real-World Case Example

Richard and Nancy Garziano contracted with Louisiana Log Home (LLH) Company for a log-cabin kit to be delivered to them in Mississippi. The contract required three install-ment payments with the final payment, due at delivery, to include the shipping costs. Two days before delivery, LLH told the buyers that those costs would be more than $2,600. The Garzianos replied that they thought the shipping costs would be lower, and refused to pay. As a result, LLH diverted the kit to a warehouse. The Garzianos filed a claim in a federal district court against LLH, alleging breach of contract. The court issued a judgment in LLH's favor. The Garzianos appealed.

Did LLH comply with its obligation to tender delivery in a reasonable manner? Yes. In a 2014 case, *Garziano v. Louisiana Log Home Co.*, the U.S. Court of Appeals for the Fifth Circuit affirmed this part of the lower court's judgment. The Garzianos contended that LLH had breached the contract by failing to inform them of the shipping costs in a timely manner. While the Garzianos may have been surprised at the size of the deliv-ery fee, LLH's notice of the delivery was not unreasonable. The Garzianos were not pre-vented from effectively taking delivery. Thus, their refusal to pay LLH was not excused.

All goods called for by a contract must be tendered in a single delivery unless the parties agree otherwise or the circumstances are such that either party can rightfully request delivery in lots. **EXAMPLE 20.2** An order for one thousand shirts cannot be delivered two at a time. If Off-the-Rack Clothing (the seller) and Trend Fashion Stores (the buyer) understand that the shirts are to be delivered as they are produced in four lots of 250 each, however, and the price can be apportioned accordingly, it may be commercially reasonable to deliver in four lots. ◄

20–1b Place of Delivery

The UCC provides for the place of delivery under a contract if the contract does not state or otherwise indicate a place.

Noncarrier Cases If the contract does not designate the place of delivery for the goods, and the buyer is expected to pick them up, the place of delivery is the *seller's place of business* or, if the seller has none, the *seller's residence*. If the contract involves the sale of *identified goods,* and the parties know when they enter into the contract that these goods are located somewhere other than at the seller's place of business (such as at a warehouse), then the *location of the goods* is the place for delivery.

Carrier Cases In many instances, circumstances or delivery terms in the contract make it apparent that the parties intend that a carrier, such as a trucking company, be used to move the goods. There are two ways a seller can complete performance of the obligation to deliver the goods in carrier cases: through a shipment contract or through a destination contract.

Shipment Contracts A shipment contract requires or authorizes the seller to ship goods by a carrier. The contract does not require that the seller deliver the goods at a particular destination. Unless otherwise agreed, the seller must do the following:

1. Put the goods into the hands of the carrier.
2. Make a contract for their transportation that is reasonable according to the nature of the goods and their value. Certain types of goods, for example, need refrigeration in transit.
3. Obtain and promptly deliver or tender to the buyer any documents necessary to enable the buyer to obtain the goods from the carrier.
4. Promptly notify the buyer that shipment has been made.

If the seller fails to notify the buyer that shipment has been made or fails to make a proper contract for transportation, and a *material loss* of the goods or a *delay* results, the buyer can reject the shipment.

Destination Contracts Under a destination contract, the seller agrees to see that conforming goods will be duly tendered to the buyer at a particular destination. The goods must be tendered at a reasonable hour and held at the buyer's disposal for a reasonable length of time. The seller must also give the buyer appropriate notice. In addition, the seller must provide the buyer with any documents of title necessary to enable the buyer to obtain delivery from the carrier.

20–1c The Perfect Tender Rule

If the goods or the tender of delivery fail in any respect to conform to the contract, the buyer or lessee has the right to accept the goods, reject the entire shipment, or accept part and reject part. This is known as the *perfect tender rule*. Because of the rigidity of the perfect tender rule, several exceptions have been created, some of which are discussed here.

Agreement of the Parties If the parties have agreed that, for example, defective goods or parts will not be rejected if the seller or lessor is able to repair or replace them within a reasonable period of time, the perfect tender rule does not apply.

Cure The term *cure* refers to the seller's or lessor's right to repair, adjust, or replace defective or nonconforming goods. When any tender or delivery is rejected because of *nonconforming goods* and the time for performance has *not yet expired,* the seller or lessor can notify the buyer or lessee promptly of the intention to cure and can then do so *within the contract time for performance.*

Once the time for performance under the contract has expired, the seller or lessor can still exercise the right to cure if he or she had *reasonable grounds to believe that the nonconforming tender would be acceptable to the buyer or lessee.*

HIGHLIGHTING THE POINT

In the past, Reddy Electronics frequently allowed the Topps Company to substitute certain electronic supplies when the goods Reddy ordered were not available. Under a new contract for the same type of goods, Reddy rejects the substitute supplies on the last day Topps can perform the contract.

Does Topps have the right to cure? Yes. Topps had reasonable grounds to believe Reddy would accept a substitute. Therefore, Topps can cure within a reasonable time, even though conforming delivery will occur after the actual time limit for performance allowed under the contract.

The right to cure substantially restricts the right of the buyer or lessee to reject. **EXAMPLE 20.3** Robinson Repair & Restore, the buyer, notices a particular defect in a shipment of hoses and pipe fittings from Commercial Hydraulics Company, the seller. Robinson refuses a tender of the hoses and fittings as nonconforming, but it does not disclose the nature of the defect to Commercial. Robinson cannot later assert the defect as a defense if the defect is one that Commercial could have cured. ◄ Generally, buyers and lessees must act in good faith and state specific reasons for refusing to accept the goods.

Substitution of Carriers An agreed-on manner of delivery (such as which carrier will be used to transport the goods) may become impracticable or unavailable through no fault of either party. If a commercially reasonable substitute is available, this substitute performance is sufficient.

installment contract
A contract in which payments due are made periodically.

Installment Contracts An **installment contract** is a single contract that requires or authorizes delivery in two or more separate lots to be accepted and paid for separately. In an installment contract, a buyer or lessee can reject an installment *only if the nonconformity substantially impairs the value* of the installment and cannot be cured. **EXAMPLE 20.4** A seller, Refrigerated Appliances, Inc., is to deliver fifteen freezers in lots of five each. In the first lot, four of the freezers have defective cooling units that cannot be repaired. The buyer in these circumstances, Home Furnishings stores, can reject the entire lot. ◄ An entire installment contract is breached only when one or more nonconforming installments *substantially* impair the value of the *whole contract.*

Commercial Impracticability Whenever occurrences unforeseen by either party when the contract was made render performance commercially impracticable, the perfect tender rule no longer holds. The unforeseen contingency must be one that would have been impossible to imagine in a given business situation.

HIGHLIGHTING THE POINT

A major oil company that receives its supplies from the Middle East has a contract to supply a buyer with one hundred thousand gallons of oil. After the contract is entered into, an oil embargo by the Organization of Petroleum Exporting Countries prevents the seller from securing oil supplies to meet the terms of the contract. Because of the same embargo, the seller cannot secure oil from any other source.

Does this situation come under the commercial impracticability exception to the perfect tender rule? Yes. Of course, the embargo must have been unforeseen by either party when the contract was made.

Destruction of Identified Goods When a casualty (such as a fire) totally destroys *identified goods* under a contract through no fault of either party and *before risk passes to the buyer or lessee,* the parties are excused from performance. If the goods are only partially destroyed, however, the buyer or lessee can inspect them and either treat the contract as void or accept the damaged goods with a reduction of the contract price.

Assurance and Cooperation If one party to a contract has "reasonable grounds" to believe that the other party will not perform as contracted, he or she may demand in writing assurance of performance from the other party. Until the assurance is received, he or she may suspend further performance. What constitutes "reasonable grounds" is determined by commercial standards. If assurance is not forthcoming within a reasonable period (not more than thirty days), the failure to respond can be considered a repudiation of the contract.

Sometimes, the performance of one party depends on the cooperation of the other. When the cooperation is not forthcoming, the first party can proceed to perform the contract in any reasonable manner or suspend his or her own performance and hold the uncooperative party in breach.

EXAMPLE 20.5 Aman is required by contract to deliver two thousand Samsung washing machines to various locations in Ohio. Deliveries are to be made on or before October 1, and the locations are to be specified later by Farrell. Aman has repeatedly requested the delivery locations, but Farrell has not responded. On October 1, the washing machines are ready to be shipped, but Farrell still refuses to give Aman the delivery locations. Aman does not ship on October 1. Aman is not liable and is excused for any resulting delay of performance because of Farrell's failure to cooperate.◀

 20–2 OBLIGATIONS OF THE BUYER OR LESSEE

Once the seller or lessor has tendered delivery, the buyer or lessee is obligated to accept the goods and pay for them according to the terms of the contract. In the absence of any specific agreements, the buyer or lessee must do the following:

LEARNING OUTCOME 2
Identify the buyer's or lessee's major duties under a contract.

1. Furnish facilities reasonably suited for receipt of the goods.
2. Make payment at the time and place the buyer *receives the goods.*

20–2a Payment

Payment can be made by any means agreed on between the parties—cash or any other method of payment generally acceptable in the commercial world. If a seller demands cash, the seller must permit the buyer reasonable time to obtain it. When a sale is made on credit, the buyer is obliged to pay according to the specified terms (for example, ninety days). The credit period usually begins on the *date of shipment.*

20–2b Right of Inspection

Unless otherwise agreed, or for collect-on-delivery goods, the buyer or lessee has an absolute right to inspect the goods before making payment. This right allows the buyer or lessee to verify, before making payment, that the goods tendered or delivered conform to the contract. If the goods are *not* what the buyer or lessee ordered (or do not conform to their description in the contract), he or she has no duty to pay. Unless otherwise agreed, inspection can take place at any reasonable place and time and in any reasonable manner. Generally, what is reasonable is determined by custom of the trade, past practices of the parties, and the like.

20–2c Revocation of Acceptance

After a buyer or lessee accepts a lot or a commercial unit, any return of the goods must be by *revocation of acceptance.* (Revocation means withdrawal.) Acceptance can be revoked if a nonconformity *substantially* impairs the value of the unit or lot and if one of the following factors is present:

1. Acceptance was predicated on the reasonable assumption that the nonconformity would be cured, and it has not been cured within a reasonable period of time.
2. The buyer or lessee does not discover the nonconformity until after acceptance, either because it was difficult to discover before acceptance or because the seller's or lessor's assurance that the goods were conforming kept the buyer or lessee from inspecting the goods.

20–3 ANTICIPATORY REPUDIATION

What if, before the time for performance, one party clearly communicates to the other the intention not to perform? Such an action is a breach of the contract by *anticipatory repudiation* (refusal to acknowledge the party's obligations under the contract). When anticipatory repudiation occurs, the aggrieved party can do the following:

1. Await performance by the repudiating party, hoping that he or she will decide to honor the contract.

2. Resort to any remedy for breach.

3. In either situation, *suspend performance* or proceed with the seller's right to resell the goods or to salvage unfinished goods (to be discussed shortly).

20–4 REMEDIES OF THE SELLER OR LESSOR

LEARNING OUTCOME 3

List the remedies available to a seller or lessor when the buyer or lessee is in breach.

Numerous remedies are available to a seller or lessor when the buyer or lessee is in breach under the UCC. Remedies—including the rights to withhold delivery, to reclaim the goods, to resell the goods, to recover the purchase price, and to recover damages—are discussed here.

20–4a The Right to Withhold Delivery

In general, sellers and lessors can withhold or stop performance of their obligations under a contract when buyers or lessees are in breach. If a buyer or lessee has wrongfully rejected or revoked acceptance, failed to make proper and timely payment, or repudiated a part of the contract, the seller or lessor can withhold delivery of the goods. If a breach results from the buyer's or lessee's *insolvency*, the seller or lessor can refuse to deliver the goods unless the buyer or lessee pays in cash.

20–4b The Right to Reclaim the Goods

Under a sales contract, if a seller discovers that the buyer has received goods on credit and is insolvent, the seller can demand return of the goods. The demand generally must be made within ten days of the buyer's receipt of the goods. The seller can demand and reclaim the goods at any time if the buyer misrepresented his or her solvency in writing within three months before the delivery.

In regard to lease contracts, if the lessee is in default (fails to make payments that are due, for example), the lessor may reclaim the leased goods that are in the possession of the lessee.

20–4c The Right to Resell the Goods

Sometimes a buyer or lessee breaches or repudiates a contract when the seller or lessor is still in possession of the goods (or when the goods have been delivered to a carrier or bailee, but the buyer or lessee has not yet received them). In this event, the seller or lessor can resell or dispose of the goods.

When the goods contracted for are unfinished at the time of breach, the seller or lessor can do one of two things: (1) cease manufacturing the goods and resell them for scrap or salvage value, or (2) complete the manufacture of the goods and resell or dispose of them. In any case, the seller or lessor can recover any deficiency between the resale price and the contract price, along with **incidental damages** (costs to the seller or lessor resulting from the breach).

incidental damages
Damages resulting from a breach of contract, including all reasonable expenses incurred because of the breach.

20–4d The Right to Recover the Purchase Price

An unpaid seller or lessor can bring an action to recover the purchase price or payments due under the contract (and incidental damages) only under one of the following circumstances:

1. When the buyer or lessee has accepted the goods and has not revoked acceptance.

2. When conforming goods have been lost or damaged after the risk of loss has passed to the buyer or lessee.

3. When the buyer or lessee has breached the contract after the contract goods have been identified and the seller or lessor is unable to resell the goods.

If a seller or lessor sues for the contract price of goods that he or she has been unable to resell or dispose of, the goods must be held for the buyer or lessee. The seller or lessor can resell at any time prior to collection of the judgment from the buyer or lessee, but the net proceeds from the sale must be credited to the buyer or lessee.

HIGHLIGHTING THE POINT

Dixon Management Consultants contracts with Gem Point to purchase one thousand laser pointers with the company name inscribed on them. Gem Point delivers the laser pointers, but Dixon refuses to accept them.

Does Gem Point have, as a proper remedy, an action for the full purchase price? Yes. Gem Point can bring an action for the purchase price because it delivered conforming goods, and Dixon refused to accept or pay for the goods. Gem Point obviously cannot resell to anyone else because the laser pointers have Dixon's business name inscribed on them.

20–4e The Right to Recover Damages

If a buyer or lessee repudiates a contract or wrongfully refuses to accept the goods, a seller or lessor can bring an action to recover the damages that were sustained. Ordinarily, the amount of damages equals the difference between the contract price or lease payments and the market price (at the time and place of tender of the goods), plus incidental damages.

Sometimes, the difference between the contract price or lease payments and the market price is too small to place the seller or lessor in the position that he or she would have been in if the buyer or lessee had fully performed. In these situations, the proper measure of damages is the seller's or lessor's lost profits, including a reasonable allowance for overhead and other incidental expenses.

20–5 REMEDIES OF THE BUYER OR LESSEE

The UCC makes numerous remedies available to the buyer or lessee in the event of a breach. Of course, the buyer or lessee can recover as much of the price as has been paid. Here, we discuss four additional remedies: the rights to reject the goods, to obtain specific performance, to obtain cover, and to recover damages.

LEARNING OUTCOME 4

State the remedies available to a buyer or lessee when the seller or lessor is in breach.

20–5a The Right of Rejection

If either the goods or the tender of the goods by the seller or lessor fails to conform to the contract in *any respect*, the buyer or lessee normally can reject the goods. If some of the goods conform to the contract, the buyer or lessee can keep the conforming goods and reject the rest.

Timeliness and Reason for Rejection Required The buyer or lessee must reject the goods within a reasonable amount of time and must notify the seller or lessor **seasonably** (in a timely fashion). Failure to do so precludes the buyer or lessee from using those defects to justify rejection or to establish breach when the seller or lessor could have cured the defects if they had been stated seasonably.

Duties of Merchant Buyers and Lessees When Goods Are Rejected If a *merchant buyer* or *lessee* rightfully rejects goods, he or she is required to follow any reasonable instructions received from the seller or lessor with respect to the goods controlled by the buyer or lessee. **EXAMPLE 20.6** Clearwater Pool & Spa Supplies, the seller, might ask North Glen Construction, the buyer, to store pool equipment that Clearwater delivered, but North Glen rejected, in its warehouse until the next day, when Clearwater can retrieve it.◄ If there are no instructions, the buyer or lessee may store the goods or reship them to the seller or lessor. In any of these situations, the buyer or lessee is entitled to reimbursement for the costs involved.

20–5b The Right to Obtain Specific Performance

A buyer or lessee can obtain specific performance—that is, exactly what was contracted for—when the goods are unique or when the buyer's or lessee's remedy at law (monetary damages) is inadequate. Specific performance may be appropriate, for example, when the contract is for the purchase of a particular work of art, a copyright, or a similarly unique item. Monetary damages may not be sufficient in these circumstances.

HIGHLIGHTING THE POINT

Sutherlin contracts to sell his antique car to Fenwick for $30,000, with delivery and payment due on June 14. Fenwick tenders payment on June 14, but Sutherlin refuses to deliver.

If Fenwick sues Sutherlin, can Fenwick obtain the car? Because the antique car is unique, Fenwick can probably obtain specific performance of the contract from Sutherlin.

20–5c The Right to Obtain Cover

In certain situations, buyers and lessees can protect themselves by obtaining **cover**—that is, by substituting goods for those that were due under the contract. This option is available to a buyer or lessee who has rightfully rejected goods or revoked acceptance. The option is also available when the seller or lessor repudiates the contract or fails to deliver the goods. After purchasing substitute goods, the buyer or lessee can recover from the seller or lessor the difference between the

---

seasonably
Within a specified time period, or if no time is specified, within a reasonable time.

cover
A remedy that allows the buyer or lessee, on the seller's or lessor's breach, to purchase or lease the goods from another seller or lessor and substitute them for the goods due under the contract.

cost of cover and the contract price, plus incidental and consequential damages, less the expenses (such as delivery costs) that were saved as a result of the breach.

Consequential damages include any loss suffered by the buyer or lessee that the seller or lessor could have foreseen (had reason to know about) at the time of the contract. **EXAMPLE 20.7** Ridgeline Construction, Inc., tells Quarry Sales Corporation, a heavy equipment manufacturer, that it needs a certain piece of equipment by July 1 to close a $50,000 deal. Quarry can foresee that if the equipment is not delivered by that date, Ridgeline will suffer consequential damages.◄

20–5d The Right to Recover Damages

If a seller or lessor repudiates the contract or fails to deliver the goods, the buyer or lessee can sue for damages. The measure of recovery is the difference between the contract price and the market price of the goods (at the place the seller or lessor was supposed to deliver) at the time the buyer or lessee *learned* of the breach. The buyer or lessee can also recover incidental and consequential damages less expenses that were saved as a result of the seller's or lessor's breach.

When the seller or lessor breaches a warranty, the measure of damages equals the difference between the value of the goods as accepted and their value if they had been delivered as warranted. For this and other types of breaches in which the buyer or lessee has accepted the goods, the buyer or lessee is entitled to recover for any loss resulting in the ordinary course of events.

ANSWERING THE LEGAL PROBLEM

In the legal problem set out at the beginning of this chapter, in San Francisco, Roger contracts to sell Arturo trucks located in a warehouse in Chicago. Nothing is said about delivery, although the parties expect Arturo to pick up the trucks.

A **What is the place for delivery?** Chicago. **How can Roger "deliver" the trucks without moving them?** Arturo will need some type of document to show the bailee (the warehouser to whom the goods are entrusted) that Arturo is entitled to the trucks. Roger can tender delivery without moving the trucks by either giving Arturo a *negotiable document of title* or obtaining the *bailee's (warehouser's) acknowledgment* that Arturo is entitled to possession.

TERMS AND CONCEPTS FOR REVIEW

conforming goods 261

cover 268

incidental damages 266

installment contract 264

seasonably 268

tender of delivery 261

CHAPTER SUMMARY—PERFORMANCE AND BREACH

LEARNING OUTCOME	
1	**Explain the seller's or lessor's major obligation under a contract.** The seller's or lessor's major obligation is to tender conforming goods to the buyer or lessee. Tender must occur at a reasonable hour and in a reasonable manner. If the seller or lessor tenders nonconforming goods and the buyer or lessee rejects them, the seller or lessor may cure—repair or replace the goods—within the contract time for performance. If the agreed-on means of delivery becomes impracticable or unavailable, a commercially reasonable substitute is sufficient.
2	**Identify the buyer's or lessee's major duties under a contract.** On a seller's or lessor's tender of conforming goods, a buyer or lessee is obligated to accept them and pay for them according to the contract. Unless the parties agree otherwise, a buyer or lessee has a right to inspect the goods before accepting them. The buyer or lessee can revoke acceptance if, among other things, a nonconformity substantially impairs the value of the goods.
3	**List the remedies available to a seller or lessor when the buyer or lessee is in breach.** When the buyer or lessee is in breach, the seller or lessor may withhold delivery, reclaim the goods, resell the goods, recover the price, or sue for damages.
4	**State the remedies available to a buyer or lessee when the seller or lessor is in breach.** When the seller or lessor is in breach, the buyer or lessee may reject the goods, sue for specific performance, obtain cover, or sue to recover damages.

ISSUE SPOTTERS

Check your answers to the *Issue Spotters* against the answers provided in Appendix C at the end of this text.

1. Mike agrees to sell one thousand espresso makers to Jenny to be delivered on May 1. Due to a strike, Mike can only deliver the espresso makers two hundred at a time over a period of ten days, with the first delivery on May 1. Does Mike have the right to deliver the goods in five lots? Explain. (See *Obligations of the Seller or Lessor*.)

2. Pic Post-Stars agrees to sell Ace Novelty five thousand posters of celebrities, to be delivered on April 1. On March 1, Pic tells Ace, "The deal's off." Ace says, "I expect you to deliver. I'll be waiting." Can Ace sue Pic without waiting until April 1? Why or why not? (See *Anticipatory Repudiation*.)

USING BUSINESS LAW

20–1. The Perfect Tender Rule. Ames contracts to ship one hundred Model Z TVs to Curley. The terms of delivery are F.O.B. Ames's city, by Green Truck Lines, with delivery on or before April 30. On April 15, Ames discovers that because of an error in inventory control, all Model Z sets have been sold. Ames has Model X, a similar but slightly more expensive unit, in stock. On April 16, Ames ships one hundred Model X sets, with notice that Curley will be charged the Model Z price. Curley (in a proper manner) rejects the Model X sets when they are tendered on April 18. Ames does not wish to be held in breach of contract, even though he has tendered nonconforming goods. Discuss Ames's options. (See *Obligations of the Seller or Lessor*.)

20–2. Remedies of the Buyer or Lessee. Lehor collects antique cars. He contracts to purchase spare parts for a 1938 engine from Beem. These parts are not made anymore and are scarce. To obtain the contract with Beem, Lehor agrees to pay 50 percent of the purchase price in advance. On May 1, Lehor sends the payment, which Beem receives on May

2. On May 3, Beem, having found another buyer willing to pay substantially more for the parts, informs Lehor that he will not deliver as contracted. That same day, Lehor learns that Beem is insolvent. Discuss fully any possible remedies available to Lehor to enable him to take possession of these parts. (See *Remedies of the Buyer or Lessee.*)

REAL-WORLD CASE PROBLEMS

20–3. The Right of Rejection. Erb Poultry, Inc., is a distributor of fresh poultry products in Lima, Ohio. CEME, LLC, does business as Bank Shots, a restaurant, in Trotwood, Ohio. CEME ordered chicken wings and "dippers" from Erb, which were delivered and for which CEME issued a check in payment. A few days later, CEME stopped payment on the check. When contacted by Erb, CEME alleged that the products were beyond their freshness date, mangled, spoiled, and the wrong sizes. CEME did not provide any evidence to support the claims or arrange to return the products. Is CEME entitled to a full refund of the amount paid for the chicken? Explain. [*Erb Poultry, Inc. v. CEME, LLC*, 20 N.E.3d 1228 (Ohio App. 2 Dist. 2014)] (See *Remedies of the Buyer or Lessee.*)

20–4. The Right to Recover Damages. Woodridge USA Properties, LP, bought eighty-seven commercial truck trailers from Southeast Trailer Mart, Inc. (STM). Gerald McCarty, an independent sales agent who arranged the deal, showed Woodridge the documents of title. They did not indicate that Woodridge was the buyer. Woodridge asked McCarty to sell the trailers, and within three months

they were sold, but McCarty did not give the proceeds to Woodridge. Woodridge—without mentioning the title documents—asked STM to refund the contract price. STM refused. Does Woodridge have a right to recover damages from STM? Explain. [*Woodridge USA Properties, LP v. Southeast Trailer Mart, Inc.*, ___ F.3d ___ (11th Cir. 2011)] (See *Remedies of the Buyer or Lessee.*)

20–5. Breach and Damages. Utility Systems of America, Inc., was doing roadwork when Chad DeRosier, a nearby landowner, asked Utility to dump 1,500 cubic yards of fill onto his property. Utility agreed but exceeded DeRosier's request by dumping 6,500 cubic yards. Utility offered to remove the extra fill for $9,500. DeRosier paid a different contractor $46,629 to remove the fill and do certain other work, and filed a suit against Utility. Because Utility charged nothing for the fill, was there a breach of contract? If so, would the damages be greater than $9,500? Could consequential damages be justified? Discuss. [*DeRosier v. Utility Systems of America, Inc.*, 780 N.W.2d 1 (Minn. App. 2010)] (See *Remedies of the Buyer or Lessee.*)

ETHICAL QUESTIONS

20–6. Commercial Impracticability. How does the doctrine of commercial impracticability attempt to balance the rights of both parties to a contract? (See *Obligations of the Seller or Lessor.*)

20–7. Assurance. Flint Hills Resources, LP, a crude oil refiner, agreed to buy "approximately one thousand barrels per day" of Mexican natural gas condensate from JAG Energy Inc., an oil broker. Four months into the contract, Flint Hills

learned that some companies might be selling stolen condensate. Flint Hills refused to accept more deliveries from JAG without proof of its title to its product. JAG promised to forward documents showing its chain of title but after several weeks had not produced the documents. Did Flint Hills have a right to demand assurance of JAG's title? Can Flint Hills cancel its agreement with JAG? Explain. [*Flint Hills Resources LP v. JAG Energy, Inc.*, 559 F.3d 373 (5th Cir. 2009)] (See *Obligations of the Seller or Lessor.*)

Chapter 20—Work Set

TRUE-FALSE QUESTIONS

_____ 1. Performance of a sales contract is controlled by the agreement between the seller and the buyer.

_____ 2. If identified goods are destroyed through no fault of either party, and risk has not passed to the buyer, the parties are excused from performance.

_____ 3. Payment is always due at the time of delivery.

_____ 4. A buyer or lessee can always reject delivered goods on discovery of a defect, regardless of previous opportunities to inspect.

_____ 5. If a buyer or lessee is in breach, the seller or lessor can cancel the contract and sue for damages.

_____ 6. If a seller or lessor cancels a contract without justification, he or she is in breach, and the buyer or lessee can sue for damages.

_____ 7. A buyer's principal obligation is to tender delivery.

_____ 8. In an installment contract, a buyer can reject any installment for any reason.

_____ 9. A seller or lessor cannot consider a buyer or lessee in breach until the time for performance has past.

MULTIPLE-CHOICE QUESTIONS

_____ 1. Standard Office Products orders one hundred tablets from National Suppliers. National promises to deliver on Tuesday. The delivery

a. must be at a reasonable hour, but it can be in any manner.
b. must be in a reasonable manner, but it can be at any time.
c. must be at a reasonable hour and in a reasonable manner.
d. is described by none of the above.

_____ 2. Bill delivers six satellite dishes to Tom, according to their contract. The contract says nothing about payment. Tom must pay for the goods

a. within thirty days of the seller's request for payment.
b. within ten days.
c. within ten business days.
d. on delivery.

_____ 3. Neal contracts to sell five laser printers to Laura. Under either a shipment or a destination contract, Neal must give Laura

a. the documents necessary to obtain the goods.
b. appropriate notice regarding delivery.
c. both a and b.
d. none of the above.

_____ 4. World Toy Company agrees to sell fifty model rockets to Tom's Hobby Shop. World tenders delivery, but Tom refuses to accept or to pay for the model rockets. If World sues Tom for damages, World could recover the difference between the contract price and the market price at the time and place of

a. contracting.
b. tender.
c. rejection.
d. none of the above.

5. Alto Corporation agrees to buy ten saxophones from Musical Equipment Warehouse (MEW). When MEW fails to deliver, Alto is forced to cover. Alto sues MEW. Alto can recover from MEW

   a. the cover price, less the contract price.
   b. incidental and consequential damages.
   c. both a and b.
   d. none of the above.

6. Pep Paints agrees to sell to Monar Painters Grade A-1 latex outdoor paint to be delivered September 8. On September 7, Pep tenders Grade B-2 paint. Monar rejects the Grade B-2 paint. If, two days later, Pep tenders Grade C-3 paint with an offer of a price allowance, Pep will have

   a. one day to cure.
   b. a reasonable time to cure.
   c. additional, unlimited time to cure.
   d. none of the above.

7. Roy's Game Town orders virtual reality helmets from Hawking, Inc. Hawking delivers, but Roy rejects the shipment without telling Hawking the reason. If Hawking had known the reason, it could have corrected the problem within hours. Roy sues Hawking for damages. Roy will

   a. win, because Hawking's tender did not conform to the contract.
   b. win, because Hawking made no attempt to cure.
   c. lose, because Roy's rejection was unjustified—Hawking could have cured.
   d. lose, because a buyer cannot reject goods and sue for damages.

8. AdamCo agrees to sell the latest version of its Go! video game to Cutter Game stores. AdamCo delivers an outdated version of Go! (nonconforming goods). Cutter's possible remedies may include

   a. recovering damages.
   b. revoking acceptance.
   c. rejecting part or all of the goods.
   d. all of the above.

 ANSWERING MORE LEGAL PROBLEMS

1. Sara contracted to buy a new Steinway Model O grand piano for $52,400 from InTune Pianos. InTune delivered a piano that had been in storage for a year and had been moved at least six times. The piano showed unacceptable damage, according to Sara.

   Could Sara reject the piano? Yes. If goods fail to _____ to a contract in any respect, the buyer can reject them. Here, the piano showed unacceptable damage. What was Sara's measure of recovery for InTune's delivery of a damaged piano? Sara was entitled to at least $52,400. If a seller fails to deliver _____ goods, the buyer is entitled to damages. The measure is the difference between the _____ price and the market price of the goods at the place the seller was supposed to deliver and at the time the buyer learned of the breach. The buyer can also recover incidental and consequential _____. In this case, these might include sales tax, delivery charges, attorneys' fees, and court costs.

2. Cal bought a 1952 Mickey Mantle Topps baseball card for $17,750 from Pete, who represented that the card was in near-mint condition. Cal put the card in a safe-deposit box. Two years later, Cal sent the card to a sports-card grading service to be evaluated. The service determined that the card was ungradable because it had been doctored and discolored.

   Could Cal reject the baseball card? Yes. If goods fail to _____ to a contract in any respect, the buyer can reject them. In this case, the card was defective—doctored and discolored. What was Cal's measure of recovery for Pete's delivery of a defective card? Cal could recover at least $17,750. When the seller breaches a _____, the measure of damages equals the difference between the value of the goods as accepted and their _____ if they had been delivered as _____. The buyer can also recover any loss resulting in the ordinary course of events. Here, Pete represented that the card was in near-mint condition, but it was not. In addition to the value of the card, Cal might recover court costs.

WARRANTIES AND PRODUCT LIABILITY

21

FACING A LEGAL PROBLEM

Shari steals merchandise from the inventory room in Miguel's Electronics Store and sells two portable smart televisions to Cory, who does not know that they are stolen. If Miguel discovers that Cory has the goods, Miguel has the right to reclaim them from her.

Q If that happens, does Cory have any recourse against Shari?

LEARNING OUTCOMES

The four Learning Outcomes below are designed to help improve your understanding of the chapter. After reading this chapter, you should be able to:

1 State when express warranties arise in a sales or lease contract.

2 Identify the implied warranties that arise in a sales or lease contract.

3 Discuss negligence as the basis of product liability.

4 List the requirements of strict product liability.

In sales and lease law, a *warranty* is an assurance by one party of the existence of a fact on which the other party can rely. The Uniform Commercial Code (UCC) has many rules governing the concept of product warranty as it relates to sales and lease contracts. These rules will be the subject matter of the first part of this chapter. A natural addition to the discussion is *product liability,* which concerns who has legal responsibility to consumers, users, and bystanders for physical harm and property damage caused by a particular good. That is the subject of the second part of this chapter.

21–1 WARRANTIES

The UCC designates several warranties that can arise in a sales or lease contract, including warranties of title, express warranties, and implied warranties.

21–1a Warranties of Title

Title warranty arises automatically in most sales contracts. There are three types of warranties of title: *good title, no liens,* and *no infringements.*

Good Title In most cases, sellers warrant that they have valid title to the goods sold and that transfer of the title is rightful. If the buyer subsequently learns that the seller did not have good title to the goods that were purchased, the buyer can sue the seller for breach of this warranty.

EXAMPLE 21.1 Alexis steals a diamond ring from Calvin and sells it to Emma, who does not know that the ring is stolen. If Calvin discovers that Emma has the ring, then he has the right to reclaim it from Emma. When Alexis sold Emma the ring, Alexis automatically warranted to Emma that the title conveyed was valid and that its transfer was rightful. Because a thief has no title to stolen goods, Alexis breached the warranty of title imposed by the UCC and became liable to Emma for appropriate damages. ◄

No Liens A second warranty of title provided by the UCC protects buyers who are unaware of any *liens*—that is, encumbrances on a property to satisfy or protect a claim for payment of a debt—against goods at the time the contract was made. This protects buyers who, for instance, unknowingly buy goods that are subject to a creditor's security interest. If a creditor repossesses the goods from a buyer who *had no knowledge of the security interest,* the buyer can recover from the seller for breach of warranty.

The buyer who has *actual knowledge* of a security interest has no recourse against a seller. If the seller is a merchant and the buyer is a "buyer in the ordinary course of business," however, the buyer is free of the security interest even if he or she knows of it. An exception occurs if the buyer knows the sale is in violation of the security interest. Then, he or she is subject to it.

No Infringements A third type of title warranty is a warranty against infringement of any patent, trademark, or copyright. In other words, a merchant is deemed to warrant that the goods delivered are free from any patent, trademark, or copyright claims of a third person. If this warranty is breached and the buyer is sued by the claim holder, the buyer *must notify the seller* of the lawsuit within a reasonable time to enable the seller to decide whether to participate in the defense against it.

Disclaimer of Title Warranty In an ordinary sales transaction, the title warranty can be disclaimed or modified only by *specific language* in a contract. **EXAMPLE 21.2** Craft Tool Corporation sells metalworking tools to Dunlap Milling Company and other manufacturing firms. Among the warranties and disclaimers that accompany the goods, Craft Tool asserts that it is transferring only the rights, title, and interest that it has in the goods. ◄

In certain cases, the circumstances of the sale are sufficient to indicate clearly to a buyer that no assurances as to title are being made. **EXAMPLE 21.3** Christian, a resident of Columbia County, borrows funds to buy a car from Town Motors. Christian defaults on the payments, however. Under a court order obtained by Town Motors, deputies from the Columbia County Sheriff's Office seize Christian's car. It is later sold to satisfy the debt. Wade, who buys the car, knows that it is not the property of the county official conducting the sale. ◄

21–1b Express Warranties

LEARNING OUTCOME 1

State when express warranties arise in a sales or lease contract.

express warranty
A promise that is included in an agreement under which the promisor assures the quality, description, or performance of the goods.

A seller or lessor can create an **express warranty** by making representations about the quality, condition, or performance potential of the goods. Express warranties arise when a seller or lessor indicates any of the following:

1. That the goods conform to any *affirmation or promise* of fact that the seller or lessor makes to the buyer or lessee about the goods. Statements such as "These drill bits will *easily* penetrate stainless steel" are express warranties.

2. That the goods conform to any *description.* A label that reads "crate contains one diesel engine" creates an express warranty.

3. That the goods conform to any *sample or model.* **EXAMPLE 21.4** Howard, a sports equipment salesperson, shows Jericho sample baseballs. Jericho orders one hundred of them. The balls that are delivered must conform to the samples. ◄

Basis of the Bargain To create an express warranty, the seller or lessor does not need to use formal words such as *warrant* or *guarantee* or to state that he or she has a specific intention to make a warranty. The UCC requires only that the affirmation, promise, description, sample, or model must become part of the "basis of the bargain." Just what constitutes the basis of the bargain is difficult to say. The UCC does not define the concept. It is a question of fact in each case whether a representation was made at such a time and in such a way that it induced the buyer or lessee to enter the contract.

Statements of Opinion If the seller or lessor makes a statement that relates to the value or worth of the goods, or makes a statement of opinion or recommendation about the goods, the seller or lessor is not creating an express warranty. EXAMPLE 21.5 Douglas, an electronics salesperson, might say that the quality of his 3D televisions is "excellent and unsurpassed." ◄ This is known as *puffery* and creates no warranty.

If the seller or lessor is an expert and gives an opinion as an expert, however, then a warranty can be created. EXAMPLE 21.6 Vincenzo, an art dealer and expert in seventeenth-century paintings, tells Lacey that a particular painting is a Rembrandt. Lacey buys the painting. Vincenzo has warranted the accuracy of his opinion. ◄

The reasonableness of the buyer's or lessee's reliance is the controlling criterion in many cases. EXAMPLE 21.7 Ruby is a salesperson for Miller Hardware. Ruby's statements that a ladder "will never break" and will "last a lifetime" are so clearly improbable that no reasonable buyer should rely on them. ◄

HIGHLIGHTING THE POINT

A salesperson for a car dealership claims, "This is the best used car to come along in years. It has four new tires and a 250-horsepower engine just rebuilt this year. It's worth a fortune—anywhere else, you'd pay $10,000 for it."

Which of these statements are express warranties, and which are opinions? The salesperson's *affirmations of fact* create a warranty: the automobile has an engine, the engine has 250 horsepower, the engine was rebuilt this year, and there are four new tires on the car. The salesperson's opinion that the vehicle is "the best used car to come along in years," however, creates no warranty. Similarly, the statements relating to the possible value of the goods ("It's worth a fortune—anywhere else, you'd pay $10,000 for it") do not create a warranty.

21–1c Implied Warranties

An **implied warranty** is one that *the law derives* by implication from the nature of the transaction or the situation or circumstances of the parties. The UCC recognizes several types of implied warranties, as discussed next.

Implied Warranty of Merchantability An **implied warranty of merchantability** automatically arises in every sale or lease of goods made *by a merchant* who deals in goods of the kind sold. EXAMPLE 21.8 Mountaintop Sports, a retailer of sports gear, makes an implied warranty of merchantability when it sells a pair of skis to Rosanna, a consumer. But Damien, Rosanna's neighbor, does not make such a warranty when he sells his skis at a garage sale. ◄

Goods that are *merchantable* are "reasonably fit for the ordinary purposes for which such goods are used." They must be of at least average, fair, or medium-grade quality. The quality must be comparable to quality that will pass without objection in the trade or market for goods of the same description. The goods must be adequately packaged and labeled. They also must conform to the promises or affirmations of fact made on the container or label, if any.

Some examples of *nonmerchantable* goods are light bulbs that explode when switched on, pajamas that burst into flames on slight contact with a stove burner, and high heels that break off under normal use. Such goods are nonmerchantable even if the merchant had no way to know about or discover their defects.

LEARNING OUTCOME 2
Identify the implied warranties that arise in a sales or lease contract.

implied warranty
A warranty that the law implies through either the situation of the parties or the nature of the transaction.

implied warranty of merchantability
A warranty by a merchant seller or lessor of goods that the goods are reasonably fit for the general purpose for which they are sold or leased.

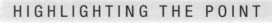

HIGHLIGHTING THE POINT

Joplin buys an ax at Gershwin's Hardware Store. No express warranties are made. The first time she chops wood with the ax, its handle breaks, and Joplin is injured. She immediately notifies Gershwin. Examination shows that the wood in the handle was rotten but that the rottenness could not have been noticed by either Gershwin or Joplin. Nonetheless, Joplin notifies Gershwin that she will hold him responsible for her medical bills.

Can Gershwin be held liable? Yes. Gershwin is responsible because a merchant seller of goods warrants that the goods he or she sells are fit for normal use. This ax was obviously not fit for normal use. Of course, Gershwin can seek recovery from the manufacturer of the ax for the award of damages and all legal costs.

implied warranty of fitness for a particular purpose
A warranty that arises when a seller knows the particular purpose for which a buyer will use the goods and knows that the buyer is relying on his or her skill and judgment to select suitable goods.

Implied Warranty of Fitness for a Particular Purpose The **implied warranty of fitness for a particular purpose** arises when *any* seller or lessor (merchant or nonmerchant) knows the particular purpose for which a buyer or lessee will use the goods *and* knows that the buyer or lessee is relying on the seller's skill and judgment to select suitable goods.

A "particular purpose of the buyer or lessee" differs from the "ordinary purpose for which goods are used" (merchantability). Goods can be merchantable but unfit for a buyer's or lessee's particular purpose. **EXAMPLE 21.9** Denzel needs a gallon of paint to match the color of his office walls—a light shade somewhere between coral and peach. He takes a sample to the local hardware store and requests a gallon of paint of that color. Instead, he is given a gallon of bright blue paint. Here, the salesperson has not breached any warranty of implied merchantability—the bright blue paint is of high quality and suitable for interior walls—but he has breached an implied warranty of fitness for a particular purpose. ◄

A seller or lessor does not need to have actual knowledge of the buyer's or lessee's particular purpose. It is sufficient if a seller or lessor "has reason to know" the purpose. The buyer or lessee, however, must have *relied* on the seller's or lessor's skill or judgment in selecting or furnishing suitable goods.

Other Implied Warranties The UCC recognizes that implied warranties can arise (or be excluded or modified) from course of dealing, course of performance, or usage of trade.

- The *course of dealing* is a sequence of conduct between the parties to a transaction that establishes a common basis for their understanding.

- *Course of performance* is the conduct that occurs under an agreement, indicating what the parties to the agreement intended for it to mean.

- *Usage of trade* is a practice or method of dealing so regularly observed as to justify an expectation that it will be observed in a particular transaction.

Thus, in the absence of evidence to the contrary, when both parties to a contract have knowledge of a well-recognized trade custom, the courts will infer that they both intended for that custom to apply to their contract. **EXAMPLE 21.10** Tri-County Cars & Trucks buys and sells new and used vehicles. If an industrywide custom is to lubricate a new car before it is delivered, and Tri-County fails to do so, it can be liable to a buyer for breach of implied warranty. ◄

21–1d Warranty Disclaimers

Because each type of warranty is created in a different way, the manner in which each one can be disclaimed or limited by the seller varies.

Express Warranties Express warranties can be excluded or limited by specific and unambiguous language, provided that this is done in a manner that protects the buyer or lessee from surprise. Therefore, a written disclaimer in language that is clear and conspicuous, and called to a buyer's or lessee's attention *at the time the sales contract is formed,* can negate all oral express warranties not included in the written sales contract.

Implied Warranties Generally speaking, unless circumstances indicate otherwise, implied warranties (merchantability and fitness) are disclaimed by the expressions "as is," "with all faults," or other similar expressions that in common understanding for *both* parties call the buyer's attention to the fact that there are no implied warranties.

The UCC also permits a seller or lessor to disclaim the implied warranty of fitness or merchantability specifically. To disclaim the implied warranty of fitness, the disclaimer *must* be in writing and be conspicuous. The word *fitness* does not have to be mentioned. It is sufficient if the disclaimer states, "There are no warranties that extend beyond the description on the face hereof." A merchantability disclaimer must be more specific. It must mention *merchantability.* It need not be written. If it is, however, the writing must be conspicuous (obvious).

Buyer's or Lessee's Refusal to Inspect If a buyer or lessee actually examines the goods (or a sample or model) as fully as desired before entering into a contract, or if the buyer or lessee refuses to examine the goods, *there is no implied warranty with respect to defects that a reasonable examination would reveal.* Failing to examine the goods and refusing to examine them are not the same. A refusal occurs only when the seller or lessor demands that the buyer or lessee examine the goods and the buyer or lessee declines to do so.

The seller or lessor remains liable for any latent (hidden) defects that ordinary inspection would not reveal. What the examination ought to reveal depends on a buyer's or lessee's skill and method of examination. **EXAMPLE 21.11** Robin an auto mechanic, is purchasing a car. He should be able to discover defects that a non-expert buyer would not be expected to find. ◄ The circumstances determine what defects an inspection should reveal.

21–1e Magnuson-Moss Warranty Act

The Magnuson-Moss Warranty Act of 1975 was designed to prevent deception in warranties by making them easier to understand. Under the act, no seller or lessor is *required* to give an express written warranty for consumer goods. If a seller or lessor chooses to do so, however, and the cost of the consumer goods is more than $25, the warranty must be labeled as "full" or "limited."

A full warranty requires free repair or replacement of any defective part. If the product cannot be repaired within a reasonable time, the consumer has the choice of either a refund or a replacement without charge. A full warranty frequently does not have a time limit on it. Any limitation on consequential damages (damages that compensate for a loss that is not direct, such as lost profits) must be *conspicuously* stated. A limited warranty arises when the written warranty fails to meet one of the requirements of a full warranty.

In addition, the warrantor must make certain disclosures completely and obviously in a single document in "readily understood language." These disclosures include the name and address of the warrantor, what specifically is warranted, procedures for enforcement of the warranty, any limitations on relief, and the fact that the buyer has legal rights.

21–2 PRODUCT LIABILITY

product liability
The legal responsibility of manufacturers and sellers to buyers, users, and sometimes bystanders for injuries or damages suffered because of defects in goods.

Manufacturers and sellers of goods can be held liable to consumers, users, and bystanders for physical harm or property damage that is caused by the goods. This is called **product liability.** Product liability may be based on the warranty theories just discussed, as well as on the theories of *negligence, misrepresentation,* and *strict liability.*

21–2a Negligence

Negligence is the failure to use the degree of care that a reasonable, prudent person would have used under the circumstances. If a seller fails to exercise such reasonable care and an injury results, he or she may be sued for negligence.

LEARNING OUTCOME 3

Discuss negligence as the basis of product liability.

Due Care Must Be Exercised Because a failure to exercise reasonable care is negligence, a manufacturer must exercise "due care" to make a product safe. Due care must be exercised in designing the product, in selecting the materials, in using the appropriate production process, in assembling and testing the product, and in placing adequate warnings on the label informing the user of dangers of which an ordinary person might not be aware. The duty of care also extends to the inspection and testing of any components that are bought from other manufacturers and used in the final product.

Privity of Contract Not Required An action based on negligence does not require *privity of contract* between the plaintiff and the defendant. A manufacturer is liable for its failure to exercise due care to any person who sustains an injury caused by a negligently made (defective) product.

21–2b Misrepresentation

When a fraudulent misrepresentation has been made to a user or consumer and that misrepresentation ultimately results in an injury, the basis of liability may be the tort of fraud. **EXAMPLE 21.12** Bright Eyes Company makes and sells cosmetics. If Bright Eyes intentionally mislabels packaged cosmetics or intentionally conceals a product's defects, it is guilty of fraudulent misrepresentation.◄ The misrepresentation must be of a material fact, and the seller must have intended to induce the buyer's reliance on the misrepresentation. In addition, the buyer must have relied on the misrepresentation.

21–2c Strict Liability

Under the doctrine of *strict liability*, people are liable for the results of their acts regardless of their intentions or their exercise of reasonable care. **EXAMPLE 21.13** Roadwork Construction uses dynamite to blast for a road. Roadwork is strictly liable for any damages that it causes, even if the company takes reasonable and prudent precautions to prevent the damages.◄ In the area of product liability, the doctrine applies to the sellers of goods (including manufacturers, processors, assemblers, packagers, bottlers, wholesalers, distributors, and retailers). Liability does not depend on privity of contract—the injured party does not have to be the buyer or a *third party beneficiary*.

Strict Product Liability and Public Policy

The law imposes strict product liability as a matter of public policy. The purpose is to ensure that the cost of injuries resulting from defective products is borne by the manufacturers rather than by the injured persons. One of the reasons for imposing the cost on the manufacturers is that they are in a better position than consumers to bear those costs. They can ultimately pass on the costs to all consumers in the form of higher prices.

The majority of states recognize strict product liability. Some state courts limit the application of the tort theory of strict product liability to situations involving personal injuries rather than property damage. In other situations, such as when the benefits of a product outweigh its adverse effects, a balance may be struck between paying a person injured by the product and protecting the product's maker because of the product's benefits.

Requirements of Strict Product Liability

Just because a person is injured by a product does not mean he or she will have a cause of action against the manufacturer. The following requirements must be met:

1. The product must be in a *defective condition* when the defendant sells it.
2. The defendant normally must be engaged in the *business of selling* that product.
3. The product must be *unreasonably dangerous* to the user or consumer because of its defective condition (in most states). A product may be **unreasonably dangerous** if it is defective to the point of threatening a consumer's health or safety. Either the product is dangerous beyond the expectation of the ordinary consumer or a less dangerous alternative was economically feasible for the manufacturer, but the manufacturer failed to produce it.
4. The plaintiff must incur *physical harm* to self or property by use or consumption of the product.
5. The defective condition must be the *proximate cause* of the harm.
6. The *goods must not have been substantially changed* from the time the product was sold to the time the injury was sustained.

LEARNING OUTCOME 4

List the requirements of strict product liability.

unreasonably dangerous
Defective to the point of threatening a consumer's health or safety.

Product Defects

How do courts determine what constitutes a "defective condition"? Three types of defects are recognized in product liability law—*manufacturing defects, design defects,* and *inadequate warnings*.

Manufacturing Defects

A product contains a manufacturing defect when the product departs from its intended design. This is true even when all possible care was exercised in the preparation and marketing of the product.

Design Defects

Unlike a product with a manufacturing defect, a product with a design defect is made in conformity with the manufacturer's design specifications but, nonetheless, results in injury to the user because the design itself is flawed. A product is defective in design when the foreseeable risks of harm posed by the product could have been reduced or avoided by the adoption of a reasonable alternative design, and the omission of the alternative design renders the product not reasonably safe.

To successfully assert a design defect, a plaintiff must show that a reasonable alternative design was available and that the defendant's failure to adopt the alternative design rendered the product unreasonably dangerous. Factors to be considered when deciding claims of design defects include the magnitude and probability of the foreseeable risks, as well as the relative advantages and disadvantages of the product as designed and as it alternatively could have been designed.

Real-World Case Example

Benjamin Riley was driving his Ford F-150 truck when it collided with a vehicle driven by Andrew Carter. The truck's driver-side door opened in the collision, and Riley was ejected. First responders found Riley's body eighty-five feet away. Riley's widow, Laura, filed a product liability suit in a South Carolina state court against Ford Motor Company. She alleged that the design of the compression rod door-latch system of the truck allowed the door to open in the collision and that it was unreasonably dangerous. She offered evidence of a reasonable alternative door-latch design. The court issued a judgment in Laura's favor. Ford appealed.

Did Laura Riley prove the existence of a reasonable alternative design for the Ford truck's defective door-latch system? Yes. In a 2014 case, *Riley v. Ford Motor Co.*, a state intermediate appellate court affirmed the lower court's ruling. Evidence showed that, among other things, Ford was aware of the rod door-latch system's safety problems. In fact, Ford had conducted a risk-utility analysis of a cable-linkage door-latch system and had concluded that it was a "feasible, if not superior, alternative" to the rod door-latch system.

Inadequate Warnings A product may also be deemed defective because of inadequate instructions or warnings. A product is defective because of inadequate instructions or warnings when the following occurs:

1. The foreseeable risks of harm posed by the product could have been reduced or avoided by the provision of reasonable instructions or warnings.

2. The omission of the instructions or warnings renders the product not reasonably safe.

Factors that courts use to decide inadequate warning claims include the obvious risks of a product, the thoroughness and accuracy of the warnings, and the basic characteristics of the product's user group.

Suppliers of Component Parts Under the rule of strict liability in tort, the basis of liability includes suppliers of component parts. **EXAMPLE 21.14** General Motors buys brake pads from a subcontractor and puts them in Chevrolets without changing their composition. If those pads are defective, both the supplier of the brake pads and General Motors will be held strictly liable for the damages caused by the defects. ◄

21–2d Defenses to Product Liability

Defendants in product liability cases can raise a number of defenses. Recovery may be limited or barred, for example, when it can be shown that the plaintiff assumed the risk of using the product or misused the product or when the plaintiff's injury was caused by his or her own comparative negligence. In addition, recovery may be limited by a danger commonly known to be associated with the product.

Assumption of Risk Assumption of risk can sometimes be used as a defense in a product liability action. For such a defense to be established, the defendant must show the following:

1. The plaintiff voluntarily engaged in the risk while realizing the potential danger.

2. The plaintiff knew and appreciated the risk created by the defect in the product.

3. The plaintiff's decision to undertake the known risk was unreasonable.

Product Misuse Similar to the defense of assumption of risk is that of product misuse, which occurs when a product is used for a purpose that was not intended. The defense of product misuse has been severely limited by the courts, and it is now recognized as a defense only when the particular use was not reasonably foreseeable. Suppliers are generally required to expect reasonably foreseeable misuses and to design products that are either safe when misused or marketed with some protective device, such as a childproof cap.

Comparative Negligence Most states consider the negligent or intentional actions of the plaintiff in the apportionment of liability and damages. This is the doctrine of *comparative negligence*. Under this doctrine, the amount of the defendant's liability is reduced in proportion to the amount by which the plaintiff's injury or damage was caused by the plaintiff's own negligence.

Commonly Known Dangers The dangers associated with certain products (such as sharp knives and guns) are so commonly known that manufacturers need not warn users of those dangers. If a defendant succeeds in convincing a court that a plaintiff's injury resulted from a commonly known danger, the defendant normally will not be liable.

ANSWERING THE LEGAL PROBLEM

In the legal problem set out at the beginning of this chapter, Shari steals goods from Miguel and sells them to Cory, who does not know about the theft. If Miguel discovers that Cory has the goods, Miguel can reclaim them.

A **Does Cory have any recourse against Shari?** Yes. Under the UCC, Cory can sue Shari for breach of warranty, because a thief has no title to stolen goods and thus cannot give good title. When Shari sold Cory the goods, Shari *automatically* warranted that the title conveyed was valid and that its transfer was rightful. Because this was not in fact the case, Shari breached the warranty of title. Shari is therefore liable to Cory for the appropriate damages.

LINKING BUSINESS LAW to Your Career

QUALITY CONTROL MANAGEMENT

Your career may lead to some aspect of quality control management. Legal issues surrounding product warranties and liability relate to quality control. Companies that have cost-effective quality control systems make products with fewer defects. As a result, these companies incur fewer warranty and product liability lawsuits. Thus, even if you are only running a very small business, you will be concerned with quality control.

Three Types of Quality Control

Most management systems involve three types of quality control—preventive, concurrent, and feedback. Preventive quality control occurs before the manufacturing process begins, concurrent control takes place during the process, and feedback control occurs afterward.

For example, preventive quality control might involve inspecting raw materials. During production, measuring and monitoring devices can assess whether a product is meeting certain

(Continued)

standards as part of a concurrent quality control system. Once the manufacturing is complete, the product can undergo a final inspection as part of a feedback quality control system.

Total Quality Management (TQM)

A concurrent quality control system known as *total quality management* (TQM) attempts to infuse quality into every activity in a company through continuous improvement.

Quality circles are a popular TQM technique. Groups of six to twelve employees meet regularly to discuss problems and solutions. A quality circle might consist of workers from different phases in the production process.

Benchmarking is a TQM technique in which a company measures its products against those of its competitors or industry leaders to identify areas for improvement. In the automobile industry, for instance, benchmarking

enabled Japanese firms to overtake U.S. automakers in terms of quality.

Another TQM system is *Six Sigma*. This approach emphasizes discipline and a relentless attempt to achieve higher quality (and lower costs) based on a five-step method of defining, measuring, analyzing, improving, and controlling. A Six Sigma program requires a major commitment from management because it involves changes throughout an entire organization.

TERMS AND CONCEPTS FOR REVIEW

express warranty 276

implied warranty 277

implied warranty of fitness
   for a particular purpose 278

implied warranty
   of merchantability 277

product liability 280

unreasonably dangerous 281

CHAPTER SUMMARY—WARRANTIES AND PRODUCT LIABILITY

LEARNING OUTCOME	
1	**State when express warranties arise in a sales or lease contract.** As part of a sale or lease, an express warranty arises when the seller or lessor (1) makes an affirmation or promise of fact, (2) provides a description of goods, or (3) shows a sample or model. Under the Magnuson-Moss Warranty Act, no seller or lessor is required to give an express *written* warranty for consumer goods. If a seller or lessor chooses to do so, and the cost of the goods is more than $25, the warranty must be labeled "full" (covering free repair, replacement, or refund of purchase price) or "limited."
2	**Identify the implied warranties that arise in a sales or lease contract.** An implied warranty of merchantability arises as part of a sale or lease when a merchant who deals in goods of the kind sold or leased warrants that the goods are properly packaged and labeled, are of proper quality, and are reasonably fit for the ordinary purposes for which such goods are used. An implied warranty of fitness for a particular purpose arises when a buyer's or lessee's purpose or use is expressly or impliedly known by the seller or lessor, and the buyer or lessee buys or leases the goods in reliance on the seller's or lessor's selection. Other implied warranties can arise as a result of course of dealing, course of performance, or usage of trade.
3	**Discuss negligence as the basis of product liability.** A manufacturer must use due care in designing a product, selecting materials, using an appropriate production process, assembling and testing a product, and placing adequate warnings on a label or product. A manufacturer is liable for failure to exercise due care to any person who sustains an injury proximately caused by a negligently made (defective) product. Privity of contract is not required.

4	**List the requirements of strict product liability.** The requirements to establish a cause of action based on strict product liability are as follows:

(1) The defendant must sell the product in a defective condition.

(2) The defendant must normally be engaged in the business of selling that product.

(3) The product must be unreasonably dangerous to the user or consumer because of its defective condition (in most states).

(4) The plaintiff must incur physical harm to self or property by use or consumption of the product (a court may also extend strict liability to include an injured bystander).

(5) The defective condition must be the proximate cause of the injury or damage.

(6) The goods must not have been substantially changed from the time the product was sold to the time the injury was sustained.

ISSUE SPOTTERS

Check your answers to the *Issue Spotters* against the answers provided in Appendix C at the end of this text.

1. General Construction Company (GCC) tells Industrial Supplies, Inc., that it needs an adhesive to do a particular job. Industrial provides a five-gallon bucket of a certain brand. When it does not perform to GCC's specifications, GCC sues Industrial, which claims, "We didn't expressly promise anything." What should GCC argue? (See *Warranties.*)

2. Anchor, Inc., makes prewrapped mattress springs. Through an employee's carelessness, an improperly wrapped spring is sold to Bloom Company, which uses it in the manufacture of a mattress. Bloom sells the mattress to Beds Unlimited, which sells it to Kay. While sleeping on the mattress, Kay is stabbed in the back by the spring. The wound becomes infected, and Kay becomes seriously ill. Can Anchor be held liable? Why or why not? (See *Product Liability.*)

USING BUSINESS LAW

21–1. Warranty Disclaimers. Tandy purchased a washing machine from Marshall Appliances. The sales contract included a provision explicitly disclaiming all express or implied warranties, including the implied warranty of merchantability. The disclaimer was printed in the same size and color as the rest of the contract. The machine never functioned properly. Tandy sought a refund of the purchase price, claiming that Marshall had breached the implied warranty of merchantability. Can Tandy recover her money, notwithstanding the warranty disclaimer in the contract? Explain. (See *Warranties.*)

21–2. Implied Warranties. Sam, a farmer, needs to place a two-thousand-pound piece of equipment in his barn. The equipment must be lifted thirty feet into a hayloft. Sam goes to Durham Hardware and tells Durham that he needs some heavy-duty rope to be used on his farm. Durham recommends a one-inch-thick nylon rope, and Sam purchases two hundred feet of it. Sam ties the rope around the piece of equipment, puts it through a pulley, and with the aid of a tractor lifts the equipment off the ground. Suddenly, the rope breaks. In the crash to the ground, the equipment is extensively damaged. Sam files suit against Durham for breach of the implied warranty of fitness for a particular purpose. Discuss how successful Sam will be with his suit. (See *Warranties.*)

REAL-WORLD CASE PROBLEMS

21–3. Implied Warranties. Bariven, S.A., agreed to buy 26,000 metric tons of powdered milk for $123.5 million from Absolute Trading Corp. The milk was to be delivered in shipments from China to Venezuela. After the first three shipments, China halted dairy exports due to the presence of melamine (a harmful chemical) in some products. Absolute assured Bariven that its milk was safe, and when China resumed its dairy exports, Absolute delivered sixteen more shipments. Sample testing of the milk revealed that it contained dangerous levels of melamine. Did Absolute breach any implied warranties? Discuss. [*Absolute Trading Corp. v. Bariven S.A.*, 2013 WL 49735 (11th Cir. 2013)] (See *Warranties*.)

21–4. Product Liability. On Interstate 40 in North Carolina, Carroll Jett became distracted by a texting system in the cab of his tractor-trailer truck and smashed into several vehicles that were slowed or stopped in front of him, injuring Barbara Durkee and others. The injured motorists filed a suit in a federal district court against Geologic Solutions,

Inc., the maker of the texting system, alleging product liability. Was the accident caused by Jett's inattention or by the texting device? Should a manufacturer be required to design a product that is incapable of distracting a driver? Discuss. [*Durkee v. Geologic Solutions, Inc.*, 2013 WL 14717 (4th Cir. 2013)] (See *Product Liability*.)

21–5. Product Liability. David Dobrovolny bought a new Ford F-350 pickup truck. A year later, the truck spontaneously caught fire in Dobrovolny's driveway. The truck was destroyed, but no other property was damaged, and no one was injured. Dobrovolny filed a suit in a Nebraska state court against Ford Motor Co. on a theory of strict product liability to recover the cost of the truck. Nebraska limits the application of strict product liability to situations involving personal injuries. Is Dobrovolny's claim likely to succeed? Why or why not? Is there another basis for liability on which he might recover? [*Dobrovolny v. Ford Motor Co.*, 281 Neb. 86, 793 N.W.2d 445 (2011)] (See *Product Liability*.)

ETHICAL QUESTIONS

21–6. Commonly Known Dangers. Should gun manufacturers be required to warn of the dangers associated with gun use? Why or why not? (See *Product Liability*.)

21–7. Inadequate Warnings. Do pharmacists have a duty to warn customers about the side effects of drugs? (See *Product Liability*.)

21–8. Assumption of Risk. Before using an Executive Tans tanning booth made by Sun Ergoline, Inc., Savannah Boles

signed a release. The form stated that the use of the booth is "at my own risk," with no liability on the part of the operator or manufacturer. Inside the booth, Boles's fingers were partially amputated by an exhaust fan. She filed a suit against Sun Ergoline, asserting strict product liability. Should a manufacturer be relieved of strict product liability for a faulty product by means of an *exculpatory clause* (see page 157)? [*Boles v. Sun Ergoline, Inc.*, 222 P.3d 724 (Colo. 2010) (See *Product Liability*.)

Chapter 21—Work Set

TRUE-FALSE QUESTIONS

_____ 1. A contract cannot involve both an implied warranty of merchantability and an implied warranty of fitness for a particular purpose.

_____ 2. A seller's best protection from being held accountable for express statements is not to make them in the first place.

_____ 3. A clear, conspicuous, written statement brought to a buyer's attention when a contract is formed can disclaim all warranties not contained in the written contract.

_____ 4. To disclaim the implied warranty of merchantability, a merchant must mention "merchantability."

_____ 5. Whether or not a buyer examines goods before entering into a contract, there is an implied warranty with respect to defects that an examination would reveal.

_____ 6. Privity of contract is required to hold a manufacturer liable in a product liability action based on negligence.

_____ 7. In a defense of comparative negligence, an injured party's failure to exercise reasonable care against a known defect will be considered in apportioning liability.

_____ 8. Under the doctrine of strict liability, a defendant is liable for the results of his or her acts only if he or she intended those results.

_____ 9. Promises of fact made during the bargaining process are express warranties.

MULTIPLE-CHOICE QUESTIONS

_____ 1. Noel's Ski Shop sells a pair of skis to Fred. When he first uses the skis, they snap in two. The cause is something that Noel did not know about and could not have discovered. If Fred sues Noel, he will likely

a. win, because Noel breached the merchant's implied duty of inspection.
b. win, because Noel breached the implied warranty of merchantability.
c. lose, because Noel knew nothing about the defect that made the skis unsafe.
d. lose, because consumers should reasonably expect to find on occasion that a product will not work as warranted.

_____ 2. Tyler Desk Corporation writes in its contracts, in large red letters, "There are no warranties that extend beyond the description on the face hereof." The disclaimer negates the implied warranty of

a. merchantability.
b. fitness for a particular purpose.
c. title.
d. all of the above.

_____ 3. Eagle Equipment sells motor vehicle parts to dealers. In response to a dealer's order, Eagle ships a crate with a label that reads, "Crate contains one 150-horsepower diesel engine." This statement is

a. an express warranty.
b. an implied warranty of merchantability.
c. an implied warranty of fitness for a particular purpose.
d. described by none of the above.

_____ 4. B&B Autos sells cars, trucks, and other motor vehicles. A B&B salesperson claims, "This is the finest car ever made." This statement is

a. an express warranty.
b. an implied warranty of merchantability.
c. an implied warranty of fitness for a particular purpose.
d. described by none of the above.

_____ 5. Sam is injured in an accident involving a defective tractor. Sam sues the maker of the tractor. To successfully claim assumption of risk as a defense, the defendant must show

a. that Sam voluntarily engaged in the risk while realizing the potential danger.
b. that Sam knew and appreciated the risk created by the defect.
c. that Sam's decision to undertake the known risk was unreasonable.
d. all of the above.

_____ 6. T&T, Inc., designs a product that is safe when used properly. Bob uses the product for an unforeseeable, improper use. If Bob sues T&T, the manufacturer will likely be held

a. liable for negligence or misrepresentation.
b. strictly liable.
c. as either a or b.
d. as none of the above.

_____ 7. Jane buys a defective product from Valu-Mart and is injured as a result of using the product. If Jane sues Valu-Mart based on strict liability, to recover damages she must prove that Valu-Mart

a. was in privity of contract with Jane.
b. was engaged in the business of selling the product.
c. failed to exercise due care.
d. defectively designed the product.

_____ 8. Fine Textiles, Inc., sells cloth to Gail by showing her a sample that Fine's salesperson claims is the same as the goods. This statement is

a. an express warranty.
b. an implied warranty.
c. a warranty of title.
d. puffery.

 ## ANSWERING MORE LEGAL PROBLEMS

1. Stella bought a cup of coffee at the Roasted Bean Drive-Thru. The coffee had been heated to 190 degrees and consequently had dissolved the inside of the cup. When Stella lifted the lid, the cup collapsed, spilling the contents onto her lap. To recover for third-degree burns on her thighs, Stella filed a suit against the Roasted Bean.

Can Stella recover for breach of the implied warranty of merchantability? Yes. An implied warranty of merchantability arises in every _____ of goods made by a merchant who deals in goods of the kind. Goods that are merchantable are _____ for the ordinary purposes for which such goods are _____. A sale of food or drink is a _____ of goods. Merchantable food is food that is _____ to eat or drink on the basis of consumer expectations. A consumer should reasonably expect hot coffee to be hot, but not to be so scaldingly hot that it causes third-degree burns.

2. Jared bought a cell phone made by WiFi Communications, Inc. Three months later, after recharging the battery through a power jack, Jared picked up the phone only to have it ignite in his hand. As a result, he suffered a severe burn. Jared filed a suit against WiFi, alleging that a design defect in the phone weakened the connection between the power jack and the motherboard, causing the wiring to overheat and creating an unreasonable safety hazard.

Could Jared succeed on his strict product liability claim? Yes. Jared can succeed with his claim if he can meet the requirements. A product is defective in design when the foreseeable _____ of harm posed by the product could have been reduced or avoided by the adoption of a reasonable alternative design, and its omission renders the product not reasonably _____. Jared must show that the phone was defective when WiFi sold it, WiFi was normally engaged in selling that product, the phone was unreasonably _____ to a user because of its defect, Jared incurred physical harm by use of the phone, the defect was the proximate _____ of the harm, and the phone was not substantially changed from the time that it was sold to the time of the injury.

CONSUMER PROTECTION

FACING A LEGAL PROBLEM

The makers of Campbell's soups advertised that "most" Campbell's soups were low in fat and cholesterol and thus were helpful in fighting heart disease. What the ad did not say was that some Campbell's soups were high in sodium (salt) and high-sodium diets may increase the risk of heart disease.

 Does this omission make the advertising deceptive?

Over time, Congress has enacted a substantial amount of legislation to protect consumers. All statutes, agency rules, and common law judicial decisions that attempt to protect the interests of consumers are classified as consumer law.

Today, countless federal and state laws attempt to protect consumers from unfair trade practices, unsafe products, discriminatory or unreasonable credit requirements, and other problems related to consumer transactions. In fact, nearly every federal agency has an office of consumer affairs, and most states have one or more such offices to help consumers.

In this chapter, we examine some of the major laws and regulations protecting consumers. It is important to note that state laws often provide more sweeping and significant protections for the consumer than do federal laws.

 ## 22–1 DECEPTIVE ADVERTISING

The Federal Trade Commission Act created the Federal Trade Commission (FTC) to carry out the broadly stated goal of preventing unfair and deceptive trade practices, including **deceptive advertising**.

deceptive advertising
Advertising that misleads consumers.

22–1a The Reasonable Consumer Test

Generally, deceptive advertising occurs if a reasonable consumer would be misled by the advertising claim. Vague generalities and obvious exaggerations—known as *puffery*—are permissible. When a claim takes on the appearance of literal authenticity, however, it may create problems.

EXAMPLE 22.1 Teak Tables posts an online ad on several furniture retailers' Web sites. The ad refers to the firm's wide selection of custom tables. Because the ad does not mention that most of Teak's tables are made from oak, it is deceptive. Online consumers could reasonably be led to assume that the tables are made of teak wood because of the company name. ◄

22–1b Forms of Deceptive Advertising

False or deceptive advertising comes in many forms. Deception may arise from a false statement or claim about a company's own products or a competitor's

LEARNING OUTCOME 1

Define what is and what is not deceptive advertising.

products. The deception may concern a product's quality, effects, price, origin, availability, or other attributes. Some advertisements contain "half-truths," meaning that the presented information is true but incomplete and therefore leads consumers to a false conclusion.

HIGHLIGHTING THE POINT

FotoFree, Inc., makes and distributes an app that allows users to send and receive photos and other digital information. The app includes a "Find" function to help senders locate their intended recipients. FotoFree's advertising states that the "Find" feature uses a recipient's mobile phone number to perform a search. But the ad does not state—and the app does not notify users—that the function also collects the names and numbers of all of the contacts in the senders' and recipients' mobile devices' address books.

Is this deceptive advertising? Yes. FotoFree advertises that its app uses a mobile number to perform a search without stating that the function also collects all of the names and numbers in the users' address books. Users are thereby misled into concluding that their privacy and personally identifiable information are protected.

Advertising that contains an endorsement by a celebrity may be deemed deceptive if the celebrity does not actually use the product. In addition, advertising that appears to be based on factual evidence but, in fact, is not reasonably supported by some evidence will be deemed deceptive. **EXAMPLE 22.2** Health Plus advertises its herbal supplements, claiming that their product wards off harmful bacteria and germs that cause the common cold. No scientific studies or research can support this claim, however. Thus, the FTC will seek an injunction to stop Health Plus from running the deceptive ads. ◄

22–1c Bait-and-Switch Advertising

One of the FTC's most important rules is contained in its "Guides against Bait Advertising." The rule is designed to prohibit **bait-and-switch advertising**—that is, advertising a very low price for a particular item that will likely be unavailable to the consumer, who will then be encouraged to purchase a more expensive item. The low price is the "bait" to lure the consumer into the store. The salesperson is instructed to "switch" the consumer to a different item.

According to the FTC guidelines, bait-and-switch advertising occurs if the seller refuses to show the advertised item, fails to have reasonably adequate quantities of it available, fails to promise to deliver the advertised item within a reasonable time, or discourages employees from selling the item.

22–1d Online Deceptive Advertising

Deceptive advertising can occur in the online environment as well. The FTC actively monitors online advertising and has identified hundreds of Web sites that have made false or deceptive claims for products ranging from medical treatments for various diseases to exercise equipment.

Generally, online ads—like all other ads—must be truthful and not misleading, and any claims made must be substantiated. FTC guidelines on Internet marketing also call for "clear and conspicuous" disclosure of any qualifying information.

Advertisers should assume that consumers will not read an entire Web page. Therefore, to satisfy the "clear and conspicuous" requirement, advertisers should

---

bait-and-switch advertising
Advertising a product at a very attractive price (the bait) and then informing the consumer that the advertised product is not available and urging him or her to purchase (switch to) a more expensive item.

place a disclosure as close as possible to the claim being qualified or include the disclosure within the claim. If that is not possible, the disclosure should appear on a section of the page to which a consumer can easily scroll. Generally, hyperlinks to a disclosure are recommended only for long disclosures or for disclosures that must be repeated in a variety of locations on a Web page.

22–1e FTC Actions against Deceptive Advertising

The FTC receives complaints about deceptive advertising from many sources, including competitors of alleged violators, consumers, consumer organizations, trade associations, Better Business Bureaus, government organizations, and state and local officials. If complaints are widespread, the FTC will investigate. If, after investigating, the FTC believes that a given advertisement is unfair or deceptive, it drafts a formal complaint, which is sent to the alleged offender.

The company may agree to settle the complaint without further proceedings. If not, the FTC can conduct a hearing. If the FTC succeeds in proving that an advertisement is unfair or deceptive, it usually issues a **cease-and-desist order** requiring that the challenged advertising be stopped. It might also require a sanction known as **counteradvertising,** which requires the company to advertise anew—in print, on radio, and on television—to inform the public about the earlier misinformation.

cease-and-desist order
An order prohibiting a person or business firm from conducting activities that an agency or court has deemed illegal.

counteradvertising
New advertising that is undertaken pursuant to a Federal Trade Commission order for the purpose of correcting earlier false claims.

22–1f False Advertising Claims under the Lanham Act

The Lanham Act, which protects trademarks, also covers false advertising claims. To state a successful claim under the act, a business must establish the following:

1. An injury to a commercial interest in reputation or sales.
2. Direct causation of the injury by false or deceptive advertising.
3. A loss of business from consumers or other buyers who were deceived by the advertising.

Real-World Case Example

Lexmark International, Inc., sells the only style of toner cartridges that work with its laser printers. Other businesses—known as remanufacturers—refurbish used Lexmark cartridges to sell in competition with the cartridges sold by Lexmark. Static Control Components, Inc., makes and sells components for the remanufactured cartridges, including microchips that mimic the chips in Lexmark's cartridges. Lexmark released ads that claimed Static's microchips infringed Lexmark's patents. Static filed a claim against Lexmark, alleging lost sales and damage to its reputation by false advertising. The court dismissed the claim. On Static's appeal, the U.S. Court of Appeals for the Sixth Circuit reversed the dismissal. Lexmark appealed.

Did Static adequately plead the elements of a cause of action for false advertising under the Latham Act? Yes. In a 2014 case, *Lexmark International, Inc. v. Static Control Components, Inc.,* the United States Supreme Court affirmed the appellate court's ruling. Businesses do not need to be direct competitors to bring an action for false advertising. To establish a claim, a plaintiff must allege an injury to a commercial interest in reputation or sales that directly flows from the false advertising. Static met this test.

22–2 Labeling and Packaging Laws

A number of federal and state laws deal specifically with the information given on labels and packages. In general, labels must be accurate, and they must use words that are understood by the ordinary consumer. In some instances, labels must specify the raw materials used in the product, such as the percentage of cotton, nylon, or other fibers used in a garment. In other instances, the products must carry a health warning, such as those required on cigarette packages and advertising.

A few examples of laws that affect labeling and packaging include the following:

- *The Fair Packaging and Labeling Act*—This act requires that food product labels identify (1) the product; (2) the net quantity of the contents and, if the number of servings is stated, the size of a serving; (3) the manufacturer; and (4) the packager or distributor. Additional requirements concern descriptions on packages, savings claims, and components of nonfood products.

- *The Energy Policy and Conservation Act*—This act requires automakers to attach an information label to every new car. This label must include the Environmental Protection Agency's fuel economy estimate for the vehicle.

- *The Nutrition Labeling and Education Act*—This act requires food labels to provide standard nutrition facts (including the amount and type of fat that the food contains) and regulates the use of such terms as *fresh* and *low fat*. These rules are updated annually.

- *The Patient Protection and Affordable Care Act*—This act requires all restaurant chains with twenty or more locations to post the caloric content of the foods on their menus, menu boards, or drive-thru menus.

22–3 Consumer Sales

A number of statutes that protect consumers in sales transactions concern the disclosure of certain terms in sales. Others provide rules governing telephone and mail-order transactions, unsolicited merchandise, and online sales.

Many states and the FTC have **"cooling-off"** laws that permit the buyers of goods sold door to door to cancel their contracts within three business days. The FTC rule further requires that consumers be notified in Spanish of this right if the oral negotiations for sale were in that language.

22–3a Telephone and Mail-Order Sales

The FTC's Mail or Telephone Order Merchandise Rule provides specific protections for consumers who purchase goods over the phone, through the mail, or online. For instance, merchants are required to ship orders within the time promised in their advertisements and to notify consumers when orders cannot be shipped on time. The rule also requires merchants to issue a refund within a specified period of time when a consumer cancels an order.

In addition, under the Postal Reorganization Act a consumer who receives *unsolicited* merchandise sent by U.S. mail can keep it, throw it away, or dispose of it in any manner that she or he sees fit. The recipient will not be obligated to the sender.

22–3b Online Sales

Many business-to-consumer sales today take place on the Internet, and it is not surprising that some involve fraudulent and deceptive sales practices. The FTC and other federal agencies have brought numerous enforcement actions against those who perpetrate online fraud. Nonetheless, protecting consumers from such practices has proved to be a challenging task. The number of consumers who have fallen prey to Internet fraud has actually grown in recent years.

Exhibit 22.1 indicates many of the areas of consumer law, including consumer sales, which are regulated by federal statutes.

22–4 CREDIT PROTECTION

Credit protection is an especially important aspect of consumer protection legislation. Nearly 80 percent of U.S. consumers have credit cards, and most carry a balance on these cards, which amounts to about $2.5 trillion of debt nationwide. In 2010, Congress established a new agency, the Consumer Financial Protection Bureau, to oversee the practices of banks, mortgage lenders, and credit-card companies. We discuss significant consumer credit protection legislation next.

22–4a The Truth-in-Lending Act

One of the most significant statutes regulating the credit and credit-card industry is Title 1 of the Consumer Credit Protection Act, commonly known as the Truth-in-Lending Act (TILA). The TILA is basically a *disclosure law* and administered by the Federal Reserve Board. It requires sellers and lenders to disclose credit terms or loan terms so that individuals can shop around for the best financing arrangements.

Application TILA requirements apply only to persons who, in the ordinary course of their business, lend money, sell on credit, or arrange for the extension of credit. Thus, sales or loans made between two consumers do not come under the protection of the act. Also, only debtors who are *natural* persons—as opposed to the artificial "person" of a corporation—are protected by this law.

Disclosure Requirements The disclosure requirements under the TILA are found in **Regulation Z**, which was issued by the Federal Reserve Board. If the contracting

EXHIBIT 22.1   Selected Areas of Consumer Law Regulated by Statutes

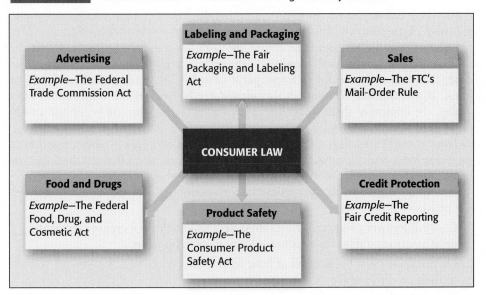

parties are subject to the TILA, the requirements of Regulation Z apply to any transaction involving an installment sales contract in which payment is to be made in more than four installments. These transactions typically include installment loans, retail and installment sales, car loans, home-improvement loans, and certain real estate loans if the amount of financing is less than $25,000.

Amendments to the TILA apply to those who lease or arrange to lease consumer goods in the ordinary course of their business, if the goods are priced at $25,000 or less and if the lease term exceeds four months. For consumers who lease automobiles and other goods, lessors are required to disclose in writing all of the material terms of the lease.

Under the provisions of the TILA, all of the terms of a credit instrument must be fully disclosed. The TILA also provides for contract rescission if a creditor fails to follow *exactly* the procedures required.

Equal Credit Opportunity Act The Equal Credit Opportunity Act (ECOA), an amendment to the TILA, prohibits the denial of credit solely on the basis of race, religion, national origin, color, gender, marital status, or age. The act also prohibits credit discrimination based in whether an individual receives certain forms of income, such as public-assistance benefits. In addition, a creditor cannot require the signature of a cosigner on a credit application if the applicant qualifies under its standards of creditworthiness for the amount and terms of the applicant's credit request.

HIGHLIGHTING THE POINT

Nikita, a contractor, applies for a loan from Home Federal Bank to finance a real estate development. He meets Home Federal's standards of creditworthiness, but the bank requires Julia, Nikita's spouse, to cosign for the loan application.

If payments are not made on the loan, can Home Federal collect the unpaid amount from Julia? No. Nikita met Home Federal's own standards of creditworthiness. Thus, Julia's signature on the loan agreement was obtained in violation of the ECOA, and the agreement is not enforceable against her.

Credit-Card Rules Under the TILA, the liability of a credit cardholder—who *solicited* (requested) the credit card from a creditor—is limited to $50 per card for unauthorized charges made before the time the creditor is notified that the card is lost. A credit-card company cannot bill a consumer for unauthorized charges if the credit card was improperly issued by the credit-card company or bank. If a consumer receives an *unsolicited* credit card in the mail that is later stolen, the company that issued the card cannot charge the consumer for any of the unauthorized charges.

If a debtor thinks that an error has occurred in billing, or wishes to withhold payment for a faulty product purchased by credit card, the TILA outlines specific procedures for settling the dispute.

Recent amendments to the credit-card protections of TILA include the following provisions:

1. Cardholders are protected from retroactive interest rate increases on existing card balances, unless the account is sixty days delinquent.

2. Cardholders must be notified at least forty-five days before changes are made to their credit-card terms.

3. A monthly bill must be sent to a cardholder at least twenty-one days before the due date.

4. The interest rate charged on a cardholder's balance can be increased only in specific situations, such as when a promotional rate ends.

5. Over-limit fees can be charged only in specific situations.

6. Cardholders' payments in excess of the minimum amount due must be applied to the higher-interest balances first (such as cash advances, which are commonly charged higher interest rates).

7. Finance charges cannot be based on a previous billing cycle. (This provision relates to a practice known as *double-cycle billing*, under which a cardholder is charged interest on the balance from a previous cycle even when that balance was paid in full.)

22–4b The Fair Credit Reporting Act

To protect consumers against inaccurate credit reporting, Congress enacted the Fair Credit Reporting Act (FCRA). This act provides that consumer credit reporting agencies may issue credit reports to users only for specified purposes, including the extension of credit. Any time a consumer is denied credit or insurance on the basis of his or her credit report, the consumer must be notified of that fact and of the name and address of the credit reporting agency that issued the report.

Consumer Requests Under the FCRA, consumers can request the source of any information used by the credit agency, as well as the identity of anyone who has received an agency's report. If a consumer discovers that the agency's files contain inaccurate information about his or her credit standing, he or she can send a written request for an investigation. The agency must then investigate the disputed information. Any unverifiable or erroneous information must be deleted within a reasonable period of time.

Liability An agency that fails to comply with the FCRA is liable for monetary damages. Creditors and others—such as lenders and insurance companies—that use information from credit reporting agencies may also be liable for violations. The FCRA also allows a court to award punitive damages for a *willful* violation.

> **LEARNING OUTCOME 4**
> Identify the federal statute aimed at preventing inaccurate credit reporting.

HIGHLIGHTING THE POINT

Diana applies for an auto insurance policy with Morris Insurance Company for her new Jeep Wrangler. Morris orders a credit report on Diana. After reviewing the credit report, Morris determines that her low credit score places her in a higher-risk category. Morris issues an insurance policy on the Jeep, but it intentionally does not disclose to Diana that she is paying higher premiums due to her credit score. After two years of making payments, Diana discovers her rates are higher because of her credit score.

Is Diana entitled to damages under the FCRA? Yes. Morris violated the FCRA by intentionally failing to inform Diana that her premium rates were higher because of her low credit score. Because this was clearly a willful violation, punitive damages may be awarded in addition to actual monetary damages.

22–4c The Fair and Accurate Credit Transactions Act

In an effort to combat rampant identity theft, Congress passed the Fair and Accurate Credit Transactions (FACT) Act of 2003. The act established a national fraud alert system so that consumers who suspect that they have been, or may be, victimized by identity theft can place an alert in their credit files.

The FACT Act requires the major credit reporting agencies to provide consumers with a free copy of their credit reports every twelve months. Another provision requires account numbers on credit-card receipts to be shortened so that merchants, employees, and others who have access to the receipts cannot obtain a consumer's name and full credit-card numbers. The act also mandates that financial institutions work with the FTC to identify "red flag" indicators of identity theft and to develop rules on how to dispose of sensitive credit information. The FACT Act also gives consumers who have been victimized by identity theft some assistance in rebuilding their credit reputations.

22–4d The Fair Debt Collection Practices Act

In 1977, Congress passed the Fair Debt Collection Practices Act (FDCPA) in an attempt to curb what were perceived to be abuses by collection agencies. The act applies only to specialized debt-collection agencies that, usually for a percentage of the amount owed, regularly attempt to collect debts on behalf of someone else. Creditors who attempt to collect debts are not covered unless, by misrepresenting themselves to the debtor, they cause the debtor to believe that they are part of a collection agency.

Requirements The act prohibits the following debt-collection practices:

1. Contacting the consumer at his or her place of employment if the employer objects, contacting the consumer at inconvenient or unusual times, or contacting the consumer if he or she has an attorney.
2. Contacting third parties other than parents, spouses, or financial advisers about the payment of a debt unless authorized by a court.
3. Using harassment and intimidation (such as using abusive language) or using false or misleading information (such as posing as a police officer).
4. Communicating with the consumer after receipt of a notice that the consumer is refusing to pay the debt, except to advise the consumer of further action to be taken by the collection agency.

validation notice
Notice to a debtor from a collection agency informing the debtor that he or she has thirty days to challenge the debt and to request verification.

Validation Notice The FDCPA also requires collection agencies to include a **validation notice** whenever they initially contact a debtor for payment of a debt or within five days of that initial contact. The notice must state that the debtor has thirty days within which to dispute the debt and to request a written verification of the debt from the collection agency. The debtor's request for debt validation must be in writing.

HIGHLIGHTING THE POINT

Roma borrows $200,000 from Suburban Mortgages to buy a house. Roma defaults on the payments, and on Suburban's behalf, Cash-Out Collection Agency initiates a foreclosure. Roma receives a validation notice that states the debt to Suburban is assumed valid unless she disputes it in writing. Roma objects.

Does Suburban's notice violate the FDCPA? Yes. Suburban violated the FDCPA by telling Roma that she could dispute the debt only in writing. There is no such requirement in the FDCPA. The form of Suburban's validation notice to Roma, however, did not violate the FDCPA.

Enforcement The enforcement of the FDCPA is primarily the responsibility of the FTC. The act allows debtors to recover civil damages, as well as attorneys' fees, in an action against a collection agency that violates provisions of the act.

22–5 PROTECTION OF HEALTH AND SAFETY

LEARNING OUTCOME 5

Describe federal health and safety protection.

The labeling and packaging laws discussed earlier are intended to promote consumer health and safety. Nevertheless, there is a significant distinction between regulating the information dispensed about a product and regulating the product's actual content. Tobacco products are the classic example. Producers of tobacco products are required to warn consumers about the hazards associated with the use of their products, but the sale of tobacco products has not been subjected to significant restrictions or banned outright despite the obvious dangers to public health. We now examine various laws that regulate the actual products made available to consumers.

22–5a The Federal Food, Drug, and Cosmetic Act

The Federal Food, Drug, and Cosmetic Act (FDCA) establishes food standards, specifies safe levels of potentially hazardous food additives, and sets classifications of food and food advertising. Most of these statutory requirements are monitored and enforced by the U.S. Food and Drug Administration (FDA). The FDCA also charges the FDA with the responsibility of ensuring that drugs are safe and effective before they are marketed to the public.

22–5b The Consumer Product Safety Act

The Consumer Product Safety Act protects consumers from unreasonable risk of injury from hazardous products. The act also created the Consumer Product Safety Commission (CPSC). Generally, the CPSC is authorized to set standards for consumer products and to ban the manufacture and sale of any product deemed potentially hazardous to consumers. The commission has the authority to remove products from the market if they are deemed imminently hazardous and to require manufacturers to report information about any products already sold or intended for sale that have proved to be hazardous.

HIGHLIGHTING THE POINT

View Clear, Inc., makes and sells a digital video recorder (DVR) that can severely overheat when it is being charged. This poses a burn threat to consumers who use the DVR and may damage their property.

Can the CPSC order a recall of View Clear's DVR? Yes. The CPSC has the authority to remove this product from the market and to require View Clear to provide information about the DVRs that have already been sold. An appropriate remedy might be a repair or a replacement of the device, or a refund of its price to a purchaser. The CPSC can also prohibit the product's further manufacture and sale.

The CPSC also has the authority to administer other acts relating to product safety, such as the Child Protection and Toy Safety Act and the Hazardous Substances Labeling Act.

22–5c The Patient Protection and Affordable Care Act

The Patient Protection and Affordable Care Act gave Americans new rights and benefits with regard to health care. The act prohibits certain insurance company practices, such as denying coverage for preexisting conditions and canceling the coverage of applicants who made inadvertent mistakes on their insurance applications.

Additionally, it protects consumers by helping more children get health coverage and allowing young adults (under the age of twenty-six) to be covered by their parents' health insurance. The act also ended lifetime limits and most annual limits on care, and it gives patients access to recommended preventive services (such as cancer screening and vaccinations) without cost.

ANSWERING THE LEGAL PROBLEM

In the legal problem set out at the beginning of this chapter, the makers of Campbell's soups stated in their advertising that most of the soups were low in fat and cholesterol and thus helped to fight heart disease. The ad did not say that some of the soups were also high in sodium (salt), which can increase the risk of heart disease.

A   **Does this omission make the advertising deceptive?** Yes. The FTC ruled that the claims were deceptive. Half-truths can lead consumers to false conclusions.

TERMS AND CONCEPTS FOR REVIEW

bait-and-switch advertising 290   counteradvertising 291   validation notice 296

cease-and-desist order 291   deceptive advertising 289

"cooling-off" law 292   Regulation Z 293

CHAPTER SUMMARY—CONSUMER PROTECTION

LEARNING OUTCOME	
1	**Define what is and what is not deceptive advertising.** Advertising is deceptive if a reasonable consumer would be misled by the advertising claim. For example, the Federal Trade Commission (FTC) prohibits bait-and-switch advertising, which occurs when a seller advertises a lower-priced product (the bait) intending not to sell the product but to lure consumers into the store and convince them to buy a higher-priced product (the switch). The FTC may issue a cease-and-desist order requiring the advertiser to stop the challenged advertising, or the FTC may order counteradvertising, in which the advertiser corrects the earlier misinformation.
2	**Recognize what information must be included on labels.** Manufacturers must comply with the labeling or packaging requirements for their specific products. In general, all labels must be accurate and not misleading.

3	**State the requirements of the Truth-in-Lending Act.** The Truth-in-Lending Act (TILA), which is administered by the Federal Reserve Board, requires sellers and lenders to disclose credit or loan terms to debtors so that the latter may shop around for the best available financing terms. Creditors who, in the ordinary course of business, lend money or sell goods on credit to consumers, or arrange for credit for consumers, are subject to the TILA. Regulation Z is a rule issued by the Federal Reserve Board of Governors to implement the TILA. Regulation Z applies to transactions involving installment sales contracts and certain real estate loans, and contains the TILA's disclosure requirements.
4	**Identify the federal statute aimed at preventing inaccurate credit reporting.** The Fair Credit Reporting Act (FCRA) is the federal statute that protects consumers against inaccurate credit reporting. The FCRA requires lenders and other creditors to report correct, relevant, and up-to-date information.
5	**Describe federal health and safety protection.** Federal laws govern the contents, as well as the processing and distribution, of food and drugs, and require explicit warnings about hazards. Products that are deemed imminently hazardous can be removed from the market. The manufacture and sale of hazardous products can be banned.

ISSUE SPOTTERS

Check your answers to the *Issue Spotters* against the answers provided in Appendix C at the end of this text.

1. Top Electronics, Inc., advertises GEM computers at a low price. Top keeps only a few in stock and tells its sales staff to switch consumers attracted by the price to more expensive brands. Top tells its staff, "If all else fails, refuse to show the GEMs, and if a consumer insists on buying one, do not promise delivery." Has Top violated a law? Explain your answer. (See *Deceptive Advertising*.)

2. Sweet Candy Company wants to sell its candy in a normal-sized package labeled "Gigantic Size." Fine Fabrics, Inc., wants to advertise its sweaters as having "That Wool Feel," but does not want to specify on labels that the sweaters are 100 percent polyester. What stops these firms from marketing their products as they would like? (See *Labeling and Packaging Laws*.)

USING BUSINESS LAW

22–1. Consumer Sales. Andrew, a resident of California, received an unsolicited advertising circular in the U.S. mail announcing a new line of regional cookbooks distributed by the Every-Kind Cookbook Co. Andrew didn't want any books and threw the circular away. Two days later, Andrew received in the mail an introductory cookbook entitled *Lower Mongolian Regional Cookbook*, as announced in the circular, on a "trial basis" from Every-Kind. Andrew was not interested but did not go to the trouble to return the cookbook. Every-Kind demanded payment of $20.95 for the *Lower Mongolian Regional Cookbook*. Discuss whether Andrew can be required to pay for the book. (See *Consumer Sales*.)

22–2. Credit-Card Rules. Maria Ochoa receives two new credit cards on May 1. She had solicited one of them from Midtown Department Store, and the other had arrived unsolicited from High-Flying Airlines. During the month of May, Ochoa makes numerous credit-card purchases from Midtown Store, but she does not use the High-Flying Airlines card. On May 31, a burglar breaks into Ochoa's home and steals both credit cards, along with other items. Ochoa notifies the Midtown Department Store of the theft on June 2, but she fails to notify High-Flying Airlines. Using the Midtown credit card, the burglar makes a $500 purchase on June 1 and a $200 purchase on June 3. The burglar then charges a vacation flight on the High-Flying Airlines card for $1,000 on June 5. Ochoa receives the bills for these charges and refuses to pay them. Discuss Ochoa's liability in these situations. (See *Credit Protection*.)

REAL-WORLD CASE PROBLEMS

22–3. Deceptive Advertising. Innovative Marketing, Inc. (IMI), sold "scareware"—computer security software. IMI's ads advised consumers that a scan of their computers had detected dangerous files—viruses, spyware, and "illegal" pornography. In fact, no scans were conducted. Kristy Ross, an IMI co-founder and vice president, reviewed and edited the ads, and was aware of the many complaints about them. An individual can be held personally liable under the Federal Trade Commission Act for deceptive acts or practices if the person (1) participated directly in the practices or had the authority to control them, and (2) had or should have had knowledge of them. Is Ross liable under this standard? Explain. [*Federal Trade Commission v. Ross, Inc.*, 743 F.3d 886 (4th Cir. 2014)] (See *Deceptive Advertising*.)

22–4. Credit-Card Rules. James McCoy held a credit card issued by Chase Bank USA, N.A. McCoy's cardholder agreement with Chase stated that he would receive preferred rates (lower interest rates) if he met certain conditions, such

as making at least the required minimum payment when due. When McCoy defaulted on a payment, Chase raised the rates on his card without informing him in advance. Did Chase violate the Truth-in-Lending Act by failing to notify McCoy of the increase until after it had taken effect? Explain. [*Chase Bank USA, N.A. v. McCoy,* 562 U.S. 195, 131 S.Ct. 871, 178 L.Ed.2d 716 (2011)] (See *Credit Protection*.)

22–5. Deceptive Advertising. Brian Cleary filed a suit against cigarette maker Philip Morris USA, Inc., claiming deceptive advertising. Cleary asserted that "light" cigarettes, such as Marlboro Lights, were advertised as being safer than regular cigarettes even though the health effects were the same. Philip Morris responded that the claim should be dismissed because the government authorized Philip Morris to advertise cigarettes. Should the court allow Cleary's claim? Why or why not? [*Cleary v. Philip Morris USA, Inc.,* 683 F.Supp.2d 730 (N.D.Ill. 2010)] (See *Deceptive Advertising*.)

ETHICAL QUESTIONS

22–6. Consumer Protection. Should consumer protection laws be strictly enforced when consumers abuse those laws? Explain your answer.

Chapter 22—Work Set

TRUE-FALSE QUESTIONS

_____ 1. Advertising will be deemed deceptive if a consumer would be misled by the advertising claim.

_____ 2. In general, labels must be accurate—they must use words as those words are understood by the ordinary consumer.

_____ 3. There is no federal legislation regulating food and drugs.

_____ 4. The Truth-in-Lending Act applies to creditors who, in the ordinary course of business, lend money or sell goods on credit to consumers.

_____ 5. Consumers may have more protection under state laws than under federal laws.

_____ 6. The Fair Debt Collection Practices Act applies to anyone who attempts to collect a debt.

_____ 7. There are no federal agencies that regulate sales.

_____ 8. One who leases consumer goods in the ordinary course of his or her business does not, under any circumstances, have to disclose all material terms in writing.

MULTIPLE-CHOICE QUESTIONS

_____ 1. Ann receives an unsolicited credit card in the mail and tosses it on her desk. Without Ann's permission, her roommate uses the card to spend $1,000 on new clothes. Ann is liable for

   a. $1,000.
   b. $500.
   c. $50.
   d. $0.

_____ 2. The ordinary business of Ace Credit Company is to lend money to consumers. Ace must disclose all credit terms clearly and conspicuously in

   a. no credit transaction.
   b. any credit transaction in which payments are to be made in more than four installments.
   c. any credit transaction in which payments are to be made in more than one installment.
   d. all credit transactions.

_____ 3. ABC Corporation sells a variety of consumer products. Generally, the labels on its products

   a. must only be accurate.
   b. must only use words as they are ordinarily understood by consumers.
   c. must be accurate and use words as they are ordinarily understood by consumers.
   d. need not conform to any of the above requirements.

_____ 4. Rich Foods Company advertises that its cereal, "Fiber Rich," reduces cholesterol. After an investigation and a hearing, the FTC finds no evidence to support the claim. To correct the public's impression of Fiber Rich, which of the following would be most appropriate?

   a. Counteradvertising.
   b. Cease-and-desist order.
   c. Civil fine.
   d. Criminal fine.

5. Hector's General Store advertises cans of Fancy brand whole tomatoes for fifty cents per can, although he does not have any in stock. When customers arrive to buy the tomatoes, Hector tells them that his stock of Fancy brand tomatoes has been sold and that he cannot obtain more at the lower price. Hector then informs the customers that he has West Gold brand tomatoes in stock, for sixty cents per can. He claims that West Gold tomatoes are far superior to Fancy tomatoes. Hector's behavior is considered

   a. counter advertising.
   b. a cease-and-desist order.
   c. bait-and-switch advertising.
   d. a violation of Regulation Z.

6. Bob takes out a student loan from the First National Bank. After graduation, Bob goes to work, but he does not make payments on the loan. The bank agrees with Ace Collection Agency that if Ace collects the debt, it can keep a percentage of the amount. To collect the debt, Ace can contact

   a. Bob at his place of employment, even if his employer objects.
   b. Bob at unusual or inconvenient times, or at any time if he retains an attorney.
   c. third parties, including Bob's parents, unless ordered otherwise by a court.
   d. Bob only to advise him of further action that Ace will take.

7. National Foods, Inc., sells many kinds of breakfast cereals. Under the Fair Packaging and Labeling Act, National must include on the packages

   a. the identity of the product only.
   b. the net quantity of the contents and number of servings only.
   c. the identity of the product, the net quantity of the contents, and the number of servings.
   d. none of the above.

8. American Doll Company begins marketing a new doll with clothes and hair that are highly flammable, and accessories small enough to choke a little child. The Consumer Product Safety Commission can

   a. order that the doll be removed from store shelves.
   b. warn consumers but cannot order that the doll be removed from stores.
   c. ban the doll's manufacture but cannot order it removed from stores.
   d. do nothing.

 ## ANSWERING MORE LEGAL PROBLEMS

1. LabTest Products, Inc., advertised that its weight-loss supplement, Drop-It, would cause users to lose weight quickly. The ad claimed that users could lose as much as fifteen pounds per week without dieting or exercising. In fact, to lose that much weight so fast, an individual would have to run fifty to seventy miles every day.

   Was LabTest's ad for Drop-It deceptive? Yes. Deceptive advertising occurs if a reasonable consumer would be _____ by the advertising claim. Puffery—vague generalities and obvious exaggerations that a reasonable person would not believe to be literally true—are permissible. When a claim appears to be based on _____ evidence, but the claim cannot be scientifically supported, the claim is deceptive. Here, LabTest's ad cannot be supported by fact. It is false and _____.

2. Greta obtained an auto loan from Ridgeline Bank, but the bank did not give her a payment schedule and refused her attempts to make payments. In fact, Ridgeline told Greta that it had not given her a loan. When the bank discovered its mistake, it demanded full payment. When payment was not forthcoming, Ridgeline declared Greta in default, repossessed her car, and forwarded adverse credit information about her to credit reporting agencies without noting that she disputed the information.

   Did Ridgeline violate the Fair Credit Reporting Act? Yes. In fact, the bank's violation may be considered willful. The Fair Credit Reporting Act protects consumers against _____ credit reporting. Here, Ridgeline forwarded adverse credit information about Greta to credit reporting agencies without noting that she disputed the information.

NEGOTIABLE INSTRUMENTS

UNIT CONTENTS

CHAPTER 23 The Essentials of Negotiability

CHAPTER 24 Transferability and Liability

CHAPTER 25 Checks and Banking in the Digital Age

LEARNING OUTCOMES

The five Learning Outcomes below are designed to help improve your understanding of the chapter. After reading this chapter, you should be able to:

❶ Identify the basic types of negotiable instruments.

❷ List the requirements of a negotiable instrument.

❸ State what may constitute a signature.

❹ Decide whether a variable-interest-rate note is negotiable.

❺ Describe a transfer by negotiation.

negotiable instrument
A written and signed unconditional promise or order to pay a specified sum of money on demand or at a definite time to order (to a specific person or entity) or to bearer.

FACING A LEGAL PROBLEM

Midwestern Style Fabrics sells $50,000 worth of fabric to D&F Clothiers, Inc., each fall on terms requiring payment to be made in ninety days. One year, Midwestern wants cash, but D&F wants the usual term of payment in ninety days.

Q What can Midwestern and D&F do so that both of their wants are satisfied?

Most commercial transactions would be inconceivable without negotiable instruments. A **negotiable instrument** is any written and signed promise or order to pay a sum of money. Drafts, checks, and promissory notes are typical examples. Negotiable instruments are transferred more readily than ordinary contract rights. Also, persons who acquire negotiable instruments are normally subject to less risk than the ordinary assignee of a contract right.

Both Article 3 and Article 4 of the Uniform Commercial Code (UCC) apply to transactions involving negotiable instruments. To understand the applicability of Article 3, it is necessary to distinguish between *negotiable* and *nonnegotiable* instruments. To qualify as a negotiable instrument, an instrument must meet special requirements relating to form and content. These requirements will be discussed later in this chapter.

When an instrument is negotiable, its transfer from one person to another is governed by Article 3 of the UCC. Indeed, the UCC defines an instrument as a "negotiable instrument." Therefore, whenever the term *instrument* is used in this book, it refers to a negotiable instrument. Transfers of nonnegotiable instruments are governed by rules of assignment of contract rights. Article 4 of the UCC governs bank deposits and collections.

23–1 TYPES OF INSTRUMENTS

The UCC specifies four types of negotiable instruments: *drafts*, *checks*, *notes*, and *certificates of deposit* (CDs). These are frequently divided into the two classifications that we will discuss in the following sections: *orders to pay* (drafts and checks) and *promises to pay* (promissory notes and CDs).

Negotiable instruments may also be classified as demand instruments. A *demand instrument* is payable when payment is requested. The instrument itself either states that it is payable on demand (or "at sight") or does not state any time for payment. Thus, because a check specifies no time for payment, a check is payable on demand. A demand instrument is payable immediately after it is *issued*. Issue is the first delivery of an instrument by the party who creates it for the purpose of giving rights in the instrument to any person.

LEARNING OUTCOME 1

Identify the basic types of negotiable instruments.

23–1a Orders to Pay—Drafts and Checks

A **draft** is an unconditional written order that involves three parties. The party creating it (the **drawer**) orders another party (the **drawee**) to pay money, usually to a third party (the **payee**). The drawee must be obligated to the drawer, either by an agreement or through a debtor-creditor relationship, for the drawee to be obligated to the drawer to *honor* (pay) the order.

Time Drafts and Sight Drafts   A *time draft* is payable at a definite future time. Exhibit 23.1 shows a typical time draft. A *sight* (or demand) *draft* is payable on sight—that is, when it is presented for payment. A sight draft may be payable on acceptance.

Acceptance is the drawee's written promise to pay the draft when it comes due. The usual manner of accepting is by writing the word *accepted* across the face of the instrument, followed by the date of acceptance and the signature of the drawee. A draft can be both a time and a sight draft. Such a draft is payable at a stated time after it is presented for payment.

Trade Acceptance   A *trade acceptance* is a draft frequently used in the sale of goods. The seller is both the drawer and the payee on this draft. Essentially, this kind of draft orders the buyer to pay a specified sum of money to the seller, usually at a stated time in the future. Trade acceptances are the standard credit instruments in sales transactions.

EXAMPLE 23.1   Jackson Street Bistro buys its restaurant supplies from Osaka Industries. When Jackson requests supplies, Osaka creates a draft ordering Jackson to pay Osaka for the supplies within ninety days. Jackson accepts the draft by signing its face and is then obligated to make the payment. This is a trade acceptance and can be sold to a third party if Osaka is in need of cash before the payment is due. ◄

Checks   The most commonly used type of draft is a **check.** The writer of the check is the drawer, the bank on which the check is drawn is the drawee, and the person to whom the check is payable is the payee. With certain types of checks, such as *cashier's checks,* the bank is both the drawer and the drawee. The bank customer

---

draft

Any instrument drawn on a drawee (such as a bank) that orders the drawee to pay a certain sum of money.

drawer

A person who initiates a draft (including a check), thereby ordering the drawee to pay.

drawee

A person who is ordered to pay a draft or check, usually a financial institution.

payee

A person to whom an instrument is made payable.

acceptance

A drawee's signed agreement to pay a draft when it comes due.

check

A draft written and signed by a drawer ordering the drawee (usually a financial institution) to pay a certain amount of money to the holder on demand.

EXHIBIT 23.1   A Typical Time Draft

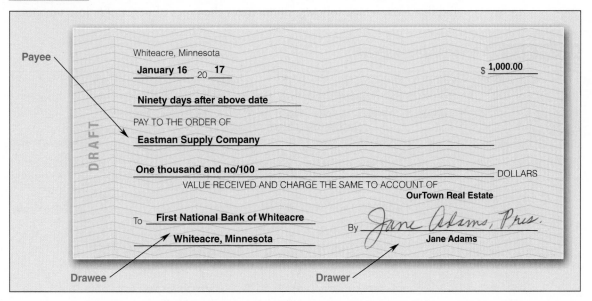

purchases a cashier's check from the bank—that is, pays the bank the amount of the check—and indicates to whom the check should be made payable. The bank, not the customer, is the drawer of the check (as well as the drawee).

23–1b Promises to Pay—Promissory Notes

promissory note
A written unconditional promise signed by a maker to pay a certain amount to a payee or a holder on demand or on a specified date.

A **promissory note** is a written promise by one party to pay another party a specified sum. The party who promises to pay is the **maker** of the note. The party to whom the promise is made is the payee.

A promissory note, which is often referred to simply as a *note*, can be made payable at a definite time or on demand. It can name a specific payee or simply be payable to **bearer**. A bearer is a person in possession of an instrument that is payable to bearer, is not payable to an identified person, does not state a payee, or is *indorsed* (signed) in blank—that is, signed without additional words.

maker
One who issues a promissory note or certificate of deposit.

EXAMPLE 23.2 On April 30, Laurence and Margaret Roberts, who are called co-makers, sign a writing unconditionally promising to pay "to the order of" the First National Bank of Whiteacre $3,000 (with 6 percent interest) on or before June 29. This writing is a promissory note.◄ A typical promissory note is shown in Exhibit 23.2.

bearer
A person in the possession of an instrument payable to bearer or indorsed in blank.

Notes are used in a variety of credit transactions and often carry the name of the transaction involved. In real estate transactions, a promissory note for the unpaid balance on a house, secured by a mortgage on the property, is called a *mortgage note*. A note payable in installments, such as for payment for a flat-screen television over a twelve-month period, is called an *installment note*.

23–1c Promises to Pay—Certificates of Deposit

certificate of deposit (CD)
An instrument evidencing a promissory acknowledgment by a bank of a receipt of money with an engagement to repay it.

A **certificate of deposit (CD)** is a type of bank note. A CD is issued when a party deposits funds with a bank that the bank promises to repay, with interest, on a certain date. The bank is the maker of the note, and the depositor is the payee. **EXAMPLE 23.3** On February 15, Sara Levin deposits $5,000 with the First National Bank of Whiteacre. The bank issues a CD, in which it promises to repay the $5,000, plus 2.25 percent annual interest, on August 15.◄

CDs are sold by savings and loan associations, credit unions, and commercial banks. Small CDs are for amounts up to $100,000, and large (or jumbo) CDs for amounts more than $100,000.

Exhibit 23.3, which follows, summarizes the types of negotiable instruments.

EXHIBIT 23.2   A Typical Promissory Note

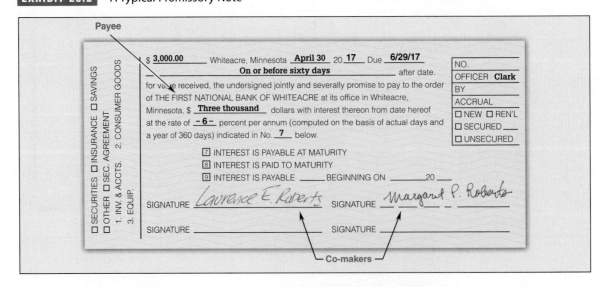

EXHIBIT 23.3   Basic Types of Negotiable Instruments

Instruments	Characteristics	Parties
ORDERS TO PAY:		
Draft	An order by one person to another person or to bearer.	Drawer—The person who signs or makes the order to pay.
Check	A draft drawn on a bank and payable on demand. (With certain types of checks, such as cashier's checks, the bank is both the drawer and the drawee.)	Drawee—The person to whom the order to pay is made. Payee—The person to whom payment is ordered.
PROMISES TO PAY:		
Promissory note	A promise by one party to pay funds to another party or to bearer.	Maker—The person who promises to pay.
Certificate of deposit	A note issued by a bank acknowledging a deposit of funds made payable to the holder of the note.	Payee—The person to whom the promise is made.

23–2 WHAT IS A NEGOTIABLE INSTRUMENT?

For an instrument to be negotiable, it must (1) be in writing, (2) be signed by the maker or the drawer, (3) be an unconditional promise or order to pay, (4) state a fixed amount of money, (5) be payable on demand or at a definite time, and (6) be payable to order or to bearer, unless it is a check.

LEARNING OUTCOME 2

List the requirements of a negotiable instrument.

23–2a Written Form

Negotiable instruments must be in written form. There are certain practical limitations concerning the writing and the substance on which the writing is placed:

1. *The writing must be on material that lends itself to permanence.* Instruments carved in blocks of ice or recorded on other impermanent surfaces would not qualify as negotiable instruments. **EXAMPLE 23.4** Suzanne writes in the sand, "I promise to pay $500 to the order of Jack." This cannot be a negotiable instrument because, although it is in writing, it lacks permanence. ◄

2. *The writing must have portability.* This is not a spelled-out legal requirement. Clearly, though, if an instrument is not movable, it cannot meet the requirement that it be freely transferable. **EXAMPLE 23.5** Charles writes on the side of a barn, "I promise to pay $500 to the order of Jason." Technically, this would meet the requirements of a negotiable instrument—except for portability. A barn cannot easily be transferred in the ordinary course of business. Thus, the "instrument" is nonnegotiable. ◄

23–2b Signatures

For an instrument to be negotiable, it must be signed by (1) the maker, if it is a note or a certificate of deposit, or (2) the drawer, if it is a draft or a check. If a person signs an instrument as the *agent* for the maker or drawer, the maker or drawer has effectively signed the instrument, provided the agent has the appropriate authority.

Extreme latitude is granted in determining what constitutes a **signature.** **EXAMPLE 23.6** A signature may consist of a symbol (such as initials or a thumbprint)

LEARNING OUTCOME 3

State what may constitute a signature.

signature

Any name, word, or mark used with the intention to authenticate a writing.

adopted by a party as his or her signature. A signature may be made manually or by means of a device (a rubber stamp) or a machine (such as those often used to write payroll checks).◄

The location of the signature on the document is unimportant. The usual place, however, is the lower right-hand corner. A *handwritten* statement in the body of the instrument, such as "I, Kamila Orlik, promise to pay Janelle Tan," is sufficient to act as a signature.

23–2c Unconditional Promise or Order to Pay

The terms of the promise or order must be included in writing in a negotiable instrument. These terms must be *unconditional*—that is, not conditioned on the occurrence or nonoccurrence of some other event or agreement.

Promise or Order For an instrument to be negotiable, it must contain an express order or promise to pay. A mere acknowledgment of the debt, which might logically *imply* a promise, is not sufficient, because the promise must be an *express* written undertaking. **EXAMPLE 23.7** The traditional I.O.U. ("I.O.U. $10 [Signed] Bobby") might logically imply a promise. It is not a negotiable instrument, however, because it does not contain an express promise to repay the debt.◄

If such words as "to be paid on demand" or "due on demand" are added, the need for an affirmative promise is satisfied. **EXAMPLE 23.8** If Francisco signs a promissory note that states, "I promise to pay $500 to the order of the seller for the purchase of an iPad Air," then the requirement for a negotiable instrument is satisfied.◄

Unconditionality of a Promise or Order Only unconditional promises or orders can be negotiable. A negotiable instrument's use as a substitute for money or as a credit device would be dramatically reduced if it had conditional promises attached to it. No one could safely purchase the instrument without first investigating whether the condition was satisfied, and doing so would be expensive and time consuming. This would also restrict the instrument's transferability. Thus, only instruments with *unconditional* promises or orders can be negotiable.

Certain necessary conditions commonly used in business transactions do not make an otherwise negotiable instrument nonnegotiable, however. Many instruments state the terms of the underlying agreement as a matter of standard business practice. Such statements are not considered conditions and do not affect negotiability. Similarly, mere reference to another agreement does not affect negotiability. Also, terms in an instrument that provide for payment only out of a particular fund or source do not render the instrument conditional—it remains negotiable.

Real-World Case Example

Sam and Odalis Groome entered into two contracts to buy alpacas from Alpacas of America, LLC (AOA). They signed two notes to finance the purchases. Within a few months, the couple stopped making payments. More than four years later, AOA filed a suit in a Washington state court to collect from them. The court ruled that the notes, which contained references to the contracts, were not negotiable instruments and applied the UCC's four-year statute of limitations on contract actions in Article 2 (instead of the six-year limit in Article 3) to dismiss the suit. AOA appealed.

> **Were the notes negotiable?** Yes. In a 2014 case, *Alpacas of America, LLC v. Groome,* a state intermediate appellate court reversed the ruling of the lower court. Despite containing references to the contracts, the notes constituted unconditional promises to pay. The notes did not include express conditions on the promises, they did not state that they were subject to or governed by another writing, and they did not indicate that the rights or obligations with respect to the promises were stated in another writing.

23–2d A Fixed Amount of Money

Negotiable instruments must state with certainty a fixed amount of money to be paid at the time the instrument is payable. This requirement promises clarity and certainty in determining the value of the instrument. In addition, to be negotiable, an instrument must be payable entirely in money.

Fixed Amount The term *fixed amount* means an amount that is ascertainable from the instrument. **EXAMPLE 23.9** Mary signs a demand note payable to Rolfe with 5 percent interest. This meets the requirement of fixed amount because its amount can be determined at the time it is payable.◄

The amount or rate of interest may be determined with reference to information that is not contained in the instrument but that is readily ascertainable by reference to a formula or a source described in the instrument. For instance, when an instrument is payable at the *legal rate of interest* (a rate of interest fixed by statute), at a *judgment rate of interest* (a rate of interest fixed by statute that is applied to a monetary judgment awarded by a court), or as fixed by state law, the instrument is negotiable.

Mortgage notes tied to a variable rate of interest, which fluctuates as a result of market conditions, can also be negotiable. Only the principal is subject to the requirement that, to be negotiable, a writing must contain a promise or order to pay a fixed amount. The interest may be stated as a variable amount.

LEARNING OUTCOME 4

Decide whether a variable-interest-rate note is negotiable.

Payable in Money Only instruments payable entirely in money are negotiable. The UCC defines *money* as "a medium of exchange authorized or adopted by a domestic or foreign government as a part of its currency." For instance, a promissory note that provides for payment in diamonds or forty hours of services is not payable in money and thus is nonnegotiable. Similarly, an instrument payable in government bonds or in shares of Facebook stock is not negotiable, because neither is a government-recognized medium of exchange.

23–2e Payable on Demand or at a Definite Time

A negotiable instrument must be payable on demand or at a definite time. Clearly, to ascertain the value of a negotiable instrument, it is necessary to know when the maker, drawee, or acceptor is required to pay. It is also necessary to know when the obligations of secondary parties will arise. Furthermore, it is necessary to know when an instrument is due in order to calculate when the statute of limitations may apply. Finally, with an interest-bearing instrument, it is necessary to know the exact interval during which the interest will accrue to determine the present value of the instrument.

Payable on Demand Instruments that are payable on demand include those that contain the words "payable at sight" or "payable on presentment" and those that say nothing about when payment is due. *Presentment* means a demand made by or on behalf of a person entitled to enforce an instrument to either pay or accept the instrument. So presentment occurs when a person brings the instrument to the appropriate party for payment or acceptance.

The nature of the instrument may indicate that it is payable on demand. A check, by definition, is payable on demand. If no time for payment is specified, and if the person responsible for payment must pay when the instrument is presented, then the instrument is payable on demand.

Payable at a Definite Time If an instrument is not payable on demand, to be negotiable, it must be payable at a definite time. An instrument is payable at a definite time if it states that it is payable (1) on a specified date, (2) within a definite period of time (such as thirty days) after being presented for payment, or (3) on a date or time readily ascertainable at the time the promise or order is issued. The maker or drawee in a time draft, for example, is under no obligation to pay until the specified time.

When an instrument is payable by the maker or drawer on or before a stated date, it is clearly payable at a definite time. The maker or drawer has the option of paying before the stated maturity date, but the holder can still rely on payment being made by the maturity date. The option to pay early does not violate the definite-time requirement. In contrast, an instrument that is undated and made payable "one month after date" is clearly nonnegotiable. There is no way to determine the maturity date from the face of the instrument.

HIGHLIGHTING THE POINT

An instrument dated February 1, 2017, states, "One year after the death of my grandfather, James Ezersky, I promise to pay to the order of Henry Ling $500. [Signed] Mary Ezersky."

Is this instrument negotiable? No. Because the date of the grandfather's death is uncertain, the maturity date is uncertain, even though his death is bound to occur eventually. Similarly, the instrument is not negotiable should the grandfather already have died, because it does not specify the time for payment.

23–2f Payable to Order or to Bearer

To ensure a proper transfer, the instrument must be "payable to order or to bearer" at the time it is issued or first comes into the possession of the holder. Note, however, that a check that meets all other requirements for negotiability is a negotiable instrument even if the words "the order of" or "bearer" are missing.

order instrument
A negotiable instrument that is payable "to the order of an identified person" or "to an identified person or order."

Order Instruments An instrument is an **order instrument** if it is payable to the order of an identified person ("Pay to the order of Sam Buke") or to an identified person or order ("Pay to Ivan Hollins or order"). This allows that person to transfer the instrument to whomever he or she wishes. Thus, the maker or drawer is agreeing to pay either the person specified or whomever that person might designate. In this way, the instrument retains its transferability.

For the instrument to qualify as order paper, the person specified must be identified with certainty, because that person must indorse the instrument to transfer it. **EXAMPLE 23.10** Teresa signs an instrument that states, "Pay to the order of my favorite cousin." The instrument is nonnegotiable, as a holder could not be sure which cousin was intended to indorse and properly transfer the instrument. ◄

Bearer Instruments A **bearer instrument** is an instrument that does not designate a specific payee. The maker or drawer of a bearer instrument agrees to pay anyone who presents the instrument for payment. An instrument containing any of the following terms is a bearer instrument:

- "Payable to the order of bearer."
- "Payable to James Jarrot or bearer."
- "Payable to bearer."
- "Payable to X."
- "Pay cash."
- "Pay to the order of cash."

 ## 23-3 TRANSFER OF INSTRUMENTS

Once issued, a negotiable instrument can be transferred by *assignment* or by *negotiation*.

23-3a Transfer by Assignment

An assignment is a transfer of rights under a contract. Under general contract principles, a transfer by assignment to an assignee gives the assignee only those rights that the assignor had. Any defenses that can be raised against an assignor normally can be raised against the assignee. When a transfer fails to qualify as a negotiation, it becomes an assignment. The transferee is then an *assignee*.

23-3b Transfer by Negotiation

Negotiation is the transfer of an instrument in such form that the transferee (the person to whom the instrument is transferred) becomes a holder. A **holder** is a person who, by the terms of a negotiable instrument, is legally entitled to payment on it. According to the UCC, a holder is a person in possession of a negotiable instrument that is either payable to that person, as identified by name, or payable to bearer.

A holder, at the very least, receives the rights of the previous possessor. Furthermore, unlike an assignment, a transfer by negotiation can make it possible for a holder to receive more rights in the instrument than the prior possessor had. (A holder who receives greater rights is known as a *holder in due course.*)

There are two methods of negotiating an instrument so that the receiver becomes a holder. The method used depends on whether the instrument is an order instrument or a bearer instrument.

Negotiating Order Instruments An order instrument contains the name of a payee capable of indorsing it, as in "Pay to the order of Elliot Goodseal." An order instrument is negotiated by delivery with any necessary indorsements. An **indorsement** is a signature placed on an instrument for the purpose of transferring ownership in the instrument.

> ### HIGHLIGHTING THE POINT
>
> Carrington Corporation issues a payroll check "to the order of Elliot Goodseal." Goodseal takes the check to the supermarket, signs his name on the back (an indorsement), gives it to the cashier (a delivery), and receives cash.

(Continued)

---

bearer instrument
A negotiable instrument that is payable to the bearer, including instruments payable to "cash."

negotiation
The transfer of a negotiable instrument to another in such form that the transferee becomes a holder.

holder
The person who, by the terms of a negotiable instrument, is legally entitled to payment on it.

LEARNING OUTCOME 5
Describe a transfer by negotiation.

indorsement
A signature placed on an instrument for the purpose of transferring ownership rights in the instrument.

Is the transfer of the check from Goodseal to the supermarket an assignment or a negotiation? A negotiation. Goodseal "delivered" the check to the supermarket with the necessary indorsement (his signature). If Goodseal had taken the check to the bank and delivered it to the teller without signing it, the transfer would not qualify as a negotiation. Instead, the transfer would be treated as an assignment, and the bank would become an assignee rather than a holder.

Negotiating Bearer Instruments If an instrument is payable to bearer, it is negotiated by delivery—that is, by transfer into another person's possession. Indorsement is not necessary. The use of bearer instruments involves more risk from loss than does the use of order instruments.

HIGHLIGHTING THE POINT

Alan Tyson writes a check "Payable to cash" and hands it to Blaine Parrington (a delivery). Tyson has issued the check to Parrington. Because no specific payee is named, the check is a bearer instrument. Parrington places the check in his wallet, which is subsequently stolen. The thief has possession of the check. At this point, negotiation has not occurred, because delivery must be voluntary on the part of the transferor.

If the thief "delivers" the check to an innocent third person, however, will negotiation be complete? Yes. Only delivery is necessary to negotiate a bearer instrument. If the thief delivers the check to an innocent third person, all rights to it pass to that third person. Parrington loses all rights to recover the proceeds of the check from that person. Of course, Parrington can recover his money from the thief if the thief can be found.

23–3c Types of Indorsements

Indorsements are required whenever the instrument being negotiated is classified as an order instrument. An indorsement is most often written on the back of the instrument itself. A person who transfers an instrument by signing (indorsing) it and delivering it to another person is an *indorser*. The person to whom the instrument is indorsed and delivered is the *indorsee*. The following are four main categories of indorsements.

Blank Indorsements A *blank indorsement* does not specify a particular indorsee and can consist of a mere signature. Hence, a check payable "to the order of Alan Luberda" is indorsed *in blank* if Luberda simply writes his signature on the back of the check. So a blank indorsement converts an order instrument to a bearer instrument, which anybody can cash.

Special Indorsements A *special indorsement* contains the signature of the indorser and identifies the person to whom the instrument is made payable—that is, it names the indorsee. For instance, words such as "Pay to the order of Clay" or "Pay to Clay," followed by the signature of the indorser, create a special indorsement. When an instrument is indorsed in this way, it is an order instrument.

Qualified Indorsements Generally, an indorser, merely by indorsing, impliedly promises to pay the holder or any subsequent indorser the amount of the instrument in the event that the drawer or maker defaults on the payment.

Usually, then, indorsements are *unqualified indorsements,* which means that the indorser is guaranteeing payment of the instrument in addition to transferring title to it. An indorser who does not wish to be liable on an instrument can use a *qualified indorsement* to disclaim this liability. The notation, "without recourse," is commonly used to create a qualified indorsement.

A qualified indorsement can be accompanied by either a special indorsement or a blank indorsement. A special qualified indorsement includes the name of the indorsee, as well as the words *without recourse.* The special indorsement makes the instrument an order instrument, and it requires an indorsement, plus delivery, for negotiation. A blank qualified indorsement makes the instrument a bearer instrument, and only delivery is required for negotiation. In either situation, the instrument can be further negotiated.

Restrictive Indorsements A *restrictive indorsement* requires the indorsee to comply with certain instructions regarding the funds involved, but it does not prohibit the further negotiation of an instrument. When payment depends on the occurrence of some event specified in the indorsement, the instrument has a conditional indorsement. **EXAMPLE 23.11** Ken Barton indorses a check, "Pay to Lars Johansen if he completes the renovation of my kitchen by June 1, 2017. [Signed] Ken Barton." Barton has created a conditional indorsement.◄

Another example of a restrictive indorsement is adding the phrase, "For deposit only," which means that the check cannot be cashed and can only be deposited in the indorser's account. For more on the potential pitfalls of different indorsements, see this chapter's *Linking Business Law to Your Career* feature.

ANSWERING THE LEGAL PROBLEM

In the legal problem set out at the beginning of this chapter, Midwestern Style Fabrics normally sells $50,000 worth of fabric to D&F Clothiers each fall on terms requiring payment in ninety days. One year, Midwestern wants cash, but D&F wants the usual ninety-day term.

A **What can Midwestern and D&F do so that both of their wants are satisfied?** Midwestern can draw a trade acceptance that orders D&F to pay $50,000 to the order of Midwestern Style Fabrics ninety days hence. D&F can accept by signing the face of the paper and returning it to Midwestern. The advantage to Midwestern of the trade acceptance is that D&F's acceptance creates an enforceable promise to pay the draft in ninety days. Midwestern can sell a trade acceptance to another party more easily than it can assign a debt to pay $50,000.

LINKING BUSINESS LAW to Your Career

WRITING AND INDORSING CHECKS

If you choose a career in business, you will certainly be writing and receiving checks. Both activities can involve pitfalls.

Checks Drawn in Blank

The danger in signing a blank check is clear. Anyone can write in an unauthorized amount and cash the check.

Although you may be able to assert lack of authorization against the person who filled in the check, subsequent holders may be able to enforce

(Continued)

the check as completed. While you are haggling with the person who inserted the unauthorized amount and who may not be able to repay it, you will also have to honor the check for the unauthorized amount to a subsequent holder in due course.

Checks Payable to "Cash"

It is equally dangerous to write out and sign a check payable to "cash" until you are actually at the bank. Checks payable to "cash" are bearer instruments.

This means that if you lose or misplace the check, anybody who finds it can present it (with proper identification) to the bank for payment.

Checks Indorsed in Blank

A negotiable instrument with a blank indorsement also presents dangers. As a bearer instrument, it may be as easily transferred as cash. When you make a bank deposit, therefore, you should indorse the back of the check in blank only in the presence of a teller who

simultaneously gives you a receipt for the deposit. If you choose to sign it ahead of time, always insert the words *For deposit only* before you sign your name.

As a precaution, you should consider obtaining an indorsement stamp from your bank. Then, when you receive a check payable to your business, you can indorse it immediately. The stamped indorsement will indicate that the check is for deposit only to your business account, specified by its number.

TERMS AND CONCEPTS FOR REVIEW

acceptance 305

bearer 306

bearer instrument 311

certificate of deposit (CD) 306

check 305

draft 305

drawee 305

drawer 305

holder 311

indorsement 311

maker 306

negotiable instrument 304

negotiation 311

order instrument 310

payee 305

promissory note 306

signature 307

CHAPTER SUMMARY—THE ESSENTIALS OF NEGOTIABILITY

LEARNING OUTCOME

1   **Identify the basic types of negotiable instruments.** The four types of negotiable instruments—drafts, checks, promissory notes, and certificates of deposit—can be classified as demand instruments, which are payable on demand when the holder presents them to the maker or drawer.

2   **List the requirements of a negotiable instrument.** To be negotiable, an instrument must:

(1) *Be in writing*—A writing can be on anything that is readily transferable and has a degree of permanence.

(2) *Be signed by the maker or drawer.*

(3) *Be an unconditional promise or order to pay*—A promise must be more than a mere acknowledgment of a debt (the words *I/We promise* or *Pay* meet this criterion). Payment cannot be expressly conditioned on the occurrence of an event or be subject to or governed by another contract.

(4) *State a fixed amount of money*—An amount can be a fixed sum even if it is payable with interest. Money is any medium of exchange recognized as the currency of a government.

(5) *Be payable on demand or at a definite time*—An instrument that is payable on sight or on presentation, or does not state any time for payment, is payable on demand. An instrument is payable at a definite time if a date is stated on the face of the instrument, even if the instrument is payable on *or before* the stated date.

(6) *Be payable to order or bearer*—An order instrument must identify the payee with certainty. An instrument that is not payable to an identified person is payable to bearer.

3	**State what may constitute a signature.** A signature can be anywhere on the face of an instrument, can be in any form (including a word, a mark, or a rubber stamp) that purports to be a signature and authenticates the writing, and can be made in a representative capacity.
4	**Decide whether a variable-interest-rate note is negotiable.** A note tied to a variable rate of interest, which fluctuates as a result of market conditions, can be negotiable. Only the principal is subject to the requirement that, to be negotiable, a writing must contain a promise or order to pay a fixed amount.
5	**Describe a transfer by negotiation.** In a transfer by negotiation, the transferee becomes a holder and can acquire more rights in the instrument than the previous possessor had. An order instrument is negotiated by indorsement and delivery. A bearer instrument is negotiated by delivery only.

ISSUE SPOTTERS

Check your answers to the *Issue Spotters* against the answers provided in Appendix C at the end of this text.

1. Jim owes Sherry $700. Sherry asks Jim to sign a negotiable instrument regarding the debt. Which of the following, if included on that instrument, would make it negotiable: "I.O.U. $700," "I promise to pay $700," or an instruction to Jim's bank stating, "I wish you would pay $700 to Sherry"? Explain why. (See *What Is a Negotiable Instrument?*)

2. Jack Caldwell gets his paycheck from his employer, indorses the back of the check by signing his name, and goes to cash it at his credit union. On the way, he loses the check. Paige finds the check. Has the check been negotiated to Paige? How might Jack have avoided any loss? (See *Transfer of Instruments*.)

USING BUSINESS LAW

23–1. Requirements of Negotiability. The following note is written by Muriel Evans on the back of an envelope: "I, Muriel Evans, promise to pay Karen Marvin or bearer $100 on demand." Is this a negotiable instrument? Discuss fully. (See *What Is a Negotiable Instrument?*)

23–2. Indorsements. Bertram writes a check for $200, payable to "cash." He puts the check in his pocket and drives to the bank to cash the check. As he gets out of his car in the bank's parking lot, the check slips out of his pocket and falls to the pavement. Jerrod walks by moments later, picks up the check, and later that day delivers it to Amber, to whom he owes $200. Amber indorses the check "For

deposit only. [Signed] Amber Dowel" and deposits it into her checking account. In light of these circumstances, answer the following questions: (See *Transfer of Instruments*.)

1. Is the check a bearer instrument or an order instrument?

2. Did Jerrod's delivery of the check to Amber constitute a valid negotiation? Why or why not?

3. What type of indorsement did Amber make?

4. Does Bertram have a right to recover the $200 from Amber? Explain.

REAL-WORLD CASE PROBLEMS

23–3. Bearer Instruments. Eligio Gaitan borrowed the funds to buy real property at 4520 W. Washington St. in Downers Grove, Illinois, and signed a note payable to Encore Credit Corp. Encore indorsed the note in blank. When Gaitan defaulted on the payments, an action to foreclose on the property was filed in an Illinois state

court by U.S. Bank, N.A. The note was in the possession of the bank, but there was no evidence that the note had been transferred or negotiated to the bank. Can U.S. Bank enforce payment of the note? Why or why not? [*U.S. Bank National Association v. Gaitan*, 2013 WL 160378 (2013)] (See *Transfer of Instruments*.)

23–4. Indorsements. Angela Brock borrowed $544,000 and signed a note payable to Amerifund Mortgage Services, LLC, to buy a house in Silver Spring, Maryland. The note was indorsed in blank and transferred several times "without recourse" before Brock fell behind on the payments. On behalf of Deutsche Bank National Trust Co., BAC Home Loans Servicing LP initiated foreclosure. Brock filed an action in a Maryland state court to block it, arguing that BAC could not foreclose because Deutsche Bank, not BAC, owned the note. Can BAC enforce the note? Explain. [*Deutsche Bank National Trust Co. v. Brock*, 430 Md. 714, 63 A.3d 40 (2013)] (See *Transfer of Instruments.*)

23–5. Negotiability. Michael Scotto borrowed $2,970 from Cindy Vinueza. Both of their signatures appeared at the bottom of a note that stated, "I, Michael Scotto, owe Cindy Vinueza $2,970 (two thousand and nine-hundred-and-seventy dollars) and agree to pay her back in full. Signed on this 26th day of September 2009." More than a year later, Vinueza filed a suit against Scotto to recover on the note. Scotto admitted that he had borrowed the money, but he contended—without proof—that he had paid Vinueza in full. Is this note negotiable? Which party is likely to prevail? Why? [*Vinueza v. Scotto*, 30 Misc.3d 1229, 924 N.Y.S.2d 312 (1 Dist. 2011)] (See *What Is a Negotiable Instrument?*)

ETHICAL QUESTIONS

23–6. Requirements for Negotiability. Should the requirements for negotiability be strictly enforced? Explain your answer. (See *What Is a Negotiable Instrument?*)

23–7. Payable on Demand or at a Definite Time. National City Bank loaned money to Reger Development, LLC, to fund development opportunities. Reger signed a promissory note that required the borrower to "pay this loan in full immediately upon Lender's demand." Later, National City asked to have some of the loan paid back. Reger—who was not in default—filed a suit against the bank, alleging breach. Was the note a demand instrument? Should the duty to act in good faith implied in every contract apply to a lender seeking payment on a demand note? Discuss. [*Reger Development, LLC v. National City Bank*, 592 F.3d 759 (7th Cir. 2010)] (See *What Is a Negotiable Instrument?*)

Chapter 23—Work Set

TRUE-FALSE QUESTIONS

_____ 1. A negotiable instrument can be transferred only by negotiation.

_____ 2. A bearer instrument is payable to whoever possesses it.

_____ 3. To be negotiable, an instrument must be in writing.

_____ 4. To be negotiable, an instrument must expressly state when payment is due.

_____ 5. An instrument that does not designate a specific payee is an order instrument.

_____ 6. Indorsements are required to negotiate order instruments.

_____ 7. An order instrument is payable to whoever properly possesses it.

_____ 8. Indorsements are required to negotiate bearer instruments.

_____ 9. To be negotiable, an instrument must include an unconditional promise to pay.

_____ 10. The person who signs or makes an order to pay is the drawer.

MULTIPLE-CHOICE QUESTIONS

_____ 1. Jasmine writes out a check payable to the order of Nancy. Nancy receives the check but wants to negotiate it further to her friend Max. Nancy can negotiate the check further by

    a. indorsing it.
    b. delivering it to the transferee.
    c. doing both a and b.
    d. none of the above methods.

_____ 2. Kurt receives from Lee a check that is made out "Pay to the order of Kurt." Kurt turns it over and writes on the back, "Pay to Adam. [Signed] Kurt." Kurt's indorsement is a

    a. blank indorsement.
    b. special indorsement.
    c. restrictive indorsement.
    d. qualified indorsement.

_____ 3. Ray is the owner of Espresso Express. Dan's Office Supplies sells Ray supplies for Espresso Express. To pay, Ray signs a check "Espresso Express" in the lower left-hand corner. The check is

    a. not negotiable, because "Espresso Express" is a trade name.
    b. not negotiable, because Ray signed the check in the wrong location.
    c. negotiable, and Ray is bound.
    d. negotiable, but Ray is not bound.

_____ 4. Alex makes out a check "Pay to the order of Mel." Mel indorses the check on the back by signing his name. Before Mel signed his name, the check was

    a. bearer paper.
    b. order paper.
    c. both a and b.
    d. none of the above.

5. Jules owes money to Vern. Vern owes money to Chris. Vern signs an instrument that orders Jules to pay to Chris the money that Jules owes to Vern. This instrument is a

a. note.
b. check.
c. certificate of deposit.
d. draft.

6. Don's checks are printed "Pay to the order of" followed by a blank space. On one of the checks, Don writes in the blank space "Mac or bearer." The check is

a. a bearer instrument.
b. an order instrument.
c. both a and b.
d. none of the above.

7. Lisa writes out a check payable to the order of Jeff. Negotiation occurs when Jeff receives the check. Jeff subsequently negotiates the check by

a. indorsing it only.
b. delivering it only.
c. indorsing and delivering it.
d. none of the above methods.

8. Ann receives an instrument that reads, "May 1, 2014. Sixty days after date, I promise to pay to the order of bearer $1,000 with interest at an annual rate of 5 percent. Due on June 30, 2014. [Signed] Bob Smith." This instrument is

a. a draft and negotiable.
b. a draft and nonnegotiable.
c. a promissory note and negotiable.
d. a promissory note and nonnegotiable.

ANSWERING MORE LEGAL PROBLEMS

1. Marit worked for Town & Garden, a landscape design service owned by Donald. Marit signed a note payable to Donald to purchase an ownership interest in Town & Garden. The note, which was undated, required installment payments, but Donald never asked for them. One year later, Marit quit Town & Garden. Donald tried to terminate Marit's interest in the business, asserting that the note had not been paid.

Was Marit's note a demand note? Yes. Instruments that are payable on demand may state "payable on demand," or the nature of an instrument may indicate that it is payable on demand. In addition, if no time for _____ is specified, then the instrument is payable on demand. Here, the note required installments but did not state a date for their _____. **Was the nonpayment of the note a proper reason for the termination of Marit's interest in Town & Garden?** No. Donald did not demand _____ on the note. Thus, Marit's obligation to make it had not arisen, and the attempted termination of her interest in Town & Garden was improper.

2. Bryce borrowed funds from Rock Canyon Bank for his education and signed a note for the amount payable to the bank. The bank indorsed the note and transferred it by delivery to the U.S. Department of Education. When Bryce did not pay the note, the government asked a court for an order to garnish his wages. Bryce argued that he had not signed any document promising to pay the government and thus its claim was invalid.

Was the government entitled to enforce the note? Yes. Negotiation is the transfer of an instrument in such form that the transferee becomes a holder—a person who, by the terms of the instrument, is entitled to enforce it. If the instrument is an order instrument, it is negotiated by delivery with any necessary indorsements. In the facts of this problem, the bank _____ the note with the necessary _____ by _____ to the government.

TRANSFERABILITY AND LIABILITY

24

FACING A LEGAL PROBLEM

Marcia Morrison issues a $500 note payable to Reinhold Smith in payment for goods. Smith negotiates the note to Judy Larson, who promises to pay Smith for it in thirty days. During the next month, Larson learns that Smith has breached the contract by delivering defective goods and that Morrison will not honor the $500 note. Smith has left town.

Q Can Larson hold Morrison liable on the note?

Problems arise when a holder seeking payment of a negotiable instrument learns that a defense to payment exists or that another party has a prior claim to the instrument. In such situations, it is important for the person seeking payment to have the rights of a *holder in due course* (HDC). An HDC takes a negotiable instrument free of all claims and most defenses of other parties.

We open this chapter by distinguishing between an ordinary holder and an HDC. We then examine the requirements for HDC status, the kinds of liability associated with negotiable instruments, and the defenses that parties may have to payment of an instrument. We conclude the chapter with a discussion of the discharge from liability on an instrument.

24–1 HOLDER VERSUS HOLDER IN DUE COURSE

A *holder* is a person who, by the terms of a negotiable instrument, is legally entitled to enforce payment of it. When a negotiable instrument is transferred, an *ordinary holder* of this kind obtains only those rights that the transferor had in the instrument. In the event that there is a conflicting, superior claim to or defense against the instrument, an ordinary holder will not be able to collect payment.

In contrast, a **holder in due course (HDC)** is a holder who, by meeting certain acquisition requirements, takes a negotiable instrument *free* of most defenses and all claims to it. Stated another way, an HDC normally can acquire a higher level of immunity than can an ordinary holder in regard to defenses against payment of the instrument and claims to ownership of the instrument by other parties.

holder in due course (HDC)
Any holder who, by meeting certain circumstances, takes a negotiable instrument free of most defenses and all claims.

24–2 REQUIREMENTS FOR HDC STATUS

First, an HDC must be a holder of a negotiable instrument. In addition, he or she must have taken the instrument under the following conditions:

1. For value.

2. In good faith.

3. Without notice that it is overdue, that it has been dishonored, that any person has a defense against it or a claim to it, or that it contains unauthorized signatures or alterations or is so irregular or incomplete as to call into question its authenticity.

24–2a Taking for Value

An HDC must have given value for the instrument. The concept of *value* in the law of negotiable instruments is not the same as the concept of *consideration* in the law of contracts. An *executory promise* (a promise to give value in the future) is valid consideration to support a contract. It does not, however, normally constitute value sufficient to make a holder an HDC.

Instead, a holder exchanging a promise for an instrument takes the instrument for value only to the extent that the promise has been performed. If the holder plans to pay for the instrument later or plans to perform the required services at some future date, the holder has not yet given value. In that case, the holder is not yet an HDC.

A holder takes an instrument for value if the holder has done any of the following:

1. Performed the promise for which the instrument was issued or transferred.

2. Acquired a security interest or other lien in the instrument (other than a lien obtained by a judicial proceeding).

3. Taken an instrument in payment of, or as security for, a preexisting debt. **EXAMPLE 24.1** Ivan owes Marta $2,000 on a past-due account. If Ivan negotiates a $2,000 note signed by Gordon to Marta, and Marta accepts it to discharge Ivan's overdue account balance, she has given value for the instrument.◄

4. Given a negotiable instrument as payment for the instrument.

5. Given, as payment, a commitment that cannot be revoked (withdrawn or recalled).

A person who receives an instrument as a gift or who inherits it has not met the requirement of value. In these situations, the person becomes an ordinary holder and does not possess the rights of an HDC.

24–2b Taking in Good Faith

The second requirement for HDC status is that the holder take the instrument in good faith. This means that the purchaser-holder must have acted honestly in acquiring the instrument. *Good faith* is honesty in fact and the observance of reasonable commercial standards of fair dealing. The good faith requirement *applies only to the holder.* It is immaterial whether the transferor acted in good faith. **EXAMPLE 24.2** Rahul issues a check payable to Paul. Laura steals the check, indorses the back, and presents it to Quick Check Service for payment. Quick's employee compares Laura's signature to the signature on her identification. Nothing indicates that the check is stolen. Quick has taken the check in good faith and may thus become an HDC.◄

Because of the good faith requirement, the purchaser, when acquiring the instrument, must have honestly believed that the instrument was not defective. The purchaser must also have observed reasonable commercial standards—that is, conformed with what others might have done. **EXAMPLE 24.3** If Rand purchases a $10,000 note for $200 from a stranger on a street corner, the issue of good faith can be raised on the grounds of the suspicious circumstances as well as the grossly inadequate consideration.◄

24–2c Taking without Notice

The final requirement for HDC status involves lack of notice that the instrument is defective. A person will not be afforded HDC protection if he or she acquires an instrument knowing, or having reason to know, that it is defective in any one of the following ways:

1. It is overdue.

2. It has been dishonored.

3. There is an uncured (uncorrected) default (failure to pay) with respect to another instrument issued as part of the same series.

4. The instrument contains an unauthorized signature or has been altered.

5. There is a defense against the instrument or a claim to the instrument.

6. The instrument is so irregular or incomplete as to call into question its authenticity.

What Constitutes Notice? A holder will be deemed to have notice if he or she has (1) actual knowledge of the defect, (2) receipt of a notice about a defect, or (3) reason to know that a defect exists, given all the facts and circumstances known at the time in question. The holder must also have received the notice at a time and in a manner that gives the holder a reasonable opportunity to act on it. A purchaser's knowledge of certain facts, such as bankruptcy proceedings against the instrument's maker or drawer, does not constitute notice that the instrument is defective.

Overdue Instruments Any negotiable instrument is either payable at a definite time *(time instrument)* or payable on demand *(demand instrument)*. What constitutes notice that an instrument is overdue will vary depending on whether it is a time or a demand instrument.

Anyone who takes a time instrument the day after its expressed due date is *on notice* that it is overdue. **EXAMPLE 24.4** Eduardo signs a promissory note due on May 15. The note must be acquired before midnight on May 15. If it is purchased on May 16, the purchaser will be an ordinary holder, not an HDC.◄ If an instrument reads, "Payable in thirty days," counting begins on the day *after* the instrument is dated. **EXAMPLE 24.5** D'Angelo signs a note dated December 1 that is payable in thirty days. This note is due by midnight on December 31.◄ If the payment date falls on a Sunday or holiday, the instrument is payable on the next business day.

Sometimes, a debt is to be paid in installments or through a series of notes. In this situation, the maker's default on any installment of principal (not interest) or on any one note of the series will constitute notice to the purchaser that the instrument is overdue.

A purchaser has notice that a demand instrument is overdue if he or she takes the instrument knowing that payment on the instrument was demanded the day before. A purchaser also has notice if he or she takes a demand instrument that has been outstanding for an unreasonable period of time after its date. A reasonable time for a check is ninety days or less. A reasonable time for other demand instruments depends on the circumstances.

Dishonored Instruments An instrument is **dishonored** when it is presented in a timely manner for payment or acceptance (whichever is required), and payment or acceptance is refused. The holder is on notice if he or she (1) has actual knowledge of the dishonor or (2) has knowledge of facts that would lead him or her to suspect that an instrument has been dishonored. Conversely, if a person purchasing an instrument does not know and has no reason to know that it has been dishonored, the person is not put on notice and can become an HDC.

dishonor
To refuse to pay or accept a negotiable instrument (whichever is required), even though the instrument is presented in a timely and proper manner.

24–3 SIGNATURE LIABILITY

The key to liability on a negotiable instrument is a signature. The general rule is that every party, except a *qualified indorser*, who signs a negotiable instrument

LEARNING OUTCOME 2

Outline the liability of parties who sign negotiable instruments.

is either primarily or secondarily liable for payment of that instrument when it comes due. Signature liability is contractual liability—no person will be held contractually liable for an instrument that he or she has not signed. A person is not liable on an instrument unless (1) the person signed the instrument, or (2) the person's agent or representative signed the instrument and the signature is binding on the represented person.

The following sections discuss the types of liability that apply to negotiable instruments and the conditions that must be met before liability can arise.

24–3a Primary Liability

A person who is primarily liable on a negotiable instrument is absolutely required to pay the instrument, subject to certain defenses. Primary liability is unconditional. The primary party's liability is immediate when the instrument is signed or issued and effective when the instrument becomes due. No action by the holder of the instrument is required.

acceptor
A drawee who accepts, or promises to pay, an instrument when it is presented later for payment.

Only makers and **acceptors** are primarily liable—that is, both have agreed to the legal obligation. The maker of a promissory note, for instance, unconditionally promises to pay the note when it becomes due. An acceptor, such as a drawee bank that indicates acceptance by signing a check, agrees to pay the check when it is presented for payment.

Even when a promissory note was incomplete at the time the maker signed it, a maker is still obligated to pay. The maker must pay according to the note's terms at the time of signing, or according to its terms when it is completed as authorized. **EXAMPLE 24.6** Tristan executes a preprinted promissory note to Sharon, without filling in the blank for a due date. If Sharon does not complete the form by adding the date, the note will be payable on demand. If Sharon subsequently fills in a due date that Tristan authorized, the note is payable on the stated due date. In either situation, Tristan (the maker) is obligated to pay the note. ◄

The drawee of a draft or check is in nearly the same position as the maker of a promissory note. When a drawee accepts a draft by signing it, the drawee becomes an acceptor and is primarily liable to all subsequent holders. The drawee's acceptance of the draft guarantees that the drawee will pay the draft when it is presented later for payment. A drawee who refuses to accept a draft that requires the drawee's acceptance has dishonored the instrument.

24–3b Secondary Liability

Drawers and indorsers have secondary liability. That is, a drawer or indorser is liable only if the party who is primarily liable for paying the instrument refuses to do so. In the case of notes, an indorser's secondary liability does not arise until the maker, who is primarily liable, has defaulted on the instrument. With regard to drafts (and checks), a drawer's secondary liability does not arise until the drawee fails to pay or to accept the instrument, whichever is required. **EXAMPLE 24.7** Liza writes a check on her account at Universal Bank payable to the order of Valerie. If Universal Bank does not pay the check when Valerie presents it for payment, then Liza is liable to Valerie. ◄

Parties who are secondarily liable on a negotiable instrument promise to pay on that instrument only if the following events occur:

1. The instrument is properly and timely presented.

2. The instrument is dishonored.

3. Timely notice of dishonor is given to the secondarily liable party.

Proper and Timely Presentment *Presentment* by a holder must be made to the proper person, must be made in a proper manner, and must be timely.

The party to whom the instrument must be presented depends on what type of instrument is involved. A note or certificate of deposit must be presented to the maker for payment. A draft is presented by the holder to the drawee for acceptance, payment, or both, whichever is required. A check is presented to the drawee-bank for payment.

Presentment can be properly made in any of the following ways, depending on the type of instrument involved:

1. By any commercially reasonable means, including oral, written, or electronic communication (but presentment is not effective until the demand for payment or acceptance is received).

2. Through a clearinghouse procedure used by banks, such as for deposited checks.

3. At the place specified in the instrument for acceptance or payment.

One of the most crucial criteria for proper presentment is timeliness. Failure to present on time is the most common cause for the discharge of *unqualified indorsers* from secondary liability. The time for proper presentment for different types of instruments is shown in Exhibit 24.1.

Dishonor and Proper Notice An instrument is dishonored when the required acceptance or payment is refused or cannot be obtained within the prescribed time. Once an instrument is dishonored, notice must be given to hold secondary parties liable. **EXAMPLE 24.8** Oman writes a check on his account at State Bank payable to Leah. Leah indorses the check in blank and cashes it at Midwest Grocery, which transfers it to State Bank for payment. If State Bank refuses to pay it, Midwest must timely notify Leah to hold her liable. ◄

Notice may be given in any reasonable manner. This includes oral, written, or electronic notice, or notice written or stamped on the instrument itself. Any necessary notice must be given by a bank before its midnight deadline (midnight of the next banking day after receipt). Notice by any party other than a bank must be given within thirty days following the day on which the person receives notice of dishonor.

24–3c Unauthorized Signatures

Unauthorized signatures arise in two situations—when a person forges another person's name on a negotiable instrument and when an agent who lacks the authority signs an instrument on behalf of a principal. The general rule is that an unauthorized signature is wholly inoperative and will not bind the person whose name is signed or forged.

EXHIBIT 24.1 Time for Proper Presentment

Type of Instrument	For Acceptance	For Payment
Time	On or before due date.	On due date.
Demand	Within a reasonable time (after date or issue or after secondary party becomes liable on the instrument).	Within a reasonable time.
Check	Not applicable.	Within thirty days of date to hold drawer secondarily liable. Within thirty days of indorsement to hold indorser secondarily liable.

There are two exceptions to this rule:

1. When the person whose name is signed ratifies (affirms) the signature, that person will be bound.

2. When the negligence of the person whose name was forged substantially contributed to the forgery, a court may not allow the person to deny the effectiveness of an unauthorized signature. **EXAMPLE 24.9** Vicente writes and signs a check, leaves blank the amount and the name of the payee, and then leaves the check in a place available to the public. Joan finds the check, fills it in, and cashes it. Vicente, on the basis of his negligence, can be prevented from denying liability for payment of the check.◄ Whatever loss occurs may be allocated, however, between certain parties on the basis of comparative negligence. If a drawer can demonstrate that the bank was negligent in paying the check, the bank may have to bear a portion of the loss as well.

An unauthorized signature operates as the signature of the unauthorized signer in favor of an HDC. For example, a person who forges a check can be held personally liable by an HDC.

24–3d Special Rules for Unauthorized Indorsements

Generally, when an indorsement is forged or unauthorized, the burden of loss falls on the first party to take the instrument with the unauthorized indorsement. The reason for this general rule is because the first party to take an instrument is in the best position to prevent the loss.

There are two exceptions to this general rule—when an indorsement is made by an *imposter* or by a *fictitious payee*.

imposter
A person who, with the intent to deceive, pretends to be somebody else.

The Imposter Rule An **imposter,** by use of the mails, telephone, the Internet, or personal appearance, induces a maker or drawer to issue an instrument in the name of an impersonated payee. If the maker or drawer believes the imposter to be the named payee at the time of issue, the indorsement by the imposter is not treated as unauthorized when the instrument is transferred to an innocent party. This is because the maker or drawer intended the imposter to receive the instrument.

In these situations, the unauthorized indorsement of a payee's name can be as effective as if the real payee had signed. The *imposter rule* provides that an imposter's indorsement will be effective—that is, not a forgery—insofar as the drawer or maker is concerned.

EXAMPLE 24.10 Carol impersonates Donna and induces Edward to write a check payable to the order of Donna. Carol, continuing to impersonate Donna, negotiates the check to First National Bank as payment on her loan there. As the drawer of the check, Edward is liable for its amount to First National Bank.◄

The comparative negligence standard mentioned in connection with the liability of banks paying over unauthorized signatures also applies in cases involving imposters. If a bank fails to exercise ordinary care in cashing a check made out to an imposter and this failure substantially contributes to the drawer's loss, the drawer may have a valid claim against the bank.

fictitious payee
A payee on a negotiable instrument whom the maker or drawer does not intend to have an interest in the instrument.

The Fictitious Payee Rule The so-called **fictitious payee** rule concerns the intent of a maker or drawer to issue an instrument to a payee who has no interest in the instrument. This most often takes place in two situations:

1. A dishonest employee deceives the employer into signing an instrument payable to a party with no right to receive the instrument.

2. A dishonest employee or agent has the authority to issue an instrument on behalf of the employer and issues a check to a person who has no interest in the instrument.

In these situations, the payee's indorsement is not treated as a forgery, and the employer can be held liable on the instrument by an innocent holder.

HIGHLIGHTING THE POINT

Dan Symes draws up the payroll list from which the salary checks for the Honsu Company's employees are written. He fraudulently adds the name Penny Trip (a friend not entitled to payment) to the payroll, thus causing checks to be issued to her. Trip cashes the checks at the Lone Star Grocery Store and shares the proceeds with Symes.

Can Lone Star hold Honsu liable on the checks? Yes. Trip's indorsement is not treated as a forgery, and Honsu can be held liable on them by Lone Star.

24–4 WARRANTY LIABILITY

In addition to the signature liability, transferors make certain implied warranties regarding the instruments that they are negotiating. Liability under these warranties is not subject to the conditions of proper presentment, dishonor, and notice of dishonor. These warranties arise even when a transferor does not indorse the instrument (as in delivery of a bearer instrument). Warranties fall into two categories: those that arise from the transfer of a negotiable instrument and those that arise on presentment.

24–4a Transfer Warranties

A person who transfers an instrument *for consideration* makes certain warranties to the transferee and, if the transfer is by *indorsement*, to all subsequent transferees and holders who take the instrument in good faith. These warranties can be disclaimed in any instruments except checks.

There are five **transfer warranties:**

1. The transferor is entitled to enforce the instrument.
2. All signatures are authentic and authorized.
3. The instrument has not been materially altered.
4. The instrument is not subject to a defense or claim of any party that can be asserted against the transferor.
5. The transferor has no knowledge of any insolvency (bankruptcy) proceedings against the maker, the acceptor, or the drawer of an unaccepted instrument.

The manner of transfer and the type of negotiation used determine how far and to whom a transfer warranty will extend. Transfer by indorsement and delivery of order instruments extends warranty liability to any subsequent holder who takes the instrument in good faith. The warranties of a person who transfers without indorsement (by delivery of bearer paper) extend only to the immediate transferee.

> **LEARNING OUTCOME 3**
> Identify transfer warranties, which extend to both signers and nonsigners of negotiable instruments.
>
> **transfer warranty**
> A guaranty made by any person who transfers a negotiable instrument for consideration to all subsequent transferees and holders who take the instrument in good faith.

HIGHLIGHTING THE POINT

Wylie forges Kim's name as a maker of a promissory note. The note is made payable to Wylie. Wylie indorses the note in blank, negotiates it to Bret, and then leaves the

(Continued)

country. Bret, without indorsement, delivers the note to Fern. Fern, in turn without indorsement, delivers the note to Rick. On Rick's presentment of the note to Kim, the forgery is discovered.

Can Rick hold Fern (the immediate transferor) liable for breach of warranty that all signatures are genuine? Yes. The note is a bearer instrument. Rick cannot hold Bret liable, however, because Bret is not Rick's immediate transferor and did not indorse the note.

24–4b Presentment Warranties

Any person who obtains payment or acceptance of an instrument makes the following warranties to any other person who in good faith pays or accepts the instrument:

1. The person obtaining payment or acceptance is entitled to enforce the draft or is authorized to obtain payment or acceptance on behalf of a person who is entitled to enforce the draft. (This is, in effect, a warranty that there are no missing or unauthorized indorsements.)

2. The draft has not been altered.

3. The person obtaining payment or acceptance has no knowledge that the signature of the drawer of the draft is unauthorized.

presentment warranty
A warranty made by any person who presents an instrument for payment or acceptance.

These warranties are often referred to as **presentment warranties,** because they protect the person to whom the instrument is presented. Like transfer warranties, these warranties can be disclaimed in any instruments except checks. A claim for breach must be given to the warrantor within thirty days after the claimant knows, or has reason to know, of the breach and the identity of the warrantor.

The second and third presentment warranties do not apply to makers, acceptors, and drawers. It is assumed that a drawer or a maker will recognize his or her own signature and that an acceptor will recognize whether an instrument has been materially altered.

24–5 DEFENSES

Defenses can bar collection from persons who would otherwise be primarily or secondarily liable on an instrument. There are two general categories of defenses—universal defenses and personal defenses.

Point out defenses against the payment of negotiable instruments.

24–5a Universal Defenses

universal defense
A defense that can be used to avoid payment to all holders of a negotiable instrument, including a holder in due course (HDC).

Universal defenses (also called *real defenses*) are valid against all holders, including holders in due course (HDCs). Universal defenses include the following:

1. *Forgery of a signature on the instrument.* A forged signature cannot bind the person whose name is used unless that person validates the signature or is barred from denying it (because the forgery was made possible by the maker's or drawer's negligence, for example). Thus, when an instrument is forged, the person whose name is forged normally has no liability to pay any holder or any HDC the value of the instrument.

2. *Fraud in the execution.* If a person is deceived into signing a negotiable instrument, believing that he or she is signing something other than a negotiable instrument (such as a receipt), fraud in the execution is committed against the signer.

3. *Material alteration.* An alteration is material if it changes the contract terms between any two parties in any way. Material alterations include completing an instrument, adding words or numbers, or making any other change in an unauthorized manner that relates to the obligation of a party.

4. *Discharge in bankruptcy.* Bankruptcy is a defense on any instrument regardless of the status of the holder, because the purpose of bankruptcy is to settle all of the insolvent party's debts.

5. *Minority.* Minority is a universal defense only to the extent that state law recognizes it as a defense to a simple contract.

6. *Illegality, mental incapacity, or extreme duress.* When the law declares that an instrument is *void* because it was issued in connection with illegal conduct, by a person who was adjudged mentally incompetent by a court, or by a person under an immediate threat of force or violence (for example, at gunpoint), the defense is universal.

24–5b Personal Defenses

Personal defenses are used to avoid payment to an ordinary holder. There are many personal defenses. They include the following:

1. *Breach of contract or breach of warranty.* When there is a breach of warranty or a breach of the contract for which the instrument was issued, the maker of a note can refuse to pay it, or the drawer of a check can stop payment.

2. *Fraud in the inducement (ordinary fraud).* A person who issues a negotiable instrument based on false statements by the other party will be able to avoid payment, unless the holder is an HDC.

3. *Illegality, mental incapacity, or ordinary duress.* If the law declares that an instrument is voidable because it was issued in connection with illegal conduct, by a person who is mentally incompetent, or by a person under ordinary duress, the defense is personal.

4. *Previous payment of the instrument.*

5. *Lack or failure of consideration.* The absence of consideration can be a successful defense in some instances. **EXAMPLE 24.11** Tony gives Cleo, as a gift, a note that states, "I promise to pay you $100,000." Cleo accepts the note. No consideration is given in return for Tony's promise. Thus, a court will not enforce the promise. ◄

personal defense
A defense that can be used to avoid payment to an ordinary holder of a negotiable instrument, but not to a holder in due course (HDC).

Real-World Case Example

Gregory Mills and Robert Chauvin were friends and attorneys, and maintained a professional and business relationship. Chauvin was an investor in Amelia Village, a real estate development project in New York. Over time, Mills paid $395,750 to Chauvin, who claimed that the funds represented an investment in the project. Mills, however, claimed that the money was a loan, and Chauvin signed a note to repay it. When the note was not paid, Mills filed a suit in a New York state court to recover. The court ruled in Mills's favor. Chauvin appealed.

Was the note unenforceable for lack of consideration? No. In a 2013 case, *Mills v. Chauvin*, a state intermediate appellate court affirmed the ruling of the lower court. Chauvin had challenged the validity of the note, claiming a lack of consideration as a defense to payment. The court did not agree: "The consideration for the promissory note was the $395,750 that Mills had provided to Chauvin."

24-6 DISCHARGE

Discharge from liability on an instrument can occur in several ways. They include payment, cancellation or surrender, and—as noted previously—material alteration. The liability of all parties is discharged when the party primarily liable on an instrument pays to a holder the full amount due. Payment by any other party discharges only the liability of that party and later parties.

The holder of a negotiable instrument can discharge any party to the instrument by cancellation. **EXAMPLE 24.12** Glenda, a loan officer for Consumer Loan Center, writes the word "Paid" across the face of an instrument. This constitutes cancellation.◄ Destruction or mutilation of a negotiable instrument is considered cancellation only if it is done with the intention of eliminating an obligation on the instrument.

Thus, if destruction occurs by accident, the instrument is not discharged, and the original terms can be established. The holder of a note may also discharge the obligation by surrendering the note to the person to be discharged, provided that the holder *intended* to eliminate the obligation.

ANSWERING THE LEGAL PROBLEM

In the legal problem set out at the beginning of this chapter, Marcia Morrison gives a $500 note to Reinhold Smith to pay for goods. Smith delivers defective goods, and Morrison refuses to pay the note. In the meantime, Smith has negotiated the note to Judy Larson, who promised to pay Smith for it in thirty days. Larson learns of Smith's breach and Morrison's refusal to pay the $500 note. Smith has left town.

A **Can Larson hold Morrison liable on the note?** That depends on whether Larson is a holder in due course (HDC). Because Larson had not yet given value at the time she learned of Morrison's defense to payment of the note (breach of contract), Larson is an ordinary holder, not an HDC. Thus, Morrison's defense is valid against Larson. If Larson had paid Smith for the note at the time of transfer, she would be an HDC and could hold Morrison liable on the note.

TERMS AND CONCEPTS FOR REVIEW

acceptor 322	holder in due course (HDC) 319	presentment warranty 326
dishonor 321	imposter 324	transfer warranty 325
fictitious payee 324	personal defense 327	universal defense 326

CHAPTER SUMMARY—TRANSFERABILITY AND LIABILITY

LEARNING OUTCOME	
1	**List the requirements for holder-in-due-course status.** To be a holder in due course, a holder must take an instrument (1) *for value,* (2) *in good faith,* and (3) *without notice.*
2	**Outline the liability of parties who sign negotiable instruments.** Every party (except a qualified indorser) who signs a negotiable instrument is either primarily or secondarily liable for payment of the instrument when it comes due. Primary liability requires payment on a negotiable instrument according to its terms. Secondary liability requires payment on an instrument only if presentment is proper and timely, the instrument is dishonored, and a timely notice of dishonor is received. Makers and acceptors are primarily liable (an *acceptor* is a drawee who promises in writing to pay an instrument when it is presented for payment at a later time). Drawers and indorsers are secondarily liable.
3	**Identify transfer warranties, which extend to both signers and nonsigners of negotiable instruments.** Any person who transfers an instrument for consideration makes certain warranties to subsequent transferees and holders. There are five transfer warranties: (1) The transferor is entitled to enforce the instrument, (2) all signatures are authentic and authorized, (3) the instrument has not been altered, (4) the instrument is not subject to a defense or claim of any party that can be asserted against the transferor, and (5) the transferor has no knowledge of any insolvency proceedings against the maker, the acceptor, or the drawer of the instrument.
4	**Point out defenses against the payment of negotiable instruments.** Universal defenses, which are valid against all holders and HDCs, include forgery, fraud in the execution, material alteration, discharge in bankruptcy, and minority (in some states), as well as illegality, mental incapacity, or extreme duress. Personal defenses, which are valid against ordinary holders but not HDCs, include breach of contract or breach of warranty, fraud in the inducement, previous payment, and lack or failure of consideration, as well as illegality, mental incapacity, or ordinary duress if under state law the contract is voidable.

ISSUE SPOTTERS

Check your answers to the *Issue Spotters* against the answers provided in Appendix C at the end of this text.

1. Adam issues a $500 note to Bill due six months from the date issued. One month later, Bill negotiates the note to Carol for $250 in cash and a check for $250. To what extent is Carol a holder in due course of the note? (See *Requirements for HDC Status.*)

2. Roy signs corporate checks for Standard Corporation. Roy makes a check payable to U-All Company, to whom Standard owes no money. Roy signs the check, forges U-All's indorsement, and cashes the check at First State Bank, the drawee. Does Standard have any recourse against the bank for the payment? Explain your answer. (See *Signature Liability.*)

USING BUSINESS LAW

24–1. Universal Defenses. Fox purchased a used car from Emerson for $1,000. Fox paid for the car with a check, written in pencil, payable to Emerson for $1,000. Emerson, through careful erasure and alterations, changed the amount on the check to read $10,000 and negotiated the check to Sanderson. Sanderson took the check for value, in good faith, and without notice of the alteration and thus met the UCC requirements for holder-in-due-course status. Can Fox successfully raise the universal defense of material alteration to avoid payment on the check? Explain. (See *Defenses.*)

24–2. Signature Liability. Marion makes a promissory note payable to the order of Perry. Perry indorses the note by writing "without recourse, Perry" and transfers the note for value to Steven. Steven, in need of cash, negotiates the note to Harriet by indorsing it with the words "Pay to Harriet, Steven." On the due date, Harriet presents the note to Marion for payment, only to learn that Marion has filed for bankruptcy and will have all debts (including the note) discharged in bankruptcy. Discuss fully whether Harriet can hold Marion, Perry, or Steven liable on the note. (See *Signature Liability and Defenses*.)

REAL-WORLD CASE PROBLEMS

24–3. Holder in Due Course. New Houston Gold Exchange, Inc., (HGE) issued a $3,500 check to Shelly McKee to buy a purportedly genuine Rolex watch. The check was *postdated*—that is, assigned a date later than the actual one. McKee indorsed the check and presented it to RR Maloan Investments, Inc., a check-cashing service. Without verifying that the check was valid, RR Maloan cashed it. Meanwhile, HGE issued a stop-payment order on the check based on information that the watch was counterfeit. When RR Maloan presented the check to HGE's bank for payment, the bank refused to honor (cash) it. Is RR Maloan entitled to payment as a holder in due course? Why or why not? [*RR Maloan Investments, Inc. v. New HGE, Inc.*, 428 S.W.3d 353 (Tex.App.—Houston 2014)] (See *Requirements for HDC Status*.)

24–4. Defenses. Thomas Klutz obtained a franchise from Kahala Franchise Corp. to operate a Samurai Sam's restaurant. Under their agreement, Klutz could transfer the franchise only if he obtained Kahala's approval and paid a transfer fee. Without telling Kahala, Klutz sold the restaurant to William Thorbecke. Thorbecke signed a note for the price. When Kahala learned of the deal, the franchisor told Thorbecke to stop using the Samurai Sam's name. Thorbecke stopped paying on the note, and Klutz filed a claim for the unpaid amount. In defense, Thorbecke asserted breach of contract and fraud. Are these defenses effective against Klutz? Explain. [*Kahala Franchise Corp. v. Hit Enterprises, LLC*, 159 Wash.App. 1013 (Div. 2 2011)] (See *Defenses*.)

24–5. Defenses. Damion and Kiya Carmichael took out a loan from Ameriquest Mortgage Co. to refinance their mortgage and signed a note to make monthly payments on the loan. Later, Deutsche Bank National Trust Co. acquired the note. The Carmichaels stopped making payments and filed for bankruptcy. Deutsche asked the court to foreclose on the mortgage. The Carmichaels asserted that they had been fraudulently induced to make the loan and sign the note. Was the bank free of this defense? Explain. [*In re Carmichael*, 443 Bankr. 698 (E.D.Pa. 2011)] (See *Defenses*.)

ETHICAL QUESTIONS

24–6. Taking in Good Faith. Why is good faith required to attain holder-in-due-course status? (See *Requirements for HDC Status*.)

24–7. Fictitious Payees. Should a bank that acts in "bad faith" be precluded from raising the fictitious payee rule as a defense? Explain your answer. (See *Signature Liability*.)

24–8. Defenses. In the wake of Hurricane Katrina, many businesses in New Orleans struggled, contending with lost files and other effects of the storm. During this period, Pyramid Title, LLC, which handled real estate closings in the city, suffered a shortfall in its account when a lender failed to fund a loan. Meanwhile, Mark Peoples, the owner of Pyramid, wrote a check on the account to pay Anthony and Alcibia Jeanmarie for the sale of their property. Peoples expected Encore Credit Corp. to deposit $130,000 in the account to cover the check. Encore failed to provide the funds, and the check was returned for insufficient funds. Should the business and personal circumstances of Pyramid and Peoples affect their liability on the check? Why or why not? [*Jeanmarie v. Peoples*, 34 So.3d 945 (La.App. 4 Cir. 2010)] (See *Defenses*.)

Chapter 24—Work Set

TRUE-FALSE QUESTIONS

_____ 1. Every person who possesses an instrument is a holder.

_____ 2. A holder who takes an instrument for value, in good faith, and without notice is a holder in due course (HDC).

_____ 3. Personal defenses can be raised to avoid payment to an HDC.

_____ 4. For HDC status, good faith means an honest belief that an instrument is not defective.

_____ 5. Knowing that an instrument has been dishonored puts a holder on notice, and he or she cannot become an HDC.

_____ 6. Generally, no one is liable on an instrument unless his or her signature appears on it.

_____ 7. Warranty liability is subject to the same conditions of proper presentment, dishonor, and notice of dishonor as signature liability.

_____ 8. Drawers are secondarily liable.

_____ 9. An unauthorized signature usually binds the person whose name is forged.

MULTIPLE-CHOICE QUESTIONS

_____ 1. Don signs a note that states, "Payable in thirty days." The note is dated March 2, which means it is due April 1. Jo buys the note on April 12. She is

a. an HDC to the extent that she paid for the note.
b. an HDC to the extent that the note is not yet paid.
c. not an HDC.
d. none of the above.

_____ 2. Jack's sister Paula steals one of Jack's checks, makes it payable to herself, signs Jack's name, and cashes it at First National Bank. Jack tells the bank that he will pay it. If Jack later changes his mind, he will

a. be liable on the check.
b. be liable only to the extent of the amount in his checking account.
c. not be liable on the check.
d. be none of the above.

_____ 3. Anna, who cannot read English, signs a promissory note after Ted, her attorney, tells her that it is a credit application. Anna has

a. a defense of fraud maintainable against a holder or an HDC.
b. a defense of fraud maintainable against a holder only.
c. a defense against payment on the note under the imposter rule.
d. no defense against payment on the note.

_____ 4. Ben contracts with Amy to fix her roof. Amy writes Ben a check, but Ben never makes the repairs. Ben negotiates the check to Carl, who knows Ben breached the contract, but Carl cashes the check anyway. Carl cannot attain HDC status in regard to

a. any defense Amy might have against payment.
b. any personal defense Amy might have against payment.
c. only Ben's breach, which is Amy's personal defense against payment.
d. none of the above.

5. Able Company issues a draft for $1,000 on July 1, payable to the order of Baker Corporation. The draft is drawn on First National Bank. Before the bank accepts the draft, who has primary liability for payment?

   a. Able Company.
   b. Baker Corporation.
   c. First National Bank.
   d. No one.

6. Bill issues a check for $4,000, dated June 1, to Ed. The check is drawn on First National Bank. Ed indorses the check and transfers it to Jane. Which of the following will trigger the liability of Bill and Ed on the check, based on their signatures?

   a. Presentment only.
   b. Dishonor only.
   c. Both presentment and dishonor.
   d. Neither presentment nor dishonor.

7. Standard Company issues a draft for $500 on May 1, payable to the order of Ace Credit Corporation. The draft is drawn on First State Bank. If the bank does not accept the draft, who is liable for payment?

   a. Standard Company.
   b. Ace Credit Corporation.
   c. First State Bank.
   d. No one.

8. United Business Corporation authorizes Vic to use company checks to buy office supplies. Vic writes a check to Wholesale Supplies, Inc., for $100 over the price of a purchase, for which the seller returns cash. When Wholesale presents the check for payment, it may recover

   a. nothing.
   b. the amount stated in the check.
   c. the amount of the overpayment only.
   d. the price of the supplies only.

 ANSWERING MORE LEGAL PROBLEMS

1. Skye asked Jim to buy a textbook for her at the County Community College campus bookstore. Skye wrote a check payable to the bookstore and left the amount blank for Jim to fill in the price of the book. The cost of the book was $100. Jim filled in the check for $200 before he got to the bookstore. The clerk at the bookstore took the check for $200 and gave Jim the book, plus $100 in cash.

   Was the bookstore a holder in due course (HDC) of Skye's check? Yes. One of the requirements for HDC status is a lack of _____ that an instrument is defective. A party will not attain this status if he or she knows, or has reason to know, that an incomplete instrument was later completed in an unauthorized manner. _____ of a defective instrument is given when a holder has reason to know that a defect exists, given all of the facts known at the time. Here, the bookstore did not have _____ that Skye's check was incomplete when it was issued. The bookstore saw only a properly completed instrument.

2. Eva bought a GMC Sierra 1500 pickup. To finance the purchase, she signed a note and an agreement to pay the note with Ranch & Farm Credit Union. After she had made half of the sixty payments on the loan, she received the agreement and the note with "Paid" stamped on the face of each document. The documents had been returned due to a clerical error in Ranch & Farm's office. The lender had not intended to discharge the note. Eva stopped making payments. Ranch & Farm filed a suit to collect.

   Was Ranch & Farm entitled to the unpaid amount of the note? Yes. The holder of a note can discharge the obligation by surrendering the note to the person to be discharged, if the holder _____ to eliminate the obligation. In this problem, Ranch & Farm delivered the agreement and the note stamped "Paid" to Eva. But the lender did not _____ to discharge the obligation. The documents were returned due to a clerical error. The surrender thus did not constitute a valid discharge of the note.

CHECKS AND BANKING IN THE DIGITAL AGE

25

FACING A LEGAL PROBLEM

O'Banion was the owner and operator of Superior Construction. When Superior ran into financial problems, O'Banion arranged with Merchants Bank to honor overdrafts on the corporate account. O'Banion continued to write checks. When the account became overdrawn, however, the bank refused to pay the checks. O'Banion developed a bad credit reputation, and Superior eventually went out of business.

Q Can O'Banion hold the bank liable for failing to pay the checks?

LEARNING OUTCOMES

The four Learning Outcomes below are designed to help improve your understanding of the chapter. After reading this chapter, you should be able to:

❶ Identify a bank's duty to honor checks.

❷ State the rules regarding liability arising from forged drawers' signatures.

❸ Outline a bank's duty to accept deposits.

❹ Define an electronic fund transfer (EFT), and name four types of EFT systems.

Checks serve as substitutes for cash and are the most common type of negotiable instruments regulated by the Uniform Commercial Code (UCC). Today, however, students tend to use debit cards and smartphones, rather than checks, for many of their retail transactions. In fact, new mobile payment services—such as Apple Pay, Google Wallet, and Softcard—are increasingly being used to pay for goods and services at both retail and online checkouts. (Also, Apply Pay and its competitors are ultimately based on debit and credit cards.) Because these mobile banking services depend on retailers and banks for their success, they have limited availability and are not yet part of the traditional banking system. Despite these new options for making payments, commercial checks remain an integral part of the American economic system and worthy of study.

This chapter identifies the legal characteristics of checks and the legal duties and liabilities that arise when a check is issued. Then it considers the check deposit-and-collection process—that is, the procedure by which checks move through banking channels, causing the underlying cash dollars to be shifted from one bank account to another.

25–1 CHECKS

A **check** is a special type of draft that is drawn on a bank, ordering the bank to pay a fixed amount of money on demand. Recall that a person who writes a check is called the *drawer*. The person to whom the check is payable is the *payee*. The bank on which the check is drawn is the *drawee*. **EXAMPLE 25.1** When Anita writes a check from her checking account to pay her college tuition, she is the drawer, her bank is the drawee, and her college is the payee. ◄

The following is a list of some special types of checks:

- *Cashier's check*—When a bank draws a check on itself, the check is called a cashier's check. It is a negotiable instrument at the moment it is issued. In effect, with a cashier's check, the bank assumes the responsibility for paying the check, thus making it more readily acceptable as a substitute for cash.

check
A special type of draft that is drawn on a bank, ordering the bank to pay a fixed amount of money on demand.

• *Certified check*—A certified check is a check that has been accepted in writing by the bank on which it is drawn. When a drawee certifies (accepts) a check, it immediately charges the drawer's account with the amount of the check and transfers those funds to its own certified checking account.

The drawer is usually a depositor in the bank on which the check is drawn. In other words, the check is based on the relationship between the bank and the drawer-customer.

25–2 THE BANK-CUSTOMER RELATIONSHIP

The bank-customer relationship begins when the customer opens a checking account and deposits funds that the bank will use to pay checks written by the customer. Essentially, three types of relationships are established:

1. A *creditor-debtor relationship* is created when, for example, a customer makes cash deposits into a checking account. When a customer makes a deposit, the customer becomes a creditor, and the bank a debtor, for the amount deposited.

2. An *agency relationship* arises between the customer and the bank when the customer writes a check. In an agency relationship, one party (an agent) agrees to represent or act for the other party (a principal). In effect, the customer orders the bank to pay the amount on the check. The bank becomes the customer's (principal's) agent and is obligated to honor the customer's request.

3. Finally, certain *contractual rights and duties* arise. The contractual rights and duties of the bank and the customer depend on the nature of the transaction. These rights and duties are discussed in detail in the following pages.

Real-World Case Example

Royal Arcanum Hospital Association of Kings County, Inc., required that its corporate checks be signed by two of three officers—Frank Vassallo, Joseph Rugilio, and William Herrnkind. The three officers were also named as signatories on the firm's account with Capital One Bank, but the terms of the account did not include the two-signature requirement. After Vassallo and Rugilio died, Herrnkind went to Capital One and opened a new $200,000 checking account in Royal Arcanum's name. The account's terms expressly permitted checks with only one signature. Over the next four years, a series of transactions emptied the accounts. Royal Arcanum filed a suit in a New York state court against Capital One to recover the funds. The court dismissed the complaint. Royal Arcanum appealed.

Was Capital One liable for the withdrawals from Royal Arcanum's account? No. In a 2014 case, *Royal Arcanum Hospital Association of Kings County, Inc. v. Herrnkind*, a state intermediate appellate court affirmed the lower court's ruling. The contractual relationship between a bank and its customer includes the understanding that the bank will pay out the customer's funds only as instructed. Royal Arcanum required two signatures on its corporate checks, but the terms of the accounts with Capital Bank did not.

25–3 HONORING CHECKS

When a bank provides checking services, it agrees to honor the checks written by its customers with the usual stipulation that there be sufficient funds available in the account to pay each check. When a drawee-bank *wrongfully* fails to honor a check, it is liable to its customer for damages resulting from its refusal to pay. When the bank properly dishonors a check for insufficient funds, it has no liability to the customer.

The customer's agreement with the bank includes a general obligation to keep sufficient funds on deposit to cover all checks written. The customer is liable to the payee or to the holder of a check in a civil suit if a check is not honored. If intent to defraud can be proved, the customer can also be subject to criminal prosecution for writing a bad check.

25–3a Overdrafts

When the bank receives an item properly payable from its customer's checking account, but there are insufficient funds in the account to cover the amount of the check, the bank can do one of two things. It can dishonor the item, or it can pay the item and charge the customer's account, creating an **overdraft.**

To hold the customer liable for the overdraft, the customer must have authorized the payment and the payment must not violate any bank-customer agreement. The bank can subtract the difference from the customer's next deposit. If there is a joint account, however, the bank cannot hold any joint-account customer liable for payment of an overdraft unless the customer has signed the check or has benefited from the proceeds of the item.

overdraft
A check written on a checking account in which there are insufficient funds to cover the check.

25–3b Stale Checks

The bank's responsibility to honor its customers' checks is not absolute. A bank is not obliged to pay a check presented for payment more than six months after its date. Commercial banking practice regards a check outstanding for longer than six months as a **stale check.** A bank has the option of paying or not paying on such a check without liability. The usual banking practice is to consult the customer, who can then ask the bank not to pay the check. If a bank pays in good faith without consulting the customer, it has the right to charge the customer's account for the amount.

stale check
A check that is presented for payment more than six months after its date.

25–3c Death or Incompetence of a Customer

Neither the death nor the mental incompetence of a customer revokes the bank's authority to pay an item until the bank knows of the situation and has had reasonable time to act on the notice. Even when a bank knows of the death of a customer, for ten days after the date of death, it can pay or certify checks drawn on or before the date of death—unless a person claiming an interest in that account, such as an heir or an executor of the estate, orders the bank to stop payment. Without this provision, banks would constantly be required to verify the continued life and competence of their drawers.

25–3d Stop-Payment Orders

A **stop-payment order** is an order by a customer to his or her bank not to pay or certify a certain check. Only a customer or a person authorized to draw on the account can order the bank to not pay the check when it is presented for payment. A customer has no right to stop payment on a check that has been certified (accepted) by a bank, however.

stop-payment order
An order by the drawer of a draft or check directing the drawer's bank not to pay the check.

Reasonable Time and Manner The customer must issue the stop-payment order within a reasonable time and in a reasonable manner to permit the bank to act on it.

Although a stop-payment order can be given orally, usually by phone, it is binding on the bank for only fourteen calendar days unless confirmed in writing. A written stop-payment order is effective for six months, at which time it must be renewed. Most banks also allow stop-payment orders to be submitted electronically via the bank's Web site.

Liability for Wrongful Payment If the bank pays the check in spite of a stop-payment order, the bank will be obligated to recredit the customer's account. In addition, if the bank's payment over a stop-payment order causes subsequent checks written on the drawer's account to "bounce," the bank will be liable for the resultant costs that the drawer incurs.

25–3e Checks with Forged Signatures

LEARNING OUTCOME 2

State the rules regarding liability arising from forged drawers' signatures.

When a bank pays a check on which the drawer's signature is forged, generally the bank suffers the loss. A bank may be able to recover at least some of the amount of the loss, however, from a customer whose negligence contributed to the forgery, from the forger of the check, or from a holder who cashes the check.

A forged signature on a check has no legal effect as the signature of a drawer. For this reason, banks require signature cards from each customer who opens a checking account. The bank is responsible for determining whether the signature on a customer's check is genuine. The general rule is that the bank must recredit the customer's account when it pays on a forged signature.

Customer Negligence When the customer's negligence substantially contributes to the forgery, the bank normally will not be obliged to recredit the customer's account for the amount of the check. The customer's liability may be reduced, however, by the amount of the loss caused by the bank's negligence—for instance, if the bank knew the customer's checks had been stolen.

HIGHLIGHTING THE POINT

Compu-Net, Inc., uses a check-writing machine to write its payroll and business checks. A Compu-Net employee—Ryan—uses the machine to write himself a check for $10,000. Compu-Net's bank subsequently honors it.

Under what circumstances can the bank refuse to recredit $10,000 to Compu-Net's account for incorrectly paying on a forged check? If the bank can show that Compu-Net failed to take reasonable care in controlling access to the check-writing equipment, Compu-Net cannot legally require the bank to recredit its account for the amount of the forged check.

Bank Statements Today, banks either mail customers monthly statements detailing activity in their checking accounts, or they make these statements available online. Either way, most banks simply provide the customer with information (such as the check number, amount, and date of payment) on the statement to allow them to reasonably identify the checks that the bank has paid. If the bank retains the canceled checks, it must keep the checks—or legible copies of the checks—for seven years. The customer can obtain a copy of a canceled check during this period of time.

Timely Examination Required A customer must examine monthly bank statements and canceled checks promptly and with reasonable care and report any forged signatures promptly. The failure to examine and report—or any carelessness by the customer that results in a loss to the bank—makes the customer liable for the loss.

Even if the customer can prove that reasonable care was taken against forgeries, discovery of such forgeries and notice to the bank must take place within one year from the date that the statement was made available for inspection. Otherwise, the customer loses the right to have the bank recredit his or her account.

A Series of Forgeries Sometimes, the same wrongdoer forges a customer's signature on a series of checks. In that situation, the customer, to recover for all the forged items, must discover and report the first forged check to the bank within thirty calendar days of the receipt of the bank statement. Failure to notify the bank within this period of time discharges the bank's liability for all similar forged checks that it pays prior to notification.

Bank Negligence If the customer can prove that the bank was also negligent, then the bank will also be liable. In this situation, the loss will be allocated between the bank and the customer on the basis of comparative negligence. In other words, even though a customer may have been negligent, the bank may have to recredit the customer's account for a portion of the loss if the bank also failed to exercise ordinary care. (*Ordinary care* means the observance of reasonable banking standards as practiced in the bank's geographical area.)

25–3f Checks Bearing Forged Indorsements

A bank that pays a customer's check bearing a forged indorsement must recredit the customer's account or be liable to the customer-drawer for breach of contract. **EXAMPLE 25.2** Simon issues a $500 check "to the order of Rosario." Charlie steals the check, forges Rosario's indorsement, and cashes the check. When the check reaches Simon's bank, the bank pays it and debits Simon's account. The bank must recredit the $500 to Simon's account because it failed to carry out Simon's order to pay "to the order of Rosario." Simon's bank can in turn recover from the bank that cashed the check when Charlie presented it. ◄

Eventually, the loss usually falls on the first party to take the instrument bearing the forged indorsement because a forged indorsement does not transfer title. Thus, no one who takes an instrument with a forged indorsement can become a holder.

The customer, in any event, has a duty to report forged indorsements promptly. Failure to report forged indorsements within a three-year period after the forged items have been made available to the customer relieves the bank of liability.

 ## 25–4 ACCEPTING DEPOSITS

Another fundamental service a bank provides for its checking-account customers is that of accepting deposits of cash and checks. This section focuses on the check after it has been deposited. Most deposited checks involve parties who do business at different banks, but sometimes checks are written between customers of the same bank. Either situation brings into play the bank collection process.

25–4a The Traditional Collection Process

The first bank to receive a check for payment is the **depositary bank.** When a person deposits an Internal Revenue Service (IRS) tax-refund check into a personal checking account at the local bank, that bank is the depositary bank. The bank on which a check is drawn (the drawee bank) is called the **payor bank.** Any bank (except the payor bank) that handles a check during some phase of the collection process is a **collecting bank.** Any bank (except the payor bank or the depositary bank) to which an item is transferred in the course of this collection process is called an **intermediary bank.**

LEARNING OUTCOME 3
Outline a bank's duty to accept deposits.

depositary bank
The first bank to receive a check for payment.

payor bank
The bank on which a check is drawn (the drawee bank).

collecting bank
Any bank handling an item for collection, except the payor bank.

intermediary bank
Any bank to which an item is transferred in the course of collection, except the depositary or payor bank.

During the collection process, any bank can take on one or more of the various roles of depositary, payor, collecting, and intermediary banks. **EXAMPLE 25.3** A buyer in New York writes a check on her New York bank and sends it to a seller in San Francisco. The seller deposits the check in her San Francisco bank account. The seller's bank is both a *depositary bank* and a *collecting bank*. The buyer's bank in New York is the *payor bank*. As the check travels from San Francisco to New York, any collecting bank handling the item in the collection process (other than the ones already acting as depositary bank and payor bank) is also called an *intermediary bank.*◄

Exhibit 25.1 illustrates how banks function in the collection process.

Check Collection between Customers of the Same Bank An item that is payable by the same bank that receives it is called an "on-us" item. In this situation, the bank is both the depositary bank and the payor bank. Usually, a bank issues a "provisional (temporary) credit" for "on-us" items within the same day. If the bank does not dishonor the check by the opening of the second banking day following its receipt, the check is considered paid.

HIGHLIGHTING THE POINT

Both Otterley and Merkowitz have checking accounts at First State Bank. On Monday morning, Merkowitz deposits into his checking account a $300 check from Otterley. That same day, the bank issues Merkowitz a provisional (temporary) credit for $300.

When is Otterley's check considered honored, and when is Merkowitz's provisional credit considered final? When the bank opens on Wednesday, Otterley's check is considered honored, and Merkowitz's provisional credit becomes a final payment.

EXHIBIT 25.1   The Check-Collection Process

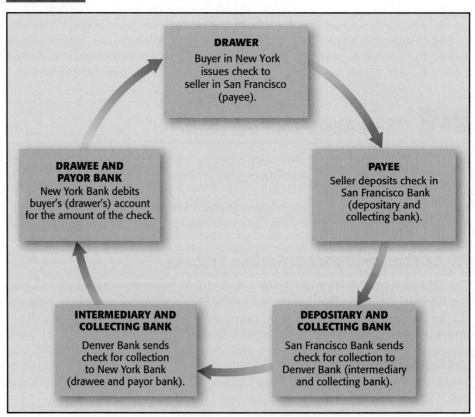

Check Collection between Customers of Different Banks Once a depositary bank receives a check, it must arrange to present it, either directly or through intermediary banks, to the appropriate payor bank. Each bank in the collection chain must pass the check on before midnight of the next banking day following its receipt. For instance, a collecting bank that receives a check on Monday must forward it to the next collection bank before midnight Tuesday.

Unless the payor bank dishonors the check or returns it by midnight on the next banking day following receipt, the payor bank is accountable for the face amount of the check. Deferred posting is permitted, however, so checks received after a certain time can be deferred for posting until the next day. (A check is *posted* when it is entered on the bank's records.). **EXAMPLE 25.4** Northwest Bank, the payor bank, defers the posting of checks received after 2:00 P.M. A check received by Northwest on Monday at 3:00 P.M. would be deferred for posting until Tuesday. Northwest's deadline for passing the check on would be midnight Wednesday. ◄

How the Federal Reserve System Clears Checks The **Federal Reserve System** is a network of twelve government banks located around the United States. Most private banks have accounts, called *reserve accounts,* in a Federal Reserve bank. This system has greatly simplified the clearing of checks—that is, the method by which checks deposited in one bank are transferred to the banks on which they were written. **EXAMPLE 25.5** Pamela Moy of Philadelphia writes a check to Jeanne Sutton in San Francisco. When Jeanne receives the check in the mail, she deposits it in her bank. Her bank then deposits the check in the Federal Reserve Bank of San Francisco, which transfers it to the Federal Reserve Bank of Philadelphia. That Federal Reserve bank then sends the check to Moy's bank, which deducts the amount of the check from Moy's account. ◄ Exhibit 25.2, which follows, illustrates this process.

Electronic Presentment In the past, most checks were processed manually—the employees of each bank in the collection chain would physically handle every check that passed through the bank for collection or payment. Today, most checks are processed electronically.

With electronic check presentment, items are encoded with information (such as the amount of the check) that is read and processed by other banks' computers. In some situations, a check may be retained at its place of deposit and only its image or description presented for payment.

A bank that encodes information on an item after the item has been issued warrants to any subsequent bank or payor that the encoded information is correct. Similarly, a bank that retains an item and presents an image or description of the item for payment warrants that the image or description is accurate.

25–4b Check Clearing and the Check 21 Act

In the traditional collection process, paper checks had to be physically transported before they could be cleared. To streamline this costly and time-consuming process and to improve the overall efficiency of the nation's payment system, Congress passed the Check Clearing in the 21st Century Act (Check 21). Check 21 is a federal law and applies to all financial institutions, other businesses, and individuals in the United States.

Before the implementation of Check 21, banks had to present the original paper check for payment in the absence of an agreement for presentment in some other form. Although the UCC authorizes banks to use other means of presentment, such as electronic presentment, a broad-based system of electronic presentment failed to develop because it required agreements among individual banks.

Check 21 changed the situation by creating a new negotiable instrument called a *substitute check.* Although the act did not require banks to change their current check-collection practices, its creation of substitute checks has certainly facilitated the use of electronic check processing.

Federal Reserve System
The central banking system of the United States, made up of twelve regional banks and headed by a board of governors.

EXHIBIT 25.2   How a Check Is Cleared

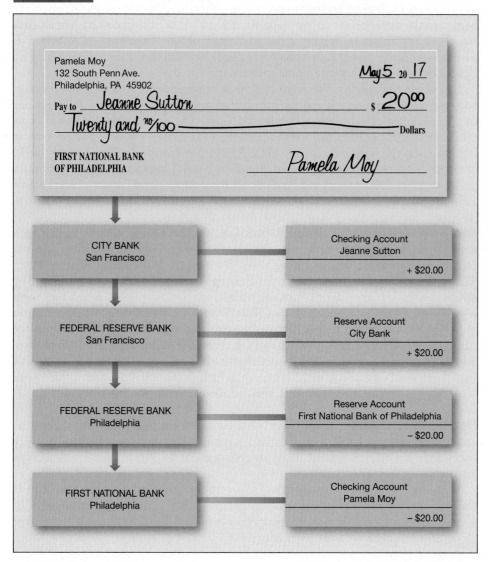

---

substitute check

A negotiable instrument that is a paper reproduction of the front and back of an original check, containing the same information required on checks for automated processing.

What Is a Substitute Check? A **substitute check** is a paper reproduction of the front and back of an original check that contains all of the same information required on checks for automated processing. Banks create a substitute check from a digital image of an original check. Every substitute check must include the following statement somewhere on it: "This a legal copy of your check. You can use it in the same way you would use the original check." See Exhibit 25.3 for an example of a substitute check.

In essence, those financial institutions that exchange digital images of checks do not have to send the original paper checks. They can simply transmit the information electronically and replace the original checks with the substitute checks. Banks that do not exchange checks electronically are required to accept substitute checks in the same way that they accept original checks.

Faster Access to Funds The Expedited Funds Availability Act requires that the Federal Reserve Board revise the availability schedule for funds from deposited checks to correspond to reductions in check-processing time. Therefore, as the speed of check processing increases under Check 21, the Federal Reserve Board will reduce the maximum time that a bank can hold funds from deposited checks before making them available to the depositor. Thus, account holders will have faster access to their deposited funds.

EXHIBIT 25.3 An Example of a Substitute Check

25–5 ELECTRONIC FUND TRANSFERS

An **electronic fund transfer (EFT)** is a transfer of funds through the use of an electronic terminal, a phone, a computer, or magnetic tape. The law governing EFTs depends on the type of transfer involved. Consumer fund transfers are governed by the Electronic Fund Transfer Act (EFTA). Commercial fund transfers are governed by Article 4A of the UCC.

Transferring funds electronically offers numerous benefits, but it also poses difficulties on occasion. For example, the possibilities for tampering with private banking information have increased.

electronic fund transfer (EFT)
A transfer of funds through the use of an electronic terminal, a phone, a computer, or magnetic tape.

25–5a Types of EFT Systems

Most banks today offer EFT services to their customers. The most common types of EFT systems include:

1. *Automated teller machines* (ATMs)—A customer inserts an ATM or debit card issued by the bank and keys in a personal identification number to access her or his accounts and conduct banking transactions.

2. *Point-of-sale systems*—Online terminals allow consumers to transfer funds to merchants to pay for purchases using a debit card.

3. *Direct deposits and withdrawals*—Customers can authorize the bank to allow another party—such as the government or an employer—to make direct deposits into their accounts. Similarly, customers can request the bank to make automatic payments to a third party at regular, recurrent intervals from the customers' funds.

4. *Online payment systems*—Many financial institutions permit their customers to access the institution's computer system via the Internet and direct a transfer of funds between accounts or pay a particular bill.

LEARNING OUTCOME 4

Define an electronic fund transfer (EFT), and name four types of EFT systems.

25–5b Consumer Fund Transfers

The Electronic Fund Transfer Act (EFTA) provides a basic framework for the rights, liabilities, and responsibilities of users of EFT systems. The EFTA governs financial institutions that offer electronic fund transfers involving consumer accounts.

Disclosure Requirements The EFTA is essentially a disclosure law benefiting consumers. The act requires financial institutions to inform consumers of their rights and responsibilities, including those listed below, with respect to EFT systems.

1. The bank must provide a monthly statement for every month in which there is an electronic transfer of funds.

2. If a customer's debit card is lost or stolen and used without his or her permission, the customer is required to pay no more than $50. The customer, however, must notify the bank of the loss or theft within two days of learning about it. Otherwise, the liability increases to $500. The customer may be liable for more than $500 if he or she does not report the unauthorized use within sixty days after it appears on the customer's statement.

3. The customer must discover any error on the monthly statement within sixty days and must notify the bank. The bank then has ten days to investigate and must report its conclusions to the customer in writing.

4. The bank must furnish receipts for transactions made through computer terminals.

Unauthorized Electronic Fund Transfers Because of the vulnerability of EFT systems to fraudulent activities, the EFTA clearly defines what constitutes an unauthorized transfer. Under the act, a transfer is unauthorized if the following conditions are met:

1. It is initiated by a person (other than the consumer) who has no actual authority to initiate the transfer.

2. The consumer receives no benefit from it.

3. The consumer did not furnish the person "with the card, code, or other means of access" to her or his account.

Unauthorized access to an EFT system constitutes a federal felony. Those convicted may be fined up to $10,000 and sentenced to as long as ten years in prison.

Violations and Damages Banks must strictly comply with the terms of the EFTA and are liable for any failure to adhere to its provisions. For a bank's violation of the EFTA, a consumer may recover both actual damages (including attorneys' fees and costs) and punitive damages. Even when a customer has sustained no actual damage, the bank may be liable for legal costs and punitive damages if it fails to follow the proper procedures outlined by the EFTA.

25–5c Commercial Transfers

Funds are also transferred electronically "by wire" between commercial parties. Commercial wire transfers are governed by Article 4A of the UCC.

EXAMPLE 25.6 Jellux, Inc., owes $5 million to Perot Corporation. Instead of sending Perot a check or some other instrument that would enable Perot to obtain payment, Jellux instructs its bank, East Bank, to credit $5 million to Perot's account in West Bank. East Bank debits Jellux's East Bank account and wires $5 million to Perot's West Bank account. In more complex transactions, additional banks would be involved. ◄

25–6 E-Money and Online Banking

digital cash (e-money)
Funds stored on microchips and other computer devices.

Electronic payments (e-payments) have the potential to replace *physical* cash—coins and paper currency—with *virtual* cash in the form of electronic impulses. This is the unique promise of **digital cash,** or **e-money,** which consists of funds stored on microchips and other computer devices. Online banking has also become common in today's world.

25–6a Stored-Value Cards and Smart Cards

The simplest kind of e-money system uses **stored-value cards.** These are plastic cards embossed with magnetic strips containing magnetically encoded data. Using a stored-value card, a person buys goods and services offered by the issuer. For instance, mass transit systems in urban areas typically sell stored-value cards that allow users to pay subway, train, or bus fares. Retail gift cards and prepaid credit, debit, and phone cards are further examples of stored-value cards.

Smart cards are plastic cards containing minute computer microchips that can hold much more information than magnetic strips. A smart card carries and processes security programming. This gives smart cards an advantage over stored-value cards. The microprocessors on smart cards can also authenticate the validity of transactions. Retailers can program electronic cash registers to confirm the authenticity of a smart card by examining a unique digital signature stored on its microchip. Common uses for smart cards are as credit or ATM cards, fuel cards, or public transportation or phone payment cards.

stored-value card
A card bearing a magnetic strip that holds magnetically encoded data, providing access to stored funds.

smart card
A card containing a microprocessor used for financial transactions and identification.

25–6b Online Banking

Today, online banking is very common. In general, online banking customers are able to do the following services via their computers or mobile devices:

1. Make online payments to various creditors.
2. Transfer funds among their accounts; for instance, transferring funds from a checking account to a savings account or vice versa.
3. Apply for loans and credit cards.

Withdrawing and depositing funds are two important banking activities not commonly available online. An exception to this rule, however, would be smart cards that are used to transfer funds on the Internet, essentially turning a personal computer into an ATM machine. Another exception is a banking app that allows customers to make check deposits via their smartphones or other mobile devices. **EXAMPLE 25.7** Bobbi, a Chase Bank customer, downloads its free mobile app called DepositQuick. This app allows Bobbi to take a photo of both sides of her endorsed check with her Android's camera, follow the on-screen instructions, and submit her check for deposit into her selected account. ◄

ANSWERING THE LEGAL PROBLEM

In the legal problem set out at the beginning of this chapter, when Superior Construction ran into financial difficulties, Merchants Bank agreed to honor Superior's overdrafts. O'Banion, Superior's owner and operator, continued to write checks. When the account became overdrawn, the bank refused to pay the checks. O'Banion developed a bad credit reputation, and Superior eventually went out of business.

A **Can O'Banion hold the bank liable for failing to pay the checks?** Yes. When a bank agrees with a customer to pay overdrafts, the bank's refusal to honor checks on an overdrawn account is a wrongful dishonor.

LINKING BUSINESS LAW to Your Career

BANKING RISKS

You may choose a career that involves running a small business, or you might be involved in the world of finance. Regardless, many careers will undoubtedly lead to transactions with banks. Your business may borrow from a bank, deposit funds with a bank, draw checks on a bank account, conduct electronic fund transfers through a bank, or engage in other financial exchanges with banks.

You should be aware that the federal government insures bank deposits. This can often have unintended consequences on bank managers' decisions.

Deposit Insurance

The Federal Deposit Insurance Corporation (FDIC) and the Federal Savings and Loan Insurance Corporation (FSLIC) were created in the 1930s to insure bank deposits. In 1971, the National Credit Union Shares Insurance Fund was added to insure credit union deposits. Although the names and form of some of these organizations have changed over the years, the principle remains the same: to insure all accounts in banks, savings and loan associations, and credit unions against losses up to a specified limit.

Unintended Consequences

Federal insurance for bank deposits may seem like a good idea, but there are problems associated with it. Depositors have little incentive to investigate the financial condition or lending activities of the depository institutions in which they have checking and savings accounts. As a result, instead of being owned and operated by individuals who are prudent, many banks are managed by those with a high tolerance for taking risks with other people's money.

Bank managers must weigh the trade-off between risk and return when deciding which loan applicants should receive funds. The riskier the loan, the higher the interest rate a lending institution will charge a borrower. Thus, managers of depository institutions have an incentive to make risky loans. In the short run, the banks make higher profits and the managers receive higher salaries and bonuses.

If some of these risky loans are not repaid, what is the likely outcome? The banks' losses are limited because the federal government—you, the taxpayer—will cover any shortfall between the banks' assets and their liabilities. Consequently, federal deposit insurance means that banks get to enjoy all of the profits of risk taking without bearing all of the consequences.

TERMS AND CONCEPTS FOR REVIEW

check 333

collecting bank 337

depositary bank 337

digital cash (e-money) 342

electronic fund transfer (EFT) 341

Federal Reserve System 339

intermediary bank 337

overdraft 335

payor bank 337

smart card 343

stale check 335

stop-payment order 335

stored-value card 343

substitute check 340

CHAPTER SUMMARY—CHECKS AND BANKING IN THE DIGITAL AGE

LEARNING OUTCOME	
1	**Identify a bank's duty to honor checks.** A bank has a duty to honor its customers' checks if the customers have sufficient funds on deposit to cover the checks. The bank is liable to its customers for actual damages proved to be due to wrongful dishonor. The bank has a right to charge a customer's account for any item properly payable, even if the charge results in an overdraft. The bank is not obligated to pay a stale check—one presented more than six months after its date. So long as the bank does not know of the death or incompetence of a customer, the bank can pay an item without liability. Even with notice, the bank can pay for ten days after the customer's death. The bank is liable for wrongful payment over a timely stop-payment order to the extent that the customer suffers a loss, with some exceptions.

2	**State the rules regarding liability arising from forged drawers' signatures or alterations.** A customer has a duty to examine account statements with reasonable care on receipt and to notify the bank promptly of any forged signatures or alterations. On a series of forged signatures or alterations by the same wrongdoer, examination and report must be made within thirty calendar days of receipt of the first statement containing a forged or altered item. The customer's failure to comply with these rules releases the bank from liability unless the bank failed to exercise reasonable care, in which case liability may be allocated according to a comparative negligence standard. Regardless of care or lack of care, the customer is barred from holding the bank liable after one year for forged customer signatures or alterations and after three years for forged indorsements.
3	**Outline a bank's duty to accept deposits.** A bank has a duty to accept deposits made by its customers into their accounts. A bank also has a duty to collect payment on any checks deposited by its customers. Funds represented by checks deposited must be made available to customers according to the following rules: (1) *Check collection between customers of the same bank*—A check payable by the same bank that receives it is an "on-us" item, and if the bank does not dishonor the check by the opening of the second banking day following its receipt, the check is considered paid. (2) *Check collection between customers of different banks*—Each bank in the collection process must pass the check on to the next appropriate bank before midnight of the next banking day following its receipt. The Federal Reserve System has greatly simplified the clearing of checks. (3) *Electronic check presentment*—When checks are presented electronically, items are encoded with information (such as the amount of the check) that is read and processed by other banks' computers. In some situations, a check may be retained at its place of deposit, with only its image or information describing it presented for payment.
4	**Define an electronic fund transfer (EFT), and name four types of EFT systems.** An EFT is a transfer of funds through the use of an electronic terminal, a phone, a computer, or magnetic type. The four most common types of EFT systems include automated teller machines, point-of-sale systems, direct deposits and withdrawals, and online payment systems.

ISSUE SPOTTERS

Check your answers to the *Issue Spotters* against the answers provided in Appendix C at the end of this text.

1. Lynn draws a check for $900 payable to the order of Jan. Jan indorses the check in blank and transfers it to Owen. Owen presents the check to First National Bank, the drawee bank, for payment. If the bank does not honor the check, is Lynn liable to Owen? Could Lynn also be subject to criminal prosecution? Explain your answers. (See *Honoring Checks*.)

2. Herb steals a check from Kay's checkbook, forges Kay's signature, and transfers the check to Will for value. Unaware that the signature is not Kay's, Will presents the check to First State Bank, the drawee. The bank cashes the check. Kay discovers the forgery and insists that the bank recredit her account. Can the bank refuse to recredit Kay's account? If not, can the bank recover the amount paid to Will? Why or why not? (See *Honoring Checks*.)

USING BUSINESS LAW

25–1. Honoring Checks. On January 5, Brian drafts a check for $3,000 drawn on Southern Marine Bank and payable to his assistant, Shanta. Brian puts last year's date on the check by mistake. On January 7, before Shanta has had a chance to go to the bank, Brian is killed in an automobile accident. Southern Marine Bank is aware of Brian's death.

On January 10, Shanta presents the check to the bank, and the bank honors the check by payment to Shanta. Later, Brian's widow, Joyce, claims that because the bank knew of Brian's death and also because the check was by date over one year old, the bank acted wrongfully when it paid Shanta. Joyce, as executor of Brian's estate and sole heir by his will, demands that Southern Marine Bank recredit Brian's estate for the check paid to Shanta. Discuss fully Southern Marine's liability in light of Joyce's demand. (See *Honoring Checks.*)

25–2. Forged Checks. Roy Supply, Inc., and R.M.R. Drywall, Inc., had checking accounts at Wells Fargo Bank. Both accounts required all checks to carry two signatures—that of Edward Roy and that of Twila June Moore, both of whom were executive officers of both companies. Between January 2006 and March 2008, the bank honored hundreds of checks on which Roy's signature was forged by Moore. On January 31, 2009, Roy and the two corporations notified the bank of the forgeries and then filed a suit in a California state court against the bank, alleging negligence. Who is liable for the amounts of the forged checks? Why? (See *Honoring Checks.*)

REAL-WORLD CASE PROBLEMS

25–3. Consumer Fund Transfers. Stephen Patterson held an account with Suntrust Bank in Alcoa, Tennessee. Juanita Wehrman—with whom Patterson was briefly involved in a romantic relationship—stole his debit card and used it for sixteen months (well beyond the length of their relationship) to make unauthorized purchases in excess of $30,000. When Patterson learned what was happening, he closed his account. The bank refused to reimburse him more than $677.46—the amount of unauthorized transactions that occurred within sixty days of the transmittal of the bank statement that revealed the first unauthorized transaction. Is the bank's refusal justifiable? Explain. [*Patterson v. Suntrust Bank*, __ S.W.3d __, 2013 WL 139315 (Tenn.App. 2013)] (See *Electronic Fund Transfers.*)

25–4. Honoring Checks. Adley Abdulwahab (Wahab) opened an account on behalf of W Financial Group, LLC, with Wells Fargo Bank. Wahab was one of three authorized signers on the account. Five months later, Wahab withdrew $1,701,250 from W Financial's account to buy a cashier's check payable to Lubna Lateef. Wahab visited a different Wells Fargo branch and deposited the check into the account of CA Houston Investment Center, LLC. Wahab was the only authorized signer on this account. Lateef never received or indorsed the check. W Financial filed a suit to recover the amount. Applying the rules for payment on a forged indorsement, who is liable? [*Jones v. Wells Fargo Bank*, 666 F.3d 955 (5th Cir. 2012)] (See *Honoring Checks.*)

25–5. Forged Drawers' Signatures. Debbie Brooks and Martha Tingstrom lived together. Tingstrom handled their finances. For five years, Brooks did not look at any statements concerning her accounts. When she finally reviewed the statements, she discovered that Tingstrom had taken $85,500 through Brooks's checking account with Transamerica Financial Advisors. Tingstrom had forged Brooks's name on six checks paid between one and two years earlier. Another year passed before Brooks filed a suit against Transamerica. Who is most likely to suffer the loss for the checks paid with Brooks's forged signature? Why? [*Brooks v. Transamerica Financial Advisors*, 57 So.3d 1153 (La.App. 2 Cir. 2011)] (See *Honoring Checks.*)

ETHICAL QUESTIONS

25–6. Forged Signatures and Unauthorized Indorsements. Why should a customer have to report a forged or unauthorized signature on a paid check within a certain time to recover the amount of the payment? (See *Honoring Checks.*)

25–7. Honoring Checks. New York City resident Esther Braunstein worked as an usher at the Lincoln Center, held an administrative position with Citibank, was a school crossing guard, and assisted disabled persons and others as a volunteer at a city hospital. Before her death, she drew a $5,000 check payable to each of her daughters, Sandra Braunstein and Carol Russo. The checks were drawn on a joint account held in the names of Esther and Sandra. Carol did not cash her check until five months after Esther's death. Sandra attempted to recover the funds paid to Carol. Was this unethical? Could Sandra have had a positive motive to want to retrieve Esther's $5,000 gift to Carol? Who is legally entitled to the funds? Discuss. [*Braunstein v. Russo*, 988 N.Y.S.2d 521 (2014)] (See *Honoring Checks.*)

Chapter 25—Work Set

TRUE-FALSE QUESTIONS

_____ 1. If a bank pays a stale check in good faith without consulting the customer, the bank cannot charge the customer's account.

_____ 2. If a bank receives an item payable from a customer's account in which there are insufficient funds, the bank cannot pay the item.

_____ 3. A bank in the collection chain must normally pass a check on before midnight of the next banking day following receipt.

_____ 4. The rights and duties of a bank and its customers are partly contractual.

_____ 5. All funds deposited in all bank accounts must be available for withdrawal no later than the next business day.

_____ 6. A forged drawer's signature on a check is effective as the signature of the person whose name is signed.

_____ 7. If a bank fails to honor a customer's stop-payment order, it may be liable to the customer for more than the amount of the loss suffered by the drawer because of the wrongful payment.

MULTIPLE-CHOICE QUESTIONS

_____ 1. Jennifer receives a check from Mary for $300. The check is drawn on a local bank. If Jennifer deposits it in her bank, the $300 will be available to her
  a. immediately.
  b. the next business day.
  c. within four days.
  d. within eight days.

_____ 2. Tom is paid with a check drawn on Pete's account at First State Bank. The check has a forged drawer's signature. Tom indorses the check to Eve, who takes it in good faith and for value, and cashes it at the bank. When Pete discovers the forgery, he notifies the bank, which recredits his account. The bank can recover the amount of its loss from Eve
  a. only if she has a bank account at any bank.
  b. only if she has an account at First State Bank.
  c. under any circumstances.
  d. under no circumstances.

_____ 3. Ann buys three $300 television sets from Gail, paying with a check. That night, one of the sets explodes. Ann phones City Bank, the drawee, and orders a stop payment. The next day, Gail presents the check to the bank for payment. If the bank honors the check, it must recredit Ann's account for
  a. $300.
  b. $900.
  c. nothing, because the stop-payment order was oral.
  d. nothing, because Gail did not present the check until the next day.

_____ 4. Colin draws a check for $500 payable to the order of Mary. Mary indorses the check in blank and transfers it to Sam. Sam presents the check to First National Bank, the drawee, for payment. If the bank does not pay the check, the bank is liable to
  a. Sam.
  b. Colin.
  c. Mary.
  d. none of the above.

5. On July 1, Liz steals two blank checks from her employer, Dave's Market. On July 3, Liz forges Dave's signature and cashes the first check. The check is returned with Dave's monthly statement from First National Bank on August 1. Dave does not examine the statement or the checks. On August 24, Liz forges Dave's signature and cashes the second check. This check is returned with Dave's monthly statement on September 1. Dave examines both statements, discovers the forgeries, and insists that the bank recredit the account for both checks. Assuming that the bank was not negligent in paying the checks, the bank must recredit Dave's account for

   a. both checks.
   b. the first check only.
   c. the second check only.
   d. neither of the checks.

6. Delta Company uses its computer system to issue payroll checks. Ed, a Delta employee, uses the system without authorization to issue himself a check for $5,000. City Bank, Delta's bank, cashes the check. The bank need not recredit Delta's account for the entire $5,000

   a. if Delta owed Ed $5,000 in unpaid wages.
   b. if the bank took reasonable care to determine whether the check was good.
   c. if Delta took reasonable care to limit access to its payroll system.
   d. under any of the circumstances.

7. Jay arranges with First National Bank to make automatic monthly payments on his student loan. More than three days before a scheduled payment, Jay can stop the automatic payments by notifying the bank

   a. orally.
   b. in writing.
   c. online.
   d. in any of the above ways.

 ## ANSWERING MORE LEGAL PROBLEMS

1. Anton, an employee of Tango Fabrication, LLC, used stolen software and blank checks to print forged company checks on his home computer. Tango's check-handling process lacked audit controls, so Tango did not discover the forgeries for more than two years. By then, the series of forged checks totaled $446,000. When the scam was discovered, Tango immediately contacted Merchants Bank and requested that it recredit the account on which the checks were drawn.

Did Merchants have to recredit Tango's account? No. When a series of forgeries by the same wrongdoer takes place, the customer, to recover for all of the forged items, must discover and _____ the first forged check to the bank within thirty days of the receipt of the bank statement. Failure to _____ the bank within this period discharges the bank's liability for all similar forged checks that it pays before being _____. Here, Tango's weak monitoring of its account meant that it did not _____ the first forged item to Merchants until at least two years after it appeared on Tango's statement. This was well beyond the thirty-day deadline.

2. On an automated teller machine (ATM) belonging to USA Bank, Sven placed a card-skimming device to pull information from the magnetic strips of users' debit cards. The device then transmitted the stolen data to thieves who used it to gain access to, and empty, the bank accounts of the users, including Megan. Megan learned of the theft the next day and promptly notified USA Bank.

Was Megan entitled to have the bank recredit her account for most of the loss due to the theft? Yes. Under the Electronic Fund Transfer Act, if a customer's debit card is lost or stolen and used without his or her permission, the customer may be required to pay no more than $50. The customer must _____ the bank of the loss or theft within two days of learning about it. Otherwise, the liability increases to $500. The customer may be liable for more than $500 if he or she does not _____ the unauthorized use within sixty days after it appears on the customer's statement. In this situation, Megan promptly _____ USA Bank, so her liability will be no more than $50.

AGENCY AND EMPLOYMENT

UNIT CONTENTS

CHAPTER 26 Agency

CHAPTER 27 Employment, Immigration, and Labor Law

CHAPTER 28 Employment Discrimination

26

AGENCY

LEARNING OUTCOMES

The five Learning Outcomes below are designed to help improve your understanding of the chapter. After reading this chapter, you should be able to:

1 Describe how an agency relationship is created.

2 List the duties of agents and principals.

3 Define the scope of an agent's authority.

4 Identify the parties' liability in agency relationships.

5 Explain how an agency relationship is terminated.

agency
A relationship between two parties in which one party (the agent) agrees to represent or act for the other (the principal).

agent
A person authorized by another to act for or in place of him or her.

principal
A person who, by agreement or otherwise, authorizes an agent to act on his or her behalf in such a way that the acts of the agent become binding on the principal.

FACING A LEGAL PROBLEM

Bruce is hired as a booking agent for an indie rock band, The Crash. As the band's agent, Bruce can negotiate and sign contracts for it to appear at concerts and other venues.

Q Are the contracts that Bruce negotiates and signs binding and thus legally enforceable against The Crash?

One of the most common, important, and pervasive legal relationships is that of **agency.** In an agency relationship between two parties, one of the parties, called the **agent,** agrees to represent or act for the other, called the **principal.** The principal has the right to control the agent's conduct in matters entrusted to the agent.

By using agents, a principal can conduct multiple business operations simultaneously in various locations. A familiar example of an agent is a corporate officer who serves in a representative capacity for the owners of a corporation. In this capacity, the officer has the authority to bind the principal (the corporation) to a contract.

26–1 AGENCY RELATIONSHIPS

In a principal-agent relationship, the parties agree that the agent will act *on behalf and instead of* the principal in negotiating and transacting business with third persons. An agent is empowered to (1) perform legal acts that are binding on the principal and (2) bind the principal in a contract with a third person.

Agency relationships commonly exist between employers and employees. Agency relationships also may sometimes exist between employers and independent contractors who are hired to perform special tasks or services.

26–1a Employer-Employee Relationships

An employee is one whose physical conduct is *controlled,* or subject to control, by the employer. Normally, all employees who deal with third parties are deemed to be agents. **EXAMPLE 26.1** Kayla, a salesperson in a department store, is an agent of the store (the principal) and acts on the store's behalf. Any sale of goods that Kayla makes to a customer is binding on the store. Similarly, most representations of fact made by Kayla with respect to the goods sold are binding on the store. ◄

Employment laws apply only to the employer-employee relationship. Statutes governing Social Security, withholding taxes, workers' compensation, unemployment compensation, workplace safety, and the like are applicable only if there is employer-employee status. *These laws do not apply to independent contractors.*

26–1b Employer–Independent Contractor Relationships

An **independent contractor** is a person who contracts with another (the principal) to do something but who is neither controlled by the principal nor subject to the principal's right to control with respect to the performance. Because those who hire independent contractors have no control over the details of their performance, independent contractors are not considered employees.

independent contractor
One who works for, and receives payment from, another (the principal) but whose working conditions and methods are not controlled by it.

Determining an Agency Relationship The relationship between a principal and an independent contractor may or may not involve an agency relationship. **EXAMPLE 26.2** Brooke, an owner of real estate, hires Tom, a real estate broker, to negotiate a sale of her property. Brooke has contracted with Tom (an independent contractor) and has established an agency relationship for the specific purpose of assisting in the sale of the property. In contrast, Henry, an owner of real estate, hires Millie, an appraiser, to estimate the value of his property. Henry does not control the conduct of Millie's work. Henry has contracted with Millie, an independent contractor, but he has not established an agency relationship. Millie has no power to transact any business for Henry and is not subject to his control with respect to the conduct of her work.◄

Determining Employee Status In determining whether a person hired by another to do a job is an employee or an independent contractor, consider that generally, the greater the employer's control over the work, the more likely it is that the worker is an employee. For a further discussion about hiring independent contractors, see this chapter's *Linking Business Law to Your Career* feature.

26–2 AGENCY FORMATION

Agency relationships normally are consensual—that is, they come about by voluntary consent and agreement of the parties. An agreement to enter into an agency relationship generally need not be in writing. There are, however, two main exceptions:

LEARNING OUTCOME 1

Describe how an agency relationship is created.

1. Whenever an agent is empowered to enter into a contract that the Statute of Frauds requires to be in writing, the agent's authority from the principal must be in writing (this is the *equal dignity rule,* which will be discussed later in this chapter).

2. A *power of attorney*—a document authorizing another to act as one's agent or attorney—must be in writing.

   A person must have *contractual capacity* to be a principal. Those who cannot legally enter into contracts directly should not be allowed to do so indirectly through an agent. Any person can be an agent, however, regardless of whether he or she has the capacity to contract.

   An agency relationship can be created for any legal purpose. One created for an illegal purpose or contrary to public policy is unenforceable. **EXAMPLE 26.3** Janelle (as principal) contracts with McKenzie (as agent) to sell illegal narcotics. This agency relationship is unenforceable because selling illegal narcotics is a crime and contrary to public policy.◄

   Agency relationships can arise by acts of the parties in one of four ways: *by agreement of the parties, by ratification, by estoppel,* or *by operation of law.*

26–2a Agency by Agreement of the Parties

Because agency is a relationship to which both parties consent, it must be based on some *affirmative* indication that the agent agrees to act for the principal and the principal agrees to have the agent so act. An agency agreement can take the form of an express written contract, or it can be oral. **EXAMPLE 26.4** Reese asks Cary, a gardener, to contract with others for the care of his lawn on a regular basis. An agency relationship has been established for the lawn care.◄

An agency agreement can also be implied from conduct. **EXAMPLE 26.5** The Dakota Springs Hotel has Boris, who is not an employee, park its guests' cars. The hotel manager tells Boris when to work and how do the tasks. The hotel's conduct implies its willingness to have Boris park its customers' cars. In turn, Boris can infer that he has the authority to act as the hotel's parking valet.◄

26–2b Agency by Ratification

ratification
The confirmation by one person of an act or contract performed or entered into on his or her behalf by another.

On occasion, a person who is in fact not an agent (or who is an agent acting outside the scope of his or her authority) may contract on behalf of another (a principal). If the principal affirms that contract by word or by action, an agency relationship is created by **ratification.** Ratification is the affirmation of a previously unauthorized contract or act. The requirements for ratification will be discussed later in this chapter.

26–2c Agency by Estoppel

A principal may cause a third person to believe reasonably that another person is his or her agent when the other person is in fact not an agent of the principal. In such a situation, the principal's actions create the *appearance* of an agency that does not in fact exist. If the third person deals with the supposed agent, the principal is estopped (barred) from denying the agency relationship with respect to that third person.

HIGHLIGHTING THE POINT

Andrew accompanies Charles to call on a customer, Steve, the proprietor of the General Seed Store. Andrew is not employed by Charles. Charles says to Steve that he wishes he had three more assistants "just like Andrew." This gives Steve reason to believe that Andrew is an agent for Charles. Steve then places seed orders with Andrew.

If Charles does not correct the impression that Andrew is an agent, will Charles be bound to fill the orders? Yes. Charles's representation to Steve creates the impression that Andrew is Charles's agent and has authority to solicit orders.

26–2d Agency by Operation of Law

In some cases, the courts find an agency relationship in the absence of a formal agreement. This may occur in family relationships. **EXAMPLE 26.6** Judy and Lee are married. If Judy purchases certain necessities and charges them to Lee's account, a court will find an agency relationship between them.◄

Agency by operation of law may also occur in emergency situations, when the agent is unable to contact the principal and the agent's failure to act outside the scope of her or his authority would cause the principal substantial loss. **EXAMPLE 26.7** Linda's car is struck by a train, and she is injured. Jake, a railroad engineer, may contract for medical care for Linda on behalf of his employer.◄

26–3 DUTIES OF AGENTS AND PRINCIPALS

In this section, we examine the duties of agents and principals. In general, for every duty of the principal, the agent has a corresponding right, and vice versa.

26–3a Agent's Duties to the Principal

The duties that an agent owes to a principal are set forth in the agency agreement or arise by operation of law. The duties are implied from the agency relationship *whether or not the identity of the principal is disclosed to a third party.* Generally, the agent owes the principal the five duties described next.

LEARNING OUTCOME 2

List the duties of agents and principals.

Performance An agent must use reasonable diligence and skill in performing the work. The degree of skill or care required of an agent is usually that expected of a reasonable person under similar circumstances. If an agent has represented himself or herself as possessing special skills (such as those that an accountant or attorney possesses), the agent is expected to use them.

Notification An agent must notify the principal of all matters that come to his or her attention concerning the subject matter of the agency. Under the law of agency, notice to the agent is notice to the principal. **EXAMPLE 26.8** Annette, the manager (the agent) of a grocery store, is notified of a spilled gallon of milk in one of the aisles. If she fails to take steps to clean up the spill and a customer is injured, the store's owner (the principal) is liable for the injury.◄

Loyalty The duty of loyalty means that the agent must act solely for the benefit of the principal and not in the interest of himself or herself, or a third party. It also means that any information (such as a customer list) acquired through the agency relationship is confidential. It would be a breach of loyalty to disclose such information either during the agency relationship or after its termination.

Furthermore, an agent employed by a principal to buy cannot buy from himself or herself. **EXAMPLE 26.9** If Verona asks Bob to buy an acre of land in a certain area of the city for her, Bob cannot take advantage of the relationship to secretly sell his own acre in that area to her.◄ Similarly, an agent employed to sell cannot become the purchaser without the principal's consent. **EXAMPLE 26.10** If Gail asks Kurt to sell her Kindle e-reader, Kurt cannot buy the e-reader without Gail's consent.◄

Obedience When an agent is acting on behalf of the principal, the agent must follow all lawful and clearly stated instructions of the principal. During emergency situations, however, when the principal cannot be consulted, the agent may deviate from the instructions if the circumstances warrant it (such as when the principal would suffer a financial loss if the agent failed to act).

Accounting The agent must keep and make available to the principal an account of all property and funds received and paid out on behalf of the principal. This includes gifts from third persons in connection with the agency. **EXAMPLE 26.11** Marta is a salesperson for Roadway Supplies. Knife River Construction gives Marta a new tablet as a gift for prompt deliveries of Roadway's paving materials. The tablet belongs to Roadway.◄ The agent must maintain separate accounts for the principal's funds and for the agent's personal funds, and the agent must not intermingle these accounts.

26–3b Principal's Duties to the Agent

The principal also has certain duties to the agent, either expressed or implied by law. Three such duties are discussed here.

Compensation The principal has a duty to pay the agent for services rendered. If the parties have agreed on the amount of compensation, the principal must pay that amount on completion of the agent's activities. If no amount is expressly agreed on, then the principal owes the agent the customary compensation for the agent's services.

Reimbursement and Indemnification When an agent disburses funds at the request of the principal or to pay for necessary expenses in the course of reasonable performance of his or her agency duties, the principal must reimburse the agent. Agents cannot recover for expenses incurred by their own misconduct, however.

A principal must also *indemnify* (compensate) an agent for liabilities incurred because of authorized acts, as well as for losses suffered by the agent or others because of the principal's failure to perform his or her duties. For instance, if an agent orders supplies on the principal's behalf and the agent is held liable for the payment, the principal must indemnify the agent for the liability.

Cooperation A principal must cooperate with the agent and assist the agent in performing his or her duties. The principal must do nothing to prevent that performance. **EXAMPLE 26.12** Peggy (the principal) creates an exclusive agency by granting Don (the agent) an exclusive territory within which Don may sell Peggy's products. If Peggy starts to sell the products herself within Don's territory—or permits another agent to do so—Peggy has not cooperated with the agent. By violating the exclusive agency, Peggy can be held liable for Don's lost sales or profits. ◄

26–4 AGENT'S AUTHORITY

LEARNING OUTCOME 3

Define the scope of an agent's authority.

The liability of a principal to third parties with whom an agent contracts depends on whether the agent had the authority to enter into legally binding contracts on the principal's behalf. An agent's authority to act can be either *actual* (express or implied) or *apparent*. If an agent contracts outside the scope of his or her authority, the principal may still become liable by ratifying the contract.

26–4a Express Authority

Express authority of an agent is embodied in that which the principal has engaged the agent to do. It can be given orally or in writing.

equal dignity rule
A rule stating that express authority given to an agent must be in writing if the contract to be made on behalf of the principal is required to be in writing.

The Equal Dignity Rule The **equal dignity rule** in most states requires that if the contract being executed is or must be in writing, then the agent's authority must also be in writing.

HIGHLIGHTING THE POINT

Zorba orally asks Parker to sell a ranch that Zorba owns. Parker finds a buyer, Gloria, and signs a sales contract on behalf of Zorba to sell the ranch. A contract for an interest in land must be in writing.

Can Gloria enforce the contract? No. The contract is unenforceable unless Zorba subsequently ratifies Parker's agency status *in writing*. Once the contract is ratified, either party can enforce rights under the contract.

Power of Attorney Giving an agent a **power of attorney** confers express authority. A power of attorney normally is a written document. It can be *special* (permitting the agent to do specified acts only), or it can be *general* (permitting the agent to transact all business dealings for the principal).

power of attorney
A document authorizing another to act as one's agent or attorney.

26–4b Implied Authority

An agent has the implied authority to do what is reasonably necessary to carry out his or her express authority and accomplish the objectives of the agency relationship. Authority can also be implied by custom or inferred from the position the agent occupies.

EXAMPLE 26.13 Crown Market employs Stephanie to manage one of its stores. Crown has not expressly stated that Stephanie has authority to contract with third persons. In this situation, though, authority to manage a business implies authority to do what is reasonably required (as is customary or can be inferred from a manager's position) to operate the business. Thus, it is reasonable to imply that Stephanie has the authority to form contracts to hire employees, to buy merchandise and equipment, and to advertise the products sold at Crown. ◄

26–4c Apparent Authority

While actual authority (express or implied) arises from what the principal makes clear *to the agent*, **apparent authority** arises when the principal, by either word or action, causes a *third party* reasonably to believe that an agent has authority to act, even though the agent has no express or implied authority. If the third party changes his or her position in reliance on the principal's representations, the principal may be estopped (barred) from denying that the agent had authority.

apparent authority
Authority that arises when the principal causes a third party to reasonably believe that an agent has authority to act on the principal's behalf.

HIGHLIGHTING THE POINT

Emily Anderson, a salesperson for Gold Products, has no authority to collect payments for orders solicited from customers. A customer, Martin Huerta, pays Anderson for an order. Anderson takes the payment to Gold's accountant, who accepts the payment and sends Huerta a receipt. This procedure is followed for other orders by Huerta. Finally, however, Anderson disappears with one of Huerta's payments.

Can Huerta claim that the payment to Anderson was authorized and thus was, in effect, a payment to Gold? Yes. Gold's repeated acts of accepting Huerta's payments through Anderson led Huerta reasonably to expect that Anderson had authority to receive payments. Although Anderson did not have authority, Gold's conduct gave her apparent authority.

26–4d Ratification

Ratification is the affirmation of a previously unauthorized contract or act involving the agent and a third party. The principal is not bound by the agent's unauthorized act unless the principal ratifies it, either expressly (by words) or impliedly (by conduct).

The requirements for ratification are as follows:

1. The one who acted as an agent must have acted on behalf of a principal who subsequently ratifies.

2. The principal must know of all material facts involved in the transaction.

3. The agent's act must be affirmed in its entirety by the principal.

4. The principal must have the legal capacity to authorize the transaction at the time the agent engages in the act and at the time the principal ratifies.

5. The principal's affirmance must occur prior to the withdrawal of the third party from the transaction or prior to the third party's change of position in reliance on the contract.

6. The principal must observe the same formalities when he or she approves the act purportedly done by the agent on his or her behalf as would have been required to authorize the act initially.

26–5 LIABILITY IN AGENCY RELATIONSHIPS

Frequently, an issue arises as to which party, the principal or the agent, should be held liable for contracts formed by the agent or torts committed by the agent. We look at this aspect of agency law next.

26–5a Liability for Agent's Contracts

An important consideration in determining liability for a contract formed by an agent is whether the principal's identity was disclosed, partially disclosed, or undisclosed to the third party.

- A **disclosed principal** is a principal whose identity is known by the third party at the time the contract is made by the agent.

- A **partially disclosed principal** is a principal whose identity is not known by the third party, but the third party knows that the agent is or may be acting for a principal at the time the contract is made. **EXAMPLE 26.14** Sarah has contracted with Raul, a real estate agent, to sell certain property. She wishes to keep her identity a secret, but Raul makes it clear to potential buyers of the property that he is acting in an agency capacity. In this situation, Sarah is a partially disclosed principal. ◄

- An **undisclosed principal** is a principal whose identity is totally unknown by the third party at the time the contract is made, and the third party has no knowledge that the agent is acting in an agency capacity.

Authorized Acts When an agent, acting within the scope of his or her authority, contracts with a third party, a disclosed principal is liable to the third party, and ordinarily the agent is not liable. In the same circumstances, a partially disclosed principal is also liable and so is the agent. An undisclosed principal is liable except in the following circumstances:

1. He or she was expressly excluded as a party to the contract.

2. The contract is a negotiable instrument, such as a check, signed by the agent with no indication that he or she is signing in a representative capacity.

3. The performance of the agent is personal to the contract (for example, the contract requires the agent, who is a famous musician, to give a concert).

In all cases, when the principal is undisclosed, the agent may be liable.

Unauthorized Acts If the agent exceeds the scope of authority, and the principal fails to ratify the contract, the principal cannot be held liable to a contract by a third party. Hence, the agent generally is liable unless the third party knew of the agent's lack of authority.

Real-World Case Example

Marvin Sussman entered into a contract with Stonhard, Inc., to install flooring at Blue Ridge Farms, a food-manufacturing facility in New York. At the time, Sussman indicated that he was acting as an agent, but he did not disclose that he was acting as an agent for the farm facility's owner, Blue Ridge Foods, LLC. When Stonhard was not paid for the work, it filed a suit in a New York state court against the farm facility, its owner, and Sussman. The court dismissed the complaint against Sussman. Stonhard appealed.

Was Sussman personally liable on the contract? Yes. In a 2014 case, *Stonhard, Inc. v. Blue Ridge Farms, LLC*, a state intermediate appellate court reversed the lower court's dismissal of Stonhard's complaint against Sussman and issued a judgment in Stonhard's favor. Sussman was acting as an agent for a partially disclosed principal—that is, the agency relationship was known, but the identity of the principal (Blue Ridge Foods) remained undisclosed. As an agent for an undisclosed principal, Sussman became personally liable to Stonhard under the contract.

26–5b Liability for Agent's Torts

A principal becomes liable for an agent's (or an employee's) torts if the torts are committed within the scope of the agency or the scope of employment. The theory of liability used here involves the doctrine of ***respondeat superior*** (pronounced ree-*spahn*-dee-uht soo-*peer*-ee-your), a Latin term meaning "let the master respond."

The doctrine of *respondeat superior* is similar to the theory of strict liability. The doctrine imposes vicarious (indirect) liability on a principal without regard to the personal fault of the principal for torts committed by an agent in the scope of the agency. **EXAMPLE 26.15** If Dan, the employee of a delivery firm, negligently runs a red light and injures Kate, a pedestrian, the *owner* of the truck is liable for Kate's injury.◄

respondeat superior
A principle of law whereby a principal or an employer is held liable for the wrongful acts committed by agents or employees acting within the scope of their agency or employment.

26–6 TERMINATION OF AGENCY RELATIONSHIPS

An agency can terminate by an act of the parties or by operation of law. Once the relationship between the principal and agent has ended, the agent no longer has the right to bind the principal.

LEARNING OUTCOME 5

Explain how an agency relationship is terminated.

26–6a Termination by Act of the Parties

An agency may be terminated by act of the parties in any of the following ways:

1. *Lapse of time.* An agency agreement may specify the time period during which the agency relationship will exist. If so, the agency ends when that period expires. If no definite time is stated, then the agency continues for a reasonable time and can be terminated by either party.

2. *Purpose achieved.* An agent is sometimes employed to accomplish a particular objective. In that situation, the agency ends when the objective is accomplished. Thus, if an agent is hired to purchase stock for a cattle rancher, the agency automatically ends after the cattle have been purchased.

3. *Occurrence of a specific event.* When an agency is created to terminate on the happening of a certain event, the agency automatically ends when the event occurs. If a principal appoints an agent to handle the principal's business while the principal is away, for instance, the agency terminates when the principal returns.

4. *Mutual agreement.* The parties can mutually agree to terminate their relationship. An agreement to terminate the agency effectively relieves the principal and the agent of the rights and duties in the relationship.

5. *Termination by one party.* As a general rule, either party can terminate an agency relationship. The agent's act of termination is a *renunciation* of authority (the agent abandons the right to act for the principal). The principal's act of termination is a *revocation* of authority (the principal takes back the right given to the agent to act on the principal's behalf).

Wrongful Termination Although both parties have the *power* to terminate an agency relationship, they may not possess the *right.* Terminating an agency relationship may require breaking an agency contract, and no one normally has the right to break a contract. Such wrongful termination can subject the canceling party to a suit for damages.

Even in an agency that either party may terminate at any time, the principal who wishes to terminate must give the agent reasonable notice. The notice must be at least sufficient to allow the agent to recoup his or her expenses and, in some situations, to make a normal profit.

Agency Coupled with an Interest An agency *coupled with an interest* is a relationship created for the benefit of the agent. The agent actually acquires a beneficial interest in the subject matter of the agency. Under these circumstances, it is not equitable to permit a principal to terminate the relationship at will. Hence, this type of agency is *irrevocable.*

HIGHLIGHTING THE POINT

Silvia Orta owns Green Hills. She needs some cash right away, so she enters into an agreement with Jack Harrington. The agreement provides that Harrington will lend her $10,000. In return, she will grant Harrington a one-half interest in Green Hills and "the exclusive right to sell" it, with the loan to be repaid out of the sale's proceeds. Harrington is Orta's agent.

Is Harrington's agency coupled with an interest? Yes. Harrington's power to sell Green Hills is coupled with a beneficial interest of one-half ownership in Green Hills. The interest was created when the loan agreement was made for the purpose of securing repayment of the loan. Thus, Harrington's agency power is irrevocable.

26–6b Termination by Operation of Law

Termination of an agency by operation of law occurs in the following circumstances:

1. *Death or insanity.* The death or mental incompetence of either the principal or the agent automatically and immediately terminates an ordinary agency relationship. Knowledge of the death is not required. **EXAMPLE 26.16** Greg sends Nina to China to purchase a rare painting. Before Nina makes the purchase, Greg dies. Nina's agent status is terminated at the moment of Greg's death, even if Nina does not know that Greg has died. ◄

2. *Impossibility.* When the specific subject matter of an agency is destroyed or lost, the agency terminates. **EXAMPLE 26.17** Katerina employs Axel to sell her house. Before any sale can be made, the house is destroyed by fire. Axel's agency and authority to sell Katerina's house terminates.◄ In addition, when it is impossible for the agent to perform the agency lawfully, the agency terminates.

3. *Changed circumstances.* When an event occurs that has such an unusual effect on the subject matter of the agency that the agent can reasonably infer that the principal will not want the agency to continue, the agency terminates. **EXAMPLE 26.18** Carter hires Rasmussen, a real estate agent, to sell a tract of land. Rasmussen learns that there is oil under the land, greatly increasing the value of the tract. The agency to sell the land is terminated.◄

4. *Bankruptcy.* Bankruptcy of the principal or the agent usually terminates the agency relationship.

5. *War.* When the principal's country and the agent's country are at war with each other, the agency is terminated, or at least suspended.

When an agency terminates by operation of law, there is no duty to notify third parties, unless the agent's authority is coupled with an interest. If the parties themselves have terminated the agency, however, it is the principal's duty to inform any third parties who know of the existence of the agency that it has been terminated. No particular form of notice of agency termination is required.

ANSWERING THE LEGAL PROBLEM

In the legal problem set out at the beginning of this chapter, Bruce is hired as a booking agent for an indie rock band, The Crash. As the band's agent, Bruce negotiates and signs contracts for The Crash to appear at concerts.

A **Are the contracts by Bruce legally enforceable against The Crash?** Yes. In their principal-agent relationship, the parties agreed that Bruce would act on behalf of The Crash when negotiating and transacting business with third persons.

LINKING BUSINESS LAW to Your Career

INDEPENDENT CONTRACTORS

In your career, you may at some point consider hiring an independent contractor. Hiring independent contractors instead of employees may help you reduce your business's potential tort liability and tax liability.

Tort Liability

One reason for using an independent contractor is that an employer usually is not liable for a tort that an independent contractor commits against a third party. Nevertheless, there are exceptions.

To minimize possible liability, you should check an independent contractor's qualifications carefully before hiring him or her. How extensively you should investigate depends on the nature of the work. For example, hiring an independent contractor to maintain the landscaping around your building should require relatively limited investigation.

A more thorough investigation is necessary when the contractor's activities will present a potential danger to the public—for example, if the contractor will be delivering explosives.

Generally, the independent contractor should assume, in a written contract, liability for harms caused to third parties by the contractor's negligence. A contractor should also buy liability insurance to cover these costs.

(Continued)

Tax Liability and Other Costs

Another reason for hiring an independent contractor is that you do not need to pay or withhold Social Security, income, or unemployment taxes on his or her behalf. Also, an independent contractor is not eligible for retirement or medical plans or other fringe benefits provided to employees.

A word of caution, though: simply designating a person an independent contractor does not make her or him one. The Internal Revenue Service (IRS) will classify an individual as an employee if it determines that he or she is an employee, regardless of your designation. The penalty in such a case may be high. Usually, you will be liable for back Social Security and unemployment taxes, plus interest and penalties. When in doubt, seek professional assistance in such matters.

To avoid these and other costs, document the independent contractor's status with his or her business identification number, business cards, and letterhead so that you can show the IRS that the contractor works independently.

TERMS AND CONCEPTS FOR REVIEW

agency 350

agent 350

apparent authority 355

disclosed principal 356

equal dignity rule 354

independent contractor 351

partially disclosed principal 356

power of attorney 355

principal 350

ratification 352

respondeat superior 357

undisclosed principal 356

CHAPTER SUMMARY—AGENCY

LEARNING OUTCOME

1

Describe how an agency relationship is created. In an agency relationship, an agent acts on behalf of, and instead of, a principal in dealing with third parties. Agency relationships may be formed by:

(1) *Agreement*—Through express consent (oral or written) or implied by conduct.

(2) *Ratification*—The principal, by act or agreement, ratifies the conduct of a person who is not an agent.

(3) *Estoppel*—The principal causes a third person to believe that another person is the principal's agent, and the third person acts to his or her detriment in reasonable reliance on that belief.

(4) *Operation of law*—May arise in family relationships or in an emergency when the agent is unable to contact the principal and failure to act would cause the principal substantial loss.

2

List the duties of agents and principals. An agent's duties include:

(1) *Performance*—An agent must use reasonable diligence and skill in performing her or his duties. An agent who has represented himself or herself as possessing special skills must use those skills.

(2) *Notification*—An agent must notify the principal of all matters that come to his or her attention concerning the subject matter of the agency.

(3) *Loyalty*—An agent has a duty to act solely for the principal's benefit and not in the interest of the agent or a third party.

(4) *Obedience*—An agent must follow all lawful and clearly stated instructions of the principal.

(5) *Accounting*—An agent must make available to the principal records of all property and funds received and paid out on the principal's behalf.

The principal's duties include:

(1) *Compensation*—A principal must pay the agreed-on value (or reasonable value) for an agent's services.

(2) *Reimbursement and indemnification*—A principal must reimburse an agent for all funds disbursed at the principal's request and for all funds an agent disburses for necessary expenses in the course of reasonable performance of agency duties.

(3) *Cooperation*—A principal must cooperate with the agent and assist the agent in performing his or her duties.

<table>
<tr>
<td>3</td>
<td>

Define the scope of an agent's authority. An agent's authority has the following sources: (1) *express authority*—can be oral or in writing but must be in writing if an agent is to execute a contract that must be in writing; (2) *implied authority*—customarily associated with the agent's position or deemed necessary for the agent to carry out expressly authorized tasks; (3) *apparent authority*—exists when a principal, by word or action, causes a third party reasonably to believe that an agent has authority to act, even though the agent has no express or implied authority; and (4) *ratification*—occurs when a principal, aware of all material facts, affirms an agent's unauthorized act or promise.

</td>
</tr>
<tr>
<td>4</td>
<td>

Identify the parties' liability in agency relationships. If a principal's identity is *disclosed* or *partially disclosed* at the time an agent forms a contract with a third party, and the agent is acting within the scope of his or her authority, the principal is liable to the third party under the contract. If the principal is disclosed, the agent is ordinarily not liable; but if the principal is partially disclosed, the agent is liable. If a principal's identity is *undisclosed* at the time of contract formation, an agent is liable to the third party under the contract, and the principal is also bound except under limited circumstances. Under the doctrine of *respondeat superior,* a principal is liable for any harm caused to another through an agent's torts if the agent was acting within the scope of employment at the time the harmful act occurred.

</td>
</tr>
<tr>
<td>5</td>
<td>

Explain how an agency relationship is terminated. An agency relationship may be terminated by *an act of the parties* in the following ways:

(1) *A lapse of time,* if a definite time for the duration of the agency was agreed on when the agency was established.
(2) *Achievement of the agency's purpose.*
(3) *Occurrence of a specified event.*
(4) *Mutual agreement.*
(5) *Revocation* by the principal or renunciation by the agent.

    An agency relationship may be terminated by *operation of law* in the following ways:

(1) *The death or mental incompetence of either party.*
(2) *Impossibility*—The purpose of the agency cannot be achieved because of an event beyond the parties' control.
(3) *Changed circumstances*—An event has such an unusual effect on the agency that the agent can reasonably infer that the principal will not want the agency to continue.
(4) *The bankruptcy of either party.*
(5) *War between the parties' countries.*

</td>
</tr>
</table>

ISSUE SPOTTERS

Check your answers to the *Issue Spotters* against the answers provided in Appendix C at the end of this text.

1. Able Corporation wants to build a new mall on a specific tract of land. Able contracts with Sheila to buy the property. When Sheila learns of the difference between the price that Able is willing to pay and the price at which the owner is willing to sell, she wants to buy the land and sell it to Able herself. Can she do this? Discuss. (See *Duties of Agents and Principals.*)

2. Marie, owner of the Consumer Goods Company, employs Rachel as an administrative assistant. In Marie's absence, and without authority, Rachel represents herself as Marie and signs a promissory note in Marie's name. Under what circumstance is Marie liable on the note? (See *Liability in Agency Relationships.*)

USING BUSINESS LAW

26–1. Agent's Duties to Principal. Iliana is a traveling sales agent. Iliana not only solicits orders but also delivers the goods and collects payments from her customers. Iliana places all payments in her private checking account and at the end of each month draws sufficient cash from her bank to cover the payments made. Giberson Corp., Iliana's employer, is totally unaware of this procedure. Because of a slowdown in the economy, Giberson tells all its sales personnel to offer 20 percent discounts on orders. Iliana solicits orders, but she offers only 15 percent discounts, pocketing the extra 5 percent paid by customers. Iliana has not lost any orders, and she is rated as one of Giberson's top salespersons. Giberson now learns of Iliana's actions. Discuss fully Giberson's rights in this matter. (See *Duties of Agents and Principals*.)

26–2. Liability for Agent's Contracts. Michael Mosely works as a purchasing agent for Suharto Coal Supply, a partnership. Mosely has authority to purchase the coal needed by Suharto to satisfy the needs of its customers. While Mosely is leaving a coal mine from which he has just purchased a large quantity of coal, his car breaks down. He walks into a small roadside grocery store for help. While there, he runs into Wiley, who owns 360 acres back in the mountains with all mineral rights. Wiley, in need of cash, offers to sell Mosely the property at $1,500 per acre. On inspection, Mosely concludes that the subsurface may contain valuable coal deposits. Mosely contracts to purchase the property for Suharto, signing the contract, "Suharto Coal Supply, Michael Mosely, agent." The closing date is set for August 1. Mosely takes the contract to the partnership. The managing partner is furious, as Suharto is not in the property business. Later, just before August 1, both Wiley and the partnership learn that the value of the land is at least $15,000 per acre. Discuss the rights of Suharto and Wiley concerning the land contract. (See *Liability in Agency Relationships*.)

REAL-WORLD CASE PROBLEMS

26–3. Determining Employee Status. Nelson Ovalles worked as a cable installer for Cox Rhode Island Telecom, LLC, under an agreement with a third party, M&M Communications, Inc. The agreement disavowed an employer-employee relationship between Cox and M&M's technicians, including Ovalles. Cox required Ovalles to designate its affiliation on his work van, clothing, and identification badge, but Cox had minimal contact with him and limited power to control the manner in which he performed his duties. Cox supplied cable wire and similar items, but the equipment was delivered to M&M, not to Ovalles. Is Ovalles an employee of Cox or an independent contractor? Explain. [*Cayer v. Cox Rhode Island Telecom, LLC*, 85 A.3d 1140 (R.I. 2014)] (See *Agency Relationships*.)

26–4. Employment Relationships. William Moore owned Moore Enterprises, a wholesale tire business. William's son, Jonathan, worked as a Moore Enterprises employee while he was in high school. Later, Jonathan started his own business, called Morecedes Tire. Morecedes regrooved tires and sold them to businesses, including Moore Enterprises. A decade after Jonathan started Morecedes, William offered him work with Moore Enterprises. On the first day, William told Jonathan to load certain tires on a trailer but did not tell him how to do it. Was Jonathan an independent contractor? Discuss. [*Moore v. Moore*, __ P.3d __ (Idaho 2011)] (See *Agency Relationships*.)

26–5. Disclosed Principal. To display desserts in restaurants, Mario Sclafani ordered refrigeration units from Felix Storch, Inc. Felix faxed a credit application to Sclafani. The application was faxed back with a signature that appeared to be Sclafani's. Felix delivered the units. When they were not paid for, Felix filed a suit against Sclafani to collect. Sclafani denied that he had seen the application or signed it. He testified that he referred all credit questions to "the girl in the office." Who was the principal? Who was the agent? Who is liable on the contract? Explain. [*Felix Storch Inc. v. Martinucci Desserts USA, Inc.*, 30 Misc.2d 1217, 924 N.Y.S.2d 308 (Suffolk Co. 2011)] (See *Liability in Agency Relationships*.)

ETHICAL QUESTIONS

26–6. Duty of Loyalty. Are there situations in which the duty of loyalty could conflict with other duties? Explain your answer. (See *Duties of Agents and Principals*.)

26–7. Duty of Loyalty. Taser International, Inc., develops and makes video and audio-recording devices. Steve Ward was Taser's vice president of marketing when he began to explore the possibility of developing and marketing devices of his own design, including a clip-on camera. Ward talked to patent attorneys and a product development company, and completed most of a business plan before he resigned from Taser. He then formed Vievu, LLC, to market the clip-on camera. Did Ward breach the duty of loyalty? Could he have taken any steps toward starting his own firm without breaching this duty? Discuss. [*Taser International, Inc. v. Ward*, 224 Ariz. 389, 231 P.3d 921 (App. Div. 1 2010)] (See *Duties of Agents and Principals*.)

Chapter 26—Work Set

TRUE-FALSE QUESTIONS

_____ 1. An agent can perform legal acts that bind the principal.

_____ 2. An agent must keep separate accounts for the principal's funds.

_____ 3. Any information or knowledge obtained through an agency relationship is confidential.

_____ 4. A disclosed principal is liable to a third party for a contract made by an agent acting within the scope of authority.

_____ 5. Generally, a principal whose agent commits a tort in the scope of his or her employment is not liable to persons injured.

_____ 6. An agent is always liable for a contract he or she enters into on behalf of an undisclosed principal.

_____ 7. Both parties to an agency have the power and the right to terminate the agency at any time.

_____ 8. The only way a principal can ratify a transaction is with a written statement.

_____ 9. When an agent enters into a contract on behalf of a principal, the principal must ratify the contract to be bound.

MULTIPLE-CHOICE QUESTIONS

_____ 1. National Supplies Company hires Linda and Brad as employees to deal with third-party purchasers and suppliers. Linda and Brad are

a. principals.
b. agents.
c. both a and b.
d. none of the above.

_____ 2. Ann gives Bill the impression that Carol is Ann's agent, when in fact she is not. Bill deals with Carol as Ann's agent. Regarding any agency relationship, Ann

a. can deny it.
b. can deny it to the extent of any injury suffered by Bill.
c. can deny it to the extent of any liability that might be imposed on Ann.
d. cannot deny it.

_____ 3. Dave is an accountant hired by Eagle Equipment Corporation to act as its agent. In acting as an agent for Eagle, Dave is expected to use

a. reasonable diligence and skill.
b. the degree of skill a reasonable person would use under similar circumstances.
c. the special skills he has as an accountant.
d. none of the above.

_____ 4. EZ Sales Company hires Jill as a sales representative for six months at a salary of $5,000 per month, plus a commission of 10 percent of sales. In matters concerning EZ's business, Jill must act

a. solely in EZ's interest.
b. solely in Jill's interest.
c. solely in the interest of the customers.
d. in none of the above ways.

5. Bass Corporation hires Ellen to manage one of its stores. Bass does not specify whether or to what extent Ellen has the authority to contract with third parties. The express authority that Bass gives Ellen to manage the store implies authority to do

   a. whatever is customary to operate the business.
   b. whatever can be inferred from the manager's position.
   c. both a and b.
   d. none of the above.

6. Ron orally engages Dian to act as his agent. During the agency, Ron knows that Dian deals with Mary. Ron also knows that Pete and Brad are aware of the agency but have not dealt with Dian. Ron decides to terminate the agency. Regarding notice of termination,

   a. Dian need not be notified in writing.
   b. Dian's actual authority terminates without notice to her of Ron's decision.
   c. Dian's apparent authority terminates without notice to Mary.
   d. Pete and Brad must be directly notified.

7. Smith Petroleum, Inc., contracts to sell oil to Jones Petrochemicals, telling Jones that it is acting on behalf of "a rich Saudi Arabian who doesn't want his identity known." Smith signs the contract, "Smith, as agent only." In fact, Smith is acting on its own. If the contract is breached, Smith may

   a. not be liable, because Smith signed the contract as an agent.
   b. not be liable, unless Jones knew Smith did not have authority to act.
   c. be liable, unless Jones knew Smith did not have authority to act.
   d. be liable, because Smith signed the contract as an agent.

8. Jill is employed by American Grocers to buy and install a computer system for American's distribution network. When the system is set up and running, the agency

   a. terminates automatically.
   b. terminates after fourteen days.
   c. continues for one year.
   d. continues indefinitely.

 ANSWERING MORE LEGAL PROBLEMS

1. Winona contracted with XtremeCast, a broadcast media firm, to cohost an Internet-streaming sports program. Winona and XtremeCast signed a new contract for each episode. In each contract, Winona agreed to work a certain number of days for a certain salary. During each broadcast, Winona was free to improvise her performance. She had no other obligation to work for XtremeCast.

Was Winona an independent contractor? Yes. Independent contractors are not employees, because those who hire them have no _____ over the details of their performance. An independent contractor is a person who contracts with another—the principal—to do something but who is neither _____ by the other nor subject to the other's right to _____ with respect to the performance. Thus, whether a person hired by another is an employee or an independent contractor depends on the extent of _____. The greater the employer's _____ over the work, the more likely it is that the worker is an employee.

2. General Retail Associates (GRA) owned Valley Mall. Reliable Property Management Company operated the mall on GRA's behalf. Reliable leased the storefronts to tenants, including GameOn, and contracted with Sweep Clean, Inc., to remove ice and snow from the sidewalks around the mall. Each contract identified GRA as the mall's owner. Kiko, a GameOn employee, slipped on a patch of ice that Sweep Clean had negligently failed to remove.

Was Reliable liable for Kiko's injury? No. A principal whose identity is known by a third party at the time that party enters into a contract with an agent is a(n) _____ principal. This type of principal is liable under a contract that an agent, acting within the scope of his or her authority, enters into with a third party on the principal's behalf. Ordinarily, the agent is not liable under the contract. In this case, because the identity of the principal (GRA) was fully _____ in the contracts that Reliable entered into on GRA's behalf, the agent could not be held liable under those contracts for Kiko's injury. Of course, GRA and Sweep Clean may be liable.

EMPLOYMENT, IMMIGRATION, AND LABOR LAW

27

FACING A LEGAL PROBLEM

A U.S. Department of Transportation rule requires employees engaged in oil and gas pipeline operations to submit to random drug testing. The rule does not require that before being tested, the individual must be suspected of drug use.

Q If the employees challenge this rule in court, will the rule be upheld?

Until the early 1900s, most employer-employee relationships were governed by the common law. Even today, under the common law employment-at-will doctrine, private employers are generally free to hire and fire workers at will, unless doing so violates an employee's contractual or statutory rights. Now, however, there are numerous statutes and administrative agency regulations that affect the workplace.

In this chapter, we look at the most significant laws regulating employment relationships. Note that these laws apply only to employers' relationships with employees, *not* to their relationships with independent contractors. We end the chapter with a discussion of immigration and labor laws.

27–1 EMPLOYMENT AT WILL

Traditionally, employment relationships have generally been governed by the **employment-at-will doctrine.** Under this doctrine, the employee or employer may terminate the employment relationship at any time and for any reason, unless doing so would violate provisions in the employment contract. Most U.S. employees are considered "at-will employees."

Because of the disruptive effects of the employment-at-will doctrine for employees, the courts have carved out various exceptions to the doctrine. For instance, federal statutes have modified the employment-at-will doctrine to protect some employees who report employer wrongdoing. Additionally, court rulings have carved out exceptions to the doctrine based on the existence of an implied employment contract or on the ground that an employee's discharge cannot violate a fundamental public policy.

27–1a Statutory Exceptions

To encourage workers to report employer wrongdoing, such as fraud, most of the states and the federal government have enacted *whistleblower* statutes. These statutes protect **whistleblowers** (those who report wrongdoing) from retaliation on the part of employers. They may also provide an incentive to disclose information by providing the whistleblower with a reward. The False Claims Reform Act of 1986 requires that a whistleblower who has disclosed information relating to a fraud

---

LEARNING OUTCOMES

The five Learning Outcomes below are designed to help improve your understanding of the chapter. After reading this chapter, you should be able to:

1 State exceptions to the employment-at-will doctrine.

2 Discuss the protection available to employees injured on the job.

3 Describe the major provisions of the Fair Labor Standards Act.

4 Distinguish between the two most important federal statutes governing immigration and employment today.

5 Identify which federal statute established employees' rights to organize unions and to engage in collective bargaining.

---

employment-at-will doctrine
A doctrine under which an employer or an employee may terminate an employment contract at any time and for any reason, unless the contract specifies otherwise.

LEARNING OUTCOME 1

State exceptions to the employment-at-will doctrine.

---

whistleblower
An employee who tells the government or the media that his or her employer is engaged in some unsafe or illegal activity.

365

perpetrated against the U.S. government receive between 15 and 25 percent of the proceeds if the government sues the wrongdoer.

HIGHLIGHTING THE POINT

Rebecca is the staff coordinator at a nursing home. One of the patients is wheelchair-bound and can be moved only by two persons using a special belt. Rebecca discovers that the patient has been improperly moved and has been injured as a result. She reports the incident to state authorities, as she is required to do by state law. Rebecca's supervisor confronts her about the report and fires her.

Is Rebecca entitled to be reinstated in her job? Yes. Even though Rebecca is an employee at will, she is protected in this instance from retaliatory discharge under her state's whistleblower statute. Because Rebecca was required by state law to report the improper treatment of the patient, she cannot be fired from her job.

27–1b Exceptions Based on an Implied Contract

Some courts have held that an implied employment contract exists between the employer and the employee. If the employee is fired outside the terms of this implied contract, he or she may succeed in an action for breach of contract.

EXAMPLE 27.1 Budge Enterprise's employee manual states that, as a matter of policy, workers will be dismissed only for good cause. Martin, an employee, reasonably expects Budge to follow this policy, but Martin is fired for no stated reason. Because there is an implied contract based on the terms stated in the employee's manual, Martin may prevail in a subsequent lawsuit.◄

27–1c Public-Policy Exceptions

The most widespread common law exception to the employment-at-will doctrine is the public-policy exception. Under this rule, an employer may not fire a worker for reasons that violate a fundamental public policy of the jurisdiction. **EXAMPLE 27.2** Rihanna works for Coastal Wholesalers. When Rihanna serves as a juror and thus misses her regular work shift, Coastal cannot fire her. Similarly, if Coastal fires Rihanna for refusing a management order to do something illegal, in most states, her firing would be held to violate public policy.◄

 ## 27–2 WORKER HEALTH AND SAFETY

LEARNING OUTCOME 2

Discuss the protection available to employees injured on the job.

Numerous state and federal statutes protect employees and their families from the risk of accidental injury, death, or disease resulting from their employment. This section discusses state workers' compensation laws and the federal Occupational Safety and Health Act.

27–2a State Workers' Compensation Laws

workers' compensation laws
State statutes establishing an administrative procedure for compensating workers for injuries that arise on the job or in the course of their employment, regardless of fault.

State **workers' compensation laws** establish an administrative procedure for compensating workers who are injured on the job or in the course of their employment, regardless of fault. Instead of suing the employer for damages, an injured worker files a claim with the administrative agency that handles local workers' compensation claims.

Requirements For the worker to recover monetary benefits, the injury must have been *accidental* and must have *occurred on the job or in the course of employment,* regardless of fault or negligence. Unlike the potential recovery in a lawsuit based on fault or negligence, recovery under a workers' compensation statute is limited to the specific amount designated in the statute for the employee's injury.

HIGHLIGHTING THE POINT

Kiana is a computer programmer for Regional Electric Corporation. After too many consecutive hours working on a computer, she begins to suffer pain in her wrists and numbness in her fingers. Howard, a Regional lineman, breaks his foot after falling from a utility pole. While working in Regional's cafeteria, Winnie, who is an assistant cook, spills a pot of boiling water on her legs, causing severe burns.

Are Kiana, Howard, and Winnie eligible for workers' compensation benefits? Yes. All three Regional employees are eligible because their injuries were accidental and occurred on the job or in the course of employment.

Non-Compensable Injuries Intentionally inflicted self-injury would not be considered accidental and hence would not be covered. Additionally, if an injury occurred while an employee was commuting to or from work, it usually would not be considered to have occurred on the job or in the course of employment and hence would not be covered by a workers' compensation law.

EXAMPLE 27.3 Fabien, an employee of Intel Electronics, drives to and from his job in his personal vehicle each workday. During one morning commute, an uninsured driver hits Fabien's car after running a red light. Fabien suffers serious injuries. His injuries are not compensable under state workers' compensation law. ◄

27–2b Federal Health and Safety Protection

At the federal level, the primary legislation for employee health and safety protection is the Occupational Safety and Health Act. The act requires that businesses be maintained free from recognized hazards. Employers with eleven or more employees are required to keep occupational injury and illness records for each employee. Whenever a work-related injury or disease occurs, employers are required to make reports directly to the Occupational Safety and Health Administration (OSHA). An employer cannot discharge an employee who files a complaint or who, in good faith, refuses to work in a high-risk area (if bodily harm or death might result).

27–3 RETIREMENT INCOME AND SECURITY

Federal and state governments participate in insurance programs designed to protect employees and their families by covering the financial impact of retirement, disability, death, hospitalization, and unemployment.

27–3a Old-Age, Survivors, and Disability Insurance

The Social Security Act of 1935 provides for old-age (retirement), survivors, and disability insurance. The act is therefore often referred to as the Old-Age, Survivors, and Disability Insurance Act. Both employers and employees must contribute under the Federal Insurance Contributions Act (FICA) to help pay for the loss of income on retirement. The basis for the employee's contribution is the employee's annual wage base—the maximum amount of an employee's wages that are subject to the tax. Benefits are fixed by statute but increase automatically with increases in the cost of living.

27–3b Medicare

The health-insurance program Medicare is administered by the Social Security Administration for people sixty-five years of age and older and for some under age sixty-five who have disabilities. Medicare covers hospital costs and other medical expenses, such as visits to doctors' offices. Both employers and employees must contribute to help pay for the cost of Medicare.

27–3c Private Retirement Plans

Significant legislation has been passed to regulate retirement plans set up by employers to supplement Social Security benefits. The major federal act covering these retirement plans is the Employee Retirement Income Security Act (ERISA). The Labor Management Services Administration of the U.S. Department of Labor enforces the ERISA provisions that cover employer-provided private pension funds.

27–3d Unemployment Compensation

The U.S. system of unemployment insurance was established by the Federal Unemployment Tax Act. The act created a state system that provides unemployment compensation to eligible individuals. Under this system, employers pay into a fund, and the proceeds are paid out to qualified unemployed workers.

To be eligible for unemployment compensation, a worker must be willing and able to work. A worker fired for misconduct or who has voluntarily left his or her job does not qualify for benefits. When disputes arise over whether an employee qualifies for benefits, courts often refer to state statutes, as well as the unique circumstances surrounding the employee's reasons for leaving, to help them make a decision.

EXAMPLE 27.4 Martha works for Baily Snowboards in Vermont. One day at work, Martha receives a text from her son saying that he has been taken to the hospital. Martha rushes to the hospital and does not return to work for several days. Bailey hires someone else for Martha's position, and Martha files for unemployment benefits. Martha's claim is denied because she left her job voluntarily and made no effort to maintain contact with her employer. ◄

27–3e Group Health Plans

The Health Insurance Portability and Accountability Act (HIPAA) establishes requirements for employers that choose to provide health-insurance coverage for their employees. Under HIPAA, an employer cannot exclude persons from coverage for "preexisting conditions" (most conditions for which medical advice, diagnosis, care, or treatment was recommended or received within the previous six months). Covered employers must also ensure that employees' health information is not disclosed to unauthorized parties.

EXAMPLE 27.5 Mack receives a medical diagnosis of diabetes. Less than six months later, Northeast Mills hires Mack. Northeast Mills cannot exclude Mack from employer-subsidized group health insurance on the basis of his preexisting condition of diabetes. ◄

27–3f COBRA

The Consolidated Omnibus Budget Reconciliation Act (COBRA) prohibits an employer from eliminating a worker's medical, optical, or dental insurance coverage on the voluntary or involuntary termination of the worker's employment. The act includes most workers who have either lost their jobs or had their hours decreased and are no longer eligible for coverage under the employer's health plan. Only workers fired for gross misconduct are excluded from protection.

HIGHLIGHTING THE POINT

Elena and Jim are employees of Kitchen Crafts, an employer subject to COBRA. Elena loses her job as part of a company-wide layoff. Jim loses his job as a consequence of hitting Laredo, his supervisor, in anger (considered a gross misconduct).

Are Elena and Jim eligible for continued health insurance coverage under COBRA? Yes for Elena. No for Jim. Workers who lose their jobs with Kitchen Crafts—or any other employer subject to COBRA—have a right to continued healthcare coverage under the company's group plan unless they are fired for gross misconduct.

If a worker chooses to continue coverage under COBRA, the employer is obligated to keep the policy active for up to eighteen months. If the worker is disabled, the employer must extend the coverage for up to twenty-nine months. The worker generally must pay the full cost of the premiums.

27–4 FAMILY AND MEDICAL LEAVE

The Family and Medical Leave Act (FMLA) of 1993 requires employers with fifty or more employees to provide employees with up to twelve weeks of unpaid family or medical leave for any twelve-month period. An eligible employee may take unpaid leave under the FMLA to care for family members for any of the following reasons:

1. To care for a newborn baby within one year of birth.

2. To care for an adopted or foster child within one year of the time the child is placed with the employee.

3. To care for the employee's spouse, child, or parent who has a serious health condition.

4. If the employee suffers from a serious health condition and is unable to perform the essential functions of her or his job.

During the employee's leave, the employer must continue the worker's health-care coverage and guarantee employment in the same position or a comparable position when the employee returns to work.

Real-World Case Example

Beverly Ballard worked for the Chicago Park District in Chicago, Illinois. She lived with her mother, Sarah, who suffered from congestive heart failure. Beverly served as Sarah's primary caregiver with support from Horizon Hospice & Palliative Care. The hospice helped Sarah plan and secure funds for a "family trip" to Las Vegas as an end-of-life goal. Beverly asked the Park District for unpaid time off under the FMLA to accompany her mother on the trip as her caregiver. The employer refused. Beverly and Sarah took the trip as planned. Later, the Park District terminated Beverly for "unauthorized absences." She filed a suit in a federal district court against her employer. The court issued a decision in Beverly's favor. The Park District appealed.

(Continued)

Was Beverly Ballard eligible for FMLA leave? Yes. In a 2014 case, *Ballard v. Chicago Park District*, the U.S. Court of Appeals for the Seventh Circuit affirmed the lower court's decision. Under the FMLA, an eligible employee is entitled to leave in order to care for a family member with a serious health condition. The care is not restricted to a particular place.

27–5 WAGE AND HOUR LAWS

LEARNING OUTCOME 3

Describe the major provisions of the Fair Labor Standards Act.

In the 1930s, Congress enacted several laws regulating the wages and working hours of employees. The most significant of these laws was the Fair Labor Standards Act (FLSA). The FLSA is concerned with child labor, minimum wages, and overtime.

27–5a Child Labor Restrictions

The FLSA sets many restrictions on the use of child labor.

- Children under fourteen years of age are allowed to do only certain types of work, such as deliver newspapers, work for their parents, and work in the entertainment and (with some exceptions) agricultural areas.

- Children who are fourteen or fifteen years of age are allowed to work, but not in hazardous occupations. There are also numerous restrictions on the number of hours per day (particularly on school days) and per week that they can work.

- Working times and hours are not restricted for persons sixteen to eighteen, but they cannot be employed in hazardous jobs or jobs detrimental to their health or well-being.

27–5b Minimum Wage Requirement

minimum wage
The lowest hourly wage that an employer can legally pay an employee.

A federal **minimum wage** of a specified amount (currently $7.25 per hour) must be paid to employees in covered industries. Congress periodically revises this minimum wage. Note that many states require a minimum wage that is higher than the federal wage. Employers must pay the higher minimum wage in those states.

EXAMPLE 27.6 Clarisa is a student worker at the Oregon State University library. Oregon's minimum wage is $9.25. Because Oregon's minimum wage is higher than the federal minimum wage of $7.25, Clarisa earns $9.25 per hour.◄

27–5c Overtime Provisions and Requirements

Under the FLSA, an employee who works more than the maximum of forty hours per week must be paid no less than 1.5 times his or her regular pay rate for all hours over forty. Employees who are covered include manual laborers and other blue-collar workers who perform tasks involving repetitive operations with their hands (nonmanagement production-line employees, for example), as well as police officers, firefighters, licensed nurses, and other public-safety workers.

Employees whose jobs are categorized as executive, administrative, or professional, as well as outside salespersons and computer employees, are exempt from the FLSA's overtime provision, although employers can give exempt employees overtime pay if they wish to. Questions may sometimes arise as to whether an employee should be classified as exempt. The answer depends on the employee's primary duty. An executive employee, for example, is one whose primary duty is management. An employee's primary duty is determined by what he or she does that is of most value to the employer, not by how much time the employee spends doing particular tasks.

HIGHLIGHTING THE POINT

Kevin, a manager at a Starbucks store, works seventy hours a week for $650 to $800, a 10 to 20 percent bonus, and paid sick leave. Kevin asks his employer to pay him overtime, claiming that he spends 70 to 80 percent of his time waiting on customers and thus is not an executive employee.

Is Kevin entitled to be paid overtime? No. Kevin is the single highest-ranking employee in his particular store and is responsible for that store's on-site day-to-day operations. Because his primary duty is managerial, Starbucks is not required to pay him overtime.

27–6 IMMIGRATION LAW

Immigration law has been in the spotlight in recent years. In 2012, for example, the United States Supreme Court struck down key parts of a controversial Arizona immigration law designed to deter illegal immigration in that state. The ruling upheld the authority of the federal government to set up immigration policy and laws.

Immigration law has also become an area of increasing concern for businesses as the number of immigrants—especially illegal immigrants—to the United States has grown. Most came to find jobs, but U.S. employers face serious penalties if they hire illegal immigrants. Thus, an understanding of immigration laws has become increasingly important for businesses. Today, the most important laws governing immigration and employment are the Immigration Reform and Control Act and the Immigration Act.

LEARNING OUTCOME 4

Distinguish between the two most important federal statutes governing immigration and employment today.

27–6a The Immigration Reform and Control Act

The Immigration Reform and Control Act (IRCA) makes it illegal to hire, recruit, or refer for a fee someone not authorized to work in this country. The federal government conducts random compliance audits and engages in enforcement actions against employers who hire illegal immigrants.

To comply with the IRCA, an employer must complete *Form I-9, Employment Eligibility Verification*, for each new hire within three days of the start of employment. The form is available from U.S. Citizenship and Immigration Services, which is part of the U.S. Department of Homeland Security. The three-day period allows an employer to check the form's accuracy and to review and verify documents establishing the worker's identity and eligibility for employment in the United States. The employer must attest that an employee produced documents establishing his or her identity and legal employability. The IRCA prohibits situations in which an employer "should have known" that the worker was unauthorized.

27–6b The Immigration Act

U.S. immigration laws have long made provisions for businesses to hire foreign workers with special qualifications. Nevertheless, limits have also been placed on this practice. The Immigration Act limits the number of legal immigrants entering the United States by capping the number of visas (entry permits) that are issued each year. Employers recruiting workers from other countries must satisfy the U.S. Department of Labor that there is a shortage of qualified U.S. workers capable of performing the required work. The employer must also establish that bringing foreign workers into this country will not adversely affect the existing labor market in the employer's particular area.

27–7 LABOR LAW

LEARNING OUTCOME 5

Identify which federal statute established employees' rights to organize unions and to engage in collective bargaining.

In the 1930s, Congress enacted several laws to protect employees' rights to join labor unions, to bargain with management over the terms and conditions of employment, and to conduct strikes. Initially, the laws were concerned with protecting the rights and interests of workers. Subsequent legislation placed some restraints on unions and granted rights to employers. We look here at four major federal statutes regulating union-employer relations.

1. *The Norris-LaGuardia Act*—This act restricts the power of federal courts to issue injunctions against unions engaged in peaceful strikes. In effect, this act declares a national policy permitting employees to organize.

2. *The National Labor Relations Act (NLRA)*—The NLRA establishes the rights of private-sector employees to form unions, to negotiate with employers over employment conditions, and to strike. The act also defines a number of unfair labor practices, which will be discussed shortly.

   Created by the NLRA, the National Labor Relations Board (NLRB) has the power to investigate employee charges of unfair labor practices and to issue complaints against employers in response to those charges. The NLRB can issue *cease-and-desist orders*—which prohibit a firm from continuing a specific practice—when violations are found.

closed shop
A firm that requires union membership as a condition of employment.

union shop
A place of employment in which all workers, once employed, must become union members within a specified period of time.

right-to-work law
State law generally providing that employees are not to be required to join a union as a condition of receiving or retaining employment.

3. *The Labor-Management Relations Act (LMRA)*—The LMRA makes illegal certain unfair union practices, such as a **closed shop,** which requires union membership as a condition of obtaining employment. The act preserves the legality of the **union shop,** which does not require membership as a prerequisite for employment but can, and usually does, require that workers join the union after a specified amount of time on the job.

   The act also allows individual states to pass their own **right-to-work laws**—laws making it illegal for union membership to be required for *continued* employment in any establishment. Thus, union shops are technically illegal in states with right-to-work laws.

4. *The Labor-Management Reporting and Disclosure Act*—This act establishes an employee bill of rights and reporting requirements for union activities to prevent corruption. The act strictly regulates internal union business procedures, such as elections for union officers.

27–7a Union Organization

authorization card
A card signed by an employee that gives a union permission to act on his or her behalf in negotiations with management.

Typically, the first step in organizing a union at a particular firm is to have the workers sign authorization cards. An **authorization card** usually states that the worker desires to have a certain union, such as the United Auto Workers, represent the workforce. If a majority of the workers sign authorization cards, the union organizers (unionizers) present the cards to the employer and ask for formal recognition of the union.

If the employer refuses to voluntarily recognize the union after a majority of the workers sign authorization cards—or if fewer than 50 percent of the workers sign authorization cards—the union organizers present the cards to the NLRB with a petition for an election.

For an election to be held, the unionizers must show that at least 30 percent of the workers to be represented support a union or an election on unionization. The proposed union must also represent an appropriate bargaining unit—that is, employees whose skills, duties, and pay are similar. The NLRB supervises the election. If the proposed union receives a majority of the votes, the NLRB certifies the union as the bargaining representative of the employees.

27–7b Collective Bargaining

After the NLRB certifies the union, the union's local office will be authorized to negotiate with management on behalf of the workers in the bargaining unit. **Collective bargaining**—the process by which labor and management negotiate the terms and conditions of employment—is at the heart of the federal labor laws.

collective bargaining
The process by which labor and management negotiate the terms and conditions of employment.

Negotiating Terms and Conditions Wages, hours of work, and certain other conditions of employment may be discussed during collective bargaining sessions. Subjects for negotiation may include workplace safety, employee discounts, health-care plans, pension funds, and apprentice programs.

Some demands are illegal in collective bargaining. Management need not bargain over a provision that would be illegal if it were included in a contract. **EXAMPLE 27.7** During negotiations with Riverside Rehabilitation Center, the Service Employees International Union presents a demand for *featherbedding*—that is, hiring more employees than are needed to do a certain project. Riverside management does not need to respond to that demand, because the practice of featherbedding is illegal under the LMRA.◄

Good Faith Once an employer and a union sit down at the conference table, they must negotiate in good faith and make a reasonable effort to come to an agreement. They are not obligated to reach an agreement. They must, however, approach the negotiations with the idea that an agreement is possible. Both parties may engage in hard bargaining, but the bargaining process itself must be geared to reaching a compromise—not avoiding a compromise.

Although good faith is a matter of subjective intent, a party's actions can be used to evaluate the party's good or bad faith. Excessive delaying tactics may be proof of bad faith, as is insistence on obviously unreasonable contract terms.

HIGHLIGHTING THE POINT

During negotiations for a new contract with Westview Energy, the Allied Power Workers Union proposes a certain pay increase. Westview rejects the proposal and does not offer a counterproposal. Westview managers also begin a campaign to undermine the union. In addition, Westview unilaterally changes the terms and conditions of employment during the collective bargaining process.

Do Westview's actions indicate bad faith in the collective bargaining process? Yes. Rejecting a proposal without making a counteroffer, campaigning to undercut union support, and changing the terms and conditions of employment during the bargaining process are indications of bad faith. Other actions that show bad faith include constantly shifting positions on disputed contract terms and sending bargainers who lack the authority to commit the company to a contract.

An employer or a union that refuses to bargain in good faith without justification commits an unfair labor practice.

Employer Unfair Labor Practices For employers, the most significant unfair labor practices include the following:

1. *Refusal to recognize and negotiate*—An employer's failure to recognize and bargain in good faith with a union over issues affecting all employees in the bargaining unit is an unfair labor practice. If the union loses the majority support of those it represents, however, an employer is not obligated to continue recognition of the union.

2. *Interference in union activities*—An employer may not interfere with, restrain, or coerce employees in the exercise of their rights to form a union and bargain collectively. Unlawful employer interference may take a variety of forms. For instance, it is an unfair practice for an employer to make threats that may interfere with an employee's decision to join a union. Even asking employees about their views on the union may be considered coercive. In addition, employers may not prohibit certain forms of union activity in the workplace. **EXAMPLE 27.8** If John has a grievance with his employer, Mayfair Trucking, Mayfair cannot prevent the union from participating in the grievance process in support of John.◄

3. *Discrimination*—Employers cannot discriminate against workers because they are union officers or are otherwise associated with a union. When workers must be laid off, for example, the company cannot consider union participation as a criterion for deciding whom to fire.

Strikes Sometimes, a union and an employer may approach the bargaining table in good faith but simply be unable to reach an agreement because of genuine differences of opinion. If the parties are deadlocked, the union may call a **strike** against the employer. The right to strike is of fundamental importance to the collective bargaining process, because it is a threat that the union can use to offset the disparity in bargaining power between management and labor.

strike
An action undertaken by unionized workers when collective bargaining fails; the workers leave their jobs, refuse to work, and (typically) picket the employer's workplace.

Picket Lines Once workers approve the plan to strike, then their services will no longer be available to the employer. Of course, an employer is not obligated to pay striking workers. Strikers have the right to form a *picket line*, in which they and other persons line up outside the workplace protesting and attempting to discourage others from entering the workplace. Workers who are not involved in the strike have the right to refuse to cross the picket line.

Replacement Workers If a strike goes on for several weeks and management finds that it is unable to maintain the production schedules needed to fulfill existing orders, then it may decide to hire replacement workers to fill the positions vacated by the strikers. An employer may hire *temporary* replacement workers during any strike. An employer may hire *permanent* replacement workers only if the dispute is an *economic strike* called by the union to pressure the employer to make concessions on wages, hours, or other terms of employment.

ANSWERING THE LEGAL PROBLEM

In the legal problem set out at the beginning of this chapter, a U.S. Department of Transportation rule requires employees engaged in oil and gas pipeline operations to submit to random drug testing. The rule does not require that before being tested, the individual must be suspected of drug use.

A **If the employees challenge this rule in court, will the rule be upheld?** Yes. The government's interest in promoting public safety in the pipeline industry outweighs the employees' privacy interests.

TERMS AND CONCEPTS FOR REVIEW

authorization card 372	minimum wage 370	whistleblower 365
closed shop 372	right-to-work law 372	workers' compensation laws 366
collective bargaining 373	strike 374	
employment-at-will doctrine 365	union shop 372	

CHAPTER SUMMARY—EMPLOYMENT, IMMIGRATION, AND LABOR LAW

LEARNING OUTCOME	
1	**State exceptions to the employment-at-will doctrine.** Under the employment-at-will doctrine, either party may terminate an employment relationship at any time and for any reason (at will). To protect employees from some of the harsh results of the doctrine, courts have made exceptions to it, which include whistleblower statutes, exceptions based on an implied contract, and public-policy exceptions.
2	**Discuss the protection available to employees injured on the job.** State workers' compensation laws compensate workers who are injured in accidents that occur on the job or in the course of employment. Under the Occupational Safety and Health Act, employers must meet safety and health standards covering working conditions for employees.
3	**Describe the major provisions of the Fair Labor Standards Act.** The Fair Labor Standards Act (FLSA) is concerned with child labor, minimum wage, and overtime provisions. Children under fourteen are restricted on the number of hours and time of day that they can work, especially on school days. A federal minimum wage must be paid to all covered employees. Employees are entitled to 1.5 times their regular hourly pay for any hours worked in excess of forty hours per workweek. Employees who are categorized as executive, administrative, or professional (such as outside salespersons) are exempt from the FLSA's overtime pay requirements.
4	**Distinguish between the two most important federal statutes governing immigration and employment today.** The most important federal statutes governing immigration and the employment of noncitizens are the Immigration Reform and Control Act (IRCA) and the Immigration Act. The IRCA prohibits the hiring of illegal immigrants. Employers must verify the employment eligibility of each new employee. The Immigration Act limits legal immigration. Under this act, to bring workers into the United States, an employer must show that there is a shortage of such workers and that the foreign workers' presence will not affect the relevant labor market.
5	**Identify which federal statute established employees' rights to organize unions and to engage in collective bargaining.** The National Labor Relations Act is the federal statute that gave employees the right to organize unions and bargain collectively. In addition, labor unions and collective bargaining are covered by the Norris-LaGuardia Act, the Labor-Management Relations Act, and the Labor-Management Reporting and Disclosure Act.

ISSUE SPOTTERS

Check your answers to the *Issue Spotters* against the answers provided in Appendix C at the end of this text.

1. American Manufacturing Company (AMC) issues an employee handbook that states that employees will be discharged only for good cause. One day, Greg, an AMC supervisor, says to Larry, "I don't like your looks. You're fired." Can AMC be held liable for breach of contract? If so, why? If not, why? (See *Employment at Will.*)

2. Erin, an employee of Fine Print Shop, is injured on the job. For Erin to obtain workers' compensation, does her injury have to have been caused by Fine Print's negligence? Does it matter whether the action causing the injury was intentional? Explain. (See *Worker Health and Safety.*)

USING BUSINESS LAW

27–1. Wages. Calzoni Boating Co. is an interstate business engaged in manufacturing and selling boats. The company has five hundred nonunion employees. Representatives of these employees are requesting a four-day, ten-hours-per-day workweek, and Calzoni is concerned that this would require paying time and a half after eight hours per day. Which federal act is Calzoni thinking of that might require this? Will the act in fact require paying time and a half for all hours worked over eight hours per day if the employees' proposal is accepted? Explain. (See *Wage and Hour Laws.*)

27–2. Workers' Compensation. Galvin Strang worked for a tractor company in one of its factories. Near his work station, there was a conveyor belt that ran through a large industrial oven. Sometimes, the workers would use the oven to heat their meals. Thirty-inch-high flasks containing molds were fixed at regular intervals on the conveyor and were transported into the oven. Strang had to walk between the flasks to get to his work station. One day, the conveyor was not moving, and Strang used the oven to cook a frozen pot pie. As he was removing the pot pie from the oven, the conveyor came on. One of the flasks struck Strang and seriously injured him. Strang sought recovery under the state workers' compensation law. Should he recover? Why or why not? (See *Worker Health and Safety.*)

REAL-WORLD CASE PROBLEMS

27–3. Unemployment Compensation. Fior Ramirez worked as a housekeeper for Remington Lodging & Hospitality, a hotel in Florida. When her father, who lived in the Dominican Republic, had a stroke, Ramirez asked her manager, Katie Berkowski, for time off to be with him. Berkowski refused the request. Two days later, Berkowski got a call from Ramirez to say that she was with her father. He died about a week later. When Ramirez returned to work, Berkowski claimed Ramierez had voluntarily abandoned her position. Ramirez then applied for unemployment compensation. Under the applicable Florida statute, "an employee is disqualified from receiving benefits if he or she voluntarily left work without good cause." Does Ramirez qualify for benefits? Explain. [*Ramirez v. Reemployment Assistance Appeals Commission*, 135 So.3d 408 (Fla.App. 2014)] (See *Retirement Income and Security.*)

27–4. Collective Bargaining. SDBC Holdings, Inc., acquired Stella D'oro Biscuit Company, a bakery in New York City. At the time, a collective bargaining agreement existed between Stella D'oro and the Bakery, Confectionary, Tobacco Workers and Grain Millers International Union, Local 50. During negotiations to renew the agreement, Stella D'oro allowed Local 50 to examine and take notes on the company's financial statement and offered the union an opportunity to make its own copy, but Stella D'oro would not give or provide Local 50 with a copy. Did Stella D'oro engage in an unfair labor practice? Discuss. [*SDBC Holdings, Inc. v. National Labor Relations Board*, 711 F.3d 281 (2d Cir. 2013)] (See *Labor Law.*)

27–5. Workers' Compensation. As a safety measure, Dynea USA, Inc., required an employee, Tony Fairbanks, to wear steel-toed boots. One of the boots caused a sore on Fairbanks's leg. The skin over the sore broke, and within a week, Fairbanks was hospitalized with a serious infection. He filed a workers' compensation claim. Dynea argued that the bacteria that had caused the infection had been on Fairbanks's skin before he came to work. What are the requirements to recover workers' compensation benefits? Does this claim qualify? Explain. [*Dynea USA, Inc. v. Fairbanks*, 241 Or.App. 311, 250 P.3d 389 (2011)] (See *Worker Health and Safety.*)

ETHICAL QUESTIONS

27–6. Workers' Compensation. Should workers' compensation be denied to a worker who is injured off the employer's premises, regardless of the reason the worker is off the premises? Why or why not? (See *Worker Health and Safety*.)

27–7. Overtime. McNeill Pediatrics is a subsidiary of Johnson & Johnson (J&J). Patty Smith was a McNeill senior professional sales representative. Her position required her to visit prescribing physicians to extoll the benefits of J&J pharmaceuticals. She targeted ten doctors per day, with revisits each quarter. Plans to maximize results were at her discretion. Her base salary was $66,000, with potential bonuses. Was Smith eligible for overtime pay? Is it fair to exempt any employees from overtime pay requirements? Why or why not? [*Smith v. Johnson and Johnson,* 593 F.3d 280 (3d Cir. 2010)] (See *Wage and Hour Laws.*)

Chapter 27—Work Set

TRUE-FALSE QUESTIONS

_____ 1. Employment "at will" means that employers can fire employees only with good cause.

_____ 2. Employers are required by federal statute to establish health-insurance and pension plans.

_____ 3. Management serves as the representative of the employees in bargaining with the union over the rights of the employees.

_____ 4. Strikes are protected under federal law.

_____ 5. In most states, an employer is justified in firing an employee who refuses to do something illegal.

_____ 6. Workers' compensation laws set up administrative procedures through which employees recover for work-related injuries.

_____ 7. Qualifying employers must provide employees with up to twelve weeks of family or medical leave during any twelve-month period.

_____ 8. A closed shop requires union membership as a condition of employment.

_____ 9. Employers must complete _Form I-9_ within three days of the start of employment by new hires to comply with the Immigration Reform and Control Act.

MULTIPLE-CHOICE QUESTIONS

_____ 1. Fast Jack is a fast-food restaurant that employs minors. Fast Jack is subject to the federal child labor, minimum wage, and overtime provisions in

    a. the Family and Medical Leave Act.
    b. the Consolidated Omnibus Budget Reconciliation Act.
    c. the Fair Labor Standards Act.
    d. none of the above.

_____ 2. Noelia works on the assembly line for Frozen Foods. Noelia and other Frozen Foods employees designate the International Union of Food Workers (IUFW) as their bargaining representative. Without violating federal labor law, Frozen Foods can

    a. contribute funds to the IUFW.
    b. discharge Noelia for supporting the IUFW.
    c. refuse to bargain with the IUFW.
    d. none of the above.

_____ 3. U.S. Goods, Inc. (USG), recruits workers from other countries to work in its U.S. plant. To comply with the Immigration Act, USG must show

    a. that there is a shortage of qualified U.S. workers to perform the work.
    b. that bringing aliens into the country will not adversely affect the existing labor market in that area.
    c. both a and b.
    d. none of the above.

_____ 4. Ron is an employee of National Sales Company. Contributions to the federal Social Security system are made by

    a. Ron only.
    b. National only.
    c. Ron and National.
    d. none of the above.

5. ABC Box Corporation provides health insurance for its 150 employees, including Diana. When Diana takes twelve weeks' leave to care for her new baby, she

   a. can continue her health insurance at her expense.
   b. can continue her health insurance at ABC's expense.
   c. loses her health insurance immediately on taking leave.
   d. is entitled to "leave pay" equal to twelve weeks of health-insurance coverage.

6. The International Brotherhood of Electrical Workers (IBEW) represents the employees of Consolidated Cable & Wire Corporation. The IBEW calls a strike to pressure Consolidated Cable to make concessions on wages. To maintain production during the strike, the employer

   a. may hire temporary replacement workers.
   b. may set up a picket line.
   c. may hire permanent replacement workers and ignore the strike.
   d. may determine the strike is an economic strike and have management staff work production shifts.

7. Norma Jean wants to unionize her fellow workers at Metro West Ambulance Company. She gets a majority of the workers who will be represented by the union to sign authorization cards, but despite this result, Metro West refuses to recognize the union. To hold an election to unionize the workforce, what percentage of the workers must have signed authorization cards?

   a. At least 25 percent.
   b. At least 30 percent.
   c. At least 50 percent.
   d. none of the above.

8. Regal Products sets up a pension fund for its employees. Regal's operation of the fund is regulated by

   a. the Federal Unemployment Tax Act.
   b. the Federal Insurance Contributions Act.
   c. the Employment Retirement Income Security Act.
   d. none of the above.

 ## ANSWERING MORE LEGAL PROBLEMS

1. Mercer Management is a consulting firm that operates an information technology (IT) center to bring greater efficiencies to other businesses and thereby help those companies cut costs. In Mercer's IT center, the firm employs a number of noncitizen temporary programmers with specialized skills, mostly recruited from India.

   Do federal immigration laws limit Mercer's hiring practices? Yes. U.S. immigration laws include provisions for businesses to hire _____ workers with _____ qualifications. But these laws also place limits on the practice. For instance, the Immigration Act caps the number of _____ that the federal government issues each year. Employers, such as Mercer, that recruit workers from other countries must show the U.S. Department of Labor that there is a shortage of qualified _____ workers who can perform the work. An employer must also show that bringing the workers into the United States will not adversely affect the existing labor market in the employer's area.

2. Serge worked for Service Attendant Corporation (SAC). He requested time off under the Family and Medical Leave Act (FMLA) from April 29 through May 31 to undergo treatment for alcoholism. For the month of May, he was hospitalized as part of the treatment. When he did not return to work on June 1, SAC fired him. SAC also counted April 29 and 30 as improper absences when it learned that Serge had been abusing alcohol on those dates.

   Did SAC violate Serge's rights under the FMLA? No. The FMLA requires qualifying employers to provide employees with up to twelve weeks of family or medical _____ for any twelve-month period. The employer must _____ employment in the same position or a comparable position when the employee returns to work. Thus, in this problem, Serge was entitled to _____ under the FMLA to obtain treatment for alcoholism. But his absence from work to abuse a substance was not a legitimate use of the _____, and his failure to return to work supported SAC's termination of his employment.

EMPLOYMENT DISCRIMINATION

28

FACING A LEGAL PROBLEM

Select Circuits, Inc., hires only applicants with high school diplomas. More members of minorities in the local labor market lack high school diplomas than do members of the majority. Thus, minorities are excluded from Select's workforce at a substantially higher rate than nonminority workers. Richard, a member of a minority who is refused a job because he does not have a high school diploma, charges the employer with discrimination.

Q What is Select's defense to the charge? Is this defense valid?

LEARNING OUTCOMES

The five Learning Outcomes below are designed to help improve your understanding of the chapter. After reading this chapter, you should be able to:

❶ Distinguish between disparate-treatment discrimination and disparate-impact discrimination.

❷ List the remedies available under Title VII of the Civil Rights Act.

❸ Identify the federal act that prohibits discrimination based on age.

❹ Note what is required of employers to avoid liability for discrimination based on disability.

❺ State three defenses to claims of employment discrimination.

Out of the 1960s civil rights movement to end racial and other forms of discrimination grew a body of law protecting employees against discrimination in the workplace. In the past several decades, judicial decisions, administrative agency actions, and legislation have restricted the ability of both employers and unions to discriminate against workers on the basis of race, color, religion, national origin, gender, age, or disability. A class of persons defined by one or more of these criteria is known as a **protected class.**

Several federal statutes prohibit **employment discrimination** against members of protected classes. Although this chapter focuses on federal statutes, many states have their own laws that protect employees against discrimination. Sometimes, these state statutes provide protection for individuals who are not covered under federal statutes. For example, gay men and lesbians not protected under federal law from discrimination for their sexual orientation may be protected under state laws.

For more information on how to avoid employment discrimination in the workplace, see the *Linking Business Law to Your Career* feature at the end of this chapter.

protected class
A class of persons with identifiable characteristics, such as age, color, gender, national origin, race, and religion, who historically have been discriminated against.

employment discrimination
Treating employees or job applicants unequally on the basis of race, color, gender, national origin, religion, age, or disability.

28–1 TITLE VII OF THE CIVIL RIGHTS ACT

Title VII of the Civil Rights Act of 1964 and its amendments prohibit job discrimination against employees, job applicants, and union members on the basis of race, color, national origin, religion, and gender at any stage of employment. Title VII applies to employers with fifteen or more employees, labor unions with fifteen or more members, labor unions that operate hiring halls (to which members go regularly to get jobs as those jobs become available), employment agencies, and state and local governing units or agencies. A special section of Title VII forbids discrimination in most federal government employment.

28–1a The Equal Employment Opportunity Commission

Compliance with Title VII is monitored by the Equal Employment Opportunity Commission (EEOC). Before filing a lawsuit, a person who alleges discrimination must file a claim with the EEOC, which investigates the facts and seeks to achieve a voluntary settlement between the employer and employee. If no settlement is reached, the EEOC may sue the employer. If the EEOC chooses not to sue—for example, if it does not believe that the complaining individual was discriminated against—the victim may bring his or her own lawsuit.

28–1b Intentional Discrimination

Title VII prohibits intentional discrimination. Intentional discrimination by an employer against an employee is known as **disparate-treatment discrimination**. The courts have established specific procedures for resolving disparate-treatment cases. A plaintiff who sues on the basis of disparate-treatment discrimination in hiring must show the following four requirements:

1. She or he is a member of a protected class.
2. She or he applied and was qualified for the job in question.
3. She or he was rejected by the employer.
4. The employer continued to seek applicants for the position or filled the position with a person not in a protected class.

If these four requirements can be met, the plaintiff makes out a *prima facie* case of illegal discrimination. (Note that *prima facie* is Latin for "at first sight." Legally, it refers to a fact that is presumed to be true, unless contradicted by evidence.)

> **disparate-treatment discrimination**
> Intentional discrimination against individuals on the basis of color, gender, national origin, race, or religion.

> **prima facie case**
> A case in which the plaintiff has produced sufficient evidence to prove his or her conclusion if the defendant produces no evidence to rebut it.

HIGHLIGHTING THE POINT

Chloe, an African American, is a loan officer for Funds Reserve Bank. She applies for the position of branch manager. Chloe meets the job's requirements, including a college degree and a minimum of five years of experience in financial services. Funds Reserve rejects her application. One month later, the bank promotes Chloe's co-worker, Garth, a white male with similar qualifications, to the position.

Can Chloe establish a *prima facie* case of illegal discrimination? Yes. Chloe is a member of two protected classes—she is an African American woman. She applied for the job of branch manager, a position for which she was qualified. Her employer rejected her, and later filled the position with Garth, a person who is not a member of a protected class.

28–1c Unintentional Discrimination

In addition to intentional discrimination, Title VII also prohibits unintentional discrimination. For instance, employers often use interviews and testing procedures to choose from among a large number of applicants for job openings. Minimum educational requirements are also common in these situations. These practices and procedures may have an unintended discriminatory impact on a protected class.

Disparate-impact discrimination occurs when a protected group of people is adversely affected by an employer's practices, procedures, or tests, even though they do not appear to be discriminatory. In a disparate-impact discrimination case, the complaining party must first show statistically that the employer's practices, procedures, or tests are discriminatory in effect. Once the plaintiff has made out a *prima facie* case, the burden of proof shifts to the employer to show that the practices or procedures in question were justified.

> **LEARNING OUTCOME 1**
> Distinguish between disparate-treatment discrimination and disparate-impact discrimination.

> **disparate-impact discrimination**
> Discrimination that results from certain employer practices or procedures that, although not discriminatory, obviously have a discriminatory effect.

EXAMPLE 28.1 Shady Cove District Fire Department administers an exam to applicants for the position of firefighter. At the exam session, one hundred white applicants take the test, and fifty pass and are hired. At the same exam session, sixty minority applicants take the test, but only twelve pass and are hired. Because the test operated to exclude members of a protected class from the department at a substantially higher rate than nonmembers, disparate-impact discrimination has occurred. ◄

28–1d Discrimination Based on Race, Color, and National Origin

Race is interpreted broadly to apply to the ancestry or ethnic characteristics of a group of persons, such as Native Americans. National origin refers to discrimination based on a person's birth in another country or their ancestry or culture, such as Hispanic.

If an employer's standards or policies for selecting or promoting employees have a discriminatory effect on employees or job applicants in these protected classes, then a presumption of illegal discrimination arises. To avoid liability, the employer must show that its standards or policies have a substantial, demonstrable relationship to realistic qualifications for the job.

EXAMPLE 28.2 Hernando, a Hispanic American, is a machinist for Dunsmire Steel Mill. Hernando argues with Jack, the plant's foreman, and refuses to follow his instructions. Dunsmire discharges Hernando and replaces him with Jim, a white worker. A presumption of illegal discrimination based on race arises—Dunsmire's termination of Hernando has a discriminatory effect on an employee who is a member of a protected class. Dunsmire can avoid liability, however, by showing that Hernando's termination was a result of his violation of a workplace policy against insubordination. ◄

28–1e Discrimination Based on Religion

Employers cannot treat employees more or less favorably based on the employees' religious beliefs or practices, nor can they require employees to participate in any religious activity (or forbid them from participating in one). **EXAMPLE 28.3** Bailey is a salesperson for Country Village Car & Truck Sales when she is discharged for failing to attend the weekly prayer meetings of the dealership's employees. Bailey has a valid claim of religious discrimination. ◄

In addition, an employer must "reasonably accommodate" the religious practices of its employees, unless to do so would cause *undue hardship* to the employer's business. **EXAMPLE 28.4** Anton is a forklift operator in the warehouse and storage yard of Timberline Lumber Company. Anton is also a Seventh Day Adventist, a religion whose followers abstain from secular work on Saturday. Anton asks Timberline not to require him to work on Saturdays. The employer must make a reasonable attempt to accommodate Anton's sincerely held religious belief. ◄

28–1f Discrimination Based on Gender

Employers are also prohibited from classifying or advertising jobs as male or female, unless the employer can prove that the gender of the applicant is essential to the job. Employers also cannot have separate male and female seniority lists or refuse to promote employees based on their gender.

Pregnancy Discrimination The Pregnancy Discrimination Act of 1978 expanded the definition of gender to include discrimination based on pregnancy. As a result, women affected by pregnancy, childbirth, or related medical conditions must be treated the same as other persons not so affected, but similar in ability to work. Thus, under this act, women cannot be discriminated against in their workplace settings for all employment-related purposes, including the receipt of benefits under employee benefit programs.

Wage Discrimination The Equal Pay Act of 1963 requires equal pay for male and female employees working at the same establishment doing similar work. To determine whether the Equal Pay Act has been violated, a court will look to the primary duties of the two jobs—the job content rather than the job description controls. If the wage differential is due to any factor other than gender, such as a seniority or merit system, then it does not violate the Equal Pay Act.

A Gender Discrimination Lawsuit To succeed in a lawsuit for gender discrimination in the workplace, a plaintiff must demonstrate that gender was a determining factor in the employer's hiring decisions or employment actions.

HIGHLIGHTING THE POINT

McKensie works in the maintenance department for Evergreen Bus Tours. She complains to Oliver, her supervisor, that Peter, an assistant manager, treats her unfairly. Oliver admits to McKensie that he is aware Peter is "harder on women." Soon after, Oliver talks to Peter about McKensie, but takes no disciplinary action. Later, Peter confronts McKensie, pushing her up against a wall and yelling at her. McKensie files a formal complaint but is subsequently fired.

Is there sufficient evidence that gender was a determining factor in McKensie's discharge? Yes. Gender was a determining factor in McKensie's losing her job with Evergreen. Peter singled her out because she was a woman, and Oliver, her supervisor, was aware of Peter's pattern of poor behavior with female employees. McKensie could pursue a gender discrimination lawsuit against her employer.

28–1g Constructive Discharge

Most Title VII complaints involve unlawful discrimination in decisions to hire or fire employees. In some situations, however, employees who leave their jobs voluntarily can claim that they were "constructively discharged" by the employer. **Constructive discharge** occurs when the employer causes the employee's working conditions to be so intolerable that a reasonable person in the employee's position would feel compelled to quit.

constructive discharge
A termination of employment brought about by making the employee's working conditions so intolerable that the employee reasonably feels compelled to leave.

EXAMPLE 28.5 Sarah's employer humiliates her in front of her co-workers by informing her that she is being demoted. Sarah's co-workers then continue to insult her about her national (Polish) origin. The employer is aware of this discriminatory treatment but does nothing to stop it, despite repeated complaints by Sarah. Sarah would likely have sufficient evidence to maintain an action for constructive discharge under Title VII.◄

28–1h Sexual and Online Harassment

Yet another category of complaints under Title VII concerns the treatment of employees in the workplace. These include complaints involving sexual harassment and online harassment, which can create a hostile work environment.

sexual harassment
The demanding of sexual favors in return for job promotion or other benefits, or language or conduct that is so sexually offensive that it creates a hostile working environment.

Sexual Harassment Title VII protects employees against **sexual harassment** in the workplace. Sexual harassment can take two forms—*quid pro quo* harassment and hostile-environment harassment. *Quid pro quo* harassment occurs when sexual favors are demanded in return for job opportunities, promotions, salary increases, or other benefits.

Hostile-environment harassment occurs when a pattern of sexually offensive conduct permeates the workplace and is sufficiently severe or pervasive to alter the conditions of employment and create an abusive working environment.

Real-World Case Example

Teresa Roberts worked for Mike's Trucking, Ltd., in Columbus, Ohio. Her supervisor was Mike's owner, Mike Culbertson. According to Roberts, Culbertson called her his "sex-retary" and constantly talked about his sex life. He often asked her if she wanted to sit on "Big Daddy's" lap, rubbed his groin against her, and asked if she needed help in the restroom. Roberts asked him to stop the behavior, to no avail. She became inse-cure and less productive, and began to suffer anxiety attacks and high blood pressure. Roberts filed a suit in an Ohio state court against Mike's. Other female employees cor-roborated Roberts's account. From a judgment in Roberts's favor, Mike's appealed.

Did Culbertson's conduct violate Title VII by creating a hostile work environment through sexual harassment? Yes. In a 2014 case, *Roberts v. Mike's Trucking, Ltd.*, a state interme-diate appellate court affirmed the lower court's judgment. The court noted that there was substantial evidence that "a reasonable person would find Culbertson's conduct created a hostile environment and Roberts found the conduct to be sufficiently severe or pervasive to affect her employment."

Sexual Harassment by Supervisors For an employer to be held liable for a supervisor's sexual harassment, the supervisor normally must have taken a *tangible employment action* against the employee. A **tangible employment action** is a significant change in employment status or benefits, such as when an employee is fired, refused a promotion, demoted, or reassigned to a position with significantly different responsibilities. A constructive discharge also qualifies as a tangible employment action.

tangible employment action
A significant change in employment status or benefit, such as occurs when an employee is fired, refused a promotion, or reassigned to a lesser position.

Employers' Defense In 1998, the United States Supreme Court issued two important rulings that established what is known as the *Ellerth/Faragher* defense to charges of sexual harassment. An employer that can prove both elements of this defense normally will not be liable for a supervisor's harassment. The elements are as follows:

1. The employer must have taken reasonable care to prevent and promptly correct any sexually harassing behavior (by establishing effective anti-harassment policies and complaint procedures, for instance).

2. The plaintiff-employee must have unreasonably failed to take advantage of preventive or corrective opportunities provided by the employer.

Online Harassment Employees' online activities can also create a hostile working environment in many ways. For instance, racial jokes, ethnic slurs, or other comments contained in e-mail, texts, blogs, and other social media platforms can lead to a claim of hostile-environment harassment or other forms of discrimination.

Employers, however, may be able to avoid liability for online harassment by taking prompt remedial action. **EXAMPLE 28.6** Bernice, an employee at Vernon

Investments, receives e-mails from Donald, another employee, containing racially harassing "jokes." After Bernice complains to her supervisor, Vernon's management warns Donald about the proper use of the company's e-mail system. Vernon's human resources manager also holds two employee meetings to discuss its e-mail policy. Because Vernon took prompt remedial action regarding Bernice's complaint, it should not be liable for Donald's racially harassing e-mails. ◄

28–1i Retaliation by Employers

Employers sometimes retaliate against employees who complain about harassment or other Title VII violations. Retaliation can take many forms. An employer might demote, fire, or otherwise change the terms, conditions, and benefits of the person's employment. Title VII prohibits retaliation.

In a *retaliation claim,* an individual asserts that she or he suffered harm as a result of making a charge, testifying, or participating in a Title VII investigation or proceeding. To prove retaliation, the plaintiff must show that the challenged action was one that would likely have dissuaded a reasonable worker from making or supporting a charge of discrimination.

HIGHLIGHTING THE POINT

Fanny and her fiancé, Greg, are employees of Pioneer Village Retirement Services. Fanny files a gender-discrimination claim against Pioneer Village with the Equal Employment Opportunity Commission. Pioneer Village then threatens to fire Greg unless Fanny withdraws her claim.

Can Greg file a retaliation claim against Pioneer Village? Yes. Pioneer Village's threat to fire Greg unless Fanny withdraws her gender-discrimination claim is unlawful. Title VII prohibits any employer action that might dissuade a reasonable employee (Greg) from making or supporting a charge of discrimination. In addition, a reasonable employee (Fanny) might be dissuaded from pursuing a claim of discrimination if she knew that her fiancé (Greg) would be fired as a result.

28–1j Remedies under Title VII

LEARNING OUTCOME 2

List the remedies available under Title VII of the Civil Rights Act.

If the plaintiff successfully proves that unlawful discrimination occurred, he or she could be awarded reinstatement, back pay, retroactive promotions, and damages. Compensatory damages are available in cases of intentional discrimination. Punitive damages may be recovered against a private employer, if the employer acted with malice or reckless indifference to an individual's rights. The total amount of compensatory and punitive damages that a plaintiff can recover ranges from $50,000 against employers with one hundred or fewer employees to $300,000 against employers with more than five hundred employees.

28–2 DISCRIMINATION BASED ON AGE

LEARNING OUTCOME 3

Identify the federal act that prohibits discrimination based on age.

Age discrimination is potentially the most widespread form of discrimination because anyone—regardless of race, color, national origin, or gender—could be a victim at some point in life. The Age Discrimination in Employment Act (ADEA) of 1967 prohibits employment discrimination on the basis of age against individuals forty years of age or older. An amendment to the act prohibits mandatory retirement for nonmanagerial workers.

28–2a Which Employers Are Covered?

For the ADEA to apply, an employer must have twenty or more employees, and the employer's business activities must affect interstate commerce. The act includes a provision that extends protections against age discrimination to federal government employers. This provision encompasses not only claims of age discrimination but also claims of retaliation for complaining about age discrimination. Thus, the ADEA protects both federal and private-sector employees from retaliation based on age-related complaints.

Generally, a state employer is immune from a private suit brought by an employee under the ADEA, unless the state consents to the suit. This immunity stems from the United States Supreme Court's interpretation of the Eleventh Amendment (see Appendix A at the end of this book).

28–2b Procedure under the ADEA

The ADEA is similar to Title VII in that it offers protection against intentional (disparate-treatment) and unintentional (disparate-impact) age discrimination. As discussed earlier, Title VII requires a plaintiff to show that an employer was motivated only *in part* by unlawful discrimination. Under the ADEA, however, a plaintiff must show that unlawful discrimination was not just a reason but *the* reason for an adverse employment action.

A *Prima Facie* Case To establish a *prima facie* case under the ADEA, a plaintiff must show that she or he was (1) a member of the protected age group, (2) qualified for the position from which she or he was discharged, and (3) discharged because of age discrimination.

EXAMPLE 28.7 Fifty-four-year-old Richard earns $25 per hour as a manager for Mid-West Soda Company. As part of Mid-West's restructuring, Richard is replaced by Tim, a younger worker with a lower salary—$15 per hour. Richard is given no opportunity to accept a lower wage or to take on additional duties to accommodate Mid-West's need to reduce costs. Instead, Richard is told, "You're too old to be working here." Based on these facts, Richard could establish a *prima facie* case under the ADEA. ◄

Employer Burden Once a *prima facie* case has been established, the burden then shifts to the employer. If the employer offers a legitimate reason for its action, then the plaintiff must show that the stated reason is only a pretext. In other words, despite the employer's stated reason, the plaintiff must show the real reason for the employer's decision was his or her age.

HIGHLIGHTING THE POINT

Victoria, who is sixty-two years old, is a longtime employee of Crooked River Outfitters. Yannick, the company's chief executive officer, fires Victoria. As the reason for her termination, Yannick refers to errors and issues with professionalism on Victoria's part. He also adds, "I need someone younger who I can pay less." Later, Zach, a younger, lower-paid employee, takes Victoria's former position with the company.

Can Victoria establish a *prima facie* case of age discrimination against Crooked River?
Yes. Victoria is a member of the protected age group and is qualified for the position from which she was discharged. Lastly, in light of her replacement, Zach, she was arguably discharged because of age discrimination.

(Continued)

Can Crooked River offer a legitimate reason for its action? Yes. When Victoria was discharged, Yannick cited errors and issues with professionalism on Victoria's part. Crooked River could offer these points as the reasons for its action. Victoria must then show that these reasons are only a pretext, which she might do by offering Yannick's comment about needing someone younger and who would work for a lower salary.

28-3 DISCRIMINATION BASED ON DISABILITY

LEARNING OUTCOME 4

Note what is required of employers to avoid liability for discrimination based on disability.

The Americans with Disabilities Act (ADA) prohibits disability-based discrimination in workplaces with fifteen or more workers. Basically, the ADA requires that employers reasonably accommodate the needs of persons with disabilities, unless doing so would cause the employer to suffer an undue hardship.

28-3a What Is a Disability?

The ADA is broadly drafted to cover persons with a wide range of disabilities. Specifically, the ADA defines disability to include any of the following:

1. A physical or mental impairment that substantially limits one or more of an individual's major life activities.

2. A record of such impairment.

3. Being regarded as having such an impairment.

Additionally, certain health conditions have been considered disabilities under the ADA. These conditions include, among others, alcoholism, blindness, cancer, cerebral palsy, heart disease, paraplegia, as well as testing positive for the human immunodeficiency virus (HIV).

A separate provision in the ADA prevents employers from taking adverse employment actions based on stereotypes or assumptions about individuals who associate with people who have disabilities. **EXAMPLE 28.8** Joan, an employer, refuses to hire Edward, who has a daughter with a physical disability. She bases her decision on the assumption that because of his daughter's disability, Edward will miss too much work or be unreliable. ◄ The ADA also prohibits employers from considering mitigating measures or medications when determining if an individual has a disability. Today, disability is often determined on a case-by-case basis.

28-3b Procedures under the ADA

To prevail on a disability claim under the ADA, a plaintiff must show that he or she (1) has a disability, (2) is otherwise qualified for the employment in question, and (3) was excluded from the employment solely because of the disability.

Filing a Claim As in Title VII cases, a plaintiff must pursue her or his claim through the EEOC before filing an action in court for a violation of the ADA. The EEOC may decide to investigate and perhaps even sue the employer on behalf of the employee. The EEOC can bring a suit against an employer for disability-based discrimination even though the employee may have previously agreed to submit any job-related disputes to arbitration. If the EEOC decides not to sue, then the employee is entitled to sue in court.

Remedies Plaintiffs in lawsuits brought under the ADA may obtain many of the same remedies available under Title VII. These include reinstatement, back pay, a limited amount of compensatory and punitive damages (for intentional discrimination), and certain other forms of relief.

28–3c Reasonable Accommodation

The ADA does not require that employers accommodate the needs of job applicants or employees with disabilities who are not otherwise qualified for the work. If a job applicant or an employee with a disability can perform essential job functions with a reasonable accommodation, however, the employer must make the accommodation. Required modifications may include installing ramps for a wheelchair, establishing more flexible working hours, creating or modifying job assignments, and creating or improving training materials and procedures. Generally, employers should give primary consideration to employees' preferences in deciding what accommodations should be made.

Undue Hardship Employers who do not accommodate the needs of persons with disabilities must demonstrate that the accommodations will cause "undue hardship" in terms of being significantly difficult or expensive for the employer. **EXAMPLE 28.9** Bryan uses a wheelchair and works for Loraine Software, which provides parking for its employees. Bryan informs Loraine supervisors that the provided parking spaces are so narrow that he is unable to extend the ramp on his van, which allows him to get in and out of the vehicle. Bryan asks his employer to reasonably accommodate his needs by paying a monthly fee for him to use a larger parking space in an adjacent lot. In this situation, it would not be an undue hardship for Loraine to pay for additional parking for Bryan.◄

Job Applications Employers must modify their job-application process so that those with disabilities can compete for jobs with those who do not have disabilities. For instance, a job announcement might be modified to allow job applicants to respond by e-mail or letter, as well as by telephone, so that the employer does not discriminate against potential applicants with hearing impairments.

 28–4 DEFENSES TO EMPLOYMENT DISCRIMINATION

Once a plaintiff succeeds in proving discrimination, the burden shifts to the employer to justify the discriminatory practice. Possible justifications, or defenses, for the employer include that the discrimination was the result of a business necessity, a bona fide occupational qualification, or a seniority system.

1. *Business necessity*—An employer may defend against a claim of disparate-impact (unintentional) discrimination by asserting that a practice that has a discriminatory effect is a **business necessity.** **EXAMPLE 28.10** EarthFix, Inc., an international consulting agency, requires its applicants to be fluent in at least one foreign language. If requiring a foreign language is shown to have a discriminatory effect, EarthFix can argue that a foreign language is necessary for its workers to perform the job at a required level of competence. If EarthFix can demonstrate a definite connection between foreign language fluency and job performance, it normally will succeed in this business necessity defense.◄

2. *Bona fide occupational qualification (BFOQ)*—Another defense applies when discrimination against a protected class is essential to a job—that is, when a particular trait is a BFOQ. Race can never be a BFOQ. Generally, courts have restricted the BFOQ defense to instances in which the employee's gender is essential to the job. For instance, a women's clothing store might legitimately hire only female sales attendants if part of an attendant's job involves assisting clients in the store's dressing rooms.

LEARNING OUTCOME 5

State three defenses to claims of employment discrimination.

business necessity
A defense in which the employer demonstrates that an employment practice that discriminates against members of a protected class is related to job performance.

3. *Seniority system*—If promotions or other job benefits are distributed according to a fair *seniority system*—in which workers with more years of service are promoted first or laid off last—an employer may have a defense against a discrimination lawsuit.

ANSWERING THE LEGAL PROBLEM

In the legal problem set out at the beginning of this chapter, Select Circuits, Inc., hires only applicants with high school diplomas. Under conditions in the local labor market, this practice has the effect of excluding minorities from Select's workforce. Richard, a member of a minority who is refused a job at Select because he does not have a high school diploma, sues Select, charging discrimination.

A **What is Select's defense to the charge?** Select might argue the defense of business necessity—specifically, that a high school education is required for workers to perform the job at a certain level of competence. **Is this defense valid?** If Select can prove that a definite connection exists between a high school education and job performance, then Select may succeed in proving the employment practice was a business necessity.

LINKING BUSINESS LAW to Your Career

HUMAN RESOURCES MANAGEMENT

Your career may lead to running a small business, to managing a small part of a larger business, or to making decisions for the operations of a big business. In any of these contexts, you may be responsible for employment decisions. As suggested in this chapter, an ill-conceived hiring or firing process can lead to a lawsuit. As a manager, you must also be sure that employees do not practice discrimination on the job. Enter the human resources management specialist.

What Is Human Resources Management?

Human resources management (HRM) is the acquisition, maintenance, and development of an organization's human resources. HRM involves the design and application of formal systems in an organization to ensure the effective and efficient use of human talent to accomplish organizational goals.

All managers need to be skilled in human resources management. Some firms require managers to play an active role in recruiting and selecting personnel, as well as in developing training programs. Those who work in a human resources department should be especially aware of the issues outlined in this chapter.

The Acquisition Phase of HRM

Acquiring talented employees is the first step in an HRM system. Recruitment must not violate any laws outlined in this chapter. For example, when evaluating a disabled job applicant, managers must make sure to consider only his or her qualifications, not the disability.

On-the-Job HRM Issues

Sexual harassment is a major concern, and you may need to work with an employment law specialist to develop antiharassment rules and policies. In addition, consider creating and supervising a reporting system so that harassment can be effectively and quickly stopped.

HRM Issues Concerning Employee Termination

Even in employment-at-will jurisdictions, lawsuits can arise for improper termination. Develop a system to protect your company, such as documenting an employee's misconduct and the employer's warnings, as well as knowing how much severance pay should be paid out on termination.

TERMS AND CONCEPTS FOR REVIEW

business necessity 389
constructive discharge 384
disparate-impact discrimination 382

disparate-treatment
    discrimination 382
employment discrimination 381
prima facie case 382

protected class 381
sexual harassment 384
tangible employment action 385

CHAPTER SUMMARY—EMPLOYMENT DISCRIMINATION

LEARNING OUTCOME	
1	**Distinguish between disparate-treatment discrimination and disparate-impact discrimination.** Intentional discrimination by an employer against an employee is known as disparate-treatment discrimination. Disparate-impact discrimination occurs when, as a result of an employer's practices, procedures, or tests, the employer's workforce does not reflect the percentages of nonwhites, women, and members of other protected classes that characterize qualified individuals in the local labor market. Disparate-impact discrimination does not require evidence of intent.
2	**List the remedies available under Title VII of the Civil Rights Act.** Remedies under Title VII include job reinstatement, back pay, retroactive promotions, and damages. Compensatory damages are available only in cases of intentional discrimination. Punitive damages may be recovered against a private employer only if the employer acted with malice or reckless indifference to an individual's rights.
3	**Identify the federal act that prohibits discrimination based on age.** The Age Discrimination in Employment Act prohibits discrimination in employment on the basis of age against individuals forty years of age or older.
4	**Note what is required of employers to avoid liability for discrimination based on disability.** The Americans with Disabilities Act requires employers with fifteen or more workers to reasonably accommodate the needs of job applicants and employees with disabilities unless to do so would cause the employer to suffer an undue hardship. In other words, an employer does not have to hire unqualified applicants with disabilities. But if an applicant with a disability can, with reasonable accommodation, perform the essential functions of the job, the employer must make the accommodation.
5	**State three defenses to claims of employment discrimination.** Employers can justify discrimination on the ground that it was a result of a business necessity, a bona fide occupational qualification, or a seniority system.

ISSUE SPOTTERS

Check your answers to the *Issue Spotters* against the answers provided in Appendix C at the end of this text.

1. Ruth is a supervisor for Subs & Suds, a restaurant. Tim is a Subs & Suds employee. The owner announces that some employees will be discharged. Ruth tells Tim that if he has sex with her, he can keep his job. Is this sexual harassment? Why or why not? (See *Title VII of the Civil Rights Act.*)

2. Koko, a person with a disability, applies for a job at Lively Sales Corporation for which she is well qualified, but she is rejected. Lively continues to seek applicants and eventually fills the position with a person who does not have a disability. Could Koko succeed in a suit against Lively for discrimination? Explain. (See *Discrimination Based on Disability.*)

USING BUSINESS LAW

28–1. Title VII Violations. Discuss fully whether any of the following actions would constitute a violation of Title VII of the 1964 Civil Rights Act:

1. Tennington, Inc., is a consulting firm with ten employees. These employees travel on consulting jobs in seven states. Tennington has an employment record of hiring only white males. (See *Title VII of the Civil Rights Act.*)

2. Novo Films, Inc., is making a film about Africa and needs to employ approximately one hundred extras for the picture. To hire these extras, Novo advertises in all major newspapers in Southern California. The ad states that only African Americans need apply. (See *Title VII of the Civil Rights Act.*)

28–2. Disparate-Impact Discrimination. Chinawa, a major processor of cheese sold throughout the United States, employs one hundred workers at its principal processing plant. The plant is located in Heartland Corners, which has a population that is 50 percent white and 25 percent African American, with the other 25 percent comprising Hispanic Americans, Asian Americans, and others. Chinawa requires a high school diploma as a condition of employment for its cleaning crew. Three-fourths of the white population completes high school, compared with only one-fourth of those in the minority groups. Chinawa has an all-white cleaning crew. Has Chinawa violated Title VII? Explain. (See *Title VII of the Civil Rights Act.*)

REAL-WORLD CASE PROBLEMS

28–3. Discrimination Based on Disability. Cynthia Horn worked as a janitor for Knight Facilities Management–GM, Inc., in Detroit, Michigan. When Horn developed a sensitivity to cleaning products, her physician gave her a "no exposure to cleaning solutions" restriction. Knight then discussed possible accommodations with her. Horn suggested that restrooms be eliminated from her cleaning route or that she be provided with a respirator. Knight explained that she would be exposed to cleaning solutions in any situation because they were airborne and concluded that there was no work available within her physician's restriction. Has Knight violated the Americans with Disabilities Act by failing to accommodate Horn's requests? Explain. [*Horn v. Knight Facilities Management–GM, Inc.,* 2014 WL 715711 (6th Cir. 2014)] (See *Discrimination Based on Disability.*)

28–4. Age Discrimination. Beginning in 1986, Paul Rangel was a sales professional for pharmaceutical company Sanofi-Aventis U.S., LLC (S-A). Rangel had satisfactory performance reviews until 2006, when S-A issued new expectations guidelines with sales call quotas and other

standards that he failed to meet. After two years of negative performance reviews, Rangel—who was then more than forty years old—was terminated as part of the company's nationwide reduction of sales professionals who had not met the expectations guidelines. The terminated salespeople included younger workers. Did S-A engage in age discrimination? Discuss. [*Rangel v. Sanofi Aventis U.S., LLC,* 2013 WL 142040 (10th Cir. 2013)] (See *Discrimination Based on Age.*)

28–5. Retaliation by Employers. Entek International hired Shane Dawson, a male homosexual. Some of Dawson's co-workers, including his supervisor, made derogatory comments about his sexual orientation. Dawson's work deteriorated. He filed a complaint with Entek's human resources department. Two days later, he was fired. State law makes it unlawful for an employer to discriminate against an individual based on sexual orientation. Could Dawson establish a claim for retaliation? Explain. [*Dawson v. Entek International,* 630 F.3d 928 (9th Cir. 2011)] (See *Title VII of the Civil Rights Act.*)

ETHICAL QUESTIONS

28–6. Employment Discrimination. Should English-only policies in the workplace be considered a form of national-origin discrimination? Explain. (See *Title VII of the Civil Rights Act.*)

28–7. Online Harassment. Should an employer's e-mail system be considered part of the workplace? Discuss your answer. (See *Title VII of the Civil Rights Act.*)

Chapter 28—Work Set

TRUE-FALSE QUESTIONS

_____ 1. Discrimination complaints under federal law must be filed with the Equal Opportunity Employment Commission.

_____ 2. All employers are subject to Title VII of the Civil Rights Act of 1964 regardless of the number of their employees.

_____ 3. Disparate-treatment discrimination occurs when an employer intentionally discriminates against an employee.

_____ 4. In a sexual-harassment case, an employer cannot be held liable if an employee did the harassing.

_____ 5. Under the Age Discrimination in Employment Act, a plaintiff must show that the unlawful discrimination was *the* reason for an adverse employment action.

_____ 6. The Americans with Disabilities Act requires that employers hire workers with disabilities whether or not they are otherwise qualified for the work.

_____ 7. Employers that do not accommodate the needs of persons with disabilities must demonstrate that the accommodations would cause undue hardship.

_____ 8. An employer may defend against a claim of unintentional discrimination by asserting that a practice that has a discriminatory effect is a business necessity.

MULTIPLE-CHOICE QUESTIONS

_____ 1. Odette believes that the Power Utility Corporation (PUC) discriminated against her on the basis of race. She files a suit against PUC under Title VII. To establish a *prima facie* case of employment discrimination, Odette must show that

    a. she is a member of a protected class.
    b. PUC has no legal defenses against the claim.
    c. discriminatory intent motivated PUC.
    d. no other firm in PUC's industry has committed a discriminatory act.

_____ 2. Inez files an employment discrimination suit against Jiffy Delivery Service, under Title VII of the Civil Rights Act, based on Jiffy's discharge of Inez. If Inez prevails in her *prima facie* case, one possible remedy for her would be

    a. an order to shutdown the employer's business.
    b. fines.
    c. imprisonment.
    d. reinstatement.

_____ 3. Tina believes that she has been discriminated against on the job because she is a woman. She attempts to resolve the dispute with her employer, who decides that her claim has no basis. Tina's best next step is to

    a. file a lawsuit.
    b. secretly sabotage company operations for revenge.
    c. ask the Equal Employment Opportunity Commission whether a claim is justified.
    d. forget about the matter.

_____ 4. Janet, who is hearing impaired, applies for a position with Alpenrose Dairy. Janet is qualified but is refused the job because, she is told, "We can't afford to accommodate you with an interpreter." If Janet sues Alpenrose, she will

    a. win, if Alpenrose has installed ramps for disabled persons.
    b. win, if an interpreter would be a "reasonable accommodation."
    c. lose, if she is not more than forty years old.
    d. lose, if Alpenrose has never done anything to accommodate any disabled person.

_____ 5. Digital Software, Inc., prefers to hire Asian Americans, because, according to its personnel director, "they're smarter and work harder" than other minorities. Showing a preference for one minority over another is prohibited by

    a. Title VII of the Civil Rights Act of 1964.

    b. the Age Discrimination in Employment Act of 1967.

    c. the Americans with Disabilities Act of 1990.

    d. none of the above.

_____ 6. Insurance Sales, Inc., requires that all its secretaries be able to type. Alice, a member of a minority, applies to Insurance Sales for a secretarial job. She cannot type but tells the company that she is willing to learn. When the firm does not hire her, she sues. She will

    a. win, if Insurance Sales workforce does not reflect the same percentage of members of a protected class that characterizes qualified individuals in the local labor market.

    b. win, because she was willing to learn and an employer is obligated to hire and train unqualified minority employees.

    c. lose, because in this case being a member of the majority is a BFOQ.

    d. lose, because Insurance Sales has a valid business necessity defense.

_____ 7. U.S. Tech, Inc., fires Mike. He believes that he was discriminated against because of his age. To bring a suit based on age discrimination, Mike must show

    a. that he is forty years old or older and is qualified for the job.

    b. that he was discharged in circumstances that imply discrimination.

    c. both a and b.

    d. none of the above.

_____ 8. National Mining Company requires job applicants to pass certain physical tests. Only a few women who apply to work for National can pass the tests, but if they pass, they are hired. National's best defense in a suit charging that the tests discriminate against women would be that

    a. gender is a BFOQ.

    b. some men cannot pass the tests.

    c. any discrimination is not intentional.

    d. passing the tests is a business necessity.

 ## ANSWERING MORE LEGAL PROBLEMS

1. Luna Boutique had a dress code that required its male salespersons to wear slacks, a shirt, and a necktie. Female salespersons were required to wear a black smock. Melissa, a female employee, refused to wear the smock. Instead, she reported to work in business attire, like the male staff, and was fired for violating the dress code. All other conditions of employment, including salary, hours, and benefits, were the same for female and male employees.

    Was Luna Boutique's dress code discriminatory? Yes. Luna's dress code policy was illegal discrimination on the basis of _____. Unlike hair and grooming codes, which are based on established social expectations, there is no justifiable basis for women to wear smocks in a workplace. There is a tendency to believe that women wearing smocks have lower professional status than their male coworkers wearing business attire. Thus, the smock requirement perpetuated a _____-based stereotype of inferiority. Therefore, the dress code policy violated the _____.

2. Cerebral palsy limits Eli's use of his legs, but with support, he can get on and off a stool. Eli applied for a cashier position at Mars Market. The job description required "no experience or qualification." Eli's application was rejected. According to Ravenna, the market's human resources manager, her decision was based on the threat that Eli posed to his safety and the safety of others. Eli claimed that Mars Market refused to hire him because of his disability.

    Can Eli prove his disability-discrimination claim? Yes. Eli needs to show that he (1) has a _____, (2) is otherwise _____ for the job, and (3) was excluded solely because of his _____. If Eli could perform the job's essential functions with _____ accommodation, Mars Market would have to make that accommodation. Eli can show that he has cerebral palsy and that he is qualified for the job, which requires "no experience or qualification." For Eli, reasonable accommodation might include a wheelchair, a stool with armrests, or a hand scanner. Additionally, it is unlikely that Mars Market could explain how Eli poses more of a safety threat to himself and others in the store.

BUSINESS ORGANIZATIONS

UNIT CONTENTS

CHAPTER 29 Sole Proprietorships, Partnerships, and Limited Liability Companies

CHAPTER 30 Formation and Termination of a Corporation

CHAPTER 31 Management and Ownership of a Corporation

29

SOLE PROPRIETORSHIPS, PARTNERSHIPS, AND LIMITED LIABILITY COMPANIES

LEARNING OUTCOMES

The four Learning Outcomes below are designed to help improve your understanding of the chapter. After reading this chapter, you should be able to:

❶ Describe doing business as a sole proprietorship.

❷ Identify the features of a general partnership.

❸ Outline the elements of a limited partnership.

❹ List the advantages of a limited liability company.

FACING A LEGAL PROBLEM

Hailey and Felix jointly own three hundred acres of farmland in northern California. They lease the land to Reese, the owner of Hillcrest Winery, who uses the land for growing his vineyards. Instead of fixed rental payments for the use of the land, Hailey and Felix receive a share of the profits from Hillcrest's operations. Only Reese pays for the losses, however.

 Are Hailey, Felix, and Reese partners?

One of the questions faced by anyone who wishes to start up a business is what form of business organization to choose. The options include a sole proprietorship, a partnership, a limited liability company, and a corporation. In this chapter, we examine the features of sole proprietorships, partnerships, and limited liability companies. See also the *Linking Business Law to Your Career* feature at the end of this chapter for more information on how to choose your business organization.

 ## 29–1 SOLE PROPRIETORSHIPS

sole proprietorship
The simplest form of business in which the owner is the business.

The simplest form of business is a **sole proprietorship.** In this form, the owner is the business. Anyone who does business without creating a separate business organization has a sole proprietorship. Sole proprietorships constitute more than two-thirds of all U.S. businesses, from informal home offices to large construction firms.

29–1a Advantages of the Sole Proprietorship

LEARNING OUTCOME 1

Describe doing business as a sole proprietorship.

A major advantage of the sole proprietorship is that the proprietor (owner) receives all the profits. In addition, it is often easier and less costly to start a sole proprietorship than to start any other kind of business, because few legal forms are involved. The sole proprietor is free to make any decision he or she wishes concerning the business—whom to hire, what kind of business to pursue, and so on.

A sole proprietor pays only personal income taxes on profits. Sole proprietors can also establish certain retirement accounts that are tax-exempt until the funds are withdrawn.

29–1b Disadvantages of the Sole Proprietorship

The major disadvantage of the sole proprietorship is that, as sole owner, the proprietor alone bears the burden of all liabilities incurred by the business. **EXAMPLE 29.1** Sheila operates a small golf shop as a sole proprietorship. One of her employees fails to secure a display of golf clubs, and they fall on Dean, a customer, and seriously injure him. If Dean sues Sheila's shop and wins, Sheila's personal liability can easily exceed the limits of her insurance policy. If this occurs, Sheila can not only lose her business, but also her house, car, and any other personal assets that can be attached to pay the judgment.◄

Another disadvantage is that the proprietor's opportunity to raise capital is limited to personal funds and the funds of those who are willing to make loans. A sole proprietorship also lacks continuity on the death of the proprietor. When the owner dies, the business is automatically dissolved. If the business is transferred to family members or other heirs, a new sole proprietorship is created.

 ## 29–2 PARTNERSHIPS

A **partnership** arises from an agreement, express or implied, between two or more persons to carry on a business for profit. A partnership is based on a voluntary contract between two or more competent persons who agree to place funds, labor, and skill in a business with the understanding that profits and losses will be proportionately shared. There are two basic types of partnerships: *general* partnerships and *limited* partnerships.

partnership
An association of two or more persons to carry on, as co-owners, a business for profit.

29–2a Agency Law and Partnership Law

Agency law governs relationships arising in partnerships. In one important way, however, partnerships are distinct from agency relationships. In a nonpartnership agency relationship, the agent usually does not have an ownership interest in the business, nor is he or she obliged to bear a portion of the ordinary business losses.

The Uniform Partnership Act (UPA) governs the operation of partnerships *in the absence of a different agreement among the partners.* The UPA has been adopted in all of the states except Louisiana, as well as in the District of Columbia.

29–2b Elements of a General Partnership

There are three essential elements to a general partnership:

1. A sharing of profits and losses.
2. A joint ownership of the business.
3. An equal right in the management of the business.

Joint ownership of property does not in and of itself create a partnership. In fact, the sharing of income and even profits from such ownership is usually not enough to create a partnership. **EXAMPLE 29.2** Claudine and Owen own a retail building in the city of Morgantown's industrial district. They lease the building to Steven, who owns and operates Bricktowne Brewery, on the premises. Instead of paying a monthly rental fee for the use of the building, Claudine and Owen agree to receive a certain portion of Bricktowne's profits, if any, on a quarterly basis. This arrangement normally does not make Claudine, Owen, and Steven partners.◄

Note, though, that while the sharing of profits from ownership of property does not prove the existence of a partnership, sharing *both profits and losses* usually does. **EXAMPLE 29.3** Jayden and his friend, Isabel, start a business that sells fruit smoothies and other beverages near Benton Community College. They open a joint bank account from which they pay for supplies and expenses, and they share the proceeds (and losses) that the business generates. If a conflict arises as to their business relationship, a court will assume that a partnership exists unless Jayden and Isabel can prove otherwise.◄

Partnership Characteristics Generally, the law of partnership recognizes a partnership as an *independent entity.* A partnership usually can sue or be sued, collect judgments, and have all accounting procedures in the name of the partnership entity. Partnership property may be held in the name of the partnership rather than in the names of the individual partners.

Tax Treatment In one circumstance (for federal income tax purposes), a general partnership is not regarded as a separate legal entity. Rather, it is treated as an aggregate (or combination) of the individual partners. In other words, a general partnership is a pass-through entity and not a tax-paying entity. A **pass-through entity** is a business entity that has no tax liability—meaning that the entity's income is passed through to the owners of the entity, who pay income taxes on it.

Thus, the income or losses a general partnership incurs are "passed through" the entity framework and attributed to the partners on their individual tax returns. The partnership itself has no tax liability and is responsible only for filing an information return with the Internal Revenue Service.

29–2c Partnership Formation

A partnership is ordinarily formed by an agreement among the parties. The law, however, recognizes another form of partnership—*partnership by estoppel*—which arises when persons who are not partners represent themselves as partners when dealing with third parties.

Partnership by Agreement Agreements to form a partnership can be *oral, written,* or *implied by conduct.* Some partnership agreements must be in writing to be enforceable under the Statute of Frauds. For instance, a partnership agreement that, by its terms, is to continue for more than one year must be in writing. Similarly, a partnership that authorizes the partners to sell real estate must be in writing.

Practically speaking, the provisions of any partnership agreement should be in writing. One disadvantage of an oral agreement is that its terms are difficult to prove. In addition, potential problems that would have been detected in the course of drafting a written agreement may go unnoticed in an oral agreement. The partnership agreement, called **articles of partnership,** usually specifies the name and location of the business, the duration of the partnership, the purpose of the business, each partner's share of the profits, how the partnership will be managed, and how assets will be distributed on dissolution, among other things.

Partnership by Estoppel Occasionally, persons who are not partners hold themselves out as partners and make representations that third parties rely on in dealing with them. In such a situation, a court may conclude that a **partnership by estoppel** exists and impose liability—but not partnership rights—on the alleged partner or partners.

Similarly, a partner in a firm may represent, expressly or impliedly, that a nonpartner is a member of the firm. When a third person has reasonably and detrimentally relied on this representation, a partnership by estoppel is deemed to exist. In this situation, the nonpartner is regarded as an agent whose acts are binding on the partnership.

29–2d Rights of Partners

In the absence of provisions to the contrary in the partnership agreement, the law imposes on partners the rights discussed next.

Management Rights In a general partnership, all partners have equal rights in managing the partnership. Each partner in an ordinary partnership has one vote in management matters *regardless of the size of his or her interest in the firm.*

---

pass-through entity
A business entity that has no tax liability. The entity's income is passed through to the owners, and they pay taxes on the income.

Identify the features of a general partnership.

articles of partnership
A written agreement that sets forth each partner's rights in, and obligations to, the partnership.

partnership by estoppel
Partnership liability imposed by a court on those who have held themselves to be partners, even though they were not.

The majority rule controls decisions in ordinary matters connected with partnership business, unless otherwise specified in the agreement. Unanimous consent of the partners is required, however, to make basic changes in the nature of the business or the partnership agreement.

Interest in the Partnership Each partner is entitled to the proportion of business profits and losses designated in the partnership agreement. If the agreement does not apportion profits or losses, profits are shared equally, and losses are shared in the same ratio as profits.

HIGHLIGHTING THE POINT

Rico and Brent establish a partnership to open a new chocolate cookie business. Their partnership agreement provides for capital contributions of $6,000 from Rico and $4,000 from Brent. The agreement is silent as to how Rico and Brent will share profits or losses.

In what proportion will Rico and Brent share profits and losses? They will share profits and losses equally. If the agreement had provided for profits to be shared in the same ratio as capital contributions, the profits would be shared 60 percent for Rico and 40 percent for Brent. If that same agreement had been silent as to losses, though, they would be shared in the same ratio as profits (60 percent and 40 percent).

Compensation Partners, in general, devote time, skill, and energy on behalf of the partnership business, and are not not generally paid for such services. Partners can, of course, agree otherwise. **EXAMPLE 29.4** Julie, the managing partner of a law firm, receives a salary in addition to her share of profits for performing special administrative duties in office and personnel management. ◄

Inspection of Partnership Books Each partner has the right to full and complete information concerning the conduct of all aspects of partnership business. Each firm keeps books in which to record such information. The books must be kept at the firm's principal business office and cannot be removed without the consent of all the partners.

Partner's Interest in the Firm A partner's interest in the firm is a personal asset consisting of a proportionate share of the profits earned and a return of capital after the partnership is terminated. On a partner's death, the partner's heirs are entitled only to the value of the partner's interest in the firm.

HIGHLIGHTING THE POINT

Oxford, Walensa, and McKee are partners. Oxford dies.

In terms of the partnership, to what are Oxford's heirs entitled? Oxford's heirs are entitled to the value of Oxford's interest in the firm. The heirs do not become partners with Walensa and McKee, nor are they entitled to specific assets of the firm. Walensa and McKee must account to the heirs, however, for the value of Oxford's interest. For instance, they might hire an accountant to determine how much the interest is worth and then pay the heirs that amount.

A partner's personal creditors can ask a court to order that payments due to the partner from the partnership be paid to them. Personal creditors may even ask a court to force the partner to sell his or her interest, but they cannot force the sale of specific partnership property.

Partnership Property Property acquired by a partnership is the property of the partnership and not of the partners individually. A partner may use or possess partnership property only on behalf of the partnership. A partner is not a co-owner of partnership property and has no interest in the property that can be transferred.

Property acquired *in the name of* the partnership or a partner is partnership property if the existence of the partnership or the person's capacity as a partner is indicated in the instrument transferring title. Even if the transferring instrument does not refer to either of these, the property is still presumed to be partnership property when it is acquired with partnership funds.

29–2e Duties and Powers of Partners

The duties and powers of partners discussed here are based on agency law. Basically, each partner owes a *fiduciary duty* to the others, and all partners exercise general agency powers.

fiduciary relationship
A relationship founded on trust and loyalty.

Fiduciary Duties Partners stand in a **fiduciary relationship**. A fiduciary relationship is one of extraordinary trust and loyalty. Each partner must act in good faith for the benefit of the partnership. Fiduciary duties include a *duty of loyalty* and a *duty of care*.

- A partner's duty of loyalty has two aspects. A partner must account to the partnership for any profit or benefit from the firm's business or the use of its property. A partner must also refrain from dealing with the firm as an adverse party or competing with it.

- A partner's duty of care is limited to refraining from negligent or reckless conduct, intentional misconduct, and violations of the law.

A partner may pursue his or her own interests without violating these duties. **EXAMPLE 29.5** Shane, a partner who owns a shopping mall, may vote against a partnership proposal to open a competing mall.◄ In addition, the partnership agreement or the unanimous consent of the partners can permit a partner to engage in any activity.

HIGHLIGHTING THE POINT

Hall, Banks, and Porter enter into a partnership. Porter undertakes independent consulting for an outside firm in competition with the partnership without the consent of Hall and Banks.

Has Porter breached the fiduciary duty that he owes to the partnership? Yes. Even with a noncompetitive activity, a partner can breach his or her fiduciary duty if the partnership suffers a loss because of the time the partner spends on that activity.

Agency Powers Partnerships, as mentioned, are governed by the principles of agency law. Each partner is an *agent* of every other partner and acts as both a principal and an agent in any business transaction within the scope of the partnership agreement. Each partner is a general agent of the partnership in carrying out the usual business of the firm. Every act of a partner concerning partnership business and every contract signed in the name of the partnership bind the firm.

Joint and Several Liability Partners are jointly and severally liable for partnership obligations, including contracts, torts, and breaches of trust. The term *severally* means separately, or individually. In other words, **joint and several liability** means that a third party may sue, at his or her option, any one or more of the partners without suing all of them or the partnership. This is true even if the partner did not participate in, ratify, or know about whatever it was that gave rise to the cause of action.

If the third party is successful, he or she may collect on the judgment only against the assets of those partners named as defendants. A judgment against only some of the partners does not extinguish the others' joint liability, however.

EXAMPLE 29.6 Brian and Julie are partners. If Tom sues Brian for a debt on a partnership contract and wins, Tom can collect the amount of the judgment against Brian only. If Tom cannot collect enough from Brian, however, Tom can later sue Julie for the difference. ◄ A partner who commits a tort that results in a judgment against the partnership may be required to repay the firm for any damages it pays.

29–2f Partner's Dissociation

Dissociation occurs when a partner ceases to be associated in the carrying on of the partnership business. Under general partnership law, when a partner left the partnership, the entire partnership had to be dissolved, or terminated—even if the other partners wanted to continue doing business together. The old partnership was forced to end, and the remaining partners were required to form a new partnership each time a partner departed from the firm. Today, however, under the law of most states, a partnership is not forced to terminate every time a partner dissociates from the firm.

Events That Cause Dissociation A partner can dissociate from the general partnership at any time by giving notice to the partnership (though the dissociation may be wrongful if it goes against the terms of a partnership agreement). A partner may dissociate by declaring bankruptcy, by assigning his or her interest in the partnership for the benefit of creditors, by incapacity through physical inability or mental incompetence, or by death.

Actions by others may also result in a partner's dissociation. A partnership agreement may specify an event that will cause dissociation. Sometimes, the other partners can expel a partner by unanimous vote. A court or an arbitrator may expel a partner for wrongful conduct that affects the partnership business, breaches the partnership agreement, or violates a duty owed to the firm or the partners.

Effects of Dissociation Dissociation normally entitles the partner to have his or her interest purchased by the partnership. On a partner's dissociation, his or her right to participate in the management and conduct of the partnership business ends, as does his or her duty of loyalty. A partner's duty of care continues only with respect to events that occurred before dissociation, unless the partner participates in *winding up* the firm's business.

joint and several liability
A doctrine under which a plaintiff may sue, and collect a judgment from, any of several jointly liable defendants.

dissociation
The severance of the relationship between a partner and a partnership.

HIGHLIGHTING THE POINT

Gwen is a partner with Brewster & Jones, an accounting firm. Gwen has been a partner with the firm for five years when she resigns to start her own accounting practice. Her work for Brewster & Jones includes unfinished business for a client, Standing Stone Shops, Inc.

Can Gwen immediately compete with Brewster & Jones for new clients? Yes. On a partner's dissociation, her right to participate in the management and conduct of

(Continued)

the partnership terminates. Her duty of loyalty to the firm also ends. Thus, Gwen can immediately compete with Brewster & Jones for new clients. In regard to Standing Stone's unfinished business, however, Gwen's duty of care continues. She must exercise care in completing the work for Standing Stone and account to Brewster & Jones for any fees received for that work.

For up to two years after a partner dissociates from a continuing partnership, the firm may be liable to a third party with whom the dissociated partner does business if the third party reasonably believes that he or she is still a partner. Similarly, a dissociated partner may be liable for partnership obligations over the same period. To avoid these circumstances, a partnership should notify its creditors of the dissociation and file a statement of dissociation in the appropriate state office. The partner should also file such a statement.

29–2g Partnership Termination

The same events that cause dissociation can result in the end of the partnership if the remaining partners no longer wish to (or are unable to) continue the partnership business. The formal termination of a partnership is referred to as **dissolution**, which essentially means the commencement of the winding up process. **Winding up** is the actual process of collecting, liquidating, and distributing the partnership assets.

dissolution
The formal disbanding of a partnership or a corporation.

winding up
The last stage of dissolution of a partnership, in which the firm collects and distributes assets and discharges liabilities.

Dissolution A partnership can be terminated by acts of the partners, by operation of law, and by judicial decree.

Acts of the Partners A partnership can be dissolved by the partners' agreement. A partnership agreement may state a fixed term or a particular business objective to be accomplished, for example. In this situation, the passing of the date or the accomplishment of the objective terminates the partnership. Furthermore, as noted, if after a partner dissociates himself or herself from the firm the remaining partners do not agree to continue the business, the partnership will terminate.

Operation of Law Any event that makes it unlawful for the partnership to continue its business will terminate the partnership. If the partners act within ninety days, however, they can decide to change the nature of their business and continue in the partnership.

HIGHLIGHTING THE POINT

Derrick and Amanda form a partnership—Norse Farms—to grow alfalfa from seed that consists of pesticide-resistant genetically modified organisms (GMO). Less than two years later, the county in which the partnership's farmland is situated bans the use of GMO seed.

Is Norse Farms terminated by operation of law? Yes. The county's enactment of a ban on the use of GMO seed makes the partnership's use of the seed unlawful. This effectively terminates the partnership. But Derrick and Amanda could continue Norse Farms if, within ninety days, they agree to change the nature of their business. They could decide to grow non-GMO alfalfa, or another non-GMO crop, or to raise cattle or other livestock, and thereby continue their partnership.

Judicial Decree A court may order a partnership to be dissolved when the court deems it impractical for the firm to continue—for example, if the business can be operated only at a loss. A partner's impropriety or fraud involving partnership business or improper behavior reflecting unfavorably on the firm may provide grounds for a judicial decree terminating the partnership. Finally, if dissension between partners becomes so persistent and harmful as to undermine the confidence and cooperation necessary to carry on the firm's business, a court may order the firm to be dissolved.

Winding up Once the partners have been notified that the partnership is ending, they cannot enter into new contracts on behalf of the partnership. Their only authority is to complete unfinished transactions and to wind up the business of the partnership. Winding up includes collecting and preserving partnership assets, discharging liabilities (paying debts), and accounting to each partner for the value of his or her interest in the partnership.

Creditors of the partnership and creditors of the individual partners can make claims on the partnership's assets at this time. Creditors of the partnership share proportionately with the partners' individual creditors in the assets of the partners' estates, which include their interests in the partnership. In sum, the priorities to a partnership's assets on dissolution are as follows:

1. Payment of debts, including those owed to partner and nonpartner creditors.

2. Return of capital contributions and distribution of profits to partners.

29–2h Limited Partnerships

A special and quite popular form of partnership is the **limited partnership (LP)**, which consists of at least one general partner and one or more limited partners. A **general partner** assumes responsibility for the management of the partnership and liability for all partnership debts. A **limited partner** has no right to participate in the management or operation of the partnership and assumes no liability for partnership debts beyond the amount of capital contributed. If limited partners participate in management, however, they risk having general-partner liability.

HIGHLIGHTING THE POINT

Leonardo, Michele, and Nicola are limited partners of Oakfield Estates, LP, a limited partnership in the business of developing real estate. Leonardo and Michele manage the firm. Without Leonardo's knowledge, Michele fraudulently transfers $500,000 of Oakfield's funds to herself to buy a house. Later, Leonardo learns of the transfer but takes no action.

Can Leonardo be held liable to Nicola for Michele's fraud? Yes. Normally, a limited partner has no liability for partnership debts beyond the amount of capital that the partner contributes to the firm. A limited partner who participates in management, however, risks being imposed with the same liability for partnership debts as a general partner. Here, Leonardo would likely be held liable to Nicola because Leonardo participated in the management of Oakfield but took no action when he learned of Michele's fraud.

Limited Partner Benefits One of the major benefits of becoming a limited partner is this limitation on liability, both with respect to lawsuits brought against the partnership and with respect to the amount at risk. The maximum amount at risk for each limited partner is defined by the LP agreement, which specifically states how much each limited partner must contribute to the partnership.

Formation of an LP The formation of an LP involves more formalities than the formation of a general partnership. The agreement to form an LP must be written. In addition, which is a *certificate of limited partnership* must be filed appropriately with a state office, usually the secretary of state's office. All states allow LPs.

29–2i Limited Liability Partnerships

limited liability partnership (LLP)
A form of partnership that allows professionals to enjoy the tax benefits of a partnership while limiting their personal liability for the malpractice of other partners.

The **limited liability partnership (LLP)** is designed for professionals who normally do business as partners in a partnership. LLPs must be formed and operated in compliance with state statutes. The appropriate form must be filled with a central state agency, usually the secretary of state's office, and the business's name must include either *Limited Liability Partnership* or *LLP*.

Advantages of an LLP The major advantage of the LLP is that it allows a partnership to continue as a pass-through entity for tax purposes but limits the personal liability of the partners. The LLP is especially attractive for two categories of businesses: professional service firms and family businesses.

Many accounting firms are organized as LLPs. An LLP allows professionals, such as attorneys and physicians, to avoid personal liability for the malpractice of other partners. A partner of an LLP, however, is still liable for his or her own wrongful acts, such as negligence.

HIGHLIGHTING THE POINT

Three physicians—Jerome, Kristin, and Loren—operate Central Point Urgent Care Clinic as a limited liability partnership. Jerome is sued by a client for malpractice and loses his lawsuit. Central Point's malpractice insurance coverage is insufficient to pay the judgment.

Can Kristin and Loren avoid personal liability for the unpaid portion of the judgment against Jerome? Yes. Because Central Point is organized as a limited liability partnership, no partner can be held liable for another partner's malpractice. Only Jerome's personal assets can be used to satisfy the judgment amount against him.

Converting to an LLP In most states, it is relatively easy to convert a general partnership into an LLP because the firm's basic structure remains the same. Additionally, all of the law governing partnerships still applies (apart from that modified by the LLP statute).

29–3 LIMITED LIABILITY COMPANIES

limited liability company (LLC)
A hybrid form of business enterprise that offers the limited liability of a corporation but the tax advantages of a partnership.

A **limited liability company (LLC)** is a hybrid that combines the limited liability of a corporation and the tax advantages of a partnership. Like an LP, an LLC must be formed and operated in compliance with state law. To form an LLC, *articles of organization* must be filed with a central state agency, such as the secretary of state's office. The business's name must include the words *Limited Liability Company* or the initials *LLC*.

29–3a Advantages of a Limited Liability Company

A major advantage of the LLC is that profits are "passed through" the LLC and taxes are paid personally by the owners of the company, who are called *members*. Another advantage is that corporations and partnerships, as well as foreign investors, can be LLC members. Additionally, there is no limit on the number of members. Members are allowed to participate fully in management activities, and the firm's managers need not be members. Yet another advantage is that the liability of the members is limited to the amount of their investments.

Finally, part of the LLC's attractiveness to businesspersons is the flexibility it offers. The members can themselves decide how to operate the various aspects of the business through a simple **operating agreement.** For example, the agreement can set forth procedures for choosing or removing members or managers.

LEARNING OUTCOME 4
List the advantages of a limited liability company.

operating agreement
In a limited liability company, an agreement in which members state how the details of the business will be managed and operated.

29–3b Disadvantages of a Limited Liability Company

One disadvantage of the LLC is that state statutes are not uniform. Therefore, businesses that operate in more than one state may not receive consistent treatment in these states. Generally, though, in dealing with a *foreign LLC*—that is, an LLC formed in another state—a state will apply the law of the state where the LLC was formed.

Real-World Case Example

Green Cab Taxi and Disabled Service Association, LLC, is a taxi service in King County, Washington. Its operating agreement requires the members to pay weekly fees. Members who do not pay are in default and must return their taxi licenses to the company. A member in default cannot withdraw from the company without the consent of all of the members. Dissatisfaction with Green Cab's management led some members who were in default, including Shumet Mekonen, to withdraw from the company without the others' consent. Both sides continued to drive under the Green Cab name.

Were the drivers in Mekonen's group in violation of Green Cab's operating agreement? Yes. In a 2014 case, *Mekonen v. Zewdu*, the court ordered Mekonen and the other drivers who had withdrawn from the company to return their taxi licenses to Green Cab. Under the provisions of the company's operating agreement, the company held all of the rights to the taxi licenses. Those members in default who withdrew without the others' consent had no right to retain and use the licenses.

ANSWERING THE LEGAL PROBLEM

In the legal problem set out at the beginning of this chapter, Hailey and Felix jointly own farmland in northern California. They lease the land to Reese, the owner of Hillcrest Winery. Instead of fixed rental payments for the use of the land, Hailey and Felix receive a share of the profits from Hillcrest's operations. Only Reese pays for the losses.

(Continued)

A **Are Hailey, Felix, and Reese partners?** No. Hailey and Felix may be partners, but Reese is not a partner with them. Only Hailey and Felix jointly own the property and have an equal right to manage it. Also, the three do not share losses. Sharing profits alone does not prove a partnership.

LINKING BUSINESS LAW to Your Career

BUSINESS FORMATION

In your career, you may find yourself in the role of an entrepreneur starting a new business. One of the most important decisions that you will make is deciding which organizational form will be the most advantageous for your business. To make the best decision, you should understand the forms and their legal and business considerations.

Number of Participants

An initial consideration in choosing a form of business organization is the number of participants involved. A sole proprietorship, for instance, is owned and operated by a single individual. In many states, a limited liability company (LLC) can also have a single member (owner). The forms of partnership—general partnership, limited partnership (LP), limited liability partnership (LLP), and limited liability limited partnership (LLLP)—must have two or more partners.

Liability Considerations

Sole proprietors and general partners share unlimited personal liability for their firm's obligations. Limited partners, the partners of LLLPs, and the members of LLCs are not liable for the obligations of their organizations beyond the amounts of their investment. The liability of the partners in an LLP varies. In some states, the partners are not exempt from personal liability for the firm's contractual obligations.

Profits and Taxes

A sole proprietor keeps all of the profits of the business and pays personal income tax on those profits. Partnerships have no income tax liability. Instead, each partner pays taxes on his or her profits from the firm. Members of LLCs and partners can decide how to split the profits of their businesses. An LLC can elect to be taxed as a partnership or as a corporation.

Professional, Personal, and Business Factors

The business in which a firm engages can be a factor in choosing an organizational form. In many states, the form of an entity that engages in a certain profession and the liability of its owners are prescribed by law. Work effort, motivation, ability, and other personal attributes can also influence the choice, as may fundamental business concerns such as a firm's expenses and debts.

Another practical factor is the willingness of others to do business with a sole proprietorship, a partnership, or a limited liability organization. For example, a supplier may not be willing to extend credit to a firm whose participants will not accept personal liability for the debt.

TERMS AND CONCEPTS FOR REVIEW

articles of partnership 398

dissociation 401

dissolution 402

fiduciary relationship 400

general partner 403

joint and several liability 401

limited liability company (LLC) 404

limited liability partnership (LLP) 404

limited partner 403

limited partnership (LP) 403

operating agreement 405

partnership 397

partnership by estoppel 398

pass-through entity 398

sole proprietorship 396

winding up 402

CHAPTER SUMMARY—SOLE PROPRIETORSHIPS, PARTNERSHIPS, AND LIMITED LIABILITY COMPANIES

LEARNING OUTCOME	
1	**Describe doing business as a sole proprietorship.** A sole proprietorship is the simplest form of business organization, used by anyone who does business without creating a separate business organization. The owner is the business. The owner pays personal income taxes on all profits and is personally liable for all business debts.
2	**Identify the features of a general partnership.** A general partnership is created by an agreement of the parties. It is treated as a pass-through entity for federal income tax purposes. Each partner has an equal voice in management, unless the partnership agreement provides otherwise. Partners share profits equally and share losses in the same ratio as they share profits. They have unlimited liability for partnership debts. A partnership can be terminated by agreement or can be dissolved by action of the partners, operation of law, or a court decree.
3	**Outline the elements of a limited partnership.** A limited partnership must be formed in compliance with statutory requirements. It can consist of one or more general partners and one or more limited partners. General partners have unlimited liability for partnership obligations. Limited partners are liable only to the extent of their contributions. Only general partners can participate in management. If limited partners participate in management, they risk having general-partner liability.
4	**List the advantages of a limited liability company.** A limited liability company (LLC) combines the limited liability of a corporation with the tax benefits of a partnership. LLC members may be corporations, partnerships, or residents of foreign countries. Members may participate in management, and nonmembers may be managers as well.

ISSUE SPOTTERS

Check your answers to the *Issue Spotters* against the answers provided in Appendix C at the end of this text.

1. Sam plans to open a sporting goods store and to hire Gil and Art. Sam will invest only his own capital. He does not expect to make a profit for at least eighteen months and to make little profit for the first three years. He hopes to expand eventually. Which form of business organization would be most appropriate? (See *Sole Proprietorships.*)

2. Hal and Gretchen are partners in a delivery business. When business is slow, without Gretchen's knowledge, Hal leases out the delivery vehicles as moving vans. The vehicles would otherwise be sitting idle in a parking lot. Can Hal keep the lease money, or does he have to account to Gretchen? (See *Partnerships.*)

USING BUSINESS LAW

29–1. Forms of Business Organization. In each of the following situations, determine whether Georgio's Fashions is a partnership or a limited partnership.

1. Georgio's defaults on a payment to supplier Dee Creations. Dee sues Georgio's and each of the owners of Georgio's personally for payment of the debt. (See *Partnerships.*)

2. Georgio's is owned by three persons, two of whom are not allowed to participate in the firm's management. (See *Partnerships*.)

29–2. Rights to Partners. Meyer, Knapp, and Cavanna establish a partnership to operate a window-washing service. Meyer contributes $10,000 to the partnership, and Knapp and Cavanna contribute $1,000 each. The partnership agreement is silent as to how profits and losses will be shared. One month after the partnership begins operation, Knapp and Cavanna vote, over Meyer's objection, to purchase another truck for the firm. Meyer believes that because he contributed $10,000, the partnership cannot make any major commitment to purchase over his objection. In addition, Meyer claims that in the absence of any provision in the agreement, profits must be divided in the same ratio as capital contributions. Discuss Meyer's contentions. (See *Partnerships*.)

REAL-WORLD CASE PROBLEMS

29–3. Partnerships. Karyl Paxton asked Christopher Sacco to work with her interior design business, Pierce Paxton Collections, in New Orleans. At the time, they were in a romantic relationship. Sacco was involved in every aspect of the business—bookkeeping, marketing, and design—but was not paid a salary. He was reimbursed, however, for expenses charged to his personal credit card, which Paxton also used. Sacco took no profits from the firm, saying that he wanted to "grow the business" and "build sweat equity." When Paxton and Sacco's personal relationship soured, she fired him. Sacco objected, claiming that they were partners. Is Sacco entitled to 50 percent of the profits of Pierce Paxton Collections? Explain. [*Sacco v. Paxton*, 133 So.3d 213 (La.App. 4th Cir. 2014)] (See *Partnerships*.)

29–4. Liability of Partners. Dan and Lori Cole operated a Curves franchise exercise facility in Angola, Indiana, as a partnership. The firm entered into a lease for commercial space from Flying Cat, LLC, for a renewable three-year term. At the end of the term, Lori signed an extension. When the Coles divorced two years later, they dissolved their partnership. At the time, Flying Cat was owed more than $21,000 on the lease. More rent went unpaid. By the end of the second term, Flying Cat was owed almost $50,000. Can Dan be held liable for the full amount? Why or why not? [*Curves for Women Angola v. Flying Cat, LLC*, 983 N.E.2d 629 (Ind.App. 2013)] (See *Partnerships*.)

29–5. Limited Liability Companies. James Williford, Patricia Mosser, Marquetta Smith, and Michael Floyd formed Bluewater Logistics, LLC, to bid on construction contracts. The operating agreement provided for a "super majority" 75 percent vote to remove a member "under any circumstances that would jeopardize the company status" as a contractor. Part of the attractiveness of an LLC as a form of business enterprise is its flexibility. Could one Bluewater member unilaterally "fire" another without providing a reason? Why or why not? [*Bluewater Logistics, LLC v. Williford*, 55 So.3d 148 (Miss. 2011)] (See *Limited Liability Companies*.)

ETHICAL QUESTIONS

29–6. Partnership Agreement. Why should partnership agreements be in writing? (See *Partnerships*.)

29–7. Partner's Dissociation. Elliot Willensky and Beverly Moran formed a partnership to buy, renovate, and sell a house. Moran agreed to finance the effort, which was to cost no more than $60,000. Willensky agreed to oversee the work, which was to be done in six months. As the project progressed, Willensky incurred excessive and unnecessary expenses, misappropriated funds for his personal use, did not pay bills on time, and did not keep Moran informed of the costs. More than a year later, Willensky walked off the project. Moran completed the renovation, which ultimately cost $311,222, and sold the house. Which of Willensky's actions breached the partnership agreement? Which of his acts were unethical? [*Moran v. Willensky*, __ S.W.3d __ (Tenn.App. 2010)] (See *Partnerships*.)

Chapter 29—Work Set

TRUE-FALSE QUESTIONS

_____ 1. In a sole proprietorship, the owner and the business are entirely separate.

_____ 2. A partnership is an association of two or more persons to carry on, as co-owners, a business for profit.

_____ 3. A general partnership cannot exist unless a certificate of partnership is filed appropriately in a state.

_____ 4. The sharing of profits from joint ownership of property is usually enough to create a partnership.

_____ 5. A writing is always necessary to form a partnership.

_____ 6. Unless a partnership agreement specifies otherwise, each partner has one vote in management matters.

_____ 7. Unless a partnership agreement specifies otherwise, profits are shared in the same ratio as capital contributions.

_____ 8. In a limited partnership, the liability of a _limited_ partner is limited to the amount of capital he or she invests in the partnership.

_____ 9. A limited liability company offers the limited liability of a corporation and the tax advantages of a partnership.

MULTIPLE-CHOICE QUESTIONS

_____ 1. Dave and Paul agree to go into business together. They do not formally declare that their business has a specific form of organization. Dave and Paul's business is

a. a proprietorship.
b. a partnership.
c. a limited liability company.
d. none of the above.

_____ 2. Greg is a general partner and Lee and Carol are limited partners in GLC Associates, a limited partnership. Lee and Carol

a. have fewer managerial powers than Greg.
b. cannot sue on behalf of the firm if Greg refuses to do so.
c. are personally liable for the debts of the firm, unlike Greg.
d. risk nothing if they participate in the management of the partnership.

_____ 3. To obtain a contract with Dick, Cindy misrepresents that she is a partner with Karl. Karl overhears Cindy's misrepresentation but says nothing to Dick. Cindy breaches the contract. Who is liable to Dick?

a. Cindy only.
b. Karl only.
c. Cindy and Karl.
d. None of the above.

_____ 4. Mark owns M Carpets, a home-furnishings store. He hires Lois as a salesperson, agreeing to pay her $8.50 per hour plus 10 percent of her sales. Mark and Lois are

a. partners, because Lois receives a share of the store's profits.
b. partners, because Lois is responsible for some of the store's sales.
c. not partners, because Lois does not have an ownership interest or management right in the store.
d. not partners, because Lois does not receive an equal share of the store's profits.

_____ 5. Greg, Kim, and Pete are partners in Northern Mines. Greg sells the ore extracted from the mines to Yukon Resources, Inc. Greg must account for the funds that he receives from Yukon for the ore to

    a. Yukon.
    b. Northern Mines.
    c. the state in which Northern Mines is located.
    d. none of the choices.

_____ 6. Dr. Jones and Dr. Smith are partners in a medical clinic. Jones manages the clinic, which is organized as a limited liability partnership. A court holds Smith liable in a malpractice suit. Jones is

    a. not liable.
    b. liable only to the extent of her share of that year's profits.
    c. liable only to the extent of her investment in the firm.
    d. liable beyond her investment in the firm, because she manages the clinic.

_____ 7. Dina is a partner in Eastman Technical Group. Dina's dissociation from the partnership will cause

    a. the automatic termination of the firm's legal existence.
    b. the immediate maturity of all partnership debts.
    c. the partnership's buyout of Dina's interest in the firm.
    d. the temporary suspension of all partnership business.

_____ 8. Jay is a limited partner in Kappa Sales, a limited partnership. Jay is liable for the firm's debts

    a. in no way.
    b. in proportion to the total number of partners in the firm.
    c. to the extent of his capital contribution.
    d. to the full extent of the debts.

_____ 9. Ava and Bud start CapCo as a limited liability company. They can participate in the firm's management

    a. only to the extent that they assume personal liability for the firm's debts.
    b. only to the extent of the amount that they invest in the firm.
    c. to any extent.
    d. to no extent.

 ## ANSWERING MORE LEGAL PROBLEMS

1. Doing business as a sole proprietorship under the name Capital Venture, Dhani offered consulting services to assist new start-ups with business structures, decision making, and customer development. Norberto paid Dhani to provide these services for Norberto's TexMex Café. When the café's customer base did not grow quickly enough, Norberto was forced to close. He filed a suit against Capital Venture and Dhani to recover lost profits.

If the court rules in Norberto's favor, could Dhani be personally liable for the amount of the judgment? Yes. The simplest form of business is a _____ proprietorship. In this form, the owner is the business. A major advantage of the _____ proprietorship is that the proprietor receives all the profits. A major disadvantage of the _____ proprietorship is that, as _____ owner, the proprietor alone bears the burden of all _____ incurred by the business. In this problem, Dhani is Capital Venture. If the court rules in Norberto's favor, Dhani is personally liable.

2. Grant was the general partner in Oil Build, LP, which he formed to construct offshore oil rigs. He asked Lucinda to invest in the company. A low bridge separated Oil Build's rig construction site from the open sea. Grant admitted that this setup could increase the cost to deliver the rigs out to sea, but he assured Lucinda that the cost increase would not be significant. Lucinda agreed to invest $10 million and became a limited partner. Oil Build's bids proved too high for the company to obtain work. Without informing Lucinda, Grant sold the limited partnership's assets and pocketed the profits.

Did Grant owe and subsequently breach a duty to Lucinda? Yes. General partners owe the partnership a duty of _____ and a duty of _____, as well as an obligation to discharge their duties in _____ _____ and in a reasonable belief that they are acting in the best _____ of the partnership. General partners owe their co-partners, including any limited partners, the highest fiduciary duty. Here, Grant was the general partner. He owed Lucinda, the firm's limited partner, this duty. He breached the duty by misrepresenting the significance of the low bridge, by selling the firm's assets without notifying her, and by pocketing the profits.

410

FORMATION AND TERMINATION OF A CORPORATION

30

FACING A LEGAL PROBLEM

Edward and Fiona wish to form a corporation to market apps designed to find goods and services for sports fans and participants in unfamiliar locales. They know that all corporations need to have an online presence to compete effectively in today's business climate. The corporate name should therefore be one that can be used as the business's Internet domain name. Edward and Fiona would like to do business as Digital Synergy; however, an existing corporation already uses that name.

  Can Edward and Fiona use the same, or a similar, name for their corporation?

LEARNING OUTCOMES

The five Learning Outcomes below are designed to help improve your understanding of the chapter. After reading this chapter, you should be able to:

❶ Summarize incorporation procedures.

❷ Describe basic corporate powers.

❸ Explain the methods of corporate financing.

❹ Identify the basic steps in a merger and a consolidation.

❺ Discuss the phases involved in the termination of a corporation.

A **corporation** is recognized by law as a "person"—an artificial, legal person—and enjoys many of the same rights under the law that natural persons enjoy. For example, corporations possess the same right of access to the courts as citizens do. The constitutional guarantees of due process, free speech, and freedom from unreasonable searches and seizures also apply to corporations. A corporation's existence generally depends on state law. Each state has its own body of corporate law, and these laws are not entirely uniform.

Corporations consist of *shareholders,* who own the corporation by virtue of holding shares of its **stock.** A board of directors, elected by the shareholders, manages the business. The board of directors normally employs officers to oversee day-to-day operations. One of the key advantages of the corporate form of business is that the shareholders' liability is limited to the amount of their investments. They are not otherwise liable for the debts of the corporation.

In this chapter, we examine various classifications of corporations. We then discuss the formation, powers, and financing of a corporation. Next, we look at the ways corporations can expand. Finally, we examine the reasons and methods for terminating a corporation.

30–1 CORPORATE CLASSIFICATIONS

We can classify corporations in various ways. The classification of a corporation may depend on its location, purpose, or ownership characteristics. A list of important corporate classifications follows:

1. *Domestic, foreign, and alien corporations*—A corporation is referred to as a **domestic corporation** by its home state (the state in which it incorporates). A corporation formed in one state but doing business in another is referred to in that other state as a **foreign corporation.** A corporation formed in another country (say, Mexico) but doing business within the United States is referred to in the United States as an **alien corporation.**

corporation
A legal business form that complies with statutory requirements.

stock
An equity or ownership interest in a corporation that is measured in units of shares.

domestic corporation
In a given state, a corporation that does business in, and is organized under the laws of, that state.

foreign corporation
In a given state, a corporation that does business in the state without being incorporated therein.

alien corporation
A designation in the United States for a corporation formed in another country but doing business in the United States.

411

2. *Public and private corporations*—A public corporation is one formed by the government to meet some political or governmental purpose. Cities and towns that incorporate are common examples. In addition, many federal government organizations, such as the U.S. Postal Service and AMTRAK, are public corporations.

   Private corporations, in contrast, are created either wholly or in part for private benefit. Most corporations are private. Although they may serve a public purpose, as a public utility does, private corporations are owned by private persons rather than by the government.

3. *Nonprofit corporations*—Corporations formed without a profit-making purpose are called *nonprofit* or *not-for-profit* corporations. Private hospitals, educational institutions, charities, religious organizations, and the like are often organized as nonprofit corporations. The nonprofit corporation is a convenient form of organization that allows various groups to own property and to form contracts without exposing the individual members to personal liability.

close corporation
A corporation whose shareholders are limited to a small group of persons or a single person.

4. *Close corporations*—Most corporate enterprises in the United States fall into the category of close corporations. A **close corporation** is one whose shares are held by a single person, members of a family, or relatively few nonrelated persons. Usually, the members of the small group constituting a close corporation are personally known to one another. Close corporations are often managed by their shareholders, who may hold the positions of directors and officers.

S corporation
A business corporation that qualifies for special income tax treatment.

5. *S corporations*—The Subchapter S Revision Act of the Internal Revenue Code divides corporations into two groups: **S corporations**, which have elected Subchapter S tax treatment, and C corporations, which are all other corporations. Certain corporations can choose to qualify under Subchapter S to avoid the imposition of income taxes at the corporate level while retaining many of the advantages of a corporation, particularly limited liability.

benefit corporation
A for-profit corporation that seeks to have a materially positive impact on society and the environment.

6. *Benefit corporations*—Recently, states have increasingly enacted legislation that creates a new corporate form called a benefit corporation. A **benefit corporation** is a for-profit corporation that seeks to have a materially positive impact on society and the environment. A benefit corporation is designed to make a profit, but its purpose is to benefit the public as a whole rather than just to provide long-term shareholder value. For instance, during the decision-making process, directors consider the impact of their decisions on society and the environment, not just on the financial bottom line.

30–2 FORMATION OF A CORPORATION

Incorporating a business is simpler today than it was in the past because most states allow businesses to incorporate online. When a businessperson wants to form a new corporation, he or she must complete all of the appropriate state's incorporation procedures, as well as adopt the new corporation's bylaws.

30–2a Incorporation Procedures

Each state has its own set of incorporation procedures, which most often, can be found on the secretary of state's Web site. There are four basic steps, however, that generally all incorporators must follow. We discuss those steps next—selecting the state in which to incorporate, securing the corporate name, and preparing and filing the articles of incorporation.

Select a State of Incorporation For reasons of convenience and cost, businesses often select to incorporate in the state in which the corporation's business will be primarily conducted.

Secure the Corporate Name Most state statutes require a search to confirm that the chosen corporate name is available. In addition, all corporate statutes require that a corporate name include a word such as *Company, Corporation,* or *Incorporated.*

If a business will have a Web site, a domain name search should be included as well to ensure its availability and avoid trade name infringement. A new corporation's name cannot be the same as, or similar to, the name of an existing corporation within the state of incorporation.

Prepare the Articles of Incorporation The primary document to incorporate a business is the **articles of incorporation.** The articles are required to include the corporation's name, the number of shares it is authorized to issue, its registered agent, and the names of its incorporators.

Other information can be included as well, such as the names of the board directors and the corporation's duration and purpose. The articles will vary in length and detail, depending on the corporation's size and type.

In essence, the articles serve as a primary source of authority for the corporation's future organization and business operations. Most notably, the articles can include the **bylaws,** which are the internal rules of management.

File the Articles of Incorporation Once the articles of incorporation have been prepared and signed properly, they are most often filed with the secretary of state's office, along with the required filing fee. Once this occurs, the new corporation officially exists.

articles of incorporation
The document filed with the appropriate governmental agency, usually the secretary of state, when a business is incorporated.

bylaws
A set of governing rules or regulations adopted by a corporation or other association.

30–2b Adoption of Bylaws

After the incorporation procedures are completed, the first organizational meeting must be held. Usually, the most important function of this meeting is the adoption of the bylaws. If the articles of incorporation named the initial board of directors, then the directors, by majority vote, call the meeting to adopt the bylaws and complete the company's organization. If the articles did not name the directors (as is typical), then the incorporators hold the meeting to elect the directors, adopt the bylaws, and complete the routine business of incorporation.

30–2c Defects in Corporate Formation

If the procedures for incorporation are not followed precisely, others may be able to challenge the existence of the corporation. If a corporation seeks to enforce a contract against a third party, for example, that party may attempt to avoid liability on the ground of a defect in the incorporation procedure. To prevent injustice, a court may attribute corporate status to an improperly formed corporation by holding it to be a *de facto* corporation. Sometimes, too, a corporation may be held to exist by estoppel.

De Jure **Corporations** If a corporation has substantially complied with all conditions of incorporation, the corporation is said to have *de jure* (rightful and lawful) existence. In most states, the secretary of state's filing of the articles of incorporation is conclusive proof of this status. Because a *de jure* corporation is one that is properly formed, neither the state nor a third party can attack its existence.

Sometimes, incorporators fail to comply with all statutory mandates. If the defect is substantial, such as failure to hold an organizational meeting to adopt bylaws, courts in some states will hold that the corporation does not legally exist.

De Facto **Corporations** In some states, however, courts recognize *de facto* (actual) corporate status. In these states, the corporation may be held to legally exist in spite of the defect if the parties have made a good faith attempt to comply with the relevant state statute and have already undertaken to do business as a corporation. A corporation with *de facto* status cannot be challenged by third persons, only by the state.

Corporation by Estoppel

Under the doctrine of *corporation by estoppel*, if a business holds itself out to be a corporation, and a third party deals with it as a corporation, neither party can raise the issue as to whether or not the corporation is validly incorporated. This usually occurs when a third party contracts with a business that claims to be a corporation but has not filed articles of incorporation or contracts with a person claiming to be an agent of a corporation that does not in fact exist. Recognition of corporate status by estoppel does not extend beyond the resolution of the problem at hand.

Piercing the Corporate Veil

pierce the corporate veil
To disregard the corporate entity and hold the shareholders personally liable for a corporate obligation.

Occasionally, the owners of a corporation use the corporate entity to perpetrate a fraud, circumvent the law, or in some other way accomplish an illegitimate objective. In these situations, the court will ignore the corporate formation and structure and **pierce the corporate veil** to expose the shareholders to personal liability.

The following are some of the factors that cause the courts to pierce the corporate veil:

1. A party is tricked or misled into dealing with the corporation rather than the individual.

2. The corporation is set up never to make a profit or always to be insolvent, or it is too "thinly" capitalized—that is, it has insufficient capital at the time of formation to meet its prospective debts or other potential liabilities.

3. Statutory corporate formalities, such as holding required corporation meetings, are not followed.

commingle
To mix funds or goods together in such a way that the funds or goods no longer have separate identities.

4. Personal and corporate interests are **commingled** (mixed together) to such an extent that the corporation has no separate identity.

Real-World Case Example

Dog House Investments, LLC, operated a dog-camp facility on property in Nashville, Tennessee, leased from Teal Properties, Inc., which was owned by its sole shareholder, Jerry Teal. Following a flood, Dog House notified Jerry that the property was unusable. Jerry assured Dog House that the damage was covered by insurance, but he took no steps to restore the property. Dog House spent $39,000 to repair the damage and asked to be reimbursed. Teal Properties received $40,000 from its insurance company for the flood repair costs but did not pay back Dog House, which ultimately filed a suit in a Tennessee state court against Jerry and his company for the funds. The court held Jerry personally liable for the repair costs, and he appealed.

Should the court pierce the corporate veil of Teal Properties to accomplish justice for Dog House? Yes. In a 2014 case, *Dog House Investments, LLC v. Teal Properties, Inc.,* a state intermediate appellate court affirmed the lower court's decision. Jerry was the sole shareholder of Teal Properties, which had no purpose other than to collect the rent on properties that he owned. Teal Properties itself owned no property and generally never held cash except the rent payments—and here, the insurance proceeds—that were disbursed on receipt to meet Jerry's personal financial obligations.

30–3 Corporate Powers

A corporation can engage in any act and enter into any contract to accomplish the purposes for which it was created. When a corporation is created, the express and implied powers necessary to achieve its purpose also come into existence.

LEARNING OUTCOME 2
Describe basic corporate powers.

30–3a Express Powers

The express powers of a corporation are found in its articles of incorporation, in the law of the state of incorporation, and in the state and federal constitutions. Corporate bylaws and the resolutions of the corporation's board of directors also grant or restrict certain powers.

The following order of priority is used when conflicts arise among documents involving corporations:

1. The U.S. Constitution.
2. State constitutions.
3. State statutes.
4. The articles of incorporation.
5. Bylaws.
6. Resolutions of the board of directors.

30–3b Implied Powers

When a corporation is created, it acquires certain implied powers. In essence, the corporation has the implied power to perform all acts reasonably appropriate and necessary to accomplish its corporate purposes. For this reason, a corporation has the implied power to borrow funds within certain limits, to lend funds, and to extend credit to those with whom it has a legal or contractual relationship.

EXAMPLE 30.1 Noble Coffee Company asks Leah, one of its employees, to drive her Ford truck to another city to pick up an overdue shipment of coffee beans. Because Noble has the implied power to reimburse her for her expenses, Leah agrees to this corporate errand. ◄

30–3c *Ultra Vires* Doctrine

The term ***ultra vires*** means "beyond the powers." Acts of a corporation that are beyond the authority given to it under its charter or under the statutes by which it was incorporated are *ultra vires* acts. Such acts may be held to be illegal.

EXAMPLE 30.2 Roberto is the chief executive officer of SOS Plumbing, Inc. The stated purpose of SOS is to install and repair plumbing. If Roberto contracts with Carl in SOS's name to purchase ten cases of brandy, he has likely committed an *ultra vires* act because the contract is not reasonably related to the corporation's purpose. ◄

Because of the *ultra vires* doctrine, corporations often adopt a very broad statement of purpose in their articles of incorporation to include almost all conceivable activities. Statutes generally permit the expression "any lawful purpose" to be a legally sufficient stated purpose in the articles of incorporation. Also, courts have held that any legal action that a corporation undertakes to profit its shareholders is allowable and proper.

ultra vires
Activities of a corporation's managers that are outside the scope of the power granted them by the corporation's charter or the laws of the state of incorporation.

30–4 Corporate Financing

To obtain financing, corporations issue **securities**—evidence of the right to repayment of funds loaned or the right to participate in earnings and the distribution of

securities
Stock certificates and bonds given as evidence of an ownership interest in the corporation or as a promise of repayment by the corporation.

corporate trusts and other property. Securities consist of *stocks* and *bonds*, both of which are sold to investors.

30–4a Stocks

Stocks represent the purchase of ownership in the business firm. Because they do not represent debt, they need never be repaid. The two major types of stocks issued by corporations are *common stock* and *preferred stock.*

LEARNING OUTCOME 3
Explain the methods of corporate financing.

common stock
True ownership of a corporation.

Common Stock **Common stock** represents the true ownership of a corporation. It provides a proportionate interest in the corporation with regard to (1) control, (2) earning capacity, and (3) net assets. A shareholder's interest is generally in proportion to the number of shares owned out of the total number of shares issued.

Control Control is exercised by common shareholders in the form of voting rights. Shareholders vote in elections for a firm's board of directors and for proposed changes in the ownership structure of a firm, such as a merger with another firm.

Dividends Common shareholders may receive *dividends,* or distributions of profit, from the firm. The firm does not have to guarantee a dividend to common shareholders, however. Indeed, some corporations never pay dividends.

Dissolution Disbursement On the firm's *dissolution* (discussed shortly), common shareholders are last in line for repayment. They are entitled only to what is left after federal and state taxes are paid and after preferred stockholders, bondholders, suppliers, employees, and other groups have been paid.

preferred stock
Classes of stock that have priority over common stock.

Preferred Stock Stock with *preferences* is **preferred stock.** This means that holders of preferred stock have priority over holders of common stock as to dividends and to payment on dissolution of the corporation. Preferred-stock shareholders may or may not have the right to vote.

In addition, preferred shareholders receive periodic dividend payments, usually established as a fixed percentage of the face amount of each preferred share. For instance, a 6 percent preferred share with a face amount of $100 would pay its owner a $6 dividend each year. These payments are not a legal obligation on the part of the firm, however.

30–4b Bonds

bond
A certificate that evidences a corporate debt. It is a security that involves no ownership interest in the issuing corporation.

Bonds (debentures) represent the long-term borrowing of funds by a firm. When bonds are issued, they almost always have a designated *maturity date*—the date when the principal or face amount of the bond is returned to the investor. The features and terms of a particular bond issue are specified in a lending agreement called a **bond indenture.** A corporate trustee, often a commercial bank trust department, represents the collective well-being of all bondholders in ensuring that the corporation meets the terms of the bond issue.

bond indenture
A contract between the issuer of a bond and the bondholder.

30–4c Alternative Financing

Some investors do not want to buy stock or bonds in a business that lacks a track record. Therefore, to obtain capital, many corporations seek alternative financing, such as venture capital and crowdfunding.

venture capital
Financing provided by professional, outside investors (venture capitalists) to new business ventures.

Venture Capital Capital provided by professional, outside investors to new business ventures is known as **venture capital.** Venture capitalists are usually groups of wealthy investors or securities firms. To obtain venture capital financing, a start-up business or other high-risk enterprise typically gives up a share of its ownership to the venture capitalists.

Crowdfunding **Crowdfunding** is a cooperative activity in which people network and pool funds and other resources via the Internet to assist a cause or invest in a venture. Sometimes, crowdfunding is used to finance budding entrepreneurs. The Securities and Exchange Commission (SEC) recently allowed companies to advertise investment opportunities to the public, and this will certainly encourage more crowdfunding in the future.

crowdfunding
A cooperative activity in which people network and pool funds and other resources via the Internet to assist a cause (such as disaster relief) or invest in a business venture.

30–5 MERGERS AND CONSOLIDATIONS

A corporation often extends its operations by combining with another corporation through a merger or a consolidation. The terms *merger* and *consolidation* are often used interchangeably, but they refer to two legally distinct proceedings. The effect of either proceeding on the rights and liabilities of the corporation, its shareholders, and its creditors is the same, however.

In either a merger or a consolidation, the surviving corporation is vested with the preexisting legal rights and obligations of the disappearing corporation (or corporations). When a merger or a consolidation takes place, the surviving corporation or newly formed corporation issues shares to pay some fair consideration to the shareholders of the corporation that ceases to exist.

LEARNING OUTCOME 4
Identify the basic steps in a merger and a consolidation.

30–5a Mergers

A **merger** involves the legal combination of two or more corporations in such a way that only one of the corporations continues to exist. **EXAMPLE 30.3** Corporation A and Corporation B decide to merge. It is agreed that A will absorb B. On merger, B ceases to exist as a separate entity, and A continues as the *surviving corporation*.◄ This process is illustrated in Exhibit 30.1.

In a merger, the surviving corporation assumes all of the assets and liabilities of the disappearing corporation. The articles of merger (the agreement between the merging corporations, which sets out the surviving corporation's name, capital structure, and so forth) amend the articles of the surviving corporation.

merger
A process whereby one corporation acquires all the assets and liabilities of another corporation, which then ceases to exist.

EXHIBIT 30.1 Merger

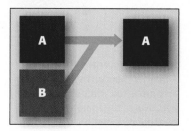

30–5b Consolidations

In a **consolidation,** two or more corporations combine in such a way that each corporation ceases to exist, and a new one emerges. **EXAMPLE 30.4** Corporation A and Corporation B consolidate to form an entirely new organization, Corporation C. In the process, A and B both terminate, and C comes into existence as a new entity.◄ This process is illustrated in Exhibit 30.2.

After a consolidation, the new corporation acquires all of the assets and liabilities of the corporations that were consolidated. The articles of consolidation (the agreement between the consolidating corporations, which sets out the new corporation's name, capital structure, and so forth) take the place of the disappearing corporations' original corporate articles and are thereafter regarded as the new corporation's corporate articles.

consolidation
A process whereby two or more corporations join to become a completely new corporation.

EXHIBIT 30.2 Consolidation

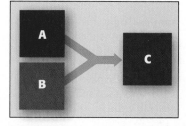

HIGHLIGHTING THE POINT

McCarty Music Corporation and Rosen Instruments, Inc., decide to consolidate to form MCR, Inc., an entirely new corporation. After the consolidation, McCarty and Rosen will cease to exist.

(Continued)

> **What happens to McCarty's assets? Who pays Rosen's creditors?** After the consolidation, MCR will be recognized as a new corporation and a single entity. MCR will assume all the rights, privileges, and powers previously held by McCarty and Rosen. Title to any assets owned by McCarty and Rosen passes to MCR without formal transfer. MCR assumes liability for all debts owed by McCarty and Rosen.

30–5c Procedure for a Merger or a Consolidation

All states have statutes authorizing mergers and consolidations for domestic (in-state) corporations. Most states also allow the combination of domestic and foreign (out-of-state) corporations. Although the procedures vary somewhat among jurisdictions, in each situation the basic requirements are as follows:

1. The board of directors of each corporation involved must approve a merger or consolidation plan.

2. The shareholders of each corporation must vote approval of the plan at a shareholders' meeting. Most state statutes require the approval of two-thirds of the outstanding shares of voting stock, although some states require only a simple majority and others require a four-fifths vote. Frequently, statutes require that each class of stock approve the merger. In that situation, the holders of nonvoting stock (such as preferred stock) must also approve. A corporation's bylaws can dictate a stricter requirement.

3. Once approved by the directors and the shareholders, the plan (articles of merger or consolidation) is filed, usually with the secretary of state.

4. When state formalities are satisfied, the state issues a certificate of merger to the surviving corporation or a certificate of consolidation to the newly consolidated corporation.

30–5d Short-Form Mergers

short-form merger
A merger that can be accomplished without the approval of the shareholders of either corporation.

Some states provide a simplified procedure for the merger of a subsidiary corporation into its parent corporation. Under these provisions, if the parent owns substantially all of the stock of the subsidiary, a **short-form merger** can be accomplished *without the approval of the other shareholders* of either corporation.

Generally, the short-form merger can be used only when the parent corporation owns at least 90 percent of the outstanding shares of each class of stock of the subsidiary corporation. The simplified procedure requires that a plan for the merger be approved by the board of directors of the parent corporation before it is filed with the state. A copy of the merger plan must be sent to each shareholder of the subsidiary corporation.

30–5e Appraisal Rights

appraisal right
A dissenting shareholder's right, if he or she objects to an extraordinary transaction of the corporation, to have his or her shares appraised and to be paid their fair value.

What if a shareholder disapproves of the merger or consolidation but is outvoted by the other shareholders? The law recognizes that a dissenting shareholder should not be forced to become an unwilling shareholder in a corporation that is new or different from the one in which the shareholder originally invested. The shareholder has the right to dissent and may be entitled to be paid the *fair value* for the number of shares held on the date of the merger or consolidation. This right is referred to as the shareholder's **appraisal right.**

An appraisal right is available only when a state statute specifically provides for it. It is normally extended to regular mergers, consolidations, short-form mergers, sales of substantially all of the corporate assets not in the ordinary course of business, and in certain states, amendments to the articles of incorporation. The appraisal right may be lost if the statutory procedures are not followed precisely. Whenever the right is lost, the dissenting shareholder must go along with the transaction despite his or her objections.

30–5f Shareholder Approval

Actions taken on extraordinary matters must be authorized by the board of directors and the shareholders. Often, modern statutes require that certain types of extraordinary matters—such as the sale, lease, or exchange of all or substantially all corporate assets outside of the corporation's regular course of business—be approved by consent of the shareholders. Hence, when any extraordinary matter arises, the corporation must proceed as authorized by law to obtain the approval of the shareholders and the board of directors.

30–5g Purchase of Assets

When a corporation acquires all or substantially all of the assets of another corporation by direct purchase, the purchasing, or *acquiring,* corporation simply extends its ownership and control over more assets. Because no change in the legal entity occurs, the acquiring corporation is not required to obtain shareholder approval for the purchase.

Although the acquiring corporation may not be required to obtain shareholder approval for such an acquisition, the U.S. Department of Justice has issued guidelines that significantly constrain, and often prohibit, mergers that could result from a purchase of assets. These guidelines are part of the federal antitrust laws.

Sales of Corporate Assets Note that a corporation that is *selling* all its assets is substantially changing its business position and perhaps its ability to carry out its corporate purposes. For that reason, the corporation whose assets are being acquired must obtain the approval of both the board of directors and the shareholders. In most states, a dissenting shareholder of the selling corporation can demand appraisal rights.

Successor Liability Generally, a corporation that purchases the assets of another corporation is not responsible for the liabilities of the selling corporation. Exceptions to this rule, however, are made in the following circumstances:

1. When the purchasing corporation assumes the seller's liabilities (or a court imposes the seller's liabilities on the purchasing corporation).
2. When the sale amounts to what in fact is a merger or consolidation.
3. When the purchaser continues the seller's business and retains the same personnel (same shareholders, directors, and officers).
4. When the sale is fraudulently executed to escape liability.

EXAMPLE 30.5 OakFabco, Inc., sold its Omni-Cast division to Precision Templates. Under the sales contract, Precision agreed to buy the assets "subject to all the liabilities connected with Omni-Cast." Weeks later, claims alleging injuries from Omni-Cast products began to arise. These claims, however, had also been made *before* the sale of the Omni-Cast division to Precision. Because the deal between OakFabco and Precision was a purchase and sale of substantially all the assets of Omni-Cast subject to "all the liabilities connected with Omni-Cast," Precision, as the successor, was liable for the consequent obligations resulting from the claims.◄

30–5h Purchase of Stock

An alternative to the purchase of another corporation's assets is the purchase of a substantial number of the voting shares of its stock. This enables the acquiring corporation to control the *target corporation*—that is, the corporation being

takeover
The acquisition of control over a corporation through the purchase of a substantial number of the voting shares of the corporation.

tender offer
An offer by the acquiring company directly to the shareholders of another company to buy those shareholders' voting shares.

acquired. The process of acquiring control over a corporation in this way is commonly referred to as a corporate **takeover.**

In a takeover attempt, the acquiring corporation deals directly with the target company's shareholders in seeking to purchase their shares. It does this by making a **tender offer** to all of the target corporation's shareholders. The tender offer can be conditioned on receipt of a specified number of shares by a certain date. To induce shareholders to accept the tender offer, the acquiring corporation generally offers them a price higher than the market price of the target corporation's shares before the announcement of the offer.

EXAMPLE 30.6 Dugan Airtel, a telecom corporation, wants to merge with Blue Ridge Communications, a television company. Before announcing its tender offer, Dugan offers to pay $40 million to acquire Blue Ridge. This means Blue Ridge shareholders will receive $25 per share—$5 in cash and $20 in Dugan stock. This $25 per share is 12 percent higher than the current market price of Blue Ridge's shares of stock.◄

30–6 TERMINATION OF A CORPORATION

Termination of a corporate life has two phases—dissolution and liquidation. We discuss these phases in further detail next.

30–6a Dissolution

LEARNING OUTCOME 5

Discuss the phases involved in the termination of a corporation.

dissolution
The formal disbanding of a partnership or a corporation.

Similar to partnerships, **dissolution** is the legal death of the artificial person of the corporation. Dissolution of a corporation can be brought about in any of the following ways:

1. An act of the state.
2. An agreement of the shareholders and the board of directors.
3. The expiration of a time period stated in the certificate of incorporation.
4. A court order.

Voluntary Dissolution Dissolution can occur voluntarily by the directors and the shareholders. State corporation statutes establish the procedures required to voluntarily dissolve a corporation. Basically, there are two possible methods: (1) by the shareholders' unanimous vote to initiate dissolution proceedings or (2) by a proposal of the board of directors that is submitted to the shareholders at a shareholders' meeting.

HIGHLIGHTING THE POINT

Dee and Jim form Home Remodeling, Inc. They are Home Remodeling's only shareholders and directors. After three years, they decide to cease business, dissolve the corporation, and go their separate ways.

Can they simply dissolve Home at will? Yes. Shareholders acting unanimously can dissolve a corporation. Also, close corporations can be dissolved by a single shareholder if the articles of incorporation provide for it.

When a corporation is dissolved voluntarily, the corporation must file articles of dissolution with the state and notify its creditors of the dissolution.

Involuntary Dissolution Sometimes, an *involuntary* dissolution is necessary. Because corporations are creatures of statute, the state can dissolve a corporation in certain circumstances, such as the following:

1. Failure to comply with administrative requirements (for example, failure to pay annual corporate taxes, to submit an annual report, or to have a designated registered agent).

2. Procurement of a corporate charter through fraud or misrepresentation.

3. Abuse of corporate powers (*ultra vires* acts).

4. Violation of the state criminal code after a demand to discontinue has been made by the secretary of state.

5. Failure to commence business operations.

6. Abandonment of operations before startup.

Sometimes, a shareholder or a group of shareholders petitions a court for corporate dissolution because of misconduct or a deadlock among its board of directors or controlling shareholders. **EXAMPLE 30.7** The Miller family—Rick, Otilia, and Breanna—operates Seven Oaks Farm in rural Virginia, as a close corporation. When Rick and Otilia are arrested for stealing from the farm's financial accounts, Breanna petitions the court for dissolution so that she can wind up Seven Oaks's business. ◄

30–6b Liquidation

Liquidation is the process by which corporate assets are converted into cash and distributed among creditors and shareholders according to specific rules of preference. When dissolution takes place by voluntary action, the members of the board of directors act as trustees of the corporate assets. As trustees, they are responsible for winding up the affairs of the corporation for the benefit of corporate creditors and shareholders. This makes the board members personally liable for any breach of their fiduciary trustee duties.

Liquidation can be accomplished without court supervision unless the members of the board do not wish to act in this capacity, or unless shareholders or creditors can show cause to the court why the board should not be permitted to assume the trustee function.

In either case, the court will appoint a receiver to wind up the corporate affairs and liquidate corporate assets. A *receiver* is a court-appointed person who receives, preserves, and manages a business or other property that is involved in the dissolution of a corporation. A receiver is always appointed by the court if the dissolution is involuntary.

liquidation
The sale of the assets of a business for cash and the distribution of that cash among creditors and shareholders.

ANSWERING THE LEGAL PROBLEM

In the legal problem set out at the beginning of this chapter, Edward and Fiona wish to form a corporation to market apps targeted at sports fans and participants. They would like to do business as Digital Synergy, although an existing corporation already uses that name.

A **Can Edward and Fiona use the same, or a similar, name for their corporation?** No. A new corporation's name cannot be the same as, or deceptively similar to, the name of an existing corporation doing business within the same state. It could cause confusion. It might also transfer some of the goodwill established by the first user to the second, infringing on the first company's trademark rights. Additionally, domain names must be distinct. For these reasons, a businessperson should check on what names are available for use *before* seeking approval for a certain name from the state of incorporation.

TERMS AND CONCEPTS FOR REVIEW

alien corporation 411	common stock 416	preferred stock 416
appraisal right 418	consolidation 417	S corporation 412
articles of incorporation 413	corporation 411	securities 415
benefit corporation 412	crowdfunding 417	short-form merger 418
bond 416	domestic corporation 411	stock 411
bond indenture 416	foreign corporation 411	takeover 420
bylaws 413	liquidation 421	tender offer 420
close corporation 412	merger 417	*ultra vires* 415
commingle 414	pierce the corporate veil 414	venture capital 416

CHAPTER SUMMARY—FORMATION AND TERMINATION OF A CORPORATION

LEARNING OUTCOME	
1	**Summarize incorporation procedures.** Exact procedures for incorporation differ among states, but the basic steps are to select a state of incorporation, secure the corporate name, and prepare and file the articles of incorporation.
2	**Describe basic corporate powers.** The powers of the corporation include the following: (1) Express powers are granted by the U.S. Constitution, state constitutions, state statutes, articles of incorporation, bylaws, and resolutions of the board of directors. (2) Implied powers exist to perform all acts reasonably appropriate and necessary to accomplish corporate purposes. (3) Any act of a corporation that is beyond its express or implied powers is an *ultra vires* act and may lead to a lawsuit by the shareholders, corporation, or state attorney general.
3	**Explain the methods of corporate financing.** Corporations obtain financing by selling stocks and bonds to investors. *Stocks* are equity securities issued by a corporation that represent the purchase of ownership in the business firm. The main types are common stock and preferred stock. *Bonds* are securities representing corporate debt—money borrowed by a corporation. Other sources of financing include venture capital and crowdfunding.

4 **Identify the basic steps in a merger and a consolidation.** In a merger, two or more corporations combine in such a way that only one of the corporations continues to exist. In a consolidation, two or more corporations combine in such a way that both cease to exist, and a new corporation emerges. In either situation, the basic steps are:

(1) The board of directors of each corporation approves the merger or consolidation plan.
(2) A majority of the shareholders of each corporation approve the plan.
(3) Articles of merger or consolidation (the plan) are filed, usually with the secretary of state.
(4) The state issues a certificate of merger (or consolidation) to the surviving (or new) corporation.

5 **Discuss the phases involved in the termination of a corporation.** The termination of a corporation involves two phases: (1) *dissolution,* the legal death of the artificial person of the corporation, which can be brought about voluntarily by the directors and shareholders or involuntarily by the state or through a court order; and (2) *liquidation,* the process by which corporate assets are converted into cash and distributed to creditors and shareholders according to specified rules. Liquidation may be supervised by members of the board of directors (when dissolution is voluntary) or by a receiver appointed by the court to wind up corporate affairs when dissolution is involuntary.

ISSUE SPOTTERS

Check your answers to the *Issue Spotters* against the answers provided in Appendix C at the end of this text.

1. In one situation, Bennett Corporation combines with Corbett Enterprises, Inc. Bennett ceases to exist, and Corbett is the surviving firm. In another scenario, Global Corporation and Hometown Company combine. Afterward, Global and Hometown cease to exist entirely. Green Springs, Inc., a new firm, functions in their place. Which of these combinations is a merger and which is a consolidation? (See *Mergers and Consolidations.*)

2. The incorporators of Consumer Investments, Inc., want their new corporation to have the authority to transact nearly any conceivable type of business. Can they grant this authority to their firm? If so, how? If not, why? (See *Corporate Powers.*)

USING BUSINESS LAW

30–1. Incorporation. Jonathan, Gary, and Ricardo are active members of a partnership called Swim City. The partnership manufactures, sells, and installs outdoor swimming pools in the states of Texas and Arkansas. The partners want to continue to be active in management and to expand the business into other states as well. They also are concerned about rather large recent judgments entered against swimming pool companies throughout the United States. Based on these facts only, discuss whether the partnership should incorporate. (See the *Introduction* and *Corporate Classifications.*)

30–2. *Ultra Vires* Doctrine. Kora Nayenga and two business associates formed a corporation called Nayenga Corp. for the purpose of selling computer services. Kora, who owned 50 percent of the corporate shares, served as the corporation's president. Kora wished to obtain a personal loan from his bank for $250,000, but the bank required the note to be cosigned by a third party. Kora cosigned the note in the name of the corporation. Later, Kora defaulted on the note, and the bank sued the corporation for payment. The corporation asserted, as a defense, that Kora had exceeded his authority when he cosigned the note. Had he? Explain. (See *Corporate Powers.*)

REAL-WORLD CASE PROBLEMS

30–3. Piercing the Corporate Veil. Scott Snapp contracted with Castlebrook Builders, Inc., which was owned by Stephen Kappeler, to remodel a house. Kappeler estimated the cost at $500,000. Eventually, however, Snapp paid Kappeler more than $1.3 million. Snapp sought to be reimbursed, but Kappeler could not provide an accounting for the project. Specifically, he could not explain double and triple charges, nor whether the amount that Snapp paid had actually been spent on the house. Meanwhile, Kappeler had commingled personal and corporate funds. As for Castlebrook, it had issued no shares of stock, and the minutes of the corporate meetings "all looked exactly the same." Are these sufficient grounds to pierce the corporate veil? Explain. [*Snapp v. Castlebrook Builders, Inc.*, 54 Ohio App.3d 361, 7 N.E.2d 574 (2014)] (See *Formation of a Corporation.*)

30–4. Purchase of Assets. Grand Adventures Tour & Travel Publishing Corp. (GATT) provided travel services. Duane Boyd, a former GATT director, incorporated Interline Travel & Tour, Inc. At a public sale, Interline bought GATT's assets. Interline moved into GATT's office building, hired former GATT employees, and began to serve GATT's customers. A GATT creditor, Call Center Technologies, Inc., sought to collect the unpaid amount on a contract with GATT from Interline. Is Interline liable? Why or why not? [*Call Center Technologies, Inc. v. Grand Adventures Tour & Travel Publishing Corp.*, 635 F.3d 48 (2d Cir. 2011)] (See *Formation of a Corporation.*)

ETHICAL QUESTIONS

30–5. Shareholder Approval. Why should shareholders be required to approve certain types of corporate actions? (See *Mergers and Consolidations.*)

30–6. Dissolution. Why should courts be reluctant to order the dissolution of a corporation? (See *Termination of a Corporation.*)

30–7. Purchase of Stock. Air Products & Chemicals, Inc., made a tender offer of $70 per share to the shareholders of Airgas, Inc. The Airgas board rejected the offer as inadequate and took defensive measures to block the bid. Some Airgas shareholders filed a suit against Airgas, seeking an order to compel the board to allow the shareholders to decide whether to accept Air Products' offer. Who should have the power to accept or reject a tender offer? Why? How can directors best fulfill their duty to act in the interest of their shareholders? [*Air Products and Chemicals, Inc. v. Airgas, Inc.*, 16 A.3d 48 (Del.Ch. 2011)] (See *Formation of a Corporation.*)

Chapter 30—Work Set

TRUE-FALSE QUESTIONS

_____ 1. A corporation is an artificial being.

_____ 2. A corporation that is formed in a country other than the United States, but which does business in the United States, is a foreign corporation.

_____ 3. When conflicts arise among documents involving corporations, resolutions of the board of directors have the highest priority.

_____ 4. Stocks represent the purchase of corporate ownership.

_____ 5. During the liquidation of a corporation, corporate assets are converted to cash and distributed to creditors and shareholders.

_____ 6. Shareholders who disapprove of a merger or a consolidation may be entitled to be paid the fair value of their shares.

_____ 7. A corporation that purchases the assets of another corporation always assumes the selling corporation's liabilities.

MULTIPLE-CHOICE QUESTIONS

_____ 1. Adam, Terry, and Victor want to form ATV Corporation. Which of the following is _not_ a step in forming the corporation?

a. selecting a state of incorporation.
b. preparing articles of incorporation.
c. adopting bylaws at a shareholders' meeting.
d. filing articles of incorporation.

_____ 2. Mike, Nora, and Paula are shareholders in National Business, Inc. All of the shareholders are National's

a. owners.
b. directors.
c. incorporators.
d. officers.

_____ 3. Responsibility for the overall management of Standard Products, Inc., a corporation, rests with its

a. owners.
b. directors.
c. incorporators.
d. officers.

_____ 4. U.S. Digital Corporation incorporated in Ohio, its only place of business. Its stock is owned by ten shareholders. Two are resident aliens. Three of the others are the directors and officers. The stock has never been sold to the public. If a shareholder wants to sell his or her shares, the other shareholders must be given the opportunity to buy them first. U.S. Digital is

a. a close corporation.
b. a foreign corporation.
c. an alien corporation.
d. none of the above.

5. General Manufacturing, Inc. (GMI), issues bonds to finance the purchase of a factory. Regarding those bonds, which of the following is *true?*

a. The bonds must be repaid.
b. The bondholders will receive interest payments only when voted by GMI directors.
c. The bonds are identical to preferred stock from an investment standpoint.
d. The bondholders will be the last investors paid on GMI's dissolution.

6. Redwood, Inc., is unprofitable. In a suit against Redwood, Inc., a court might order dissolution if the firm does *not*

a. buy its stock from its shareholders.
b. declare a dividend.
c. make a profit this year.
d. pay its taxes.

7. Macro Corporation and Micro Company combine, and a new organization, MM, Inc., takes their place. This is

a. a consolidation.
b. a merger.
c. a purchase of assets.
d. a purchase of stock.

8. Mary and Adam are the directors and majority shareholders of U.S. Imports, Inc., and Overseas Corporation. U.S. Imports owes $5,000 to International Transport, Inc. To avoid the debt, Mary and Adam vote to sell all of U.S. Imports' assets to Overseas. If International sues Overseas on the debt, International will

a. win, because an acquiring firm always assumes a selling corporation's liabilities.
b. win, because the sale was fraudulently executed to avoid liability.
c. lose, because Overseas refused to assume U.S. Imports' debt.
d. lose, because U.S. Imports has ceased to exist.

ANSWERING MORE LEGAL PROBLEMS

1. Mountainview Resort made annual contributions to its employees' pension fund. During the latest recession, business began to decline. Mountainview's owners obtained a loan from Investco Bank. Two years later, the resort closed due to poor business. Investco—which was still owed $14 million by Mountainview—instituted foreclosure proceedings. At the foreclosure sale, Investco bought the resort and reopened it under new management with new employees.

   As the resort's new owner, was Investco obligated to pay into the pension fund? No. An acquiring corporation will be held to have assumed the _____ of the selling corporation when (1) the purchasing corporation expressly or impliedly assumes the seller's _____, (2) the sale is in effect a merger or consolidation of the two companies, (3) the purchaser continues the seller's business and retains the same _____, or (4) the sale is entered into fraudulently to avoid liability. Here, Mountainview ceased operations before Investco bought it. Under the new owner, there was a new _____. The company was not a continuation of the previous operation.

2. Jeremy incorporated FormFit Concrete, Inc., but did not file its first annual report, so the state involuntarily dissolved the firm. Unaware of this, Jeremy contracted with Market Square to lay the foundations for a commercial building project. After the work was complete, Market Square refused to pay. To recover, Jeremy filed a claim as "FormFit Concrete, Inc." Market Square asked the court to dismiss the claim on the ground that the state had dissolved that firm. Jeremy immediately filed new articles of incorporation for "FormFit Concrete, Inc."

   Can Jeremy recover from Market Square? Yes. Under the doctrine of corporation by _____, if a business holds itself out as a corporation, and a third party deals with it as a corporation, neither party can raise the issue as to whether or not the corporation is validly _____. In this problem, Jeremy fulfilled the contract in good faith, as indicated by his lack of awareness of the dissolution, his continuing to act as a corporation, and his filing of new articles under the same corporate name immediately on learning of the involuntary dissolution. Market Square dealt with FormFit as a _____ and accepted the benefit of its performance.

MANAGEMENT AND OWNERSHIP OF A CORPORATION

31

FACING A LEGAL PROBLEM

Tim Rodale, one of the directors of the First National Bank, attends no board of directors' meetings in five and a half years, never inspects any of the bank's books or records, and generally fails to supervise the efforts of the bank president and the loan committee. Meanwhile, the bank president makes various improper loans and permits large overdrafts.

Q Can Rodale be held liable to the bank for losses resulting from the unsupervised actions of the bank president and the loan committee?

A corporation joins together the efforts and resources of a large number of individuals for the purpose of producing greater returns than those persons could have produced individually. This chapter focuses on the roles and responsibilities of corporate directors, officers, and *shareholders*—those who own stock in the corporation. No one individual shareholder or director bears sole responsibility for the corporation and its actions.

31–1 CORPORATE MANAGEMENT— DIRECTORS AND OFFICERS

Every corporation is governed by a board of directors, which is its ultimate authority. Directors have responsibility for all policymaking decisions necessary to the management of corporate affairs. The corporation's officers and other executive employees are hired by the board of directors to manage those policies and to make daily business decisions.

31–1a Election of Directors

The number of directors is set forth in the corporation's articles of incorporation or bylaws. Historically, the minimum number of directors has been three, but many states today permit fewer. The initial board of directors is normally appointed by the incorporators on the creation of the corporation. The initial board serves until the first annual shareholders' meeting. Subsequent directors are elected by a majority vote of the shareholders.

The term of office for a director usually is one year—from annual meeting to annual meeting. Longer and staggered terms are permissible under most state statutes. A common practice is to elect one-third of the board members each year for a three-year term. In this way, there is greater management continuity.

Removal of Directors A director can be removed *for cause* (breach of duty or other misconduct), either as specified in the articles or bylaws or by shareholder action.

427

The board of directors itself may be given power to remove a director for cause, subject to shareholder review. In most states, unless the corporation has previously authorized such an action, a director cannot be removed without cause.

Vacancies Sometimes, vacancies occur on the board of directors due to death or resignation. In addition, new positions may be created through amendment of the articles or bylaws. When a vacancy exists, either the shareholders or the board itself can fill the position, depending on state law or on the provisions of the bylaws.

31–1b Board of Directors' Meetings

The board of directors conducts business by holding formal meetings with recorded minutes. Most often, the date at which regular meetings are held is established in the articles and bylaws or by board resolution. No further notice is customarily required. Special meetings can be called with notice sent to all directors. Most states allow directors to participate in board meetings from remote locations via telephone or Web conferencing.

quorum
The number of members of a decision-making body that must be present before business may be transacted.

Quorum Requirements Normally, a majority of the board of directors must be present to constitute a *quorum*. A **quorum** is the minimum number of members of a body of officials or other group that must be present before business can be transacted validly. Quorum requirements vary among jurisdictions. Many states leave the decision to the corporate articles or bylaws. If the articles or bylaws do not state quorum requirements, most states provide that a quorum is a majority of the number of directors authorized in the articles or bylaws.

Voting Once a quorum is present, the directors transact business and vote on issues affecting the corporation. Each director has one vote. Ordinary matters generally require a majority vote. Certain extraordinary issues may require a greater-than-majority vote.

31–1c Directors' Responsibilities

LEARNING OUTCOME 2

Discuss directors' management responsibilities and directors' and officers' fiduciary duties.

The general areas of responsibility of the board of directors include the following:

1. Authorization for major corporate policy decisions. **EXAMPLE 31.1** The board of directors of Catalina Swimwear approves the company's new product lines every season. It also oversees the contract negotiations with the companies that will manufacture the new swimsuits and other swim apparel.◄

2. Appointment, supervision, and removal of corporate officers and other managerial employees and determination of their compensation.

3. Financial decisions, such as the declaration and payment of dividends to shareholders or the issuance of authorized shares (stocks) or bonds.

The board of directors can delegate some of its functions to an executive committee or to corporate officers. Corporate officers and managerial personnel are then empowered to make decisions relating to ordinary, daily corporate affairs within well-defined guidelines. The board retains its overall responsibility for directing the corporation's affairs, however.

HIGHLIGHTING THE POINT

The board of directors for Shire Pharmaceuticals has a dozen members. To manage the many complex issues facing the company, the board creates an executive committee and an audit committee. The board appoints directors to serve on these committees. The executive committee is authorized to make management decisions between board meetings. The audit committee is charged with the selection, compensation, and oversight of the independent public accountants who audit the firm's financial records.

Can a board of directors delegate these responsibilities to committees? Yes. When a board has a large number of members who must deal with complex issues, meetings can become unwieldy. The boards of large corporations typically create committees of directors to focus on specific subjects and increase company efficiency. Thus, it is quite common for a board to form executive and audit committees.

31–1d The Role of Corporate Officers

Corporate officers manage the day-to-day operations of a corporation. At a minimum, most corporations have a president, one or more vice presidents, a secretary, and a treasurer. In most states, an individual can hold more than one office, such as president and secretary, and can be both an officer and a director of the corporation. In addition to carrying out the duties spelled out in the bylaws, corporate and managerial officers act as agents of the corporation, and the ordinary rules of agency normally apply to their employment.

The rights of corporate officers and other high-level managers are defined by employment contracts, because officers and managers are employees of the company. Regardless of the terms of their employment contract, the board of directors normally can remove corporate officers at any time with or without cause. If the board removes an officer in violation of an employment contract, however, the corporation may be liable for breach of contract.

31–1e Duties of Directors and Officers

Directors and officers are fiduciaries of the corporation. A *fiduciary* is a person with a duty to act primarily for another's benefit. Thus, the relationship of directors and officers with the corporation and its shareholders is one of trust and confidence.

The fiduciary duties of the directors and officers include the *duty of care* and the *duty of loyalty*. These duties also play a role in the *business judgment rule*.

Duty of Care Directors are obligated to be honest and to use prudent business judgment in the conduct of corporate affairs. They must exercise the same degree of care that reasonably prudent people use in conducting their own personal affairs. In addition, they must carry out their responsibilities in an informed, business-like manner and act in accordance with their own knowledge and training.

Directors can be held answerable to the corporation and to the shareholders for breaching their duty of care. When directors delegate work to corporate officers and employees, they are expected to use a reasonable amount of supervision. Otherwise, they will be held liable for negligence or mismanagement of corporate personnel.

HIGHLIGHTING THE POINT

Imani is a board member for Viral Fashions, an online clothing designer. For two years, Imani does not attend any board meetings, inspect any of the corporate books, or meet

(Continued)

with the research and development (R&D) committee. She co-chairs the R&D committee with Sydney. In Imani's absence, Sydney secretly steals original dress designs from the company's computers and sells them to competitors for personal financial gain.

As a ViralFashion board director, is Imani breaching her duty of care? Yes. Imani is failing to use a reasonable amount of supervision over Viral Fashions' personnel. In this situation, Imani can be held liable to the corporation for losses resulting from Sydney's unsupervised actions.

Duty of Loyalty *Loyalty* can be defined as faithfulness to one's obligations and duties. In the corporate context, the duty of loyalty requires directors and officers to subordinate their personal interests to the corporation's welfare. Directors cannot use corporate funds or confidential information for personal advantage and must refrain from self-dealing. **EXAMPLE 31.2** Reyna is a member of the board of directors for Coal Creek Creamery, Inc. When Seattle Cheese Company makes a tender offer to merge with Coal Creek, Reyna cannot oppose it simply because she will lose her board position. If, however, the tender offer is not in Coal Creek's best interest, then her duty of loyalty justifies her opposition. In short, Reyna's loyalty is to Coal Creek, not herself.◄

Sometimes, a corporation enters into a contract or engages in a transaction in which an officer or director has a personal interest. When this situation occurs, the director or officer must make a *full disclosure* of any conflict of interest and must abstain from voting on the proposed transaction.

The Business Judgment Rule Directors and officers are expected to exercise due care and to use their best judgment in guiding corporate management, but they are not insurers of business success. Under the **business judgment rule,** a corporate director or officer will not be liable to the corporation or to its shareholders for honest mistakes of judgment and bad business decisions. For the rule to apply, the directors or officers must act within their managerial authority and within the powers of the corporation. They must also exercise due care.

Generally, if there is a reasonable basis for a business decision, a court will not likely interfere with that decision, even if it causes the corporation to suffer. In fact, unless there is evidence of bad faith, fraud, or a clear breach of fiduciary duties, most courts will apply the business judgment rule to protect directors and officers from liability for their bad business decisions.

business judgment rule
A rule that immunizes corporate management from liability for actions that are undertaken in good faith.

HIGHLIGHTING THE POINT

Sterling Software announces its intention to acquire Nifty Apps. Nifty's directors, however, do very little to prepare for the possible merger. They fail to research Nifty's market value and make no attempt to seek out other potential buyers. A $60 million cash merger is negotiated and finalized in less than a week—and Nifty's directors meet for only seven hours to discuss it. As a result, Nifty's shareholders do not get as much financial gain as they possibly could have from the merger with Sterling.

Are the Nifty directors liable for potential lost financial gains due to a breach of their fiduciary duties by failing to maximize Nifty's sales price? No. Even though the Nifty shareholders are not ultimately pleased with the Sterling merger, there is no indication of bad faith, fraud, or a breach of fiduciary duties in these facts. Thus, Nifty's directors are protected by the business judgment rule.

31–2 CORPORATE OWNERSHIP—SHAREHOLDERS

The acquisition of a share of stock makes a person an owner and shareholder of a corporation. Shareholders thus own the corporation. One of the hallmarks of the corporate organization is that shareholders are not personally liable for the debts of the corporation. The only exception to this protection from personal liability is if the shareholders commit fraud, commingle funds, undercapitalize, or are careless in observing corporate formalities. In these instances, a court may "pierce the corporate veil" and hold shareholders responsible for any corporate debts.

As a general rule, shareholders have no responsibility for the corporation's daily management. They are, however, ultimately responsible for choosing the board of directors, which does have that control (through its appointment of officers). If the corporation fails, shareholders can lose their investments, but that is generally the limit of their liability.

Here, we look at the powers and voting rights of shareholders, which are generally established in the articles of incorporation and the state's general incorporation law.

31–2a Shareholders' Powers

Shareholders must approve fundamental changes affecting the corporation before the changes can be implemented. Hence, shareholders must approve amendments to the articles of incorporation and bylaws, a merger or dissolution of the corporation, or the sale of all or substantially all of the corporation's assets. Some of these actions are subject to prior board approval.

Shareholders elect and remove the directors of the corporation. The first board of directors is either named in the articles of incorporation or chosen by the incorporators to serve until the first shareholders' meeting. From that time on, selection and retention of directors are exclusively shareholder functions.

Shareholders have the inherent power to remove a director from office *for cause* by a majority vote. Some state statutes permit removal of directors *without cause* by the vote of a majority of the holders of outstanding shares entitled to vote. Some corporate charters expressly provide that shareholders, by majority vote, can remove a director at any time without cause.

31–2b Shareholders' Meetings

Shareholders' meetings must occur at least annually. Additionally, special meetings can be called to take care of urgent matters. Some states provide that the unanimous written consent of shareholders is a permissible alternative to holding a shareholders' meeting. Because it is not practical for owners of only a few shares of stock to attend shareholders' meetings, such stockholders normally give third parties a written authorization to vote their shares at the meeting. This authorization is called a **proxy**.

31–2c Rights of Shareholders

Shareholders possess many rights, including voting rights and the right to receive stock certificates and dividends. We discuss several other important shareholder rights in this section.

Voting Rights Shareholders exercise ownership control through the power of their votes. Each shareholder is entitled to one vote per share. The articles of incorporation can exclude or limit voting rights, particularly to certain classes of shares. For instance, owners of *preferred stock* usually are denied the right to vote.

Quorum Requirements For shareholders to act during a meeting, a quorum must be present. Generally, a quorum exists when shareholders holding more than

proxy
A written agreement between a stockholder and another under which the stockholder authorizes the other to vote the stockholder's shares in a certain manner.

LEARNING OUTCOME 3
List shareholders' rights.

50 percent of the outstanding shares are present, but state laws often permit the articles of incorporation to set higher or lower quorum requirements.

Real-World Case Example

Sink & Rise, Inc., had eighty-four shares of voting common stock outstanding. James Case owned twenty shares. In addition, he and his estranged wife, Shirley, jointly owned another sixteen shares. Three different individuals owned sixteen shares each. During a shareholders' meeting, James was the only shareholder present. He elected himself and another shareholder to be directors, replacing Shirley as Sink & Rise's secretary. Shirley sued to set aside the election, claiming the sixteen shares that she owned jointly with James should not have been counted for quorum purposes.

Could the shares held jointly by James and Shirley be counted for purposes of a quorum? Yes. In a 2013 case, *Case v. Sink & Rise, Inc.*, the Wyoming Supreme Court affirmed a lower court's judgment. Corporate bylaws required that, in determining a quorum, the shares had to be entitled to vote and represented in person or by proxy. Because the sixteen shares that were jointly held were indeed represented in person by James at the shareholders' meeting, they could be counted for quorum purposes. Consequently, the actions taken at the meeting were accomplished with authority, and Shirley was no longer the company's secretary.

Passing Resolutions Once a quorum is present, voting can proceed. Corporate business matters are presented in the form of resolutions, which shareholders vote to approve or disapprove. A straight majority vote of the shares represented at the meeting is usually required to pass resolutions.

Cumulative Voting for Directors Shareholders, as mentioned, also vote for directors. Sometimes, each director is elected by a simple majority vote of the shareholders present at the meeting. Most states permit, however, and some states require, shareholders to elect directors by *cumulative voting*. This method of voting allows minority shareholders to obtain representation on the board of directors.

When cumulative voting is used, the number of members of the board to be elected is multiplied by the total number of voting shares held. The result equals the number of votes a shareholder has. The shareholder can cast this total number of votes for one or more nominees for director.

HIGHLIGHTING THE POINT

Tam Corporation has 10,000 outstanding shares. Three members of the board are to be elected. A majority of the shareholders (holding 7,000 shares) favor Acevedo, Barkley, and Craycik. The other shareholders (3,000 shares) favor Drake.

Can Drake be elected by the minority shareholders? If cumulative voting is allowed, the answer is yes. The minority shareholders have 9,000 votes among them (the number of directors to be elected times the number of shares is 3 times 3,000, which equals 9,000 votes). All of these votes can be cast to elect Drake. The majority shareholders have 21,000 votes (3 times 7,000 equals 21,000 votes), but these votes have to be distributed among their three choices. No matter how the majority shareholders cast their votes, they cannot elect all three directors if the minority shareholders cast all of their votes for Drake. (See Exhibit 31.1.)

EXHIBIT 31.1 Results of Cumulative Voting

Ballot	Majority Shareholders' Votes			Minority Shareholders' Votes	Directors Elected
	Acevedo	Barkley	Craycik	Drake	
1	10,000	10,000	1,000	9,000	Acevedo/Barkley/Drake
2	9,001	9,000	2,999	9,000	Acevedo/Barkley/Drake
3	6,000	7,000	8,000	9,000	Barkley/Craycik/Drake

Stock Certificates A **stock certificate** is a certificate issued by a corporation that evidences ownership of a specified number of shares in the corporation. In jurisdictions that require the issuance of stock certificates, shareholders have the right to demand that the corporation issue a certificate and record their names and addresses in the corporate stock record books.

stock certificate
A certificate issued by a corporation evidencing the ownership of a specified number of shares.

Preemptive Rights A shareholder who has a **preemptive right** obtains a preference over all other purchasers to subscribe to, or purchase, a prorated share of a new issue of stock. This allows the shareholder to maintain his or her portion of control, voting power, and financial interest in the corporation. **EXAMPLE 31.3** Sheri, a shareholder who owns 10 percent of a company and who has preemptive rights, can buy 10 percent of any new issue (to maintain her 10 percent position). Thus, if Sheri owns 100 shares of 1,000 outstanding shares, and the corporation issues 1,000 more shares, she can buy 100 of the new shares.◄

preemptive right
A shareholder's right to purchase new shares of a corporation's stock—equal in percentage to shares already held—before the stock is offered to others.

Dividends A **dividend** is a distribution of corporate profits or income *ordered by the directors* and paid to the shareholders in proportion to their respective shares in the corporation. Dividends can be paid in cash, property, stock of the corporation that is paying the dividends, or stock of other corporations.

State laws vary, but every state determines the circumstances and legal requirements under which dividends are paid. Generally, dividends are allowed so long as the corporation can continue to pay its debts as they come due and the amount of the dividends does not exceed the corporation's *net worth*—that is, its total assets minus its total liabilities. Once declared, a cash dividend becomes a corporate debt enforceable at law like any other debt.

dividend
A distribution of profits or income to shareholders, disbursed in proportion to the number of shares held.

Inspection Rights Shareholders have a right to inspect and copy corporate books and records for a *proper purpose*, provided they request access to the books and records in advance. Either the shareholder can inspect in person, or an attorney, agent, accountant, or other type of assistant can do so.

HIGHLIGHTING THE POINT

Laila, the majority shareholder of Market Mogul, Inc., sells the firm's assets to herself and sets up another corporation, Nano Research. Laila then tells Market Mogul's minority shareholders that she is dissolving Market Mogul because it is failing financially. Kurt, a minority shareholder, asks to inspect the corporate records so that he can determine Market Mogul's financial condition, the value of its stock, and whether any misconduct has occurred.

Is Kurt entitled to inspect Market Mogul's books and records? Yes. Kurt has expressed a proper purpose for the inspection and should be allowed access to Market Mogul's

(Continued)

records. A shareholder can be denied access to corporate records to prevent harassment or to protect trade secrets or other confidential corporate information, but that is not the situation here—Kurt is not abusing his right to inspect.

Transfer of Shares Corporate stock represents an ownership right in intangible (nonphysical) personal property. The law generally recognizes the right of an owner to transfer property to another person, unless there are valid restrictions on its transferability. Sometimes, corporations or their shareholders restrict transferability by reserving the option to purchase any shares offered for resale by a shareholder.

The Shareholder's Derivative Suit When the corporation is harmed by the actions of a third party, the directors can bring a lawsuit in the name of the corporation against that party. If the corporate directors fail to bring a lawsuit, shareholders can do so "derivatively" in what is known as a **shareholder's derivative suit.**

The right of shareholders to bring a derivative action is especially important when the wrong suffered by the corporation results from the actions of corporate directors or officers. This is because the directors and officers would most likely not be willing to sue themselves.

When shareholders bring a derivative suit, they are not pursuing rights or benefits for themselves personally but are acting as guardians of the corporate entity. Therefore, if the suit is successful, any damages recovered normally go into the corporation's treasury, not to the shareholders personally.

31–2d Duties of Majority Shareholders

In some instances, a majority shareholder is regarded as having a fiduciary duty to the corporation and to the minority shareholders. This occurs when a single shareholder (or a few shareholders acting in concert) owns a sufficient number of shares to exercise *de facto* (actual) control over the corporation. In these situations, majority shareholders owe a fiduciary duty to the minority shareholders.

When a majority shareholder breaches her or his fiduciary duty to a minority shareholder, the minority shareholder can sue for damages. A breach of fiduciary duties by those who control a *close corporation* normally constitutes what is known as *oppressive conduct*. A common example of a breach of fiduciary duty occurs when the majority shareholders "freeze out" the minority shareholders and exclude them from the benefits of participating in the firm.

EXAMPLE 31.4 Jamil, Jordan, and Barbara form a close corporation to operate a machine shop. Each own one-third of the company, and all three are directors. After disagreements arise, Jamil asks the company to purchase his shares, but his requests are refused. A few years later, Jamil dies, and his wife inherits his shares. Jordan and Barbara refuse to perform a valuation of the company, deny her access to the corporate information she requests, do not declare any dividends, and refuse to elect her as a director. In this situation, the majority shareholders have violated their fiduciary duty to Jamil's wife, the minority shareholder. ◄

ANSWERING THE LEGAL PROBLEM

In the legal problem set out at the beginning of this chapter, Tim Rodale, one of the directors of the First National Bank, attends no board meetings in five and a half years, never inspects any of the bank's books or records, and fails to supervise the bank president

LEARNING OUTCOME 4

Explain how a shareholder's derivative suit can help a corporation.

shareholder's derivative suit
A suit brought by a shareholder to enforce a corporate cause of action against a third person.

and the loan committee. Meanwhile, the bank president makes improper loans and permits large overdrafts.

A **Can Rodale be held liable to the bank for losses resulting from the actions of the president and the loan committee?** Yes. The director has breached his duty of care and may be held liable to the bank for the losses.

TERMS AND CONCEPTS FOR REVIEW

business judgment rule 430

dividend 433

preemptive right 433

proxy 431

quorum 428

shareholder's derivative suit 434

stock certificate 433

CHAPTER SUMMARY—MANAGEMENT AND OWNERSHIP OF A CORPORATION

LEARNING OUTCOME	
1	**State how directors are elected and the requirements to hold a board meeting.** The first board of directors usually is appointed by the incorporators. Thereafter, directors are elected by the shareholders. The board conducts business by holding formal meetings with recorded minutes. The date of regular meetings generally is established in the corporate articles or bylaws. Special meetings can be called after notice is sent to all directors. Quorum requirements vary. Usually, a quorum is a majority of the directors. In ordinary matters, a majority vote of the directors present is required.
2	**Discuss directors' management responsibilities and directors' and officers' fiduciary duties.** Directors' management responsibilities include (1) authorization of major corporate policy-making decisions, (2) appointment, supervision, compensation, and removal of corporate officers and other management employees, and (3) declaration and payment of corporate dividends to shareholders and issuance of authorized shares or bonds. Directors may delegate some of their responsibilities to executive committees or officers and executives. Directors and officers have a fiduciary duty to use care in conducting corporate business and subordinate their own interests to those of the corporation in corporate matters. They must fully disclose any potential conflicts of interest between their personal interests and those of the corporation.
3	**List shareholders' rights.** Shareholders have many rights, which may include voting rights, the right to a stock certificate, preemptive rights, the right to obtain a dividend (at the discretion of the directors), the right to inspect the corporate records, the right to transfer shares (this right may be restricted), and the right to sue on behalf of the corporation (bring a shareholder's derivative suit) when the directors fail to do so.
4	**Explain how a shareholder's derivative suit can help a corporation.** If the directors refuse to act in order to redress a wrong suffered by the corporation, the shareholders can act on its behalf by filing a shareholder's derivative suit. Any monetary damages recovered by such a lawsuit goes into the corporation's coffers.

ISSUE SPOTTERS

Check your answers to the *Issue Spotters* against the answers provided in Appendix C at the end of this text.

1. Glen is a director and shareholder of Diamond Corporation and of Emerald, Inc. If a resolution comes before the Emerald board to compete with Diamond, what is Glen's responsibility? (**See** *Corporate Management— Directors and Officers.*)

2. Joe is a director and officer of United Products, Inc. Joe makes a decision about the marketing of United's products that results in a dramatic decrease in profits for United and its shareholders. The shareholders accuse Joe of breaching his fiduciary duty to the corporation. What is Joe's best defense? (See *Corporate Management—Directors and Officers*.)

USING BUSINESS LAW

31–1. Rights of Shareholders. Dmitri has acquired one share of common stock of a multimillion-dollar corporation with more than 500,000 shareholders. Dmitri's ownership is so small that he is questioning what his rights are as a shareholder. For example, he wants to know whether this one share entitles him to attend and vote at shareholders' meetings, inspect the corporate books, and receive periodic dividends. Discuss Dmitri's rights in these matters. (See *Corporate Ownership—Shareholders*.)

31–2. Duties of Directors. Starboard, Inc., has a board of directors consisting of three members, Ellsworth, Green, and Morino. The corporation has approximately five hundred shareholders. At a regular meeting of the board, the board selects Tyson as president of the corporation by a unanimous vote. Later, during an audit, it is discovered that Tyson is a former convict and has openly embezzled $500,000 from Starboard. This loss is not covered by insurance. The corporation wants to hold Ellsworth, Green, and Morino liable. Discuss the personal liability of the directors to the corporation. (See *Corporate Management—Directors and Officers*.)

REAL-WORLD CASE PROBLEMS

31–3. Liability of Shareholders. Country Contractors, Inc., contracted to provide excavation services for A Westside Storage of Indianapolis, Inc., but did not complete the job and later filed for bankruptcy. Stephen Songer and Jahn Songer were Country's sole shareholders. The Songers had not misused the corporate form to engage in fraud, the firm had not been undercapitalized, personal and corporate funds had not been commingled, and Country had kept accounting records and minutes of its annual board meetings. Are the Songers personally liable for Country's failure to complete its contract? Explain. [*Country Contractors, Inc. v. A Westside Storage of Indianapolis, Inc.*, 4 N.E.3d 677 (Ind.App. 2014)] (See *Corporate Ownership—Shareholders*.)

31–4. Duty of Loyalty. Kids International Corp. produced children's wear for Walmart and other retailers. Gila Dweck was a Kids director and its chief executive officer. Because she felt that she was not paid enough for the company's success, she started Success Apparel to compete with the firm. Success operated out of Kids' premises, used its employees,

borrowed on its credit, took advantage of its business opportunities, and capitalized on its customer relationships. As an "administrative fee," Dweck paid Kids 1 percent of Success's total sales. Did Dweck breach any fiduciary duties? Explain. [*Dweck v. Nasser*, 2012 WL 161590 (Del. Ch.2012)] (See *Corporate Management—Directors and Officers*.)

31–5. Duties of Majority Shareholders. Bill McCann was the president and chief executive officer of McCann Ranch & Livestock Co. He and his brother Ron each owned 36.7 percent of the stock, but Ron had been removed from the board of directors on their father's death and was not authorized to work for the firm. Their mother, Gertrude, owned the rest of the stock, which was to pass to Bill on her death. The corporation paid Gertrude's personal expenses in an amount that represented about 75 percent of the net corporate income. Bill received regular salary increases. The corporation did not issue a dividend. Was Ron the victim of a freeze-out? Discuss. [*McCann v. McCann*, __ P.3d __ (Idaho 2012)] (See *Corporate Ownership—Shareholders*.)

ETHICAL QUESTIONS

31–6. Board of Directors' Meetings. Should state corporation laws allow board of directors' meetings to be held in cyberspace? Discuss. (See *Corporate Management—Directors and Officers*.)

31–7. Duty of Loyalty. Under what circumstances might a director's sale of corporate property to himself or herself be justified? (See *Corporate Management—Directors and Officers*.)

31–8. The Business Judgment Rule. Robert Henrichs was elected the chairman of the board of Chugach Alaska Corp. During his term, Henrichs held board meetings with only

his supporters present. He also refused to follow bylaws that required a special meeting of shareholders on a certain matter and acted without board discussion or approval. In addition, he ignored board rules in the conduct of meetings and retaliated against directors who challenged his decisions by excluding them from the board. Do these acts fall under the business judgment rule? Do they constitute a breach of ethics? Discuss. [*Henrichs v. Chugach Alaska Corp.*, 250 P.3d 531 (Alaska 2011) (See *Corporate Management—Directors and Officers*.)

Chapter 31—Work Set

TRUE-FALSE QUESTIONS

_____ 1. Both directors and officers may be immunized from liability for poor business decisions under the business judgment rule.

_____ 2. Officers have the same fiduciary duties as directors.

_____ 3. The rights of shareholders are established only in the articles of incorporation.

_____ 4. Dividends can be paid in cash or property.

_____ 5. Damages recovered in a shareholder's derivative suit are normally paid to the shareholder who brought the suit.

_____ 6. As a general rule, shareholders are not personally responsible for the debts of the corporation.

_____ 7. Officers, but not directors, owe a duty of loyalty to the corporation.

_____ 8. The business judgment rule makes a director liable for losses to the firm that result from the director's authorized, good faith business decisions.

_____ 9. Cumulative voting allows minority shareholders to obtain representation on the board of directors.

MULTIPLE-CHOICE QUESTIONS

_____ 1. Jill is a shareholder of United Manufacturing Company. As a shareholder, Jill's rights include all of the following _except_ a right to

a. one vote per share.
b. access to corporate books and records.
c. transfer shares.
d. sell corporate property when directors are mishandling corporate assets.

_____ 2. The board of directors of U.S. Goods Corporation announces that the corporation will pay a cash dividend to its shareholders. Once declared, a cash dividend is

a. a corporate debt.
b. a personal debt of the directors.
c. a personal debt of the shareholders.
d. an illusory promise.

_____ 3. Julio and Gloria are officers of World Export Corporation. As corporate officers, their rights are set out in

a. state corporation statutes.
b. World Export's certificate of authority.
c. their employment contracts with World Export.
d. international agreements with nonresident shareholders.

_____ 4. The board of Consumer Sales Corporation delegates work to corporate officers and employees. If the directors do not use a reasonable amount of supervision, they could be held liable for

a. negligence only.
b. mismanagement of corporate personnel only.
c. negligence or mismanagement of corporate personnel.
d. none of the above.

_____ 5. The management of National Brands, Inc., is at odds with the shareholders over some recent decisions. To redress a wrong suffered by National from the actions of management, the shareholders may

a. exercise their preemptive rights.
b. exercise their inspection rights.
c. file a shareholder's derivative suit.
d. issue a proxy.

_____ 6. Federated Products Corporation uses cumulative voting in its elections of directors. Mary owns 3,000 Federated shares. At an annual meeting at which three directors are to be elected, how many votes may Mary cast for any one candidate?

a. 1,000.
b. 3,000.
c. 9,000.
d. 2,700.

_____ 7. Local Corporation invests in intrastate businesses. In Local's state, as in most states, the minimum number of directors that must be present before a board can transact business is

a. all of the directors authorized in the articles.
b. a majority of the number authorized in the articles or bylaws.
c. any odd number.
d. one.

_____ 8. Nationwide Company's chief financial officer resigns. After a personnel search, an investigation, and an interview, the board of directors hires Ed. Ed turns out to be dishonest. Nationwide's shareholders sue the board. The board's best defense is

a. the business judgment rule.
b. the directors' duty of care.
c. the directors' duty of loyalty.
d. a shareholder's derivative suit.

_____ 9. Ron is a director of Standard Company. Ron has a right to

a. compensation for his efforts on Standard's behalf.
b. transfer shares of Standard stock.
c. participate in Standard board meetings.
d. preemptive rights to buy Standard shares on any new issue.

ANSWERING MORE LEGAL PROBLEMS

1. The directors of Urban Credit Corp.—a consumer, corporate, and investment bank—voted to invest in subprime lending. Soon after, the housing market declined, foreclosures increased, and other subprime lenders collapsed. Subsequently, Urban Credit suffered significant losses.

   Were Urban Credit's directors liable for their decision to engage in this course of business? No. Directors are not insurers of business success. Honest mistakes of judgment and poor business decisions on their part do not make them liable to the corporation or its shareholders for damages. This is the _____ _____ rule. For the rule to apply, directors and officers must act within their _____ authority and within the _____ of the corporation. They must also exercise _____ _____. Here, the directors of Urban Credit did not disregard their duties or act in bad faith.

2. Brent, Jon, and Kenzie owned Kenzie's Lemonade Corp., which made and sold fruit drinks. Each owned one-third of the shares of the corporate stock, and each was a director. A disagreement arose over the direction of the business. Kenzie asked Brent and Jon to buy her shares, but they refused. They also denied her access to the company's books and records, did not declare a dividend, and did not reelect her as a director.

   Did Brent and Jon, as majority shareholders, breach their fiduciary duty to Kenzie? Yes. When a few shareholders acting together own a sufficient number of shares to exercise _____ over a corporation, they owe a _____ duty to the minority shareholders. A breach of this duty occurs when the majority shareholders of a close corporation _____ _____ the minority shareholder or shareholders, whom they exclude from the benefits of the firm. A minority shareholder's remedy for this oppressive conduct is to sue for _____.

CREDIT AND RISK

UNIT CONTENTS

CHAPTER 32 Secured Transactions

CHAPTER 33 Creditors' Rights and Remedies

CHAPTER 34 Bankruptcy

CHAPTER 35 Insurance

secured transaction
Any transaction in which the payment of a debt is guaranteed by personal property.

FACING A LEGAL PROBLEM

Home State Bank lends funds to Moran Manufacturing, Inc. As part of the deal, Moran gives Home State the right to take possession of its equipment if the loan is not repaid. The agreement between Home State and Moran describes the equipment in detail, including each item's serial number. To inform other creditors of the interest that Home State has in the equipment, the bank files a statement in a state office that exists for that purpose.

Q In this statement, can the bank use the same description of the equipment that it used in the loan agreement?

Whenever the payment of a debt is guaranteed, or *secured*, by personal property owned by the debtor or in which the debtor has a legal interest, the transaction is known as a **secured transaction.** Personal property can be *tangible* (physical, such as a building or a vehicle) or *intangible* (nonphysical, such as stocks or patents).

The concept of a secured transaction is as basic to modern business practice as the concept of credit. Logically, sellers and lenders want to get paid for their goods and services, so they usually will not sell goods or lend funds unless payment is somehow guaranteed. Indeed, business as we know it could not exist without laws permitting and governing secured transactions.

32–1 THE TERMINOLOGY OF SECURED TRANSACTIONS

The Uniform Commercial Code (UCC) provides the law covering secured transactions. A brief summary of the UCC's definitions of terms relating to secured transactions follows:

1. A *security interest* is every interest in personal property that secures (guarantees) the payment or performance of an obligation.

2. A *secured party* is a lender, a seller, or any person in whose favor there is a security interest. The terms *secured party* and *secured creditor* are used interchangeably.

3. A *debtor* is the party who owes payment or performance of the secured obligation.

4. A *security agreement* is the agreement that creates or provides for a security interest between the debtor and a secured party.

5. *Collateral* is the property subject to a security interest (the property that secures the payment or performance of the obligation).

6. A *financing statement*—referred to as Form UCC-1—gives notice to the public that the creditor has a secured interest in collateral belonging to the debtor named in the statement. The secured creditor prepares Form UCC-1 and then files it with the appropriate state or local official, usually the secretary of state.

32–2 CREATING A SECURITY INTEREST

Before a creditor can become a secured party, the creditor must have a security interest in the collateral of the debtor. Three requirements must be met for a creditor to have an enforceable security interest:

1. Either the collateral must be in the possession of the secured party, or there must be a written security agreement. In most situations, a written security agreement is used. The agreement must be signed by the debtor and must contain a description that reasonably identifies the collateral.

2. The secured party must give value to the debtor. Normally, the value takes the form of a direct loan or a commitment to sell goods on credit.

3. The debtor must have rights in the collateral.

Once these requirements are met, the creditor's rights *attach* to the collateral. This means that the creditor has a security interest against the debtor that is enforceable. **Attachment** ensures that the security interest between the debtor and the secured party is effective.

EXAMPLE 32.1 Roma applies for a credit card at Sears. The application contains a clause giving Sears a security interest in any goods that Roma buys with the card until she pays for them in full. This signed application meets the first requirement for a security interest. Sears's commitment to sell goods to Roma on credit constitutes value, which is the second requirement. The goods that Roma buys with the card are the collateral, and her right in them is her ownership interest, which is the third requirement. Thus, all the requirements for an enforceable security interest are met. When Roma buys something with the credit card, the store's rights attach to it. ◄

The concept under which a debtor-creditor relationship becomes a secured transaction and the terminology involved are illustrated in Exhibit 32.1.

32–3 PERFECTING A SECURITY INTEREST

Even though a security interest has attached, the secured party must take steps to protect its claim to the collateral in the event that the debtor *defaults*—that is, fails to

> **LEARNING OUTCOME 1**
>
> Explain how an enforceable security interest can be created and perfected.

> **attachment**
> In a secured transaction, the process by which a security interest in the property of another becomes enforceable.

EXHIBIT 32.1 Secured Transactions—Concept and Terminology

In a security agreement, a debtor and a creditor agree that the creditor will have a security interest in collateral in which the debtor has rights. In essence, the collateral secures the loan and ensures the creditor of payment should the debtor default.

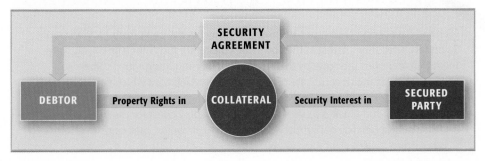

perfection
The method by which a secured party obtains priority by notice that his or her security interest in the debtor's collateral is effective against the debtor's subsequent creditors.

pay the debt as promised. **Perfection** is the legal process by which secured parties protect themselves against the claims of third parties who may wish to have their debts satisfied out of the same collateral. This sort of conflict may occur, for example, in bankruptcy proceedings when many creditors are making claims for monies owed them by the debtor who is filing for bankruptcy.

32–3a Perfection by Filing a Financing Statement

In most situations, a secured party perfects a claim by filing a financing statement, or Form UCC-1, with the appropriate state or local official. The financing statement must contain the following:

- The signature of the debtor.
- The addresses of the debtor and the creditor.
- A description of the collateral by type or item.

Also, to avoid problems arising from different descriptions, the secured party can repeat the security agreement's description in the financing statement or file the two together.

Where to File Where or how a security interest is perfected sometimes depends on the type of collateral, which can be classified as either tangible or intangible. Depending on the classification of the collateral, filing is done either centrally with the secretary of state, locally with the county clerk or other official, or both. In general, financing statements for timber to be cut, fixtures, or items to be extracted—such as oil, coal, gas, and minerals—are filed with the county clerk. Other kinds of collateral require filing with the secretary of state.

Effectiveness of a Financing Statement A financing statement is effective for five years from the date of filing. If a *continuation statement* is filed *within six months* before the expiration date, the effectiveness of the original statement is continued for another five years, starting with the expiration date of the first five-year period. The effectiveness of the statement can be continued in the same manner indefinitely.

32–3b Improper Filing of a Financing Statement

Improper filing of the financing statement can render the security interest unperfected and reduce the secured party's claim in bankruptcy proceedings to that of an unsecured creditor. For instance, if extra papers or lists are attached to the financing statement and *not* referred to in the form itself, that would most likely be considered misleading. Additionally, if the debtor's name on a financing statement is seriously misleading or if the collateral is not sufficiently described, the filing may not be effective.

HIGHLIGHTING THE POINT

Nick and Bianca operate a ranch in Texas. They buy twenty cows from Judy on credit. To perfect a security interest in the cows (the collateral), Judy files a financing statement that identifies the cows by their names and ear-tag designations. She also gives Nick and Bianca a certificate of registration for each cow, which features the same information. Nick and Bianca remove the ear tags, sell the cows, and then file for bankruptcy. Judy makes a claim with the bankruptcy court for the debt Nick and Bianca owe her. The bankruptcy court's trustee, however, maintains that Judy's security interest in the cows is not perfected, because the financing statement does not describe the cows in sufficient detail.

Are the cows' descriptions in the financing statement reasonably sufficient to perfect Judy's security interest in them?   Yes. Both the statement and the certificates of registration contain the cows' names and ear-tag numbers. This is sufficient information to permit any party to easily identify which cows are covered by the security interest.

32–4 THE SCOPE OF A SECURITY INTEREST

A security agreement can cover various types of property in addition to collateral already in the debtor's possession—(1) the *proceeds of the sale of collateral,* (2) *after-acquired property,* and (3) *future advances.*

LEARNING OUTCOME 2
Define the scope of a security interest.

32–4a Proceeds

Proceeds include whatever cash or property is received when collateral is sold, exchanged, collected, or disposed of. A secured party has an interest in the proceeds of the sale of collateral.

proceeds
Whatever is received when collateral is sold, exchanged, collected, or disposed of.

HIGHLIGHTING THE POINT

A bank has a perfected security interest in the inventory of a retail seller of heavy farm machinery. The retailer sells a tractor out of this inventory to a farmer, a buyer in the ordinary course of business. The farmer agrees, in a retail security agreement, to make monthly payments for twenty-four months.

If, two months later, the retailer should go into default on the loan from the bank, is the bank entitled to the remaining payments the farmer owes to the retailer?   Yes. These payments are proceeds. They are what the retailer was to receive for the collateral. The bank, as a secured party, has an interest in such proceeds.

A security interest in proceeds perfects automatically on the perfection of the secured party's security interest in the original collateral and remains perfected for twenty days after the debtor receives the proceeds. One way to extend the twenty-day automatic perfection period is to provide for extended coverage in the original security agreement or financing statement. This is typically done when the collateral is the type that is likely to be sold, such as a retailer's inventory of digital tablets or smartphones. A security interest in identifiable cash proceeds is also able to remain perfected after twenty days.

32–4b After-Acquired Property

After-acquired property is property that the debtor acquired after the execution of the security agreement. To cover after-acquired property, the security agreement must provide for the coverage. This provision often accompanies security agreements covering a debtor's inventory.

after-acquired property
Property of the debtor that is acquired after a secured creditor's interest in the debtor's property has been created.

HIGHLIGHTING THE POINT

Amato buys factory equipment from Bronson on credit, giving as security an interest in all of her equipment—both what she is buying and what she already owns. The security agreement with Bronson contains an after-acquired property clause. Six months later, Amato pays cash to another seller for other equipment. Six months after that, Amato goes out of business before she has paid off her debt to Bronson.

Does Bronson's security interest cover the equipment bought from the other seller? Yes. Under the after-acquired property clause, Bronson has a security interest in all of Amato's equipment, even the equipment bought from the other seller.

32–4c Future Advances

Often, a debtor arranges with a bank to have a continuing *line of credit* under which the debtor can borrow funds intermittently. Advances against lines of credit can be subject to a perfected security interest in identified collateral. The security agreement may provide that any future advances made against that line of credit are also subject to the security interest in the same collateral.

HIGHLIGHTING THE POINT

Stroh is the owner of a small manufacturing plant with equipment valued at $1 million. He has an immediate need for $50,000 of working capital, so he secures a loan from Midwestern Bank and signs a security agreement, putting up all his equipment as security. The security agreement provides that Stroh can borrow up to $500,000 in the future, using the same equipment as collateral for any future advances.

Is it necessary to execute a new security agreement and perfect a security interest in the collateral each time an advance is made to Stroh? No. Stroh has a line of credit with the bank, and the security agreement that he signed gives the bank a security interest in any advances made against the line of credit.

32–4d The Floating-Lien Concept

floating lien
A security interest retained in collateral even when the collateral changes in character, classification, or location.

When a security agreement provides for the creation of a security interest in proceeds of the sale of after-acquired property or future advances, or both, the security interest is referred to as a **floating lien.** Floating liens commonly arise in the financing of inventories. A creditor is not interested in specific pieces of inventory, because they are constantly changing. Thus, the lien "floats" from one item to another as the inventory changes.

HIGHLIGHTING THE POINT

Cascade Sports, Inc., a cross-country ski dealer, has a line of credit with Portland First Bank to finance an inventory of cross-country skis. Cascade and Portland First enter into a security agreement that provides for coverage of proceeds, after-acquired inventory, present inventory, and future advances. Portland First perfects the security interest by filing centrally (with the secretary of state). One day, Cascade sells a new pair of cross-country skis and receives a used pair in trade. The same day, it buys two new pairs of skis from a local manufacturer with a new advance of funds from Portland First.

Does Portland First have a perfected security interest in the used skis, the new skis, and the advance? Yes. All of this is accomplished under the original perfected security interest. The bank has a perfected security interest in the used skis under the proceeds clause, in the new skis under the after-acquired property clause, and in the advance under the future-advance clause. Hence, Portland First has a floating lien.

 ## 32–5 PRIORITIES AMONG SECURITY INTERESTS

When more than one party claims an interest in the same collateral, which one has priority? The UCC sets out detailed rules to answer this question. Although in many situations the party who has a perfected security interest will have priority, there are exceptions.

32–5a General Rules

In most situations, the following rules apply when more than one party, or creditor, claims rights in the same collateral:

1. *Conflicting unperfected security interests*—When two conflicting security interests are unperfected, the first to attach (be created) has priority. This is sometimes called the "first-in-time" rule.

2. *Perfected security interests versus unperfected interests*—When a security interest is perfected, it has priority over any unperfected interests.

3. *Conflicting perfected security interests*—When two or more creditors have perfected security interests in the same collateral, the first to perfect (by filing or taking possession of the collateral) generally has priority.

> **LEARNING OUTCOME 3**
> Set out the priorities among perfected and unperfected security interests.

32–5b Buyers in the Ordinary Course of Business

An exception to these general rules concerns a buyer in the ordinary course of business. Such a buyer takes the goods free from any security interest created by the seller even if the security interest is perfected and the buyer knows of its existence. In other words, a buyer in the ordinary course has priority even if a perfected security interest exists as to the goods.

The Definition A *buyer in the ordinary course of business* is defined as a person who in good faith—and without knowledge that the sale violates the rights of another in the goods—buys in ordinary course from a person in the business of selling goods of that kind. Note that the buyer can know about the existence of a perfected security interest, so long as he or she does not know that buying the goods violates the rights of any third party.

Of course, the seller of the goods must have valid title to them. If the goods are stolen, the seller's title is void. In that situation, the buyer acquires no title, and the real owner can reclaim the goods from the buyer.

The Rationale for the Exception The rationale for the exemption regarding buyers in the ordinary course of business is obvious. If buyers could not buy the goods free and clear of any security interests, the free flow of goods in the marketplace would be hindered.

Most customers of any business are buyers in the ordinary course of business. **EXAMPLE 32.2** Destiny buys clothes regularly at Urban Outfitters in the Fashion West Mall. She takes those items free of any security interest that a creditor (such as a bank or the store's supplier) has in them. This is true even if Destiny knows that Urban Outfitters borrows the money to buy its inventory and uses that inventory—including the clothes that she buys—to guarantee repayment of the loan.◄

32–6 Rights and Duties of the Debtor and Creditor

LEARNING OUTCOME 4

List the rights and duties of the debtor and creditor in a secured transaction.

The security agreement determines most of the rights and duties of the debtor and creditor. Rights and duties that apply in the absence of a security agreement to the contrary include the following:

- *Reasonable care of collateral*—Collateral may sometimes be in the secured party's possession. In this situation, the secured party must use reasonable care in preserving it. If the collateral increases in value, the secured party can hold this increased value as additional security unless it is in the form of cash, which must be paid to the debtor or applied toward reducing the debt. The debtor must pay for all reasonable charges incurred by the secured party in caring for the collateral.

- *Termination statement*—When a secured debt is paid, the secured party may send a termination statement to the debtor or file such a statement with the filing officer to whom the original financing statement was given. In situations involving most types of goods, a termination statement must be filed or sent within twenty days after the debt is paid. If it is not, the secured party is liable to the debtor for $500, plus any loss to the debtor.

32–7 Default

Any breach of the terms of a security agreement can constitute default. Most commonly, *default* occurs when the debtor fails to meet the scheduled payments that the parties have agreed on or when the debtor becomes bankrupt.

32–7a Basic Remedies

LEARNING OUTCOME 5

State the secured party's options on a debtor's default.

The rights and remedies of secured parties are *cumulative*—that is, if a creditor is unsuccessful in enforcing rights by one method, he or she can pursue another method. Generally, a secured party's remedies can be divided into the two basic categories: *repossession of the collateral* and *judicial remedies*.

Repossession of the Collateral When a debtor defaults, a secured party can take *peaceful* possession of the collateral without going to court. The general rule is that the collateral has been taken *peacefully* if the secured party can take possession without committing (1) trespass onto land, (2) assault and/or battery, or (3) breaking and entering. On taking possession, the secured party may either retain the collateral for satisfaction of the debt or resell the goods and apply the proceeds toward the debt.

Judicial Remedies Alternatively, a secured party can relinquish the security interest and use any judicial remedy available, such as obtaining a judgment on the underlying debt. **EXAMPLE 32.3** Gillian loans funds to Caleb to buy a Steinway Boston grand piano, using the piano as collateral. Caleb fails to repay the loan. Gillian can sue him for the funds. If that proves unsuccessful, she can repossess the piano. In other words, Gillian's attempt to sue Caleb does not prevent her from repossessing the piano if the suit does not result in satisfaction of the debt.◄

32–7b Retaining or Disposing of the Collateral

Once default has occurred and the secured party has obtained possession of the collateral, the secured party can retain the collateral or can sell, lease, or otherwise dispose of it in any commercially reasonable manner.

Retention of the Collateral by the Secured Party A secured party's right to retain the collateral is subject to several conditions. Written notice must be sent to the debtor unless the debtor signed a statement renouncing or modifying his or her rights after default. In the case of consumer goods, no other notice need be given. In all other cases, notice must be sent to any other secured creditor from whom the secured party has received written notice of a claim to the collateral. If, within twenty days, the debtor or other secured creditor objects to the retention of the collateral, the secured party must sell or otherwise dispose of it.

Disposition of the Collateral by the Secured Party A secured party who does not choose to retain the collateral must dispose of it in a *commercially reasonable* manner. Selling the collateral by the same method normally used for selling similar property fulfills this requirement. The sale can be public or private. It can be conducted in any manner, place, and time and according to any terms, as long as it is commercially reasonable and in good faith.

Real-World Case Example

Bradley Smith, on his own behalf and that of the John J. Smith Revocable Living Trust, borrowed funds from Firstbank Corporation secured with pledges of Sparton Corporation stock and other collateral. When the loans were not paid, Firstbank sold the stock in private sales, returned the other collateral, and remitted the excess funds to Smith and the trust. Alleging that the Sparton stock sales were commercially unreasonable—because a higher price might have been obtained for them in public sales—Smith and the trust sued Firstbank in a Michigan court. The court ruled in the Firstbank's favor. The plaintiffs appealed.

Were Firstbank's sales of the debtors' Sparton stock commercially reasonable? Yes. In a 2013 case, *Smith v. Firstbank Corp.*, a state intermediate appellate court affirmed the lower court's judgment in the bank's favor. The court noted that, "The defendant had valid reasons for choosing a private sale, and made efforts to obtain a reasonable price for the shares. In fact, the method chosen by Firstbank allowed the plaintiffs to retain over five million dollars of collateral, as well as a net surplus on the sale of the stock."

The secured party must notify the debtor and other specified parties in writing ahead of time about the sale or disposition of the collateral. Notification is not required if the collateral is perishable, will decline rapidly in value, or is of a type customarily sold on a recognized market. The debtor may waive the right to receive this notice, but only after default.

When the collateral is consumer goods, such as a car or boat, and the debtor has paid 60 percent or more of the purchase price, the secured party *must* sell or otherwise dispose of the repossessed collateral within ninety days. Failure to comply opens the secured party to a legal action for *conversion* or other liability. To avoid such action, however, the consumer-debtor has to have signed a written statement *after default* renouncing or modifying the right to demand the sale of the goods.

Note that if a debtor has paid less than 60 percent of the purchase price, the secured party has the option to repossess the collateral in a commercially reasonable manner, but is not required to do so.

Proceeds from Disposition Proceeds from the disposition must be applied in the following order:

1. Reasonable expenses incurred by the secured party in repossessing, storing, and reselling the collateral.

2. Satisfaction of the balance of the debt owed to the secured party.

3. Subordinate security interests of creditors whose written demands are received prior to the completion of distribution of the proceeds.

4. Any surplus to the debtor.

deficiency judgment
A judgment against a debtor for the amount of a debt remaining unpaid after the collateral has been repossessed and sold.

Deficiency Judgment Often, after proper disposition of the collateral, the secured party has not collected all that the debtor still owes. Unless otherwise agreed, the debtor is liable for any deficiency, and the creditor can obtain a **deficiency judgment** from a court to collect the remaining unpaid amount. **EXAMPLE 32.4** Randy buys a new Honda FourTrax Rancher ATV for $6,000 from PowerPlay Motors on credit. Randy begins making payments, but defaults six months into the sales contract. PowerPlay then repossesses the ATV, and to recover Randy's remaining $5,500 debt, the store sells it at auction for $4,000. PowerPlay can then obtain a deficiency judgment against Randy for $1,500, because he is still liable for what he owes the store.◄

Redemption Rights Any time before the secured party disposes of the collateral or enters into a contract for its disposition, or before the debtor's obligation has been discharged through the secured party's retention of the collateral, the debtor (or any other secured party, if there is one) can exercise the right of *redemption*. This is done by tendering performance of all obligations secured by the collateral, by paying the expenses reasonably incurred by the secured party (including, if provided in the security agreement, reasonable attorneys' fees and legal expenses), and by retaking the collateral and maintaining its care and custody.

    EXAMPLE 32.5 Lerner borrows the funds to buy a car and gives the car as security for the loan but fails to make the payments. The lender, Valley River Bank, repossesses the car and plans to sell it to get back some of what Lerner borrowed. Before the car is sold (or before Valley River Bank has contracted to sell it), Lerner can exercise his right of redemption—that is, he can pay the bank what he owes, plus expenses, and take back the car.◄

ANSWERING THE LEGAL PROBLEM

In the legal problem set out at the beginning of this chapter, Home State Bank loaned funds to Moran Manufacturing, Inc., taking a security interest in Moran's equipment. The security agreement described the equipment in detail, including each item's serial number.

A   **Can the bank use the same description in the financing statement?** Yes. In fact, to avoid problems that could arise from variations in descriptions, a secured party may repeat exactly the security agreement's description in the financing statement, file the security agreement itself as a financing statement (if it otherwise meets the requirements), or file a combination security agreement and financing statement.

TERMS AND CONCEPTS FOR REVIEW

after-acquired property 443

attachment 441

deficiency judgment 448

floating lien 444

perfection 442

proceeds 443

secured transaction 440

CHAPTER SUMMARY—SECURED TRANSACTIONS

LEARNING OUTCOME	
1	**Explain how an enforceable security interest can be created and perfected.** *Creating* an enforceable security interest involves three requirements: (1) The creditor must possess the collateral, or there must be a written security agreement signed by the debtor and reasonably identifying the collateral; (2) the secured party must give value to the debtor; and (3) the debtor must have rights in the collateral. The most common method of *perfecting* a security interest is filing a financing statement that contains the names and addresses of the secured party and the debtor, describes the collateral by type or item, and is signed by the debtor.
2	**Define the scope of a security interest.** Beyond the collateral already in the debtor's possession, a security agreement can cover (1) proceeds from a sale, exchange, collection, or disposition of secured collateral; (2) after-acquired property—property acquired after the execution of the security agreement; and (3) future advances—future advances made against a line of credit.
3	**Set out the priorities among perfected and unperfected security interests.** The following rules apply when more than one creditor claims rights in the same collateral: (1) When two conflicting security interests are unperfected, the first to attach has priority. (2) A perfected security interest takes priority over an unperfected security interest. (3) When both security interests are perfected, the interest that was first to perfect generally has priority. A secured creditor does not prevail against a buyer in the ordinary course of business.
4	**List the rights and duties of the debtor and creditor in a secured transaction.** The security agreement determines most of the rights and duties of the debtor and creditor. In the absence of a security agreement to the contrary, rights and duties include the following: (1) If a secured party is in possession of the collateral, he or she must use reasonable care in preserving it. (2) When a debt is paid, the secured party generally must send a termination statement to the debtor or file one with the filing officer to whom the original financing statement was given.
5	**State the secured party's options on a debtor's default.** On a debtor's default, a secured party who does not already have possession of the collateral identified in the security agreement can take possession. The secured party can then retain the collateral or sell it. A secured party can also relinquish the security interest and use any judicial remedy available. In the case of retention, the secured party must generally send written notice to the debtor and to any other secured parties who have claimed an interest in the collateral. In the case of a sale, the secured party must sell the collateral in a commercially reasonable manner and generally must notify the debtor and other specified parties of the sale.

ISSUE SPOTTERS

Check your answers to the *Issue Spotters* against the answers provided in Appendix C at the end of this text.

1. Adam needs $500 to buy textbooks and other supplies. Beth agrees to loan Adam $500, accepting as collateral Adam's iPad. They put their agreement in writing. How can Beth let other creditors know of her interest in the iPad? (See *Perfecting a Security Interest.*)

2. First National Bank loans $5,000 to Gail to buy a car, which is used as collateral to secure the loan. Gail has paid less than 50 percent of the loan when she defaults. First National could repossess and keep the car, but the bank does not want it. What are some alternatives? (See *Default.*)

USING BUSINESS LAW

32–1. Priority Disputes. Redford is a seller of electric generators. He purchases a large quantity of generators from a manufacturer, Mallon Corp., by making a down payment and signing an agreement to make the balance of payments over a period of time. The agreement gives Mallon Corp. a security interest in the generators and the proceeds. Mallon Corp. files a financing statement on its security interest centrally. Redford receives the generators and immediately sells one of them to Garfield with payment to be made in twelve equal installments. At the time of sale, Garfield knows of Mallon's security interest. Two months later, Redford goes into default on his payments to Mallon. Discuss Mallon's rights against purchaser Garfield in this situation. (See *Priorities among Security Interests.*)

32–2. The Scope of a Security Interest. Edward owned a retail sporting goods shop. A new ski resort was being created in his area, and to take advantage of the potential business, Edward decided to expand his operations. He borrowed a large sum of money from his bank, which took a security interest in his present inventory and any after-acquired inventory as collateral for the loan. The bank properly perfected the security interest by filing a financing statement. A year later, just a few months after the ski resort had opened, an avalanche destroyed the ski slope and lodge. Edward's business consequently took a turn for the worse, and he defaulted on his debt to the bank. The bank sought possession of his entire inventory, even though the inventory was now twice as large as it had been when the loan was made. Edward claimed that the bank had rights to only half of his inventory. Is Edward correct? Explain. (See *The Scope of a Security Interest.*)

REAL-WORLD CASE PROBLEMS

32–3. Disposition of Collateral. With a loan of 1.4 million euros from Barclays Bank, Thomas Poynter bought a yacht. The loan agreement gave Barclays multiple stand-alone options on default. One option required that it give ten days' advance notice of a sale. A different option permitted the bank to avoid this requirement. When Poynter did not repay the loan, Barclays repossessed the yacht, notified Poynter that it would be sold—but did not specify a date, time, or place—and sold it two months later. Barclays got less than what Poynter owed. Is Barclays entitled to collect the deficiency even though it did not give Poynter ten days' advance notice of the sale? Explain. [*Barclays Bank PLC v. Poynter*, 710 F.3d 16 (1st Cir. 2013)] (See *Default.*)

32–4. Perfecting a Security Interest. Thomas Tille owned M.A.T.T. Equipment Co. To operate the business, Tille borrowed funds from Union Bank. For each loan, Union filed a financing statement that included Tille's signature and address, the bank's address, and a description of the collateral. The first loan covered all of Tille's equipment, including "any after-acquired property." The second loan covered a truck crane "whether owned now or acquired later." The third loan covered a "Bobcat mini-excavator." Did these financing statements perfect Union's security interests? Explain. [*Union Bank Co. v. Heban*, 2012-Ohio-30 (6 Dist. 2012)] (See *The Scope of a Security Interest.*)

32–5. Disposition of Collateral. PRA Aviation, LLC, borrowed $3 million from Center Capital Corp. to buy a Gates Learjet 55B. Center perfected a security interest in the plane. Later, PRA defaulted on the loan, and Center obtained possession of the jet. The jet's value was estimated at $1.45 million based on the market, design, and mechanical condition of similar aircraft. The jet was marketed in trade publications, on the Internet, and by direct advertising to select customers for $1.6 million. There were three offers. Center sold the jet to the highest bidder for $1.3 million. Was the sale commercially reasonable? Explain. [*Center Capital Corp. v. PRA Aviation*, LLC, __ F.Supp.2d __ (E.D.Pa. 2011)] (See *Default.*)

ETHICAL QUESTIONS

32–6. Taking Possession of the Collateral. Does the potential harm of allowing a creditor to repossess collateral on a debtor's default, without going to court, outweigh the benefit? Discuss. (See *Default.*)

32–7. Priorities. James Cavazos bought a Mercedes S550 from Mercedes-Benz of Sugar Land with funds that he borrowed from JPMorgan Chase Bank. Chase perfected a security interest in the car. Cavazos forged a release of the debt and obtained a certified copy of the title. In reliance on that copy, NXCESS Motor Cars, Inc., bought the car and sold it to Xavier Valeri, who paid with a loan from U.S. Bank. The bank filed a financing statement to perfect its security interest. Later, Cavazos's forgery was discovered. Who has the right to possess the car? Explain. [*NXCESS Motor Cars, Inc. v. JPMorgan Chase Bank, N.A.*, 317 S.W.3d 462 (Tex.App.—Houston 2010)] (See *Priorities among Security Interests.*)

Chapter 32—Work Set

TRUE-FALSE QUESTIONS

_____ 1. Attachment gives a creditor an enforceable security interest in collateral.

_____ 2. To be valid, a financing statement does not need to contain a description of the collateral.

_____ 3. When a secured debt is paid, the secured party does not need to file a termination statement in all cases.

_____ 4. The security agreement determines most of the parties' rights and duties concerning the security interest.

_____ 5. Default occurs most commonly when a debtor fails to repay the loan for which his or her property served as collateral.

_____ 6. After a default, and before a secured party disposes of the collateral, a debtor cannot exercise the right of redemption.

_____ 7. When two secured parties have perfected security interests in the same collateral, generally the last to perfect has priority.

MULTIPLE-CHOICE QUESTIONS

_____ 1. Hudson National Bank files a financing statement regarding a transaction with EcoVibes. To be valid, the financing statement must contain all of the following except

    a. a description of the collateral.
    b. the debtor's name.
    c. the reason for the transaction.
    d. the secured party's name.

_____ 2. Austin Transport, Inc., buys a forklift, but does not make a payment on it for five months. The seller, Baker Equipment Company, repossesses it by towing it from a public street. Austin sues Baker for breach of the peace. Able will likely

    a. not prevail, because Baker did not use judicial process.
    b. not prevail, because the repossession was not a breach of the peace.
    c. prevail, because Able did not default on the loan.
    d. prevail, because the repossession was a breach of the peace.

_____ 3. Dan owns Parkside Café, which he uses as collateral to borrow $10,000 from First State Bank. To be effective, the security agreement must include

    a. a description that reasonably identifies the collateral only.
    b. Dan's signature only.
    c. a description that reasonably identifies the collateral and Dan's signature.
    d. none of the above.

_____ 4. Irma defaults on a loan from Jiffy Loan Corporation. Jiffy takes possession of the collateral and would like to keep it. Kwik Kapital, which also has an interest in the collateral, sends Jiffy notice of its claim. Jiffy may

    a. be forced to sell the collateral and pay Kwik.
    b. be forced to sell the collateral if Kwik objects to the retention.
    c. not retain the collateral, because doing so would violate Kwik's interest.
    d. retain the collateral if it sends notice to Kwik.

_____ 5. Kappa Credit, Inc., has a security interest in the proceeds from the sale of collateral owned by Local Stores Company. This interest may remain perfected for longer than twenty days after Local receives the proceeds

    a. only if a filed financing statement covers the proceeds.
    b. only if the proceeds are identifiable cash proceeds.

c. if a filed financing statement extends coverage of the proceeds or the proceeds are identifiable cash proceeds.

d. under any circumstances.

_____ **6.** Nick borrows $5,000 from Modern Financial Corporation (MFC). MFC files a financing statement on May 1, but Nick does not sign a security agreement until he receives the funds on May 5. He also borrows $5,000 from Omega Bank, which advances funds, files a financing statement, and signs a security agreement on May 2. He uses the same property as collateral for both loans. On Nick's default, in a dispute over the collateral, MFC will

a. lose, because Omega perfected first.

b. lose, because Omega's interest attached first.

c. win, because it filed first.

d. win, because its interest attached first.

_____ **7.** Peak Electronics Stores borrows $10,000 from Quick Loan Company. The loan is secured by Peak's inventory, which includes appliances sold to consumers on installment payment plans. Peak defaults. Quick is entitled to

a. all of the inventory sold to consumers.

b. any remaining installment payments.

c. both a and b.

d. none of the above.

_____ **8.** Safe Loans, Inc., wants to perfect its security interest in Tech Corporation's inventory for sale or lease. Most likely, Safe should file a financing statement with

a. a city manager.

b. a county clerk.

c. a federal loan officer.

d. the appropriate state or local official, usually the secretary of state.

ANSWERING MORE LEGAL PROBLEMS

1. Good Buy Co. sold consumer electronics. To operate its business, Good Buy borrowed funds from Capital Bank and Business Credit, Inc. Good Buy granted Capital Bank a security interest in "all Apple products," which attached on May 1. Business Credit's interest in "all Good Buy's inventory" attached on May 10. Business Credit perfected the interest by filing a financing statement on May 15. Capital filed a financing statement on May 20. One week later, Alexis bought an iPad from Good Buy. EZ Lending, LLC, loaned Good Buy funds on May 31 for an interest in "all Good Buy's equipment, whenever acquired." Before EZ Lending filed a financing statement, Good Buy filed for bankruptcy.

What is the priority to Good Buy's assets among these security interests? _____ has first priority. _____ is second, _____ is third, and _____ is last. When a security interest is perfected, it has priority over any _____ interests. When two or more creditors have perfected security interests in the same collateral, the interest that was the _____ to attach has priority. A buyer in the ordinary course of business—any person who in good faith, and without knowledge that a sale is in violation of a security interest, buys in ordinary course from a person in the business of selling goods

of that kind—has priority over a _____ security interest.

2. North Star Motors, Inc., sold used cars. To finance the purchase of the used cars, North Star borrowed funds from ReFinance Co. When North Star defaulted on its loans, ReFinance took possession of the dealer's inventory and notified it that the cars would be sold. In the auto industry, there are many ways to resell cars, including individual retail sales and wholesale sales of sets of vehicles. Most of North Star's repossessed vehicles were sold individually, but those that had high mileage or were in poor condition were sold to wholesalers in batches. The total sales did not amount to the full debt, so ReFinance held North Star liable for the difference.

Were these sales commercially reasonable? Yes. Once default occurs, the secured party can obtain possession of the collateral. A secured party who does not choose to retain the collateral must dispose of it in a commercially reasonable manner. Selling the collateral using the same _____ that is typical for selling similar property fulfills this requirement. Generally, _____ of the sale must be sent to the debtor. After the disposition of the collateral, a secured party who does not collect all that is owed by the debtor can hold the debtor liable for any _____.

CREDITORS' RIGHTS AND REMEDIES

33

FACING A LEGAL PROBLEM

Ethan and Raney Sword own a summer cabin in the Poconos Mountains. The Swords contract with Adrian, a local painter, to paint the cabin before the summer season. They agree on a price of $5,000, including labor and materials. Adrian completes the job on time, but the Swords claim financial hardship and only pay him $2,000 of the charges.

 Q Can Adrian obtain the rest of what he is owed from the Swords?

LEARNING OUTCOMES

The five Learning Outcomes below are designed to help improve your understanding of the chapter. After reading this chapter, you should be able to:

❶ Distinguish different types of liens.

❷ Define garnishment and creditors' composition agreements.

❸ Define suretyship and guaranty contracts.

❹ State what a mortgage is and how to protect a creditor's interest in it.

❺ Identify state law exemptions from writs of attachment and execution.

Normally, creditors have no problem collecting the debts owed to them. When disputes arise over the amount owed, however, or when the debtor simply cannot or will not pay, what happens? What remedies are available to creditors when debtors default?

In this chapter, we focus on some basic laws that assist the debtor and creditor in resolving their dispute.

33–1 LAWS ASSISTING CREDITORS

The law creates many rights and remedies for creditors, including liens, garnishment, creditors' composition agreements, suretyship and guaranty, and mortgage agreements. We discuss these rights and remedies in this section.

33–1a Liens

A **lien** is an encumbrance on (claim against) property to satisfy a debt or protect a claim for the payment of a debt. Liens may arise in various ways. *Mechanic's liens* derive from statutory law, while *artisan's liens* were recognized at common law. *Judicial liens* result from legal actions of creditors against debtors.

Liens are a very important tool for creditors because they generally take priority over other claims against the same property. In fact, mechanic's liens and artisan's liens normally take priority even over perfected security interests in the property.

Mechanic's Lien When a person contracts for labor, services, or material to be furnished for the purpose of making improvements on real property but does not immediately pay for the improvements, a creditor can place a **mechanic's lien** on the property. This creates a special type of debtor-creditor relationship in which the real estate itself becomes security for the debt—that is, the property can be taken and held to guarantee payment of the debt, or it can be sold through foreclosure proceedings to effect actual payment. The lienholder, however, must give notice to the property owner before foreclosure and sale.

EXAMPLE 33.1 Kim owns the Lake Valley Ranch. To remove tree stumps on her lower ten acres, she hires Mountain View Excavation. When she refuses to pay for

lien
A claim against specific property to satisfy a debt or to protect a claim for debt payment.

LEARNING OUTCOME 1
Distinguish different types of liens.

mechanic's lien
A statutory lien on the real property of another created to ensure priority of payment for work performed.

the completed work, Mountain View places a mechanic's lien on the ranch. If Kim does not pay the lien, the property can be sold to satisfy the debt.◄

Artisan's Lien   An **artisan's lien** is a security device created at common law through which a creditor can recover payment from a debtor for labor and materials furnished in the repair of personal property. In contrast to a mechanic's lien, an artisan's lien is *possessory*. This means that the lienholder ordinarily must have retained possession of the property and have expressly or impliedly agreed to provide the services on a cash, not a credit, basis. The artisan's lien exists as long as the lienholder maintains possession. The lien ends when possession is voluntarily surrendered.

> **EXAMPLE 33.2** Selena leaves her diamond ring at the jeweler's to be repaired and to have her initials engraved on the band. In the absence of an agreement, the jeweler can keep the ring until Selena pays for the services. Should she fail to pay, the jeweler has a lien on Selena's ring for the amount of the bill and normally can sell the ring in satisfaction of the lien.◄

Modern statutes permit the holder of an artisan's lien to foreclose and sell the personal property subject to the lien to satisfy payment of the debt. As with the mechanic's lien, the lienholder is required to give notice to the owner of the property prior to foreclosure and selling. The sale proceeds are used to pay the debt and the costs of the legal proceedings. The surplus, if any, is paid to the former owner.

Judicial Liens   When a debt is past due, a creditor can bring a legal action against the debtor to collect the debt. If the creditor succeeds in the action, the court awards the creditor a judgment against the debtor. The amount of the judgment is usually the amount of the debt, plus interest and legal costs. Frequently, however, the creditor is unable to collect the awarded amount.

To ensure that a judgment in the creditor's favor will be collectible, the creditor can request that certain property of the debtor be seized to satisfy the debt. A court's order to seize the debtor's property is known as a *writ of attachment* if it is issued before a judgment. If it is issued after a judgment, it is referred to as a *writ of execution*. Note, however, that because of exemption laws (discussed later in this chapter) and bankruptcy laws, many judgments are uncollectible for all intents and purposes.

Writ of Attachment   **Attachment** is a court-ordered seizure of property before the securing of a judgment for a past-due debt. (Note that *attachment* has a different meaning in regard to secured transactions.) Normally a *prejudgment* remedy, attachment occurs either at the time of or immediately after the commencement of a lawsuit and before the entry of a final judgment.

To use attachment as a remedy, the creditor must have an enforceable right to payment of the debt under law and must follow certain procedures. The creditor must file an *affidavit* with the court. An **affidavit** states that the debtor is in default and the statutory grounds under which attachment is sought. The creditor must also post a bond to cover at least court costs, the value of the loss of use of the good suffered by the debtor, and the value of the property attached.

When the court is satisfied that all the requirements have been met, it issues a **writ of attachment,** which directs the sheriff or other officer to seize the debtor's property. If the creditor prevails at trial, the seized property can be sold to satisfy the judgment.

Writ of Execution   If the creditor wins at trial and the debtor will not or cannot pay the judgment, the creditor is entitled to go back to the court and obtain a **writ of execution.** This order, usually issued by the clerk of the court, directs the sheriff to seize and sell the debtor's property. The property must be located within the court's

---

artisan's lien
A possessory lien given to a person who has made improvements and added value to another person's personal property as security for payment for services performed.

attachment
The legal process of seizing another's property under a court order to secure satisfaction of a judgment yet to be rendered.

affidavit
A statement of facts confirmed by the oath or affirmation of the party making it and made before a person having the authority to administer the oath or affirmation.

writ of attachment
A writ used to enforce obedience to an order or judgment of the court.

writ of execution
A writ that puts in force a court's decree or judgment.

geographical jurisdiction (usually the county in which the courthouse is located). The proceeds of the sale are used to pay off the judgment and the costs of the sale. Any excess is paid to the debtor. The debtor can pay the judgment and redeem the property any time before the sale takes place.

33–1b Garnishment

Garnishment occurs when a creditor is permitted to collect a debt by seizing property of the debtor (such as wages or funds in a bank account) that is being held by a third party (such as an employer or a bank). As a result of a garnishment proceeding, the debtor's employer may be ordered by the court to turn over a portion of the debtor's wages to pay the debt.

Procedures Garnishment operates differently from state to state. According to the laws in some states, the judgment creditor (the creditor who obtains the garnishment order) needs to obtain only one order of garnishment. The order will then continuously apply to the weekly wages of the judgment debtor (the debtor whose wages will be garnished) until the entire debt is paid. In other states, the judgment creditor must go back to court for a separate order of garnishment for each pay period.

Limitations Both federal laws and state laws limit the amount that can be garnished from a debtor's weekly take-home pay. Federal law provides a minimal framework to protect debtors from losing all their income in order to pay judgment debts. State laws also provide dollar exemptions, and these amounts are often larger than those provided by federal law. State and federal statutes can be applied together. Under federal law, an employer cannot dismiss an employee because the employee's wages are being garnished.

> ### HIGHLIGHTING THE POINT
>
> Colleen is an independent contractor working for Dash Delivery Service as a driver. She receives medical treatment for a knee injury from Eastside Orthopedic Specialists. When she does not pay for the treatment, Eastside asks a court to issue a garnishment order to Dash Delivery to withhold an appropriate amount from Colleen's earnings until the debt is paid.
>
> **Can Colleen's earnings be garnished to pay this debt?** Yes. Colleen is working as an independent contractor for Dash Delivery, but its payments for her services fall within the definition of earnings. Dash Delivery can be ordered to turn over Colleen's earnings to pay her debt to Eastside, subject to the federal and state limits on the amount that can be garnished.

33–1c Creditors' Composition Agreements

Creditors may contract with a debtor to discharge the debtor's liquidated debts on payment of a sum less than that owed. (*Liquidated debts* are debts that are definite, or fixed, in amount.) These agreements are called **creditors' composition agreements** and are usually enforceable.

33–1d Suretyship and Guaranty

When a third person promises to pay a debt owed by another in the event the debtor does not pay, either a *suretyship* or a *guaranty* relationship is created. In a

garnishment
A legal process whereby a creditor appropriates a debtor's property or wages that are in the hands of a third party.

LEARNING OUTCOME 2
Define garnishment and creditors' composition agreements.

creditors' composition agreement
An agreement between a debtor and his or her creditors in which the creditors agree to accept a lesser sum than that owed by the debtor in full satisfaction of the debt.

Define suretyship and guaranty contracts.

suretyship

A contract in which a third party to a debtor-creditor relationship (the surety) promises to be primarily responsible for the debtor's obligation.

surety

A third party who agrees to be primarily responsible for the debt of another.

suretyship contract, creditors have the right to seek payment from the third party as soon as the debt is due. A guaranty provides creditors with the right to seek payment from the third party if the principal debtor defaults on her or his obligations. Exhibit 33.1 illustrates the relationship between a suretyship or guaranty party and the creditor.

Surety A contract of strict **suretyship** is a promise made by a third person to be responsible for a debtor's obligation. It is an express contract between the **surety** (a third party, other than the debtor, who agrees to assume the debt) and the creditor. The surety is *primarily* liable for the debt of the principal debtor—that is, the creditor can demand payment from the surety from the moment that the debt is due. The creditor need not exhaust all legal remedies against the principal debtor before holding the surety responsible for payment. Surety agreements are usually in writing, although not all states require a writing.

HIGHLIGHTING THE POINT

Robert Delmar wants to borrow funds from the bank to buy a used car. Because Robert is still in college, the bank will not lend him the funds unless his father, Joseph Delmar, who has dealt with the bank before, will cosign the note. By adding his signature to the note, Joseph becomes jointly liable for payment of the debt.

When Joseph cosigns the note, is he primarily liable to the bank?　Yes. Once he signs the note, Joseph is a surety. On the note's due date, the bank can seek payment from Robert, his father, or both jointly.

guarantor

A third party who agrees to satisfy the debt of another (the debtor) only if and when the debtor fails to pay the debt.

Guaranty With a suretyship arrangement, the surety is *primarily* liable for the debtor's obligations. With a guaranty arrangement, the **guarantor**—the third person making the guaranty—is *secondarily* liable. The guarantor can be required to pay the obligation *only after the debtor defaults*, and default usually takes place only after the creditor has made an attempt to collect from the debtor.

Real-World Case Example

To buy and develop a piece of property in Delaware, Brandywine Partners, LLC, borrowed $15.9 million from HSBC Realty Credit Corp. (USA). As part of the deal, Brian O'Neill, principal for Brandywine, signed a guaranty that designated him the "primary obligor" for $8.1 million of the loan. Brandywine defaulted, and HSBC filed a suit in a federal district court against O'Neill to recover on the guaranty. From a judgment in HSBC's favor, O'Neill appealed.

Is a guarantor bound to the clear, unambiguous terms of the guaranty?　Yes. In a 2014 case, *HSBC Realty Credit Corp. (USA) v. O'Neill*, the U.S. Court of Appeals for the First Circuit affirmed the lower court's judgment in favor of HSBC. O'Neill argued that HSBC induced him to sign the guaranty by misrepresenting the value of the property. But the guaranty expressly stated that O'Neill was familiar with the value, that he was not relying on the property as an inducement to sign the guaranty, and that HSBC made no representations to induce him to sign. The guaranty also provided that HSBC could enforce its rights against the primary obligor without trying to recover on the property first.

EXHIBIT 33.1 Suretyship and Guaranty Relationships

In a suretyship or guaranty arrangement, a third party promises to be responsible for a debtor's obligations. A third party who agrees to be responsible for the debt (even if the principal debtor does not default) is known as a surety. A third party who agrees to be *secondarily* responsible for the debt—that is, responsible only if the principal debtor defaults—is known as a guarantor.

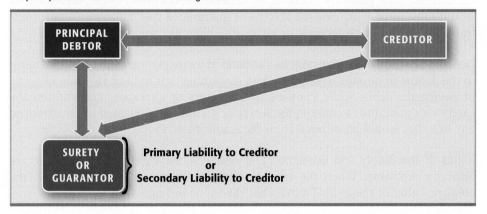

A guaranty contract between the guarantor and creditor must be in writing to be enforceable unless the *main purpose rule* applies. Briefly, this exception provides that if the main purpose of the guaranty agreement is to benefit the guarantor, then the contract need not be in writing to be enforceable.

Defenses of the Surety and Guarantor Generally, the surety or guarantor can assert any of the defenses available to a principal debtor to avoid liability on the obligation to the creditor. A few exceptions do exist, however. The surety or guarantor cannot assert the principal debtor's incapacity or bankruptcy as a defense, nor can the surety or guarantor assert the *statute of limitations* as a defense. The following discussion illustrates how the defenses of the surety and guarantor are basically the same.

Modification of the Contract between the Debtor and Creditor Any material change made in the terms of the original contract between the principal debtor and the creditor, including the awarding of a binding extension of time for making payment without first obtaining the consent of the surety or guarantor will discharge the surety or guarantor either completely or to the extent that the surety or guarantor suffers a loss.

EXAMPLE 33.3 Roxanne agrees to act without compensation as a surety for Stewart's loan from Scott Valley Bank. Later, without Roxanne's knowledge, Stewart and Scott Valley agree to postpone one year of payments and add their accrued interest to the balance due. This modification extends the time for payment of the loan and thereby discharges Roxanne's obligation as a surety completely. If she had accepted compensation to act as a surety, her obligation would have been discharged only to the extent that she suffered a loss under the contract as modified. ◄

Payment of the Obligation or Tender of Payment If the principal obligation is paid by the debtor or by another person on behalf of the debtor, the surety or guarantor is discharged from the obligation. Similarly, if valid tender of payment is made, and the creditor for some reason rejects it with knowledge of the surety's or guarantor's existence, then the surety or guarantor is released from any obligation on the debt.

Principal Debtor's Defenses Generally, any defenses available to a principal debtor can be used by the surety or guarantor to avoid liability on the obligation to the creditor. The ability of the surety or guarantor to assert any defenses the debtor may have against the creditor is the most important concept in suretyship because most of the defenses available to the surety or guarantor are also those of the debtor.

Surety's Own Defenses A surety or guarantor may have his or her own defenses. If the creditor fraudulently induced the surety or guarantor to guarantee the debt of the debtor, the surety or guarantor can assert fraud as a defense. In most states, the creditor has a legal duty to inform the surety or guarantor, before the formation of the suretyship or guaranty contract, of material facts known by the creditor that would substantially increase the surety's or guarantor's risk. Failure to so inform is fraud and makes the suretyship or guaranty obligation voidable.

Creditor's Surrender or Impairment of the Collateral If a creditor surrenders the collateral to the debtor or impairs it—that is, does something that reduces its value in terms of paying the debt—while knowing of the surety or guarantor and without the surety's or guarantor's consent, the surety or guarantor is released to the extent of any loss that would be suffered from the creditor's actions.

Rights of the Surety and Guarantor The rights of the surety and guarantor are basically the same. When the surety or guarantor pays the debt owed to the creditor, either of these third parties has the following rights.

right of subrogation
The right of a person to stand in the place of (be substituted for) another, giving the substituted party the same legal rights that the original party had.

The Right of Subrogation The surety or guarantor has the legal **right of subrogation.** Simply stated, this means that any right the creditor had against the debtor becomes the right of the surety or guarantor. Included are creditor rights in bankruptcy, rights to collateral possessed by the creditor, and rights to judgments secured by the creditor. In short, the surety or guarantor stands in the shoes of the creditor and may pursue any remedies that were available to the creditor against the debtor.

right of reimbursement
The legal right of a person to be restored, repaid, or indemnified for costs, expenses, or losses incurred or expended on behalf of another.

The Right of Reimbursement The surety or guarantor has a **right of reimbursement** from the debtor. Basically, the surety or guarantor is entitled to receive from the debtor all outlays made on behalf of the suretyship or guaranty arrangement. Such outlays can include expenses incurred as well as the actual amount of the debt paid to the creditor.

co-surety
One who assumes liability jointly with another surety for the payment of an obligation.

right of contribution
The right of a co-surety who pays more than his or her proportionate share on a debtor's default to recover the excess paid from other co-sureties.

The Right of Contribution Two or more sureties on the same obligation are called **co-sureties.** When one co-surety pays more than his or her proportionate share on a debtor's default, she or he is entitled to recover from the other co-sureties the excess amount paid. This is the **right of contribution.** Generally, a co-surety's liability either is determined by agreement or, in the absence of agreement, is set at the maximum liability under the suretyship contract. A co-guarantor has the same right.

HIGHLIGHTING THE POINT

Two co-sureties—Jeremiah and Veda—are obligated under a suretyship contract to guarantee the debt of Jules. Veda's maximum liability is $15,000, and Jeremiah's is $10,000. Jules owes $10,000 and is in default. Veda pays the creditor the entire $10,000.

Can Veda recover anything from Jeremiah? Yes. **How much?** In the absence of an agreement to the contrary, Veda can recover $4,000 from Jeremiah. The amount of the debt that Jeremiah agreed to cover is divided by the total amount that Veda and Jeremiah together agreed to cover. The result is multiplied by the amount of the default, yielding the amount that Jeremiah owes—($10,000 ÷ $25,000) × $10,000 = $4,000.

mortgage
A written document that gives the creditor (the mortgagee) an interest in, or lien on, the debtor's (mortgagor's) real property as security for a debt.

33–1e Mortgages

When individuals purchase real property, they typically borrow from a financial institution most of the funds needed to pay the purchase price. A **mortgage** is a written instrument that gives the creditor an interest in, or lien on, the debtor's real property as security for payment of a debt. The creditor is the *mortgagee*, and the debtor is the *mortgagor*.

Types of Mortgages Among the many different types of mortgages, a basic distinction is whether the interest rate is fixed or variable. A *fixed-rate mortgage* has a fixed, or unchanging, rate of interest. This means the debtor's monthly payment remains the same for the duration of the loan. With an *adjustable-rate mortgage (ARM)*, however, the rate of interest paid by the borrower changes periodically. Typically, the initial interest rate for an ARM is a low fixed rate for a specified period, but later, the rate is usually adjusted annually or by some other time period.

LEARNING OUTCOME 4

State what a mortgage is and how to protect a creditor's interest in it.

EXAMPLE 33.4 Bryan borrows $250,000 from Community Credit Bank to finance the purchase of a house. The loan is an ARM. According to its terms, the initial interest rate is 3.75 percent for the first three years. Beginning in the fourth year, the amount of the monthly payments is to be adjusted annually by adding up to three percentage points to the appropriate economy-wide index rate. ◄

Creditor Protections When creditors extend mortgages, they are advancing a significant amount of funds for a number of years. Consequently, creditors take a number of steps to protect their interest.

Mortgage Insurance One precaution is to require debtors to obtain private mortgage insurance if they do not make a down payment—the part of the purchase price that is paid up front in cash—of at least 20 percent of the purchase price. With private mortgage insurance, the debtor (borrower) pays the premiums, but the creditor (lender) is the beneficiary. **EXAMPLE 33.5** After providing a $10,000 down payment, Marina borrows $190,000 from Northwest Timber Credit Union to buy a house for $200,000. Because Marina's down payment is only 5 percent of the purchase price, Northwest makes her obtain private mortgage insurance. Then, if Marina later defaults on the mortgage loan the insurance company ensures that Northwest is paid in full. ◄

Recording the Mortgage Another precaution is for the creditor to record the mortgage with the appropriate office in the county where the property is located. Recording the mortgage ensures that the creditor is officially on record as holding an interest in the property.

Contract Provisions In addition, creditors can also include provisions in the mortgage contract that are aimed at protecting their investment.

HIGHLIGHTING THE POINT

Aaron borrows $300,000 from Bank of the Hudson Valley to finance the purchase of a house. In the mortgage contract, the bank includes a *prepayment penalty clause*, which requires Aaron to pay a penalty if he pays off the mortgage in full within a certain period. In the contract, the bank also requires Aaron to maintain homeowner's insurance on the mortgaged property.

Do these provisions protect the bank's investment in Aaron's property? Yes. A prepayment penalty helps to protect the lender should the borrower refinance within a short time after obtaining a mortgage. Homeowner's insurance on mortgaged property promises to reimburse the lender for its investment if the property is damaged or destroyed.

foreclosure
A legal proceeding in which a mortgagee takes title to or forces the sale of the mortgagor's property to satisfy a debt.

Mortgage Foreclosure Another important creditor protection is foreclosure. **Foreclosure** is the legal process by which the lender repossesses and auctions off the property that has secured the loan. If the homeowner defaults, or fails to make the mortgage payments, the lender has the right to foreclose on the mortgaged property. If the sale proceeds from the property are not enough to pay the mortgage loan, in most states, the lender can ask a court for a deficiency judgment, which is a court order against the borrower to cover the rest of the debt.

33–2 LAWS ASSISTING DEBTORS

homestead exemption
A law allowing an owner to designate his or her house and adjoining land as a homestead and thus exempt it from liability for his or her general debt.

The law protects debtors as well as creditors. Certain property of the debtor, for example, is exempt from creditors' actions. Consumer protection statutes also protect debtors' rights. Of course, bankruptcy laws are designed specifically to assist debtors in need of help.

In most states, certain types of property are exempt from writs of attachment and execution. Probably the most familiar of these exemptions is the **homestead exemption.** Each state permits the debtor to retain the family home, either in its entirety or up to a specified dollar amount, free from the claims of unsecured creditors or trustees in bankruptcy.

HIGHLIGHTING THE POINT

Van Cleave owes Acosta $40,000. The debt is the subject of a lawsuit, and the court awards Acosta a judgment of $40,000 against Van Cleave. Van Cleave's homestead is valued at around $50,000. There are no outstanding mortgages or other liens. To satisfy the judgment debt, Van Cleave's family home is sold at public auction for $45,000. Assume that the homestead exemption is $25,000.

How are the proceeds of the sale distributed? First, Van Cleave is given $25,000 as his homestead exemption. Second, Acosta is paid $20,000 toward the judgment debt, leaving a $20,000 deficiency that can be paid from any other nonexempt property that Van Cleave has, if permitted by state law.

Various types of personal property may also be exempt from satisfaction of judgment debts. Personal property that is most often exempt under state law includes the following:

1. Household furniture up to a specified dollar amount.
2. Clothing and certain personal possessions, such as family pictures or religious items.
3. A vehicle (or vehicles) for transportation (at least up to a specified dollar amount).
4. Certain classified animals, usually livestock and pets.
5. Equipment that the debtor uses in a business or trade, such as tools or professional instruments, up to a specified dollar amount.

ANSWERING THE LEGAL PROBLEM

In the legal problem set out at the beginning of this chapter, Adrian agreed to paint Ethan and Raney Sword's summer cabin for $5,000 to cover labor and materials. The Swords could only pay $2,000 of the charges.

(A) **Can Adrian get the rest of what he is owed from the Swords?** Yes. A mechanic's lien against the property could be created. Adrian would be the lienholder. The property would be subject to the mechanic's lien for the amount owed ($3,000). If the Swords did not pay the lien, their cabin could be sold to satisfy the debt.

TERMS AND CONCEPTS FOR REVIEW

affidavit 454

artisan's lien 454

attachment 454

co-surety 458

creditors' composition
 agreement 455

foreclosure 460

garnishment 455

guarantor 456

homestead exemption 460

lien 453

mechanic's lien 453

mortgage 458

right of contribution 458

right of reimbursement 458

right of subrogation 458

surety 456

suretyship 456

writ of attachment 454

writ of execution 454

CHAPTER SUMMARY—CREDITORS' RIGHTS AND REMEDIES

LEARNING OUTCOME	
1	**Distinguish different types of liens.** A *mechanic's lien* is a lien on real estate for labor, services, or materials furnished to make improvements on the property. An *artisan's lien* is a possessory lien on personal property for labor performed or value added. *Judicial liens* include (1) *attachment*, which is a court-ordered seizure of property before a court's final determination of the creditor's rights to the property, and (2) *writ of execution*, which is a court order directing the sheriff to seize and sell a debtor's nonexempt real or personal property to satisfy a court's judgment in the creditor's favor.
2	**Define garnishment and creditors' composition agreements.** *Garnishment* is a collection remedy that allows a creditor to attach a debtor's property (such as wages owed or bank accounts) that is held by a third person. A *creditors' composition agreement* is a contract between a debtor and his or her creditors discharging the debtor's debts on payment of a sum less than the amount actually owed.
3	**Define suretyship and guaranty contracts.** Under a suretyship or guaranty contract, a third person agrees to be primarily or secondarily liable for the debt owed by the principal debtor. A creditor can turn to this third person for satisfaction of the debt.
4	**State what a mortgage is and how to protect a creditor's interest in it.** A mortgage is a written document that gives a creditor (the mortgagee) an interest in, or lien on, a debtor's (mortgagor's) real property as security for a debt. Steps that a creditor can take to protect his or her interest in the mortgage include requiring debtors to obtain private mortgage insurance, recording a mortgage with the appropriate county office, and inserting certain protective provisions in the mortgage contract. If a debtor defaults, a creditor can also foreclose on the property—repossess and sell it—and obtain a judgment against the debtor for any deficiency.
5	**Identify state law exemptions from writs of attachment and execution.** Certain property of a debtor is exempt from creditors' actions under state laws. Each state permits a debtor to retain the family home, either in its entirety or up to a specified dollar amount, free from the claims of unsecured creditors or trustees in bankruptcy (homestead exemption). The personal property that is most often exempt, up to a specified amount, from satisfaction of judgment debts includes household furniture, clothing, personal possessions, vehicles, certain animals, and equipment that a debtor uses in a business or trade.

462 UNIT 7 *Credit and Risk*

ISSUE SPOTTERS

Check your answers to the *Issue Spotters* against the answers provided in Appendix C at the end of this text.

1. Joe contracts with Larry of Midwest Roofing to fix Joe's roof. Joe pays half of the contract price in advance. Larry and Midwest complete the job, but Joe refuses to pay the rest of the price. What can Larry and Midwest do to get the remainder of what Joe owes? (See *Laws Assisting Creditors.*)

2. Al owes Don $5,000 and refuses to pay. Don obtains a garnishment order and serves it on Al's employer. If the employer complies with the order and Al stays on the job, is one order enough to garnish all of Al's wages for each pay period until the debt is paid? Why or why not? (See *Laws Assisting Creditors.*)

USING BUSINESS LAW

33–1. Creditors' Remedies. In what circumstances would a creditor resort to each of the following remedies when trying to collect on a debt? (See *Laws Assisting Creditors.*)

   1. Mechanic's lien.   **4.** Writ of execution.

   2. Artisan's lien.   **5.** Garnishment.

   3. Writ of attachment.

33–2. Creditors' Remedies. Kanahara is employed by Cross-Bar Packing Corp. and earns take-home pay of $400 per week. He is $2,000 in debt to Holiday Department Store for goods purchased on credit over the past eight months. Most of this property is nonexempt and is located in Kanahara's apartment. Kanahara is in default on his payments to Holiday. Holiday learns that Kanahara has a girlfriend in another state and that he plans on giving her most of this property for Christmas. Discuss what actions should be taken by Holiday to collect the debt owed by Kanahara. (See *Laws Assisting Creditors.*)

REAL-WORLD CASE PROBLEMS

33–3. Guaranty. Timothy Martinez, owner of Koenig & Vits, Inc. (K&V), guaranteed K&V's debt to Community Bank & Trust. The guaranty stated that the bank was not required to seek payment of the debt from any other source before enforcing the guaranty. K&V defaulted. The bank sought payment of $536,739.40 from Martinez. Martinez argued that the bank could not enforce his guaranty while other funds were available to satisfy K&V's debt—for example, the debt might be paid out of the proceeds of a sale of corporate assets. Is this an effective defense to a guaranty? Why or why not? [*Community Bank & Trust v. Koenig & Vits, Inc.,* 346 Wis.2d 279, 827 N.W.2d 928 (Wis.App. 2013)] (See *Laws Assisting Creditors.*)

33–4. Homestead Exemption. Bill and Betty Ma owned half of a two-unit residential building. Betty lived in the unit, but Bill did not. To collect a judgment against the Mas, Mei-Fang Zhang obtained a writ of execution directing the sheriff to seize and sell the building. State law allowed a $100,000 homestead exemption if the debtor lived in the home and $175,000 if the debtor was also disabled and "unable to engage in gainful employment." Bill argued that he could not work because of physical ailments. How much of an exemption were the Mas entitled to? Why? [*Zhang v. Tse,* __ F.Supp.2d __ (N.D.Cal. 2011)] (See *Laws Assisting Debtors.*)

ETHICAL QUESTIONS

33–5. Guaranty. Should a promise of collateral signed by a corporate officer to secure a corporate debt always create personal liability? Explain your answer. (See *Laws Assisting Creditors.*)

33–6. Guaranty. 73-75 Main Avenue, LLC, agreed to lease commercial property to PP Door Enterprise, Inc., which was owned by Ping Ying Li. A signed lease and guaranty agreement were faxed to 73-75. When the monthly rental payments ceased after five months, 73-75 sought to recover from Li. Li claimed to have no knowledge of the lease and denied signing it. Was the guaranty enforceable against Li? Should she be held liable even if the guaranty is not enforceable against her? Discuss. [*73-75 Main Avenue, LLC v. PP Door Enterprise Inc.,* 120 Conn.App. 150, 991 A.2d 650 (2010)] (See *Laws Assisting Creditors.*)

Chapter 33—Work Set

TRUE-FALSE QUESTIONS

_____ 1. A mechanic's lien always involves real property, and an artisan's lien always involves personal property.

_____ 2. Federal and state laws limit the amount that can be garnished from wages, but they cannot be applied together to determine how much is exempt.

_____ 3. Generally, to avoid liability, a surety or a guarantor cannot use any defenses available to the principal debtor.

_____ 4. Foreclosure allows a lender to legally repossess and auction off the property securing a loan.

_____ 5. A surety or guarantor is discharged from his or her obligation when the principal debtor pays the debt.

_____ 6. A writ of execution is issued before the entry of a final judgment.

_____ 7. An employer can dismiss an employee due to garnishment.

MULTIPLE-CHOICE QUESTIONS

_____ 1. Jan leaves her necklace with Gold Jewelers to be repaired. When Jan returns to pick up the necklace, she says, "I don't have the money now, but I'll pay you for the repairs later." Gold

   a. can keep the necklace until Jan pays for the repairs.
   b. can keep the necklace for a reasonable time but must then return it to Jan even if she does not pay for the repairs.
   c. cannot keep the necklace.
   d. cannot keep the necklace or do a or b.

_____ 2. Don owes Barb $500 but refuses to pay. To collect, Barb files a suit against Don and wins. Don still refuses to pay. To collect the amount of the judgment, Barb can use

   a. an artisan's lien.
   b. a creditor's composition agreement.
   c. a foreclosure.
   d. a writ of execution.

_____ 3. John is a cabinet maker. Tammy contracts with John to make and install a custom bookcase in Tammy's house for $4,000. John completes the bookcase, but Tammy does not pay. To obtain the amount that is owed, John can use

   a. an artisan's lien.
   b. a creditor's composition agreement.
   c. a mechanic's lien.
   d. a writ of execution.

_____ 4. Dian's $6,000 debt to Ace Credit Company is past due, and Ace files suit. Before the judge hears the case, Ace learns that Dian has hidden some of her property from Ace. Ace believes that Dian is about to hide the rest of her property. To ensure there will be some assets to satisfy the debt if Ace wins the suit, Ace can use

   a. garnishment.
   b. a mechanic's lien.
   c. an artisan's lien.
   d. attachment.

_____ 5. Ed's $2,500 debt to Owen is past due. Ed does not own a house and has very little personal property, but he has a checking account, a savings account, and a job. To reach these assets to satisfy the debt, Owen can use

   a. garnishment.
   b. a mechanic's lien.
   c. an artisan's lien.
   d. attachment.

_____ 6. Bob obtains a judgment for $30,000 and a writ of execution against Mary. To enforce the writ, Mary's home is sold for $60,000. The homestead exemption is $35,000. All of Mary's personal property is exempt except two motorcycles, which are sold for $5,000. After applying the appropriate amounts to payment of the debt, how much of the debt will be unpaid?

    a. $25,000.

    b. $10,000.

    c. $5,000.

    d. $0.

_____ 7. L&R Computers, Inc., wants to obtain a loan from First National Bank. The bank refuses to lend L&R the funds unless Lee, L&R's sole stockholder, agrees to assume liability if L&R does not pay off the loan. Lee agrees. When the first payment is due, the bank can seek payment from L&R

    a. but not Lee, because Lee is a guarantor.

    b. but not Lee, because Lee is a surety.

    c. or Lee, because Lee is a surety.

    d. or Lee, because Lee is a guarantor.

_____ 8. Giordana borrows $225,000 from Hearthstone Credit Union to buy a home, which secures the loan. Five years into the term, Giordana stops making payments. Hearthstone repossesses and sells the property, but the proceeds are not enough to cover the unpaid amount of the loan. In most states, the lender could now obtain

    a. a deficiency judgment.

    b. a redemption.

    c. a short sale.

    d. nothing more.

ANSWERING MORE LEGAL PROBLEMS

1. Nguyen applied to Venture Source, LLC, a business lender, for a loan to finance the development of an innovative series of apps for mobile devices, such as cell phones, tablets, and handheld game players. Nguyen had a good employment record with a major game arts marketer and a solid business plan for his own newly formed company, APPlications, Inc.

What steps should Venture Source take to guarantee payment of the loan? Venture Source should have _____ sign the loan documents on behalf of APPlications, Inc., and also sign a personal _____. Signing the loan documents for the company is, of course, a requirement for the _____ of their terms if the firm defaults on the loan. Default usually occurs only after the creditor, Venture Source, attempts to collect from the debtor unsuccessfully. With the personal _____, the guarantor, _____, is secondarily liable. He can be required to pay the obligation if the principal debtor, APPlications, Inc., defaults.

2. Dulcy graduated from AgriState University in May, obtained employment with Bountiful Fields Food Corp.

in June, and was issued a credit card by Union Co-op Bank in July. Over the next year, Dulcy saved a small percentage of each paycheck in a bank account and used her credit card to buy clothing, electronics, and vacations. The card soon reached its limit. After a time, Dulcy stopped making the minimum payment on the monthly credit-card bill.

Which remedies could Union Co-op pursue to recover the amount that Dulcy owes on her card? The credit-card issuer could avail itself of _____, _____, or _____. When a debt is past due, a creditor can begin legal action against a debtor. Once a legal action is brought, the debtor's property can be seized to satisfy the debt. If the property is seized before a trial, the seizure is an _____. If the seizure occurs after a court judgment in the creditor's favor, the court's order to seize the property is a writ of _____. _____ occurs when a creditor collects a debt by seizing the property of a debtor, such as wages or funds in a bank account, that is held by a third party, such as an employer or a bank.

BANKRUPTCY

FACING A LEGAL PROBLEM

G&M Trucking borrows funds from Middleton Bank to buy two trucks, giving the bank a security interest in the trucks. G&M fails to make its monthly payments for two months and files a petition in bankruptcy. Under bankruptcy law, the bank is prevented from repossessing the trucks. The trucks are rapidly falling in resale value, however, and will soon be worth much less than the balance due on the loan.

 Is there anything that the bank can do to protect itself?

LEARNING OUTCOMES

The four Learning Outcomes below are designed to help improve your understanding of the chapter. After reading this chapter, you should be able to:

❶ Identify the debtor, procedures, and advantages in a Chapter 7 liquidation.

❷ List the duties and powers of a bankruptcy trustee.

❸ Identify the debtor and procedures in a Chapter 11 reorganization.

❹ Identify the debtor, procedures, and advantages in a Chapter 13 adjustment.

Historically, debtors had few rights. Today, in contrast, debtors have many rights. In this chapter, we look at another significant right of debtors: the right to petition for bankruptcy relief under federal law. You will read about the different types of relief offered under federal bankruptcy law and about the basic bankruptcy procedures required for specific types of relief.

34–1 THE BANKRUPTCY CODE

The U.S. Constitution gave Congress the power to establish uniform laws on bankruptcy. Bankruptcy law in the United States has two goals:

1. To protect a debtor by giving him or her a fresh start from creditors' claims.

2. To ensure equitable treatment of creditors who are competing for a debtor's assets.

The federal bankruptcy law is known as the Bankruptcy Code (the Code). Although bankruptcy law is federal, state laws on secured transactions, liens, judgments, and exemptions also play a role in federal bankruptcy proceedings. Bankruptcy proceedings are held in federal **bankruptcy courts,** which are under the authority of U.S. district courts. Rulings from bankruptcy courts can be appealed to the district courts.

When the debtor is a *consumer-debtor*—one whose debts result primarily from the purchase of goods for personal, family, or household use—the clerk of the court must offer information about the purposes, benefits, and costs of the various types of bankruptcy before the start of the bankruptcy proceeding. The clerk must also provide information on the services of credit counseling agencies.

The most frequently used bankruptcy plans are contained in specific chapters of the Code: Chapter 7, liquidations; Chapter 11, reorganizations; and Chapter 13, adjustments of debt. See Exhibit 34.1 for a visual comparison of these three types of bankruptcies.

bankruptcy court
A federal court of limited jurisdiction that handles only bankruptcy proceedings.

EXHIBIT 34.1 Bankruptcy—A Comparison of Chapters 7, 11, and 13

Issue	Chapter 7	Chapter 11	Chapter 13
Who Can Petition	Debtor (voluntary) or creditors (involuntary).	Debtor (voluntary) or creditors (involuntary).	Debtor (voluntary) only.
Who Can Be a Debtor	Any "person" (including partnerships and corporations) except railroads, insurance companies, banks, savings and loan institutions, investment companies licensed by the U.S. Small Business Administration, and credit unions. Farmers and charitable institutions cannot be involuntarily petitioned.	Any debtor eligible for Chapter 7 relief; railroads are also eligible.	Any individual (not partnerships or corporations) with regular income who owes fixed (liquidated) unsecured debts of less than $383,175 or fixed secured debts of less than $1,149,525.
Procedure Leading to Discharge	The voluntary or involuntary filing of a petition in bankruptcy court. Nonexempt property is sold with proceeds to be distributed to priority groups. Dischargeable debts are terminated.	Reorganization plan is submitted. If it is approved and followed, debts are discharged.	Repayment plan is submitted and must be approved if the value of the property to be distributed equals the amount of the claims or if the debtor turns over disposable income for a three- or five-year period. If the plan is followed, debts are discharged.

34–2 CHAPTER 7—LIQUIDATION

liquidation
The sale of the assets of a business or an individual for cash and the distribution of the cash received to creditors, with the balance going to the owner(s).

discharge
The termination of a debtor's obligation.

LEARNING OUTCOME 1

Identify the debtor, procedures, and advantages in a Chapter 7 liquidation.

insolvent
A condition in which a person cannot pay his or her debts as they become due or ceases to pay debts in the ordinary course of business.

Liquidation under Chapter 7 is the most familiar type of bankruptcy proceeding and is often referred to as an *ordinary,* or *straight, bankruptcy.* Put simply, debtors in straight bankruptcies state their debts and turn their assets over to a bankruptcy trustee, who sells the assets and distributes the proceeds to creditors. With certain exceptions, the remaining debts are then **discharged,** and the debtor is relieved of his or her obligation to pay the debts. This gives the debtor an opportunity for a fresh start.

Any *person*—defined as including individuals, partnerships, and corporations—may be a debtor under Chapter 7. Railroads, insurance companies, banks, savings and loan associations, credit unions, and investment companies licensed by the U.S. Small Business Administration *cannot* be Chapter 7 debtors. Other chapters of the Bankruptcy Code or other federal or state statutes apply to them.

A straight bankruptcy may be commenced by the filing of either a voluntary or an involuntary petition.

34–2a Voluntary Bankruptcy

A voluntary petition is brought by the debtor, who files official forms designated for that purpose in the bankruptcy court. A debtor does not have to be **insolvent** to file a petition. In addition, a husband and wife can file jointly for bankruptcy under a single petition.

Chapter 7 Schedules The voluntary petition must include a list of the debtor's **secured creditors** and **unsecured creditors,** their addresses, and the amount of debt owed to each. It must also include a list of all of the debtor's property, income, and expenses, as well as other information. The official forms must be completed accurately, sworn to under oath, and signed by the debtor. To conceal assets or knowingly supply false information is a crime.

With the petition, a consumer-debtor must include a certificate proving that he or she has received credit counseling from an approved agency within the last six months. The debtor must also state, at the time of filing, that he or she understands the relief available under other chapters of the Code and has chosen to proceed under Chapter 7.

secured creditor
A lender or seller who has a security interest in collateral that secures a debt.

unsecured creditor
A creditor whose debt is not backed by any collateral.

Means Test A debtor filing for bankruptcy must complete a *means test* to determine whether he or she qualifies for Chapter 7. If the debtor's average monthly income is below the median income in the geographic area in which the person lives, the debtor's petition for a Chapter 7 bankruptcy will most likely be allowed.

If the debtor's average monthly income is above the median, his or her disposable income is calculated by subtracting living expenses and secured debt payments from monthly income. The purpose is to determine whether the debtor can repay some of his or her unsecured debts.

HIGHLIGHTING THE POINT

Sylvie, who is twenty-eight years old, owns a home and a car and is currently employed earning $50,000 per year. She also has $12,000 in credit-card debt. Sylvie files a Chapter 7 bankruptcy petition that lists monthly net income of $2,900 and expenditures of $3,000, for a deficit of $100. In making this calculation, she excluded a $300 monthly contribution to a retirement plan.

Is Sylvie's petition likely to be dismissed? Yes. The bankruptcy court is likely to disallow the retirement contribution and dismiss Sylvie's petition. Her retirement contribution is not reasonably necessary based on her age and financial circumstances. With this amount included in the calculation of her disposable income, it is clear that she can afford to pay at least some of her unsecured debt.

Other Grounds for Dismissal A court can dismiss a debtor's voluntary petition for Chapter 7 relief for failing to provide the necessary documents. A court might also dismiss a Chapter 7 petition if the debtor has been convicted of a violent crime or a drug-trafficking offense, or if the debtor has not paid a domestic-support obligation, such as child and spousal support.

Order for Relief If the petition for bankruptcy is found to be proper, the filing of the petition will itself constitute an **order for relief.** This order relieves the debtor of having to pay the debts listed in the petition.

order for relief
A court's grant of assistance to a complainant.

34–2b Involuntary Bankruptcy

An involuntary bankruptcy occurs when the debtor's creditors force the debtor into bankruptcy proceedings. Such a case cannot be commenced against a farmer or a charitable institution. Nor can it be filed unless one of the following two requirements is met:

1. If the debtor has twelve or more creditors, three or more of those having unsecured claims adding up to at least $14,425 must join in the petition.

2. If the debtor has fewer than twelve creditors, one or more creditors having an unsecured claim of $14,425 may file.

Sometimes, a debtor challenges the involuntary petition. The court will listen to the debtor's arguments, but it will go ahead with the bankruptcy proceeding if it finds either of the following:

1. That the debtor is generally not paying debts as they become due.

2. That a custodian took possession of, or was appointed to take charge of, substantially all of the debtor's property within 120 days before the filing of the petition.

34–2c Automatic Stay

automatic stay
A suspension of all judicial proceedings on the occurrence of an independent event.

The filing of a petition, either voluntary or involuntary, operates as an **automatic stay** on (suspension of) almost all litigation and other action by creditors against the debtor or the debtor's property. Once a petition is filed, creditors cannot commence or continue most legal actions against the debtor to recover claims. Nor can they take any action to repossess property in the hands of the debtor.

HIGHLIGHTING THE POINT

Soon after graduating from Applied Science University (ASU), Britta files a Chapter 7 bankruptcy petition. Before the court finds that Brett's petition is proper and enters an order for relief, she requests a transcript from the university. ASU refuses her request, claiming that she owes more than $6,000 in unpaid tuition.

Can Britta obtain her transcript despite the unpaid ASU tuition? Yes. ASU is violating the automatic stay when it refuses to provide the transcript, because the school is attempting to collect an unpaid tuition debt. An automatic stay prohibits a creditor from taking any action to collect, assess, or recover a claim against the debtor that arose before the filing of his or her bankruptcy petition.

There are some exceptions, however. A secured creditor can petition the bankruptcy court for relief from the automatic stay in certain circumstances. Also, the automatic stay does not apply to paternity, alimony, spousal maintenance, or child-support debts or to related proceedings.

34–2d Creditors' Meeting

Within a reasonable time after the order for relief is granted (not less than twenty days or more than forty days), the court must call a meeting of creditors. At this meeting, a trustee is elected to take over the assets of the debtor.

The debtor must attend the creditors' meeting (unless excused by the court) and must submit to an examination under oath by the creditors and the trustee. A debtor who fails to appear when required or who makes false statements under oath may be denied a discharge of his or her debts in the bankruptcy proceeding.

At the meeting, the trustee ensures that the debtor is aware of the potential consequences of bankruptcy and of his or her ability to file for bankruptcy under a different chapter. Proof of claims by creditors must normally be filed within ninety days of this meeting.

34–2e Estate in Property

On the commencement of a Chapter 7 proceeding, an **estate in property** is created. The estate consists of all the debtor's property, together with certain jointly owned property, property transferred in a transaction voidable by the trustee, and proceeds and profits from the property. Interests in certain property—such as gifts, inheritances, property settlements (divorce), or life insurance death proceeds—to which the debtor becomes entitled *within 180 days after filing* may also become part of the estate.

estate in property
All of the property owned by a person, including real estate and personal property.

34–2f The Bankruptcy Trustee

Promptly after the order for relief has been entered, a bankruptcy trustee is appointed. The **bankruptcy trustee** sells the debtor's assets and distributes the proceeds to creditors.

Trustee Duties The basic duty of the trustee is to collect the debtor's property and reduce it to money for distribution, preserving the interests of both the debtor and the unsecured creditors. In other words, the trustee is accountable for administering the debtor's estate.

Initially, the trustee determines whether the debtor's financial situation warrants relief based on a comparison of the debtor's income with the income of other families in the same state. The trustee must notify the creditors of this determination. The trustee must then either (1) file a motion to dismiss the petition or convert it to a Chapter 13 bankruptcy proceeding or (2) explain to the court why such a motion would not be appropriate.

bankruptcy trustee
A person appointed by the bankruptcy court to sell the assets of a debtor and distribute the proceeds to creditors.

Trustee Powers To enable a trustee to accomplish his or her duties, the Code provides certain powers. These powers enable the trustee to exercise, in some situations, the same rights as creditors. A trustee can ask the court for a *writ of execution*. This is an order directing the sheriff to seize and sell the debtor's property. Proceeds of the sale are used to pay off creditors. This power gives a trustee priority over an unsecured creditor.

LEARNING OUTCOME 2

List the duties and powers of a bankruptcy trustee.

Fraudulent Transfers A trustee also has the power to avoid (cancel) certain types of transactions or obligations. For instance, a trustee can cancel fraudulent transfers that were made by the debtor within two years of the filing of the petition with the intent to hinder, delay, or defraud a creditor.

In addition, transfers made for less than reasonably equivalent consideration are also recoverable. **EXAMPLE 34.1** Marilyn is planning to petition for bankruptcy, so she sells her gold jewelry, worth $10,000, to her friend Diana for $500. Diana agrees that in the future, she will "sell" the jewelry back to Marilyn for the same amount. The trustee can undo this fraudulent transaction.◄

Lastly, a trustee can also cancel transactions that the debtor could rightfully cancel, such as those involving fraud on the part of someone other than the debtor, and obtain the return of the debtor's property.

HIGHLIGHTING THE POINT

Rob sells his boat to Inga. Inga gives Rob a check, knowing that her bank account does not contain enough funds to cover the check. Inga has committed fraud. Within a month, Rob files a bankruptcy petition.

Can Rob cancel the transfer of the boat to Inga? Yes. Rob has the right to avoid that transfer and recover the boat from Inga, because she committed fraud. **Could the trustee of Rob's estate cancel the transfer of the boat?** Yes. Once an order for relief has been entered for Rob, the trustee can exercise Rob's right to recover the boat from Inga.

preference
In bankruptcy proceedings, the debtor's favoring of one creditor over others by making payments or transferring property to that creditor at the expense of the rights of other creditors.

Preferences Another power that the trustee has is to avoid **preferences**. A preference occurs when a debtor transfers property or money—generally within ninety days of filing the petition in bankruptcy—favoring one creditor over others. The trustee is allowed to recover payments made both voluntarily and involuntarily to one creditor in preference over another.

34–2g Exemptions under Chapter 7

The trustee takes control over the debtor's property, but an individual debtor is entitled to exempt certain property from the bankruptcy. The Code allows the exemption of the following properties:

1. Up to $22,975 in equity in the debtor's residence and burial plot (the homestead exemption).
2. Interest in a motor vehicle, up to $3,675.
3. Interest in household goods and furnishings, wearing apparel, appliances, books, animals, crops, or musical instruments. The amount of this exemption is limited to $550 for any particular item or $12,250 for all items together.
4. Interest in any tools of the debtor's trade, up to $2,300.
5. The right to receive Social Security and certain welfare benefits, alimony and support payments, certain retirement funds and pensions, and certain education savings accounts.

State versus Federal Exemptions The states can pass legislation to prevent debtors in their states from using the federal exemptions. A majority of the states have done this. In those states, debtors must use the state exemptions. In the rest of the states, a debtor can choose between the exemptions provided under the applicable state law and the federal exemptions.

Federal Limits on State Homestead Exemption The federal Code does set limits on a debtor's use of a state's homestead exemption, however. If a home was acquired less than three and a half years before the filing of the petition, the exemption generally is limited to $155,675. If the debtor has lived in the state fewer than two years, and in some other circumstances, no amount of home equity is exempt.

34–2h Property Distribution

In the next step of a Chapter 7 bankruptcy, the trustee distributes the bankruptcy estate to the creditors. The right of a creditor to be paid from the property of the estate depends on whether the creditor is secured or unsecured.

Secured Creditors A secured creditor has a security interest in collateral that secures the debt. If the collateral is surrendered to the secured creditor, the creditor can enforce the security interest either by accepting the property in full satisfaction of the debt or by selling the collateral and using the proceeds to pay off the debt. Should the collateral be insufficient to cover the secured debt owed, the secured creditor becomes an unsecured creditor for the difference.

Unsecured Creditors Unsecured creditors, of course, do not have security interests in collateral. These creditors are paid in a certain order of priority. They are divided into classes, and each class must be fully paid before the next class is entitled to any of the proceeds. The highest-priority class comprises claims for domestic support, such as child-support and alimony. These claims must be paid first.

If there are insufficient funds to pay an entire class, the proceeds are distributed *proportionately* to each creditor in the class. Classes lower in priority on the list receive nothing.

In almost all Chapter 7 bankruptcies, the proceeds are insufficient to pay all creditors. If any amount remains after the priority classes of creditors have been satisfied, however, it is turned over to the debtor.

34–2i Discharge under Chapter 7

Once the proceeds have been distributed, the debtor's remaining debts are discharged. Certain debts, however, are not dischargeable in bankruptcy. Also, certain debtors may not qualify to have all their debts discharged. These situations are discussed next.

Exceptions to Discharge Discharge of a debt may be denied because of the nature of the claim or the conduct of the debtor. Claims that are not dischargeable in bankruptcy include the following:

- Claims that are based on a debtor's willful or malicious conduct or fraud.
- Claims related to property or funds that the debtor obtained by false pretenses, embezzlement, or larceny.
- Any monetary judgment against the debtor for driving while intoxicated.
- Claims by creditors who were not notified of the bankruptcy—meaning that the claims did not appear on the required forms that accompany the debtor's petition and, thus, the creditors did not know about the bankruptcy proceedings.
- Claims for amounts due to the government for taxes accruing within three years, fines, or penalties, as well as any amounts borrowed to pay these debts.
- Domestic-support obligations and property settlements arising from a divorce or separation.
- Certain student loans (unless payment of the loans imposes an undue hardship on the debtor).
- Claims for amounts due on a retirement account loan.

Objections to Discharge In addition to the exceptions to discharge just described, the following circumstances (relating to the debtor's *conduct* and not to the debt) will cause a discharge to be denied:

1. The debtor's concealment or destruction of property with the intent to hinder, delay, or defraud a creditor.
2. The debtor's fraudulent concealment or destruction of records, or failure to keep adequate records, of his or her financial condition.

3. The grant of a discharge to the debtor within eight years of the filing of the current petition.

4. The debtor's failure to attend a required consumer education course.

5. Proceedings in which the debtor could be found guilty of a felony.

When a discharge is denied under these circumstances, the assets of the debtor are still distributed to the creditors. After the bankruptcy proceeding, however, the debtor remains liable for the unpaid portions of all claims.

Effect of a Discharge The primary effect of a discharge is to void, or set aside, any judgment on a discharged debt and prohibit any action to collect it. A discharge may be revoked (taken back) within one year, however, if it is discovered that the debtor acted fraudulently or dishonestly during the bankruptcy proceeding. In that situation, a creditor whose claim was not satisfied in the distribution of the debtor's property can proceed with his or her claim against the debtor.

34–3 CHAPTER 11—REORGANIZATION

reorganization
A plan for the readjustment of a corporation and its debt, the submission of the plan to a bankruptcy court, and the court's approval or rejection of the plan.

In a Chapter 11 **reorganization,** the creditors and the debtor—usually a corporation—formulate a plan under which the debtor pays a portion of the debts and is discharged of the remainder. Then the debtor is allowed to continue in business. Although this type of bankruptcy is commonly a corporate reorganization, any debtor who is eligible for Chapter 7 relief is eligible for Chapter 11 relief (with the exception of railroads, which are eligible under Chapter 11).

The same principles that govern the filing of a Chapter 7 petition apply to Chapter 11 proceedings. The petition may be filed either voluntarily or involuntarily. The same principles govern the entry of the order for relief. The automatic-stay provision also applies.

34–3a Creditors' Committees

LEARNING OUTCOME 3

Identify the debtor and procedures in a Chapter 11 reorganization.

Soon after the entry of the order for relief, a creditors' committee of unsecured creditors is appointed. This committee often is composed of the biggest suppliers to the business. The committee may consult with the trustee or the debtor concerning the administration of the case or the formulation of the plan. Additional creditors' committees may be appointed to represent special interest creditors.

Generally, no orders affecting the estate will be entered without the consent of the committee or after a hearing in which the judge is informed of the committee's position. Businesses with debts of less than $2.19 million that do not own or manage real estate can avoid creditors' committees. In these cases, orders for relief can be entered without a committee's consent.

34–3b The Reorganization Plan

The next step is to establish a reorganization plan. The plan is intended to conserve and administer the debtor's assets in the hope of an eventual return to successful operation and solvency.

Filing the Plan Only the debtor may file a plan within the first 120 days after the date of the order for relief. (This period may be extended up to 18 months.) If the debtor does not meet the deadline, or if the debtor fails to obtain creditor consent for the plan within 180 days, any party with a sufficient interest may propose a plan. This party's plan can be filed up to 20 months from the date of the order for relief. If a small-business debtor chooses to avoid creditors' committees, the time for the debtor's filing is shortened to 100 days, and any other party's plan must be filed within 180 days.

The Plan's Criteria The plan must be fair and equitable. It also must do the following:

1. Designate classes of creditors under the plan.
2. Specify the treatment to be afforded the classes of creditors. (The plan must provide the same treatment for each claim in a particular class.)
3. Provide an adequate means for the plan's execution.
4. Provide for payment of tax claims over a five-year period.

Acceptance of the Plan Once the plan has been developed, it is submitted to each class of creditors for acceptance. Even if all classes of creditors accept the plan, the court may refuse to confirm it if it is not "in the best interests of the creditors." Conversely, even if only one class of creditors accepts the plan, the court may still confirm it under the Code's so-called *cram-down provision*. In other words, the court may confirm the plan over the objections of creditors.

Discharge of the Plan The plan is binding on confirmation. The law provides, however, that confirmation of a plan does not discharge an individual debtor. *For individual debtors, the plan must be completed before discharge will be granted,* unless the court orders otherwise. For all other debtors, the court may order discharge at any time after the plan is confirmed. At this time, the debtor is given a reorganization discharge from all claims not protected under the plan. This discharge does not apply to any claims that would be denied discharge under Chapter 7 liquidation.

 34–4 CHAPTER 13—ADJUSTMENT

Under Chapter 13 of the Code, debtors with a regular income can have their debts adjusted. Individuals (not partnerships or corporations) with regular income who owe fixed, unsecured debts of less than $383,175 or fixed, secured debts of less than $1,149,525 can take advantage of Chapter 13. Sole proprietors and individuals on welfare, Social Security, fixed pensions, or investment income are included.

Filing a Chapter 13 plan is less expensive and less complicated than a Chapter 11 reorganization or a Chapter 7 liquidation. Also, the debtor in a Chapter 13 bankruptcy continues in business or in possession of most of his or her assets. The majority of debts are discharged within three years.

A Chapter 13 case can be initiated only by the filing of a voluntary petition by the debtor or by the conversion of a Chapter 7 petition. A trustee must be appointed.

34–4a The Individual's Repayment Plan

Only the debtor may file a plan under Chapter 13. This plan may provide for the payment of all obligations in full or for payment of an amount less than 100 percent. The plan must provide for the following:

1. The turnover of such future earnings or income of the debtor to the trustee as is necessary for execution of the plan.
2. Full payment of all claims entitled to priority, such as taxes. Payments must be completed within three to five years, depending on the debtor's family income. The debtor is allowed to deduct certain expenses to arrive at family income, including expenses for food, housing, and transportation.
3. The same treatment of each claim within a particular class of claims.

LEARNING OUTCOME 4

Identify the debtor, procedures, and advantages in a Chapter 13 adjustment.

Good Faith Requirement The Code imposes the requirement of good faith on a debtor at the time of the filing of the petition and the time of the filing of the plan. If the circumstances indicate bad faith, the court can dismiss the debtor's petition.

Real-World Case Example

David and Sharon Welsh filed a Chapter 13 petition. The bankruptcy trustee objected to the Welshes' proposed plan. The trustee argued that it was not proposed in good faith because of "minuscule" payments to unsecured claims while the Welshes lived in a $400,000 home and bought unnecessary items. The trustee also argued that the couple failed to commit 100 percent of their disposable income to the plan—specifically, they excluded their Social Security income. As a result, the plan would pay only about $14,700 of $180,500 of their unsecured debt. From a judgment in the Welshes' favor, the trustee appealed.

Did the Welshes propose their plan in good faith? Yes. In a 2013 case, *In re Welsh*, the U.S. Court of Appeals for the Ninth Circuit affirmed the judgment in the Welshes' favor. A plan prepared in accord with the Bankruptcy Code is considered proposed in good faith. Under the Code, the calculation of disposable income requires certain expenses to be subtracted from a debtor's "current monthly income." The Code's definition of "current monthly income" excludes Social Security income.

Confirmation of the Plan After the plan is filed, the court holds a hearing at which interested parties (such as creditors) can object to the plan. Unsecured creditors do not have a vote, however. The court will confirm the plan with respect to each claim of a secured creditor under any of the following circumstances:

1. The secured creditors have accepted the plan.
2. The plan provides that secured creditors retain their liens until there is full payment or a discharge.
3. The debtor surrenders the collateral to the creditors.

purchase-money security interest (PMSI)
The security interest that arises when a seller or lender extends credit for part or all of the purchase price of goods bought by a buyer.

Purchase-Money Security Interests In addition, for confirmation, the plan must make certain provisions for creditors with a **purchase-money security interest (PMSI)**. (A PMSI is created when a seller or lender agrees to extend credit for part or all of the purchase price of the goods that a debtor is buying.) For a motor vehicle purchased within 910 days before the petition was filed, the plan must provide that a creditor with a PMSI retains its lien until the entire debt is paid. For other PMSIs, the plan must cover debts incurred within one year preceding the filing.

34–4b Discharge under Chapter 13

After the completion of all payments under the plan, the court grants a discharge of the debts provided for by the plan. All debts are dischargeable *except* claims not provided for by the plan, certain long-term debts provided for by the plan, certain tax claims, payments on retirement accounts, and claims for domestic-support obligations.

In addition, under current law, debts related to injury or property damage caused while driving under the influence of alcohol or drugs are not dischargeable. Certain student loan debts can be discharged under Chapter 13, but only if the court finds that payment of the debts would constitute an undue hardship for the debtor. Furthermore, a discharge can be revoked if it is discovered that the debtor acted fraudulently or dishonestly.

ANSWERING THE LEGAL PROBLEM

In the legal problem set out at the beginning of this chapter, G&M Trucking borrows funds from Middleton Bank to buy two trucks, giving the bank a security interest in the trucks. G&M fails to make its payments for two months and files a petition in bankruptcy. Under bankruptcy law, Middleton is prevented from repossessing the trucks. This is the automatic stay. The trucks are rapidly falling in resale value, however, and will soon be worth much less than the balance due on the loan.

A **Is there anything that Middleton can do to protect itself?** Yes. The bank can ask the court to require G&M to make a one-time cash payment or periodic cash payments (or to provide additional collateral) to the extent that the trucks are losing value. If G&M cannot provide adequate protection, the court may vacate (cancel) the automatic stay and allow the bank to repossess the trucks.

TERMS AND CONCEPTS FOR REVIEW

automatic stay 468

bankruptcy court 465

bankruptcy trustee 469

discharge 466

estate in property 469

insolvent 466

liquidation 466

order for relief 467

preference 470

purchase-money security
   interest (PMSI) 474

reorganization 472

secured creditor 467

unsecured creditor 467

CHAPTER SUMMARY—BANKRUPTCY

LEARNING OUTCOME	
1	**Identify the debtor, procedures, and advantages in a Chapter 7 liquidation.** In a Chapter 7 liquidation, a debtor may be any "person" (including individuals, partnerships, and corporations) except railroads, insurance companies, banks, savings and loan institutions, credit unions, and investment companies licensed by the U.S. Small Business Administration. A petition may be filed by the debtor (voluntary) or by creditors (involuntary). Farmers and charitable institutions cannot be involuntarily petitioned. A creditors' meeting is held, and a trustee is elected. Nonexempt property is sold, and proceeds are distributed (in order) to priority groups. Most debts are discharged, and the debtor has an opportunity for a fresh start.
2	**List the duties and powers of a bankruptcy trustee.** A bankruptcy trustee's basic duty is to administer the debtor's estate by collecting the property of the estate and reducing it to money for distribution. The trustee first determines whether the debtor is entitled to relief under Chapter 7 or Chapter 13. The trustee has the power to exercise the same rights as creditors. The trustee also has the power to avoid certain transactions, including fraudulent transfers, preferences, and those that the debtor could rightfully cancel.
3	**Identify the debtor and procedures in a Chapter 11 reorganization.** In a Chapter 11 reorganization, the debtor may be any debtor eligible for Chapter 7 relief. Railroads are also eligible. A petition may be filed by the debtor (voluntary) or by creditors (involuntary). A reorganization plan is submitted to creditors. If the creditors do not accept the plan, it may be "crammed down" on them by the court. If the plan is approved and followed, the debts are discharged, and the business continues.
4	**Identify the debtor, procedures, and advantages in a Chapter 13 adjustment.** In a Chapter 13 adjustment, the debtor may be any individual (not partnerships or corporations) with regular income who owes fixed unsecured debts of less than $383,175 or fixed secured debts of less than $1,149,525. A Chapter 13 case can be initiated only by the filing of a voluntary petition by the debtor or by the conversion of a Chapter 7 petition. The debtor files a plan that may provide for payment of all obligations in full or for payment of less than 100 percent. If the plan is followed, the debtor makes payments for three to five years, and after that, most debts are discharged. The significant advantage of a Chapter 13 adjustment is that the debtor continues in business or in possession of assets.

ISSUE SPOTTERS

Check your answers to the *Issue Spotters* against the answers provided in Appendix C at the end of this text.

1. Al's Retail Store is a sole proprietorship. Smith & Jones is an advertising partnership. Roth & Associates, Inc., is a professional corporation. First State Savings & Loan is a savings and loan association. Which of these is not eligible for reorganization under Chapter 11? (See *Chapter 11—Reorganization.*)

2. After graduating from college, Tina works briefly as a salesperson before filing for bankruptcy. As part of her petition, Tina reveals that her only debts are student loans, taxes accruing within the last year, and a claim against her based on her misuse of customers' funds during her employment. Are these debts dischargeable in bankruptcy? Explain. (See *Chapter 7—Liquidation.*)

USING BUSINESS LAW

34–1. Debts under Chapter 7. Darin is experiencing personal financial problems. The amount of income he receives from his corporation is barely sufficient to cover his living expenses, the payments due on his mortgage, various credit-card debts, and some loans that he took out to pay for his son's college tuition. He would like to file for Chapter 7 liquidation just to be rid of the debts entirely, but he knows that he could probably pay them off over a four-year period if he really budgeted and used every cent available to pay his creditors. Darin decides to file for bankruptcy relief under Chapter 7. Are all of Darin's debts dischargeable under Chapter 7, including the debts incurred for his son's education? Given the fact that Darin could foreseeably pay off his debts over a four-year period, will the court allow Darin to obtain relief under Chapter 7? Why or why not? (See *Chapter 7—Liquidation.*)

34–2. Preferences. At the beginning of a new year, Paulo starts a greenhouse and nursery business. In February, Quail Springs Nursery Supply extends credit to Paulo. Because Paulo is short of capital, he uses all of the credit. In June, Quail Springs asks for payment, and on July 1, Paulo pays half of the debt. On September 1, Paulo files a voluntary petition for a Chapter 7 bankruptcy, listing Quail Springs and many other creditors. Can the bankruptcy trustee avoid Paulo's payment to Quail Springs? Discuss. (See *Chapter 7—Liquidation.*)

REAL-WORLD CASE PROBLEMS

34–3. Discharge. Michael and Dianne Shankle divorced. An Arkansas state court ordered Michael to pay Diane alimony and child support and half of the couple's $184,000 in their investment accounts. Instead, he withdrew more than half of the investment funds and spent them on himself. Over the next several years, the court repeatedly held Michael in contempt for failing to pay Dianne. Six years later, Michael filed for Chapter 7 bankruptcy, including in the petition's schedule the debt to Dianne of the unpaid alimony, child support, and investment funds. Is Michael entitled to a discharge of this debt, or does it qualify as an exception? Why or why not? [*In re Shankle*, 2014 WL 486208 (5th Cir. 2014)] (See *Chapter 7—Liquidation.*)

34–4. Discharge. Barbara Hann financed her education partially through $22,500 in loans. Hann believed that she had repaid the loans, but when she later filed a Chapter 13 petition, Educational Credit Management Corp. (ECMC) filed an unsecured proof of claim based on the loans. Hann

objected. At a hearing at which ECMC failed to appear, Hann submitted correspondence from the lender that indicated the loans had been paid. The court entered an order sustaining Hann's objection. Can ECMC now resume its effort to collect on Hann's loans? Explain. [*In re Hann*, 711 F.3d 235 (1st Cir. 2013)] (See *Chapter 13—Adjustments.*)

34–5. Discharge. Caroline McAfee loaned $400,000 to Carter Oaks Crossing. Joseph Harman, Carter's president, signed a personal guaranty for the loan. Later, Harman obtained a discharge in bankruptcy under Chapter 7 for his personal debts. His petition did not list the guaranty among the debts. When Carter defaulted on the loan, McAfee sought to collect the unpaid amount from Harman based on the guaranty. Harman argued that the guaranty had been discharged in his bankruptcy proceedings. Is Harman correct? Why or why not? [*Harman v. McAfee*, 302 Ga.App. 698, 691 S.E.2d 586 (2010)] (See *Chapter 7—Liquidation.*)

ETHICAL QUESTIONS

34–6. Voluntary Bankruptcy. What are some of the factors that might be considered in deciding whether a debtor should be allowed to declare bankruptcy? (See *Chapter 7—Liquidation.*)

34–7. Discharge. Monica Sexton filed a petition for Chapter 13 reorganization. One of her creditors was Friedman's Jewelers. Her petition misclassified Friedman's claim as $800 of unsecured debt. Within days, Friedman's filed proof of a secured claim for $300 and an unsecured claim for $462. Eventually, Friedman's was sent payments of about $300 by check. None of the checks were cashed. By then, Friedman's had filed its own petition under

Chapter 11, Bankruptcy Receivables Management (BRM) had bought Friedman's unpaid accounts, and the checks had not been forwarded. Sexton received a discharge on the completion of her plan. BRM was not notified. BRM wrote to Sexton's attorney to ask about the status of her case, but received no response. BRM demanded that Sexton surrender the collateral on its claim. Sexton asked the court to impose sanctions on BRM for violating the discharge order. Was Sexton's debt to Friedman's dischargeable? Should BRM be sanctioned? Discuss. [*In re Sexton*, __ Bankr. __ (E.D.N.C. 2011)] (See *Chapter 11—Reorganization.*)

Chapter 34—Work Set

TRUE-FALSE QUESTIONS

_____ 1. A debtor must be insolvent to file a voluntary petition under Chapter 7.

_____ 2. Debtors are protected from losing the value of their property as a result of the automatic stay.

_____ 3. The same principles cover the filing of a Chapter 7 petition and a Chapter 11 proceeding.

_____ 4. A bankruptcy may be commenced by involuntary petition under Chapter 13.

_____ 5. Generally, in a bankruptcy proceeding, any creditor's claim is allowed.

_____ 6. When a business debtor files for Chapter 11 protection, the debtor is not allowed to continue in business.

_____ 7. No small business can avoid creditors' committees under Chapter 11.

_____ 8. Bankruptcy proceedings are held in federal bankruptcy courts.

_____ 9. A discharge obtained by fraud can be revoked within one year.

MULTIPLE-CHOICE QUESTIONS

_____ 1. Jill's monthly income is $2,000, her monthly expenses are $2,800, and her debts are nearly $40,000. To obtain a fresh start, Jill could file for bankruptcy under

a. Chapter 7.
b. Chapter 11.
c. Chapter 13.
d. none of the above.

_____ 2. Pat files a Chapter 7 petition for a discharge in bankruptcy. Pat may be denied a discharge on which of the following grounds?

a. Concealing property with the intent to defraud a creditor.
b. Paying for services received in the ordinary course of business.
c. Having obtained a bankruptcy discharge twelve years earlier.
d. Both a and c.

_____ 3. Carol is the sole proprietor of Beekman Café, which owes debts in an amount more than Carol believes she and the café can repay. The creditors agree that liquidating the business would not be in their best interests. To stay in business, Carol could file for bankruptcy under

a. Chapter 7 only.
b. Chapter 11 only.
c. Chapter 13 only.
d. Chapter 11 or Chapter 13.

_____ 4. Jerry's monthly income is $2,500, his monthly expenses are $2,100, and his debts are nearly $15,000. If he applied the difference between his income and his expenses to pay off the debts, they could be eliminated within three years. The provision in the Bankruptcy Code that covers this plan is

a. Chapter 7.
b. Chapter 11.
c. Chapter 12.
d. Chapter 13.

_____ 5. General Supplies Corporation (GSC) has not paid any of its fifteen creditors, six of whom have unsecured claims of more than $18,000. Under which chapter of the Bankruptcy Code can the creditors force GSC into bankruptcy?

    a. Chapter 7 only.
    b. Chapter 11 only.
    c. Chapter 13 only.
    d. Chapter 7 or Chapter 11.

_____ 6. Bob files a bankruptcy petition under Chapter 7 to have his debts discharged. If Bob's plan is approved, the debts most likely to be discharged include claims for

    a. back taxes accruing within three years before the petition was filed.
    b. certain fines and penalties payable to the government.
    c. domestic support.
    d. student loans, if the payment would impose undue hardship on Bob.

_____ 7. National Stores, Inc., decides to file for bankruptcy. Under which chapter of the Bankruptcy Code can a corporation file a petition for bankruptcy?

    a. Chapter 7 only.
    b. Chapter 11 only.
    c. Chapter 13 only.
    d. Chapter 7 or Chapter 11.

ANSWERING MORE LEGAL PROBLEMS

1. Lorenzo was a Realtor. For a few years, he made a substantial income. During and after the Great Recession, however, his income matched the drop in property values and numbers of sales. As his business floundered, Lorenzo found himself unable to pay his debts. He approached Rosanna, a bankruptcy attorney, to explore his options. Rosanna suggested that filing a petition for bankruptcy under Chapter 7 might be Lorenzo's best course.

What are the requirements for filing a voluntary Chapter 7 bankruptcy petition? The debtor must be a _____—an individual, partnership, or corporation—not otherwise prohibited from using Chapter 7. The debtor must file a _____ that includes certain information, including a list of the debtor's creditors and the amounts owed to each. The forms must be completed accurately, sworn to under oath, and signed by the debtor. A _____-debtor must include a certificate proving that he or she received _____ _____ from an approved agency within the last six months. The debtor must not be seeking an advantage over a creditor, and the debtor's financial situation must warrant relief. Finally, the court must find that the _____ is proper.

2. Pauline borrowed funds from Student Loan Corp. to attend flight school, where she learned to be a pilot. After graduation, Pauline started a business she called Otto Airshows with a helicopter decorated as "Otto the Clown." When Student Loan Corp. tried to collect the amount of Pauline's unpaid loan from the assets of Otto Airshows, she formed Prop Aviation, Inc., and leased the Otto equipment to Prop. She then filed a Chapter 13 bankruptcy petition without noting the unpaid loan and the equipment lease.

Is the court likely to allow Pauline's petition to proceed? No. The court is likely to _____ the petition due to _____ _____. The Bankruptcy Code imposes the requirement of good faith at the time of the filing of a petition and the time of the filing of a repayment plan under Chapter 13. Pauline did not include all of her assets and liabilities in her petition. For this reason, even if the petition was allowed to proceed, and a discharge was granted, the student loan debt would not be included. There would have been no finding that payment of the debt constituted _____ _____.

INSURANCE

FACING A LEGAL PROBLEM

Tanya and Miguel are married and have two children. When they divorce, Tanya gives her interest in their house to Miguel and moves out. Miguel dies, leaving the house to the children. Because the children are minors, Tanya moves back into the house with them. She keeps the house in good repair and takes out an insurance policy on the property. When the house is destroyed in a fire, the insurance company refuses to pay, arguing that Tanya could not legally take out insurance on the house because she did not own it—her children did.

 Is Tanya entitled to payment under the insurance policy?

Protecting against loss is a foremost concern of all property owners. No one can predict whether an accident or a fire will occur, so individuals and businesses typically protect their personal and financial interests by obtaining insurance, which is the topic of this chapter.

Insurance is a contract in which the insurance company (the insurer) promises to pay a sum of money or give something of value to another (either the insured or a beneficiary) to compensate the other for a particular, stated loss. Insurance protection may compensate for the injury or death of the insured or another, for damage to the insured's property, or for other types of losses, such as those resulting from lawsuits.

By insuring their property, individuals and businesses protect themselves against damage and loss. Most individuals insure both real and personal property (as well as their lives). Businesses almost always insure their real and personal property.

 ## 35–1 INSURANCE TERMINOLOGY AND CONCEPTS

Insurance has its own terminology and concepts. A knowledge of these matters is essential to understanding insurance law.

35–1a Insurance Terminology

An insurance contract is called a **policy.** The consideration paid to the insurer is called a **premium.** The insurance company is sometimes called an **underwriter.**

The parties to an insurance policy are the *insurer* (the insurance company) and the *insured* (the person covered by the policy's provisions or the holder of the policy). Insurance contracts are usually obtained through an *agent*, who ordinarily works for the insurance company, or through a *broker*, who ordinarily is an independent contractor. A *beneficiary* receives proceeds under the policy.

LEARNING OUTCOMES

The five Learning Outcomes below are designed to help improve your understanding of the chapter. After reading this chapter, you should be able to:

1 Define important insurance terms and concepts.

2 Discuss insurance as a component of risk management.

3 State when the coverage on an insurance policy begins.

4 Explain how courts interpret insurance provisions.

5 Identify defenses an insurance company may have against payment on a policy.

insurance
A contract in which, for a stipulated consideration, one party agrees to compensate the other for loss on a specific subject caused by a specified peril.

LEARNING OUTCOME 1
Define important insurance terms and concepts.

policy
In insurance law, the contract between the insurer and the insured.

premium
In insurance law, the price for insurance protection for a specified period of time.

underwriter
In insurance law, the one assuming a risk in return for the payment of a premium.

When a broker deals with an applicant for insurance, the broker is, in effect, the applicant's agent. By contrast, an insurance agent is an agent of the insurance company, not of the applicant. As a general rule, the insurance company is bound by the acts of its agents when they act within the agency relationship. A broker, however, has no relationship with the insurance company and is an agent of the insurance applicant.

A person can insure anything in which he or she has an *insurable interest*. Without this insurable interest, there is no enforceable contract, and a transaction to insure would have to be treated as a wager. The existence of an insurable interest is a primary concern in determining liability under an insurance policy.

35–1b Risk Management

Risk can be described as a prediction concerning potential loss based on known and unknown factors. Basically, insurance is an arrangement for *transferring and allocating risk*. This concept is known as **risk management.** The most common method of risk management is the transfer of certain risks from an individual or business to an insurance company. (For a discussion of risk management in cyberspace, see this chapter's *Linking Business Law to Your Career* feature).

Risk Pooling All types of insurance companies use the principle of *risk pooling*. That is, they spread the risk among a large number of people—the pool—to make the premiums small compared with the coverage offered. For instance, life insurance companies know that only a small proportion of the individuals in any particular age group will die in any one year. If a large percentage of this age group pays premiums to the company in exchange for a benefit payment in case of death, there will be enough funds to pay the beneficiaries of the policyholders who die.

Determining Rates Through the extensive correlation of data over a period of time, insurers can estimate fairly accurately the total amount they will have to pay if they insure a particular group. With this estimate, insurers can determine the rates they will have to charge each member of the group so that they can make the necessary payments and still show a profit.

35–1c Classifications of Insurance

Insurance is classified according to the nature of the risk involved. Fire insurance, casualty insurance, life insurance, and title insurance apply to different types of risk. Furthermore, policies of these types differ in relation to the persons and interests that they protect. This is reasonable because the types of losses that are expected and the types that are foreseeable or unforeseeable vary with the nature of the activity.

See Exhibit 35.1 for a list of various insurance classifications.

35–1d Insurable Interest

In the case of real and personal property, an **insurable interest** exists when the insured derives a financial benefit from the preservation and continued existence of the property. Put another way, you have an insurable interest in property if you would sustain a financial loss from its destruction. This interest in property must exist when the loss occurs.

In the case of life insurance, for instance, a person must have a reasonable expectation of benefit from the continued life of another in order to have an insurable interest in that person's life. The benefit may be financial, as in the case of *key person insurance*. An organization may buy this sort of insurance to protect itself against the loss of employees considered especially important to the organization's success. Or the benefit may be founded on the relationship between the parties, as in the case of blood relationships and marital relationships.

LEARNING OUTCOME 2

Discuss insurance as a component of risk management.

risk
A specified contingency or peril.

risk management
Planning undertaken to protect one's interest should some event threaten to undermine its security.

insurable interest
A substantial, financial interest either in a person's life or well-being or in property.

EXHIBIT 35.1 Examples of Insurance Classifications

Type of Insurance	Coverage
Automobile	May cover damage to automobiles resulting from specified hazards or occurrences (such as fire, vandalism, theft, or collision); normally provides protection against liability for personal injuries and property damage resulting from the operation of the vehicle.
Disability	Replaces a portion of the insured's monthly income from employment in the event that illness or injury causes a short- or long-term disability. Some states require employers to provide short-term disability insurance. Benefits typically last a set period of time, such as six months for short-term coverage or five years for long-term coverage.
Employer's liability	Insures employers against liability for injuries or losses sustained by employees during the course of their employment; covers claims not covered under workers' compensation insurance.
Fidelity or guaranty	Provides indemnity against losses in trade or losses caused by the dishonesty of employees, the insolvency of debtors, or breaches of contract.
Fire	Covers losses caused to the insured as a result of fire.
Group	Provides individual life, medical, or disability insurance coverage; obtainable by persons who are members of certain groups; when the group consists of employees, the policy premium is paid either entirely by the employer or partially by the employer and partially by the employees.
Health	Covers expenses incurred by the insured resulting from physical injury or illness and other expenses relating to health and life maintenance.
Homeowners'	Protects homeowners against some or all risks of loss to their residences and the residences' contents or liability related to such property.
Key-person	Protects a business in the event of the death or disability of a key employee.
Liability	Protects against liability imposed on the insured resulting from injuries to the person or property of another.
Life	Covers the death of the policyholder. On the death of the insured, an amount specified in the policy is paid by the insurer to the insured's beneficiary.
Malpractice	Protects professionals (doctors, lawyers, and others) against malpractice claims brought against them by their patients or clients; a form of liability insurance.

The insurable interest in life insurance must exist at the time the policy is obtained. This is exactly the opposite of property insurance, for which the insurable interest must exist at the time the loss occurs and not necessarily when the policy is purchased.

35–2 THE INSURANCE CONTRACT

An insurance contract is governed by the general principles of contract law, although the insurance industry is heavily regulated by each state. Customarily, a party offers to purchase insurance by submitting an application to an insurance company. The company can either accept or reject the offer. Sometimes, the insurance company's acceptance is conditional—on the results of a life insurance applicant's medical examination, for example. For the insurance contract to be binding, consideration (in the form of a premium) must be given, and the parties forming the contract must have the required contractual capacity to do so.

35–2a The Application

The filled-in application form for insurance is usually attached to the policy and made a part of the insurance contract. Thus, an insurance applicant is bound by any false statements that appear in the application (subject to certain exceptions).

Because the insurance company evaluates the risk factors based on the information included in the insurance application, misstatements or misrepresentations can void a policy, especially if the insurance company can show that it would not have extended insurance if it had known the facts.

35–2b The Effective Date

LEARNING OUTCOME 3

State when the coverage on an insurance policy begins.

The effective date of an insurance contract—that is, the date on which the insurance coverage begins—is important. In some instances, the insurance applicant is not protected until a formal written policy is issued. In other situations, the applicant is protected between the time an application is received and the time the insurance company either accepts or rejects it. Facts that should be kept in mind include the following:

1. A broker is merely the agent of an applicant. Therefore, until the broker obtains a policy, the applicant normally is not insured.

2. A person who seeks insurance from an insurance company's agent usually is protected from the moment the application is made, provided—in the case of life insurance—that some form of premium has been paid. Between the time the application is received and either rejected or accepted, the applicant is covered (possibly subject to a medical examination). Usually, the agent writes a memorandum, or **binder**, indicating that a policy is pending and stating its essential terms.

binder
A written, temporary insurance policy.

3. If the parties agree that the policy will be issued and delivered at a later time, the contract is not effective until the policy is issued and delivered or sent to the applicant, depending on the agreement. Thus, any loss sustained between the time of application and the delivery of the policy is not covered.

HIGHLIGHTING THE POINT

McNeal pays a premium to CPB Insurance Company for a life insurance policy that is expressly contingent on McNeal's passing a medical examination. If McNeal passes the examination, the policy coverage will date from the payment of the premium. McNeal dies before having the medical examination.

Can McNeal's beneficiary collect on the policy? Yes. To collect, however, the beneficiary must show that McNeal would have passed the examination had he not died.

In sum, coverage on an insurance policy can begin when a binder is written, when the policy is issued, or, depending on the terms of the contract, after a certain period of time has elapsed.

35–2c Provisions and Clauses

LEARNING OUTCOME 4

Explain how courts interpret insurance provisions.

Some important provisions and clauses in insurance contracts are listed and defined in Exhibit 35.2. The courts realize that most people do not have the special training necessary to understand the intricate terminology used in insurance policies. So courts interpret the words used in an insurance contract according to their ordinary meanings and in light of the nature of the coverage involved. When there is an ambiguity in the policy, the provision is interpreted against the insurance company.

In some situations, it may be unclear whether an insurance contract actually exists because the written policy has not been delivered. Here, too, the uncertainty will be determined against the insurance company. The court will presume that the policy is in effect unless the company can show otherwise.

Real-World Case Example

Burt Hoey owns a farmers' market that offers hayrides. Western World Insurance Company insures Hoey's business under a commercial general liability policy. The policy does not apply to an injury to an employee. Hoey hired Mary Armbruster to run the hay wagon for eight weekends. An accident with the wagon crushed Armbruster's spine. She sought to recover for the injury from Western World. Western World denied coverage. A federal district court ruled that the policy did not cover Armbruster's claim because she fit the common understanding of the word *employee*.

Was Armbruster an employee according to the ordinary meaning of the word and in light of the nature of the coverage involved? Yes. In a 2014 case, *Western World Insurance Co. v. Hoey*, the U.S. Court of Appeals for the Sixth Circuit affirmed the lower court's ruling. The language of the policy was clear, and as a result, Armbruster's injuries were not covered by the policy. The normal purpose of a commercial general liability policy is to provide coverage for injuries that occur to the "public-at-large," not to a business's workers. Businesses maintain workers' compensation insurance to cover injuries that occur to employees.

35–2d Cancellation

The insured can cancel a policy at any time, and the insurer can cancel under certain circumstances. When an insurance company can cancel its insurance contract, the policy or a state statute usually requires that the insurer give advance written notice of the cancellation to the insured.

EXHIBIT 35.2 Insurance Contract Clauses and Descriptions

Type of Clause	Description
Antilapse clause	An antilapse clause provides that the policy will not automatically lapse if no payment is made on the date due. Ordinarily, under such a provision, the insured has a *grace period* of thirty or thirty-one days within which to pay an overdue premium before the policy is canceled.
Appraisal clause	Insurance policies frequently provide that if the parties cannot agree on the amount of a loss covered under the policy or the value of the property lost, either party can demand an appraisal, or estimate, by an impartial and qualified third party.
Arbitration clause	Many insurance policies include clauses that call for arbitration of disputes that arise between the insurer and the insured concerning the settlement of claims.
Incontestability clause	An incontestability clause provides that after a policy has been in force for a specified length of time—usually two or three years—the insurer cannot contest statements made in the application.
Multiple insurance	Many insurance policies include a clause providing that if the insured has multiple insurance policies that cover the same property and the amount of coverage exceeds the loss, the loss will be shared proportionately by the insurance companies.

HIGHLIGHTING THE POINT

As part of an employee benefits package, the Bobcat Company pays for a group life insurance plan. To cut back on its financial risk, however, Eagle Insurance Company cancels the policy. A state statute requires written notice of the cancellation, but an Eagle employee merely telephones Bobcat to tell it about the cancellation. No written notice is sent to Bobcat or Bobcat's employees. When Meade, a Bobcat employee, dies, Eagle refuses to pay on the policy.

Can the company be required to pay on Meade's policy? Yes. The state statute requires written notice. A telephone call is not sufficient.

An insurer can cancel a policy for various reasons, depending on the type of insurance. Some examples include the following:

1. Automobile insurance can be canceled for nonpayment of premiums or suspension of the insured's driver's license.

2. Property insurance can be canceled for nonpayment of premiums or for other reasons, including the insured's fraud, negligence, or conviction for a crime that increases the risk to the insurer.

3. Life and health policies can be canceled due to false statements made by the insured in the application.

An insurer cannot cancel—or refuse to renew—a policy for discriminatory or other reasons that violate public policy or because the insured has appeared as a witness in a case against the company.

35–2e Defenses against Payment

LEARNING OUTCOME 5

Identify defenses an insurance company may have against payment on a policy.

An insurance company can raise any of the defenses that would be valid in an ordinary action on a contract, as well as the following defenses:

1. *Fraud or misrepresentation*—If the insurance company can show that the policy was procured through fraud or misrepresentation, it may have a valid defense for not paying on a claim. (The insurance company may also have the right to disaffirm, or rescind, the insurance contract.) **EXAMPLE 35.1** Haller Systems sells and installs upscale office furniture. To cover any loss of its inventory, Haller obtains an insurance policy from Regency. When completing Regency's application, Haller intentionally overstates the number of items in its warehouse. Later, Haller files a claim to recover the difference between the inflated figure and the actual count. If Regency can prove the fraud, it has a valid defense for not paying Haller's claim. Regency may also have the right to cancel the policy.◄

2. *Lack of insurable interest*—An absolute defense exists if the insurer can show that the insured lacked an insurable interest—thus rendering the policy void from the beginning.

3. *Illegal actions*—Improper actions, such as those that are against public policy or that are otherwise illegal, can also give the insurance company a defense against the payment of a claim or allow it to rescind the contract. **EXAMPLE 35.2** Montrose Chemical obtains an insurance policy from Greenhaven Insurance to cover liability imposed on Montrose as a result of injuries to nonemployees or damage to their property. Following an explosion at Montrose's plant, a release of toxic chemicals results in injuries to nearby residents. An investigation reveals that the explosion was likely caused by Montrose's failure to comply with government

regulations for the safe handling of the chemicals. Greenhaven can assert this misconduct as a defense against payment on Montrose's policy.◄

An insurance company may not act in bad faith, however. For instance, if an insurer denied coverage without a reasonable basis, the insured could file a bad faith tort action to recover. An insurer has a duty to investigate to determine the facts and provide reasons for any decision to deny or reduce coverage of a particular claim.

In some situations, the insurance company may be prevented from asserting defenses that normally are available. For instance, an insurance company ordinarily cannot escape payment on the death of an insured on the ground that the person's age was stated incorrectly on the application. Also, *incontestability clauses* (see Exhibit 35.2) prevent the insurer from asserting certain defenses.

ANSWERING THE LEGAL PROBLEM

In the legal problem set out at the beginning of this chapter, Tanya and Miguel are married and have two children. When they divorce, Tanya gives her interest in their house to Miguel and moves out. Miguel dies, leaving the house to the children. Because the children are minors, Tanya moves back into the house with them. She keeps the house in good repair and takes out an insurance policy on the property. When the house is destroyed in a fire, the insurance company refuses to pay, arguing that Tanya could not legally take out insurance on the house because she did not own it—her children did.

A **Is Tanya entitled to payment under the insurance policy?** Yes. Tanya had an insurable interest in the house. The funds she spent to keep the house in repair, the loss she suffered in having to obtain other housing, and the loss she suffered as guardian of the children indicate that Tanya had an insurable interest in the house, even if she did not own it.

LINKING BUSINESS LAW to Your Career

RISK MANAGEMENT IN CYBERSPACE

Your career may require you to evaluate risks to your business and obtain insurance against those risks. If your company does business online, you may be confronting risks that are not covered by traditional types of insurance.

Insurance for Web-Related Risks

Insurance to cover Web-related incidents frequently is referred to as *network intrusion insurance*. Such insurance protects companies from losses stemming from hackers and computer viruses; programming errors; network and Web site disruptions; theft of electronic data and assets, including intellectual property; Web-related defamation, copyright infringement, and false advertising; and violations of users' privacy rights.

Customized Policies

Unlike traditional insurance policies, which generally are drafted by insurance companies and presented to insurance applicants on a take-it-or-leave-it basis, cyberinsurance policies usually are customized to provide protection against specific risks faced by a particular type of business.

For example, an Internet service provider will face different risks than an online merchant, and a banking institution will face different risks than a law firm. The specific business-related risks are taken into consideration in determining the policy premium.

(Continued)

Qualifying Criteria

Many companies that offer network intrusion insurance require applicants to meet high security standards. Some companies assess an applicant's Web-related security system before underwriting a policy.

For instance, an insurer might assess the applicant's security measures and refuse to provide coverage unless the business scores higher than 60 percent according to certain criteria. If the business does not score that high, it can contract with the company to improve its Web-related security.

Considering Coverage

When procuring any type of insurance coverage, you should read the policy carefully, including any exclusions contained in the fine print, before committing to it. It is wise to pay attention to details when it comes to insurance.

Though coverage may seem expensive, it may be less costly than the loss of intellectual property or the cost of defending against a lawsuit. Opting for higher deductibles can reduce premiums.

TERMS AND CONCEPTS FOR REVIEW

binder 484

insurable interest 482

insurance 481

policy 481

premium 481

risk 482

risk management 482

underwriter 481

CHAPTER SUMMARY—INSURANCE

LEARNING OUTCOME	
1	**Define important insurance terms and concepts.** The *policy* is the insurance contract. The *premium* is the consideration paid to the insurer for a policy. The *underwriter* is the insurance company. The parties include the *insurer* (the insurance company), the *insured* (the person covered by insurance), an *agent* (a representative of the insurance company) or a *broker* (ordinarily an independent contractor), and a beneficiary (a person to receive proceeds under the policy). An *insurable interest* exists whenever an individual or entity benefits from the preservation of the health or life of the insured or the property to be insured.
2	**Discuss insurance as a component of risk management.** Insurance is an arrangement for transferring and allocating certain risks from individuals to insurance companies. Insurance is based on the principle of pooling risks—spreading risk among a large number of people to make the premiums small compared with the coverage offered.
3	**State when the coverage on an insurance policy begins.** Coverage on an insurance policy can begin when a *binder* (a written memorandum indicating that a formal policy is pending and stating its essential terms) is written, when the policy is issued, when the contract is formed, or when a condition specified in the contract—such as passage of a certain period of time—is met.
4	**Explain how courts interpret insurance provisions.** Words will be given their ordinary meanings, and any ambiguity in the policy will be interpreted against the insurance company. When the written policy has not been delivered and it is unclear whether an insurance contract actually exists, the uncertainty will be resolved against the insurance company. The court will presume that the policy is in effect unless the company can show otherwise.
5	**Identify defenses an insurance company may have against payment on a policy.** Defenses that an insurance company may have against payment to the insured include (1) misrepresentation or fraud, (2) lack of an insurable interest, or (3) illegal actions.

ISSUE SPOTTERS

Check your answers to the *Issue Spotters* against the answers provided in Appendix C at the end of this text.

1. Neal applies to Farm Insurance Company for a life insurance policy. On the application, Neal understates his age. Neal obtains the policy, but for a lower premium than he would have had to pay had he disclosed his actual age. The policy includes an incontestability clause. Six years later, Neal dies. Can the insurer refuse payment? Why or why not? (See *The Insurance Contract*.)

2. Al is divorced and owns a house. Al has no reasonable expectation of benefit from the life of Bea, his former spouse, but applies for insurance on her life anyway. Al obtains a fire insurance policy on the house, then sells the house. Ten years later, Bea dies and the house is destroyed by fire. Can Al obtain payment for these events? Explain your answers. (See *Insurance Terminology and Concepts*.)

USING BUSINESS LAW

35–1. Timing of Insurance Coverage. On October 10, Joleen Vora applied for a $50,000 life insurance policy with Magnum Life Insurance Co. She named her husband, Jay, as the beneficiary. Joleen paid the insurance company the first year's policy premium on making the application. Two days later, before she had a chance to take the physical examination required by the insurance company and before the policy was issued, Joleen was killed in an automobile accident. Jay submitted a claim to the insurance company for the $50,000. Can Jay collect? Explain. (See *The Insurance Contract*.)

35–2. Insurable Interest. Shelley is the chief financial officer for Ready Auto Parts Corporation. Shelley also heads the corporate IT department, which is responsible for managing the company's inventory to closely time acquisitions, distribution, and sales. Ready considers Shelley especially important to the firm's success and obtains an insurance policy on Shelley's life from United Insurance Company. Is Ready entitled to recover under the policy? Why or why not? (See *Insurance Terminology and Concepts*.)

REAL-WORLD CASE PROBLEMS

35–3. Insurable Interest. Donald Breeden and Willie Buchanan were married in Marion County, Mississippi. They lived in a home in Sandy Hook. Nationwide Property & Casualty Insurance Co. insured the home under a policy bought by Breeden that named him as the insured. The policy provided that the spouse of the named insured was covered as an insured. After eight years of marriage, Breeden and Buchanan divorced. Breeden transferred his interest in the home to Buchanan as part of the couple's property settlement. Less than a year later, a fire completely destroyed the home. A claim was filed with Nationwide. Who is entitled to the proceeds? Why? [*Breeden v. Buchanan*, 2014 WL 1292462 (Miss.App. 2014)] (See *Insurance Terminology and Concepts*.)

35–4. Provisions and Clauses. Darling's Rent-a-Car carried property insurance on its cars under a policy issued by Philadelphia Indemnity Insurance Co. The policy listed Darling's as the "insured." Darling's rented a car to Joshuah Farrington. In the rental contract, Farrington agreed to be

responsible for any damage to the car and declined the optional insurance. Later, Farrington collided with a moose. Philadelphia paid Darling's for the damage to the car and sought to collect this amount from Farrington. Farrington argued that he was an "insured" under Darling's policy. How should "insured" be interpreted in this case? Why? [*Philadelphia Indemnity Insurance Co. v. Farrington*, 37 A.3d 305 (Me. 2012) (See *The Insurance Contract*.)

35–5. Defenses against Payment. Leo and Mary Deters owned Deters Tower Service, Inc. The firm obtained a liability policy from USF Insurance Co. to cover its officers, including Leo. One afternoon, two Deters Tower employees were servicing a tower when they fell to their deaths. The workers' families filed a negligence suit against Leo. USF refused to defend Leo against the suit or to pay any claim and did not provide a reason for this response. Is USF liable to Leo for this refusal? If so, on what basis, and how much might Leo recover? [*Deters v. USF Insurance Co.*, 797 N.W.2d 621 (Iowa App. 2011)] (See *The Insurance Contract*.)

ETHICAL QUESTIONS

35–6. Insurance Agent. Should an insurance agent be held to a duty to advise applicants about coverage? Why or why not? (See *Insurance Terminology and Concepts*.)

35–7. Defenses against Payment. James Bubenik, a dentist, had medical malpractice insurance with Medical Protective Co. (MPC). The policy required MPC to defend Bubenik against any malpractice claim and required Bubenik to cooperate in the defense of such a claim. When a patient filed a claim against Bubenik for malpractice, however, he refused to submit to depositions, answer interrogatories, testify at trial, or communicate with MPC. Instead, he agreed to help the patient obtain a payment. Under these circumstances, did MPC have a legal or ethical duty to defend against the claim? Could MPC refuse to pay it? Explain. [*Medical Protective Co. v. Bubenik*, 594 F.3d 1047 (8th Cir. 2010)] (See *The Insurance Contract*.)

Chapter 35—Work Set

TRUE-FALSE QUESTIONS

_____ 1. Risk management involves the transfer of certain risks from an individual or a business to an insurance company.

_____ 2. Insurance is classified by the nature of the person or interest protected.

_____ 3. An insurance broker is an agent of an insurance company.

_____ 4. An insurance applicant is usually protected from the time an application is made, if a premium has been paid, possibly subject to certain conditions.

_____ 5. A person can insure anything in which he or she has an insurable interest.

_____ 6. An application for insurance is not part of the insurance contract.

_____ 7. The insurable interest in life insurance must exist at the time the policy is obtained.

_____ 8. An antilapse clause provides that an insurance policy lapses if the insured does not pay a premium exactly on time.

_____ 9. In courts, the words used in an insurance policy are given special meaning.

MULTIPLE-CHOICE QUESTIONS

_____ 1. Satellite Communications, Inc., takes out an insurance policy on its plant. For which of the following reasons could the insurer cancel the policy?

   a. Satellite's president appears as a witness in a case against the company.
   b. Satellite begins using grossly careless manufacturing practices.
   c. Two of Satellite's drivers have their driver's licenses suspended.
   d. All of the above.

_____ 2. Sue applies for a fire insurance policy for her warehouse from A&I Insurance Company. To obtain a lower premium, she misrepresents the age of the property. The policy is granted. After the warehouse is destroyed by fire, A&I learns the truth. In this situation, A&I

   a. can refuse to pay on the ground of fraud in the application.
   b. can refuse to pay on the ground that the warehouse has been destroyed by fire.
   c. cannot refuse to pay, because an application is not part of an insurance contract.
   d. cannot refuse to pay, because the warehouse has been destroyed by fire.

_____ 3. Technon Corporation manufactures computers. To cover injuries to consumers if the products prove defective, Technon should buy

   a. group insurance.
   b. liability insurance.
   c. major medical insurance.
   d. life insurance.

_____ 4. Jim is an executive with E-Tech Corporation. Because his death would cause a financial loss to E-Tech, the firm insures his life. Later, Jim resigns to work for MayCom, Inc., one of E-Tech's competitors. Six months later, Jim dies. Regarding payment for the loss, E-Tech

   a. can collect, because its insurable interest existed when the policy was obtained.
   b. cannot collect, because its insurable interest did not exist when a loss occurred.
   c. cannot collect, because it suffered no financial loss from the death of Jim, who resigned to work for one of its competitors.
   d. None of the above.

5. Tom takes out a mortgage with First National Bank to buy a house. Tom obtains a fire insurance policy, partially payable to the bank. After Tom makes the last mortgage payment, the house is destroyed by fire. Regarding payment for the loss, the bank

   a. can collect, because its insurable interest existed when the policy was obtained.
   b. can collect, because its mortgage required Tom to take out the policy.
   c. cannot collect, because its insurable interest did not exist when a loss occurred.
   d. cannot collect, because its mortgage required Tom to take out the policy.

6. Ace Manufacturing, Inc., has property insurance with National Insurer, Inc. When Ace suffers a loss in a burglary, Ace and National cannot agree on the amount of recovery. Under an appraisal clause,

   a. only Ace can demand an appraisal by a third party.
   b. only National can demand an appraisal by a third party.
   c. either party can demand an appraisal by a third party.
   d. the government sets the value of the loss, which both parties must accept.

7. Lee buys BizNet, a company that provides Internet access, and takes out property insurance with InsCo to cover a loss of the equipment. Two years later, Lee sells BizNet. Six months after the sale, BizNet's equipment is stolen. Under InsCo's policy, Lee can recover

   a. the total amount of the insurance.
   b. the total amount of the loss.
   c. InsCo's proportionate share of the loss to the total amount of insurance.
   d. nothing.

8. Insurance premiums are small relative to the coverage offered because

   a. the risks are spread among a large number of people.
   b. agents and brokers receive only a small percentage of the premiums.
   c. insurance companies rarely have to pay any claims.
   d. the government guarantees insurance payments up to a certain amount.

 ## ANSWERING MORE LEGAL PROBLEMS

1. Trimpoint Maintenance, Inc. (TMI), a property maintenance service, leased storage and office space at Hilltop Corporate Complex. TMI also maintained and operated the complex's lighting, ventilation systems, and common areas. Marketplace Insurance Co. insured TMI against losses caused by damage to "property owned, leased, used, or controlled" by TMI. When fire destroyed Hilltop, TMI filed a claim with Marketplace.

   Was TMI entitled to recover for the loss of its Hilltop operations? Yes. TMI was entitled to compensation for the loss of all of its operations at Hilltop. For property insurance, an insurable interest must exist at the time that the _____ _____. TMI's Marketplace policy included coverage for property that the insured "owned, leased, used, or controlled." At the time of the loss at Hilltop, TMI _____ an insurable interest in the storage and office space that it leased in the buildings, as well as the common areas that it maintained and on which its income depended.

2. Marco applied to Commercial Insurance Co. for a policy to cover Hooligan's, Marco's nightclub. The application indicated that the premises had a sprinkler system. Commercial issued a policy that required such a system. One year later, when Hooligan's sustained more than $250,000 in fire damage, Marco filed a claim for payment under the policy. Before paying the claim, Commercial learned that there was no sprinkler system.

   Could Commercial refuse to pay Marco's claim and cancel the policy? Yes. Commercial can refuse to pay the claim and cancel the policy. An insurance company can raise any of the defenses that would be valid in an ordinary action on a contract, as well as others. If an insurance company can show that a policy was procured through _____ or _____, it may have a valid defense for not paying. In the application for insurance, Marco _____ that Hooligan's had a sprinkler system.

UNIT 8

PROPERTY

UNIT CONTENTS

CHAPTER 36 Personal Property and Bailments

CHAPTER 37 Real Property

CHAPTER 38 Landlord and Tenant Law

CHAPTER 39 Wills and Trusts

36 PERSONAL PROPERTY AND BAILMENTS

LEARNING OUTCOMES

The five Learning Outcomes below are designed to help improve your understanding of the chapter. After reading this chapter, you should be able to:

1 Explain the nature of personal property.

2 Identify different types of property ownership.

3 State how ownership of personal property is acquired.

4 Discuss who gets title to lost, mislaid, and abandoned property.

5 Outline the elements of a bailment.

FACING A LEGAL PROBLEM

Cameron has a new flat-screen TV and would like to watch cable broadcasts without paying for them. He lives in an apartment building in which many of the tenants subscribe to Apollo Communications, a local cable service. Cameron carefully splices into a cable line that runs into the other tenants' apartments so that he can connect his set to the line without Apollo's knowledge.

Q Has Cameron committed a theft of personal property?

Property consists of the legally protected rights and interests a person has in anything with an ascertainable value that is subject to ownership. The law defines the right to use property, to sell or dispose of it, and to prevent trespass onto it.

In this chapter, we look at the nature and different types of *personal property*, the methods of acquiring ownership of personal property, and issues relating to mislaid, lost, and abandoned personal property. We also look at *bailments*, in which personal property is temporarily placed in the care of another.

LEARNING OUTCOME 1

Explain the nature of personal property.

personal property
Property that is movable; any property that is not real property.

36–1 THE NATURE OF PERSONAL PROPERTY

Property is divided into two categories. *Real property* consists of the land and everything permanently attached to the land. When structures are permanently attached to the land, then everything attached permanently to the structures is also real property, or realty. All other property is **personal property,** or *personalty*.

Personal property can be tangible or intangible. *Tangible* personal property, such as a flat-screen TV or a car, has physical substance. *Intangible* personal property represents some set of rights and interests but has no real physical existence. Stocks and bonds, patents, and copyrights are intangible personal property.

In a dynamic society, the concept of personal property must expand to take account of new types of ownership rights. Gas, water, and telephone services are considered personal property for the purpose of criminal prosecution when they are stolen or used without authorization.

In addition, federal and state statutes protect against the copying of musical compositions. For example, it is a crime to engage in the illegal downloading of copy-protected digital music files. Similarly, the theft of iPhone app software is a theft of personal property.

36–2 PROPERTY OWNERSHIP— RIGHTS OF POSSESSION

LEARNING OUTCOME 2
Identify different types of property ownership.

Ownership of property—both real and personal property—can be viewed as a bundle of rights, including the right to possess the property and to dispose of it by sale, gift, lease, or other means. The right of ownership in property is often referred to as *title*.

36–2a Fee Simple

A person who holds the entire bundle of rights to property is said to be the owner in **fee simple**. The owner in fee simple is entitled to use, possess, or dispose of the property as he or she chooses during his or her lifetime. On death, the interests in the property passes to his or her heirs. **EXAMPLE 36.1** Emily owns stock in ETC Mobile and Dickson Entertainment. Based on Emily's ownership of ETC stock, she exercises her shareholder's right to vote in an election for the directors. Later, she decides to sell half of her ETC shares and use the proceeds to increase the number of her shares in Dickson. On Emily's death, her interest in the stock of the two companies will pass to her heirs. ◄

fee simple
A form of property ownership entitling the property owner to use, possess, or dispose of the property as he or she chooses during his or her lifetime.

36–2b Concurrent Ownership

Persons who share ownership rights simultaneously in particular property are said to be *concurrent* owners. There are two principal types of *concurrent ownership:* tenancy in common and joint tenancy. A less common type of concurrent ownership exists when owners hold community property.

Tenancy in Common In a **tenancy in common,** each co-owner owns an undivided, fractional interest in the property. The fractional interests do not need to be equal. When one tenant dies, that party's interest passes to his or her heirs.

tenancy in common
Co-ownership of property in which each party owns an undivided interest that passes to his or her heirs at death.

HIGHLIGHTING THE POINT

Rosalind and Vlad own a rare art collection as tenants in common. Each of them owns one-half of the collection. If Rosalind sells her interest to Fred, Fred and Vlad will be co-owners of the art collection as tenants in common.

If, instead, Rosalind dies before selling her interest to Fred, will her heirs become tenants in common with Vlad? Yes. On Rosalind's death, one-half of the art collection will become the property of Rosalind's heirs. They, in turn, will own the property with Vlad as tenants in common.

Joint Tenancy In a **joint tenancy,** each co-owner owns an undivided interest in the property, and a deceased co-owner's interest passes to the surviving co-owner or co-owners. This "right of survivorship" is the main feature distinguishing a joint tenancy from a tenancy in common.

joint tenancy
Co-ownership of property in which each party owns an undivided portion of the property. On the death of one of the joint tenants, his or her interest automatically passes to the others.

A joint tenancy can be terminated at any time by gift or by sale before a joint tenant's death. If termination occurs, the co-owners become tenants in common. If no termination occurs, then on the death of a joint tenant, his or her interest transfers to the remaining joint tenants, not to the heirs of the deceased joint tenant.

In most states, it is presumed that a tenancy is a tenancy in common unless it is clear that the parties intended to establish a joint tenancy. In those states, specific language is necessary to create a joint tenancy.

EXAMPLE 36.2 Jean and Perry are songwriters. They sign a contract that provides they own the rights to their songs as joint tenants. The contract clearly expresses the intent to create a joint tenancy. It states, "Jean and Perry as joint tenants with rights of survivorship." Jean and Perry each have a spouse, but if Jean dies, her interest in the songs automatically passes to Perry rather than to her spouse.◄

Community Property In a few states, property can be held by a married couple as **community property.** Each spouse technically owns an undivided one-half interest in the property. This type of ownership applies to most property acquired by the husband or the wife during the course of their marriage. It does not apply to most property acquired before the marriage or to property acquired by gift or inheritance during the marriage. After divorce, community property is divided equally in some states and according to the discretion of a court in other states.

community property
A form of concurrent ownership in which each spouse owns an undivided one-half interest in most property acquired during the marriage.

36–3 ACQUIRING OWNERSHIP OF PERSONAL PROPERTY

The most common way to acquire personal property is to purchase it. **EXAMPLE 36.3** Snap Tech owns a number of patents in digital cameras and the software that operates them. Rad App Corporation buys Snap Tech and thereby acquires the patents. Tony, a consumer, buys a Snap Tech–brand camera and so acquires the camera.◄ Often, personal property is acquired by will or inheritance. Here, we look at additional ways to acquire ownership of personal property, including acquisition by possession, production, gift, accession, and confusion.

LEARNING OUTCOME 3

State how ownership of personal property is acquired.

36–3a Possession

Sometimes, a person can become the owner of personal property merely by possessing it. An interesting example of acquiring ownership by possession is the capture of wild animals. Wild animals belong to no one in their natural state, and the first person to take possession of a wild animal normally owns it. The killing of a wild animal amounts to assuming ownership of it.

There are two exceptions to this basic rule. First, any wild animals captured by a trespasser are the property of the landowner, not the trespasser. Second, if wild animals are captured or killed in violation of wild game statutes, the state, and not the capturer, obtains title to the animals.

Those who find lost or abandoned property can also acquire ownership rights through mere possession of the property, as discussed later in this chapter.

36–3b Production

Production—the fruits of labor—is another means of acquiring ownership of personal property. Writers, inventors, and manufacturers all produce personal property and thereby acquire title to it. (In some situations, however, the producer does not own what is produced. For instance, a researcher hired by a company to develop a new product may not own the product developed.)

36–3c Gifts

A **gift** is another fairly common means of both acquiring and transferring ownership of real and personal property. A gift is essentially a voluntary transfer of property ownership. It is not supported by legally sufficient consideration (the value—such as money—given in return for a promise) because the very essence of a gift is transferring without consideration.

In addition, a gift must be transferred or delivered in the present rather than in the future. In other words, a *promise* to make a gift tomorrow or next year is *not* a gift.

For a gift to be effective, three requirements must be met: (1) donative intent on the part of the *donor* (the one giving the gift), (2) delivery, and (3) acceptance by the *donee* (the one receiving the gift). Until these requirements are met, no effective gift has been made. **EXAMPLE 36.4** Daisy tells Elmore that she is going to give him a Fender Stratocaster electric guitar with a cherry heritage finish on his next birthday. Daisy has made a promise to make a gift. But there is no gift until the guitar is delivered and accepted.◄

Donative Intent There must be evidence of the donor's intent to give the donee the gift. Donative intent is determined from the language of the donor and the surrounding circumstances.

When a gift is challenged in court, the court may look at the relationship between the parties and the size of the gift in relation to the donor's other assets to determine intent. A gift to a mortal enemy is viewed with suspicion. Likewise, when a gift represents a large portion of a person's assets, the courts scrutinize the transaction closely to determine the mental capacity of the donor and the possibility of fraud or extreme duress.

Delivery An effective delivery requires giving up complete control of, and **dominion** over, the subject matter of the gift. *Dominion* refers to ownership rights.

Delivery is obvious in most situations. In some circumstances, however, when the physical object cannot be delivered, a symbolic, or constructive, delivery is sufficient. **Constructive delivery** is a general term for all those acts that the law holds to be equivalent to acts of real delivery. The delivery of intangible property—such as stocks, bonds, insurance policies, contracts, and so on—is always accomplished by symbolic, or constructive, delivery. This is because the documents represent rights and are not, by themselves, the true property.

EXAMPLE 36.5 Geneva wants to make a gift to Harlan of gold coins that she has stored in a safe-deposit box. Of course, she cannot deliver the box itself to Harlan, and she does not want to take the coins out of the bank. Geneva can deliver the key to the box to Harlan and authorize his access to the box and its contents. This is a constructive delivery of the contents of the box.◄

Delivery may be accomplished by means of a third party. If the third party is the agent of the donor, the delivery is effective when the agent delivers the gift to the donee. If the third party is the agent of the donee, then the gift is effectively delivered when the donor delivers the property to the donee's agent.

Acceptance The final requirement of a valid gift is acceptance by the donee. This rarely presents any problems, as most donees readily accept their gifts. The courts generally assume acceptance unless shown otherwise.

---

gift
Any voluntary transfer of property ownership made without consideration, past or present.

dominion
The right to own, use, and possess property.

constructive delivery
An act equivalent to the physical delivery of property that cannot be physically delivered because of difficulty or impossibility.

gift *inter vivos*
A gift made during one's lifetime and not in contemplation of imminent death.

gift *causa mortis*
A gift made in contemplation of imminent death.

Gifts *Inter Vivos* and Gifts *Causa Mortis* A gift made during one's lifetime is a **gift *inter vivos***. A **gift *causa mortis*** (a so-called *deathbed gift*) is made in contemplation of imminent death from a specific cause, such as a particular illness.

To be effective, a gift *causa mortis* must meet the three requirements discussed earlier—donative intent, delivery, and acceptance by the donor. The gift is revocable at any time up to the death of the donor. It does not become absolute until the donor dies from the contemplated cause, and it is automatically revoked if the donor recovers or if the donee dies before the donor.

36–3d Accession

accession
An addition that increases the value of property (such as the addition of a diamond to a ring).

An **accession** occurs when someone adds value to a piece of personal property by supplying either labor or materials. Generally, there is no dispute about who owns the property after accession has occurred, especially when the accession is accomplished with the owner's consent. **EXAMPLE 36.6** Martin buys all the materials necessary to customize his Corvette. He hires Zach, a customizing specialist, to come to his house to perform the work. Martin pays Zach for the value of the labor, obviously retaining title to the property.◄

Bad Faith If accession occurs without the permission of the owner, the courts tend to favor the owner over the improver—the one who improved the property—if the accession took place wrongfully and in bad faith. In addition, many courts deny the wrongdoer any compensation for the value added. **EXAMPLE 36.7** Patti steals a car and puts expensive new tires on it. If Ivan, the rightful owner, later recovers the car, he obviously will not be required to compensate Patti, a car thief, for the value of the new tires.◄

Good Faith If the accession is performed in good faith and the improvement was made due to an honest mistake of judgment, the owner normally still retains title to the property but usually must pay for the improvement. In rare instances, when the improvement greatly increases the value of the property or changes its identity, the court may rule that ownership has passed to the improver. In those rare situations, the improver must compensate the original owner for the value of the property before the accession occurred.

36–3e Confusion

confusion
The mixing together of goods belonging to two or more owners so that the independent goods cannot be identified.

Confusion is defined as the commingling (mixing together) of goods to such an extent that one person's personal property cannot be distinguished from another's. Confusion frequently occurs with *fungible goods,* such as grain and oil, that consist of identical units.

If confusion is caused by a person who wrongfully and willfully mixes goods for the purpose of rendering them indistinguishable, the innocent party acquires title to the whole. If confusion occurs as a result of agreement, an honest mistake, or the act of some third party, the owners share ownership as tenants in common and share any loss in proportion to their shares of ownership of the property. **EXAMPLE 36.8** Five farmers enter into a cooperative arrangement. Each fall, the farmers harvest the same amount of number 2–grade yellow corn and store it in silos that are held by the cooperative. Each farmer thus owns one-fifth of the total corn in the silos. If a fire burns down one of the silos, each farmer will bear one-fifth of the loss.◄

36–4 MISLAID, LOST, AND ABANDONED PROPERTY

If you find another's property, it is important to learn whether the owner mislaid, lost, or abandoned the property. This is because the legal effect differs in each case. We discuss each of these three categories in the next subsections.

LEARNING OUTCOME 4
Discuss who gets title to lost, mislaid, and abandoned property.

36–4a Mislaid Property

Property that has been placed somewhere by the owner voluntarily and then inadvertently forgotten is **mislaid property.** Because it is highly likely that the true owner will return for property that is mislaid, the finder does not obtain title to the goods. Instead, the finder is obligated to return the property to the true owner.

EXAMPLE 36.9 Michelle goes to the theater. While paying for popcorn at the concessions stand, she sets her smartphone on the counter and then leaves it there, where an employee finds it. The smartphone is mislaid property, and the theater owner is entrusted with the duty of taking reasonable care of it—that is, taking the same care as would any reasonable person in similar circumstances. ◄

mislaid property
Property that the owner has voluntarily parted with and then cannot find or recover.

36–4b Lost Property

Lost property is property that is left involuntarily and forgotten. A lost property's finder can claim title to it against the whole world, *except the true owner.* If a third party attempts to take possession of the property from the finder, the third party cannot assert a better title than the finder.

lost property
Property with which the owner has involuntarily parted and then cannot find or recover.

> ### HIGHLIGHTING THE POINT
>
> Karina works in a hotel. On her way home one evening, she finds a piece of gold jewelry in the courtyard of the hotel. Covered with dust and dirt, the piece appears to have been lost. The piece also looks like it has several precious stones in it. Karina takes it to Lawrence Jewelry to have it appraised. While pretending to weigh the jewelry, a Lawrence employee removes several of the stones. When Karina discovers that the stones are missing, she sues Lawrence.
>
> **Will Karina win her lawsuit?** Yes. Karina will win, because she found lost property and holds valid title against everyone except the true owner. Because the property was lost, rather than mislaid, the owner of the hotel is *not* the caretaker of the jewelry. Instead, Karina acquires title good against the whole world (except the true owner).

Conversion of Lost Property If the true owner of the lost property demands that it be returned, the finder must return it. In fact, many states require the finder to make a reasonably diligent search to locate the true owner. When a finder of lost property knows the true owner's identity and fails to return the property to that person, the finder has committed the tort of *conversion.*

Estray Statutes Many states have **estray statutes,** which encourage and facilitate the return of property to its true owner and then reward the finder for honesty

estray statute
A statute defining finders' rights in property when the true owners are unknown.

if the property remains unclaimed. These laws provide an incentive for finders to report their discoveries by making it possible for them, after the passage of a specified period of time, to acquire legal title to the property they found. Generally, the item must be lost property, not merely mislaid property, for estray statutes to apply. Estray statutes usually require the finder or the county clerk to advertise the property in an attempt to help the owner recover what has been lost.

36–4c Abandoned Property

abandoned property
Property that has been discarded by the owner, who has no intention of recovering it.

Property that has been discarded by the true owner, who has no intention of reclaiming title to it, is **abandoned property.** Someone who finds abandoned property acquires title to it, and this title is good against the whole world, *including the original owner.* An owner of lost property who eventually gives up any further attempt to find the lost property is frequently held to have abandoned the property.

EXAMPLE 36.10   Whitney is hiking a section of the Pacific Coast Trail and drops her Garmin GPS watch. She retraces her route and searches for the watch, but she cannot find it. She finally gives up her search and proceeds to her destination thirty miles down the trail. When Max later finds the watch along the trail, he acquires title to it that is good even against Whitney. By completely giving up her search, Whitney abandoned the watch just as effectively as if she had intentionally discarded it.◄

Note that if a person finds abandoned property while trespassing on the property of another, title vests in the owner of the land, not in the finder.

 # 36–5 BAILMENTS

Almost every business is affected by the law of bailments at one time or another (and sometimes even on a daily basis). When individuals deal with bailments, whether they realize it or not, they are subject to the obligations and duties that arise from the bailment relationship.

bailment
An agreement in which the personal property of a bailor is entrusted to a bailee, who is obligated to return the bailed property or dispose of it as directed.

A **bailment** is formed by the delivery of personal property, without transfer of title, by one person (called a **bailor**) to another (called a **bailee**), usually under an agreement for a particular purpose (for example, storage, repair, or transportation). On completion of the purpose, the bailee is obligated to return the bailed property to the bailor or to a third person, or to dispose of it as directed.

bailor
One who entrusts goods to a bailee.

36–5a The Creation of a Bailment

Most bailments are created by agreement, but not necessarily by contract because many bailments do not include all of the elements of a contract.   **EXAMPLE 36.11**   If Anjali loans her mountain bike to a friend, a bailment is created, but there is no contract because there is no consideration.◄ Many commercial bailments, such as the delivery of a suit or dress to the cleaner's for dry cleaning, are based on contract, however.

bailee
One to whom goods are entrusted by a bailor.

36–5b The Elements of a Bailment

Not all transactions involving the delivery of property from one person to another create a bailment. For such a transfer to become a bailment, the following three conditions must be met:

1. The property involved must be personal property.

2. The property must be delivered to the bailee.

3. An agreement for the return or disposal of the property must be made.

LEARNING OUTCOME 5

Outline the elements of a bailment.

Personal Property Requirement A bailment involves only personal property. Neither a person nor real property can be the subject of a bailment. **EXAMPLE 36.12** Grace is traveling to New York on business. When she checks her luggage at the airport, a bailment of her luggage is created when it is transported by the airline. As a passenger, though, Grace is not the subject of a bailment. ◄

Delivery of Possession Possession of the property must be transferred to the bailee in such a way that (1) the bailee is given both exclusive possession of the property and control over it, and (2) the bailee *knowingly* accepts the property. In other words, the bailee must *intend* to exercise control over it. If either of these conditions for effective *delivery of possession* is lacking, there is no bailment relationship.

Physical versus Constructive Delivery Either *physical* or *constructive delivery* will result in the bailee's exclusive possession of and control over the property. As discussed earlier in this chapter, in the context of gifts, constructive delivery is a substitute, or symbolic, delivery. What is delivered to the bailee is not the actual property bailed (such as a car) but something so related to the property (such as the car keys) that the requirement of delivery is satisfied.

Involuntary Bailments In certain unique situations, a bailment is found despite the apparent lack of the requisite elements of control and knowledge. One example of such a situation occurs when the bailee acquires the property accidentally or by mistake—as in finding someone else's lost or mislaid property. A bailment is created even though the bailor did not voluntarily deliver the property to the bailee. Such bailments are called *constructive* or *involuntary bailments*.

EXAMPLE 36.13 Several corporate managers attend an urgent meeting at the law firm of Jacobs & Matheson. One of the managers, Kyle Gustafson, inadvertently leaves his briefcase at the firm at the conclusion of the meeting. In this situation, a court could find that an involuntary bailment was created, even though Gustafson did not voluntarily deliver the briefcase and the law firm did not intentionally accept it. ◄

The Bailment Agreement A bailment agreement can be *express* or *implied*. No written agreement is required for bailments of less than one year—that is, the Statute of Frauds does not apply. Nevertheless, it is a good idea to have one, especially when valuable property is involved.

The bailment agreement expressly or impliedly provides for the return of the bailed property to the bailor or to a third person, or it provides for disposal by the bailee. The agreement presupposes that the bailee will return the identical goods originally given by the bailor.

In certain types of bailments, however, such as bailments of fungible goods, only equivalent property must be returned. **EXAMPLE 36.14** Holman stores his grain (fungible goods) at Central Valley Grange's facilities. At the end of the storage period, Central Valley is not obligated to return the exact same grain that Holman originally stored. As long as Central Valley returns grain of the same type, grade, and quantity, the company has performed its obligation as the bailee. ◄

36–5c The Rights and Duties of the Bailee

Certain rights are implicit in the bailment agreement. Generally, the bailee has the right to take possession of the property, to utilize the property for accomplishing the purpose of the bailment, to receive some form of compensation, and to limit her or his liability for the bailed goods. These rights of the bailee are present (with some limitations) in varying degrees in all bailment transactions.

The bailee has two basic responsibilities: (1) to take appropriate care of the property and (2) to surrender the property to the bailor or dispose of it in accordance with the bailor's instructions at the end of the bailment.

The Duty of Care The bailee must exercise *reasonable care* in preserving the bailed property. What constitutes reasonable care in a bailment situation normally depends on the nature and circumstances of the bailment. Generally speaking, there are three types of bailments, and each calls for a different level of care.

1. A *bailment for the sole benefit of the bailor* exists for the convenience and benefit of the bailor. Basically, the bailee is caring for the bailor's property as a favor. In this type of bailment, the bailee need exercise only a slight degree of care and will be liable only if grossly negligent in caring for the property.

2. A *bailment for the sole benefit of the bailee* exists for the convenience and benefit of the bailee. Typically, this sort of bailment arises when the bailor lends an article to the bailee. Because the bailee is borrowing the item for her or his own benefit, the bailee owes a duty to exercise the utmost care and will be liable for even slight negligence.

3. A *bailment for the mutual benefit of the bailee and the bailor,* the most common type of bailment, involves some form of compensation for storing items or holding property. Here, the bailee must exercise ordinary care, which is the care that a reasonably careful person would use under the circumstances. If the bailee fails to exercise reasonable care, he or she will be liable for ordinary negligence.

Real-World Case Example

Hornbeck Offshore Service engaged R&R Marine, Inc., to repair the ship *Erie Service* at R&R's shipyard on Lake Sabine in Port Arthur, Texas. While repairs were being made, the National Weather Service issued a tropical storm warning for Port Arthur. R&R's personnel left the shipyard without preparing the *Erie Service* for the storm.

During the night, rain and water from Lake Sabine swamped the vessel. R&R's insurer, National Liability & Fire Insurance Company, asked a federal district court to declare that it was not required to pay the salvage cost. Hornbeck filed a claim with the court against R&R. The court issued a judgment in Hornbeck's favor. R&R appealed.

Was R&R negligent in failing to secure the *Erie Service* and to protect the ship from damage by the storm? Yes. In a 2014 case, *National Liability & Fire Insurance Co. v. R&R Marine, Inc.*, the U.S. Court of Appeals for the Fifth Circuit affirmed the lower court's judgment. Hornbeck established a *prima facie* case of negligence. The *Erie Service* was delivered to R&R afloat, R&R had full custody of the vessel, and the ship sank while in R&R's care. The weather conditions in Port Arthur were not of unexpected severity but were those that had been forecast. R&R could point to no act it took to show that it had exercised ordinary care. The insurance company wasn't liable.

Exhibit 36.1 illustrates these concepts.

The Duty to Return Bailed Property At the end of the bailment, the bailee normally must hand over the original property to either the bailor or someone the bailor

EXHIBIT 36.1   Degree of Care Required of a Bailee

Bailment for the Sole Benefit of the Bailor	Mutual-Benefit Bailment	Bailment for the Sole Benefit of the Bailee
DEGREE OF CARE →		
SLIGHT	REASONABLE	GREAT

designates, or must otherwise dispose of it as directed. This is usually a *contractual* duty arising from the bailment agreement. Failure to give up possession at the time the bailment ends is a breach of contract and could result in the tort of conversion or an action based on bailee negligence.

If the bailed property has been lost or is returned damaged, a court will presume that the bailee was negligent. The bailee's obligation is excused, however, if the property was destroyed, lost, or stolen through no fault of the bailee (or claimed by a third party with a superior claim).

ANSWERING THE LEGAL PROBLEM

In the legal problem set out at the beginning of this chapter, Cameron has a new flat-screen TV and wants to watch cable programs without paying for them. He lives in an apartment building in which many of the tenants subscribe to Apollo Communications, a local cable service. Cameron splices into a cable line that runs into the other tenants' apartments so that he can connect his TV without Apollo's knowledge.

A **Is this a theft of personal property?** Yes. Although Apollo and Cameron's neighbors may not know what he has done, cable services are personal property for the purpose of criminal prosecution when they are used without permission.

TERMS AND CONCEPTS FOR REVIEW

abandoned property 500

accession 498

bailee 500

bailment 500

bailor 500

community property 496

confusion 498

constructive delivery 497

dominion 497

estray statutes 499

fee simple 495

gift 497

gift *causa mortis* 498

gift *inter vivos* 498

joint tenancy 495

lost property 499

mislaid property 499

personal property 494

tenancy in common 495

CHAPTER SUMMARY—PERSONAL PROPERTY AND BAILMENTS

LEARNING OUTCOME	
1	**Explain the nature of personal property.** Personal property (personalty) includes all property not classified as real property (realty). Personal property can be tangible (such as a car) or intangible (such as stocks or bonds).
2	**Identify different types of property ownership.** *Fee simple* exists when an individual has the right to use, possess, or dispose of the property as he or she chooses during his or her lifetime and to pass on the property to his or her heirs at death. *Concurrent ownership* includes the following: (1) *Tenancy in common*—Co-ownership in which two or more persons own an undivided interest in property. On one tenant's death, that tenant's property interest passes to his or her heirs (2) *Joint tenancy*—Co-ownership in which two or more persons own an undivided interest in property. On the death of a joint tenant, that tenant's property interest transfers to the remaining tenant or tenants, not to the heirs of the deceased. (3) *Community property*—A form of co-ownership between a husband and wife in which each spouse technically owns an undivided one-half interest in property acquired during the marriage. This type of ownership exists in only some states.
3	**State how ownership of personal property is acquired.** In addition to purchase and inheritance, property can be acquired in the following ways: (1) *Possession*—Ownership can be acquired by possession if no other person has ownership title to the property (for example, by capturing wild animals or finding abandoned property). (2) *Production*—Any item produced by an individual (with minor exceptions) becomes the property of that individual. (3) *Gift*—A gift is a voluntary transfer of property. It requires evidence of *intent* to make a gift, *delivery* (physical or constructive) of the gift to the donee or the donee's agent, and *acceptance* by the donee or the donee's agent. (4) *Accession*—When someone adds value to an item of personal property through the use of labor or materials, the original owner of the property generally retains ownership. Good faith accessions that substantially increase the property's value or change the identity of the property may, on rare occasions, cause title to pass to the improver. (5) *Confusion*—If a person wrongfully and willfully commingles fungible goods with those of another in order to render them indistinguishable, the innocent party acquires title to the whole. Otherwise, the owners become tenants in common of the commingled goods.
4	**Discuss who gets title to lost, mislaid, and abandoned property.** *Mislaid property* is property that is placed somewhere voluntarily by the owner and then inadvertently forgotten. A finder of mislaid property does not acquire title to the goods, and the owner of the place where the property was mislaid becomes a caretaker of the mislaid property. *Lost property* is property that is involuntarily left and forgotten. A finder of lost property can claim title to the property against the whole world *except the true owner. Abandoned property* is property that has been discarded by the true owner, who has no intention of claiming title to the property in the future. A finder of abandoned property can claim title to it against the whole world, *including the original owner.*
5	**Outline the elements of a bailment.** The elements of a bailment are as follows: (1) *Personal property*—Bailments involve only personal property. (2) *Delivery of possession*—The bailee (the one receiving the property) must be given exclusive possession and control over the property. In a voluntary bailment, the bailee must knowingly accept the personal property. (3) *Bailment agreement*—The agreement provides for the return of the bailed property to the bailor or a third party, or for the disposal of the bailed property by the bailee.

ISSUE SPOTTERS

Check your answers to the *Issue Spotters* against the answers provided in Appendix C at the end of this text.

1. Dave and Paul share ownership rights in a multimedia computer. When they acquired the computer, they agreed in writing that if one dies, the other inherits his interest. Are Dave and Paul tenants in common or joint tenants? Explain. (See *Property Ownership—Rights of Possession.*)

2. Bob leaves his clothes with Corner Dry Cleaners to be cleaned. When the clothes are returned, some are missing, and others are greasy and smell bad. Is Corner liable? Why or why not? (See *Bailments.*)

USING BUSINESS LAW

36–1. Found Property. Bill Heise is a janitor for the First Mercantile Department Store. While walking to work, Bill finds an expensive watch lying on the curb. Bill gives the watch to his son, Otto. Two weeks later, Martin Avery, the true owner of the watch, discovers that Bill found the watch and demands that Otto return it. Explain who is entitled to the watch and why. (See *Mislaid, Lost, and Abandoned Property.*)

36–2. Requirements of a Bailment. Calvin is an executive on a business trip to the West Coast. He has driven his car on this trip and checks into the Hotel Ritz. The hotel has a guarded underground parking lot. Calvin gives his car keys to the parking-lot attendant but fails to notify the attendant that his wife's $10,000 diamond necklace is in a box in the trunk. The next day, on checking out, he discovers that his car has been stolen. Calvin wants to hold the hotel liable for both the car and the necklace. Discuss the probable success of his claim. (See *Bailments.*)

REAL-WORLD CASE PROBLEMS

36–3. Gifts. Jennifer Koerner adopted a dog—the Stig—from the Anti-Cruelty Society in Chicago, Illinois, for $95. Koerner wrote a poem and presented it to Kent Nielsen, her live-in boyfriend. In the poem, she expressed her intent to give the Stig to him as a gift. While Koerner and Nielsen lived together, they were both involved in the Stig's day-to-day care. They ended their relationship a year later, and Nielsen agreed to leave their shared residence. Can Nielsen take the Stig with him, or is Koerner the Stig's rightful owner? Explain. [*Koerner v. Nielsen*, 8 N.E.3d 161 (Ill.App. 1 Dist. 2014)] (See *Acquiring Ownership of Personal Property.*)

36–4. Bailment Obligation. Bob Moreland left his plane at Don Gray's aircraft repair shop to be painted. Disappointed by the quality of the paint job, Moreland refused to pay Gray and flew the plane to another shop to have the work redone. Gray sued to collect, contending that Moreland had no right to take the plane to another shop without giving

Gray a chance to fix any defects. Gray further argued that by taking the plane, Moreland had accepted Gray's work. Moreland counterclaimed for his expenses. Which party should be awarded damages and why? [*Gray v. Moreland*, 2010 Ark.App. 207 (2010)] (See *Bailments.*)

36–5. Gifts. John Wasniewski opened a brokerage account with Quick and Reilly, Inc., in his son James's name. Twelve years later, when the balance was $52,085, the account was closed, and the funds were transferred to an account in John's name alone. Only after the transfer, when James was notified that the account had been closed, did he learn of its existence. He filed a suit against Quick and Reilly, arguing that John's opening of the account had constituted a gift. Is James entitled to the amount that was in the account on its closing? Explain. [*Wasniewski v. Quick and Reilly, Inc.*, 292 Conn. 98, 971 A.2d 8 (2009)] (See *Acquiring Ownership of Personal Property.*)

ETHICAL QUESTIONS

36–6. The Bailment Agreement. What standard of care over bailed property should be expected of bailees? (See *Bailments.*)

Chapter 36—Work Set

TRUE-FALSE QUESTIONS

_____ 1. Generally, those who produce personal property have title to it.

_____ 2. If goods are confused due to a wrongful act and the innocent party cannot prove what percentage is his or hers, all of the goods belong to the wrongdoer.

_____ 3. To constitute a gift, a voluntary transfer of property must be supported by consideration.

_____ 4. One who finds abandoned property acquires good title to the property against the whole world, except the true owner.

_____ 5. Co-ownership in which each of two or more persons owns an undivided, fractional interest in the property is a tenancy in common.

_____ 6. Gas, water, and other utility services are considered personal property.

_____ 7. If an object cannot be physically delivered, it cannot be a gift.

_____ 8. Any delivery of personal property from one person to another creates a bailment.

MULTIPLE-CHOICE QUESTIONS

_____ 1. Eve designs an Internet home page to advertise her services as a designer of home pages. Tim hires her to design a home page for his business. Eve has title to

a. her home page only.
b. Tim's home page only.
c. her home page, Tim's home page, and any other home page she creates.
d. none of the above.

_____ 2. Dan sells his multimedia system to Paul and Amy. Each takes a one-half interest in it. Paul and Amy are not married. Nothing is said about the form of the buyers' ownership. They own the system as

a. tenants in common.
b. joint tenants.
c. community property.
d. a and b.

_____ 3. Nancy sells her boat to Chris and Nora. Chris and Nora are not married. The contract of sale says that each of the buyers has a right of survivorship in the boat. Chris and Nora own the boat as

a. tenants in common.
b. joint tenants.
c. community property.
d. b and c.

_____ 4. Meg wants to give Lori a pair of diamond earrings that Meg has in her safe-deposit box at First National Bank. Meg gives Lori the key to the box and tells her to go to the bank and take the earrings from the box. Lori does so. Two days later, Meg dies. To whom do the earrings belong?

a. Lori.
b. Meg's heirs.
c. First National Bank.
d. The state government.

_____ 5. Carol goes to Don's Salon for a haircut. Behind a plant on a table in the waiting area, Carol finds a wallet containing $5,000. The party entitled to possession of the wallet is

a. Carol.
b. Don.
c. the owner of the building in which the salon is located.
d. the state.

_____ 6. Jane, Mark, and Guy are farmers who store their grain in three silos. Jane contributes half of the grain, Mark a third, and Guy a sixth. A tornado hits two of the silos and scatters the grain. If each farmer can prove how much he or she deposited in the silos, how much of what is left belongs to each?

a. Jane owns half, Mark a third, and Guy a sixth.
b. Because only a third is left, Mark owns it all.
c. Because Jane and Mark lost the most, they split what is left equally.
d. Jane, Mark, and Guy share what is left equally.

_____ 7. Doug wants to give Kim a laptop computer that is stored in a locker at the airport. Doug gives Kim the key to the locker and tells her to take the laptop from the locker. Kim says that she doesn't want the computer and leaves the key on Doug's desk. The next day, Doug dies. Who gets the computer?

a. Kim.
b. Doug's heirs.
c. The airport.
d. The state government.

_____ 8. Eve parks her car in an unattended lot behind Bob's store, which is closed. Eve locks the car and takes the keys. This is _not_ a bailment, because

a. no money is involved.
b. no personal property is involved.
c. there is no transfer of possession.
d. neither party signed a contract.

ANSWERING MORE LEGAL PROBLEMS

1. Hobie and Colleen designed and developed a smart phone app called Do It. Do It is a game in which players cooperate rather than compete to complete a task, such as draw a picture, play a tune, or score a point. Documents evidence each party's investment, ownership, and share of profits and losses in the app. In the documents, Hobie and Colleen are referred to as "joint owners" and "tenants."

   Is the ownership interest of each party a tenancy in common or a joint tenancy? The ownership interest of each party is a _____ _____ _____. With this type of co-ownership, each of two or more persons owns an undivided, fractional interest in the property, and on one tenant's death that interest passes to his or her heirs. In contrast, with a _____ _____, each of two or more persons owns an undivided interest, and a deceased owner's interest passes to the surviving co-owner or co-owners. In most states, it is presumed that a tenancy is a _____ _____ _____ unless it is clear that the parties intended to establish a _____ _____. Under that rule, Hobie and Colleen did not state or otherwise make clear that they intended to share the ownership of their business in a _____ _____.

2. On learning that Sébastien planned to travel abroad, Roslyn asked him to deliver $25,000 in cash to her family in Mexico. During a customs inspection at the border, Sébastien told the customs inspector that he carried less than $10,000. The officer discovered the actual amount of cash that Sébastien was carrying, seized it, and arrested Sébastien. Roslyn asked the government to return what she claimed was her money, arguing that the arrangement with Sébastien was a bailment and that she still held title to the cash.

   Is Roslyn entitled to the return of the money? Yes. A bailment is formed by the delivery of personal property, without transfer of _____, by one person (the bailor) to another (the bailee), usually under an agreement for a particular purpose. On completion of the purpose, the bailee is obligated to deliver the property to the bailor or a third person, or to dispose of it as directed. Here, Roslyn delivered the cash to Sébastien for the purpose of delivering it to her family in Mexico. She did not transfer _____ to the money to Sébastien. Thus, she had the right to assert her _____ to it against any person, including the government.

REAL PROPERTY

37

FACING A LEGAL PROBLEM

Rosa and Santiago are neighbors living in rural northern California. On her property, Rosa plants grapes and begins to operate a vineyard and winery. A few years later, Santiago, who operates a small gravel pit on his land, wants to enlarge his business. The expanded excavation will throw more dust into the air, and large trucks and other equipment will come and go from Santiago's property more often. The increased dust and vibrations will harm Rosa's agricultural operation.

Q Can Santiago use his property as he sees fit, regardless of the effect on his neighbor's business?

LEARNING OUTCOMES

The five Learning Outcomes below are designed to help improve your understanding of the chapter. After reading this chapter, you should be able to:

❶ Discuss the nature of real property.

❷ Identify the most common types of real property ownership.

❸ Explain how the ownership of real property can be transferred.

❹ List the elements for acquiring real property by adverse possession.

❺ Describe the government's right of eminent domain.

From earliest times, property has provided a means for survival. Primitive peoples lived off the fruits of the land, eating the vegetation and wildlife. Later, as the wildlife was domesticated and the vegetation cultivated, property provided pasturage and farmland. Throughout history, property has continued to be an indicator of family wealth and social position. Indeed, the protection of people's right to their property became, and remains, one of their most important rights.

In this chapter, we look at real property and the various ways in which real property can be owned. We also examine how ownership rights in real property are transferred from one person to another.

37–1 THE NATURE OF REAL PROPERTY

Personal property generally is movable. In contrast, *real property*—also called *real estate* or *realty*—normally is immovable. **Real property** consists of land and the buildings, plants, and trees that it contains. It also includes subsurface and air rights. Personal property that has become permanently attached to real property (such as a mobile home that is connected to utilities and otherwise anchored to the land) is also considered part of the land.

real property
Land and everything attached to it, such as trees and buildings.

LEARNING OUTCOME 1
Discuss the nature of real property.

37–1a Land

Land includes the soil on the surface of the earth and the natural or artificial structures that are attached to the land. It further includes all the waters contained on or under the surface and much, but not necessarily all, of the airspace above it. The exterior boundaries of land extend straight down to the center of the earth and straight up to the sky (subject to certain qualifications).

37–1b Airspace Rights and Subsurface Rights

The owner of real property has relatively exclusive rights to the airspace above the land, as well as to the soil and minerals underneath it. Significant limits on air or subsurface rights normally must be indicated on the deed or other document transferring title to the land.

Airspace Rights Early cases involving airspace rights dealt with matters such as whether a telephone wire could be run across a person's property when the wire did not touch the property and whether a bullet shot over a person's land constituted trespass.

Today, airspace-rights cases involve the right of commercial and private planes to fly over property, as well as the right of individuals and governments to seed clouds and produce artificial rain. Flights over private land normally do not violate the property owners' rights unless the flights are low and frequent, causing a direct interference with the enjoyment and the use of the land.

Subsurface Rights Subsurface rights can be extremely valuable, as they include the ownership of minerals and, in most states, oil and natural gas. In many states, the owner of the surface of a parcel of land is not necessarily the owner of the subsurface. Hence, the land ownership can be separated. When the ownership is separated into surface and subsurface rights, each owner can pass title to what he or she owns without the consent of the other.

In some cases, conflicts arise between a surface owner's use and the subsurface owner's need to extract minerals, oil, or natural gas. An owner of subsurface rights has a right to go onto the surface of the land to, for example, find and remove minerals. The owner of the surface, however, has a right to have the land maintained in its natural condition. The subsurface owner cannot excavate in a way that causes the surface to collapse. In many states, a subsurface owner who excavates is also responsible for any damage that the excavation causes to buildings on the surface. State statutes typically provide exact guidelines as to the requirements for excavations.

37–1c Plant Life and Vegetation

Plant life, both natural and cultivated, is also considered real property. In many instances, natural vegetation, such as trees, adds greatly to the value of realty. When a parcel of land is sold and the land has growing crops on it, the sale includes the crops, unless otherwise specified in the sales contract. When crops are sold by themselves, however, they are considered personal property. Consequently, the sale of crops is a sale of goods. It is governed by the Uniform Commercial Code rather than by real property law.

37–1d Fixtures

Certain personal property can become so closely associated with the real property to which it is attached that the law views it as real property. Such property is known as a **fixture**—a thing *affixed* to realty. A thing is affixed to realty when it is attached to the realty by roots, embedded in it, or permanently attached by means of cement, plaster, bolts, nails, or screws.

In addition, the fixture can be physically attached to real property or attached to another fixture. It can even be an item, such as a statue, which is not physically attached to the land in any way. The most important factor in determining whether an item is a fixture is the *intent* of the owners, however.

Within Land Sales Fixtures are included in the sale of land if the sales contract does not provide otherwise. The sale of a house includes the land and the house and garage on it, as well as the built-in cabinets, plumbing, and windows. Because

fixture
An item of personal property that is attached to real property in such a way that it takes on the characteristics of real property and becomes part of that real property.

these are permanently affixed to the property, they are considered to be a part of it. Unless otherwise agreed, however, the curtains and throw rugs are not included. Items such as drapes and window-unit air conditioners are difficult to classify. Thus, a contract for the sale of a house or commercial realty should indicate which items of this sort are included in the sale.

Fixture versus Personal Property Sometimes, a question arises as to whether an item is a fixture or whether it is personal property. Generally, to determine whether an item is a fixture, a court examines the intention of the party who placed the object on the real property. If the facts indicate that the person intended the item to be a fixture, then it is normally considered a fixture. **EXAMPLE 37.1** Julie and Mark DeBolt are selling their home. When potential buyers come to visit the property, they often ask if the unique birdbath in the front yard is included in the sale. Because the birdbath is not attached to the ground and is a family heirloom, it is not a fixture nor is it intended to be part of the home sale. The tile and wall-to-wall carpeting in the house, however, are intended as fixtures because they are permanently attached to the floor. ◄

37–2 Ownership Interest

Ownership of property is an abstract concept that cannot exist independently of the legal system. No one can actually possess or *hold* a piece of land, the air above, the earth below, and all the water contained on it. Instead, the legal system recognizes certain rights and duties that constitute ownership interests in real property.

Property ownership is often viewed as a bundle of rights. One who possesses the entire bundle of rights is said to hold the property in *fee simple*. When some of the rights in the bundle are transferred to another person, the effect is to limit the ownership rights of both the one transferring the rights and the one receiving them.

We look first at ownership rights held in fee simple. Then we examine how these rights can be limited through certain types of real property transfers.

LEARNING OUTCOME 2
Identify the most common types of real property ownership.

37–2a Ownership in Fee Simple

The most common type of property ownership today is the fee simple. Generally, the term *fee simple ownership* designates a **fee simple absolute,** in which the owner has the greatest aggregation of rights, privileges, and power possible. The fee simple is owned absolutely by a person and his or her heirs and is assigned forever without limitation or condition.

fee simple absolute
An estate or interest in land with no time, disposition, or descendibility limitations.

Rights of Owner The rights that accompany a fee simple include the right to use the land for whatever purpose the owner sees fit. Of course, certain laws, including applicable zoning, noise, and environmental laws, may limit the owner's ability to use the property in certain ways. A person cannot use his or her property in a manner that unreasonably interferes with others' right to use or enjoy their own property.

HIGHLIGHTING THE POINT

An area is zoned as a residential district with small businesses permitted so long as they do not adversely affect the character of the neighborhood. Within the district, Harmony Bank owns property in fee simple on which it wants to build and open a

(Continued)

branch office. The bank shows the local zoning board that the office, parking lot, and landscaping will conform to the style of the surrounding properties.

Can Harmony Bank use its land in a residential zone to operate a branch office? Most likely, yes. A fee simple owner can use his or her property for whatever purpose the owner sees fit. Zoning laws can restrict an owner's ability to use property in certain ways, however. In this situation, the law permits a different use if the property owner shows that it will not harm the immediate neighborhood. The bank shows that its desired use will conform to the style of the surrounding properties.

Duration A fee simple is potentially infinite in duration. The owner can dispose of it by deed or by will (by selling or giving it away). When there is no will, the fee simple passes to the owner's legal heirs. The owner of a fee simple absolute also has the rights of *exclusive possession* and use of the property.

Fee Simple Defeasible Ownership in fee simple may become limited when the property is transferred to another *conditionally*. When this occurs, the fee simple is known as a **fee simple defeasible** (*defeasible* means "capable of being terminated"). The original owner retains a *partial* ownership interest. If the specified condition occurs, the land reverts, or returns, to the original owner. If the original owner is not living at the time, the land passes to his or her heirs.

fee simple defeasible
An estate that can be taken away by the grantor on the occurrence or nonoccurrence of a specified event.

HIGHLIGHTING THE POINT

Avril conveys (transfers) a plot of land "to Rocio Lopez and her heirs as long as the land is used for charitable purposes." For thirty years, Rocio uses the land to generate income that she donates to various charities. After both Avril and Rocio die, however, Rocio's son Kevin begins to keep the income from the property for himself.

Now that the property is no longer being used for "charitable purposes," does ownership of it return to Avril's heirs? Yes. The original conveyance (transfer) of the land creates a fee simple defeasible, because ownership of the property is conditioned on its being used for charitable purposes. Avril retains a partial ownership interest. If the condition does not occur (if the land is not used for charitable purposes), then the land reverts to her. Because Avril is not living at the time the land use changes, the land passes to her heirs.

37–2b Life Estates

life estate
An interest in land that exists only for the duration of the life of some person.

A **life estate** is an estate that lasts for the life of a specified individual. For instance, a conveyance "to Alvin Mueller for his life" creates a life estate. The rights of the holder of a life estate, called a *life tenant*, cease to exist on the life tenant's death.

The life tenant has the right to use the land, provided that he or she does not use the land in a manner that would adversely affect its value. **EXAMPLE 37.2** Julius, who is a life tenant, can use the land to harvest crops. If mines and oil wells are already on the land, Julius can extract minerals and oil from it, although he cannot further exploit the land by creating new wells or mines. ◄

The life tenant has the right to mortgage the life estate and create leases and other interests. A mortgage or other interest, however, cannot extend beyond the life of the tenant. Also, with few exceptions, the owner of a life estate has an exclusive right to possession during his or her life.

Along with these rights, the life tenant also has some duties—to keep the property in repair and to pay property taxes. In short, the owner of the life estate has the same rights as a fee simple owner except that the life tenant must do the following:

- Maintain the value of the property during his or her tenancy, less the decrease in value resulting from normal use of the property.

- Not sell the property or pass it to his or her heirs.

37–2c Nonpossessory Interests

Some interests in land do not include any rights to possess the property. These interests are therefore known as *nonpossessory interests*. They include easements, profits, and licenses. Easements and profits are similar, and the same rules apply to both.

Easements and Profits An **easement** is the right of a person to make limited use of another person's real property without taking anything from the property. For example, an easement can be the right to walk across a neighbor's property. In contrast, a **profit** is the right to go onto land owned by another and take away some part of the land itself or some product of the land. **EXAMPLE 37.3** Akmed owns Sandy View. Akmed gives Kathy the right to go there to remove all the sand and gravel that she needs for her cement business. Kathy has a profit. ◄

Most easements and profits are created by an express grant in a contract, a deed, or a will.

easement
A nonpossessory right to use another's property.

profit
The right to enter onto and remove things from the property of another (for example, the right to enter onto a person's land and remove sand).

Real-World Case Example

Walnut Bowls, Inc., owned land in Lebanon, Missouri. Its deed expressly reserved an easement to an adjacent farm owned by James and Linda Baker, but it did not fix a precise location. On learning of the easement, a potential buyer of Walnut's property refused to go through with the sale. Walnut then put steel cables across its driveway entrances, installed a lock and chain on an access gate, and bolted a "No Trespassing" sign facing the Bakers' property. The Bakers filed a suit in a Missouri state court to determine the location of the easement. Citing the lack of an express location, the court held that there was no easement. The Bakers appealed.

Did the Bakers have an easement despite the lack of an express location? Yes. In a 2014 case, *Baker v. Walnut Bowls, Inc.*, a state intermediate appellate court reversed the judgment of the lower court. If a grant or other agreement does not precisely fix an easement's location, "it is the trial court's obligation to fix the location of the easement so as to provide the easement holder with convenient, reasonable and accessible use."

Licenses Like an easement, a **license** involves the right of a person to come onto another person's land. Unlike an easement, however, a license is a personal privilege that arises from the consent of the owner of the land and that can be withdrawn or recalled by the owner.

license
In real property law, a revocable privilege to enter onto another's land.

Carlotta buys a ticket to attend a movie at a Cineplex Sixteen theater. When she tries to enter the theater, Glenn, the manager, refuses to admit Carlotta because she is not wearing any shoes. Carlotta argues that she has a ticket, which guarantees her the same right as an owner to come onto the property. Glenn explains that a ticket is a right that he, as the representative of the owner, can take back.

Is Glenn correct? Yes. A movie ticket is only a license, not a conveyance of an interest in property. A ticket holder has no right to force his or her way into a theater.

37–3 TRANSFER OF OWNERSHIP

LEARNING OUTCOME 3

Explain how the ownership of real property can be transferred.

Ownership of real property can pass from one person to another in a number of ways. Commonly, ownership interests in land are transferred by sale. In that case, the terms of the transfer are specified in a real estate sales contract. We look here at some of the ways in which ownership rights in real property can be transferred.

37–3a Deeds

When real property is sold or transferred as a gift, title to the property is conveyed by means of a **deed**—the instrument of conveyance of real property. A valid deed must contain the following elements:

deed
A document by which title to property is passed.

1. The names of the buyer (*grantee*) and seller (*grantor*).
2. Words indicating an intent to convey (transfer) the property (for example, "I hereby bargain, sell, grant, or give").
3. A legally sufficient description of the land.
4. The grantor's and usually the spouse's signature.
5. Delivery of the deed.

Warranty Deeds Different types of deeds provide different degrees of protection against defects of title. A defect of title exists, for example, if an undisclosed third person has an ownership interest in the property. A **warranty deed** contains the most covenants, or promises, of title and thus provides the greatest protection for the buyer, or grantee. In most states, special language is required to create a warranty. Generally, a warranty deed must include a written promise to protect the buyer against all claims of ownership of the property.

warranty deed
A deed under which the grantor provides a number of guarantees to the grantee concerning title.

Warranty deeds also commonly include the **covenant of quiet enjoyment**. This covenant guarantees that the buyer will not be disturbed in his or her possession of the land by the seller or any third persons.

covenant of quiet enjoyment
A promise by the grantor of real property that the grantee will not be disturbed in his or her possession of the property by the grantor or anyone having a lien against the property or superior title to it.

Julio sells a two-acre lot and office building by warranty deed to the Lynn Company. Subsequently, Perkins shows that he, not Julio, actually owns the property and proceeds to evict the business. The Lynn Company sues Julio on the ground that he has breached the covenant of quiet enjoyment.

Will the Lynn Company succeed in its suit? Yes. The covenant of quiet enjoyment has been breached. Thus, the Lynn Company can recover the purchase price of the lot and building, plus any other damages incurred as a result of the eviction.

Quitclaim Deeds A **quitclaim deed** offers the least amount of protection against defects in the title. Basically, a quitclaim deed conveys to the grantee whatever interest the grantor had. Therefore, if the grantor had no interest, then the grantee receives no interest. Quitclaim deeds are often used when the seller, or grantor, is uncertain as to the extent of his or her rights in the property.

quitclaim deed
A deed intended to pass any title, interest, or claim that the grantor may have in the premises but not professing that such title is valid and not containing any warranty.

37–3b Will or Inheritance

Property that is transferred on an owner's death is passed either by will or by state inheritance laws. If the owner of land dies with a will, the property that the owner had prior to death passes in accordance with the terms of the will. If the owner dies without a will, state inheritance statutes prescribe how and to whom the property will pass.

37–3c Adverse Possession

Adverse possession is a means of obtaining title to land without delivery of a deed. Essentially, when one person possesses the property of another for a certain statutory period of time (three to thirty years, depending on state law, with ten years being most common), that person, called the *adverse possessor,* acquires title to the land and cannot be removed from it by the original owner. The adverse possessor is vested with title to the property, just as if there had been a conveyance by deed.

adverse possession
The acquisition of title to real property by occupying it openly, without the consent of the owner, for a period of time specified by state statutes.

LEARNING OUTCOME 4

List the elements for acquiring real property by adverse possession.

For property to be held adversely, four elements must be satisfied:

1. Possession must be *actual and exclusive*—that is, the possessor must take sole physical occupancy of the property.
2. The possession must be *open, visible, and notorious*—that is, it must be so conspicuous that the owner can be presumed to know of it—not secret or clandestine. The possessor must occupy the land for all the world to see.
3. Possession must be *continuous and peaceable for the required period of time.* The possessor must not have been interrupted in the occupancy by the true owner or by the courts.
4. Possession must be *hostile and adverse.* In other words, the possessor must claim the property as against the whole world. He or she cannot be living on the property with the permission of the owner.

HIGHLIGHTING THE POINT

Katya and Leopold own adjacent commercial buildings in which they operate different businesses—Katya's Culinary Arts, a cooking school, and Leopold's Coast-to-Coast Shipping, a truck and transport dispatch service. Katya believes that she owns the parking lot behind the buildings. For more than thirty years, she has paid taxes on the lot, posted signs claiming its exclusive use for her students, and towed away vehicles that did not belong to those students. Leopold has always believed that he owns the lot, however, and claims he has never expressly consented to Katya's use of the parking lot. Finally, Leopold challenges Katya's possession of the parking lot.

(Continued)

> **Does Katya own the parking lot by adverse possession?** Yes. Katya has used the lot exclusively for more than thirty years. The use has been open, visible, and conspicuous. The possession has been against the whole world and without Leopold's permission.

37–3d Eminent Domain

Even ownership in fee simple absolute is limited by a superior ownership. The government has an ultimate ownership right in all land. This right, known as **eminent domain,** is sometimes referred to as the condemnation power of the government to take land for public use. It gives a right to the government to acquire possession of real property in the manner directed by the U.S. Constitution and the laws of the state whenever the public interest requires it. Property may be taken only for public use. Note, though, that "public use" may include use for economic development involving private developers, as discussed in this chapter's *Linking Business Law to Your Career* feature.

The Taking When the government takes land owned by a private party for public use, it is referred to as a **taking.** The government must compensate the private party. Under the so-called takings clause of the Fifth Amendment to the U.S. Constitution, private property may not be taken for public use without "just compensation."

EXAMPLE 37.4 Bosque Systems proposes to build a liquefied natural gas pipeline across the property of more than two hundred landowners in Franklin County, Iowa. Some property owners consent to this use and accept Bosque's offer of compensation. Others object to this use and refuse the firm's offer. Bosque's use of the owners' land to lay its pipeline is construed as a public use. Under the Fifth Amendment, the government can "take" the land, provided the Franklin County property owners are justly compensated for the taking.◄

Condemnation The power of eminent domain generally is invoked through condemnation proceedings. For instance, when a new public highway is to be built, the government decides where to build it and how much land to condemn. After the government determines that a particular parcel of land is necessary for public use, it brings a judicial proceeding to obtain title to the land. Then, in another proceeding, the court determines the *fair value* of the land, which usually is approximately equal to its market value.

ANSWERING A LEGAL PROBLEM

In the legal problem set out at the beginning of the chapter, Rosa and Santiago are adjacent property owners. Rosa operates a vineyard and winery. Santiago wants to expand a small gravel pit on his land. The increased dust and vibrations of a more extensive mining operation will harm Rosa's business.

A **Can Santiago use his property as he sees fit, regardless of the effect on his neighbor's business?** No. Property owners can use their property for whatever purpose they see fit so long as the use does not unreasonably interfere with a neighbor's use or enjoyment of his or her own property. The negative impact of an expanded gravel-mining operation on a neighbor's vineyard and winery would likely result in an injunction or an imposition of damages.

LINKING BUSINESS LAW to Your Career

EMINENT DOMAIN AND COMMERCIAL DEVELOPMENT

Your career may include real property acquisition and commercial development. You might, for example, be responsible for buying land to build a shopping center. The owner of the land can exchange it for a payment that you or your company agrees to make. If the owner does not believe that the payment is sufficient, then the sale does not occur. This is the principle of voluntary exchange, which is the basis of all market economic systems.

Forced Sales

There is a thriving real estate market in the United States, even when prices are falling. Real property is bought and sold every day. But the private ownership of land is limited by a superior ownership interest—the government's power of eminent domain. The government can exercise this power to condemn, or take, privately owned land for a public use. An owner can thereby be forced to sell his or her property. There is a clear conflict between the economic principle of voluntary exchange and the power of eminent domain, which can be used to force an involuntary transfer.

Bad Results

Businesses, which might include your company, use financial projections to tell them whether a real estate development is worthwhile. You might notice, for example, that one area of town appears undervalued. You think it might be profitable to buy the land, including the houses, and then tear the houses down and build a shopping center. You will use financial projections to determine whether, considering the estimated costs and revenues, the project will likely be profitable.

Costs therefore are an important consideration in your decision.

If the government forces the homeowners in that area to sell their land to the government, which then resells it to you, then you may obtain the land at a lower price than if you had gone directly to the private homeowners. In essence, the local government is forcing the homeowners to subsidize your project.

We often assume that when the government exercises its power of eminent domain, the use of the condemned property will benefit the community more than the forced transaction will hurt the previous owner. But any use of eminent domain that involves a taking of private property to be sold to a private company will have some adverse economic consequences that may not be completely justified.

TERMS AND CONCEPTS FOR REVIEW

adverse possession 515

covenant of quiet enjoyment 514

deed 514

easement 513

eminent domain 516

fee simple absolute 511

fee simple defeasible 512

fixture 510

license 513

life estate 512

profit 513

quitclaim deed 515

real property 509

taking 516

warranty deed 514

CHAPTER SUMMARY—REAL PROPERTY

LEARNING OUTCOME	
1	**Discuss the nature of real property.** Real property (also called real estate or realty) is immovable. It includes land, subsurface and airspace rights, plant life and vegetation, and fixtures.
2	**Identify the most common types of real property ownership.** *Fee simple absolute* is the most complete form of real property ownership. A *life estate* is an estate that lasts for the life of a specified individual, during which time the individual is entitled to possess, use, and benefit from the estate. The life tenant's ownership rights in the life estate end on her or his death. A *nonpossessory interest* is an interest that involves the right to use real property but not to possess it. Easements, profits, and licenses are nonpossessory interests.

3	**Explain how the ownership of real property can be transferred.** Real property can be transferred by:
	(1) *Deed*—When real property is sold or transferred as a gift, title to the property is conveyed by means of a deed. A *warranty deed* warrants the most extensive protection against defects of title. A *quitclaim deed* conveys to the grantee only whatever interest the grantor had in the property.
	(2) *Will or inheritance*—If an owner dies after having made a valid will, the land passes as specified in the will. If the owner dies without having made a will, the heirs inherit according to state inheritance statutes.
	(3) *Adverse possession.*
	(4) *Eminent domain.*
4	**List the elements for acquiring real property by adverse possession.** When a person possesses the property of another for a statutory period of time (ten years is the most common), that person acquires title to the property by *adverse possession,* provided the possession is actual and exclusive, open and visible, continuous and peaceable, and hostile and adverse (without the permission of the owner).
5	**Describe the government's right of eminent domain.** By exercising the right of *eminent domain,* the government can take land for public use, with just compensation, when public interest requires the taking.

ISSUE SPOTTERS

Check your answers to the *Issue Spotters* against the answers provided in Appendix C at the end of this text.

1. Eve and Frank own twenty acres of land. On the land, there is a warehouse surrounded by a fence. What is the most important factor in determining whether the fence is a fixture? (See *The Nature of Real Property.*)

2. Sam owns an acre of land on Red River. The government dams the river. A lake forms behind the dam, covering Sam's land. Does the government owe Sam anything? If so, what? If not, why? (See *Transfer of Ownership.*)

USING BUSINESS LAW

37–1. Property Ownership. Antonio is the owner of a lakeside house and lot. He deeds the house and lot "to my wife, Angela, for life, then to my son, Charles." Given these facts, answer the following questions: (See *Ownership Interest.*)

    1. Does Antonio have any ownership interest in the lakeside house after making these transfers? Explain.

    2. What is Angela's interest called? Is there any limitation on her rights to use the property as she wishes?

    3. What is Charles's interest called? Why?

37–2. Deeds. Wiley and Gemma are neighbors. Wiley's lot is extremely large, and his present and future use of it will not involve the entire area. Gemma wants to build a single-car garage and driveway along the present lot boundary. Because of ordinances requiring buildings to be set back fifteen feet from an adjoining property line, and because of the placement of her existing structures, Gemma cannot build the garage. Gemma contracts to purchase ten feet of Wiley's property along their boundary line for $3,000. Wiley is willing to sell but will give Gemma only a quitclaim deed, whereas Gemma wants a warranty deed. Discuss the differences between these deeds as they would affect the rights of the parties if the title to this ten feet of land later proved to be defective. (See *Transfer of Ownership.*)

REAL-WORLD CASE PROBLEMS

37–3. Real Estate Sales Contracts. A California state statute requires sellers to provide a real estate "Transfer Disclosure Statement" (TDS) to buyers of residential property. Required disclosures include information about significant defects, including hazardous materials, encroachments, easements, fill, settling, flooding, drainage problems, neighborhood noise, damage from natural disasters, and lawsuits. Mark Hartley contracted with Randall Richman to buy Richman's property in Ventura, California. The property included a commercial building and a residential duplex. Richman did not provide a TDS, claiming that it was not required because the property was "mixed-use." Hartley refused to go through with the deal. Did Hartley breach their contract, or did Richman's failure to provide a TDS excuse Hartley's non-performance? Discuss. [*Richman v. Hartley*, 224 Cal.App.4th 1182, 169 Cal.Rptr.3d 475 (2 Dist. 2014)] (See *Transfer of Ownership*.)

37–4. Eminent Domain. Under an agreement with the town of Monroe, North Carolina, the town of Midland began to acquire the rights to local land for the installation of a natural gas pipeline. When the owners refused to sell, Midland used its eminent domain authority to condemn the property. Fifteen owners challenged the action in court. They claimed that Midland's condemnation was not for a public benefit, because the town did not plan to tap into the line to provide natural gas for its citizens. Did Midland act within its rights? Discuss. [*Town of Midland v. Morris*, 704 S.E.2d 329 (N.C.App. 2011)] (See *Transfer of Ownership*.)

37–5. Adverse Possession. Charles Scarborough and Mildred Rollins owned adjoining properties. Rollins believed that their common boundary ran along the far edge of a grassy area on the north side of a gravel road. Her deed indicated that she owned the grassy area and the road. For more than thirty-five years, she and her predecessors had used it exclusively and paid taxes on it, and no one else had claimed it. Scarborough, however, believed that the property was his. Under the principles of adverse possession, who owns the property? Explain. [*Scarborough v. Rollins*, 44 So.3d 381 (Miss.App. 2010)] (See *Transfer of Ownership*.)

 ETHICAL QUESTIONS

37–6. Adverse Possession. What public policies underlie the doctrine of adverse possession? (See *Transfer of Ownership*.)

37–7. Eminent Domain. Should eminent domain be used to promote private developments? Discuss your answer. (See *Transfer of Ownership*.)

37–8. Adverse Possession. Alana Mansell built a garage on her property that encroached on the property of her neighbor, Betty Hunter, by fourteen feet. Hunter knew of the encroachment and informally agreed to it, but she did not transfer ownership of the property to Mansell. A survey twenty-eight years later confirmed the encroachment, and Hunter sought the removal of the garage. Mansell asked a court to declare that she was the owner of the property by adverse possession. Did Mansell obtain title by adverse possession? Was her conduct in any way unethical? Discuss. [*Hunter v. Mansell*, 240 P.3d 469 (Colo.App. 2010)] (See *Transfer of Ownership*.)

Chapter 37—Work Set

TRUE-FALSE QUESTIONS

_____ 1. A fee simple absolute is potentially infinite in duration and can be disposed of by deed or by will.

_____ 2. The owner of a life estate has the same rights as a fee simple owner.

_____ 3. An easement allows a person to use land and take something from it, but a profit allows a person only to use land.

_____ 4. Deeds offer different degrees of protection against defects of title.

_____ 5. The government can take private property for *public* use without just compensation.

_____ 6. The government can take private property for *private* uses only.

_____ 7. A license is a revocable right of a person to come onto another person's land.

_____ 8. When real property is sold, the title to the property is conveyed by a deed.

MULTIPLE-CHOICE QUESTIONS

_____ 1. Lou owns two hundred acres next to Brook's lumber mill. Lou sells to Brook the privilege of removing timber from his land to refine into lumber. The privilege of removing the timber is

a. an easement.
b. a profit.
c. a license.
d. none of the above.

_____ 2. Evan owns an apartment building in fee simple. Evan can

a. give the building away.
b. sell the building for a price or transfer it by a will.
c. do both a and b.
d. do none of the above.

_____ 3. Gina conveys her warehouse to Sam under a warranty deed. Later, Hannah appears, holding a better title to the warehouse than Sam's. Hannah proceeds to evict Sam. Sam can recover from Gina

a. the purchase price of the property.
b. damages from being evicted.
c. both a and b.
d. none of the above.

_____ 4. Metro City wants to acquire undeveloped land within the city limits to convert into a public park. Metro City brings a judicial proceeding to obtain title to the land. This is

a. adverse possession.
b. an easement.
c. constructive eviction.
d. the power of eminent domain.

_____ 5. Dan owns a half acre of land that fronts on Blue Lake. Rod owns the property behind Dan's land. No road runs to Dan's land, but Rod's driveway runs between a road and Dan's property, so Dan uses Rod's driveway. The right-of-way that Dan has across Rod's property is

a. an easement.
b. a profit.
c. a license.
d. none of the above.

6. Dave owns an office building. Dave sells the building to P&I Corporation. To be valid, the deed that conveys the property from Dave to P&I must include a description of the property and

a. only Dave's name and P&I's name.

b. only words evidencing Dave's intent to convey.

c. only Dave's signature (witnessed and acknowledged).

d. words evidencing Dave's intent to convey, Dave's name, P&I's name, and Dave's signature (witnessed and acknowledged).

7. Lana owns a cabin on Long Lake. Bob takes possession of the cabin without Lana's permission and puts up a sign that reads "No Trespassing by Order of Bob, the Owner." The statutory period for adverse possession is ten years. Bob is in the cabin for eleven years. Lana sues to remove Bob. She will

a. win, because she sued Bob after the statutory period for adverse possession.

b. win, because Bob did not have permission to take possession of the cabin.

c. lose, because the no-trespassing sign misrepresented ownership of the cabin.

d. lose, because Bob acquired the cabin by adverse possession.

8. Ron sells his house and yard to Jill. When Jill arrives to take possession, she learns that Ron has removed the kitchen cabinets from the house and the plastic lawn furniture from the yard. Jill is entitled to the return of

a. the lawn furniture only.

b. the cabinets only.

c. the lawn furniture and the cabinets.

d. none of the above.

9. Betty owns a farm. On the land are a barn and other farm buildings. Under the surface of the land are valuable minerals. Betty's deed does not indicate any significant limits on her rights to the realty. Betty owns

a. only the surface of the land.

b. only the surface of the land and the buildings on it.

c. the surface of the land, the buildings on it, and the minerals beneath the surface.

d. none of the above.

 ANSWERING MORE LEGAL PROBLEMS

1. Cici owned a building in Whitewater Village. She lived in the building and operated Cici's Canyon Wall Flower Shop there. Declan owned the building next door, in which he operated Declan's Sandspit Steak House & Brew Pub. The noise from Sandspit kept Cici awake at night. When the two neighbors were unable to come to an accommodation, Cici filed a suit against Declan.

Was Cici entitled to relief from a neighbor's noise? Yes. Cici is entitled to an injunction to reduce the effect of the operation of Declan's business on Cici's enjoyment of her property. The owner of a fee simple absolute has the greatest aggregation of rights, privileges, and power with respect to the _____. The rights that accompany this ownership include the right to use the land for whatever purpose the owner sees fit. The owner cannot, however, use his or her property in a way that interferes with others' right to use or enjoy their own property. Declan owned his building in fee simple absolute, but he is subject to the restriction that he may not use his land to _____ annoy his neighbor.

2. Sloan operated ChoCo, a gourmet chocolate factory. When the business doubled and then tripled in size,

Sloan wanted to expand ChoCo's facilities. To accomplish the expansion, Sloan needed to buy fifty feet of the adjacent property, which was owned by Corporate Park Holdings, Inc. Sloan made an offer to which Corporate Park agreed, and the parties arranged to exchange Sloan's payment for a deed to the fifty feet.

Would a buyer of real property prefer a warranty deed or a quitclaim deed, and why? A buyer would most likely prefer a _____ deed. Different types of deeds provide different degrees of protection against defects of title. A _____ deed contains the most covenants, or promises, of title and thus provides the greatest protection for the owner. These promises include the covenant of quiet enjoyment, which guarantees that the owner will not be disturbed in his or her possession of the land by any other persons. Generally, the deed must state a promise to protect the owner against all others' claims of ownership of the property. A _____ deed offers the least amount of protection against defects in title. A _____ deed conveys only whatever interest the grantor had in the property. If the grantor had no interest, no interest is conveyed.

LANDLORD AND TENANT LAW

38

LEARNING OUTCOMES

The four Learning Outcomes below are designed to help improve your understanding of the chapter. After reading this chapter, you should be able to:

1 Identify different types of tenancies.

2 Describe a lease agreement.

3 Outline the landlord's and tenant's rights and duties under a lease agreement.

4 Discuss the transfer of rights to leased property.

FACING A LEGAL PROBLEM

Darryl Katz signs a one-year lease to occupy an apartment. The lease does not contain a renewal clause. Eleven months and two weeks later, the landlord tells Katz that the apartment has been rented to someone else and he must move out at the end of the month. Katz argues that the landlord did not give him enough notice.

Q Does Katz have to move out at the end of the month?

Much real property is used by people who do not own it. A **lease** is a contract by which the owner (the landlord) grants someone else (the tenant) an exclusive right to use and possess the land, usually for a specified period of time, in return for rent or some other form of payment. In this chapter, we discuss leased property and landlord-tenant relationships.

lease
A transfer of real property by a landlord to a tenant for a period of time for the payment of rent.

38–1 LEASEHOLD ESTATES

A tenancy, or **leasehold estate**, is created when a real property owner or lessor (landlord) agrees to convey the right to possess and use the property to a lessee (tenant) for a certain period of time. In every leasehold estate, the tenant has a *qualified* right to exclusive possession (qualified by the right of the landlord to enter onto the premises to ensure that no damage is being done). The tenant can use the land—for example, by harvesting crops—but cannot injure the land through such activities as extracting oil.

Several types of leasehold estates, or tenancies, can be created when real property is leased. They include fixed-term tenancy, periodic tenancy, tenancy at will, and tenancy at sufferance.

leasehold estate
An estate held by a tenant under a lease. The tenant has a qualified right to possess and use the land.

LEARNING OUTCOME 1
Identify different types of tenancies.

38–1a Fixed-Term Tenancy

In a **fixed-term tenancy**, also known as a *tenancy for years*, property is leased for a specified period of time, such as a month or a year. The tenancy is created by an *express contract*—one stated orally or in written words—that specifies the lease period. At the end of the specified period, the lease ends without notice, and possession of the property returns to the landlord. If the tenant dies during the period of the lease, the lease interest passes to the tenant's heirs as personal property. Often, such leases include provisions for renewal or extension.

fixed-term tenancy
A lease for a specified period of time, after which the interest reverts to the landlord.

38–1b Periodic Tenancy

A **periodic tenancy** is created by a lease that does not specify how long it is to last but does specify that rent is to be paid at certain intervals. This type of tenancy is automatically renewed for another rental period unless properly terminated.

periodic tenancy
A lease for an indefinite period involving payment of rent at fixed intervals.

523

EXAMPLE 38.1 Jewell enters into a lease with Capital Properties. The lease states, "Rent is due on the tenth day of every month." This provision creates a periodic tenancy from month to month◄ A periodic tenancy can also be from week to week or from year to year. Sometimes, a periodic tenancy arises when a landlord allows a tenant under a fixed-term tenancy to hold over and continue paying monthly or weekly rent.

To terminate a periodic tenancy, the landlord or tenant must give at least one period's notice to the other party. **EXAMPLE 38.2** If Grecia's tenancy is month to month, she must give at least one month's notice to her landlord before moving out.◄

38–1c Tenancy at Will

tenancy at will
A type of tenancy that either party can terminate without notice.

With a **tenancy at will**, either party can terminate without notice. This type of tenancy can arise if a landlord rents property to a tenant "for as long as both agree" or allows a person to live on the premises without paying rent. Certain events—such as the death of either party or the voluntary commission of **waste** by the tenant—automatically terminate a tenancy at will.

waste
The abuse or destructive use of real property by someone who is in rightful possession of the property but does not hold title to it.

Tenancies at will are rare today because most state statutes require a landlord to provide some period of notice to terminate a tenancy. States may also require a landowner to have sufficient cause to end a residential tenancy.

38–1d Tenancy at Sufferance

tenancy at sufferance
Tenancy by one who, after rightfully being in possession of leased premises, continues (wrongfully) to occupy the property after the lease has been terminated.

The possession of land without right is called a **tenancy at sufferance**. A tenancy at sufferance is not a true tenancy because it is created by a tenant's *wrongfully* retaining possession of property. When a fixed-term tenancy or a periodic tenancy ends and the tenant continues to retain possession of the premises without the owner's permission, a tenancy at sufferance is created.

When a tenant wrongfully retains possession, the landlord is entitled to damages. Typically, the damages are based on the fair market rental value of the premises after the expiration of the lease. If the landlord can show that another tenant was ready to rent the property at a higher rent, the proper standard of damages is the higher rental rate (rather than the existing rate).

38–2 THE LANDLORD-TENANT RELATIONSHIP

The lease agreement creates a landlord-tenant relationship. Traditionally, such relationships have been governed by contract law, but today, state or local laws often dictate permissible lease terms. For instance, a statute or ordinance might prohibit the leasing of a structure that is not in compliance with local building codes. Next, we look at how landlord-tenant relationships are created and at the respective rights and duties of landlords and tenants.

38–2a The Lease Agreement

LEARNING OUTCOME 2
Describe a lease agreement.

A lease agreement may be oral or written. An oral lease may be valid, but as with most oral agreements, a party who seeks to enforce an oral lease may have difficulty proving its existence. Furthermore, in most states, some leases must be in writing (such as those for terms exceeding one year). To ensure the validity of a lease agreement, it should be in writing. In addition, it should do the following:

1. Express an intent to establish the relationship.

2. Provide for the transfer of the property's possession to the tenant at the beginning of the term.

3. Provide for the landlord's future interest, which entitles the landlord to retake possession at the end of the term.

4. Describe the property—for example, give its street address.

5. Indicate the length of the term, the amount of the rent, and how and when the rent is to be paid.

Real-World Case Example

Lynwood Place, LLC, owns an office building in Newtown, Connecticut. Sandy Hook Hydro, LLC, agreed to lease part of the building. The lease required Sandy Hook to pay annual rent of $1,500 and provided that this amount could be adjusted each year by adding 6 percent of any increase in operating expenses incurred by the landlord. "Operating expenses" included all costs of maintenance and repair related to the premises. When Sandy Hook did not pay rent in accord with this provision, Lynwood Place filed a suit in a Connecticut state court to take immediate possession of the property. The court issued a judgment in the landlord's favor. The tenant appealed.

Did the lease clearly and unambiguously indicate the amount of the rent? Yes. In a 2014 case, *Lynwood Place, LLC v. Sandy Hook Hydro, LLC,* a state intermediate appellate court affirmed the judgment of the lower court. Sandy Hook admitted that it had not paid 6 percent of any increase in the costs to operate the building, but it argued that its share should have been 1.77 percent in proportion to its space in the building. The lease was clear and unambiguous on this point, however, and Sandy Hook understood that its share would be 6 percent when it agreed to the lease's terms.

As noted, state or local laws often dictate additional lease terms. A statute might prohibit the leasing of property for a particular purpose. For instance, Oregon law prohibits gambling houses. Thus, if a landlord and a tenant intend to house an illegal betting operation in a leased property, their lease is unenforceable.

Just as the parties to any contract may later agree to modify the contract's terms, the parties to a lease can later agree to change the terms of the lease. **EXAMPLE 38.3** Beverly and Vickie have a five-year lease agreement, but two years into the lease, they agree to end the tenancy at the end of the current year. ◄

Unconscionability The *unconscionability concept* is one of the most important of the contract doctrines applied to leases. Under this doctrine, a court may declare an entire contract, or any of its clauses, unenforceable and thus illegal. This may occur when one party, as a result of his or her disproportionate bargaining power, is forced to accept terms that unfairly benefit the other party.

HIGHLIGHTING THE POINT

Waterbury Properties, Inc., owns a number of residential buildings in which it leases space. Waterbury provides each tenant with a lease that contains a clause claiming to absolve Waterbury from all responsibility for interruptions in such essential services as central heating or air-conditioning.

(Continued)

If the systems break down, will the tenants be able to hold Waterbury liable? Yes. The clause in Waterbury's lease will not shield it from liability if the heating and air-conditioning systems break down when they are needed the most. Under the unconscionability doctrine, a court can declare the clause unenforceable, on the ground that the parties have unequal bargaining power. Waterbury is a corporation that can refuse to lease to those who do not accept its terms. Its tenants are individuals whose power to bargain over the terms of their individual leases is generally limited.

Antidiscrimination A property owner cannot legally discriminate against prospective tenants on the basis of age, disability, race, color, religion, national origin, or gender. Obviously, the public policy underlying this prohibition is to treat all people equally.

Often, rental properties are leased by agents of the owners. Under the theory of *respondeat superior*, a principal (a landlord, with respect to leases) is liable for the wrongful actions of his or her agent if the actions occurred within the scope of employment. Thus, a landlord can be held liable for his or her agent's discrimination against potential tenants.

Similarly, a tenant cannot legally promise to do something counter to laws prohibiting discrimination. **EXAMPLE 38.4** Cavill Manufacturing leases commercial property. Cavill cannot legally promise the property owner that it will do business only with white men. ◄

38–2b Rights and Duties of Landlords and Tenants

LEARNING OUTCOME 3

Outline the landlord's and tenant's rights and duties under a lease agreement.

The rights and duties of landlords and tenants generally pertain to four broad areas of concern—the possession, use, and maintenance of leased property and, of course, rent.

Possession of the Leased Property The landlord has a duty to deliver possession of the leased property to the tenant at the beginning of the lease term. The tenant has a corresponding right to obtain possession and retain it until the lease expires.

Covenant of Quiet Enjoyment The covenant of quiet enjoyment also applies to leased premises. Under this covenant, the landlord promises that during the lease term, neither the landlord nor any third party with an unlawful claim will interfere with the tenant's use and enjoyment of the property. This covenant forms the essence of the landlord-tenant relationship. If it is breached, the tenant can terminate the lease and sue for damages.

eviction
Depriving a person of the possession of property that he or she leases.

Eviction When the landlord deprives the tenant of possession of the leased property or interferes with the tenant's use or enjoyment of it, an **eviction** occurs. **EXAMPLE 38.5** Enrique is the landlord at Sunrise Meadow Apartments. One day, Enrique changes the locks on Emily's apartment door and refuses to give her a new key. Enrique has evicted Emily from her apartment. ◄

constructive eviction
Depriving a person of the possession of property that he or she leases by rendering the premises unfit or unsuitable for occupancy.

Constructive Eviction A **constructive eviction** occurs when the landlord wrongfully performs or fails to perform any of the undertakings the lease requires, thereby making the tenant's further use and enjoyment of the property exceedingly difficult or impossible. **EXAMPLE 38.6** Peter, the landlord at Rocky Butte Estates in Anchorage, Alaska, has failed to fix the central heating system in David's rental house for months. As a result, David has had to sleep next to a wood stove in his living room. Once winter arrives, he leaves to stay at his parents' home. This is a constructive eviction. ◄

Use and Maintenance of the Leased Property If the parties' agreement does not limit the uses to which the property may be put, the tenant may make any use of it, as long as the use is legal. The use also must reasonably relate to the purpose for which the property is adapted or ordinarily used and must not injure the landlord's interest.

The tenant is responsible for all damage that he or she causes, intentionally or negligently. The tenant may be held liable for the cost of returning the property to the physical condition it was in when the lease began. Unless the parties have agreed otherwise, the tenant is not responsible for ordinary wear and tear or for the property's consequent depreciation in value.

HIGHLIGHTING THE POINT

BRB Restaurants, Inc., leases property from Dahl Enterprises, Inc. The lease provides for lower payments of rent than normal but requires BRB to return the property in the condition in which BRB received it. On the property, BRB operates a restaurant. When the lease expires, BRB moves off the property, leaving it in a state of disrepair. Dahl replaces the roof, the air-conditioning unit, and the restroom fixtures. Dahl also repaves the parking lot.

Is BRB liable for the cost of these repairs? Yes. Except for ordinary wear and tear, a tenant is responsible for all damage that he or she causes, intentionally or negligently. In addition, BRB and Dahl—parties of "equal bargaining power"—signed a lease in which BRB agreed to pay the cost of returning the property to the physical condition it was in at the beginning of the lease.

Compliance with Ordinances Usually, the landlord must comply with state statutes and city ordinances that delineate specific standards for the construction and maintenance of buildings. Typically, these codes contain structural requirements common to the construction, wiring, and plumbing of residential and commercial buildings. In some jurisdictions, landlords of residential property are required by statute to maintain the premises in good repair.

Implied Warranty of Habitability The **implied warranty of habitability** requires a landlord who leases residential property to ensure that the premises are habitable—that is, in a condition that is safe and suitable for people to live in—at the beginning of a lease term and to maintain the premises in that condition for the lease's duration. Some state legislatures have enacted this warranty into law. In other jurisdictions, courts have based the warranty on the existence of a landlord's statutory duty to keep leased premises in good repair, or they have simply applied it as a matter of public policy.

EXAMPLE 38.7 Carol and Gary Cooper own a house within the city limits of Redmond. The house does not have a proper sewer system. A Redmond public health regulation requires all residential rental properties to have an approved sewer system before anyone, including tenants, can live in the house. Thus, the Coopers' house is not legally habitable. ◄

Generally, this warranty applies to major—or *substantial*—physical defects that the landlord knows or should know about and has had a reasonable time to repair—for example, a large hole in the roof. An unattractive or annoying feature, such as a crack in the wall, may be unpleasant, but unless the crack is a structural defect or affects the residence's heating capabilities, it is probably not sufficiently substantial to make the place uninhabitable.

implied warranty of habitability
A presumed promise by the landlord that rented residential premises are fit for human habitation.

Rent for the Leased Property *Rent* is the tenant's payment to the landlord for the tenant's occupancy or use of the landlord's real property. Usually, the tenant must pay the rent even if she or he refuses to occupy the property or moves out, as long as the refusal or the move is unjustified and the lease is in force.

EXAMPLE 38.8 Lifetime Insurance Agency enters into a lease with Mallory for a suite of offices in Mallory's building. Lifetime's revenue is less than the company had projected, however, and the rent is now more than it wants to pay. Lifetime vacates the offices before the end of the lease. In terms of the landlord-tenant relationship, the move is unjustified and the lease remains in force. Lifetime must continue to pay the rent. ◄

Under the common law, if the leased premises were destroyed by fire or flood, the tenant still had to pay rent. Today, however, if an apartment building burns down, most state's laws do not require tenants to continue to pay rent.

In some situations, such as when a landlord breaches the implied warranty of habitability, a tenant may be allowed to withhold rent as a remedy. When rent withholding is authorized under a statute, the tenant must usually put the amount withheld into an *escrow account*. This account is held in the name of the depositor (the tenant) and an *escrow agent* (usually the court or a government agency). The funds are returnable to the tenant if the landlord fails to make the premises habitable.

38–2c Transferring Rights to Leased Property

Either the landlord or the tenant may wish to transfer his or her rights to the leased property during the term of the lease.

Transferring the Landlord's Interest Just as any other real property owner can sell, give away, or otherwise transfer his or her property, so can a landlord—who is, of course, the leased property's owner. If complete title to the leased property is transferred, the tenant becomes the tenant of the new owner. The new owner may collect subsequent rent and normally must also abide by the terms of the existing lease.

Transferring the Tenant's Interest The tenant's transfer of his or her entire interest in the leased property to a third person is an *assignment of the lease*. A lease assignment is an agreement to transfer all rights, title, and interest in the lease to the assignee. It is a complete transfer.

Assignment Requirements Many leases require that the assignment have the landlord's written consent. An assignment that lacks consent can be voided by the landlord, and the assignee can be evicted. A landlord who knowingly accepts rent from the assignee, however, will be held to have waived the requirement.

A tenant does not end his or her liabilities on a lease on assignment, because the tenant may assign rights but not duties. Thus, even though the assignee of the lease is required to pay rent, the original tenant is not released from the contractual obligation to pay the rent if the assignee fails to do so.

sublease
A lease executed by the lessee of real estate to a third person, conveying the same interest that the lessee enjoys, but for a shorter term than that held by the lessee.

Sublease A tenant may also transfer all or part of the premises for a period shorter than the lease term. This arrangement is called a **sublease**. The same restrictions that apply to an assignment of the tenant's interest in leased property apply to a sublease.

EXAMPLE 38.9 Derek, a student, leases an apartment for a two-year period. Although Derek had planned on attending summer school, he decides to accept a job offer in Europe for the summer months instead. Derek obtains his landlord's consent to sublease the apartment to Ava. Ava is bound by the same terms of the lease as Derek, and the landlord can hold Derek liable if Ava violates the lease terms. ◄

38–2d Terminating the Lease

Usually, a lease terminates when its term ends. The tenant surrenders the property to the landlord, who retakes possession. If the lease states the time it will end, the landlord is not required to give the tenant notice. The lease terminates automatically. In contrast, as explained earlier, a periodic tenancy renews automatically unless one of the parties gives timely notice of termination (usually one rental period).

Once the lease terminates, the tenant has no right to remain unless the parties have agreed that the tenant will stay on. If the lease is renewable and the tenant decides to exercise the option, the tenant must comply with any conditions requiring notice to the landlord.

Suppose that a tenant abandons the premises—that is, moves out completely with no intention of returning before the lease expires. In this situation, the tenant, in many states, remains obligated to pay the rent for the remainder of the term. In a growing number of jurisdictions, the landlord is required to mitigate his or her damages, meaning that the landlord must make a reasonable attempt to lease the property to another party. **EXAMPLE 38.10** Artisan Creations, a jewelry store, leases space in Gray Meadows Mall from Cascade Commercial Properties. With six months still remaining in the lease term, Artisan vacates the mall premises. Cascade seeks a new tenant. Three months later, Betty's Beads agrees to move into the space. Artisan owes Cascade rent for the time between when it left the space and when Betty's Beads took possession of it. ◄

If a tenant terminates a fixed-term tenancy before the end of the term, such as a one-year lease, then the tenant has breached the lease contract. Exceptions to this would be if the landlord wrongfully evicted the tenant or rendered the premises uninhabitable.

ANSWERING THE LEGAL PROBLEM

In the legal problem set out at the beginning of this chapter, Darryl Katz signs a one-year lease to occupy an apartment. The lease does not contain a renewal clause. Eleven months and two weeks later, the landlord tells Katz that the apartment has been rented to someone else and he must move out at the end of the month. Katz argues that the landlord did not give him enough notice.

A **Does Katz have to move out at the end of the month?** Yes. The lease signed by Katz and the landlord creates a fixed-term tenancy. At the end of the period specified in the lease, the lease ends without notice, and possession of the property returns to the landlord. Although leases often include renewal provisions, this lease did not.

TERMS AND CONCEPTS FOR REVIEW

constructive eviction 526

eviction 526

fixed-term tenancy 523

implied warranty
   of habitability 527

lease 523

leasehold estate 523

periodic tenancy 523

sublease 528

tenancy at sufferance 524

tenancy at will 524

waste 524

CHAPTER SUMMARY—LANDLORD AND TENANT LAW

LEARNING OUTCOME	
1	**Identify different types of tenancies.** Types of tenancies (leasehold estates) include: (1) *Fixed-term tenancy*—A tenancy for a period of time stated by express contract. (2) *Periodic tenancy*—A tenancy for a period determined by the frequency of rent payments; automatically renewed unless proper notice is given. (3) *Tenancy at will*—A tenancy for as long as both parties agree. No notice of termination is required. (4) *Tenancy at sufferance*—Possession of land without legal right.
2	**Describe a lease agreement.** A lease agreement creates the landlord-tenant relationship. The agreement may be oral or written, but to ensure its validity, it should be in writing. It should express an intent to establish a landlord-tenant relationship, provide for transfer of possession to the tenant, provide for the landlord's future interest, describe the property, and indicate the term of the lease and the rent. State or local laws may dictate additional lease terms.
3	**Outline the landlord's and tenant's rights and duties under a lease agreement.** The rights and duties that arise under a lease agreement generally pertain to: (1) *Possession*—The tenant has an exclusive right to possess the leased premises, which must be available to the tenant at the agreed-on time. Under the covenant of quiet enjoyment, the landlord promises that during the lease term neither the landlord nor anyone having superior title to the property will disturb the tenant's use and enjoyment of the property. (2) *The use and maintenance of the premises*—Unless the parties agree otherwise, the tenant may make any legal use of the property. The tenant is responsible for any damage that he or she causes. The landlord must comply with laws that set specific standards for the maintenance of real property. The implied warranty of habitability requires that a landlord furnish and maintain residential premises in a habitable condition—that is, in a condition safe and suitable for human life.
4	**Discuss the transfer of rights to leased property.** If the landlord transfers complete title to the leased property, the tenant becomes the tenant of the new owner. The new owner may then collect the rent but must abide by the existing lease. Generally, in the absence of an agreement to the contrary, tenants may assign their rights (but not their duties) under a lease contract to a third person. Tenants may sublease leased property to a third person, but the original tenant is not relieved of any obligations to the landlord under the lease. In either situation, the landlord's consent may be required.

ISSUE SPOTTERS

Check your answers to the *Issue Spotters* against the answers provided in Appendix C at the end of this text.

1. Ann leases an office in Ted's building for a one-year term. At the end of the period specified in the lease, the lease ends without notice, and possession of the office returns to Ted. If Ann dies during the period of the lease, what happens to the leased property? (See *Leasehold Estates*.)

2. Eve orally agrees to rent an apartment to Nancy for a six-month term. Is this lease enforceable if it is not in writing? (See *The Landlord-Tenant Relationship*.)

USING BUSINESS LAW

38–1. Tenant's Rights and Responsibilities. You are a college student and plan to attend classes for nine months. You sign a twelve-month lease for an apartment. Answer fully each of the following questions:

1. You have a summer job in another town and wish to assign the balance of your lease (three months) to a fellow student who will be attending summer school. Can you do so? (See *The Landlord-Tenant Relationship*.)

2. You are graduating in May. The lease will have three months remaining. Can you terminate the lease without liability by giving a thirty-day notice to the landlord? (See *The Landlord-Tenant Relationship*.)

38–2. Constructive Eviction. James owns a three-story building. He leases the ground floor to Juan's Mexican restaurant. The lease is to run for a five-year period and contains an express covenant of quiet enjoyment. One year later, James leases the top two stories to the Upbeat Club. The club's hours run from 5:00 P.M. to 11:00 P.M. The noise from the Upbeat Club is so loud that it is driving customers away from Juan's restaurant. Juan has notified James of the interference and has called the police on a number of occasions. James refuses to talk to the owners of the Upbeat Club or to do anything to remedy the situation. Juan abandons the premises. James files suit for breach of the lease agreement and for the rental payments still due under the lease. Juan claims that he was constructively evicted and files a countersuit for damages. Discuss who will be held liable. (See *The Landlord-Tenant Relationship*.)

REAL-WORLD CASE PROBLEMS

38–3. Rent. Flawlace, LLC, leased unfinished commercial real estate in Las Vegas, Nevada, from Francis Lin to operate a beauty salon. The lease required Flawlace to obtain a "certificate of occupancy" from the city to commence business. This required the installation of a fire protection system. The lease did not allocate responsibility for the installation to either party. Lin voluntarily undertook to install the system. After a month of delays, Flawlace moved out. Three months later, the installation was complete, and Lin leased the premises to a new tenant. Did Flawlace owe rent for the three months between the time that it moved out and the new tenant moved in? Explain. [*Tri-Lin Holdings, LLC v. Flawlace, LLC*, 2014 WL 1101577 (Nev. 2014)] (See *The Landlord-Tenant Relationship*.)

38–4. Maintenance of the Leased Premises. Gi Hwa Park entered into a lease with Landmark HHH, LLC, for space in the Plaza at Landmark, a shopping center. The lease required the landlord to keep the roof "in good repair." In the space, Park opened a store—The Four Seasons—specializing in imported men's clothing. Within a month,

water began leaking intermittently through the roof, causing damage. Nearly eight years later, Landmark installed a new roof, but water continued to leak. On a night of record rainfall, The Four Seasons suffered substantial water damage, and Park was forced to close the store. Who is liable for the loss? Why? [*Landmark HHH, LLC v. Gi Hwa Park*, 277 Va. 50, 671 S.E.2d 143 (2009)] (See *The Landlord-Tenant Relationship*.)

38–5. Tenancy at Sufferance. S&V Liquor, Inc., leased retail space from the Charles Downey Family Limited Partnership for a five-year term for $3,333.33 per month. Four months before the end of the term, Downey offered to renew the lease at a new rate of $9,167.67 per month. S&V did not respond. Five days before the lease expired, S&V told Downey that it would remain as a tenant for six months and then move out. Which monthly rental rate should apply? Explain. [*Charles Downey Family Limited Partnership v. S&V Liquor, Inc.*, 880 N.E.2d 322 (Ind.App. 2008)] (See *Leasehold Estates*.)

ETHICAL QUESTIONS

38–6. Maintenance of the Leased Premises. What is a landlord's ethical duty with respect to keeping rental premises "fit for human habitation"? (See *The Landlord-Tenant Relationship*.)

38–7. Rent. Perry Armstrong owned the Monona Center, a mall. One of the mall's eight tenants, Ring's All-American Karate, occupied about one-third of the space under a five-year lease. Ring's began to experience financial difficulties, and Armstrong agreed to reduce its rent for nine months. Ring's failed to pay, nonetheless, and when the amount of unpaid rent exceeded $13,000, Ring's vacated Monona Center. What obligation, if any, did Ring's have to Armstrong after defaulting on the lease? Why? [*Kailin v. Armstrong*, 2002 WI App. 70, 252 Wis.2d 676, 643 N.W.2d 132 (2002)] (See *The Landlord-Tenant Relationship*.)

Chapter 38—Work Set

TRUE-FALSE QUESTIONS

_____ 1. A covenant of quiet enjoyment guarantees that a tenant will not be disturbed in his or her possession of leased property by the landlord or any third person.

_____ 2. If the covenant of quiet enjoyment is breached, the tenant can sue the landlord for damages.

_____ 3. Generally, a tenant must pay rent even if he or she moves out, if the move is unjustifiable.

_____ 4. A tenant does not have to pay rent if there is anything wrong with leased property, no matter how slight the defect.

_____ 5. A fixed-term tenancy is a lease for a specified period of time.

_____ 6. When a landlord sells leased premises to a third party, any existing leases terminate automatically.

_____ 7. When a tenant assigns a lease to a third party, the tenant's obligations under the lease terminate automatically.

_____ 8. A landlord who leases residential property must deliver the premises in a condition that is safe and suitable for people to live in.

MULTIPLE-CHOICE QUESTIONS

_____ 1. Reuben leases an apartment from Maria. With Maria's consent, Reuben assigns the lease to Nell for the last two months of the term, after which Nell exercises an option under the original lease to renew for three months. One month later, Nell moves out. Regarding the rent for the rest of the term,

a. no one is liable.
b. Reuben can be held liable.
c. only Nell is liable.
d. Maria is liable.

_____ 2. Dian leases an apartment from Tom. The lease provides that Tom is not liable for any injury if the heating system fails to function. In midwinter, the system breaks down. Dian becomes seriously ill. If Dian sues Tom, she will

a. win, because Dian is the tenant.
b. win, because the clause absolving Tom of liability is unconscionable.
c. lose, because the lease absolves Tom of responsibility.
d. lose, because Tom is the landlord.

_____ 3. Paul rents an office from John for an eighteen-month term. Their lease

a. must be oral to be enforceable.
b. must be in writing to be enforceable.
c. is enforceable whether or not it is in writing.
d. is not enforceable whether or not it is in writing.

_____ 4. Sahil signs a one-year lease for an apartment. Kim is the landlord. Six months later, Sahil moves out of the apartment leaving it in a state of extreme disrepair, including ripped up flooring and holes in the walls. Sahil will be

a. liable for the cost of returning the apartment to its original condition.
b. able to sue Kim for damages.
c. given a constructive eviction by Kim.
d. none of the above.

5. Andrei rents an apartment from Sue. Two months later, Andrei moves out and arranges with Lee for Lee to move in and pay the rent to Sue for the rest of the term. This is

   a. an assignment.
   b. a sublease.
   c. both a and b.
   d. none of the above.

6. Ray operates the Apple Spice Restaurant in space that he leases in Village Mall. Village Mall is owned by VM Associates. VM Associates sells the mall to BB Properties. For the rest of the lease term, Ray owes rent to

   a. VM Associates.
   b. BB Properties.
   c. the Apple Spice Restaurant.
   d. none of the above.

7. Natasha signs a lease for an apartment, agreeing to make rental payments before the fifth of each month. The lease does not specify a termination date. This tenancy is

   a. a periodic tenancy.
   b. a fixed-term tenancy.
   c. a tenancy at will.
   d. a tenancy at sufferance.

8. Max leases a house from Nina for a two-year term. To ensure the validity of the lease, it should include

   a. a description of the premises.
   b. a due date for the payment of the property taxes.
   c. a requirement that Max perform structural repairs to the house.
   d. a requirement that Nina carry liability insurance.

 ## ANSWERING MORE LEGAL PROBLEMS

1. Jasper leased commercial space from Retro Enterprises for a three-year term. In the space, Jasper opened Suite Potato, a restaurant. The building's plumbing was defective, and six months into the term, a pipe connected to the upstairs restrooms burst, spewing sewage into the kitchen. Jasper was forced to close and did not pay rent for the remainder of the lease.

   Can Jasper recover damages from Retro? Yes. The covenant of _____ _____ applies to leased premises. Under this covenant, the landlord promises that during the lease term, the landlord will not interfere with the tenant's _____ and _____ of the property. If this covenant is breached, the tenant can terminate the lease and sue for damages. A landlord must comply with state and city codes that specify standards for structural requirements, such as plumbing. Here, it can be assumed that Retro did not comply with the codes. This failure interfered with Jasper's _____ and _____ of the premises. This breach of the lease allows Jasper to sue for damages.

2. McKenna leased ten thousand square feet of space in Midtown Lofts to Home Gallery, an interior design firm, for a five-year term. Less than two years into the term, Home Gallery ceased doing business. Without McKenna's consent, Home Gallery assigned its lease to Cloud Cover, a small server farm. Cloud Cover paid rent to McKenna, who accepted it. With eight months left in the original lease term, Cloud Cover abandoned the premises. Before the term expired, McKenna unsuccessfully attempted to re-lease the premises.

   Can McKenna recover the unpaid rent from Home Gallery? Yes. The tenant's transfer of the entire interest in the leased property to a third party is an assignment of the lease. Many leases require that an assignment have the landlord's _____, and without it, the assignment can be _____. But a landlord who knowingly accepts rent from the assignee will be held to have waived the requirement. A tenant's _____ on a lease do not end on an assignment. If the assignee fails to pay the rent, the _____ _____ is required to pay it. In some jurisdictions, the landlord is required to mitigate the damages on a tenant's abandonment of the leased premises. McKenna made the attempt, but it proved to be unsuccessful.

WILLS AND TRUSTS

39

FACING A LEGAL PROBLEM

Fran's will provides that $100,000, which at the time of her death is one-tenth of her estate, is to be divided among a group of local charities. These charities include a food bank, a homeless shelter, a refuge for victims of domestic abuse, and an animal-rescue facility. The charities are listed in a written memorandum that Fran gives to her lawyer on the same day the will is signed.

Q Is this list a valid part of Fran's will?

As the adage says, "You can't take it with you." After you die, all of the real and personal property that you own will be transferred to others. In this chapter, we examine how property is passed on the death of its owner. Our laws require that on death, the rights to ownership of all of the property of the *decedent* (the one who has died) must be transferred somewhere. This transfer can be done by will, through state laws prescribing distribution of property among heirs or next of kin, or through trusts.

39–1 WILLS

A **will** is the final declaration of how a person wishes to have his or her property disposed of after death. A will is a formal instrument that must follow exactly the requirements of state law to be effective. The reasoning behind such a strict requirement is obvious. A will becomes effective only *after* death. No attempts to modify it after death are allowed because the court cannot ask the deceased to confirm the attempted changes.

39–1a Terminology of a Will

A person who makes out a will is known as a **testator.** After the testator dies, his or her will is subject to *probate*. To probate a will means to establish its validity and to carry the administration of the estate through a court process. The court that oversees this process is called a **probate court.**

A *personal representative* of the decedent's estate often becomes involved in probate. The personal representative settles the affairs of the deceased, such as collecting and taking inventory of the deceased's assets, getting appraisals, and sorting out creditor claims. An **executor** is a personal representative named in a will. An **administrator** is a personal representative appointed by a court for a decedent who dies without a will, who fails to name an executor in the will, who names an executor lacking the capacity to serve, or who writes a will that the court refuses to accept.

LEARNING OUTCOMES

The five Learning Outcomes below are designed to help improve your understanding of the chapter. After reading this chapter, you should be able to:

❶ Outline the requirements of a will.

❷ Discuss methods of revoking or modifying a will.

❸ Describe the distribution of the property of a person who dies without a will.

❹ List the essential elements of a trust.

❺ State how different types of express and implied trusts are created or arise.

will
An instrument directing what is to be done with the testator's property on his or her death, made by the testator.

testator
One who makes and executes a will.

probate court
A court having jurisdiction over proceedings concerning the settlement of a person's estate.

executor
A person appointed by a testator to see that his or her will is administered appropriately.

administrator
A person appointed by a court to handle the disposition of a person's estate under certain circumstances, such as if the person dies without a will.

devise
A gift of real property by will.

legacy
A gift of personal property by a will; also called a *bequest.*

devisee
A person who inherits real property under a will.

legatee
A person who inherits personal property under a will.

A gift of real estate by will is generally called a **devise.** A gift of personal property by will is called a **legacy** or a *bequest.* The recipient of a gift by will is a **devisee** or a **legatee,** depending on whether the gift was a devise or a legacy.

39–1b Types of Gifts

Gifts by will can be specific, general, or residuary. A *specific* devise or legacy describes particular property that can be distinguished from all the rest of the testator's property. For example, a specific devise may consist of a particular piece of real estate.

A *general* devise or bequest (legacy) does not single out any particular item of property to be transferred by will. Instead, it usually specifies the property's value in monetary terms (such as "two diamonds worth $10,000") or simply states a sum of money ("$10,000").

Abatement If the assets of an estate are insufficient to pay in full all general bequests provided for in the will, an *abatement* takes place. In an abatement, the legatees receive reduced benefits. **EXAMPLE 39.1** Sergey's will leaves $15,000 each to his children, Tamara and Kevin. On Sergey's death, only $10,000 is available to honor these bequests. By abatement, each child will receive $5,000. ◄

Lapsed Legacy If a legatee dies before the testator dies or before the legacy is payable, a *lapsed legacy* results, and the legacy may fail. The legacy may not lapse, however, if the legatee has a certain blood relationship to the testator (such as child or sibling) and has a surviving descendant. If a provision in the will addresses lapsed legacies, a court will normally enforce it according to the testator's intent.

Residuary Clause Sometimes, a will provides that any assets remaining after gifts are made and debts are paid are to be distributed through a *residuary* clause. This is necessary when the exact amount to be distributed cannot be determined until all other gifts and payouts are made.

39–1c Requirements of a Valid Will

A will must comply with statutory formalities designed to ensure that the testator understood his or her actions at the time the will was made. These formalities are intended to help prevent fraud. Unless they are followed, the will is declared void, and the decedent's property is distributed according to state laws.

For a valid will, most states require proof of the following:

LEARNING OUTCOME 1

Outline the requirements of a will.

1. The testator's capacity.
2. The testator's intent.
3. A written document.
4. The testator's signature.
5. The signatures of persons who witnessed the testator sign the will.
6. Publication.

Testamentary Capacity The testator must have capacity. In other words, the testator must be of legal age and sound mind *at the time the will is made.* The legal age for executing a will varies. In most states, the minimum age is eighteen years. The "sound mind" requirement refers to the testator's ability to formulate and understand a personal plan for the disposition of property. Further, a testator must intend the document to be his or her will, comprehend the kind and character of the property being distributed, and remember the names of family and friends. In all states, the testator must have capacity.

Real-World Case Example

Marjorie Sirgo executed a will in which she left her estate equally to her children, Susie and Rene. The next year, Marjorie, suffering from Parkinson's disease and diabetes, began living at Chateau Living Center, a nursing home in Kenner, Louisiana. She stayed there until August 2005, when she was evacuated with Susie due to Hurricane Katrina. In October, while Marjorie was a resident of Poplar Springs Nursing Center, Susie took her to execute another will. This will left her entire estate to Susie. Marjorie died, and Susie filed a petition in a Louisiana state court to probate her mother's second will. Rene objected. The court declared the second will void and ordered the probate of Marjorie's first will. Susie appealed.

Did Marjorie lack testamentary capacity when she executed the second will? Yes. In a 2014 case, *In re Succession of Sirgo*, a state intermediate appellate court affirmed the order of the lower court. Nurses' notes in Marjorie's medical records at Poplar Springs indicated that she suffered from cognitive impairment and lacked the ability to make even small decisions. In October 2005, the month in which she executed the second will, it was noted that Marjorie suffered from "short-term and long-term memory problems"—for instance, she was unable to recall the current season, the location of her room, or that she was in a nursing home facility.

Testamentary Intent A valid will is one that represents the maker's intention to transfer and distribute her or his property. Generally, a testator must be able to do the following:

- Know the nature of the act (of making a will).
- Comprehend and remember the "natural objects of his or her bounty" (usually, family members and persons for whom the testator has affection).
- Know the nature and extent of her or his property.
- Understand the distribution of assets called for by the will.

Undue Influence When it can be shown that the decedent's plan of distribution was the result of fraud or undue influence, the will is declared invalid. If the testator ignored blood relatives and named as a beneficiary a nonrelative who was in constant close contact with the testator, for instance, a court might infer undue influence. **EXAMPLE 39.2** Walter's third wife, Laura, has him change his will to leave his entire estate to her. This new will now ignores Walter's two adult sons from his first marriage, who were to split Walter's estate with Laura after his death. After Walter dies, his two sons contend that the last will is invalid because of Laura's undue influence as their father's primary caregiver. ◄

Disinheritance There is no requirement that testators give their estate to their family and other blood relatives. A testator may decide to disinherit, or leave nothing to, a certain relative or individual for various reasons. Most states have laws that attempt to prevent accidental disinheritance, however. Therefore, the testator's intent to disinherit needs to be made clear in his or her will for it to be upheld in court should a dispute arise.

Writing Requirements A will must be in writing. The writing can be informal. **EXAMPLE 39.3** Earl writes out his will on a scrap of paper before going into

holographic will
A will written entirely in the testator's handwriting and usually not witnessed.

emergency surgery.◄ A will that is completely in the handwriting of the testator is called a **holographic will**. A will can also refer to a written memorandum that itself is not in the will but that contains information necessary to carry out the will and is in existence when the will is signed.

Signature Requirements A formal, nonholographic (not handwritten) will must be signed by the testator. The testator's signature must appear in the will, generally at the end. Each jurisdiction dictates by statute and court decision what constitutes a signature. Initials, an "X" or other mark, and words such as "Mom" have all been upheld as valid when the testators intended them to be signatures.

Witness Requirements A formal, nonholographic (not handwritten) will normally must be witnessed. A will must be attested (affirmed to be genuine) by two, and sometimes three, witnesses. The number of witnesses, their qualifications, and the manner in which the witnessing must be done are generally set out in a statute. Some states require a witness to be disinterested—that is, not a beneficiary under the will. There are no age requirements. Witnesses must be mentally competent, however.

Publication Sometimes, a will must be published. A will is "published" by an oral declaration of the testator to the witnesses that the document they are about to sign is his or her will. In most states, publication is not necessary.

39–1d Revocation of a Will

Discuss methods of revoking or modifying a will.

The testator can revoke an executed will at any time during his or her life, either by a physical act or by a subsequent writing. Wills can also be revoked by operation of law. Revocation can be partial or complete, and must follow certain strict formalities.

Revocation by a Physical Act of the Maker Revocation by an act of the testator can be effected by a physical act. The physical acts by which a testator can revoke a will include intentionally burning it; intentionally tearing, canceling, obliterating, or destroying it; or having someone else perform such an act in the presence of the testator and at the testator's direction.

In some states, partial revocation by physical act is recognized. Thus, those portions of a will lined out or torn away are dropped, and the remaining parts of the will are valid. In no case, however, can a provision be crossed out and an additional or substitute provision written in. To add new provisions, the testator and witnesses must sign the will again.

codicil
A formal written supplement or modification to a will.

Revocation by a Subsequent Writing A will may be wholly or partially revoked by a **codicil**, a written instrument separate from the will that amends or revokes provisions in the will. A codicil eliminates the need to redraft an entire will merely to add to it or amend it. It can also be used to revoke an entire will. The codicil must be executed with the same formalities required for a will, and it must refer expressly to the will.

A second will, or new will, may revoke a prior will. The second will must use specific language, such as "This will hereby revokes all prior wills." If such an express *declaration of revocation* is missing, then both wills are read together. If any of the dispositions made in the second will are inconsistent with the prior will, the second will controls.

Revocation by Operation of Law Revocation by operation of law occurs when marriage, divorce or annulment, or the birth of a child takes place after a will has been made.

Marriage In most states, when a testator marries after making a will that does not include the new spouse, the spouse can still receive the amount he or she would have taken had the testator died without a valid will. The rest of the estate is distributed according to the terms of the will. If, however, the testator intentionally omitted the future spouse from the existing will or otherwise provided for the spouse in the will (or through a transfer of property outside the will), the omitted spouse will not receive a share.

EXAMPLE 39.4 Keyari is not married and has no children. She executes a will, disposing of her estate to "my brother and sister, Henry and Liliana." Later, Keyari marries Jason. They have no children. Keyari does not execute a new will before she dies. On her death, Jason is entitled to receive her entire estate. ◄

Divorce Divorce does not necessarily revoke an entire will. A divorce or an annulment occurring after a will has been written revokes those dispositions of property made under the will to the former spouse.

EXAMPLE 39.5 Cynthia executes a will, leaving her estate to "my husband, Donald, but if he should predecease me, then to our children, Evan and Faye, in equal shares." Later, Cynthia and Donald divorce. Cynthia dies without executing a new will. The divorce revokes the disposition of Cynthia's property to Donald. Her entire estate descends to Evan and Faye. ◄

Children If a child is born after a will has been executed and if it appears that the testator would have made a provision for the child, then the child is entitled to receive whatever portion of the estate he or she is allowed under state intestacy laws (discussed next). Most states allow a child to receive some portion of the estate if no provision is made in a will, unless it appears from the terms of the will that the testator intended that the child receive nothing.

EXAMPLE 39.6 Xavier executes a will, providing that "if my wife, Jayla, should predecease me, my estate is to descend to my children, Teresa and David, in equal shares." Later, Xavier's third child, Alexia, is born. Jayla predeceases Xavier, who subsequently dies without executing a new will. Because it appears from the language of the will that Xavier would have provided for a share of his estate to descend to Alexia, she is entitled to a portion of the estate. ◄

39–2 INTESTACY LAWS

Statutes of descent and distribution regulate how property is distributed when a person dies **intestate**—that is, without a will. These statutes—called **intestacy laws**—attempt to carry out the likely intent and wishes of the decedent.

39–2a Order of Distribution

Intestacy laws specify the order in which the heirs of an intestate share in the estate. First, the debts of the decedent must be paid out of his or her estate. Then the remaining assets pass to the surviving spouse and to the decedent's children. When there is no surviving spouse or child, then grandchildren, brothers and sisters, and, in some states, parents of the decedent are next in line. These relatives are usually called *lineal heirs*. If there are no lineal heirs, then *collateral heirs*—nieces, nephews, aunts, and uncles of the decedent—are the next group.

If the decedent has no surviving relatives in these groups, most statutes provide that the property will be distributed among the next of kin of any collateral heirs. Stepchildren are not considered kin. Legally adopted children, however, are recognized as lawful heirs of their adoptive parents. If no heirs exist, then the property reverts to the state—that is, the state assumes ownership of the property.

LEARNING OUTCOME 3
Describe the distribution of the property of a person who dies without a will.

intestate
As a noun, one who has died without having created a valid will; as an adjective, without a will.

intestacy laws
State laws determining the descent and distribution of the property of one who dies intestate (without a will).

39–2b Surviving Spouse and Children

Usually, state statutes provide that the estate first must be used to satisfy the debts of the decedent. Then, the remaining assets pass to the surviving spouse and to the children. A surviving spouse usually receives only a share of the estate—one-half, if there is also a surviving child, and one-third, if there are two or more children. Only if no children or grandchildren survive the decedent will a surviving spouse be entitled to the entire estate.

HIGHLIGHTING THE POINT

Mario dies intestate and is survived by his wife, Delia, and his children, Francisco and Tara. Mario's property passes according to intestacy laws.

Do Delia and the children receive any of Mario's property? Yes. After Mario's outstanding debts are paid, Delia will receive the homestead and usually one-third of all other property. The remaining real and personal property will pass to Francisco and Tara in equal portions.

39–2c Grandchildren

When an intestate is survived by descendants of deceased children, a question arises as to what share the descendants (that is, grandchildren of the intestate) will receive. There are two methods of dividing the assets of intestate decedents: the *per stirpes* method and the *per capita* method.

***Per Stirpes* Distribution** Under the *per stirpes* method, a class or group of distributees (for example, grandchildren) take the share that their deceased parent would have been entitled to inherit had that parent lived. Thus, a grandchild with no siblings inherits all of his or her parent's share, while grandchildren with siblings divide their parent's share. (See Exhibit 39.1.)

***Per Capita* Distribution** An estate may also be distributed on a *per capita* basis, which means that each person in a class or group takes an equal share of the estate. For instance, if a grandfather's estate is distributed *per capita* to three grandchildren,

per stirpes
A Latin term meaning "by the roots." A method of distributing an intestate's estate in which a class or group of distributees take the share to which their deceased ancestor would have been entitled.

per capita
A Latin term meaning "per person." A method of distributing the property of an intestate's estate by which all the heirs receive equal shares.

EXHIBIT 39.1   *Per Stirpes* Distribution

Under this method of distribution, an heir takes the share that his or her deceased parent would have been entitled to inherit, had the parent lived. This may mean that a class of distributees—the grandchildren in this example—will not inherit in equal portions. Note that Becky and Holly receive only one-fourth of Michael's estate while Paul inherits one-half.

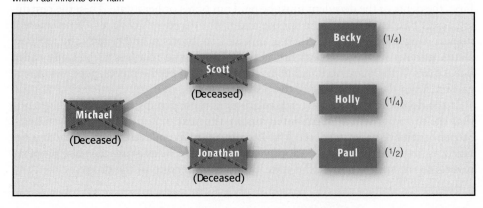

each grandchild will receive a one-third share of the estate. Exhibit 39.2, which follows, illustrates the *per capita* method of distribution.

39–3 TRUSTS

A **trust** is any arrangement through which property is transferred from one person to a trustee to be administered for the first person's or another party's benefit. A trust can also be defined as a right or property held by one party for the benefit of another.

The essential elements of a trust are as follows:

1. A designated beneficiary.
2. A designated trustee.
3. A fund sufficiently identified to enable title to pass to the trustee.
4. Actual delivery by the settlor or grantor (the person who creates the trust) to the trustee with the intention of passing title.

A trust can be express or implied.

39–3a Express Trusts

An *express trust* is one created or declared in definite terms, usually in writing. Here, we discuss two types of express trusts: *living trusts* and *testamentary trusts*.

Living Trusts A **living trust** is created by a grantor to be effective during the grantor's lifetime. It is also called an *inter vivos* trust, after a Latin term for "between or among the living." Living trusts have become a popular estate-planning option because at the grantor's death, assets held in a living trust can pass to the heirs without going through probate.

Note, however, that living trusts do not shelter assets from estate taxes, and the grantor may still have to pay income taxes on trust earnings—depending on whether the trust is revocable or irrevocable.

Revocable Living Trusts In a *revocable* living trust, which is the most common type, the grantor retains control over the trust property during her or his lifetime. The grantor deeds the property to the trust but retains the power to amend, alter, or revoke the trust. The grantor may also serve as a trustee or co-trustee and can arrange to receive income earned by the trust assets. Because the grantor controls

trust
An arrangement in which title to property is held by one person (a trustee) for the benefit of another (a beneficiary).

LEARNING OUTCOME 4

List the essential elements of a trust.

living trust
A trust created by a grantor (settlor) and effective during the grantor's lifetime.

LEARNING OUTCOME 5

State how different types of express and implied trusts are created or arise.

EXHIBIT 39.2 *Per Capita* Distribution

Under this method of distribution, all heirs in a certain class—in this example, the grandchildren—inherit equally. Note that Becky and Holly in this situation each inherit one-third, as does Paul.

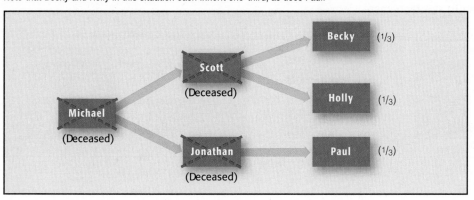

the funds, she or he is required to pay income taxes on the trust earnings. Unless the trust is revoked, the principal of the trust is transferred to the trust beneficiaries on the grantor's death.

EXAMPLE 39.7 James Cortez owns and operates a large farm. After his wife dies, James decides to create a living trust for the benefit of his three children, Alicia, Emma, and Jayden. He contacts his attorney, who prepares the documents creating the trust, executes a deed conveying the farm to the trust, and transfers the farm's bank accounts into the name of the trust. The trust designates James as the trustee and names his son, Jayden, as the *successor trustee,* who will take over the management of the trust when James dies or becomes incapacitated.

Each of the children will receive income from the trust while James is alive, and when James dies, the farm will pass to them without having to go through probate. By holding the property in a revocable living trust, James still has control over the farm during his life. This trust arrangement is illustrated in Exhibit 39.3.◄

Irrevocable Living Trusts In an *irrevocable* living trust, in contrast, the grantor permanently gives up control over the property to the trustee. The grantor executes a trust deed, and legal title to the trust property passes to the named trustee. The trustee has a duty to administer the property as directed by the grantor for the benefit and in the interest of the beneficiaries. The trustee must preserve the trust property; make it productive; and, if required by the terms of the trust agreement, pay income to the beneficiaries, all in accordance with the terms of the trust. Because the grantor has, in effect, given over the property for the benefit of the beneficiaries, he or she is no longer responsible for paying income taxes on the trust earnings.

testamentary trust
A trust that is created by will and therefore does not take effect until the death of the testator.

Testamentary Trusts A **testamentary trust** is created by a will and comes into existence on the settlor's death. After the death, a trustee takes title to the trust property, but his or her actions are subject to judicial approval. The legal responsibilities of this trustee are the same as those of the trustee of a living trust. The trustee of a testamentary trust can be named in the will or be appointed by the court.

If the will setting up a testamentary trust is invalid, then the trust will also be invalid. The property that was supposed to be in the trust will then pass according to intestacy laws, not according to the terms of the trust.

39–3b Implied Trusts

Sometimes, a trust is imposed by law in the absence of an express trust. Customarily, these *implied trusts* are of two types: *constructive trusts* and *resulting trusts.*

constructive trust
A trust created by operation of law against one who wrongfully holds a legal right to property that that person should not, in equity and good conscience, hold and enjoy.

Constructive Trusts A **constructive trust** is imposed by a court in the interests of fairness and justice. In a constructive trust, the owner of the property is declared

EXHIBIT 39.3   A Revocable Living Trust Arrangement

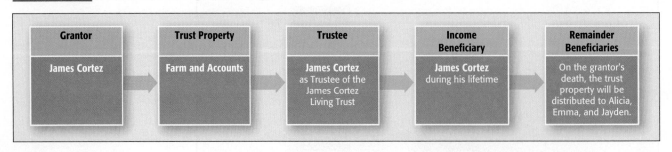

to be a trustee for the parties who are, in equity, actually entitled to the benefits that flow from the property. If someone wrongfully holds legal title to property—because the property was obtained through fraud or in breach of a legal duty, for example—a court may impose a constructive trust. Courts often impose constructive trusts when someone who is in a confidential or fiduciary relationship with another person, such as a guardian of a ward, has breached a duty to that person.

Resulting Trusts A **resulting trust** arises from the conduct of the parties, indicating an apparent intention to create a trust. When circumstances raise an inference that the party holding legal title to the property does so for the benefit of another, a trust is created.

resulting trust
A trust implied in law from the intentions of the parties to a given transaction.

EXAMPLE 39.8 Garrison wants to put one acre of land she owns on the market for sale. Because she is going out of the country for two years and will not be able to deed the property to a buyer during that period, Garrison conveys (transfers) the property to her good friend Oswald. Oswald can then attempt to sell the property while Garrison is gone. Because the transaction in which Garrison conveyed the property to Oswald is neither a sale nor a gift, the property will be held in trust (a resulting trust) by Oswald for the benefit of Garrison. On Garrison's return, Oswald will be required either to deed the property back to Garrison or, if the property has been sold, to turn over the proceeds to her.◄

ANSWERING THE LEGAL PROBLEM

In the legal problem set out at the beginning of this chapter, Fran's will provides that a certain sum of money is to be divided among a group of charities named in a written memorandum that Fran gives to her lawyer on the same day her will is signed.

A   **Is this list a valid part of Fran's will?** Yes. The written list of charities will be "incorporated by reference" into the will. It is in existence when the will is signed, and it is sufficiently described in the will so that it can be identified.

TERMS AND CONCEPTS FOR REVIEW

administrator 535	intestacy laws 539	probate court 535
codicil 538	intestate 539	resulting trust 543
constructive trust 542	legacy 536	testamentary trust 542
devise 536	legatee 536	testator 535
devisee 536	living trust 541	trust 541
executor 535	*per capita* 540	will 535
holographic will 538	*per stirpes* 540	

CHAPTER SUMMARY—WILLS AND TRUSTS

LEARNING OUTCOME	
1	**Outline the requirements of a will.** The requirements of a will include the following: (1) The testator must have capacity—that is, be of legal age and sound mind at the time the will is made. (2) A will must represent the maker's intention to transfer and distribute his or her property. (3) A will must be in writing. A holographic will is completely in the handwriting of the testator. (4) A nonholographic (not handwritten) will must be signed by the testator. What constitutes a signature varies from jurisdiction to jurisdiction. (5) A nonholographic will must be witnessed in the manner prescribed by state statute. (6) A will may have to be published—that is, the testator may be required to announce to witnesses that it is his or her will.
2	**Discuss methods of revoking or modifying a will.** A testator can revoke or modify a will through a physical act, such as intentionally burning or tearing up all (or part) of the will. A testator can also revoke or modify a will through a subsequent writing, such as a codicil or a new will. Revocation by operation of law occurs when marriage, divorce or annulment, or the birth of a child takes place after a will has been written. In general, it is assumed that the testator would wish to provide for the new spouse and for the new child and to revoke any provisions for the former spouse.
3	**Describe the distribution of the property of a person who dies without a will.** Intestacy laws (statutes of descent and distribution) vary widely from state to state. Usually, the law provides that the surviving spouse and children inherit the property of the decedent (after the decedent's debts are paid). If there is no surviving spouse or child, then lineal heirs (grandchildren, brothers and sisters, and sometimes parents of the decedent) inherit. If there are no lineal heirs, then collateral heirs (nieces, nephews, aunts, and uncles of the decedent) inherit.
4	**List the essential elements of a trust.** The essential elements of a trust are a beneficiary, a trustee, a fund sufficiently identified to enable title to pass to the trustee, and delivery to the trustee with the intention of passing title.
5	**State how different types of express and implied trusts are created or arise.** *Express trusts* are created by the use of definite terms, usually in writing. They include (1) the *living trust,* which is created by a grantor during her or his lifetime, and (2) the *testamentary trust,* which is created by a will and comes into existence on the death of the grantor. *Implied trusts* are imposed by law. They include (1) the *constructive trust,* which arises by operation of law when a person wrongfully takes title to property, and (2) the *resulting trust,* which arises from the conduct of the parties when an *apparent intention* to create a trust is present.

ISSUE SPOTTERS

Check your answers to the *Issue Spotters* against the answers provided in Appendix C at the end of this text.

1. Sheila makes out a will, leaving her property in equal thirds to Mark and Paula, her children, and Carol, her niece. Two years later, Sheila is adjudged mentally incompetent, and that same year, she dies. Can Mark and Paula have Sheila's will revoked on the ground that she did not have the capacity to make a will? Explain. (See *Wills.*)

2. Lee's will provides for a distribution of his property. First, the assets must be collected and inventoried, however. They may also need to be appraised. Creditors' claims must be sorted out. Federal and state income taxes must be paid. Finally, the assets must be distributed. Who performs these tasks? (See *Wills.*)

USING BUSINESS LAW

39–1. Estate Distribution. While single, James made out a will naming his mother, Carol, as sole beneficiary. Later, James married Lisa. (See *Intestacy Laws.*)

1. If James died while married to Lisa without changing his will, would the estate go to his mother, Carol? Explain.
2. Assume that when James married Lisa, he made out a new will leaving his entire estate to her. Later, he divorced Lisa and married Mandis, but he did not change his will. Discuss the rights of Lisa and Mandis to his estate after his death.

3. Assume that James divorced Lisa, married Mandis, and changed his will, leaving his estate to Mandis. Later, a daughter, Claire, was born. James died without having included Claire in his will. Discuss fully whether Claire has any rights in the estate.

REAL-WORLD CASE PROBLEMS

39–2. Requirements of a Will. Sherman Hemsley was a well-known actor from the 1970s. Most notably, he played George Jefferson on the television shows "All in the Family" and "The Jeffersons." He was born to Arsena Chisolm and William Thornton. Thornton was married to another woman, and Hemsley never had a relationship with his father or that side of the family. Hemsley never married and had no children. He lived with Flora Bernal, his business manager. Diagnosed with cancer, Hemsley executed a will naming Bernal the sole beneficiary of his estate. At the signing, Hemsley indicated that he knew he was executing his will and that he had deliberately chosen Bernal, but he did not discuss his relatives or the nature of his property with his attorney or the witnesses. After his death, the Thorntons challenged the will. Was Hemsley of sound mind? Discuss. [*In re Estate of Hemsley*, __ S.W.3d __, 2014 WL 5854220 (Tex.App.–El Paso 2014)] (See *Wills.*)

39–3. Undue Influence. Susie Walker executed a will that left her entire estate to her grandson. When her grandson died,

Susie executed a new will that named her great-grandson her sole beneficiary and specifically disinherited her son, Tommy. At the time, Tommy's ex-wife was living with Susie. After Susie died, Tommy filed a suit, claiming that her will was the product of undue influence on the part of his ex-wife. Several witnesses testified that Susie had been mentally competent when she executed her will. Does undue influence appear likely based on these facts? Explain. [*In re Estate of Walker*, 80 A.D.3d 865, 914 N.Y.S.2d 379 (3 Dept. 2011)] (See *Wills.*)

39–4. Requirements of a Will. Katherine Hagan executed a will that left her estate to various charitable organizations, such as the Humane Society, and expressly excluded her relatives. When Hagan died, her estate was worth $1.48 million. Janice Benjamin and other Hagan relatives objected to the will. They argued that it was invalid because Hagan had not been of "sound mind" and that the funds should pass to them by intestacy. Should the will be declared void? Why or why not? [*Benjamin v. JPMorgan Chase Bank, N.A.*, 305 S.W.3d 446 (Ky.App. 2010)] (See *Wills.*)

ETHICAL QUESTIONS

39–5. Requirements of a Will. Under what circumstances might it be appropriate to ignore the provisions in a will? (See *Wills.*)

39–6. Constructive Trusts. Stella Jankowski added her niece, Genevieve Viarengo, as a joint owner on Jankowski's bank accounts. In executing a will, Jankowski told her attorney, John Wabiszczewicz, that she wanted her estate divided

equally among her ten nieces, nephews, and cousins. Neither she nor Viarengo mentioned the joint accounts. After Jankowski's death, her estate totaled about $600,000. The joint accounts were valued at about $500,000. Viarengo claimed that those accounts were hers. Jankowski's relatives filed a suit against Viarengo. Should the court impose a constructive trust? Discuss. [*Garrigus v. Viarengo*, 112 Conn.App. 655, 963 A.2d 1065 (2009)] (See *Trusts.*)

Chapter 39—Work Set

TRUE-FALSE QUESTIONS

_____ 1. A will is revocable only after the testator's death.

_____ 2. The testator generally must sign a will.

_____ 3. If a person dies without a will, all of his or her property automatically passes to the state in which that person lived most of his or her life.

_____ 4. A legacy (_inter vivos_) trust is created by a grantor during his or her lifetime.

_____ 5. A testamentary trust is created by will and begins on the settlor's death.

_____ 6. If a person marries after executing a will that does not include the spouse, the spouse gets nothing when the person dies.

_____ 7. If a will setting up a testamentary trust is invalid, the trust is also invalid.

_____ 8. A constructive trust does not differ from an express trust.

MULTIPLE-CHOICE QUESTIONS

_____ 1. Joe's will provides for specific items of property to be given to certain individuals, including employees of Joe's business. The will also provides for certain sums of money to be given to Joe's daughters, Gail and Laura. Because Joe's assets are insufficient to pay in full all of the bequests,

    a. all of the property must be sold and the proceeds distributed to the heirs.
    b. the employees, who are not in a blood relationship with Joe, get nothing.
    c. Gail and Laura get nothing.
    d. the gifts to Gail and Laura will be reduced proportionately.

_____ 2. Donna dies without a will, but with many relatives—a spouse, children, adopted children, sisters, brothers, uncles, aunts, cousins, nephews, and nieces. Who gets what is determined by the state's

    a. intestacy law.
    b. Statute of Frauds.
    c. trustee, who is appointed by Donna's executor.
    d. personal representative, who is appointed by a probate court.

_____ 3. Paul executes a will that leaves all his property to Dave. Two years later, Paul executes a will that leaves all his property to Nora. The second will does not expressly revoke the first will. Paul dies. Who gets his property?

    a. Dave, because he was given the property in the first will.
    b. Dave, because the second will did not expressly revoke the first will.
    c. Nora, because the first will was revoked by the second will.
    d. Nora, because two years separated the execution of the wills.

_____ 4. Tony dies intestate, survived by Lisa, his mother; Grace, his wife; Abby and Selena, his two daughters; and Brock, his grandson. Brock is the son of Cliff, Tony's son, who has already died. Under intestacy laws,

    a. Grace receives one-third of Tony's estate, and Abby, Selena, and Brock receive equal portions of the rest.
    b. Abby and Selena receive half of Tony's estate, and Grace receives the rest.
    c. Lisa and Grace receive equal portions of Tony's estate.
    d. Grace receives all of Tony's estate.

_____ 5. Kate wants Bev and Nina, her daughters, to get the benefit of her farm when she dies. She does not believe that her daughters can manage the farm effectively, because they live in other states. She can provide for them to get the farm's income, under another party's management, by setting up

a. a constructive trust.
b. a resulting trust.
c. a testamentary trust.
d. none of the above.

_____ 6. Al's will provides, "I, Al, leave all my computer equipment to my good friend, Ray." When Al dies, the personal representative gives Ray the computer equipment. Ray is

a. a devisee.
b. a legatee.
c. a residuary.
d. none of the above.

_____ 7. Joan, a nurse, cares for Ted for one year before Ted's death. Joan is named the sole beneficiary under Ted's will, to the exclusion of Ted's family members. Ted's family may challenge the will on the basis of

a. the state's intestacy laws.
b. undue influence.
c. both a and b.
d. none of the above.

_____ 8. Bob's will provides that each of his lineal heirs living at the time of his death is to take an equal share of his estate. This means that Bob intends for his estate to be distributed on

a. a _per capita_ basis.
b. a _per stirpes_ basis.
c. a residuary basis.
d. the basis of none of the above.

_____ 9. Eve dies without a will but is survived by her brother, Frank; her daughter, Gail; and her parents. The party with the first priority to receive Eve's estate is

a. Eve's brother, Frank.
b. Eve's daughter, Gail.
c. Eve's parents.
d. the state.

ANSWERING MORE LEGAL PROBLEMS

1. After the death of his wife, Thorne executed a will that transferred all of his assets to a trust for the benefit of his only daughter, Evelin. Later, Thorne married Dyan. Fourteen months into the marriage, Thorne died. Dyan objected to the will, asserting that Thorne had intended to provide for her financial security through a trust. She claimed that he had been prevented from creating this trust by Evelin, who had improperly pressured her father.

Is Dyan entitled to a share of Thorne's estate? It depends. A valid will is one that represents the testator's _____ to transfer and distribute his or her property. When the decedent's plan of distribution results from improper pressure by another person, the will is _____. Fraud or undue influence may be inferred when a testator ignores a spouse in favor of a third party who was in a position to influence the terms. Here, if Dyan can prove that Thorne _____ to give her a share of his assets in the form of a trust and was prevented from doing so by Evelin, the will is _____. In that circumstance, Dyan is entitled

to a share of Thorne's estate under the _____ laws.

2. Michael and Barbara wanted to set up a $150,000 trust fund to provide funds for their grandson, Tanner, to attend Eastern State University or a similar accredited institution.

What type of trust would this be, how would it be created, and how would it be administered? A trust created by a grantor to be effective during his or her lifetime is a _____ trust. The essential elements of a trust are a designated beneficiary, a designated trustee, property sufficiently identified to enable title to pass to the _____, and delivery of the property by the grantor to the _____ with the intent of passing title. The grantor signs a trust deed, and the ownership of the trust property passes to the _____. The trustee administers the property as directed by the grantor for the benefit of the beneficiary and in the beneficiary's interest. The trustee does this by preserving the trust property, making it productive, and paying the income from it as directed.

SPECIAL TOPICS

UNIT CONTENTS

CHAPTER 40 Administrative Law

CHAPTER 41 Antitrust Law

CHAPTER 42 International Law

40 ADMINISTRATIVE LAW

administrative agency
A federal or state government agency established to perform a specific function.

administrative law
The body of law that administrative agencies create in order to carry out their duties and responsibilities.

enabling legislation
Statutes enacted by Congress that authorize the creation of an administrative agency and specify the name, purposes, functions, and powers of the agency being created.

FACING A LEGAL PROBLEM

The federal Occupational Safety and Health Administration (OSHA) issues a rule to protect healthcare workers from viruses that can be transmitted in the blood of patients. Before issuing the rule, OSHA asks whether the restrictions materially reduce a significant workplace risk to human health without imperiling the existence of, or threatening massive dislocation to, the healthcare industry.

The American Dental Association (ADA) objects to the rule on the ground that OSHA did not prove that dental workers are sufficiently at risk to benefit from the rule.

 Can the proposed OSHA rule be set aside because of the ADA's objection?

In its early years, the United States had a simple, nonindustrial economy with little regulation. As the economy has grown and become more complex, the size of government has also increased, and so has the number of **administrative agencies.**

In some instances, new agencies have been created in response to a crisis. In the wake of the financial crisis that led to the recent Great Recession, for example, Congress enacted the Dodd-Frank Wall Street Reform and Consumer Protection Act. Among other things, this statute created the Financial Stability Oversight Council to identify and respond to emerging risks in the financial system. It also created the Consumer Financial Protection Bureau to protect consumers from abusive practices by financial institutions.

As the number of agencies has multiplied, so have the rules, orders, and decisions that they issue. Today, there are rules covering almost every aspect of a business's operations (see the *Linking Business Law to Your Career* feature at the end of this chapter). The regulations that administrative agencies issue make up the body of **administrative law.** In this chapter, we explain how these agencies exercise their authority.

 ## 40–1 AGENCY CREATION

Congress creates federal administrative agencies. Because Congress cannot possibly oversee the actual implementation of all the laws it enacts, it must delegate such tasks to others, particularly when the issues relate to highly technical areas, such as air and water pollution.

To create an administrative agency, Congress passes **enabling legislation,** which specifies the name, purposes, functions, and powers of the agency being created. For example, in 1914, Congress created the Federal Trade Commission (FTC) by enacting the Federal Trade Commission Act. This act does the following:

1. Prohibits unfair and deceptive trade practices.
2. Outlines the procedures the agency must follow to charge persons or organizations with violations of the act.
3. Provides for judicial review of agency orders.

Through similar enabling acts, state legislatures create state administrative agencies. Most often, a state agency is created as a parallel to a federal agency. For example, state pollution-control agencies parallel the U.S. Environmental Protection Agency. Federal regulations take precedence over conflicting state regulations.

There are two basic types of administrative agencies: *executive agencies* and *independent regulatory agencies*.

40–1a Executive Agencies

At the national level, executive agencies include the cabinet departments of the executive branch and the subagencies within the cabinet departments. For instance, the Food and Drug Administration is within the U.S. Department of Health and Human Services. Executive agencies are subject to the authority of the president, who has the power to appoint and remove the agencies' officers. Exhibit 40.1 lists a selection of cabinet departments and their most important subagencies.

40–1b Independent Regulatory Agencies

Independent regulatory agencies are outside the federal executive departments. They include the FTC, the Securities and Exchange Commission, and the Federal Communications Commission. The president has somewhat less power over independent regulatory agencies, whose officers serve for fixed terms and cannot be removed without just cause. Exhibit 40.2, which follows, lists selected independent agencies and their principal functions.

EXHIBIT 40.1   Selected Executive Departments and Important Subagencies

Department and Year Formed	Important Subagencies
Treasury—1789	Internal Revenue Service; U.S. Mint
Interior—1849	U.S. Fish and Wildlife Service; National Park Service; Bureau of Indian Affairs; Bureau of Land Management
Justice—1870	Federal Bureau of Investigation; Drug Enforcement Administration; Bureau of Prisons; U.S. Marshals Service
Commerce—1913	Bureau of the Census; Bureau of Economic Analysis; Minority Business Development Agency; U.S. Patent and Trademark Office; National Oceanic and Atmospheric Administration
Labor—1913	Occupational Safety and Health Administration; Bureau of Labor Statistics; Employment Standards Administration; Office of Labor-Management Standards; Employment and Training Administration
Defense—1949	National Security Agency; Joint Chiefs of Staff; Departments of the Air Force, Navy, Army; service academies
Transportation—1967	Federal Aviation Administration; Federal Highway Administration; National Highway Traffic Safety Administration; Federal Transit Administration
Health and Human Services—1980	Food and Drug Administration; Centers for Medicare and Medicaid Services; Centers for Disease Control and Prevention; National Institutes of Health
Veterans Affairs—1989	Veterans Health Administration; Veterans Benefits Administration; National Cemetery System
Homeland Security—2002	U.S. Citizenship and Immigration Services; Directorate of Border and Transportation Services; U.S. Coast Guard; Federal Emergency Management Agency

EXHIBIT 40.2   Selected Independent Regulatory Agencies

Name of Agency and Year Formed	Principal Duties
Federal Reserve System Board of Governors—1913	Guides monetary policy for the United States, such as determining interest rates, credit availability, and the money supply; analyzes domestic and international economic and financial conditions; and exercises supervisory control over the financial services industry.
Federal Trade Commission (FTC)—1914	Prevents businesses from engaging in unfair trade practices; stops the formation of monopolies in the business sector; protects consumer rights.
Securities and Exchange Commission (SEC)—1934	Regulates the nation's stock exchanges, in which shares of stock are bought and sold; enforces the securities laws, which require full disclosure of the financial profiles of companies that wish to sell stock and bonds to the public.
Federal Communications Commission (FCC)—1934	Regulates all communications by telegraph, cable, telephone, radio, satellite, and television.
National Labor Relations Board (NLRB)—1935	Protects employees' rights to join unions and bargain collectively with employers; attempts to prevent unfair labor practices by both employers and unions.
Equal Employment Opportunity Commission (EEOC)—1964	Works to eliminate discrimination in employment based on religion, gender, race, color, disability, national origin, or age; investigates claims of discrimination.
Environmental Protection Agency (EPA)—1970	Undertakes programs aimed at reducing air and water pollution; works with state and local agencies to help fight environmental hazards.
Nuclear Regulatory Commission (NRC)—1975	Ensures that electricity-generating nuclear reactors in the United States are built and operated safely; regularly inspects operations of such reactors.

40–2 THE ADMINISTRATIVE PROCESS

The basic functions of an administrative agency include making rules, investigating activities regulated by the agency, enforcing the agency's rules, and adjudicating disputes between the agency and those who are subject to its rules. These functions make up what is called the **administrative process**, which is the administration of law by administrative agencies. In contrast, the *judicial process* involves the administration of law by the courts.

An integral part of the administrative process is the Administrative Procedure Act (APA). The APA imposes requirements that all federal agencies must follow.

40–2a Rulemaking

The major function of an administration agency is **rulemaking**. We look here at the most common rulemaking procedure, called **notice-and-comment rulemaking**. This procedure involves three basic steps: (1) notice of the proposed rulemaking, (2) a comment period, and (3) publication of the final rule.

Notice of the Proposed Rulemaking When a federal agency decides to create a new rule, the agency publishes a notice of the proposed rulemaking proceedings in the *Federal Register,* a daily publication of the executive branch that prints government orders, rules, and regulations. The notice states where and when the proceedings will be held, the agency's authority for making the rule (usually its enabling legislation), and the terms or subject matter of the proposed rule.

Comment Period Following the publication of the notice of the proposed rulemaking proceedings, the agency allows time for persons to comment on the

administrative process
The procedure used by administrative agencies in the administration of law.

LEARNING OUTCOME 2

Outline the rulemaking, investigative, and adjudicative functions of administrative agencies.

rulemaking
The actions undertaken by administrative agencies when formally adopting new regulations or amending old ones.

notice-and-comment rulemaking
A procedure in agency rulemaking that requires notice, an opportunity for comment, and a published draft of the final rule.

proposed rule. The comments may be in writing or, if a hearing is held, may be given orally.

EXAMPLE 40.1 Cross Country Trucking learns that the U.S. Department of Transportation is considering a new regulation that will have a negative impact on its ability to do business and on its bottom line. A notice of the rulemaking is published in the *Federal Register*. Later, a public hearing is held so that proponents and opponents can offer evidence and question witnesses. At this hearing, Cross Country expresses its opinion about the pending rule. ◄

The agency need not respond to all comments, but it must respond to significant comments that bear directly on the proposed rule. The agency responds by either modifying its final rule or explaining, in a statement accompanying the final rule, why it did not make any changes.

The Final Rule After the agency reviews the comments, it drafts the final rule and publishes it in the *Federal Register*. The final rule is later compiled with the rules and regulations of other federal agencies in the *Code of Federal Regulations* (CFR). Final rules have binding legal effect unless the courts later overturn them. If an agency failed to follow proper rulemaking procedures, for instance, the final rule may not be binding.

EXAMPLE 40.2 The Drug Enforcement Administration (DEA) allows the production of hemp products that contain trace amounts of THC, a component of marijuana. These products include food products made by members of the Hemp Industries Association (HIA). Without following formal rulemaking procedures, the DEA publishes rules that effectively ban the possession and sale of HIA's food products as controlled substances. A court will most likely overturn the rules, holding that they are unenforceable because the DEA did not follow formal rulemaking procedures. ◄

40–2b Investigation

Administrative agencies conduct investigations of the entities that they regulate. During the rulemaking process, agencies investigate to obtain information about a particular industry so that any rule they issue is based on a consideration of relevant factors. After final rules are issued, agencies conduct investigations to monitor compliance with the rules.

Inspections and Tests Many agencies gather information through on-site inspections. Sometimes, inspecting an office, a factory, or some other business facility is the only way to obtain the evidence needed to prove a regulatory violation. Administrative inspections and tests cover a wide range of activities, including safety inspections of mines, safety tests of equipment, and environmental monitoring of potentially harmful emissions. An agency may also ask a firm or individual to submit certain documents or records to the agency for examination.

If a business firm refuses to comply with an agency request to inspect facilities or business records, the agency may resort to the use of a subpoena or a search warrant.

Subpoenas There are two basic types of subpoenas. The subpoena *ad testificandum*—which means "to testify" and is pronounced "add tes-*tee-fee*-can-dum"—is the technical term for an ordinary subpoena. It is a writ, or order, compelling a witness to appear at an agency hearing. The subpoena *duces tecum*—which means "bring it with you" and is pronounced "*doo*-suhs *tee*-kum"—compels an individual or organization to hand over books, papers, records, or documents to the agency.

There are limits on what an agency can demand. To determine whether an agency is abusing its discretion in its pursuit of information, a court may consider such factors as the following:

1. *The purpose of the investigation.* An investigation must have a legitimate purpose. An improper purpose is, for instance, harassment.
2. *The relevance of the information.* Information is relevant if it reveals that the law is being violated or if it assures the agency that the law is not being violated.
3. *The specificity of the demand for testimony or documents.* A subpoena, for example, must adequately describe what is being sought.
4. *The burden of the demand on the party from whom the information is sought.* For instance, in responding to a request for information, a business need not reveal trade secrets.

HIGHLIGHTING THE POINT

Natalie is a director of First National Bank when it is declared *insolvent* (unable to pay debts as they fall due). As part of an investigation into the bank's finances, the Federal Deposit Insurance Corporation (FDIC) issues a subpoena to Natalie for personal financial records relating to gains and losses in her assets. She objects that the subpoena intrudes on her privacy. The FDIC says that it needs to determine whether she used bank funds for her personal benefit and asks a court to enforce the subpoena.

Will the court enforce the subpoena? Yes. When personal documents of individuals are the subject of an administrative subpoena, privacy concerns must be considered. But there is a significant public interest in promptly resolving the affairs of insolvent banks on behalf of their creditors and depositors. The FDIC has a reasonable need to gain access to some of Natalie's records to determine whether she improperly used bank funds for her personal benefit.

Search Warrants The Fourth Amendment protects against unreasonable searches and seizures. It does this by requiring that, in most instances, a physical search for evidence be conducted under the authority of a search warrant. An agency's *search warrant* is an order directing law enforcement officials to search a specific place for a specific item and present it to the agency.

Agencies can conduct warrantless searches in several situations. Warrants are not required to conduct searches in highly regulated industries. Firms that sell firearms or liquor, for example, are automatically subject to inspections without warrants. Sometimes, a statute permits warrantless searches of certain types of hazardous operations, such as coal mines. Also, a warrantless inspection in an emergency situation is normally considered reasonable.

Of course, a warrant is not required if a business has no reasonable expectation of privacy in what is being searched. For instance, a party who puts trash on a curb for pick-up has no reasonable expectation of privacy regarding the trash, even if it is placed in a black plastic bag. This is because any passerby can rummage through the trash until the trash collector takes it, and even then, the collector can sift through the bag as well.

40–2c Adjudication

adjudication
A proceeding in which an administrative law judge hears and decides issues that arise when an administrative agency charges a person or a firm with an agency violation.

After conducting an investigation of a suspected rule violation, an agency may begin to take administrative action against an individual or organization. Most administrative actions are resolved through negotiated settlements at their initial stages. When no settlement can be reached, the dispute is resolved through a hearing conducted by the agency—a proceeding called **adjudication**.

Negotiated Settlements Depending on the agency, negotiations may take the form of a simple conversation or a series of informal conferences. The purpose is to correct the problem to the agency's satisfaction and eliminate the need for additional proceedings.

Formal Complaints If attempts at a settlement fail, the agency may issue a formal *complaint* against the suspected violator. In response, the suspected violator will file an *answer*. After this exchange, if the agency and the suspected violator still cannot agree on a settlement, the case will be heard in a trial-like setting before an **administrative law judge (ALJ)**.

EXAMPLE 40.3 The Environmental Protection Agency (EPA) finds that McAndrews Fish Factory is polluting groundwater in violation of federal pollution laws. The EPA issues a complaint against McAndrews in an effort to bring it into compliance with federal regulations. McAndrews answers, but no settlement is reached, so the matter goes to formal adjudication. ◄

The Role of an ALJ The ALJ presides over the hearing and has the power to administer oaths, take testimony, rule on questions of evidence, and make determinations of fact. The law requires an ALJ to be unbiased.

Certain safeguards prevent bias on the part of the ALJ and promote fairness in the proceedings. For example, the APA requires that the ALJ be separate from an agency's investigative and prosecutorial staff. The APA also prohibits private communications between the ALJ and any party to an agency proceeding. Finally, provisions of the APA protect the ALJ from agency disciplinary actions, unless the agency can show good cause for such an action.

Hearing Procedures Hearing procedures vary widely from agency to agency. Often, disputes are resolved through informal proceedings. **EXAMPLE 40.4** The Federal Trade Commission (FTC) charges Good Foods, Inc., with deceptive advertising. Representatives of Good Foods and the FTC, their counsel, and the ALJ meet at a table in a conference room to resolve the dispute informally. ◄

A formal hearing, in contrast, resembles a trial. Before the hearing, for example, the parties are permitted to undertake extensive discovery. During the hearing, the parties may give testimony, present other evidence, and cross-examine witnesses.

One difference between a trial and an agency hearing is that, normally, much more information can be introduced as evidence during an administrative hearing. This can include *hearsay*—that is, secondhand information offered for its truth.

Agency Orders Following a hearing, the ALJ renders an **initial order**, or decision. Either party may appeal the ALJ's decision to the board or commission that governs the agency. If a party does not agree with the commission's initial order, it can appeal to a federal court of appeals. **EXAMPLE 40.5** If McAndrews Fish Factory is dissatisfied with the ALJ's decision, it may appeal the decision to the commission that governs the EPA. If the factory is dissatisfied with the commission's decision, it may appeal the decision to a federal court of appeals. ◄

If no party appeals, the ALJ's decision becomes the **final order** of the agency. If a party appeals and the decision is reviewed, the final order comes from the commission's decision or that of the reviewing court. If a party appeals and the commission and the court decline to review the case, the ALJ's decision also becomes final.

The administrative adjudication process is illustrated in Exhibit 40.3.

40–3 AGENCY POWERS

Administrative agencies are unusual because they exercise powers that normally are divided among the three branches of government. Agencies' powers include

---

administrative law judge (ALJ)
One who presides over an administrative agency hearing and has the power to administer oaths, take testimony, rule on questions of evidence, and make determinations of fact.

initial order
An administrative agency's disposition in a matter other than a rulemaking.

final order
The final decision of an administrative agency on an issue.

LEARNING OUTCOME 3

State the limitations on agency powers.

EXHIBIT 40.3 The Process of Formal Administrative Adjudication

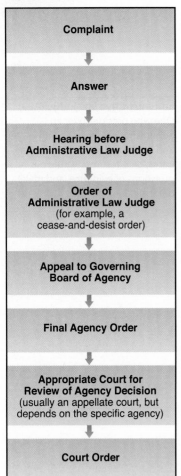

EXHIBIT 40.3 The Process of Formal Administrative Adjudication

Complaint

↓

Answer

↓

Hearing before
Administrative Law Judge

↓

Order of
Administrative Law Judge
(for example, a
cease-and-desist order)

↓

Appeal to Governing
Board of Agency

↓

Final Agency Order

↓

Appropriate Court for
Review of Agency Decision
(usually an appellate court, but
depends on the specific agency)

↓

Court Order

functions associated with the legislature (rulemaking), the executive branch (enforcement), and the courts (adjudication). For instance, agencies can make rules that are as legally binding as laws passed by Congress.

The constitutional principle of checks and balances allows each of the three branches of government to act as a check on the actions of the other two. Yet the Constitution does not specifically refer to administrative agencies, and this principle does not apply to them. Because administrative agencies function relatively independently, they are sometimes referred to as the fourth branch of the U.S. government.

An important governmental concern is to prevent agencies from abusing their extensive powers without hindering the agencies as they carry out their prescribed duties. To address this concern, all three branches of the government exercise certain controls over agency powers and functions.

40–3a Executive Controls

The executive branch of government exercises control over agencies through the president's powers to appoint federal officers and through the president's veto powers. For example, the president may veto enabling legislation presented by Congress or congressional attempts to modify an existing agency's authority.

40–3b Legislative Controls

Congress exercises authority over agency powers in several ways. As noted earlier, Congress gives power to an agency through enabling legislation. An agency may not, however, exceed the power that Congress gives to it. Through later legislation, Congress can take away that power or even abolish an agency altogether. Congressional authority is required to fund an agency, and enabling legislation usually sets time and monetary limits relating to particular programs. Congress can always change these limits. In addition, Congress can investigate the agencies that it creates.

The question that a court faces when confronted with an agency's interpretation of a statute it administers is always whether the agency has acted within the extent of the authority given to it by Congress.

Real-World Case Example

Responding to concern about the performance of some paid tax-return preparers, the Internal Revenue Service (IRS) issued a new rule. The rule required paid preparers to pass an initial certification exam, pay annual fees, and complete fifteen hours of continuing education courses each year. As authority for the rule, the IRS relied on a statute enacted in 1884 that authorizes the agency to "regulate the practice of representatives of persons before the Department of the Treasury." Three preparers filed a suit in a federal district court against the IRS, challenging the rule. The court ruled in the plaintiffs' favor. The IRS appealed.

Did the IRS's rule regulating tax-return preparers exceed the agency's authority? Yes. In a 2014 case, *Loving v. Internal Revenue Service*, the U.S. Court of Appeals for the D.C. Circuit affirmed the lower court's ruling. The IRS interpreted the statute to empower the agency "for the first time to regulate hundreds of thousands of individuals in the multi-billion dollar tax-preparation industry." Nothing in the statute's text, history, structure, or context "contemplates that vast expansion of the IRS's authority."

40–3c Judicial Controls

The judicial branch of the government exercises control over agency powers through the courts' review of agency actions. The APA provides for judicial review of most agency decisions.

Requirements for Judicial Review Agency actions are not automatically subject to judicial review. Parties seeking review must meet certain requirements, including the following:

1. *The action must be reviewable by the court.* The APA provides that unless proven otherwise, agency actions are reviewable, making this requirement easy to satisfy.

2. *The party must have standing to sue the agency.*

3. *The party must have exhausted all possible administrative remedies.* Each agency has its "chain of review," and the party must follow agency appeal procedures before a court will review the case. **EXAMPLE 40.6** The Federal Trade Commission (FTC) claims that Happy Trails Travel Agency uses deceptive advertising and orders the firm to run new ads correcting the misstatements. Happy Trails contends that its ads are not deceptive. To challenge the order, Happy Trails must go through the entire FTC appeal process before it can ask a court to review the case.◄

The Arbitrary and Capricious Test The APA provides that courts should "set aside" agency actions found to be "arbitrary, capricious, an abuse of discretion, or otherwise not in accordance with law." Under this standard, parties can challenge regulations as contrary to law or so irrational as to be arbitrary and capricious.

The arbitrary and capricious standard does not have a precise definition, but in applying it, courts typically consider whether the agency has done any of the following:

1. Failed to provide a rational explanation for its decision.

2. Changed its prior policy without justification.

3. Considered legally inappropriate factors.

4. Failed to consider a relevant factor.

5. Rendered a decision plainly contrary to the evidence.

HIGHLIGHTING THE POINT

Under the Clean Air Act (CAA), the Environmental Protection Agency (EPA) is authorized to regulate any pollutants that in its judgment "cause, or contribute to, air pollution." Calling global warming "the most pressing environmental challenge of our time," a group of private organizations asks the EPA to regulate carbon dioxide and other "greenhouse gas" emissions from new motor vehicles. The EPA refuses, stating that Congress last amended the CAA in 1990 without authorizing new, binding auto emissions limits.

Is the EPA's refusal to regulate greenhouse gases arbitrary and capricious? Yes. The EPA has the authority under the CAA to regulate the emission of greenhouse gases from new motor vehicles. Nothing in the statute suggests that Congress meant to curtail the agency's power to treat greenhouse gases as air pollutants. The EPA can avoid issuing regulations only if the agency determines that greenhouse gases do not contribute to purported climate change, or if the agency reasonably explains why it cannot or will not determine whether they do.

40–4 PUBLIC ACCOUNTABILITY

LEARNING OUTCOME 4

Describe federal laws that make agencies accountable through public scrutiny.

Several laws make agencies more accountable through public scrutiny. Next, we discuss the most significant of these laws.

40–4a Freedom of Information Act

Enacted in 1966, the Freedom of Information Act (FOIA) requires the federal government to disclose certain records to any person on request, even if the person does not give any reason for the request. For most records, a request need include only a reasonable description of the information sought. An agency's failure to comply with a request may be challenged in a federal district court.

The media, public-interest groups, and even companies seeking information about competitors can obtain information from government agencies under this law. Some records are exempt, however, such as those containing confidential business or personal information. **EXAMPLE 40.7** Juanita, a reporter from *Healthy-Works* magazine, makes an FOIA request to the Centers for Disease Control and Prevention for a list of people who have contracted a highly contagious virus. The Centers for Disease Control and Prevention will not have to comply, because the requested information is confidential and personal.◄

40–4b Government in the Sunshine Act

The Government in the Sunshine Act requires that "every portion of every meeting of an agency" be open to "public observation." Closed meetings are permitted, however, under the following circumstances:

1. The subject of the meeting concerns accusing any person of a crime.

2. Open meetings would frustrate implementation of future agency actions.

3. The meeting involves matters relating to future litigation or rulemaking.

Nonetheless, courts interpret these exceptions to allow open access whenever possible.

40–4c Regulatory Flexibility Act

Congress passed the Regulatory Flexibility Act in 1980. Under this act, whenever a new regulation will have a "significant impact upon a substantial number" of small businesses, the agency must conduct a regulatory flexibility analysis. The analysis must measure the cost that the rule would impose on small businesses and must consider less burdensome alternatives. The act also contains provisions to alert small businesses about forthcoming regulations.

40–4d Small Business Regulatory Enforcement Fairness Act

The Small Business Regulatory Enforcement Fairness Act (SBREFA) allows Congress to review new federal regulations for at least sixty days before they take effect. This period gives opponents of the rules time to present their arguments to Congress.

The SBREFA also requires federal agencies to prepare guides that explain in "plain English" how small businesses can comply with regulations. The act set up the Office of the National Ombudsman at the U.S. Small Business Administration to receive comments from small businesses about their dealings with federal agencies. Based on these comments, regional small-business fairness boards rate the agencies and publicize their findings.

ANSWERING THE LEGAL PROBLEM

In the legal problem set out at the beginning of this chapter, the federal Occupational Safety and Health Administration (OSHA) issues a rule to protect health-care workers from viruses that can be transmitted in the blood of patients. Before issuing the rule, OSHA asks whether the restrictions materially reduce a significant workplace risk to human health without imperiling the existence of, or threatening massive dislocation to, the health-care industry.

The American Dental Association (ADA) objects to the rule on the ground that OSHA did not prove that dental workers are sufficiently at risk to benefit from the rule.

A **Can the proposed OSHA rule be set aside because of the ADA's objection?** No. To be sure, OSHA cannot impose burdensome requirements on an entire industry if the safety or health of its workers is not really at risk. The agency is not required, however, to issue separate rules for each workplace. If an agency provides a rational explanation for its rules, the rules will not be set aside.

LINKING BUSINESS LAW to Your Career

DEALING WITH ADMINISTRATIVE LAW

In your career, whether you end up owning your own business or working for another, you will be dealing with multiple aspects of administrative law. All federal, state, and local government agencies create rules that have the force of law. As a manager, you will have to learn about the rules that pertain to your business activities.

Participate in the Rulemaking Process

All federal agencies and many state agencies invite public commentary on proposed rules. Suppose that your state occupational safety agency proposes to require all construction-site employees to wear hearing protection. If you manage a construction company, you may believe that such a rule will lead to a less safe environment because your employees will not be able to communicate easily with each other.

Should you spend time offering comments to the agency proposing this rule? As an efficient manager, you would make a trade-off calculation: What is the value of the time that you would spend in an attempt to prevent or alter the proposed rule? You would compare this cost with your estimate of the benefits your company would receive if the rule was not put into place.

Prepare for Investigations and Enforcement of Rules

All agencies have investigatory powers. Investigators usually have the power to search business premises. As a manager, if you receive investigators on a routine basis, you may opt to cooperate fully. In contrast, if your business is rarely investigated, you may decide that an inspection is overreaching.

If an agency cites you for a violation, you will probably negotiate a settlement rather than take your case to an administrative law judge. Again, as a manager, you have to weigh the cost of the negotiated enforcement with the potential cost of fighting the violation.

Stay Flexible

Throughout your career, you will face hundreds of administrative rules, investigations, and perhaps enforcement proceedings for violations. Accept these as part of the legal environment in which you work and remain flexible in your outlook on administrative laws.

TERMS AND CONCEPTS FOR REVIEW

adjudication 554

administrative agency 550

administrative law 550

administrative law judge (ALJ) 555

administrative process 552

enabling legislation 550

final order 555

initial order 555

notice-and-comment
rulemaking 552

rulemaking 552

CHAPTER SUMMARY—ADMINISTRATIVE LAW

LEARNING OUTCOME	
1	**Identify how administrative agencies are created.** Administrative agencies are created by enabling legislation, which usually specifies the name, purposes, functions, and powers of the agency.
2	**Outline the rulemaking, investigative, and adjudicative functions of administrative agencies.** (1) *Rulemaking*—Agencies are authorized by their enabling legislation to create new regulations. Notice-and-comment rulemaking is the most common rulemaking procedure. It begins with the publication of the proposed regulation in the *Federal Register*. Publication of the notice is followed by a comment period to allow private parties to comment on the proposed rule. (2) *Investigation*—Agencies investigate the entities that they regulate. Investigations are conducted during the rulemaking process to obtain information and after rules are issued to monitor compliance. The most important investigative tools available to an agency are (1) inspections and tests and (2) subpoenas that direct individuals to appear at a hearing or to hand over specified documents. In seeking information, the agency must have a legitimate purpose. In addition, the information sought must be relevant, and the demands made must be specific and not unduly burdensome. Search warrants are usually required for on-site inspections. (3) *Adjudication*—After a preliminary investigation, an agency may initiate an administrative action against an individual or organization. Most such actions are resolved by negotiated settlement at this initial stage. If there is no settlement, the case is presented to an administrative law judge (ALJ) in a proceeding similar to a trial. After a proceeding is concluded, the ALJ renders an initial order, which may be appealed by either party to a federal appeals court. If no appeal is taken or the case is not reviewed, then the order becomes the final rule.
3	**State the limitations on agency powers.** (1) *Executive controls*—The president can control agencies through appointments of federal officers and through vetoes of legislation creating or affecting agency powers. (2) *Legislative controls*—Congress can give power to an agency, take it away, increase or decrease the agency's funding, or abolish the agency. (3) *Judicial controls*—Agencies are subject to the judicial review of the courts. For an agency action to be reviewed, it must be reviewable by the court, the party seeking review must have standing to sue, and the parties must have exhausted all possible administrative remedies. Courts can "set aside" agency actions that are found to be arbitrary and capricious.
4	**Describe federal laws that make agencies accountable through public scrutiny.** (1) *Freedom of Information Act*—Requires that the government disclose certain records to any person on request. (2) *Government in the Sunshine Act*—Requires that every portion of every meeting of an agency be open to "public observation." (3) *Regulatory Flexibility Act*—Requires a regulatory flexibility analysis whenever a new regulation will have a "significant impact upon a substantial number" of small businesses. (4) *Small Business Regulatory Enforcement Fairness Act*—Allows Congress sixty days to review new regulations, requires federal agencies to explain in "plain English" how to comply with regulations, and empowers the U.S. Small Business Administration to rate federal agencies based on comments from small businesses.

ISSUE SPOTTERS

Check your answers to the *Issue Spotters* against the answers provided in Appendix C at the end of this text.

1. The Securities and Exchange Commission (SEC) makes rules regarding what must be in a stock prospectus, prosecutes and adjudicates alleged violations, and prescribes punishment. This gives the SEC considerable power. What checks are there against this power? (See *Agency Powers.*)

2. Itex Corporation would like to know what information federal agencies have about its business operations so that it will know what its competitors may be able to learn about it. Under what federal law can Itex require the agencies to disclose whatever information they may have concerning the company? (See *Public Accountability.*)

USING BUSINESS LAW

40–1. Rulemaking Procedures. Assume that the Food and Drug Administration (FDA), using proper procedures, adopts a rule covering future investigations involving the FDA's regulation of food additives. According to the new rule, the FDA will not regulate food additives without giving food companies an opportunity to cross-examine witnesses. Some time later, the FDA regulates methylisocyanate, a food additive. In its investigation of methylisocyanate, the FDA has not allowed producers to cross-examine witnesses. Producers protest, saying that the FDA promised cross-examination. The FDA responds that the Administrative Procedure Act does not require such cross-examination and that it can freely withdraw the promise made in its new rule. If the producers challenge the FDA in a court, on what basis could the court rule in their favor? (See *The Administrative Process.*)

40–2. Rulemaking and Adjudication Powers. For decades, the Federal Trade Commission (FTC) resolved fair trade and advertising disputes through individual adjudications. In the 1960s, the FTC began making rules that defined fair and unfair trade practices. In cases involving violations of these rules, the due process rights of participants were more limited than in the past and did not include cross-examination. Although anyone found violating a rule would receive a full adjudication, the legitimacy of the rule itself could not be challenged in the adjudication. Any party charged with violating a rule was almost certain to lose the adjudication. Affected parties complained to a court, arguing that their rights before the FTC were unduly limited by the new rules. What will the court examine to determine whether to uphold the new rules? (See *The Administrative Process.*)

REAL-WORLD CASE PROBLEMS

40–3. Adjudication. Mechanics replaced a brake assembly on the landing gear of a CRJ–700 plane operated by GoJet Airlines, LLC. They installed gear pins to lock the assembly in place during the repair but then failed to remove one of the pins. After takeoff on the plane's next flight, a warning light alerted the pilots that the landing gear would not retract. There was a potential for danger, but the pilots safely flew the CRJ–700 back to the departure airport. No one was injured, and no property was damaged. The Federal Aviation Administration (FAA) cited GoJet for violations of FAA regulations by "carelessly or recklessly operating an unairworthy airplane." GoJet objected to the citation. To which court can GoJet appeal for review? On what ground might that court decline to review the case?

[*GoJets Airlines, LLC v. Federal Aviation Administration,* 743 F.3d 1168 (8th Cir. 2014)] (See *The Administrative Process.*)

40–4. Judicial Controls. Michael Manin, an airline pilot, was twice convicted of disorderly conduct, a minor misdemeanor. To renew his flight certification with the National Transportation Safety Board (NTSB), Manin filed an application that asked him about his criminal history. He did not disclose his two convictions. When these came to light more than ten years later, Manin argued that he had not known that he was required to report convictions for minor misdemeanors. The NTSB's policy was to consider an applicant's understanding of what information a question sought before determining whether an answer was false. But without explanation, the agency departed from this policy, refused to consider Manin's argument, and revoked his certification. Was this action arbitrary or capricious? Explain. [*Manin v. National Transportation Safety Board*, 627 F.3d 1239 (D.C. Cir. 2011)] (See *Agency Powers*.)

40–5. The Freedom of Information Act. Sikorsky Aircraft Corp. contracted with the U.S. Department of Defense (DoD). Under the Freedom of Information Act, a reporter asked the DoD for copies of all DoD requests that

Sikorsky fix problems with its Black Hawk helicopter. Sikorsky objected that the documents would expose trade secrets about its business operations. The DoD promised to remove sensitive information, but the copies given to the reporter revealed trade secrets. Sikorsky filed a suit, arguing that the DoD's decision to release the documents was arbitrary and capricious. Was the reporter's request legal? Was the DoD's response sufficient? Explain. [*United Technologies Corp. v. U.S. Department of Defense*, 601 F.3d 557 (D.C. Cir. 2010)] (See *Public Accountability*.)

ETHICAL QUESTIONS

40–6. Judicial Controls. Should an individual or organization sue an agency before the agency takes formal enforcement action? Discuss your answer. (See *Agency Powers*.)

40–7. Judicial Controls. The Federal Communications Commission (FCC) monitors *indecent speech*—that is, "language that describes, in terms patently offensive as measured by contemporary community standards for the broadcast medium, sexual or excretory activities and organs." The FCC had long ignored so-called fleeting expletives. During a television broadcast of the Golden

Globe Awards, the rock band U2's lead singer, Bono, commented, "This is really, really, f***ing brilliant." The FCC issued a complaint about Bono's comment, stating that any use of "the F-Word" falls within the scope of the indecency definition. Children are often exposed to indecent language in various media. Does this mean that we need more—or less—stringent regulation? Explain. [*Federal Communications Commission v. Fox Television Stations, Inc.*, 556 U.S. 502, 129 S.Ct. 1800, 173 L.Ed.2d 738 (2009)] (See *Agency Powers*.)

Chapter 40—Work Set

TRUE-FALSE QUESTIONS

_____ 1. Enabling legislation specifies the powers of an agency.

_____ 2. Federal courts are part of the executive branch of government.

_____ 3. Congress creates federal administrative agencies.

_____ 4. After an agency adjudication, the administrative law judge's order must be appealed to become final.

_____ 5. The Administrative Procedure Act provides for judicial review of most agency actions.

_____ 6. When a new regulation will have a significant impact on a substantial number of small entities, an analysis must be conducted to measure the costs imposed on small businesses.

_____ 7. State administrative agency operations prevail over federal agency actions.

_____ 8. An agency cannot conduct a search without a warrant.

_____ 9. Agency rules are not as legally binding as the laws that Congress enacts.

_____ 10. Congress has no power to influence agency policy.

MULTIPLE-CHOICE QUESTIONS

_____ 1. Congress has the power to establish administrative agencies to perform which of the following functions?

a. Make administrative rules.
b. Adjudicate disputes arising from administrative rules.
c. Investigate violations of administrative rules.
d. All of the above.

_____ 2. An agency may obtain information concerning activities and organizations that it oversees through

a. a subpoena only.
b. a search only.
c. a subpoena and a search.
d. neither a subpoena nor a search.

_____ 3. The Occupational Safety and Health Administration (OSHA) issues a subpoena for Triplex Corporation to hand over all of its files. Triplex's possible defenses against the subpoena include which of the following?

a. OSHA is a federal agency, but Triplex only does business locally.
b. An administrative agency cannot issue a subpoena.
c. The demand is not specific enough.
d. None of the above.

_____ 4. In making rules, an agency's procedure normally includes

a. notice.
b. opportunity for comments by interested parties.
c. publication of the final draft of the rule.
d. all of the above.

5. The National Oceanic and Atmospheric Administration (NOAA) is a federal agency. To limit the authority of NOAA, the president can

a. abolish the agency.
b. take away the agency's power.
c. veto legislative modifications to the agency's authority.
d. refuse to appropriate funds for the agency.

6. The Bureau of Indian Affairs (BIA) wants to close a series of its meetings to the public. To open the meetings, a citizen would sue the BIA under the

a. Freedom of Information Act.
b. Government in the Sunshine Act.
c. Regulatory Flexibility Act.
d. Administrative Procedure Act.

7. The U.S. Fish and Wildlife Service orders Bill to stop using a certain type of fishing net from his boat. Before a court will hear Bill's appeal of the order, Bill must

a. exhaust all administrative remedies.
b. bypass all administrative remedies and appeal directly to the court.
c. appeal simultaneously to the agency and the court.
d. ignore the agency and continue using the net.

8. The Federal Trade Commission (FTC) issues an order relating to the advertising of Midtron Corporation. Midtron appeals the order to a court. The court may review whether the FTC has

a. exceeded its authority.
b. taken an action that is arbitrary, capricious, or an abuse of discretion.
c. violated any constitutional provisions.
d. done any of the above.

9. The Environmental Protection Agency (EPA) publishes notice of a proposed rule. When comments are received about the rule, the EPA must respond to

a. all of the comments.
b. any significant comments that bear directly on the proposed rule.
c. only comments by businesses engaged in interstate commerce.
d. none of the comments.

ANSWERING MORE LEGAL PROBLEMS

1. OptiWire makes plastic-coated wire. The process generates acidic and alkaline wastewater. OptiWire has a system in its plant to treat the wastewater. The water then flows into an open pit outside the plant and through a pipe that connects with the public sewer system three hundred feet away. Without a search warrant or OptiWire's express consent, agents for the Environmental Protection Agency (EPA) took samples from the pit. Based on the samples, OptiWire is charged with violations of the Clean Water Act.

Does the EPA agents' sampling of the water in the pit constitute a reasonable search? Yes. The U.S. Constitution's Fourth Amendment protects against _____ searches. The EPA agents' "search" was not _____. OptiWire had no _____ expectation of privacy in the wastewater, and therefore, it had no Fourth Amendment _____ with respect to the agents' sampling of it. The water in the pit flows into the public sewer, which is only three hundred feet away. Once the wastewater reaches that point, any member of the public can take a sample.

2. The Federal Trade Commission (FTC) issued a subpoena to athletic shoemaker Sleek Feet to investigate the company's claims about the benefits of its shoes—which purportedly helped their wearers lose weight, tone their bodies, and fight heart disease. After a hearing, the FTC decided that the claims were unsubstantiated. Sleek Feet wants to appeal the decision.

What are the requirements for the judicial review of an agency decision? A party seeking the review of an agency decision must meet certain requirements. (1) The action must be _____ by the court. Unless proven otherwise, agency actions are _____. (2) The party seeking review must have _____ to sue the agency. (3) The party must have _____ all possible administrative remedies.

ANTITRUST LAW

41

FACING A LEGAL PROBLEM

A group of independent oil producers in Texas and Louisiana are caught between falling demand due to bad economic times and increasing supply from newly discovered oil fields in the region.

In response to these conditions, a group of major refining companies agree to buy excess supplies from the independents so as to dispose of the excess in an "orderly manner."

It is clear that the purpose is to limit the supply of gasoline on the market and thereby raise prices. In a lawsuit challenging the agreement, the oil producers claim that under the circumstances, the agreement is reasonable.

Q Does the agreement violate antitrust law?

LEARNING OUTCOMES

The four Learning Outcomes below are designed to help improve your understanding of the chapter. After reading this chapter, you should be able to:

❶ List anticompetitive activities prohibited by the Sherman Act.

❷ List anticompetitive activities outlawed by the Clayton Act.

❸ State who enforces the antitrust laws.

❹ Define the extraterritorial reach of U.S. antitrust laws.

Antitrust legislation is an important area of business regulation. This legislation is based on the desire to foster competition. Antitrust legislation was initially created—and continues to be enforced—because of our belief that competition leads to lower prices, more product information, and a better distribution of wealth between consumers and producers.

Laws that regulate economic competition are referred to as **antitrust laws.** Today's antitrust laws are the direct descendants of common law actions intended to limit **restraints of trade** (agreements between firms that have the effect of reducing competition in the marketplace). Concern arose following the Civil War over the growth of large corporate enterprises and their attempts to reduce or eliminate competition. At the national level, the government recognized the problem and passed the Sherman Act in 1890. In 1914, Congress passed the Clayton Act, as well as the Federal Trade Commission Act, to further curb anticompetitive business practices.

antitrust law
Laws protecting commerce from unlawful restraints.

restraint of trade
Any conspiracy or combination that unlawfully eliminates competition or facilitates the creation of a monopoly or monopoly pricing.

41–1 THE SHERMAN ACT

The Sherman Act is the most important antitrust law. Sections 1 and 2 contain its main provisions:

1: Every contract, combination in the form of trust or otherwise, or conspiracy, in restraint of trade or commerce among the several States, or with foreign nations, is hereby declared to be illegal [and is a crime punishable by fine and/or imprisonment].

2: Every person who shall monopolize, or attempt to monopolize, or combine or conspire with any other person or persons, to monopolize any part of the trade or commerce among the several States, or with foreign nations, shall be deemed guilty of a felony [and is similarly punishable].

LEARNING OUTCOME 1

List anticompetitive activities prohibited by the Sherman Act.

565

Any activity that substantially affects interstate commerce (trade between two or more states) falls under the Sherman Act. The Sherman Act also extends to U.S. nationals abroad who are engaged in activities that affect U.S. foreign commerce.

41–1a Section 1 of the Sherman Act

The underlying assumption of Section 1 of the Sherman Act is that society's welfare is harmed if rival firms are permitted to join in an agreement that consolidates their market power or otherwise restrains competition. Not all agreements between rivals, however, result in enhanced market power or *unreasonably* restrain trade.

rule of reason
A test by which a court balances the reasons for an agreement against its potentially anticompetitive effects.

The Rule of Reason Under what is called the **rule of reason**, anticompetitive agreements that supposedly violate Section 1 of the Sherman Act are analyzed with the view that they may, in fact, constitute reasonable restraints of trade. When applying this rule, the court considers several factors. These factors include the purpose of the agreement, the parties' market ability to implement the agreement to achieve that purpose, and the effect or potential effect of the agreement on competition. If the court deems that legitimate competitive benefits outweigh the anticompetitive effects of the agreement, it will be held lawful.

Some business situations that have the rule of reason applied to them include trade associations, territorial restrictions, and resale price maintenance agreements.

Trade Associations Businesses in the same general industry or profession frequently organize trade associations to pursue common interests. The joint activities of the trade association may include exchanges of information, representation of the members' business interests before governmental bodies, advertising campaigns, and the setting of regulatory standards to govern the industry or profession.

Generally, the rule of reason is applied to these actions. If a court finds that a trade association practice or agreement that restrains trade is sufficiently beneficial both to the association and to the public, it may deem the restraint reasonable. Other trade association agreements may have such substantially anticompetitive effects that the court will consider them to be in violation of Section 1.

Territorial or Customer Restrictions In arranging for the distribution of its products, a manufacturer often wishes to insulate its dealers from direct competition with one another. To this end, it may institute territorial restrictions or attempt to prohibit wholesalers or retailers from reselling the product to certain classes of customers, such as competing retailers. Territorial and customer restrictions are judged under the rule of reason, because there may be legitimate reasons for such restrictions.

EXAMPLE 41.1 Goodspeed Machine Manufacturing wishes to prevent Hillsboro Mechanics, one of its dealers, from cutting costs and undercutting other Goodspeed dealers by selling Goodspeed's products at lower prices. By not including Goodspeed's promotional and customer services in their prices—and relying on others to provide these same services at lower costs—Hillsboro reaps the benefits paid for by other Goodspeed dealers and may harm Goodspeed's reputation. ◄

resale price maintenance agreement
An agreement between a manufacturer and a distributor or retailer in which the manufacturer specifies what the retail prices of its products must be.

Resale Price Maintenance Agreements An agreement between a manufacturer and a distributor or retailer in which the manufacturer specifies what the retail prices of its products must be is referred to as a **resale price maintenance agreement**. This type of agreement may violate Section 1 of the Sherman Act. Such agreements are evaluated under the rule of reason.

***per se* violation**
A type of anticompetitive agreement that is considered to be so injurious to the public that there is no need to determine whether it actually injures market competition.

***Per Se* Violations** Some agreements are so blatantly and substantially anticompetitive that they are deemed illegal *per se* (inherently) under Section 1. If an agreement is deemed a ***per se* violation**, a court is prevented from determining whether the agreement's benefits outweigh its anticompetitive effects. Some important types of *per se* violations under Section 1 are discussed next.

Price-Fixing Agreements A **price-fixing agreement** is an agreement among competitors to set prices. Any agreement that restricts output or artificially fixes prices is considered a *per se* violation under Section 1.

price-fixing agreement
An agreement between competitors to fix the prices of products or services at a certain level.

HIGHLIGHTING THE POINT

The chief executive officers (CEOs) of the largest U.S. book publishers meet four times a year in private to discuss industry issues, including pricing policies and strategies. When e-books are introduced to the market, the publishers appear to be acting together. The releases of e-books are delayed for a certain window of time to facilitate the sales of the printed versions. When the e-books are released, they all sell for the same price as the printed versions. Echo Electronics makes and sells e-book readers. Echo's CEO meets with the publishers' CEOs, who agree to sell their e-books through Echo's new online store. The prices of e-books subsequently rise.

Do these circumstances indicate an illegal price-fixing agreement? Yes. The meetings of the CEOs include discussions of pricing policies and strategies. The prices of the printed versions of books and their e-book forms appear to rise in concert, thereby eliminating retail price competition. These circumstances meet the requirements of a *per se* illegal price-fixing agreement—that is, concerted action between at least two competitors that constitutes an unreasonable, anti-competitive restraint of trade.

Group Boycotts A **group boycott** is an agreement by two or more sellers to boycott, or refuse to deal with, a particular person or firm. Section 1 has been violated if it can be demonstrated that the boycott or joint refusal to deal was undertaken with the intention of eliminating competition or preventing entry into a given market.

group boycott
The refusal of a group of competitors to deal with a particular person or firm.

Market Divisions It is a *per se* violation of Section 1 for competitors to divide up market territories or customers. **EXAMPLE 41.2** Alred Office Supplies, Belmont Business Services, and Carlton Biz Network compete against each other in Kansas, Nebraska, and Oklahoma. These three firms agree that Alred will sell office products only in Kansas, Belmont will sell only in Nebraska, and Carlton will sell only in Oklahoma. This concerted action reduces marketing costs and allows all three to raise the price of the goods sold in their respective states. (This situation assumes there is no other competition and ignores online competitors.)◄

41–1b Section 2 of the Sherman Act

Section 1 of the Sherman Act prohibits certain concerted, or joint, activities that restrain trade. In contrast, Section 2 condemns "every person who shall monopolize, or attempt to monopolize." Thus, two distinct types of behavior are subject to sanction under Section 2: *monopolization* and *attempts to monopolize*.

One tactic that may be involved in either offense is **predatory pricing**. Predatory pricing involves an attempt by one firm to drive its competitors from the market by selling its product at prices substantially *below* the normal costs of production. Once the competitors are eliminated, the firm will attempt to recapture its losses and go on to earn higher profits by driving prices up far above their competitive levels.

predatory pricing
The pricing of a product below cost with the intent to drive competitors out of the market.

Monopolization **Monopolization** involves the following two elements:

1. The possession of monopoly power in the relevant market.

2. The willful acquisition or maintenance of that power as distinguished from growth or development as a consequence of a superior product, good business judgment, or historic accident.

monopolization
The possession of monopoly power in the relevant market and the willful acquisition or maintenance of that power.

A violation of Section 2 requires that both these elements—*monopoly power* and *an intent to monopolize*—be established.

Monopoly Power The Sherman Act does not define *monopoly*. In theory, *monopoly* refers to control of a single market by a single entity. It is well established in antitrust law, however, that a firm may be deemed a monopolist even though it is not the sole seller in a market. Additionally, size alone does not determine whether a firm is a monopoly. **EXAMPLE 41.3** Stage Stop Store, a "mom and pop" business located in the isolated town of Happy Camp, Wyoming, is the only grocery store serving that market. Thus, Stage Stop Store is a monopolist. Size in relation to the market is what matters because monopoly involves the power to affect prices. ◄

To prove monopoly power indirectly, the plaintiff must show that the firm has a dominant share of the relevant market and that there are significant barriers for new competitors entering that market.

Relevant Market In determining the extent of a firm's market power, courts often use the **market-share test**, which measures the firm's percentage share of the *relevant market*. The relevant market consists of two elements:

1. A relevant product market.

2. A relevant geographic market.

The relevant product market includes all products that have identical attributes, such as tea. Because products that are not identical may sometimes be substituted for one another—coffee may be substituted for tea, for example—these products are also considered to be part of the same relevant product market.

For products that are sold nationwide, the relevant geographic market encompasses the entire United States. A producer and its competitors may sell in a more limited area, however, in which their customers do not have access to other sources of the product. In that situation, the relevant geographic market is limited to that area.

Defining the relevant product market narrowly can enhance the degree of a firm's market power.

market-share test
The primary measure of monopoly power. A firm's market share is the percentage of the relevant market that the firm controls.

HIGHLIGHTING THE POINT

White Whale Apps acquires Springleaf Apps, its main competitor in nationwide Android-based mobile phone apps. White Whale maintains that the relevant product market consists of all mobile phone apps online retailers. The Federal Trade Commission (FTC), however, argues that the relevant product market consists of only "app retailers specific to Android mobile phones."

Does the FTC's view of the relevant product market enhance measured White Whale's market power? Yes. Under the FTC's more narrow definition of the relevant product market, White Whale can be seen to have a dominant share of the Android-based mobile phone app retail market. Because the merger with Springleaf has already taken place, the FTC can order White Whale to divest—that is, sell or give up control over—some of its retail outlets. This divesture could include former Springleaf online retail Web sites.

The Intent Requirement Monopoly power, in and of itself, does not constitute the offense of monopolization under Section 2 of the Sherman Act. The offense also requires an *intent* to monopolize. A dominant market share, as suggested earlier, may result from the development of a superior product or the exercise of good business judgment. Or, it may simply result from a historic accident. In these situations, the acquisition of monopoly power is not an antitrust violation.

If a firm possesses market power as a result of carrying out some purposeful act to acquire or maintain that power through anticompetitive means, however, then it is in violation of Section 2. In most monopolization cases, intent can be inferred from evidence that the firm had monopoly power and engaged in anticompetitive behavior.

Refusals to Deal Group boycotts, discussed earlier, are also known as joint refusals to deal—sellers acting as a group jointly refuse to deal with another business or individual. These refusals to deal, as mentioned, are subject to close scrutiny under the Sherman Act. Normally, though, a single seller acting unilaterally is free to deal, or not to deal, with anyone it chooses.

Nevertheless, in limited circumstances, a unilateral refusal to deal violates antitrust laws. These instances involve offenses prohibited under Section 2 of the Sherman Act and occur only if (1) the firm refusing to deal has—or is likely to acquire—monopoly power and (2) the refusal is likely to have an anticompetitive effect on a particular market.

EXAMPLE 41.4 Clark Industries, the owner of three of the four major downhill ski areas in Blue Hills, Idaho, refuses to continue participating in a jointly offered six-day "all Blue Hills" lift ticket. Clark's refusal to cooperate with its smaller competitor is a violation of Section 2 of the Sherman Act. Because Clark owns three-fourths of the local ski areas, it has monopoly power, and thus its unilateral refusal has an anticompetitive effect on the market. ◂

Attempts to Monopolize Cases involving attempts to monopolize are concerned with the following:

1. Actions that are intended to exclude competitors and garner monopoly power.

2. Actions that have a dangerous probability of success.

The probability cannot be dangerous unless the alleged offender possesses some degree of market power. In other words, only serious threats of monopolization are condemned as violations.

HIGHLIGHTING THE POINT

Big Deal, Inc., owns five rock-format radio stations in Cincinnati and is a major concert promoter in the area. Big Deal's relevant market share in terms of ad revenue is about 90 percent. Big Deal's stations refuse to accept ads for performers who do not contract with Big Deal to promote their concerts. This refusal intimidates many artists into contracting exclusively with Big Deal.

Do Big Deal's activities represent an attempt to monopolize the market in violation of Section 2 of the Sherman Act? Yes. Companies enter into exclusive or favored arrangements with other firms every day. Such arrangements are lawful in most cases but may be unlawful when used by a monopolist. Big Deal is a monopolist in its relevant market. How the firm uses its monopoly power and how its actions affect competition make its practices illegal. The effects may include an increase in ticket prices and a decreasing market share for the firm's competitors.

41–2 THE CLAYTON ACT

In 1914, Congress attempted to strengthen federal antitrust laws by enacting the Clayton Act. The Clayton Act is aimed at three specific anticompetitive or monopolistic practices that are not covered by the Sherman Act. These practices are price discrimination, exclusionary practices and certain mergers. The Clayton

LEARNING OUTCOME 2

List anticompetitive activities outlawed by the Clayton Act.

Act makes these practices illegal only if they substantially lessen competition or tend to create monopoly power.

41–2a Price Discrimination

price discrimination
Setting prices in such a way that two competing buyers pay two different prices for an identical product or service.

A seller that charges different prices to different buyers for identical goods is practicing **price discrimination.** The Clayton Act prohibits certain classes of price discrimination that cannot be justified by differences in production or transportation costs. Under the act, sellers are prohibited from reducing prices to levels substantially below those charged by their competitors unless they can justify the reduction by demonstrating that they charged the lower price "in good faith to meet an equally low price of a competitor."

41–2b Exclusionary Practices

Under the Clayton Act, sellers or lessors cannot condition the sale or lease of a product on the buyer's or lessee's promise not to use or deal in the goods of the seller's competitors. This effectively prohibits two types of agreements: *exclusive-dealing contracts* and *tying arrangements*.

exclusive-dealing contract
An agreement under which a producer of goods agrees to sell its goods exclusively through one distributor.

Exclusive-Dealing Contracts A contract under which a seller forbids a buyer to purchase products from the seller's competitors is called an **exclusive-dealing contract.** An exclusive-dealing contract is prohibited if the effect of the contract is to lessen competition substantially or to tend to create a monopoly.

tying arrangement
An agreement between a buyer and a seller under which the buyer of a specific product or service is obligated to purchase additional products or services from the seller.

Tying Arrangements When a seller conditions the sale of a product (the tying product) on the buyer's agreement to purchase another product (the tied product) produced or distributed by the same seller, a **tying arrangement** results. The legality of such an agreement depends on many factors, particularly the purpose of the agreement and the agreement's likely effect on competition in the relevant markets.

Real-World Case Example

James Batson walked up to the box office of Live Nation Entertainment, Inc., at the Charter One Pavilion in Chicago, Illinois, and bought a nonrefundable concert ticket. The price included a $9 parking fee. Batson did not have a car to park. He filed a suit in a federal district court against Live Nation. He argued that the "bundled" ticket for the concert admittance and the parking fee was unfair. He claimed consumers were forced to pay a parking fee or forego the concert. He asserted that this was an illegal tying arrangement. The court dismissed the suit. Batson appealed.

Is bundling a fee for parking with the price of a concert ticket a permissible tying arrangement? Yes. In a 2014 case, *Batson v. Live Nation Entertainment, Inc.*, the U.S. Court of Appeals for the Seventh Circuit affirmed the lower court's dismissal of Batson's claim. A tying arrangement is illegal only if a seller has sufficient power in the tying product market so that forcing the buyer to accept a second product restrains competition in the market for the tied product. The court could not identify a product market in which Live Nation had sufficient power to force consumers who wanted to attend a concert (the tying product) to buy "useless parking rights" (the tied product). Lastly, there was no evidence that Live Nation's parking tie-in restrained competition for parking in Chicago.

41–2c Mergers

A *merger* occurs when one business firm absorbs the assets and liabilities of another, so that the other ceases to exist. Under the Clayton Act, a business organization cannot merge with another if the effect may be to lessen competition substantially.

A crucial consideration is **market concentration,** which refers to the market shares among the various firms in a market. For instance, if the four largest grocery stores in Chicago account for 80 percent of all retail food sales, that market is concentrated in those four firms. If one of these stores absorbs the assets and liabilities of another, so that the other ceases to exist, the result is a merger that would further concentrates the market and thereby possibly diminishes competition.

Competition is not necessarily diminished solely as a result of market concentration. Other factors will be considered in determining whether a merger violates the Clayton Act. One such factor, for example, is whether the merger will make it more difficult for potential competitors to enter the market.

market concentration
A situation that exists when a small number of firms share the market for a particular good or service.

41–3 ENFORCEMENT OF ANTITRUST LAWS

The federal agencies that enforce the federal antitrust laws are the U.S. Department of Justice (DOJ) and the Federal Trade Commission (FTC). The FTC was established by the Federal Trade Commission Act in 1914. Section 5 of that act prohibits all forms of anticompetitive behavior that are not covered under other federal antitrust laws.

LEARNING OUTCOME 3
State who enforces the antitrust laws.

41–3a Enforcement by Federal Agencies

The DOJ can prosecute violations of the Sherman Act as either criminal or civil violations. Violations of the Clayton Act are not crimes, and the DOJ can enforce that statute only through civil proceedings. The various remedies that the DOJ has asked the courts to impose include **divestiture** (making a company give up one or more of its operating functions) and dissolution. For example, the DOJ might force a meat packer to divest itself of control or ownership of butcher shops.

The FTC also enforces the Clayton Act and has sole authority to enforce violations of the Federal Trade Commission Act. The FTC does not enforce the Sherman Act.

divestiture
The act of selling one or more of a company's parts, such as a subsidiary or manufacturing plants.

41–3b Enforcement by Private Parties

A private party can sue for treble (triple) damages and attorneys' fees under the Clayton Act if the party is injured as a result of a violation of any of the federal antitrust laws, except the Federal Trade Commission Act. A person wishing to sue under the Sherman Act must prove the following:

1. The antitrust violation either caused or was a substantial factor in causing the injury that was suffered.
2. The unlawful actions of the accused party affected business activities of the plaintiff that were protected by the antitrust laws.

41–3c Exemptions from Antitrust Laws

There are many legislative and constitutional limitations on antitrust enforcement. For example, one exemption covers professional baseball teams. Another permits agricultural cooperatives and fisheries to set prices.

One of the most significant antitrust enforcement exemptions covers joint efforts by businesspersons to obtain government action. For instance, movie producers, DVD makers and sellers, and video-streaming companies can jointly lobby Congress to extend the period of copyright protection. Additionally, they can jointly make changes to other provisions of intellectual property law without being liable for attempting to restrain trade.

See Exhibit 41.1 for a more detailed listing of exemptions to antitrust enforcement.

 # 41–4 U.S. ANTITRUST LAWS IN THE GLOBAL CONTEXT

LEARNING OUTCOME 4

Define the extraterritorial reach of U.S. antitrust laws.

Section 1 of the Sherman Act provides for the extraterritorial effect of the U.S. antitrust laws. In other words, these laws may apply outside U.S. territory. Thus, any conspiracy that has a *substantial effect* on U.S. commerce is within the reach of the Sherman Act. The violation may even occur outside the United States, and foreign governments as well as individuals can be sued for violation of U.S. antitrust laws.

EXHIBIT 41.1   Exemptions to Antitrust Enforcement

Exemption	Source and Scope
Labor	Clayton Act—Permits unions to organize and bargain without violating antitrust laws and specifies that strikes and other labor activities normally do not violate any federal law.
Agricultural associations	Clayton Act and Capper-Volstead Act—Allow agricultural cooperatives to set prices.
Fisheries	Fisheries Cooperative Marketing Act—Allows the fishing industry to set prices.
Insurance companies	McCarran-Ferguson Act—Exempts the insurance business in states in which the industry is regulated.
Exporters	Webb-Pomerene Act—Allows U.S. exporters to engage in cooperative activity to compete with similar foreign associations. Export Trading Company Act—Permits the U.S. Department of Justice to exempt certain exporters.
Professional baseball	The United States Supreme Court has held that professional baseball is exempt because it is not "interstate commerce."
Oil marketing	Interstate Oil Compact—Allows states to set quotas on oil to be marketed in interstate commerce.
Defense activities	Defense Production Act—Allows the president to approve, and thereby exempt, certain activities to further the military defense of the United States.
Small businesses' cooperative research	Small Business Administration Act—Allows small firms to undertake cooperative research.
State actions	The United States Supreme Court has held that actions by a state are exempt if the state clearly articulates and actively supervises the policy behind its action.
Regulated industries	Industries (such as airlines) are exempt when a federal administrative agency (such as the Federal Aviation Administration) has primary regulatory authority.
Businesspersons' joint efforts to seek government action	Cooperative efforts by businesspersons to obtain legislative, judicial, or executive action are exempt unless it is clear that an effort is "objectively baseless" and is an attempt to make anticompetitive use of government processes.

Before U.S. courts will exercise jurisdiction and apply antitrust laws extraterritorially, it must be shown that the alleged violation had a substantial effect on U.S. commerce. U.S. jurisdiction is automatically invoked when a *per se* violation occurs.

For instance, if a domestic firm joins a foreign cartel to control the production, price, or distribution of goods, and this cartel has a substantial effect on U.S. commerce, a *per se* violation may exist. Hence, both the domestic firm and the foreign cartel could be sued for violation of U.S. antitrust laws. Likewise, if a foreign firm doing business in the United States enters into a price-fixing or other anticompetitive agreement to control a portion of U.S. markets, a *per se* violation may exist.

ANSWERING THE LEGAL PROBLEM

In the legal problem set out at the beginning of this chapter, a group of independent oil producers in Texas and Louisiana are caught between falling demand due to bad economic times and increasing supply from newly discovered oil fields in the region.

In response to these conditions, a group of major refining companies agrees to buy excess supplies from the independents so as to dispose of the excess in an "orderly manner."

It is clear that the purpose is to limit the supply of gasoline on the market and thereby raise prices. In a lawsuit challenging the agreement, the oil producers claims that under the circumstances, the agreement is reasonable.

A **Does the agreement violate antitrust law?** Yes. Any agreement among competitors to restrict output or fix prices constitutes a *per se* violation of Section 1 of the Sherman Act. The "reasonableness" of a price-fixing agreement is never a defense.

TERMS AND CONCEPTS FOR REVIEW

antitrust law 565

divestiture 571

exclusive-dealing contract 570

group boycott 567

market concentration 571

market-share test 568

monopolization 567

per se violation 566

predatory pricing 567

price discrimination 570

price-fixing agreement 567

resale price maintenance
agreement 566

restraint of trade 565

rule of reason 566

tying arrangement 570

CHAPTER SUMMARY—ANTITRUST LAW

LEARNING OUTCOME	
1	**List anticompetitive activities prohibited by the Sherman Act.** The Sherman Act prohibits contracts, combinations, and conspiracies in restraint of trade, as well as monopolies and attempts to monopolize. The act applies only to activities that have a significant impact on interstate commerce. The rule of reason applies when an anticompetitive agreement may be justified by legitimate benefits. The *per se* rule applies to restraints of trade that are so inherently anticompetitive that they cannot be justified and are deemed illegal as a matter of law.
2	**List anticompetitive activities outlawed by the Clayton Act.** The Clayton Act prohibits price discrimination (charging different buyers different prices for identical goods), exclusionary practices (exclusive-dealing contracts and tying arrangements), and mergers that may substantially lessen competition.
3	**State who enforces the antitrust laws.** Federal agencies that enforce antitrust laws are the Department of Justice and the Federal Trade Commission, which was established by the Federal Trade Commission Act. Private parties who have been injured as a result of violations of the Sherman Act or Clayton Act may also bring civil suits. If successful, they may be awarded treble damages and attorneys' fees.
4	**Define the extraterritorial reach of U.S. antitrust laws.** Section 1 of the Sherman Act provides for the global effect of U.S. antitrust laws. A violation may occur outside the United States, and foreign governments as well as individuals can be sued for violations. It must be shown that the violation had a substantial effect on U.S. commerce.

ISSUE SPOTTERS

Check your answers to the *Issue Spotters* against the answers provided in Appendix C at the end of this text.

1. Maple Corporation conditions the sale of its syrup on the buyer's agreement to buy Maple's pancake mix. What type of arrangement is this? What factors would a court consider to decide whether this arrangement violates antitrust law? (See *The Clayton Act*.)

2. Under what circumstances would Pop's Market, a small store in an isolated town, be considered a monopolist? If Pop's is a monopolist, is it in violation of Section 2 of the Sherman Act? Discuss your answer. (See *The Sherman Act*.)

USING BUSINESS LAW

41–1. Section 1 of the Sherman Act. Allitron, Inc., and Donovan, Ltd., are interstate competitors selling similar appliances, principally in the states of Illinois, Indiana, Kentucky, and Ohio. Allitron and Donovan agree that Allitron will no longer sell in Ohio and Indiana and that Donovan will no longer sell in Kentucky and Illinois. Have Allitron and Donovan violated any antitrust laws? If so, which law or laws? Explain. (See *The Sherman Act*.)

41–2. Section 1 of the Sherman Act. An agreement that is blatantly and substantially anticompetitive is deemed a *per se* violation of Section 1 of the Sherman Act. Under what rule is an agreement analyzed if it appears to be anticompetitive but is not a *per se* violation? In making this analysis, what factors will a court consider? (See *The Sherman Act*.)

REAL-WORLD CASE PROBLEMS

41–3. Section 1 of the Sherman Act. The National Collegiate Athletic Association (NCAA) and the National Federation of State High School Associations (NFHS) set a standard for non-wood baseball bats to ensure that aluminum and composite bats performed like wood bats in an effort to enhance player safety and reduce technology-driven homeruns and other big hits. Marucci Sports, LLC, makes nonwood bats. Under the NCAA and NFHS's standard, four of Marucci's eleven products were decertified for use in high school and collegiate games. But many certified bats—including seven of Marucci's products—were available. Marucci's competitors did not drop out of the market, bat prices were not significantly changed, and bat quality was not affected. Did the NCAA and NFHS's standard violate the Sherman Act? Explain. [*Marucci Sports, LLC v. National Collegiate Athletic Association,* 751 F.3d 368 (5th Cir. 2014)] (See *The Sherman Act.*)

41–4. Price Discrimination. Dayton Superior Corp. makes and distributes commercial concrete construction products. Dayton's customers, including Spa Steel Products, Inc., compete with each other to sell Dayton's products. Spa Steel's customers begin to buy Dayton's products from competitors whose prices for the same products are 10 to 15 percent lower than Spa Steel's prices. Consequently, Spa Steel loses sales. Can Spa Steel successfully allege price discrimination under the Clayton Act? Why or why not? [*Dayton Superior Corp. v. Spa Steel Products, Inc.,* 2012 WL 113663 (N.D.N.Y. 2012)] (See *The Clayton Act.*)

41–5. Monopolization. E.I. du Pont de Nemours and Co. manufactures a special fiber that is used to make body armor, fiber-optic cables, and other products. In fact, DuPont controls more than 70 percent of the U.S. market for this fiber. DuPont imposes multiyear agreements on customers for the fiber, requiring them to purchase from 80 to 100 percent of the fibers they need from DuPont. This limits the ability of other producers of the fiber to compete. Do these agreements constitute monopolization and attempt to monopolize in violation of the Sherman Act? Explain. [*E.I. du Pont de Nemours and Co. v. Kolon Industries, Inc.,* 637 F.3d 435 (4th Cir. 2011)] (See *The Sherman Act.*)

ETHICAL QUESTIONS

41–6. The Rule of Reason. Should all commercial arrangements subject to the antitrust laws be evaluated under the rule of reason? Discuss. (See *The Sherman Act.*)

41–7. The Sherman Act. NBC Universal, Inc., and other owners of television channels sell their products only in multichannel packages. Comcast and other distributors of cable and satellite programming buy the packages and then sell them to consumers. Each package includes a mix of channels with high and low viewership. Consumers are forced to pay for all of the channels in a package and are not allowed to buy or cancel some channels. Meanwhile, the growth of online programming by Netflix and other firms continues to foster competition for viewers. Does the bundling of programming in multichannel packages violate the Sherman Act? Discuss. [*Brantley v. NBC Universal, Inc.,* 675 F.3d 1192 (9th Cir. 2012)] (See *The Sherman Act.*)

Chapter 41—Work Set

TRUE-FALSE QUESTIONS

_____ 1. Monopoly power is market power sufficient to control prices and exclude competition.

_____ 2. An exclusive-dealing contract is a contract under which competitors agree to divide up territories or customers.

_____ 3. Price discrimination occurs when a seller forbids a buyer from buying products from the seller's competitors.

_____ 4. An agreement between competitors to fix prices is a *per se* violation of antitrust law.

_____ 5. A merger between firms that compete with each other in the same market is not a violation of antitrust law.

_____ 6. A relevant product market consists of all products with identical attributes and products that are sufficient substitutes for each other.

_____ 7. An agreement that is inherently anticompetitive is illegal *per se*.

_____ 8. Under the rule of reason, conduct is unlawful if its anticompetitive harms outweigh its competitive benefits.

_____ 9. A unilateral refusal to deal cannot violate antitrust law.

MULTIPLE-CHOICE QUESTIONS

_____ 1. The National Coal Association (NCA) is a group of independent coal mining companies. Demand for coal falls, so the price drops. The Coal Refiners Association, a group of coal-refining companies, agrees to buy NCA's coal and sell it according to a schedule that will increase the price. This agreement is

   a. exempt from the antitrust laws.
   b. subject to evaluation under the rule of reason.
   c. a *per se* violation of the Sherman Act.
   d. none of the above.

_____ 2. Federated Tools, Inc., charges Jack's Hardware five cents per item and Eve's Home Store ten cents per item for the same product. Jack's Hardware and Eve's Home Store are competitors. If this practice substantially lessens competition, it constitutes

   a. a market division.
   b. an exclusionary practice.
   c. price discrimination.
   d. none of the above.

_____ 3. American Goods, Inc., and Consumer Products Corporation are competitors. They merge, and after the merger, Consumer Products is the surviving firm. To assess whether the merger is in violation of the Clayton Act requires a look at

   a. market division.
   b. market concentration.
   c. market power.
   d. none of the above.

_____ 4. International Sales, Inc. (ISI), is charged with a violation of antitrust law. ISI's conduct is a *per se* violation

   a. if the anticompetitive harm outweighs the competitive benefits.
   b. if the competitive benefits outweigh the anticompetitive harm.
   c. if the conduct is blatantly anticompetitive.
   d. only if it qualifies as an exemption.

_____ 5. Techno, Inc., sells its brand-name computer equipment directly to its franchised retailers. Depending on how existing franchisees do, Techno may limit the number of franchisees in a given area to reduce intrabrand competition. Techno's restrictions on the number of dealers is

   a. a *per se* violation of the Sherman Act.
   b. exempt from the antitrust laws.
   c. subject to continuing review by the appropriate federal agency.
   d. subject to the rule of reason.

_____ 6. Gamma Corporation is charged with a violation of antitrust law that requires evaluation under the rule of reason. The court will consider

   a. only the purpose of the conduct.
   b. only the effect of the conduct on trade.
   c. only the power of the parties to accomplish what they intend.
   d. the purpose of the conduct, the effect of the conduct on trade, and the power of the parties to accomplish what they intend.

_____ 7. Omega, Inc., controls 80 percent of the market for telecommunications equipment in the southeastern United States. To show that Omega is monopolizing that market in violation of the Sherman Act requires proof of

   a. only the possession of monopoly power in the relevant market.
   b. only the willful acquisition or maintenance of monopoly power.
   c. the possession of monopoly power in the relevant market and the willful acquisition or maintenance of that power.
   d. none of the above.

ANSWERING MORE LEGAL PROBLEMS

1. Pharma, Inc., made Cancera, a prescription drug that helped in the treatment of certain forms of cancer. When Cancera's patent was about to expire, Synthetic Chemix Corp. developed a generic version of Cancera and prepared to enter the market. Within weeks of this drug's debut, Pharma offered to pay Synthetic $50 million per year *not* to market the generic version. Synthetic accepted the offer.

   Was the agreement between Pharma and Synthetic a violation of antitrust law? Yes. One *per se* violation of Section 1 of the Sherman Act is a _____-_____ agreement—an agreement among competitors to set prices. Although the agreement between Pharma and Synthetic included no specific statement as to price, its purpose was to limit the supply of the generic version of Cancera and thus maintain or increase the price of the brand-name drug. This _____-_____ agreement between rival firms also restrained _____ by delaying the entry of the generic version of Cancera into the market. Under these circumstances, the agreement was a *per se* violation of the Sherman Act.

2. Choice Foods Market, Inc., is the largest national chain of supermarkets selling high-end organic food. Choice Foods wanted to acquire the assets of its main competitor, Naturally Select Markets, Inc. The relevant product market was defined to consist of only premium natural and organic supermarkets rather than all supermarkets. Under this narrow definition, Choice Foods had an 80 percent share of the market, and Naturally Select had a 15 percent share.

   Did this proposed acquisition constitute monopolization and thereby violate the Sherman Act? Yes. Monopolization involves two elements: (1) the possession of monopoly _____ in the relevant market and (2) the willful acquisition or maintenance of that _____. In determining the extent of a firm's market _____, the market-share test measures the firm's percentage share of the relevant market. This consists of the relevant product market and the relevant geographic market. The relevant product market can include all products with identical attributes. For products that are sold nationwide, the relevant geographic market is the entire United States. In this problem, the largest chain of high-end organic supermarkets wanted to acquire its main competitor. The merger would have given Choice Foods a 95 percent share of the defined relevant market—a significant increase in monopoly _____ acquired willfully.

INTERNATIONAL LAW

42

LEARNING OUTCOMES

The five Learning Outcomes below are designed to help improve your understanding of the chapter. After reading this chapter, you should be able to:

❶ Identify important international principles and doctrines.

❷ Discuss how business is done internationally.

❸ Explain common provisions used in international contracts.

❹ Outline the regulation of international business activities.

❺ State examples of U.S. laws applied in a global context.

FACING A LEGAL PROBLEM

Café Rojo, a Colombian firm, agrees to sell coffee beans to Black Bear Coffee Company, a U.S. firm. Black Bear accepts the beans, but refuses to pay. Café Rojo sues Black Bear in a Colombian court and is awarded damages, but Black Bear's assets are in the United States.

Q Is a U.S. court likely to enforce the Colombian court's judgment?

International business transactions are not unique to the modern world. Indeed, commerce has always crossed national borders. What is new is the dramatic growth in world trade and the emergence of a global business community. Because exchanges of goods, services, and intellectual property on a global level are now routine, students of business law and the legal environment need to be familiar with the laws pertaining to international business transactions.

In this chapter, we first examine the legal context of international business transactions. We also look at some selected areas relating to business activities in a global context, including exporting and manufacturing, international sales contracts, payment procedures, and regulation. We conclude the chapter with a discussion of the application of certain U.S. laws in the international setting.

42–1 INTERNATIONAL PRINCIPLES AND DOCTRINES

International law is defined as a body of law—formed as a result of international customs, **treaties,** and organizations—that governs relations among or between nations. *National law,* in contrast, is the law of a particular nation, such as Brazil or Germany.

Here, we look at some legal principles and doctrines of international law that the courts of various nations have employed to resolve or reduce conflicts that involve a foreign element. The three important legal principles and doctrines discussed in the following subsections are based primarily on courtesy and respect, and are applied in the interests of maintaining harmonious relations among nations.

42–1a The Principle of Comity

Under the principle of **comity,** one nation will defer and give effect to the laws and judicial decrees of another country as long as those laws and decrees are consistent with the law and public policy of the accommodating nation.

One way to understand the principle of comity is to consider the relationships among the states in our federal form of government. Each state honors the contracts, property deeds, wills, and additional legal obligations formed in other

treaty
A formal written agreement negotiated between two or more nations.

LEARNING OUTCOME 1

Identify important international principles and doctrines.

comity
The principle by which one nation defers and gives effect to the laws and judicial decrees of another nation. This recognition is based primarily on respect.

579

states. On a worldwide basis, nations similarly attempt to honor judgments rendered in other countries when it is feasible to do so.

42–1b The Act of State Doctrine

The **act of state doctrine** provides that the judicial branch of one country will not examine the validity of public acts committed by a recognized foreign government within its own territory. This doctrine can have important consequences for individuals and firms doing business with, and investing in, other countries.

The act of state doctrine frequently is employed in situations involving *expropriation* or *confiscation*. **Expropriation** occurs when a government seizes a privately owned business or privately owned goods for a proper public purpose and awards just compensation. When a government seizes private property for an illegal purpose or without just compensation, the taking is referred to as a **confiscation.** The line between these two forms of taking is sometimes blurred because of differing interpretations of what is illegal and what constitutes just compensation.

EXAMPLE 42.1 Flaherty, Inc., a U.S. company, owns a mine in Venezuela. The government of Venezuela seizes the mine for public use and claims that the profits that Flaherty has already realized from the mine constitute just compensation. Flaherty disagrees, but the act of state doctrine may prevent the company's recovery in a U.S. court. ◄ Note that in a case alleging that a foreign government has wrongfully taken the plaintiff's property, the defendant government has the burden of proving that the taking was an expropriation, not a confiscation.

42–1c The Doctrine of Sovereign Immunity

When certain conditions are satisfied, the doctrine of **sovereign immunity** protects foreign nations from the jurisdiction of U.S. courts. In 1976, Congress codified this rule in the Foreign Sovereign Immunities Act (FSIA). The FSIA governs the circumstances in which an action may be brought in the United States against a foreign nation.

According to the FSIA, a foreign state is not immune from the jurisdiction of U.S. courts in the following situations:

1. When the foreign state has waived its immunity either explicitly or by implication.

2. When the foreign state has engaged in commercial activity within the United States or in commercial activity outside the United States that has a direct effect in the United States.

3. When the foreign state has committed a tort in the United States or has violated certain international laws.

Under the FSIA, a *foreign state* includes both a political subdivision of a foreign state and an instrumentality of a foreign state. An *instrumentality* may be any department or agency of any branch of the foreign state's government.

 42–2 DOING BUSINESS INTERNATIONALLY

A U.S. domestic firm can engage in international business transactions in a number of ways. The simplest way is to seek out foreign markets for domestically produced products or services. In other words, U.S. firms can **export** their goods and services to markets in other countries. For a discussion on global marketing management, see the *Linking Business Law to Your Career* feature at the end of this chapter.

Alternatively, a U.S. firm can establish foreign production facilities so as to be closer to the foreign market or markets in which its products are sold. The

---

act of state doctrine
A doctrine providing that the judicial branch of one country will not examine the validity of public acts committed by a recognized foreign government within its own territory.

expropriation
The seizure by a government of a privately owned business or personal property for a proper public purpose and with just compensation.

confiscation
A government's taking of a privately owned business or personal property without a legal public purpose or an award of just compensation.

sovereign immunity
A doctrine that immunizes foreign nations from the jurisdiction of U.S. courts when certain conditions are satisfied.

export
To sell products to buyers located in other countries.

advantages may include lower labor costs, fewer government regulations, and lower taxes and trade barriers. A domestic firm can also obtain revenues by licensing its technology to an existing foreign company or by expanding abroad by selling franchises to overseas entities.

42–2a Exporting

Most U.S. companies make their initial foray into international business through exporting. Exporting can take two forms: direct exporting and indirect exporting.

LEARNING OUTCOME 2
Discuss how business is done internationally.

Direct Exporting In *direct exporting*, a U.S. company signs a sales contract with a foreign purchaser that provides for the conditions of shipment and payment for the goods. (How payments are made in international transactions will be discussed later in this chapter.)

Indirect Exporting If sufficient business develops in a foreign country, a U.S. corporation may set up a specialized marketing organization in that foreign market by appointing a foreign agent or a foreign distributor. This is called *indirect exporting.*

Foreign Agent When a U.S. firm wishes to limit its involvement in an international market, it normally establishes an agency relationship with a foreign firm. In an agency relationship, one person (the agent) agrees to act on behalf of another (the principal). The *foreign agent* is thereby empowered to enter into contracts in the agent's country on behalf of the U.S. company.

Foreign Distributor When a substantial market exists in a foreign country, a U.S. firm may wish to appoint a distributor located in that country. The U.S. firm and the distributor enter into a **distribution agreement,** which is a contract between the seller and the distributor setting out the terms and conditions of the distributorship. These include price, currency of payment, availability of supplies, and method of payment.

distribution agreement
A contract between a seller and a distributor of the seller's products setting out the terms and conditions of the distributorship.

42–2b Manufacturing Abroad

An alternative to direct or indirect exporting is the establishment of foreign manufacturing facilities. Typically, U.S. firms establish manufacturing plants abroad if they believe that doing so will reduce their costs—particularly for labor, shipping, and raw materials—and enable them to compete more effectively in foreign markets. A U.S. firm can manufacture goods in other countries in several ways, including those discussed next.

Licensing In a *licensing agreement,* the owner of intellectual property (the *licensor*) gives another party (the *licensee*) certain rights in the property. A license can be restricted to certain specified purposes and can be limited to the licensee only. Thus, a U.S. firm (or any domestic firm) can license its formula, product, or process to a foreign concern to avoid its theft or piracy. (*Piracy* is the unauthorized use of another's production, patent, trademark, or copyright.) The foreign firm obtains the right to make and market the product according to the formula (or the right to use the process) and agrees to keep the necessary information secret and to pay royalties to the licensor.

For instance, the Coca-Cola Bottling Company licenses firms worldwide to use (and keep confidential) its secret formula for the syrup used in its soft drink. In return, the foreign firms licensed to make the syrup pay Coca-Cola a percentage of the income (royalties) earned from the sale of the soft drink.

Licensing is also one of the best ways to protect intellectual property on the Internet. Because the Internet does not have any geographical boundaries, a licensing agreement should be made in consideration of all U.S., foreign, and international laws.

Franchising Franchising is a well-known form of licensing. A **franchise** is any arrangement in which the owner of a trademark, trade name, or copyright (the *franchisor*) licenses another (the *franchisee*) to use the trademark, trade name, or copyright under certain conditions or limitations in the selling of goods or services. In return, the franchisee pays a fee, which usually is based on a percentage of gross or net sales. International franchises include Hilton Hotels, Starbucks, and McDonald's.

Subsidiaries and Joint Ventures Another way to expand into a foreign market is to establish a wholly owned subsidiary firm in a foreign country. When a wholly owned subsidiary is established, the parent company, which remains in the United States, retains complete ownership of all the facilities in the foreign country, as well as complete authority and control over all phases of the operation.

A U.S. firm can also expand into international markets through a joint venture. In a joint venture, the U.S. company owns only part of the operation. The rest is owned either by local owners in the foreign country or by another foreign entity. All of the firms involved in a joint venture share responsibilities, as well as profits and liabilities.

 ## 42–3 INTERNATIONAL CONTRACT PROVISIONS

Language and legal differences among nations can create special problems for parties to international contracts when disputes arise. It is possible to avoid these problems by including special provisions designating the official language of the contract, the legal forum (court or place) in which disputes under the contract will be settled, and the substantive law that will be applied in settling any disputes. Parties to international contracts should also indicate what acts or events will excuse the parties from performance under the contract and whether disputes will be arbitrated or litigated.

Including these provisions greatly simplifies dispute resolution. If no choice of language, forum, or law is specified in the contract, and no arbitration clause is included, legal proceedings will be more complex and will be attended by much more uncertainty.

42–3a Choice-of-Language Clause

A deal struck between a U.S. company and a company in another country normally involves two languages. Typically, many phrases in one language are not readily translatable into another. Consequently, the complex contractual terms involved may not be understood equally well by the parties. To make sure that no disputes arise out of this language problem, an international sales contract should have a **choice-of-language clause** designating the official language by which the contract will be interpreted in the event of disagreement.

42–3b Forum-Selection Clause

When parties from several countries are involved, litigation may be pursued in courts in different nations. No universally accepted rules govern which court has

---

franchise
Any arrangement in which the owner of a trademark, trade name, or copyright licenses another to use it under specified conditions in the selling of goods or services.

LEARNING OUTCOME 3

Explain common provisions used in international contracts.

choice-of-language clause
A clause in a contract designating the official language by which the contract will be interpreted in the event of a future disagreement over the contract's terms.

jurisdiction over particular subject matter or parties to a dispute. Consequently, parties to an international transaction should always include a **forum-selection clause** in the contract, which indicates what court, jurisdiction, or tribunal will decide disputes arising under the contract. It is especially important to indicate the specific court that will have jurisdiction. The forum does not have to be within the geographic boundaries of the home nation of either party.

forum-selection clause
A contract provision identifying the court or jurisdiction that will decide any disputes.

HIGHLIGHTING THE POINT

Garware, Ltd., which is based in India, makes plastics. Intermax Corporation, which is based in New York, is Garware's U.S. agent. The parties execute a written agreement that provides, "The courts of India have jurisdiction to hear suits on all claims relating to this agreement." Intermax buys goods from Garware, warehouses them in the United States, and resells them. When Intermax fails to pay for the goods, Garware files a suit in a U.S. court to collect.

Does the forum-selection clause require the dismissal of this suit? Yes. The parties' agreement contains a valid and enforceable forum-selection clause, which applies to this suit.

42–3c Choice-of-Law Clause

A contractual provision designating the applicable law—such as the law of Germany or California—is called a **choice-of-law clause.** Every international contract usually includes a choice-of-law clause. Generally, parties are allowed to choose the law that will govern their contractual relationship, provided that the law chosen is the law of a jurisdiction that has a substantial relationship to the parties and to the international business transaction.

choice-of-law clause
A clause in a contract designating the law—such as the law of a particular state or nation—that will govern the contract.

42–3d *Force Majeure* Clause

Every contract, particularly those involving international transactions, should have a **force majeure clause.** *Force majeure* is a French term meaning "impossible or irresistible force"—sometimes loosely identified as "an act of God." In international business contracts, *force majeure* clauses commonly stipulate that acts of God, such as floods, fires, or catastrophic accidents, may excuse a party from liability for nonperformance. A number of other eventualities, such as government orders or embargoes, may do the same.

force majeure clause
A provision in a contract stipulating that certain unforeseen events—such as war, political upheavals, or acts of God—will excuse a party from liability for nonperformance of contractual obligations.

42–3e Arbitration Clause

International contracts frequently include arbitration clauses. By means of such clauses, the parties agree in advance to be bound by the decision of a specified third party in the event of a dispute. The third party may be a neutral entity (such as the International Chamber of Commerce), a panel of individuals representing both parties' interests, or some other group or organization.

Foreign arbitration awards are usually easier to enforce than foreign court judgments. The enforcement of court judgments normally depends on the principle of comity and bilateral agreements providing for such enforcement. An international agreement—the Convention on the Recognition and Enforcement of Foreign Arbitral Awards (also known as the New York Convention)—provides for the enforcement of foreign arbitration provisions and awards.

42–4 PAYMENT ON INTERNATIONAL TRANSACTIONS

Currency differences among nations and the geographic distance between parties to international sales contracts add a degree of complexity to international sales. Because international contracts involve greater financial risks, special care must be taken in drafting these contracts to specify both the currency in which payment is to be made and the method of payment.

42–4a Foreign Exchange Markets

An important factor is the *convertibility* of a currency. Currencies are convertible when they can be freely exchanged one for the other at some specified market rate in a **foreign exchange market.** Foreign exchange markets make up a worldwide system for the buying and selling of most foreign currencies.

In unrestricted foreign exchange markets, the foreign exchange rate is set by the forces of supply and demand. The foreign exchange rate is simply the price of a unit of one country's currency in terms of another country's currency. For example, if today's exchange rate is one hundred Japanese yen for one U.S. dollar, anybody with one hundred yen can obtain one dollar, and vice versa.

foreign exchange market
A worldwide system in which foreign currencies are bought and sold.

42–4b Correspondent Banks

Frequently, a U.S. company can rely on its domestic bank to take care of all international transfers of funds. Commercial banks often transfer funds internationally through their **correspondent banks** in other countries.

EXAMPLE 42.2 Scottsdale Corporation, a customer of Citibank, wishes to pay a bill in euros to Française Mécanique, a company in Paris. Citibank can draw a bank check payable in euros on its account in Crédit Agricole, a Paris correspondent bank, and then send the check to Française Mécanique, to which its customer, Scottsdale, owes the funds. Alternatively, Scottsdale can request a wire transfer of the funds to Française Mécanique. Citibank will then instruct Crédit Agricole by wire to pay the necessary amount in euros. ◄

correspondent bank
A bank in which another bank has an account (and vice versa) for the purpose of facilitating fund transfers.

42–5 REGULATION OF INTERNATIONAL BUSINESS ACTIVITIES

International business activities can affect the economies, foreign policies, domestic policies, and other national interests of the countries involved. For this reason, nations impose laws to restrict or facilitate international business. Controls may also be imposed by international agreements. Next, we discuss how different types of international activities are regulated.

LEARNING OUTCOME 4

Outline the regulation of international business activities.

42–5a Investment Protection

Firms that invest in a foreign nation face the risk that the foreign government may take possession of the investment property. Expropriation, as already mentioned, occurs when property is taken and the owner is paid just compensation. Expropriation does not violate generally observed principles of international law. Such principles are normally violated, however, when a government confiscates property without compensation (or without adequate compensation). Few remedies are available for confiscation of property by a foreign government. When U.S. firms are involved, claims are often resolved by lump-sum settlements after negotiations between the United States and the taking nation.

To counter the deterrent effect that the possibility of confiscation may have on potential investors, many countries guarantee that foreign investors will be compensated if their property is taken. A guaranty can take the form of national constitutional or statutory laws or provisions in international treaties. As further protection for foreign investments, some countries provide insurance for their citizens' investments abroad.

42–5b Export Controls

The U.S. Constitution provides in Article I, Section 9, that "No Tax or Duty shall be laid on Articles exported from any State." Thus, Congress cannot impose any export taxes. Congress can, however, use a variety of other devices to control exports. Congress may set export quotas on various items, such as grain being sold abroad. Under the Export Administration Act, the flow of technologically advanced products and technical data can be restricted.

While restricting certain exports, the United States uses devices such as export incentives and subsidies to stimulate other exports and thereby aid domestic businesses. Under the Export Trading Company Act, U.S. banks are encouraged to invest in export trading companies, which are formed when exporting firms join together to export a line of goods. The Export-Import Bank of the United States provides financial assistance, consisting primarily of credit guaranties given to commercial banks that in turn lend funds to U.S. exporting companies.

42–5c Import Controls

All nations have restrictions on imports, and the United States is no exception. Restrictions include strict prohibitions, quotas, and tariffs. Under the Trading with the Enemy Act, for instance, no goods may be imported from nations that have been designated enemies of the United States. Other laws prohibit the importation of illegal drugs, books that urge insurrection against the United States, and agricultural products that pose dangers to domestic crops or animals.

Quotas and Tariffs Limits on the amounts of goods that can be imported are known as **quotas.** At one time, for example, the United States had legal quotas on the number of automobiles that could be imported from Japan. Today, Japan "voluntarily" restricts the number of automobiles exported to the United States.

quota
A set limit on the amount of goods that can be imported.

Tariffs are taxes on imports. A tariff usually is a percentage of the value of the import, but it can be a flat rate per unit (for example, per barrel of oil). Tariffs raise the prices of goods, causing some consumers to purchase less expensive, domestically manufactured goods.

tariff
A tax on imported goods.

For instance, Mexico imposed tariffs of 10 to 20 percent on ninety products exported from the United States into Mexico—$2.4 billion of U.S. goods annually. This led to a rise in the prices of those goods in Mexico and a decrease in sales. Mexico agreed to suspend the tariffs when the United States agreed to allow Mexican truckers to enter the United States (subject to certain requirements).

Dumping The United States has specific laws directed at what it sees as unfair international trade practices. **Dumping,** for example, is the sale of imported goods at "less than fair value." *Fair value* usually is determined by the price of those goods in the exporting country. Foreign firms that engage in dumping in the United States hope to undersell U.S. businesses to obtain a larger share of the U.S. market. To prevent this, an extra tariff—known as an *antidumping duty*—may be assessed on the imports.

dumping
The selling of goods in a foreign country at a price below the price charged for the same goods in the domestic market.

Minimizing Trade Barriers Restrictions on imports are known as *trade barriers*. The elimination of trade barriers is sometimes seen as essential to the world's economic well-being.

Most of the world's leading trade nations are members of the World Trade Organization (WTO). To minimize trade barriers among nations, each member country of the WTO is required to grant **normal-trade-relations (NTR) status** to other member countries. This means that each member is obligated to treat other members at least as well as it treats the country that receives its most favorable treatment with regard to imports or exports.

Various regional trade agreements and associations also help to minimize trade barriers between nations. They include the following:

1. *The European Union (EU)*—The EU is a single integrated trading unit made up of twenty-eight European nations. Governing bodies within the EU issue regulations, or directives, that define EU law in various areas, such as environmental law.

2. *The North American Free Trade Agreement (NAFTA)*—NAFTA created a regional trading unit consisting of Canada, Mexico, and the United States. The goal of NAFTA is to eliminate tariffs among these three countries on substantially all goods by reducing the tariffs incrementally over a period of time.

3. *The Central America–Dominican Republic–United States Free Trade Agreement (CAFTA-DR)*—CAFTA-DR was formed by Costa Rica, the Dominican Republic, El Salvador, Guatemala, Honduras, Nicaragua, and the United States. Its purpose is to reduce tariffs and improve market access among all of these nations.

4. *The Republic of Korea–United States Free Trade Agreement (KORUS FTA)*—KORUS is the first U.S. free trade agreement with South Korea. The treaty's provisions will eliminate 95 percent of each nation's tariffs on industrial and consumer exports from other nations within five years.

42–5d Bribing of Foreign Officials

The United States also regulates payments to foreign officials. Giving cash or in-kind benefits to foreign government officials to obtain business contracts and other favors is often considered normal practice. To reduce such bribery among representatives of U.S. corporations, Congress enacted the Foreign Corrupt Practices Act.

 ## 42–6 U.S. Laws in a Global Context

The internationalization of business raises questions about the extraterritorial application of a nation's laws—that is, the effect of the country's laws outside its boundaries. Here, we look at the extraterritorial application of U.S. antitrust laws and U.S. laws prohibiting employment discrimination.

42–6a Antitrust Laws

U.S. antitrust laws have a wide application. They may *subject* persons in foreign nations to their provisions, as well as *protect* foreign consumers and competitors from violations committed by U.S. citizens. Consequently, *foreign persons*—a term that by definition includes foreign governments—may sue under U.S. antitrust laws in U.S. courts.

Section 1 of the Sherman Act provides for the extraterritorial effect of the U.S. antitrust laws. Before U.S. courts will exercise jurisdiction and apply antitrust laws extraterritorially, however, it must be shown that the alleged violation had a substantial effect on U.S. commerce. Jurisdiction is automatically invoked when a *per se* violation, such as a price-fixing agreement, occurs.

HIGHLIGHTING THE POINT

Able Corporation, a U.S. firm, joins a cartel of foreign companies to control the production, price, and distribution of the goods that the members of the cartel produce.

Can Able and the foreign cartel be sued for a violation of the U.S. antitrust laws? Yes. If the cartel has a substantial effect on U.S. commerce, a *per se* violation of U.S. antitrust laws may exist, and both Able and the cartel may be sued for this violation. Likewise, if foreign firms doing business in the United States enter into a price-fixing or other anticompetitive agreement to control a portion of U.S. markets, a *per se* violation may exist, and those firms may be sued for their illegal actions.

42–6b International Tort Claims

All nations have laws governing torts, but there are significant variations in the application and effect of the laws. In the United States, the Alien Tort Claims Act (ATCA) allows foreign citizens to bring suits in U.S. courts for injuries allegedly caused by violations of international tort law. Some cases have involved violations of human rights. Some have alleged environmental crimes. There are limits, however, to the jurisdiction of U.S. courts over events that occur in countries outside the United States.

Real-World Case Example

Twenty-two residents of Argentina filed a suit in a federal district court in California against Daimler AG, a German company. The plaintiffs alleged that Mercedes-Benz Argentina (MB Argentina), a subsidiary of Daimler, collaborated with state security forces to kidnap, detain, torture, and kill certain MB Argentina workers, including the plaintiffs and their relatives. These claims were asserted under the ATCA. Personal jurisdiction was based on the California contacts of Mercedes-Benz USA, LLC (MBUSA), a Daimler subsidiary incorporated in Delaware, with its principal place of business in New Jersey. The district court dismissed the suit for lack of jurisdiction. The U.S. Court of Appeals for the Ninth Circuit reversed the dismissal. Daimler appealed.

Is there a limit to the authority of a U.S. court to entertain a claim brought by foreign plaintiffs against a foreign defendant based on events occurring entirely outside the United States? Yes. In a 2014 case, *Daimler AG v. Bauman*, the United States Supreme Court reversed the federal appellate court's decision. The issue is whether a corporation's connections with a state are so continuous and systematic as to render it at home there. Neither Daimler nor MBUSA was incorporated in California, neither had its principal place of business there, and there was no California connection to the atrocities, perpetrators, or victims described in the complaint. Thus, the federal district court in California could not exercise jurisdiction over Daimler in this case.

42–6c Antidiscrimination Laws

Federal laws in the United States prohibit discrimination on the basis of race, color, national origin, religion, gender, age, or disability. These laws, as they affect employment relationships, generally apply extraterritorially.

The Age Discrimination in Employment Act covers U.S. employees working abroad for U.S. employers. The Americans with Disabilities Act, which requires employers to accommodate the needs of workers with disabilities, also applies to U.S. nationals working abroad for U.S. firms. Title VII of the Civil Rights Act applies extraterritorially to all U.S. employees working for U.S. employers abroad. Generally, U.S. employers must abide by U.S. antidiscrimination laws unless to do so would violate the laws of the country in which their workplaces are located. This "foreign laws exception" allows an employer to avoid being subjected to conflicting laws.

ANSWERING THE LEGAL PROBLEM

In the legal problem set out at the beginning of this chapter, Café Rojo, a Colombian firm, sells coffee beans to Black Bear Coffee Company, a U.S. firm. When Black Bear accepts the beans but refuses to pay for them, Café Rojo sues Black Bear in a Colombian court and is awarded damages.

Because Black Bear's assets are in the United States, Café Rojo must ask a U.S. court to enforce the Colombian court's judgment.

A **Is a U.S. court likely to grant this request?** Yes. Under the principle of comity, a U.S. court defers and gives effect to foreign laws and judicial decrees that are consistent with U.S. law. The collection of the judgment in this case should not present any problems.

LINKING BUSINESS LAW to Your Career

GLOBAL MARKETING MANAGEMENT

Your career may involve global marketing; therefore, you must understand how to market on a global basis.

Legal and Economic Constraints on Going Global

If you are the global marketing manager for your company, be aware of the following legal considerations outlined in this chapter:

• **Tariffs**—Determine what tariffs may be imposed on your company's products. If your company must pay relatively high tariffs and compete against domestic producers who face no tariffs, you may be wasting your time.

• **Quotas**—The United States has strict quotas on imports of textiles, sugar, and many dairy products. Other countries have quotas, too. If those quotas are highly restrictive, there is no point in trying to sell your company's products in those countries.

• **Trade agreements**—Some countries may have signed bilateral or international trade agreements that make it particularly attractive for you to attempt to market your company's products in those countries. Find out precisely how those agreements can help your company.

Consider Each Culture Separately

No matter how "small" the world has become, countries still have different sets of shared values that affect their citizens' preferences. Therefore, it is important to become intimately acquainted with the cultures of the countries where you conduct marketing campaigns.

TERMS AND CONCEPTS FOR REVIEW

act of state doctrine 580

choice-of-language clause 582

choice-of-law clause 583

comity 579

confiscation 580

correspondent bank 584

distribution agreement 581

dumping 585

export 580

expropriation 580

force majeure clause 583

foreign exchange market 584

forum-selection clause 583

franchise 582

normal-trade-relations (NTR) status 586

quota 585

sovereign immunity 580

tariff 585

treaty 579

CHAPTER SUMMARY—INTERNATIONAL LAW

LEARNING OUTCOME	
1	**Identify important international principles and doctrines.** Important international principles and doctrines include: (1) *The principle of comity*—Under this principle, nations give effect to the laws and judicial decrees of other nations for reasons of courtesy and international harmony. (2) *The act of state doctrine*—A doctrine under which U.S. courts avoid passing judgment on the validity of public acts committed by a recognized foreign government within its own territory. (3) *The doctrine of sovereign immunity*—When certain conditions are satisfied, foreign nations are immune from U.S. jurisdiction. The doctrine is codified in the Foreign Sovereign Immunities Act.
2	**Discuss how business is done internationally.** U.S. firms engage in international business transactions through (1) exporting, which may involve foreign agents or distributors, and (2) manufacturing abroad through licensing arrangements, franchising operations, wholly owned subsidiaries, or joint ventures.
3	**Explain common provisions used in international contracts.** International business contracts often include choice-of-language, forum-selection, and choice-of-law clauses to reduce the uncertainties associated with interpreting the language of the agreement and dealing with legal differences. Most domestic and international contracts include *force majeure* clauses. They commonly stipulate that certain events may excuse a party from liability for nonperformance of the contract. Arbitration clauses are also frequently found in international contracts.
4	**Outline the regulation of international business activities.** National laws regulate foreign investments, exporting, and importing. The World Trade Organization attempts to minimize trade barriers among nations, as do regional trade agreements and associations.
5	**State examples of U.S. laws applied in a global context.** U.S. antitrust laws may be applied beyond the borders of the United States if it can be shown that the alleged violation had a substantial effect on U.S. commerce. U.S. tort laws may be applied to wrongful acts that occur in foreign jurisdictions. Foreign citizens can bring civil suits in U.S. courts for violations of international tort law. The major U.S. laws prohibiting employment discrimination, including Title VII of the Civil Rights Act, the Age Discrimination in Employment Act, and the Americans with Disabilities Act, cover U.S. employees working abroad for U.S. firms—*unless* to apply the U.S. laws would violate the laws of the host country.

ISSUE SPOTTERS

Check your answers to the *Issue Spotters* against the answers provided in Appendix C at the end of this text.

1. Hi-Cola Corporation, a U.S. firm, markets a popular soft drink. The formula is secret, but with careful chemical analysis, its ingredients could be discovered. What can Hi-Cola do to prevent its product from being pirated abroad? (See *Doing Business Internationally*.)

2. Gems International, Ltd., is a foreign firm that has a 12 percent share of the U.S. market for diamonds. To capture a larger share, Gems offers its products at a below-cost discount to U.S. buyers (and inflates the prices in its own country to make up the difference). How can this attempt to undersell U.S. businesses be defeated? (See *Regulation of International Business Activities*.)

USING BUSINESS LAW

42–1. Doing Business Internationally. Macrotech, Inc., develops an innovative computer chip and obtains a patent on it. The firm markets the chip under the trademarked brand name "Flash." Macrotech wants to sell the chip to Nitron, Ltd., in Pacifica, a foreign country. Macrotech is concerned, however, that after an initial purchase, Nitron will duplicate the chip, pirate it, and sell the pirated version to computer manufacturers in Pacifica. To avoid this possibility, Macrotech could establish its own manufacturing facility in Pacifica, but it does not want to do this. How can Macrotech, without establishing a manufacturing facility in Pacifica, protect against Flash's being pirated by Nitron? (See *Doing Business Internationally*.)

42–2. Sovereign Immunity. Taconic Plastics, Ltd., is a manufacturer incorporated in Ireland with its principal place of business in New York. Taconic enters into a contract with a German firm, Werner Voss Architects and Engineers, acting as an agent for the government of Saudi Arabia, to supply special material for a tent project designed to shelter religious pilgrims visiting holy sites in Saudi Arabia. Most of the material is made in, and shipped from, New York. The German company does not pay Taconic and files for bankruptcy. Taconic files a suit in a U.S. court against the government of Saudi Arabia, seeking to collect $3 million. The defendant files a motion to dismiss the suit based on the doctrine of sovereign immunity. Under what circumstances does this doctrine apply? What are its exceptions? Should this suit be dismissed? Explain. (See *International Principles and Doctrines*.)

REAL-WORLD CASE PROBLEMS

42–3. Import Controls. The Wind Tower Trade Coalition is an association of domestic manufacturers of utility-scale wind towers. The coalition filed a suit in the U.S. Court of International Trade against the U.S. Department of Commerce, challenging its decision to impose only *prospective* antidumping duties, rather than *retrospective* (retroactive) duties, on imports of utility-scale wind towers from China and Vietnam. The Commerce Department had found that the domestic industry had not suffered any "material injury" or "threat of material injury," and that it would be protected by a prospective assessment. Can an antidumping duty be assessed retrospectively? If so, should it be assessed here? Discuss. [*Wind Tower Trade Coalition v. United States*, 741 F.3d 89 (Fed. Cir. 2014)] (See *Regulation of International Business Activities*.)

42–4. Sovereign Immunity. Technology Incubation and Entrepreneurship Training Society (TIETS) is an association made up of members of a local community in India. TIETS contracted with Mandana Farhang, a resident of California, to develop and market certain technology. Later, Farhang filed a suit against TIETS in a U.S. court, claiming breach of contract when the defendant "abandoned all efforts to further the technology." Assuming that TIETS qualifies a "foreign state," is it immune from Farhang's suit under the doctrine of sovereign immunity? Why or why not? [*Farhang v. Indian Institute of Technology*, ___ F.Supp.2d ___ (N.D.Cal. 2012)] (See *International Principles and Doctrines*.)

42–5. The Act of State Doctrine. Spectrum Stores, Inc., a gasoline retailer, filed a suit against Citgo Petroleum Corp. in a U.S. court. Spectrum alleged that Citgo conspired with other oil production companies to fix the prices of petroleum products sold in the United States, primarily by limiting the production of crude oil. The government of Venezuela owns Citgo, and a government controls the resources within its territory. Does the act of state doctrine prevent a U.S. court from considering Spectrum's claim? Explain. [*Spectrum Stores, Inc. v. Citgo Petroleum Corp.*, 632 F.3d 938 (5th Cir. 2011)] (See *International Principles and Doctrines*.)

ETHICAL QUESTIONS

42–6. Choice of Language. Would it be ethical for a U.S. firm to choose *not* to do business in a foreign country that requires the use of its own language in the legal documents that govern the firm's business transactions? Discuss. (See *International Contract Provisions*.)

42–7. Sovereign Immunity. Bell Helicopter Textron, Inc., makes and sells helicopters. Its Model 206 Series includes the Jet Ranger. All of Bell's helicopters have a distinctive design that identifies them as Bell aircraft. Thirty-six years after Bell developed the Jet Ranger, the Islamic Republic of Iran began to make and sell counterfeit Model 206 Series helicopters. Iran's versions—the Shahed 278 and the Shahed 285—used Bell's design. Can Bell successfully sue Iran in a U.S. court, or is Iran—a foreign nation—exempt from the court's jurisdiction? Explain. [*Bell Helicopter Textron Inc. v. Islamic Republic of Iran*, 764 F.Supp.2d 122 (D.D.C. 2011)] (See *International Principles and Doctrines*.)

Chapter 42—Work Set

TRUE-FALSE QUESTIONS

_____ 1. All nations must give effect to the laws of all other nations.

_____ 2. Under the act of state doctrine, foreign nations are subject to the jurisdiction of U.S. courts.

_____ 3. Under the doctrine of sovereign immunity, foreign nations are subject to the jurisdiction of U.S. courts.

_____ 4. The Foreign Sovereign Immunities Act states the circumstances in which the United States can be sued in foreign courts.

_____ 5. A member of the World Trade Organization must usually grant other members normal-trade-relations status with regard to trade.

_____ 6. Congress cannot tax exports.

_____ 7. U.S. employers with workplaces abroad must generally comply with U.S. antidiscrimination laws.

_____ 8. Under a _force majeure_ clause, a party may be excused from liability for nonperformance.

_____ 9. U.S. courts cannot exercise jurisdiction over foreign entities under U.S. antitrust laws.

_____ 10. Under a license, one party is allowed to use another's patented product.

MULTIPLE-CHOICE QUESTIONS

_____ 1. Johnston International, a U.S. firm, signs a contract with Irkut, Ltd., a Russian company, to give Irkut the right to sell Johnston's products in Russia. This is

    a. a distribution agreement.
    b. a joint venture.
    c. direct exporting.
    d. licensing.

_____ 2. China, which governs Hong Kong, seizes the property of Mack Enterprises, Inc., a U.S. firm doing business in Hong Kong, without paying the owners just compensation. This is

    a. a confiscation.
    b. a dumping.
    c. a licensing.
    d. an expropriation.

_____ 3. To obtain new computers, Liberia accepts bids from U.S. firms, including Macro Corporation and Micro, Inc. Macro wins the contract. Alleging impropriety, Micro files a suit in a U.S. court against Liberia and Macro. The court may decline to hear the suit under

    a. the act of state doctrine.
    b. the doctrine of sovereign immunity.
    c. the principle of comity.
    d. the World Trade Organization.

_____ 4. A South African seller and a U.S. buyer form a contract, which the buyer later breaches. The seller sues in a South African court and wins damages, but the buyer's assets are in the United States. If a U.S. court enforces the judgment, it will be because of the

    a. act of state doctrine.
    b. doctrine of sovereign immunity.
    c. principle of comity.
    d. World Trade Organization.

_____ 5. A contract between Moss Energy, a U.S. firm, and Electronique, S.A., a French company, provides that disputes between the parties will be adjudicated in a specific British court. This clause is

a. a forum-selection clause.
b. a choice-of-law clause.
c. a *force majeure* clause.
d. an arbitration clause.

_____ 6. Kenya issues bonds to finance the construction of an international airport. Kenya sells some of the bonds in the United States to Larry. A terrorist group destroys the airport, and Kenya refuses to pay the interest or principal on the bonds. Larry files a suit in a U.S. court. The court will hear the suit

a. if Kenya's acts constitute a confiscation.
b. if Kenya's acts constitute an expropriation.
c. if Kenya's selling bonds is a "commercial activity."
d. under no circumstances.

_____ 7. Digital, Inc., makes supercomputers that feature advanced technology. To inhibit Digital's export of its products to other countries, Congress can

a. confiscate all profits on exported supercomputers.
b. expropriate all profits on exported supercomputers.
c. set quotas on exported supercomputers.
d. tax exported supercomputers.

_____ 8. Auto Corporation makes cars in the United States. To boost the sales of Auto Corporation and other domestic car-makers, Congress can

a. neither set quotas nor tax imports.
b. only set quotas on imports.
c. only tax imports.
d. set quotas and tax imports.

 ## ANSWERING MORE LEGAL PROBLEMS

1. Hong Electronics, a state-owned factory in the People's Republic of China, made counterfeit parts that were misrepresented as genuine and sold in the United States. Integrated Technology Corp., a U.S. company that made and sold the genuine parts in the U.S. market, filed a suit in a U.S. court against Hong, alleging violations of trademark and patent law.

Does the doctrine of sovereign immunity prevent the U.S. court from hearing Integrated's suit? No. The doctrine of sovereign immunity exempts foreign nations from the jurisdiction of U.S. courts, subject to certain conditions. The Foreign Sovereign Immunities Act governs the circumstances in which an action may be brought in a U.S. court against a foreign state, its political _____, or any of its _____ or _____. A foreign state is not immune from the jurisdiction of U.S. courts when it engages in _____ activity that takes place within the United States or that has a _____ effect in the United States. Here, Hong engaged in _____ activity when it sold its counterfeit parts in the United States. Thus, a U.S. court can exercise jurisdiction.

2. Mobile Processes, Inc., a U.S. company, made network management devices. To test the demand for the devices in Asia, Mobile exported the products to Asian markets. When the test proved successful, Mobile decided to expand its operations to India.

What are Mobile's options for engaging in further international business transactions? Mobile can continue to export its goods to foreign markets. In _____ exporting, a seller signs a contract with a foreign buyer that provides for the conditions of shipment and payment. In _____ exporting, the seller sets up a marketing organization in a foreign market by appointing a foreign agent or distributor. An alternative is to _____ a manufacturing plant abroad. This would likely reduce the costs of labor, shipping, and raw materials and enable the seller to _____ more effectively in foreign markets. The seller can also obtain business abroad by _____ a foreign company to use copyrighted, patented, or trademarked intellectual property or trade secrets. Another way to expand into a foreign market is to establish a wholly owned _____ in a foreign country and thereby retain complete ownership, authority, and control over the operation.

The Constitution of the United States

PREAMBLE

We the People of the United States, in Order to form a more perfect Union, establish Justice, insure domestic Tranquility, provide for the common defence, promote the general Welfare, and secure the Blessings of Liberty to ourselves and our Posterity, do ordain and establish this Constitution for the United States of America.

ARTICLE I

Section 1. All legislative Powers herein granted shall be vested in a Congress of the United States, which shall consist of a Senate and House of Representatives.

Section 2. The House of Representatives shall be composed of Members chosen every second Year by the People of the several States, and the Electors in each State shall have the Qualifications requisite for Electors of the most numerous Branch of the State Legislature.

No Person shall be a Representative who shall not have attained to the Age of twenty five Years, and been seven Years a Citizen of the United States, and who shall not, when elected, be an Inhabitant of that State in which he shall be chosen.

Representatives and direct Taxes shall be apportioned among the several States which may be included within this Union, according to their respective Numbers, which shall be determined by adding to the whole Number of free Persons, including those bound to Service for a Term of Years, and excluding Indians not taxed, three fifths of all other Persons. The actual Enumeration shall be made within three Years after the first Meeting of the Congress of the United States, and within every subsequent Term of ten Years, in such Manner as they shall by Law direct. The Number of Representatives shall not exceed one for every thirty Thousand, but each State shall have at Least one

Representative; and until such enumeration shall be made, the State of New Hampshire shall be entitled to chuse three, Massachusetts eight, Rhode Island and Providence Plantations one, Connecticut five, New York six, New Jersey four, Pennsylvania eight, Delaware one, Maryland six, Virginia ten, North Carolina five, South Carolina five, and Georgia three.

When vacancies happen in the Representation from any State, the Executive Authority thereof shall issue Writs of Election to fill such Vacancies.

The House of Representatives shall chuse their Speaker and other Officers; and shall have the sole Power of Impeachment.

Section 3. The Senate of the United States shall be composed of two Senators from each State, chosen by the Legislature thereof, for six Years; and each Senator shall have one Vote.

Immediately after they shall be assembled in Consequence of the first Election, they shall be divided as equally as may be into three Classes. The Seats of the Senators of the first Class shall be vacated at the Expiration of the second Year, of the second Class at the Expiration of the fourth Year, and of the third Class at the Expiration of the sixth Year, so that one third may be chosen every second Year; and if Vacancies happen by Resignation, or otherwise, during the Recess of the Legislature of any State, the Executive thereof may make temporary Appointments until the next Meeting of the Legislature, which shall then fill such Vacancies.

No Person shall be a Senator who shall not have attained to the Age of thirty Years, and been nine Years a Citizen of the United States, and who shall not, when elected, be an Inhabitant of that State for which he shall be chosen.

The Vice President of the United States shall be President of the Senate, but shall have no Vote, unless they be equally divided.

The Senate shall chuse their other Officers, and also a President pro tempore, in the Absence of the

Vice President, or when he shall exercise the Office of President of the United States.

The Senate shall have the sole Power to try all Impeachments. When sitting for that Purpose, they shall be on Oath or Affirmation. When the President of the United States is tried, the Chief Justice shall preside: And no Person shall be convicted without the Concurrence of two thirds of the Members present.

Judgment in Cases of Impeachment shall not extend further than to removal from Office, and disqualification to hold and enjoy any Office of honor, Trust, or Profit under the United States: but the Party convicted shall nevertheless be liable and subject to Indictment, Trial, Judgment, and Punishment, according to Law.

Section 4. The Times, Places and Manner of holding Elections for Senators and Representatives, shall be prescribed in each State by the Legislature thereof; but the Congress may at any time by Law make or alter such Regulations, except as to the Places of chusing Senators.

The Congress shall assemble at least once in every Year, and such Meeting shall be on the first Monday in December, unless they shall by Law appoint a different Day.

Section 5. Each House shall be the Judge of the Elections, Returns, and Qualifications of its own Members, and a Majority of each shall constitute a Quorum to do Business; but a smaller Number may adjourn from day to day, and may be authorized to compel the Attendance of absent Members, in such Manner, and under such Penalties as each House may provide.

Each House may determine the Rules of its Proceedings, punish its Members for disorderly Behavior, and, with the Concurrence of two thirds, expel a Member.

Each House shall keep a Journal of its Proceedings, and from time to time publish the same, excepting such Parts as may in their Judgment require Secrecy; and the Yeas and Nays of the Members of either House on any question shall, at the Desire of one fifth of those Present, be entered on the Journal.

Neither House, during the Session of Congress, shall, without the Consent of the other, adjourn for more than three days, nor to any other Place than that in which the two Houses shall be sitting.

Section 6. The Senators and Representatives shall receive a Compensation for their Services, to be ascertained by Law, and paid out of the Treasury of the United States. They shall in all Cases, except Treason, Felony and Breach of the Peace, be privileged from Arrest during their Attendance at the Session of their respective Houses, and in going to and returning from the same; and for any Speech or Debate in either House, they shall not be questioned in any other Place.

No Senator or Representative shall, during the Time for which he was elected, be appointed to any civil Office under the Authority of the United States, which shall have been created, or the Emoluments whereof shall have been increased during such time; and no Person holding any Office under the United States, shall be a Member of either House during his Continuance in Office.

Section 7. All Bills for raising Revenue shall originate in the House of Representatives; but the Senate may propose or concur with Amendments as on other Bills.

Every Bill which shall have passed the House of Representatives and the Senate, shall, before it become a Law, be presented to the President of the United States; If he approve he shall sign it, but if not he shall return it, with his Objections to the House in which it shall have originated, who shall enter the Objections at large on their Journal, and proceed to reconsider it. If after such Reconsideration two thirds of that House shall agree to pass the Bill, it shall be sent together with the Objections, to the other House, by which it shall likewise be reconsidered, and if approved by two thirds of that House, it shall become a Law. But in all such Cases the Votes of both Houses shall be determined by Yeas and Nays, and the Names of the Persons voting for and against the Bill shall be entered on the Journal of each House respectively. If any Bill shall not be returned by the President within ten Days (Sundays excepted) after it shall have been presented to him, the Same shall be a Law, in like Manner as if he had signed it, unless the Congress by their Adjournment prevent its Return in which Case it shall not be a Law.

Every Order, Resolution, or Vote, to which the Concurrence of the Senate and House of Representatives may be necessary (except on a question of Adjournment) shall be presented to the President of the United States; and before the Same shall take Effect, shall be approved by him, or being disapproved by him, shall be repassed by two thirds of the Senate and House of Representatives, according to the Rules and Limitations prescribed in the Case of a Bill.

Section 8. The Congress shall have Power To lay and collect Taxes, Duties, Imposts and Excises, to pay the Debts and provide for the common Defence and general Welfare of the United States; but all Duties, Imposts and Excises shall be uniform throughout the United States;

To borrow Money on the credit of the United States;

To regulate Commerce with foreign Nations, and among the several States, and with the Indian Tribes;

To establish an uniform Rule of Naturalization, and uniform Laws on the subject of Bankruptcies throughout the United States;

To coin Money, regulate the Value thereof, and of foreign Coin, and fix the Standard of Weights and Measures;

To provide for the Punishment of counterfeiting the Securities and current Coin of the United States;

To establish Post Offices and post Roads;

To promote the Progress of Science and useful Arts, by securing for limited Times to Authors and Inventors the exclusive Right to their respective Writings and Discoveries;

To constitute Tribunals inferior to the supreme Court;

To define and punish Piracies and Felonies committed on the high Seas, and Offenses against the Law of Nations;

To declare War, grant Letters of Marque and Reprisal, and make Rules concerning Captures on Land and Water;

To raise and support Armies, but no Appropriation of Money to that Use shall be for a longer Term than two Years;

To provide and maintain a Navy;

To make Rules for the Government and Regulation of the land and naval Forces;

To provide for calling forth the Militia to execute the Laws of the Union, suppress Insurrections and repel Invasions;

To provide for organizing, arming, and disciplining, the Militia, and for governing such Part of them as may be employed in the Service of the United States, reserving to the States respectively, the Appointment of the Officers, and the Authority of training the Militia according to the discipline prescribed by Congress;

To exercise exclusive Legislation in all Cases whatsoever, over such District (not exceeding ten Miles square) as may, by Cession of particular States, and the Acceptance of Congress, become the Seat of the Government of the United States, and to exercise like Authority over all Places purchased by the Consent of the Legislature of the State in which the Same shall be, for the Erection of Forts, Magazines, Arsenals, dock-Yards, and other needful Buildings;—And

To make all Laws which shall be necessary and proper for carrying into Execution the foregoing Powers, and all other Powers vested by this Constitution in the Government of the United States, or in any Department or Officer thereof.

Section 9. The Migration or Importation of such Persons as any of the States now existing shall think proper to admit, shall not be prohibited by the Congress prior to the Year one thousand eight hundred and eight, but a Tax or duty may be imposed on such Importation, not exceeding ten dollars for each Person.

The privilege of the Writ of Habeas Corpus shall not be suspended, unless when in Cases of Rebellion or Invasion the public Safety may require it.

No Bill of Attainder or ex post facto Law shall be passed.

No Capitation, or other direct, Tax shall be laid, unless in Proportion to the Census or Enumeration herein before directed to be taken.

No Tax or Duty shall be laid on Articles exported from any State.

No Preference shall be given by any Regulation of Commerce or Revenue to the Ports of one State over those of another: nor shall Vessels bound to, or from, one State be obliged to enter, clear, or pay Duties in another.

No Money shall be drawn from the Treasury, but in Consequence of Appropriations made by Law; and a regular Statement and Account of the Receipts and Expenditures of all public Money shall be published from time to time.

No Title of Nobility shall be granted by the United States: And no Person holding any Office of Profit or Trust under them, shall, without the Consent of the Congress, accept of any present, Emolument, Office, or Title, of any kind whatever, from any King, Prince, or foreign State.

Section 10. No State shall enter into any Treaty, Alliance, or Confederation; grant Letters of Marque and Reprisal; coin Money; emit Bills of Credit; make any Thing but gold and silver Coin a Tender in Payment of Debts; pass any Bill of Attainder, ex post facto Law, or Law impairing the Obligation of Contracts, or grant any Title of Nobility.

No State shall, without the Consent of the Congress, lay any Imposts or Duties on Imports or Exports, except what may be absolutely necessary for executing its inspection Laws: and the net Produce of all Duties and Imposts, laid by any State on Imports or

Exports, shall be for the Use of the Treasury of the United States; and all such Laws shall be subject to the Revision and Controul of the Congress.

No State shall, without the Consent of Congress, lay any Duty of Tonnage, keep Troops, or Ships of War in time of Peace, enter into any Agreement or Compact with another State, or with a foreign Power, or engage in War, unless actually invaded, or in such imminent Danger as will not admit of delay.

ARTICLE II

Section 1. The executive Power shall be vested in a President of the United States of America. He shall hold his Office during the Term of four Years, and, together with the Vice President, chosen for the same Term, be elected, as follows:

Each State shall appoint, in such Manner as the Legislature thereof may direct, a Number of Electors, equal to the whole Number of Senators and Representatives to which the State may be entitled in the Congress; but no Senator or Representative, or Person holding an Office of Trust or Profit under the United States, shall be appointed an Elector.

The Electors shall meet in their respective States, and vote by Ballot for two Persons, of whom one at least shall not be an Inhabitant of the same State with themselves. And they shall make a List of all the Persons voted for, and of the Number of Votes for each; which List they shall sign and certify, and transmit sealed to the Seat of the Government of the United States, directed to the President of the Senate. The President of the Senate shall, in the Presence of the Senate and House of Representatives, open all the Certificates, and the Votes shall then be counted. The Person having the greatest Number of Votes shall be the President, if such Number be a Majority of the whole Number of Electors appointed; and if there be more than one who have such Majority, and have an equal Number of Votes, then the House of Representatives shall immediately chuse by Ballot one of them for President; and if no Person have a Majority, then from the five highest on the List the said House shall in like Manner chuse the President. But in chusing the President, the Votes shall be taken by States, the Representation from each State having one Vote; A quorum for this Purpose shall consist of a Member or Members from two thirds of the States, and a Majority of all the States shall be necessary to a Choice. In every Case, after the Choice of the President, the Person having the greater Number of Votes of the Electors shall be the Vice President. But if there should remain two or more who have equal Votes, the Senate shall chuse from them by Ballot the Vice President.

The Congress may determine the Time of chusing the Electors, and the Day on which they shall give their Votes; which Day shall be the same throughout the United States.

No person except a natural born Citizen, or a Citizen of the United States, at the time of the Adoption of this Constitution, shall be eligible to the Office of President; neither shall any Person be eligible to that Office who shall not have attained to the Age of thirty five Years, and been fourteen Years a Resident within the United States.

In Case of the Removal of the President from Office, or of his Death, Resignation or Inability to discharge the Powers and Duties of the said Office, the same shall devolve on the Vice President, and the Congress may by Law provide for the Case of Removal, Death, Resignation or Inability, both of the President and Vice President, declaring what Officer shall then act as President, and such Officer shall act accordingly, until the Disability be removed, or a President shall be elected.

The President shall, at stated Times, receive for his Services, a Compensation, which shall neither be increased nor diminished during the Period for which he shall have been elected, and he shall not receive within that Period any other Emolument from the United States, or any of them.

Before he enter on the Execution of his Office, he shall take the following Oath or Affirmation: "I do solemnly swear (or affirm) that I will faithfully execute the Office of President of the United States, and will to the best of my Ability, preserve, protect and defend the Constitution of the United States."

Section 2. The President shall be Commander in Chief of the Army and Navy of the United States, and of the Militia of the several States, when called into the actual Service of the United States; he may require the Opinion, in writing, of the principal Officer in each of the executive Departments, upon any Subject relating to the Duties of their respective Offices, and he shall have Power to grant Reprieves and Pardons for Offenses against the United States, except in Cases of Impeachment.

He shall have Power, by and with the Advice and Consent of the Senate to make Treaties, provided two thirds of the Senators present concur; and he shall nominate, and by and with the Advice and Consent of the Senate, shall appoint Ambassadors, other public Ministers and Consuls, Judges of the supreme Court, and all other Officers of the United States, whose Appointments are not herein otherwise provided for, and which shall be established by Law; but the Congress may by Law vest the Appointment of such inferior Officers, as they think proper, in the President alone, in the Courts of Law, or in the Heads of Departments.

The President shall have Power to fill up all Vacancies that may happen during the Recess of the Senate, by granting Commissions which shall expire at the End of their next Session.

Section 3. He shall from time to time give to the Congress Information of the State of the Union, and recommend to their Consideration such Measures as he shall judge necessary and expedient; he may, on extraordinary Occasions, convene both Houses, or either of them, and in Case of Disagreement between them, with Respect to the Time of Adjournment, he may adjourn them to such Time as he shall think proper; he shall receive Ambassadors and other public Ministers; he shall take Care that the Laws be faithfully executed, and shall Commission all the Officers of the United States.

Section 4. The President, Vice President and all civil Officers of the United States, shall be removed from Office on Impeachment for, and Conviction of, Treason, Bribery, or other high Crimes and Misdemeanors.

ARTICLE III

Section 1. The judicial Power of the United States, shall be vested in one supreme Court, and in such inferior Courts as the Congress may from time to time ordain and establish. The Judges, both of the supreme and inferior Courts, shall hold their Offices during good Behaviour, and shall, at stated Times, receive for their Services a Compensation, which shall not be diminished during their Continuance in Office.

Section 2. The judicial Power shall extend to all Cases, in Law and Equity, arising under this Constitution, the Laws of the United States, and Treaties made, or which shall be made, under their Authority;—to all Cases affecting Ambassadors, other public Ministers and Consuls;—to all Cases of admiralty and maritime Jurisdiction;—to Controversies to which the United States shall be a Party;—to Controversies between two or more States;—between a State and Citizens of another State;—between Citizens of different States;—between Citizens of the same State claiming Lands under Grants of different States, and between a State, or the Citizens thereof, and foreign States, Citizens or Subjects.

In all Cases affecting Ambassadors, other public Ministers and Consuls, and those in which a State shall be a Party, the supreme Court shall have original Jurisdiction. In all the other Cases before mentioned, the supreme Court shall have appellate Jurisdiction, both as to Law and Fact, with such Exceptions, and under such Regulations as the Congress shall make.

The Trial of all Crimes, except in Cases of Impeachment, shall be by Jury; and such Trial shall be held in the State where the said Crimes shall have been committed; but when not committed within any State, the Trial shall be at such Place or Places as the Congress may by Law have directed.

Section 3. Treason against the United States, shall consist only in levying War against them, or, in adhering to their Enemies, giving them Aid and Comfort. No Person shall be convicted of Treason unless on the Testimony of two Witnesses to the same overt Act, or on Confession in open Court.

The Congress shall have Power to declare the Punishment of Treason, but no Attainder of Treason shall work Corruption of Blood, or Forfeiture except during the Life of the Person attainted.

ARTICLE IV

Section 1. Full Faith and Credit shall be given in each State to the public Acts, Records, and judicial Proceedings of every other State. And the Congress may by general Laws prescribe the Manner in which such Acts, Records and Proceedings shall be proved, and the Effect thereof.

Section 2. The Citizens of each State shall be entitled to all Privileges and Immunities of Citizens in the several States.

A Person charged in any State with Treason, Felony, or other Crime, who shall flee from Justice, and be found in another State, shall on Demand of the executive Authority of the State from which he fled, be delivered up, to be removed to the State having Jurisdiction of the Crime.

No Person held to Service or Labour in one State, under the Laws thereof, escaping into another, shall, in Consequence of any Law or Regulation therein, be discharged from such Service or Labour, but shall be delivered up on Claim of the Party to whom such Service or Labour may be due.

Section 3. New States may be admitted by the Congress into this Union; but no new State shall be formed or erected within the Jurisdiction of any other State; nor any State be formed by the Junction of two or more States, or Parts of States, without the Consent of the Legislatures of the States concerned as well as of the Congress.

The Congress shall have Power to dispose of and make all needful Rules and Regulations respecting the Territory or other Property belonging to the United States; and nothing in this Constitution shall be so construed as to Prejudice any Claims of the United States, or of any particular State.

Section 4. The United States shall guarantee to every State in this Union a Republican Form of Government, and shall protect each of them against Invasion; and on Application of the Legislature, or of the Executive (when the Legislature cannot be convened) against domestic Violence.

ARTICLE V

The Congress, whenever two thirds of both Houses shall deem it necessary, shall propose Amendments to this Constitution, or, on the Application of the Legislatures of two thirds of the several States, shall call a Convention for proposing Amendments, which, in either Case, shall be valid to all Intents and Purposes, as part of this Constitution, when ratified by the Legislatures of three fourths of the several States, or by Conventions in three fourths thereof, as the one or the other Mode of Ratification may be proposed by the Congress; Provided that no Amendment which may be made prior to the Year One thousand eight hundred and eight shall in any Manner affect the first and fourth Clauses in the Ninth Section of the first Article; and that no State, without its Consent, shall be deprived of its equal Suffrage in the Senate.

ARTICLE VI

All Debts contracted and Engagements entered into, before the Adoption of this Constitution shall be as valid against the United States under this Constitution, as under the Confederation.

This Constitution, and the Laws of the United States which shall be made in Pursuance thereof; and all Treaties made, or which shall be made, under the Authority of the United States, shall be the supreme Law of the Land; and the Judges in every State shall be bound thereby, any Thing in the Constitution or Laws of any State to the Contrary notwithstanding.

The Senators and Representatives before mentioned, and the Members of the several State Legislatures, and all executive and judicial Officers, both of the United States and of the several States, shall be bound by Oath or Affirmation, to support this Constitution; but no religious Test shall ever be required as a Qualification to any Office or public Trust under the United States.

ARTICLE VII

The Ratification of the Conventions of nine States shall be sufficient for the Establishment of this Constitution between the States so ratifying the Same.

AMENDMENT I [1791]

Congress shall make no law respecting an establishment of religion, or prohibiting the free exercise thereof; or abridging the freedom of speech, or of the press; or the right of the people peaceably to assembly, and to petition the Government for a redress of grievances.

AMENDMENT II [1791]

A well regulated Militia, being necessary to the security of a free State, the right of the people to keep and bear Arms, shall not be infringed.

AMENDMENT III [1791]

No Soldier shall, in time of peace be quartered in any house, without the consent of the Owner, nor in time of war, but in a manner to be prescribed by law.

AMENDMENT IV [1791]

The right of the people to be secure in their persons, houses, papers, and effects, against unreasonable searches and seizures, shall not be violated, and no Warrants shall issue, but upon probable cause, supported by Oath or affirmation, and particularly describing the place to be searched, and the persons or things to be seized.

AMENDMENT V [1791]

No person shall be held to answer for a capital, or otherwise infamous crime, unless on a presentment or indictment of a Grand Jury, except in cases arising in the land or naval forces, or in the Militia, when in actual service in time of War or public danger; nor shall any person be subject for the same offence to be twice put in jeopardy of life or limb; nor shall be compelled in any criminal case to be a witness against himself, nor be deprived of life, liberty, or property, without due process of law; nor shall private property be taken for public use, without just compensation.

AMENDMENT VI [1791]

In all criminal prosecutions, the accused shall enjoy the right to a speedy and public trial, by an impartial jury of the State and district wherein the crime shall have been committed, which district shall have been previously ascertained by law, and to be informed of the nature and cause of the accusation; to be confronted with the witnesses against him; to have compulsory process for obtaining witnesses in his favor, and to have the Assistance of Counsel for his defence.

AMENDMENT VII [1791]

In Suits at common law, where the value in controversy shall exceed twenty dollars, the right of trial by jury shall be preserved, and no fact tried by jury, shall be otherwise re-examined in any Court of the United States, than according to the rules of the common law.

AMENDMENT VIII [1791]

Excessive bail shall not be required, nor excessive fines imposed, nor cruel and unusual punishments inflicted.

AMENDMENT IX [1791]

The enumeration in the Constitution, of certain rights, shall not be construed to deny or disparage others retained by the people.

AMENDMENT X [1791]

The powers not delegated to the United States by the Constitution, nor prohibited by it to the States, are reserved to the States respectively, or to the people.

AMENDMENT XI [1795]

The Judicial power of the United States shall not be construed to extend to any suit in law or equity, commenced or prosecuted against one of the United States by Citizens of another State, or by Citizens or Subjects of any Foreign State.

AMENDMENT XII [1804]

The Electors shall meet in their respective states, and vote by ballot for President and Vice-President, one of whom, at least, shall not be an inhabitant of the same state with themselves; they shall name in their ballots the person voted for as President, and in distinct ballots the person voted for as Vice-President, and they shall make distinct lists of all persons voted for as President, and of all persons voted for as Vice-President, and of the number of votes for each, which lists they shall sign and certify, and transmit sealed to the seat of the government of the United States, directed to the President of the Senate;—The President of the Senate shall, in the presence of the Senate and House of Representatives, open all the certificates and the votes shall then be counted;—The person having the greatest number of votes for President, shall be the President, if such number be a majority of the whole number of Electors appointed; and if no person have such majority, then from the persons having the highest numbers not exceeding three on the list of those voted for as President, the House of Representatives shall choose immediately, by ballot, the President. But in choosing the President, the votes shall be taken by states, the representation from each state having one vote; a quorum for this purpose shall consist of a member or members from two-thirds of the states, and a majority of all states shall be necessary to a choice. And if the House of Representatives shall not choose a President whenever the right of choice shall devolve upon them, before the fourth day of March next following, then the Vice-President shall act as President, as in the case of the death or other constitutional disability of the President.—The person having the greatest number of votes as Vice-President, shall be the Vice-President, if such number be a majority of the whole number of

Electors appointed, and if no person have a majority, then from the two highest numbers on the list, the Senate shall choose the Vice-President; a quorum for the purpose shall consist of two-thirds of the whole number of Senators, and a majority of the whole number shall be necessary to a choice. But no person constitutionally ineligible to the office of President shall be eligible to that of Vice-President of the United States.

AMENDMENT XIII [1865]

Section 1. Neither slavery nor involuntary servitude, except as a punishment for crime whereof the party shall have been duly convicted, shall exist within the United States, or any place subject to their jurisdiction.

Section 2. Congress shall have power to enforce this article by appropriate legislation.

AMENDMENT XIV [1868]

Section 1. All persons born or naturalized in the United States, and subject to the jurisdiction thereof, are citizens of the United States and of the State wherein they reside. No State shall make or enforce any law which shall abridge the privileges or immunities of citizens of the United States; nor shall any State deprive any person of life, liberty, or property, without due process of law; nor deny to any person within its jurisdiction the equal protection of the laws.

Section 2. Representatives shall be apportioned among the several States according to their respective numbers, counting the whole number of persons in each State, excluding Indians not taxed. But when the right to vote at any election for the choice of electors for President and Vice President of the United States, Representatives in Congress, the Executive and Judicial officers of a State, or the members of the Legislature thereof, is denied to any of the male inhabitants of such State, being twenty-one years of age, and citizens of the United States, or in any way abridged, except for participation in rebellion, or other crime, the basis of representation therein shall be reduced in the proportion which the number of such male citizens shall bear to the whole number of male citizens twenty-one years of age in such State.

Section 3. No person shall be a Senator or Representative in Congress, or elector of President and Vice President, or hold any office, civil or military, under the United States, or under any State, who having previously taken an oath, as a member of Congress, or as an officer of the United States, or as a member of any State legislature, or as an executive or judicial officer of any State, to support the Constitution of the United States, shall have engaged in insurrection or rebellion against the same, or given aid or comfort to the enemies thereof. But Congress may by a vote of two-thirds of each House, remove such disability.

Section 4. The validity of the public debt of the United States, authorized by law, including debts incurred for payment of pensions and bounties for services in suppressing insurrection or rebellion, shall not be questioned. But neither the United States nor any State shall assume or pay any debt or obligation incurred in aid of insurrection or rebellion against the United States, or any claim for the loss or emancipation of any slave; but all such debts, obligations and claims shall be held illegal and void.

Section 5. The Congress shall have power to enforce, by appropriate legislation, the provisions of this article.

AMENDMENT XV [1870]

Section 1. The right of citizens of the United States to vote shall not be denied or abridged by the United States or by any State on account of race, color, or previous condition of servitude.

Section 2. The Congress shall have power to enforce this article by appropriate legislation.

AMENDMENT XVI [1913]

The Congress shall have power to lay and collect taxes on incomes, from whatever source derived, without apportionment among the several States, and without regard to any census or enumeration.

AMENDMENT XVII [1913]

Section 1. The Senate of the United States shall be composed of two Senators from each State, elected by the people thereof, for six years; and each Senator shall have one vote. The electors in each State shall have the qualifications requisite for electors of the most numerous branch of the State legislatures.

Section 2. When vacancies happen in the representation of any State in the Senate, the executive authority of such State shall issue writs of election to fill such vacancies: Provided, That the legislature of any State may empower the executive thereof to make temporary appointments until the people fill the vacancies by election as the legislature may direct.

Section 3. This amendment shall not be so construed as to affect the election or term of any Senator chosen before it becomes valid as part of the Constitution.

AMENDMENT XVIII [1919]

Section 1. After one year from the ratification of this article the manufacture, sale, or transportation of intoxicating liquors within, the importation thereof into, or the exportation thereof from the United States and all territory subject to the jurisdiction thereof for beverage purposes is hereby prohibited.

Section 2. The Congress and the several States shall have concurrent power to enforce this article by appropriate legislation.

Section 3. This article shall be inoperative unless it shall have been ratified as an amendment to the Constitution by the legislatures of the several States, as provided in the Constitution, within seven years from the date of the submission hereof to the States by the Congress.

AMENDMENT XIX [1920]

Section 1. The right of citizens of the United States to vote shall not be denied or abridged by the United States or by any State on account of sex.

Section 2. Congress shall have power to enforce this article by appropriate legislation.

AMENDMENT XX [1933]

Section 1. The terms of the President and Vice President shall end at noon on the 20th day of January, and the terms of Senators and Representatives at noon on the 3d day of January, of the years in which such terms would have ended if this article had not been ratified; and the terms of their successors shall then begin.

Section 2. The Congress shall assemble at least once in every year, and such meeting shall begin at noon on the 3d day of January, unless they shall by law appoint a different day.

Section 3. If, at the time fixed for the beginning of the term of the President, the President elect shall have died, the Vice President elect shall become President. If the President shall not have been chosen before the time fixed for the beginning of his term, or if the President elect shall have failed to qualify, then the Vice President elect shall act as President until a President shall have qualified; and the Congress may by law provide for the case wherein neither a President elect nor a Vice President elect shall have qualified, declaring who shall then act as President, or the manner in which one who is to act shall be selected, and such person shall act accordingly until a President or Vice President shall have qualified.

Section 4. The Congress may by law provide for the case of the death of any of the persons from whom the House of Representatives may choose a President whenever the right of choice shall have devolved upon them, and for the case of the death of any of the persons from whom the Senate may choose a Vice President whenever the right of choice shall have devolved upon them.

Section 5. Sections 1 and 2 shall take effect on the 15th day of October following the ratification of this article.

Section 6. This article shall be inoperative unless it shall have been ratified as an amendment to the Constitution by the legislatures of three-fourths of the several States within seven years from the date of its submission.

AMENDMENT XXI [1933]

Section 1. The eighteenth article of amendment to the Constitution of the United States is hereby repealed.

Section 2. The transportation or importation into any State, Territory, or possession of the United States for delivery or use therein of intoxicating liquors, in violation of the laws thereof, is hereby prohibited.

Section 3. This article shall be inoperative unless it shall have been ratified as an amendment to the Constitution by conventions in the several States, as provided in the Constitution, within seven years from the date of the submission hereof to the States by the Congress.

AMENDMENT XXII [1951]

Section 1. No person shall be elected to the office of the President more than twice, and no person who has held the office of President, or acted as President, for more than two years of a term to which some other person was elected President shall be elected to the office of President more than once. But this Article shall not apply to any person holding the office of President when this Article was proposed by the Congress, and shall not prevent any person who may be holding the office of President, or acting as President, during the term within which this Article becomes operative from holding the office of President or acting as President during the remainder of such term.

Section 2. This article shall be inoperative unless it shall have been ratified as an amendment to the Constitution by the legislatures of three-fourths of the several States within seven years from the date of its submission to the States by the Congress.

AMENDMENT XXIII [1961]

Section 1. The District constituting the seat of Government of the United States shall appoint in such manner as the Congress may direct:

A number of electors of President and Vice President equal to the whole number of Senators and Representatives in Congress to which the District would be entitled if it were a State, but in no event more than the least populous state; they shall be in addition to those appointed by the states, but they shall be considered, for the purposes of the election of President and Vice President, to be electors appointed by a state; and they shall meet in the District and perform such duties as provided by the twelfth article of amendment.

Section 2. The Congress shall have power to enforce this article by appropriate legislation.

AMENDMENT XXIV [1964]

Section 1. The right of citizens of the United States to vote in any primary or other election for President or Vice President, for electors for President or Vice President, or for Senator or Representative in Congress, shall not be denied or abridged by the United States, or any State by reason of failure to pay any poll tax or other tax.

Section 2. The Congress shall have power to enforce this article by appropriate legislation.

AMENDMENT XXV [1967]

Section 1. In case of the removal of the President from office or of his death or resignation, the Vice President shall become President.

Section 2. Whenever there is a vacancy in the office of the Vice President, the President shall nominate a Vice President who shall take office upon confirmation by a majority vote of both Houses of Congress.

Section 3. Whenever the President transmits to the President pro tempore of the Senate and the Speaker of the House of Representatives his written declaration that he is unable to discharge the powers and duties of his office, and until he transmits to them a written declaration to the contrary, such powers and duties shall be discharged by the Vice President as Acting President.

Section 4. Whenever the Vice President and a majority of either the principal officers of the executive departments or of such other body as Congress may by law provide, transmit to the President pro tempore of the Senate and the Speaker of the House of Representatives their written declaration that the President is unable to discharge the powers and duties of his office, the Vice President shall immediately assume the powers and duties of the office as Acting President.

Thereafter, when the President transmits to the President pro tempore of the Senate and the Speaker of the House of Representatives his written declaration that no inability exists, he shall resume the powers and duties of his office unless the Vice President and a majority of either the principal officers of the executive department or of such other body as Congress may by law provide, transmit within four days to the President pro tempore of the Senate and the Speaker of the House of Representatives their written declaration that the President is unable to discharge the powers and duties of his office. Thereupon Congress shall decide the issue, assembling within forty-eight hours for that purpose if not in session. If the Congress, within twenty-one days after receipt of the latter written declaration, or, if Congress is not in session, within twenty-one days after Congress is required to assemble, determines by two-thirds vote of both Houses that the President is unable to discharge the powers and duties of his office, the Vice President shall continue to discharge the same as Acting President; otherwise, the President shall resume the powers and duties of his office.

AMENDMENT XXVI [1971]

Section 1. The right of citizens of the United States, who are eighteen years of age or older, to vote shall not be denied or abridged by the United States or by any State on account of age.

Section 2. The Congress shall have power to enforce this article by appropriate legislation.

AMENDMENT XXVII [1992]

No law, varying the compensation for the services of the Senators and Representatives, shall take effect, until an election of Representatives shall have intervened.

Appendix B

Article 2 of the Uniform Commercial Code

Article 2—Sales

Part 1 Short Title, General Construction and Subject Matter

§ 2–101. Short Title.

This Article shall be known and may be cited as Uniform Commercial Code—Sales.

§ 2–102. Scope; Certain Security and Other Transactions Excluded From This Article.

Unless the context otherwise requires, this Article applies to transactions in goods; it does not apply to any transaction which although in the form of an unconditional contract to sell or present sale is intended to operate only as a security transaction nor does this Article impair or repeal any statute regulating sales to consumers, farmers or other specified classes of buyers.

§ 2–103. Definitions and Index of Definitions.

(1) In this Article unless the context otherwise requires
    (a) "Buyer" means a person who buys or contracts to buy goods.
    (b) "Good faith" in the case of a merchant means honesty in fact and the observance of reasonable commercial standards of fair dealing in the trade.
    (c) "Receipt" of goods means taking physical possession of them.
    (d) "Seller" means a person who sells or contracts to sell goods.

(2) Other definitions applying to this Article or to specified Parts thereof, and the sections in which they appear are:
    "Acceptance". Section 2–606.
    "Banker's credit". Section 2–325.

    "Between merchants". Section 2–104.
    "Cancellation". Section 2–106(4).
    "Commercial unit". Section 2–105.
    "Confirmed credit". Section 2–325.
    "Conforming to contract". Section 2–106.
    "Contract for sale". Section 2–106.
    "Cover". Section 2–712.
    "Entrusting". Section 2–403.
    "Financing agency". Section 2–104.
    "Future goods". Section 2–105.
    "Goods". Section 2–105.
    "Identification". Section 2–501.
    "Installment contract". Section 2–612.
    "Letter of Credit". Section 2–325.
    "Lot". Section 2–105.
    "Merchant". Section 2–104.
    "Overseas". Section 2–323.
    "Person in position of seller". Section 2–707.
    "Present sale". Section 2–106.
    "Sale". Section 2–106.
    "Sale on approval". Section 2–326.
    "Sale or return". Section 2–326.
    "Termination". Section 2–106.

(3) The following definitions in other Articles apply to this Article:
    "Check". Section 3–104.
    "Consignee". Section 7–102.
    "Consignor". Section 7–102.
    "Consumer goods". Section 9–109.
    "Dishonor". Section 3–507.
    "Draft". Section 3–104.

(4) In addition Article 1 contains general definitions and principles of construction and interpretation applicable throughout this Article.
    As amended in 1994 and 1999.

§ 2–104. Definitions: "Merchant"; "Between Merchants"; "Financing Agency".

(1) "Merchant" means a person who deals in goods of the kind or otherwise by his occupation holds himself

out as having knowledge or skill peculiar to the practices or goods involved in the transaction or to whom such knowledge or skill may be attributed by his employment of an agent or broker or other intermediary who by his occupation holds himself out as having such knowledge or skill.

(2) "Financing agency" means a bank, finance company or other person who in the ordinary course of business makes advances against goods or documents of title or who by arrangement with either the seller or the buyer intervenes in ordinary course to make or collect payment due or claimed under the contract for sale, as by purchasing or paying the seller's draft or making advances against it or by merely taking it for collection whether or not documents of title accompany the draft. "Financing agency" includes also a bank or other person who similarly intervenes between persons who are in the position of seller and buyer in respect to the goods (Section 2–707).

(3) "Between merchants" means in any transaction with respect to which both parties are chargeable with the knowledge or skill of merchants.

§ 2–105. Definitions: Transferability; "Goods"; "Future" Goods; "Lot"; "Commercial Unit".

(1) "Goods" means all things (including specially manufactured goods) which are movable at the time of identification to the contract for sale other than the money in which the price is to be paid, investment securities (Article 8) and things in action. "Goods" also includes the unborn young of animals and growing crops and other identified things attached to realty as described in the section on goods to be severed from realty (Section 2–107).

(2) Goods must be both existing and identified before any interest in them can pass. Goods which are not both existing and identified are "future" goods. A purported present sale of future goods or of any interest therein operates as a contract to sell.

(3) There may be a sale of a part interest in existing identified goods.

(4) An undivided share in an identified bulk of fungible goods is sufficiently identified to be sold although the quantity of the bulk is not determined. Any agreed proportion of such a bulk or any quantity thereof agreed upon by number, weight or other measure may to the extent of the seller's interest in the bulk be sold to the buyer who then becomes an owner in common.

(5) "Lot" means a parcel or a single article which is the subject matter of a separate sale or delivery, whether or not it is sufficient to perform the contract.

(6) "Commercial unit" means such a unit of goods as by commercial usage is a single whole for purposes of sale and division of which materially impairs its character or value on the market or in use. A commercial unit may be a single article (as a machine) or a set of articles (as a suite of furniture or an assortment of sizes) or a quantity (as a bale, gross, or carload) or any other unit treated in use or in the relevant market as a single whole.

§ 2–106. Definitions: "Contract"; "Agreement"; "Contract for Sale"; "Sale"; "Present Sale"; "Conforming" to Contract; "Termination"; "Cancellation".

(1) In this Article unless the context otherwise requires "contract" and "agreement" are limited to those relating to the present or future sale of goods. "Contract for sale" includes both a present sale of goods and a contract to sell goods at a future time. A "sale" consists in the passing of title from the seller to the buyer for a price (Section 2–401). A "present sale" means a sale which is accomplished by the making of the contract.

(2) Goods or conduct including any part of a performance are "conforming" or conform to the contract when they are in accordance with the obligations under the contract.

(3) "Termination" occurs when either party pursuant to a power created by agreement or law puts an end to the contract otherwise than for its breach. On "termination" all obligations which are still executory on both sides are discharged but any right based on prior breach or performance survives.

(4) "Cancellation" occurs when either party puts an end to the contract for breach by the other and its effect is the same as that of "termination" except that the cancelling party also retains any remedy for breach of the whole contract or any unperformed balance.

§ 2–107. Goods to Be Severed From Realty: Recording.

(1) A contract for the sale of minerals or the like (including oil and gas) or a structure or its materials to be removed from realty is a contract for the sale of goods within this Article if they are to be severed by the seller but until severance a purported present sale thereof which is not effective as a transfer of an interest in land is effective only as a contract to sell.

(2) A contract for the sale apart from the land of growing crops or other things attached to realty and capable of severance without material harm thereto but not described in subsection (1) or of timber to be cut is a contract for the sale of goods within this Article

whether the subject matter is to be severed by the buyer or by the seller even though it forms part of the realty at the time of contracting, and the parties can by identification effect a present sale before severance.

(3) The provisions of this section are subject to any third party rights provided by the law relating to realty records, and the contract for sale may be executed and recorded as a document transferring an interest in land and shall then constitute notice to third parties of the buyer's rights under the contract for sale.

As amended in 1972.

Part 2   Form, Formation and Readjustment of Contract

§ 2–201.   Formal Requirements; Statute of Frauds.

(1) Except as otherwise provided in this section a contract for the sale of goods for the price of $500 or more is not enforceable by way of action or defense unless there is some writing sufficient to indicate that a contract for sale has been made between the parties and signed by the party against whom enforcement is sought or by his authorized agent or broker. A writing is not insufficient because it omits or incorrectly states a term agreed upon but the contract is not enforceable under this paragraph beyond the quantity of goods shown in such writing.

(2) Between merchants if within a reasonable time a writing in confirmation of the contract and sufficient against the sender is received and the party receiving it has reason to know its contents, its satisfies the requirements of subsection (1) against such party unless written notice of objection to its contents is given within ten days after it is received.

(3) A contract which does not satisfy the requirements of subsection (1) but which is valid in other respects is enforceable

(a) if the goods are to be specially manufactured for the buyer and are not suitable for sale to others in the ordinary course of the seller's business and the seller, before notice of repudiation is received and under circumstances which reasonably indicate that the goods are for the buyer, has made either a substantial beginning of their manufacture or commitments for their procurement; or

(b) if the party against whom enforcement is sought admits in his pleading, testimony or otherwise in court that a contract for sale was made, but the contract is not enforceable under this provision beyond the quantity of goods admitted; or

(c) with respect to goods for which payment has been made and accepted or which have been received and accepted (Sec. 2–606).

§ 2–202.   Final Written Expression: Parol or Extrinsic Evidence.

Terms with respect to which the confirmatory memoranda of the parties agree or which are otherwise set forth in a writing intended by the parties as a final expression of their agreement with respect to such terms as are included therein may not be contradicted by evidence of any prior agreement or of a contemporaneous oral agreement but may be explained or supplemented

(a) by course of dealing or usage of trade (Section 1–205) or by course of performance (Section 2–208); and

(b) by evidence of consistent additional terms unless the court finds the writing to have been intended also as a complete and exclusive statement of the terms of the agreement.

§ 2–203.   Seals Inoperative.

The affixing of a seal to a writing evidencing a contract for sale or an offer to buy or sell goods does not constitute the writing a sealed instrument and the law with respect to sealed instruments does not apply to such a contract or offer.

§ 2–204.   Formation in General.

(1) A contract for sale of goods may be made in any manner sufficient to show agreement, including conduct by both parties which recognizes the existence of such a contract.

(2) An agreement sufficient to constitute a contract for sale may be found even though the moment of its making is undetermined.

(3) Even though one or more terms are left open a contract for sale does not fail for indefiniteness if the parties have intended to make a contract and there is a reasonably certain basis for giving an appropriate remedy.

§ 2–205.   Firm Offers.

An offer by a merchant to buy or sell goods in a signed writing which by its terms gives assurance that it will be held open is not revocable, for lack of consideration, during the time stated or if no time is stated for a reasonable time, but in no event may such period of irrevocability exceed three months; but any such term of assurance on a form supplied by the offeree must be separately signed by the offeror.

§ 2–206.   Offer and Acceptance in Formation of Contract.

(1) Unless other unambiguously indicated by the language or circumstances

(a) an offer to make a contract shall be construed as inviting acceptance in any manner and by any medium reasonable in the circumstances;

(b) an order or other offer to buy goods for prompt or current shipment shall be construed as inviting acceptance either by a prompt promise to ship or by the prompt or current shipment of conforming or nonconforming goods, but such a shipment of non-conforming goods does not constitute an acceptance if the seller seasonably notifies the buyer that the shipment is offered only as an accommodation to the buyer.

(2) Where the beginning of a requested performance is a reasonable mode of acceptance an offeror who is not notified of acceptance within a reasonable time may treat the offer as having lapsed before acceptance.

§ 2–207. Additional Terms in Acceptance or Confirmation.

(1) A definite and seasonable expression of acceptance or a written confirmation which is sent within a reasonable time operates as an acceptance even though it states terms additional to or different from those offered or agreed upon, unless acceptance is expressly made conditional on assent to the additional or different terms.

(2) The additional terms are to be construed as proposals for addition to the contract. Between merchants such terms become part of the contract unless:

(a) the offer expressly limits acceptance to the terms of the offer;

(b) they materially alter it; or

(c) notification of objection to them has already been given or is given within a reasonable time after notice of them is received.

(3) Conduct by both parties which recognizes the existence of a contract is sufficient to establish a contract for sale although the writings of the parties do not otherwise establish a contract. In such case the terms of the particular contract consist of those terms on which the writings of the parties agree, together with any supplementary terms incorporated under any other provisions of this Act.

§ 2–208. Course of Performance or Practical Construction.

(1) Where the contract for sale involves repeated occasions for performance by either party with knowledge of the nature of the performance and opportunity for objection to it by the other, any course of performance accepted or acquiesced in without objection shall be relevant to determine the meaning of the agreement.

(2) The express terms of the agreement and any such course of performance, as well as any course of dealing and usage of trade, shall be construed whenever reasonable as consistent with each other; but when such construction is unreasonable, express terms shall control course of performance and course of performance shall control both course of dealing and usage of trade (Section 1–303).

(3) Subject to the provisions of the next section on modification and waiver, such course of performance shall be relevant to show a waiver or modification of any term inconsistent with such course of performance.

§ 2–209. Modification, Rescission and Waiver.

(1) An agreement modifying a contract within this Article needs no consideration to be binding.

(2) A signed agreement which excludes modification or rescission except by a signed writing cannot be otherwise modified or rescinded, but except as between merchants such a requirement on a form supplied by the merchant must be separately signed by the other party.

(3) The requirements of the statute of frauds section of this Article (Section 2–201) must be satisfied if the contract as modified is within its provisions.

(4) Although an attempt at modification or rescission does not satisfy the requirements of subsection (2) or (3) it can operate as a waiver.

(5) A party who has made a waiver affecting an executory portion of the contract may retract the waiver by reasonable notification received by the other party that strict performance will be required of any term waived, unless the retraction would be unjust in view of a material change of position in reliance on the waiver.

§ 2–210. Delegation of Performance; Assignment of Rights.

(1) A party may perform his duty through a delegate unless otherwise agreed or unless the other party has a substantial interest in having his original promisor perform or control the acts required by the contract. No delegation of performance relieves the party delegating of any duty to perform or any liability for breach.

(2) Except as otherwise provided in Section 9–406, unless otherwise agreed, all rights of either seller or buyer can be assigned except where the assignment would materially change the duty of the other party, or increase materially the burden or risk imposed on him by his contract, or impair materially his chance of obtaining return performance. A right to damages for

breach of the whole contract or a right arising out of the assignor's due performance of his entire obligation can be assigned despite agreement otherwise.

(3) The creation, attachment, perfection, or enforcement of a security interest in the seller's interest under a contract is not a transfer that materially changes the duty of or increases materially the burden or risk imposed on the buyer or impairs materially the buyer's chance of obtaining return performance within the purview of subsection (2) unless, and then only to the extent that, enforcement actually results in a delegation of material performance of the seller. Even in that event, the creation, attachment, perfection, and enforcement of the security interest remain effective, but (i) the seller is liable to the buyer for damages caused by the delegation to the extent that the damages could not reasonably by prevented by the buyer, and (ii) a court having jurisdiction may grant other appropriate relief, including cancellation of the contract for sale or an injunction against enforcement of the security interest or consummation of the enforcement.

(4) Unless the circumstances indicate the contrary a prohibition of assignment of "the contract" is to be construed as barring only the delegation to the assignee of the assignor's performance.

(5) An assignment of "the contract" or of "all my rights under the contract" or an assignment in similar general terms is an assignment of rights and unless the language or the circumstances (as in an assignment for security) indicate the contrary, it is a delegation of performance of the duties of the assignor and its acceptance by the assignee constitutes a promise by him to perform those duties. This promise is enforceable by either the assignor or the other party to the original contract.

(6) The other party may treat any assignment which delegates performance as creating reasonable grounds for insecurity and may without prejudice to his rights against the assignor demand assurances from the assignee (Section 2–609).

As amended in 1999.

Part 3 General Obligation and Construction of Contract

§ 2–301. General Obligations of Parties.

The obligation of the seller is to transfer and deliver and that of the buyer is to accept and pay in accordance with the contract.

§ 2–302. Unconscionable Contract or Clause.

(1) If the court as a matter of law finds the contract or any clause of the contract to have been unconscionable at the time it was made the court may refuse to enforce the contract, or it may enforce the remainder of the contract without the unconscionable clause, or it may so limit the application of any unconscionable clause as to avoid any unconscionable result.

(2) When it is claimed or appears to the court that the contract or any clause thereof may be unconscionable the parties shall be afforded a reasonable opportunity to present evidence as to its commercial setting, purpose and effect to aid the court in making the determination.

§ 2–303. Allocations or Division of Risks.

Where this Article allocates a risk or a burden as between the parties "unless otherwise agreed", the agreement may not only shift the allocation but may also divide the risk or burden.

§ 2–304. Price Payable in Money, Goods, Realty, or Otherwise.

(1) The price can be made payable in money or otherwise. If it is payable in whole or in part in goods each party is a seller of the goods which he is to transfer.

(2) Even though all or part of the price is payable in an interest in realty the transfer of the goods and the seller's obligations with reference to them are subject to this Article, but not the transfer of the interest in realty or the transferor's obligations in connection therewith.

§ 2–305. Open Price Term.

(1) The parties if they so intend can conclude a contract for sale even though the price is not settled. In such a case the price is a reasonable price at the time for delivery if

(a) nothing is said as to price; or

(b) the price is left to be agreed by the parties and they fail to agree; or

(c) the price is to be fixed in terms of some agreed market or other standard as set or recorded by a third person or agency and it is not so set or recorded.

(2) A price to be fixed by the seller or by the buyer means a price for him to fix in good faith.

(3) When a price left to be fixed otherwise than by agreement of the parties fails to be fixed through fault of one party the other may at his option treat the contract as cancelled or himself fix a reasonable price.

(4) Where, however, the parties intend not to be bound unless the price be fixed or agreed and it is not fixed or agreed there is no contract. In such a case the buyer must return any goods already received or if unable so to do must pay their reasonable value at the time of

delivery and the seller must return any portion of the price paid on account.

§ 2–306. Output, Requirements and Exclusive Dealings.

(1) A term which measures the quantity by the output of the seller or the requirements of the buyer means such actual output or requirements as may occur in good faith, except that no quantity unreasonably disproportionate to any stated estimate or in the absence of a stated estimate to any normal or otherwise comparable prior output or requirements may be tendered or demanded.

(2) A lawful agreement by either the seller or the buyer for exclusive dealing in the kind of goods concerned imposes unless otherwise agreed an obligation by the seller to use best efforts to supply the goods and by the buyer to use best efforts to promote their sale.

§ 2–307. Delivery in Single Lot or Several Lots.

Unless otherwise agreed all goods called for by a contract for sale must be tendered in a single delivery and payment is due only on such tender but where the circumstances give either party the right to make or demand delivery in lots the price if it can be apportioned may be demanded for each lot.

§ 2–308. Absence of Specified Place for Delivery.

Unless otherwise agreed

(a) the place for delivery of goods is the seller's place of business or if he has none his residence; but

(b) in a contract for sale of identified goods which to the knowledge of the parties at the time of contracting are in some other place, that place is the place for their delivery; and

(c) documents of title may be delivered through customary banking channels.

§ 2–309. Absence of Specific Time Provisions; Notice of Termination.

(1) The time for shipment or delivery or any other action under a contract if not provided in this Article or agreed upon shall be a reasonable time.

(2) Where the contract provides for successive performances but is indefinite in duration it is valid for a reasonable time but unless otherwise agreed may be terminated at any time by either party.

(3) Termination of a contract by one party except on the happening of an agreed event requires that reasonable notification be received by the other party and an agreement dispensing with notification is invalid if its operation would be unconscionable.

§ 2–310. Open Time for Payment or Running of Credit; Authority to Ship Under Reservation.

Unless otherwise agreed

(a) payment is due at the time and place at which the buyer is to receive the goods even though the place of shipment is the place of delivery; and

(b) if the seller is authorized to send the goods he may ship them under reservation, and may tender the documents of title, but the buyer may inspect the goods after their arrival before payment is due unless such inspection is inconsistent with the terms of the contract (Section 2–513); and

(c) if delivery is authorized and made by way of documents of title otherwise than by subsection (b) then payment is due at the time and place at which the buyer is to receive the documents regardless of where the goods are to be received; and

(d) where the seller is required or authorized to ship the goods on credit the credit period runs from the time of shipment but post-dating the invoice or delaying its dispatch will correspondingly delay the starting of the credit period.

§ 2–311. Options and Cooperation Respecting Performance.

(1) An agreement for sale which is otherwise sufficiently definite (subsection (3) of Section 2–204) to be a contract is not made invalid by the fact that it leaves particulars of performance to be specified by one of the parties. Any such specification must be made in good faith and within limits set by commercial reasonableness.

(2) Unless otherwise agreed specifications relating to assortment of the goods are at the buyer's option and except as otherwise provided in subsections (1)(c) and (3) of Section 2–319 specifications or arrangements relating to shipment are at the seller's option.

(3) Where such specification would materially affect the other party's performance but is not seasonably made or where one party's cooperation is necessary to the agreed performance of the other but is not seasonably forthcoming, the other party in addition to all other remedies

(a) is excused for any resulting delay in his own performance; and

(b) may also either proceed to perform in any reasonable manner or after the time for a material part of his own performance treat the failure to specify or to cooperate as a breach by failure to deliver or accept the goods.

§ 2–312. Warranty of Title and Against Infringement; Buyer's Obligation Against Infringement.

(1) Subject to subsection (2) there is in a contract for sale a warranty by the seller that

(a) the title conveyed shall be good, and its transfer rightful; and

(b) the goods shall be delivered free from any security interest or other lien or encumbrance of which the buyer at the time of contracting has no knowledge.

(2) A warranty under subsection (1) will be excluded or modified only by specific language or by circumstances which give the buyer reason to know that the person selling does not claim title in himself or that he is purporting to sell only such right or title as he or a third person may have.

(3) Unless otherwise agreed a seller who is a merchant regularly dealing in goods of the kind warrants that the goods shall be delivered free of the rightful claim of any third person by way of infringement or the like but a buyer who furnishes specifications to the seller must hold the seller harmless against any such claim which arises out of compliance with the specifications.

§ 2–313. Express Warranties by Affirmation, Promise, Description, Sample.

(1) Express warranties by the seller are created as follows:

(a) Any affirmation of fact or promise made by the seller to the buyer which relates to the goods and becomes part of the basis of the bargain creates an express warranty that the goods shall conform to the affirmation or promise.

(b) Any description of the goods which is made part of the basis of the bargain creates an express warranty that the goods shall conform to the description.

(c) Any sample or model which is made part of the basis of the bargain creates an express warranty that the whole of the goods shall conform to the sample or model.

(2) It is not necessary to the creation of an express warranty that the seller use formal words such as "warrant" or "guarantee" or that he have a specific intention to make a warranty, but an affirmation merely of the value of the goods or a statement purporting to be merely the seller's opinion or commendation of the goods does not create a warranty.

§ 2–314. Implied Warranty: Merchantability; Usage of Trade.

(1) Unless excluded or modified (Section 2–316), a warranty that the goods shall be merchantable is implied in a contract for their sale if the seller is a merchant with respect to goods of that kind. Under this section the serving for value of food or drink to be consumed either on the premises or elsewhere is a sale.

(2) Goods to be merchantable must be at least such as

(a) pass without objection in the trade under the contract description; and

(b) in the case of fungible goods, are of fair average quality within the description; and

(c) are fit for the ordinary purposes for which such goods are used; and

(d) run, within the variations permitted by the agreement, of even kind, quality and quantity within each unit and among all units involved; and

(e) are adequately contained, packaged, and labeled as the agreement may require; and

(f) conform to the promises or affirmations of fact made on the container or label if any.

(3) Unless excluded or modified (Section 2–316) other implied warranties may arise from course of dealing or usage of trade.

§ 2–315. Implied Warranty: Fitness for Particular Purpose.

Where the seller at the time of contracting has reason to know any particular purpose for which the goods are required and that the buyer is relying on the seller's skill or judgment to select or furnish suitable goods, there is unless excluded or modified under the next section an implied warranty that the goods shall be fit for such purpose.

§ 2–316. Exclusion or Modification of Warranties.

(1) Words or conduct relevant to the creation of an express warranty and words or conduct tending to negate or limit warranty shall be construed wherever reasonable as consistent with each other; but subject to the provisions of this Article on parol or extrinsic evidence (Section 2–202) negation or limitation is inoperative to the extent that such construction is unreasonable.

(2) Subject to subsection (3), to exclude or modify the implied warranty of merchantability or any part of it the language must mention merchantability and in case of a writing must be conspicuous, and to exclude or modify any implied warranty of fitness the exclusion must be by a writing and conspicuous. Language to exclude all implied warranties of fitness is sufficient if it states, for example, that "There are no warranties which extend beyond the description on the face hereof."

(3) Notwithstanding subsection (2)

(a) unless the circumstances indicate otherwise, all implied warranties are excluded by expressions like "as is", "with all faults" or other language which in common understanding calls the buyer's attention to the exclusion of warranties and makes plain that there is no implied warranty; and

(b) when the buyer before entering into the contract has examined the goods or the sample or model as fully as he desired or has refused to examine the goods there is no implied warranty with regard to defects which an examination ought in the circumstances to have revealed to him; and

(c) an implied warranty can also be excluded or modified by course of dealing or course of performance or usage of trade.

(4) Remedies for breach of warranty can be limited in accordance with the provisions of this Article on liquidation or limitation of damages and on contractual modification of remedy (Sections 2–718 and 2–719).

§ 2–317. Cumulation and Conflict of Warranties Express or Implied.

Warranties whether express or implied shall be construed as consistent with each other and as cumulative, but if such construction is unreasonable the intention of the parties shall determine which warranty is dominant. In ascertaining that intention the following rules apply:

(a) Exact or technical specifications displace an inconsistent sample or model or general language of description.

(b) A sample from an existing bulk displaces inconsistent general language of description.

(c) Express warranties displace inconsistent implied warranties other than an implied warranty of fitness for a particular purpose.

§ 2–318. Third Party Beneficiaries of Warranties Express or Implied.

Note: If this Act is introduced in the Congress of the United States this section should be omitted. (States to select one alternative.)

Alternative A

A seller's warranty whether express or implied extends to any natural person who is in the family or household of his buyer or who is a guest in his home if it is reasonable to expect that such person may use, consume or be affected by the goods and who is injured in person by breach of the warranty. A seller may not exclude or limit the operation of this section.

Alternative B

A seller's warranty whether express or implied extends to any natural person who may reasonably be expected to use, consume or be affected by the goods and who is injured in person by breach of the warranty. A seller may not exclude or limit the operation of this section.

Alternative C

A seller's warranty whether express or implied extends to any person who may reasonably be expected to use, consume or be affected by the goods and who is injured by breach of the warranty. A seller may not exclude or limit the operation of this section with respect to injury to the person of an individual to whom the warranty extends.

As amended 1966.

§ 2–319. F.O.B. and F.A.S. Terms.

(1) Unless otherwise agreed the term F.O.B. (which means "free on board") at a named place, even though used only in connection with the stated price, is a delivery term under which

(a) when the term is F.O.B. the place of shipment, the seller must at that place ship the goods in the manner provided in this Article (Section 2–504) and bear the expense and risk of putting them into the possession of the carrier; or

(b) when the term is F.O.B. the place of destination, the seller must at his own expense and risk transport the goods to that place and there tender delivery of them in the manner provided in this Article (Section 2–503);

(c) when under either (a) or (b) the term is also F.O.B. vessel, car or other vehicle, the seller must in addition at his own expense and risk load the goods on board. If the term is F.O.B. vessel the buyer must name the vessel and in an appropriate case the seller must comply with the provisions of this Article on the form of bill of lading (Section 2–323).

(2) Unless otherwise agreed the term F.A.S. vessel (which means "free alongside") at a named port, even though used only in connection with the stated price, is a delivery term under which the seller must

(a) at his own expense and risk deliver the goods alongside the vessel in the manner usual in that port or on a dock designated and provided by the buyer; and

(b) obtain and tender a receipt for the goods in exchange for which the carrier is under a duty to issue a bill of lading.

(3) Unless otherwise agreed in any case falling within subsection (1)(a) or (c) or subsection (2) the buyer must seasonably give any needed instructions for making delivery, including when the term is F.A.S. or F.O.B. the loading berth of the vessel and in an appropriate case its name and sailing date. The seller may treat the

failure of needed instructions as a failure of cooperation under this Article (Section 2–311). He may also at his option move the goods in any reasonable manner preparatory to delivery or shipment.

(4) Under the term F.O.B. vessel or F.A.S. unless otherwise agreed the buyer must make payment against tender of the required documents and the seller may not tender nor the buyer demand delivery of the goods in substitution for the documents.

§ 2–320.   C.I.F. and C. & F. Terms.

(1) The term C.I.F. means that the price includes in a lump sum the cost of the goods and the insurance and freight to the named destination. The term C. & F. or C.F. means that the price so includes cost and freight to the named destination.

(2) Unless otherwise agreed and even though used only in connection with the stated price and destination, the term C.I.F. destination or its equivalent requires the seller at his own expense and risk to

(a) put the goods into the possession of a carrier at the port for shipment and obtain a negotiable bill or bills of lading covering the entire transportation to the named destination; and

(b) load the goods and obtain a receipt from the carrier (which may be contained in the bill of lading) showing that the freight has been paid or provided for; and

(c) obtain a policy or certificate of insurance, including any war risk insurance, of a kind and on terms then current at the port of shipment in the usual amount, in the currency of the contract, shown to cover the same goods covered by the bill of lading and providing for payment of loss to the order of the buyer or for the account of whom it may concern; but the seller may add to the price the amount of the premium for any such war risk insurance; and

(d) prepare an invoice of the goods and procure any other documents required to effect shipment or to comply with the contract; and

(e) forward and tender with commercial promptness all the documents in due form and with any indorsement necessary to perfect the buyer's rights.

(3) Unless otherwise agreed the term C. & F. or its equivalent has the same effect and imposes upon the seller the same obligations and risks as a C.I.F. term except the obligation as to insurance.

(4) Under the term C.I.F. or C. & F. unless otherwise agreed the buyer must make payment against tender of the required documents and the seller may not

tender nor the buyer demand delivery of the goods in substitution for the documents.

§ 2–321.   C.I.F. or C. & F.: "Net Landed Weights"; "Payment on Arrival"; Warranty of Condition on Arrival.

Under a contract containing a term C.I.F. or C. & F.

(1) Where the price is based on or is to be adjusted according to "net landed weights", "delivered weights", "out turn" quantity or quality or the like, unless otherwise agreed the seller must reasonably estimate the price. The payment due on tender of the documents called for by the contract is the amount so estimated, but after final adjustment of the price a settlement must be made with commercial promptness.

(2) An agreement described in subsection (1) or any warranty of quality or condition of the goods on arrival places upon the seller the risk of ordinary deterioration, shrinkage and the like in transportation but has no effect on the place or time of identification to the contract for sale or delivery or on the passing of the risk of loss.

(3) Unless otherwise agreed where the contract provides for payment on or after arrival of the goods the seller must before payment allow such preliminary inspection as is feasible; but if the goods are lost delivery of the documents and payment are due when the goods should have arrived.

§ 2–322.   Delivery "Ex-Ship".

(1) Unless otherwise agreed a term for delivery of goods "ex-ship" (which means from the carrying vessel) or in equivalent language is not restricted to a particular ship and requires delivery from a ship which has reached a place at the named port of destination where goods of the kind are usually discharged.

(2) Under such a term unless otherwise agreed

(a) the seller must discharge all liens arising out of the carriage and furnish the buyer with a direction which puts the carrier under a duty to deliver the goods; and

(b) the risk of loss does not pass to the buyer until the goods leave the ship's tackle or are otherwise properly unloaded.

§ 2–323.   Form of Bill of Lading Required in Overseas Shipment; "Overseas".

(1) Where the contract contemplates overseas shipment and contains a term C.I.F. or C. & F. or F.O.B. vessel, the seller unless otherwise agreed must obtain a negotiable bill of lading stating that the goods have been loaded on board or, in the case of a term C.I.F. or C. & F., received for shipment.

(2) Where in a case within subsection (1) a bill of lading has been issued in a set of parts, unless otherwise agreed if the documents are not to be sent from abroad the buyer may demand tender of the full set; otherwise only one part of the bill of lading need be tendered. Even if the agreement expressly requires a full set

(a) due tender of a single part is acceptable within the provisions of this Article on cure of improper delivery (subsection (1) of Section 2–508); and

(b) even though the full set is demanded, if the documents are sent from abroad the person tendering an incomplete set may nevertheless require payment upon furnishing an indemnity which the buyer in good faith deems adequate.

(3) A shipment by water or by air or a contract contemplating such shipment is "overseas" insofar as by usage of trade or agreement it is subject to the commercial, financing or shipping practices characteristic of international deep water commerce.

§ 2–324. "No Arrival, No Sale" Term.

Under a term "no arrival, no sale" or terms of like meaning, unless otherwise agreed,

(a) the seller must properly ship conforming goods and if they arrive by any means he must tender them on arrival but he assumes no obligation that the goods will arrive unless he has caused the non-arrival; and

(b) where without fault of the seller the goods are in part lost or have so deteriorated as no longer to conform to the contract or arrive after the contract time, the buyer may proceed as if there had been casualty to identified goods (Section 2–613).

§ 2–325. "Letter of Credit" Term; "Confirmed Credit".

(1) Failure of the buyer seasonably to furnish an agreed letter of credit is a breach of the contract for sale.

(2) The delivery to seller of a proper letter of credit suspends the buyer's obligation to pay. If the letter of credit is dishonored, the seller may on seasonable notification to the buyer require payment directly from him.

(3) Unless otherwise agreed the term "letter of credit" or "banker's credit" in a contract for sale means an irrevocable credit issued by a financing agency of good repute and, where the shipment is overseas, of good international repute. The term "confirmed credit" means that the credit must also carry the direct obligation of such an agency which does business in the seller's financial market.

§ 2–326. Sale on Approval and Sale or Return; Rights of Creditors.

(1) Unless otherwise agreed, if delivered goods may be returned by the buyer even though they conform to the contract, the transaction is

(a) a "sale on approval" if the goods are delivered primarily for use, and

(b) a "sale or return" if the goods are delivered primarily for resale.

(2) Goods held on approval are not subject to the claims of the buyer's creditors until acceptance; goods held on sale or return are subject to such claims while in the buyer's possession.

(3) Any "or return" term of a contract for sale is to be treated as a separate contract for sale within the statute of frauds section of this Article (Section 2–201) and as contradicting the sale aspect of the contract within the provisions of this Article or on parol or extrinsic evidence (Section 2–202).

As amended in 1999.

§ 2–327. Special Incidents of Sale on Approval and Sale or Return.

(1) Under a sale on approval unless otherwise agreed

(a) although the goods are identified to the contract the risk of loss and the title do not pass to the buyer until acceptance; and

(b) use of the goods consistent with the purpose of trial is not acceptance but failure seasonably to notify the seller of election to return the goods is acceptance, and if the goods conform to the contract acceptance of any part is acceptance of the whole; and

(c) after due notification of election to return, the return is at the seller's risk and expense but a merchant buyer must follow any reasonable instructions.

(2) Under a sale or return unless otherwise agreed

(a) the option to return extends to the whole or any commercial unit of the goods while in substantially their original condition, but must be exercised seasonably; and

(b) the return is at the buyer's risk and expense.

§ 2–328. Sale by Auction.

(1) In a sale by auction if goods are put up in lots each lot is the subject of a separate sale.

(2) A sale by auction is complete when the auctioneer so announces by the fall of the hammer or in other customary manner. Where a bid is made while the hammer is falling in acceptance of a prior bid the auctioneer may in his discretion reopen the bidding

or declare the goods sold under the bid on which the hammer was falling.

(3) Such a sale is with reserve unless the goods are in explicit terms put up without reserve. In an auction with reserve the auctioneer may withdraw the goods at any time until he announces completion of the sale. In an auction without reserve, after the auctioneer calls for bids on an article or lot, that article or lot cannot be withdrawn unless no bid is made within a reasonable time. In either case a bidder may retract his bid until the auctioneer's announcement of completion of the sale, but a bidder's retraction does not revive any previous bid.

(4) If the auctioneer knowingly receives a bid on the seller's behalf or the seller makes or procures such as bid, and notice has not been given that liberty for such bidding is reserved, the buyer may at his option avoid the sale or take the goods at the price of the last good faith bid prior to the completion of the sale. This subsection shall not apply to any bid at a forced sale.

Part 4   Title, Creditors and Good Faith Purchasers

§ 2–401.   Passing of Title; Reservation for Security; Limited Application of This Section.

Each provision of this Article with regard to the rights, obligations and remedies of the seller, the buyer, purchasers or other third parties applies irrespective of title to the goods except where the provision refers to such title. Insofar as situations are not covered by the other provisions of this Article and matters concerning title became material the following rules apply:

(1) Title to goods cannot pass under a contract for sale prior to their identification to the contract (Section 2–501), and unless otherwise explicitly agreed the buyer acquires by their identification a special property as limited by this Act. Any retention or reservation by the seller of the title (property) in goods shipped or delivered to the buyer is limited in effect to a reservation of a security interest. Subject to these provisions and to the provisions of the Article on Secured Transactions (Article 9), title to goods passes from the seller to the buyer in any manner and on any conditions explicitly agreed on by the parties.

(2) Unless otherwise explicitly agreed title passes to the buyer at the time and place at which the seller completes his performance with reference to the physical delivery of the goods, despite any reservation of a security interest and even though a document of title is to be delivered at a different time or place; and in particular and despite any reservation of a security interest by the bill of lading

(a) if the contract requires or authorizes the seller to send the goods to the buyer but does not require him to deliver them at destination, title passes to the buyer at the time and place of shipment; but

(b) if the contract requires delivery at destination, title passes on tender there.

(3) Unless otherwise explicitly agreed where delivery is to be made without moving the goods,

(a) if the seller is to deliver a document of title, title passes at the time when and the place where he delivers such documents; or

(b) if the goods are at the time of contracting already identified and no documents are to be delivered, title passes at the time and place of contracting.

(4) A rejection or other refusal by the buyer to receive or retain the goods, whether or not justified, or a justified revocation of acceptance revests title to the goods in the seller. Such revesting occurs by operation of law and is not a "sale".

§ 2–402.   Rights of Seller's Creditors Against Sold Goods.

(1) Except as provided in subsections (2) and (3), rights of unsecured creditors of the seller with respect to goods which have been identified to a contract for sale are subject to the buyer's rights to recover the goods under this Article (Sections 2–502 and 2–716).

(2) A creditor of the seller may treat a sale or an identification of goods to a contract for sale as void if as against him a retention of possession by the seller is fraudulent under any rule of law of the state where the goods are situated, except that retention of possession in good faith and current course of trade by a merchant-seller for a commercially reasonable time after a sale or identification is not fraudulent.

(3) Nothing in this Article shall be deemed to impair the rights of creditors of the seller

(a) under the provisions of the Article on Secured Transactions (Article 9); or

(b) where identification to the contract or delivery is made not in current course of trade but in satisfaction of or as security for a pre-existing claim for money, security or the like and is made under circumstances which under any rule of law of the state where the goods are situated would apart from this Article constitute the transaction a fraudulent transfer or voidable preference.

§ 2–403.   Power to Transfer; Good Faith Purchase of Goods; "Entrusting".

(1) A purchaser of goods acquires all title which his transferor had or had power to transfer except that

a purchaser of a limited interest acquires rights only to the extent of the interest purchased. A person with voidable title has power to transfer a good title to a good faith purchaser for value. When goods have been delivered under a transaction of purchase the purchaser has such power even though

(a) the transferor was deceived as to the identity of the purchaser, or

(b) the delivery was in exchange for a check which is later dishonored, or

(c) it was agreed that the transaction was to be a "cash sale", or

(d) the delivery was procured through fraud punishable as larcenous under the criminal law.

(2) Any entrusting of possession of goods to a merchant who deals in goods of that kind gives him power to transfer all rights of the entruster to a buyer in ordinary course of business.

(3) "Entrusting" includes any delivery and any acquiescence in retention of possession regardless of any condition expressed between the parties to the delivery or acquiescence and regardless of whether the procurement of the entrusting or the possessor's disposition of the goods have been such as to be larcenous under the criminal law.

(4) The rights of other purchasers of goods and of lien creditors are governed by the Articles on Secured Transactions (Article 9), Bulk Transfers (Article 6) and Documents of Title (Article 7).

As amended in 1988.

Part 5 Performance

§ 2–501. Insurable Interest in Goods; Manner of Identification of Goods.

(1) The buyer obtains a special property and an insurable interest in goods by identification of existing goods as goods to which the contract refers even though the goods so identified are non-conforming and he has an option to return or reject them. Such identification can be made at any time and in any manner explicitly agreed to by the parties. In the absence of explicit agreement identification occurs

(a) when the contract is made if it is for the sale of goods already existing and identified;

(b) if the contract is for the sale of future goods other than those described in paragraph (c), when goods are shipped, marked or otherwise designated by the seller as goods to which the contract refers;

(c) when the crops are planted or otherwise become growing crops or the young are conceived if the contract is for the sale of unborn young to be born within twelve months after contracting or for the sale of crops to be harvested within twelve months or the next normal harvest season after contracting whichever is longer.

(2) The seller retains an insurable interest in goods so long as title to or any security interest in the goods remains in him and where the identification is by the seller alone he may until default or insolvency or notification to the buyer that the identification is final substitute other goods for those identified.

(3) Nothing in this section impairs any insurable interest recognized under any other statute or rule of law.

§ 2–502. Buyer's Right to Goods on Seller's Insolvency.

(1) Subject to subsections (2) and (3) and even though the goods have not been shipped a buyer who has paid a part or all of the price of goods in which he has a special property under the provisions of the immediately preceding section may on making and keeping good a tender of any unpaid portion of their price recover them from the seller if:

(a) in the case of goods bought for personal, family, or household purposes, the seller repudiates or fails to deliver as required by the contract; or

(b) in all cases, the seller becomes insolvent within ten days after receipt of the first installment on their price.

(2) The buyer's right to recover the goods under subsection (1)(a) vests upon acquisition of a special property, even if the seller had not then repudiated or failed to deliver.

(3) If the identification creating his special property has been made by the buyer he acquires the right to recover the goods only if they conform to the contract for sale.

As amended in 1999.

§ 2–503. Manner of Seller's Tender of Delivery.

(1) Tender of delivery requires that the seller put and hold conforming goods at the buyer's disposition and give the buyer any notification reasonably necessary to enable him to take delivery. The manner, time and place for tender are determined by the agreement and this Article, and in particular

(a) tender must be at a reasonable hour, and if it is of goods they must be kept available for the period reasonably necessary to enable the buyer to take possession; but

(b) unless otherwise agreed the buyer must furnish facilities reasonably suited to the receipt of the goods.

(2) Where the case is within the next section respecting shipment tender requires that the seller comply with its provisions.

(3) Where the seller is required to deliver at a particular destination tender requires that he comply with subsection (1) and also in any appropriate case tender documents as described in subsections (4) and (5) of this section.

(4) Where goods are in the possession of a bailee and are to be delivered without being moved

(a) tender requires that the seller either tender a negotiable document of title covering such goods or procure acknowledgment by the bailee of the buyer's right to possession of the goods; but

(b) tender to the buyer of a non-negotiable document of title or of a written direction to the bailee to deliver is sufficient tender unless the buyer seasonably objects, and receipt by the bailee of notification of the buyer's rights fixes those rights as against the bailee and all third persons; but risk of loss of the goods and of any failure by the bailee to honor the non-negotiable document of title or to obey the direction remains on the seller until the buyer has had a reasonable time to present the document or direction, and a refusal by the bailee to honor the document or to obey the direction defeats the tender.

(5) Where the contract requires the seller to deliver documents

(a) he must tender all such documents in correct form, except as provided in this Article with respect to bills of lading in a set (subsection (2) of Section 2–323); and

(b) tender through customary banking channels is sufficient and dishonor of a draft accompanying the documents constitutes non-acceptance or rejection.

§ 2–504.   Shipment by Seller.

Where the seller is required or authorized to send the goods to the buyer and the contract does not require him to deliver them at a particular destination, then unless otherwise agreed he must

(a) put the goods in the possession of such a carrier and make such a contract for their transportation as may be reasonable having regard to the nature of the goods and other circumstances of the case; and

(b) obtain and promptly deliver or tender in due form any document necessary to enable the buyer to obtain possession of the goods or otherwise required by the agreement or by usage of trade; and

(c) promptly notify the buyer of the shipment. Failure to notify the buyer under paragraph (c) or to make a proper contract under paragraph (a) is a ground for rejection only if material delay or loss ensues.

§ 2–505.   Seller's Shipment under Reservation.

(1) Where the seller has identified goods to the contract by or before shipment:

(a) his procurement of a negotiable bill of lading to his own order or otherwise reserves in him a security interest in the goods. His procurement of the bill to the order of a financing agency or of the buyer indicates in addition only the seller's expectation of transferring that interest to the person named.

(b) a non-negotiable bill of lading to himself or his nominee reserves possession of the goods as security but except in a case of conditional delivery (subsection (2) of Section 2–507) a non-negotiable bill of lading naming the buyer as consignee reserves no security interest even though the seller retains possession of the bill of lading.

(2) When shipment by the seller with reservation of a security interest is in violation of the contract for sale it constitutes an improper contract for transportation within the preceding section but impairs neither the rights given to the buyer by shipment and identification of the goods to the contract nor the seller's powers as a holder of a negotiable document.

§ 2–506.   Rights of Financing Agency.

(1) A financing agency by paying or purchasing for value a draft which relates to a shipment of goods acquires to the extent of the payment or purchase and in addition to its own rights under the draft and any document of title securing it any rights of the shipper in the goods including the right to stop delivery and the shipper's right to have the draft honored by the buyer.

(2) The right to reimbursement of a financing agency which has in good faith honored or purchased the draft under commitment to or authority from the buyer is not impaired by subsequent discovery of defects with reference to any relevant document which was apparently regular on its face.

§ 2–507.   Effect of Seller's Tender; Delivery on Condition.

(1) Tender of delivery is a condition to the buyer's duty to accept the goods and, unless otherwise agreed, to his duty to pay for them. Tender entitles the seller to acceptance of the goods and to payment according to the contract.

(2) Where payment is due and demanded on the delivery to the buyer of goods or documents of title, his right as against the seller to retain or dispose of them is conditional upon his making the payment due.

§ 2–508. Cure by Seller of Improper Tender or Delivery; Replacement.

(1) Where any tender or delivery by the seller is rejected because non-conforming and the time for performance has not yet expired, the seller may seasonably notify the buyer of his intention to cure and may then within the contract time make a conforming delivery.

(2) Where the buyer rejects a non-conforming tender which the seller had reasonable grounds to believe would be acceptable with or without money allowance the seller may if he seasonably notifies the buyer have a further reasonable time to substitute a conforming tender.

§ 2–509. Risk of Loss in the Absence of Breach.

(1) Where the contract requires or authorizes the seller to ship the goods by carrier

 (a) if it does not require him to deliver them at a particular destination, the risk of loss passes to the buyer when the goods are duly delivered to the carrier even though the shipment is under reservation (Section 2–505); but

 (b) if it does require him to deliver them at a particular destination and the goods are there duly tendered while in the possession of the carrier, the risk of loss passes to the buyer when the goods are there duly so tendered as to enable the buyer to take delivery.

(2) Where the goods are held by a bailee to be delivered without being moved, the risk of loss passes to the buyer

 (a) on his receipt of a negotiable document of title covering the goods; or

 (b) on acknowledgment by the bailee of the buyer's right to possession of the goods; or

 (c) after his receipt of a non-negotiable document of title or other written direction to deliver, as provided in subsection (4)(b) of Section 2–503.

(3) In any case not within subsection (1) or (2), the risk of loss passes to the buyer on his receipt of the goods if the seller is a merchant; otherwise the risk passes to the buyer on tender of delivery.

(4) The provisions of this section are subject to contrary agreement of the parties and to the provisions of this Article on sale on approval (Section 2–327) and on effect of breach on risk of loss (Section 2–510).

§ 2–510. Effect of Breach on Risk of Loss.

(1) Where a tender or delivery of goods so fails to conform to the contract as to give a right of rejection the risk of their loss remains on the seller until cure or acceptance.

(2) Where the buyer rightfully revokes acceptance he may to the extent of any deficiency in his effective insurance coverage treat the risk of loss as having rested on the seller from the beginning.

(3) Where the buyer as to conforming goods already identified to the contract for sale repudiates or is otherwise in breach before risk of their loss has passed to him, the seller may to the extent of any deficiency in his effective insurance coverage treat the risk of loss as resting on the buyer for a commercially reasonable time.

§ 2–511. Tender of Payment by Buyer; Payment by Check.

(1) Unless otherwise agreed tender of payment is a condition to the seller's duty to tender and complete any delivery.

(2) Tender of payment is sufficient when made by any means or in any manner current in the ordinary course of business unless the seller demands payment in legal tender and gives any extension of time reasonably necessary to procure it.

(3) Subject to the provisions of this Act on the effect of an instrument on an obligation (Section 3–310), payment by check is conditional and is defeated as between the parties by dishonor of the check on due presentment.

As amended in 1994.

§ 2–512. Payment by Buyer Before Inspection.

(1) Where the contract requires payment before inspection non-conformity of the goods does not excuse the buyer from so making payment unless

 (a) the non-conformity appears without inspection; or

 (b) despite tender of the required documents the circumstances would justify injunction against honor under this Act (Section 5–109(b)).

(2) Payment pursuant to subsection (1) does not constitute an acceptance of goods or impair the buyer's right to inspect or any of his remedies.

As amended in 1995.

§ 2–513. Buyer's Right to Inspection of Goods.

(1) Unless otherwise agreed and subject to subsection (3), where goods are tendered or delivered or identified to the contract for sale, the buyer has a right before payment or acceptance to inspect them at any

reasonable place and time and in any reasonable manner. When the seller is required or authorized to send the goods to the buyer, the inspection may be after their arrival.

(2) Expenses of inspection must be borne by the buyer but may be recovered from the seller if the goods do not conform and are rejected.

(3) Unless otherwise agreed and subject to the provisions of this Article on C.I.F. contracts (subsection (3) of Section 2–321), the buyer is not entitled to inspect the goods before payment of the price when the contract provides

　(a) for delivery "C.O.D." or on other like terms; or

　(b) for payment against documents of title, except where such payment is due only after the goods are to become available for inspection.

(4) A place or method of inspection fixed by the parties is presumed to be exclusive but unless otherwise expressly agreed it does not postpone identification or shift the place for delivery or for passing the risk of loss. If compliance becomes impossible, inspection shall be as provided in this section unless the place or method fixed was clearly intended as an indispensable condition failure of which avoids the contract.

§ 2–514. When Documents Deliverable on Acceptance; When on Payment.

Unless otherwise agreed documents against which a draft is drawn are to be delivered to the drawee on acceptance of the draft if it is payable more than three days after presentment; otherwise, only on payment.

§ 2–515. Preserving Evidence of Goods in Dispute.

In furtherance of the adjustment of any claim or dispute

　(a) either party on reasonable notification to the other and for the purpose of ascertaining the facts and preserving evidence has the right to inspect, test and sample the goods including such of them as may be in the possession or control of the other; and

　(b) the parties may agree to a third party inspection or survey to determine the conformity or condition of the goods and may agree that the findings shall be binding upon them in any subsequent litigation or adjustment.

Part 6   Breach, Repudiation and Excuse

§ 2–601.   Buyer's Rights on Improper Delivery.

Subject to the provisions of this Article on breach in installment contracts (Section 2–612) and unless otherwise agreed under the sections on contractual limitations of remedy (Sections 2–718 and 2–719), if the goods or the tender of delivery fail in any respect to conform to the contract, the buyer may

　(a) reject the whole; or

　(b) accept the whole; or

　(c) accept any commercial unit or units and reject the rest.

§ 2–602.   Manner and Effect of Rightful Rejection.

(1) Rejection of goods must be within a reasonable time after their delivery or tender. It is ineffective unless the buyer seasonably notifies the seller.

(2) Subject to the provisions of the two following sections on rejected goods (Sections 2–603 and 2–604),

　(a) after rejection any exercise of ownership by the buyer with respect to any commercial unit is wrongful as against the seller; and

　(b) if the buyer has before rejection taken physical possession of goods in which he does not have a security interest under the provisions of this Article (subsection (3) of Section 2–711), he is under a duty after rejection to hold them with reasonable care at the seller's disposition for a time sufficient to permit the seller to remove them; but

　(c) the buyer has no further obligations with regard to goods rightfully rejected.

(3) The seller's rights with respect to goods wrongfully rejected are governed by the provisions of this Article on Seller's remedies in general (Section 2–703).

§ 2–603.   Merchant Buyer's Duties as to Rightfully Rejected Goods.

(1) Subject to any security interest in the buyer (subsection (3) of Section 2–711), when the seller has no agent or place of business at the market of rejection a merchant buyer is under a duty after rejection of goods in his possession or control to follow any reasonable instructions received from the seller with respect to the goods and in the absence of such instructions to make reasonable efforts to sell them for the seller's account if they are perishable or threaten to decline in value speedily. Instructions are not reasonable if on demand indemnity for expenses is not forthcoming.

(2) When the buyer sells goods under subsection (1), he is entitled to reimbursement from the seller or out of the proceeds for reasonable expenses of caring for and selling them, and if the expenses include no selling commission then to such commission as is usual in the trade or if there is none to a reasonable sum not exceeding ten per cent on the gross proceeds.

(3) In complying with this section the buyer is held only to good faith and good faith conduct hereunder is neither acceptance nor conversion nor the basis of an action for damages.

§ 2–604. Buyer's Options as to Salvage of Rightfully Rejected Goods.

Subject to the provisions of the immediately preceding section on perishables if the seller gives no instructions within a reasonable time after notification of rejection the buyer may store the rejected goods for the seller's account or reship them to him or resell them for the seller's account with reimbursement as provided in the preceding section. Such action is not acceptance or conversion.

§ 2–605. Waiver of Buyer's Objections by Failure to Particularize.

(1) The buyer's failure to state in connection with rejection a particular defect which is ascertainable by reasonable inspection precludes him from relying on the unstated defect to justify rejection or to establish breach

  (a) where the seller could have cured it if stated seasonably; or

  (b) between merchants when the seller has after rejection made a request in writing for a full and final written statement of all defects on which the buyer proposes to rely.

(2) Payment against documents made without reservation of rights precludes recovery of the payment for defects apparent on the face of the documents.

§ 2–606. What Constitutes Acceptance of Goods.

(1) Acceptance of goods occurs when the buyer

  (a) after a reasonable opportunity to inspect the goods signifies to the seller that the goods are conforming or that he will take or retain them in spite of their nonconformity; or

  (b) fails to make an effective rejection (subsection (1) of Section 2–602), but such acceptance does not occur until the buyer has had a reasonable opportunity to inspect them; or

  (c) does any act inconsistent with the seller's ownership; but if such act is wrongful as against the seller it is an acceptance only if ratified by him.

(2) Acceptance of a part of any commercial unit is acceptance of that entire unit.

§ 2–607. Effect of Acceptance; Notice of Breach; Burden of Establishing Breach After Acceptance; Notice of Claim or Litigation to Person Answerable Over.

(1) The buyer must pay at the contract rate for any goods accepted.

(2) Acceptance of goods by the buyer precludes rejection of the goods accepted and if made with knowledge of a non-conformity cannot be revoked because of it unless the acceptance was on the reasonable assumption that the non-conformity would be seasonably cured but acceptance does not of itself impair any other remedy provided by this Article for non-conformity.

(3) Where a tender has been accepted

  (a) the buyer must within a reasonable time after he discovers or should have discovered any breach notify the seller of breach or be barred from any remedy; and

  (b) if the claim is one for infringement or the like (subsection (3) of Section 2–312) and the buyer is sued as a result of such a breach he must so notify the seller within a reasonable time after he receives notice of the litigation or be barred from any remedy over for liability established by the litigation.

(4) The burden is on the buyer to establish any breach with respect to the goods accepted.

(5) Where the buyer is sued for breach of a warranty or other obligation for which his seller is answerable over

  (a) he may give his seller written notice of the litigation. If the notice states that the seller may come in and defend and that if the seller does not do so he will be bound in any action against him by his buyer by any determination of fact common to the two litigations, then unless the seller after seasonable receipt of the notice does come in and defend he is so bound.

  (b) if the claim is one for infringement or the like (subsection (3) of Section 2–312) the original seller may demand in writing that his buyer turn over to him control of the litigation including settlement or else be barred from any remedy over and if he also agrees to bear all expense and to satisfy any adverse judgment, then unless the buyer after seasonable receipt of the demand does turn over control the buyer is so barred.

(6) The provisions of subsections (3), (4) and (5) apply to any obligation of a buyer to hold the seller harmless against infringement or the like (subsection (3) of Section 2–312).

§ 2–608. Revocation of Acceptance in Whole or in Part.

(1) The buyer may revoke his acceptance of a lot or commercial unit whose non-conformity substantially impairs its value to him if he has accepted it

  (a) on the reasonable assumption that its nonconformity would be cured and it has not been seasonably cured; or

  (b) without discovery of such non-conformity if his acceptance was reasonably induced either by the difficulty of discovery before acceptance or by the seller's assurances.

(2) Revocation of acceptance must occur within a reasonable time after the buyer discovers or should have discovered the ground for it and before any substantial change in condition of the goods which is not caused by their own defects. It is not effective until the buyer notifies the seller of it.

(3) A buyer who so revokes has the same rights and duties with regard to the goods involved as if he had rejected them.

§ 2–609.   Right to Adequate Assurance of Performance.

(1) A contract for sale imposes an obligation on each party that the other's expectation of receiving due performance will not be impaired. When reasonable grounds for insecurity arise with respect to the performance of either party the other may in writing demand adequate assurance of due performance and until he receives such assurance may if commercially reasonable suspend any performance for which he has not already received the agreed return.

(2) Between merchants the reasonableness of grounds for insecurity and the adequacy of any assurance offered shall be determined according to commercial standards.

(3) Acceptance of any improper delivery or payment does not prejudice the party's right to demand adequate assurance of future performance.

(4) After receipt of a justified demand failure to provide within a reasonable time not exceeding thirty days such assurance of due performance as is adequate under the circumstances of the particular case is a repudiation of the contract.

§ 2–610.   Anticipatory Repudiation.

When either party repudiates the contract with respect to a performance not yet due the loss of which will substantially impair the value of the contract to the other, the aggrieved party may

> (a) for a commercially reasonable time await performance by the repudiating party; or
>
> (b) resort to any remedy for breach (Section 2–703 or Section 2–711), even though he has notified the repudiating party that he would await the latter's performance and has urged retraction; and
>
> (c) in either case suspend his own performance or proceed in accordance with the provisions of this Article on the seller's right to identify goods to the contract notwithstanding breach or to salvage unfinished goods (Section 2–704).

§ 2–611.   Retraction of Anticipatory Repudiation.

(1) Until the repudiating party's next performance is due he can retract his repudiation unless the aggrieved party has since the repudiation cancelled or materially changed his position or otherwise indicated that he considers the repudiation final.

(2) Retraction may be by any method which clearly indicates to the aggrieved party that the repudiating party intends to perform, but must include any assurance justifiably demanded under the provisions of this Article (Section 2–609).

(3) Retraction reinstates the repudiating party's rights under the contract with due excuse and allowance to the aggrieved party for any delay occasioned by the repudiation.

§ 2–612.   "Installment Contract"; Breach.

(1) An "installment contract" is one which requires or authorizes the delivery of goods in separate lots to be separately accepted, even though the contract contains a clause "each delivery is a separate contract" or its equivalent.

(2) The buyer may reject any installment which is non-conforming if the non-conformity substantially impairs the value of that installment and cannot be cured or if the non-conformity is a defect in the required documents; but if the non-conformity does not fall within subsection (3) and the seller gives adequate assurance of its cure the buyer must accept that installment.

(3) Whenever non-conformity or default with respect to one or more installments substantially impairs the value of the whole contract there is a breach of the whole. But the aggrieved party reinstates the contract if he accepts a non-conforming installment without seasonably notifying of cancellation or if he brings an action with respect only to past installments or demands performance as to future installments.

§ 2–613.   Casualty to Identified Goods.

Where the contract requires for its performance goods identified when the contract is made, and the goods suffer casualty without fault of either party before the risk of loss passes to the buyer, or in a proper case under a "no arrival, no sale" term (Section 2–324) then

> (a) if the loss is total the contract is avoided; and
>
> (b) if the loss is partial or the goods have so deteriorated as no longer to conform to the contract the buyer may nevertheless demand inspection and at his option either treat the contract as voided or

accept the goods with due allowance from the contract price for the deterioration or the deficiency in quantity but without further right against the seller.

§ 2–614. Substituted Performance.

(1) Where without fault of either party the agreed berthing, loading, or unloading facilities fail or an agreed type of carrier becomes unavailable or the agreed manner of delivery otherwise becomes commercially impracticable but a commercially reasonable substitute is available, such substitute performance must be tendered and accepted.

(2) If the agreed means or manner of payment fails because of domestic or foreign governmental regulation, the seller may withhold or stop delivery unless the buyer provides a means or manner of payment which is commercially a substantial equivalent. If delivery has already been taken, payment by the means or in the manner provided by the regulation discharges the buyer's obligation unless the regulation is discriminatory, oppressive or predatory.

§ 2–615. Excuse by Failure of Presupposed Conditions.

Except so far as a seller may have assumed a greater obligation and subject to the preceding section on substituted performance:

(a) Delay in delivery or non-delivery in whole or in part by a seller who complies with paragraphs (b) and (c) is not a breach of his duty under a contract for sale if performance as agreed has been made impracticable by the occurrence of a contingency the nonoccurrence of which was a basic assumption on which the contract was made or by compliance in good faith with any applicable foreign or domestic governmental regulation or order whether or not it later proves to be invalid.

(b) Where the causes mentioned in paragraph (a) affect only a part of the seller's capacity to perform, he must allocate production and deliveries among his customers but may at his option include regular customers not then under contract as well as his own requirements for further manufacture. He may so allocate in any manner which is fair and reasonable.

(c) The seller must notify the buyer seasonably that there will be delay or non-delivery and, when allocation is required under paragraph (b), of the estimated quota thus made available for the buyer.

§ 2–616. Procedure on Notice Claiming Excuse.

(1) Where the buyer receives notification of a material or indefinite delay or an allocation justified under the preceding section he may by written notification to the seller as to any delivery concerned, and where the prospective deficiency substantially impairs the value of the whole contract under the provisions of this Article relating to breach of installment contracts (Section 2–612), then also as to the whole,

(a) terminate and thereby discharge any unexecuted portion of the contract; or

(b) modify the contract by agreeing to take his available quota in substitution.

(2) If after receipt of such notification from the seller the buyer fails so to modify the contract within a reasonable time not exceeding thirty days the contract lapses with respect to any deliveries affected.

(3) The provisions of this section may not be negated by agreement except in so far as the seller has assumed a greater obligation under the preceding section.

Part 7   Remedies

§ 2–701. Remedies for Breach of Collateral Contracts Not Impaired.

Remedies for breach of any obligation or promise collateral or ancillary to a contract for sale are not impaired by the provisions of this Article.

§ 2–702. Seller's Remedies on Discovery of Buyer's Insolvency.

(1) Where the seller discovers the buyer to be insolvent he may refuse delivery except for cash including payment for all goods theretofore delivered under the contract, and stop delivery under this Article (Section 2–705).

(2) Where the seller discovers that the buyer has received goods on credit while insolvent he may reclaim the goods upon demand made within ten days after the receipt, but if misrepresentation of solvency has been made to the particular seller in writing within three months before delivery the ten day limitation does not apply. Except as provided in this subsection the seller may not base a right to reclaim goods on the buyer's fraudulent or innocent misrepresentation of solvency or of intent to pay.

(3) The seller's right to reclaim under subsection (2) is subject to the rights of a buyer in ordinary course or other good faith purchaser under this Article (Section 2–403). Successful reclamation of goods excludes all other remedies with respect to them.

§ 2–703. Seller's Remedies in General.

Where the buyer wrongfully rejects or revokes acceptance of goods or fails to make a payment due on or before delivery or repudiates with respect to a part or the whole, then with respect to any goods directly affected and, if the breach is of the whole contract (Section 2–612), then also with respect to the whole undelivered balance, the aggrieved seller may

(a) withhold delivery of such goods;

(b) stop delivery by any bailee as hereafter provided (Section 2–705);

(c) proceed under the next section respecting goods still unidentified to the contract;

(d) resell and recover damages as hereafter provided (Section 2–706);

(e) recover damages for non-acceptance (Section 2–708) or in a proper case the price (Section 2–709);

(f) cancel.

§ 2–704. Seller's Right to Identify Goods to the Contract Notwithstanding Breach or to Salvage Unfinished Goods.

(1) An aggrieved seller under the preceding section may

(a) identify to the contract conforming goods not already identified if at the time he learned of the breach they are in his possession or control;

(b) treat as the subject of resale goods which have demonstrably been intended for the particular contract even though those goods are unfinished.

(2) Where the goods are unfinished an aggrieved seller may in the exercise of reasonable commercial judgment for the purposes of avoiding loss and of effective realization either complete the manufacture and wholly identify the goods to the contract or cease manufacture and resell for scrap or salvage value or proceed in any other reasonable manner.

§ 2–705. Seller's Stoppage of Delivery in Transit or Otherwise.

(1) The seller may stop delivery of goods in the possession of a carrier or other bailee when he discovers the buyer to be insolvent (Section 2–702) and may stop delivery of carload, truckload, planeload or larger shipments of express or freight when the buyer repudiates or fails to make a payment due before delivery or if for any other reason the seller has a right to withhold or reclaim the goods.

(2) As against such buyer the seller may stop delivery until

(a) receipt of the goods by the buyer; or

(b) acknowledgment to the buyer by any bailee of the goods except a carrier that the bailee holds the goods for the buyer; or

(c) such acknowledgment to the buyer by a carrier by reshipment or as warehouseman; or

(d) negotiation to the buyer of any negotiable document of title covering the goods.

(3) (a) To stop delivery the seller must so notify as to enable the bailee by reasonable diligence to prevent delivery of the goods.

(b) After such notification the bailee must hold and deliver the goods according to the directions of the seller but the seller is liable to the bailee for any ensuing charges or damages.

(c) If a negotiable document of title has been issued for goods the bailee is not obliged to obey a notification to stop until surrender of the document.

(d) A carrier who has issued a non-negotiable bill of lading is not obliged to obey a notification to stop received from a person other than the consignor.

§ 2–706. Seller's Resale Including Contract for Resale.

(1) Under the conditions stated in Section 2–703 on seller's remedies, the seller may resell the goods concerned or the undelivered balance thereof. Where the resale is made in good faith and in a commercially reasonable manner the seller may recover the difference between the resale price and the contract price together with any incidental damages allowed under the provisions of this Article (Section 2–710), but less expenses saved in consequence of the buyer's breach.

(2) Except as otherwise provided in subsection (3) or unless otherwise agreed resale may be at public or private sale including sale by way of one or more contracts to sell or of identification to an existing contract of the seller. Sale may be as a unit or in parcels and at any time and place and on any terms but every aspect of the sale including the method, manner, time, place and terms must be commercially reasonable. The resale must be reasonably identified as referring to the broken contract, but it is not necessary that the goods be in existence or that any or all of them have been identified to the contract before the breach.

(3) Where the resale is at private sale the seller must give the buyer reasonable notification of his intention to resell.

(4) Where the resale is at public sale

(a) only identified goods can be sold except where there is a recognized market for a public sale of futures in goods of the kind; and

(b) it must be made at a usual place or market for public sale if one is reasonably available and except in the case of goods which are perishable or threaten to decline in value speedily the seller must give the buyer reasonable notice of the time and place of the resale; and

(c) if the goods are not to be within the view of those attending the sale the notification of sale must state the place where the goods are located and provide for their reasonable inspection by prospective bidders; and

(d) the seller may buy.

(5) A purchaser who buys in good faith at a resale takes the goods free of any rights of the original buyer even though the seller fails to comply with one or more of the requirements of this section.

(6) The seller is not accountable to the buyer for any profit made on any resale. A person in the position of a seller (Section 2–707) or a buyer who has rightfully rejected or justifiably revoked acceptance must account for any excess over the amount of his security interest, as hereinafter defined (subsection (3) of Section 2–711).

§ 2–707. "Person in the Position of a Seller".

(1) A "person in the position of a seller" includes as against a principal an agent who has paid or become responsible for the price of goods on behalf of his principal or anyone who otherwise holds a security interest or other right in goods similar to that of a seller.

(2) A person in the position of a seller may as provided in this Article withhold or stop delivery (Section 2–705) and resell (Section 2–706) and recover incidental damages (Section 2–710).

§ 2–708. Seller's Damages for Non-Acceptance or Repudiation.

(1) Subject to subsection (2) and to the provisions of this Article with respect to proof of market price (Section 2–723), the measure of damages for non-acceptance or repudiation by the buyer is the difference between the market price at the time and place for tender and the unpaid contract price together with any incidental damages provided in this Article (Section 2–710), but less expenses saved in consequence of the buyer's breach.

(2) If the measure of damages provided in subsection (1) is inadequate to put the seller in as good a position as performance would have done then the measure of damages is the profit (including reasonable overhead) which the seller would have made from full performance by the buyer, together with any incidental damages provided in this Article (Section 2–710), due allowance for costs reasonably incurred and due credit for payments or proceeds of resale.

§ 2–709. Action for the Price.

(1) When the buyer fails to pay the price as it becomes due the seller may recover, together with any incidental damages under the next section, the price

(a) of goods accepted or of conforming goods lost or damaged within a commercially reasonable time after risk of their loss has passed to the buyer; and

(b) of goods identified to the contract if the seller is unable after reasonable effort to resell them at a reasonable price or the circumstances reasonably indicate that such effort will be unavailing.

(2) Where the seller sues for the price he must hold for the buyer any goods which have been identified to the contract and are still in his control except that if resale becomes possible he may resell them at any time prior to the collection of the judgment. The net proceeds of any such resale must be credited to the buyer and payment of the judgment entitles him to any goods not resold.

(3) After the buyer has wrongfully rejected or revoked acceptance of the goods or has failed to make a payment due or has repudiated (Section 2–610), a seller who is held not entitled to the price under this section shall nevertheless be awarded damages for non-acceptance under the preceding section.

§ 2–710. Seller's Incidental Damages.

Incidental damages to an aggrieved seller include any commercially reasonable charges, expenses or commissions incurred in stopping delivery, in the transportation, care and custody of goods after the buyer's breach, in connection with return or resale of the goods or otherwise resulting from the breach.

§ 2–711. Buyer's Remedies in General; Buyer's Security Interest in Rejected Goods.

(1) Where the seller fails to make delivery or repudiates or the buyer rightfully rejects or justifiably revokes acceptance then with respect to any goods involved, and with respect to the whole if the breach goes to the whole contract (Section 2–612), the buyer may cancel and whether or not he has done so may in addition to recovering so much of the price as has been paid

(a) "cover" and have damages under the next section as to all the goods affected whether or not they have been identified to the contract; or

(b) recover damages for non-delivery as provided in this Article (Section 2–713).

(2) Where the seller fails to deliver or repudiates the buyer may also

(a) if the goods have been identified recover them as provided in this Article (Section 2–502); or

(b) in a proper case obtain specific performance or replevy the goods as provided in this Article (Section 2–716).

(3) On rightful rejection or justifiable revocation of acceptance a buyer has a security interest in goods in his possession or control for any payments made on their price and any expenses reasonably incurred in their inspection, receipt, transportation, care and custody and may hold such goods and resell them in like manner as an aggrieved seller (Section 2–706).

§ 2–712. "Cover"; Buyer's Procurement of Substitute Goods.

(1) After a breach within the preceding section the buyer may "cover" by making in good faith and without unreasonable delay any reasonable purchase of or contract to purchase goods in substitution for those due from the seller.

(2) The buyer may recover from the seller as damages the difference between the cost of cover and the contract price together with any incidental or consequential damages as hereinafter defined (Section 2–715), but less expenses saved in consequence of the seller's breach.

(3) Failure of the buyer to effect cover within this section does not bar him from any other remedy.

§ 2–713. Buyer's Damages for Non-Delivery or Repudiation.

(1) Subject to the provisions of this Article with respect to proof of market price (Section 2–723), the measure of damages for non-delivery or repudiation by the seller is the difference between the market price at the time when the buyer learned of the breach and the contract price together with any incidental and consequential damages provided in this Article (Section 2–715), but less expenses saved in consequence of the seller's breach.

(2) Market price is to be determined as of the place for tender or, in cases of rejection after arrival or revocation of acceptance, as of the place of arrival.

§ 2–714. Buyer's Damages for Breach in Regard to Accepted Goods.

(1) Where the buyer has accepted goods and given notification (subsection (3) of Section 2–607) he may recover as damages for any non-conformity of tender the loss resulting in the ordinary course of events from the seller's breach as determined in any manner which is reasonable.

(2) The measure of damages for breach of warranty is the difference at the time and place of acceptance between the value of the goods accepted and the value they would have had if they had been as warranted, unless special circumstances show proximate damages of a different amount.

(3) In a proper case any incidental and consequential damages under the next section may also be recovered.

§ 2–715. Buyer's Incidental and Consequential Damages.

(1) Incidental damages resulting from the seller's breach include expenses reasonably incurred in inspection, receipt, transportation and care and custody of goods rightfully rejected, any commercially reasonable charges, expenses or commissions in connection with effecting cover and any other reasonable expense incident to the delay or other breach.

(2) Consequential damages resulting from the seller's breach include

(a) any loss resulting from general or particular requirements and needs of which the seller at the time of contracting had reason to know and which could not reasonably be prevented by cover or otherwise; and

(b) injury to person or property proximately resulting from any breach of warranty.

§ 2–716. Buyer's Right to Specific Performance or Replevin.

(1) Specific performance may be decreed where the goods are unique or in other proper circumstances.

(2) The decree for specific performance may include such terms and conditions as to payment of the price, damages, or other relief as the court may deem just.

(3) The buyer has a right of replevin for goods identified to the contract if after reasonable effort he is unable to effect cover for such goods or the circumstances reasonably indicate that such effort will be unavailing or if the goods have been shipped under reservation and satisfaction of the security interest in them has been made or tendered. In the case of goods bought for personal, family, or household purposes, the buyer's right of replevin vests upon acquisition of a special property, even if the seller had not then repudiated or failed to deliver.

As amended in 1999.

§ 2–717. Deduction of Damages From the Price.

The buyer on notifying the seller of his intention to do so may deduct all or any part of the damages resulting from any breach of the contract from any part of the price still due under the same contract.

§ 2–718. Liquidation or Limitation of Damages; Deposits.

(1) Damages for breach by either party may be liquidated in the agreement but only at an amount which is reasonable in the light of the anticipated or actual harm caused by the breach, the difficulties of proof of loss, and the inconvenience or nonfeasibility of otherwise obtaining an adequate remedy. A term fixing unreasonably large liquidated damages is void as a penalty.

(2) Where the seller justifiably withholds delivery of goods because of the buyer's breach, the buyer is entitled to restitution of any amount by which the sum of his payments exceeds

(a) the amount to which the seller is entitled by virtue of terms liquidating the seller's damages in accordance with subsection (1), or

(b) in the absence of such terms, twenty per cent of the value of the total performance for which the buyer is obligated under the contract or $500, whichever is smaller.

(3) The buyer's right to restitution under subsection (2) is subject to offset to the extent that the seller establishes

(a) a right to recover damages under the provisions of this Article other than subsection (1), and

(b) the amount or value of any benefits received by the buyer directly or indirectly by reason of the contract.

(4) Where a seller has received payment in goods their reasonable value or the proceeds of their resale shall be treated as payments for the purposes of subsection (2); but if the seller has notice of the buyer's breach before reselling goods received in part performance, his resale is subject to the conditions laid down in this Article on resale by an aggrieved seller (Section 2–706).

§ 2–719. Contractual Modification or Limitation of Remedy.

(1) Subject to the provisions of subsections (2) and (3) of this section and of the preceding section on liquidation and limitation of damages,

(a) the agreement may provide for remedies in addition to or in substitution for those provided in this Article and may limit or alter the measure of damages recoverable under this Article, as by limiting the buyer's remedies to return of the goods and repayment of the price or to repair and replacement of nonconforming goods or parts; and

(b) resort to a remedy as provided is optional unless the remedy is expressly agreed to be exclusive, in which case it is the sole remedy.

(2) Where circumstances cause an exclusive or limited remedy to fail of its essential purpose, remedy may be had as provided in this Act.

(3) Consequential damages may be limited or excluded unless the limitation or exclusion is unconscionable. Limitation of consequential damages for injury to the person in the case of consumer goods is prima facie unconscionable but limitation of damages where the loss is commercial is not.

§ 2–720. Effect of "Cancellation" or "Rescission" on Claims for Antecedent Breach.

Unless the contrary intention clearly appears, expressions of "cancellation" or "rescission" of the contract or the like shall not be construed as a renunciation or discharge of any claim in damages for an antecedent breach.

§ 2–721. Remedies for Fraud.

Remedies for material misrepresentation or fraud include all remedies available under this Article for non-fraudulent breach. Neither rescission or a claim for rescission of the contract for sale nor rejection or return of the goods shall bar or be deemed inconsistent with a claim for damages or other remedy.

§ 2–722. Who Can Sue Third Parties for Injury to Goods.

Where a third party so deals with goods which have been identified to a contract for sale as to cause actionable injury to a party to that contract

(a) a right of action against the third party is in either party to the contract for sale who has title to or a security interest or a special property or an insurable interest in the goods; and if the goods have been destroyed or converted a right of action is also in the party who either bore the risk of loss under the contract for sale or has since the injury assumed that risk as against the other;

(b) if at the time of the injury the party plaintiff did not bear the risk of loss as against the other party to the contract for sale and there is no arrangement between them for disposition of the recovery, his suit or settlement is, subject to his own interest, as a fiduciary for the other party to the contract;

(c) either party may with the consent of the other sue for the benefit of whom it may concern.

§ 2–723. Proof of Market Price: Time and Place.

(1) If an action based on anticipatory repudiation comes to trial before the time for performance with respect to some or all of the goods, any damages based

on market price (Section 2–708 or Section 2–713) shall be determined according to the price of such goods prevailing at the time when the aggrieved party learned of the repudiation.

(2) If evidence of a price prevailing at the times or places described in this Article is not readily available the price prevailing within any reasonable time before or after the time described or at any other place which in commercial judgment or under usage of trade would serve as a reasonable substitute for the one described may be used, making any proper allowance for the cost of transporting the goods to or from such other place.

(3) Evidence of a relevant price prevailing at a time or place other than the one described in this Article offered by one party is not admissible unless and until he has given the other party such notice as the court finds sufficient to prevent unfair surprise.

§ 2–724.   Admissibility of Market Quotations.

Whenever the prevailing price or value of any goods regularly bought and sold in any established commodity market is in issue, reports in official publications or trade journals or in newspapers or periodicals of general circulation published as the reports of such market shall be admissible in evidence. The circumstances of the preparation of such a report may be shown to affect its weight but not its admissibility.

§ 2–725.   Statute of Limitations in Contracts for Sale.

(1) An action for breach of any contract for sale must be commenced within four years after the cause of action has accrued. By the original agreement the parties may reduce the period of limitation to not less than one year but may not extend it.

(2) A cause of action accrues when the breach occurs, regardless of the aggrieved party's lack of knowledge of the breach. A breach of warranty occurs when tender of delivery is made, except that where a warranty explicitly extends to future performance of the goods and discovery of the breach must await the time of such performance the cause of action accrues when the breach is or should have been discovered.

(3) Where an action commenced within the time limited by subsection (1) is so terminated as to leave available a remedy by another action for the same breach such other action may be commenced after the expiration of the time limited and within six months after the termination of the first action unless the termination resulted from voluntary discontinuance or from dismissal for failure or neglect to prosecute.

(4) This section does not alter the law on tolling of the statute of limitations nor does it apply to causes of action which have accrued before this Act becomes effective.

Answers to *Issue Spotters*

Chapter 1

1A: Case law includes courts' interpretations of statutes, constitutional provisions, and administrative rules. Statutes often codify common law rules. For these reasons, a judge might rely on the common law as a guide to the intent and purpose of a statute.

2A: No. The U.S. Constitution is the supreme law of the land and applies to all jurisdictions. A law in violation of the Constitution (in this question, the First Amendment to the Constitution) will be declared unconstitutional.

Chapter 2

1A: Maybe. On the one hand, it is not the company's "fault" when a product is misused. Also, keeping the product on the market is not a violation of the law, and stopping sales would hurt profits. On the other hand, suspending sales could reduce suffering and could stop potential negative publicity that might occur if sales continued.

2A: When a corporation decides to respond to what it sees as a moral obligation to correct for past discrimination by adjusting pay differences among its employees, an ethical conflict is raised between the firm and its employees and between the firm and its shareholders. This dilemma arises directly out of the effect such a decision has on the firm's profits. If satisfying this obligation increases profitability, then the dilemma is easily resolved in favor of "doing the right thing."

Chapter 3

1A: Before a court will hear a case, it must be established that the court has subject-matter and personal jurisdiction and that the matter at issue is justiciable. The party bringing the suit must also have standing to sue.

2A: Yes. Whenever a suit involves citizens of different states, diversity of citizenship exists, and the suit can be brought in a federal court. In diversity-of-citizenship suits, Congress has set an additional requirement—the amount in controversy must be more than $75,000.

Chapter 4

1A: No. Even if commercial speech is not related to illegal activities and is not misleading, it may be restricted if a state has a substantial interest that cannot be achieved by less restrictive means. In this case, the interest in energy conservation is substantial, but it could be achieved by less restrictive means. That would be the utilities' defense against the enforcement of this state law.

2A: Yes. The tax would limit the liberty of some persons (out-of-state businesses), so it is subject to a review under the equal protection clause. Protecting local businesses from out-of-state competition is not a legitimate government objective. Thus, such a tax would violate the equal protection clause.

Chapter 5

1A: Yes. Adam is guilty of battery—an unexcused, harmful, or offensive physical contact intentionally performed. A battery may involve contact with any part of the body and anything (a blouse, in this problem) attached to it.

2A: No. As long as competitive behavior is bona fide, it is not wrongful, even if it results in the breaking of a contract. The public policy that favors free competition in advertising outweighs any instability that bona fide competitive activity causes in contractual or business relations.

  To constitute wrongful interference with a contractual relationship, there must be (1) a valid, enforceable contract between two parties; (2) the knowledge of a third party that this contract exists; and (3) the third party's intentionally causing the breach of the contract (and damages) to advance that party's interest.

Chapter 6

1A: This is patent infringement. A software maker in this situation might best protect its product, save litigation costs, and profit from its patent by the use of a license. In the context of this problem, a license would grant permission to sell a patented item. (A license can be limited to certain purposes and to the licensee only.)

2A: Yes. Roslyn has committed theft of trade secrets. Lists of suppliers and customers cannot be patented, copyrighted, or trademarked, but the information is protected against appropriation by others as trade secrets. And most likely, Roslyn signed a contract, agreeing not to use this information outside her employment by Organic. But even without this contract, Organic could have made a convincing case against Roslyn for a theft of trade secrets.

Chapter 7

1A: Karl may have committed trademark infringement. Search engines compile their results by looking through Web sites' keyword fields. Key words, or meta tags, increase the likelihood that a site will be included in search engine results, even if the words have no connection to the site. A site that appropriates the key words of other sites with more frequent hits will appear in the same search engine results as the more popular sites. But using another's trademark as a key word without the owner's permission normally constitutes trademark infringement.

Of course, some uses of another's trademark as a meta tag may be permissible if the use is reasonably necessary and does not suggest that the owner authorized or sponsored the use.

2A: Yes. This may be an instance of trademark dilution. Dilution occurs when a trademark is used, without permission, in a way that diminishes the distinctive quality of the mark. Dilution does not require proof that consumers are likely to be confused by the use of the unauthorized mark. The products involved do not have to be similar. Dilution does require, however, that a mark be famous when the dilution occurs.

Chapter 8

1A: Yes. Forgery is the fraudulent making or altering of any writing that changes the legal liability of another.

2A: Yes. Federal law makes it a crime to use the mails, a telegram, a telephone, a radio, or a television to defraud. Carl has committed a violation of federal wire fraud statutes.

Chapter 9

1A: No. This contract, although not fully executed, is for an illegal purpose and therefore is void. A void contract gives rise to no legal obligation on the part of any party. A contract that is void is no contract. There is nothing to enforce.

2A: Yes. A person who is unjustly enriched at the expense of another can be required to account for the benefit under the theory of quasi contract. Alison and Jerry did not have a contract, but the law will impose one to avoid the unjust enrichment.

Chapter 10

1A: No. Revocation of an offer may be implied by conduct inconsistent with the offer. When the corporation hired someone else, and the offeree learned of the hiring, the offer was revoked. The acceptance was too late.

2A: Dani has entered into an enforceable contract to subscribe to *E-Profit*. In this set of facts, the offer to deliver the newsletter via e-mail was presented by *E-Profit* (the offeror) with a statement of how to accept. This statement specified that clicking on the "SUBSCRIBE" button was an acceptance of the offer. Dani (the offeree) had an opportunity to decline the offer by *not* clicking on the button before making the contract. This is a click-on agreement.

Chapter 11

1A: Yes. The original contract was executory. The parties rescinded it and agreed to a new contract. If the employee had broken the contract to accept a contract with another employer, she might have been held liable for damages for the breach.

2A: Yes. Under the doctrine of promissory estoppel (or detrimental reliance), Maria, the promisee, is entitled to payment of the promised amount when she graduates. There was a promise, she relied on it, and her reliance was substantial and definite. She went to college for nearly four years, incurring considerable expenses. It would only be fair to enforce the promise.

Chapter 12

1A: No. Joan may disaffirm this contract. Because the apartment was a necessary, however, she remains liable for the reasonable value of her occupancy of the apartment.

2A: A minor may effectively ratify a contract after he or she reaches the age of majority either expressly or impliedly. Failing to disaffirm an otherwise enforceable contract within a reasonable time after reaching the age of majority would also effectively ratify it. Nothing a minor does before attaining majority, however, will ratify a contract.

Chapter 13

1A: No. A contract that calls for something that is prohibited by statute is illegal and thus void and unenforceable.

2A: No. Generally, an exculpatory clause—a clause attempting to absolve parties of negligence or other wrongs—is not enforced if the party seeking its enforcement is involved in a business that is important to the public as a matter of practical necessity, such as an airline. Because of the essential nature of these services, such a party has an advantage in bargaining strength and could insist that anyone contracting for its services agree not to hold it liable.

Chapter 14

1A: No. Brad exerted economic duress on Dina. The threat to break a contract on the eve of the deadline in this problem was sufficiently coercive to constitute duress. Duress involves coercive conduct—forcing a party to enter into a contract by threatening the party with a wrongful act.

2A: Yes. Rescission may be granted on the basis of fraudulent misrepresentation. The elements of fraudulent misrepresentation include intent to deceive, or *scienter*. *Scienter* exists if a party makes a statement recklessly, without regard to whether it is true or false, or if a party says or implies that a statement is made on some basis such as personal knowledge or personal investigation when it is not.

Chapter 15

1A: No. Under the UCC, a contract for a sale of goods priced at $500 or more must be in writing to be enforceable. In this case, the contract is not enforceable beyond the quantity already delivered and paid for.

2A: The court might conclude that under the doctrine of promissory estoppel, the employer is estopped from claiming the lack of a written contract as a defense. The oral contract may be enforced because the employer made a promise on which the employee justifiably relied in moving to New York, the reliance was foreseeable, and injustice can be avoided only by enforcing the promise. If the court strictly enforces the Statute of Frauds, however, the employee may be without a remedy.

Chapter 16

1A: Yes. When one person makes a promise with the intention of benefiting a third person, the third person can sue to enforce it. This is a third party beneficiary contract. The third party in this problem is an intended beneficiary.

2A: Yes. Generally, if a contract makes it clear that a right is not assignable, no assignment will be effective, but there are exceptions, and assignment of the right to receive funds cannot be prohibited.

Chapter 17

1A: Ron, the buyer, is entitled to the benefit of the bargain that was made with George, the contractor—that is, Ron is entitled to be put in as good a position as he would have been in if the contract had been fully performed. The measure of the benefit is the cost to complete the work ($500). These are compensatory damages.

2A: No. To recover damages that flow from the consequences of a breach but that are caused by circumstances beyond the contract (consequential damages), the breaching party must know, or have reason to know, that special circumstances will cause the nonbreaching party to suffer the additional loss. That was not the situation in this problem, as stated in the facts.

Chapter 18

1A: A shipment of nonconforming goods constitutes an acceptance and a breach, unless the seller seasonably notifies the buyer that the nonconforming shipment does not constitute an acceptance and is offered only as an accommodation. Without the notification, the shipment is an acceptance and a breach. Thus, here, the shipment was both an acceptance and a breach.

2A: Yes. In a transaction between merchants, the requirement of a writing is satisfied if one of them sends to the other a signed written confirmation that indicates the terms of the agreement, and the merchant receiving it has reason to know of its contents. If the merchant who receives it does not object in writing within ten days after receipt, the writing will be enforceable against him or her even though he or she has not signed anything.

Chapter 19

1A: Buyers and sellers can have an insurable interest in identical goods at the same time. If the buyer (Silk & Satin) bore the risk, it must pay and seek reimbursement from its insurance company. If the seller (Adams Textiles) bore the risk, it must seek reimbursement from its insurance company and may still have an obligation to deliver the identified goods (the fabric) to Silk & Satin.

2A: George (the buyer) suffers the loss of the goods (Blaze, the horse). If a bailee—in this case, the stable—holds goods for a seller (Paula), and the goods are to be delivered without being moved, the risk of loss passes when the bailee (the stable) acknowledges the buyer's (George's) right to possess the goods (Blaze). The stable acknowledged George's right to possess the horse when the stable said, "Okay," in response to Paula's call about the sale.

Chapter 20

1A: Yes. Normally, goods must be tendered in a single delivery, but the parties can agree otherwise, or the circumstances may be such that either party can rightfully request delivery in lots. The seller's (Mike's) proposal to work around the circumstances in this problem seems reasonable.

2A: Yes. In a case of anticipatory repudiation, as in this problem, a buyer can resort to any remedy for breach even though the buyer told the seller—the repudiating party in this problem—that the buyer would wait for the seller's performance.

Chapter 21

1A: General Construction, the buyer, should argue that Industrial Supplies, the seller, breached an implied warranty of fitness for a particular purpose. An implied warranty of fitness for a particular purpose arises when a seller knows the particular purpose for which a buyer will use goods and that the buyer is relying on the seller's skill and judgment to select suitable goods.

2A: Yes. Anchor, Inc., as the manufacturer of the component part, may be held liable. The strict liability doctrine has been expanded to include suppliers of component parts.

Chapter 22

1A: Yes. The Federal Trade Commission (FTC) has issued rules to govern advertising techniques, including rules designed to prevent bait-and-switch advertising. Under the FTC guidelines, bait-and-switch advertising occurs if the seller refuses to show the advertised item, fails to have in stock a reasonable quantity of the item, fails to promise to deliver the advertised item within a reasonable time, or discourages employees from selling the item.

2A: A number of federal and state laws deal specifically with information given on labels and packages. These laws include the Fair Packaging and Labeling Act and the Nutrition Labeling and Education Act.

Chapter 23

1A: "I promise to pay $700" would make the instrument negotiable. "I.O.U. $700" or an instruction to Jim's bank stating, "I wish you would pay $700 to Sherry," would render the instrument nonnegotiable. To be negotiable, an instrument must contain an express promise to pay. An I.O.U. is only an acknowledgment of indebtedness. An order stating, "I wish you would pay," is not sufficiently precise.

2A: Yes. When Jack signed the back of his check, he converted it to a bearer instrument, which anyone can cash. Because a bearer instrument can be negotiated by delivery alone, the check was negotiated to Paige (the finder). Jack could have avoided this loss by indorsing the check with a restrictive indorsement, such as "For Deposit Only"—which means the check could not have been cashed, but only deposited into his credit union account. In addition, Jack could have simply waited until he reached the credit union's teller counter before indorsing (signing the back of his check).

Chapter 24

1A: Carol is an HDC to the full extent of the note. One of the requirements for becoming an HDC is taking an instrument for value. A party may attain HDC status to the extent that she or he gives value for the instrument. Paying with cash or with a check is giving value.

2A: No. When a drawer's employee provides the drawer with the name of a fictitious payee—that is, a payee whom the drawer does not actually intend to have any interest in an instrument—a forgery of the payee's name is effective to pass good title to subsequent transferees.

Chapter 25

1A: Yes to both questions. In a civil suit, a drawer is liable to a payee or to a holder of a check that is not honored. If intent to defraud can be proved, the drawer can also be subject to criminal prosecution for writing a bad check.

2A: The general rule is that the bank must recredit a customer's account when it pays on a forged signature. The bank has no right to recover from a holder who, without knowledge, cashes a check bearing a forged drawer's signature. Thus, the bank in this problem can collect from neither its customer nor the party who cashed the check. The bank's recourse is to look for the thief.

Chapter 26

1A: No. Sheila, as an agent, is prohibited from taking advantage of the agency relationship to obtain property that the principal (Able Corporation) wants to purchase. This is the *duty of loyalty* that arises with every agency relationship.

2A: Marie would be liable on the note only if she ratifies it when she returns. Remember that ratification is the affirmation of a previously unauthorized contract or act. In this situation, the unauthorized act was Rachel's representing Marie when signing the promissory note.

Chapter 27

1A: Yes. Some courts have held that an implied employment contract exists between employer and employee when an employee handbook states that employees will be dismissed only for good cause. An employer who fires a worker contrary to this promise can be held liable for breach of contract.

2A: Workers' compensation laws establish a procedure for compensating workers who are injured on the job. Instead of suing to collect benefits, an injured worker notifies the employer of the injury and files a claim with the appropriate state agency. The right to recover is normally determined without regard to negligence or fault, but intentionally inflicted injuries are not covered. Unlike the potential for recovery in a lawsuit based on negligence or fault, recovery under a workers' compensation statute is limited to the specific amount designated in the statute for the employee's injury.

Chapter 28

1A: Yes. One type of sexual harassment occurs when a request for sexual favors is a condition of employment, and the person making the request is a supervisor or acts with the authority of the employer. A tangible employment action, such as continued employment, may also lead to the employer's liability for the supervisor's conduct. That the injured employee is a male and the supervisor a female, instead of the other way around, would not affect the outcome. Same-gender harassment is also actionable.

2A: Yes. Koko could succeed in a discrimination suit if she can show that she was not hired solely because of her disability. The other elements for a discrimination suit based on a disability are that the plaintiff (1) has a disability and (2) is otherwise qualified for the job. Both of these elements appear to be satisfied in this scenario.

Chapter 29

1A: The most appropriate form for doing business for Sam may be a sole proprietorship. This is because his business is relatively small and is not diversified, employs relatively few people, has modest profits, and is not likely to expand significantly or require extensive financing in the immediate future.

2A: Under the partners' fiduciary duty, a partner must account to the partnership for any personal profits or benefits derived without the consent of all the partners in connection with the use of any partnership property. Thus, in this scenario, Hal may not keep the lease money.

Chapter 30

1A: The first combination of Bennett Corporation and Corbett Enterprises, Inc., is a merger. Corbett absorbed Bennett and is the surviving company.

The second combination of Global Corporation and Hometown Company is a consolidation. Neither Global nor Hometown continues after the combination. Rather, the new firm, Green Springs, Inc., continues in their place.

2A: Yes. Broad authority to conduct business can be granted in a corporation's articles of incorporation. For example, the phrase "any lawful purpose" is often used. This can be important because acts of a corporation that are beyond the authority given to it in its articles or charter (or state statutes) are considered illegal, *ultra vires* acts.

Chapter 31

1A: A director cannot support a business that competes directly with a corporation on the board of which the director sits. The director's fiduciary duty requires him to fully disclose the conflict of interest, and he must abstain from voting on the proposed transaction.

2A: The best defense in this context is the business judgment rule. As long as a director or officer acts in good faith, in what he or she considers to be the best interests of the corporation, and with the care that an ordinarily prudent person would use in similar circumstances, he or she is not liable simply because the decision had a negative result.

Chapter 32

1A: A creditor can put other creditors on notice by perfecting its interest by filing a financing statement in the appropriate public office or by taking possession of the collateral until the debtor repays the loan.

2A: When collateral consists of consumer goods, and the debtor has paid less than 60 percent of the debt or the purchase price, the creditor has the option of disposing of the collateral in a commercially reasonable manner. This generally requires notice of the place, time, and manner of sale.

A debtor can waive the right to notice, but only *after default*. Before the disposal, a debtor can redeem the collateral by tendering performance of all of the obligations secured by the collateral and by paying the creditor's reasonable expenses in retaking and maintaining the collateral.

Chapter 33

1A: Each of the parties (Larry and Midwest Roofing) can place a mechanic's lien on the debtor's (Joe's) property. If Joe does not pay what is owed, the property can be sold to satisfy the debt.

2A: No. In some states, a creditor must go back to court for a separate order of garnishment for each pay period. Also, federal and state laws limit the amount that can be garnished from a debtor's pay.

Chapter 34

1A: The savings and loan association is not eligible to file a bankruptcy petition under Chapter 11. Debtors that can file under Chapter 11 are generally the same as those that can file under Chapter 7—any person, including individuals, partnerships, and corporations, except railroads, insurance companies, banks, savings and loan associations, and credit unions.

2A: No. Besides the claims listed in this problem, the debts that cannot be discharged in bankruptcy include amounts borrowed to pay back taxes, goods obtained by fraud, debts that were not listed in the bankruptcy's petition, domestic-support obligations, and others.

Chapter 35

1A: No. An incorrect statement as to the age of an insured is a misrepresentation and would be considered a valid defense for Farm Insurance Company. Under an incontestability clause, however, after a policy has been in force for a certain time (usually two or three years), the insurer cannot cancel the policy or avoid a claim on the basis of statements made in the application.

2A: No. To obtain insurance, one must have a sufficiently substantial interest in whatever is to be insured. A person has an insurable interest in property if she or he would suffer a financial loss from its destruction. This interest in *property* must exist *when the loss occurs*.

To obtain insurance on another's life, a person must have a reasonable expectation of benefit from the continued life of the other. The benefit may be founded on a relationship, but an "ex-spouse" alone is not such a relationship. An interest in someone's life must exist *when the policy is obtained*.

Chapter 36

1A: Dave and Paul are joint tenants. The main distinguishing feature between a tenancy in common and a joint tenancy is that a joint tenancy includes a right of survivorship. This is what the owners in this problem provided for themselves when they acquired their property.

2A: Yes. A bailment agreement expressly or impliedly provides for the return of the bailed property to the bailor (or a third person), or it provides for the disposal of the goods. This agreement presupposes that the bailee will return the identical goods given by the bailor and in acceptable condition. An ordinary bailee owes a duty to take proper care of the items left in its charge.

Chapter 37

1A: The most important factor in determining whether an item is a fixture is the intent of the owners. Other factors include whether the item can be removed without damaging the real property and whether the item is sufficiently adapted so as to have become a part of the real property. If removal would irreparably damage the property, the item may also be considered a fixture.

2A: Yes. The government can take private property for public use (a taking), but it cannot do so, under the Fifth Amendment to the U.S. Constitution, without paying the property owner just compensation. In some cases, to obtain title, a condemnation proceeding is brought before the property is taken. In a separate proceeding, a court determines the property's fair value (usually market value) to be paid to the owner.

Chapter 38

1A: The tenant's heirs inherit the lease and can fulfill its term. (A lease passes to a tenant's heirs as personal property.) This rule protects the landlord's interest, which is to realize the full benefits of the lease, and the tenant's interest, which is also to realize the benefits of the lease. Of course, both parties must continue to abide by the terms of the lease.

2A: Yes. A lease may be oral. In most states, however, some leases must be in writing (such as those that cannot be completed within a year, which must be in writing under the Statute of Frauds). As with other oral agreements, a party who wants to enforce an oral lease may have a hard time proving its existence.

Chapter 39

1A: No. At the time that a will is made, the testator must comprehend the kind and character of the property

being distributed, and understand and formulate a plan for disposing of the property. In this problem, Sheila, the testator, passes the test. Mental incompetency did not occur until after the will was made.

2A: The will may name an *executor* to administer the estate. If the will does not name an executor, or if there is no will, the court must appoint an *administrator*. The term *personal representative* refers to either an executor or an administrator.

Chapter 40

1A: Checks against the arbitrary use of agency power include the courts' power to review agency actions. Among other things, Congress can create, restrict, or abolish an agency. Congress can also limit the funds that it gives to an agency. The president can exercise control over an agency through the appointment of its officers.

2A: Itex Corporation can use the Freedom of Information Act (FOIA) to require the federal government to reveal certain "records" to "any person" on request. Under the FOIA, a business firm can learn what information federal agencies possess about it.

Chapter 41

1A: This agreement is a tying arrangement. The legality of a tying arrangement depends on the purpose of the agreement, the agreement's likely effect on competition in the relevant markets (the market for the tying product and the market for the tied product), and other factors. Tying arrangements for commodities are subject to Section 3 of the Clayton Act. Tying arrangements for services can be agreements in restraint of trade in violation of Section 1 of the Sherman Act.

2A: Size alone does not determine whether a firm is a monopoly—size in relation to the market is what matters. A small store in a small, isolated town is a monopolist if it is the only store serving that market. Monopoly involves the power to affect prices and output. If a firm has sufficient market power to control prices and exclude competition, that firm has monopoly power. Monopoly power in itself is not a violation of Section 2 of the Sherman Act. The offense also requires an intent to acquire or maintain that power through anticompetitive means.

Chapter 42

1A: A U.S. firm (or any domestic firm) can license its formula, product, or process to a foreign concern to avoid its theft. The foreign firm obtains the right to make and market the product according to the formula (or the right to use the process) and agrees to keep the necessary information secret and to pay royalties to the licensor.

2A: The practice described in this scenario is known as dumping, which is regarded as an unfair international trade practice. Dumping is the sale of imported goods at "less than fair value." Based on the price of those goods in the exporting country, an extra tariff can be imposed on the imports. This is known as an anti-dumping duty.

A

abandoned property   Property that has been discarded by the owner, who has no intention of recovering it.

acceptance   In contract law, a voluntary act by the offeree that shows assent, or agreement, to the terms of an offer. In negotiable instruments, a drawee's signed agreement to pay a draft when it comes due.

acceptor   A drawee who accepts, or promises to pay, an instrument when it is presented later for payment.

accession   An addition that increases the value of property (such as the addition of a diamond to a ring).

accord and satisfaction   An agreement and payment (or other performance) between two parties, one of whom has a right of action against the other.

action   A proceeding by one person against another in a court to obtain the enforcement or protection of a right, the redress or prevention of a wrong, or the punishment of a public offense.

act of state doctrine   A doctrine providing that the judicial branch of one country will not examine the validity of public acts committed by a recognized foreign government within its own territory.

actual malice   A defamatory statement made about a public figure with knowledge of its falsity or with reckless disregard for the truth.

adhesion contract   A standard-form contract in which the stronger party dictates the terms.

adjudication   A proceeding in which an administrative law judge hears and decides issues that arise when an administrative agency charges a person or a firm with an agency violation.

administrative agency   A federal or state government agency established to perform a specific function.

administrative law   A body of law in the form of rules, orders, and decisions created by administrative agencies in order to carry out their duties and responsibilities.

administrative law judge (ALJ)   One who presides over an administrative agency hearing and has the power to administer oaths, take testimony, rule on questions of evidence, and make determinations of fact.

administrative process   The procedure used by administrative agencies in the administration of law.

administrator   A person appointed by a court to handle the disposition of a person's estate under certain circumstances, such as if the person dies without a will.

adverse possession   The acquisition of title to real property by occupying it openly, without the consent of the owner, for a period of time specified by state statutes.

affidavit   A statement of facts confirmed by the oath or affirmation of the party making it and made before a person having the authority to administer the oath or affirmation.

after-acquired property   Property of the debtor that is acquired after a secured creditor's interest in the debtor's property has been created.

agency   A relationship between two parties in which one party (the agent) agrees to represent or act for the other (the principal).

agent   A person authorized by another to act for or in place of him or her.

agreement   A meeting of two or more minds in regard to the terms of a contract.

alien corporation   A designation in the United States for a corporation formed in another country but doing business in the United States.

alternative dispute resolution (ADR)   The resolution of disputes in ways outside the traditional judicial process, such as negotiation, mediation, and arbitration.

answer   Procedurally, a defendant's response to a complaint.

antitrust law   Laws protecting commerce from unlawful restraints.

apparent authority   Authority that arises when the principal causes a third party to reasonably believe that an agent has authority to act on the principal's behalf.

appellant   The party who takes an appeal from one court to another.

appellee   The party against whom an appeal is taken— that is, the party who opposes setting aside or reversing the judgment.

appraisal right   A dissenting shareholder's right, if he or she objects to an extraordinary transaction of the corporation, to have his or her shares appraised and to be paid their fair value.

arbitration   The settling of a dispute by submitting it to a disinterested third party who renders a decision.

articles of incorporation   The document filed with the appropriate governmental agency, usually the secretary of state, when a business is incorporated.

articles of partnership   A written agreement that sets forth each partner's rights in, and obligations to, the partnership.

artisan's lien   A possessory lien given to a person who has made improvements and added value to another person's personal property as security for payment for services performed.

assault   Any word or action intended to make another person fearful of immediate physical harm.

assignment   The act of transferring to another all or part of one's rights arising under a contract.

assumption of risk   A defense against negligence that can be used when the plaintiff is aware of a danger and voluntarily assumes the risk of injury from that danger.

attachment   In a secured transaction, the process by which a security interest in the property of another becomes enforceable. The legal process of seizing another's property under a court order to secure satisfaction of a judgment yet to be rendered.

authorization card   A card signed by an employee that gives a union permission to act on his or her behalf in negotiations with management.

automatic stay   A suspension of all judicial proceedings on the occurrence of an independent event.

B

bailee   One to whom goods are entrusted by a bailor.

bailment   An agreement in which the personal property of a bailor is entrusted to a bailee, who is obligated to return the bailed property or dispose of it as directed.

bailor   One who entrusts goods to a bailee.

bait-and-switch advertising   Advertising a product at a very attractive price (the bait) and then informing the consumer that the advertised product is not available and urging him or her to purchase (switch to) a more expensive item.

bankruptcy court   A federal court of limited jurisdiction that handles only bankruptcy proceedings.

bankruptcy trustee   A person appointed by the bankruptcy court to sell the assets of a debtor and distribute the proceeds to creditors.

battery   The intentional touching of another.

bearer   A person in the possession of an instrument payable to bearer or indorsed in blank.

bearer instrument   A negotiable instrument that is payable to the bearer, including instruments payable to "cash."

benefit corporation   A for-profit corporation that seeks to have a materially positive impact on society and the environment.

bilateral contract   A contract that includes the exchange of a promise for a promise.

bilateral mistake   A mistake that occurs when both parties to a contract are mistaken as to a material fact.

Bill of Rights   The first ten amendments to the U.S. Constitution.

binder   A written, temporary insurance policy.

blue sky law   State law that regulates the offer and sale of securities.

bond   A certificate that evidences a corporate debt. It is a security that involves no ownership interest in the issuing corporation.

bond indenture   A contract between the issuer of a bond and the bondholder.

breach   The failure to perform a legal obligation.

breach of contract   Failure, without legal excuse, of a promisor to perform the obligations of a contract.

brief   A written summary or statement prepared by one side in a lawsuit to explain its case to the judge.

business ethics   A consensus of what constitutes right or wrong behavior in the world of business and how moral principles are applied by businesspersons.

business invitee   A person, such as a customer or a client, who is invited onto business premises by the owner for business purposes.

business judgment rule   A rule that immunizes corporate management from liability for actions that are undertaken in good faith.

business necessity   A defense in which the employer demonstrates that an employment practice that discriminates against members of a protected class is related to job performance.

business tort   A tort occurring only within the business context.

bylaws   A set of governing rules or regulations adopted by a corporation or other association.

C

case law   Rules of law announced in court decisions.

categorical imperative   An ethical framework in which an action is evaluated in terms of what would happen if everybody else in the same situation, or category, acted in the same way.

causation in fact   An act or omission without which an event would not have occurred.

cause of action   A situation or state of facts that gives a person a right to initiate a judicial proceeding.

cease-and-desist order   An order prohibiting a person or business firm from conducting activities that an agency or court has deemed illegal.

certificate of deposit (CD)   An instrument evidencing a promissory acknowledgment by a bank of a receipt of money with an engagement to repay it.

check   A draft written and signed by a drawer ordering the drawee (usually a financial institution) to pay a certain amount of money to the holder on demand.

checks and balances   The system by which each of the three branches of the national government exercises a check on the actions of the others.

choice-of-language clause   A clause in a contract designating the official language by which the contract will be interpreted in the event of a future disagreement over the contract's terms.

choice-of-law clause   A clause in a contract designating the law—such as the law of a particular state or nation—that will govern the contract.

civil law   The branch of law dealing with the definition and enforcement of all private and public rights, as opposed to criminal matters.

civil law system   A system of law derived from that of the Roman Empire and based on a code rather than case law.

class-action lawsuit   A suit in which a number of persons join together to bring an action.

click-on agreement   An agreement entered into online when a buyer indicates his or her acceptance of an offer by clicking on a button that reads "I agree."

close corporation   A corporation whose shareholders are limited to a small group of persons or a single person.

closed shop   A firm that requires union membership as a condition of employment.

cloud computing   The delivery to users of on-demand services from third-party servers over a network.

codicil   A formal written supplement or modification to a will.

collateral promise   A secondary promise, such as a promise made by one person to pay the debts of another if the latter fails to perform.

collecting bank   Any bank handling an item for collection, except the payor bank.

collective bargaining   The process by which labor and management negotiate the terms and conditions of employment.

comity   The principle by which one nation defers and gives effect to the laws and judicial decrees of another nation. This recognition is based primarily on respect.

commerce clause   The provision in Article I, Section 8, of the U.S. Constitution that gives Congress the power to regulate interstate commerce.

commercial impracticability   A doctrine that may excuse the duty to perform a contract when it becomes much more difficult or costly due to forces neither party could control at the time of contract formation.

commingle   To mix funds or goods together in such a way that the funds or goods no longer have separate identities.

common law   The body of law developed from custom or judicial decisions in English and U.S. courts.

common stock   True ownership of a corporation.

community property   A form of concurrent ownership in which each spouse owns an undivided one-half interest in most property acquired during the marriage.

comparative negligence   A doctrine in tort law under which the liability for injuries resulting from negligent acts is shared by all parties who were negligent (including the injured party), on the basis of each person's proportionate negligence.

compensatory damages   A money award equivalent to the actual value of injuries or damages sustained by the aggrieved party.

complaint   The pleading made by a plaintiff or a charge made by the state alleging wrongdoing on the part of the defendant.

computer crime   Any act that is directed against computers and computer parts or that uses computers as instruments of crime.

concurrent jurisdiction   Jurisdiction that exists when two different courts have the power to hear a case.

confiscation   A government's taking of a privately owned business or personal property without a legal public purpose or an award of just compensation.

conforming goods   Goods that conform to contract specifications.

confusion   The mixing together of goods belonging to two or more owners so that the independent goods cannot be identified.

consequential damages   Special damages that compensate for a loss that is not direct or immediate.

consideration   The value given in return for a promise or performance in a contractual agreement.

consolidation   A process whereby two or more corporations join to become a completely new corporation.

constructive delivery   An act equivalent to the physical delivery of property that cannot be physically delivered because of difficulty or impossibility.

constructive discharge   A termination of employment brought about by making the employee's working conditions so intolerable that the employee reasonably feels compelled to leave.

constructive eviction   Depriving a person of the possession of property that he or she leases by rendering the premises unfit or unsuitable for occupancy.

constructive trust   A trust created by operation of law against one who wrongfully holds a legal right to property that that person should not, in equity and good conscience, hold and enjoy.

contract   A set of promises constituting an agreement between parties, giving each a legal duty to the other and also the right to seek a remedy for the breach of the promises or duties.

contractual capacity   The legal ability to enter into a contractual relationship.

conversion   The wrongful taking, using, or retaining possession of personal property that belongs to another.

cookie   A small file sent from a Web site and stored in a user's Web browser to track the user's Web-browsing activities.

"cooling-off" law   A law that allows a buyer three business days in which to cancel a door-to-door sales contract.

copyright   The exclusive right of an author to publish, print, or sell an intellectual production for a statutory period of time.

corporate social responsibility   The idea that those who run corporations can and should act ethically and be accountable to society for their actions.

corporation   A legal business form that complies with statutory requirements.

correspondent bank   A bank in which another bank has an account (and vice versa) for the purpose of facilitating fund transfers.

cost-benefit analysis   A decision-making technique that involves weighing the costs of a given action against the benefits of the action.

co-surety   One who assumes liability jointly with another surety for the payment of an obligation.

counteradvertising   New advertising that is undertaken pursuant to a Federal Trade Commission order for the purpose of correcting earlier false claims.

counteroffer   An offeree's response to an offer in which the offeree rejects the original offer and at the same time makes a new offer.

course of dealing   A sequence of previous conduct between the parties to a particular transaction that establishes a common basis for their understanding.

course of performance   The conduct that occurs under the terms of a particular agreement indicating what the parties to an agreement intended it to mean.

covenant not to compete   A contractual promise of one party to refrain from competing in business with another party for a certain period of time and within a specified geographical area.

covenant not to sue   An agreement to substitute a contractual obligation for some other type of action.

covenant of quiet enjoyment   A promise by the grantor of real property that the grantee will not be disturbed in his or her possession of the property by the grantor or anyone having a lien against the property or superior title to it.

cover   A remedy that allows the buyer or lessee, on the seller's or lessor's breach, to purchase or lease the goods from another seller or lessor and substitute them for the goods due under the contract.

creditors' composition agreement   An agreement between a debtor and his or her creditors in which the creditors agree to accept a lesser sum than that owed by the debtor in full satisfaction of the debt.

crime   A wrong against society proclaimed in a statute and punishable by society through fines, imprisonment, or death.

criminal law   Law that governs and defines those actions that are crimes and that subject the convicted offender to punishment imposed by the government.

cross-examination   The questioning of an opposing witness during the trial.

crowdfunding   A cooperative activity in which people network and pool funds and other resources via the Internet to assist a cause (such as disaster relief) or invest in a business venture.

cure   The right of a party who tenders nonconforming performance to correct his or her performance within the contract period.

cyber crime   A crime that occurs in the virtual community of the Internet, as opposed to the physical world.

cyber fraud   Any misrepresentation knowingly made over the Internet with the intention of deceiving another for the purpose of obtaining property or funds.

cybersquatting   The act of registering a domain name that is the same as, or confusingly similar to, the trademark of another and then offering to sell that domain name back to the trademark owner.

cyberterrorist   A hacker whose purpose is to exploit a target computer to create a serious impact.

cyber tort   A tort committed via the Internet.

D

damages   Money sought as a remedy for a breach of contract or for a tortious (wrongful) act.

deceptive advertising   Advertising that misleads consumers.

deed   A document by which title to property is passed.

defamation   Anything published or publicly spoken that causes injury to another's good name, reputation, or character.

default judgment   A judgment entered by a court against a defendant who has failed to appear in court to answer or defend against the plaintiff's claim.

defendant   A person against whom a lawsuit is brought.

defense   A reason offered by the defendant in an action or lawsuit as to why the plaintiff should not recover or establish what he or she seeks.

deficiency judgment   A judgment against a debtor for the amount of a debt remaining unpaid after the collateral has been repossessed and sold.

delegation   The transfer of a contractual duty to a third party.

depositary bank   The first bank to receive a check for payment.

deposition   A generic term that refers to any evidence verified by oath.

destination contract   A contract for the sale of goods in which the seller assumes liability for any losses or damage to the goods until they are tendered at the destination specified in the contract.

devise   A gift of real property by will.

devisee   A person who inherits real property under a will.

digital cash (e-money)   Funds stored on microchips and other computer devices.

direct examination   The examination of a witness by the attorney who calls the witness to testify on behalf of the attorney's client.

disaffirmance   The repudiation (avoidance) of an obligation.

discharge   The termination of one's obligation under a contract.

disclosed principal   A principal whose identity and existence as a principal is known by a third person at the time a contract is made by an agent.

discovery   A method by which opposing parties obtain information from each other to prepare for trial.

dishonor   To refuse to pay or accept a negotiable instrument (whichever is required), even though the instrument is presented in a timely and proper manner.

disparagement of property   Economically injurious falsehoods about another's product or property.

disparate-impact discrimination   Discrimination that results from certain employer practices or procedures that, although not discriminatory, obviously have a discriminatory effect.

disparate-treatment discrimination   Intentional discrimination against individuals on the basis of color, gender, national origin, race, or religion.

dissociation   The severance of the relationship between a partner and a partnership.

dissolution   The formal disbanding of a partnership or a corporation.

distributed network   A network that can be used by persons located (distributed) around the country or the globe to share computer files.

distribution agreement   A contract between a seller and a distributor of the seller's products setting out the terms and conditions of the distributorship.

diversity of citizenship   A basis for federal court jurisdiction over a lawsuit between citizens of different states and countries.

divestiture   The act of selling one or more of a company's parts, such as a subsidiary or manufacturing plants.

dividend   A distribution of profits or income to shareholders, disbursed in proportion to the number of shares held.

document of title   Paper exchanged in the regular course of business that evidences the right to possession of goods.

domain name   The series of letters and symbols used to identify site operators on the Internet; Internet "addresses."

domestic corporation   In a given state, a corporation that does business in, and is organized under the laws of, that state.

dominion   The right to own, use, and possess property.

double jeopardy   A situation occurring when a person is tried twice for the same criminal offense.

draft   Any instrument drawn on a drawee (such as a bank) that orders the drawee to pay a certain sum of money.

drawee   A person who is ordered to pay a draft or check, usually a financial institution.

drawer   A person who initiates a draft (including a check), thereby ordering the drawee to pay.

due process clause   The provisions of the Fifth and Fourteenth Amendments to the Constitution that guarantee that no person shall be deprived of life, liberty, or property without due process of law.

dumping   The selling of goods in a foreign country at a price below the price charged for the same goods in the domestic market.

duress   Unlawful, forceful pressure brought to bear on a person, overcoming that person's free will and causing him or her to do what he or she otherwise would not have done.

duty of care   The duty of all persons, as established by tort law, to exercise a reasonable amount of care in their dealings with others.

E

easement   A nonpossessory right to use another's property.

e-contract   A contract entered into online.

e-evidence   A type of evidence that consists of all computer-generated or electronically recorded information.

electronic fund transfer (EFT)   A transfer of funds through the use of an electronic terminal, a phone, a computer, or magnetic tape.

emancipation   In regard to minors, the act of being freed from parental control.

embezzlement   The fraudulent appropriation of money or other property by a person to whom the money or property has been entrusted.

eminent domain   The power of a government to take land for public use from private citizens for just compensation.

employment-at-will doctrine   A doctrine under which an employer or an employee may terminate an employment contract at any time and for any reason, unless the contract specifies otherwise.

employment discrimination   Treating employees or job applicants unequally on the basis of race, color, gender, national origin, religion, age, or disability.

enabling legislation   Statutes enacted by Congress that authorize the creation of an administrative agency and specify the name, purposes, functions, and powers of the agency being created.

entrapment   A claim that a defendant was induced by a police officer or other public official to commit a crime that he or she would not otherwise have committed.

entrustment rule   A rule stating that transferring goods to a merchant who deals in goods of that kind gives that merchant the power to transfer those goods and all rights to them to a buyer in the ordinary course of business.

equal dignity rule   A rule stating that express authority given to an agent must be in writing if the contract to be made on behalf of the principal is required to be in writing.

equal protection clause   The provision in the Fourteenth Amendment to the Constitution that guarantees that a state may not "deny to any person within its jurisdiction the equal protection of the laws."

e-signature   An electronic sound, symbol, or process attached to or logically associated with a record and executed or adopted by a person with the intent to sign the record.

establishment clause   The provision in the First Amendment to the Constitution that prohibits Congress from creating any law "respecting an establishment of religion."

estate in property   All of the property owned by a person, including real estate and personal property.

estray statute   A statute defining finders' rights in property when the true owners are unknown.

ethics   Moral principles and values applied to social behavior.

eviction   Depriving a person of the possession of property that he or she leases.

exclusionary rule   Evidence obtained in violation of rights under the Fourth, Fifth, and Sixth Amendments—and evidence derived from illegally obtained evidence—is not admissible in court.

exclusive-dealing contract   An agreement under which a producer of goods agrees to sell its goods exclusively through one distributor.

exclusive jurisdiction   Jurisdiction that exists when a case can be heard only in a particular court or type of court.

exculpatory clause   A clause that releases a party to a contract from liability for his or her wrongful acts.

executed contract   A contract that has been completely performed by both parties.

executor   A person appointed by a testator to see that his or her will is administered appropriately.

executory contract   A contract that has not yet been fully performed.

export   To sell products to buyers located in other countries.

express contract   A contract that is stated in words, oral or written.

express warranty   A promise that is included in an agreement under which the promisor assures the quality, description, or performance of the goods.

expropriation   The seizure by a government of a privately owned business or personal property for a proper public purpose and with just compensation.

F

federal form of government   A system of government in which the states form a union and the sovereign power is divided between a central government and the member states.

federal question   A question that pertains to the U.S. Constitution, acts of Congress, or treaties. A federal question provides jurisdiction for federal courts.

Federal Reserve System   The central banking system of the United States, made up of twelve regional banks and headed by a board of governors.

fee simple   A form of property ownership entitling the property owner to use, possess, or dispose of the property as he or she chooses during his or her lifetime.

fee simple absolute   An estate or interest in land with no time, disposition, or descendibility limitations.

fee simple defeasible   An estate that can be taken away by the grantor on the occurrence or nonoccurrence of a specified event.

felony   A crime that carries the most severe sanctions, usually ranging from one year in prison to death.

fictitious payee   A payee on a negotiable instrument whom the maker or drawer does not intend to have an interest in the instrument.

fiduciary relationship   A relationship founded on trust and loyalty.

filtering software   A computer program that screens in order to block access to certain Web sites.

final order   The final decision of an administrative agency on an issue.

firm offer   An offer (by a merchant) that is irrevocable without consideration for a period of time (not longer than three months). A firm offer by a merchant must be in writing and must be signed by the offeror.

fixed-term tenancy   A lease for a specified period of time, after which the interest reverts to the landlord.

fixture   An item of personal property that is attached to real property in such a way that it takes on the characteristics of real property and becomes part of that real property.

floating lien   A security interest retained in collateral even when the collateral changes in character, classification, or location.

forbearance   The act of refraining from an action that one has a legal right to undertake.

force majeure **clause**   A provision in a contract stipulating that certain unforeseen events—such as war, political upheavals, or acts of God—will excuse a party from liability for nonperformance of contractual obligations.

foreclosure   A legal proceeding in which a mortgagee takes title to or forces the sale of the mortgagor's property to satisfy a debt.

foreign corporation   In a given state, a corporation that does business in the state without being incorporated therein.

foreign exchange market   A worldwide system in which foreign currencies are bought and sold.

forgery   The fraudulent making or altering of any writing in a way that changes the legal rights and liabilities of another.

formal contract   A contract that by law requires a specific form for its validity.

form   The manner observed in creating a legal agreement, as opposed to the substance of the agreement.

forum-selection clause   A contract provision identifying the court or jurisdiction that will decide any disputes.

franchise   Any arrangement in which the owner of a trademark, trade name, or copyright licenses another to use it under specified conditions in the selling of goods or services.

fraudulent misrepresentation   Any misrepresentation, either by misstatement or by omission of a material fact, knowingly made with the intention of deceiving another and on which a reasonable person would and does rely to his or her detriment.

free exercise clause   The provision in the First Amendment to the Constitution that prohibits Congress from making any law "prohibiting the free exercise" of religion.

fungible goods   Goods that are alike by physical nature, by agreement, or by trade usage.

G

garnishment   A legal process whereby a creditor appropriates a debtor's property or wages that are in the hands of a third party.

general partner   A partner who assumes responsibility for the management of the partnership and liability for all partnership debts.

gift   Any voluntary transfer of property ownership made without consideration, past or present.

gift *causa mortis*   A gift made in contemplation of imminent death.

gift *inter vivos*   A gift made during one's lifetime and not in contemplation of imminent death.

good faith purchaser   A purchaser who buys without notice of any circumstance that would cause a person of ordinary prudence to inquire as to whether the seller has valid title to the goods being sold.

group boycott   The refusal of a group of competitors to deal with a particular person or firm.

guarantor   A third party who agrees to satisfy the debt of another (the debtor) only if and when the debtor fails to pay the debt.

H

hacker   A person who uses one computer to break into another.

holder in due course (HDC)   Any holder who, by meeting certain circumstances, takes a negotiable instrument free of most defenses and all claims.

holder   The person who, by the terms of a negotiable instrument, is legally entitled to payment on it.

holographic will   A will written entirely in the testator's handwriting and usually not witnessed.

homestead exemption   A law allowing an owner to designate his or her house and adjoining land as a homestead and thus exempt it from liability for his or her general debt.

I

identification   In the sale or lease of goods, the express designation of the goods provided for in the contract.

identity theft   The act of stealing another's identifying information and using that information to access the victim's financial resources.

implied contract   A contract formed in whole or in part from the conduct of the parties.

implied warranty   A warranty that the law implies through either the situation of the parties or the nature of the transaction.

implied warranty of fitness for a particular purpose   A warranty that arises when a seller knows the particular purpose for which a buyer will use the goods and knows that the buyer is relying on his or her skill and judgment to select suitable goods.

implied warranty of habitability   A presumed promise by the landlord that rented residential premises are fit for human habitation.

implied warranty of merchantability   A warranty by a merchant seller or lessor of goods that the goods are reasonably fit for the general purpose for which they are sold or leased.

impossibility of performance   A doctrine under which a party to a contract is relieved of the duty to perform when performance becomes impossible or totally impracticable.

imposter   A person who, with the intent to deceive, pretends to be somebody else.

incidental beneficiary   A third party who incidentally benefits from a contract but has no rights in it and cannot sue the promisor if it is breached.

incidental damages   Damages resulting from a breach of contract, including all reasonable expenses incurred because of the breach.

independent contractor   One who works for, and receives payment from, another (the principal) but whose working conditions and methods are not controlled by it.

indictment   A charge or formal accusation by a grand jury that a named person has committed a crime.

indorsement   A signature placed on an instrument for the purpose of transferring ownership rights in the instrument.

informal contract   A contract that does not require a specific form for its validity.

initial order   An administrative agency's disposition in a matter other than a rulemaking.

injunction   A court decree ordering a person to do or to refrain from doing a certain act.

insolvent   A condition in which a person cannot pay his or her debts as they become due or ceases to pay debts in the ordinary course of business.

installment contract   A contract in which payments due are made periodically.

insurable interest   A property interest in goods that is sufficiently substantial to permit a party to insure against damage to the goods. A substantial, financial interest either in a person's life or well-being or in property.

insurance   A contract in which, for a stipulated consideration, one party agrees to compensate the other for loss on a specific subject caused by a specified peril.

intangible property   Property that cannot be seen or touched but exists only conceptually (such as corporate stocks).

integrated contract   A written contract that constitutes the final expression of the parties' agreement.

intellectual property   Property resulting from intellectual, creative processes.

intended beneficiary   A third party for whose benefit a contract is formed and who can sue the promisor if it is breached.

intentional tort   A wrongful act knowingly committed.

intermediary bank   Any bank to which an item is transferred in the course of collection, except the depositary or payor bank.

international law   The law that governs relations among nations.

Internet service provider (ISP)   A business or organization that offers users access to the Internet and related services.

interrogatory   A series of written questions for which written answers are prepared and then signed under oath by the plaintiff or the defendant.

intestacy laws   State laws determining the descent and distribution of the property of one who dies intestate (without a will).

intestate   As a noun, one who has died without having created a valid will; as an adjective, without a will.

J

joint and several liability   A doctrine under which a plaintiff may sue, and collect a judgment from, any of several jointly liable defendants.

joint tenancy   Co-ownership of property in which each party owns an undivided portion of the property. On the death of one of the joint tenants, his or her interest automatically passes to the others.

jurisdiction The authority of a court to hear and decide a specific action.

L

larceny The wrongful taking and carrying away of another person's personal property with the intent to permanently deprive the owner of the property.

law A body of rules of conduct with legal force and effect, set forth by the government of a society.

lawsuit A judicial proceeding for the resolution of a dispute between parties in which rights are enforced or protected, wrongs are prevented or redressed, or public offenses are prosecuted.

lease A transfer of real property by a landlord to a tenant for a period of time for the payment of rent.

lease agreement An agreement in which one person (the lessor) agrees to transfer the right to the possession and use of the property or goods to another person (the lessee) in exchange for rental payments.

leasehold estate An estate held by a tenant under a lease. The tenant has a qualified right to possess and use the land.

legacy A gift of personal property by a will; also called a *bequest*.

legatee A person who inherits personal property under a will.

lessee A person who acquires the right to the possession and use of another's goods in exchange for rental payments.

lessor A person who transfers the right to the possession and use of goods to another in exchange for rental payments.

liability The state of being legally responsible (liable) for something, such as a debt or an obligation.

libel Defamation in written form.

license An agreement permitting the use of a trademark, patent, copyright, or trade secret for certain limited purposes. In real property law, a revocable privilege to enter onto another's land.

lien A claim against specific property to satisfy a debt or to protect a claim for debt payment.

life estate An interest in land that exists only for the duration of the life of some person.

limited liability company (LLC) A hybrid form of business enterprise that offers the limited liability of a corporation but the tax advantages of a partnership.

limited liability partnership (LLP) A form of partnership that allows professionals to enjoy the tax benefits of a partnership while limiting their personal liability for the malpractice of other partners.

limited partner A partner who contributes capital to the partnership but has no right to participate in the daily operations of the business.

limited partnership (LP) A partnership consisting of one or more general partners and one or more limited partners.

liquidated damages An amount, stipulated in a contract, that the parties to the contract believe to be a reasonable estimate of the damages that will occur in the event of a breach.

liquidation The sale of the assets of a business or an individual for cash and the distribution of the cash received to creditors, with the balance going to the owner(s).

living trust A trust created by a grantor (settlor) and effective during the grantor's lifetime.

long arm statute A state statute that permits a state to exercise jurisdiction over nonresident defendants.

lost property Property with which the owner has involuntarily parted and then cannot find or recover.

M

mailbox rule A rule providing that an acceptance of an offer becomes effective on dispatch.

maker One who issues a promissory note or certificate of deposit.

market concentration A situation that exists when a small number of firms share the market for a particular good or service.

market-share test The primary measure of monopoly power. A firm's market share is the percentage of the relevant market that the firm controls.

mechanic's lien A statutory lien on the real property of another created to ensure priority of payment for work performed.

mediation A method of settling disputes outside of court by using a neutral third party who acts as a communicating agent between the parties to help them negotiate a settlement.

merchant A person who is engaged in the purchase and sale of goods.

merger A process whereby one corporation acquires all the assets and liabilities of another corporation, which then ceases to exist.

metadata Data that are automatically recorded by electronic devices and provide information about who created a file and its history.

meta tag A key word used in online coding that gives Internet browsers specific information about a Web site, often increasing its frequency in search engine results.

minimum wage   The lowest hourly wage that an employer can legally pay an employee.

mirror image rule   A common law rule that requires, for a valid contractual agreement, that the terms of the offeree's acceptance adhere exactly to the terms of the offeror's offer.

misdemeanor   A lesser crime than a felony, usually punishable by a fine or imprisonment for up to one year.

mislaid property   Property that the owner has voluntarily parted with and then cannot find or recover.

mitigation of damages   A rule requiring a plaintiff to have done whatever was reasonable to minimize the damages caused by the defendant.

monopolization   The possession of monopoly power in the relevant market and the willful acquisition or maintenance of that power.

moral minimum   The minimum degree of ethical behavior expected of a business firm.

mortgage   A written document that gives the creditor (the mortgagee) an interest in, or lien on, the debtor's (mortgagor's) real property as security for a debt.

motion for a directed verdict   A motion for the judge to direct a verdict for the moving party on the ground that the other party has not produced sufficient evidence to support his or her claim.

motion to dismiss   A pleading in which a defendant admits the facts as alleged by the plaintiff but asserts that the plaintiff's claim has no basis in law.

N

necessaries   Necessities required for life, such as food, shelter, clothing, and medical attention.

negligence   The failure to exercise the standard of care that a reasonable person would exercise in similar circumstances.

negotiable instrument   A written and signed unconditional promise or order to pay a specified sum of money on demand or at a definite time to order (to a specific person or entity) or to bearer.

negotiation   A process in which parties attempt to settle their dispute without going to court, with or without attorneys to represent them. In the context of negotiable instruments, the transfer of a negotiable instrument to another in such form that the transferee becomes a holder.

normal-trade-relations (NTR) status   A status granted through an international treaty by which each member nation must treat other members at least as well as it treats the country that receives its most favorable treatment.

notice-and-comment rulemaking   A procedure in agency rulemaking that requires notice, an opportunity for comment, and a published draft of the final rule.

novation   The substitution, by agreement, of a new contract for an old one, with the rights under the old one being terminated.

O

objective theory of contracts   The view that contracting parties shall be bound only by terms that can objectively be inferred from promises made.

offer   A promise or commitment to perform or refrain from performing some specified act in the future.

offeree   A person to whom an offer is made.

offeror   A person who makes an offer.

online dispute resolution (ODR)   The resolution of disputes with the assistance of organizations that offer dispute-resolution services via the Internet.

operating agreement   In a limited liability company, an agreement in which members state how the details of the business will be managed and operated.

option contract   A contract under which the offeror cannot revoke his or her offer for a stipulated time period and the offeree can accept or reject the offer during this period.

order for relief   A court's grant of assistance to a complainant.

order instrument   A negotiable instrument that is payable "to the order of an identified person" or "to an identified person or order."

overdraft   A check written on a checking account in which there are insufficient funds to cover the check.

P

parol evidence rule   A rule of contracts under which a court will not receive into evidence oral statements that contradict a written agreement.

partially disclosed principal   A principal whose identity is unknown by a third person, but the third person knows that the agent is or may be acting for a principal at the time the contract is made.

partnership   An association of two or more persons to carry on, as co-owners, a business for profit.

partnership by estoppel   Partnership liability imposed by a court on those who have held themselves to be partners, even though they were not.

pass-through entity   A business entity that has no tax liability. The entity's income is passed through to the owners, and they pay taxes on the income.

past consideration   An act completed in the past, which ordinarily, by itself, cannot be consideration for a later promise to pay for the act.

patent A government grant that gives an inventor the exclusive right or privilege to make, use, or sell his or her invention for a limited time period.

payee A person to whom an instrument is made payable.

payor bank The bank on which a check is drawn (the drawee bank).

peer-to-peer (P2P) networking The sharing of resources (such as files, hard and flash drives, and processing styles) among multiple computers without the requirement of a central network server.

penalty A sum named in a contract as punishment for a default.

per capita A Latin term meaning "per person." A method of distributing the property of an intestate's estate by which all the heirs receive equal shares.

perfection The method by which a secured party obtains priority by notice that his or her security interest in the debtor's collateral is effective against the debtor's subsequent creditors.

performance The fulfillment of one's duties arising under a contract.

periodic tenancy A lease for an indefinite period involving payment of rent at fixed intervals.

per se violation A type of anticompetitive agreement that is considered to be so injurious to the public that there is no need to determine whether it actually injures market competition.

personal defense A defense that can be used to avoid payment to an ordinary holder of a negotiable instrument, but not to a holder in due course (HDC).

personal property Property that is movable; any property that is not real property.

per stirpes A Latin term meaning "by the roots." A method of distributing an intestate's estate in which a class or group of distributees take the share to which their deceased ancestor would have been entitled.

phishing An e-mail scam in which the message appears to be from a legitimate business to induce individuals to reveal personal financial data, passwords, or other information.

pierce the corporate veil To disregard the corporate entity and hold the shareholders personally liable for a corporate obligation.

plaintiff A person who initiates a lawsuit.

pleadings Statements by the plaintiff and the defendant that detail the facts, charges, and defenses of a case.

police powers Powers possessed by states as part of their inherent sovereignty.

policy In insurance law, the contract between the insurer and the insured.

power of attorney A document authorizing another to act as one's agent or attorney.

precedent A court decision that furnishes an example or authority for deciding subsequent cases involving identical or similar facts.

predatory pricing The pricing of a product below cost with the intent to drive competitors out of the market.

preemption A doctrine under which certain federal laws preempt, or take precedence over, conflicting state or local laws.

preemptive right A shareholder's right to purchase new shares of a corporation's stock—equal in percentage to shares already held—before the stock is offered to others.

preference In bankruptcy proceedings, the debtor's favoring of one creditor over others by making payments or transferring property to that creditor at the expense of the rights of other creditors.

preferred stock Classes of stock that have priority over common stock.

premium In insurance law, the price for insurance protection for a specified period of time.

prenuptial agreement An agreement entered into in contemplation of marriage, specifying the rights and ownership of the parties' property.

presentment warranty A warranty made by any person who presents an instrument for payment or acceptance.

price discrimination Setting prices in such a way that two competing buyers pay two different prices for an identical product or service.

price-fixing agreement An agreement between competitors to fix the prices of products or services at a certain level.

prima facie case A case in which the plaintiff has produced sufficient evidence to prove his or her conclusion if the defendant produces no evidence to rebut it.

principal A person who, by agreement or otherwise, authorizes an agent to act on his or her behalf in such a way that the acts of the agent become binding on the principal.

principle of rights The principle that human beings have certain fundamental rights. A key factor in determining whether an action is ethical is how it affects others' rights.

privilege In tort law, immunity from liability for an action that would otherwise be a tort.

privity of contract The relationship that exists between the promisor and the promisee of a contract.

probable cause Reasonable grounds for believing that a search will reveal a specific illegality.

probate court A court having jurisdiction over proceedings concerning the settlement of a person's estate.

proceeds   Whatever is received when collateral is sold, exchanged, collected, or disposed of.

product liability   The legal responsibility of manufacturers and sellers to buyers, users, and sometimes bystanders for injuries or damages suffered because of defects in goods.

profit   The right to enter onto and remove things from the property of another (for example, the right to enter onto a person's land and remove sand).

promise   A declaration that binds the person who makes it (promisor) to do or not to do a certain act.

promisee   A person to whom a promise is made.

promisor   A person who makes a promise.

promissory estoppel   A doctrine that can be used to enforce a promise when the promisee has justifiably relied on it, and justice will be better served by enforcing it.

promissory note   A written unconditional promise signed by a maker to pay a certain amount to a payee or a holder on demand or on a specified date.

protected class   A class of persons with identifiable characteristics, such as age, color, gender, national origin, race, and religion, who historically have been discriminated against.

proximate cause   Legal cause that exists when the connection between an act and an injury is strong enough to justify imposing liability.

proxy   A written agreement between a stockholder and another under which the stockholder authorizes the other to vote the stockholder's shares in a certain manner.

puffery   A salesperson's claims concerning the quality of property offered for sale. Such claims involve opinions rather than facts and are not legally binding promises or warranties.

punitive damages   Compensation in excess of actual or consequential damages awarded to punish the wrongdoer.

purchase-money security interest (PMSI)   The security interest that arises when a seller or lender extends credit for part or all of the purchase price of goods bought by a buyer.

Q

quasi contract   An obligation or contract imposed by law, in the absence of agreement, to prevent unjust enrichment.

quitclaim deed   A deed intended to pass any title, interest, or claim that the grantor may have in the premises but not professing that such title is valid and not containing any warranty.

quorum   The number of members of a decision-making body that must be present before business may be transacted.

quota   A set limit on the amount of goods that can be imported.

R

ratification   The confirmation by one person of an act or contract performed or entered into on his or her behalf by another.

real property   Land and everything attached to it, such as trees and buildings.

reformation   A court-ordered correction of a written contract so that it reflects the true intentions of the parties.

Regulation Z   A set of rules issued by the Federal Reserve System's Board of Governors to implement the provisions of the Truth-in-Lending Act.

release   An agreement in which one party gives up the right to pursue a legal claim against another party.

remedy   The relief given to innocent parties, by law or by contract, to enforce a right or to prevent or compensate for a wrong.

reorganization   A plan for the readjustment of a corporation and its debt, the submission of the plan to a bankruptcy court, and the court's approval or rejection of the plan.

resale price maintenance agreement   An agreement between a manufacturer and a distributor or retailer in which the manufacturer specifies what the retail prices of its products must be.

rescission   A remedy whereby a contract is terminated and the parties are returned to the positions they occupied before the contract was made.

respondeat superior   A principle of law whereby a principal or an employer is held liable for the wrongful acts committed by agents or employees acting within the scope of their agency or employment.

restitution   A remedy under which a person is restored to his or her original position prior to the formation of a contract.

restitution   The restoration of goods, property, or funds previously conveyed; necessary to rescind a contract.

restraint of trade   Any conspiracy or combination that unlawfully eliminates competition or facilitates the creation of a monopoly or monopoly pricing.

resulting trust   A trust implied in law from the intentions of the parties to a given transaction.

revocation   In contract law, the withdrawal of an offer by an offeror. Unless the offer is irrevocable, it can be revoked at any time before acceptance without liability.

right of contribution   The right of a co-surety who pays more than his or her proportionate share on a debtor's default to recover the excess paid from other co-sureties.

right of reimbursement   The legal right of a person to be restored, repaid, or indemnified for costs, expenses, or losses incurred or expended on behalf of another.

right of subrogation   The right of a person to stand in the place of (be substituted for) another, giving the substituted party the same legal rights that the original party had.

right-to-work law   State law generally providing that employees are not to be required to join a union as a condition of receiving or retaining employment.

risk   A specified contingency or peril.

risk management   Planning undertaken to protect one's interest should some event threaten to undermine its security.

robbery   The act of forcefully and unlawfully taking personal property of any value from another.

rulemaking   The actions undertaken by administrative agencies when formally adopting new regulations or amending old ones.

rule of reason   A test by which a court balances the reasons for an agreement against its potentially anticompetitive effects.

S

sale   The passing of title to property from the seller to the buyer for a price.

sale on approval   A conditional sale that becomes absolute only when the buyer approves, or is satisfied with, the goods sold.

sale or return   A conditional sale wherein title and possession pass from the seller to the buyer. The buyer, however, retains the option to rescind or return the goods during a specified period even though the goods conform to the contract.

sales contract   A contract to sell goods.

scienter   The knowledge by the misrepresenting party that material facts have been falsely represented or omitted with an intent to deceive.

S corporation   A business corporation that qualifies for special income tax treatment.

search warrant   An order from a judge or other public official that authorizes a search or seizure of particular property.

seasonably   Within a specified time period, or if no time is specified, within a reasonable time.

secured creditor   A lender or seller who has a security interest in collateral that secures a debt.

secured transaction   Any transaction in which the payment of a debt is guaranteed by personal property.

securities   Stock certificates and bonds given as evidence of an ownership interest in the corporation or as a promise of repayment by the corporation.

service mark   A mark used in the sale or advertising of services to distinguish the services of one person or company from the services of others.

sexual harassment   The demanding of sexual favors in return for job promotion or other benefits, or language or conduct that is so sexually offensive that it creates a hostile working environment.

shareholder's derivative suit   A suit brought by a shareholder to enforce a corporate cause of action against a third person.

shipment contract   A contract for the sale of goods in which the buyer assumes liability for any losses or damage to the goods on the seller's delivery of the goods to a carrier.

short-form merger   A merger that can be accomplished without the approval of the shareholders of either corporation.

shrink-wrap agreement   An agreement expressed on the inside or the outside of a box in which goods are packaged.

signature   Any name, word, or mark used with the intention to authenticate a writing.

slander   Defamation in oral form.

slander of quality   Publication of false information about another's product, alleging it is not what its seller claims; also referred to as *trade libel*.

slander of title   The publication of a statement that denies or casts doubt on another's legal ownership of any property, causing financial loss to that property's owner.

small claims court   A special inferior trial court in which parties litigate small claims (usually claims involving $2,500 or less).

smart card   A card containing a microprocessor used for financial transactions and identification.

social media   Forms of communication through which users create and share information, ideas, messages, and other content via the Internet.

sole proprietorship   The simplest form of business in which the owner is the business.

sovereign immunity　A doctrine that immunizes foreign nations from the jurisdiction of U.S. courts when certain conditions are satisfied.

spam　Bulk, unsolicited (junk) e-mail.

specific performance　An equitable remedy requiring exactly the performance that was specified in a contract.

stale check　A check that is presented for payment more than six months after its date.

standing to sue　The requirement that an individual have a sufficient stake in a controversy before he or she can bring a lawsuit.

stare decisis　A doctrine of the courts under which judges are obligated to follow the precedents established within their jurisdictions.

Statute of Frauds　A state statute under which certain types of contracts must be in writing to be enforceable.

statute of limitations　A statute setting the maximum time period during which a certain action can be brought.

statutory law　Laws enacted by a legislative body.

stock　An equity or ownership interest in a corporation that is measured in units of shares.

stock certificate　A certificate issued by a corporation evidencing the ownership of a specified number of shares.

stop-payment order　An order by the drawer of a draft or check directing the drawer's bank not to pay the check.

stored-value card　A card bearing a magnetic strip that holds magnetically encoded data, providing access to stored funds.

strict liability　Liability regardless of fault.

strike　An action undertaken by unionized workers when collective bargaining fails; the workers leave their jobs, refuse to work, and (typically) picket the employer's workplace.

sublease　A lease executed by the lessee of real estate to a third person, conveying the same interest that the lessee enjoys, but for a shorter term than that held by the lessee.

substantial government interest　A significant connection or concern of the government that is required to justify restrictions on commercial speech.

substitute check　A negotiable instrument that is a paper reproduction of the front and back of an original check, containing the same information required on checks for automated processing.

summary judgment　A judgment entered by a trial court before trial that is based on the valid assertion by one of the parties that there are no disputed issues of fact that would necessitate a trial.

supremacy clause　The provision in Article VI of the Constitution that the Constitution, laws, and treaties of the United States are "the supreme Law of the Land."

surety　A third party who agrees to be primarily responsible for the debt of another.

suretyship　A contract in which a third party to a debtor-creditor relationship (the surety) promises to be primarily responsible for the debtor's obligation.

symbolic speech　Nonverbal expressive conduct.

T

takeover　The acquisition of control over a corporation through the purchase of a substantial number of the voting shares of the corporation.

taking　The taking of private property by the government for public use and for just compensation.

tangible employment action　A significant change in employment status or benefit, such as occurs when an employee is fired, refused a promotion, or reassigned to a lesser position.

tangible property　Property that has physical existence (such as a car).

tariff　A tax on imported goods.

tenancy at sufferance　Tenancy by one who, after rightfully being in possession of leased premises, continues (wrongfully) to occupy the property after the lease has been terminated.

tenancy at will　A type of tenancy that either party can terminate without notice.

tenancy in common　Co-ownership of property in which each party owns an undivided interest that passes to his or her heirs at death.

tender　A timely offer or expression of willingness to pay a debt or perform an obligation.

tender of delivery　A seller's or lessor's act of placing conforming goods at the disposal of the buyer or lessee and providing whatever notification is reasonably necessary to enable the buyer or lessee to take delivery.

tender offer　An offer by the acquiring company directly to the shareholders of another company to buy those shareholders' voting shares.

testamentary trust　A trust that is created by will and therefore does not take effect until the death of the testator.

testator　One who makes and executes a will.

third party beneficiary　One who is not a party to a contract but for whose benefit a promise is made in the contract.

tort　A civil wrong not arising from a breach of contract.

tortfeasor　One who commits a tort.

trademark　A word, symbol, sound, or design that has become sufficiently associated with a good or has been registered with a government agency.

trade name A name used in commercial activity to designate a particular business.

trade secret Information or a process giving a business an advantage over competitors who do not know the information or process.

transfer warranty A guaranty made by any person who transfers a negotiable instrument for consideration to all subsequent transferees and holders who take the instrument in good faith.

treaty A formal written agreement negotiated between two or more nations.

trespass to land The entry onto, above, or below the surface of land owned by another without the owner's permission or legal authorization.

trespass to personal property The unlawful taking or harming of another's personal property; interference with another's right to the exclusive possession of his or her personal property.

trust An arrangement in which title to property is held by one person (a trustee) for the benefit of another (a beneficiary).

tying arrangement An agreement between a buyer and a seller under which the buyer of a specific product or service is obligated to purchase additional products or services from the seller.

typosquatting A form of cybersquatting that relies on mistakes, such as typographical errors, made by Internet users when inputting information into a Web browser.

U

ultra vires Activities of a corporation's managers that are outside the scope of the power granted them by the corporation's charter or the laws of the state of incorporation.

unconscionable contract or clause A contract or clause that is void because one party is forced to accept terms that are unfairly burdensome and that unfairly benefit the other party.

underwriter In insurance law, the one assuming a risk in return for the payment of a premium.

undisclosed principal A principal whose identity is unknown by a third person, and the third person has no knowledge that the agent is acting in an agency capacity at the time the contract is made.

undue influence Persuasion that is less than actual force but more than advice and that induces a person to act according to the will or purposes of the dominating party.

unenforceable contract A valid contract having no legal effect because of a statute or law.

unilateral contract A contract that includes the exchange of a promise for an act.

unilateral mistake A mistake that occurs when one party to a contract is mistaken as to a material fact.

union shop A place of employment in which all workers, once employed, must become union members within a specified period of time.

universal defense A defense that can be used to avoid payment to all holders of a negotiable instrument, including a holder in due course (HDC).

unreasonably dangerous Defective to the point of threatening a consumer's health or safety.

unsecured creditor A creditor whose debt is not backed by any collateral.

usage of trade Any practice or method of dealing having such regularity of observance in a place, vocation, or trade as to justify an expectation that it will be observed.

usury Charging an illegal rate of interest.

utilitarianism An approach to ethical reasoning in which an action is evaluated in terms of its consequences for those whom it will affect. A "good" action is one that results in the greatest good for the greatest number of people.

V

validation notice Notice to a debtor from a collection agency informing the debtor that he or she has thirty days to challenge the debt and to request verification.

valid contract A properly constituted contract having legal strength or force.

venture capital Financing provided by professional, outside investors (venture capitalists) to new business ventures.

vested The condition in which rights have taken effect and cannot be taken away.

voidable contract A contract that may be legally avoided at the option of one of the parties.

void contract A contract having no legal force or binding effect.

voluntary consent The knowledge of, and genuine assent to, the terms of a contract.

W

warranty deed A deed under which the grantor provides a number of guarantees to the grantee concerning title.

waste The abuse or destructive use of real property by someone who is in rightful possession of the property but does not hold title to it.

whistleblower An employee who tells the government or the media that his or her employer is engaged in some unsafe or illegal activity.

white-collar crime Nonviolent crime committed by individuals or corporations to obtain a personal or business advantage.

will   An instrument directing what is to be done with the testator's property on his or her death, made by the testator.

winding up   The last stage of dissolution of a partnership, in which the firm collects and distributes assets and discharges liabilities.

workers' compensation laws   State statutes establishing an administrative procedure for compensating workers for injuries that arise on the job or in the course of their employment, regardless of fault.

writ of attachment   A writ used to enforce obedience to an order or judgment of the court.

writ of *certiorari*   A writ from a higher court asking the lower court for the record of a case.

writ of execution   A writ that puts in force a court's decree or judgment.

Table of Cases

For your convenience and reference, here is a list of all the cases mentioned in this text. The cases in the *Real-World Case Examples* for each chapter are given special emphasis by having their titles appear in **boldface**.

A

Absolute Trading Corp. v. Bariven S.A., 286
Aceves v. U.S. Bank, 154
Adams Associates, LLC v. Frank Pasquale Limited Partnership, 27
Air Products and Chemicals, Inc. v. Airgas, Inc., 424
Aleris International, Ltd., *In re*, 258
Alexander v. Lafayette Crime Stoppers, Inc., 143
Allan v. Nersesova, 213
Allied Concrete Co. v. Lester, 46
Allied Erecting and Dismantling Co. v. Genesis Equipment & Manufacturing, Inc., 27
Alpacas of America, LLC v. Groome, 308–309
Already, LLC v. Nike, Inc., 151
American Civil Liberties Union of Ohio Foundation, Inc. v. DeWeese, 61
Application of the United States of America for an Order Pursuant to 18 U.S.C. Section 2703(d), *In re*, 104
Ashley County, Arkansas v. Pfizer, Inc., 27
Austin Rare Coins, Inc. v. Acoins.com, 103

B

Baker v. Walnut Bowls, Inc., 513
Balboa Island Village Inn, Inc. v. Lemen, 62
Ballard v. Chicago Park District, 369–370
Barclays Bank PLC v. Poynter, 450
Batson v. Live Nation Entertainment, Inc., 570
Bell Helicopter Textron Inc. v. Islamic Republic of Iran, 591
Benjamin v. JPMorgan Chase Bank, 545
Bishop v. Housing Authority of South Bend, 176
Blackford v. Prairie Meadows Racetrack and Casino, 143

Blackwell Publishing, Inc. v. Custom Copies, Inc., 90
Bluewater Logistics, LLC v. Williford, 408
Boles v. Sun Ergoline, Inc., 286
Bowen v. Gardner, 244
Brantley v. NBC Universal, Inc., 575
Braunstein v. Russo, 346
Breeden v. Buchanan, 489
Brooks v. Transamerica Financial Advisors, 346
Brothers v. Winstead, 39
Brown & Brown, Inc. v. Johnson, 171
B-Sharp Musical Productions, Inc. v. Haber, 229
B.S. International, Ltd. v. JMAM, LLC, 244
Byrd v. Maricopa County Sheriff's Department, 118

C

Call Center Technologies, Inc. v. Grand Adventures Tour & Travel Publishing Corp., 424
Capitol Records, Inc. v. Thomas-Rasset, 103
Carmichael, *In re*, 330
Case v. Sink & Rise, Inc., 432
Cayer v. Cox Rhode Island Telecom, LLC, 362
Center Capital Corp. v. PRA Aviation, LLC, 450
Charles Downey Family Limited Partnership v. S&V Liquor, Inc., 531
Chase Bank USA, N.A. v. McCoy, 300
Citizens United v. Federal Election Committee, 53
Cleary v. Philip Morris USA, Inc., 300
Cohen v. Seinfeld, 229
Coleman v. Retina Consultants, 176
Community Bank & Trust v. Koenig & Vits, Inc., 462
Country Contractors, Inc. v. A Westside Storage of Indianapolis, Inc., 436
Covenant Health & Rehabilitation of Picayune, LP v. Lumpkin, 46

Crilow v. Wright, 142
Cronkelton v. Guaranteed Construction Services, LLC, 183
Curves for Women Angola v. Flying Cat, LLC, 408

D

Daimler AG v. Bauman, 587
Dawson v. Entek International, 392
Dayton Superior Corp. v. Spa Steel Products, Inc., 575
DeRosier v. Utility Systems of America, Inc., 271
Desgro v. Pack, 176
Deters v. USF Insurance Co., 489
Deutsche Bank National Trust Co. v. Brock, 316
Dobrovolny v. Ford Motor Co., 286
Doe 1 v. AOL, LLC, 12
Dog House Investments, LLC v. Teal Properties, Inc., 414
Drury v. Assisted Living Concepts, Inc., 165
Durkee v. Geologic Solutions, Inc., 286
Dweck v. Nasser, 436
Dynea USA, Inc. v. Fairbanks, 376

E

E.I. du Pont de Nemours and Co. v. Kolon Industries, Inc., 575
Erb Poultry, Inc. v. CEME, LLC, 271
Estate v. _____. *See name of party*
Experience Hendrix, LLC v. Hendrixlicensing.com, Ltd., 6–7

F

Faden v. Merit Systems Protection Board, 46
Family Winemakers of California v. Jenkins, 12
Farhang v. Indian Institute of Technology, 590
Federal Communications Commission v. Fox Television Stations, 562

Federal Trade Commission v. Ross, Inc., 300

Felix Storch Inc. v. Martinucci Desserts USA, Inc., 362

Flint Hills Resources LP v. Jag Energy, Inc., 271

Foley v. Grigg, 214

Fox & Lamberth Enterprises, Inc. v. Craftsmen Home Improvement, Inc., 244

G

Garrigus v. Viarengo, 545

Garziano v. Louisiana Log Home Co., 262

Gianelli, *In re*, 90

Glass, *In re*, 26

GoJets Airlines, LLC v. Federal Aviation Administration, 561

Goldberg v. UBS AG, 12

Gray v. Moreland, 505

Green, State of New York v., 118

Gyabaah v. Rivlab Transportation Corp., 135

H

Hall, United States v., 61

Hanjuan Jin, United States v., 90

Hann, *In re*, 477

Harman v. McAfee, 477

Hassan, United States v., 104

Havensure, LLC v. Prudential Insurance Co. of America, 27

Hemsley, Estate of, *In re*, 545

Henderson v. National Railroad Passenger Corp., 78

Henrichs v. Chugach Alaska Corp., 436

Hibbard v. McMillan, 143

Horn v. Knight Facilities Management–GM, Inc., 392

HSBC Realty Credit Corp. (USA) v. O'Neill, 456

Humble v. Wyant, 228

Hunter v. Mansell, 519

I

Inhale, Inc. v. Starbuzz Tobacco, Inc., 85

In re _____. See name of party

J

Jeanmarie v. Peoples, 330

Jensen v. International Business Machines Corp., 130

Jones v. Wells Fargo Bank, 346

J. T. v. Monster Mountain, LLC, 165

K

Kahala Franchise Corp. v. Hit Enterprises, LLC, 330

Kailin v. Armstrong, 532

Kazery v. Wilkinson, 213

Kemper v. Brown, 142

Kincaid v. Dess, 213

Koerner v. Nielsen, 505

Kolodin v. Valenti, 221

L

LabMD, Inc. v. Tiversa, Inc., 104

Lake County Grading Co. v. Village of Antioch, 208–209

Landmark HHH, LLC v. Gi Hwa Park, 531

Lexmark International, Inc. v. Static Control Components, Inc., 291

Lhotka v. Geographic Expeditions, Inc., 176

Loving v. Internal Revenue Service, 556

Lynwood Place, LLC v. Sandy Hook Hydro, LLC, 525

M

Main Avenue, LLC v. PP Door Enterprise Inc., 462

Manin v. National Transportation Safety Board, 562

Marcum, State of Oklahoma v., 110

Marriage of Tuttle, *In re*, 199

Marucci Sports, LLC v. National Collegiate Athletic Association, 575

Maxwell's Pic-Pac, Inc. v. Dehner, 57

May v. Chrysler Group, LLC, 12

McCann v. McCann, 436

Medical Protective Co. v. Bubenik, 490

Medtronic, Inc. v. Hughes, 78

Mekonen v. Zewdu, 405

Miller v. Miller, 130

Mills v. Chauvin, 327–328

Moore v. Moore, 362

Moran v. Willensky, 408

N

National Football League Players Association v. National Football League Management Council, 46

National Liability & Fire Insurance Co. v. R&R Marine, Inc., 502

Nationwide Mutual Insurance Co. v. Wood, 164

Nautilus Insurance Co. v. Cheran Investments LLC, 235

Newmark & Co. Real Estate Inc. v. 2615 East 17 Street Realty, LLC, 199

Northpoint Properties, Inc. v. Charter One Bank, 186

NXCESS Motor Cars, Inc. v. JPMorgan Chase Bank, N.A., 450

NYKCool A.B. v. Pacific Fruit, Inc., 193

O

Oakley Fertilizer, Inc. v. Continental Insurance Co., 244

Omole, United States v., 118

OneBeacon Insurance Co. v. Haas Industries, Inc., 258

P

PAK Foods Houston, LLC. v. Garcia, 158

Panenka v. Panenka, 130

Pan Handle Realty, LLC v. Olins, 123

Parker v. Williams, 200

Patterson v. Suntrust Bank, 346

PEMS Co. International, Inc. v. Temp-Air, Inc., 176

People v. _____. See name of opposing party

Person v. Bowman, 251

Pervis, *In re*, 186

Philadelphia Indemnity Insurance Co. v. Farrington, 489

Planned Pethood Plus, Inc. v. KeyCorp, Inc., 229

R

Ramirez v. Reemployment Assistance Appeals Commission, 376

Ramsey v. Allstate Insurance Co., 130

Rangel v. Sanofi Aventis U.S., LLC, 392

Rawls v. Progressive Northern Insurance Co., 78

Reger Development, LLC v. National City Bank, 316

Richman v. Hartley, 519

Riley v. F. A. Richards & Associates, 165

Riley v. Ford Motor Co., 282

Roberts v. Mike's Trucking, Ltd., 385

Rosenzweig v. Givens, 186

Royal Arcanum Hospital Association of Kings County, Inc. v. Herrnkind, 334

Royal & Sun Alliance Insurance, PLC v. International Management Services Co., 258

RR Maloan Investments, Inc. v. New HGE, Inc., 330

S

Sacco v. Paxton, 408

Scarborough v. Rollins, 519

Scott v. Carpanzano, 18

SDBC Holdings, Inc. v. National Labor Relations Board, 376
Sexton, *In re*, 477
Shankle, *In re*, 477
Sharabianlou v. Karp, 154
Simkin v. Blank, 186
Simpson, United States v., 118
Singletary, III v. P&A Investments, Inc., 258
Sisuphan, People v., 118
Smith Kline Beecham Corp. v. Abbott Laboratories, 61
Smith v. Firstbank Corp., 447
Smith v. Johnson and Johnson, 377
Snapp v. Castlebrook Builders, Inc., 424
Sniezek v. Kansas City Chiefs Football Club, 154
Southern Prestige Industries, Inc. v. Independence Plating Corp., 46
Spectrum Stores, Inc. v. Citgo Petroleum Corp., 591
State v. _____. *See name of opposing party*
Stonhard, Inc. v. Blue Ridge Farms, LLC, 357
Succession of Sirgo, *In re*, 537

T

Taser International, Inc. v. Ward, 362
Testa v. Ground Systems, Inc., 228
Town of Midland v. Morris, 519
Tri-Lin Holdings, LLC v. Flawlace, LLC, 531

U

UMG Recordings, Inc. v. Augusto, 90
Union Bank Co. v. Heban, 450
United Fabrics International, Inc. v. C & J Wear, Inc., 90
United States v. _____. *See name of opposing party*
United Technologies Corp. v. U.S. Department of Defense, 562
U.S. Bank National Association v. Gaitan, 315

V

Vinueza v. Scotto, 316

W

Walker, Estate of, *In re*, 545
Wasniewski v. Quick and Reilly, Inc., 505

Watkins v. Schexnider, 199
Welco Electronics, Inc. v. Mora, 72
Welsh, *In re*, 474
Western Surety Co. v. APAC-Southeast, Inc., 213
Western World Insurance Co. v. Hoey, 485
Wind Tower Trade Coalition v. United States, 590
Wood Care Centers, Inc. v. Evangel Temple Assembly of God of Wichita Falls, 199
Wooden, State v., 61
Woodridge USA Properties, LP v. Southeast Trailer Mart, Inc., 271

Y

Yelp v. Hadeed Carpet Cleaning, 99

Z

Zhang v. Tse, 462
Zurenda v. Zurenda, 164

A

Abandoned property, 500
Abatement, 536
Abuse of process, 70
Abusive litigation, 70
Acceptance
  authorized means of, 139
  communication of, 138–139, 237–238
  conditioned on offeror's assent, 239
  contractual, 138–139
  defined, 138
  of delivered goods, 265
  deposited acceptance rule, 138
  drafts and checks, 305
  e-contract, 139–140
  of gifts, 497
  lease contracts, 237–239
  mailbox rule, 138–139
  methods of, 237–238
  mirror image rule, 137, 138, 238
  mode of, 138–139
  notice of, 238
  online for e-contracts, 139–140
  as requirement of contract, 123
  requirements of, 138–139
  revocation of, 265
  sales contracts, 237–239
  silence as, 138
  substitute means of, 139
  timeliness of, 138
  trade acceptance, 305
  unequivocal, 138
Acceptor, 322
Accession, 498
  bad and good faith, 498
Accommodation, nonconforming goods
    shipped as, 238
Accord, satisfaction and, 150, 220
Accounting
  agent's duty to, 353
  managerial, 24–25
  of partnership assets or profits, 399
  requirements to prevent bribes of
    foreign officials, 24
  Sarbanes-Oxley Act and, 17
Action, 5
Act(s)
  authorized and unauthorized, by agent,
    356
  promise for, 124
  of state doctrine, 580
Actual (express or implied) authority,
    354–355
Actual malice, 69
Adequacy of consideration, 148
Adhesion contract, 172

Adjudication, 554–555
Adjustable-rate mortgage, 459
Administrative agencies
  adjudication, 554–555
  agency orders, 555
  arbitrary and capricious test, 557
  creation of, 550–551
  defined, 8, 550
  enabling legislation, 550–551
  executive agencies, 551
  formal complaints, 555, 556
  independent regulatory agencies,
    551–552
  investigation, 553–554
  negotiated settlements, 555
  powers of, 555–557
  public accountability, 558
  rulemaking, 552–553
  social media and, 98
  types of, 551–552
Administrative employees, overtime
    wages, 370–371
Administrative law
  defined, 8, 550
  as source of American law, 5, 8
Administrative law judge (ALJ), role of, 555
Administrative Procedure Act (APA), 552,
    555, 557
Administrator, 535
Admission
  exception to Statute of Frauds, 193
  oral contract and, 240
  request for, 40
Advances, future, 444
Adverse possession, 515–516
Advertisements
  bait-and-switch advertising, 290
  based on half-truths, 290
  clear and conspicuous disclosure,
    290–291
  counteradvertising, 291
  deceptive advertising, 289–291
  FTC actions, 291
  as invitation to negotiate, 134
  Lanham Act and false advertising
    claims, 291
  online deceptive, 290–291
  protections under First Amendment, 53
  puffery, 289
Affidavit, 454
Affirmation, express warranty and, 276
Affirmed judgment, 41
After-acquired property, 443–444
Age
  discrimination based, 386–387
  of majority, 157

misrepresentation of, and
    disaffirmance, 159
replacing older workers with
    younger, 387
Age Discrimination in Employment Act
    (ADEA), 588
  procedures under, 387
  replacing older workers with
    younger, 387
  state employees not covered by, 387
Agency relationship, 350–360
  agent's authority
    apparent, 355
    express, 354–355
    implied, 355
    ratification, 355–356
  bank-customer relationship as, 334
  coupled with an interest, 358
  defined, 350
  duties in, 353–354
  employer-employee relationships, 350
  employer-independent contractor
    relationships, 351
  employment status determination, 351
  equal dignity rule, 351
  with foreign firm, 581
  formation of, 351–352
    by agreement, 351–352
    contractual capacity and, 351
    by estoppel, 352
    by operation of law, 352
    by ratification, 352
    writing requirement exceptions, 351
  liability in
    for contracts, 356–357
    for torts, 357
  partners, 400
  partnership and, 397
  termination of, 357–359
Agents
  acts of
    authorized, 356
    unauthorized, 356
  authority of
    apparent, 355
    equal dignity rule, 354
    express, 354–355
    implied, 355
    power of attorney, 355
    ratification, 355–356
  bankruptcy, agency termination and,
    359
  corporate officers and directors as, 429
  of corporation, 350
  death or insanity, agency termination
    and, 358

Agents (*continued*)
  defined, 350
  duties of
    accounting, 353
    loyalty, 353
    notification, 353
    obedience, 353
    performance, 353
    to principal, 353
  insurance agent, 481–482
  principal's duties to, 354
  termination of agency, 357–359
  torts of, 357
Agreements
  acceptance, 138–140
  agency formation by, 351–352
  click-on agreement, 140
  contract discharge by, 219–220
  contractual, 123, 133–141
  creditors' composition, 455
  as element of bailment, 501
  lease, 236
  noncompete, 150
  offer requirement, 133–135
  offer termination, 136–137
  partnership by, 398
  prenuptial agreement, 192
  price-fixing, 567
  as requirement of contract, 123
  resale price maintenance
      agreement, 566
  shrink-wrap agreement, 140
  that lack consideration, 148–149
Airspace rights, 510
Alien corporation, 411
Alien Tort Claims Act (ATCA), 587
Alternative dispute resolution (ADR)
  advantages of, 42
  arbitration, 43
  defined, 42
  mediation, 43
  negotiation, 42
  online dispute resolution (ODR), 44
Ambiguous terms, 195
America Invents Act, 84
Americans with Disabilities Act
      (ADA), 588
  disability defined, 388
  procedures under, 388–389
  reasonable accommodations, 389
Answer, 38
Anticipatory repudiation, 266
Anti-Counterfeiting Trade Agreement
      (ACTA), 87
Anticybersquatting Consumer Protection
      Act (ACPA), 94
Antidumping duty, 585
Antilapse clause, 485
Antitrust law, 565–573
  Clayton Act, 569–571
  defined, 565
  enforcement of, 571–572
  exclusionary practices, 570
  exemptions from, 571–572
  extraterritorial application of, 572
  global context and, 586–587
  global context for, 572–573

group boycott, 567
  historical perspective on, 565
  market divisions, 567
  mergers, 571
  monopolization, 567–569
  per se violations and rule of reason,
      566–567
  predatory pricing, 567
  price discrimination, 570
  price-fixing agreement, 567
  restraints of trade and, 565
  Sherman Antitrust Act, 565–569
Apparent authority, 355
Appeals
  filing, 41
  process of, in lawsuit, 41
Appellant, appellee, 41
Appellate (reviewing) courts
  federal, 34–36
  final review, 41
  state, 33–34
  types of rulings, 41
Apple Pay, 333
Appraisal clause, 485
Appraisal rights, 418–419
Appropriation, 69
Arbitrary and capricious test, 557
Arbitrary trademark, 82
Arbitration
  award, 43
  nonbinding, 43
Arbitration clause, 485
Arbitration clauses, 583
Arbitrator, 43
Aristotle, 2
Articles of incorporation
  defined, 413
  filing, 413
  preparing, 413
Articles of organization, formation of
      LLC and, 404
Articles of partnership, 398
Artisan's lien, 454
Assault, 67
Assets
  accounting of, in partnerships, 399
  distribution of
    in partnership dissolution, 403
    purchase of, and merger/consolidation,
      419
Assignment, 203–206
  of all rights, 208
  defined, 203
  effect of, 204
  extinguished rights, 204
  of lease, 528
  notice of, 205–206
  rights that cannot be assigned, 205
  transfer of negotiable instruments
      by, 311
  uses of, 204
Assignor, assignee, 204
Assumption of risk defense, 75
  to product liability, 282
Assurance
  merchant's firm offer, 237
  right of, 264–265

Attachment
  defined, 454
  in security transaction, 441
  writ of, 454
Auctions
  contractual offers versus, 134–135
  as invitation to bid, 134–135
  online, 135
  with and without reserve, 134–135
Authority
  actual, 354
  of agent, 355–356
  apparent, 355
  equal dignity rule, 354
  express, 354–355
  implied, 355
Authorization card, 372
Automated teller machines (ATMs)
  as electronic fund transfer, 341
Automatic stay, 468
Automobile insurance, 483
Award, in arbitration, 43

B

Bad faith
  accession and, 498
  insurance policy payment and, 487
Bailee
  defined, 252, 500
  goods held by, 253
  rights and duties of, 501–503
Bailment
  constructive, 501
  creation of, 500
  defined, 500
  elements of
    agreement, 501
    delivery of possession, 501
    personal property requirement, 501
  involuntary, 501
  rights and duties of bailee, 501–503
  types of, 502
Bailor, 500
Bait-and-switch advertising, 290
Bankruptcy, 465–475
  agency termination and, 359
  automatic stay, 468
  courts, 465
  cram-down provision, 473
  credit counseling and, 467
  creditors' claims, 470–471
  creditors' committees, 472
  creditors' meeting, 468–469
  as defense to surety/guarantor, 457
  discharge in, 466, 471–472, 473, 475
  distribution of property in, 470–471
  estate in property, 469
  exemptions in, 470
  fraudulent transfers, 469
  involuntary, 468
  law governing, 465
  liquidation proceedings, 466–472
  means test, 467
  order for relief, 467
  ordinary, 466
  petition in, 466–467

preferences in, 470
reorganizations, 372–373, 472–473
straight, 466
trustee in, 469–470
as universal defense, 327
voluntary, 466–467
Bankruptcy Code
Chapter 7 of (liquidation proceedings), 466–472
Chapter 11 of (reorganization), 466, 472–473
Chapter 13 of (adjustment of debts by individuals), 466, 473–475
comparison of, 466
defined, 465
Bankruptcy trustee, 469–470
Banks
accepting deposits in check-collection process
check clearing and Check 21 Act, 339–341
traditional process, 337–339
bank-customer relationship, 334
banking risks, 344
collecting bank, 337
correspondent bank, 584
deposit insurance, 344
depository bank, 337
electronic funds transfers, 341–342
e-money, 342–343
honoring checks, 334–337
intermediary bank, 337
online banking, 343
payor bank, 337
Bargained-for exchange, 148
Bargaining unit, 373
Basis of bargain, 276
Battery, 67
Bearable instrument, 311
negotiating, 312
Bearer
defined, 306
payable to, 310–311
Benchmarking, 284
Beneficiary
creditor, 209
defined, 208
donee, 209
incidental, 209–210
insurance and, 481
intended, 208–209
third party, 203, 208–210
Benefit corporation, 412
Bentham, Jeremy, 20
Bequest, 536
Berne Convention, 87
Beyond a reasonable doubt, 107–108
Bilateral contracts, 124
Bilateral (mutual) mistake, 180–181
Bill of lading, 249, 253
Bill of Rights. See also individual amendments
business and, 52–55
defined, 52
freedom of religion, 54–55
freedom of speech, 53–54

limits of federal and state actions, 52–55
summary of, 52
Binder, 484
Blackstone, William, 2
Blank indorsement, 312
Blue sky law, 174
Board of directors. See Directors, corporate
Bona fide occupational qualification (BFOQ), 389
Bond indenture, 416
Bonds
defined, 416
maturity date, 416
securities fraud, 113
Breach, 3
Breach of contract
damages for, 222–226
defined, 217
material, 218
as personal defense, 327
sales or lease
remedies for, 266–269
risk of loss, 254
statute of limitations and, 220
Bribes/bribery
commercial bribery, 112
of foreign officials, 23, 112–113, 586
of public officials, 112
as white-collar crime, 112
Brief, 41
Broker
insurance, 481–482
Burden of proof, civil law compared to criminal law, 107–108
Businesses
Bill of Rights and, 52–55
crimes affecting, 110–113
search and seizure, 109
wrongful interference with, 70–71
Business ethics, 15–27. See also Ethics
codes of conduct, 16
conflicts and trade-offs, 17
corporate compliance program, 16–17
corporate social responsibility, 21–22
defined, 15
duty-based ethics, 19–20
ethical leadership, 16
Foreign Corrupt Practices Act, 22–23
on global level, 22–23
importance of, 15
international business and, 22–230–92
laws and relationship to, 17–18
monitoring practice of foreign suppliers, 22–23
moral minimum, 17
outcome-based ethics, 20–21
regulations and, 18
Sarbanes-Oxley Act, 17
setting right ethical tone, 16–17
social media and, 22
Business invitee, 74
Business judgment rule, 430
Business necessity, as defense to employment discrimination, 389
Business organization
choosing best form, 406

limited liability company, 404–405
limited liability partnership, 404
limited partnership, 403–404
partnerships, 397–403
sole proprietorship, 396–397
Business torts, 70–71
Buyer
breach of contract, and risk of loss, 254
insurable interest of, 255
obligation of, 265
in the ordinary course of business, 445–446
remedies for, 267–269
Bylaws, 413

C

Capacity, contractual, 123, 157–163
defined, 157
intoxicated persons, 160–161, 163
mentally incompetent persons, 161–162
minors and, 157–160, 162–163
Capper-Volstead Act, 572
Care
due
product liability, 280
duty of
bailees, 502, 503
breach of, 73–74
corporate directors, 429
corporate officers, 429
defined, 73
partnerships, 400
reasonable care of collateral, 446
reasonable person standard, 73
Carrier
delivery via, 262–263
substitution of, 263
Carrier cases, 251–252
Case law
common law doctrine and, 7
defined, 7
Cashier's check, 305–306, 333
Categorical imperative, 20
Causation
in fact, 74–75
foreseeability, 75
legal cause, 75
negligence and, 74–75
proximate cause, 74–75
Cause of action, 6
Cease-and-desist order, 291
Central America–Dominican Republic–United States Free Trade Agreement (CAFTA-DR), 586
Certificate of deposit (CD)
defined, 306
as negotiable instrument, 307
Certificate of limited partnership, 404
Certified check, 334
Chancellor, 6
Chapter 7 (liquidation proceedings)
automatic stay, 468
credit counseling and, 467
creditors' meeting, 468–469
discharge in, 471–472

Chapter 7 (liquidation proceedings) (continued)
estate in property, 469
exemptions in, 470
fraudulent transfers, 469
grounds for dismissal, 467
involuntary bankruptcy, 468
means test, 467
order for relief, 467
preferences in, 470
property distribution, 470–471
schedules of, 467
trustee in, 469–470
voluntary bankruptcy, 466–467
Chapter 11 (reorganization)
cram-down provision, 473
creditors' committees, 472
reorganization plan, 472–473
Chapter 13 (adjustment of debts by individuals)
discharge in, 475
filing petition, 473
good faith requirement, 474
purchase-money security interest (PMSI), 474
repayment plan, 473–474
Charitable institutions
involuntary bankruptcy, 468
Check Clearing in the 21st Century Act (Check 21), 339–341
Checks, 333–344
accepting deposits in check-collection process
check clearing and Check 21 Act, 339–341
between customers of different banks, 339
between customers of same bank, 338
electronic presentment, 339
Federal Reserve System clears checks, 339
substitute check, 339–341
traditional collection process, 337–339
bank-customer relationship, 334
bank honoring, 334–337
checks with forged indorsements, 337
checks with forged signatures, 336–337
death or incompetence of customer, 335
overdrafts, 335
stale checks, 335
stop-payment orders, 335–336
cashier's check, 305–306, 333
certified check, 334
defined, 333
drawn in blank, 313–314
as negotiable instrument, 304, 307
payable to cash, 314
substitute check, 339–341
as type of draft, 305–306
writing and indorsing, 313–314
Checks and balances, 50
administrative agencies and, 556

Chick-fil-A restaurant chain, 15
Child labor, 370
Child Protection and Toy Safety Act, 297
Children
intestacy and, 540
revocation of will, 539
Children's Internet Protection Act (CIPA), 54
Choice-of-language clause, 582
Choice-of-law clause, 583
Cicero, 2
C.I.F. or C.&F. (cost, insurance, and freight or just cost and freight), 252
Civil law
burden of proof, 107–108
compared to criminal law, 8–9, 107, 108
defined, 8
Civil Rights Act of 1964, 588
Title VII, 381–386
Claims
accord and satisfaction, 150
covenant not to sue, 151
proof of, 469
release, 151
settlement of, 150–151
Class Action Fairness Act (CAFA), 66
Class-action lawsuits, 66
Clayton Act, 569–571, 572
exclusionary practices, 570
mergers, 571
price discrimination, 570
Clean Air Act (CAA), 557
Clear and conspicuous disclosure, 290–291
Click-on agreement, 140
Close corporation
defined, 412
oppressive conduct, 434
Closed shop, 372
Closing argument, 41
Cloud computing, 97
Coca-Cola Bottling Company, 581
Code law, 9
Code of Federal Regulations (CFR), 553
Codes of conduct, 16
Codicil, 538
Collateral
attachment, 441
bankruptcy property distribution and, 471
defined, 440
disposition of, 447–448
deficiency judgment, 448
proceeds from, 448
redemption rights, 448
peaceful possession of, 446
proceeds of sale of, 443
reasonable care of, 446
repossession of, 446
retention of, 447
surrender of, to release surety/guarantor, 458
Collateral heirs, 539
Collateral promise, 191–192
Collecting bank, 337
Collective bargaining, 373–374

Color, discrimination based on, 383
Comity, of principle, 579–580
Comment period
in rulemaking, 552–553
Commerce, Department of, 551
Commerce clause
dormant commerce clause, 51
national powers, 50
regulatory powers of states, 50–51
Commercial bribes, 112
Commercial impracticability, 221, 264
Commercial reasonableness
UCC and, 261
Commercial speech, 53
Commercial wire transfers, 342
Commingled interests, 414
Common law
acceptance and, 237, 238
artisan's lien, 454
defined, 5
employment-at-will doctrine, 365
restraints of trade and, 565
as source of American law, 4–7, 31
stare decisis, 5
today, 7
tradition of, 5–7
Commonly known dangers defense, 283
Common stock, 416
Communication
of acceptance, 138–139, 237–238
of offer, 135
privileged communication and defamation, 69
stored electronic, 101
Communications Decency Act (CDA), 99–100
Community property, 469, 496
Comparative negligence, 67, 75–76
as defense to product liability, 283
Compensation
principal's duty of, 354
Compensatory damages, 222–223
Competitive practices, 70
Complaint
defined, 37–38
elements of, 37
formal, in administrative law, 555, 556
Complete performance, 218
Compliance program
for ethical codes of conduct, 16–17
Composition agreements, 455
Computer crime, 114. See also Cyber crimes
Computer Fraud and Abuse Act (CFAA), 115
Computer Software Copyright Act, 86
Concurrent jurisdiction, 36
Concurrent ownership, 495–496
Condemnation power, 516–517
Conduct
code of, 16
in implied contract, 125
misrepresentation by, 182
Confederate form of government, 49
Confessions, constitutional rights and, 110
Confiscation, 580, 584–585

Conflicts of interest, corporate officers
   and directors, 430
Conforming goods, 261
Confusion, 498
Congress
   control over administrative
      agencies, 556
   enabling legislation, 550–551
   taxing and spending powers, 51–52
Consent
   as defense to intentional tort, 66–67
   voluntary, 124
Consequential damages, 223
Consideration
   adequacy of, 148
   bargained-for exchange, 148
   defined, 147
   elements of, 147–148
   illusory promises, 150
   lack or failure of
      as personal defense, 327
   lease contracts, 239
   legally sufficient value, 147
   noncompete agreement and, 150
   option-to-cancel clauses, 150
   past consideration, 149–150
   preexisting duty, 148–149
   problems with, 150–152
   promissory estoppel, 151–152
   as requirement of contract, 123
   rescission and new contract, 149
   sales contracts, 239
   settlement of claims, 150–151
   unforeseen difficulties and, 149
Consistent additional terms, 241
Consolidated Omnibus Budget
      Reconciliation Act (COBRA),
      368–369
Consolidations
   appraisal rights, 418–419
   defined, 417
   procedure for, 418
   purchase of assets, 419
   purchase of stocks, 419–420
   shareholder approval and, 419
Constitution, states, 7
   as primary source of law, 31
Constitutional Convention, 49
Constitutional law. See also United States
      Constitution
   as source of American law, 4–5, 7
Constructive bailments, 501
Constructive delivery, 497, 501
Constructive discharge, 384
Constructive eviction, 526
Constructive trust, 542–543
Consumer-debtor
   defined, 465
   special bankruptcy requirements
      for, 466
Consumer Financial Protection Bureau
      (CFPB), 293, 550
Consumer law, 289–298
   credit protection, 293–297
   deceptive advertising, 289–291
   defined, 289
   health and safety protection, 297–298

labeling and packaging, 292
   sales, 292–293
Consumer Product Safety Act, 297
Consumer Protection Act, 550
Contests, as unilateral contract, 124
Continuation statement
   of financing statement, 442
Continuity, sole proprietorship and lack
      of continuity, 397
Contracts, 122–175. See also Agreements;
      Lease contracts; Sales contracts
   acceptance in, 123, 138–140
   adhesion, 172
   agency relationship and, 356
   agreement in, 123, 133–141
   ambiguity and, 128
   arbitration clauses, 583
   assignments, 203–206
   bank-customer relationship as, 334
   bilateral, 124
   breach of, 217, 218, 220, 222–226
   capacity in, 157–163
   choice-of-language clause, 582
   choice-of-law clause, 583
   consideration in, 123, 147–152
   contractual capacity in, 123
   contrary to public policy, 170–173
   contrary to statute, 169–170
   defined, 122
   delegation, 203, 206–208
   destination contract, 248, 252, 263
   discharge of, 217–222
   e-contract, 127, 139–140
   e-mail, 197
   enforceability of, 126–127
   enforcement of, defenses to, 123–124
   exclusive-dealing contract, 570
   exculpatory clauses, 172–173
   executed, 126
   executory, 126
   express, 125
   force majeure clause, 583
   formal, 126
   formation of, 124–127
   form of, 124, 189
   forum-selection clause, 582–583
   implied (implied-in-fact), 125
   informal, 126
   installment, 264
   insurance, 483–487
   integrated, 196
   international law and, 582–583
   interpretation of, 127–128
   intoxication and, 160–161
   involving interests in land, 190
   law governing, 234
   legality of, 123, 169–174
   mental incompetence, 161–162
   minors and, 157–160
   mirror image rule, 137, 138, 238
   objective theory of, 122–123, 133
   offer in, 123, 136–137
   one-year rule, 190–191
   option contract, 136
   performance of, 126, 218–219
   plain meaning rule, 128
   privity of, 203, 280

promise, 122
   proposed, supervening illegality, offer
      termination, 137
   quasi, 125–126, 225
   ratification of, 126–127
   requirements for valid, 123–124
   rescission, 149
   in restraint of trade, 170–172
   for sale of goods, 192
   shipment contract, 248, 252, 262–263
   simple, 126
   of subsequent modification, 195
   terms in, 135
   third party beneficiaries, 203, 208–210
   types of, 124–127
   unconscionable, 171–172
   unilateral, 124
   voidable, 126–127, 169, 195
   void contract, 127, 195
   voluntary consent in, 124, 179–184
   writing requirements, 189–195
   wrongful interference with, 70
Contract theory, exceptions to
      employment-at-will, 366
Contractual capacity, 157–163
   defined, 157
   intoxicated persons, 160–161, 163
   mentally incompetent persons, 161–162
   minors and, 157–160, 162–163
   for principal, in agency formation, 351
   as requirement of contract, 123
Contribution, right of, 458
Controlling the Assault of Non-Solicited
      Pornography and Marketing
      (CAN-SPAM) Act, 93–94
Controversy, justiciable, 37
Conversion, 72
   of lost property, 499
Cookies, 101
Cooling-off laws, 292
Cooperation
   duty of, 264–265
   principal's duty of, 354
Copyright, 84–86
   defined, 84
   digital information and, 96–98
   fair use doctrine, 85–86
   idea exclusions, 85
   infringement of, 85–86, 96–97
   material that can be, 84–85
   remedies for, 85–86
   of software, 86
Copyright Act, 84, 85
Corporate citizenship approach to
      corporate social responsibility, 21
Corporate officers. See Officer, corporate
Corporate social responsibility (CSR),
      21–22
Corporate veil, piercing, 414
Corporations
   agent of, 350
   classification of, 411–412
      alien, 411
      benefit corporation, 412
      close, 412, 434
      domestic, 411
      foreign, 411

Corporations (*continued*)
    nonprofit (not-for-profit), 412
    private, 412
    public, 412
    S corporations, 412
  corporate name, selecting, 413
  de facto, 413–414
  defined, 411
  de jure, 413
  directors of, 411, 427–430
  dissolution disbursement, 416
  by estoppel, 414
  executives, 429
  financing, 415–417
    bonds, 416
    crowdfunding, 417
    stocks, 416
    venture capital, 416
  formation of, 412–414
    adoption of bylaws, 413
    defects in, 413–414
    incorporation procedures, 412–413
  jurisdiction over, 32
  as legal person, 411
  mergers and consolidations
    appraisal rights, 418–419
    defined, 417
    procedures for, 418
    purchase of assets, 419
    purchase of stock, 419–420
    shareholder approval, 419
    short-form merger, 418
  officers of, 411, 427–430
  parent corporation, 418
  personnel of, 411
  pierce corporate veil, 414
  political speech, 53
  powers of, 415
    express, 415
    implied, 415
    ultra vires doctrine, 415
  reorganizations, 472–473
  shareholders of, 411, 431–434
  social responsibility, 21–22
  subsidiary corporation, 418
  surviving corporation, 417
  takeover, 420
  target corporation, 419–420
  termination of
    dissolution, 420–421
    liquidation, 421
Correspondent bank, 584
Cost-benefit analysis, 20
Co-sureties, 458
Counteradvertising, 291
Counterclaim, 38
Counterfeit Access Device, 115
Counterfeit goods, 83
Counteroffer, 137
Course of dealings, 241
  implied warranties and, 278
Course of performance, 241
Court procedures, 37–41
  appeals, 41
  cyber courts, 41–42
  discovery, 39–40
  pleading, 37–38

  pretrial motions, 38–39
  standing to sue, 37
  trial procedures, 40–41
Courts
  bankruptcy, 465
  cyber courts, 41–42
  early English, 5
  of equity, 6
  federal courts, 34–36
  jurisdiction, 31–36
  king's *(curiae regis)*, 5
  of law, 6
  procedures of, 37–41
  small claims, 33
  state courts, 32–34
Covenant
  not to compete, 171–172
  not to sue, 151
  of quiet enjoyment, 514, 526
Cover, 268–269
Cram-down provision, 473
Credit cards, 293
  consumer protection laws, 293–297
  double-cycle billing, 295
  TILA rules for, 294–295
  Truth-in-Lending Act (TILA)
    requirements, 294–295
Credit counseling, 467
Creditor beneficiary, 209
Creditor-debtor relationship
  bank-customer relationship as, 334
Creditors
  bankruptcy property distribution,
    470–471
  claims of
    in bankruptcy, 469
    dissolution of partnership and, 403
  committees of, 472
  credit protection laws, 293–297
  default
    remedies of, 446–448
  Fair and Accurate Credit Transactions
    (FACT) Act, 295–296
  fair debt collection practices, 296–297
  garnishment, 455
  guaranty, 455–458
  laws assisting, 453–460
  liens, 453–455
  main purpose rule, 191–192
  meeting of, 468–469
  mortgage protection, 459–460
  preferred, 470
  rights and duties of, 446
  secured, 467
  security interest creation, 441
  suretyship, 455–458
  termination statement, 446
  unsecured, 467
Creditors' composition agreements, 455
Credit protection
  Consumer Financial Protection
    Bureau, 293
  Equal Credit Opportunity Act
    (ECOA), 294
  Fair and Accurate Credit Transactions
    (FACT) Act, 295–296
  Fair Credit Reporting Act (FCRA), 295

  Fair Debt Collection Practices Act
    (FDCPA), 296–297
  Truth-in-Lending Act (TILA),
    293–295
Credit report, notification and inaccurate
    information, 295
Crimes
  affecting businesses, 110–113
  bribery, 112–113
  classification of, 108
  computer, 114
  contract to commit, 169–170
  criminal act, 108
  criminal prosecution compared to tort
    lawsuit, 65–66
  cyber, 114–116
  cyber fraud, 114
  cyberterrorism, 115
  defined, 107
  embezzlement, 111
  forgery, 111
  identity theft, 114–115
  intent to commit, 108–109
  larceny, 111
  mail and wire fraud, 112
  racketeering, 113
  robbery, 111
  state of mind, 108–109
  white-collar, 110–113
Criminal act, 108
Criminal investigations, social media
    and, 98
Criminal law
  beyond a reasonable doubt, 107–108
  burden of proof, 107–108
  compared to civil law, 8–9, 107, 108
  Constitutional safeguards, 109–110
  criminal liability, 108–109
  cyber crime and, 114–116
  defenses for, 113–114
  defined, 9
  exclusionary rule, 110
  informing suspects of their rights, 110
  searches and seizure, 109
  types of crimes, 110–113
Criminal liability, 108–109
  defenses to, 113–114
  elements of, 108–109
Cross-examination, 40
Crowdfunding, 417
Cruel and unusual punishment, 109
Cumulative voting, 432–433
Cure, 254
  perfect tender rule and, 263–264
Customary practices, 195
Customer restrictions, 566
Cyber courts, 41–42
Cyber crimes, 114–116
  cyber fraud, 114
  cyberterrorism, 115
  defined, 114
  hacking, 115
  identity theft, 114–115
  jurisdiction and, 115
  network intrusion insurance, 487–488
  phishing, 115
  prosecuting, 115–116

Cyber fraud, 114
Cybersquatting, 94–95
Cyberterrorism, 115
Cyber torts, 99–100

D

Damages
  for breach of contract, 222–226
  buyer's or lessee's right to recover, 268
  compensatory, 222–223
  consequential, 223
  damage vs. damages, 65
  defined, 6, 65, 222
  exemplary damages, 223
  incidental, 223, 266
  liquidated, 224
  mitigation of, 224
  punitive, 184, 223
  seller's or lessor's right to recover, 267
  from shareholder's derivative suit., 434
  special, 223
  substantial performance, 218
  tenancy at sufferance, 524
  for tort action, 65
  treble damages, 571
  trespass to land, 71
  types of, 222–224
Danger, commonly known dangers, 283
Death
  of customer, and check payment, 335
  offer termination and, 137
  of party to personal contract, 221
  of principal or agent, agency
      termination and, 358
Deathbed gift, 498
Debt collection practices, 296–297
Debtors
  consumer-debtors, 465
  credit protection laws, 293–297
  default
      remedies of, 446–448
  default of, 453
  defined, 440
  duties of, 446
  guaranty, 455–458
  homestead exemption, 460
  mortgage, 458–460
  personal property exemption, 460
  protection for, 460 (See also
      Bankruptcy)
  rights of, 446, 465
  suretyship, 455–458
  termination statement, 446
Debts, liquidated, 455
Deceive, intent to, 182–183
Deceptive advertising, 289–291
  bait-and-switch advertising, 290
  based on half-truths, 290
  cease-and-desist order, 291
  clear and conspicuous disclosure,
      290–291
  counteradvertising, 291
  forms of, 289–290
  Lanham Act and false advertising
      claims, 291
  online, 290–291

  puffery, 289
  reasonable consumer test, 289
Declaration, 37
Deeds
  defined, 514
  quitclaim deed, 515
  requirements of, 514
  warranty deed, 514
De facto corporation, 413–414
Defamation
  defenses, 69
  defined, 68
  liability of Internet service providers
      (ISPs) for, 99–100
  online, 99–100
  privileged communications, 69
  public figures and, 69
  requirements of, 68–69
  as unprotected speech, 54
Default
  of debtor, 453
  of security agreement
      basic remedies, 446
      retaining or disposing of collateral,
          447–448
Default judgment, 38
Defendant, 37
Defense, Department of, 551
Defense Production Act, 572
Defenses
  assignment and, 204
  collection of negotiable instruments,
      326–327
  to defamation, 69
  defined, 66
  Ellerth/Faragher affirmative defense, 385
  to employment discrimination, 389–390
  to enforceability of contract, 123–124
  to insurance payment of policy,
      486–487
  against intentional tort against persons,
      66–67
  against negligence, 67
  for negligence, 75–76
  personal, 327
  to product liability, 282–283
  real, 326
  for sexual harassment, 385
  to surety/guarantor, 457–458
  for tort, 66–67
  trespass of land, 71
  universal, 326–327
  voluntary consent, 179
  wrongful interference, 71
Deficiency judgment, 448
De jure corporation, 413
Delegation, 203, 206–208
  defined, 206
  duties that cannot be delegated,
      206–207
  effect of, 207
  liability of delegatee, 207
Delegator, delegatee, 206
Delivery
  C.I.F. or C.&F. (cost, insurance, and
      freight or just cost and freight), 252
  constructive, 497, 501

  delivery ex-ship (delivery from the
      carrying vessel), 252
  in destination contracts, 248, 252
  as element of bailment, 501
  F.A.S. (free alongside), 252
  F.O.B. (free on board), 252
  of gifts, 497
  with movement of goods (carrier cases),
      248, 251–252
  physical, 501
  place of, 262–263
  seller's or lessor's right to withhold, 266
  in shipment contract, 248, 252
  substitution of carrier, 263
  symbolic, 497
  tender of, 248, 253, 256, 261–262
  terms, 251–252
  via carrier, 262–263
  without movement of goods, 249,
      252–253
Demand, payable on, 309–310
Demand instrument
  defined, 305
  issue of, 305
  negotiable instruments as, 305, 321
  overdue, 321
Denial
  as misrepresentation by conduct, 182
Deposited acceptance rule, 138
Depositions, 39–40
Depository bank, 337
Deposits
  bank accepting for checking accounts,
      337–341
Design defects, 281
Destination contract, 248, 252, 263
Detrimental reliance, 152
Devise, devisee, 536
Digital cash (e-money), 342–343
  smart cards, 343
  stored-value card, 343
Digital Millennium Copyright Act
      (DMCA), 96–97
  fair use exception, 97
  file-sharing methods, 97
  ISP limited liability, 97
Dilution, of trademark, 81–82, 96
Direct deposits/withdrawals
  as electronic fund transfer, 341
Directed verdict, motion for, 41
Direct examination, 40
Direct exporting, 581
Directors, corporate
  agency relationship, 429
  approval of, and mergers and
      consolidations, 419
  business judgment rule, 430
  conflicts of interest, 430
  cumulative voting for, 432–433
  defined, 411
  duties of, 429–430
      of care, 429
      of loyalty, 430
  election of, 427–428
  fiduciary duties of, 429–430
  initial, 427
  liabilities of, 430

Directors, corporate (*continued*)
  meetings of, 428
  in mergers and consolidations
      procedures, 418
  number of, 427
  quorum requirements, 428
  removal of, 427–428
  responsibilities of, 428
  roles of, 427
  sale of corporate assets and, 419
  shareholders voting for, 416
  term of office, 427
  vacancies on board, 428
  voting, 428
Disability
  defined, 388
  discrimination based on, 388–389
  job applications and physical
      exams, 389
  reasonable accommodations, 389
Disability insurance, 483
Disaffirmance, 158–159
  duty of restitution, 158–159
  exceptions to, 159–160
  liability for necessaries, 159–160
  misrepresentation of age, 159
Discharge
  in bankruptcy, 466, 471–472, 473, 475
  constructive, 384
  effect of, 472
  exceptions to, 471
  from liability of negotiable
      instruments, 328
  objections to, 471–472
Discharge of contract
  by accord and satisfaction, 220
  by agreement, 219–220
  by breach of contract, 217
  defined, 217
  by failure of a condition, 217–218
  by mutual rescission, 219
  by novation, 219
  by operation of law, 220–222
  by performance, 218–219
Disclosed principal, 356
Disclosure law, 293–295
Discovery, 39–40
  compliance with requests, 40
  defined, 39
  depositions, 39–40
  e-evidence for, 40
  interrogatory, 40
  social media and, 98
Discrimination
  based on
      age, 386–387
      color, 383
      disability, 388–389
      gender, 383–384
      national origin, 383
      pregnancy, 383–384
      race, 383
      religion, 383
  disparate-impact discrimination,
      382–383
  disparate-treatment discrimination, 382
  intentional, 382
  international business and, 587–588

lease agreement and
    antidiscrimination, 526
  prima facie case, 382
  unintentional discrimination, 382–383
  against union workers, 374
  wage discrimination, 384
Dishonored instruments, 321, 323
Disinheritance, 537
Dismissals, 38, 41
Disparagement of property, 72–73
Disparate-impact discrimination,
    382–383
Disparate-treatment discrimination, 382
Disposable income, 467
Disposition of collateral, 447–448
Dispute resolution, online, 44
Dissociation
  defined, 401
  effects of, 401–402
  events that cause, 401
  of partners, 401–402
Dissolution
  of corporation
      involuntary, 421
      voluntary, 420
  of partnerships, 402–403
Distributed network, 97
Distribution agreement, 581
Distribution of property
  in bankruptcy, 471
  intestate, 539–541
  trusts, 541–543
  wills, 535–539
Diversity of citizenship, 36
Divestiture, 571
Dividends
  defined, 433
  sources paid from, 433
  stock, 416
Divorce
  community property and, 496
  revocation of will, 539
Documents
  requests for, 40
  of title, 249, 253
Dodd-Frank Wall Street Reform, 550
Domain names
  defined, 94
  online dispute resolution and, 44
  registering, 95
  tracking, 94–95
Domestic corporation, 411
Domestic relations courts, 33
Dominion, 497
Donative intent, 497
Donee beneficiary, 209
Dormant commerce clause, 51
Double jeopardy, 109
Dow Chemical Company, 24
Down payment, 459
Drafts
  acceptance, 305
  check as, 305–306
  defined, 305
  as negotiable instrument, 304, 307
  sight draft, 305
  time draft, 305
  trade acceptance, 305

Drawer, drawee, 305, 333
Drugs
  consumer protection and, 297
Due care
  product liability and, 280
Due process, 109
  procedural, 55
  substantive, 56
Dumping, 585
Duress
  as defense to enforcement of
      contract, 184
  defined, 184
  economic, 184
  extreme, as universal defense, 327
  ordinary, as personal defense, 327
  voidable contracts, 127
  voluntary consent and, 184
Duty-based ethics, 19–20
Duty(ies)
  in agency relationships, 353–354
  antidumping, 585
  of bailee, 501–503
  of care
      bailee, 502, 503
      corporate directors, 429
      corporate officers, 429
      partnerships, 400
      reasonable care of collateral, 446
  of cooperation, 264–265
  of corporate directors, 429–430
  of corporate officer, 429–430
  of creditors, 446
  of debtors, 446
  delegation of, 203, 206–208
  fiduciary, 400
  of landlords, 526–529
  of landowners, 73–74
  of loyalty, 430
      agent, 353
      partnerships, 400
  of partners, 400
  preexisting duty and lack of
      consideration, 148–149
  of professionals, 74
  reasonable person standards, 73
  of restitution, and disaffirmance,
      158–159
  of shareholders, 434
  of tenants, 526–529
  trustee in bankruptcy, 469
  to warn
      business invitees of risks, 74
DVDs, file-sharing and, 97

E

Easement, 513
Economic development, eminent domain
    used for, 517
Economic duress, 184
Economic Espionage Act, 87
Economic strike, 374
E-contracts
  acceptance, 139–140
  click-on agreement, 140
  defined, 127
  offer, 139

requirements of, 139
shrink-wrap agreement, 140
Uniform Electronic Transactions Act, 127, 140
E-evidence, 40
Effective date, insurance contract, 484
Eighth Amendment, 52, 109
Elderly, undue influence in, 184
Electronic Communications Privacy Act (ECPA), 58, 100–101
business-extension exception to, 100
reasonable expectation of privacy, 100–101
stored communication, 101
Electronic Fund Transfer Act (EFTA), 341–342
Electronic fund transfers (EFT)
commercial, 342
consumer, 341–342
defined, 341
disclosure requirements, 342
types of, 341
unauthorized transfers, 342
violations and damages, 342
Electronic payments (e-payments), 342–343
Electronic Signatures in Global and National Commerce Act (E-SIGN Act), 195
Eleventh Amendment, 387
Ellerth/Faragher affirmative defense, 385
E-mail
as enforceable contract, 197
spam, 93–94
tips for writing precise, 197
Emancipation, minors, 160
Embezzlement, 111
Eminent domain, 516–517
commercial development and, 517
process of, 516
E-money, 342–343
Employee Retirement Income Security Act (ERISA), 368
Employees
agency relationship, 350
at-will employees, 365
child labor, 370
discrimination of (*See* Employment discrimination)
employer-employee relationships, 350
federal health and safety protection, 367
health and safety, 366–368
immigration law and, 371–372
income security, 367–369
overtime, 370–371
retirement income and security, 367–369
sexual harassment of, 384–386
social media and, 98–99
status as, determining, 351
unions (*See* Unions)
wages of, 370–371
workers' compensation laws, 366–367
Employers
agency relationship, 350–351
employer-employee relationships, 350

employer-independent contractor relationships, 351
prima facie case of age discrimination, 387
retaliation by, for sexual harassment complaints, 386
social media and, 98–99
unfair labor practices, 374
discrimination against union workers, 374
interference with unions, 374
refusal to recognize or negotiate with union, 374
Employer's liability insurance, 483
Employment, 365–371
determining status of, 351
discrimination in (*See* Employment discrimination)
employment-at-will doctrine, 365–366
family and medical leave, 369
federal health and safety protection, 367
health insurance, 368–369
human resource management, 390
immigration law and, 371–372
retirement income and security, 367–369
wage and hour laws, 370–371
workers' compensation laws, 366–367
Employment-at-will doctrine, 365–366
Employment contracts
covenant not to compete, 171
implied, 366
Employment discrimination, 381–390
based on
age, 386–387
color, 383
disability, 388–389
gender, 383–384
national origin, 383
race, 383
religion, 383
defenses to, 389–390
defined, 381
disparate-impact discrimination, 382–383
disparate-treatment discrimination, 382
intentional discrimination, 382
international business and, 588
prima facie case, 382
remedies, 386
retaliation by employers, 386
sexual and online harassment, 384–386
Title VII of Civil Rights Act, 381–386
unintentional discrimination, 382–383
wage discrimination, 384
Enabling legislation, 550–551
Energy Policy and Conservation Act, 292
Enforceability, of contract, 126–127
Entrapment, as defense for criminal liability, 114
Entrustment rule, 250–251
Environmental Protection Agency (EPA), 557
duties of, 552
Equal Credit Opportunity Act (ECOA), 294
Equal dignity rule, 351, 354

Equal Employment Opportunity Commission (EEOC)
duties of, 552
role of, 381–382
Equal Pay Act, 384
Equal protection clause
intermediate scrutiny, 57
rational basis test, 56
strict scrutiny, 57
Equitable remedies, 6
specific performance, 225
Equity
courts of, 6
defined, 6
Escrow account, 528
Escrow agent, 528
E-signature, 194–195
Establishment clause, 54–55
Estate
in bankruptcy, 469
in property, 469
Estoppel
agency formation by, 352
corporations by, 414
partnership by, 398
promissory, 151–152
Estray statutes, 499–500
Ethics, 15–27. *See also* Business ethics
codes of conduct, 16
conflicts and trade-offs, 17
cost-benefit analysis, 20
defined, 15
duty-based ethics, 19–20
Foreign Corrupt Practices Act, 22–23
laws and relationship to, 17–18
outcome-based ethics, 20–21
principle of rights, 20
religious ethical principles, 19
Sarbanes-Oxley Act, 17
setting right ethical tone, 16–17
utilitarianism, 20
European Union (EU), 586
antitrust law and, 572–573
Eviction, 526
Evidence
e-evidence, 40
exclusionary rule, 110
parol evidence rule, 195–196
Examination
cross-examination, 40
direct, 40
request for, 40
of witnesses, 40
Exclusionary practices, 570
Exclusionary rule, 110
Exclusive-dealing contract, 570
Exclusive jurisdiction, 36
Exculpatory clauses, 172–173
Executed contract, 126
Execution, writ of, 454–455, 469
Executive agencies, 551
Executive branch
checks and balances, 50
control over administrative agencies, 556
separation of powers, 50
Executive employees, overtime wages, 370–371

Executives, corporate, 429
Executor, 535
Executory contract, 126
Exemplary damages, 223
Exemptions
    in bankruptcy, 470
    homestead, 460, 470
    personal property, 460
Existing goods, 247
Expedited Funds Availability Act, 340
Export Administration Act, 585
Exporting
    controls on, 585
    direct or indirect, 581
    distributorship, 581
Export Trading Company Act, 585
Express authority
    of agent, 354–355
Express contracts, 125
Express powers, 415
Express ratification, 160
Express trusts, 541–542
    living trusts, 541–542
    testamentary trust, 542
Express warranty, 276–277
    basis of bargain, 276
    disclaimers, 279
    statements of opinion, 277
Expropriation, 580, 584–585
Extreme duress
    as universal defense, 327

F

Facebook, 98, 99, 101
Fact(s)
    affirmation of, 276
    causation in, 74–75
    false statement of, 68
    justifiable ignorance of, 173–174
    material, 179
    misrepresentation of a material fact,
        181–182
    mistake of, 113, 179–181
    objective, and intent to form contract,
        122–123
Fair and Accurate Credit Transactions
    (FACT) Act, 295–296
Fair Credit Reporting Act (FCRA), 295
Fair Debt Collection Practices Act
    (FDCPA), 296–297
Fair Labor Standards Act (FLSA), 370
Fair Packaging and Labeling Ac, 292
Fair use doctrine, 85–86
Fair use exception, 97
Fair value of goods, 585
False advertising. See Deceptive
    advertising
False Claims Reform Act, 365–366
False imprisonment, 68
False light, 69
Family and medical leave, 369
Family and Medical Leave Act
    (FMLA), 369
Fanciful trademark, 82
Farmers, involuntary bankruptcy, 468
F.A.S. (free alongside), 252

Featherbedding, 373
Federal Circuit, 35
Federal Communications Commission
    (FCC), 552
Federal court system, 34–36. See also
    United States Supreme Court
    appellate courts of, 34–36
    jurisdiction of, 36
    structure of, 34
    trial (district) courts of, 34, 35
Federal Deposit Insurance Corporation
    (FDIC), 344
Federal government, 49–52
    commerce clause, 50–51
    expansion of powers of, under
        commerce clause, 50–51
    labor laws, 372–374
    limits on, and Bill of Rights, 52–55
    powers of, 49–50
    separation of powers, 50
    supremacy clause, 51
    taxation, 51–52
Federal Insurance Contributions Act
    (FICA), 367
Federal question, 36
Federal Register, 552, 553
Federal Reserve Board
    duties of, 552
    Expedited Funds Availability Act, 340
    Truth-in-Lending Act (TILA),
        293–295
Federal Reserve System
    clearing checks, 339
Federal Savings and Loan Insurance
    Corporation (FSLIC), 344
Federal Trade Commission (FTC), 551
    bait-and-switch advertising, 290
    cease-and-desist order, 291
    clear and conspicuous disclosure,
        290–291
    cooling-off laws, 292
    counteradvertising, 291
    creation of, 289, 550–551
    duties of, 552
    enforcement of antitrust law, 571
    formal complaint, 291
    Mail or Telephone Order Merchandise
        Rule, 292
    privacy violation complaints, 101
Federal Trade Commission Act, 289,
    550–551
Federal Trademark Dilution Act, 81
Fee simple, 495
Fee simple absolute, 511
Fee simple defeasible, 512
Felonies, 108
Fictitious payee rule, 324–325
Fidelity insurance, 483
Fiduciary duties
    of corporate directors and officers,
        429–430
    of majority of shareholders, 434
    of partners, 400
Fiduciary relationship
    defined, 400
    partnership as, 400
    undue influence in, 184

Fifth Amendment, 52, 55, 58
    due process and, 109
    self-incrimination, 110, 114
File-sharing methods, 97
Filtering software, 54
Final order, 555
Final review, 41
Financial Stability Oversight Council, 550
Financing statement (Form UCC-1)
    continuation statement, 442
    defined, 441
    effectiveness of, 442
    elements of, 442
    improper filing of, 442–443
    location for filing, 442
    perfection by filing, 442
Fire insurance, 483
Firm offer, 237
First Amendment, 52–55, 58
First-in-time rule for security
    interests, 445
Fisheries Cooperative Marketing Act, 572
Fixed-rate mortgage, 459
Fixed-term tenancy, 523
Fixture, 190
    compared to personal property, 511
    defined, 510
    within land sales, 510–511
Floating-lien, 444–445
F.O.B. (free on board), 252
Food, Drug, and Cosmetic Act
    (FDCA), 297
Food and Drug Administration
    (FDA), 551
    food safety, 297
    safety of new drugs, 297
Food labeling, 292
Forbearance, 147
Force majeure clause, 583
Foreclosure
    artisan's lien and, 454
    defined, 460
    mechanic's lien and, 453
Foreign corporation, 411
Foreign Corrupt Practices Act (FCPA)
    accounting requirements, 24
    penalties for violations, 24
    prohibition against bribery of foreign
        officials, 23
Foreign exchange market, 584
Foreign investors, limited liability
    company and, 405
Foreign officials, bribery of, 112, 586
Foreign Sovereign Immunities Act
    (FSIA), 580
Foreign state, 580
Foreseeability, 75
Forgery, 111
    checks with forged signatures, 336–337
    of signature, as universal defense, 326
Form, contract, 189
Formal contracts, 126
Form UCC-1. See Financing statement
    (Form UCC-1)
Forum-selection clause, 582–583
Forum shopping, 66
Fourteenth Amendment, 52, 55, 56

Fourth Amendment, 52, 55, 58, 554
  probable cause, 109
  protections under, 109, 110
  search warrant, 109
Franchises
  manufacturing abroad, 582
Franchisee, franchisor, 582
Fraud
  cyber, 114
  as defense to insurance policy
      payment, 486
  defined, 114
  elements of, 181–184
  in execution, as universal defense, 326
  fraudulent misrepresentation, 69–70,
      181–184
  in the inducement, as personal
      defense, 327
  injury to innocent party, 184
  intent to deceive, 182–183
  mail and wire fraud, 112, 113
  misrepresentation has occurred,
      181–182
  reliance on misrepresentation, 183
  securities, 113
  surety/guarantor defense, 458
  voidable contracts, 127
Fraudulent misrepresentation, 69–70,
      181–184
Freedom
  of religion, 54–55
  of speech, 53–54
Freedom of Information Act (FOIA),
      58, 558
Free exercise clause, 54, 55
Frivolous litigation, 70
Fundamental right, 56
Fungible goods, 248
  confusion and, 498
Future advances, 444
Future goods, 248

G

Gambling, 170
Garnishment, 455
Gender
  discrimination based on, 383–384
  pregnancy discrimination, 383–384
  wage discrimination, 384
General jurisdiction
  defined, 33
  state trial courts and, 32, 33
General partner, 403
Gifts
  acceptance of, 497
  causa mortis (deathbed gift), 498
  defined, 497
  delivery of, 497
  donative intent, 497
  inter vivos, 498
  ownership by, 497–498
  requirements of, 497
  by will, 536
Global environment
  antitrust laws in, 572–573
  business ethics and, 22–23

  monitoring practice of foreign
      suppliers, 22–23
Global warming, 557
Good faith
  accession and, 498
  Chapter 13 and, 474
  collective bargaining and, 373
  defined, 239
  good faith purchaser and voidable
      title, 250
  sales contracts and, 239
  taking in, and holder in due course, 320
  UCC and, 261
Goods
  associated with real estate, 235
  buyer's right
    obtain cover, 268–269
    to obtain specific performance, 268
    recover damages, 269
    to reject, 268
  compensatory damages for breach of
      contract, 223
  conforming, 261
  counterfeit, 83
  defined, 235
  destruction of, 264
  existing, 247
  fair value of, 585
  fungible, 248, 498
  future, 248
  goods and services combined, 235
  held by bailee, 253
  held by lessor, 253
  held by seller, 253
  identification, 247–248
  intangible property, 235
  from a larger mass, 248
  lessee's rights
    obtain cover, 268–269
    to obtain specific performance, 268
    recover damages, 269
    to reject, 268
  lessor's rights, to resell of dispose
      of, 266
  location of, 262
  merchantable, 277
  nonconforming, 263
  nonmerchantable, 277
  owners in common, 248
  prohibited from importing, 585
  right to reclaim, 266
  sale of, contracts for, 192
  seller's rights, to resell of dispose of, 266
  specially manufactured, exception to
      Statute of Frauds, 240
  tangible property, 235
Goodwill
  covenants not to compete and sale of
      ongoing business, 171
Google, 101
Google+, 98
Google Wallet, 333
Government
  form of
    confederal, 49
    federal, 49–52
  powers of, constitutional, 49–52

Government in the Sunshine Act, 558
Gramm-Leach-Bliley Act, 59
Grandchildren, intestacy and, 540–541
Greenhouse gases, 557
Gross negligence, 180
Group boycott, 567
Group insurance, 483
Guarantor, 456
Guaranty, 455–458
  actions that release, 457–458366
  defenses of, 457–458
  defined, 456
  relationship with creditor and debtor,
      456, 457
  rights of, 458
  writing requirement exception, 457
Guaranty insurance, 483

H

Hacking, 115
  protecting company against, 116
Harassment
  hostile-environment harassment, 385
  online, 385–386
  quid pro quo harassment, 384–385
  sexual, 384–385
Harm, standing to sue, 37
Hazardous Substances Labeling Act, 297
Health
  consumer protection and, 297–298
  food safety, 297
Health and Human Services, Department
  of, 551
Health insurance, 483
  COBRA, 368–369
  controlling costs of, 298
  employee-sponsored, 368
  expanded coverage, 298
  Medicare, 368
Health Insurance Portability and
    Accountability Act (HIPAA),
    58, 368
Heirs
  collateral, 539
  lineal, 539
Hiring procedures, social media and
    ethics, 22
Holder
  compared to holder in due course, 319
  defined, 312, 319
  in due course, 312
  ordinary, 319
Holder in due course, 319–325
  compared to ordinary holder, 319
  defined, 319
  requirements for, 319–321
    taking for value, 320
    taking in good faith, 320
    taking without notice, 320–321
Holmes, Oliver Wendell, Jr., 2
Holographic will, 538
Homeland Security, Department of, 551
Homeowners' insurance, 483
Homestead exemption, 460, 470
Hostile-environment harassment, 385
Human resource management, 390

I

I-9 verifications, 371
Idea, copyright and, 85
Identification, 247–251
    defined, 247
    existing goods, 247
    future goods, 248
    passage of title, 248–251
Identified goods
    destruction of, 264
    insurable interest in, 255
Identity theft, 114–115
Illegal actions
    as defense to insurance policy payment,
        486–487
Illegal contracts
    contrary to public policy, 170–173
    contrary to statute, 169–170
    justifiable ignorance of the facts,
        173–174
    members of protected classes, 174
    withdrawal from, 174
Illegality
    as personal defense, 327
    as universal defense, 327
Illusory promises, 150
Immigration Act, 371–372
Immigration law, 371–372
    I-9 verifications, 371
    Immigration Act, 371–372
    Immigration Reform and Control Act
        (IRCA), 371
Immigration Reform and Control Act
        (IRCA), 371
Immunity
    as defense for criminal liability, 114
    sovereign, 580
Implied authority, of agent, 355
Implied contracts, 125
Implied-in-fact contract, 125
Implied powers, 415
Implied ratification, 160
Implied trusts, 542–543
    constructive trust, 542–543
    resulting trust, 543
Implied warranties, 277–278
    course of dealings, 278
    course of performance, 278
    defined, 277
    disclaimers, 279
    of fitness for particular purpose, 278
    of habitability, 527
    of merchantability, 277
    usage of trade, 278
Imports
    dumping, 585
    prohibited goods, 585
    quotas and tariffs, 585
Impossibility, agency termination and, 359
Impossibility of performance
    commercial impracticability, 221
    defined, 220
    objective, 220
    subjective, 220
    temporary, 221–222
Imposter rule, 324
Incidental beneficiary, 209–210

Incidental damages, 223, 266
Income
    disposable, 467
    means test in Chapter 7, 467
    retirement income, 367–369
Income security, 367–369
Incontestability clause, 485, 487
Incorporation procedures
    defects in corporate formation,
        413–414
    prepare/file articles of
        incorporation, 413
    secure corporate name, 413
    select state of incorporation, 412
Incorporators, 413
Indemnification, principal's duty of, 354
Independent contractors
    agency relationship and, 351
    defined, 351
    employer-independent contractor
        relationships, 351
    tax liability and, 360
    tort liability, 359
Independent regulatory agencies, 551–552
Indictment, 52
Indirect exporting, 581
Indorsement
    blank, 312
    of checks, 313–314
    checks with forged, 337
    defined, 312
    of negotiable instruments, 311–313
    qualified, 312–313
    restrictive, 313
    special, 312
    unqualified, 313
Indorser, indorsee, 312
Infant (minor), 157
Informal contracts, 126
Information return, 398
Infringement
    of copyright, 85–86, 96–97
    file-sharing, 97
    of patents, 84
    of trademark, 81, 83, 94, 95–96
    warranty of title and, 276
Inheritance
    transfer of real property and, 515
Initial order, 555
Injunction, 6
Injury
    to innocent party and fraud, 184
    legally recognizable, 74
    negligence and requirement of, 74
    workers' compensation laws, 366–367
Insanity. *See also* Mental incompetence
    as defense for criminal liability,
        113–114
    tests for, 114
Insolvent, 249, 466
Inspections
    by administrative agencies, 553
    implied warranty disclaimer and, 279
    right of, 433
        buyer or lessee, 265
Installment contract, 264
Installment note, 306

Instrumentality, 580
Insurable interest
    of buyer or lessee, 255
    defined, 482
    lack of, as defense to insurance policy
        payment, 486
    life insurance, 482–483
    in property, 482
    of seller or lessor, 255
    sufficient interest, 255
Insurance, 481–487
    broker vs. agent, 482
    classifications of, 482, 483
    contract
        application, 483–484
        cancellation, 485–486
        defenses against payment, 486–487
        effective date, 484
        provisions and clauses, 484–485
    for cyber losses, 116
    defined, 481
    determining rates for, 482
    Federal insurance for bank
        deposits, 344
    insurable interest, 254–255, 482–483
    mortgage, 459
    network intrusion insurance, 487–488
    online business and, 487–488
    policy, 481
    premium, 481
    risk management, 482
    terminology for, 481–482
    underwriter, 481
    unemployment insurance, 368
Insurer, insured, 481
Intangible property, 235, 440, 494
Integrated contracts, 196
Intellectual property, 81–90
    copyright, 84–86
        digital information, 96–98
    counterfeit goods, 83
    defined, 81
    international protection for, 87–88
    licensing, 84, 581–582
    patents, 83–84
    service marks, 83
    trademarks, 81–83
    trade names, 83
    trade secrets, 86–87
Intended beneficiary, 208–209
Intent, intention
    advertisements, 134
    contract and, 122–123, 133–135
    to deceive, 182–183
    expressions of opinion, 134
    monopoly and, 568–569
    offer and, 133–135
    serious intent, 134
    tort law, 67
    valid will and, 537
Intentional discrimination, 382
Intentional torts
    against person
        abusive or frivolous litigation, 70
        assault, 67
        battery, 67
        defamation, 68–69

defined, 67
false imprisonment, 68
fraudulent misrepresentation, 69–70
invasion of privacy, 69
against property
conversion, 72
disparagement of property, 72–73
trespass to land, 71
trespass to personal property, 71–72
Interest, usury and, 169
Interest rate
judgment rate, 309
legal rate of, 309
Interior, Department of, 551
Intermediary bank, 337
Intermediate scrutiny, 57
Internal Revenue Code
Subchapter S of, 412
Internal social networks, 98–99
International business
business ethics and, 22–23
contract provisions, 582–583
distributorship, 581
dumping, 585
exporting, 581
Foreign Corrupt Practices Act, 22–23
franchising, 582
joint venture, 582
licensing, 581–582
manufacturing abroad, 581–582
monitoring employment practices of
foreign suppliers, 22–23
payment on transactions, 584
protection for intellectual property,
87–88
regulations on, 584–586
subsidiaries, 582
International contracts
arbitration clauses, 583
choice-of-language clause, 582
choice-of-law clause, 583
force majeure clause, 583
forum-selection clause, 582–583
International law
antidiscrimination law, 587–588
defined, 9
export controls, 585
import controls, 585–586
investment protections, 584–585
minimizing trade barriers, 585–586
principles and doctrines
act of state doctrine, 580
comity principle, 579–580
sovereign immunity doctrine, 580
sources of, 9
tort claims, 587
treaties and agreements, 579
U.S. antitrust law, 586–587
Internet
clear and conspicuous disclosure for
advertisements, 290–291
copyright and, 96–98
cyber courts and, 41–42
cyber crimes, 114–116
cyber fraud, 114
cybersquatting, 94–95
data collection and cookies, 101

deceptive advertising, 290–291
domain names, 94
DVDs and file-sharing, 97
e-contracts, 127, 139–140
file-sharing methods, 97
identity theft, 114–115
Internet companies' privacy
policies, 101
jurisdiction and, 32
licensing on, 95–96
meta tags, 95
network intrusion insurance, 487–488
obscene materials on, 54
online acceptance, 139–140
online auctions, 135
online banking, 343
online defamation, 99–100
online dispute resolution (ODR), 44
online harassment, 385–386
online offers, 139
online payment systems, 341
phishing, 115
privacy rights, 100–101
risk management for, 487–488
sales online, 292–293
sliding-scale standard, 32
social media and legal issues, 98–100
software copyright protection, 86
spam, 93–94
trademark dilution, 96
typosquatting, 95
Internet Corporation for Assigned Names
and Numbers (ICANN), 94
Internet service providers (ISPs)
defined, 97
liability for online defamation,
99–100
limited liability for copyright
infringement, 97
Interrogatory, 40
Interstate commerce, 50
dormant commerce clause and, 51
Sherman Act and, 566
Interstate Oil Compact, 572
Inter vivos trust, 541
Intestacy laws
defined, 539
grandchildren, 540–541
order of distribution, 539
per capita distribution, 540–541
per stirpes distribution, 540
surviving spouse and children, 540
Intestate, 539
Intoxication, contractual capacity and,
160–161, 163
Invasion of privacy, 69
Investigation
by administrative agencies, 553–554
Investments, in foreign nations, 584–585
Invitation to submit bids, 134
Involuntary bailment, 501
Involuntary bankruptcy, 468
Involuntary dissolution, of
corporation, 421
Irresistible-impulse test, 114
Issue
demand instrument, 305

J

Joint and several liability, 401
Joint liability, 401
Joint tenancy, 495–496
Joint venture, 582
Judgment rate of interest, 309
Judgments
affirmed, 41
default, 38
as a matter of law, 41
on the pleadings, 39
reversed, 41
summary, 39, 41
Judicial branch
checks and balances, 50
control over administrative
agencies, 557
separation of powers, 50
Judicial lien, 454–455
Judicial review, 557
Jurisdiction, 31–36
concurrent, 36
cyber crimes and, 115
in cyberspace, 32
defined, 31
diversity of citizenship, 36
exclusive, 36
of federal courts, 36
general, 33
limited, 33
long arm statute, 32
minimum contacts, 32
over corporations, 32
over person (in personam),
31–32
over property (in rem), 32
sliding-scale standard, 32
Justice, Department of, 551
enforcement of antitrust law, 571
Justiciable controversy, 37
Justifiable ignorance of the facts,
173–174
Justifiable reliance, 183

K

Kant, Immanuel, 19–20
Key-person insurance, 482, 483

L

Labels
food labeling, 292
laws affecting, 292
Labor, Department of, 551
Labor law, 372–374. See also Unions
child labor, 370
collective bargaining, 373–374
major federal labor laws, 372
right to-work laws, 372
strikes, 374
unfair labor practices, 374
union organization, 372–373
Labor-Management Reporting and
Disclosure Act (LMRDA), 372
Labor Management Services
Administration, 368

Land. *See also* Real property
  contract for sale of, 190
  contracts involving, and writing
      requirement, 190
  defined, 190, 509
  fixture, 190
  as real property, 509
  request for entry upon, 40
  sale of, as specific performance, 225
  sales of
      fixtures and, 510–511
  structures on, 509
  subsurface rights, 510
  trespass to, 71
Landlord
  lease agreement, 524–526
      antidiscrimination, 526
      elements of, 524–525
      unconscionability concept, 525
  leasehold estate, 523–524
      fixed-term tenancy, 523
      periodic tenancy, 523–524
      tenancy at sufferance, 524
      tenancy at will, 524
  rights and duties of
      compliance with ordinances, 527
      covenant of quiet enjoyment, 526
      eviction, 526
      implied warranty of habitability, 527
      possession of leased property, 526
      rent, 528
      transferring rights, 528–529
      use and maintenance of leased prop-
          erty, 527
  terminating lease, 529
Landowners, duty of, 73–74
Lanham Act, 81, 94
  false advertising claims under, 291
Lapsed legacy, 536
Larceny, 111
Law(s)
  affecting single business transaction, 3
  bankruptcy, 465
  case (*See* Case law)
  civil (*See* Civil law)
  codified, 9
  common (*See* Common law)
  consulting legal expert on, 10
  consumer (*See* Consumer law)
  cooling-off laws, 292
  courts of, 6
  creditors and assisting, 453–460
  criminal (*See* Criminal law)
  debtors and assisting, 460
  defined, 2
  disclosure, 293–295
  due process of (*See* Due process)
  international (*See* International law)
  labor, 372–374
  misrepresentation by, 182
  mistake of, 113
  national, 9, 579
  operation of (*See* Operation of law)
  remedies at, 6
  right to-work laws, 372
  sources of, 4–8
  statutory (*See* Statutory law)

tort (*See* Torts)
  uniform, 8
Lawsuits
  appeals, 41
  class-action, 66
  defined, 3
  discovery, 39–40
  pleading, 37–38
  pretrial motions, 38–39
  standing to sue, 37
  summary of stages, 42
  trial procedures, 40–41
Lease
  assignment of, 528
  defined, 523
  sublease, 528–529
  terminating, 529
Lease agreement, 236, 524–526
  antidiscrimination, 526
  elements of, 524–525
  unconscionability concept, 525
Lease contracts, 234–242
  acceptance, 237–239
  breach of
      remedies for, 266–269
      risk of loss, 254
  consideration, 239
  firm offer, 237
  formation of, 236–242
  identification, 247–251
  insurable interest, 254–255
  modification in good faith, 239
  modification without consideration, 239
  offer, 237
  parol evidence rule, 240–241
  performance of, 261–266
  risk of loss, 251–254
  Statute of Frauds, 239–240
  UCC Article 2A and, 236–242
  unconscionability, 241–242
  warranties, 275–280
Leasehold estate, 523–524
Legacy, 536
Legal advice, consulting expert for, 10
Legal cause, 75
Legality, of contracts, 169–174
Legally sufficient value, 147
Legal rate of interest, 309
Legatee, 536
Legislative branch
  checks and balances, 50
  control over administrative
      agencies, 556
  separation of powers, 50
Lending institutions, assignment, 204, 211
Lessee
  breach of contract, and risk of loss, 254
  defined, 236
  insurable interest of, 255
  obligation of, 265
  remedies for, 267–269
Lessor
  breach of contract, and risk of loss, 254
  defined, 236
  entrustment rule, 250–251
  good faith purchaser and voidable
      title, 250

goods held by, 253
  insurable interest of, 255
  obligation of, 261–265
  remedies for, 266–267
Letters of credit, 126
Liability
  agency relationships
      for contracts, 356
      for torts, 357
  corporate asset sale, and successor
      liability, 419
  of corporate directors, 430
  of corporate officer, 430
  defined, 67
  joint, 401
  joint and several, 401
  in limited liability partnership, 404
  of members of LLC, 405
  for necessaries, 159–160
  negotiable instrument, 321–325
  of parents', and minors, 160
  of partners, 401
  of partners in limited partnership,
      403–404
  primary liability, 322
  product, 76
  secondary liability, 322–323
  of shareholders, 411, 431
  signature liability, 321–325
  sole proprietorship and, 396–397
  strict, 76
  without fault, 76
Liability insurance, 483
Libel, 68
  trade libel, 72–73
License, licensing
  contracts with unlicensed person, 170
  defined, 84, 513
  of intellectual property, 84
  manufacturing abroad, 581–582
  as nonpossessory interest, 513
  online, 95–96
  trademark, 95–96
Licensee, 84, 581
Licensor, 581
Liens, 453–455
  artisan's, 454
  defined, 453
  floating-lien, 444–445
  judicial, 454–455
  mechanic's, 453–454
  title and, 275–276
Life estates, 512–513
Life insurance, 483
  insurable interest, 482–483
Life tenant, 512
Limited jurisdiction
  defined, 33
  state trial courts, 32, 33
Limited liability company (LLC), 404–405
  advantages of, 405
  defined, 404
  disadvantages of, 405
  foreign investors and, 405
  formation of, 404
  liability of members, 405
  management of, 405

nature of, 404
taxation, 405
Limited liability partnership (LLP)
advantages of, 404
converting to, 404
defined, 404
liability in, 404
Limited partner, 403
Limited partnership (LP), 403–404
benefits of, 403–404
defined, 403
formation of, 404
liability of, 403–404
Lineal heirs, 539
Line of credit
continuing, 444
LinkedIn, 98
Liquidated damages, 224
compared to penalty, 224
Liquidated debts, 455
Liquidation. *See also* Chapter 7
(liquidation proceedings)
of corporation, 421
defined, 421, 466
Litigation
appeals, 41
discovery, 39–40
pleading, 37–38
pretrial motions, 38–39
standing to sue, 37
trial procedures, 40–41
Living trusts, 541–542
Long arm statute, 32
Loss
risk of, 251–254
sharing of, in partnerships, 397
Lost property
conversion, 499
defined, 499
estray statutes, 499–500
Lotteries, as unilateral contract, 124
Loyalty
defined, 430
duty of, 430
agent, 353
corporate officers and directors, 430
partnerships, 400

M

Magnuson-Moss Warranty Act, 279–290
Mailbox rule, 138–139
Mail fraud, 112, 113
Mail Fraud Act, 112
Mail-order sales, 292
Mail or Telephone Order Merchandise
Rule, 292
Main purpose rule, 191–192
Maker, of promissory note, 306
Malice, actual, 69
Malicious prosecution, 70
Malpractice insurance, 483
Management
ethical leadership, 16
of limited liability company, 405
management rights of partners, 398–399
Managerial accounting, 24–25

Manufacturing
abroad, 581–582
Manufacturing defects, 281
Market, relevant, 568
Market divisions, 567
Market-share test, 568
Marriage
prenuptial agreement, 192
promise made in consideration of, 192
revocation of will by, 539
Material alteration
as universal defense, 327
Material fact, 179
McCarran-Ferguson Act, 572
Means test, bankruptcy, 467
Mechanic's lien, 453–454
Mediation
advantages of, 43
as form of ADR, 43
Medical information, privacy rights and, 58
Medical leave, 369
Medical malpractice
tort reform and, 66
Medicare, 368
Members (of LLC), 405
Memorandums, written
defined, 194
essential terms, 194
Mental incapacity
as personal defense, 327
as universal defense, 327
Mental incompetence
contractual capacity and, 161–162
of customer, and check payment, 335
as defense for criminal liability, 113–114
of principal or agent, agency
termination and, 358
Merchant
both parties as, 238
defined, 236
entrustment rule, 250–251
firm offer, 237
special rules for contract between, 240
Merchantability, implied warranty of, 277
Mergers
appraisal rights, 418–419
Clayton Act and, 571
defined, 417
market concentration and, 571
procedure for, 418
purchase of assets, 419
purchase of stocks, 419–420
shareholder approval and, 419
short-form merger, 418
surviving corporation, 417
target corporation, 419–420
Metadata, 40
Meta tags, 95
Mill, John Stuart, 20
Minimum contacts, 32
Minimum wages, 370
Minority, as universal defense, 327
Minors
age of majority, 157
contractual capacity and, 157–160,
162–163
disaffirmance, 158–159

emancipation and, 160
misrepresentation of age, 159
parents' liability and, 160
ratification, 160
undue influence in, 184
voidable contracts, 127
Mirror image rule, 137, 138
UCC and, 238
Misdemeanors, 108
Mislaid property, 499
Misrepresentation
by conduct, 182
as defense to insurance policy
payment, 486
fraudulent, 69–70, 181–184
injury, 184
by law, 182
product liability based on, 280
by silence, 182
voluntary consent and, 181–184
by words, 181–182
Mistake
bilateral (mutual), 180–181
as defense for criminal liability, 113
email contract and, 197
of fact, 113, 179–181
of law, 113
unilateral, 179–180
of value or quality, 179, 181
voidable contracts, 127
voluntary consent and, 179–181
Mitigation of damages, 224
Money
defined by UCC, 309
digital cash (e-money), 342–343
negotiable instruments payable in, 309
Monopoly/monopolization, 567–569
attempted, 569
defined, 567
elements of, 567
intent requirement, 568–569
predatory pricing and, 567
relevant market, 568
unilateral refusals to deal, 569
Monopoly power, 568
Moral minimum, 17
Mortgage, 458–460
adjustable-rate, 459
creditor protections in, 459
defined, 458–459
down payment, 459
fixed-rate, 459
foreclosure, 460
insurance for, 459
recording of, 459
types of, 459
Mortgagee, Mortgagor, 459
Mortgage note, 306, 309
Motions
for directed verdict, 41
to dismiss, 38, 41
for judgment as matter of law, 41
for judgment on the pleadings, 39
for new trial, 41
posttrial, 41
pretrial, 38–39
for summary judgment, 39, 41

Motion to dismiss, 38, 41
Multiple insurance clause, 485
Music, file-sharing of, 97, 494
Mutual rescission, 219
MySpace, 101

N

National Conference of Commissioners on Uniform State Laws (NCCUSL), 8
National Information Infrastructure Protection Act, 115
National Labor Relations Act (NLRA), 372
　union election supervision, 373
National Labor Relations Board (NLRB)
　cease-and-desist order, 372
　duties of, 552
　workers protected by, 372
National law, 9, 579
National origin, discrimination based on, 383
Necessaries
　defined, 159
　liability for, and disaffirmance, 159–160
Negligence, 73–76
　causation, 74–75
　checks with forged signatures and, 336–337
　comparative, 75–76
　　as defense to product liability, 283
　comparative negligence, 67
　defense against, 67
　defenses to, 75–76
　defined, 73
　duty of care and its breach, 73–74
　elements of, 73
　gross, 180
　injury requirement, 74
　product liability based on, 280
Negotiable instruments, 126
　checks as, 333–344
　compared to nonnegotiable instruments, 304
　defenses
　　personal defenses, 327
　　universal defenses, 326–327
　defined, 304
　as demand instrument, 305
　discharge, 328
　dishonored instruments, 321, 323
　holder, 312
　holder in due course, 319–328
　overdue instruments, 321
　proper and timely presentment, 322–323
　requirements of
　　fixed amount of money, 309
　　payable on demand or at a definite time, 309–310
　　payable to order or to bearer, 310–311
　　signatures, 307–308
　　unconditional promise or order to pay, 308–309
　　written form, 307

signature liability, 321–325
　primary liability, 322
　secondary liability, 322–323
　unauthorized signatures, 323–324
transfer of
　by assignment, 311
　indorsements of, 312–314
　by negotiation, 311–312
types of
　certificates of deposit, 306
　drafts and checks, 305–306
　orders to pay, 305–306
　overview, 304, 307
　promises to pay, 306
　promissory notes, 306
UCC and, 304
value, 320
warranty liability
　presentment warranties, 326
　transfer warranties, 325
Negotiated settlement, 555
Negotiation
　as form of ADR, 42
　preliminary, 134
　transfer of negotiable instruments by, 311–312
Network intrusion insurance, 487–488
Ninth Amendment, 52, 58
Nonbinding arbitration, 43
Noncompete agreements, 150
Nonconforming goods, 263
Nonmerchant, contract rules for, 238
Nonnegotiable instruments
　compared to negotiable instruments, 304
Nonpossessory interests, 513–514
Nonprofit (not-for-profit) corporation, 412
Normal trade relations (NTR) status, 586
Norris-LaGuardia Act, 372
North American Free Trade Agreement (NAFTA), 586
Note. See Promissory note
Notice, 320–321
　dishonored instruments, 321
　overdue instruments, 321
　taking without, and holder in due course, 320–321
　validation, 296
Notice-and-comment rulemaking, 552–553
Notification
　agent's duty to, 353
　collection agency and, 296
Novation, discharge by, 219
Nuclear Regulatory Commission (NRC), 552
Nutrition Labeling and Education Act, 292

O

Obedience, agent's duty to, 353
Objective theory of contracts, 122–123, 133
Obligation
　primary, 191
　secondary, 191

Obligee, obligor, 204
Obscenity
　defined, 54
　online, 54
Occupational Safety and Health Act, 366, 367
Occupational Safety and Health Administration (OSHA)
　reporting work-related injuries, 367
Offer
　auctions, 134–135
　communication of, 135
　contractual, 123, 133–137
　counteroffer, 137
　defined, 133
　definiteness of terms, 135
　e-contracts, 139
　elements of, 133–135
　firm, 237
　intention, 133–135
　irrevocable, 136
　lease contracts, 237
　online for e-contracts, 139
　open terms, 237
　preliminary negotiations, 134
　rejection, 137
　as requirement of contract, 123
　revocation of, 136
　　for unilateral contract, 124
　sales contracts, 237
　termination of, 136–137
　　by operation of law, 137
Offeree
　counteroffer by, 137
　death or incompetence of, offer termination and, 137
　defined, 124, 133
　rejection of offer by, 137
Offeror
　death or incompetence of, offer termination and, 137
　defined, 124, 133
　revocation of offer by, 136
Officer, corporate
　agency relationship, 429
　business judgment rule, 430
　conflicts of interest, 430
　defined, 411
　duties of, 429–430
　　of care, 429
　　of loyalty, 430
　fiduciary duties of, 429–430
　liabilities of, 430
　removal of, 429
　roles of, 427, 429
Old-Age, Survivors, and Disability Insurance Act, 367
One-year rule, 190–191
Online banking, 343
Online contracts. See E-contracts
Online dispute resolution (ODR), 44
Online payment systems
　as electronic fund transfer, 341
Opening statement, 40
Open term, open quantity, 237
Operation of law
　agency formation by, 352

contract discharge by, 220–222
termination by, 358–359
Opinions
expression of, 134
statement of, 277
Oppressive conduct, 434
Option contract, 136
Option-to-cancel clauses, 150
Oral contract
admissions and, 240
partial performance, 240
promissory estoppel, 193–194
for specially manufactured
goods, 240
Orally agreed-on condition, 196
Order, payable to, 310
Order for relief, 467
Order instrument, 310
negotiating, 311
Orders
final, 555
initial, 555
Orders to pay
checks as, 305–306
drafts as, 305
negotiable instruments, 305–306
express order, 308
unconditionality of, 308
Ordinances, 8
landlords and compliance with, 527
Ordinary duress, as personal
defense, 327
Ordinary holder, 319
Outcome-based ethics, 20–21
Overdraft, 335
Overdue instruments, 321
Overtime, 370–371
Ownership in personal property
acquiring
accession, 498
confusion, 498
gifts, 497–498
possession, 496
production, 496–497
rights of possession
concurrent ownership, 495–496
fee simple, 495
Ownership in real property
in fee simple, 511–512
leasehold estate, 523–524
life estates, 512–513
nonpossessory interests, 513–514
transfer of
adverse possession, 515–516
deed, 514–515
eminent domain, 516–517
intestate, 539–541
trusts, 541–543
will or inheritance, 515, 535–539
Owners in common, 248

P

Packaging
laws affecting, 292
Parent corporation, 418
Paris Convention, 87

Parol evidence rule
consistent additional terms, 241
course of dealings, 241
course of performance, 241
defined, 195
exceptions to, 195–196
sales and lease contracts, 240–241
usage of trade, 241
Partially disclosed principal, 356
Partners. *See also* Partnerships
agency power, 400
compensation of, 399
dissociation of, 401–402
fiduciary duties of, 400
general, 403
inspection of books, 399
liability of, 401
limited, 403
property rights, 400
rights of, 398–400, 401
Partnerships (traditional general),
397–404. *See also* Partners
accounting of assets/profits, 399
agency concept and, 397
by agreement, 398
articles of, 398
defined, 397
dissolution, 402–403
duration of, 398
duties and powers of partners,
400–401
entity vs. aggregate of individuals,
397–398
essential elements of, 397
by estoppel, 398
formation of, 398
interest in firm, 399–400
interest in partnership, 399
joint ownership and, 397
laws governing, 397
limited liability partnership, 404
limited partnership, 403–404
management rights, 398–399
profits and losses of, 397
taxes and, 398
for a term, 398
termination of, 402–403
Uniform Partnership Act (UPA), 397
winding up and distribution of assets,
402–403
Pass-through entity, 398, 405
Past consideration, 149–150
Patents
defined, 83
infringement of, 84
licensing, 84
patentable requirements, 83
Patient Protection and Affordable Care
Act, 292
Payee, 305
Payment
on international transactions, 584
lessor's right of recover when
due, 267
obligation of buyer or lessee, 265
tender of, 457
Payor bank, 337

Peer-to-peer (P2P) networking, 97
Penalty
compared to liquidated damages, 224
defined, 224
Pension plans, private, 368
Per capita distribution, 540–541
Perfection
defined, 442
by filing financing statement, 442
Perfect tender rule, 263–265
Performance
accord and satisfaction, 220
agent's duty to, 353
anticipatory repudiation, 266
complete, 218
consideration and, 147
of contract, 126
course of, 195, 241, 278
defined, 217
discharge of contract by, 218–219
impossibility of, 220–222
installment contracts, 264
of lease contracts, 261–266
obligations of buyer or lessee, 265
obligations of seller or lessor, 261–265
one-year rule and, 190–191
partial, exception to Statute of
Frauds, 193
perfect tender rule, 263–265
place of delivery, 262–263
revocation of acceptance, 265
right of inspection, 265
right to obtain specific, 268
of sales contract, 261–266
to satisfaction of another, 218–219
specific, 193, 225
substantial, 218
tender of delivery, 261–262
Periodic tenancy, 523–524
Per se violations, 566–567
Person
in Chapter 7 (liquidation
proceedings), 466
corporation as, 411
jurisdiction over, 31–32
legal, 411
Personal defenses, 327
Personal property
abandoned, 500
acquiring
accession, 498
confusion, 498
gifts, 497–498
possession, 496
production, 496–497
bailment of, 500–503
defined, 71, 494
exemption, 460
fixture and, 190, 511
intangible, 440, 494
lost, 499–500
mislaid, 499
nature of, 494
ownership rights
community property, 496
concurrent ownership, 495–496
fee simple, 495

Personal property (*continued*)
　tangible, 440, 494
　trespass to, 71–72
Personal service contract, specific
　　performance and, 225
Per stirpes distribution, 540
Petition, 37
　in bankruptcy, 466–467
Petitioner, 41
Phishing, 115
Physical delivery, 501
Picket line, 374
Pierce the corporate veil
　commingled interests, 414
　defined, 414
　factors in, 414
Pinterest, 98
Piracy, 581
Plain meaning rule, 128
Plaintiff, 37
Plant life, real property, 510
Plato, 2
Pleading
　answer, 38
　complaint, 37–38
　defined, 37
　motion to dismiss, 38
　summons, 38
Point-of-sale systems
　as electronic fund transfer, 341
Police powers, of states, 50–51
Policy, insurance, 481
Pornography, online, 54
Possession
　artisan's lien and, 454
　of leased property, 526
　ownership by, 496
Postal Reorganization Act, 292
Posttrial motions, 41
Power of attorney
　of agent, 355
　defined, 355
　express authority, 355
　general, 355
　special, 355
　writing requirement for, 351
Powers
　condemnation, 516–517
　express, 415
　implied, 415
　monopoly, 568
　police, 50–51
　of shareholders, 431
　trustee in bankruptcy, 469–470
Precedent
　civil law system and, 9
　defined, 5
Predatory behavior, 70
Predatory pricing, 567
Predominant-factor test, 235
Preemption, 51
Preemptive rights, 433
Preexisting duty rule, 148–149
Preference, in bankruptcy, 470
Preferred stock, 416
　voting rights and, 431
Pregnancy Discrimination Act, 383

Prejudgment remedy, 454
Premium, insurance, 481
Prenuptial agreement, 192
Preponderance of evidence, 107
Presentation, payable on, 309–310
Presentment
　electronic, 339
　proper and timely, 322–323
Presentment warranties, 326
Pretexting, 59
Pretrial motions, 38–39
Pretrial procedures
　discovery, 39–40
　pleadings, 37–38
　pretrial motions, 38–39
Price
　predatory pricing, 567
　price discrimination, 570
　resale price maintenance
　　agreement, 566
　seller's right to recover purchase
　　price, 267
Price-fixing agreement, 567
Prima facie case, 382, 387
Primary liability, 322
Primary obligation, 191
Principal
　agent's duties to, 353
　bankruptcy, agency termination
　　and, 359
　contractual capacity, 351
　death or insanity, agency termination
　　and, 358
　defined, 350
　disclosed, 356
　duties of, to agent, 354
　　compensation, 354
　　cooperation, 354
　　reimbursement and
　　　indemnification, 354
　partially disclosed, 356
　termination of agency, 357–359
　undisclosed, 356
Principle of rights, 20
Prior dealings, 195
Privacy Act, 58
Privacy/privacy rights
　Constitution and, 57–58
　data collection and cookies, 101
　Electronic Communications Privacy Act
　　(ECPA), 100–101
　Internet and, 100–101
　Internet companies' privacy policies, 101
　invasion of, 69
　medical information and, 58
　pretexting and, 59
　statutes affecting, 58
　stored communications, 101
Private corporation, 412
Privilege, 69
Privity of contract
　defined, 203
　exceptions to
　　assignments, 203–206
　　delegations, 203, 206–208
　　third-party beneficiaries, 203, 208–210
　product liability and, 280

Probable cause
　detention after shoplifting and, 68
　search warrant and, 109
　search warrants, 109
Probate courts, 33, 535
Procedural due process, 55
Procedural rules, 37
Procedural unconscionability, 172
Proceeds, security interest in, 443
　order of application, 448
Production, ownership by, 496–497
Product liability
　based on misrepresentation, 280
　based on negligence, 280
　defenses to, 282–283
　defined, 76, 280
　due care, 280
　inadequate warnings, 282
　privity of contract and, 280
　public policy and, 281
　quality control management and,
　　283–284
　requirements for, 281
　strict liability and, 280–282
Product misuse, 283
Products
　defective condition, 281
　defects of, 281–282
　　design, 281
　　manufacturing, 281
　unreasonably dangerous, 281
Professionals, duty of, 74
Profit(s)
　accounting of, in partnerships, 399
　as nonpossessory interest in land, 513
　sharing of, in partnerships, 397
Promise
　for an act, 124
　collateral, 191–192
　consideration and, 147–152
　defined, 122
　express warranty and, 276
　illusory promises, 150
　made in consideration of marriage, 192
　negotiable instruments, 306
　　express promise, 308
　　unconditionality of, 308
　to pay
　　certificates of deposit, 306
　　promissory notes, 306
　for a promise, 124
　to ship, and acceptance, 237
Promisor/promisee, 122
Promissory estoppel, 151–152, 193–194
Promissory note
　defined, 306
　example of, 306
　installment note, 306
　maker of, 306
　mortgage note, 306
　as negotiable instrument, 304, 306, 307
　uses of, 306
Property
　abandoned, 500
　after-acquired, 443–444
　community, 469, 496
　conversion, 72

defined, 494
disparagement of, 72–73
distribution of
    in bankruptcy, 470–471
    intestate, 539–541
    trusts, 541–543
    wills, 535–539
estate in, 469
homestead exemption, 460
insurable interest in, 482
intangible property, 235, 494
intellectual (*See* Intellectual property)
intentional tort against
    conversion, 72
    disparagement of property, 72–73
    trespass to land, 71
    trespass to personal property,
        71–72
joint ownership, and partnership, 397
jurisdiction over, 32
lost, 499–500
mislaid, 499
ownership of
    partnership and, 400
    rights of, 495–496
personal, 71
    acquiring, 496–498
    bailments, 500–503
    exemption, 460
    mislaid, lost and abandoned,
        499–500
    nature of, 494
    rights of possession, 495–496
private, taken by foreign governments,
    580, 584–585
real, 71, 494
    limitations on rights of property
        owners, 516–517
    nature of, 509–511
    ownership in, 511–514
    transfer of ownership, 514–516
surrender of, to release surety/
    guarantor, 458
tangible property, 235, 494
writ of attachment, 454
writ of execution, 454
Protected class, 381
    illegal contracts and, 174
Proximate cause, 74–75
Proxy, 431
Publication requirement
    of libel, 68
    of valid will, 538
Public Company Accounting Oversight
    Board, 17
Public corporation, 412
Public figures, defamation and, 69
Public officials, bribery of, 112
Public policy
    contracts contrary to, 170–173
    exceptions to employment-at-will, 366
    strict product liability and, 281
Puffery, 70, 277, 289
Punitive damages, 184, 223
Purchase-money security interest
    (PMSI), 474
Purpose, particular, 278

Q

Qualified indorsement, 312–313
Quality
    mistake of, 179, 181
    slander of, 72–73
Quality circles, 284
Quality control management, 283–284
Quantity, open term, 237
Quasi contracts, 125–126
    liability for necessaries and, 159–160
    recovery based on, 225
Quid pro quo harassment, 384–385
Quiet enjoyment, covenant of, 526
Quitclaim deed, 515
Quorum requirements
    board of directors' meetings and, 428
    defined, 428
    shareholders and, 431
Quotas, 585

R

Race
    discrimination based on, 383
    as suspect trait, 57
Racketeer Influenced and Corrupt
        Organizations Act (RICO)
    federal crimes under, 113
    implications of, 113
Racketeering activity, 113
Ratification
    agency formation by, 352
    of agent's unauthorized acts,
        355–356
    of contract, 126–127
    defined, 160, 352
    express, 160
    implied, 160
    minors and, 160
Rational basis test, 56
Real defenses, 326
Real estate
    defined, 509
    goods associated with, 235
Real property
    contract for sale of land and, 190
    defined, 71, 494, 509
    limitation of rights of, 516–517
    nature of
        airspace rights and subsurface
            rights, 510
        fixtures, 510–511
        land, 509–510
        plant life and vegetation, 510
    ownership in
        in fee simple, 511–512
        leasehold estate, 523–524
        life estates, 512–513
        nonpossessory interests, 513–514
    transfer of ownership
        adverse possession, 515–516
        deed, 514–515
        deeds, 514–515
        eminent domain, 516–517
        will or inheritance, 515
    waste, 524
Realty, 509

Reasonable accommodations
    for employees with disability, 389
    for religious practices, 383
Reasonable duty
    trespass to land and, 71
Reasonable person standard
    assault and battery, 67
    detention after shoplifting, 68
    duty of care, 73
    objective facts, 122–123
Rebuttal, 40–41
Record on appeal, 41
Redemption rights, 448
Reformation, 172
Registration, of trademark, 83
Regulations
    administrative agencies, 8, 551–552
    ethical issues and, 18
    independent regulatory agencies,
        551–552
    by states, 50–51
Regulation Z, 293–294
Regulatory Flexibility Act, 558
Reimbursement
    principal's duty of, 354
    right of, 458
Rejection, right of, 268
Rejoinder, 41
Release, 151
Relevant market, 568
Religion
    discrimination based on, 383
    establishment clause, 54–55
    ethical principles and, 19
    freedom of, 54–55
    free exercise clause, 54, 55
    reasonable accommodations, 383
Remanded case, 41
Remedy(ies)
    for breach of contract, 222–226
        sales or lease contracts, 266–269
    for copyright infringement, 85–86
    damages, 222–224
    of default, 446–448
    defined, 6, 222
    for employment discrimination, 386
    equitable, 6
    in equity, 6
    of law, 6
    of lessor, 266–267
    prejudgment, 454
    recovery based on quasi contract, 225
    rescission and restitution, 224
    of seller, 266–267
    specific performance, 225
Rent, for leased property, 528
Renunciation, agent's termination of
        agency relationship, 358
Reorganization, 472–473
Repayment plan, Chapter 13, 473–474
Replacement workers, 374
Reply, 38
Republic of Korea–United States Free Trade
        Agreement (KORUS FTA), 586
Reputation
    covenants not to compete and sale of
        ongoing business, 171

Resale price maintenance agreement, 566
Rescission
    of contract, 224
    defined, 149
    discharge of contract by, 219
    mutual, 219
    new contract and, 149
    restitution and, 224
Reserve accounts, 339
Residuary clause, 536
Respondeat superior
    defined, 357
    liability of agent's torts, 357
Respondent, 41
Restitution, 224
    defined, 159
    duty of, 158–159
Restraint of trade
    contracts in, 170–172
    covenant not to compete,
        171–172
    defined, 565
Restrictive indorsement, 313
Resulting trust, 543
Retaliation claim, 386
Retention of collateral, 447
Retirement income, 367–369
    private retirement plans, 368
Reversed judgment, 41
Revocation
    defined, 124, 136
    of offers, 136
    of offers for unilateral contract, 124
    principal's termination of agency
        relationship, 358
    of will, 538–539
Rights
    airspace, 510
    appraisal, 418–419
    assignments, 203–206
    of bailee, 501–503
    of contribution, 458
    of creditors, 446
    of debtors, 446
    fundamental right, 56
    of inspection, 433
    of ownership, 511–514
    of partners, 398–400
    preemptive rights, 433
    principle of, 20
    of redemption, 448
    of reimbursement, 458
    of shareholders, 431–434
    to strike, 374
    of subrogation, 458
    subsurface, 510
    of surety and guarantor, 458
    vested, 209
Right to-work laws, 372
Risk
    assumption of, as defense, 75, 282
    banking risks, 344
    defined, 482
    of loss, 251–254
    negligence and, 73
    of personal assets and sole
        proprietorship, 396–397
    product warnings and, 282

risk management, 256
    to warn business invitees of risks, 74
Risk management
    in cyberspace, 487–488
    defined, 482
    risk pooling, 482
Risk of loss
    conditional sales, 253–254
    delivery with movement of goods
        (carrier case), 251–252
    delivery without movement of goods,
        252–253
    when contract is breached, 254
Risk pooling, 482
Robbery, 111
Royalties, 85
Rulemaking
    comment period in, 552–553
    defined, 552
    final rule, 553
    notice of proposed rulemaking, 552
Rule of four, 36
Rule of reason
    defined, 566
    per se violations and, 566–567
    resale price maintenance agreement, 566
    territorial or customer restrictions, 566

S

Safety
    drug safety, 297
    food safety, 297
Safe Web Act, 94
Sales
    conditional, 253–254
    consumer protection and, 292–293
    cooling-off laws, 292
    defined, 234
    of goods, 223
        written requirement, 192
    of land, 225
        fixtures and, 510–511
    mail-order, 292
    of ongoing business, and covenant not
        to compete, 171
    online, 292–293
    sale on approval, 253–254
    sale or return, 254
    telephone, 292
Sales contracts, 234–242
    acceptance, 237–239
    breach of
        compensatory damages, 223
        remedies for, 266–269
        risk of loss, 254
    consideration, 239
    course of dealings, 241
    course of performance, 241
    defined, 234
    firm offer, 237
    formation of, 236–242
    good defined, 235
    good faith, 239
    identification, 247–251
    insurable interest, 254–255
    law governing, 234
    letters of credit, 126

merchant defined, 236
mirror image rule, 238
modification in good faith, 239
modification without consideration, 239
offer, 237
parol evidence rule, 240–241
performance of, 261–266
predominant-factor test, 235
risk of loss, 251–254
sales defined, 234
Statute of Frauds, 192, 239–240
UCC Article 2 and, 234, 236–242
unconscionability, 241–242
usage of trade, 241
warranties, 275–280
Sarbanes-Oxley Act, 17
Satisfaction, accord and, 220
Scienter, 182–183
S corporations, 412
Search and seizure
    by administrative agencies, 554
    Fourth Amendment protections, 109
Search warrant
    administrative agencies and, 554
    Fourth Amendment protections, 109
    probable cause and, 109
    scope of, 109
Seasonably, 238, 268
Second Amendment, 52
Secondary liability, 322–323
Secondary meaning of trademark, 82–83
Secondary obligation, 191
Second level domain (SLD), 94
Secured creditor, 467
    defined, 440
    distribution to, 471
Secured party, 440
Secured transaction. *See also* Security
        interest
    attachment, 441
    defined, 440
    terminology of, 440–441
Securities
    blue sky law, 174
    bonds, 416
    defined, 415
    securities fraud, 113
    stocks, 416
Securities and Exchange Commission
        (SEC), 551, 552
Security agreement, 440
Security interest
    attachment, 441
    creating, 441
    default
        basic remedies, 446
        retaining or disposing of collateral,
            447–448
    defined, 255, 440
    perfecting
        defined, 442
        by filing financing statement, 442
        improper filing, 442–443
    priorities among
        buyers in ordinary course of business,
            445–446
        first-in-time rule, 445
        general rules for, 445

rights and duties of debtor/creditor, 446
scope of
after-acquired property, 443–444
floating-lien concept, 444–445
future advances, 444
proceeds, 443
warranty of title and, 276
Self-incrimination, 109, 114
Seller
breach of contract, and risk of loss, 254
good faith purchaser and voidable title, 250
goods held by, 253
insurable interest of, 255
obligation of, 261–265
place of business, 262
remedies for, 266–267
residence, 262
Seller's talk, 70
Seniority system, as defense to employment discrimination, 390
Separation of powers, 50
Service mark, 83, 88
Services
goods and services combined, 235
predominant-factor test, 235
Settlements, negotiated, 555
Seventh Amendment, 52
Sexual harassment
Ellerth/Faragher affirmative defense, 385
forms of, 384–385
human resource management and, 390
by supervisors, 384
tangible employment action, 385
Shareholders
appraisal right, 418–419
approval of, and mergers and consolidations, 419
common, 416
cumulative voting for directors, 432–433
defined, 411
derivative suit of, 434
dissolution disbursement, 416
dissolution of corporation, 420–421
dividends and, 433
duties of, 434
inspection rights, 433
liability of, 411, 431
majority of, fiduciary duties of, 434
meetings of, 431
in mergers and consolidations procedures, 418
minority, 434
passing resolutions, 432
powers of, 431
preemptive rights, 433
preferred, 416
proxy and, 431
quorum requirements, 431
rights of, 431–434
sale of corporate assets and, 419
stock certificates, 433
takeover, 420
tender offer, 420
transfer of shares, 434
voting by, 418
voting rights, 416, 431

Sherman Act, 586
group boycott, 567
historical perspective on, 565
jurisdictional requirements of, 566
market divisions, 567
monopolization, 567–569
overview of, 565–566
per se violations, 566–567
predatory pricing, 567
price-fixing agreement, 567
rule of reason, 566
Ship, promise to, 237
Shipment
date of, 265
prompt, and acceptance, 237
Shipment contract, 248, 252, 262–263
Shoplifting
detention after, and probable cause, 68
Short-form merger, 418
Shrink-wrap agreement, 140
Sight draft, 305
Signature liability, 321–325
primary liability, 322
secondary liability, 322–323
unauthorized signatures, 323–324
Signature requirements
for valid will, 538
Signatures
checks with forged, 336–337
defined, 307–308
electronic, 194–195
indorsement, 312
liability, 321–325
of negotiable instruments, 307–308
unauthorized, 323–325
fictitious payee rule, 324–325
imposter rule, 324
for written contracts, 194–195
Silence
as acceptance, 138
misrepresentation by, 182
Simple contracts, 126
Six Sigma system, 284
Sixth Amendment, 52, 109, 110
Slander, 68
of quality, 72–73
of title, 73
Sliding-scale standard, 32
Small Business Administration (SBA)
Office of the National Ombudsman, 558
Small Business Administration Act, 572
Small businesses
legal issues in managing, 4
partnerships, 397–403
Regulatory Flexibility Act, 557
sole proprietorship, 396–397
Small Business Regulatory Enforcement Fairness Act (SBREFA), 558
Small claims courts, 33
Smart cards, 343
Social media
business ethics and, 22
company social media networks, 98–99
criminal investigations and litigation, 98
defined, 98

Electronic Communications Privacy Act (ECPA), 100–101
hiring procedures and, 22
legal issues and, 98–99
workplace media policies, 98
Social Security, 367
Social Security Act, 367
Social Security Administration, 368
Softcard, 333
Software, copyright protection of, 86
Sole proprietorship, 396–397
advantages of, 396
defined, 396
disadvantages of, 396–397
lack of continuity, 397
personal assets at risk, 396–397
taxes and, 396
Sovereign immunity, doctrine of, 580
Spam, 93–94
Special damages, 223
Special indorsement, 312
Specific performance
contracts for personal services, 225
defined, 193
as equitable remedy, 225
right to obtain, 268
sale of land as, 225
Speech
commercial, 53
corporate political, 53
freedom of, 53–54
reasonable restrictions, 53
substantial government interest, 53
symbolic, 53
unprotected, 54
Spouse
intestacy and, 540
revocation of will by marriage, 539
Stakeholder approach to corporate social responsibility, 21
Stale check, 335
Standing to sue, 37
Stare decisis
civil law system and, 9
common law tradition and, 5
defined, 5
State court system, 32–34
appellate courts, 33–34
structure of, 33, 34
supreme (highest) courts of, 33–34
trial courts of, 33
Statements
false statement of fact, 68
of opinion, 181, 277
of value, 277
States/state government
commerce clause, 50–51
laws of
ordinances, 8
uniform laws, 8
limited liability companies, 405
limits on, and Bill of Rights, 52–55
mergers and consolidation procedures, 418
police powers, 50–51
powers of, 7
regulation by, 50–51
spam, 93

States/state government (*continued*)
  selecting state of incorporation, 412
  supremacy clause, 51
  workers' compensation laws, 366–367
Statute of Frauds
  collateral promises, 191–192
  contract for sales of goods, 192
  contracts involving interests in
      land, 190
  defined, 189
  exceptions to, 192–194, 240
    admissions, 193
    partial performance, 193
    promissory estoppel, 193–194
    special exceptions under UCC, 194
  main purpose rule, 191–192
  one-year rule, 190–191
  promises made in consideration in
      marriage, 192
  purpose of, 189
  types of contracts, 189–192
  UCC and, 192, 239–240
  writing requirement
    of contracts, 239–240
    partnership agreements, 398
Statute of limitations
  contracts and, 220
  surety/guarantor defense, 457
Statutes, 5
  contracts contrary to, 169–170
  long arm statute, 32
  as primary source of law, 8, 31
  state, 8
Statutory law, 7
  defined, 8
  as primary source of law, 8
  as source of American law, 5, 8
  trademark protection and, 81
Stock certificates, 433
Stocks
  blue sky law, 174
  common, 416
  defined, 411
  dividends, 416
  preferred, 416
  purchase of, and mergers/
      consolidations, 419–420
  securities fraud, 113
  takeover and, 420
  tender offer, 420
  transfer of shares, 434
Stop-payment order, 335–336
Stored Communications Act (SCA), 101
Stored-value card, 343
Strict liability
  defined, 76
  product liability and, 280–282
Strict product liability
  defenses to, 282–283
  inadequate warnings, 282
  product defects, 281–282
  public policy and, 281
  requirements for, 281
Strict scrutiny, 57
Strike
  defined, 374
  picket line, 374

replacement workers, 374
  right to, 374
Subchapter S of IRS code, 412
Sublease, 528–529
Subpoenas
  by administrative agencies, 553–554
  ad testificandum, 553
  duces tecum, 553
Subrogation, right of, 458
Subsidiary corporation, 418, 582
Substantial government interest
  commercial speech and, 53
  defined, 53
  due process and, 56
Substantial performance, 218
Substantive due process, 56
Substantive unconscionability, 172
Substitute check, 339–341
Subsurface rights, 510
Sufficient interest, 255
Suggestive trademark, 82
Summary judgment, 39, 41
Summons, 38
Sunshine Act, 558
Supervisors, sexual harassment by, 385
Suppliers
  of component parts, and strict product
      liability, 282
  monitoring practice of foreign,
      22–23
Supremacy clause, 51
Supreme court, state, 34
Surety, 456
Suretyship, 455–458
  actions that release, 457–458
  defenses of, 457–458
  defined, 456
  relationship with creditor and debtor,
      456, 457
  rights of, 458
Surviving corporation, 417
Survivorship
  right of, 495–496
Suspect trait, 57
Symantec Corporation, 24
Symbolic delivery, 497
Symbolic speech, 53

T

Takeover, 420
Taking, 516
Tangible employment action, 384
Tangible property, 235, 440, 494
Target corporation, 419–420
Tariffs, 585
Taxes/taxation
  congressional power to, 51–52
  on imported goods, 585
  independent contractors, 360
  information return, 398
  of limited liability company, 405
  Medicare, 368
  partnerships and, 398
  pass-through entity, 398, 405
  S corporations, 412
  Social Security, 367

sole proprietorship and, 396
  tariffs, 585
Telephone Records and Privacy Protection
      Act, 59
Telephone sales, 292
Tenancy
  in common, 495
  fixed-term, 523
  joint, 495–496
  lease agreement, 524–526
    antidiscrimination, 526
    elements of, 524–525
    unconscionability concept, 525
  life estates and, 512–513
  periodic, 523–524
  rights and duties of
    compliance with ordinances, 527
    covenant of quiet enjoyment, 526
    eviction, 526
    possession of leased property, 526
    rent, 528
    transferring rights, 528–529
    use and maintenance of leased prop-
        erty, 527
  at sufferance, 524
  terminating lease, 529
  waste, 524
  at will, 524
  for years, 523
Tender
  defined, 218
  of delivery, 248, 253, 261–262
  of payment, 457
  perfect tender rule, 263–265
  of performance, 218
Tender offer, 420
Tenth Amendment, 7, 52
  police powers, 50–51
Termination
  of agency
    by act of parties, 357–358
    operation of law, 358–359
  of corporation, 420
  of lease, 529
  of offer, 136–137
  by operation of law, 358–359
  wrongful, 358
Termination statement, 446
Term(s)
  additional, 238–239
  ambiguous, 195
  consistent additional terms, 241
  definiteness of, 135
  delivery, 251–252, 256
  essential, 194
  open, 237
  partnership for a, 398
  shrink-wrap and agreement, 140
Territorial restrictions, 566
Terrorism
  cyberterrorism, 115
Testamentary trust, 542
Testator
  capacity of, 536
  defined, 535
  intent of, 537
Third Amendment, 52, 58

Third party
  assignment, 203–206
  delegation, 206–208
  liability to, and partner
    dissociation, 402
  third party beneficiary contract, 203,
    208–210
Third party beneficiary, 203, 208–210
Time
  acceptance and, 138
  offer and lapse of, 137
  payable at a definite time, 310
  in proper presentment, 323
  reasonable, 137, 261, 268
  stop-payment orders, 335
Time draft, 305
Time instrument, 321
Title
  deeds and defect of, 514
  defined, 234
  disclaimer of title warranty, 276
  document of, 249
  entrustment rule, 250–251
  good title, 275
  lost property, 499–500
  mislaid property, 499
  negotiable/nonnegotiable document
    of, 253
  no infringements, 276
  no liens, 275–276
  passage of, 248–251
    delivery without movement of
      goods, 249
    destination contract and, 248
    identified goods and, 248
    sale on approval, 253
    sale or return, 254
    sales or leases by nonowners,
      249–251
    shipment contracts and, 248
  as right of ownership, 495
  slander of, 73
  voidable, 249–250
  void title, 248, 249
  warranties, 275–276
Title VII of Civil Rights Act, 381–386
  Equal Employment Opportunity
    Commission (EEOC), 381–382
  intentional discrimination, 382
  international business and, 22
  unintentional discrimination, 382–383
Top-level domain (TLD), 94
Tortfeasor, 67
Torts, 65–78
  of agent, 357
  basis of, 65
  business
    wrongful interference with a contrac-
      tual relationship, 70–71
    wrongful interference with business
      relationship, 70–71
  compared to criminal prosecution, 65
  cyber torts, 99–100
  damages available to, 65
  defenses, 66–67
  defined, 65
  of independent contractor, 359

intentional against person
  abusive or frivolous litigation, 70
  assault, 67
  battery, 67
  defamation, 68–69
  defenses, 66–67
  defined, 67
  false imprisonment, 68
  fraudulent misrepresentation, 69–70
  invasion of privacy, 69
intentional against property
  conversion, 72
  disparagement of property, 72–73
  trespass to land, 71
  trespass to personal property, 71–72
international claims, 587
reform of, 66
unintentional (negligence)
  causation, 74–75
  defenses to, 75–76
  duty of care and its breach, 73–74
  injury requirements and
    damages, 74
Total quality management, 284
Trade
  contracts in restraint of, 170–172
  minimizing barriers to, 585–586
  restraints of, 565
  usages of, and implied warranties, 278
Trade acceptance, 305
Trade associations
  rule of reason and, 566
Trade libel, 72–73
Trademark, 81–83
  abbreviations, 88
  catchy phrases, 88
  counterfeit goods and, 83
  defined, 81
  dilution of, 81–82, 96
  distinctiveness of mark, 82
  domain names and, 94
  fanciful and arbitrary, 82
  infringement of, 81, 83, 94, 95–96
    meta tags, 95
  licensing, 95–96
  meta tags and, 95
  ornamental colors and designs, 88
  registration of, 83
  secondary meaning of, 82–83
  shape of, 88
  statutory protection of, 81
  strong marks, 82
  suggestive, 82
  when to protect, 88
Trade name, 83
  securing corporate name and, 413
Trade-Related Aspects of Intellectual
    Property Rights (TRIPS), 87
Trade secrets
  company-wide social networks and
    protection of, 99
  defined, 86
  penalties for stealing, 87
Trading with the Enemy Act, 585
Transfers
  in bankruptcy, 469
  fraudulent, 469

  in leased property rights, 528–529
  of negotiable instruments, 311–312
Transfer warranties, 325
Transportation, Department of, 551
Treasury, Department of, 551
Treaty, 579
Treble damages, 571
Trespass
  to land, 71
  to personal property, 71–72
Trial courts
  federal (district), 34
  state, 32, 33
Trials
  closing argument, 41
  examination of witnesses, 40
  motion for new, 41
  motions at, 41
  opening statement, 40
  posttrial motions, 41
  rebuttal, 40–41
  rejoinder, 41
TRIPS agreement, 87
Trustee, bankruptcy and, 469–470
Trusts
  constructive trust, 542–543
  defined, 541
  essential elements of, 541
  express, 541–542
  implied, 542–543
  inter vivos trust, 541
  living trusts, 541–542
  resulting trust, 543
  testamentary trust, 542
Truth-in-Lending Act (TILA),
    293–295
Twitter, 98, 99, 101
Tying arrangement, 570
Typosquatting, 95

U

Ultra vires doctrine, 415
Unauthorized signatures
  defined, 323
  exceptions to, 324
  fictitious payee rule, 324–325
  imposter rule, 324
Unconscionability
  of contracts or clauses, 172
  lease agreements and, 525
  procedural, 172
  of sales or lease contracts, 241–242
  substantive, 172
Undertaking Spam, Spyware, and Fraud
    Enforcement with Enforcers
    Beyond Borders Act, 94
Underwriter, 481
Undisclosed principal, 356
Undue hardship
  reasonable accommodations for
    disabilities, 389
  reasonable accommodations for
    religious practices and, 383
Undue influence
  valid will and, 537
  voidable contracts, 127

Undue influence, voluntary consent
    and, 184
Unemployment compensation, 368
Unenforceable contract, 127
Unequivocal acceptance, 138
Unfair labor practices, 374
Unforeseen difficulties
    as exceptions to preexisting duty
        rule, 149
Uniform Commercial Code (UCC)
    acceptance, 237–239
    adoption of, 8
    anticipatory repudiation, 266
    Article 2 (sales contracts), scope of,
        234, 236–242
    Article 2A (leases), scope of, 236–242
    Article 3 and 4 (negotiable
        instruments), 304
    commercial reasonableness, 261
    communication of acceptance, 237–238
    consideration, 239
    consistent additional terms, 241
    course of dealings, 241
    course of performance, 241
    creation of, 8
    customary practices, 195
    entrustment rule, 250–251
    essential terms, 194
    firm offer, 237
    goal of, 234
    good faith and, 261
    identification, 247–251
    insolvent, 249–250
    insurable interest, 254–255
    merchant defined, 236
    mirror image rule, 238
    money definition, 309
    negotiable instruments, 304
    open terms, 237
    oral contract, 193
    passage of title, 248–251
    perfect tender rule, 263–265
    place of delivery, 262–263
    priorities among security interests, 445
    risk of loss, 251–254
    secured transaction term definitions,
        440–441
    Statute of Frauds, 192, 239–240
        exceptions to, 194
    terms between merchants, 238–239
    unconscionability, 241–242
    usage of trade, 241
    warranties under, 275–280
Uniform Electronic Transactions Act
    (UETA), 127, 140
    E-SIGN Act, 195
    signatures on electronic records,
        194–195
Uniform laws, 8, 31
Uniform Partnership Act (UPA), 397
Unilateral contracts, 124
Unilateral mistake, 179–180
Unintentional discrimination, 382–383
Unintentional torts (negligence)
    causation, 74–75
    defenses to, 75–76
    duty of care and its breach, 73–74
    injury requirements and damages, 74

Unions
    authorization card, 372
    closed shop, 372
    collective bargaining, 373–374
    decision to form or select, 372
    elections, 373
    employer's discrimination against union
        workers, 374
    employer's domination of union, 374
    employer's interference with, 374
    employer's refusal to recognize or
        negotiate with, 374
    featherbedding, 373
    federal laws regarding, 372–374
    good faith bargaining, 373
    negotiating terms and conditions, 373
    right to-work laws, 372
    strikes, 374
    unfair labor practices, 374
    union shop, 372
Union shop, 372
United States Constitution
    administrative agencies and, 556
    checks and balances, 50
    commerce clause, 50–51
    criminal liability and safeguards
        of, 109
    cruel and unusual punishment, 109
    double jeopardy, 109
    due process clause, 55–56, 109
    equal protection clause, 56–57
    establishment clause, 54–55
    excessive fines, 109
    exclusionary rule, 110
    federal courts under, 36
    federal form of government, 49–52
    freedom of religion, 54–55
    freedom of speech, 53–54
    free exercise clause, 54, 55
    powers of government and, 49–52
    as primary source of law, 31, 49
    privacy rights and, 57–58
    search and seizure, 109
    self-incrimination, 109, 114
    separation of powers, 50
    supremacy clause, 51
    as supreme law of the land, 7
    taxation, 51–52
    trial jury, 109
United States Supreme Court
    appeals to, 35
    justices, 35
    petitions granted by, 35
    rule of four, 36
Universal defenses, 326–327
Unjust enrichment
    quasi contracts and, 125–126
Unprotected speech, 54
Unqualified indorsement, 313
Unreasonably dangerous products, 281
Unsecured creditor, 467
Unsecured creditors, distribution
    to, 471
Usage of trade, 195, 241
U.S. Circuit Courts of Appeals, 34
U.S. Copyright Office, 84
U.S. Court of Appeals, geographic
    boundaries of, 35

U.S. District Courts
    geographic boundaries of, 35
    jurisdiction, 34
U.S. Patent and Trademark Office, 83
U.S. Safe Web Act, 94
Usury, 169
Utilitarianism, 20

V
Validation notice, 296
Valid contract, 126–127
Value
    legally sufficient value, 147
    mistake of, 179, 181
    in negotiable instruments, 320
    statement of, 277
    taking for, and holder in due course, 320
Vegetation, real property, 510
Venture capital, 416
Verdict
    motion for directed, 41
Vested
    defined, 209
    intended beneficiary rights, 209
Veterans Affairs, Department of, 551
Voidable contract, 126–127, 195
Voidable title, 249–250
Void contract, 127, 195
Void title, 248, 249
Voluntary consent
    as defense to contract's
        enforceability, 179
    defined, 179
    duress, 184
    email contract and, 197
    fraudulent misrepresentation, 181–184
    mistake, 179–181
    undue influence, 184
Voluntary dissolution, of corporation, 420
Voting, by shareholders, 416
    cumulative, 432–433

W
Wages
    collective bargaining and, 373
    garnishment, 455
    laws governing, 370–371
    minimum, 370
    overtime provision and exemptions,
        370–371
    wage discrimination, 384
War, agency termination and, 359
Warehouse receipt, 249, 253
Warnings, product liability and, 282
Warranties
    breach of, as personal defense, 327
    defined, 275
    disclaimers, 279
    express, 276–277
    implied, 277–278
        of habitability, 527
    Magnuson-Moss Warranty Act,
        279–290
    presentment warranties, 326
    quality control management and,
        283–284

in sales and lease contracts, 275–280
  title, 275–276
  transfer warranties, 325
Warranty deed, 514
Waste, 524
Webb-Pomerene Act, 572
Whistleblowing, 365–366
White-collar crimes
  bribery, 112–113
  defined, 110
  embezzlement, 111
  forgery, 111
  larceny, 111
  mail and wire fraud, 112
  Racketeer Influenced and Corrupt
    Organizations Act (RICO), 113
  racketeering activity, 113
  robbery, 111
Will
  disinheritance, 537
  holographic will, 538
  requirements of valid, 536–538
    publication, 538
    signature requirements, 538
    testamentary capacity, 536
    undue influence, 537
    witness requirements, 538
    writing requirements, 537–538
  revocation of, 538–539
    by operation of law, 538–539
    by physical act of maker, 538

subsequent writing, 538
transfer of real property and, 515
types of gifts, 536
Wills, 535–539
  defined, 535
  terminology of, 535–536
Winding up
  of partnerships, 402–403
Wire fraud, 112
Witnesses
  cross-examination of, 40
  direct examination of, 40
  as valid will requirement, 538
Women
  gender discrimination, 383–384
  global environment and
    discrimination, 22
  pregnancy discrimination, 383–384
  sexual harassment of, 384–386
  wage discrimination, 384
Workers' compensation laws, 366–367
Workplace safety, OSHA
  requirements, 367
World Trade Organization (WTO), 586
Writing, requirements
  assurance of due performance,
    264–265
  confirmation between merchants and,
    240
  of contract, 189–195
  email contract and, 197

equal dignity rule, 351, 354
guaranty, 457
limited partnership agreement, 404
merchant's firm offer, 237
modifications without
  consideration, 239
of negotiable instruments, 307
partnership agreement, 398
Statute of Frauds, 189–195, 239–240
for valid will, 537–538
Writs
  of attachment, 454
  of *certiorari*, 35–36
  of execution, 454–455, 469
Written contracts, 189–195
  integrated contracts, 196
  parole evidence rule, 195–196
  Statute of Frauds
    collateral promises, 191–192
    contract for sales of
      goods, 192
    exceptions to, 192–194
    main purpose rule, 191–192
    one-year rule, 190–191
    promises made in consideration in
      marriage, 192
  sufficiency of writing
    essential terms, 194
    memorandums, 194
    signatures, 194–195
Wrongful interferences, 70–71